THE CLARENDON EDITION OF THE WORKS OF JOHN LOCKE



# THE CORRESPONDENCE

# THE CORRESPONDENCE OF John Locke

EDITED BY E. S. DE BEER

IN EIGHT VOLUMES

*Volume One*

INTRODUCTION

LETTERS NOS. 1–461

OXFORD
AT THE CLARENDON PRESS
1976

*Oxford University Press, Ely House, London W. 1*

GLASGOW NEW YORK TORONTO MELBOURNE WELLINGTON
CAPE TOWN IBADAN NAIROBI DAR ES SALAAM LUSAKA ADDIS ABABA
DELHI BOMBAY CALCUTTA MADRAS KARACHI DACCA
KUALA LUMPUR SINGAPORE HONG KONG TOKYO

ISBN 0 19 824396 0



*Printed in Great Britain*
*at the University Press, Oxford*
*by Vivian Ridler*
*Printer to the University*

# PREFACE

THE present work contains the texts of all the extant letters from and to John Locke so far as they are known to and have been accessible to me. They are printed from the original manuscripts when they have been available or, failing them, from the most reliable manuscript or printed copies. The texts are accompanied by translations where desirable and by notes. The principles of transcription and presentation are set out at length in the introduction.

The letters are enumerated; the system used is set out in the introduction. The primary reason for enumeration in the present case is its usefulness for forward citations: it makes it possible in connection with any letter to cite in short form a letter of later date. When relevant letters follow in rapid succession the forward citations could be by volume and page; when letters much later in date are to be cited the citations would for practical reasons have to be by date, with perhaps the correspondents' names also. The gain is apparent especially when any particular correspondence is required: the successive letters can be found with little interruption and without recourse to any index. The disadvantage of enumeration is that new letters will almost certainly come to light; a few have done so since the present enumeration was established and have had to be tagged in. This does not seem to outweigh the gains. In the index citations will normally be by volume and page.

Since 1956, when I began to edit the correspondence, much Locke material has been published, and many books and articles relating to him and his writings. These publications have influenced me, but the increasing cumulation of typescript copies of the letters has been more important. As it became easy to bring together the various letters relating to particular issues, statements which I had accepted previously ceased to be valid; Locke's life and circumstances were changing and my opinions have changed accordingly. The process has been gradual. As a result there is some unevenness in the notes. While I have tried to pay proper attention to all subjects of interest within my competence the importance of some of them and the significance of some notices were not immediately apparent. In the course of revision I have removed some deficiencies but a fundamental reconsideration of the whole correspondence is impracticable for me.

Some notes are provisional for another reason. While at work on the correspondence I have consulted freely other parts of Locke's manuscript heritage, but I have not made a systematic survey of everything that has been accessible to me, and some part of the heritage has been inaccessible or not readily accessible. The project now on foot for the complete publication of the heritage, of which this edition of the correspondence forms a part, will include miscellaneous and personal memoranda and papers. As they are published some of my notes will prove erroneous or inadequate. While some of them could be corrected or improved by further work on the manuscripts the resultant gains would not compensate for the requisite expenditure of time.

# ACKNOWLEDGEMENTS

FOR permission to publish and use the letters and other documents belonging to them I am indebted to the custodians of libraries and of the manuscript collections of other institutions, and to private owners; to many of them I am indebted also for facsimiles of one kind or another. Above all to the Bodleian Library, the holder of the finest and largest collection of manuscript and printed materials for Locke; further, to the Public Record Office in London, which holds as a component of the Shaftesbury papers part of Locke's literary heritage; to the Amsterdam University Library, which has by devolution Philippus van Limborch's correspondence; to the British Library, which has the majority of Locke's letters to Nicolas Toinard as well as other letters and papers of his; to the Royal Library in Copenhagen, where the bulk of J. G. Grævius's correspondence has come to rest; for permission to reprint sixty-five letters to the Carl and Lily Pforzheimer Foundation, Inc., on behalf of the Carl H. Pforzheimer Library; and for twenty-seven letters to the Pierpont Morgan Library.

For smaller holdings or single letters to the following:

Libraries, institutions, and societies: the Boston (Massachusetts) Public Library; the Staatsbibliothek Preussischer Kulturbesitz, Berlin; the Henry E. Huntington Library; His Grace the Lord Archbishop of Canterbury and the Trustees of the Lambeth Palace Library; the Marciana; the Moscow State Historical Museum; the Newberry Library; the Henry W. and Albert A. Berg Collection of the New York Public Library, Astor, Lenox, and Tilden Foundations; the Bank of England; the Royal Society; Colonial Williamsburg Inc., Williamsburg, Virginia; the Historical Society of Pennsylvania; the Museum of the History of Science, Oxford; the Victoria and Albert Museum.

Universities and colleges: Basel; the William Andrews Clark Library of the University of California, Los Angeles; King's College, Cambridge; the Houghton Library, Harvard; Leiden; the Governing Body of Christ Church, Oxford; the Robert H. Taylor Collection, Princeton; the Manuscripts Division, Department of Special Collections, Stanford University Libraries; the Hanley Collection, the Humanities Research Center Library, University of Texas at Austin; the Waller Collection, Uppsala.

County Record Offices: Berkshire (deposits); Derbyshire; East Riding (deposit); East Sussex; Kent (deposit); Somerset.

Private owners: N. Forbes Adams, Esq.; the Marquess of Bath; the Marquess of Downshire; Mrs. Donald Hyde; the Earl of Lovelace; Dr. Paul Mellon; Dr. James Marshall Osborn; Dr. G. K. Woodgate.

I am indebted to the British Academy for grants from the Pilgrim Trust Fund towards the cost of transcription, translation, and typing.

I learnt from Professor Thomas W. Copeland, first in discussion and later by the example of the *Check-list* of Burke's correspondence (1955), how to record the individual letters in Locke's correspondence; though I adopted a different plan, closer to that of Mme Labrousse's *Inventaire* of Bayle's correspondence (1961), it was thanks to him that I was able from the outset to keep control of the texts.

For help with transcription of the letters I am indebted principally to Mr. Philip Long, Mr. G. F. T. Jones, and the late A. S. Treves; in all cases I have checked their transcripts. I am also indebted for transcripts of single letters whose originals I have not seen to Mr. Ivor P. Collis, County Archivist of Somerset, and Mr. N. Higson, County Archivist of the East Riding.

The translations of almost all the Latin letters and passages, and of the one Greek letter, were made by the late Professor Walter M. Edwards; he provided also many valuable remarks on them, and explanations of the occasional pieces of Hebrew. In revising the translations I was helped greatly by Mr. R. H. Barrow, who translated no. 390A. Dr. Graham Speake translated no. *1024A*. The Dutch letter, no. *1024*, was translated by Dr. Pieter Seuren; Sir George Clark helped me to revise it. In all cases I am responsible for the published versions.

The typing of the transcripts and sub-editorial work were done by the late Mrs. Dorinda Kirby and by Dr. Isabel Kenrick.

Mrs. Kirby consulted books for me in the Bodleian Library and rendered other services for me there; Mrs. Graham Speake has latterly done the same work. Without their help it would have been impossible for me to prepare this edition in any reasonable length of time.

I have done much of my work in the London Library. It has

provided open access to the primary books in almost every subject that crops up in the correspondence; very frequently it has provided the particular books, and editions of books, requisite for precision in the elucidation of the notices. Its *Subject-index* (1909–55) has proved invaluable; it has enabled me to pursue inquiries, and sometimes to perceive subjects of inquiry, where without it I should have been at a standstill. I am indebted to many booksellers, and especially to Mr. Arnold Muirhead, for providing me with copies of indispensable books, and to the Bibliothèque Nationale and the Newberry Library for microfilm of a large part of Nicolas Toinard's correspondence and of Esther Masham's letter-book.

I must express my gratitude to librarians, archivists, and custodians in the various institutions where I have worked for their helpfulness and kindliness to an exacting scholar; and to those who have answered my inquiries for letters of Locke or for other information. I must name in particular Mr. Philip Long, who for many years was in charge of the Lovelace Collection in the Bodleian and who is the author of its invaluable *Summary Catalogue* (1959).

Of other books the most important for the correspondence has been *The Library of John Locke*, by John Harrison and Peter Laslett (1965; second edition 1971); it has led me into many parts of Locke's literary environment. I have profited by very many of the books and articles on Locke that I have read or examined. They vary in quality; many are good; a few, the reverse. What matters for an editor of documents is the contents of a book and not its quality. Anything may be grist that comes to his mill. My judgement and my sense of obligation are, or should be, independent of one another. So, whatever my opinions about their performances, I recognize my debts to many of my fellow workers in this field.

For most of the eighteen years during which I have been engaged with it, Locke's correspondence has been almost without interruption either uppermost in my mind or within easy call. As a result I have discussed it, or matters arising from or related to it, with a large number of persons: the scholars in this and related fields; students in various stages of their training; friends; and am indebted to them for help of one sort or another, for information, correction, or suggestion. It is impossible for me to name everyone; more especially the various persons who have answered my questions about the possible existence of letters in their ownership or charge, or who have called my attention to letters and texts which might otherwise have escaped me.

I am more especially indebted for frequent consultation, help, and information, to the late Rosalie Colie, Mr. John Harrison, Mr. Peter Laslett, Mr. R. C. Latham, Professor Peter Nidditch, Professor Caroline Robbins, Dr. Robert Shackleton, Mr. J. S. G. Simmons, the late Dr. C. Louise Thijssen-Schoute, Professor Robert Voitle, Dr. W. von Leyden, and Professor John W. Yolton.

I have received special information or other help from, or consulted occasionally, the late C. Kingsley Adams (portraits of Locke), Dr. G. Ahlström (the Lapland picture), Mr. Raymond G. Astbury (Stationers' Company monopoly of the classics), Mlle C. Avignon, Mr. J. L. Axtell (education), Mr. Alan Bell (the Saltoun papers, etc.), Mr. John C. Biddle (Locke and religion), Mr. E. G.W. Bill (Christ Church, etc.), Professor C. R. Boxer (voyages), Professor J. S. and Mrs. Bromley, Mr. Barry M. Burrows, Dr. Herbert Cahoon, Miss Margaret Candee (Toland), Professor Leland H. Carlson, Mr. W. R. Chadwick (Wycherley), Sir George N. Clark, Dr. Allison Coudert (F. M. van Helmont), Professor Maurice Cranston, the late Professor Gladys Dickinson, Mr. John Dunn (the Sanford manuscripts, etc.), Mr. Roger Ellis, Mr. F. G. Emmison (Bexwells), Mlle C.-E. Engel, Mr. Robert G. Frank, jnr., Mr. Jocelyn Gibb, Professor Nigel Glendinning (*Don Quixote*), Dr. Friedrich Gorissen (Cleves), Professor Janice L. Gorn (education, etc.), Professor K. H. D. Haley (the first Shaftesbury, etc.), Professor A. Rupert Hall (Oldenburg), Mr. Roland Hall, Professor Ragnhild Hatton, Mrs. Patricia M. Henson, Mr. P. Hepworth (the Rebecca Collier letter), Dr. W. J. von Hoboken (Guenellon), Dr. R. W. Hunt, the late William A. Jackson (Locke manuscripts at Harvard), Mr. Nicholas Jolley (Thomas Burnett of Kemney), Mr. Patrick Kelly (Locke and the recoinage), Sir Geoffrey Keynes (the medical notices), Miss L. M. Labowsky (the Marciana letter; through Mr. Long), Dr. W. Lamont, the late Professor Douglas McKie, Miss M. Macleod (editions of the Bible), Mr. J. C. Maxwell, Mr. A. Taylor Milne, Mr. David R. J. Neave, Mr. D. G. Neill (Locke bibliography), Mr. J. H. P. Pafford (the Goldsmiths' Library manuscripts), Dr. L. F. Powell, Professor Jacob M. Price (London merchants), Miss B. J. Rahn (Sir Robert Peyton, etc.), Professor Patrick Romanell (Locke and medicine), Professor Nicolai Rubinstein, Miss Margaret Rumbold (Pierre Coste), Mr.

Henry Schankula, the late Dr. J. F. Scott (Newton), Mr. Anthony W. Shipps (Pheidon), Mr. Frank T. Smallwood (the St. John family), M. and Mme John Storms, Mrs. M. A. Thomson, Mr. Willis Van Devanter (Locke's library, etc.), Mr. Peter Walne, Mr. John Wilders (*Hudibras*), Professor Neal Wood.

E. S. de B.

*London*, 1974

# CONTENTS

# INTRODUCTION

## GENERAL SURVEY OF THE CORRESPONDENCE

LOCKE'S extant correspondence consists of about 3,650 items. Of these about a thousand are letters from him; most of the rest are letters to him; there are a few miscellaneous documents and letters between third parties. Of the letters from him about 880 are letters sent; about a hundred are drafts for letters; texts not at present available, fragments, and some miscellaneous items bring the present total number of items emanating from him to 1,023. About 350 persons are participants in the correspondence, mainly for single or very few letters or for small exchanges, but three exchanges each rise to above 200 letters. Most of the letters are in English, but several hundred are in French or Latin or a combination of the two languages; there are a few in Dutch and one in Greek. The letters range in date from 1652 to 1704. The survival of those addressed to him depended in part on their interest or importance to him, in part on his movements; that of those written by him, on the recipients' habits and the chances of preservation of whatever papers they kept. The relative number of surviving letters to or from him increases from the beginning of 1687; towards the end of his life he kept a large proportion of those that he received. Most of the letters are from England; several hundred, from France and the Netherlands; a few, from America, the East Indies, and elsewhere.

The correspondence provides evidence for Locke's biography: for the course of events in it and for the social, intellectual, and moral environments in which he lived. He belonged in time to the phase of the culture of Western Europe which Paul Hazard called the crisis of European thought; he was a citizen of what Bayle called the République des Lettres; in Locke's own rendering, the Commonwealth of Learning. The expansion of Western Europe from the fifteenth century onwards had promoted the growth of the educated laity. The correspondence illustrates the social and economic circumstances of this class, and some incidents in its growth; the discoveries resulting from, and the scientific and technical advances requisite for, the expansion; and their impact on the conduct of thought and ultimately on religious belief.

Locke's interest in and contributions to this advancement emerge in his published and unpublished writings, his extant correspondence, his journals and notebooks, and his library. These materials have their various limitations. The particular weakness of the correspondence is that it fails—and, even if everything were preserved, almost inevitably would fail—to give a complete account of Locke's relations with his friends.[1] Where there was personal intercourse there would be at most only occasional letters; in such cases our knowledge must depend on incidental notices in letters between Locke and other correspondents or in his other papers or in extraneous materials. It is impracticable to give a general account of the extant correspondence without some reference to the lost letters and to the fallow periods when no letters were written.

Many of the letters are of minimal interest as individuals. They bear on Locke only indirectly; they relate mainly to his time, and not so much to its distinctive characteristics or outstanding developments as to the ordinary circumstances of life. The tenant farmers and cottagers on Locke's property in Somerset; the carrier services to Oates; the ways in which savings can be invested: their analogues are to be found most readily in naturalistic fiction. Locke from 1689 onwards lives the orderly life of the lesser English gentry from the seventeenth century to the early nineteenth, the daily life of the House Beautiful or Longbourn or Hartfield, as yet untouched by the Industrial Revolution, a life in which the differences between wealth and poverty, between education and illiteracy, are softened by neighbourliness and charity. It is to the accompaniment of this synthesis that the letters possessing greater individual interest are to be read.

The English letters in the correspondence belong to the age of Dryden. As a young man Locke read, in English translations, the letters in the French romances and probably those of Balzac.[2] These could serve as models for complimentary and sententious

[1] The exchange between Locke and William Molyneux is virtually complete (the unprinted passages amount to little) and the two men did not meet until shortly before it ended. But there were several intermediaries to carry oral messages between them and to describe the one to the other. There were further their common culture, now largely lost to us, and their experiences in regard to the great political and military events of their time.

[2] Jean-Louis Guez, sieur de Balzac: no. 66.

letters; Balzac in addition would teach him to write with point. For more serious letters clarity and precision were requisite, qualities that Locke was later to find indispensable for his published works; on suitable occasions he indulged in a liking for dialect words and pungent phrases. His correspondents belonged to various social and intellectual levels; the older writers of the earliest letters are separated by some seventy years from the younger writers of the latest. Some of the writers are old-fashioned or provincial or ill-educated; some are careless; but the better-educated in general show the same concern as Locke for effective communication. There is also a noticeable improvement in the orthography of writers who reach manhood about 1690 over that of their elders.

The correspondence opens with Locke's family life in Somerset and his studentship at Christ Church in Oxford. Many items in this early period are problematical. There are many drafts, and the existence of a draft provides no assurance that a letter was sent, or, if one was sent, that it resembled the draft. In many cases the writers of letters and the persons for whom drafts were intended are unnamed or indicated only by initials or fanciful designations. Many items are undated or incompletely dated. There are plenty of questionable allusions and unidentifiable persons in the texts. As a result of these factors the treatment here of many items prior to June 1661 is constructive or conjectural. I have set out as far as may be the reasons for my decisions and explanations so that readers may test them for themselves.

The Locke family in Somerset was armigerous but belonged socially to the middle rank of the countryside. Locke's father, also John Locke, was an attorney; his uncle Peter Locke was probably a tanner. His father owned some land in Pensford, some six miles south-east of Bristol. On his death in 1661 it was inherited by Locke and was managed for him by Peter Locke, then by Peter's son-in-law William Stratton, and finally by an attorney Cornelius Lyde. In his earliest letters to his father Locke seems unduly submissive for a man nearly twenty years old. This has disappeared in his succeeding extant letters, dating from 1656 and later years; Locke was still an affectionate and dutiful son, but writes as a friend to a friend. He visited Somerset on several occasions between 1655 and 1661 and kept in touch with the family connections and friends; notably with John Strachey, a man two years younger than himself, of higher social standing, and with some legal training. Where Locke's other Somerset friends are apt to be bucolic and drop out of the correspondence after a year or two, Strachey had more acquaintance than Locke with the world at large. He was his principal non-academic friend until his death in 1675.

Locke's father served in the Civil War as a captain under Alexander Popham, one of the leading men in Somerset. Thanks to him Locke was admitted to Westminster School. From there he went in 1652 to Christ Church in Oxford. He corresponded with students[1] and young graduates, among them William Godolphin, the future diplomatist. He made friends also with men from other colleges, including Gabriel Towerson, with whom he discussed the Law of Nature, and two men who were to contribute later to his fortunes, David Thomas, who became a physician and settled at Salisbury, and James Tyrrell, a grandson of Archbishop Ussher. Locke himself studied medicine; he appears to have made some progress by 1660; and it may have been through this that he became acquainted with Robert Boyle the scientist. About the beginning of 1659 he was introduced to a household of fugitives from Ireland then residing at Black Hall in St. Giles outside the North Gate of Oxford. With one of them, Elinor Parry, he engaged in a protracted and abortive love-affair; she came again into his life in 1689 as Mrs. Hawkshaw, again a fugitive from Ireland.

It is questionable whether social intercourse such as Black Hall provided would have been available for young dons in Oxford before the Civil War or for many years after the Restoration; as among the resident members of the university only heads of houses and professors were allowed to marry, young women of suitable standing may have been scarce. Locke and several of his friends were welcome visitors to the house. They used nicknames, Scribelia and others; Locke may already have been Atticus. This may have been in imitation of the French *précieuses*. The best-known English group of the kind is that associated with Katherine Philips, 'the matchless Orinda'. For Locke and his companions the object was probably to make manners less formal; Mrs. Parry could be addressed as 'Scribelia' but not as 'Elinor'. A few years later Locke, Dr. and Mrs. Thomas, Tyrrell, and others were using

[1] The students of Christ Church correspond roughly to the fellows and scholars of other colleges. See the note on Christ Church, pp. 3–4 of this volume.

names derived from the novels of Charles Sorel. Later occurrences suggest that Locke liked using nicknames in this way.

At Christ Church for two or three years after the Restoration Locke had a number of pupils. Their parents' letters show what was expected of him as tutor; those of two of them, Sir Charles Berkeley and John Alford, the affection that he elicited from them. But to retain his studentship he would ordinarily be required to take holy orders. Strachey advised him against doing so. His Somerset property did not yield an adequate income. He was averse to practising medicine. Late in 1665 when an envoy was sent to the Elector of Brandenburg at Cleves Locke, probably through the good offices of William Godolphin, was appointed his secretary. He sent political news to Godolphin, narrations of his experiences to Strachey, and to Boyle an account of religious toleration as he witnessed it at Cleves. He probably owed to Boyle his conviction that toleration was desirable, and to Cleves his conviction that it was practicable.

Returning to Oxford in February 1666 Locke refused another diplomatic appointment. If he was still uncertain about his future livelihood he was relieved from anxiety in June, when David Thomas introduced him to Lord Ashley, the future first earl of Shaftesbury. It was probably through his influence that Locke obtained a dispensation enabling him to retain his studentship at Christ Church without taking orders. He joined Shaftesbury's household in 1667, serving as man of affairs and physician, and ranking about on a level with the chaplain, the steward, and the countess's principal attendants. Shaftesbury is generally envisaged almost exclusively as a ruthless politician, guilty above all others of the blood of the innocent victims of the Popish Plot: if not himself engaged in treason, a friend or associate of future conspirators and rebels. Locke's correspondence shows other sides of his character, his interest in his family and property, the love and loyalty of his third wife and of the principal members of his household. Beyond this: if the reign of Charles II is to be regarded as a duel between the king and Shaftesbury the king was the immediate victor but the future was Shaftesbury's. His aims included the limited monarchy, religious toleration, the establishment of London as a great financial and commercial centre, overseas expansion; Locke's later correspondence shows them all in process of achievement.

Shaftesbury—still Lord Ashley—was one of the original proprietors of the colony of Carolina. In 1669 he prepared the Fundamental Constitutions of Carolina, Locke acting as his amanuensis and assisting him probably with the wording and perhaps with some part of the matter. Locke seems from this time to have acted as his secretary for Carolina; he was concerned also in some of his other colonizing ventures. In 1672 Shaftesbury became president of a newly instituted Council of Trade and Foreign Plantations. When a vacancy occurred in the autumn of 1673 he appointed Locke as secretary. This might appear to provide permanently for him, but Shaftesbury fell from favour in November of that year and the Council was abolished in December 1674.

Locke was elected a fellow of the Royal Society in 1668. He seems to have taken little part in its activities. Old friendships continued: with John Strachey, with David Thomas, who was now settled in Salisbury, and with James Tyrrell. The then Lady Ashley (Shaftesbury) was a first cousin of the countess of Northumberland, the wife of Josceline, the eleventh earl. Locke became a friend of Margaret Beavis, later Mrs. Blomer, one of Lady Northumberland's principal attendants, and through her of Dr. John Mapletoft and Mrs. Anne Grigg. Mapletoft was a physician; in that capacity he helped Locke with advice when Lady Northumberland was ill. The friendship apparently came to an end about 1679. Mrs. Grigg was the widow of a clergyman who was probably a nephew of Peter Locke's wife. Left with an infant son, she supplemented her small means by employment apparently chiefly as supervisor of young children. Very devout, she attached herself in 1689 to the non-jurors and acted as an intermediary for the deprived bishops; she was saddened when her son decided to take orders in the Established Church. Despite the differences in their opinions she and Locke were fond of one another; he might think her piety misdirected but had to appreciate her clear and observant mind. Shaftesbury's household provided Locke with a transient friendship with Thomas Stringer his steward. Locke's acquaintance with Edward Clarke may have been due to Clarke's attaching himself to Shaftesbury; alternatively it may have been due to Clarke's marriage to Mary Jepp, with whose mother Locke called cousins; her father was a half-brother of John Strachey.

During these years Locke's health was deteriorating. Late in 1675 he went in quest of good air to Montpellier. There or in

Provence he found other English residents and among them Denis Grenville, William Charleton (an alias; his real surname was Courten), and Thomas Herbert, the future eighth earl of Pembroke. Grenville was a divine; he was indebted to his aristocratic birth for preferments for which he was not suited by character or ability; and was now in France on account of his debts. Locke wrote for him what are in effect essays on moral subjects. Charleton was living abroad under this assumed name on account of a contested heritage. He brought together natural history and other objects of virtu, forming a collection that was acquired after his death by Sir Hans Sloane and so became the nucleus of the British Museum. Locke helped him with this. The absence of letters between the two men after 1688 does not imply a termination of the friendship; by that time Charleton was living in London and there would be opportunities of meeting that would suffice for it. Herbert was perhaps a forlorn young man; his elder brother, the seventh earl, was notoriously hard-drinking and violent; he would look to Locke for comfort and advice. Locke found in him excellent character and great intellectual ability. It was natural that he should appeal to him in 1684 when he was deprived of his studentship and that he should dedicate to him the *Essay concerning Human Understanding*. Despite the absence of letters the friendship continued until Locke's death. It is in respect of his relations with Pembroke that the limitations of the extant correspondence, and of correspondence inherently, bear most grievously.

Thomas Stringer kept Locke informed of events in England. Early in 1677 Locke learnt that Sir John Banks, a London businessman, wanted him to take charge of his son Caleb, who was to spend some time in France; Shaftesbury himself wrote asking Locke to do so. Locke went to Paris to meet the young man, and for the next two years received frequent letters from Sir John, telling him what his son might or might not do. In Paris at this time Henri Justel, a Protestant, with the assistance of Nicolas Toinard, a Catholic, held at his house gatherings, probably weekly, of men interested in all branches of science, theoretical or applied, without distinction of creed or nationality. Locke was admitted and established a lasting friendship with Toinard. The latter had one great ambition, to construct a harmony of the Gospels. All the resources of scholarship, in every relevant field, were to contribute. Toinard printed a version in 1678 for his private use, but was dissatisfied with it; he tried continually to improve it but always found openings for fresh improvements, and at the same time had too many other interests, especially in voyages and the ancillary sciences; the harmony was not published until after his death. Locke valued the friendship highly; it was he who reopened the correspondence in 1697 after an intermission due to eight years of war. To Toinard probably Locke owed his introduction to the Parisian scientists at the Observatoire. Justel wrote him news of the Commonwealth of Learning until 1681, when he sought refuge in England. This friendship apparently ended in 1685.

In the autumn of 1678 Locke made a second tour of France, this time with Caleb Banks. Their banker at Lyons, Jacques Selapris, provided Locke with a servant, a Swiss boy, Sylvester Brounower. With one short interruption Syl remained in Locke's service until 1696, when he married and was appointed a clerk to the newly established Commission for Trade and Plantations. From 1684 or earlier he acted as Locke's amanuensis. There is only one letter from him prior to his retirement; occasional notices show Locke's and his friends' regard for him.

Locke returned to London with Caleb Banks and Syl on 30 April 1679. For a time his correspondence was mainly with his French friends or with men whom he had met in France, the last including Dr. John Covel, sometime chaplain to the Levant Company in Constantinople and to become in 1688 Master of Christ's College in Cambridge. Among old friends there were Dr. Thomas and Mrs. Grigg, who spent about a year in France with her son and another boy in 1680 and 1681, and informed Locke about the increasing maltreatment of the Huguenots. In Somerset Peter Locke was handing over the management of Locke's land to his son-in-law William Stratton. At Oxford several friends had looked after Locke's property; now Dr. John Fell, Dean of Christ Church and bishop of Oxford, consulted him about the University's press.

In 1680 and the next three years Locke was in close contact with James Tyrrell; he visited him frequently at his house at Oakley near Oxford; each of them composed a refutation of Sir Robert Filmer's *Patriarcha*; and they combined to controvert Dr. Edward Stillingfleet's attacks on the Nonconformists. The closeness was a result of the political circumstances of the time rather than of an affinity of character. Tyrrell was eager to find proofs of opinions that he had formed without much inquiry; he was a devoted Whig and when he wrote medieval history it had to prove that the Whigs were always in the right. He prided himself too much on being Archbishop Ussher's grandson; he overrated his ability; he was officious, tiresome, and pettish. Locke treated him badly. He accepted important services from him and gave too little in return; he did not allow sufficiently for Tyrrell's weaknesses. The long gap between 1696 and 1701 in the extant correspondence does not imply a complete breach of intercourse. Tyrrell perhaps became more diffident; there were fewer opportunities for him to irritate Locke; old liking resumed and he succeeded in coaxing him into a good temper when in 1704 Locke was hesitating whether to make his second gift of books to the Bodleian Library.

Early in 1681 when he was lying ill at Oakley Locke was requested by Shaftesbury to find accommodation for him for the parliament that was shortly to be held in Oxford. There are few other traces in the extant correspondence of the great political crisis of the year; there was little need for news of it in private letters; when Locke was out of London newspapers and newsletters would keep him informed. In August Shaftesbury fell dangerously ill and Locke was summoned to London. It was there probably that he became acquainted with Damaris Cudworth, the future Lady Masham.

She was the daughter of Dr. Ralph Cudworth, the Cambridge Platonist. Now nearly 22 years old, she was lodging in London perhaps on account of her health. From the start she used the nickname Philoclea; Locke, at any rate when they exchanged verses, was Damon. Flattered by his attention, she was eager to discuss the Platonists' views with him; she consulted him also about her family affairs. In 1685 she married Sir Francis Masham, a widower with eight sons and one daughter; she bore him a son, Francis Cudworth Masham. From 1691 she and Sir Francis provided Locke with a home at Oates in Essex. No letters from her after 1688 survive; his letters to her are represented only by drafts and fragmentary copies. The account of him which she wrote for Jean Le Clerc shows how great her affection for him had become by the time of his death.

In the winter of 1681 she appears to have lodged in the same house as Edward Clarke, the husband of Locke's cousin Mary Jepp. Clarke had an estate at Chipley near Taunton in Somerset. He had studied law. He was a Whig but was not as yet engaged in politics. Shaftesbury appointed him a trustee for himself, his countess, and his grandson, the future third earl of Shaftesbury. Locke may have been acquainted with him by 1675 but it was not until 1682 that they became close friends. Locke was concerned about Clarke's ill health and his children's welfare. When, as a sequel to Shaftesbury's death early in 1683, Locke decided to go abroad, he entrusted the superintendence of his affairs and the collection and remittance of money to Clarke. James Tyrrell took into safe-keeping his books and other goods in Oxford.

Locke went to the Netherlands. At Amsterdam, where he settled in September, he found Pieter Guenellon, a physician of French parentage, whom he had met in Paris in 1678. Guenellon was a member of a 'collegie', a group of seven friends meeting for study, all of them physicians except one, the divine and theologian Philippus van Limborch. They were all Remonstrants in religion, followers of Arminius who rejected Calvinistic dogmas about predestination. From the start the Remonstrants held Erasmian views on toleration; in their early days they had suffered persecution; now, although they differed from them in their views on the Trinity, they went so far as to admit the Socinians to their communion. Van Limborch had corresponded with Cudworth; the English Latitudinarians valued his teaching. He and Locke became friends; it was for him that Locke wrote the *Epistola de Tolerantia.* The friendship continued until Locke's death and when van Limborch's son came to England to seek a livelihood as a merchant Locke was active on his behalf.

It was probably through van Limborch that Locke met Jean Le Clerc, a fugitive from Genevan orthodoxy who had found a haven in Amsterdam. He ought to have given his whole life to scholarship but was forced to earn his living as a man of letters and a lecturer. He was disappointed that the world would not take scholarship, and particularly his own scholarship, at his valuation; and, while he was quick to tear the work of other scholars to pieces, he regarded any questioning of his own work as an outcome of personal malignity. His letters to Locke do him an injustice. They are the complaints of a man who has accepted his lot while believing that he deserves something better. He is to be judged by his works. He is not among the greatest scholars but, apart from some failures due to his overrating his powers, his works are noteworthy for their quality and quantity, the products of devotion to learning and unceasing industry.

While Locke was in the Netherlands he and Edward Clarke in their correspondence frequently designated persons by nicknames, initials, or descriptive or allusive words or phrases. Tyrrell and Dr. Thomas commonly used designations of the kind; so little survives of Clarke's correspondence before September 1683 that it is impossible to say whether or not he used them. In January 1685, immediately after Locke had learnt of his expulsion from Christ Church, he called Clarke Mr. Somerton; although the letters were addressed to Mr. Clarke the designation continued in use until Locke's return to England in 1689. These designations appear to have been in use almost exclusively for friends; men such as Mr. Stratton were always given their surnames. This private nomenclature does not seem to have been adopted as a safeguard against espionage or interference by the English government.[1] The principal reason for its use, apart from the fact that Locke and at any rate some of his friends liked it, seems to have been that it would be a safeguard if letters should go astray; if the persons mentioned were not identifiable they could not be the subjects of discussion. This seems to be the reason why, when Locke wrote to Clarke in April 1689, it was 'my cousin Somerton' whom he wanted to be appointed Auditor to the queen.

Locke spent much of his time working on the *Essay concerning Human Understanding*; he was also engaged in writing to Edward and Mrs. Clarke letters and instructions about the care and education of their children, materials which he later adapted and published as *Some Thoughts concerning Education.* At the end of 1684 he was deprived of his studentship at Christ Church. About the same time he moved to Utrecht, where he became acquainted with J. G. Grævius, the classical scholar. In May 1685, when Monmouth was preparing his invasion, the English envoy to the States General applied for the expulsion or arrest of a number of English or Scots

[1] In February 1684 Tyrrell addressed a letter for Locke to 'Mr. John Lynne' (no. *775*). Lynne was an agent for Clarke in London. Tyrrell used his name again for Locke's on 20 January 1686 (no. *842*). Dr. Thomas used it on 26 December 1686; Tyrrell, writing on the same day, addresses his letter to Locke (nos. *888–9*). Thomas used Lynne again on 17 July 1687 (no. *946*). The name does not occur in other extant addresses. Its use seems to be fortuitous. Clarke uses the name 'Pieter de la Nove' on 25 January 1687 (no. *900*); Locke may have thought that he was in danger at that time, but there is nothing in the extant correspondence to show that he asked Clarke to use a false name.

Lady Masham and some other correspondents addressed their letters simply 'For Mr. Locke'. Presumably an agent in London sent them to Locke in the Netherlands, perhaps in packages addressed to his own correspondents.

conspirators or rebels resident in the United Provinces; Locke was included in the list. He went for shelter to his Remonstrant friends in Amsterdam; he then revisited Cleves; and then returned to Amsterdam and Utrecht. In the summer of 1686 there were some English visitors: Dr. Thomas; Sir Walter Yonge and his brother-in-law and sister, Richard and Mrs. Duke; and John Freke. Yonge and Freke were friends of Edward Clarke and former associates of Shaftesbury; like Clarke they had been detained during Monmouth's rebellion. Mrs. Duke wrote to Locke about her travels and her health; Freke, waywardly and warily about Locke's affairs, about their common friends, and about his desire to emigrate to Pennsylvania. The increasing political tension is illustrated by Tyrrell's accounts of the proceedings against Magdalen College in Oxford; the feeling aroused by it, by Mrs. Grigg in a letter written at the time of the trial of the Seven Bishops.

At the end of 1686 a fresh alarm drove Locke from Utrecht. Two months later he found a lodging with Benjamin Furly, an English merchant in Rotterdam; he spent most of his time there until his return to England in 1689. He was perhaps introduced to Furly by Freke or Yonge. Novelty captivated Furly, whether in thought or religion or politics. He had been a Quaker but no rules, however slight, could bind him. His house was open to speculators in religion and innovators in politics; he had received Algernon Sidney formerly; now he was befriending Baron Franciscus Mercurius van Helmont, the propounder of a new system of metempsychosis. Locke and Furly were members, probably founders, of the Lantern, a club of friends holding meetings for discussion. Late in 1687 Furly obtained control of a report of the proceedings of the Inquisition at Toulouse between 1307 and 1323. The dragonnades made the report immediately relevant. It was entrusted for publication to van Limborch, who prefixed to it an account of the Inquisition in which he demonstrated the evil of all religious persecution.

Locke's sojourn in Rotterdam was broken by a visit to Amsterdam at the end of 1687. As he completed drafts of the four books of the *Essay* he sent copies of them to Clarke. He was able to send him a copy of that for the fourth book in December 1686, and perhaps sent him an improved version some weeks later. He also prepared an abridgement. Le Clerc translated this into French and Locke came to Amsterdam to superintend its printing for Le Clerc's periodical the *Bibliotheque universelle*; there was also an offprint which he dedicated to Pembroke. On this visit he tried to find a bookseller who would publish the report of the Inquisition in Toulouse. In 1688 Locke was visited by Dr. Thomas and, later, by Edward and Mrs. Clarke and their daughter Betty; on both occasions he accompanied his visitors to Amsterdam and so had further opportunities of seeing his friends there.

It was perhaps through Furly that Locke met Lord Mordaunt, the future earl of Monmouth and third earl of Peterborough, the general. Mordaunt was vigorous and outspoken, fiery and unstable. At this time he was in the Netherlands urging William of Orange to invade England. Lady Mordaunt was a badly educated and raffish court lady. In her company Locke sailed to England on the ship that brought Princess Mary to England. Locke owed to Mordaunt's patronage his appointment as a Commissioner of Appeals in Excise. There were other acts of kindness. The friendship lasted until Locke's death.

When he returned to London there were old friendships to be resumed and new acquaintances to be made. When leaving England in 1683 he had entrusted a small part of his possessions to Rabsy Smithsby. Now he went to lodge with her for a time; later she prepared chocolate for his use and made shirts and caps for him. About September 1690 Locke moved to the house of Robert Pawling. Locke knew him at Oxford where he had been in trade as a mercer; he was mayor in 1679–80. He was well informed, a Whig, and anti-clerical. In 1694 he was appointed Comptroller of the new Stamp Office. Though after 1690 Locke was spending more and more of his time at Oates he kept his London lodging probably until his death. Pawling attended to some of Locke's private affairs. He looked after his clothing and watch, and paid his tax as Commissioner of Appeals; he could also do Locke's business with Locke's friends and had sufficient standing to be received by Lord Pembroke. At a lower level, mainly for the purchase and dispatch of household goods, Locke relied on his first cousin John Bonville, a pewterer in Houndsditch. When Sylvester Brounower settled in London he also attended to Locke's needs. A kinsman, Samuel Locke, an East India merchant, sent him presents of wine. Edward Clarke supervised his Somerset property. The brothers Awnsham and John Churchill, the booksellers, acted as his bankers. In his last years his cousin Peter King managed his investments.

There were new friends to be made. He heard about Somers, the future Lord Chancellor, from Freke in 1686 or 1687. They met first in 1689. For a time Locke was Somers's political mentor, advising him on his duty as a member of parliament. In 1693 when Somers was promoted to be Lord Keeper Locke apparently fancied that he, Somers, Freke, and Clarke, might form a junto. Somers could scarcely permit this but consulted Locke on specific questions and notably on the state of the currency in 1694 and the recoinage of 1696–9; it was at his request that Locke wrote *Further Considerations concerning Raising the Value of Money*; and it was probably owing to him that Locke was appointed a Commissioner for Trade and Plantations in 1696.

Locke and Newton may have met early in 1675; they are unlikely to have done so at any other time before the Revolution. Locke perhaps wrote the account of the *Principia* that appeared in the *Bibliotheque universelle* for March 1688. But he was neither a mathematician nor a physicist; what he and Newton discussed principally was the text of the Bible. Newton wrote his paper on the two corruptions in the New Testament for Locke; Locke submitted to him his paraphrases of St. Paul's epistles. Newton also appealed to Locke during his illness in 1692 and 1693.

Locke may have met William Popple at Bordeaux in 1677 or 1678. Popple was for many years a wine-merchant there. He returned to London in 1688. His views on religious matters were similar to Locke's. Both were concerned to defend Christianity against Deism; for both it was a rational and moralistic Christianity. Popple translated Locke's *Epistola de Tolerantia* into English; he agreed with Locke about the limits of toleration, but was more outspoken in his claim for liberty. He was a friend of Furly and the third earl of Shaftesbury. He was a leading member of a club founded by Locke in 1692 for the discussion of religion and morals. He apparently supervised the publication of Locke's *Some Thoughts concerning Education*, and perhaps that of other books by Locke. When the Commission for Trade and Plantations was established in 1696 Locke was apparently concerned in securing Popple's appointment as its secretary. A few letters from him show Locke's great interest in the Commission's work.

One of Locke's tasks while he was a member of the first earl of Shaftesbury's household was to oversee the health and education of Shaftesbury's grandson, the future third earl, the philosopher. The boy had a difficult life. He was cared for by his grandparents while his brothers and sisters remained with their parents. His father was a weakling physically and the son inherited a poor physique. No love was lost between his mother and the dowager countess. After the first earl's death his schoolfellows made the grandson pay for the grandfather's misdeeds. Relief came in 1687 when at the age of sixteen he was allowed to travel on the Continent. He visited Locke at Rotterdam and made friends with Furly. He returned to England in the summer of 1689 and reattached himself to Locke. Though ultimately he rejected Locke's views he found in his and Lady Masham's company at Oates a sympathy and serenity of which he had known so little.

Locke visited Lady Masham at Oates in the summer of 1690. His health would not bear the London winters. In January 1691 she received him as a lodger. He spent increasingly longer periods at Oates, and in his last years remained there altogether. He participated in the family life, taking a special interest in Lady Masham's son Francis Cudworth Masham. Sir Francis Masham was a grandson of a first cousin of Oliver Cromwell. In the reigns of William III and Queen Anne relations of Cromwell are noticeable in English political life. It is impossible to say how far the kinsfolk were cohesive socially; it is certain, however, that Locke's acquaintance with some of them sprang from his association with Sir Francis. The most prominent of them in the correspondence is Martha Lockhart—by courtesy Mrs. or Madame Lockhart—a great-niece of Cromwell and one of Queen Mary's Bedchamber Women. She in her turn, as a daughter of a Scotsman, introduced him to, or advanced his acquaintance with, several of her fellow countrymen, including Thomas Burnett of Kemney, the friend of Leibniz, and James Johnstoun, 'Secretary Johnstoun'.

When Locke was at Leiden in 1684 he met a student of medicine from Dublin, Thomas Molyneux. In 1692 Thomas's brother William Molyneux sent Locke a copy of his *Treatise of Dioptricks*. He had complimented Locke in the dedication; Locke in response invited his friendship. William was a leading member of the Philosophical Society of Dublin, a body akin to the Royal Society; he was interested also in moral questions and in the prosperity of Ireland. He was one of the best of Locke's correspondents. He was the most capable of appreciating Locke's writings: van Limborch was debarred from most of them by language; Le Clerc was fully occupied with his own work; Clarke's intellect was too limited;

Toinard was disqualified on all three counts; others were too busy, too set in their ways of thought, or too self-centred, to give them the time and concentration requisite for mastery. Locke and Molyneux did not meet until the latter visited England in the summer of 1698. He died a few days after his return to Dublin.

In November 1694, as a new session of parliament was beginning, Locke, Freke, and Clarke joined in close alliance for political ends. Freke and Clarke together formed 'the College'. They corresponded with Locke (sometimes called 'the Castle') about current affairs. Freke, who had Somers's ear, could keep them in touch with him; Clarke voiced their views in the house of commons. They were concerned mainly with the liberation of publishing from the control of the Licensing Act and with the recoinage of 1696 and the following years. They were active principally in 1695 and 1696; although the College is mentioned as late as 1701 the underlying friendship had long since dwindled.

While it was in full force a new friendship was building up. Peter King, a grandson of Locke's uncle Peter Locke, was born in 1669. Locke seems to have taken very little notice of him until 1691 when King published a book on the early Church, a compilation from the writings of the Fathers designed to settle questions at issue between Anglicans and Nonconformists about its nature and practices. Locke is said to have persuaded King's father to send the young man to study at Leiden. Returning in 1694 he was admitted to the Middle Temple. A letter of 1696, a chance survivor, shows a repetition of Locke's standing with his own father: what had begun as kinship is maturing into friendship. By 1696 Locke was becoming rich; King assisted him with his investments. When King entered parliament Locke advised him on his duties and conduct as a member. Locke made him his principal heir and his literary executor.

Locke's correspondence illustrates the growth of three heterodox religious movements during the last two decades of the seventeenth century: Socinianism, which accepted the miraculous birth of Jesus, but rejected his divinity and the Trinity; Unitarianism, which rejected the miraculous birth and the Trinity; and Deism, which rejected Christian revelation. These are crude distinctions; the tenets were never defined rigorously; there were no obligatory articles of belief; the names were frequently used as terms of abuse. Whatever Locke may have thought about the doctrine of the Trinity he could appreciate the intellectual difficulties which led men to reject it; but his belief in the Bible was too strong for him to extend his sympathy to Deism. Its advance led him in 1695 to publish *The Reasonableness of Christianity*.

His theme is that Christian doctrine, as it is stated in the New Testament, conforms to the dictates of reason; a single article of belief is requisite for salvation, that Jesus is the Messiah. The book was attacked bitterly and scurrilously by John Edwards. In 1697 his attacks brought Locke a new friend and nearly lost him an old one. Samuel Bold, a Dorset parson, had been penalized in 1682 on account of a sermon that he had preached on toleration. He was treated kindly by Awnsham Churchill (another Dorset man) and the brothers published most of his books. When Bold replied to Edwards early in 1697 Edwards counter-attacked. Locke expressed his thanks to Bold in the *Second Vindication of the Reasonableness of Christianity*, whereupon Bold wrote to him. He visited Locke at Oates once or twice; without being embittered by his loneliness he was glad of the intellectual companionship that neither his parishioners at Steeple nor the neighbouring clergy could provide. Locke, while appreciating Bold's publications in his defence, feared lest they should lead to further proceedings against him.

Dr. John Covel, who had succeeded Cudworth as Master of Christ's College, was a friend of Lady Masham. In 1697 Edwards obtained from him and three other Cambridge grandees commendatory signatures for a book with an innocuous title containing a virulent attack on Locke. When Locke saw the book he lost his temper completely. He drafted a letter to Covel in which he threatened to expose a shameful incident in Covel's past; although the worst passages in the draft were omitted the letter that Locke sent is disgraceful. Covel apologized and Locke was appeased. While he was at no time intimate with Covel there are no traces in their later letters of any residual ill feeling.

Along with his scurrility Edwards brought against Locke the opprobrious charge of Socinianism. In an age of strong religious belief any questioning of the doctrine of the Trinity would appear blasphemous to orthodox believers in it. The hanging of Thomas Aikenhead in Edinburgh was a terrible example of the savagery of the zealots. In view of his subject, the essentials of Christianity, Locke could not ignore Edwards, abusive as he was. A more potent antagonist was to succeed him. John Toland in *Christianity not Mysterious* (1696) used Locke's *Essay* to reach rationalist conclusions far beyond anything that Locke had foreseen. Edward Stillingfleet, bishop of Worcester, was bound when he attacked Toland to challenge the *Essay* also. The ensuing controversy figures in the correspondence only in incidental notices. Locke's friends, while declaring him victorious, praise his courtesy to Stillingfleet.

Locke was appointed a Commissioner for Trade and Plantations in May 1696. The commission established a new board (the Board of Trade) with powers similar to, but more limited than, those of the Council of Trade and Foreign Plantations whose secretary Locke had been some twenty years earlier. Locke attended meetings as often as his health permitted. Some business was assigned to him on account of his special knowledge. Friends and acquaintances sent him questions or reports bearing on matters of concern for themselves. The most exacting matters for the board in his time were the great increase of piracy about the time of the Treaty of Ryswick and the Scots settlement in Darien. He was allowed to resign in June 1700.

When he was appointed a commissioner Locke already had an annual income of at least £450.[1] He was thrifty; he dressed well but disliked extravagance; apart from his modest living his principal expenditure was on books. The new Commission brought him an addition of £1,000 per annum less some deductions; this lasted for four years. This increase in his fortune coincided with the establishment of new opportunities for investment. The earlier Stuarts had never achieved a trustworthy and efficient system of national finance; crown and parliament in close alliance now inspired confidence in the repayment of the loans required for the war against France. The newly created Bank of England required capital; overseas ventures were maturing, and the East Indian trade had grown to such an extent that in 1698 a new East India Company was instituted to be a rival to the old; several smaller companies were engaged in manufactures. The London stock-market came into being about this time; from 1697 it had its own paper. Locke was too old to feel completely satisfied with dealings in stocks and shares; mortgages seemed more reliable. Peter King belonged to the new regime; a cousin of his was a leading stock-jobber; Locke's money therefore went mainly into the new kind of investment.

[1] His salary as a Commissioner of Appeals £200 less some deductions; his annuities from Shaftesbury and Clarke (this apparently continued) £100 each; his Somerset property £50 and more; literary earnings and perhaps interest from loans.

About August 1697 there was an addition to the household at Oates, Pierre Coste, a young French Protestant, who came from Amsterdam to be tutor to the young Francis Cudworth Masham. He had previously translated *Some Thoughts concerning Education* and *The Reasonableness of Christianity* into French; now he translated the *Essay* under Locke's supervision. As Locke spent most of his time at Oates in these later years there can have been few occasions for letter-writing. The few letters from Coste that survive show his assiduity as a translator; and that, thanks to his other correspondence, he was able to keep Locke informed of the progress of learning in the Netherlands.

The war that broke out between England and France in 1689 interrupted Locke's correspondence with Toinard. Toinard continued to write until June 1690 but apparently with no responses from Locke. With the help of Grævius at Utrecht there was a short exchange in 1694. When peace came in 1697 Locke wrote to Toinard. The correspondence resumed. Toinard was much the same as before, unable or unwilling to complete his chosen task the Harmony of the Gospels, scattering his interests in too many fields. But now his patrimony was dwindling and, among other projects, he tried to improve it by investing in the lotteries for Greenwich Hospital. The friendship was perhaps living on its past rather than flourishing in the present. To Toinard in these later years, however, Locke was indebted for an acquaintance with J.-B. Du Bos, who visited him in London in 1698 and kept him posted about new publications in France and elsewhere. Locke's correspondence with France was again interrupted by the outbreak of war in 1702. When a letter from Du Bos reached him in 1703 he was alarmed lest he should be charged with communicating with the enemy. A final letter from Toinard came in 1704 to remind Locke of the happy early years of their long-lived friendship.

It is regrettable that very little survives of Locke's correspondence with Awnsham Churchill before 1700. Locke was acquainted with him in 1682, when he was starting in bookselling on his own account. Churchill took his brother John into partnership in 1690; they and Jacob Tonson became the leading Whig booksellers. When Awnsham published the first editions of the *Letter concerning Toleration* (the translation) and *Two Treatises of Government* it is by no means certain that Locke disclosed his authorship to him; it is possible that Locke never owned up to *Two Treatises* to him;

he is likely to have claimed the *Letter* in 1690 when he entrusted the publication of the *Second Letter concerning Toleration* to the brothers. By 1694 they were acting as agents and bankers for him. In the surviving letters Awnsham consults Locke about a cherished project, the great *Collection of Voyages* that goes under the brothers' name. A letter from Locke shows his regard for and confidence in him.

The publication of the French and Latin translations in 1700 and 1701 enabled van Limborch to read Locke's *Essay*. He was concerned with men's liberty to accept or reject divine grace, one of the principal tenets distinguishing the Remonstrants from the Calvinists. He discussed the subject with Locke in letters seeking agreement; as a result Locke added a passage to the *Essay* to clarify one of his statements.

Locke resigned from the Commission for Trade and Plantations in 1700 and visited London for the last time in June 1702. In his last years there were many visitors to Oates: Peter King, Edward and Mrs. Clarke, Awnsham Churchill, Samuel Bold, two of Benjamin Furly's sons, Francis Limborch, John Bonville; perhaps Newton, Covel, and the third earl of Shaftesbury; Lord and Lady Peterborough, a brief visit; and in 1703 and 1704 a new friend, Anthony Collins the Deist. He was a younger man than King and recently widowed. His wealth provided him with leisure to render services to Locke which could not fairly be asked of King with his professional engagements and parliamentary duties; his attachment to Locke made the rendering of these services a pleasure to him. Locke also perhaps preferred him to King for the discussion of some religious subjects; he was more open-minded where King might be constricted by his piety. Locke showed his reliance on him when he appointed him, along with King and Awnsham Churchill, as a trustee for his bequest to Francis Cudworth Masham.

The last months of the correspondence are melancholy reading. Locke's health was declining; little vigour remained. His friends knew it and their letters are tinged by their knowledge. Locke bore his infirmity patiently. There was one great occasion for rejoicing. King had found a bride. He was married in September; he and his wife came to Oates a few days later for a wedding feast. There was a little more business to attend to; Collins visited him again; Awnsham Churchill sent a proof of his *Paraphrase and Notes on the Epistle of St. Paul to the Galatians* for him to inspect; final instructions for King were to be written. He finished the last task on 25 October. He died three days later while listening to Lady Masham reading the Psalms.

## THE PRESERVATION OF THE LETTERS

The great majority of the surviving letters received by Locke and of his drafts for letters are preserved in one or other of two repositories: the Bodleian Library and the Public Record Office in London. The letters from him descended in a few cases to the descendants or representatives of the persons to whom they were addressed and have survived as groups to this day. The heritages from other recipients have been dispersed; letters from them and isolated survivors from the letters addressed to other persons are preserved in English, European, and American collections. A few of the letters written by him are known only from printed texts.

Locke apparently tended to keep the letters that he received and drafts for some letters that he wrote. It was not always easy to keep them, as when he was travelling; some he probably tore up out of hand for lack of interest or enduring importance; and he is likely to have weeded the accumulation from time to time. It is easy to guess reasons for some survivals. Locke kept letters relating to property and money; letters containing information such as he noted in his Journal while travelling in France; letters relating to books and the Commonwealth of Learning; letters belonging to political, philosophical, and literary discussions. He evidently kept drafts or copies of his letters to Edward Clarke on the education of his son; these are lost but were used in the writing of *Some Thoughts concerning Education.* Personal affection is likely to be responsible for the preservation of some letters; others apparently owe their survival to vagaries or chance.

The question arises whether Locke destroyed any part of his correspondence for political reasons: letters addressed to him that might endanger either him or their writers. Little can be known about what lost letters he received from his correspondents in England before 1679, and extremely little, if anything, about their contents; rather more information could perhaps be brought together from Locke's extant letters for the period from 1679 to 1689; but the total is so small that any statement about it must be tentative. Now there is very little in the correspondence relating to current English politics before 1689. Such notices as there are are occasional and general; the only notable exceptions are James Tyrrell's account of the Ecclesiastical Commissioners' proceedings against Magdalen College in 1687 and Mrs. Grigg's letter at the time of the proceedings against the Seven Bishops. (Thomas Stringer's letters containing news of Shaftesbury and his household and associates are personal rather than political.) In 1681 he was concerned to find accommodation for Lord Shaftesbury for the Oxford Parliament; this was the service of a client to his patron and did not imply political involvement. Shaftesbury and his associates probably discussed politics frequently. There is no indication that Locke was ever in any inner ring and for considerable periods after his return to London in 1679 he and Shaftesbury lived in separate towns. Apart from his readiness to reply to Filmer's *Patriarcha* and Stillingfleet's *The Mischief of Separation* there is very little to show any interest on Locke's part in current politics before the Revolution. There are notable gaps in the extant correspondence where there can be no suspicion that the letters contained anything relating to politics: Nicolas Toinard's letter announcing the Abbé Gendron's death; Philippus van Limborch's letters in 1687. The question of destruction for political reasons can scarcely arise for the many demonstrable gaps from 1689 onwards.

When Locke left England in 1675 he left his private papers probably either in two divisions, the one at Christ Church in Oxford or with a friend in or near Oxford, the other at one of Lord Shaftesbury's residences (probably Exeter House in London); or all of them together at Shaftesbury's residence; if all together, he recovered some part of them on his return to England in 1679 or during the next few years. When he left England in 1683 he left some of his papers with his friend James Tyrrell at Oakley near Oxford, and when he was expelled from Christ Church in 1684 Tyrrell doubtless took charge of any papers remaining there; Locke perhaps left other papers with other friends, in London or elsewhere. There is nothing to show when he recovered his papers after his return to England in 1689; some of those left with Tyrrell perhaps not until 1692; the papers remaining after 1683 in Lord Shaftesbury's residence never. He may have kept some papers in his London lodgings, with Mrs. Rabsy Smithsby or Robert Pawling. He is likely to have had the bulk of his surviving papers, apart from the Shaftesbury deposit, with him at Oates when he died in 1704. If he left any papers in London they have been incorporated later in the main group or are lost.

Locke bequeathed his 'Manuscripts' to his cousin Peter King and, apart from specific legacies to King and others, the rest of his goods and chattels to King. His 'Manuscripts' were drafts for compositions; he discusses them in his valedictory letter to King. His private papers were evidently reckoned among his goods, and were received by King in due course.

King was created Baron King of Ockham in 1725. The manuscripts and papers were preserved by him and his descendants (from 1838 earls of Lovelace) until 1942, when they were deposited in the Bodleian Library for safe keeping. Almost all the correspondence and many of the other papers were acquired in 1947 by the Bodleian Library, where they are known as the Lovelace Collection. Further instalments of Locke's papers were given to the Bodleian by Dr. Paul Mellon in 1960 and 1963.

The principal known escape from the King heritage is the bulk of the letters from William and Thomas Molyneux and Ezekiel Burridge. These were published in *Some Familiar Letters* in 1708 and have come to rest in the Carl H. Pforzheimer Library in New York. In 1836 five letters from Dr. Richard Burthogge were lent to Burthogge's descendant Charles Babbage; the manuscripts have disappeared. I have noticed only one letter from the heritage in trade. Locke apparently placed a few letters loose in printed books; others were pasted in by him or his successors. The total loss in this way is probably slight.[1]

King added to the heritage such letters from Locke to himself as he had kept; apparently a very good sequence from March 1698 to the end. Strictly these are King and not Locke papers. Forty-seven were included in the collection acquired by the Bodleian in 1947; the remaining 165 were acquired in 1953.

There is nothing to show when or how the Shaftesbury deposit came to Wimborne St. Giles, in Dorset, the seat of the earls of Shaftesbury. It was apparently amalgamated with the family papers, which were presented by the seventh earl of Shaftesbury, the philanthropist, to the Public Record Office in 1871. Some of

[1] The principal escape, apart from correspondence, is Locke's Adversaria, 1661, now belonging to Arthur A. Houghton, jnr. There are notebooks and drafts for compositions in collections in America and elsewhere. They may never have belonged to the Lovelace heritage; some of them, if kept among Locke's printed books, may have belonged to Francis Cudworth Masham.

the letters are private letters to Locke and there are some other papers of his; but perhaps some of the letters from America that are addressed to him, and probably the 'Essay concerning Toleration', should be regarded as Shaftesbury papers; and his letters to members of the family are Shaftesbury and not Locke papers. Some of the last have found their way to the Forster Collection in the Victoria and Albert Museum, perhaps a gift from Lord Shaftesbury or W. D. Christie to John Forster.

The fate of the letters written by Locke depended on the conduct of the recipients and the chances of survival of their heritages. In general letters addressed to noblemen and landed gentlemen are more likely to survive than those addressed to townsmen. The families of the former are sedentary; if they keep their papers at all they are likely to leave them undisturbed in muniment rooms or unused chests. If the latter do not change houses themselves their children are likely to do so, and with the removal old papers will be destroyed. There is nothing to show whether or not Robert Pawling or Dr. Pieter Guenellon kept Locke's letters; if they did so it is extremely unlikely that the letters survived long after their deaths. These are generalizations; there are exceptions; some of the principal survivals of Locke's letters are due to townsmen.

The accumulation of material for the Commonwealth of Learning, so far as it was provided by correspondence, was a motive for the preservation of letters that influenced Locke and notably two of his correspondents, Nicolas Toinard and J. G. Græevius. After Toinard's death in 1706 his collection of letters appears to have been kept together until the nineteenth century. It was then broken up. A large part, but including no letters from Locke, was acquired in 1870 by the Bibliothèque Nationale, where it now forms MSS. N. Acq. fr. 560–3. Some of the letters from Locke belonged for a time to J.-C. Brunet, the bibliographer. They were sold by auction in 1868; the British Museum acquired fifty of them and copies of nine more. Other letters from Locke were detached from the collection either before Brunet came into possession of his holding or by him; these are scattered among various libraries and private collections. On account of the dispersal it is impossible to decide how assiduous Toinard was in keeping Locke's letters; he was careful as a rule but seems occasionally to have been careless.

Græevius was probably more systematic than Toinard. After passing through various hands his great collection of letters was bequeathed in 1785 to the Royal Library in Copenhagen. A few letters, notably those from Newton, were detached during its wanderings. It contains eight letters from Locke and several, among them some from Toinard, relating to him.

A number of leading Remonstrants preserved their correspondence probably in part for religious, in part for political, reasons: the letters would contribute to the definition of their doctrines and would provide some evidence for their conduct in a hostile environment. These motives are likely to have influenced Philippus van Limborch; as far as Locke was concerned there was also strong affection. Van Limborch's collection came either on his death in 1712 or later to the Remonstrants' Church in Amsterdam, and thence to the Amsterdam University Library. He seems to have kept every letter that he received from Locke with one exception, an ill-tempered letter which he probably destroyed soon after he received it (its contents are known from Locke's draft); the mutilation of another letter is likely to have been his work. There appear to have been very few escapes from the collection. Further van Limborch kept copies of many of his letters to Locke.

Edward Clarke owned an estate at Chipley in Somerset. Locke wrote for him the letters which he transformed into *Some Thoughts concerning Education*; later Locke maintained a vigorous political correspondence with him and their common friend John Freke (these two constituted 'the College'). Some of the letters written for the two together were perhaps kept by Freke; it is unlikely that Clarke ever had complete ownership of this part of the correspondence. It is clear that Clarke kept many of the letters that he received from Locke, but the history of the collection makes impossible any precise statement about this. The collection passed to his successors, first Clarke at Chipley, later Sanford at Nynehead. Thomas Birch acquired 42 letters presumably from one of them; he bequeathed them with his other collections of manuscripts to the British Museum in 1766. In the nineteenth century at least two letters from the collection were given away. In 1915 Col. E. A. Sanford sold five letters; these are dispersed among various collections. A large part of the collection was sold in 1922. It was bought later by J. H. Whitehouse, who bequeathed it to Bembridge School in the Isle of Wight; it was acquired by the Bodleian Library in 1963. There was loss of unknown extent through decay. Benjamin Rand, who had access to the collection shortly before 1914, recorded a few letters whose condition rendered them illegible; it is possible that some were thrown away before his time. Apparently about 57, many in bad condition, remain at Nynehead.

The brothers William and Thomas Molyneux and William's friend Ezekiel Burridge preserved Locke's letters carefully. They, apart from an early letter to Thomas, were published in 1708, in conjunction with their letters to Locke, as the first section of *Some Familiar Letters*. About 1840 the letters to Thomas became available for, if not into the possession of, Dr. (later Sir) William R. W. Wilde, who published the early letter and fresh transcripts of some of the others. The early letter now belongs to Dr. G. K. Woodgate; all the other letters to the two brothers and to Burridge are with one exception in a private collection in England.

Benjamin Furly, the merchant with whom Locke lodged in Rotterdam from 1687 to 1689, formed a large library which was sold after his death. He kept some letters, including some from Locke, his descendant Thomas (I. M.) Forster publishing a collection in 1830, and later two more letters from Locke to Furly and one to Furly's son Benjohan. The originals of seven of these, and an additional letter from Locke to Furly, have come to light in recent years and were acquired by the Bodleian Library in 1962.

Anthony Collins kept some, if not all, of the letters that he received from Locke; many of them were published, with Collins's co-operation, by Pierre Desmaizeaux in *A Collection of Several Pieces* (1720). The collection was broken up at an unknown date; the larger part of it was acquired by the Pierpont Morgan Library; a few letters are scattered in other collections. A letter not published by Desmaizeaux has appeared recently; it is impossible to say whether or not it was still in Collins's possession in 1720.

Peter King kept Locke's letters apparently almost invariably from March 1698 until Locke's death. There is a single earlier letter, dated 28 November 1696. It is unlikely that Locke did not write to King again until 1698; and it is probable that Locke wrote to him before 1696. The implication is that a large number of letters to King have been lost, whether he failed to keep them on receipt or by destruction at some date unknown.

Robert Boyle and Dr. John Mapletoft kept at any rate some of the letters that they received; the letters, or selections of them, were published in the eighteenth century and the manuscripts have disappeared. An associate collected some of the letters addressed to Denis Grenville; the collection is now in the Bodleian Library. Esther Masham, when tearing up old letters, copied a few of them, adding some notes; her letter-book is now in the Newberry Library, Chicago. The letters from Locke to Richard King were published by Edmund Curll in 1714; the originals have disappeared. Sir Hans Sloane acquired the natural history, art, and miscellaneous collections formed by William Charleton or Courten, and with them apparently some of the letters addressed to Charleton; these, including some from Locke, are now in the British Museum. Other letters from Locke to Charleton have passed into the autograph market. (Sir) William Godolphin and William and Mrs. Stratton apparently kept the letters that they received from Locke; they have come into the market but there is nothing to show from what source.

There are many other small collections or single letters, either forming part of heritages whose history is clear or strays having no pedigree; the statements of provenance prefixed to the individual letters should provide sufficient information about them.

Locke corresponded with several persons whom one would expect to have kept letters carefully, his among them, and who have left no surviving heritage of his letters. Thus James Tyrrell: he, however, may have been careless from the start. Sir John Banks: he is likely to have kept Locke's letters from France for a time; either he or one of his descendants may have destroyed them. Lord Pembroke: apparently no private papers survive. Lady Masham: presumably destroyed with the decay of Oates or after transfer to some other house.[1] Somers and Olaus Rømer: destroyed by fire in 1752 and 1728 respectively. Some of these losses must be regarded as grievous. In some cases it is possible to guess the contents of what has been lost; in others—notably the letters to Pembroke, Lady Masham, and Somers—it is likely that we should have had fuller and clearer illustrations of the more amiable parts of Locke's character.

## PREVIOUS PUBLICATIONS OF THE CORRESPONDENCE

Publication of Locke's correspondence began shortly after his death with a collection of letters brought together by two or three of his friends and his cousin Peter King. It has continued since then

[1] J. Harrison and P. Laslett, *The Library of John Locke*, 2nd ed., 1971, pp. 58–61.

as letters have become accessible. The motive for publication is interest in Locke. This has varied from time to time in amount and nature. Editors and publishers had to consider its limits. Thus Bishop Law in his preface to the eighth edition of Locke's *Works* (1777): 'We have not room to insert' Locke's thirteen letters to Dr. John Mapletoft 'as they contain very few matters of literature, to which our enquiries are chiefly confined at present . . . Forty Letters to *Edward Clarke*, Esq; M.P. are among Dr. *Birch*'s papers in the Museum, but of like unimportance'; Law, however, printed one 'as a specimen'. Thomas Forster, in the preface to his *Original Letters* of Locke, Algernon Sidney, and the third Lord Shaftesbury (1830), states that his grandfather, who died in 1812, 'used to say, that what one man believed or thought, could be no business of any other man's, and that private letters and sentiments, however ancient, ought not to be divulged to the public by posterity'; Forster himself was hesitant. Philippus van Limborch's views and practice are more reasonable. He considered that Vossius's correspondence, as published by P. Colomiès (1690), contained too much trivial matter. When editing his own correspondence with Locke he was selective: he omitted some letters or parts of letters on account of lack of interest and suppressed all passages that could offend or injure living persons. He could not foresee the growth of historical interest and the desire to know all aspects of the everyday life of the past.

Almost all the former editors had to contend with one great impediment. They saw only one side of the correspondence and their work suffered consequently from lack of information: it was easy to go astray with badly written proper names or dates. The editors of *Some Familiar Letters* and T. J. de Boer had very nearly full access to both sides of the correspondence that they edited. Rand was less fortunate, failing to see about forty letters that are relevant to the correspondence between Locke and Clarke. In many cases only one side of an exchange survives; here, however, the letters to or from other correspondents are apt to be relevant. In judging an editor's performance this lack of information must always be borne in mind.

The individual publications[1] begin with *Some Familiar Letters*

[1] Some further information about reprints and translations is given in H. O. Christophersen, *A Bibliographical Introduction to the Study of John Locke*, 1930, pp. 81–3.

*between Mr. Locke, and Several of his Friends*, published by Awnsham and John Churchill in 1708. This contains almost all Locke's letters to and from the brothers William and Dr. Thomas Molyneux, with a letter from Locke to William's friend Ezekiel Burridge, and a selection from the letters between Locke and Philippus van Limborch. There is nothing to show who projected the book; it was perhaps Locke's principal heir Peter King (the future Lord Chancellor and first Baron King of Ockham) in conjunction with the Churchills. There is a short unsigned epistle to the reader. The letters 'contain not only such civil and polite conversation as friendship produces among men of parts, learning, and candour; but several matters relating to literature, and more particularly to Mr. *Locke*'s notions, in his *Essay concerning Human Understanding*, and in some of his other works'; although some readers would like more intimate information the writer considers that this is what the public wants; the book is a supplement to Locke's published writings rather than an independent biographical collection. The letters in the first part must have been contributed principally by Peter King and Samuel Molyneux, William Molyneux's son. Comparison with the originals shows that the orthography was modified, probably to bring it into conformity with the style of the printing house, and that there are a few slight omissions, mainly for privacy.[1] The second part was the work of van Limborch. He and Locke wrote to one another in Latin. He had available almost all Locke's letters to him and copies of some of his letters to Locke. From these materials he made a selection. Almost everything of general interest was to be retained, and notably anything bearing on religious toleration and the discussion of the activity of the human will. The principal sacrifice was van Limborch's discussion with the young woman who preferred Judaism to Christianity. Locke's personal adventures were omitted, and almost everything relating to van Limborch and his family. The texts were transcribed carefully. This part is especially good, but the whole book is one of the finest achievements among the publications of Locke's correspondence.

[1] Thanks to the generosity of Mr. Carl H. Pforzheimer I am able to print the letters to Locke from the originals. By the courtesy of the present owner I have seen Xerox reproductions of all but one of the letters from Locke printed in this part of this volume.

Some letters between Awnsham Churchill and Samuel Molyneux relating to this publication are preserved among the Southampton Corporation muniments: H.M.C., *Rep.* xi, App. iii. 34–8.

It was reprinted in the first edition of Locke's *Works* (1714) and in all later editions.[1]

The next publication, *The Remains of John Locke Esq;* (1714), was probably a simple commercial venture. Edmund Curll the bookseller obtained from Richard King five letters from Locke, one to Humphry Smith about Dr. Edward Pococke, the remainder to King; he published these with such of Locke's poems as he could collect and Locke's will. The five letters were reprinted by Pierre Desmaizeaux in *A Collection of Several Pieces of Mr. John Locke* (1720). According to the title-page of the second edition Desmaizeaux published the *Collection* 'under the Direction' of Anthony Collins, and he included in it, besides the five letters, thirty-two letters from Locke to Collins and a letter apiece from him to Henry Oldenburg and to Lady Calverley. Curll is unlikely to have bothered about Locke's orthography; Desmaizeaux modernized freely. Desmaizeaux also supplied some notes. The *Collection* was reprinted in 1739 and then in the fourth edition of Locke's *Works* (1740) and in all later editions.

There followed a century of occasional or incidental publication. Thomas Birch, publishing his edition of Robert Boyle's *Works* (1744), included Boyle's correspondence, and among the letters ten from Locke to Boyle. Birch was an outstanding textuary, diligent and exact, the best of all who have published Locke's English letters. These letters are not mentioned by the later editors of Locke's *Works* or by Lord King; it was Fox Bourne who first paid them due attention.

Next came two single letters of note: one to Samuel Bold, published in *The Museum* in 1746; the other to Catherine Trotter, later Mrs. Cockburn, which Birch included in his edition of her *Works* (1751). Bishop Law included these two letters in the eighth edition of Locke's *Works* (1777), and added a single letter from Locke to Edward Clarke. The three were reprinted in the ninth edition (1794). No further letters were added despite an important addition to the corpus. A grandson of Dr. John Mapletoft offered Law thirteen letters from Locke to Mapletoft. Law refused to publish them. The letters were published eventually with letters from other persons to Mapletoft in the *European Magazine*, vols. xiv and xv (1788–9). The transcription is good. Four letters between Locke and William Charleton were printed in the article on the latter in the *Biographia Britannica*, 2nd ed., vol. iv (1789).

[1] There were also separate editions in 1737 and 1742.

These were the last of the eighteenth-century publications. There were now in print, in whole or in part, 212 letters from or to Locke.

About the end of the century there emerges a new impulse for interest in Locke and his writings. The Unitarians, many of them middle-class intellectuals, were finding increasingly irksome the civil disabilities imposed on them by the Test Acts; the penalties imposed by the Blasphemy Act on denial of the Trinity, if never exacted, were an invidious pronouncement on their creed. In Locke they saw a champion: he had written for religious toleration and a simple form of Christian belief more or less reconcilable with their own; the social contract as the foundation for political society could serve as an argument for a wide and equable suffrage if not, as in America, for universal democracy. A reprint of Locke's letter to Samuel Bold by Robert Goadby in *The Moral and Entertaining Magazine*, vol. ii (1778), was due perhaps to local interest (Bold was rector of Steeple in Dorset); but Goadby was not an orthodox Anglican and may have reprinted the letter on account of its religious content; that it attracted the Unitarians is shown by a further reprint by J. H. Bransby, a Unitarian divine, in the *Christian Reformer*, vol. ii (1835). The earliest certain manifestation of the Unitarian interest is the publication in the *Monthly Repository*, vols. xiii and xiv (1818–19), of translations by J. T. Rutt of the first forty-four of the letters between Locke and van Limborch that the latter had contributed to *Some Familiar Letters*. Rutt, a radical in politics, would appreciate van Limborch's friendliness to the Socinians; while he added nothing new to the corpus of the correspondence he opened an important part of it to a non-academic public.

Lord King published the first edition of his *Life* of Locke in 1829. King had at his disposal his heritage of Locke's papers. He was not an orthodox Anglican; he was eager to vindicate Locke in relation to Bishop Fell and to promote Locke's religious and political views. His book, despite its title, is less a connected biography than a collection of documents. Among them are 40 ostensible letters or excerpts from letters from Locke and 40 letters and 10 excerpts to him. The latter are accurately printed, the texts being modernized. With the former King took great liberties, omitting passages without indication, sometimes combining parts of two or more letters to form a single letter. This was acceptable practice at the time. Apart from it there appear to be few positive errors. The second edition, 1830, retains all the defects of the first but has an important addition. At the instance of Dr. Thomas Rees, a Unitarian divine, King appended nine letters from van Limborch to Locke and the passage omitted from *Some Familiar Letters* narrating his discussion with the young woman who preferred Judaism to Christianity, and one letter from Locke to van Limborch; the letters from van Limborch from the originals in King's possession and that to him from Locke's draft. On account of the language these letters probably attracted little attention. King added also excerpts from five letters to Locke.[1] Rees also published a translation of an unpublished letter from van Limborch in the *Christian Reformer*, vol. ii (1835).

Thomas Forster, a descendant of Locke's friend Benjamin Furly, perhaps inspired by King's *Life* of Locke, published in 1830 *Original Letters of Locke; Algernon Sidney; and Anthony Lord Shaftesbury, Author of the "Characteristics."* Drawing from his family heritage he printed in whole or in part eleven letters from Locke to Furly and a note of the contents of another; he added thirteen letters from Locke to Edward Clarke and four to Sir Hans Sloane, all from the British Museum. He was fairly successful in reproducing the original spelling but modernized the punctuation. With a letter wrongly dated by Locke to mislead him he went astray when supplying the years of two incompletely dated letters. He printed two further letters to Furly and one to his son Benjohan in his *Epistolarium*, 1845, and included them in the second edition of *Original Letters*, 1849.

After 1830 there followed another period of occasional or incidental publication. About 1840 Locke's letters to Dr. (later Sir) Thomas Molyneux became accessible to, if not the property of, Dr. (later Sir) William R. W. Wilde, the father of Oscar Wilde. Wilde was writing a life of Thomas Molyneux which he published in the *Dublin University Magazine*, vols. xviii–xix (1841–2). He included one new letter from Locke to Thomas Molyneux and fresh transcripts of three that had been published in *Some Familiar Letters*. He kept closer than most of his predecessors to Locke's orthography.[2] Lord Campbell printed excerpts from four unpublished

[1] He reprinted also three of Locke's letters to Mapletoft from the *European Magazine*.

[2] An unprinted part of one of the letters in *Some Familiar Letters* was published by Wilde's son William Wilde in *Notes and Queries*, 8th ser. ix (1896), 381. Dr. Wilde printed also Locke's letter to E. Burridge, 27 October 1698.

letters from Locke to Peter King and from three letters from King to Locke in *The Lives of the Lord Chancellors* (1845–69), vol. iv.

About 1870 the opening of the Shaftesbury papers to W. D. Christie and their subsequent transfer to the Public Record Office, and the dispersal of Nicolas Toinard's papers, made new developments possible. The publications of the Royal Commission on Historical Manuscripts from 1870 onwards added a few letters, mainly isolated or in small groups. It is impracticable to list the publications of single letters after this time.

First, two authors of biographies. Neither was concerned in the first place with the publication of letters; excerpts or summaries would suffice for their purpose; modernized orthography was more suitable than the original. W. D. Christie for his *Life of Anthony Ashley Cooper, First Earl of Shaftesbury*, 1871, had free access to the Shaftesbury heritage and obtained some letters from Lord Lovelace, formerly Baron King of Ockham; he was thus able to print 27 letters from or to Locke, or parts of them, many of them new. For him Locke was incidental; Locke is the central figure of H. R. Fox Bourne's *Life of John Locke*, 1876. Fox Bourne was unable to use the Lovelace heritage; in other directions his achievement is remarkable. He brought together what he could find in the Shaftesbury heritage; the British Museum, and notably its recently acquired letters to Toinard; van Limborch's papers in Amsterdam; Esther Masham's letter-book; and what he could find in the Bodleian Library, the Lambeth Palace Library, and the Public Record Office. He was not editing the letters; any texts that he printed were to be accurate; but they were to be incorporated in his narrative and were not to be printed for their own sake as more or less independent ornaments. On the whole he was accurate and careful with the texts of the English letters. His outstanding defect is his mistranslation of some of the Latin letters. He reckoned that earlier publications had provided him with 356 letters or extracts from letters from and to Locke. He was able to make use of 218 hitherto unprinted letters, 176 of them written by Locke and 42 to him.

A new period in the publication of Locke's correspondence begins about the end of the century. It opens with *The Life, Unpublished Letters, and Philosophical Regimen of Anthony, Earl of Shaftesbury, Author of the "Characteristics"*, edited by Benjamin Rand, 1900. In this Rand printed twelve letters from Shaftesbury to

Locke from the originals in the Lovelace heritage. It is impossible to determine what he was shown. He did not reprint letters that had been printed by King and, if he was shown them, it was reasonable to omit some short business letters. The absence of some other letters is regrettable; presumably he did not see the manuscripts; but his work does not inspire confidence in his conduct. The orthography is modernized; the transcription is good.

Next there came the publication by Charles Bastide in the *Revue international de l'enseignement*, vol. lv (1908), of the eight letters from Locke to J. G. Græevius. The texts were carefully transcribed and added punctuation is distinguished as such; a notably fine achievement where there has been so much indifferent or shoddy work. In the same year Henry Ollion published *Notes sur la correspondance de John Locke*, in which he printed thirty-two letters from Locke to Toinard from the British Museum manuscripts. He added a list of the letters or parts of letters known to him, in all about 600 items.

Four years later Ollion published *Lettres inédites de John Locke*, 1912, until that time by far the most important publication of Locke's correspondence since *Some Familiar Letters*. Ollion evidently projected the volume. It contains 59 letters to Toinard and 29 to Edward Clarke; another section comprises 80 letters or parts of letters to van Limborch. Forty-four letters from Locke to him had been published in *Some Familiar Letters*. In all cases the addresses were omitted; in many of them, postscripts and occasional short passages; in some, substantial passages. These omitted fragments were now printed, but for the rest of these letters the reader has to turn to *Some Familiar Letters*.

Ollion was responsible for the letters to Toinard and Clarke. At his best he is excellent and he provides many interesting notes to the letters. But he was in too much of a hurry and was too fond of short cuts. His transcription is good in the main but when in difficulties it may degenerate into guesswork. For the letters to Toinard, with only one side of the correspondence before him, it was impossible for him to explain correctly the more or less allusive notices and he was bound to have difficulties with some proper names. But when all allowances are made he seems to have been satisfied with the first answers to his questions; to have failed to search for alternative answers and in general to have done too little subsidiary work (he seems not to have consulted the letters to

Toinard in the Bibliothèque Nationale); to have pondered wider problems insufficiently. The planning of the section for van Limborch, which I take to be his work (it was executed by T. J. de Boer) is symptomatic. Besides Locke's letters to van Limborch van Limborch's copies of many of his letters were available; de Boer printed some passages from them in his notes. It is impossible not to feel that a great opportunity was lost. The division of the texts between *Some Familiar Letters* and *Lettres inédites* disrupts the intellectual continuity; de Boer was debarred from commenting on the passages printed in the earlier work; no notice is taken of them in the index to the later book. De Boer's notes are less expansive than Ollion's, but are closer to the matter in hand; in his introduction he gives an excellent account of van Limborch and the Remonstrants.

At some date before 1914 Benjamin Rand obtained access to the letters from Locke to Edward and Mrs. Clark belonging to Col. E. A. Sanford at Nynehead in Somerset, and the right to publish them. Lord Lovelace allowed him to copy almost all the letters from Clarke, his wife, and children, to Locke in his possession.[1] Locke's letters to Clarke in the British Museum were also available, and he found one or two letters elsewhere. Rand brought together in all 384 letters; he saw also a number so decayed as to be illegible. War came in 1914. During and after the war Col. Sanford sold a large part of his collection; when, after the end of the war, Rand wanted to check his transcripts the new owner of the greater part of the collection, who himself wanted to edit the letters, refused him access. He had bad luck in another direction also. When in 1695–7 Locke corresponded with Clarke and John Freke as members of 'the College' the replies, whether signed by Clarke and Freke or by Freke alone, were kept in the Lovelace collection with Freke's letters. Rand, who was not allowed to inspect the collection, could not know this; as a result he failed to obtain thirty-four relevant texts. He published his assemblage in 1927 as *The Correspondence of John Locke and Edward Clarke.*

Rand modernized the orthography. His transcripts were probably fairly good, but he did not try hard enough for decayed and faded passages. When there is any question about the dates of letters what he supplies is unreliable. There are few notes and the

[1] A few letters appear to have been out of place in the collection, and so were not shown to Rand. Clearly the intention was that he should see and copy everything.

introduction is too general in character to provide much help. Some allowance must be made for the book's misadventures between projection and publication but it is impossible not to consider Rand incompetent and irresponsible. He shows little concern for future scholars. His *Shaftesbury* went without an index; that for *Locke and Clarke* is bad. The tasks that he undertook require exacting attention to detail; Rand was either unaware of the requirement or found no difficulty in neglecting it.

This was the last publication of Locke's correspondence prior to the acquisition of the Lovelace Collection by the Bodleian Library in 1947. Since it became available a number of scholars have published from it or from other collections: Gabriel Bonno has published the letters from J. B. Du Bos, Pierre Coste, and Jean Le Clerc; Dr. Kenneth Dewhurst, medical letters, those from Thomas Sydenham and Dr. William Cole, and those relating to Lady Northumberland's trigeminal neuralgia; H. W. Turnbull and J. F. Scott, the letters between Locke and Newton. Maurice Cranston published many letters or excerpts from letters in his *John Locke*, 1957; further he edited Locke's exchange with John Aubrey in 1694 and ran to earth Esther Masham's letter-book and edited Locke's letters to her in exemplary fashion. Single or isolated letters have been published incidentally in connection with other writings by Locke, notably by J. Lough, W. von Leyden, and P. Abrams.[1]

## THE PRESENT EDITION

The present edition contains the texts of all available private letters from and to Locke; of drafts of letters from him; of some relevant third-party letters; and some miscellaneous documents. Further it contains enumerated headings for letters likely to exist but not at present accessible and for some letters that are excluded on other grounds. It contains also notes of four letters that have been attributed to Locke. It excludes printed pieces called a 'Letter' or a 'Reply' and printed dedications or similar compositions; it enumerates but does not print some manuscript dedications; two complimentary letters to Locke as Censor of Moral Philosophy at

[1] I have found writing some of these judgements on my predecessors an invidious task. I am indebted to almost all of them at some points. But unless a bare list is to be regarded as sufficient some criticism is inescapable.

Christ Church; letters written to or received by Locke in an official capacity as secretary to the Council of Trade and Foreign Plantations in 1673–4; and Newton's dissertation on two corruptions in the New Testament (no. *1338*).

Subject to adjustments required by printing, the texts of the letters are given as they left the writers' hands. All markings on them by the recipients, apart from the endorsements and similar notes, are recorded in the critical notes. This applies even to components of dates. Addresses and endorsements are printed, and postmarks are recorded, at the ends of the letters. The treatment of the texts is set out in detail below.

Private letters, like any other kind of writings, have their peculiar characteristics. A private letter is addressed by an individual or small group of individuals to an individual or small group of individuals. It conveys one or more messages: information, whether of external events or of the writer's or writers' opinions or feelings about some matter or matters; including perhaps thanks to or censure of the person or persons addressed; and commands, requests, or refusals. Writer or writers and person or persons addressed have some common knowledge or common interests. A letter will be relevant for both; hence allusions, nicknames or designations other than proper names, incomplete dates, will suffice for its purpose. There are elements of diplomatic. A letter generally consists of date, stating the place and time of writing; salutation; text; subscription; and address; there may be also one or more postscripts. Individual writers have their own habits in the writing: notably in subscriptions, less markedly in dates and addresses; they may also have characteristic words in certain situations. In general writers date their letters correctly and mean what they write. If they convey information they believe it to be trustworthy information; if they make a request it is one that they expect to be fulfilled.

By the late seventeenth century there were regular postal services in most countries of Western and Central Europe. The evidence suggests that they were reliable. Communications between England and the Continent were necessarily subject to the weather. A letter from Amsterdam could be stamped at the General Post Office in London on the third day after the date of writing; if the weather were unfavourable it might take two or three weeks in transit. The objection to using the postal services was that they were expensive. For the ordinary English post the minimum charge was 2*d.* to carry a single sheet for not more than eighty miles. This has to be measured against other ordinary expenses of the time. In England some charges could be evaded by franking. Inland letters to and from members of parliament during sessions and for some weeks before and after were carried free of charge; this privilege was frequently abused. Whenever possible letters were sent by private conveyance.

Letters that have been preserved often show signs of their treatment by their recipients. There is frequently an endorsement. This usually contains the writer's name and the date of writing or, failing that, of receipt; it may contain also a note of the contents of the letter and the date of reply. In some cases there are marginal or other markings, to call attention to particular passages; notes of the subjects may be made in the margins.[1]

A letter usually consisted of a single sheet of paper which was folded and held together by a seal; the address was written on the outside. If the part of the sheet on which the address was written contained no part of the text it might be torn off for further use. If the letter was sealed carelessly it might be torn when it was opened, with in some cases the loss of part of the text. Further a recipient might mutilate a letter deliberately. He might delete particular words and passages with pen and ink; or he might cut away parts of the paper, regardless of what was written on the back of what he set out to destroy.

## THE TEXTS

The texts of the letters fall into two principal divisions: those printed from the original manuscripts and those printed from printed versions or old copies. The first division is divided further into two classes: letters sent and drafts for letters. The treatment of the two classes is similar, but the drafts require greater freedom of treatment than the letters sent.

### *The original manuscripts: the letters sent*

i. The general aim is to reproduce the manuscript 'as closely as typography admits'.[2] If letters are carefully written this is simple; there may be a few customary adjustments to be made, such as the

[1] Markings on the manuscripts made after Locke's time are readily distinguishable. They are ignored here apart from the editorial markings on the letters of William Molyneux that were printed in *Some Familiar Letters*.

[2] R. W. Chapman, ed., *The Letters of Samuel Johnson*, 1952, vol. i, p. viii.

expansion of abbreviations, but no further interference is requisite. But many letters are written by careless or incompetent writers. The recipients are used to deficiencies and make allowances for them, the more so because reading cursive handwriting is generally slower than reading print. They see the accidental features of the manuscripts, the false starts and deletions, the interlineations, the ends of the lines and pages, the places where the writers have paused. It is impracticable if not impossible to reproduce all these features in print. If then the printed text is to do justice to the writers there must be some interference with their punctuation.

The reader of the printed text is further to be considered in regard to some of the writers' errors. Writers are apt to omit, misplace, or duplicate words, and to spell badly. Seventeenth-century English spelling was commonly irregular and variable; some writers are consistent in their spelling; others are inconsistent. This the reader must accept. But writers occasionally exceed all possible latitude. Wild spellings of the kind, like misprints in modern books, throw the reader out; while he gropes for the correct word he loses the thread of the sentence. As a rule of thumb: if a bad mistake occurs in the first three letters of a word the reader must be helped; if it occurs later in the word he is likely to have anticipated what was intended. The correct words must be inserted in the text but distinguished as departures from the manuscripts, and the spellings of the manuscripts must be immediately available for the reader.

It is desirable that there should be a minimum of interference anywhere and that for some writers it should be restricted to the provision of a stop at the turnover of a leaf. John Bonville had no notion of orthography; to impose corrections on his text will be to falsify it; he conveys his meaning best when left to himself. Similarly Peter Locke is best left to himself. When Locke makes mistakes or writes carelessly, it is another matter. If he writes under stress, that is to be stated. The reader is to be enabled to grasp his meaning unhindered by fortuitous lapses. This applies also to the great majority of Locke's correspondents. The treatment of the texts must vary in some degree with the competence of the writers.

## ii. Handwriting and transcription

In general the handwriting of the letters should present few difficulties to an experienced transcriber. Writers have their habits in the formation and combination of the letters of the alphabet, and in the marking of accents and punctuation. These must be mastered; if little of a particular writer survives it may be impossible to establish his habits, so that some readings must be doubtful. The capital and small forms of some letters of the alphabet are distinguished only by their size; it is frequently impossible to be certain which form a writer uses; in such cases a transcriber must depend on his judgement. For altered words there is apt to be no true reading; all that the transcriber can do is to guess. Where proper names or unusual words occur it is desirable to know what the writer ought to have written. This brings a risk that the transcriber will force a wrong reading on to the text; without this knowledge there may be needless and misleading errors.

All these are casual difficulties. Where manuscripts have been carefully preserved the principal obstacles to accurate transcription are careless and dashing writing and the use of pale ink and rough paper. One would scarcely make identical transcripts of Lady Mordaunt's letters on two successive days; a passage in J. Schard's letter could be deciphered only by placing beside it the text that he copied.[1]

Where manuscripts are badly faded, rubbed, water-stained, or torn, there will be difficulties in transcription. Statements about the condition of the manuscript should provide sufficient warning.

Locke deleted some words or passages in letters that he received by writing over them a looping line or other words. In a few cases it is possible to recover some of either the deleted or the covering words.

## iii. Authorship and person addressed

Most of the surviving letters to Locke were signed. Some letters to him have lost the signature by damage. If these are left aside the letters without signature fall into two main groups: the strictly anonymous and those that did not require a signature as their authorship would be recognized by Locke immediately.

The strictly anonymous include at least one series of letters that were all written by the same writer; while it is impossible to fix a name, the writer is in other respects a clearly defined person.

[1] I have not transcribed it. This is the one passage that has defeated me. When transcribing prescriptions I have kept beside me the appropriate pharmacopoeias; when in difficulties with proper names and unusual words I have consulted whatever seemed likely to help.

There can be no reasonable doubt about the authorship of many of the unsigned or mutilated letters. Many unsigned letters can be attributed to Nicolas Toinard on account of their resemblance to signed letters by him. They agree with the signed letters so closely in handwriting, contents, language, style, and orthography, that, if they are attributed to some other writer, the letters signed by Toinard must be taken from him and attributed to the same writer. This applies also to the mutilated letters from Edward Clarke.

In a few cases authorship must be argued.[1] Where there is no positive evidence the arguments can produce no more than an acceptable probability.

Many of the letters in the Lovelace Collection are without addresses. It is to be assumed that they were addressed to Locke unless there is some indication to the contrary. He kept a few letters between third parties, so that some of these letters without addresses may also have been addressed to other persons.

It is sometimes possible to state to whom a letter that has lost its address is likely to have been addressed. This occurs when it can be associated with a letter to Locke as antecedent or answer.[2] The identification at best is not more than an acceptable probability.

## iv. Dates of letters

A date is complete when it states the day of the month, the month, and the year. When it is understood that in the absence of a day or month from the date a particular day or month is intended the date is still complete. This occurs in some of Toinard's letters when the absent month is invariably January.

Incomplete dates commonly state the day of the month and the month, omitting the year. Sometimes they state simply a day of the week, as Monday. Sometimes there is no date at all. These deficiencies are generally due to the writers and only rarely to damage.

The correspondence includes letters with wrong or questionable dates. Deliberate false dates with intention to mislead are rare.[3] Wrong dates, stating the day of dispatch instead of the day of

[1] The most notable is no. *2207*. The original letter is lost; only a copy survives.
[2] So no. 1743. Similarly the drafts nos. 18 and 20.
[3] The enclosure in no. *2481* is an example.

writing, occur among Locke's letters from Oates; as the letters were to be taken away early in the morning they had to be written on the preceding day. Most of the wrong dates are due to error alone.

The means of supplying, completing, and checking the dates of the letters are identical.

First: endorsements and notes by the persons addressed. From 1667 Locke habitually endorsed the letters that he received with the writer's name and the date of writing; from about the end of 1686 he notes also the date of his answer. If the writer's date were incomplete Locke might complete it. When he received an undated letter he sometimes endorsed it with what appears to have been the date on which he received it. Some of his correspondents had similar habits; thus van Limborch and Edward Clarke. Just as the dates on the letters, so those in the endorsements are subject to human error.

Secondly: mention in answering or other letters. A specific mention of a letter with or without its date in a completely dated or reliably dated letter.

Thirdly: postmarks. All letters passing through the General Post Office in London from 1661 onwards were stamped at some moment during their transit through the office with a mark showing the month and day of the month. These marks, so far as they appear on the letters and are legible, are reliable; I have found in the Locke correspondence only one fully legible mark that appears to be open to question.

Fourthly: external events. A certain mention of an event whose date is certain. This may be a public or a private event: a battle or a death in the family; the mention must be so distinctive that it can apply to it alone. The dates of some of Mrs. Lockhart's letters depend on combining her incomplete dates (the day of the week or of the month) with the dates of securely dated events mentioned in her letters; there may be further assistance from endorsements by Locke.

These means of dating letters or checking dates are all reliable and in most cases should provide close dates. There are also looser means, such as addresses or mentions of past events. An address does not prove that the person addressed was at the place mentioned in it at any particular time, but the place can scarcely be named before the person addressed is associated with it and is unlikely to be named long after his dissociation from it. There are altogether very few undated or incompletely dated letters for which no limiting dates can be suggested.[1]

For all supplied dates or parts of dates, and for dates differing from those given by the writers, the reasons for the dates given here are set out in the head-notes.

v. Treatment of the texts

Spelling

I have retained the spelling of the manuscripts as far as possible; the exceptions are where words are abridged (for these see below) and where there are wild spellings. If such a spelling is likely to throw the reader out the correct or customary spelling is given in the text in angle brackets, and the writer's spelling in a critical note.

In the French letters I have not supplied accents where there are none in the manuscripts. I may have occasionally read an undifferentiated accent as grave or acute when the writer intended it to be read as the other.

Abbreviations and Suspensions, etc.

Current abbreviations, such as 'Mr.', are retained; others are expanded silently, as in Sir John Banks's letters. Where there can be any reasonable doubt there is a note.

Suspensions are reproduced as they stand in the manuscripts. Similarly initials such as 'the K', 'C', or 'Sir W. Y.' are retained as they stand; explanations are supplied in the notes where necessary.

Ampersands are always silently expanded to 'and' or 'et'; similarly '&c.' becomes 'etc.' Similarly in Latin letters 'n' is silently expanded to 'enim'.

Superior letters, as in 'M$^{r}$', are printed in line, except where ambiguity would result. The treatment of these letters in the case of weights and money-sums has varied slightly from letter to letter; any loss is limited to the writing and does not affect meaning.

Chemical symbols representing substances or processes are replaced in the printed texts by the names of the substances or processes in square brackets. Symbols indicating quantities and that for 'Recipe' are retained in the printed texts.[2]

[1] I can find no means of dating no. *90*; the dates here suggested for nos. *131–2*, *152*, *295*, and others, are limited to a few years. The arguments for the dating of Locke's early drafts are set out below. They apply also to some letters.

[2] There is a table of the symbols, with their meanings, in J. R. Partington, *A History of Chemistry*, vol. ii, 1961, p. 769. The symbols retained are ℞ (Recipe); ℥ (an ounce); ʒ (a drachm); ℈ (a scruple).

Superseded and deleted words, false starts, etc.

The treatment is selective; only those that appear to be substantive are recorded.

Punctuation

(i) The punctuation reproduces that of the manuscripts with certain relaxations. Reading handwriting is slower than reading print; if the writing is bad or unusual it is very much slower. Again, the reader of a manuscript checks at the end of a line, at false starts and deleted words, and at interlineations; the sight of the manuscript will show where the writer has changed his speed or paused. The manuscript was not written for printing; for the writer it was the final product; the roughness would scarcely trouble the reader for whom it was written.

When the letter is printed some allowance must be made for those features in the manuscript which the reader does not see and which can scarcely be recorded in print. In practice it is desirable to supply some punctuation, and in texts of the present kind to supply it silently except where it may affect meaning. It is to be kept to a minimum and must conform to the writer's own system or habits of punctuation; it is wrong to impose a modern system on an idiosyncratic writer of the past. Writers for whom punctuation is meaningless must not have it forced upon them; as their spelling in any case will make reading slow this should provide no hardship for the reader.

Jean Le Clerc sometimes leaves a short blank space in a line when he has finished with one subject and starts another. There should be a proper paragraph break, the new subject starting with a new line; Le Clerc perhaps wanted to save paper. I have kept these internal paragraph breaks when the printed text allows for them; when they come at the ends of lines in the printed text the following lines are indented for new paragraphs in the usual way.

The incidence of the supplied punctuation is mainly at the ends of lines in the manuscripts, where there are deletions or interlineations, and before words beginning with capital letters that plainly start new sentences (sometimes these are preceded in the manuscripts by very short blank spaces). I have not interfered with the punctuation of such writers as Peter Locke and John Bonville.

(ii) Brackets of three kinds occur in the texts.

(*a*) Round brackets. These are the brackets that writers generally use. Here they are always the writers' brackets except where a writer has failed to close a parenthesis and a closing bracket is supplied.

(*b*) Angle brackets. These are used for editorial departures from the manuscripts, as for replacement of wild spellings or supply of words omitted by the writers or lost through decay or tearing of the manuscripts. The reason for their use is explained invariably.

(*c*) Square brackets. These occur for various reasons:

1. The writer of the letter uses them. That they are his is stated when they occur.
2. For marginalia that are brought into the text for printing. These are accounted for where they occur.
3. Replacement of chemical symbols: see above, p. lvii.
4. Interpolated words in some of the translations.
5. Locke noted in the margins of some letters from Toinard and Justel the contents of each paragraph, and then combined all the marginal notes in a list at the end of the letter. The marginal notes are not reproduced here; any that Locke omitted from the terminal lists are inserted in them in square brackets.
6. To distinguish enclosures and the various parts of letters consisting of sections written by two or more writers. The word enclosure or the writer's name is placed in square brackets at the head of the enclosure or section.
7. Where texts of letters or passages from them are summarized.
8. In abbreviated addresses of letters to Locke at Oates.[1]

Subscriptions

The concluding words of letters and the signatures are commonly written in three or four lines. Where there is a greater spread I have reduced it by joining the short lines.

Addresses, postmarks, and endorsements

These are printed or recorded at the ends of the letters. If none is mentioned nothing is present on the manuscript of the letter as it now exists.

All addresses are printed in full except those later than 28 August 1690 (no. *1311*) which take the form of 'For Mr. John

[1] For the use of square brackets in texts printed from print or old copies and in headings of items see below, pp. lxii, lxiv–lxv.

Locke at Sir Francis Masham's at Oates. To be left at Mr. Joslyn's, a shopkeeper in Bishops Stortford in Essex'. This form, regardless of variant spellings and small variations in wording, is summarized as 'For Mr. John Locke [at Oates, by Joslyn, Bishops Stortford]'.

All postmarks are recorded. The various marks that occur in the correspondence are described below, pp. lxxvii–lxxix. For marks other than the ordinary marks of the General Post Office in London and the London receiving offices the office of origin is stated and any indications of place, date, and cost. The ordinary General Post Office mark is circular, the month reduced to two capital letters above, the day of the month (one or two arabic numerals) below; the London receiving office marks consist usually of one or two initials, sometimes in a frame. These marks, or such parts of them as are decipherable, are indicated only by the letters and numerals contained in them: e.g. DE 31; LV. If they are fragmentary or smudged I have indicated their presence as G.P.O. (or London receiving office) imperfect or indecipherable.

Impressions are frequently imperfect. As they were made from metal stamps the choice of reading of the letters or numerals is limited. Where enough of a letter or numeral is present for its identification to be certain I have disregarded the imperfection; if too little is present the deficiency is indicated by a dash.

Endorsements are printed in full. Miscellaneous notes on the backs of letters are printed in full or summarized according to their merits.

*The original manuscripts: the drafts*

Most of the drafts in the Locke correspondence were written by Locke. The existence of a draft does not prove that a letter was sent, or, if sent, that it bore much resemblance to the draft. Many of the drafts can, however, be associated with letters sent to Locke; these drafts belong with the letters to him. It seems better to bring into the general sequence than to relegate to an appendix those for which no association can be found.

i. Rendering in print

The handwriting of a draft is likely to be worse than that of a letter sent. There is more scribbling. There are more deletions, false starts, interlineations, and marginal additions, than in a letter written for a reader. In many drafts there is a distinguishing feature, the presence of alternative versions of a single passage. Where they occur it may be difficult to establish the writer's final intention and the connection of the various parts of his sentence. Unless there is to be a type-facsimile an editor must construct or reconstruct what he believes to be a valid text; if the writer's changes are important the alternative versions must be printed.[1]

In other respects the treatment of the drafts is the same as that of the letters sent.[2]

ii. The persons for whom the projected letters were intended

Where a person is named no question arises; where the draft is headed by initials or a nickname the question of identification belongs with the general question of these designations. Where no person is named or indicated allusions or connections with other letters may supply a name or a distinct but nameless personality.

iii. Dates of drafts

Many of the drafts are undated or incompletely dated. Some can be dated by association with completely dated or reliably datable letters. Those that appear to belong to the period ending at the close of 1661 must be dated mainly by tenuous arguments.

First: survival. Among the early letters there are some addressed to Locke's father; they are to be omitted from this argument. Taking only the dated and securely datable letters and drafts, the survival varies from year to year. For 1653 there are none; for 1654, three; for 1655, seven; for 1656, one; for 1657, two; for 1658, four; for 1659, seventeen; for 1660, ten; for 1661, twelve. Where the survival of the dated and datable items is relatively good the survival of the undated is likely also to be relatively good.

Secondly: place. Locke's usual place of residence between 1652 and 1667 may be assumed to have been Oxford. In view of the difficulty of movement, if he is found at a place more than a day's journey from Oxford on two days say a month apart, it can reasonably be assumed that he stayed there or in the neighbourhood during that month. Apart from a few exceptional letters from London Locke's dated letters or drafts, if he names the place, are dated from Oxford or from the country, that is, his father's house at Pensford in Somerset. Some of the dated or closely datable

[1] In the critical notes 'or' signifies different possible readings of a word; 'alternatively', a choice of words provided by the writer.

[2] I have not used square brackets to distinguish marginal additions in the drafts.

letters to him are addressed to him at Pensford or, where the address is lacking, imply that they are being sent from Oxford to the country. Locke can be placed at Pensford by date and datable letters and drafts for what appear to be autumn vacations in 1655, 1656, 1659, and 1660. He was there apparently very little after his father's death early in 1661. He seems to have stayed in Oxford in 1657; nothing survives for autumn 1658. His known movements have some bearing on the dates of letters and drafts in which place is mentioned or implied.

Thirdly: repetitions of phrases; echoes of one kind or another. If these occur between a dated letter to Locke and an undated draft from him, or between two undated pieces, a relationship between the two is possible; they may belong to the same period.

These arguments are rickety and insecure. Survival depends on chance. We know where Locke was on some particular days in the course of eight or nine years; for all the other days we must rely on inference or assumption. Repetitions and echoes provide poor foundations for argument. When nothing better is available one must resort to these vague indications. For all the incompletely dated drafts the reasons for the date to which they are attributed are set out in the head-notes.

*Texts printed from print or old manuscript copies*

The copy-texts are reproduced faithfully apart from alterations for manifest errors. These departures are kept to a minimum: the printers or transcribers had seen the original manuscripts, and at least some errors may have been present in them. The substituted words are incorporated in the texts in angle brackets, the readings of the copy-texts being shown in the critical notes.

The square brackets in the texts reprinted from Rand's edition of the correspondence of Locke and Edward Clarke occur in his texts; they apparently indicate that the words have been supplied by Rand on account of either loss of words through damage to the manuscript or omission of words by Locke.

The square brackets in Burthogge's letters are those of Babbage's transcripts.

Esther Masham made some notes to accompany the transcripts in her letter-book. Those on the letters from it that are printed here are reproduced with her initials in square brackets to distinguish them.

## ARRANGEMENT

The letters are arranged as far as is possible in a single chronological sequence, the date assigned to the letter being the latest date written on it by the writer; for undated letters and drafts, the date based on the considerations set out above.

The dates are those of the old-style or Julian calendar with one modification: the new year is assumed to begin on 1 January and not on 25 March. While legal practice retained 25 March until the adoption of the new-style or Gregorian calendar in 1752 ordinary English usage from the Restoration onwards seems to have favoured 1 January. Where there is a possibility of ambiguity I have given the double year: thus William and Mary accepted the throne on 13 February 1688/9. The Julian calendar was ten days behind the Gregorian from the institution of the latter in 1582 until 28 February 1700; the year 1700 being a leap-year in the Julian but not in the Gregorian, the Julian was henceforward until 1800 eleven days behind. When a letter bears a new-style date both old- and new-style dates are given in the heading; the letter is placed in accordance with the old-style date.

When there are two or more letters written on the same day I have generally given precedence to the letter or letters written by Locke; then to the letters that he is likely to have received sooner and then to those that he is likely to have received later. But the arrangement is variable. Where it is manifest that he wrote a letter after receiving one written on the same day I have followed the sequence.

Forwarded letters, that is, letters written by or to Locke and transmitted by agents, whether or not the agents enclose them in letters of their own, are treated as independent letters and placed according to their dates of writing. Enclosures are letters not written to Locke that are sent to him by correspondents of his as components of their letters, or not written by him that he sent to correspondents of his as parts of his letters; they are treated as components of the enclosing letters and their dates are disregarded in the arrangement.

Composite letters, that is, letters written by two or more persons severally, whether or not the sections bear the same date, are treated as units and are placed according to the latest date of writing.

## ENUMERATION

The items are enumerated in a single numerical sequence. On account of the late emergence of some letters and of a change in plan a few letters bear numbers followed by capital letters (no. 183A, etc.).

The numerals for letters from and drafts written by Locke are in roman arabic; those for letters to him and for letters between third parties are in italic arabic.

Letters bearing more than one date of writing and composite letters written by two or more persons are regarded as units and enumerated according to their position in the chronological sequence.

## HEADINGS OF LETTERS

The heading of a simple letter or draft consists of its number, the writer's name, the name of the person addressed, the date of the letter, the number of the immediately preceding letter between the correspondents, and that of the immediately succeeding letter between them.

For a joint letter, that is one written by one writer and signed by him and another, and for a composite letter in which the writers write separate sections, the names are given together, as no. *459*, 'George Walls and Nathaniel Hodges to Locke'.

The correspondents' names are given in sufficient detail for quick recognition. Locke is always Locke. For ordinary men the Christian name when available and the surname are given (if there are two Christian names they are commonly reduced to initials); for doctors, knights, and baronets, their dignities; for peers their Christian and family names and their ultimate titles, titles held temporarily being given only when required by the correspondence. Ordinary unmarried women have their names without qualification; married women appear as 'Mrs.' unless they possess titles; women who change their surnames on marriage and appear under both names as correspondents have both names in the headings so far as they are requisite for continuity.[1]

Supplied names and identifications of correspondents that are not based on explicit statements in the letters or other clear evidence are enclosed in square brackets. If an identification is doubtful the name is followed by a query; if no name is available that is indicated by a rule.

[1] Unmarried women were commonly addressed as 'Mrs.'; sometimes probably as 'Madam'. I have adopted this usage in my notes for Mrs. Smithsby and Mrs. Lockhart.

If the writer began to write on one date and finished on another the two dates are given. If two writers wrote on different days the names and dates are distinguished. The dates are those of the writers of the letters. Any departure from the writer's date is given in square brackets; similarly if there is no date the date supplied is given in square brackets. Wherever there is doubt a query is inserted.

In the headings of composite letters the immediately preceding and succeeding letters are cited for each writer in the order in which he is listed in the heading. The joint letters written by Edward Clarke and John Freke on the one side and Locke on the other between 1694 and 1700 (the 'College' letters) are all brought into the Clarke sequence (begin no. *1821*; end no. *2686*). When three numbers occur in the citations the middle number is that of an item other than a draft or a letter to or from Locke.

HEAD-NOTES

The head-note contains the following information so far as it is requisite: the source of the text printed here (the copy-text); if it is a manuscript other than the letter sent its status (draft or copy); the handwriting; the condition of the manuscript; drafts or old manuscript copies; the earliest printing of the text or passages from it (when only unimportant passages are omitted the printing is generally regarded as complete; printings after 1947 are recorded selectively); any independent printings; where the name of the writer or person addressed is concealed or disguised the reason for any identification; the reason for any departure from the date of the letter as stated by the writer or for any date, or part of a date, supplied; the transmission of the letter; the relation of the letter to other letters between Locke and the correspondent; a biographical note on, or identification of, the correspondent; general remarks on the contents of the letter.

The source of the text is stated precisely. If it is transcribed from a facsimile (Xerox print, photostat, etc.) that is stated. The handwriting is described mainly when it is likely to make the transcription uncertain. The condition is described for much the same reason and to account for lacunae.

I have recorded such old manuscript copies as I have found. I have given only the first printings except when later editors went back to the manuscripts. This did not occur until the nineteenth and twentieth centuries. Sir William R. W. Wilde printed fresh versions of four letters from Locke to Dr. Thomas Molyneux and Ezekiel Burridge that were printed first in *Some Familiar Letters*; and Benjamin Rand printed fresh versions of letters from Locke to Edward Clarke that had been printed previously by Thomas Forster or Henry Ollion.

If a letter is forwarded by another writer or is carried by anyone of note or is unduly slow in transit that is stated. If it is an answer to, or an antecedent of, any other letter or letters, that is stated, regardless of the citations of preceding and succeeding letters in the heading.

The writer or person addressed is the subject of a biographical note only if there has been no previous biographical note for him; there may be supplementary notes. There is a general note on the contents of a letter when some introduction to them is desirable.

## TRANSLATIONS

The texts of the Latin letters, the Latin passages in other letters, and the texts of the solitary Greek letter and of one of the Dutch letters, are accompanied by translations. The Dutch letters for which there are no translations are domestic or complimentary in character.

The translations are to be regarded as companions to the original texts and not as substitutes for them. An exact translation is possible only where words are defined rigorously. Few words can be so limited. Though their primary meanings may be identical Latin and English words will have different connotations and perhaps different associations. The absence of articles in Latin occasionally leads to ambiguities. Moreover men's thought is influenced by their own languages. Locke and van Limborch were competent Latinists, writing freely and making no more errors than they would if they wrote in their own languages. When composing their letters they may have thought in Latin rather than translated their matter from their own languages into Latin; they will attach slightly divergent meanings to their utterances. I have tried to exclude from the translations anything that is not in the originals and to avoid forcing particular meanings on to comprehensive statements; in other respects the translations can only approximate to the meanings of the originals.

ANNOTATION

The general purpose of the annotation is to provide information for the immediate understanding of the correspondence and guidance for its further study. To these ends authorities are cited for all substantive statements in the notes: to serve as a means of testing their reliability and to indicate the available materials for their elaboration. The meanings of unusual words are explained; persons, places, religious bodies and movements, historical events, scientific and technical developments, voyages, coins and currency, and books are identified. There are omissions in practice, due to the specialized nature or limited interest of the matter, to my ignorance of some subjects, to the impracticability of searching all possible sources, or to the absence of studies. Thus I have left Locke's tenants in Somerset to local historians and have not tried to identify mortgagors; I have not penetrated far into medicine or Hebrew philology; I have not run to earth some quotations or anecdotes; on account of the lack of bibliographies and secondary works the treatment of cartography is unsatisfactory.

Some subjects attract more attention than others. This is due primarily to the importance attached to them by Locke and his correspondents. The notices bearing on some subjects are not capable of adequate elucidation without some comprehensive statement; there are therefore extensive introductory notes for them. A few persons take such important parts in the correspondence as to require biographical accounts at length rather than the summary statements that suffice for most persons.

The notes are based mainly on printed materials. I have consulted manuscripts when I knew that they contained, or were likely to contain, relevant matter: thus the letters from Nicolas Toinard to J. G. Grævius in the Royal Library in Copenhagen. In selecting editions of books for citation or quotation I have usually preferred original editions to modern reprints, but this always depends on the particular case.

In citations of books I have tried to give recognizable designations; except when a book is cited for the first time these are generally the author's surname and an abbreviated title; full titles, as far as necessary, are given in a finding-list.[1] In page

[1] I have introduced round brackets where I have omitted the opening words of a title, and for condensations such as 'Buckinghamshire' for 'the county of Buckingham'.

citations where an asterisk accompanies the page-number either the page is so numbered in the book or the required page is misnumbered in the book; in the latter case the number given is the correct number by the count.

*Probability*

Many notes, especially those relating to the identifications of persons, contain expressions of doubt: 'probably', 'perhaps', 'identifiable as', and so on. These notes range from the almost certain to reasonable guesses. The certainty is the historian's certainty; it is based on what are believed to be trustworthy sources of information. There are the chances of misunderstanding of the notice and of defects in the historical record. Occasionally there are difficulties with the meaning of words. Where there can be any reasonable doubt about the validity of a statement it is proper to indicate its existence.

There is one caveat. A statement indicated as doubtful is apt in a repetition overleaf to be treated as certain. I have tried to guard against using these unqualified repetitions in the construction of arguments, and in general for the more doubtful statements some indication of doubt is retained.

For some notices there is no obvious elucidation. The best that can be provided is a line of inquiry. It must comply with any data provided by the text and must not conflict with any requirements of the text. The justification for inserting guesses of this kind is editorial experience.

*Words and phrases; proverbs*

The English of Locke and most of his correspondents is that of the educated Englishmen of their time, such as Dryden or Halifax. The writing is sometimes colloquial, and Locke is fond of dialect or racy words. The English of the older and less educated correspondents is closer to that of the Authorized Version of the Bible. They have some difficulty in constructing their sentences, but none in finding appropriate words for them.

I assume that the reader has little difficulty with the books that Locke published and that he has some acquaintance with English prose from Hobbes to Addison. Very few sentences in the correspondence call for explanation. For words I have used as a rough guide the *Concise Oxford Dictionary of Current English* (more precisely, the edition of 1929). The meanings of a few words that are absent from it will be obvious; a few words that are in it will require definition if their context is to be understood. For definitions I have used the *Oxford English Dictionary*; the great collections of quotations that accompany the definitions are invaluable. I have supplemented it with the various editions of the dictionaries of the time, more especially Thomas Blount, *Glossographia*, 1656, etc.; Edward Phillips, *The New World of English Words*, 1658, etc.; and *Glossographia Anglicana Nova*, 1707, etc. For dialect I have used Joseph Wright, *The English Dialect Dictionary*, 1898–1905.

For proverbs I have used W. G. Smith, *The Oxford Dictionary of English Proverbs*, 2nd ed., 1948. I have not cited it for those in current use.

The great difficulty is to recognize phrases that were formerly in vogue and that have long since ceased to be current. Some may be quotations or altered quotations, but have been too ephemeral for the dictionaries.

The principal difficulties in the French letters are provided by Nicolas Toinard's spelling reforms and Locke's erratic use of the language. Basically the spelling, which includes the use of accents, is that of the late seventeenth-century dictionaries. Writers were careless in marking accents; an undifferentiated stroke over the letter was to be read as grave or acute; or the accent might be omitted altogether in words that in print were habitually provided with one; slow reading will overcome this. For the meanings of words I have taken the *Concise Oxford French Dictionary* (reprint 1957) as a guide. I have assumed that, apart from a few out-of-the-way words, the reader will not require interpretations of the words contained in it. For obsolete or unusual words I have used mainly Randle Cotgrave, *A Dictionarie of the French and English Tongues*, 1632, and Abel Boyer, *Dictionnaire royal, françois et anglois*, 1702; and further P. Richelet, *Dictionnaire de la langue françoise*, 3 vols., 1740.[1]

For Latin, besides modern dictionaries, I have used occasionally T. Holyoke, *A Large Dictionary*, 1677, and more frequently Adam Littleton, *Linguæ Latinæ Liber Dictionarius Quadripartitus*, 4th ed., 1703.

For Dutch, besides the great *Woordenboek* of M. de Vries and others, I have used Henry Hexham, *A Copious English and Netherdutch Dictionary*, 1675, 1672, and W. Sewel, *A Large Dictionary English and Dutch*, 1708.

[1] When reproducing print I have retained the use of accents of the originals.

*Persons*

Subject to the limitation mentioned above, all persons concerned in the correspondence, whether writers of letters, persons to whom letters are addressed, or persons mentioned in the texts, are identified as far as possible. If biographical statements have been published they are cited; if none exist short statements are provided. Many persons are elusive. Some are sufficiently identified by their occupations. If notices relating to them are readily available there will be a note. I have not searched parish registers or rate-books. On account of their importance in the correspondence a few persons are the subjects of longer notes; these are apt to be concerned with the general bearings of their activities as well as with their immediate careers.

Citations are of the great national and international biographical dictionaries so far as they are available; where they fail, occasionally of encyclopedias; frequently of peerages, alumni lists, and similar compilations. In general I assume that the most recent biographical dictionary will provide the most serviceable account; sometimes, however, an older work will be more informative. Where this occurs I have cited either both works or the older one alone. I have not cited biographies and other works published more recently than the dictionaries and other compilations unless they are required for the elucidation of statements in the texts. When there is a disagreement about dates or other matter between a dictionary and a peerage or similar compilation I have followed silently that which appeared to be the more reliable.[1]

*Places*

The majority of the place-names occurring in the correspondence do not require elucidation; such matters as the areas, populations, communications, and political situations, of the places themselves must in general be left to the reader. The names of some areas have, however, changed so greatly in their application, or, if they have disappeared from the modern map, have become so vague, as to require elucidation: thus the West Indies or Tartary. The principal geographical dictionary is M. A. Baudrand, *Geographia Ordine Litterarum Disposita* (1682–1).

[1] I have set out my principles regarding biographical statements and citations at greater length in the introduction to my edition of Evelyn's *Diary*: i. 123–6.

I have stated the distances between places where they are required by notices in the texts. For those in England I have used generally *Cary's New Itinerary*, 1798.

*Religious bodies and movements*

The correspondence bears witness to the struggle of a strong inherited religious belief to adapt itself to new intellectual and scientific foundations; to the rise of new systems of belief and to the growth of toleration. It illustrates also the need of the Huguenots of the dispersal to define the beliefs for which they had left their homes.

The great guide is *The Oxford Dictionary of the Christian Church*, edited by F. L. Cross, first published in 1957 (I have used the reprint of 1963), a comprehensive and informative work, objective in a field in which prejudice is almost always present. Among more general works I have used for religion in the Netherlands L. Knappert, *Geschiedenis der Hervormde Kerk onder de Republiek en het Koningrijk der Nederlanden*, 1911–12, and the regrettably incomplete *Biographisch woordenboek van protestantsche godgeleerden in Nederland* by J. P. de Bie and J. Loosjes, 1919– ; for the Huguenot refugees E. and E. Haag, *La France protestante*, 10 vols., 1846–59, and the incomplete second edition, 6 vols. (to Gasparin), 1877–88; and Erich Haase, *Einführung in die Literatur des Refuge*, 1959; for the Socinians and Unitarians the two books by E. M. Wilbur, *A History of Unitarianism: Socinianism and its Antecedents*, 1946, and *A History of Unitarianism: in Transylvania, England, and America*, 1952.

*Natural science and technology*

Most of my notes are little more than citations of original or recent authorities. I have paid some attention to mensuration, a subject in which, as his Journals show, Locke was greatly interested. I have not tried to investigate Nicolas Toinard's theory of the variation of the compass.

*Voyages and exploration*

Most of the notes are bibliographical. Almost all the writers are stay-at-home. Their sources of information, the authorities for their statements, if they themselves do not name them, are still readily identifiable. I have tried to check statements for which I have failed to find a printed or manuscript source. For the bibliography I have usually started with G. Boucher de la Richarderie,

*Bibliothèque universelle des voyages*, 6 vols., 1808. This is a well-arranged descriptive catalogue but is unreliable on account of deficiencies and misprints.

*Coins and currency; Finance*

The correspondence contains little that bears on the composition of Locke's writings on the recoinage of 1696–9 but many notices for the recoinage itself, the price of guineas, and the rate of exchange with Amsterdam. The most important of the books on the English coinage is J. Keith Horsefield, *British Monetary Experiments 1650–1710*, 1960; it contains a remarkable bibliography of the contemporary pamphlets and other literature on the subject. Tables for the variations in the Amsterdam exchange and the price of guineas are given in J. E. Thorold Rogers, *The First Nine Years of the Bank of England*, 1887 (for the dates of the quotations in these see Horsefield, p. 254 n.).

In Locke's correspondence with Peter King there is frequent mention of his dealings in Bank of England and New East India Company shares. These questions, instructions, and reports show how he was affected by the establishment of trustworthy government finance and the growth of commercial enterprise; they show the beginning of the London stock-market. For the general setting I have relied on P. G. M. Dickson, *The Financial Revolution in England*, 1967, a full and lucid account of what is for most readers a difficult subject.

*Books and booksellers; Periodicals*

Locke was author, book-collector, and friend of several booksellers: men who were at once publishers and retailers. The notices in Locke's correspondence and Journals are of great interest for the history of particular books; there are notices relating to the trade in England and the Netherlands; and there are important series of letters from two booksellers, J. H. Wetstein and Awnsham Churchill.

For English publications there is a union catalogue, Donald Wing, *Short-title Catalogue of Books printed in England, Scotland, Ireland, Wales, and British America, and of English Books printed in Other Countries, 1641–1700*, 3 vols., 1945–51 (a new edition is now appearing). Periodical lists of new publications were published in the series reprinted by Edward Arber as *The Term Catalogues, 1668–*

*1709 A.D.*, 3 vols., 1903–6; and in *Bibliotheca Annua*, four volumes extending from January 1699 to 25 March 1704. There are further lists in *The History of the Works of the Learned*, a monthly that ran from 1699 to 1712 (there may be lists in earlier periodicals also; they are likely to be poor). Close dates of publication are to be found chiefly in newspaper advertisements. There are notices of books in various periodicals, including the *Philosophical Transactions* of the Royal Society. Biographical notices of the booksellers are contained in H. R. Plomer, *A Dictionary of the Booksellers and Printers who were at work in England, Scotland, and Ireland from 1641 to 1667*, 1907, and *A Dictionary of the Printers and Booksellers . . . from 1668 to 1725*, 1922 (Bibliographical Society publications); these can be supplemented by P. G. Morrison, *Index of Printers, Publishers and Booksellers in Donald Wing's Short-title Catalogue*, 1955.

English newspapers and other periodicals are listed in *The New Cambridge Bibliography of English Literature*, vol. ii, 1971. R. T. Milford and D. M. Sutherland, *A Catalogue of English Newspapers and Periodicals in the Bodleian Library 1622–1800*, 1936, gives catalogue entries for one of the leading English collections.

For publications in France I have used Henri-Jean Martin, *Livre, pouvoirs et société à Paris au XVIIe siècle*, 2 vols., 1969, which contains much incidental information about the booksellers. I have used further the lists of new books and notices in the *Journal des Sçavans*.

Booksellers in the United Provinces were working largely for export. Many of their publications were in French or Latin; Dutch was reserved for books whose principal circulation was at home. Very few books in Dutch are mentioned in the correspondence. For the French and Latin publications I have depended on the printed catalogues of the great libraries and the contemporary periodicals. The Amsterdam booksellers and their activities are the subject of I. H. van Eeghen, *De Amsterdamse boekhandel, 1680–1725*, in progress, 1960– , a work based on archival and other contemporary material. For the great output of pamphlets I have used the *Catalogus van de pamfletten-verzameling berustende in de Koninklijke Bibliotheek* by W. P. C. Knuttel, 9 vols. in 11, 1889–1920 (here cited as Knuttel and by number of item). I have not seen the pamphlets themselves, but what I have required here is mainly evidence of publication.

Cologne in imprints in this period is suspect; when the publisher is Pierre Marteau the books are usually the work of Dutch, mainly

Amsterdam, booksellers, who wanted either to avoid inquiry or to call attention to a book.[1] There is an incomplete list of these publications in P. G. Brunet, *Imprimeurs imaginaires et libraires supposés*, 1866.[2]

There are important illustrative documents for the international trade in *The Notebook of Thomas Bennet and Henry Clements (1686–1719)*, edited by Norma Hodgson and Cyprian Blagden, 1956 (Oxford Bibliographical Society, new ser. vol. vi); the editors give an account of the trade, drawing especially on the papers of Samuel Smith (Bodleian Library, Rawlinson MSS., Letters 114).

The Commonwealth of Learning depended largely on periodicals for the diffusion of knowledge and thought. They ranged in character from those containing mainly original articles with a few notices of books to those consisting almost exclusively of notices. Locke's friend Jean Le Clerc was for a time editor and principal author of one, and was responsible later for two successors to it. Locke used two or three periodicals as guides to book-buying. I have cited them freely in my notes to notices of books on account of their importance in the intellectual life of the time. The following are the principal periodicals that I have used:[3]

*Le Journal des Sçavans*, 5 January 1665 N.S.–1753 and continuations. Publication was very irregular until the end of 1677 on account of royal interference; after that there were some further fluctuations and a long interruption in 1687. It then becomes a weekly with a long autumn vacation, so that there are about 42 issues each year. This continues until after 1704, but the issues increase in length, so that the volumes after 1701 are nearly half as long again as the immediately preceding volumes. The contents are notices of books, astronomical and other scientific observations, miscellaneous notices, mainly of scientific interest, and lists of new books. I have used the Amsterdam reprints, published generally as annual volumes from 1669 onwards.

*Philosophical Transactions*, 6 March 1665– (still continuing). The periodical of the Royal Society; officially recognized from the start but not conducted by the Society until 1753. Publication was irregular. It broke off in 1678 after the issue of no. 142 (part of

[1] Van Eeghen, ii. 35–6.

[2] pp. 112–45. The latest is dated 1834. After 1715 they are mainly erotic.

[3] I regret that I have not seen C. Juncker, *Schediasma Historicum de Ephemeridibus, sive Diariis Eruditorum*, 1692. There is a notice of it in *Bibliotheque universelle*, xxii. 423–9.

vol. xii); in the next three years there were seven issues of *Philosophical Collections*; it resumed in 1683, but there were no issues in 1688–90. Until 1704 and later it contains mainly original contributions or reports; there are some reviews of books. For work I have used mainly the second edition of the abridgement by John Lowthorp (3 vols., 1716), but citations are of the original issues.

*Acta Eruditorum*, Leipzig, 1682–1731, 50 volumes, with 'Supplementa', 10 vols., 1692–1734, and decennial indexes, 1693–1733; continued by *Nova Acta Eruditorum*, 1732–76, with supplements and indexes. Monthly. The contents are similar in range to those of the *Journal des Sçavans*, but the original scientific articles are more substantial.

*Nouvelles de la Republique des Lettres*, Rotterdam, March 1684–February 1687. Monthly. By Pierre Bayle with some items from contributors. Mainly notices of books; some articles and reports on scientific subjects; some obituary notices. I have used the reprint in Bayle, *Œuvres diverses*, The Hague, 1727, vol. i. There was a continuation by D. de Larroque and others, 1687–9; then a revival by Jacques Bernard, January 1699–July 1710.

*Bibliotheque universelle et historique*, Amsterdam, January 1686–December 1693. Quarterly (each volume divided into three months). 25 volumes. By Jean Le Clerc and others (vols. i–ix, Le Clerc and J. Cornand de la Croze; vol. x, Le Clerc; vol. xi, Cornand; vols. xii, xiii arts. 8 and 15, xiv–xix, and part of xx, Le Clerc; vols. xx–xxv, Jacques Bernard). Index volume, 1718. Almost entirely literary; mainly notices of books; some original articles; two contributions by Locke. This is for Locke's correspondence the most important of the periodicals. I have used a set consisting partly of original, partly of second or third, editions of the various volumes.

*The History of the Works of the Learned*, January 1699–December 1711 (13 volumes). Monthly. By Samuel Parker, jnr., and others. Reviews of books, news of the learned world, lists of new publications. Some passages apparently taken from foreign periodicals.

*Memoires pour l'histoire des sciences et des beaux arts*, January 1701–1762. The so-called 'Journal de Trévoux'. For it and its Amsterdam reprints see van Eeghen, *De Amsterdamse boekhandel*, ii. 128–34.

*Bibliotheque choisie*, Amsterdam, 1703–13 (27 volumes). Twice or thrice a year. By Jean Le Clerc. Index volume, 1718. Notices and digests of books, essays, obituary notices. It is less concerned than the *Bibliotheque universelle* with recent publications. Le Clerc used it frequently to defend his own writings.

For the particular notices of books in the correspondence I have cited, if they appear in it, the catalogue of books owned by Locke in John Harrison and Peter Laslett, *The Library of John Locke*, 2nd ed., 1971 (it is cited as L.L. and by number of item). This catalogue has also been of value for tracing the sources of information of statements which writers made without naming their authority; I have accordingly cited it in the notes when I have cited books contained in it. I have also used Locke's Journals.[1]

### CRITICAL NOTES

Manuscript readings recorded in the critical notes are signalled by superior letters in the text. Where two successive words govern a single note the same superior letter follows both words. Where three or more words are affected, the first and last words only are followed by superior letters with dashes after and before ([a–] [–a]), and the note is keyed to them in the form [a–a] (see, for example, note [c–c] on i. 24 and in the text: but[c–] the warmth[–c]).

## APPENDIX I: FOREIGN EXCHANGE

Notices in the correspondence relating to coins and currencies are explained as they occur. The only foreign currencies for which there are notices relating to the rate of exchange are the French and the Dutch.

The French used as monies of account livres, sols tournois, and deniers; the livre of 20 sols; the sol of 12 deniers. The principal coins were the louis d'or and the silver écu (crown). The weight and standard of these coins remained constant. The louis in 1660 was valued at 10 livres; in 1669 at 11; in 1685 at 11 livres 5 sols; in 1689 at 12 livres 10 sols; in 1693 at 14 livres; in 1704 at 15. The écu in 1660 was valued at 3 livres (i.e. 60 sols); in 1689 at 3 livres 6 sols; in 1693 at 3 livres 12 sols; in 1701 at 3 livres 16 sols; and in 1704 at 4 livres. Exchange was stated in terms of the écu of 60 sols tournois. Par was 1 écu = 54 pence. At this rate £1 = 13 livres 6 sols 8 deniers. I have found no tables showing the fluctuations in the rate. Apparently it could range to 1 écu = 60 pence. At this rate £1 = 12 livres.

[1] I have also benefited by the lists of books in John Lough, 'Locke's Reading during his Stay in France' (*The Library*, 5th ser. viii (1953), 229–58), and G. Bonno, *Les Relations intellectuelles de Locke avec la France*, 1955, pp. 175–208. These lists should ultimately be overtaken by the publication of the manuscript materials on which they are based, and especially of the Journals; hence their absence from my citations.

The principal Dutch coins are:

Ducatoon (Dukaton) = 63 stuivers.
Three gulden piece = 60 stuivers.
Gulden = 20 stuivers.
Stuiver = 2 grooten.

Exchange was stated in terms of schillings of 6 stuivers ('shillings Fleems'). Par was £1 = $37\frac{1}{27}$ schillings (= 11 gulden $2\frac{2}{9}$ stuivers). The exchange from January 1695 to July 1696 ranged generally between 27 and 32 schillings; from July 1696 to October 1701, between 35 and 37 schillings.

The principal authorities are Alexander Justice, *A General Treatise of Monies and Exchanges*, 1707, which makes some use of a book by S. Ricard: *Le Nouveau Negociant*, 1686, or *Traité general du commerce* (I have seen only the second edition, 1705); and J. E. Thorold Rogers, *The First Nine Years of the Bank of England*, 1887, pp. 37, 165–8 (for his table see Horsefield, *British Monetary Experiments*, pp. 254–5); for the French coinage, J. A. Blanchet and A. Dieudonné, *Manuel de numismatique française*, 1912–36, vol. ii.

## APPENDIX II: POSTMARKS; FRANKING

The only postmarks occurring in the Locke correspondence are those of the General Post Office in London; the London receiving offices; the London Penny Post; and an office or offices in Amsterdam.

The marks were made by a stamp (presumably of metal) and were commonly called stamps until the word was transferred (about 1840) to the printed adhesive labels of our time.

1. The General Post Office was established by act of parliament in 1657. At the Restoration this act, like other acts enacted since 1641, was held to be void, but a new act, passed in 1660, put the office on a permanent footing.

From 1661 letters were stamped at some point during their transit through the office with a distinctive mark. It was a circle divided into two halves by a bar; in the upper the month was indicated by two capital letters (IA, FE, MR, AP, MA, IV, IY, AV, SE, OC, NO, DE); in the lower, the day of the month. No marks of this kind were used in Locke's time anywhere except in the London General Post Office.

The foreign office used also two special marks. One is a small rectangle divided into two compartments; the upper contains a letter, S or D; the lower, a number; this was the amount of postage to be paid by the recipient. The mark occurs only on incoming foreign letters between 1663 and 1667 (it occurs on no. *198*).[1] The other is a large circular mark bearing the word FRANCHES surrounding a rose. It was used on outgoing foreign correspondence from 1667 until about 1720. There are impressions, all rather poor, on nos. *308*, *309*, *312*, *314*, *323*, and *324*.

2. Of the London receiving offices nothing appears to be known except what can be derived from their marks. They were presumably shops or houses that took in letters and carried them at appropriate times to the General Post Office; if any payments were to be made to the General Post Office they must have received the money for them with the letters. Their marks generally consist of a ring enclosing sometimes one, sometimes two, capital letters. These marks occur frequently in the correspondence; the general positions of one or two of the offices can be deduced from them. Two letters, nos. 284, *308*, bear a circular mark with OFF in the upper half and 4 in the lower; this mark also is believed to have belonged to a London receiving office.

3. The London Penny Post was inaugurated by William Dockwra, a London merchant, in March 1680. The duke of York (the future James II), who had been granted the profits of the General Post Office in 1663, claimed that the Penny Post infringed his monopoly. He proceeded against Dockwra and judgement was given in his favour on 23 November 1682. The service started again on 11 December; it was conducted by a special organization, separate from the General Post Office.

Dockwra established seven sorting houses and four or five hundred receiving houses (these were shops, coffee-houses, etc.). Letters were stamped with two marks: a triangular mark inscribed along the sides 'Penny Post Paid' and in an inner triangle the initial letter of the sorting house; and a heart-shaped mark inscribed 'Mor' or 'Af' and the hour at which the letter or package was received. There are impressions of the two stamps on nos. *677*, *719*.

The new organization had six sorting houses. It generally stamped letters with two marks: a triangular mark much as before, inscribed 'Peny Post Payd' and in the inner triangle a single

[1] Another design may also have been in use to show postage due.

letter indicating the sorting house and two or three letters to give the day of the week; and a circular mark inscribed with a large initial indicating the office from which the letter was carried for delivery and 'Mor' or 'Af' and the hour at which it was handed to the letter carrier. Sometimes there is a dotted heart-shaped mark to indicate transfer from the General Post Office to the Penny Post. A few letters in the correspondence bear the new organization's marks.

4. An English local mark, occurring on no. *668*.

5. There is an Amsterdam mark, a circle enclosing the city's arms; above them is a post-horn with the letter R; and on either side 3 and S. This mark occurs on nos. 905, 913, etc. Another mark, also circular, with AMSTERDAM in a ring surrounding probably the city's arms, occurs on nos. *745*, *1197*.

Franking was a concession to all members of both houses of parliament. First proposed apparently in 1650, it was established by royal warrant of 14 May 1661. Single inland letters from or to them were to be carried free of charge. The privilege did not extend to packets or foreign letters. On 4 March 1693 it was restricted to the principal secretaries of state and three other persons of similar standing; two days later it was re-established for all members of both houses during the sessions of parliament and for forty days before and forty days after them; members were to write their names on the covers of their letters and to seal them; and to provide the Postmaster General with specimen signatures and impressions of their seals.

The leading authority for the English postal service is Howard Robinson, *The British Post Office: a history*, 1948.[1] On the early G.P.O. stamps I have followed C. H. L'Estrange Ewen, *The Earliest Postal Stamps*, 1939. For the receiving offices I have used F. Bagust, *Some Notes on the Small Post-offices of London in the Seventeenth and Eighteenth Centuries*, 1937. For the London Penny Post the principal books are T. Todd, *William Dockwra . . . the Story of the London Penny Post, 1680–82*, 1952 (this reprints the relevant documents); and F. Staff, *The Penny Post, 1680–1918*, 1964. There are lists of the English post-towns and of the places served by the London Penny Post in Strype's Stow, v. 402–4.

[1] Robinson's book is now in part superseded by R. M. Willcocks, *England's Postal History*, 1975. I am indebted to Dr. Barrie Jay for calling my attention to this book and for examining this appendix.

# FINDING-LIST OF BOOKS CITED BY SHORT TITLES, ETC.


Aaron, R. I. *John Locke*. 3rd ed. 1971.

Aaron and Gibb. *An Early Draft of Locke's Essay together with Excerpts from his Journals*. Edited by R. I. Aaron and Jocelyn Gibb. 1936.

*Abstracts of Somersetshire Wills, etc.* From the manuscript collections of Frederick Brown. Edited by F. A. Crisp. 6 vols. 1887–90.

*Account of Several late Voyages and Discoveries to the South and North, An*. 1694.

Acres, W. Marston. *The Bank of England from Within, 1694–1900*. 2 vols. 1931.

*Acts and Ordinances of the Interregnum, 1642–1660*. Edited by C. H. Firth and R. S. Rait. 3 vols. 1911.

*A.D.B. Allgemeine deutsche Biographie*. 56 vols. 1875–1912.

Aitzema, L. van. *Saken van Staet en Oorlogh, in, ende omtrent de Vereenigde Nederlanden*. 7 vols. fol. 1669–72.

Álvaro Dória, A. *A Rainha D. Maria Francisca de Sabóia*. 1944.

Anderson, R. C. The Society for Nautical Research: Occasional publications no. 5: *Lists of men of war, 1650–1700*. Part 1: *English ships, 1649–1702*. Compiled by R. C. Anderson. 1935. [Cited by number.]

Ascoli, G. *La Grande Bretagne devant l'opinion française au* XVII$^{e}$ *siècle*. 2 vols. 1930.

Atterbury, Francis, bishop of Rochester. *Epistolary Correspondence* . . . 5 vols. 1783–90 (1798).

Avaux, J. A. de Mesmes, comte d'. *Négociations de Monsieur le Comte d'Avaux en Hollande* [1679–88]. 6 vols. 1752–3.

Baillie, G. H. *Watchmakers and Clockmakers of the World*. 1969.

Baker, George. *The History . . . of (Northamptonshire)*. 2 vols. fol. 1822–41.

Barker and Stenning. G. F. Russell Barker and A. H. Stenning. *The Record of old Westminsters: a Biographical List of all those . . . Educated at Westminster School, to 1927*. 2 vols. 1928. [Vol. iii, for the years 1883–1960, by J. B. Whitmore and others, 1972.]

Barnes, Mrs. Annie. *Jean Le Clerc (1657–1736) et la République des Lettres*. 1938.

Barnouw, P. J. *Philippus van Limborch*. 1963.

Baudrand, M.-A. *Geographia, ordine litterarum disposita*. 2 vols. fol. Paris. 1682, 1681.

Baxter, S. B. *The Development of the Treasury, 1660–1702*. 1957.

—— *William III*, 1966.

BAYLE, PIERRE. His correspondence is cited as 'Labrousse, no. —', the reference being to E. Labrousse, *Inventaire critique de la correspondance de Pierre Bayle*, 1961, which will be superseded by Mme Labrousse's edition of the correspondence; when a letter is quoted the source of the quotation is specified.

—— *Dictionaire historique et critique*. I have used the third edition, 4 vols., fol., Rotterdam, 1720.

BEAVEN, A. B. *The Aldermen of the City of London*. 2 vols. 1908–13.

BENNET and CLEMENTS. *The Notebook of Thomas Bennet and Henry Clements (1686–1719)*. Edited by N. Hodgson and C. Blagden (Oxford Bibliographical Society, new ser., vol. vi, 1953).

BENOIST, E. *Histoire de l'Édit de Nantes*. 3 vols. in 5. Delft. 1693–5.

BERNIER, FRANÇOIS. *Histoire de la derniere revolution des Etats du Grand Mogol*. Paris. 1670. *Evenemens particuliers*. Paris. 1670. *Suite des Memoires*. Paris. 1671.

*Bibliotheque choisie*. Jean Le Clerc. 28 vols. (Vol. xxviii index.) Amsterdam. 1703–13; 1718.

*Bibliotheque universelle et historique*. Jean Le Clerc and others. 26 vols. (Vol. xxvi index.) Amsterdam. 1686–93; 1718.

*Biographie universelle* (Michaud). New ed. 45 vols. 1852–66.

BIRCH, THOMAS. *The History of the Royal Society of London*. 4 vols. 1756–7.

—— *The Life of the Honourable Robert Boyle*. 8°. 1744.

—— *The Life of the Most Reverend Dr. John Tillotson, Lord Archbishop of Canterbury*. 2nd ed. 1753.

BISCHOFF, E. *Kritische Geschichte der Thalmud-Übersetzungen*. 1899.

BITTNER and GROSS. *Repertorium der diplomatischen Vertreter aller Länder seit dem Westfälischen Frieden (1648)*. Edited by L. Bittner and L. Gross. Vol. i, 1648–1715. 1936.

B.L. Bodleian Library.

BLAGDEN, C. *The Stationers' Company*. 1960.

BLEGNY, NICOLAS DE (A. du Pradel). *Le Livre commode des adresses de Paris pour 1692*. Edited by E. Fournier. 2 vols. 1878.

BLOMEFIELD, F. *(History) of Norfolk*. 11 vols. 8°. 1805–10.

BLOUNT, THOMAS. *Glossographia*. 1656 and later editions. [Cited as 'Blount' with date of edition.]

BLOXAM, J. R., ed. *Magdalen College and King James II, 1686–1688*. (Oxford Historical Society, vol. vi, 1886).

—— *Register of Members (of Magdalen College, Oxford)*. 8 vols. 1853–85.

B.M. British Library by its former name, British Museum, *Catalogue of the Pamphlets . . . Collected by George Thomason, 1640–1661*. 2 vols. 1908.

—— *Handbook of the Coins of Great Britain and Ireland*. By H. A. Grueber. 1899.

—— *List of Catalogues of English Book Sales 1676–1900 now in the British Museum*. 1915.

B.M. *Medallic Illustrations of the History of Great Britain and Ireland.* Compiled by E. Hawkins, etc. 2 vols. 1885.

B.N. Bibliothèque Nationale.

BOHUN, EDMUND. *The Diary and Autobiography of Edmund Bohun.* Edited by S. W. Rix. 1853.

BONNO, *Le Clerc. Lettres inédites de Le Clerc à Locke.* Edited by Gabriel Bonno. University of California publications in modern philology, vol. lii. Berkeley and Los Angeles. 1959.

BOSSUET, J.-B. *Correspondance.* Edited by C. Urbain and E. Levesque (Les grands écrivains de la France). 15 vols. 1909–25.

BOURGEOIS, É., and L. ANDRÉ. *Les Sources de l'histoire de France . . . (1610–1715).* 8 vols. 1913–35.

BOYER, ABEL. *Dictionnaire royal, françois et anglois.* 2 vols. The Hague. 1702.

BOYLE, ROBERT. *Works.* Edited by Thomas Birch. 5 vols. fol. 1744.

BRADY, W. MAZIERE. *Clerical . . . Records of Cork, Cloyne and Ross.* 3 vols. 1863–4.

BRAITHWAITE, W. C. *The Beginnings of Quakerism.* 2nd ed., edited by H. J. Cadbury. 1955.

BRAYLEY, E. W., and J. BRITTON. *The History of the Ancient Palace and Late Houses of Parliament at Westminster.* 1836.

BREWSTER, SIR DAVID. *Memoirs of the Life . . . of Sir Isaac Newton.* 2 vols. 1855.

BRICE, GERMAIN. *Description nouvelle de ce qu'il y a de plus remarquable dans la ville de Paris.* 2 vols. 1684.

BRITISH LIBRARY, formerly BRITISH MUSEUM. See B.M.

BROWN, HARCOURT. *Scientific Organizations in Seventeenth Century France, 1620–1680.* 1934.

BROWN, LLOYD A. *The Story of Maps.* 1951.

BROWN, LOUISE FARGO. *The First Earl of Shaftesbury.* 1933.

BROWNE (BROWN), EDWARD, M.D. *An Account of several Travels through a Great Part of Germany.* 1677.

—— *A Brief Account of some Travels.* 2nd ed. 1685.

BROWNING, ANDREW. *Thomas Osborne, Earl of Danby.* 3 vols. 1944–51.

BRUCE, JOHN. *Annals of the Honourable East-India Company . . . (1600–1708).* 3 vols. 1810.

BURNET, GILBERT, bishop of Salisbury. *Bishop Burnet's History of His Own Time.* 6 vols. 1833.

BURTCHAELL, G. D., and T. U. SADLEIR, edd. *Alumni Dublinenses.* 1935.

CALAMY, EDMUND. *An Historical Account of My Own Life.* Edited by J. T. Rutt. 2 vols. 1829.

*Calendar of State Papers: Colonial Series.* 1860– . [Cited as *Cal. S.P., Col.*, and by volume and number of item. The earlier volumes in the series are not numbered; those cited here are *America and West Indies*: vols. vii, 1669–74; xiv, 1693–6; xv, 1696–7; xvi, 1697–8; xvii, 1699; and xviii, 1700.]

*Calendar of State Papers: Domestic Series*. 1856– . [Cited as *Cal. S.P., Dom.*, and by dates covered by volume and page, except for the volumes for 1685–8, where the citation is by dates covered by volume and number of item.]

*Calendar of the Clarendon State Papers preserved in the Bodleian Library*. 5 vols. 1869–1970.

*Calendar of Treasury Books*, 1660– . 1904– .

CAMPBELL, JOHN, Baron Campbell. *The Lives of the Lord Chancellors and Keepers of the Great Seal*. 8 vols. 1845–69.

CARPENTER, EDWARD F. *Thomas Tenison, Archbishop of Canterbury*. 1948.

CARSTARES, WILLIAM. *State-papers and Letters addressed to William Carstares*. Edited by J. M'Cormick. 1774.

CASTRIES, H. DE. *Les Sources inédites de l'histoire du Maroc de 1530 à 1845*. 20 vols. in 22. 1905–48.

*C.B.E.L. The Cambridge Bibliography of English Literature*. 4 vols. 1940.

C., G. E.: see G. E. C.

CHAMBERLAYNE, EDWARD. *Angliæ notitia*. 1669 and later editions; continued after 1703 by John Chamberlayne, and after 1707 as *Magnæ Britanniæ notitia*. [Bibliography in I.H.R., *Bull.* xv (1938), 24–6; for office holders editions are cited by date without page citations; general information contained in several editions is usually indicated as such, with a citation of a particular edition by date and page.]

CHAUFFEPIÉ, J. G. de. *Nouveau Dictionnaire historique et critique*. 4 vols. fol. Amsterdam. 1750–6.

CHRISTIE, W. D. *A Life of Anthony Ashley Cooper, First Earl of Shaftesbury*. 2 vols. 1871.

CHRISTOPHERSEN, H. O. *A Bibliographical Introduction to the Study of John Locke*. Oslo. 1930.

CHURCHILL, A. and J. *A Collection of Voyages and Travels*. 4 vols. fol. 1704. Two further volumes were added for the second edition, 1732.

CHURCHILL, (SIR) WINSTON L. SPENCER. *Marlborough: his Life and Times*. 4 vols. 1933–8.

*C.J. Journals of the House of Commons*. fol. *c.* 1742– . [Citations are not specific if the date of the proceedings is stated in text or notes unless the entry for the day occupies several pages, in which case a page reference is given.]

CLAPHAM, SIR JOHN. *The Bank of England*. 2 vols. 1944.

CLARENDON, HENRY HYDE, second earl of. *The Correspondence of Henry Hyde, Earl of Clarendon, and of his Brother Laurence Hyde, Earl of Rochester; with the Diary of Lord Clarendon from 1687 to 1690*. Edited by S. W. Singer. 2 vols. 1828. [Cited as 'Clarendon, *Correspondence*, ed. Singer'.]

CLARK, E. A. G. *The Ports of the Exe Estuary, 1660–1860*. 1960.

CLARK, SIR GEORGE (N.). *A History of the Royal College of Physicians of London*. 2 vols. 1964–6. [Vol. iii, by A. M. Cooke, 1972.]

CLARK, RUTH. *Anthony Hamilton.* 1921.

CLARKE, T. E. S., and H. C. FOXCROFT. *A Life of Gilbert Burnet, Bishop of Salisbury.* 1907.

CLOWES, SIR WILLIAM LAIRD, and others. *The Royal Navy.* 7 vols. 1897–1903.

CLUTTERBUCK, R. *The History . . . of (Hertfordshire).* 3 vols. fol. 1815–27.

COCKBURN, MRS. CATHERINE. *Works.* Edited by T. Birch. 2 vols. 1751.

COLBERT, J.-B. *Lettres, instructions et mémoires.* Edited by P. Clément. 8 vols. in 9. 1861–82.

COLEMAN, D. C. *Sir John Banks.* 1963.

*A Collection of Several Pieces of Mr. John Locke, never before printed, or not extant in his Works.* Edited by Pierre Desmaizeaux. 1720.

COLLINS, ARTHUR. *Collins's Peerage of England.* Edited by Sir E. Brydges. 9 vols. 1812.

COLLINSON, J. *The History . . . of Somerset.* 3 vols. 1791.

*Conway Letters.* Edited by M. H. Nicolson. 1930.

COOPER, C. H. *Annals of Cambridge.* 5 vols. 1842–1908.

CORDIER, HENRI. *Bibliotheca Indosinica.* 5 vols. 1912–32.

—— *Bibliotheca Sinica.* 2nd ed. 5 vols. 1904–24.

*Correspondentie van Willem III en van Hans Willem Bentinck, eersten Graaf van Portland.* Edited by N. Japikse. 5 vols. (Rijksgeschiedkundige Publicatiën, Kleine serie, nos. 23–4, 26–8, 1927–37.)

COTGRAVE, RANDLE. *A Dictionarie of the French and English Tongues.* 1632.

CRANSTON, MAURICE. *John Locke.* 1957.

CRATON, M. *A History of the Bahamas.* 1962.

CUNDALL, F. *The Governors of Jamaica in the Seventeenth Century.* 1936.

DALLAWAY, J. *A History of the Western Division of . . . Sussex.* 2 vols. in 3. 1815–32.

DALRYMPLE, SIR JOHN. *Memoirs of Great Britain and Ireland . . .* [1681–1702]. New ed. 3 vols. 1790.

DALTON, CHARLES, ed. *English Army Lists and Commission Registers, 1661–1714.* 6 vols. 1892–1904.

DANGEAU, P. DE COURCILLON, marquis de. *Journal.* Edited by E. Soulié and others. 19 vols. 1854–60.

DAS, HARIHAR. *The Norris Embassy to Aurangzib (1699–1702).* 1959.

DAUMAS, M. *Les Instruments scientifiques aux XVII^e^ et XVIII^e^ siècles.* 1953.

DAVIES, GODFREY. *The Restoration of Charles II, 1658–1660.* 1955.

DAVIES, K. G. *The Royal African Company.* 1957.

*D.B.F. Dictionnaire de biographie française.* 1933– .

DEAN, C. G. T. *The Royal Hospital, Chelsea.* 1950.

DE BIE, J. P., and J. LOOSJES. *Biographisch woordenboek van protestantsche godgeleerden in Nederland.* 1919– .

DELAMBRE, J.-B.-J. *Histoire de l'astronomie moderne.* 2 vols. 1821.

DES AMORIE VAN DER HOEVEN, A. *De Joanne Clerico et Philippo Limborch dissertationes duae.* 1843.

DEWHURST, KENNETH. *Dr. Thomas Sydenham (1624–1689).* 1966.

—— *John Locke (1632–1704), Physician and Philosopher.* 1963.

DICKSON, P. M. G. *The Financial Revolution in England, 1688–1756.* 1967.

*Dictionary of American Biography.* 22 vols. 1928–44.

*Dictionary of Canadian Biography.* 1966– .

*Dizionario biografico degli Italiani.* 1960– .

*D.N.B. Dictionary of National Biography.* Reissue. 22 vols. 1908–9.

DOUGLAS, SIR ROBERT. *The Scots Peerage.* Edited by Sir J. B. Paul. 9 vols. 1904–14.

DRAKE'S HASTED. See Hasted.

DROSTE, COENRAET. *Overblyfsels van Geheugchenis.* Edited by R. Fruin. 2 vols. 1879.

DUMONT, JEAN, baron de Carlscroon. *Corps universel diplomatique.* 8 vols. in 16. fol. 1726–31.

EASTON, C. *Les Hivers dans l'Europe occidentale.* 1928.

EHRMAN, JOHN. *The Navy in the War of William III, 1689–1697.* 1953.

ELIZABETH CHARLOTTE, duchess of Orleans. *Aus den Briefen der Herzogin Elisabeth Charlotte von Orléans an die Kurfürstin Sophie von Hannover.* Edited by E. Bodemann. 2 vols. 1891.

*Ellis Correspondence, The: Letters . . . (1686–8) to John Ellis.* Edited by G. Agar Ellis. 2 vols. 1829.

*Encyclopaedia Judaica.* 16 vols. 1971–2.

ERASMUS. *Opera omnia.* Edited by J. Le Clerc. 10 vols. in 11. fol. 1703–6.

ERSKINE, JOHN, of Carnock. *Journal (1683–7).* Edited by W. Macleod. (Scottish History Society, vol. xiv, 1893.)

ESTRADES, GODEFROI, comte d'. *Lettres, mémoires . . .* 9 vols. 1743.

EVELYN, JOHN. *The Diary of John Evelyn.* Edited by E. S. de Beer. 6 vols. 1955. [Citations by volume and page are of notes in this edition. Citations by date are of Evelyn's text.]

EWEN, C. H. L'ESTRANGE. *Lotteries and Sweepstakes.* 1932.

—— *Witch Hunting and Witch Trials.* 1929.

*Familiae minorum gentium.* Compiled by Joseph Hunter; edited by J. W. Clay. (Harleian Society, vols. xxxvii–xl, 1894–6.)

FAULKNER, T. *An Historical . . . Description of Chelsea.* [2nd ed.] 2 vols. 1829.

—— *History . . . of Kensington.* 8°. 1820.

FEAVEARYEAR, SIR A. *The Pound Sterling*. 2nd ed., edited by E. V. Morgan. 1963.

FEILING, SIR KEITH. *British Foreign Policy, 1660–1672*. 1930.

FIENNES, CELIA. *The Journeys of Celia Fiennes*. Edited by C. Morris. 1947.

FIRTH, SIR CHARLES HARDING. *The Regimental History of Cromwell's Army*. 2 vols. 1940.

—— *The Last Years of the Protectorate*. 2 vols. 1909.

—— and S. C. LOMAS. *Notes on the Diplomatic Relations of England and France, 1603–1688*. 1906.

FLOQUET, A. *Bossuet précepteur du Dauphin*. 1864.

FOORD, A. S. *Springs, Streams and Spas of London*. 1910.

FORSTER. *Original Letters of Locke; Algernon Sidney; and Anthony Lord Shaftesbury, Author of the 'Characteristics'*. Edited by Thomas (I. M.) Forster. 1830. [The second edition, 1847, is cited for additional matter only.]

FOSS, EDWARD. *The Judges of England*. 9 vols. 1848–64.

FOSTER, JOSEPH. *Alumni Oxonienses: the Members of the University of Oxford, 1500–1714*. Early series. 4 vols. 1891–2. [Cited as 'Foster' when the note relates expressly to a member of the university; otherwise as 'Foster, *Alumni*'.]

—— *Register of Admissions to Gray's Inn, 1521–1889*. 1889.

FOX BOURNE, H. R. *The Life of John Locke*. 2 vols. 1876.

FOXCROFT, H. C. *The Life and Letters of Sir George Savile, Bart., First Marquis of Halifax*. 2 vols. 1898.

—— ed. *A Supplement to Burnet's History of My Own Time*. 1902.

FRANKLIN, ALFRED. *Les Anciennes Bibliothèques de Paris*. 3 vols. 1867–73. (Histoire générale de Paris.)

—— *Histoire de la Bibliothèque Mazarine*. 1860.

—— *Précis de l'histoire de la Bibliothèque du Roi, aujourd'hui Bibliothèque Nationale*. 2nd ed. 1875.

FULTON, J. F. *A Bibliography of the Honourable Robert Boyle*. 2nd ed. 1961.

GARDINER, S. R. *History of the Commonwealth and Protectorate, 1649–1656*. New ed. 4 vols. 1903.

—— *History of the Great Civil War, 1642–1649*. New ed. 4 vols. 1893. [Cited from new impression, 1904–5.]

G. E. C. G. E. COKAYNE. *The Complete Peerage*. New ed., edited by V. Gibbs and others. 14 vols. 1910–59.

G. E. C., *Baronetage*. G. E. COKAYNE. *The Complete Baronetage*. 6 vols. 1900–9.

GOODISON, N. *English Barometers, 1680–1860*. 1969.

GREY, ANCHITELL. *Debates of the House of Commons from 1667 to 1694*. 10 vols. 1769.

GREY, FORDE, Lord Grey of Warke, etc. *The Secret History of the Rye-House Plot*. 1754.

HAAG, E. and E. *La France protestante.* 10 vols. 1846–59. 2nd ed., vols. i–vi (to Gasparin). 1877–88.

HAASE, E. *Einführung in die Literatur des Refuge.* 1959.

HALEY, K. H. D. *The First Earl of Shaftesbury.* 1968.

HALLEY, EDMOND. *Correspondence and Papers.* Edited by E. F. MacPike. 1932.

HARBEN, H. A. *A Dictionary of London.* 1918.

HARLOW, V. T. *Christopher Codrington, 1668–1710.* 1928.

—— *A History of Barbados, 1625–1685.* 1926.

HARRIS, F. R. *The Life of Edward Mountagu, K.G., First Earl of Sandwich.* 2 vols. 1912.

HARTLEY, SIR HAROLD, ed. *The Royal Society: its Origins and Founders.* 1960.

HASTED, EDWARD. *The History . . . of Kent.* 4 vols. fol. 1778–99.

—— *Hasted's History of Kent* . . . Edited by H. H. Drake. Part i, The hundred of Blackheath. 1886. [Cited as 'Drake's Hasted'.]

HATTON, EDWARD. *A New View of London.* 2 vols. 1708.

*Hatton Correspondence. Correspondence of the family of Hatton, 1601–1704.* Edited by (Sir) Edward Maunde Thompson. 2 vols. (Camden Society, new ser. vols. xxii–xxiii, 1878.)

HAWKINS, E. *Medallic Illustrations.* See B.M.

HEAL, SIR AMBROSE. *The London Goldsmiths, 1200–1800.* 1935.

HEARNE, THOMAS. *Remarks and Collections of Thomas Hearne.* Edited by C. E. Doble and others. 11 vols. (Oxford Historical Society, vols. ii, etc., 1885–1921.)

HEDGES, SIR WILLIAM. *The Diary of William Hedges, Esq. . . . 1681–1687.* Edited by R. Barlow. 3 vols. (Hakluyt Society, vols. lxxiv, lxxv, lxxviii, 1887–9.)

HERBERT, A. S. *Historical Catalogue of Printed Editions of the English Bible, 1525–1961.* 1968.

HEXHAM, HENRY. *A Copious English and Netherdutch Dictionary.* New ed., edited by Daniel Manby. 2 vols. Rotterdam. 1675, 1672.

HILL, RICHARD. *The Diplomatic Correspondence of . . . Richard Hill . . . (1703–6).* Edited by W. Blackley. 2 vols. 1845.

HILL, S. CHARLES. *Notes on Piracy in Eastern Waters.* 1923.

HIRSCH, AUGUST. *Biographisches Lexikon der Aertzte aller Zeiten und Völker.* 2nd ed. 6 vols. 1929–35.

*Histoire des evenemens tragiques d'Angleterre.* Cologne. 1686.

H.M.C. Historical Manuscripts Commission.

HOARE, SIR RICHARD COLT. *The History of Modern Wiltshire.* 6 vols. fol. 1822–44.

HOLMES, GEOFFREY. *British Politics in the Age of Anne.* 1967.

HOOKE, ROBERT. *The Diary of Robert Hooke . . . 1672–1680.* Edited by H. W. Robinson and W. Adams. 1935.

HOPPEN, K. T. *The Common Scientist in the Seventeenth Century: a Study of the Dublin Philosophical Society, 1683–1708.* 1970.

HORN, D. B., ed. *British Diplomatic Representatives, 1689–1789.* (Royal Historical Society, Camden third series, vol. xlvi, 1932.)

HORSEFIELD, J. K. *British Monetary Experiments, 1650–1710.* 1960. [This includes a bibliography of books on money, etc., published mainly between 1690 and 1700; citations by number refer to it.]

HÜBNER, J. *Genealogische Tabellen.* 4 vols. oblong 4°. 1727–37. Supplement. 1822–4.

HUDSON'S BAY COMPANY. *Minutes, 1671–4.* Edited by E. E. Rich. (Champlain Society, Hudson's Bay series, vol. v, 1942.)

HULL, WILLIAM I. *Benjamin Furly and Quakerism in Rotterdam.* 1941.

HUTCHINS, JOHN. *The History . . . of Dorset.* 3rd ed., edited by W. Shipp and J. W. Hodson. 4 vols. fol. 1861–70.

HUYGENS, CHRISTIAAN. *Œuvres complètes.* 22 vols. 1888–1950.

HUYGENS, CONSTANTIJN, jnr. *Journaal, 1688–96.* 2 vols. (Historisch Genootschap te Utrecht, Werken, new ser. vols. xxiii, xxv, 1876–7). Indexes 2 vols. (ibid., 3rd ser., vols. xxii, xxxv, 1906, 1915).

I.H.R., *Bull.* Institute of Historical Research (University of London). *Bulletin.* 1925– .

JAPIKSE, N. *Prins Willem III: de Stadhouder-Koning.* 2 vols. 1930–3.

*Journal des Sçavans*, Paris, 1665–1753, etc. [Here cited by the date of issue and by the page numbers in the Amsterdam reprint, which started in 1669.]

KEMBLE, J. M., ed. *State Papers and Correspondence . . . (1686–1707).* 1857.

KENYON, J. P. *Robert Spencer, Earl of Sunderland.* 1958.

KING, PETER, seventh Baron King. *The Life of John Locke.* 1829. [Citations are always of this first edition except for the additional matter printed in the second edition, 2 vols., 1830, when it is specified: 'King, 1830, . . .']

KLOPP, ONNO. *Der Fall des Hauses Stuart.* 14 vols. 1875–88.

KNAPPERT, L. *Geschiedenis der Hervormde Kerk onder de Republiek en het Koningrijk der Nederlanden.* 2 vols. 1911–12.

KNUTTEL. *Catalogus van de pamfletten-verzameling berustende in de Koninklijke Bibliotheek* (at The Hague). Compiled by W. P. C. Knuttel. 9 vols. in 11. 1889–1916. [Cited as 'Knuttel' with number of item.]

LABROUSSE, ELISABETH. *Pierre Bayle.* 2 vols. 1963–4.

—— For citations of Bayle's correspondence as 'Labrousse, no. —' see Bayle.

LA CHENAYE-DESBOIS, F.-A. AUBERT DE, and BADIER. *Dictionnaire de la noblesse.* 3rd ed. 19 vols. 1863–76.

LAMBERTY, G. DE. *Memoires pour servir à l'histoire du* XVIII*e siecle.* 14 vols. (vols. i–v, 2nd ed.). Amsterdam. 1733–40.

LANE-POOLE, S. *Aurangzíb.* 1901.

LA RONCIÈRE, C. B. DE. *Histoire de la marine française.* 6 vols. 1899–1932.

LASCELLES, R. *Liber munerum publicorum Hiberniæ, 1152–1827.* 2 vols. fol. [1824–30.]

LAVISSE, ERNEST, and others. *Histoire de France.* 9 vols. in 18. 1900–11.

L.C.C. *Survey of London.* Vols. i– . 1900– .

LEIBNIZ, G. W. *Correspondance de Leibniz avec l'électrice Sophie.* Edited by O. Klopp. 3 vols. [*c.* 1873.]

—— *Die philosophischen Schriften.* Edited by C. I. Gerhardt. 7 vols. 1875–90.

—— *Sämtliche Schriften und Briefe.* Published by the Deutsche Akademie der Wissenschaften zu Berlin. 1923– . [The first series contains the general, historical, and political correspondence; vol. viii, published in 1970, the latest available (1973), contains that of the year 1692. Cited as Leibniz, *S.S.*]

LE NEVE, JOHN. *Monumenta Anglicana: being Inscriptions on the Monuments of several Eminent Persons . . .* 5 vols. 1717–19. [The volumes are cited by the years to which they relate.]

LE NEVE, PETER. *Le Neve's Pedigrees of the Knights made by King Charles II . . . Queen Anne.* Edited by G. W. Marshall. (Harleian Society, vol. viii, 1873.)

LESLIE, J. B. *Ossory Clergy and Parishes.* 1933.

LETI, GREGORIO. *Il teatro brittanico.* 5 vols. 1684.

LÉVY-VALENSI, J. *La Médecine et les médecins français au xvii^e^ siècle.* 1933.

LI, MING-HSUN. *The Great Recoinage of 1696 to 1699.* 1963.

LILLYWHITE, BRYANT. *London Coffee Houses.* 1963. [Cited by number.]

LIPSCOMB, GEORGE. *The History . . . of (Buckinghamshire).* 4 vols. 1847.

LITTLETON, ADAM. *Linguæ Latinæ liber dictionarius quadripartitus.* 4th ed. 1703. [First published in 1678.]

*L.J. Journals of the House of Lords.* fol. *c.* 1767– .

L.L., no. —. *The Library of John Locke.* By John Harrison and Peter Laslett. 2nd ed. 1971. [Cited in this form to show Locke's possession of particular books.]

LOCKE, JOHN. [Citations of his works are from the original editions or, when he made alterations in successive editions, from the editions specified by date. For *Some Thoughts concerning Education* in connection with his letters to Edward Clarke the first five editions are distinguished as A, B, C, D, and E.]

—— *Essays on the Law of Nature.* Edited by W. von Leyden. 1954.

—— Herbarium. Bodleian Library, MSS. Locke c. 41; b. 7. [Cited for Locke's pupils at Christ Church; list printed in *Bodleian Library Record*, vii (1967), 190–3.]

—— Journal. Bodleian Library, MSS. Locke f. 1–10, and British Museum, Add. MS. 15,642. [Cited by date or by Locke's pagination according to circumstances.]

—— *Two Tracts on Government.* Edited by Philip Abrams. 1967.

*London Inhabitants within the Walls, 1695.* Introd. by D. V. Glass. (London Record Society, vol. ii, 1966.)

LONG, PHILIP. *Summary Catalogue of the Lovelace Collection of the Papers of John Locke in the Bodleian Library*, 1959. (Oxford Bibliographical Society, new ser. vol. viii.)

LOUGH, JOHN, ed. *Locke's Travels in France, 1675–1679.* 1953.

LÜTHY, H. *La Banque protestante en France.* 2 vols. 1959–61.

LUTTRELL, NARCISSUS. *A Brief Historical Relation of State Affairs . . . (1678–1714).* 6 vols. 1857. [Cited by volume and page or by date of entry according to circumstances.]

LYSONS, DANIEL. *The Environs of London.* 2nd ed. 2 vols. in 4. 1811.

MACAULAY, T. B., Lord Macaulay. *The History of England from the Accession of James the Second.* 5 vols. 1849–61; later editions.

MCKENZIE, D. F. *The Cambridge University Press, 1696–1712.* 2 vols. 1966.

MACKINTOSH, SIR JAMES. *History of the Revolution in England in 1688.* 1834.

MACRAY, W. D. *Annals of the Bodleian Library.* 2nd ed. 1890.

MADAN, FALCONER. *Oxford Books* [1468–1680]. 3 vols. 1895–1931. [Vols. ii and iii (1641–80) are generally cited by number of item; by volume and page for miscellaneous notices. There are subsidiary enumerations of the contributions to some of the Oxford congratulatory volumes.]

MAGDALEN COLLEGE. See Bloxam, J. R.

MANNING, OWEN, and W. BRAY. *The History . . . of Surrey.* 3 vols. fol. 1804–14.

*Marriage Bonds for the Diocese of Bristol.* Vol. i, 1637–1700. Edited by E. Ralph. (Bristol and Gloucestershire Archaeological Society, Records Section, vol. i, 1952.)

MARTIN, C. T. *Catalogue of the Archives . . . of All Souls' College.* 1877.

MARTIN, H.-J. *Livre, pouvoirs et société à Paris au xvii^e siècle.* 2 vols. 1969.

MARY II, QUEEN. *Lettres et mémoires.* Edited by Mechtild, Countess Bentinck. 1880.

—— *Memoirs . . . (1689–93).* Edited by R. Doebner. 1886.

MATTHEWS, A. G. *Calamy Revised.* 1934.

—— *Walker Revised.* 1948.

MAYOR, J. E. B., ed. *Cambridge in the Seventeenth Century.* 3 pts. 1855–71.

*Middle Temple Records: Minutes of Parliament.* Edited by C. T. Martin. 4 vols. 1904–5.

MISSON, HENRI, DE VALBOURG. H. M. de V., *Memoires . . . en Angleterre.* 1698.

MONK, J. H. *The Life of Richard Bentley*, 2nd ed. 2 vols. 1833.

MORANT, PHILIP. *The History . . . of Essex.* 2 vols. fol. 1768.

MORE, L. T. *The Life and Works of . . . Robert Boyle.* 1944.

MORRISON, P. G. *Index of Printers, Publishers and Booksellers in Donald Wing's Short-title Catalogue.* 1955.

MORSE, H. B. *The Chronicles of the East India Company Trading to China, 1635–1834.* 5 vols. 1926–9.

MUNK, WILLIAM. *The Roll of the Royal College of Physicians.* 2nd ed. 3 vols. 1878. [Vol. iv, for the years 1826–1925, by G. H. Brown, 1955.]

NASH, T. R. *Collections for the History of Worcestershire.* 2 vols. fol. 1781–99.

*N.B.G. Nouvelle biographie générale* (Didot). Edited by F. Hoefer. 46 vols. 1855–66.

NEWTON, SIR ISAAC. *The Correspondence of Isaac Newton.* Edited by H. W. Turnbull, J. F. Scott, and others. 1959– .

—— Monetary tables. [Here quoted from the reprint in J. Ede, *A View of the Gold and Silver Coins of all Nations, c.* 1808.]

NICHOLS, JOHN. *The History . . . of (Leicestershire).* 4 vols. in 8. fol. 1795–1815.

*N.N.B.W. Nieuw Nederlandsch biographisch woordenboek.* Edited by P. C. Molhuysen and others. 10 vols. 1911–37.

NOBLE, MARK. *Memoirs of the Protectoral-house of Cromwell.* 3rd ed. 2 vols. 1787.

NORTH, ROGER. *The Life of . . . Francis North, Baron of Guilford.* 1742.

*O.D.C.C. The Oxford Dictionary of the Christian Church.* Edited by F. L. Cross. 1957 (corrected reprint 1963).

*O.E.D. The Oxford English Dictionary.* Edited by James A. H. Murray and others. Corrected reissue with supplement. 13 vols. 1933.

OLDENBURG, H. *The Correspondence of Henry Oldenburg.* Edited by A. R. and M. B. Hall. 1965– .

OLLION. *Lettres inédites de John Locke à ses amis Nicolas Thoynard, Philippe van Limborch et Edward Clarke.* Edited by Henry Ollion with the collaboration of T. J. de Boer. 1912.

—— *Notes.* H. Ollion, *Notes sur la correspondance de John Locke suivies de trente-deux lettres inédites de Locke à Thoynard (1678–1681).* 1908.

*Oxford Dictionary of English Proverbs, The.* Compiled by W. G. Smith. 2nd ed. 1948.

PAPILLON, A. F. W. *Memoirs of Thomas Papillon.* 1887.

PARTINGTON, J. R. *A History of Chemistry.* 4 vols. 1961–70.

PASCAL, BLAISE. *Œuvres.* Edited by L. Brunschvicg and P. Boutroux, etc. (Les grands écrivains de la France). 14 vols. 1908–21.

PASTOR, LUDWIG VON. *Geschichte der Päpste seit dem Ausgang des Mittelalters.* 16 vols. in 22. 1901–33.

PAULY, A. F. VON. *Paulys Real-Encyclopädie der classischen Altertumswissenschaft.* New ed. Edited by G. Wissowa. 1894– .

PEILE, JOHN. *Biographical Register of Christ's College.* 2 vols. 1910–13.

PERWICH, W. *The Despatches of William Perwich.* Edited by M. B. Curran. (Royal Historical Society, Camden Third Series, vol. v, 1903).

PHILLIPS, EDWARD. *The New World of English Words*. 1658 and later editions. [Cited as 'Phillips' with date of edition.]

PIGANIOL DE LA FORCE, J.-A. *Description de Paris*. New ed. 8 vols. 1742.

PIPER, DAVID. *Catalogue of Seventeenth-Century Portraits in the National Portrait Gallery*. 1963.

PLOMER, H. R. *A Dictionary of the Booksellers and Printers . . . (1641–67)*; *A Dictionary of the Printers and Booksellers . . . (1668–1725)* (Bibliographical Society, 1907, 1922).

PRIDEAUX, *Letters*. *Letters of Humphrey Prideaux . . . to John Ellis . . . 1674–1722*. Edited by (Sir) Edward Maunde Thompson. (Camden Society, new ser., vol. xv, 1875.)

RAND. *The Correspondence of John Locke and Edward Clarke*. Edited by Benjamin Rand. 1927.

—— *Shaftesbury*. *The Life, Unpublished Letters, and Philosophical Regimen of Anthony*, [*Third*] *Earl of Shaftesbury*. Edited by Benjamin Rand. 1900.

RAVAISSON, FRANÇOIS. *Archives de la Bastille*. 19 vols. 1866–1904.

REDLICH, O. *Geschichte Österreichs*, vol. vi, 1921 (Geschichte der europäischen Staaten).

RERESBY, SIR JOHN. *Memoirs*. Edited by Andrew Browning. 1936.

RICHELET, PIERRE. *Dictionnaire de la langue françoise*. 3 vols. fol. 1740. [For the first edition, 1680, see no. *505* etc.]

ROBBINS, CAROLINE. *The Eighteenth-Century Commonwealthman*. 1959.

ROBINSON, HOWARD. *The British Post Office*. 1948.

ROGERS, J. E. THOROLD. *The First Nine Years of the Bank of England*. 1887. [Cited as 'Thorold Rogers'.]

RONAN, C. A. *Edmond Halley*. 1970.

ROUTH, E. M. G. *Tangier: England's Lost Atlantic Outpost, 1661–1684*. 1912.

RUSSELL, RACHEL, LADY. *Letters*. Edited by Lord John Russell. 2 vols. 1853.

SAINT-SIMON, LOUIS DE ROUVROY, duc de. *Mémoires*. Edited by A. de Boislisle (Les grands écrivains de la France). 43 vols. 1879–1930.

SALMON, W. *Seplasium. The Compleat English Physician*. 1693.

SAUGRAIN, C.-M. *Nouveau voyage de France*. By M. L. R. Dernière éd. 1723.

*Savile Correspondence*. Edited by W. D. Cooper. (Camden Society, vol. lxxi, 1858.)

SCHICKLER, BARON F. DE. *Les Églises du Refuge en Angleterre*. 3 vols. 1892.

SCOTT, W. R. *The Constitution and Finance of English, Scottish and Irish Joint-Stock Companies to 1720*. 3 vols. 1910–12.

SÉVIGNÉ, MME DE. *Lettres*. Edited by L.-J.-N. de Monmerqué (Les grands écrivains de la France). 14 vols. 1862–6.

SEWEL, WILLIAM. *A Large Dictionary English and Dutch. . . Groot woordenboek der Engelsche en Nederduytsche taalen*. 2 vols. 1708.

SHAW, W. A. *The Knights of England*. 2 vols. 1906.

*Shrewsbury Correspondence. Private and Original Correspondence of Charles Talbot, Duke of Shrewsbury* . . . Edited by William Coxe, 1821.

SMITH, R. W. INNES. *English-Speaking Students of Medicine at . . . Leyden*. 1932.

SMYTH, RICHARD. *The Obituary of Richard Smyth . . . from 1627 to 1674*. Edited by Sir Henry Ellis. (Camden Society, vol. xliv, 1849.)

*Some Familiar Letters*. John Locke, *Some Familiar Letters between Mr. Locke, and Several of his Friends*. 1708.

SOMMERVOGEL. *Bibliothèque de la Compagnie de Jésus*. New ed., edited by C. Sommervogel. 11 vols. 1890–1932.

STATUTES. [Statutes are cited by regnal year and chapter, with further specification as required, from *Statutes of the Realm* [1101–1713], 9 vols. fol. 1810–22.]

STEELE, I. K. *Politics of Colonial Policy: the Board of Trade . . . 1696–1720*. 1968.

STEELE, R. R. *Tudor and Stuart Proclamations, 1485–1714*. 2 vols. 1910. [Cited by the numbers of the proclamations.]

STOETT, F. A. *Nederlandsche spreekwoorden*. 3rd ed. 2 vols. 1915–16.

STORY, R. H. *William Carstares*. 1874.

STRICKLAND, AGNES. *The Lives of the Seven Bishops*. 1866.

STRYPE'S STOW. John Stow, *A Survey of the Cities of London and Westminster*, edited by John Strype. 6 books in 2 vols. fol. 1720.

SURTEES, R. *The History . . . of the County Palatine of Durham*. 4 vols. fol. 1816–40.

*T.C.* See *Term Catalogues*.

TEMPLE, SIR WILLIAM. *Works*. [Citations are from the edition in four volumes, octavo, 1770.]

*Term Catalogues, The, 1668–1709*. Edited by E. Arber. 3 vols. 1903–6. [Citations following a book-title: '*T.C.*', with volume and page; general citations: '*Term Catalogues*', with volume and page; citations of particular issues: 'the Term *Catalogue* for' with month and page.]

THÉVENOT, M. *Relations de divers voyages curieux*. 4 vols. fol. 1663–72.

THIEME, *Lexikon*. Ulrich Thieme and F. Becker. *Allgemeines Lexikon der bildenden Künstler*. 37 vols. 1907–50.

THIJSSEN-SCHOUTE, C. LOUISE. *Nederlands Cartesianisme*. 1954.

—— *Uit de republiek der letteren*. 1967.

THOMPSON, H. L. *Christ Church*. 1900.

THOROLD ROGERS. See under Rogers.

TOLAND, JOHN. *A Collection of Several Pieces*. Edited by Pierre Desmaizeaux. 2 vols. 1726.

TREVELYAN, G. M. *England under Queen Anne*. 3 vols. 1930–4. [The first two volumes are cited as 'Trevelyan, *Blenheim*' and 'Trevelyan, *Ramillies*'.]

UFFENBACH, Z. C. VON. *Merkwürdige Reisen.* 3 vols. 1753–4.

UNDERWOOD, *Apothecaries.* C. Wall, H. C. Cameron, and E. A. Underwood, *A History of the Worshipful Society of Apothecaries of London.* Vol. i. 1963.

VAILLÉ, E. *Histoire générale des postes françaises.* 6 vols. in 7. 1947–55.

VAN DER AA, A. J. *Biographisch woordenboek der Nederlanden.* 21 vols. [1852–78.]

VAN EEGHEN, I. H. *De Amsterdamse Boekhandel, 1680–1725.* 1960– .

VARENNES, C. DE. *Le Voyage de France.* 1639. [The edition of 1667 is cited in no. 400 n.]

*V.C.H.* —. *Victoria History of the County of* —.

VENN, J. and J. A. *Alumni Cantabrigienses: a Biographical List of All Known Students . . . at the University of Cambridge . . . to 1900.* Part I. From the earliest times to 1751. 4 vols. 1922–7. [Cited as 'Venn' when the note relates expressly to a member of the university; otherwise as Venn, *Alumni.*]

VERTUE, GEORGE. *Vertue Note Books.* 6 vols. (Walpole Society, 1930–47.)

VIVIAN, J. L. *The Visitations of the County of Devon.* [1895.]

VRIES, M. DE, and others. *Woordenboek der Nederlandsche taal.* 1882– .

WAFER, LIONEL. *A New Voyage and Description of the Isthmus of America.* Edited by L. E. Elliot Joyce. (Hakluyt Society, 2nd ser., no. 73. 1934.)

WAGENAAR, J. *Vaderlandsche historie.* 24 vols. 1790–6.

WALKER, D. P. *The Decline of Hell.* 1964.

WARD, E. F. *Christopher Monck, Duke of Albemarle.* 1915.

WARD, JOHN. *The Lives of the Professors of Gresham College.* 1740.

WEAVER, F. W., ed. *Somerset Incumbents.* 1889.

WELD, C. R. *A History of the Royal Society.* 2 vols. 1848.

*Westminster Abbey Registers. The Marriage, Baptismal and Burial Registers of the Collegiate Church or Abbey of St. Peter, Westminster.* Edited and annotated by J. L. Chester. (Harleian Soc., vol. x. 1876.)

WHEATLEY, H. B. *London Past and Present.* 3 vols. 1891.

WILBUR, E. M. *A History of Unitarianism: in Transylvania, England, and America.* 1952.

WILKINS, JOHN, bishop of Chester. *An Essay towards a Real Character, and a Philosophical Language.* 1668.

WILKINSON, H. C. *The Adventurers of Bermuda.* 2nd ed. 1958.

WILLIAM III. See *Correspondentie.*

WILLIAMSON, SIR J. *Letters . . . to Sir Joseph Williamson . . . in 1673 and 1674.* Edited by W. D. Christie. 2 vols. (Camden Soc., new ser., vols. viii, ix, 1874).

WILSON, WALTER. *The History and Antiquities of Dissenting Churches and Meeting-houses in London.* 4 vols. 1808–14.

WING, DONALD. *Short-title Catalogue of Books Printed in England, Scotland, Ireland, and British America and of English Books Printed in Other Countries,*

*1641–1700*. 3 vols. 1945–51. Cited as Wing. [All citations are of this edition. See also Morrison, P. G.]

WOOD, ANTHONY (À). *Athenæ Oxonienses . . . the Fasti*. Edited by P. Bliss. 4 vols. 1813–20. The *Fasti* form the latter parts of vols. ii and iv. [All citations are of this edition.]

—— *The History and Antiquities of the Colleges and Halls in the University of Oxford . . . with a Continuation to the Present Time*. Edited by John Gutch. 1786.

—— *The Life and Times of Anthony Wood . . . Described by Himself*. Edited by Andrew Clark. 5 vols. (Oxford Historical Society, vols. xix, xxi, xxvi, xxx, xl, 1891–1900.)

WOOD, F. A. *Collections for a Parochial History of Chew Magna*. 1903.

WOODHEAD, J. R. *The Rulers of London, 1660–1689*. 1965.

WOOTTON, A. C. *Chronicles of Pharmacy*. 2 vols. 1910.

WOTTON, THOMAS. *The English Baronets*. 3 vols. 1727.

WREN SOCIETY. Edited by A. T. Bolton and H. D. Hendry. 20 vols. 1924–43.

WRIGHT, JOSEPH. *The English Dialect Dictionary*. 6 vols. 1898–1905.

WRIGHT, W. B. *The Ussher Memoirs*. 1889.

YOLTON, J. W. *John Locke and the Way of Ideas*. 1956. [Cited as 'Yolton'.]

—— ed. *John Locke: Problems and Perspectives*. 1969.

YONGE, JAMES. *The Journal of James Yonge [1647–1721] Plymouth Surgeon*. Edited by F. N. L. Poynter. 1963.

YOUNG, SIDNEY. *The Annals of the Barber-Surgeons of London*. 1890.

ZEDLER, J. H. *Grosses vollständiges Universal-Lexicon aller Wissenschaften und Künste*. 64 vols. fol. 1732–*c*. 1750. Supplement, 4 vols. 1751–4.

# LOCKE'S LIFE: PRINCIPAL DATES FOR THIS VOLUME

THIS table is planned to provide dates that should be serviceable to readers of the correspondence. It is not a chronological framework for Locke's life.

The principal difficulty in its compilation is that for many incidents in his life precise dates do not exist. Thus, if the mention is accurate, Locke was acquainted with Robert Boyle on 20 May 1660; there is nothing to show how much earlier the acquaintance was made. Unsatisfactory as many of them are, the dates are the best available.

In the dates *a.* (for *ante*) is to be taken to imply shortly before. In the dates for books when a precise date accompanies the word 'published' it is to be taken as the date of the earliest notice that the book had been, was, or was about to be, published, and not necessarily as the day of publication.

| | |
|---|---|
| 1632 | 29 August. Locke born. |
| 1646? | Locke admitted to Westminster School. |
| 1652 | Locke elected to a studentship at Christ Church, Oxford. From this time until 1667 Oxford was Locke's usual place of residence. |
| 1656 | 14 February. Locke graduates B.A. |
| 1658 | 29 June. Locke graduates M.A. |
| 1659 | *c.* 16 February. Locke's first extant letter to Elinor Parry. |
| 1660 | 20 May. Locke's acquaintance with Robert Boyle is first mentioned. |
| | 11 December. Locke's first treatise on the Civil Magistrate. |
| 1661 | 13 February. Locke's father dies. |
| 1661 or 1662 | Locke's second treatise on the Civil Magistrate. |
| 1664 | Locke Censor of Moral Philosophy at Christ Church. The Essays on the Law of Nature. |
| 1665 | November–February 1666. Locke's visit to Cleves. |
| 1666 | 9 July. Locke is recommended to Lord Ashley (the future first earl of Shaftesbury). |
| | 14 November. Locke granted dispensation to retain his studentship without taking holy orders. |
| 1667 | Spring? Locke joins Ashley's household in London. From this time until November 1675 Locke apparently resided usually in London. An Essay concerning Toleration. |
| 1668 | 12 June. The operation on Ashley. |
| | 23 November. Locke elected F.R.S. |
| 1670 | 1 March. The Fundamental Constitutions of Carolina sealed. |

## *Locke's Life: Principal Dates for this Volume*

1671 The first drafts of Locke's *Essay Concerning Human Understanding*. From this year until 1675 Locke appears to have been secretary to the Lords Proprietors of Carolina.

1672 October–November. Locke visits Paris.

1673 15 October–21 December 1674. Locke secretary to the Council of Trade and Foreign Plantations.

1675 6 February. Locke graduates M.B.

12 November. Locke goes to France.

25 December/4 January 1676–15/25 March 1677. Locke resides usually at Montpellier.

1676 Autumn? Locke translates Nicole's three essays.

22 September/2 October. Locke mentions for the first time Thomas Herbert, the future eighth earl of Pembroke.

1677 23 May/2 June–29 June/9 July 1678. Locke resides usually in Paris.

27 September/7 October. Locke mentions Henri Justel for the first time.

1678 11/21 April. Locke mentions Nicolas Toinard for the first time.

29 June/9 July–18/28 November. Locke's second tour of France.

4/14 November. Locke engages Sylvester Brounower.

18/28 November–22 April/2 May 1679. Locke resides in Paris.

# GENEALOGICAL TABLES

# GRIGG

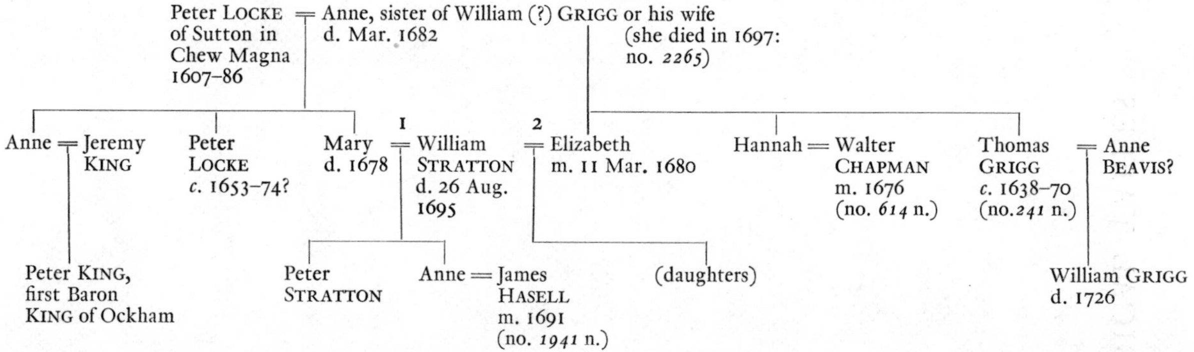


The Revd. Thomas Grigg, d. 1670, was probably a nephew of Mrs. Peter Locke, the wife of Locke's uncle. Mrs. Grigg mentions in her letters her 'Uncle Locke and cousin Stratton', meaning Peter Locke and his daughter Mary or son-in-law William Stratton: no. *313*; her sister Betty, meaning Elizabeth Grigg, second wife of William Stratton: nos. *539*, *555*; and her cousin King, meaning Peter King, the future first Lord King, Peter Locke's grandson: no. *3231*. She calls Locke brother, but neither she nor her son William Grigg claims kinship with him. Mrs. Elizabeth Stratton mentions her sister Grigg: nos. *550*, *614*, *630*; with 'our nephew', meaning William Grigg: no. *2137* (where 'our' probably refers to her late husband William Stratton); her cousin Grigg, meaning her nephew William Grigg: no. *2247*; and 'my uncle Locke', meaning Peter Locke, whom she might have regarded as her father-in-law: no. *630*. Locke, when asking to be remembered to Mrs. Grigg, mentions 'her and my uncle Locke', meaning Peter Locke: no. 260; and, writing to Mrs. Stratton, mentions 'your cousin William Grigg', meaning her nephew: no. 2020. Locke and Mrs. Stratton call one another cousin; she was entitled to do so by her marriage with Stratton, himself a cousin by marriage.

These statements imply that Thomas Grigg and Mrs. Elizabeth Stratton were brother and sister, and nephew and niece, through one or other parent, of Mrs. Peter Locke.

# KEENE

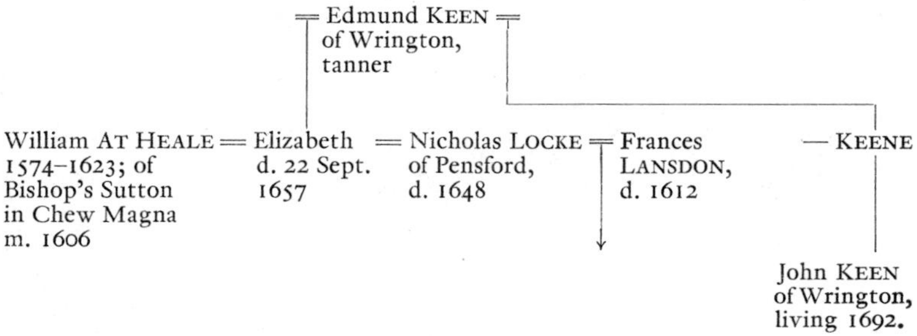


From John at Heale's pedigree in *Notes and Queries for Somerset and Dorset*, xxiv (1946), 107. (Edmund Keen is wrongly called 'a plumber' in Fox Bourne, i. 4 n.)

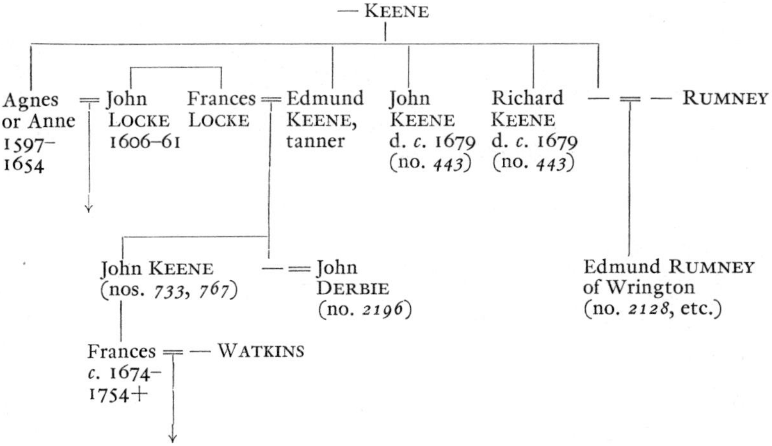


Agnes, wife of John Locke, is said by Fox Bourne to have been a niece of Elizabeth, wife of Nicholas Locke: i. 4. For Frances Locke and her descendants see ibid. i. 4 n.

John Derbie writes to Locke about 'our Kinsman John Keen' in 1697: no. *2196*. By his statement this John Keen would be about 16 years old.

Edmund Rumney may have been a great nephew rather than a nephew of Mrs. Agnes Locke.

# THE CORRESPONDENCE

## CHRIST CHURCH

Locke was elected to a studentship at Christ Church in Oxford in May 1652 and matriculated on 27 November of that year. From that time until 1666 or 1667 Christ Church was his principal place of residence; thenceforward he resided there occasionally until 1683. His studentship also provided him with an income until his expulsion in 1684.

Henry VIII established the see of Osney in 1542 and removed it to Oxford in 1545. By his charter in 1546 Henry granted to the Dean and canons of the cathedral and their successors the site and buildings of the college formerly established by Cardinal Wolsey and since dissolved, and part of the properties belonging to it. The Dean and eight canons were to maintain a number of persons partly for the cathedral services, partly for study; and among them more especially a number soon fixed at one hundred and known as students (one further studentship was added by private benefaction in 1664). The Dean and canons were appointed normally by the crown; between 1649 and 1660 by the Parliamentary visitors of the university. The government of the college was entrusted to them; they managed its revenues and elected to studentships. In practice most of the canons were generally absentees and the day-by-day control, especially in academic business, was exercised by the Dean. It was he who admitted undergraduates and allotted tutorships and rooms. There were no fellows as there were in the other colleges. The students had no standing in the government of the college.

The hundred students were divided into three classes: forty Discipuli, forty Philosophi, and twenty Theologi. Tenure of a studentship was for life, subject to certain requirements. By statute of Elizabeth I three of the Discipuli were to be elected annually from Westminster School; one was a nominee of Lord Vernon; the remainder were appointed from among the undergraduates by the Dean and canons. The next class, the Philosophi, were graduates, either masters or bachelors, depending on their length of residence, and were only occasionally in holy orders. The first four Philosophi were termed Faculty students, two of them studying law and two medicine (the new studentship of 1664 was also a Faculty place). The twenty Theologi had to be in holy orders. When a vacancy occurred among them the senior Philosophus, other than the four Faculty students, was promoted and was obliged to take orders if he had not done so already; otherwise he would forfeit his studentship.

The governmental system worked well for three hundred years. A contributory factor was that many of the canons had been students previously. There was some friction between the canons and the students in 1659. This was perhaps due to the appointments made by the Parliamentary visitors; when they had to replace the men whom they had expelled or men who had died, most of the new men came from other colleges.

Christ Church was much concerned in one university activity, the publication of congratulatory and commemorative volumes of poems written by members of the university. The earliest volume of the kind appears to be one for the death of Elizabeth I; the practice continued into the eighteenth century. For the volume addressed to Cromwell in 1654 on the peace with the United Provinces more than a third of the contributors were Christ Church men; nearly half, in that of 1661 for the death of Princess Mary of Orange. Generally the proportion of Christ Church to other men was lower, but rarely less than one to five. Most of the poems are in Latin; a few in English and other languages.

*Authorities.* The best account of the old government of Christ Church is Mr. Bill's opening chapter in E. G. W. Bill and J. F. A. Mason, *Christ Church and Reform, 1850–1867*, 1970. Further: Anthony Wood, *The History and Antiquities of the Colleges and Halls in the University of Oxford*, edited by J. Gutch, 1786; *The Register of the Visitors of the University of Oxford, 1647–58*, ed. M. Burrows, Camden Soc., new ser., vol. xxix, 1881; Anthony Wood, *Life and Times*, ed. Andrew Clark, Oxford Hist. Soc., vols. xix, etc., 1891–1900; Humphrey Prideaux, *Letters . . . to John Ellis*, ed. E. Maunde Thompson, Camden Soc., new ser., vol. xv, 1875; Falconer Madan, *Oxford Books* (1468–1680), 1895–1931.

## 1. LOCKE: Latin oration or letter, [*c.* 1650–1652]

B.L., MS. Locke c. 24, ff. 1, 2. Drafts. f. 1 is neatly written, but with many alterations and additions; these are written by Locke, and perhaps the text also. f. 2 is a fair copy with some corrections. I have copied f. 2 with help from f. 1, but ignoring everything except the final text. This and no. 2 appear to have been written in Locke's school-days. They may be academic exercises rather than letters.

Certum est quod ubique jactatum, exundante Euphrate Assyriam fœcundari; quippe quod flumen illud admirabile non tantum aquas, sed et semina secum invehit, unde et serere orientem dicitur et rigare: Liceat obsecro idem de te, nec portentosum est, asserere, cujus quotannis huc influxus scholam hanc nostram difficili partu laborantem opportunè beat, et sterilescentem quasi stercorat. Hic iam maturi (si fas sit ita cogitare) ad manus succrescunt fructus; quin exultat uberior seges talem habitura te messorem, tale repositorium Academiam. Quin animadvertas, obsecro, quàm se in-

---

It is certain, as is everywhere affirmed, that Assyria is fertilized by the overflow of the Euphrates; for that wonderful river not only brings its waters there but also seeds with it, whence it is said both to sow and to irrigate the East. I beg that I may be allowed to say the same of you, and it is no outrageous assertion; for your annual inflow here is a seasonable blessing to this our school in its difficult travail and as it were manures it if it grows sterile. There are now ripe fruits, if it may be right to think so, growing up here to your hands; nay, the crop leaps up in fuller abundance at the prospect of finding such a reaper as you and such a granary as the University. Observe, I pray you, how the nodding ears bow themselves at your feet,

curvant ad pedes nutantes Aristæ, quàm declinant aridum caput ne miserè derelictæ prorsus emarcescant. Noli itaque me tanquam inutilem urticam præterire, sed manu tuâ collige, et bene olentem suavissimumque florem influentiâ tuâ me dabis.

---

how they hang their parched heads for fear of being miserably abandoned and utterly withering away. Do not therefore pass me by as a useless nettle, but gather me with your hand, that you may by your influence present me as a fragrant and pleasing flower.

## 2. LOCKE to ——, [*c.* 1650–1652?]

B.L., MS. Locke c. 24, f. 16. Draft or copy? The upper margin of the leaf torn away. See head-note to no. 1.

*Εὐπράττειν*

Si aliud quicquam ad ⟨virt⟩utem[a] animos magis excitare possit quam ipsa virtus, certe hoc illud esset posse a Te (Vir Colendissime) munera sperare. nisi quod etiam in hoc virtus sibi præmium esset, quum a Te qui sine illâ nihil agis, et a virtute beneficium accipere idem putetur. Noli igitur mirari si abs Te impensius efflagito libertatem, munus plane inter mortales maximum, ideoque dignum quod Tu patronus donares, quod Tuus expectaret cliens, Quid enim a Te sperare non licet? Quum virtutem donum illud quod in terris perfectissimum et pulcherrimum fecerunt dii, pulchriorem Tu adhuc et magis optabilem reddere possis? Quod tot tantaque jam a Te petii, quod tam multa obtinui, qui Te ignorant mirentur fortassis alii, ego quidem quod plura nondum

[a] *Page torn.*

---

Greetings

If there is anything that could better incite men's minds to virtue than virtue itself, this would assuredly be the possibility of hoping for favours from you, most honoured Sir; save that even in this case virtue would be its own reward, since to receive a benefit from you, who do nothing without virtue, and from virtue itself may be considered the same thing. Do not therefore be surprised if I beg you so earnestly for liberty, which is clearly the greatest of gifts among mortal men, and therefore worthy to be bestowed by you as patron and to be hoped for by your client. For what may one not hope for from you, seeing that you are able to make virtue, that most perfect and fairest gift of the gods to men on earth, yet fairer and more desirable? That I have already asked you for so many and great favours, and that I have obtained so many, may perhaps be wondered at by others, who do not know you; I for my part only wonder that I have not asked for more; for many as

rogaverim; plurimis enim beneficiorum Tuorum multitudo concessa fuerit, ⟨satietas⟩[a] nulli. Parce igitur ambitioni isti cujus ipse necessitatem imposueris, nam quis unquam se Tuis (nostri hujus orbis Phœbe) beatum sensit radiis. qui solem propius accedere non ⟨desideraret⟩?[b] qui se altiore Gradu non optaret sublevatum? ubi majori liberius frueretur influentiâ. Sic videmus vapores ipsos e terrâ extractos, ubi semel solarem experti sunt virtutem, non contenti humiles reliquisse sedes, ascendunt continuo, nec stationem figunt, donec ad ipsum a quo primum evecti sunt appropinquant Phœbum lucemque[c]– ab eo mutuantur–[c] mundoque (quod mihi spero futurum) ostendunt quantum sit ad solem accedere.

Favoris Tui studiosissimus

J. Locke.

f. 16[v]: Epistola[d]

[a] *MS.* sasietas? [b] *MS.* desiderarit [c–c] *Interlined; last word doubtful.*
[d] *Also* Elect *expunged.*

---

they are to whom your countless benefits have been granted, no one feels that he has received enough. Look kindly, then, on the importunity which you yourself have made necessary; for who is there who has ever felt himself blessed by your rays, who are the Phoebus of this our world, and has not desired to approach the sun more closely and to be raised to a higher level where he might enjoy its intenser influence in greater freedom? Thus we see that the very vapours which are drawn from the earth, when they have once felt the power of the sun, are not content merely to have left their lowly station but mount forthwith, not coming to rest until they come nearer to that Phoebus by whom they were first drawn forth, and by borrowing light from him show to the world (as I hope will be my own case) how great a thing it is to draw near to the sun.

In earnest hope of your favour

J. Locke.

## 3. Locke to John Locke, sen., 4 May 1652 (4)

B.L., MS. Locke c. 24, ff. 165–6. John Locke the elder, 1606–61; of Beluton in Pensford, Somerset; an attorney; a captain of horse under Colonel Alexander Popham in the Parliamentary army in the Civil War: H. R. Fox Bourne, *The Life of John Locke*, 1876, i. 1–11, etc.; Maurice Cranston, *John Locke*, 1957, pp. 3–17; letters below.

The present letter and no. 4 relate to the annual election of scholars from Westminster School to Christ Church, Oxford, and Trinity College, Cambridge. The election was held probably on the Monday, Tuesday, and Wednesday preceding Rogation Sunday; this year on 17–19 May: J. Welch, *List of the Queen's Scholars of St. Peter's College, Westminster*, new ed., 1852, preface.

Most deare and ever lovein father

My humble duty remembred unto. yours by Mr Wheeler I have received, and according to former order sent your letters only Those for Mr Stapleton[1] which as yet I have that for Lieutenant Generall Fleetwood[2] I sent to Captaine Smyth[3] who hath promised me to doe his utmost I doubt not much of the election with the help of some freinds which I shall diligently labour for. your letter to Mr Busby[4] I have delivered and he hath promised me to doe what he can which I can not doubt of haveing soe many assureances of his love he hath made choice of my oration before any of the rest to be perhaps spoken at the Election. Pray remember my humble duty to my mother[5] and love to the rest of my freinds Thus desireing your prayers sum

Tuus obedientissimus filius

JOHN LOCKE

Westminster 4° Maij 1652

My brother[6] is well and remembers his humble duty to you and my mother

Address: For my ever loveing father Mr John Locke, at Pensford. Leave this at Mr Michaell Paxtons in st Thomas street Bristoll

Note on cover in another hand: mr Voxen did come to bristoll Thursday last and is yet in bristoll

## 4. LOCKE to JOHN LOCKE, sen., 11 May 1652 (3, 29)

B.L., MS. Locke c. 24, ff. 167–8.

Most deare and ever loveing father

My humble duty remembred unto you, I have to my utmost donne what lyes in me for the preparation both of my selfe and

[1] No one of this name is associated with Westminster School or with Christ Church at this time.

[2] Charles Fleetwood, d. 1692, the Parliamentary commander: *D.N.B.* He was now a governor of Westminster School: *Acts and Ordinances of the Interregnum*, ed. C. H. Firth and R. S. Rait, 1911, ii. 257.

[3] pp. 8, 44. A man named Henry Smith was one of the governors of Westminster School: ibid. ii. 257; he is more likely to have been the regicide (*D.N.B.*), who was not a soldier, than this captain.

[4] Richard Busby, 1606–95; D.D. 1660; master of Westminster School from 1640: *D.N.B.*

[5] Agnes Keene, 1597–1654; of Wrington, Somerset; married Locke's father 1630: Fox Bourne, i. 4; Cranston, pp. 3–6, 37.

[6] Thomas Locke, 1637–63; he was apparently admitted to Westminster School in 1651, but his name does not appear in the school register: Cranston, pp. 13, 23, 79.

freinds for the election, Captain Smith I finde most ready and willing to lay out himselfe for the accomplishment there of neither is Mr Busby any way wanting he haveing spoken to the Electors in my behalfe, and although my lattine oration be not spoken yet he hath promised me that my Hebrew one which I made seince shall which I would desire you to be silent of for there hath beene some thing already spoken abrode more then hath beene for my good. If I bee not elected (but I have good hopes) pray send me word what I shall doe, for we heare that there will be very few chosen. Pray remembr my humble duty to my mother and love to the rest of my freinds thus desireing your prayers sum

Tuus obedientissimus filius

JOHN LOCKE

Westminster 11 May 1652

Address: For my loveing father Mr John Locke at Pensford. Leave this at Mr Michell Paxtons in st Thomas street Bristoll.

## 5. LOCKE to ——, [May 1652?]

B.L., MS. Locke c. 32, f. 8. Fair copy of draft. Apparently intended for one of the examiners at Westminster, of whom the principal were Dr. John Owen, Dean of Christ Church (p. 30, n. 3), Thomas Hill, Master of Trinity College, Cambridge (*D.N.B.*), and Busby.

Post decennalis belli pericula, post immensos pelagi labores, placuit tandem Minervæ Ulyssis misereri et ad Penelopen suam salvum reducere. Ego itidem (Vir dignissime) quum aliquot jam annis sub Grammaticæ vexillis militaverim, quum[a] Iliada ⟨Homericam⟩[b] expugnaverim, Academiam (Ithacam illam tuam) peto, Philosophiam (desideratiorem utique Penelopen) ambire gestio. nos certè cum Ulysse exulavimus, cum Ulysse planximus, similes dolores sustinuimus; sentiamus obsecro numinis non minus propi-

[a] *Doubtful reading.* [b] *MS.* Homericum

After his perils in the ten years' war and his boundless labours on the sea Minerva was at last pleased to take pity on Ulysses and to bring him safe home to his Penelope. In the same way I, most honourable Sir, having now served for some years under the standards of Grammar, and having mastered the *Iliad* of Homer, am seeking to reach that Ithaca of yours, the University, where it is my ambition to court Philosophy, assuredly a more desirable Penelope. I have certainly suffered exile with Ulysses, have bewailed my lot with him, and have endured similar woes; let me, I beseech you, experience

tii auxilium. Idem Homerus illum exulem canit et reducem; eadem Odyssea in exteris periclitantem[a] nationibus eadem in patriâ sospitem et incolumem commemorat. Tu itidem (o patrone) me ab Athenis tuis dilectissimâ literatorum omnium patriâ exulantem, benignè quasi domum revoca. Suffragii tui vox (quam nullâ ego vendo Iliade,[1] totâ mihi odysseâ non minus grata) Gymnasii me modo asperitatibus miserè jactatum, in plenissimo quietis et tranquilitatis loco, Academiâ, reponat.

Undâ obruisset Xanthus Æaciden suâ
⟨Si non⟩[b] marini dextra fortior dei
Opem tulisset.[2] sic premente numine,
Propitius alter sæpe subvenit deus.
Mihi sed patronus unus admoveat manum
Cujus caditve statve judicio gravi
Fortuna nostra.[c] ⟨tu meis⟩[d] votis fave
Ne te premente nullus auxilium ferat

Endorsed by Locke: $\overset{\circ}{\wedge}$. Electio

[a] *Last letter doubtful.* [b] *MS.* Sinon [c] *Stop supplied.* [d] *MS.* tumeis

---

the aid of a not less propitious deity. The same Homer sings Ulysses both in exile and on his return; the same *Odyssey* describes him facing dangers among strange peoples and safe and sound in his own country. Do you likewise, my patron, have pity on me, who am in exile from that Athens of yours, the beloved fatherland of all men of learning, and of your kindness recall me as it were to my home. Let your favouring voice, which I would barter for no *Iliad*,[1] and which is no less welcome to me than a whole *Odyssey*, set me, after my wretched buffeting as it were in the rough handling of the wrestling-school, in a place of perfect peace and tranquillity, the University.

Xanthus had whelmed Achilles with his wave
Had not the sea-god with his mightier hand
Brought help.[2] So when one godhead presses sore
Oft comes another with propitious aid.
To me may my one patron reach his hand;
For 'tis by his grave judgement stands or falls
My fortune. O, do thou regard my prayers,
Lest, if thou failest, none should bring me aid.

---

[1] Adapted from Persius, *Satires*, i. 122–3.

[2] This alludes to *Iliad*, xxi. 284 ff.

## 6. Locke to [Alexander Popham?], [May 1652?] (8)

B.L., MS. Locke c. 32, f. 9. Fair copy of draft with fresh alterations. Alexander Popham, *c.* 1605–69; matriculated from Balliol College, Oxford, 1621; M.P. for Bath in Short and Long Parliaments, 1654, 1660, 1661; for Somerset 1656; for Minehead 1659; member of the Council of State 1649–52, 1660; one of Cromwell's lords 1657; in favour with Charles II. He owned seats at Houndstreet (Hunstrete) in Marksbury, about 2 miles SE. of Pensford, and at Littlecote in Wiltshire: G.E.C., iv. 629; *D. N. B.*, art. Popham, Sir Francis; Fox Bourne, i. 5–9, 16–17; Mark Noble, *Memoirs of the Protectoral-house of Cromwell*, 3rd ed., 1787, i. 408–12. It was thanks to him that Locke was admitted to Westminster School; he had no known connection with it.

Improbum fortasse aliis videbitur (præsul amplissime) apud virum illum a quo tot jam beneficia acceperim novis adhuc precibus instare. at ego ingenui potius animi minimeque ingrati existimo cui multum debeas ei adhuc amplius debere velle.[1] solebant veteres ad illorum frequentius deorum aras provolvi, iisque fidentius supplicare, quos maximè et præ aliis sibi propitios olim senserant. Et certè pristina beneficia, uti clientibus gratitudinis ità et patronis novæ adhuc munificentiæ argumentum suggerunt. Recorderis itaque (ô Mæcenas optime) quo amore qua benevolentiâ quibus etiam officiis me hactenus complexus es et prosecutus. Reminiscaris obsecro cujus suffragio cujus manuductione olim in hosce parietes sum immissus et ex veteris beneficientiæ commemoratione liceat tuum etiamnum sperare et acre sollicitare patrocinium.

---

Others perhaps will think it presumptuous in me, most excellent patron, to be still importuning with fresh prayers one from whom I have already received so many kindnesses. But I consider it to be rather the mark of a candid and not ungrateful mind to wish to owe yet more to one to whom one owes so much.[1] The men of old were wont more frequently to bow down at the altars and more confidently to solicit the blessings of those gods whom they had previously found above others propitious to them. And assuredly former benefits, just as they are a reason for gratitude in clients, so they afford to patrons a reason for fresh munificence. Bethink yourself therefore, O best of Maecenases, of all the affection, all the benevolence, all the good offices, too, with which you have hitherto encompassed and accompanied me. Remember, I beseech you, by whose supporting voice and by whose introduction I was once placed within these walls, and let me be permitted on the ground of that old favour now also to hope for and earnestly to solicit your patronage.

---

[1] Adapted from Cicero: 'Est . . . animi ingenui, cui multum debeas, eidem plurimum velle debere': *Epistolæ ad Familiares*, II. vi. There are other adaptations in nos. 556 and *3128*.

*7. J. Heane to John Locke, sen., 14 September 1652*

Numinibus faciunt populi sua vota benignis
  Oscula dant saxis ingeminantque preces
Optatisque vident siquando pondus inesse
  Nil reddunt præter thura precesque novas.
Numina et hinc fiunt, parcas tu multa petenti,
  Te nostrum ostendo sæpe rogando deum.

At foot of page: Needham[1]
Endorsed by Locke: (i) Electio. Ep:
(ii): Ep. Elect.
Some scribbles, etc., on reverse, including: Julius.

---

To gods proved kind do suppliants most repair;
They kiss the stones, redoubling prayer on prayer.
Then, when they see their wishes prospering,
New prayers, new incense are the thanks they bring.
By these, too, gods are made; do thou condone
My often asking; thus my god you're shown.

## 7. Col. JAMES HEANE to JOHN LOCKE, sen., 14 September 1652

B.L., MS. Locke c. 11, ff. 180–1. The writer is identifiable as James Heane, 1613–55, soldier; at this time governor of Jersey. He was born at Little Dean in Gloucestershire: *Miscellanea Genealogica et Heraldica*, 2nd ser. ii (1888), 201–2, 209–10; Sir C. H. Firth, *The Regimental History of Cromwell's Army*, 1940, pp. 718–20.

Noble Hart

Your Lynes are Receaved as soe Many Carrecters of Love and Vertue, The unexpected favour of a Sheete of paper with the Inscription of your Name Raised my Collour And gave mee the Happynes that Attends the Remembrance of a true Frend, The Leviathan seemes to whisper through those Craggy Rocks. I now Live on: That true Frendshipp Exceedes All Neptunes Tresure, Boreas whistles as yf it wold favour mee, in Carryeing these Lynes uppon its wings as a Gratefull Salutation to you: whom I desire to Scatter my Love (According to the Ripenes and truth of it) towards Bristoll and Horfeild[2] Amongest our fast Frends. Deare

[1] Perhaps Walter Needham, 1631?–91; at Westminster School; elected to Trinity College, Cambridge, 1650; M.D. 1664; physician: *D.N.B.*

[2] In Gloucestershire; now part of Bristol.

Hart, Distance of Station is a Greate Confirmation of Affection and true Love, from

Sir

your Faithfull Servant

JA: HEANE[a]

Jersey this 14th of Sept 1652

Address: To his Much Honoured Frend Mr. John Lock in Pensford in Com Somerset These

Leave this with Mr Maddox in waymouth who is Desired to send this as abovesaid by Ja: Heane[b]

## 8. LOCKE to P. A [Alexander Popham?], [late 1652?] (4, 96)

B.L., MS. Locke c. 24, f. 289ᵛ. Draft. Written on one of six leaves torn from one or more notebooks. There is little to show when or in what order the drafts on them were written. They perhaps belong to two groups: (i) the two halves of one draft (TAE; no. 10) are on ff. 288ʳ, 289ʳ; the two halves of another (GOW; no. 9) are on ff. 288ᵛ, 290ʳ; (ii) the two halves of another (BE; no. 14) are on ff. 291ʳ, 292ʳ; the drafts for two closely related letters (TGR; nos. 18, 20) are on ff. 291ᵛ, 293ᵛ. On the remaining sides there are further drafts; their positions suggest that they divide between the two groups: (i) on f. 289ᵛ (PA; no. 8); on f. 290ᵛ (a detached sentence here attached to no. 9); (ii) on f. 292ᵛ (AM; no. 13); on f. 293ʳ (N; no. 12). By the general appearance of the writing all the drafts may be early. There are indications of dates in the second group: no. 12 (diplomatists); no. 13 (Quakers); nos. 18, 20 (Grenfeild). I can find none in the first group.

The present draft appears to belong to Locke's early time in Oxford, perhaps not long after he matriculated on 27 November 1652. It was perhaps intended for Alexander Popham. The language is comparable with that of no. 96.

P. A

Were there not to be found here more then ordinary advantages, and did not this place yeeld dayly increase and the most desireable thing in the world, I might well dislike my stay here as affording noething answerable, to my first days injoyment, wherein you were pleasd to afford your company an happinesse with which theres non can stand in competition but that of learning. and truly had you at your returne left me here lesse then all the worthys and most admird persons of former ages to converse with I might have well repind at the change

[a] *This could be read alternatively as* Heans   [b] *Or* Heans

## 9. LOCKE to G O W [William (later Sir William) Godolphin?] [early 1653?] (*25*)

B.L., MS. Locke c. 24, ff. 288$^{v}$, 290$^{r}$, 290$^{v}$? Draft. See p. 12 n. If this was intended for (Sir) William Godolphin (no. *25*) it dates probably from within a few months of Locke's matriculation.

G. O. W

Tis noe more then I expected from you that that eloquence which hath soe often left the most judicious silencd with admiration should not give me leave to speake, nor leave me the liberty of telling you handsomely how[a] much[a] I honour you without I borrowd the expressions from your self. this I confesse I might doe but twould be a strang kinde of vanity to make ostentation of borrowd riches before the owner. I can be content therefor to have my mouth stopt by one who assures me he is my freind and I am bound to thinke my freind, for I dare beleeve what e're you say, and am not so much enemy to my self to be spareing of my faith to those words that make soe much to my advantage and bring soe glorious a frendship. Give me leave to admire your bounty which is able to bestow more then army ever fought for or the most touring ambition ever aimd at, which at most is but a crowne,[b] but it hath placd me ⟨above⟩[c] the state of kings who in their highest pitch doe homage unto fortune as subjects to her empire, but that blinde goddesse hath now noe longer any power over me, nor is it in her reach whilst I posesse your freindship to make me miserable. I see you can bestow. what e're I want and what you say I have you'l make me master of. now indeed you have found a title which I dare glory in. If that language by signes which you mention did always speake thus pleasingly I should repent the time I have spent at schoole, and noe longer seeke pleasing rhetorick in an university amongst mutes and those that nature left imperfect and be soe uncharitable to my self as to wish all my freinds dumb, but tis not to a dumb man I owe soe much happinesse but one whose words give me the greatest cause to thank nature for my eares and to blesse that man that first invented wrighting. tis the part of my love to seeke out actions wherin to expresse its self and therefor I shall be greedy to imbrace all occasions you shall

[a] *Doubtful reading; the two words are run together.* [b] *MS.* crowene ?
[c] *MS.* a bause

afford me to[a-] evidence to you by all the signes I can[-a] make[b-] me a gift of the Indies and the riches of Pactolus and those streams which floud more plentifully in the heads then purses of the poets I could not be more then I am[-b]

## 10. Locke to T A E, [1653?]

B.L., MS. Locke c. 24, ff. 288ʳ, 289ʳ. Draft. See p. 12 n. This can be dated only by association with no. 9.

T A E

I would not willingly renew in your memory the sad thoughts of your late losse and instead of drying your eys draw fresh tears into them when time and reason hath wiped them away. laid your sorrows for a misery which if you rightly consider it may perhaps deserves a better name. I doubt not but you desird his company to[c] well to be willing to part with him, but would you wish for it always, you lovd him well but did you love him soe well? as to wish him the miserys of old age: would you have had stay with you till he had not beene able to know you nor to see those things that were dearest to him till had been a burden to him self. some years more must needs have brought him to this and doe you grieve that he ⟨died⟩[d] before he came to a sense of these evils and that he left the world, before his miserys had forced a license from your wishes and his owne to have[e] him out of it. Consider you under goe a fate soe common that that very thought might comfort you, see how many ⟨of⟩[f] your neibours ⟨are⟩[g] in the same condition ⟨of⟩[f] widow hood. how many without parents wives brother sister scarce one free from the losse of one freind or other yet you see they live and if it be not their owne faults comfortably. be not more dejected then they. you suffer noe more then kings and princes doe, and you can greive for noething unlesse it be that you have not a greater priviledg then they. you cannot rationaly be sorry for that which a bridges you not a one of your wishes and I dare say were all your interests joynd to gether they could not put into your heart one desire that should call him back againe. I hope my letter will come to[h] late to you and you will not stand in need of any consolation

[a–a] *Alternatively* by as evident signes as I can [b–b] *This sentence (on f. 290ᵛ) may not belong with the rest of the draft.* [c] *Doubtful reading; written above* very [d] *An illegible word.* [e] *Doubtful reading.* [f] *MS.* o. [g] *MS.* r [h] *Or* so

## 11. Locke to Louis Thiery, [autumn 1653?]

B.L., MS. Locke c. 24, ff. 272–3. Transcribed by Professor W. M. Edwards. The date is a guess. The letter appears to be in young man's style. The vocabulary appears to be influenced by Rabelais; hence a date fairly soon after the publication of Sir Thomas Urquhart's translation about June 1653. A Mr. Lewis Thiery is named as the authority for a plaster for corns in Locke's father's notebook, B.M., Add. MS. 28,273, f. 143. I cannot identify the writer of the prescription.

*Ἡ βαρβάρη σου ἐπιστολὴ (Ὦ σε χειρουργότατον φημὶ ἄν ἢ μᾶλλον πανουργότατον) τὰ τῆς μητρυίας πήματα καὶ τὴν ἀπάτην τὴν σὴν ἧκέ μοι φέρουσα, εἰπέν δε ἁπεπανούργηκας, καὶ ὅντινα τρόπον τὴν πενθερὰν τὴν οἰνοβαρῆ καὶ παμμέγιστον γραὺν ἔλαθες θὀιμάτιον ἀποσυλήσας, ὥστε μὴ ἐν τῷ χειμῶνι τριβώνιον ἔχοντα ῥιγώσειν, ταῦτα μεν ἀνελεγόμην ἐπιγελῶν, καί τοιγέ μέ τι ⟨προυργιαίτερον⟩[a] ἀπησχόλει τὰ δε λοιπὰ τῆς δέλτου σολοικιζούσης οὐ ξυνίην ἀναλεγόμενος, τοσαύτην ἄραγε τοῦ διηγήματος καὶ τῆς φλυαρίας χάριν ἔχω, ὅσην ἐν τῇ ἐπιστολῇ ταύτῃ δύνασαι βάρβαρός ὢν ἀκριβώσας ἀνευρηκέναι*

*Ἰωάννης ὁ Λῶκ*

Address: Amico suo *πολυγλώττῳ καὶ* Monsieurissimo Ludovico Thiery Gallo = Anglo = Anglo = Gallo
in
Eutopia

[a] *MS. προυργαίτερον*

Your barbarous letter ('O you master-craftsman' I would say, or rather 'O you consummate rascal') arrived bringing me the woes of the step-mother and your deceitful behaviour; it told me of all your knavery and how you managed undetected to rob the mother-in-law, that bibulous and enormous old woman, of her cloak, so that you would not have to shiver in the winter (or storm?) in your threadbare garment. I read all this with amusement, although I was busy with a more important matter; but the rest of your letter, with all its solecisms, I could not understand when I read it; I am grateful, at least, for so much of your story and your chatter as you were able, in your barbarism, to contrive with sufficient accuracy in this letter

John Locke.

Address: To his polyglot friend and Monsieurissimo Louis Thiery, the Franco-English-Anglo-Frenchman.
Happyland.

## 12. Locke to N, [January–February 1654?]

B.L., MS. Locke c. 24, f. 293r. Draft: see p. 12 n. Part of the commencement of several lines is torn away; the damage suggests that the draft was written before the leaf was torn from the notebook. Evidently written at Oxford for someone at Pensford. The mention of the diplomatists suggests a date early in 1654.

N

Theres scarce any thing can exceed my expectation founded on your last letter in greatnesse but the benefitt is promisd in it. by which my desirs are raisd to a pitch scarce alowable by the rule of duty and decency seing noething can satisfy them except you take a journy of above 50 miles.[1] I should be affraid to be soe unmannerly to utter them did not your grant authorise it. or to lett you see how prowd my wishes[a] seeme to looke when the comeing ambassadour from France or Agent from holland[2] would be inconsiderable to them in respect of his[b] presence;[b] but I am glad. that my desires how great and irregular soe ⟨e⟩ver[c] they seeme suit with your intentions and ⟨r⟩each[c] at noething but what you are able and ⟨o⟩fferd[c] to afford them. I hope mr Greenfeild[3] will accompany ⟨y⟩ou[c] and though here be little new and unknowne to him which may ⟨in⟩vite[c] him hither yet here is a better pulpit then St ⟨Tho⟩mas[c4] and an auditery more worthy of him. let not the feare of undoe⟨ing⟩[c] a poore scholer hinders them from comeing as it doth not me from inviteing them[d] and as for them, I doubt not to ⟨doe⟩[c] well enough with 'em. If i can doe it noe other way I'll fill their bellys at their ⟨ with⟩[c] the sight of colledges gardens librarys books more then the best stomaks in England are able ⟨to di⟩sgest[c] and theyl meet with one from ⟨L⟩ondon[c] will satisfy them plentifully by their ears, and I'le season a short messe with rules and commendation ⟨of⟩[e] temperance that if they'l

[a] *Here* what is wont to satisfy kings *interlined.* [b] *Doubtful reading; substituted for* what I expect, *which is only partially deleted.* [c] *Page torn.* [d] *Doubtful reading.* [e] *Word omitted by Locke.*

---

[1] The distance between Oxford and Pensford by the shortest possible route appears to be about 60 miles.

[2] Antoine de Bordeaux-Neufville, who came to England in 1652 as a French agent, was raised to the rank of ambassador in March 1654: C. H. Firth and S. C. Lomas, *Notes on the Diplomatic Relations of England and France 1603–1688*, 1906, p. 40. Four Dutch agents came to England in June 1653 to negotiate peace; after some going and coming two of them returned here on 28 February 1654 to rejoin the third: S. R. Gardiner, *History of the Commonwealth and Protectorate*, 1903, iii. 40, 45, 67.

[3] No. 18.

[4] Pensford church is dedicated to St. Thomas.

venture their stomacks I'le dare venture a commons. and I dust promise to doe them one noe meane ⟨courtesy⟩[a] to send them home well furnishd with what many would purchase at a considerable rate, good stomacks.

## 13. Locke to A M, [early 1654?]

B.L., MS. Locke c. 24, f. 292$^{v}$. Draft. See p. 12 n. The opening cross is Locke's. Perhaps to 'Cousin Martine': no. 21. Apparently written from Oxford; the mention of the Quakers suggests a date early in 1654.

A M.

X

I know not what leger de maine the Carrier plays with me who puts tricks not only with my intentions to send but consent there in also, and maks me glad that I have omitted my duty, and not conveyd this inclosed to you according to your expectation. untill I sent a contradiction with it. If ever I were glad that an untruth came from me it might be now. the inclosed brings sad news to you, but such as pamplets were wont to doe of victorys which[b] were to be understood by the contrary. and therefor ought not to be beleivd. neither indeed had I sent it had it not beene to let you see what reports we have here and that Aristotle and Scotus cannot secure us from lys and deceivers whereof we have an other experiment. in the quakers here amongst us.[1] were all fashons used like this, not sufferd to manifest its self till it brougt its condemer with it we might hope for more truth and sincerity. which I feare the renewing[c] of the higest and most honourable customes of this nation yea that which puts crowns on the mortals heads will not bring backe and revive

[a] *The first letters illegible; some other word may be intended.* [b] *MS.* wh. *or* who
[c] *Doubtful reading.*

[1] The Quakers are said to have come to Oxford first in 1652, or, more likely, in 1654: Anthony Wood, *Life and Times*, ed. A. Clark (Oxford Hist. Soc., vols xix, etc., 1891–1900), i. 190–1. See further p. 84, n. 1.

## 14. Locke to B E, [1654 or 1655?]

B.L., MS. Locke c. 24, ff. 291$^r$, 292$^r$. Draft. See p. 12 n. Evidently intended for a lady. The language is comparable with that of no. 45, but it is unlikely that the two drafts were intended for the same person.

B E

I doubt not but what I doe will seeme very extravagant and I foresee you will account it a strange thing to receive a letter from one that never saw you but consider that your beauty being extraordinary must have extraordinary effects and ought in ⟨its⟩[a] operations to keepe the common rode as little as nature did when she framd it I have often[b] receivd such hansome characters of you with delight and admiration from Mr L[1] his lips, that I cannot without injustice deny you that homage which if the fairest and most ⟨excellent⟩[c] ought to command you may exact from all the world. I must confesse that though mr L. hath ever had an absolute command over me yet he could never dispose of my affections to any other object but him self besides you, to whome I now wholy resigne 'em, see hence what an empire you have that you know not of and how celestiall you ⟨are⟩[d] who like those hevenly bodys have soe strong an influenc on those that you never saw and are soe far distant from you. I never see any thing stampt with the marke of beauty or excellency but I suppose it to be an emblem of you, and I draw soe many hansome picture of you in my minde that could they be seene they might be copys to the most expert limerers of their fairest peices, and yet I think them to be as far short ⟨of⟩[e] you that I never saw as they excell all others hansome things that I have seene, you are therefor if I flatter not my self very much obleiged to me for takeing soe much pains for the sake of one who in requitall never soe much as bestoud a thought upon me nor once wishd me well, and one from whome your little dog hath receivd more curtesys. but yet from this obligation doe not thinke I pretend to any thanks noe I have offended and therefor have reason to write to you to beg your pardon M my ignorance detained this puf[f] which was sooner destind to you, which I now resigne fild with sweets that it might be a fit present fit for you

[a] *MS.* is it  [b] *Here* 2 *interlined.*  [c] *MS.* excellenting?  [d] *MS.* r
[e] *MS.* c  [f] *Doubtful reading.*

[1] If not Locke himself, probably Thomas Lockey (p. 48, n. 2).

and something resembling you and with it I have sent my wishes for as many blessing to you as there are dusts of pouder in it, use it therefor and let not that haire which is to be the chaines ⟨of⟩[a] soe many soules want its ornament and sweetnesse, I must confesse twas a strange boldnesse in me to keepe any thing that was yours but consider I beseech you that if you will be angry for[b] deteining[b] that which was only intended yours, you may also take it ill that I present not my self to you since I[c]– am as much destined to your service–[c] as ever this was and be confident that amongst all those that know you not there is not one that honours you with halt that respect that I doe, and I dare assure you that amongst those that ⟨are⟩[d] happy in your acquaintance there is not one more then I am

## 15. Locke to ——, 1 May 1654

B.L., MS. Locke c. 24, ff. 3–4. This consists of f. 3: text of letter (signature cut away); f. 4[v]: address (cut away, apart from three letters); f. 3[v]: draft of a letter (here printed as no. 16). Remains of a seal.

No. 15 appears to have been prepared for dispatch and then held back. It is addressed to a man who has a wife and who arranged Locke's reception at Hampton Court by another family. Mr. Cranston suggests that it was intended for Cousin Martine (no. 21): p. 34. Nos. 16 and 17 are closely connected with no. 15, perhaps as alternative drafts for a new version of it; but one or both may be for separate letters, and they are here printed separately.

Sir

As I owe all those courtesies I received at Hampton[e] Court[e1] unto your freindshipp, soe must I my thanks for them too, which I must convey backe the same way I reeceivd those favours, that is throug you and spetially unto you. For although Fortune my niggard Stepdame hath denied me an abilitye to acquitt my selfe of those many obligations, the bounty of Hampton[e] Court[e] did lately lay upon me. yet herein I must confesse her favourable, that she hath brought all my debts into one hand soe that all those favours I receivd from others I must owe partly and primarily unto you as

[a] *MS.* c [b] *MS.* for / fordeteining [c–c] *Alternatively* I am as much yours
[d] *MS.* r [e] *Concealed by Locke, who scribbled over these words, presumably some time after the letter was written.*

[1] The palace now belonged to Cromwell.

author and procurer. The first part therefor of my gratitude must be my thanks unto your selfe, the means, whereby I injoyed soe much happinesse, not excludeing one part of your selfe (I meane) your Lady. Next which pray present my humble service respects and thankfulnesse unto all the members and spetially the heads of that most happy family, and lett them know I am fuller of gratefull thoughts then they can suppose me; For if for each severall courtesie they should expect (as it deserves) a particular acknowledgment. I'm sure my sence and experience and every part about me loden with theire kindenesse would and must needs suggest more favours to my remembrance, then theire memory did register, when they soe free and carelessly bestowed them. But these my thankfull thoughts, are but empty shadows, vaine things, and little answerable to those great and reall favours I receivd. And indeed I must confesse they could not have sowne theire favours in soe strange a soile for noe where could they have taken deeper roote and beene more firmely fixt then in my breast and yet have floureshed and appeard soe little outwardly and as it were above ground, and yeild soe little fruit unto their expectation, the strangenesse whereof will perhaps begett some wonder, but I feare its fruitlessnesse noe acceptation. I should not therefor have dar'd to returne this barren kinde of gratitude, had not my confidence assured me that where there was soe much bounty in bestowing there was also, a like clemency in forgiveing and freenesse in accepting, But this had scarce provd a sufficient argument unto my doubting thoughts, had I not also beleiv'd that your delivery might adde some merit to my worthlesse thanks and soe procure theire entertainment, which will be one new favour more added to that vast heape of your courtesies for all which I am only able to say that I am

Sir your most gratefull and obleiged servant[a]

Oxon: Ch: Ch: 1° May 1654

Address: [this is entirely cut away, except the letters -ine or -me][1]
Endorsed by Locke: Letters to H. C

[a] *Signature cut away.*

---

[1] If the reading '-ine' is correct, it is perhaps a remnant of Martine.

## 16. Locke to ——, [1 May 1654?]

B.L., MS. Locke c. 24, f. 3v. Draft. See p. 19 n. The letter may be intended for a woman; the word 'Sir' as used here could apply to persons of either sex: *O.E.D.*

When such sharp eys and soe many accurat and criticall judgments are to scan the rude impolisht lines what could I expect but some severe sentence but that I know those breast will ententertaine all virtues cannot exclude that most beneficiall one to your servants clemency and aptnesse to forgive, though I must confesse I least deserv't of any and may justly expect a particular doome from each of you for thus crouding up my thanks into one little paper, when whole volums would come short of conteining[a] a gratitude equall to the merits of one of you, but consider Sir[b] that your abounding favours have made me bankptrupt and unable to pay your deserts with answerable thanks and services, and besids by this short way I have savd you the pains of reading longer storys and freed you from the trouble of more laughter or vexation ⟨which⟩[c] particular acknowledgment might have causd in you, for my thinks I see into what posture this little hath putt you into,[d] she[e] condems it with a censorious pish the sound[f] wherof alarms up her[g] hands into a posture redy to strike the offender were he present My Cosin Ms[1] ready to brand it[h] with the title of a lye and is apt to suspect each word carrys an untruth int and hath scarce patience to heare it out. MA[i] hes laught his eys out at it and will not see to read the rest, M sentences it with a smile and saye your naught your very naugt and soe leaves of, M condems it with a silent froun R vext with these ilturnd wourds pleasth her self with her owne harmony and sings away her anger, wheareas when you read this what an agony must I needs be in, nor can the influence of such a constellation as you make up doe lesse then reach hether and wreak its fury on me, but a little to alay your anger, what I want in thanks Il make up in washes, wherein I will I will soe suit with you, that you shall renounce your owne thoughts or else be angry at them as well as me therfor appeased in particular

[a] *Substituted for* expressing [b] *Substituted for* L. [c] *MS.* with [d] *Followed by* Mr V *deleted.* [e] *Perhaps* he, *preceded by a stroke.* [f] *Substituted for* winde [g] *Or* his [h] *Here* this letter *interlined.* [i] *Followed by* she *del.*

[1] It is apparently to her that Locke wishes a child. She may be the Cousin Martine who had recently become a mother in August 1655: no. 21.

to the first I wish something beyond a servant[1] to the second a sonne or if heavens pleas a daughter might it be like the mother. 3 that whereof she has good store mirth, and a companion to increase it, to the 4 a better valentine,[2] to 4 to Ra. life as quiet as her thoughts and as sweet as her owne voice, I wish her too pitty on the[a–] nitingas that she mai not killem all wither her . . . melody.[–a3] and if any thing can be more agreeable to your severall desirs I wish you your owne wishes You see Im loth to leave such good company and therfor prolength my letter . . .[b] y'r weary wit share it amongst you unlesse it be condemnd to the fire, however as you excell all your sex in all the accomplishment of it, soe lett me see that you have this one property of it let (viz) reveng which may prompt you vent your spleen in sending answers too,

J

## 17. Locke to ——, 1 May 1654

B.L., MS. Locke c. 24, f. 5. Two pieces are cut out of the text, and the part of the page containing the salutation ('Sir', etc.) has been torn away. Draft. Neatly written. See p. 19 n.

The same greatnesse of those favours I receivd from every one, but espetially from your selfe, at my being with you, which exacts a more then ordinary returne of thanks, the same ⟨a⟩lsoe[c] pleads an excuse for the delay of my acknowledgment. Small and common courtesies cause as little difficulty in makeing a returne as they lay slender obligations on the receiver, but those which are of a greater bulke, and of that vast magnitude those were, that you confer'd on me. o'rewhelme and fill the soule, and leave noe roome for any other thoughts then of theire greatnesse, which rather amaze the minde, then compose it for a due returne of thanks. Soe that the receiver cannot presently performe that duty which his gratitude would prompt him to, such large favours require a time suitable to theire greatnesse, for theire acknowledgment. Wherefore these empty expressions of my thanks how void soever, of what

[a–a] *Most readings doubtful; one word unreadable.* [b] *Two short unreadable words.* [c] *Page torn.*

[1] In this context a professed lover: *O.E.D.* Similarly below, pp. 102, 109, etc.

[2] A person of the opposite sex chosen or drawn by lot on St. Valentine's day (14 February) as a special friend; the relationship continued during the ensuing year: *O.E.D.* See further no. 48 below.

[3] Perhaps alluding to the poem by Famiano Strada; for it and English imitations see R. Crashaw, *Poems*, ed. L. C. Martin, 2nd ed., 1957, pp. 438–40.

e're else may be answerable to your obligations, have this of greatnesse in them, that they have taken up a large roome in time, and have been long in preparation. Haveing therefor scarce shaken off the astonishment possest me, (that soe great blessings should be granted to one soe undeserveing) and hardly yet recollected my selfe, you need not wonder, if instead of a gratefull acknowledgment, I only yet seeme to talke idle, whereby you may suppose my thoughts distracted, and soe may finde an excuse for the empty vanity of these verball thanks the fruits of lightnesse. But besides the largenesse of your courtesies the smalnesse of my ability to make a retalliation even in words, will suggest an Apologie for me, it being a kinde of satisfaction in a poore man that he is able to pay noething but an acknowledgment he is indebted. For[a] I write soe ill and my letters are soe empty and light, they want something to goe along with them, to adde unto theire weight, and bespeake your entertainment: and my presents (if they may deserve that name) are soe meane that they need commendatory letters to begg your acceptation, which either single would despaire, and togeather I feare will but cause a greater injury from me and greater trouble to and dislike in you. Yet both I have adventured to send you: the one to tell you why the other came. when I last saw you you were pleasd to say you would willingly spend some howers in the study of heraldry, a study wherein I must confesse my ignorance and therefor knew not what booke was most fitt for your perusall. but this if its name or the information of others deceive me nott, cannot be unfitt for a beginer, which when you have perus'd or in the meane time, if any other shall please you better, you will vouchsafe to lett me know it, you will thereby conferre a new happinesse on him who esteems this his greatest to be

your[b] most faithfull and most affectionate servant

JOHN LOCKE

Oxford. Ch. Ch. 1° Maij 1654

The tediousnesse of this would need another letter to begge your pardon, but that the excuse would only augment the crime. yet I must adde one petition that if you will not please to burne that paper (I dare not call it letter) I soe often begg'd, you would take out a leafe of clean paper inserted at the begining of this booke

[a] *A hole is cut in page at beginning of next line; there is room for* Sir, *but scarcely for* Madam. [b] *Preceded by hole cut in page.*

and when you are alone warme it very hott by the fire.[1] beyond this I dare not trouble you, though my gratefull thoughts prompt me to intreat you to present my service and my thanks to all those your relations I am soe much obleigd to, whome if I should name particularly with their severall favors I must send a rheme not sheet of paper

## 18. LOCKE to G.R, [Thomas Grenfeild?], [July 1655?] (*19*)

B.L., MS. Locke c. 24, f. 291v. Draft. See p. 12 n. Apparently a draft for the antecedent of no. *19*; hence the person to whom it is addressed and the date to which it is attributed.

Thomas Grenfeild, *c.* 1618–71?; son of Joseph Grenfeild, vicar of Combe St. Nicholas, Somerset, 1617–43. Matriculated at Oxford 1635; B.A. 1639; M.A. 1641. Vicar of Combe St. Nicholas 1643–71?; minister at Publow and Pensford 1657; preacher at Lincoln's Inn 1658–63?; canon of Exeter 1662–71: A. G. Matthews, *Walker Revised*, 1948, pp. 313–14; F. W. Weaver, ed., *Somerset Incumbents*, 1889, p. 339; W. Melmoth, *The Great Importance of a Religious Life*, 1849, pp. 255–6; etc.

G. R,[a]

X

You will not admire my long delay if you consider that besides common helps he will stand in need not only of the lively[b] genius and serenity of the spring but[c–] the warmth[–c] and vigor of somer that writes to you. you are[d] not of[e] the number of[e] those with home every scribling that brings a name and seale with it will passe for an obligation, who will not be satisfid with my love remembred unto you hopeing that you are[d] in good health[2] nor such an one to whome one is not beholding for reading and answering letters. I am better acquainted with your accuratenesse, but setting aside that, which I must not hope to satisfy, doe you thinke tis every days businesse to talke with an Imbassador and ⟨the imbassador⟩[f] from heaven or to interrup a dispenser of Oracles. The Ancients indeed had often to doe with holy men but it was by expecting their counsels in an uninterrupted silense and such an

[a] *Preceded by* T, *apparently obliterated.* [b] *Doubtful reading, possibly a noun replacing* genius [c–c] *Alternative for* and the advantage [d] *MS.* r [e] *MS.* c [f] *MS.* yibassador *?; words interlined.*

[1] Heating the paper would reveal writing on it in lemon-juice or a similar liquid.
[2] So in no. 93.

one as hath accompanid my waiting for a continuance of your directions. Thinke not Sir that[a] I have put my self out of your protection either out of security or desire of change, swarmes of dangers forbid the former and the number of good men are[b] soe few and pretious that we may be satisfid in the posession of one without thoughts of variety. Tis confest ⟨the⟩[c] place where I am is the great luminary of the land[1] but the neare vicinity of[d] the sun may

## *19.* THOMAS GRENFEILD to LOCKE, 2 August 1655 (18, 20)

B.L., MS. Locke c. 10, f. 54. Answers no. 18; answered by no. 20.

Sir

If your remembrances had come to mee in a playner dresse, they had bin more wellcome to him, that now studyes playnesse, more than ever quayntnesse heretofore: were you not my freind, on the exuberancy of whose affection I must father this luxury of language, I should playnly give your letter the same lye, which my thoughts give mee, if I should dare to owne what you asperse me with: what ever you thinke mee, I am but a poore Gibeonite of the Countrey, condemned to the courser worke of Israel, and fitt for noe other,[2] (if for that:) It argues yet, that a good spiritt mixes itselfe with that high Genius of your university, that you stoope to the notice of him, who has allmost forgotten, he was ever there; and can hardly give any other Testimony of it, then the names of Colledges, and formes of streets:

But however: I should judge it a far greater Courtesy, if I might heare of my defects from you: and should kisse that letter, that would lay mee low; for I am apt to fly high enough, (too high) in my owne conceipts, without the breath of others prayses: Yet I pardon you; because you have such a redundancy of learninge and goodnesse, that (like one of our teeminge springes here,) you will choose rather to rivulet it out on undeservinge grounds, then be a niggard of your own store: soe have I seene pregnant witts, (rather then want imployment) spend themselves on the contemptible thinges of nature, the fly, the flea, etc.—and such, whose

[a] *Here* ... 'tis distance ... hinderd me not from hopeing for *interlined.* [b] *MS.* r
[c] *Word omitted by Locke.* [d] *Doubtful reading.*

[1] Oxford. [2] Joshua 9: 3–27.

pigmy-beinges came not within the honour of humane observation, 'till theyre witts had made them famous:

Yet I promise you, though you have mispent soe much on mee, It shall not be wholly lost; but lookt on, as Tessera tuæ amicitiæ, Calcar meæ diligentiæ:[1] It's strange, you, that live soe neere the Sun, should thus appeale to a poore Comett here for Direction: If you love ignorance, and error, make use of mee, who am now good for nothinge, but to stand as the deplored ruines of one, that would be a schollar, but was wrackt in the Attempt: The only use you can make of mee, I conceive is only to gayne greater luster to yourselfe, by lookinge on mee; and as men looke on rockes,[2] to learne by mee, not to decline: I am now rendred beneath all, but wishinge well to you, and your endeavours; for the blessinge of which, though my Directions must, my prayers shall not be Absent: Tis our hopes, to see you here shortly, when that great argument 'twixt us (of my worth) will more neerly be debated; and I beleive you will then be forced to conclude that in the Neg. which now you prove only in the way of a sophister. Till then, I must crave leave to b⟨e⟩[a] angry with you: But then, (if you Retract) you shall have my pardon: pray Sir, Remember, your Busynesse at Oxford is to learne Truth; and acquaynt yourselfe with it:

Your freinds here are well: and soe is hee that is

your true lover, and Freind

THO. GRENFEILD

Pensford. Aug. 2. 55

Endorsed by Locke: Mr Grenfeild letter

## 20. LOCKE to T.G.V. [Thomas Grenfeild?], [mid-August 1655?] (*19*, *40*)

B.L., MS. Locke c. 24, f. 293v. Draft. See p. 12 n. Apparently a draft for an answer to no. *19*; hence the date to which it is attributed.

T. G. V.

Were I not well acquainted with a sincerity in you worthy of your function. and had I not large proofs of your freindship to me

[a] *Page torn.*

[1] 'A token of your friendship and a spur to my diligence'. Source not found; perhaps made up by Grenfeild.

[2] Apparently a mis-spelling of wracks or wrecks.

I might now well suspect it. since you deale with me noe better then some niggardly misers are wont to doe with their pore suppliants deny them theyr request by telling them they are rich enough already. Nay since it is necessary for all that know you to love and esteeme you you would deprive me of the only advantage I have over plowmen which is to tell you soe after a little better manner then they doe soe. Sir That you make plainesse your study I doe not doubt. and that it is a pains to you to be understood by your Pensfordians. I durst beleeve any thing you say but when you speake of that which most consearns you your self: your modesty is too injuryous but I see you will not part with any virtue though you keepe it to your owne prejudice. Sir Tis not without reason you say you vould kisse that letter which would shew you your defects. to such a rarity you might well expresse particular indearments and he that had soe accurate a judgment as to performe that might well deserve a more then ordinary entertainment. but Sir

## 21. LOCKE to COUSIN MARTINE, 11 August 1655

B.L., MS. Locke c. 24, f. 188. Draft? On five occasions about 1650 Locke received money from 'my cousin Gabriel Martin', £4 5*s*. in all: B.L., MS. Locke f. 11, pp. 1, 83, 84. See also pp. 17 n., 19 n., 21 n. 1.

Madame

I have scarce soe much charity left as to congratulate the late great blessing you receivd from heaven: and I give you noe small proofs of a good nature and the power you have over me, to be able soe to overcome those resentments your cruell silence might have wrought in me, as to give you this testimony that I very much rejoyce in your happinesse; the relation whereof wanted noething of being the welcomest news that ever I receiv'd, but that it came not from your selfe, which was the only condition it wanted to make it perfect. Me thinks the name of mother hath wrought a change upon your disposetion, and you begin with a more then ordinary forwardnesse to put on the providence of a carefull parent. How else comes it to passe that you are soe much altred from that former freenesse which appeard in all your actions, as that when you were possess'd of the happinesse of haveing a first-borne, a joy large enough to spread its self into more soules then yours, you could be soe niggardly, as not to afford him any part of it? who in spight of all your neglects is resolv'd to be

Madame

Your most affectionate freind and faithfull servant

JOHN LOCKE

Oxford 11° Aug. 1655.

If you are resolvd to save your inke and paper, and not to write to me yet pray spend a little of your breath for me in presenting my respects to your parents. as for your sisters I intend them particular remembrances.

Endorsed by Locke: To my Cosin Martine

## 22. LOCKE to [SAMUEL TILLY?], [early September 1655?] (*23*)

B.L., MS. Locke c. 24, f. 276. Draft written on the cover of a letter bearing the address 'For Mr Samuell Tilly at his chamber in Hart Hall Oxford'. Apparently a draft for the antecedent of no. *23*; hence the date to which it is attributed.

Tilly was a son of Samuel Tillie, vicar of Keynsham 1625–39, rector of Compton Martin 1639–74 (the former is 4 miles north, the latter, 6½ miles south, of Pensford). Tilly matriculated from Wadham College on 22 March 1651; B.A., Hart Hall, 1654; M.A. 1657; vicar of Kingsbury Episcopi 1664–85; rector of East Lambrook 1670–85 (both in Somerset): Foster, *Alumni Oxonienses*; Weaver, *Somerset Incumbents*, pp. 273, 262, 389, 393.

If in freindship there be any sympathy you cannot but be sensible that I suffer in my absence from that place where you are,[1] and all those gaurds your virtue affords you from the assalts and evils would but ill preserve you from my envye of that happinesse you plentifully injoy in your self and whereof seperation permits me soe small a share, were it not that I necessarily love you above my self ⟨seing⟩[a] what hath most good in it challenges the greatest affection. I can be content therefor your injoyment should be greater then mine, soe long as I exceede you in that which men esteeme the greatest happinesse of their lives, that I have a better freind then you can hope for I meane Sir your self from whose freindship besids common and familiar offices I can expect miracles such as these, that you should make me sensible of some delight ⟨whilst⟩[b]

[a] *MS.* senig  [b] *MS.* whist

[1] Locke evidently writes from Pensford to Tilly at Oxford.

I am away from you, this you can doe[a] by the same way that hath sett all most all the world in an uprore and at varience, writeing; whereby you may make it possible that I may rejoyce in my absence if you will afford me ⟨as⟩[b] frequent a converse with you as your retirednesse would alow me at Ox. that is once a weeke, there in I shall have this advantage too that in this your language will be more lasting, and I shall be able to injoy your discoorse as often as I please, these are but the ⟨smallest⟩[c] part of your power, you can change languages make Aristotle and Demosthenes speake ⟨English⟩,[d] remove mountains or what is equivalent send Oxford library[1] hither in a sheet. Such are the priviledges your learning and worth afford you above ordinary mortals, amongst which pray suffer me to rank this of mine, that you give me leave to take unto me the title of what I most desire to be

Endorsed by Locke: To S T To S. T

## *23.* SAMUEL TILLY to LOCKE, 11 September 1655 (22, 24)

B.L., MS. Locke c. 20, ff. 175–6. Part of f. 176 (the cover) is torn away. On f. 175[v] is the draft of Locke's answer. Answers no. 22; answered by no. 24.

Sir

To be able to reveal their thought's by only willing their discoverie, is (they say) the priviledge of Angel's; whether other's share in't, I know not, sure I am, it fall's not to my lot; for I should then from your Charitie, being inform'd of my resolutions to write, have obtaind the advantage of sending the first letter. Insufficiencie in power, you know, is often supplied by prudence, in the improvement of favouring advantages: How unhappie then am I, who being destitute of abilitie to send what might be worthie your acceptance, have neither had the discretion, to embrace an opportunitie, that might have rendred my letter deserving. But, Sir, I know to whome I am writing, and tho your former favourable inclinations towards me, challeng a larger acknowledgment, then may be compriz'd within the narrow limits of a letter, so that the superaddition of this, which I have this morning receiv'd, might

[a] *Here* quit settle my spirit *is interlined.* [b] *Replaced in MS. by* a more [c] *MS.* smalls [d] *MS.* Engligh

[1] The Bodleian.

render me altogether silent, yet Jam repeto assiduè mecum, sicu⟨t⟩[a] meus est mos, Qualia! Quæ! Quam multa! quibus debentur et a me jure peti possunt[1]—I shall employ the Carrier's allotment, which is one halfe houre, to make some offer towards an acknowledgment. Sir those favourable expressions concerning me, which I finde multiplied in your letter, I shall presume to receive from your affection, tho I am far from pretending to them by my desert. 'Twere easie for me, to be large in expressing the realitie of my respects to you, but I hope your assurance will render such attempt's as needlesse, as was his, who that he might have somewhat to doe, would needs print a new Almanack for the old yeare: To colour over realities with painted expressions, were but to gild gold, which I shall leave for such, as are willing to render it suspected. I will not be injurious to your expectation, to bribe your acceptance of this, with the promise of a second letter from hence, because I am speedily to come into the Countrey, so that, tho what I write will not have the travail of a long journey to commend it, yet I shall be capable of endeavouring to supplie that defect, by quantitie and number. To leave Oxford now troubles me not, since I have undergon the losse of your companie in it, elce might I deservedly be thought as preposterous, as old Phedon,[2] who was not griev'd so much, that he must die, as that the expence of his funeral would cost him 4s. Now that I may not dismisse my letter, without sending you some newes, know that your reverend Deane,[3] who came the last night from London, is (they say) that his honour may be proportionate to his person, and merit, resolv⟨ed⟩[a] on to continue Vice-chancellour another yeare; we have also lately lost one of our flowers, (him I meane that kept the Gallerie at St Maries)[4] cropt by death to make it a posie, I hope your more southern climate protects those with you from the like fate,

[a] *Page torn.*

[1] 'I now assiduously call to mind, as my way is, what, how great and how many are the debts I owe and to whom I owe them, debts which I might justly be called upon to pay.' The words make 2½ hexameter lines, possibly in imitation of Horace, who has the phrase 'ut meus est mos' in *Satires*, I. ix. 1, and similar phrases elsewhere.

[2] Pheidon the miser occurs in the *Greek Anthology*, xi. 170. Tilly perhaps follows a post-classical derivative rather than the original poem. The name, deriving from the king of Argos who introduced standards of weights and measures, was applied to stingy or niggardly old men: Theophrastus, *Characters*, trans., etc., by R. C. Jebb and J. E. Sandys, 1909, p. 131 n.

[3] John Owen, *c.* 1615–83; D.D. 1653; Dean of Christ Church 1651–60: *D.N.B.* He was vice-chancellor from September 1652 to October 1657.

[4] St. Mary the Virgin.

although indeed I may well doubt it, having not of late heard thence. Some time since, I receivd a letter, I need not tell you from whome, and indeed what tis, I can't tell you, for tis above my apprehension: to have rendred it profitable it should have brought a Paraphrase, for truly the text it selfe is so intricate and mysterious, that I feare even time it selfe will not be able to write its commentari⟨e⟩.[a] As to your receiving the Librarie Epitomiz'd, had your letter come somewhat sooner I might have bin more capable of answearing your desire, the Bishop of Armagh[1] being lately here, who without a Metaphor almost might have bin so term'd. As for those other impossibilities when they fall within the compasse of my capacitie, you shall not meet with a readyer complyance from any, then from him, that without complement or vanitie subscribes himself

Sir

Your friend and servant

SAMUEL TILLY

Oxon: Sep: 11 —55

Present my service to your father.

Address: These For mr John Lock at his father's house in Pensford. To be left at Mr Thomas Day's[2] in st Thomas street in Bristoll to be Convey'd as abovesaid.

Endorsed by Locke: Mr Tillys letter & answer

[Besides the draft of Locke's answer (no. 24) there is on f. 176 a note written by Locke, a cure 'For the spleen'.]

## 24. LOCKE to [SAMUEL TILLY?], [late September 1655?] (*23, 35*)

B.L., MS. Locke c. 20, f. 175$^{v}$. Draft or copy. Written on reverse of no. *23* which it answers. Badly written with poor ink.

you ar too coviteous of victory either[b]– to much distrust your owne strength–[b] wish[c] me overcome before I was prepard for an

[a] *Page torn.* [b–b] *Written above first line.* [c] *Preceded by* to desire *or* or desire, *both words expunged.*

[1] James Ussher, 1581–1656; archbishop of Armagh 1625: *D.N.B.*

[2] Day was perhaps a common surname in Bristol; letters from a Thomas Day of Bristol, and from another Thomas Day, perhaps his son, are printed below, nos. *1221*, *1382*, *2887*. A Mr. Day is mentioned in nos. *614*, *1258*; and Alderman Sir Thomas Day in nos. *1426*, *2993*. It is impossible to determine to how many men the notices relate.

assault and to desire that I should be deprivd of[a] those pore shifts I have to keepe the lists with you and *you*[b–] *use me to severely*[–b] to but I thank my Fortune and good genius I have gott an advantage which unlesse time turne back his wheele I shall keepe and shall yeeld unto you with this confort that I gave the first blow. envye me not this tis all I can boast of from whenc I can raise unto my self noe greater[c] then that soldier that for[d] shooting of the first gunn was wounded and taken, wonder not Sir that I write in so quarlesome and martiall a dialect Freindship to hath its scirmishes and you may well give me leave to call it a war soe long as I leave you the victory. Could you be soe injurious when you have ⟨so⟩[e] cleare a title to all other precedency to bethink me that of[d] true[d] in[f–] all one.[–f] this you might have allowd methinks one soe.

⟨You could⟩[g] have alowd this with a great deale of safety when herein you had but followd[h] the best guide nature who if we may beleeve yonger[i] brothers,[i] often permits that which hath least worth to be first borne.[1] or did you soe much feare my ability and the slacknesse of my duty and affection as to think I would not pay my respects to you without a summons and a patterne, your letter gives me just ground to beleeve soe for I cannot suppose you guilty of soe much flattery that you should meane ⟨this⟩[j] letter for me unless[k–] it were[–k] for a coppy to sugget what I should write to you. thus you doubly oblige me in giving me 100 large proofs of your freindship and telling me how to preserve it.[l] That you lately received a mysterious letter I can easily beleeve since your owne is soe, wherein I finde many things above my reach which require a strong faith to be their interpreter, for what reason can perswade me that you are[m] soe much indebted as you speake of to one whose utmost indeavours could scarce reach to an acknowledgment of your favours.[g] you being away every thing that may invite one to stay. I[n–] see noe reason but[–n] you may be willing to leave Oxford since you leave not your self there you may be well

[a] *Here and below Locke uses a symbol for* of [b–b] *Underlined perhaps to denote deletion.* [c] *Followed by* from whence I can ? *deleted.* [d] *Doubtful reading.* [e] *MS.* sto*?* [f–f] *Interlined and doubtful.* [g] *Two words expunged here.* [h] *Interlined above* imitated [i] *Substituted for* the proverb [j] *In MS. a vague scribble.* [k–k] *Repeated in MS.* [l] *This sentence is partly interlined, partly written in the margin.* [m] *Here and below Locke uses a symbol for* are [n–n] *Added in margin.*

[1] Either, 'The younger brother hath the more wit' or 'is the better gentleman': *Oxford Dictionary of English Proverbs.*

content to goe any whether soe long as you have such good company. methings you seeme very much to share in that Angelicall priviledg whereof you professe the want sing things alter according to your will and your very intentions are able to make a place more amiable, and I am unwilling now to leave Somerset not soe much because It gave me first entertainment in the world as because you purpose it shall give entertainment shortly to you. Sir you are soe accustomd to baffle all opposers[a][1] that it is become a property attending on your person, and your very actions have learnd to confute receivd opinions which would perswade us that the happinesse of a place consists[b]– in a–[b] firtill soil under a favourable constelation,[2] both which contribute little if you or your like be left out. Sir were there more such we might hope for the golden[c] age againe only with this difference that twould be more learned.

Tis a resolution worthy your self to restore the Muses to a country where religion hath almost jostld then out of doores I thinke that it may its self the sooner follow, tis a dangerous signe of giveing up house where the servants are turnd away. I need not tell you what people you are to come amongst neare Bristoll but this lett me tell you they are such as I shall have reason to envy, when they shall injoy your presence a happinesse which I sighth after and which they are as unworthy of as they are unworthy. it will concearne[d] you when you are where all things suit with your desires to wish and endeavour my absence for such is the greatnesse of my ill fortune that[e] should I take a journy on purpose to see you I should loose my labour and my indeavours to be with you would drive you forth. but Sir tis an happinesse large enough for me to have this converse with you, and I need not murmur soe long as you permitt me to professe my self to be what I really am

[a] *Followed by* that your actions have learnt it to which*? deleted.* [b–b] *MS.* consists in in a [c] *MS* gd [d] *Interlined above* behove [e] *Followed by* my resolutions to be with you would drive you forth *deleted.*

---

[1] In academic disputations.

[2] I have not found this statement elsewhere. A place cannot be said to be under a particular constellation in the current sense, a group of fixed stars; the word must be used in the obsolete sense, the position of the planets in regard to one another at a particular time.

## 25. WILLIAM (later Sir William) GODOLPHIN to LOCKE, 18 February 1656 (9, *60*)

B.L., MS. Locke c. 10, ff. 15–16.

William Godolphin, 1634–96, a second cousin of Sidney Godolphin, the Lord High Treasurer and first earl of Godolphin; at Westminster School; matriculated from Christ Church 21 June 1651; M.A. 1661; D.C.L. 1663; contributed a poem to *Musarum Oxoniensium 'Ἐλαιοφορία*, 1654 (F. Madan, *Oxford Books*, 1895–1931, vol. iii, no. 2243 (52)); perhaps in Arlington's employ after the Restoration; M.P. for Camelford 1665–78; diplomatist, first as secretary to Lord Sandwich, ambassador to Spain 1666–8; knighted 1668; envoy extraordinary to Spain 1669–72; ambassador 1672–80; became a Roman Catholic and died in Spain: *D.N.B.*; V. Barbour, *Henry Bennet, Earl of Arlington*, 1914; F. R. Harris, *The Life of Edward Mountagu, K.G., First Earl of Sandwich*, 1912; etc.; letters below.

Mr Locke

I was ever of Opinion that Merit is the best Honour; and that to doe well is more noble, then to have many Titles usher in our Name; Such Nobility the Purse gives oftner then the Soule, of which the most unworthy are not sometimes uncapable; the Splendour of this Externall Renowne being like that of the Sun which with Equall vigour spreads it-selfe upon the humble Cottage and most stately Palace, to whose Perfection it gives no Encrease, but shows only what it had before. By this I would insinuate, that the new Prefix you have obtained gives no Credit to your Name, but your Name to it, and that you are not so much promoted as your fellow-Batchelours, whose quality is thought worthy to comprehend a Person of so good Abilityes.[1] For my part, I cannot now consider my Degree[2] without some Pride, who never before Gloryed in any Title, but when I was call'd

Mr Locke's most humble Servant

WM GODOLPHIN

Inner Temple Febru: 18 1655

Address: To Mr John Locke Batchelour of Arts in Christ-Church Oxon:

Endorsed by Locke: Mr Godolphin's letter

[1] Locke was created bachelor of arts on 14 February of this year.

[2] There is no record that Godolphin graduated as B.A.

## *26.* [DR. AYLIFFE IVYE to a German doctor], [summer 1656?] (*97*)

B.L., MS. Locke c. 12, f. 8. Draft written by Locke. With it are associated ff. 3–7 of the same volume; they are not printed here. Folio 3 is a draft or copy of a Latin letter from Ivye to the person for whom no. *26* was intended, or the letter itself, completed but not dispatched; it is signed by Ivye. Folio 4 is neatly written by Locke; the text is the same as that of f. 3, and it may be either a copy of it or the original composition for it. Folios 5–6 are another version of this letter, written by Locke in Latin, with considerable variations, some very free, from the preceding version. Folio 7 is yet another version, also written by Locke in Latin. If f. 3 is Ivye's copy from f. 4 his poor command of Latin would explain the use of English in no. *26*. From f. 7 it is clear that the person addressed was a German. The date is tentative; no. 29 shows that Locke was in Somerset in September 1656.

I have not found Ivye outside Locke's correspondence. He was perhaps a son of Thomas Ivye, who married Mary, daughter of John Aileffe of Brinkworth, Wilts.: *Wiltshire Visitation Pedigrees, 1623*, ed. G. D. Squibb (Harleian Soc., vols. cv–cvi, 1954), pp. 1–2.

Feareing that the language of learning should be as far beyond your capacity as learning its self and that your shallow braines (stufd only with the fragments pickd up from the severall countrys your vagabond life hath led you through) should have as little Latine in them as they have physick, I have taken the paines to shew you your self in a more familiar language and to draw your picture in black and white (not as Madam Ber: is wont with a dawbing pencill who is supposd can as well paint her owne as others faces, and can teach her customers the most lively way of makeing their pictures,) and were I only to have to doe with that mishapen body which hath beene driven out of all countrys least your conversation amongst teeming women might discompose their phansys and the thoughts of their Doctor might stamp deformity on their conceptions and make them produce apes instead of men, one great blott would serve the turne, or else to take a more suitable way it would be but the transforming somebody into your country man that is makeing him drunke who should thereby be inabld to draw a german picture of you, and spew as handsome shape as nature ⟨made⟩[a] for you or your wife for others. But I leave your outside to the lash of beddles and titheing men[1] who had noe doubt long ere this (according to our wholsome laws provided

[a] *MS.* mades, *altered from* makes

[1] Petty constables: *O.E.D.*; nos. 50, *952*.

against straglers and runagates) whipt you home from titheing to titheing could there have beene any place found that would have owned the originall of such a creature. well whereever you were borne Bristoll it seems must maintayne you. there you have sett downe your packe and all your trinkets where what ever else you want of a scholler you arivd I'm sure in this like a philosopher (with your omnia mea mecum porto),[1] that you carried your whole stock along with you which I thinke you might well doe without any great trouble of carriage since all you brought with you besides an empty head and pockets was a well traveld cloak, your old companion, half a dozen storys of the wonders you had seene and donne, 2 or 3 musicall airs, (which in plaine English we call old songs) and a wife all of them things Light enough. It pittys me to see the poor citizens guld by your more then Mountebank impostures, but you have too well studied and too long practisd the cheat to suffer any one to scape you. you have traps ready baited for all the sences, temptations fitted to all humors you have musick to catch the ears and pictures for the eys nor are you unprovided for those that delight in feeling. at your house the merry meet with songs and for the Melancholy the costivenesse of your owne German countenance is a suitable entertainment: and certainely those that get of from you with their decaid healths will have reason always to look on it as a deaths head with a memento mori. with the gaudy you trade in Jewels and with the credulous in storys and for the lusty joviall youth you have a danceing schoole and as it is supposd a vaulting schoole[2] too. why soe many arts soe many callings is your skill in physick soe weake and infirme that it will not stand without these poor supports, whither I pray leads all this but only hither that you may draw to you a great many that are sick or such as may be perswaded to be made soe. your painteing wife forsooth cannot draw any ones picture to the best advantage till your physick hath purgd their bloud and cleard their beauty, danceing may be dangerous and breed distempers unlesse the bad humors be carried off by your pills and potions. It shames me to see the profession of physick discredited by these ill artifices, and soe noble a science thus disgracefully prostituted, to finde any one that ownes the name of Doctor runne about lik[a] a Tinker

[1] 'I carry all my possessions with me': Cicero, *Paradoxa*, i. 8. A saying of Bias of Priene; for it see the edition by M. Schneider, 1891.
[2] A brothel: *O.E.D.*

with a brazen face offering to cure crazy vessells and with like successe mending one crack and makeing two. Indeed you had not unfitly[a] chosen out painting and danceing to accompany your physick, if when your hackney prescriptions have discolourd your patients faces your wives fucus's could recover them againe or when your ill applyd medicens have cast them into convulsions her skil could compose these irregular motions and reduce them to the order of a dance. but I wonder your folly should mak choise of England to sett up your trades in, since we are not troubled here with frisking frenzies, methinkes Italy had beene a more hopefull place where you might have not dispaird at one time or other to have curd the Tarantula with a Coranto.[1] Methinks when I consider your fiddle and your physick togeather I see the story of Orpheus perfectly inverted whose musick brought backe one person from the other world yours leads many thither. But I passe by this as being sufficiently knowne in the whole citty to come to the exercellency of your skill which is raileing the only faculty where in you have commencd Doctor. I omitt your saying that these parts had neither chymist nor physitian, this was uncharitably donne to see the want and not supply it, for I'm sure you brought neither with you. I tell thee thou scurrilous Vagabond wanderer that hast traveld beyond all good manners and civility, whose mouth is fouler then the close stooles of thy patients and dost there with take a liberty to bespatter every one, hadst thou the least spark of ingenuity, that tongue which had imployd its self to confesse submit recant and ask forgivenesse for its owne impudent slanders would for the future have beene bridled. But he that beleevs when he sees a dog fawne that he will not barke againe will be sure to be mistaken. and indeed it would be well if you had a tongue as inoffensive and usefull as our doggs have then possibly we might expect from it more cures then wounds, and we might finde some part about endued with the gift of healeing. I wonder not at all to finde my self as well as others within the reach of your obloquies and I receive it as a just recompense for misplaceing soe many civilitys on an ingratefull stragler. I shall only mention of many others that disgracefull language you lett fall on me at

[a] *Doubtful reading; page rubbed.*

[1] A tune in triple time accompanying the dance called the coranto: *O.E.D.* The tarantula here is the bite of the spider, and so tarantism, which was believed to be curable by dancing: ibid.

Cadnam when Mr Hungerford[1] was sending for me to a sick gentlewoman. there you were (as indeed what doore stands open where you will not thrust yourself in?) pretending to deale for pictures and Jewels, ways you take to insinuate your self into the Gent of the country and to begge custome ways soe unworthy soe far beneath the temper of a gent. a scholler or an Englishman that they are only to be found in a sneakeing ignorant Mountebank German. there, upon the mention of my name you take occasion to Characterize me to the company to disgrace my practise and villify my skill and out of a very tender care and zeale for the Ladys recovery or your owne gaine by a sad relation of many that miscaried in my hands and a prophesie of her certaine death if she came into them you deterr her from makeing use of me. you tell them all my practise was confinde to one poore vomit which usually brought the desease and the patient to an end togeather, and that by this dose she was sure to be sent after those two or 3 I had kild with it allready, what did you thinke me soe fond and doateing on your most reverend Doctorship that I had given away all my medicens (as I did too many) to you and left only this for my self. or that after you had disgracd many of them by your unskilfull applications did you suppose I would never owne them againe, this language, these calumnys deserve a severer scourge then my pen I doe here repeat them only not reward them. But if the Cittizens who begin to sent your fallacys, if the magistrates who are chary of Englishmens lives and are carefull to secure them from the attempts of unlicenced Empiricks, if the officers that looke after fugitives doe not prevent me I shall take order that you shall not long triumph in the reproaches that you have cast on him that is noe more

Y

## 27. FRANCIS ATKINS to LOCKE, [summer 1656?] (*32*)

B.L., MS. Locke c. 3, f. 55. The writer is not identifiable. A man named Francis Atkins, born *c.* 1611, a son of John Atkins of Chard, was incumbent of Chard from 1661 to 1672; he matriculated from Wadham College in 1629; B.A. 1632; M.A. 1635; fellow 1639–48: Foster. Both nos. *27* and *32* appear to be written by a young man to a young man; hence the divine is unlikely

[1] Probably Edward Hungerford, 1600?–67, of Cadenham, near Calne, Wilts.: John Evelyn, *Diary*, ed. E. S. de Beer, 1955, iii. 100–1 and nn.

to be the writer. There was a tenant named James Atkins on the Pensford estate in 1674 and later: nos. 293, *848*; see also no. *568*.

The dates for this and Atkins's other letter are conjectural. The postscript to the present letter perhaps alludes to the widow in that of no. *54*; in that case its date would be summer 1659.

Deare Soule,

My calamityes leave mee this only unhappie way of expressing my love to my Friends, by making bold with them: as the men of Russia (they say) have no better way to demonstrate their affection to their wives, then by beating of them. Had you come, according to your purpose, upon Friday, you had made the obtaining of this request from you, more easie to my hopes, then now the streightnes of the time will suffer it, bee: howbeit, a little difficulty, I know, will but adde spurrs to thy resolution; and therfore I shall dare adventure it to thy censure.

My Ladie hath commaunded mee, to doe a little busines for her at Chard[1] upon Tuesday next: and though I am but badly hors'd, yet, if I may obtaine thy companie, I shall not want a caroach. I did the more greedily fasten upon this commaund, because it sorts luckily to my owne desires: it may bee Cupid may bee one of the Actors in our comicall journey: and to that purpose I have sent alreadie a footboy to my Mistresse to meet mee Tuesday, or Wednesday night at Chard. Shee's one of thine owne sect; and if shee errs, doth it out of pure zeale, and simplicity of soule. I cannot promise you shee's handsome; but this; though I think shee has the more scarlet in her cheek oth'two, yet you shal be her Judge.

Cloris[2] is just Agrippa-like,[3] almost perswaded to goe too: and if your consent bee had, certainly ther's little doubt to bee made of his, notwithstanding, the young horse, and the cockes eye[4] out, and I know not what else, bee coldly, and perfunctorily objected.

If you dissent, then one sad word will be doome enough, but if otherwise then I shall desire to meet you at the place next the coalpitts, wher wee last parted, when I came from Pensford:[5] about 4 a clock ith'afternoone. Ther wee'l have a little

[1] Chard is about 40 miles SW. of Pensford. The name here is perhaps an abbreviated version of some other place-name, such as Orchardleigh.

[2] By the name this should be a woman, but here a man; perhaps Thomas Grenfeild (p. 24 n.) from the Greek χλωρός, green.

[3] Acts 26: 28.

[4] I have not found the expression elsewhere.

[5] Pensford is in the Somerset coalfield: p. 413, etc.

Love-revell, and Cloris his gravity shall dance a part. Meane while love and prosperity are wish't thee from,

Thy entire Friend
FRANC: ATKINS

My service to thy bedfellow,[1] for so I think shee is at this time.

Address: To my deserving Friend, Mr John Lock these at Pensford

## *28.* JOHN LOCKE, sen., to ——, [summer 1656?]

B.L., MS. Locke c. 14, f. 169. Draft, apparently written by Locke. The date is conjectural.

Sir

He that brings you this brings you alsoe a person whose carrage has beene soe good in these times as to deserve the envy of some of his neigbours which higthend with private malice would perswade others to a beleefe of that malignancy in him which neither the feares or advantages of an adverse party could perswade him to, and since his estate and life lye out of theire reach they would robbe him of the title of well affected to the commonwealth, for which he hath not spareingly venturd both. his name William Masye of Wrington[2] [Liuet: of my regiment][a] one better knowne to me by the courage and faithfulnesse of his services, then conspicuousnesse of his person, who might he finde a suitable reward to his merit would be soe far from deserveing that character which the biasd of ill will would draw on him, that he might stand in the first ranke of those are[b] esteemd[b] weldeserveing, Sir should his faithfulnesse finde soe ill a recompence as to be listed in the number of offenders, we should find few that could promise to themselves security from their former services, and twould be an ill incouragement to future indeavours should necessity at any time call for them. Did his cause want any thing to help it, I should make use of my intreatys in his behalfe, but I will not be soe injurious to the justice of it as to mix it with any alay of favour and respect, knowing that his inocence before inteligent persons is enough to secure him without interposeing of the mediation of

[a] *Added in margin, possibly not by Locke.* [b] *Interlined, probably not by Locke, over deleted word.*

[1] See head-note.

[2] I have failed to identify Masye. Wrington was the home of Locke's mother and his birth-place.

## 29. LOCKE to JOHN LOCKE, sen., 25 October 1656 (4, 30)

B.L., MS. Locke c. 24, ff. 169–70.

Most deare father

The next morning after I sent home Tom: Watts[1] I tooke coach at Bathe, which brought to London three persons besides my self of the English size and one woman of the race of the Anakime,[2] soe that in all I may count six in our company, for that mountaine of flesh that cald herself a merchants wife, by her tongue and her body may well be taken for two, shee was soe grosse that shee turnd my stomack and made me sick the two first mornings and the third[3] I was like to be buried, for had the coach (as it might) overturnd and shee fell upon me I should have been dead and buried at a time, but I thank god after that and a thousand squeeses which my place some time alotted me to I came safe to London and tooke up my quarters at Mr Knights. and the next morning saw our Senators enter the house which a stranger would have mistaken for a fenceing schoole there were soe many swords worne into it. I beleeve this councell is not to be parraleld in Europe if you compare either their ages or faces. What is beyond that was not obvious to my eys.[4] but noe more, The news of Digby is contradicted[5] and that of the prize either not come hither yet, for perhaps it keeps its native Spanish pace or else dead before I came hither.[6] the most remarkable thing I have met with since I came hither was a company of quakers in Westminster hall this afternoone, one whereof being brought the last terme to the chancery to give testimony there, refuseing to put of his hat, had it strooke of, for a marke of which persecution he hath gonne ever since bare, and this day came to complaine to the Lords Commissioners and to have redresse for the injury, I saw him walke bare headed in the Hall which he might well doe haveing come soe out of Yorkeshire, The rest of his breathren may doe well to immitate him, the keepeing

[1] Mentioned again in no. *54*.
[2] Numbers 13: 33, etc.
[3] Bath is about 110 miles distant from London.
[4] The first session of Cromwell's second parliament opened on 17 September. There was a preliminary purge of about a third of its members; of the rest between a third and a half were drawn from the army: C. H. Firth, *The Last Years of the Protectorate*, 1909, i. 1–23; W. C. Abbott, *The Writings and Speeches of Oliver Cromwell*, 1937–47, iv. 282–3.
[5] Presumably Sir Kenelm: see *D.N.B.*
[6] This refers to a ship captured in Admiral Richard Stayner's action off Cadiz on 9 September. News of the capture reached London on 1 October; the prize was brought to Portsmouth about 28 October: Firth, *Last Years*, i. 49–57.

the head to hott being dangerous for mad folks,[1] I have donne noething in my owne busensse yet,[2] there haveing been soe continued a raine since I came hither that I have not adventured farther then Westminster hall or the Abby. I have noe more at present but to subscribe my self

Your most obedient sonne

J LOCKE

Westminster 25° Oct. 1656

My love to my brother[3] and the rest of my freinds Mr Jo: Burges[4] remembers you

Address: For Mr John Locke at Pensford
Leave this at Mr Thomas Days[5] in st Thomas street Bristoll.

## 30. LOCKE to JOHN LOCKE, sen., 15 November 1656 (29, 43)

B.L., MS. Locke c. 24, f. 171. The central portion of the letter has been cut away in such a way as to leave the postscript intact; hence some parts of the letter (as distinct from the postscript) survive, mainly ends of lines. I have transcribed the surviving words, but not single letters. The lost part of the letter apparently related to Locke's endeavour to be admitted to one of the Inns of Court.

Most dear⟨e⟩

. . . yours by
. . . being with
. . . ⟨o⟩portunity to
. . . -ham hinderd
. . . ⟨m⟩y last (if it
. . . -t what progress
. . . Colonell. From
. . . ⟨r⟩eceivd more
. . . I could expect
. . . Inns of Court

[1] The Lords Commissioners are those of the Great Seal; the court of Chancery sat in Westminster Hall. The Quaker is not identifiable.

[2] Locke was probably preparing to apply for admission to one of the Inns of Court. He was admitted to Gray's Inn on 10 December: *The Register of Admissions to Gray's Inn, 1521–1889*, ed. Joseph Foster, 1889, p. 280.

[3] p. 7, n. 6.

[4] Persons of this surname are mentioned in nos. 64, *98*, 1962, etc.; no. *1950* is written by Mary Burges.

[5] p. 31, n. 2.

. . . -r soe willing
. . . ⟨pr⟩omises will
. . . I know he is
. . . -h interest
. . . -es to deceive
. . . maintenance
. . . how imprudent it would be to cast my self on the necessity of depending on them and how unhandsome such a course would be, enough to diswade me from it, were the uncertainty away. I will therefor once more try what I can doe, that if it may be, I may ease you of that from which I know you desire to disingage your self as well as rid my self of a farther unsetlednesse . . . ⟨en⟩deavours and
. . . crosd and repeted
. . . you have
. . . affords me yet
. . . you may not
. . . often your
. . . -arted with
. . . ⟨br⟩eathe, I must
. . . not thinke
. . . since this
. . . -ted from you
. . . in any thing
. . . the greatest
. . . -e desires of
. . . obedient sonne
J. LOCKE

I came just now from heareing the examination of Nayler and his Proselites who haveing before the Committee upon reexamination own'd what he receivd and they what they gave him as Christ, after all being askd what he had to say made this evasion (which I pickd as well as I could out of his uncouth and unusuall expression, whose canting language with that of his disciples I made an hard shift some times to understand) That Christ being the same to day and for ever what honour was given to him at Jerusalem might be given to him where and in whomesoever he is manifested from god. His owning of the name of Jesus of the sonne of god, of the prophet of the most high god, of haveing him his father whome we call our god and his disciples owing the attributeing of these to him, Sir the shortnesse of my paper and the consideration of the presse which I beleeve will shortly better informe you, adviseth me to leave out. only this, after their examination I went to the roome by the painted chamber whether the committee orderd them to retire where I found Nailer one man more and 3 or 4 women of the tribe all with white gloves and the womens heads in white baggs. their carriage was strange to me, one of the women made a continued humming noise longer then the reach of an ordinari breath without motion either of lips or breath that I who stood next her could perceive, shee ceaseing another sung holy holy holy with the addition of some other words, then the other (her song being donne) gave some of their ordinary exhortacon[a] with their common mixture of judgment and threatning and after a little pause they went over the same round, without answering any questions which by the standers by were proposd, and those which by the committee were urgd. I observd they either not answerd or did it with a great deale of suttlety besides the cover and cunning of that language which others and I beleeve they them selves scarce understand,[1] but I am weary of the Quakers and returne to my freinds with you, to home I desire to be remembred, not thinke when I began that this subject should have soe long kept my pen from them

Captain Smith[2] remembers you.

Westminster 15° Novem:[b] 1656

I would gladly receive that letter to Colonel Popham[3] which by my last I desird from you if it may bee with speed as conceiveing it very materiall to my affairs.

Endorsed by Locke: Nayler *56*.

[a] *A final* -s *perhaps torn away.* [b] *Altered from* 6° Decem:

[1] In the earlier part of this year James Nayler (1617?–60) and his followers had created disturbances at Bristol; later some of them called him Jesus or the Lamb of God; and on 24 October he made a triumphant entry into Bristol in imitation of Christ's entry into Jerusalem. The matter was brought before Parliament on 31 October, and on 15 November Nayler and his followers were examined by a committee of members in the Painted Chamber. In December he was adjudged guilty of blasphemy and was severely punished: *D.N.B.*; Firth, *Last Years*, i. 84–106; W. C. Braithwaite, *The Beginnings of Quakerism*, 2nd ed., ed. H. J. Cadbury, 1955, pp. 241–78. William Grigge, the author of *The Quaker's Jesus*, 1658, which is based on the examination of Nayler at Bristol on 25 October, was probably a connection of Locke's, perhaps a brother-in-law of Peter Locke. At least two lives of Nayler were published in December. [2] p. 7 and n. 3. [3] p. 10 n.

## *31.* W. C. to My Lord P: Secretary, [1656/1657?]

B.L., MS. Locke c. 24, f. 26. Draft written by Locke. Roughly written. W. C. may be William Carr (no. *33*, etc.); my Lord P. may be the Protector; but the heading may be fictitious.

For W. C. to My Lord P: Secretary

Sir

That my resentments have beene silent soe long is oweing to their greatnesse, neith would your favours be what they are, nor my acknowledgments such as they should be could I sooner have spoken them. even trees that pay noething for the influence and droppings from heaven but leaves require time for that too and doe not presently make returns of their fruitlesse verdure. could I hope to proportion my thanks to your favours it were necessary that I studyed some new way of gratitude and ought to be as extraordinary in my acknowledgment as you have beene in obligeing. Tis not enough to assure you that you have gott one more to the number of your servants, you have beene to much accustomd to triumphs and dwelt to long neare conquerors to glory in soe triviall an acquisition and since by the nobler way of conquereing you assaile men with the same successe and take in soules with the same ease that those you converse amongst doe towns and castles. It would appeare rather my priviledg then gratitude to ranke my self in the list of your Trophes. were it not that I might be thought too insensible silence in this case would be my best refuge and most suitable to that wonder and transport wherewith I receivd your courtesy, from which I have not yet recoverd those setled and undesturbed thoughts as are[a] requisit to one that would speake him self gratefull and I can only get leave of my amasement to stammer out a few unjoynted and broken expressions and mak faint signes instead of perfect returns of acknowledgment. your favours like those from heaven great unmeritted and at a distance are most fitly entertained like those with a silent admiration. and when the piety of the ancients made the highest returns it was only some breathings from their alters and an handfull of Frankinsense satisfyd for a whole harvest. Sir my returns are forcd to beare the same proportion as unsuitably to your merits as my owne desires: my gratidue cannot out reach their devotion all therefor that this paper will bring unto you will be some small marks of my indeavors and inclinations to assure you that I am

Sir

[a] *MS.* r

## *32.* FRANCIS ATKINS to LOCKE, 15 April [1657?] (*27*)

B.L., MS. Locke c. 3, ff. 53–4. The year is conjectural. Locke was at Pensford in April 1661 after his father's death, but the letter is inappropriate for that period. He is not known to have visited Pensford in any other April in these years; a visit in any of them is possible.

Sir

Upon the mention of your name, and an opportunity of conveighance (together with the enthusiams of the sack which I am now drinking your health in) methinks I begin to be inspir'd; and cannot chuse but talke light. If you have the luck to receive this paper in such a place, and temper as it is written in, I am confident wee are agreed, and I may save the labour of further Apologie: but if it should chance to arrive at such an howre, when your severer imployments, shall superciliate or furrow your then threatning ⟨brow⟩;[a] I hope you will but burne the innocent paper, and acquit the principall malefactour; and your Justice shall be applauded.

I wish thee joy, money; Friends, and if thou know'st what to wish thy self more, that, and Heav'n to boote, from

Thy true Friend
FRANC: ATKINS

The horsshooe Taverne in Covent Garden
Aprill the 15th.

Address: For my Friend Mr John Lock at Pensford

## *33.* WILLIAM CARR to [LOCKE?], 3 July [1657?] (37)

B.L., MS. Locke c. 5, f. 13. The writer, d. 1689, was the son of William Carr, brother(?) of Robert Ker, first earl of Ancrum (Scotland; *D.N.B.*). He was admitted to Gray's Inn 15 December 1655; matriculated from Christ Church 1 April 1656; fellow of All Souls, 1658; B.C.L. 15 October 1664; barrister, Gray's Inn, 1663; Cursitor Baron of the Exchequer 1689; married Anne, daughter of Philip Wharton, fourth Baron Wharton (*D.N.B.*), by his second wife Jane Goodwin; buried at Woburn, Bucks. His sister Lettice married Alexander Popham; his other sister, Anne, married first Popham's brother Admiral Edward Popham (d. 1651; *D.N.B.*), and secondly, in 1661, as his third wife, the fourth Lord Wharton: *Genealogist*, ii (1878), 290–1; Sir R. Douglas, *The Scots Peerage*, ed. Sir J. B. Paul, 1904–14, v. 463; J. Le Neve, *Monumenta Anglicana . . . 1680 to . . . 1699*, 1718, pp. 106–7; G. E. C., art. Wharton; Foster; etc.

The year and place of writing of the letter are problematical. It could belong to any year between Carr's matriculation in 1656 and his leaving

[a] *MS.* bow;

Oxford at some date after August 1660. The writing is closer to letters from Carr datable in 1658 and 1660 than to one datable in 1664 (nos. *39*, *92*, *166*). The formal opening and subscription are similar to those of no. *39*; in February 1660 and 1664 Carr writes in a more familiar manner: nos. *92*, *166*.

I have failed to find a place named Wiccham or anything similar approximately 50 miles from Oxford. There is a hamlet Whitcombe (Whitcomb) near Popham's seat at Littlecote, which is about 41 miles from Oxford; and modern maps show Wick Farm near Houndstreet, conventionally about 50 miles from Oxford: no. 12, etc. Wickham in Hampshire (no. *51* n.) is 70 miles from Oxford.

Carr's brother is probably his brother-in-law Alexander Popham. If the fee sent by him is to be associated with his son Francis's admission at Oxford (no. 96 n.) the year must be 1660; but as M.P. for Bath Popham is likely to have been in London rather than in the country on 3 July 1660. Carr was perhaps in Oxford early in July 1659: no. *60*. The letter appears not to belong to the same summer as no. *44*, which belongs probably to 1658.

Act Monday fell in 1656 on 14 July; in the next three years on 13, 12, and 11 July. It fell on 9 July 1660, but no act was held; as this was not decided until 30 June, Carr might not have heard of the cancellation: Wood, *L. and T.* i. 320.

Sir

I would not have you harbour shuch a thought as to thinke that 50 miles distance can in the least diminish the service I owe unto you; I should have trowlled you with a relation of sume passages that I have meet with sence I came into this country but that my time is so short and your occasions so urgent that they will not give me leave. My Brother hath sent 20sh. by this bearer for the Keepers fee,[1] and desiers you to send this letter away with all speed and after you have read it to seale it. I doubt that the Doctors perswasions and my sisters will keepe me here til after the Act,[2] so that I shall not waite on my friends as I thought I should, Deare Sir give me leave to break off abruptly, but still to remaine

Your humble servant

W. CARR.

Wiccham[a] July 3

My service to mr Ward[3]

Endorsed by Locke: Mr Cars letter;

[a] *Or* Wiceham

---

[1] Presumably the Keeper of the Archives at Oxford.

[2] This consisted mainly of the final, but mostly formal, exercises for the degrees of M.A. and of doctor in the faculties. It was held on the next Monday after 7 July and on the two days before the Monday: Evelyn, *Diary*, ed. de Beer, iii. 104 n.

[3] Probably Isaiah Ward: no. *44*.

## *34.* THOMAS SYMES to [LOCKE?] [*c.* July 1657?] (67)

B.L., MS. Locke c. 19, f. 177. The writer matriculated from Christ Church on 21 April 1657. He was perhaps from Poundisford, near Taunton, Somerset, and barrister, Lincoln's Inn, 1666: Foster. Date: Symes was absent from Oxford shortly before 20 August of this year: no. *35*. Later years are also possible.

Sir

I had not left Oxford without taking a more solem leave of you, would my buisnesse have allowed of a longer stay; Yet I was about to have dispensed with my occasions to have waited on you, but that I knew by experience it would be difficult for me to part from you so suddenly; your company is so pleasing and delightfull to me, that I can never leave you without exercising some violence upon my Inclinations. Sir It greives me, that I could not keep my word with you, to send you Albovine,[1] though if lawfull excuses might exempt duty, I am absolved of my promise; I had heard such commendations of Salisbury and Wilton house from Mr Locky,[2] that made me desire to see it, and I had such faire profers made me if I would accompanie a freind of mine thither that I accepted of them, and went the second day after I came home; but left the booke in the hands of a servant to be sent by the next carrier, who (I beleive) forgot it, though he doth impute the fault to others. I have sent him by this ther is a leave torne out of him in my absense. I am Yours

THO. SYMES.

my service to Mr Tilly.[3] I thought I should have heard from him long ere this, and mr Hastings[4] if he be returned: pray deliver the inclosed key to Mr Locky with my humble service:

[1] Probably *The Tragedy of Albovine, King of the Lombards*, by Sir William Davenant, first published in 1629.

[2] Thomas Lockey, 1602–79; student of Christ Church 1621; B.D. 1634; D.D. 1660; Bodley's Librarian 1660–5: *D.N.B.* He was resident in Oxford and active as a tutor 'in the time of Usurpation'; and contributed a poem (no. 14) to *Musarum Oxoniensium 'Ελαιοφορία*, 1654: Anthony Wood, *Fasti Oxonienses*, ed. Bliss, ii. 242; Madan, no. 2243 (14); see also p. 18, n. 1.

[3] Probably Samuel Tilly of Wadham: p. 28 n. There was a Henry Tilly at Christ Church from 1654 to 1660: G. F. R. Barker and A. H. Stenning, *The Record of Old Westminsters*, 1928.

[4] Not traceable in Foster; presumably a man admitted to Christ Church who did not matriculate, like Henry Guy (p. 54, n. 3) and Henry Savile (p. 86, n. 8).

## *35.* SAMUEL TILLY to [LOCKE?], 20 August 1657 (24, *36*)

B.L., MS. Locke c. 20, f. 177.

Sir

To offer you a defensive of the passion you thinke me to entertain, were to suppose you ignorant of the power that caused it, whereof how sensible you are, I have no need to expect assurance, having receiv'd your letter, which, however dated the 29th of July, came not to my hands until Sunday last. It troubled me not a litle, that I was no sooner capable, as of answering your expectations by a more early return, so to crave your exposition for my right understanding of those Mysterious passages towards the closure of your letter, which if they can but affoord satisfaction proportionable to the hopes they have begotten, how acceptable their knowledge will be I must leave you to imagine. Can that goodnesse, which hath such a Commanding power, reward obedience with any thing that lookes like an approbation! Since I came thence I have in my travels (for I have hitherto bin litle at home) bin sollicited for a western voyage,[1] the design's not unknowne to you; but indeed to steer my course by any other then that northern Pole-starre,[2] were to shipwrack my contentment, the impression of whose influence hath bin so lasting, that 'tis now become complexional in me, like that which at Nativities, Astrologers use to attribute to the starrs then Culminant. Although I can in my esteem preferre nothing to an equalitie with this Ladie's favour, yet the realitie of those respects I owe you is such, as that I am even ready to say as Scipio (sueing for the Consu⟨ls⟩hip,[a] and finding Pompey his friend opposing it) said of himselfe eum Consulatum sibi non tam gloriæ futurum si adipisceretur, quam, si refragante Pompeio, consequeretur, molestum, et inauspicatum.[3]

[a] *Page torn.*

[1] To Devon and Cornwall.

[2] Presumably one of the residents at Black Hall in St. Giles, Oxford, one of the Evelegh or one of the Parry sisters: p. 74, n. 4. The star in nos. *71*, *104*, and *105*, is probably Anne Evelegh.

[3] 'That this Consulship, if he secured it, would not be so glorious for him as it would be troublesome and ill omened if he achieved it against the wishes of Pompey.' Tilly perhaps took this from Erasmus, *Apophthegmata* (in *Opera*, ed. Le Clerc, 1703–6, iv. 267), a book apparently known to him: no. *36* n. Erasmus does not give his authority. Scipio is identifiable as Quintus Caecilius Metellus Pius Scipio, consul 52 B.C.: A. F. von Pauly, *Paulys Real-Encyclopädie der classischen Altertumswissenschaft*, ed. G. Wissowa, 1894– , s.v. Caecilius 99.

I intend verie shortly to return, if not to Oxford, yet so neere it as may revive those impressions I have receivd. Wer't not that I have at present a more direct conveyance, I should trouble you to present her with a letter, to whome, if, before you see me you have an opportunitie be pleasd to present my most affectionate service. I shall not fail for the future of performing my promise altho for the time past my occasions abroad have disabled me. I cannot but promise my selfe your sudden answer to this because it will conduce so much to the contentment of

your cordial friend

SAM: TILLY

Compton Martin Aug: 20 —57

My service to mr Baldwin[1] and to litle Sims,[2] if returnd, whose letter I am expecting.

Endorsed by Locke: Mr Tillys Lett:
[Also on verso a calculation about money.]

## *36.* SAMUEL TILLY to [LOCKE?], 4 September 1657 (*35, 123, 127*)

B.L., MS. Locke c. 20, f. 178.

Affectionate Sir

I expected a Comment and behold a text more difficult then the former; waiting for light, I had not traveld far in your letter, but I found my selfe o're-cast by a thicker cloud, as if your former lines had not bin obscure enough, unlesse you had now farther added the darknesse of a shaddow. But that you may not thinke I quarrel with your Similitude I assure you there's no fault in't save only its disparitie, for tho 'tis but a slender subsistence that's yet to much to shaddow out what you pretend to expresse thereby (scil. your being so a servant to etc.) that indeed lookes to much like nothing, to have power to scare me who therefore can safely conclude, that sure ther's no danger in't. But as I passe on, I finde a name, which I had yet bin at a losse whome to have applied it to, had not you own'd it for yours, 'tis since therefore you'l challenge it, that you may see how much I tender the successe of your

[1] William Baldwin, armiger; matriculated from Christ Church 23 July 1656: Foster.
[2] Thomas Symes.

affection, you shall not want all incouragement I can affoord, who can assure you, I thinke it as possible for two each of us wholy to possess some third persons affection, as for Cæsar and Pompey to get the same consulship together, which I presume never any two at once obtaind, unlesse in Bibulus's yeare, when both Julius and Cæsar was Consul.[1] As for that provision you have sent for my supply, whilst absent, what thankes would I return you! 'Twas no Physick for Aristotle of which his Physician did render him no reason;[2] tho his example might in this case also warrant it, yet the ingredients here are to numerous to expect it of all particulars, resolve me in this one, why you make roome for codlings in such a Compound, and then ther's but one Quere more, and I shall fall to, 'tis this, If her eies were those suns that boild the Pap whence was that heat that boil'd them to Codlings! As for that freezing cold of that northern starre[3] you insinuate, ther's no need of any caution; those influences that had warmth enough to enliven will never be to cold to cherrish those hopes they have produc'd; nor is there cause to feare least by the conjunction of any malignant planet they should, like those of Mercurie, suffer alteration, to thinke so, were not lesse to prejudice her virtue, then to contradict my owne former experience. And now I am come to your needlesse Apologie for the length of your letter, for what Plinie said of Tullies orations I ever thought of your letters, the longest to be best,[4] it had bin more proper for your excuse in that you added no more, for I must confesse I found that at length left out at the end of your letter which I lookd for in the beginning. How ever I'le not stile that a delusion which yet may possibly proove but a delay, intended not to defeat my expectations but to deferr them. And now deare Sir that I have traveld thus far give me leave at length to rest in your shaddow, which could I believe it accompanied that noble substance that terminates my thoughts, I might then use your attendance, to present her with my choicest respects. But because her splendor is such, as no shaddow comes neere, unlesse favour'd by some bodie interposing, therefore, to the end there may be roome for you, Ile suddenly take that office upon me,

[1] M. Calpurnius Bibulus, consul 59 B.C.: Pauly, *Real-Encyc.*, s.v. Calpurnius 28. Tilly alludes to Suetonius, *De Vita Caesarum*, Divus Julius, cap. 20, § 2 (Teubner edition, i. 9).

[2] The anecdote is given by Erasmus in his *Apophthegmata* (in *Opera*, ed. Le Clerc, 1703–6, iv. 368).

[3] p. 49 and n. 2.

[4] The younger Pliny; *Epistolae*, i. 20.

that therein I may have the happinesse as to wait on so deserving a Ladie, so to testifie how much Sir

I am

your real friend and servant

SAM: TILLY

C. M.[1] 4 Sept. 1657.

Let not my two last lines furnish you with an excuse to deprive me of the happinesse of your letters, for that would be lesse currant then mine that carried the stamp of real necessitie. And if you please let the vizard be a litle laid aside, that you may breake through the mist of similies and metaphors, so as I may clearly apprehend what return was made to your intended inquiries, at those lodgings neer Christchurch westwards.[2] Unlesse my Nomenclator fail you are mistaken in her name, who was partly the subject[a] of your letter

Vale Vige Scribe[3]

If you see litle Sims be pleas'd to tell him, I am in the storm's til he please to vousafe me a Covert.

Endorsed by Locke: Mr Tillys Letter

## 37. LOCKE to [WILLIAM CARR], 23 January 1658 (*33, 39*)

B.L., MS. Locke c. 24, ff. 6–7. Possibly the letter sent. Apparently the antecedent of no. *39*.

Sir

Had not I beene possest with a zeale to obey your commands, which acknowledges noe subjection to cold and winter, you might have dispensd with my not sending you a letter from this frozen climate and benumd fingers. and when you shall consider how many watermans blows it cost my hands, before I could bring them to a limbernesse that could direct my pen; and that it put me to the expence of a three halfpenny faggot to thaw my inke, I hope you will judg this letter hath meritt enough in it to deserve an answer.[4] Had I had confidence enough to beleeve that story,

[a] *MS.* subt

[1] Compton Martin. [2] Not identifiable.

[3] 'Good-bye, keep flourishing, and write.'

[4] The winter of 1657–8 was rigorous throughout western Europe: C. Easton, *Les Hivers dans l'Europe occidentale*, 1928.

which tells us that in some countrys neare the pole mens words are arested by the frost asoone as they peepe out of their mouths, and may be heard in the same place the next thaw;[1] I had now an oportunity to make an experiment, and had undoubtedly only spoke my letter into a box and sent you my minde in frozen aire, which would have given you an account verbatim by your Hownestreet fires.[2] Certainely how far soever Winter extends his territorys this is his head quarters, and he forbids the approach of any fire to affront his empire unlesse it be here and there the flame of a rush candle. Report tels us that Mr George[3] is dead and though I see no teares droping to this death yet I cannot impute it soe much to want of sorrow, as care of theire eys, which should this cold weather finde wet with tears it would undoubtedly freeze them up and blinde them with their owne Isicles and they must not hope to see till the next thaw. The truth is I have found soe much cold since I came hither that I have almost forgot what it is to be warme, and had not my vexation at the necessity that hurried me away from you, and from the warme summer of that country, unchild me some times with a fitt of anger, I thinke ere this time I had beene little short of a statue. Sir if your expectation promisd you any jockes from Mr Nurse's declamation[4] you must be content with the rest of the howse to goe without 'em for however he was formerly predicant he is now a silenc'd Parson and that I thinke for feare he should be Malignant. His theame was Melancholici non sunt igeniosi this was all that was sufferd to be knowne he being prohibited to speake in the hall, which I know not wheather it were out of a care of his jests, which they were afraid to let venter abrode this cold weather. Besides this, news which I know you were greedy of, the howse, or university affords me none that may deserve to detaine you any longer, unlesse you will be content to know, that when you come hither next, you must resolve to

[1] The story occurs first in Plutarch, *Moralia*, c. 79. Locke perhaps knew the version in B. Castiglione, *Il Libro del Cortegiano*, ii. 55.

[2] Hunstrete or Houndstreet, near Pensford, a seat of Carr's brother-in-law Alexander Popham: p. 10 n.

[3] Identifiable as William George, student of Christ Church 1651; B.A. 1656; he was buried at Garsington on 5 April: Foster; Wood, *L. and T.* i. 242–3; Madan, nos. 2160, 2243 (58).

[4] Either John Nourse: at Westminster School; matriculated from Christ Church 27 November 1650; B.A. 1655; M.A. 1657; or George Nourse: at Westminster School; matriculated from Christ Church 2 June 1652; B.A. 1656; M.A. 1658; contributed a poem (no. 72) to Oxford volume *Britannia Rediviva*, 1660 (Madan, no. 2466; L.L., no. 2162): Barker and Stenning.

shroud your head under a round bonnet; the late command of the Proctor haveing ordaind caps to be worne.[1] By that time you come hither I thinke you will be sufficiently tir'd with reading soe tedious a scribling but if this be too long pray let it goe for two, since all I shall ever write to you will be but the same with this which is to assure you that I am

Sir

Your most faithfull servant

JOHN LOCKE

Ch: Ch: 23° Jan 1657

Mr Ward[2] returnes his kind remembrance to you. I should tell you too of commendations from Great Guy[3] and little Robin,[4] did not the Oxford ague begin to benum my hands and command a period

f. 7v: In hand probably not Locke's: Jhem[a] Lithe[a] Love Love

## *38.* JOHN STRACHEY to LOCKE, 23 January 1658 (*47*)

B.L., MS. Locke c. 18, f. 188. John Strachey, 1634–75 (11 Feb. 1674/5); of Sutton Court, about 3 miles SW. of Pensford; his mother's (no. *107*) first husband, Samuel Jepp, perhaps related to Locke; matriculated from Lincoln College, Oxford, 1 April 1653; B.A. 2 April 1653; barrister, Gray's Inn, 1660 (1661?); married, December 1662, Jane, 1643–1727, daughter of George Hodges of Great Wedmore, Somerset, etc.; children Jane (died young), Elizabeth (married William Jones of Stowey), and John (1671–1743): *Virginia Magazine of History and Biography*, lix (1951), 275–96.

Sir

What Forrainers throw on the Inglish in way of disparagement may in a different sence bee spoken in your comendation, (They are strangers at home): for could my unworthy pen present you a mapp of your owne rich parts, your eyes I see would wander in a Terra incognita, or looke on it as a Lady lookinglasse that reflects you fairer then nature made you. But by your modesties leave if

[a] *Doubtful reading.*

[1] This was part of a return to academic dress after Dr. John Owen's attempt to abolish it: Wood, *L and T.* i, 359; p. 62, n. 1

[2] Presumably Isaiah (Esay) Ward: pp. 47, n. 3, 63 n.

[3] Perhaps Henry Guy the politician: no. *1715*; he apparently spent some time at Christ Church, but did not matriculate: Wood, *Fasti*, ii. 272.

[4] Perhaps Robert South, the divine: p. 153, n. 5.

any errataes were in the last edition, twa's in not giving you what your deserts might challenge, and why should the title of Honourable trouble you, unlesse you feare that good extraction and high endowments are the only Remora's in a voyage for the other house;[1] but Honors[a] are not derivd from Crownes nor tied to acres; they are none of frindships by blowes, but the Legitimat offspring of thy meritts. But least this duty prove poison soe swell you into a Mogul or some of the other Bug bares, thus you may scare your freinds soe that they dare not come neere you, Ile deale noe more in your Court Comodities, but will awake you out of this pleasant dreame with a how dee. Faith Jack I am now falling into the sweete sin of love and unles thou helpe mee I must needes bee lost, and though I have Ovids and Osbornes better remedium amoris by mee,[2] yett I am perswaded my Flame is soe much allyed to lightninge that none but the Bristoll milke[3] can quench it. Not to deale in fancy lett mee have what your reason suggests on this occasion, if thou refuse this courtesie, know you are guilty of my perishing, and what a terrible blow that may strike on thy conscience I leave thee to thinke I can't speake it. Some have proposed the visiting of Bawdy houses, but tis ineffectuall, for these divells raise my mind to the contemplation of Angells by the same workings that Atheists have beene scard into a divine worship, and serve to noe other purpose then my Ladys patches viz to sett off her beauty with a greater lustre. Now if a strong opinion of the Doctors ability hath as greate an operation in the cure of the patiente disease as the very physick, you may presume the cure halfe perfected, for hee can embrace noe ones prescriptions then yours with greater greedinesse who is

your frind and servant
J STRACHEY

Janu 23. 1657

Endorsed by Locke: Mr Strachys Letter

[a] *Spelling doubtful; last letters rewritten.*

[1] Cromwell's 'other House' met for the first time on 20 January of this year; its members were styled Lords. The remora or sucking-fish was believed to have the power of staying any ship to which it attached itself; hence the word was used for an impediment, obstruction, etc.: *O.E.D.*

[2] It was Ovid who wrote the *Remedium Amoris*; the book by Francis Osborne is *Advice to a Son*, first published anonymously in 1656 (1655). The first edition to bear the author's name, the sixth, was published this year: *D.N.B.*, art. Osborne; Madan, nos. 2278, 2396, etc.

[3] Sherry.

## *39.* William Carr to Locke, 30 January [1658] (37, *92*)

B.L., MS. Locke c. 5, f. 8. Year from contents. Answers no. 37.

Dear Sir

I know that you cannot expect that this sheet should be so crowded with witt a⟨s⟩[a] yours was; I hope you have a better consideration of the ayre and the person that writts it. When I read your letter I wondred that the sawsie winter should so sharply assaylte you, yet he hath been so mearsifull that althought he hath keept your outward parts prisoners and benumed your limbs, yet he gives your witt leave to runn fluently; I suppose we should have had the same privilige here in Somersetshire if we had any to flow. Your news of George's departure causeth as few tears here as at Oxford; and I could wish that those who had the greatest hand in advansing capps were also with him: Capt: Bird through my perswasions is going next weeke to Bristol to teach a free schole,[1] and hath undertaken to bring-up scholars that shall have more manners then all the Universitie of Oxford can show: Sir tis time now to breake off my folly and to sit doune and lament your departure which can never enough be lamented by him who is

Your most faithfull servant
W Carr

My service to all my friends in generall and if you can spare so much time as to present my service to little Robin I shall be further engaged to you

Jan: 30

Endorsed by Locke: Mr Carres Letter

[a] *Page torn.*

[1] Free schools had some endowment and were probably under some kind of public control. They provided education free of charge, but the masters were allowed to receive voluntary gifts from the boys' parents: *O.E.D.*, s.vv. Free, *a.*, 32b, especially quotations of 1512 and 1727, and Public School; examples in *Essex Papers*, vol. i (Camden Soc., new ser., no. xlvii, 1890), pp. 113–17; E. Hatton, *New View of London*, 1708, p. 657 (list of the London free schools at p. 661); modern statement in W. A. L. Vincent, *The Grammar Schools*, 1969, pp. 40–57.

## *40.* THOMAS GRENFEILD to LOCKE, 18 March 1658 (20)

B.L., MS. Locke c. 10, f. 55.

Sir

'Tis noe marvell, I have not heard from you, nor you from mee, in a tyme, when, I thinke, all thinges were frozen. For my part: it has byn soe cold with mee, that I could doe nothinge with my fingers, but warme them: And I beleive, the very dutch-men themselves, with you, could not play the theife in your libraryes at that rate of longe-writinge,[1] as they use to doe in milder weather: Yet, you must wonder that I, fell into a very burninge feaver, in the mydst of all your cold, (at London);[2] and as one was reported to bee a walkinge Library,[3] soe was I a walkinge fyre, and wondringe that others put theyre fingers in the very flames, when I wisht my selfe in the water: It was a pretty provision, my distempered nature made mee; that in all this cold weather, I had fyre enough; and was warmed at noe other Expence, then for somewhat to coole it:

I was non-plus't in my Intellectuals for some houres; as you may guesse by the remnants of it in this paper. but doe hope, yet to treat you with as much reason, as your next veiw will make you pitty the ruines of:

I question not, how you have shifted at Oxford; hopinge you have had a hott tyme on't this Lent, 'tis impossible to be cold in a schoole; and indeed; I thinke it an excellent refuge from the frost, when well heated with a disputation: Well Sir: whatever the incomposednesse of this is, I hope you will pardon it, when you consyder, and are desyred to beleive, it comes from one, who wishes very well to your studyes, and shall take it for noe small favour, if that accurate pen of yours will please to trouble itselfe in a Lyne to

your assured Freind
THO. GRENFEILD

Pensford. Mar. 18vo. —57

Endorsed by Locke: Mr Gren: letter

[1] The converse of shorthand. Wood mentions a number of Germans, Swedes, etc., who worked in the Bodleian about 1655–7: *Fasti*, ii. 190–1, 197, 213.
[2] Grenfeild was now preacher at Lincoln's Inn.
[3] The phrase goes back to Classical Antiquity: *O.E.D.*, s.v. Walking, *ppl. a.* 5.

## 41. LOCKE to M. J. [John Maggs?], [late March 1658?] (*42*)

B.L., MS. Locke c. 24, f. 187. Draft. The initials at the head suggest that it was written to Maggs. It appears to be in response to an apology for not writing rather than to a letter from Maggs. It may be for the antecedent of no. *42*, which Locke appears to have received by 6 April, the probable date of no. 43.

In 1661 a man named John Maggs rented land in Pensford or Publow from Locke: B.L., MS. Locke c. 26, ff. 15, 16. He was perhaps the witness of Thomas Locke's nuncupative will in 1663: Cranston, p. 79; see further nos. *614* and *1484*. A man named Thomas Maggs was a benefactor to Pensford: J. Collinson, *History . . . of Somerset*, 1791, ii. 429.

M. J.[a]

Sir

What every day ingraveing lines upon old downe and never drawing any on paper, an imployment more suitable to your ingenuity and the Genius of a sociable man? and from which you may expect an harvest too, though not of corne yet of thanks, which though they have not soe much sollid stuffing and belly timber in them as the sheaf, yet have more of sauce and a delicate relish. doe you use the same method in your amity as husbandry hide it under, the clods and bury your freindship in your furrows to increase it? and must we look to heare noe more of it till the next harvest? and expect intelligence from the approaches of the sun not carrier. I am willing to beleeve you are a carefull manurer of freindship, but closenesse and silence will not improve it, tis of too sublime and heavenly a makeing to begge[b]– it preservation–[b] from a spareing providence and to stand in neede of time to ripen it the more you spend the more you have of it and prodigality is its best improvement. this flame must have roome to expand and shew its self, and if you goe to close and lock it up you loose it The morall of this is easy, when you have walkd your morning rounds and bestowd your care on your cattle, after the sheep and oxen have shard your visit alow then some moments to the memory of your freinds, at least tune the violl, strike up a coranto and seale him up in a letter and send him hither you know not how it may revive us and how suitable it will be to those who are ⟨accustomd⟩[c] to live upon little besides air. twill be as good as fretting away two

[a] *Preceded by* T *expunged.* [b–b] *Interlined;* it *is perhaps a slip for* its, *but an obsolete or dialect usage is possible.* [c] *MS.* accustomds

howers at wisk[1] and after twenty murrens manjes and poisons to pay tups for being beaten. or at most get a victory to be celebrated with the[a] discharge[a] ⟨of⟩ a canon of ale[2] and the bonefire of a Tabacopipe. whilst we perhaps are labouring for a pore lively whood amongst the bare bones of a sheepe and murning the absence of our freinds in colledg beare. had you any regards for despicable forlorne people in such a condition I should oftener heare from you and you would quickly eccho back I am your lov

## 42. John Maggs to [Locke?], [*c.* 1 April 1658?] (41)

B.L., MS. Locke c. 15, f. 197. Roughly datable from Popham's accident. Perhaps the letter from Maggs mentioned in no. 43. Perhaps written in answer to a letter for which no. 41 was a draft.

Deere Sir

I envye not your retiredness, but if it weare or might be lawfull for me to wish a change, I should wish me your selfe, for to live retired was never but safe, and very pleaseinge to som Constitutions, but in theise times far better as the world is worse: att Penceford we nothinge but Toyle and labour and sweet, like Asses groaneinge under our burthens, and knowe not how soone wee shall be deprived of those outward Injoyements, but Christs Church is a safe shelter from outward discontentments: I have little to write unto you for matter of newes from this dull Cell, onlye that Collonell Popham is verye well recovered from a verye dangerous Fall from his horse,[3] Mr Greenefeild is at present with us,[4] and if I am not much mistaken wee shall within a minuit or two after the writeinge hereof, tuch your right hand puls with a Cupp of heart reviveinge sack, noe more at present but that I am

your moste Cordiall Friend and servant:

Joh Maggs:

Endorsed by Locke: Mr Maggs his letter

[a] *Interlined; the word* of *supplied.*

---

[1] Whisk, a card-game; apparently the earlier name for whist: *O.E.D.* Tups appears to be Locke's abbreviation for twopence.

[2] Presumably the same as a gun, a flagon: *O.E.D.*, s.v. Gun, *sb.* 9.

[3] In a letter written probably in London on 2 April Popham was said to be ill from a fall from his horse: *Cal. Clarendon State Papers*, iv. 36. If Popham was at Houndstreet news of his recovery might take some time to reach London.

[4] See p. 57.

## 43. LOCKE to JOHN LOCKE, sen., [6 April 1658?] (30, *54*)

B.L., M.S. Locke c. 24, f. 172. Locke's date is wrong; the approximate date is fixed by Fisher's speech, the insurrections, etc., and the cold winter (that of 1658–9 was mild). I assume that Locke is mistaken about the month, but that he gives the day correctly.

Honoured Sir

I have long impatiently expected that treasure of good news the carrier this last weeke brought me. and though your letters carried satisfaction enough in them to excuse an ordinary fault, yet I could not but quarrell with them for staying soe long for one anothers company. There arivd at my hands two packets togeather, though one of them set out a month before the other. In these I had found a perfect gladnesse had there not beene one rubb to alay it, one cloud to marre the serenity which I hope will be blowne over since there is noe more requird to it, then one mans breath. and such an one who cannot but doe it, if he either consider himself, or you. I must confesse this news contradicting my perswasion and setled beleefe, somewhat startld me, and set me at variance with all man kinde: and I was on the point to looke upon them, as an heard of untrusty creatures, not worth ones love, or regard, since he hath faild soe poorely who was lookd on as one of the best. I was ready to bewaile Virtue and Noblenesse as quite lost and banishd, since not to be found in him who was thought to have given them harbor and a retreat. Should the businesse stick, It will hasten my journy into the country sooner then my intention, and if it should miscary (which I hope not) I shall disclaime all greatnesse and slight those swelling baggs and titles, as mansions only of pride and vanity, and uninhabited by worth and virtue. However it will teache me this caution, to withdraw my dependences from such windy props, to forbid my hopes and feares a commerce with their frowns, or promises, and to use them as they use us, only as long as serviceable. I cannot overvalue those accidentall differences that chance doth place on men, and are noe reall ones, but as they are usd. Pardon me Sir if I have dwelt to long on this and perhaps to hotly. But I cannot see your services soe rewarded, repeated promises so slighted and jugling in a great man without being movd.[1] well there be some acres left yet

[1] Perhaps Alexander Popham, with whom the elder Locke had been associated. He was now one of Cromwell's Lords; at the same time the Royalists hoped that he would join in their projected rising: Firth, *Last Years*, ii. 63.

which may at last (if all faile) be coind, and I shall be unwilling to keepe them when they may be serviceable to him that gave them. If you health stick at any thing I beleeve tis only at this rub: which therefor I have double desires to have removd, however the Doctors advice cannot but be very requisite this spring and I hope (both your Physicians contributeing their help) you will shortly finde noe thoughts nor viands which you will not be easily able to digest.

Insurrections and Invasions fly about here to on the wings of fame.[1] and I have had such information of it as some men upon the like would beleeve it more then probable. this report I thinke I may safely entertaine with this prayer that we may be preservd from oppression and bloud. I wonder to finde the Vicar Generall the Ubiquitary Parson[2] again at Pensford. certainely there is some secreat loadestone holds him there. and I am confident there is noe thing but gold can draw and fix that Mercury. I had thought that Pensford Litton.[3] Lincolns Inne etc had beene places enough for him to ⟨s⟩kip[a] up and downe in, without frisking from one world to another. but he may well goe once into a coffin and out againe, who hath fetchd soe many turnes in a Vault. Tis noe wonder to finde all the whole college of deseases in him who if we may beleeve a sicke man hath usualy more maladys in him then a spittle[4] and if I mistake not hath some incurable beyond the art of Physitians. I have sent him here inclosd some gilded pills to strengthen his weake stomacke after his sicknesse. Honest ⟨Mr⟩[b] Maggs his letter[5] I take extreame kindely, and have sent him an answer, which I hope will appease his grumbling gizard. and I intend should force a smile though his head hung on toe' side. Had he felt at Oxford the cold of winter and skermishes of lent,[6] possibly he might be induced to beleeve Pensford a warmer and securer place. what a deale of skin and stuff hath beene torne this Campania. scarce a face or gowne but hath stood in need of Chirurgery. On wednesday last Ch: Ch: party fild with mighty valour and potentiall ale. stormd Corpus christi the then randesvouz of the contrary side. fought their way in, and beat them all great and small into their chambers and after that the Proctor of that howse comeing

[a] *Hole in page.* [b] *MS.* Mrs

[1] Ibid. ii. 67–71. [2] Grenfeild.
[3] About 6 miles south of Pensford.
[4] Spital, hospital, especially one 'occupied by persons of a low class or afflicted with foul diseases': *O.E.D.*
[5] Probably no. *42*. [6] Easter Day fell on 11 April this year.

into Ch: Ch: something beyond the bounds of his power, found that his authority was not able to preserve him and his squire from being bangd in the enemy quarters.[1] Some few days since Pagan Fisher my L Protectors poet made a speech in Ch: Ch: hall in commendation of my Lord Bishop of Armagh (being denyd to doe it in the schooles though he came downe from London on purpose) for which he was out of the meare affection of his auditors abondantly laughd at, and almost josseld to death, never did any man take soe much pains to be ridiculous. the particulars would fill a volume, which I keepe to make you laugh when I come into the Country.[2] Since the great stir on wednesday last we have beene all confinde within the bounds of our Colledg which we cannot passe without leave or a sconce.[3] and were not our limitts pretty wide I should tell you we are all close prisoner. I perceive by Mr Car. who overtooke his letter here the last weeke,[4] and told me that he receivd but one of mine, that the Carrier hath very much abusd you and me too. There is an other whome I usualy imploy more carefull and constant then the other who lys at the swan in st Mary pole street[5] whome I desire you send by to prevent my want of intelligence, and those doubts and feares which are most able to trouble me here sensibly. and in your silence are justly due from

your most obedient sonne

J Locke

Ch: Ch: 6º Feb: 1658

[1] On 9 October 1657 the Independent Dr. John Owen, Dean of Christ Church (p. 30, n. 3), was succeeded as vice-chancellor by the Presbyterian Dr. John Conant (*D.N.B.*), who, as one of his reforms, re-established the use of academic dress (pp. 53–4 and n.). On 17 February of this year a Keeper of the Archives was elected. The candidates were Dr. Richard Zouche (*D.N.B.*) and Dr. John Wallis (p. 280, n. 1); Conant secured the latter's election by keeping the poll open until his friends could be brought in. Samuel Byfield (Foster), the senior proctor (of the university; but each college in turn elected one of the proctors; Byfield belonged to Corpus Christi, so 'of that howse' is correct in fact, but misleading) supported Wallis; Henry Stubbe of Christ Church (p. 109 n.) wrote against him: Wood, *Athenae*, ed. Bliss, iii. 1073–6 (not in earlier editions); Madan, nos. 2325, 2371; P. Abrams, ed., Locke, *Two Tracts on Government*, 1967, pp. 32–3. I have found no other notices of the fight between the colleges.

[2] Payne Fisher (1616–93; *D.N.B.*), who regarded himself as the Protector's laureate, delivered his commemorative oration on Ussher on 26 March: *Publick Intelligencer*, 4 April 1658, pp. 429–30; this notice and the jeering are mentioned by S. Woodford, poem prefixed to *Naps upon Parnassus*, 1658 ('advertisement to the reader' dated 30 May; Madan, no. 2363). The speech was printed as *Armachanus Redivivus*, 1658.

[3] A fine imposed for a breach of university or college discipline (an Oxford word): *O.E.D.*

[4] William Carr: p. 46 n.

[5] Perhaps a slip for St. Mary le Port Street in Bristol.

## 44. ISAIAH WARD to LOCKE, 14 September [1658?] (68)

B.L., M.S. Locke c. 23, ff. 59–60. The year is not earlier as Locke did not graduate M.A. until 29 June 1658. The letter suggests that Ward had been absent from Oxford for some time; nos. *60* and *99*, that he was there in July 1659 and July 1660.

Isaiah (Esay) Ward, born *c.* 1629; matriculated from Christ Church 1647; B.A. 1650; M.A. 1652; incorporated at Cambridge 1655: probably a contributor to Oxford congratulatory volumes 1654, 1660 (Madan, nos. 2243 (25), 2466 (70)); probably the physician of this name who died in London in 1674: Foster; Venn, *Alumni*; Wood, *L. and T.* i. 314, 316, 474; pp. 218–19 and n.

Mr Locke

If you can looke on mee as haveing any thing of reall friendship, you will not take it ill that I have been boldest with you, and deferred the civility of answering yours, untill better opportunity, and, as I hope, more likelihood of recovery. And yet in the meane while, without application, to give order for your trouble, with a scholler or two of mine, if need should bee. Indeed my disease hangs on mee faster, then I imagined it would, after the first shocke: every night it visits mee, with inquietude, and great sweatings. Yet my feavourish stomach desires mee to eate and drinke; and I have obeyed it a late to see whether I can possibly regaine my strength, soe strangely decayed. If I could with reason presume my selfe to bee able for travaile, I would (Deo Volente) venture unto you. Well, it may bee shortly. for I phansie that the society of my merry friends there might bee very Instrumentall to the cure. Pray therefore condescend to send for my servitour (unto whom I have noe other thing now, but thanks for his good will towards mee) and tell him I would have him take up of Mr Fifield[1] money, and with the assistance of Evan provide a very good load of billet, and lett it bee cut short and small. for where I come I bring a winter in my bones; and taking cold, I thinke hath caused many petty relapses in mee. Mee thinkes I have found out much of the mysteries of Agues; and could write a booke of Paradoxes[2] about them, enough to make mee famous for ever, but let it alone, untill amendment, lest the event disparage all. One of my sadnesses is that I neither see, nor heare, soe many of my

[1] Thomas Fyfeild, head-butler of Christ Church at the time of his death in 1662: Wood, *L. and T.* i. 459.

[2] In the older sense, statements or tenets contrary to received opinion or belief; often with the implication that they are marvellous or incredible; used both favourably and unfavourably: *O.E.D.*

goode friends persons, or welfare; especially since I find cheerfullnes a great ingredient to my ease. upon this account I have lately essayed to putt now and then a glasse of sacke in the place of small beere: (and hitherto I see noe cause to repent:) and that according to my principles of the nature of the disease. Now, Sir, you see you have it at length, what was due in promise long since; and will believe there can be no failing in one thats mindfull. Commendations now to be divided among my good friends; there is an inconvenience in particular reciteing, in mee who am dozed with long sickness; I rather give you generall commission; and then twill bee your fault to forgett any. bee sure of Mr Car: Mr Garrett,[a][1] and Mr Hoskins,[2] (out of our rank of Stud.) if they are with you.

See then; measure my respect for you by my tediousnes; which I could make almost infinite, when I thinke of Oxford, where my hart is. The Lord keepe us all; and never withold his Grace and Mercy from us, prayes

Your assured Fr.
ESAY WARD.

Enfield, Sept: 14.

Address: These For my singular good Fr. Mr. Jo: Locke, Master of Arts, and Student of Chr. Chu. in Oxford.

In his absence to bee delivered to Mr. Jo. Parry;[3] at his Chamb: in Ch. Ch.[b]

Endorsed by Locke: Mr Wards letter

## 45. LOCKE to a lady, [1658/1659?]

B.L., MS. Locke c. 24, f. 13. Draft. Written on cover of a letter to Locke. Irregular writing. It does not fit in with Locke's extant correspondence with Ann Evelegh or Elinor Parry (P. E.) in 1659.

Madam

To catch the eys of forward gazers, or by degrees to fire a heart that courts its flames is the effect of an ordinary face, As what fire

[a] *Doubtful reading.* [b] *The leaf on which the letter is written also bears the following address, written probably by Locke*: for Mr Isaiah Ward at Nicholas Raintons Esq att Enfeild to bee left att Mr Websters Cutler att the Starr next the Horn Taverne Fleet-street.

[1] Probably John Garrard, 1638–1701; of Lamer, Herts.; subscribed, Christ Church, 18 March 1657; third baronet 1685: G. E. C., *Baronetage*, i. 189.

[2] p. 112 n.

[3] Servitor; matriculated from Christ Church 23 July 1656; B.A. 1659; M.A. 1662: Foster.

is there that cannot warme him that nearely approaches it, But M. to Captivate at a distance and takeing a heart (that supposd it self well fortified) without either surprise or seige is the priviledg only of your beauty which scorns to conquer ordinary ways, which nature it seems designd to doe miracles as well as be one, and with the brightnesse of Heaven gave to your eys its influence too which at a distance secreatly commands and controls our fates without the assistance of our sences. this then being the easy though uncommon method of your victorys thinke it not strange that you finde at your feet an unknowne captive, who may be permitted to submitt to a passion hee had noe means left him to resist and can noe more conceale then those flames that comeing from heaven are more violent then others and seldome burne slow or secreatly. Pardon then the bold declaration which I here make of it, which yet my respects forbad till after I had debated with my self whether I ought to erect altars to you only in my breast and dye your silent votary which certainely I had endeavourd to doe had I not thought it necessary to give the world this testimony of your pour. Slight ⟨not⟩[a] therefore I beseech you[b] your conquest because soe easy, and think not my heart deserves the lesse to hold by you because it yeilded without summons. You cannot loose againe what you have once made yours, absence (the great destroyer of others Love) that could not hinder will not be able to impaire mine, nor will time ever be able to blott out that bright Idea I have of you in my heart since there is no faire object I meet with which I think not some representation of you, every thing handsome and excellent bring you to my thoughts and certainely should your severity doome me to death even that its self with all its Ice and coldnesse would not be able to extinguish my flame, since my soule must needs carry with it that faire image and its adoration of it into the other world which it borrowd not from any object in this Since then what ever becomes of me it is necessary that I love you give leave to assure you that there is not any one either in this or the other world that knows you lesse or adores you more

then

On reverse: For Mr John Locke in C: Church Oxon.

[a] *Word omitted by Locke.*
[b] *MS.* beseech ʸ your, *the* y *being inserted after* your *was written.*

## *46.* —— to —— ('Sine fuco aut fraude', no. 1), 24 January 1659 (*56*)

B.L., MS. Locke c. 14, f. 166. The letter sent? This letter and no. *56* belong together. The handwriting, the subscriptions, and the style in general, diverge from Locke's. The first letter appears to be written by an Oxonian to someone in London; it is perhaps from Somerset, and, if so, can scarcely be by Locke. The second appears to be from London to Somerset or vice versa; again it is unlikely to be by Locke. The letters were perhaps written by an amanuensis of Locke's father on his own account. They appear to be intended for someone other than Locke.

What have you chid your self out of breath and are you grown speechless indeed Or is it a quality in Choler after it hath suffic⟨iently⟩[a] vented it self on freinds to bury them in oblivion and disrespect also. I have known som who puft with that passion after som[b] furious breathings have husht themselves into a quiet and well composed calm and have been soe far (after a short heat) from iterateing and irritating the supposed Causes of disquiet that they became the readiest servants in all freindly offices. If you are dumb thats noe place for you to abide in and if you are dead why doe you not write mee when and where you died and what offices of freindship I must bee honourd withall as to your self or others but if you are alive Why soe sullen why soe silent What not a lettre not a word in six long weary wett windy weeks Wher's the fault? sure I think now I think ont 'tis in my selfe that have not woorth enough in mee to deserve such a favour. Well Ile bee content with these neglects and endeavour for the future to bee more deserving. Heers noe newes but good I wish the like from you about sennight since Aquinas[1] was with mee and told mee of you meeting in London. Old Volpone lies still and hath exchangd his Choplen for a pittifull Chiplen I have not seen him since I saw you tis thought the Choplen wilbee an University Proctor.[2] The canvas for Parliament[c] men there hath inraged the Heads of howses

[a] *Interlined; MS.* suffic, *perhaps with mark to indicate abbreviation.* [b] *Followed by* ventilation *underlined, perhaps as an alternative.* [c] *MS.* Parlt

[1] No. *56* is to be carried by 'Dr. Aquinas'. Perhaps the Revd. Thomas Grenfeild, who had incumbencies in both Somerset and London.

[2] I have found no other application of the name Volpone to anyone in Oxford in this period. Here it may indicate Dr. Thomas Barlow (p. 294, n. 1). He was Provost of Queen's College from 1658 to 1677; George Phillips of Queen's (Foster) was elected one of the two proctors about March of this year. Wood writes about Barlow's 'base false spirit', time-serving, and so on, abusively but with some justification: *L. and T.* i. 364–5.

against the masters and tis thought the Deane of Chr Ch: is gon to your Town to get amunition to chardg the Cannons against those furious Fellowes who dare thwart them in their suffrages.[1] I suppose twill bee best for them to beat away all the Students that they may receive and rule without controll but this by the By. Our Parliament men are coming. I heartily wish good success. I am sorry Major Long[2] is not elected. Had I bin chosen (pardon the supposall) I would have wayted on you insteed of this lettre which brings you my cordiall respects and this addiconall assureance that I am

Sir

yours[a]– sine fuco aut fraude–[a3]

S L[b]

24 Jan: 58

Start of address: To his

## *47*. John Strachey to Locke, 4 February 1659 (*38, 49*)

B.L., MS. Locke c. 18, ff. 189–90.

Domine

Amore meo tibi commendato, per hoc intelligas, quod benè valeam, et te quoque benè valere sperem.[4]

Sir Wanting a facing to your letter, I have presumed to clap on this thread bare one, yett soe disguised, that I am confident, it will passe for a new mode, especially since it weares an outlandish visage. But to leave figures, the short and the long is, I intended this paper as a Hue and Crie to pursue one Mr John Locke, who hath robd mee of all the good company I enjoyd in the Country,

a–a *Substituted for* your unfeigned freind and servant    b *Doubtful reading.*

1 Richard Cromwell's parliament met on 27 January. Owen was in London in February: ibid. i. 268. I have found nothing further about the present dispute. See further nos. 55, 59.

2 I have failed to identify him.

3 'Without pretence or deceit'. Perhaps made up from recollections of such phrases as 'sine fuco ac fallaciis' (Cicero, *Ad Atticum*, I. i).

4 'I send you my love, and you may understand from this that I am well and hope you are too.' Perhaps a variation of the common heading 'S.T.V.E.V.' or something similar.

and run away with it to Oxford. Pray Sir entreate the Vice-Chancellour to bestow him in Bocardo,[1] for the rogue hath quite undon mee, and when I appeare at his triall, I beleive hee wo'nt have the Impudence to pleade not guilty. But why doe I lye all this while, I protest the primary purpose was to provoke you to send mee a few lines, which will mightily refresh mee, I have given you the first blow, if you strike not againe, I will post you for the arrantest Coward as ever handled such a dangerous Instrument as a pen, but I hope you will not deale soe unkindly with him as not to afford him a love stroake who is

your humble servant
JO: STRACHY

Feb: 4th 58

Address: For Mr John Locke Master of Arts att his Chamber in Christ Church Colledg in Oxford these.

## 48. LOCKE to P E [Elinor Parry later Mrs. Hawkshaw?], [*c.* 16 February 1659?] (69)

B.L., MS. Locke c. 24, f. 208. Draft. Date: The letter appears to be addressed to a newly appointed valentine (p. 22, n. 2.) and probably belongs a day or two after St. Valentine's day. The likeliest years are 1657, 1658, 1659, and 1660: there is no known association with Black Hall before 1657 (p. 49, n. 2); 1661, when Locke was at Pensford during his father's last illness, is most unlikely; later years seem too late. Locke had a valentine in 1659, someone other than Anne Evelegh (pp. 130, 131). If the dates here proposed for the letters to P. E., nos. 69–89 *passim*, are acceptable, she is presumably the valentine; hence the year for this letter. Locke's known connection with Black Hall was strongest in 1659.

The identification of P. E. depends mainly on the connection between two groups of letters: the draft letters to P. E. and the group associated with Scribelia. The drafts for P. E., despite occasional variations from 'Madam' to 'Sir', are apparently all intended for one person. The Scribelia group, consisting of letters signed 'Elia', 'Berelisa', 'Scribelia', and 'Tho. Willson', and the unsigned 'Oxford Gazette', appear all to be written by the same hand; their style and contents are compatible with a single authorship. The two groups are linked by nos. *121* and 122; the latter, a draft for P. E., is clearly for an answer to no. *121*, which, although unsigned, is in Scribelia's hand (it in its turn apparently answers no. 120, another draft for P. E.). The identification of Scribelia depends on her association with John Parry (nos. *217*, 219–20, *225*). Additional evidence is supplied by the reversed initials P E and by the name ParryoCalistan in no. 87.

[1] The city prison in Oxford.

## 48. *Elinor Parry, 16 February 1659*

Edward Parry, bishop of Killaloe 1647–50, was father of John Parry, who was born in 1634 or earlier; Benjamin, baptized in 1635; a daughter, perhaps Mary, later Mrs. Flood alias Bulkeley, baptized in 1636; and at least two more sons and a daughter; the last is Elinor, who was born late in 1640 or later. John was educated at Trinity College, Dublin, and at Jesus College, Oxford, of which he was now a fellow. He became dean of Christ Church, Dublin, in 1666, and bishop of Ossory in 1672. He died in 1677; in his will he mentions his sisters Mary Flood, alias Bulkeley, and Elinor Hawkshaw. He was succeeded as bishop by his brother Benjamin, who died in 1678.

Elinor married Richard Hawkshaw of Dublin probably about 1670 and had several children by him. He died in 1687. She came to England as a refugee in 1689 and was buried in Dublin in 1690: *D.N.B.*, arts. Edward, John, and Benjamin Parry; P. Dwyer, *The Diocese of Killaloe*, 1878, pp. 252–62, 581; J. B. Leslie, *Ossory Clergy and Parishes*, 1933, pp. 19–21; *The Registers of . . . St. Michan, Dublin*, ed. H. F. Berry (Parish Register Soc. of Dublin, vols. iii and vii, 1907–9), p. 365, etc.; letters below.

To P E.

Had your choise alone bestowd on me what I now partly owe to chance I had wanted noething of perfect happinesse. however as it is my condition is too glorious to lett me be insensible of it and I will be content with the enjoyment of a blessing without examineing how I came by it. I have an overflow of happinesse and honour in being yours though a Lottery made me soe, and you have given noe small proofs of an excellent and obleigeing nature in accepting such a trifle from the hand of fortune. I cannot with moderation and without extasy consider where and by whome my name hath been worne and written; and methinks tis but reasonable I should pride my self in it, with lesse then this have the great actions of Heros beene rewarded, they were well satisfyd for all their toyls and dangers did but fame record their names and scatter them in the world, but tis you not Fame have writt mine and raisd me above the ambition of princes, who contended themselves with lesse then you have bestowd on me, since there is as much difference betweene what you and Fame doe as betweene Fame and Virtue. Nor is my obligacon to you the lesse because Fortune had an hand in it, only I learne from hence to esteeme you above her since your virtue hath given you a command over her, I[a] see you can make her smile on whome you list, that she can be kinde to me when ever you please to assist her, and that if she would obleige me by a choise favour which I ough to prize she

[a] *Preceded by* that *probably deleted.*

must make use of your hand to bestow it. In the condicon to which your goodnesse hath advancd me twould be a strange vanity to thinke of thanks such pore things must be reservd for meaner persons and meaner merits, noe you have robd me of the only virtue I flatterd my self to be owner of, and yet I must blesse you for it, you have undone and beggard my gratitude, should I endeavour any returns I should be but lavish of what is already yours. Fortune hath given me into your possession and disposd of me too much to my owne advantage and likeing for me to endeavour to recall her grant, what soever therfor this paper brings with it, will not looke like thanks to you but I must beseech you to accept but in homage to custome, which must be my apologie for this boldnesse, I hope you will not condemne me for being an exact observer of the fashon of my country and[a]– since your owne practise hath justifyd part of it and given it a repute,–[a] allow it with all its circumstances. I would not willingly by the neglect of any thing forfeit that title I have received from it with a great satisfaction, when I see you next twill be to beg the continuance of it to kisse those hands that will be but to ill rewarded for the honour they have donne me and to assure you

Marked on f. 208v: Electio.

## 49. John Strachey to Locke, 26 February 1659 (47, 50)

B.L., MS. Locke c. 18, ff. 191–2. On f. 192 is Locke's draft for his answer, no. 50.

Sir

I perceive you have with much nimblenesse skipt over my letter and twisted all into one line, I guesse by the last that if you prove soe exellent in enlarginge as you doe in summing up, though you can bee noe dispenser of seasons, yett you may make a notable dealer of the word. The Ocean you speake of was a Pensford quagmire where a certaine Levite[1] and I by the helpe of Don Quixotts brainepan imagining ourselves in good company stucke soe fast

a–a *Inserted in margin.*

[1] A cleric; perhaps Grenfeild; p. 73.

all night like Dun in the mire,[1] that Apollo was faine to bringe his coach and horses the next morning to draw us out. You say you travaild the Alpes in reading mine, yours Ile assure you placed mee upon the mountaines of Tenariff (I thinke those are the highest in the world)[2] sure I am I was lifted above the midle region with the meere bravery of the expression; had I beene the Composer of those lines, a young Master of Artes with all his formalities[3] on in this Lent vacation too had beene nothing to mee in conceite, nay I suppose I should have overlookt its very Deaneship of Christ Church, though it bee Cozen Germane to the mountaines. But to returne to our Author I know not how good a preacher you make, but methinkes you are but a bad Expositor, or else you would never vary from the literall sence of Hue and Cry, rogue and Bocardo. I thought I had spoake Inglish, but notwithstanding you dissemble the understandinge, when you talke of stripping yourselfe for the combat you would needes betray the sence you had of it, for that I conceive was in Charity to the Beadle, whome you were both to putt to too much trouble of making the back bare and then lashing of it. Goe you are whipt and soe I leave you

your humble servant

J STRACHEY

Febr 26th 58

If you had ballasted your letter with newes out of Aristotle, in good faith you had gravaild mee.

Address: For Mr John Locke att his Chamber in Christ Church Colledge in Oxford these.

## 50. LOCKE to JOHN STRACHEY, [*c.* 1 March 1659] (*49*, *55*)

B.L., MS. Locke c. 18, f. 192. Draft, written on blank page of no. *49*, which it answers. Hence its probable date.

Sir

Whatever agility you ascribe to me in skiping over your letter you have undoubtedly gott the credit of the better Jumper, and

[1] 'Dun is in the mire' was a proverbial expression: *Oxford Dict. English Proverbs*; no. 3573A.

[2] Until the eighteenth century or later the Peak was reputed to be the highest mountain in the world.

[3] Robes; here academic dress: *O.E.D.*

have as far outleapd me as from hence to the Canarys in[a–] downe right length besids some advantage in heith too.[–a] I must confesse you are the most exquisite valter I ever heard of but pray have a care of such dareing Levaltos.[1] the next frisk possibbly you may leape over the moone, and then what would become of you or how we should hold intelligence I cannot guesse ⟨since⟩[b] in all my readings I meet with noe account of any that went soe far all my story lys on this side should you miscarry twill not excuse you to your freinds nor to me who am like to goe a great share in the losse. to impute it to the impulse of my letter, certainly I send neither pouder nor engines there that should soe hoise you my lines are not strong enough to crane you up to that heigth, and all you will finde in them will be to low for you to take a rise for such a Jump. I am rather inclind to thinke that your charioteer Phœbus when he came to draw you out of the mire conveyd you thither, you tooke coach with him and he set you downe on Tenariff as the nearest lodging to his rode. or is it not possible that since your Ocean was *noething* but a pott of Ale, the Tenariff you talke of was noething but the tost erected[c] in it The spirit of Don Quixot that[d–] could turne windemills into giants and who then wrought wonders with you,[–d] might possibly be the author too of this Metamorphosis and soe by your being above the middle region I thinke you meane[e] noe thing but fudling in a cockloft. possibly your freind Sanco[2] who was with you in the adventure. and if you will keepe to the story must always be dull enough to call things by their common names will incline to my interpretation. but here I feare I shall be accusd againe for not understanding english. I must confesse hugh and cry and rogue are plaine enough however if you must be understood according to the litterall sense and you will needs be thought to have beene among the starrs which[f–] I thinke is something out of the way of your profession[3] and hath to doe with thing of the earth.[–f] I wonder how you mett in my letter with such spirits as could waft you thither, certainely the days of enchantments are long since ended and the way of travelling throug the

[a–a] *Interlined.* [b] *MS.* sine [c] *Interlined above* that stood [d–d] *Locke altered the arrangement of these two clauses; they should perhaps read* . . . giants who then . . . with you and might . . . [e] *Blotted; reading doubtful.* [f–f] *Interlined above* a strange place for men of your robe

---

[1] Lavoltas. The lavolta was a dance for two persons, consisting largely of high and active bounds: *O.E.D.*

[2] Probably the same man as on p. 82. [3] The law.

aire is quite forgotten, however could I like you send spells that dispose of us as they please, or as you doe scatter irrisistable charms I might hope to doe wonders, but Sir my pen is wingd for noe such flights, my thoughts trace noe such lofty steps as to lead you to those heights, and therefore must be excusd if not arrivd to that pitch. as to looke downe with contempt on the formalitys of a MA. we have other opinions of them here, we think they cary as much honour with them as a lawe gowne and a greate deale more honesty. and were you here wee should quickly make you feele that the autority that attends them is not contemptible and now sir I have past all but your whiping and that I am loth to come to. I[a] surfett.[a] I wonder what made you twist your lines into whip cord thus, with such a knot at the ende of it, which I must confesse I cannot untie, indeed your letter is like an epigram in prose, good all over with the sting in the taile, but what maks you talke of such lashess I cannot surmise unlesse the Levite you mention[1] hath made you his usher and soe it being your profession ⟨you⟩[b] are naturally inclind to talk of it or are you Tutor to the Titheing-man of Stowy?[2] and by reading lectures to him on penall statutes, by expouding the stocks and whiping post have gott an habit in this dialect? if soe you are to be excusd and I must beare it and truly I beleeve I shall never complaine severely of your lash. I will be content you should imploy your lines to what use you please upon me. I shall look upon them inly as strong ties of obligation to you and would I were whipt if I be not.

## *51.* William Uvedale to Locke, [mid-March 1659?] (52)

B.L., MS. Locke c. 22, f. 173. What appears to be the draft for Locke's answer, no. 52, was written in Lent, when the spring was advancing. Uvedale's succeeding letter, no 57, which contains an allusion to no. 52, was probably written early in June 1659. Easter Day, old style, fell in 1659 on

[a] *Interlined.* [b] *MS.* yo

[1] p. 70. An usher suggests a school or an assistant teacher.

[2] Stowey is about 3 miles south of Pensford, and close to Sutton Court. The manor was owned by Richard Jones (1605–92; no. *306*, etc.), father of Sir William Jones the lawyer (1631–82; *D.N.B.*) and other children. William Jones, a nephew of Sir William, married Strachey's daughter Elizabeth; and Sir William's sister Sarah married William Lyde of Stowey Court: F. A. Wood, *Chew Magna*, 1903, pp. 173–8. The Tithingman here is probably a petty constable: *O.E.D.*; p. 35; no. *952*.

3 April; hence no. *51* was written probably about the middle of March, and no. 52 near the end.

William Uvedale was born probably at Wickham or Bishop's Waltham, Hants. He matriculated from Queen's College, 10 November 1651; B.A. 1654; M.A. 1660; fellow of All Souls *c.* November 1659–64; later of Horton, Dorset; contributed poems to Oxford commemorative volumes, 1660, 1661 (Madan, nos. 2466 (121), 2543): *Surrey Archaeological Collections*, iii (1865), 123–4, (189); J. Hutchins, *Hist. . . . of Dorset*, 3rd ed., ed. W. Shipp and J. W. Hodson, 1861–70, iii. 143–9; Foster; C. T. Martin, ed. *Catalogue of the Archives . . . of All Souls' College*, 1877, p. 382.

Mr. Lock

Least you should Thinke I have as bad a memory as Mr. Tilly,[1] and can forgette my Friends assoone as He, I have sent This to assure you of the contrary, and withall to tell you that I can not but Thinke my selfe very unfortunate in being Thus long banished from Christ-church, I mean from you, for had not you a Chamber there, itt would be noe more to me then the english Colledge at Doway,[2] and I should have as little Affections for That as This. you may easily guesse by This how much I long to returne to a place which your society ha⟨s⟩[a] soe far endeared to me, and where I may againe enjoy your ingenious company (you know to whom I allude as Dr. Goodwin[3] said) which is very much prized by your humble servant

UVEDALE

I dare not fold up my Letter without enclosing in itt a very low salute to the three Ladies shall I say or Goddesses at B.H.:[4] and desiring you to convey itt to them

[a] *Page torn.*

---

[1] Probably Locke's friend Samuel Tilly of Wadham rather than Henry Tilly of Christ Church (p. 48, n. 3).

[2] Douai; the principal seminary for English Roman Catholic missionary priests.

[3] Thomas Goodwin, D.D., 1600–80, Independent divine; President of Magdalen 1650–60: *D.N.B.* I have not traced the story.

[4] Identifiable as Black Hall, now Queen Elizabeth House, in St. Giles's outside the North Gate of Oxford. It was now occupied by John Eveleigh, vicar of Knockmourne, etc., co. Cork, 1620–34; dean of Ross 1664–78. He had five daughters: W. Maziere Brady, *Clerical . . . Records of Cork, Cloyne and Ross*, 1863–4, ii. 308, 427; Wood, *L. and T.* i. 279 and n. The three ladies appear to be Anne Evelegh (no. 63), Elinor Parry (no. 48), and a sister of one or other of them.

## 52. Locke to U. W. [William Uvedale], [late March 1659?] (*51*, *57*)

B.L., MS. Locke c. 24, f. 280. Draft. The prefixed initials indicate that it was intended for Uvedale; the remark about Tilly links it with no. *51*; the country delights, with no. *57*. For the date see no. *51*.

U. W.

Sir

Whatever reason Mr Tillys silence hath given me to quarrell with him, I am yet perfectly reconcild to[a–] him as[–a] often as I consider that tis to him I owe the happinesse of your freindship,[b] and he well securd him self against my anger however provokd by his neglects when he bestowd on me in you an acquaintance more obleigeing and more mindefull of his freinds then himself. I never suspected that you would faile your promise though you had his example to authorise it and it shall be to that if ⟨you⟩[c] please that I will acknowledg the favour you have donne me without being guilty of soe much vanity as to think I could be an argument to draw your thoughts or your self towourds Oxford. Ch. Ch. much lesse my chamber holds not anything in't that may be an invitation to men taken up with better thoughts and better company and when I consider what violence you must needs doe your self in removeing your thoughts from your country delights to place them in soe forlorne a thing as I am in your absence I cannot but looke on your letter as a very great favour and an high act of a generous pitty, did you consider how your absence hath put me in a condition that stands in need of all manner of comforts you would be inclind to continue this bounty and would not be spareing of such restorative to one that languisheth till he sees you; all these faire days that make every thing flourish recovers not my droopeing. The noise of lent scarce wakens me from my melancorly and were it not that the company at B H and the mention and memory of you that I finde there doth sometimes revive me. I should be as miserable as doubtlesse you are happy. but how long these remedys will be able to support me against soe importunate a maladie I cannot provise[1] you are dispenser of my quiet and comfort. my spring and happy days of gaiety depend upon yours

[a–a] *MS.* to him / him as [b] *Alternatively* acquaintance [c] *MS.* your

[1] Foresee: *O.E.D.*, where the verb is said to be rare.

not the approaches of the . . . and I am doomd to sadnesse till I shall . . .[a] to your face that I am.

## 53. Locke to a lady, [spring 1659?]

B.L., MS. Locke c. 24, f. 9. Draft. It appears to belong to the springtime. There is nothing to indicate the person addressed or the year.

Madam[b]

After the bestowing on me this title where in I very much pride my self I fore see I shall make but a poor returne ⟨in⟩[c] presenting you with the mines of a plunderd garden and when all the Flowers both of Nature and Rhetorick gatherd into one bundle would be little enough to pay my thanks, tis with shame I finde my self reducd to the necessity of sending only the refuse of others ransacking. What these bare leaves may produce though[d–] I who am usd not to value things by there outsides and doe as much esteeme the plaine carelesnesse of a morning dresse as the curious diligence of an afternoone gaity have sent these trifles out of this confidence that this playne greene now in the spring may have a midsomer bravery yet I cannot promise[–d] since, if those hands which carried away their fellows were as skilfull to choose as forward to take I have reason to suspect these are none of the best. but should they proove soe contrary to my desires that when the sun and you have[e] ripened them into flower they should offer nothing fit to take your eye. or reward your care I wish they[f] may rather hide their heads in the earth and finde their graves there where every good thing flourishes then grow there to upbraid the poornesse of my thanks and cumber your garden with common trifles, yet if they will be perswaded to prove suitable to my wishes and the person they are sent to they will be faire and sweet and every way excellent. this is my comfort that what ever be the issue I shall be in noe other condition I have been a long time and tis noe new thing to me to receive obligations from you beyond the hopes of gratitude well the adventure is made and we must take the chance of the lottery and if when they come hereafter to display them blues and court your favour, they shew noething but a comely yellow or an unmixt read pray impute it to the change of

[a] *Page torn.* [b] *Altered from* Sir? [c] *MS.* ne? [d–d] *Added in margin; some doubtful readings; MS. has* esteeme the the plaine [e] *MS.* have have [f] *MS.* they they

soyle or unseasonablenesse of weather or the secreat influence or the Stars and be soe charitable[a] that your new planted kindred may grow and flourish as well as your garden as to lay the fault any where rather then on him that is

## 54. JOHN LOCKE, sen., to LOCKE, 21 May 1659 (43, 59)

B.L., MS. Locke c. 14, ff. 167–8. Perhaps written by an amanuensis. The inner pages contain pencil drafts by Locke for nos. 64 and 65. Answered by no. 59.

Yours by Tom Watts[1] I received and another of the 17 instant (which came to my hands this morning) wherunto and for your better satisfaction you may understand by this (and a former delivered by Fra: Gullock[2] to Mr Jo: Oliver[3] of Midsomer Norton for you) that my desires (on behalf of my freinds and neighbours of Norton) are lymitted to the civilities of Advice of them in what with conveniency you may and more particularly in asisting this Gent the bearer Mr Nathaniell TillAdam[4] in his and their desires of obteyning that Church for him. The little acquaintance I have with him and the reports which I have received from honest and juditious persons concerning him are to mee sufficient grownds for such desires. It seems to mee by your last that previous reports have possest you that som unsuitable Comaunds in this affaire should or would proceed from mee, but I was soe far from the thoughts of what you suggest that I could not have ymagin'd any such thing unless by such a relation. The civilities you shall afford Mr TillAdam wilbee very acceptable to mee by whom or Mr Oliver I shall expect to rec⟨eive⟩[b] from you. Contynue your paper visits, and (if possible) alter your phrase, for these (although too much truths) are unpleasing, un-welcom. I praise God we are in good health, and in peace. Deliver or convey thinclosed. I am in a

[a] *Abbreviated; the expansion, which is doubtful, is based on a deleted variant of the present clause.* [b] *MS.* rec, *perhaps with mark to indicate abbreviation.*

---

[1] Mentioned on p. 41.

[2] A man of this name was later one of Locke's tenants at Pensford.

[3] Perhaps the person for whom no. 101 was intended. Midsomer Norton is 6 miles SE. of Pensford.

[4] Matriculated from St. John's 1650; scholar 1653; incumbent of Midsomer Norton 1662; of Compton Dando 1665–88; etc.: Foster; Weaver, *Somerset Incumbents*, pp. 144, 261, 287.

possibility of procureing a good peece of Cloth for you when I shall know the quantity you expect from mee.

I am yours

J L

Saterday 21 May 59.

Prepare to be heer after the Act[1] where a Widow young, childless, handsom, with 200l per Annum and 1000l in her purse may possibly occasion your stay heer, but more of this heerafter.

Address: To Mr John Locke att his Chamber in Ch: Ch: Oxon this.

## 55. John Strachey to Locke, 28 May 1659 (50, *98*, *103*)

B.L., MS. Locke c. 18, ff. 193–4.

Sir

The first part of your letter lookt soe bigg, that it surely had frighted mee into the Aldermans condition,[2] had not the ensuing lines given mee sufficient assurance you intended noe duell, for to speake trueth I should bee loth to encounter soe daring an enemy that sticks not to charge a whole roe of Cannons,[3] and who is soe powerfull as to adhærents, that there is noe heart but is absolutely gaind at the very first addresses. As to the crimes I stand Indicted of, I shall rather choose to throw myselfe at your feete for pardon then stand a tryall, having to deale with one whose Rhetoricke is able to charme the audience and make even kindnesses appeare injuries. Refuse not the present opportunity of exercisinge your goodnesse, for feare you never have the like occasion, for I resolve hereafter to hold soe strickt a Correspondence with you in matters of freindship, that you shall[a-] never bee able[-a] to pick a quarrell with my actions. Now seeing our piety doth consist rather in our penitence then innocence, I hold my selfe cleare of that guilt I lay

[a-a] *MS.* shall bee never / bee able

[1] The days for the Act this year were 9, 10, and 11 July. It appears to have been held despite the decision of Convocation mentioned in no. 59.

[2] Sir Thomas Atkin or Atkyn; London alderman 1638–61; M.P. 1640, etc.; Lord Mayor 1644–5; knighted by Cromwell 1657; an unpleasant mishap subjected him to much royalist ridicule: J. R. Woodhead, *The Rulers of London, 1660–1689*, 1965; below, p. 92.

[3] This alludes to the disputes in Christ Church: pp. 67, 84.

under, and I hope not bee esteemed a man of a seard conscience, if I can sometimes enjoy myselfe surrounded with briske wine and merry companions. Amonge all these changes and alterations wherein fortune never shewed soe much of her fickelness before,[1] meethinkes I keepe my footing, and nither find my selfe in a worse or better ⟨condition⟩,[a] I am one her Ladyshipp hath small thoughts off, and had I but thy company I would never complaine of her injustice. I am glad I find you a man for the good old cause, for then I hope you will freely part with your penny halfe penny commons to satisfie the poore and hungry stomacks of the famous asserters of the nations liberties.[2] Pray when you have an occasion to dispute next, let the question bee, ⟨An⟩[b] Cedant arma togæ.[3] It is verily beleived here, that the Lawyers and the Logitians Gownes will bee hunge upp by the Scots colours in Westminster Hall,[4] but if all the Lawyers themselves suffer the like fate, I conceive you will hardly find him amonge them, that subscribes ⟨hi⟩m-selfe[c]

your frind and servant
J: STRACHEY

May 28 59.

Address: For Mr John Locke att his Chamber in Christ Church Colledge in Oxford these.

## 56. —— to —— ('Sine fuco aut fraude', no. 2), [late May 1659?] (*46*)

B.L., MS. Locke c. 14, f. 165. The letter sent? By the same writer, and presumably addressed to the same person, as no. *46*. The allusion to law-reform

[a] *MS.* condion *altered to* condiotion [b] *MS.* A [c] *Page torn.*

[1] Richard Cromwell had been superseded; his submission to the new government was announced to parliament on 25 May.

[2] The Rump had reassembled on 7 May.

[3] 'Whether arms should yield to the gown.' From a verse quoted in Cicero, *De Officiis*, i. 77.

[4] The flags captured by the Parliamentary army at Preston, Dunbar, and Worcester, were hung up in the hall; they were removed at the Restoration: Gardiner, *Commonwealth and Protectorate*, ii. 1; John Stow, *A Survey of the Cities of London and Westminster*, ed. J. Strype, 1720, vi. 49. The courts of justice sat in the hall. Law reform and the reform of the universities were being discussed about this time: Godfrey Davies, *The Restoration of Charles II, 1658–60*, 1955, pp. 92–3; Madan, nos. 2424, 2430; Anthony Wood, *Hist. . . . of the University of Oxford*, ed. Gutch, 1792–6, ii. 695–6.

suggests a date near that of no. 55, and the statement about the fields agrees. Apparently written from London or Oxford to Pensford.

Sir

Haveing this faire opportunity by doctor Aquinas[1] blame mee not if I have assumed this boldness to greet you and to let you know if you know it not already that I have received none from you since your arrivall there. I shalbee very glad and am greedy to bee informd of your good health in these times of soe much sickness and of your peace quiet and welfare amidst such perturbations. Your Lettre from Bathe[a] I received and have given order accordingly which I beleeve wilbee readily observed. If you expect Newes you may please to understand that the heavens drop fatnes and the frequent showres make the meadowes smile and the Feilds to laugh and sing yet wee sinfull mortalls on whom and for whom these blessings are powred down remayn still ingratefull to God and injurious each to other. What the deportments and disposicons of people are there I cannot tell but Im too sure bad enough heere. They talkt heertofore of takeing away the long Robes[2] from som persons but now they speak of eradicacon. I have som hopes things wilbee amended bec⟨ause⟩[b] I heare that your good freind C J P[3] is com amongst you. Nothing els at present but the tender of my deerest affection resting in expectacon to heare from you

yours sine fuco aut fraude

S L[c]

The World is now with mee the Flesh visited mee this morning and the Divell is expected this day the World is busied in carrying of Muck the Flesh gratifying friends[d] with Fish and the Divell is compassing the Earth

## 57. William Uvedale to Locke, [early June 1659?] (52, *61*)

B.L., MS. Locke c. 22, f. 180. A strip has been torn off at the foot of the sheet; some words may be lost. Date from the notice relating to Black Hall; It might, however, refer to some other death affecting the household. Pre-

[a] *Doubtful reading.* [b] *MS.* bec, *perhaps with mark to indicate abbreviation.*
[c] *The same initials as in no. 46.* [d] *MS.* fds*?*

[1] See no. *46*. [2] Of the lawyers. [3] I have failed to identify him.

sumably written from Uvedale's home in Hampshire. The opening passage alludes to the 'country delights' of no. 52.

Mr. Lock.

I know not what delightes you meet with in the country, but I find none here ether to recompense or alleviate soe ⟨considerable⟩[a] a Losse as that of your company; All my pleasures here are confined to a River or a Hill, where the gentle murmurs of the one, and the larger prospect on the other, are the onely delightes nature Thought fit to provide here; which Though They are not soe ravishing, are yet more innocent Then Those that are in Courtes, or citys, And there is lesse danger of a Temptation in the musick of a country voice, or conversing with the pretty Innocence of a simple girl, Then in the staring upon a more beuteous and artificiall face, or frequenting onely masks, and Revells. When I am weary of These litle pleasures, I have noe other diversion but what my Booke or my Thoughts afford mee, and being almost sequestred from All the world, I cannot yet deny but that each of them yeild mee at least a phantasticall or imaginary cont⟨ent, i⟩f[b] not a reall one; and I had rather be soe alone then in some company; yet for All This I am not soe much in Love with solitude as that I would live like a Hermitt, and converse with none, but stocks, and stones, or men as dull as They; I am sensible enough of that Affliction the Absence of friendis inseparably brings along with itt, and soe shall endeavour to come out of itt as soone as I can; Wherein if I consult my owne Interest I feare to be Injurious to you, by bringing you one who is soe much a Lover of your company, that he is resolved to tire you out with his often visitts, and soe regaine that time he has lost fro⟨m the⟩[b] embraces of

your friend, and servant

W. U.

I know not how to present a complement to B.H. because I heare tis all in mourning.[1]

Address: For his respected friend Mr. John Lock att Christchurch.

[a] *MS.* condiderable [b] *Page torn.*

[1] The only son of a man identifiable as John Eveleigh, the future dean, died on 31 May 1659: Wood, *L. and T.* i. 279 and n.

## 58. LOCKE to a lady, 4 June 1659

B.L., MS. Locke c. 24, f. 12. Draft or copy. There is nothing to identify the person addressed.

Madam

Cleopatra[1] comes once more to attend you, and it is but fitt that the most lively and curious Shadow should wait on the most perfect and excellent Substance. This and your glasse give your eys the fittest imployment, since the one shews you the beautys of your face the other of your minde. This (Madam) and a great deale more to this purpose I could tell you without any appearance of a Complement. and undoubtedly love to truth and the infinite pleasure I finde in talkeing with you, had perswaded my pen to expatiate in soe just and pleaseing a discourse, had you not made me know that I am not to procure my satisfaction at the expence of your time or patience, both which I am too regardlesse of, whilst I take the liberty to tell you any thing but that I am

Madam

Your most faithfull and obedient servant

J L:

4° June 59.

## 59. LOCKE to JOHN LOCKE, sen., 22 June [1659] (*54*, 91)

B.L., MS. Locke c. 24, ff. 173–4. Year from contents. Answers no. *54*.

Sir

Yours by Sancho[2] with all its retinue came safely to my hand and brought me noe small satisfaction in the account it gave me of your health and quiet which is a blessing this tumbling world is very spareing of, though I cannot remember any days of my life

[1] *La Cléopâtre*, by G. de Costes de la Calprenède, was first published in twelve volumes in 1646–57. Locke possessed copies of the first four: L.L., no. 1650[c]. An English translation, by R. Loveday and others, entitled *Hymen's Præludia*, appeared in instalments in 1652–9; pts. vii–x are advertised in *Mercurius Politicus*, 17 Feb. 1659, p. 237 (repeated 3 March, p. 268); pts. xi and xii (the last part), in the issue for 5 May, p. 413. If nos. 58 and 62 are to the same lady, the present letter probably relates to pt. x of the translation, and whatever was issued with it. Locke probably knew little French before 1672: p. 370; in the dedication of his translations from Nicole, which date from 1676 or shortly afterwards, he says that he 'had but begun to learn French': *Discourses Translated from Nicole's Essays*, ed. T. Hancock, 1828, p. xxiii; W. von Leyden, ed., Locke, *Essays on the Law of Nature*, 1954, pp. 252–4.

[2] p. 72.

wherein I have injoyd more. and all these tossings have servd but to rock me into a pleasant slumber, whilst others dreame, (for our life is noething else) of noe thing but fire sword and ruine, but you may easily guesse what sort of hott headed men they are whose brains are troubld with such distempers. I hope I shall not be thought unsensible for this serenity which I thinke ought to be the endeavour of every one that remembers there is a god to rest on, and an other world to retire into. I have taught my hopes to overlooke my fears and suppresse those troublers, and as I doe not credit all the glorious promises and pretences of the one side. soe neither am I scared with those threats of danger and destruction which are soe perremptorily asserted by a sort of men which would perswade us that the cause of god suffers when ever they are disappointed of their ambitious and coviteous ends. I hope I am to be pardond on both sides if I[a] am not quick sighted enough to see either that glorious fabrick of liberty and happinesse, or those goblins of warre and bloud which either side would perswade us they behold over our heads ready to drop downe on us, that which I looke to is the hand that governs all things, that manages our Chaos and will bring out of it what will be best for us and what we ought to acquiesce in, I have long since learnd not to rely on men. These bubles however swolne and glittering, soft and inviteing are not yet fit to be[b] lean'd[b] on and who ever shall make them his support shall finde them noething but a little guilded aire, But I wander beyond my intention, which designd something that you did not know not what you are well acquainted with allready, and a comment on these times is as dangerous as to you uselesse, and therefor fitt for noething but the fire. If Norton men enquire after their businesse they may be informd that Mr Fowler[1] of CCC. interposd and undertooke to returne the answer. We have beene long since acquainted with the Railery of the Quakers and it would be strange if we alone of all the people in England should not be sported with, for I looke on such papers as noething but a sceane of mirth, if there were any such people and such usage here

[a] *Followed by* cannot *deleted.* [b] *MS.* belean'd

[1] Edward Fowler, 1632–1714; matriculated from Corpus Christi College 1650; B.A. 1653; M.A. 1656; D.D. 1681; bishop of Gloucester 1691: *D.N.B.* He does not appear to have been connected with Midsomer Norton (no. 54); the patron was generally the Dean and Chapter of Christ Church: Weaver, *Somerset Incumbents*, p. 144.

in some particulars it comes very short of their story and aggravations and if such people (who cannot in their carrage and raptures be thought any other then madd or jugglers) fall into the hands of young men that have not yet learned of them a personated sobriety what can be expected but some such usage, or what accusation will arise hence against the university from the extravigancys of youth, not authorizd nor countenanced by the governors or goverment of the place.[1] Yesterday the Students of Ch: Ch: accosted the Cannons with 3 sheets of proposalls very materiall and such as it is supposd had but an ill relish. and possibly this is the only time wherein upon a meeting the Students lookd cheerfull, the Cannons dejected, the one with guilt the other with confidence in their countenances, Their answer is expected in a fortnight, wherein twill be difficult either to grant or deny.[2]

There were 3 Convocations in order to the Act and after twice being confirmd it was a third time proposd. (an unusuall way of proceeding) and voted against.[3] Seldens books are at last confirmd to us, and will shortly dwell in the west end of the Library if those books that are in the library allready be sufferd to keepe their habitation.[4]

The Dash in your letter seems to point at something in reference to Stanton.[5] but I shall not pry any farther then you permitt me. but I should be glad to heare whether your resolution to remove thither is like to take effect. since the many conveniences I see in it prompt me to wish it.

22° June.

[1] The Quakers participated in the current attack on the universities, George Fox himself writing against them: p. 79, n. 4; Madan, no. 2424. They were treated roughly by the undergraduates on their coming to Oxford in 1654: p. 17, n. 1; Madan, nos. 2245, 2250. There may have been undergraduate attacks in the following years, but there is no specific evidence for it.

[2] See nos. 46 and 55. The canons are attacked in *Sundry Things from Severall Hands Concerning the University of Oxford*, which was circulating about 29 June (Madan, no. 2430). The writer proposes the abolition of the canons; the governors of Westminster School are to govern the college; several of the canons are attacked by name. It is not clear whether the proposals are serious or satirical (they include the teaching of Cartesian mathematics, natural and physical sciences, etc.); in either case they are evidence of discontents at this time but are unlikely to be the proposals mentioned in Locke's letter.

[3] See p. 78, n. 1.

[4] John Selden the jurist (*D.N.B.*) died in 1654. Some manuscripts and printed books apparently came to the Bodleian Library shortly afterwards; the remainder, apart from some losses, in September of this year. Since they were placed there the west end of the library has been known as Selden End: W. D. Macray, *Annals of the Bodleian Library*, 2nd ed., 1890, pp. 110–23; Wood, *L. and T.* i. 282; D. M. Barratt in *Bodleian Library Record*, iii (1951), 128–42, etc.

[5] Identifiable as Stanton Drew, 1½ miles west of Pensford.

I gave you an account in my last that I desird you not to trouble your self for the cloth. for which I must not be unmindfull to returne my thanks

Address: These For Mr John Locke at Pensford To be left at Mr Thomas Days in St Thomas street Bristoll

## *60.* WILLIAM (later Sir William) GODOLPHIN to LOCKE, 7 July 1659 (*25*, 66)

B.L., MS. Locke c. 10, ff. 17–18. Answered by no. 66.

Dear Sir

I receiv'd long ago both your letters with as much joy and Satisfaction, as I doe now with shame reflect on their date: And if at that time I blush'd to see my-selfe Commended by a Pen which seemes fashion'd to illustrate the Noblest Theames, how much more am I provok'd therunto by considering my Negligence in not sooner thanking you for the honour you have done mee. I hope you have a better opinion of mee then to beleive that I consent by my Silence to those high Expressions you give mee, which I never consider'd otherwise then as your modest way of instructing mee; the benefit wherof I shall bee better able to acknowledge, when I have in any measure attain'd the least of those qualityes you attribute to mee, which I can by no better title claime then that I have not Vanity enough to own them. In the mean time I give you leave to make such use of mee, as Sir Tho: More did of (what never was) his Utopia, which hee made the Subject of those Excellent formes of Government his brain had contriv'd, therby teaching the World not what really was, but what ought to bee. I shall bee as litle angry, as any of the Utopians, for being the Name of your Romance, and shall lend my-selfe at any time to so good purpose, as is the receiving your Precepts, and the Characters which you make of Virtue. But I am very sorry that I am not able to returne to you Conceptions of the same Nature, unlesse I would make some other Person the Subject therof, since to describe you is not so much the Worke of Invention as of Memory, and needs only to recollect what I have known and Observ'd concerning You. But such an Undertaking would render this not a Letter, but History, and I should therin doe like Sir Tho: Smith who being well acquainted with the Country hee lov'd, and preferring the Reality of its Policy before the Imaginations of Others, made an Exact description therof to Posterity, either out of Gratitude, or designe to give a Pattern to the rest of the World of an Exact Government.[1] Wheras you have chosen to imitate Mr Harrington, who having fancy'd a Modell borrow'd a Name to bee a title to his Conceptions.[2] But I beg your pardon for not remembring how you spend your time, while I detain you with a second side;[3] of which Errour I am so sencible, that I fear to tell you why I have delay'd thus long the rendring you an account of the businesse you desir'd of mee in your Brother's behalfe,[4] which I desire you would not think to bee for want of Industry therin, but through my inconstant resolutions of seeing You, which have so often deceiv'd mee, that I have (for fear of my-selfe) surrendred up the power of Commanding mee to my Cousin Trevanion,[5] whom I shall attend on Monday[6] towards Oxon: wher I hope yet doubt of finding You, and ther I shall supply the defects which great hast makes mee guilty of at present. I am

(Sir)

your most Affectionate freind to serve

WM GODOLPHIN

I crave your favour to present my humble service to Mr Ward[7] and Mr Carr whose Letter I have dismiss'd to Savile.[8]

Lond: July 7th —59

Address: To my honor'd Freind Mr John Locke at Christs-Church in Oxford Leave this in his absence with Mr Esay Ward of Ch: Ch:

[1] Sir Thomas Smith (1513–77; *D.N.B.*), *De Republica Anglorum. The Maner of Governement of England*, first published in 1583. The most recent edition was that of 1640; of a Latin translation (first published in 1610?), that of 1641.

[2] James Harrington (1611–77; *D.N.B.*), *The Common-wealth of Oceana*, 1656; new edition 1658. About this time Harrington's views were much discussed. Locke possessed a copy of the edition by John Toland, 1700: L.L., no. 1388.

[3] The second page of the letter.

[4] No. 3.

[5] Presumably Charles Trevanion, second son of Hugh Trevanion of Gerrans, Cornwall; matriculated from Christ Church 1 April 1656; barrister, Gray's Inn, 1663: Foster. I have failed to trace his kinship with Godolphin; there was a family connection: F. G. Marsh, *The Godolphins*, 1930, p. 7.

[6] 11 July.

[7] Isaiah Ward: no. *44*, etc.

[8] Apparently Henry Savile, 1642–87, diplomatist and brother of Sir George, the future first marquis of Halifax; although he did not matriculate he is said to have been a gentleman commoner of Christ Church: *D.N.B.*; Wood, *L. and T.* iii. 483.

## *61.* WILLIAM UVEDALE to LOCKE, [about July 1659?] (*57, 73*)

B.L., MS. Locke c. 22, f. 179. The letter appears to have been written at a time when Locke might have recently left, or might soon leave, Oxford; the likeliest times are soon after the Act and before Christmas. The mention of Black Hall (no. *51* n.) suggests 1659 as the year.

Mr. Lock

I know not how they have improved att Black-Hall those hints I lef there concerning your selfe, and mr. Towerson,[1] but I make noe question you have possessd them by this time with strange suspicions and jealousys of mee; and in requitall shall promise you onely to be even with you at my Returne, if your absence give me the same opportunity as mine doth at present to you; This is the onely revenge I intend, and therefore I give you free leave to say what you please, as being resolved to take the same Liberty my selfe; but least Mr. Towerson should beare noe part in the comedy I have suggested to them that he weares his Mistress[a] Picture on his left side next his heart; and when you meet next together at B.H: you may take some occasion to desire them to search him, and you will there really find something worth your discovery. I have not patience to write with this pen, and Inke any longer; when you see your charge let me desire you to doe your selfe and mee one curtesy that is to kisse her; As you proceed I pray doe the same to Scribelia, Solacia,[b] Tartania, Duckelia,[2] which I thinke will hardly be soe pleasing to you as the former; but I beleeve her lips are as soft as any of the others as having noe teeth to make them set out. Pray let me know soone[c] if you will be so curteous as to afford me a letter, how all the litle brood doth, about the house; and whether the poore cock that was like to be burned be in heath or not. but to be serious. Sir I have returned your coate with a great many thankes, and a very strick commad to Odes that he should not smell ether of Lobsters, or whitings. With that I hope he will be no more offensive to you at his Returne then he was when he parted from you; When I returne my selfe I shall

[a] *MS.* Mrs [b] *Or* Iolacia? [c] *Doubtful reading; altered from* fr—?

[1] Gabriel Towerson: no. *104*. He was a contemporary of Uvedale at Queen's. There is nothing to show when he became acquainted with Locke.

[2] Locke's charge may be a young girl; Scribelia is probably Elinor Parry (no. 48, etc.); Solacia and Tartania may be the other two ladies of Black Hall; Duckelia appears to be an infant or an old woman.

renew my thankes if your occasions call you not before that out of Oxford, which I wish they may not, as knowing how much your absence will take of from that delight I naturally have to a place where I hope to find you; If they doe, let me conjure you in Scribelias name to hasten your returne as soone as tis possible, both to her, and

your friend
W. UVEDALE.

## 62. LOCKE to a lady, [about July 1659?]

B.L., MS. Locke c. 24, f. 11. Draft or copy. Date: Cleopatra and Cæsario part in pt. x. of *Hymen's Præludia.* If this draft was intended for the same lady as no. 58, and if that relates to pt. x, the date depends on the time that she required to read pt. x and whatever accompanied it. A month should have sufficed for the whole of pts. vii–x for a reader who had an hour or two daily for reading.

Madam.

Cleopatra is safely returnd hither and commands me to thank you for the kind entertainment you gave her and to tell you that she hath this one injury more to charge on her Fortune that she is forcd to leave you. Cæsario is the only person she ever parted with with an equall regrett, and she cannot but reckon this a new misfortune to be taken from the company of a person that really possesses more excellent qualitys, then could be phansy'd in her. She hath learnt from you to hope some period of her troubles, and is perswaded by your example to beleive that virtue is not always miserable. She is glad she hath learnt to speake English, since it hath furnishd her with an oportunity of giveing you some diversion, and she is sufficiently rewarded for her travells over the whole world since it hath brought her to an acquaintance with the most accomplishd person in't. She bids me assure you that tis her Love only and not beauty or any other ornament where in she hath an advantage over you, t'was that that spread her fame and tooke her up an esteeme and welcome in all places where she came, and she whisperd me in the eare, that when ever you please to lay by your aversion to that, she hath not one excellence left that she dares dispute with you. 'twas this flame that stuck a glory and luster on ⟨al⟩l[a] her other perfections which made them dazle the eys of the

[a] *Page torn.*

whole world. She would have hasted to entertaine you with the remains of her adventurs, had she not beene allready ingagd But her sister Cassandra[1] (for you must know they had both one father) hasts to supply her roome. This is that I am to tell you from Cleopatra, which you cannot suspect of Flattery since it comes from one soe like your self and one of the most excellent persons that ever nature and virtue bestoud all their skill on to make a masterpeice. But from my self I am to tell you, That durst I oppose my judgment to Cleopatras I should assure you that I thinke it not at all derogateing from your merit and perfection that you have not a minde to ingage in that passion which cost her soe many sighes and soe many misfortunes and that you content your self with a Love more refind (and as it is cald Platonick) and seated above those stormes, a flame soe pure as raises noe mists to cloud its beautys. But Madam whilst I consider your happinesse not to forgett my owne that I hold of you, give me leave to tell you that Cleopatra and all her storys have not any thing soe pleaseing and admirable in them, as that little note accompanyd them hither. Tis you alone Madam practise those virtues which others only discourse of. Tis you alone are owner of a Gallantry which ingrosses all obligations, you will not only bestow your favours without merit but your thanks too and acknowledg your self a debtor where you are only a benefactor, for which I am to assure you that all the passion and Eloquence in this booke is not able to expresse to you[a]

## 63. LOCKE to [ANNE EVELEGH?], [mid-July 1659?] (65)

B.L., MS. Locke c. 24, f. 10. Draft or copy. Lower part of leaf torn away. Reverse blank. It appears to be intended for the same person as no. 65 and to precede it. There are identifiable but not completely legible pencil drafts for nos. 64 and 65 on the inner pages of no. 54; that for no. 65 appears to have been written later than no. 64. I assume that the pencil drafts were written within a few days of one another, and that, as no. 64 is dated 21 July 1659, they were written shortly before or about that day. No. 65 may then have been written a few days after it, and no. 63 on that day or a few days before.

[a] *The rest torn away.*

---

[1] La Calprenède's *Cassandre* was first published in 1642–5; an English translation, by Sir Charles Cotterell (*D.N.B.*), appeared in 1652 (five parts; in six parts 1661; another English translation, of part of the first book only, also appeared in 1652).

The absence of the letters 'P E' suggests that the drafts were intended for a young woman other than Elinor Parry. They agree in tone with the extant letters between Anne Evelegh and Locke, and a passage in no. 65 is echoed in no *71*; but there may have been other young women on a similar footing with him.

Anne Evelegh, the dean's second daughter (no. *51* n.), married Benjamin Cross of Chester. He matriculated at Cambridge 1657; B.A. 1661; precentor of Cloyne 1664–83; rector of Spettisbury, Dorset, 1680–4?: Venn; Brady, *Cork*, etc. ii. 308, 427; Dorset Natural Hist. and Archaeol. Soc., *Proc.* lxxxiii (1951), 162.

Madam

I send this letter as a spye to gaine intelligence where you are lodgd, and as a scout to discover how approaches may be made to you. I must confesse this is usually the methode of hostility and certainely if to disturbe the mirth of holydays, if to plunder me of my content and quiet, if to conquer and take captive, if to wound incureablely, and to fire that which is dearer to me then houses and lumber, and in truth to carry fire and sword, (you cannot have forgott those two edgd eys I have often told you of) to ones most inmost retirements be the actions of an enemy I may well looke on you as the greatest of mine. This now methinks lookes either like a challenge or a loveletter, but it cannot with reason be thought that I should send a challenge to one, to whome I owe an entire submission or a Loveletter to a Platonick. Though lett me tell you, those that write to you will finde it some difficulty to avoid that suspition and tis not easie to talke with you without letting fall some expressions of an extraordinary emotion. This (Madam) is not the least of those mischeefs you doe me in robing me of the use of my reason, which possibly would dictate other things, and were I my self when absent from you, I should neither quarrell nor court you after this fashon. You cannot expect I should swallow all these provocations without some disgust, which forces me to tell you, that the retreat you have made from hence shall not be able to secure you from my persecution, nor gard you from my revenge. But stay: this forward courage begins to faile me. I can noe longer endure to consider you as an enemy and though I had an hundred things more to say to you, yet I cannot forbeare any longer to tell you, that you must not beleeve any of these quarlesome words, nor any thing else, but what may assure you that I am most affectionately[a]

[a] *Rest of leaf torn away.*

## 64. Locke to Mrs. Sarah Edwards, 21 July 1659

B.L., MS. Locke c. 24, ff. 39–40. Fair copy, presumably intended for dispatch but not sent. For a pencil draft see no. 63 n. I cannot identify Mrs. Edwards or Captain Burges.

Mrs Edwards

I am sorry you had not the clouts I promisd you sooner since I heare you had lately soe much need of 'em. But who could guesse that you should be soe soone brought to bed with a youngster that should want diteing[1] and indanger your linin? but god give you joy on't tis a chopping boy god blesse it, and though its loosnesse may sometimes offend the sheets, and it be troubld with the usuall infirmity of children yet age and whiping may mend that, and tis not to be despaird but by that time it comes to be threescore it may grow cleanly espetially if it feed on dry meate, and beware of soluble[2] ale. Had I knowne the babe your bedfellow had wanted wipers at Stanton[3] I doubt not but my interest could have prevaild with Captain Burges for his saile cloth rather then he should have been destitute. What pitty 'twas that Jack Constable had not made use of his authority to prevent such mischeef, undoubtedly the cheif man of a whole hundred had power enough to restraine such miscarrages, and keepe in offenders from breakeing prison at such a time as that, were it not to be feard that the man of worship himself were guilty of the scape. Had such a thinge been donne at Westbury[4] assuredly the cleanly officers of that place had severly punishd such a loose companion and your quick sented husband would have smelt out the Transgressor, and the stocks and whiping post he soe much talkd on had beene his guerdon. But poore man his authority reachd not soe far as Stanton, and he that at Westbury usd to scourge the hinder parts of others had not there the command of his owne. The truth is being lately in the country I wonderd to finde him returnd to the necessity of clouts and swathbands, and could scarce beleeve that those infirmitys should hang on him at his full age with all his honours and offices about him which uses to

[1] Probably a variant of dighting, making ready, adorning, etc.; in Scottish and north English dialect it can also mean wiping clean or dry, apparently the sense in which Locke uses it here: *O.E.D.*; J. Wright, *The English Dialect Dictionary*, 1898–1905.

[2] In the obsolete sense, laxative: *O.E.D.*

[3] Probably Stanton Drew: no. 59.

[4] There are three places of the name within 20 miles of Pensford, the nearest Westbury-on-Trym, 3 miles NW. of Bristol. Westbury, Wilts., was a parliamentary borough, but it is not clear that 'your corporation' (p. 92) refers to it.

leave children before seven. They should have conceald it from me had it been possible but murder and — will out, besids it was too manifest in its ill consequences my Cosin Besse[1] and some of the family haveing been ill ever since he was there, whose distempers must needs be oweing to the infection and fowlenesse of the aire, which how it was occasiond I leave him to guesse. well! should any of them miscarry pray god he be not found guilty, I feare it would lye heavy on his conscience should the Jury acquitt him. If he scape 'twill be noe small advantage to your corporation, who when they choose Burgeses next need not be troubld to seeke far for a Parliament man, since they have at home a grave man of office and one of a free utterance, he will be very fitt to make a member of Parliament, but what member lett any one judg, I shall not name it. He and his brother alderman Atkins[2] will make sweet worke in the house when they come to hold forth before the assembly, and undoubtedly we shall have a fruitfull and flourishing land under their manureing. Pray tell Mr Constable 'twas noe ill grounded conjecture that I told him when I saw him last that he was in the way to preferment: I then smelt advancement in his breeches and his luck was sure to be good according to the proverb.[3] I should say something to excuse him were it to any purpose but ten sheets would not be sufficient to make him cleane. I wish his preferment prove noe hindrance to his trade since I feare one fulling mill will be little enough to keepe him cleane, wherin you will be faine constantly to scoure him and soe keep him fitt for conversation, Oburne earth[4] and fresh water well set on with the stocks may doe much. but I leave him to your discretion whose long practise in Nursery gives you more skill in those affairs only I wish the reformation of that loose liver and consequently the sweet and happy life of you both. which is the desire of

Your freind and servant

J LOCKE.

Oxford. 21° July 1659

Address: These for Mrs Sarah Edwards at Westbury.

[1] I have failed to identify her.

[2] No. 55 n.

[3] 'Shitten luck is good luck': *Oxford Dict. English Proverbs*.

[4] Apparently earth from Oborne near Sherborne, perhaps that locally called stone rush: Hutchins, *Dorset*, iv. 200.

## 65. LOCKE to [ANNE EVELEGH?], [late July 1659?] (63, *71*)

B.L., MS. Locke c. 24, f. 15. Draft. For a pencil draft, date, and person addressed, see no. 63 n. The passage about 'flowers of rhetorick' and 'raretys' is echoed in no. *71*.

Those undeservd Elogiums[1] you were pleasd soe carelesly to lavish away upon me have given me the confidence to write again, not that I shall ever have vanity enough to be perswaded by such commendations, though[a]– ⟨pronouncd⟩[b] by the fairest and most eloquent mouth in the world,–[a] but to redeeme you out of the only error you are guilty of, and since you have endeavourd to perswade me into a better opinion of my self then either Justice or you can allow, you will finde your ponishment in being ingagd to read what you have nicknamd good. I know I shall appeare strangely malicious in professing my self the persecutor of the most virtuous person of the age whose crime was only an excesse of goodnesse. But pray M[c] Consider, when I had but only one good quality, Modesty, should I be content to be robd of that by a force irresistable. and a pen that is able to doe all things without shewing some resentment of it. Can I take it well that you should endeavour the ruine of that virtue in another which is the darling you most of all cherish in your self and soe often favour to the prejudice of your other perfections. Noe M[c] if I doe seem mischeevous in these paper persecutions you must looke on me as provokd and you are noe longer to expect from one whome you have taught to be proud, that he should keepe him self within the limits of civility or any longer by a complaysant carrage study your quiet or satisfaction. These words are noe sooner out but I wish[d]– em in againe–[d] and consider twill be noe discretion to proclaime often wars with one that can look me dead and stands in need of noe other engine to ruine but her owne wishes. Noe M[c] althoug I know that you cannot but rank my letters amongst those importunate troubles you would be easd of, yet Il assure you that noe designe of reveng guided my pen, but my admiration of your extraordinary accomplishments. among the rest I might justly wonder at that Prodigality where with you Cast away those flowers of rhetorick upon me did I not consider that those raretys grow naturally and

a–a *Interlined*; world *is represented by a symbol* ○. b *MS.* pronound c *Substituted for* Sir d–d *Interlined above* recant, *which is not deleted.*

1 Elogies; here commendations: *O.E.D.*

flourish continually in you which barrener soules after much cultivation produce but faintly and at certaine seasons, you know undoubtedly that there is noe injoyment of life out of your company and therefor have usd the same charity to me they doe commonly to the dead, you have sprinkld flowers on one that hath not life enough to thanke you, you have dresd up a dull peice of clay in most choise ornaments. were my hand fitt for such an imployment and did I know where to furnish my self I would make a garland of such flowers to present to my conqueror and the fairest peice of nature should not finde herself[a] in my letter but in the most curious dresse of words but[b–] I have not art enough to polish my rude papers into such mirrors as may represent you to yourself[–b] and since I am to despair of that and that you may receive something from me that is not altogeather unhandsome. I doe[c] here inclosd present you with a coppy of verses generally approvd both for their subject and witt where in there is a testimony given to the excellency of your sex which to those arts that men bost of hath its owne peculiar ones super added, you can with your scisars and needls when you please paint and engrave and out doe the artists and which is more draw indelible pictures with your looks,[d] but these are but your sports but the guilt and outside of those richer endowments nature hath culd out to store up in you. but why should I recon up the riches of others who am so pore my self that I am forcd to make you my presents out of other mens treasurs, and have noe thing to pride my self in but that I am

## 66. LOCKE to G W [William (later Sir William) Godolphin], [*c.* August 1659?] (*60*, *176*)

B.L., MS. Locke c. 24, f. 49. Draft, evidently for an answer to no. *60*. As it is written from the country it is presumably later than no. 64.

G W

Sir

When I lately revisd[1] your letter which I carried into the country as a spell against Barbarisme and a fence against the incroachments

[a] *Altered from* himself [b–b] *Substituted for* but my rough papers [*substituted for* things] are not polishd enough to be a lookeing glasse to represent you to your self [c] *Substituted for* have [d] *Or* locks

[1] Looked at again: *O.E.D.*

of rusticity I wish'd for the Genius or letters of Balzac[1] without one of which it is impossible to returne an answer, certainely had I had his volume by me I had thence transcribd an answer since it is fitt that I should borrow or pilfer from anothers treasure then returne you my owne brasse for your gold.[2] and I may be permitted rather to be carelesse of my owne credit then[a]– to be insensible of your favour–[a] or not indeavour make some returne. as often as I reade your letter I examine my self what great things I have donne whether I ever yet releivd cittys and conquerd armys, whether I ever yet made the Turk tremble, and made some other place out sound Lepanto, for methinks tis requisite that I should have worne[b] laurells and rode at least 3 times in triumph all[c]– ⟨as⟩ preparations–[c] and gradations to your panagyricks, and I very much doubt if fortune should have raisd me to such a greatnesse whether yet your complements would not be to large for me. Sir these are the re-creations of your pen when ever you please to sport your self with your owne eloquence, and frame a world better peopld then that you dwele in, and since this age is not able to entertaine you with persons of equall worth you are faine to retire into your owne thoughts, and to fashon to your self fitt companions. and you[d] would[d] converse with things excellent it must be either your self or your owne workemanship. I cannot but be sensible of this great honour that you will take the pains to disguise me under one of these handsome ⟨shapes⟩,[e] and make choise of me to weare soe glorious a livery, and to mak me a fitt objet for your thoughts, this is like the sun to guild every thing you cast your eye on, and with your reflection to clothe dull earth with flowers and gayety. After this I cannot wonder to finde my self ranke with Harrington and More, I know you are able to fashon me into what shape you please, and as if you were Deucalion like to new people the world what would be but a shapeless ⟨lump⟩[f] in anothers hand prooves a compleat and accomplishd man when it parts from yours. but

[a–a] *Substituted for* then not to be sensible of the honour you have donne me
[b] *Followed by* an 100 *del.* [c–c] *Altered incorrectly from* all as degrees and preparations
[d] *Substituted for* to [e] *MS. has* Ideas shape, *both words deleted.* [f] *MS.* lup

[1] Jean-Louis Guez, sieur de Balzac, 1597–1654, miscellaneous writer: *D.B.F.* His letters were published as models of epistolary style, the first collection in 1624, and the others following it; the first English translation in 1634: Jean Robertson (Mrs. J. S. Bromley), *The Art of Letter-writing*, 1942, pp. 42–3; L.L., nos. 183–4, 186[b], 186[c]. Locke's complimentary letters were perhaps influenced by Balzac's.

[2] A reversal from the Greek: no. 473, etc.

you have not only compard me to them but taught me ⟨a way⟩[a] to exceed those Politick contrivers whose curious modells though they may impale[1] some part of the wide world yet leave the inhabitants wild still noe! I could easily frame a happier Uptopia then either only by makeing you the patterne of my citizens. Such a country would want noe more law then we are now governed by. But I feare it is not the way to make us a glorious[b] Oceana. I cannot hope that we shall[c] ever be able to trace your steps and therefor shall need some other rule to guide us besides every mans private[d] moralls. out of this confidence I am encouraged to repeate my request to you in behalf of my brother who is willing to become a votary to the law at a time when others forsake her, this tottering condition it now appears in doth not at all deterr me being confident that noethinge can be able to crush it but the ruins of the whole nation.

## 67. Locke to S T [Thomas Symes?], [August 1659?] (*34*)

B.L., MS. Locke c. 24, f. 266. Draft. On same sheet as f. 267, also a draft, here printed as no. 68. The two drafts appear to have been written about the same time. The date is tentative. Carr appears to have resided in London early in 1660, but may have returned to Oxford later. Locke and his father appear both to have been ill in the late summer of 1659; there is no evidence for earlier years or for 1660; Locke himself was apparently in good health in the first months of 1661. The compliment to Hoskins and that possibly to him in no. 68 are consistent with a period two or three weeks before his letter of 13 September 1659 (no. *76*); there would have to be some interval as that letter answers a letter of Locke's that would have to be later than the present compliments.

The initials S T suggest Thomas Symes.

S T

Sir

The testimonys I was able to give with what esteeme I receivd the honour of your amity have beene soe fewe and weake, and I have soe ill performd the dutys of freindship on my side that I cannot wonder you should admitt[e] an accusation against me

[a] *MS.* away [b] *Followed by* people *del.* [c] *Followed by* all *del.* [d] *Substituted for* particular [e] *Alternatively* alow

[1] In the obsolescent sense, fence in with stakes: *O.E.D.*

which possibly defects of my owne actions and my much want of meritt may seeme to evidence, and my weake indeavours have beene able to adde soe little strength to a freindship which I hold mearely of your bounty that I can easily beleeve the breath of a report may be able to shake ⟨it⟩[a] and though I have not beene able to spruce up my affection to you in that trim language and courtly fashon which others possibly can command yet I can satisfy my self of its reality. and that the readinesse of my inclination hath not beene wanting however my words or actions may have faild to second them. But Sir that you should thinke I could consent to throw away the happinesse of my life, or voluntarily to reject a blessing which I ought to have labourd for with the services of my whole live[b] deserves my wonder, possibly now your eys may begin to open upon my defects which may make you willing to retract[c] your misplact bounty,[d] and by withdrawing your freindship let me see that that relation is only for such whose worth and other advantages raise them nearer to an equality and soe teach[b] that affecction which I shall ever have for you more[b] humble addresse and a more becomeing ⟨distance⟩.[e] Sir I have carefully scand all my actions and certainely he was a stricter observer of them then my self that could finde any one soe criminall against my happinesse as report gives it if there should be any soe guilty as to be capable to be wrested towards a breach it stole from me without the consent of my knowledg or alowance of my will. and I dare confidently assure you that however ugly it may be represented to you others tongues licked into that shape which it was not borne in. yet should your letter speake your thoughts which I would rather flatter my self is but a more freindly admonition to quicken my diligence and awaken my duty, I should be really miserable since with[f]– the injoyment of your freindship I was not blest with discretion or good fortune to defend me from your suspition–[f] and since I suffer in your opinion this imputed guilt sets me at variance with my self and armes all my former injoyments against. This is all the satisfaction I have left that I know my accuser and though ignorant of my crime I shall yet doe pennance for it in my absence till I returne either to ⟨acquit⟩[g] my self of this chardg or be convicted of a crime which noe body shall more severely ponish on me

[a] *Struck out in MS.* [b] *Doubtful reading.* [c] *Alternatively* recall [d] *Alternatively* favours [e] *MS.* distane [f–f] *Alternatively* that goodnesse made me happy was not resolvd to continue me soe [g] *MS.* acquid?

Let[a] Mr Tilly[1] know I gladly receive his remembrances but I expected a letter and pray deliver my thanks to mr Car in the same language you would your owne and let mr Hoskins[2] see if you please the assureance I heare give in that I doe not more gladly receive the honour of his remembranc then I shall willingly imbrace all occasions to serve and thanke and serve him

## 68. Locke to W J [Isaiah Ward?], [August 1659?] (*44*)

B.L., MS. Locke c. 24, f. 267. Draft. For date see no. 67. The initials W J suggest Isaiah Ward.

W J

If my silence appeare criminall to you as I cannot expect you should erre soe much in favour of me as to think otherwise I hope you will pardon it to the distraction of my owne and my fathers sicknesse[3] at least I shall mollify your sentence by the ⟨assureance⟩[b] I here give you that ⟨ever⟩[c] since I came into the contry I have beene either not well or not at rest and I perceive that when I left you I left my health and quiet, I am sure much of my content but I shall ⟨forbeare⟩[d] to make my losses more sensibly by repeateing them yet did you consider your self, and these animals that in exchange I am often ⟨forced⟩[e] to converse with here you would thinke I stood in need of all your pitty whilst I stay and all your welcome at my returne. I am in the midst of a company of mortall that know noething but the price of corne and sheepe that can entertaine discourse of noething fatting of beast and dugging[f] of ground and never thanke god for any thing but a fruitfull yeare and fat[g] bacon.[g] besids these here are the quakers, the people of Goshen . . .,[h] with light in their breast and smoake in their mouth[4] and mak up the company a degree of clowns beyond these you cannot therefor but thinke how willing I am to returne to you and in that to the injoyment of learning civility etc. but I spare your modesty and content my self with the treasure without boasting of it. the expectation of my fathers health is all now that stays me. from

[a] *This postscript may belong with Locke's letter to W. J., rather than to this one.*
[b] *MS.* assureane [c] *MS.* evever? [d] *MS.* frbeare [e] *MS.* foced
[f] *Altered from* dungging [g] *Doubtful reading.* [h] *Illegible word.*

[1] pp. 28 n., 48 n. 3, etc. [2] p. 112 n.
[3] No. *71* implies that Locke was ailing in August.
[4] Alluding apparently to Moses and Aaron when they came from the land of Goshen, where the Israelites dwelt, to announce the plagues to Pharaoh.

bringing back to his attendance one of your servant and see and injoy againe my fellow collegiates of curtaine hall[1] C. W.[2] to whome I desire you to present my service and lett them know that the west of England holds not one that is more their servant then I. and now Sir if you will admitt my affection in our country dresse and downeright somerset know that I love you heartily and am

You[a] cannot doe me a greater favour then to continue in the memory and good opinion of Mr H[3] what my little acquaintance and lesse desert doth but ill assure and let him know that I never thinke of Oxford but him the best part of it and when my thoughts wander over other things they fix on him as the most ingageing object, but I doe not pretend to oblige him by this noe more then I should an hansome face by delighting my eyes with it

letters

## 69. Locke to P E [Elinor Parry, later Mrs. Hawkshaw?], [August 1659?] (48, 70)

B.L., MS. Locke c. 24, f. 217. Draft. Evidently written soon after Locke had left Oxford for the country; assignable to 1659 on account of the mention of Black Hall.

P E

Evils seldome come single. I'm sure my severe Fortune is always soe fruitfull in them as to produce twins. you must redresse me against her cruelty, you have a command over your vassall and can force to be kinder when you please. lett it suffice that I am at distance without being banishd and treated as an Outlaw with whome there is held noe commerce. to give this condicon any softer name then death were to flatter my self and grow fond of my misery. I am already gott into the land of forgetfullnesse and the grave cannot have a more perfect silence, methinks every house that lodges me is but a larger coffin that shuts me up from all correspondence with the liveing, and forbids all hopes of intelligence with those persons that made me[b–] sensible of my life.[–b] The best things

[a] *This postscript may belong with Locke's letter to S. T., rather than to this one; or may be independent of both.* [b–b] *These words are underlined, perhaps for deletion or for an intended alternative.*

[1] There was an Oxford bookseller Amos Curteyne, traceable from 1652 to 1683; John Curteyne, probably his brother, was an intruded fellow of Lincoln from 1650 to 1660: Wood, *L. and T.*; Madan, iii. 424, 426.

[2] Carr? and Thomas Westrowe? (p. 122 n.).

[3] Hoskins? (p. 98); or Hastings? (p. 48); or Nathaniel Hodges? (p. 260, n. 3).

I converse with are to me noe better then shades since those that had a reall and substantiall good in them have forsaken me. when I left Ox: I did not intend my journy soe far as the other world, I thought to have gonne noe farther then carriers and letters might come to me, but since you that ordaine our fates are pleasd to set me at a greater distance and suffer me to have noe longer converse with the liveing I will give you some account of the place I am in, and what is the condicon of the shades in the other world. at my entrance I found as great variety as in the other world for the shades have their old passions sticking to 'em and the same flames torment 'em here that scorch them above and the fire that ladies eys kindle is of such a nature that death hath not coldnesse enough to extinguish it, it pleasd me to see a truer[a] distribution of Justice for here the constant lovers ⟨are⟩[b] crownd with garlands and the fickle have their continuall fits of heat and cold. that which most supprisd me were a company of frozen hearts which some hasty lover such as inamourd[c] at first sight with suddain blasts that were soon kindled and as soone out endeavourd to thaw but al in vaine though they were blowne too with the continuall sighs of despairers. The most content and Joviall were the Platonicks from whome death hath tooke noething but the earth which they regarded not and they are but only disrobd[d][1] the more freely to enjoy one another. I enquird for elyzium but they told me I had left that at B H[2] and since our torment here is proportionate to that happinesse and those good things we left behinde I am concluded the most miserable since none of them were acquainted at B H but I. this sad estate am I destind to grone under till you please to redeeme me tis the priviledg of your vertue alone, the fame and authority where of is not limitted to one world but hath extended it self hither too and the shades that have bid adue to all other things of your world pay still a reverence to that. your letter alone will enlarge me and you may be obeyd in both worlds when you please. you will beleeve me when I tell you that I am weary of this melancholy condicon, I cannot get myself in love with shades and ⟨silence⟩,[e] I long to be againe a man of that world which I am sure hath not one that is

[a] *Doubtful reading; perhaps* freer [b] *MS.* and [c] *Doubtful reading.*
[d] *Or, less likely,* disribd [e] *MS.* sile; *end of line.*

---

[1] Apparently alluding to Plato, *Gorgias*, 523–4. [2] Black Hall.

## 70. Locke to P E [Elinor Parry, later Mrs. Hawkshaw?], [late August 1659?] (69, 72)

B.L., MS. Locke c. 24, f. 211. Draft. By its contents the successor to no. 69.

P E.

I finde with sorrow that tis a shorter journy from the other world hither then from hence to Oxford, the inhabitants of this world are clogd with dull earth which obeys not the nibler motion of their spirits, else m you had beene ere this a witnesse of my resurrection and I had not made use of these slow pacd messengers to convey my thanks, but I must patiently acquiese in the same condicon with my fellow Mortalls. and must be content as well as others to carry about a luggage of clay,[1] and whilst I (that is my soule) snaile like beare about my howse with me it will be unavoidable that my removvall should be snaile pacd too. tis well for you that it is soe for could my body remove with my thoughts I beleeve you would have reasone to complaine of my too frequent visits, and possibly some times at midnight you would finde other company at B H[2] besides sleep and pleasant dreams. I am sorry I cannot give you that account of the other world you desire I have naturally a bad memory and tis a great way to bring any remembrances, and you may easily guesse that that place is something to darke to take notes in besides the joy to be againe upon the same earth with you and to returne to soe pleaseing a conversation[3] hath quite effacd all those Ideas and the consideration where I am allows me not leisure to reflet where I have beene or how I was treated, yet you know if they placd me according to justice I ought to be ranck among the Platonicks. I beleeve had I power to recollect my self I might give you a more exact narrative, but my thoughts have an aversion to travell soe far as the other world soe long as they have better objects in this, and you cannot thinke it strange. that they should be unwilling to returne to sprits and leave the company of Angells such ⟨as⟩[a] are the inhabitants of that Elyzium I told you of. But if yet your curiosity be unsatisfied they are soe much at your comaund[b] that they shall take a journy thither once more to fetch

[a] *MS.* in [b] *Doubtful spelling.*

[1] The house of clay, deriving from Job 4: 19, was a commonplace in Locke's time; he alludes to it or to the cognate tabernacle (2 Corinthians 5: 1–4; 2 Peter 1: 13–14) in several letters.

[2] Black Hall.

[3] In the obsolete sense, society or intercourse: *O.E.D.*

you a description and map of the country. I finde by those excellent epithites you misplace upon me that you thinke I am improvd by this journy and that it is like travelling beyond sea from whence they returne more accomplishd. I[a–] am sorry it hath fard otherwise with me.[–a] those flames have not a jott refin'd me. I am the same rough thing still that I was when I left you and I feare I shall grow worse in a country famous for rusticks. which however it may endanger that small stock of civility I am owner of yet it shall never impair that esteeme I have for you nor alter my resolution of being.

## 71. Anne Evelegh to Locke, 30 August 1659 (65, *83*)

B.L., MS. Locke c. 8, ff. 77–8.

Worthy Sir

you are not able to immagine with what content and satisfaction I read over your Civell and most obliging letter: and to find my selfe not quite banished your thoughts: nay and to see I am mistress of the most accomplished Person in the universe: I know not what your thoughts are: but I can with a great deale of justice complaine that I am Robd of my servant. and your absence is a famine to me: therefore had I the Power of a mistress I would Command you back to oxford that I might have the pleasure of your sweet society and Pleasing Company: for permit me to tell you without flattery or a complement that my thoughts are wholy one you: and to see how avers fortune is to us all here: that on a sudden so much vertue as wee all injoyed in your presence was snatched from us in a moment: but why bewaile I my owne misfortune since it is to great a happinesse for me to injoy: you are pleased to tell me that it is a punishment to be absent because you cannot give your attendance: that word punishment ⟨might⟩[b] justly be attributed to me who hath a los in loosing the best of servants: nay I might say the best of men: for had I so much vanity as to beleive that I had a traine of servants which you fancy yet you may justly boast if there were any conquest in it that you have won the prise: therefore insteed of a check I could wish I had a

[a–a] *Substituted for* but pray Sir undeceive your self, *which is only partially deleted.*
[b] *MS.* migh

Romantick[1] Pen that might give you: your due in expresing your perfections in a more quicke and lively dresse: I am sorry to heare that you rid out of your way: and resent with greife that I should be the cause of it: for I will assure you it was my prayers that you might have a happie journy: but I beleive there is som mistery in it: in your saying the star of oxford[2] misled you: I could wish I knew that star that had so taken up your thoughts: for I am Confident it is som exquisite Person which liveth not with us mortalls below: I could wish my blunt pen could drop forth so much rarity and Rhetorick, which you would faine make me beleive I am capable of: no, no, Sir I am none of those wites which can speak and write high laungauge when thay please: no you are better acquainted with my dull soule: which hath nothing of ingenuity: but I have a high esteeme for you: which shall last eternally, but though you are no souldier yet you can doe more then an army of men for when you please you can conquer. I am sorry to heare of the indisposition of your body: I wish wee could prove good Phisitians that wee might send somthing that might be restorative: Good sir excuse these rude lines of mine but I have sent them to make you laugh: and to serve for a diversion in the country: thus with my fathers and mothers and sisters respects unto you who all honers you

I Remaine your Cordiall frind
ANNE EVELEGH

Blackhall the 30th of August 1659

Address: For my Esteemed frind mr: John Lock these.

## 72. LOCKE to P E [Elinor Parry, later Mrs. Hawkshaw?], [early September 1659?] (70, 74)

B.L., MS. Locke c. 24, f. 210. Draft. The 'two letters' mentioned in this letter are probably the 'two other Letters' of no. *73*; if so, Locke probably received them in the week ending Saturday 3 September. If no. *71* is one of the two the present draft, although it is not for an answer to it, must date from after Locke received it, probably very early in September.

P E.

Tis certaine that the Genious of the University flourishes and is more vigerous and sprightly now then ever and tis with injustice

[1] The word was coming into use by 1650: *Times Literary Supplement*, 1933, p. 909.
[2] This may be Anne herself: p. 49, n. 2.

that some complaine of the decay of learning there such confident censurers would be silencd had they but read those two letters I lately receivd from thence and would soone be of another minde when they did see that there be ladys in Oxford that write things now which the Doctors of former ages would have envid, such evidences as these would easily perswade the most obstinate that the Muses dwell still in Oxford and that B H holds at least two of them. and I should not at all nick name things if I cald your mount, Parnassus. Well my faire Urania.[1] must noething be wanting to your perfection and must rhetorick be added to all your other accomplishments, is it not enough that you have a minde above the ordinary rate of mortalls, that vertue stamps grandure on all your actions, that your eys cary authority in them and can looke us into subjection, But must every part have the priviledg to command and be ordaind for empire. who would not be proud to be guided by that hand which soe easily converts a pen into a scepter. tis you that justify the dareing fictions of the Poets which will now begin to appeare true history and the tale of Orpheus shall noe more be reckond amongst the fabulous. since your quill[2] strikes an harmony whose soveraignety doth greater wonders wherewith you absolutely command the wilde and savage part of man that pays[a] noe homage to Laws and reason. those unruly affections that rebell against all other commands readily obey yours we hope and feare are merry or sad just as you please to order us, and have noe other passions but those that you please to imploy. and tis you that can reach out comfort to on that is two days journy from his happinesse[3]

I wonder with what spell it is that you convert your inke into soe efficacious a balsame. that when I thought myself in a condition destind to misery beyond remedy and beyond comfort behold two or three drops have revivd me. Is it not strang that when my minde was over cast with sadnesse and all my joys darkend and dampd with melancholy day should breake to me but M[4] twas

[a] *MS.* paiys ?, *altered from* pains

[1] Urania, princess of Cappadocia, is a character in *Hymen's Præludia* (p. 82, n. 1), IV. iii. She discovers that Philadelph, whose father wishes him to marry her, is in love with another lady (Delia), and accepts the position. She is beautiful, eloquent, and sensible. The name would be a compliment.

[2] Here both the pen and the plectrum for a musical instrument: *O.E.D.*

[3] Also in no. 79. So 50 miles in nos. 12, 74, 80, 119.

[4] Madam.

from your standish, who could produce light and sune shine out[a–] of such a place[–a] but you, and that which in an other hand would be but blots and blacknesse in yours becomes rays and splendor. thus you and Nature are able to raise the brightnesse and beautys of the morning out of night[b] obscurity. I could loose my self in these thoughts and look my self blinde in this dazleing radiancy. but there is something else that more affects me, is it not a strange priviledg and such as I ought to be satisfide with that the sun should shine on me alone when those that are round about me live in darkenesse, but you can doe more then this when you please to exercise your bounty.[c] tis time I admire the gallantry and composure of your expressions,[d] but tis that veine of goodnesse that runs throug it that I take my self to be concearnd in.

and tis this that makes me adore the Graces of your letter that they are kinde as well as handsome, and that you have made them smile upon me.

the ⟨brightnesse⟩[e] of the gould you send me I must confesse dazles and delights but tis the cordiall int that comforts me and[f–] you have been carefull not to separate'm.[–f] were it not for this mixture those glorious words and your shineing eloquence would noe more refresh me then the brightest sunbeams a sickly temper. after this all the gratitude I can putt into a letter will be but a poore returne and it would concearnment to bring ⟨my⟩[g] self to Oxford to thank you. but I am not at my commands.[h] I am under the disposure of a power which I must not dispute;[1] and I cannot tell when it will license me to come and tell you that I am

## 73. WILLIAM UVEDALE to LOCKE, [September 1659] (*61, 85*)

B.L., MS. Locke c. 22, f. 174. Datable from Newton's death.

Mr. Locke;

The newes of your leaving oxford which I met with att Black-Hall was soe litle agreable to my wishes, That I shall never be perfectly reconciled to the place untill Itt requite me with as great

[a–a] *Interlined; should perhaps follow* but you [b] *Interlined.* [c] *Doubtful reading.* [d] *Substituted for* letter [e] *Deleted in MS.* [f–f] *Interlined.* [g] *MS.* me [h] *Substituted for* owne disposeing

[1] Presumably Locke's father.

a happynesse as that I have now lost; soe That unlesse you intend I should be as great a stranger att Black-Hall as Mr. Tilly is, you must hasten your Returne, and soe take of That aversion I have att present to a place, where I first learnt my misfortune; were I lesse sensible of itt, I should need noe better Remembrancers then I meet with There, in whose memory you are soe constantly preserved, that I can reade their misfortunes, and mine in their Faces, and instead of complayning of itt, wee can onely sit still, and looking melancholy upon one Another sigh out in a pitifull Tone, Ah mr. Lock! By this you may see how absolutely necessary your Returne is for our Content, wherein noe body can be more concerned Then

Sir

Your very humble servant

W. U.

Sir I supposed you were soe taken up the last weeke with the Ingenuity of two other Letters,[1] that I could not but Thinke mine would come very impertinently, and therefore forbore to send itt untill now; and now mr. Newtons death[2] hath made itt short.

## 74. LOCKE to P E [Elinor Parry, later Mrs. Hawkshaw?], [mid-September 1659?] (72, 79)

B.L., MS. Locke c. 24, f. 219. Draft. The mentions of the verdure and of autumn suggest a date about the first half of the old-style September. The year is based on association with other drafts to P E.

P E

Sir

That you are a person altogether extraordinary I have beene a long time assurd and now I finde your power proportionate to it. there is noething receivd Sir soe undoubted a truth[a] which you are not able to confute, and the generall consent of both the learned and experiencd will be little able to secure our maximes[b3] when you appeare against them. soe that where you come you assume an

[a] *Substituted for* maxime [b] *Substituted for* opinions (*MS.* opiōns)

[1] See p. 103 n.

[2] Humphrey Newton, born *c.* 1614; B.C.L. 1641; fellow of All Souls 1636; died on 6 September: Foster; Wood, *L. and T.* i. 282.

[3] 'There are a sort of Propositions, which under the name of *Maxims* and *Axioms*, have passed for Principles of Science': Locke, *Essay*, IV. vii. 1.

empire over the whole soule and our ⟨opinions⟩[a] as well as the rest loose their freedome and cease to be at our owne ⟨disposure⟩.[b] Doe not thinke that all this is a groundless flattery, tis not my phancy which entertaines you with fine courtship, but my sad experience that tell you truth and doth but too sufficiently prove it. I wonder since I last left Oxford and you int that people should place pleasur and satisfaction in variety, and should be soe simple to beleeve that ones happinesse can lye in[c–] the renewd converse of absent[–c] freinds. I laugh at those their maximes and impute their mistakes to their ignorance of you. I could tell them of injoyments that grow not old and can never cloy with constancy, which disgrace variety, and need not the poore helps of change to adde a relish to them. Such are those that are to be found in your conversation, and you were made to conferre that unwearying happinesse in this which the poets with all their invention could bring noe nearer to us then the other world. he that hath once arivd at this condition cannot change but to his losse, he that hath once injoyd your company cannot enter into other's without prejudice and dislike this methinks should perswade you to allow him some roome in your thoughts whose content you have ruind every where else, and you are concearnd to preserve a sure freindship for him whome you have set at variance with all the world besides. I[d] cannot but be frighted at the imbraces of my acquaintance which looke methinks more like the violence of enemys then welcome of freinds, who thus make me their prisoner and keepe me from a place of greater happinesse their entertainments want their wonted relish and the country ceases to be a place of delight. tis true the feilds may present me with their various and flourishing verdure but with noe pleasure whilst I languish only the more sensibly to finde the common earth worth my envy. what is it the neere[1] that the Sun bestows his warmth and light as freely here as at Oxford. if in the meane time I want another influence that did use to quicken me more then this? and Autumne though he spread here the treasures of his plenty cannot move in me the least satisfaction. and the remembrance of those ravishing riches I have mett with in one little garden makes me slight all he loads

[a] *MS.* opions [b] *MS.* diposure [c–c] *Substituted for* in the welcome of country [d] *Here* This makes me *interlined.*

[1] Nearer to one's end or purpose: *O.E.D.*, s.v. Near, *adv.*[1], 5.

the earth with. I could enlarge on[a] these thoughts and my melancholy is great enough would I permitt it to be infectious at 50 miles distance, but my misery hath not yet made me malicious and I shall ever be cautious not to drive mirth and content from that place where alone I can hope to finde them they are confind to your company. I wish you may always uninterrupted injoy that large stock of happinesse you have in your self, but that[b] not with soe niggardly a closenesse as not sometimes to thinke on me and wish me a little. I know you your remembrances are not to be purchasd, but yet I have learnt from one that best knows you what things are fittest to suggest them. to have sent you common gold had beene barely to follow others examples and to doe noe more then everyone might. noe[c] Sir I have summond a[d] miracle[d] to assist me. and though perhaps the memento your brother[1] left may have more worth in it these have more wonder which being stampd silver have put on a new shape to appeare before you, observe what a country you neglected to see whose very waters have the virtue of the soe much ⟨sought⟩[e] philosophers stone, and let not Bath any longer be accounted amongst ordinary places whose springs are able to cure the palenesse of our bullion as well as our bodys and mak them both appeare in their most lovely complexions. were I in the Indies as god be thanked I am not soe far I could but send you the gold of that place and soe I doe of this.[2] doe not reject then the best things of a country not the most contemptible, but allow them some roome in your cabinet and have some regard for silver gold as well as for silken flowers and ⟨learne⟩[f] of me to value these as I doe them which I esteeme the higer because they were not of the suns makeing, wel if after all this you will thinkem but trifles I cannot help it, yet I dare say it is one of the statelyest fowerpenny presents that ever was made you this I am sure the mind wherewith they are presented ought to gaine their acceptance and you cannot be displeasd with a confidence soe suitable to a reall freindship which will not be tide always to the ceremonious rules and complement and courtship. and you will allow me this freedom with you since I am sincerly

[a] *Or* in [b] *MS.* y[t], *perhaps for* yet [c] *Followed by* mad *? del.* [d] *Perhaps deleted in MS.* [e] *MS.* sough [f] *MS.* learnen

[1] John or Benjamin Parry: p. 69 n.

[2] The process of colouring the money is described by J. Childrey, *Britannia Baconica*, 1661, p. 33. He adds that 'the colour is but pale and faint, and will quickly wear off'.

## 75. LOCKE to S H [Henry Stubbe], [mid-September? 1659]

B.L., MS. Locke c. 27, f. 12. Draft. Badly written and with many alterations. Printed, with omissions, by P. Abrams, ed., Locke, *Two Tracts on Government*, 1967, pp. 242–4. It is intended for Henry Stubbe or Stubbes (1632–76; *D.N.B.*), author and physician. Stubbe's father, Henry Stubbes, was minister about 1650–3 at Chew Magna, some 3 miles west of Pensford: A. G. Matthews, *Calamy Revised*, 1934; *Walker Revised*, 1948, p. 315. Stubbe went from Westminster School to Christ Church in 1649, and was now M.A. and a student of Christ Church. His book is *An Essay in Defence of the Good Old Cause; or a discourse concerning the rise and extent of the power of the civil magistrate in reference to spiritual affairs*, etc. (L.L., no. 2800[a]). It was published about September of this year: B.M., *Catalogue of the Pamphlets . . . Collected by George Thomason*, 1908, ii. 258; a deleted part of a note written by Locke, with the date 5 September 1659, suggests that he obtained the book early in the month: B.M., Add. MS. 28,273, f. 12; hence the date here assigned to the letter.

S H

Sir

The same messengar that carryd my letter the last weeke to Bristoll returnd with your booke which I have read with very much satisfaction and the only pauses I made in my hasty perusal were to reflect with admiration the strength and vigor of your stile checkerd embelishd seasond with many poinant passages of witt and sharp sallys, and that clearnesse of reason and plenty of matter wherewith every part is stuffd. had some sort of men had but the tithe of soe many arguments they should have beene musterd to one and thirtiethly beloved and their numerous though unarmd files should have beene marshalld with ostentation. this is the only deficient I complaine of. If I may be permitted to complaine after satisfaction, which I doe not that I thinke your weapon less sharpe if you doe not every where shew where the point lys or think you noe good champion because you hold it in that very posture and manage it with that regulated motion which a pedanticall fenser would prescribe you, But because that party you more particulary designe it against are soe blinded with prejudice and ⟨ignorance⟩[a] that they will not be able to discover them unlesse a figure or hand in the margent direct their purblind observation. you must tell them what is arg: ab impossibli what ab incongruo if you will have them take notice and they will never beleeve you have any forces unlesse you draw them up into batallions and shew them where

[a] *MS.* ignorane

they lye encampd, they are soe generall habituated to that play of primus secundus tertius the only thing one may confidently presume they brought[a] from[a] schoole that unlesse you deale with them in the same methode. they will not thinke them selves concearnd. they will not conceive it ⟨possible⟩[b] they should be mett with by a man that travells not in the same tract, and it will fare with you as it did with a Gentlewoman, who receiveing a⟨n⟩ addresse[c] from her servant cond out of the Schoole of Complements answerd what she thought pertinent which the overlearnd Inamorato findeing not to agree with his lesson nor to be the same he had gott without booke told her she answerd amisse and concluded her a very ill courtier because she was not able to maintaine the dialouge ⟨by⟩[d] rote.[1] to this I must adde that I am sorry that you continued not your history of toleration downe to these times, and given us an account of Holland France Poland[2] etc. since nearest examples have the greatest influence and we are most easily perswaded to tread in those fresh steps which time hath least defacd and men will travell in that road which is most beaten though Carriers only be their guides, when you have added the authority of dayly experience that men of different professions may quietly unite (antiquity the testimony)[e] under the same government and unanimously cary the same civill intrest and hand in hand march to the same end of peace and mutuall society though they take different way towards heaven[3] you will adde noe small strength to your cause and be very convinceing to those to whome

[a] *Alternative for* learned at [b] *MS.* possille [c] *Alternative for* complement [d] *MS.* be [e] *Interlined.*

[1] Locke probably follows John Davies (*D.N.B.*), the translator of Charles Sorel, *The Extravagant Shepherd*, 1653, etc.: 'I heard of a Country-Gentleman, that having bought the *Academy of Complements*, came to court his Mistress, where after he had pass'd his Complement, he wondered she did not answer him as it was in the Book. The next time he came to London he bought one for her, that so she might be able to continue the Dialogue with him': The Translator to the Reader, Second Book. There was a book *The Academy of Complements*, by John Gough, 1640 and later editions (no. *114* n.), from which Davies may have taken his title. *The Schoole of Complement* is the title of a play by James Shirley, 1631, etc.; it does not contain a relevant scene. In 1669 Locke and some of his friends were using fanciful names derived from *The Extravagant Shepherd*: p. 324, n. 1.

[2] Dr. W. von Leyden holds that 'the mentioning of Poland intimates Locke's early interest in Socinianism': ed. Locke, *Essays on the Law of Nature*, 1954, p.22 n. But there had been toleration in Poland for a time; the Protestants were now being persecuted; in May 1658 Cromwell authorized a collection to be made for the victims. There seems to be no other evidence for Locke's interest in Socinianism at this time.

[3] There are similar expressions in Locke's tract 'Question: Whether the Civil Magistrate': *Two Tracts on Government*, p. 161, and in no. 175.

what you have already said hath left noething to doubt but wither it be now practicable. But this I expect from the promise of a second edition, however you must be sure to reserve me one more of this, for I beleeve the importunity of many here will not lett me bring back this to Oxford.

The only scruple I have is how the liberty you grant the Papists[a] can consist with the security of the Nation (the end of goverment) since I cannot see how they can at the same time obey two different authoritys carrying on contrary intrest espetially where that which is destructive to ours ith backd with an opinion of infalibility and holinesse supposd by them to be immediatly derivd from god founded in the scripture and their owne equally sacred tradition, not limitted by any contract and therefor not accountable to any body, and you know how easy it is under pretence of spirituall jurisdiction to hooke[b] in all secular affairs since in a commonwealth wholy Christian[c] it is noe small difficulty to set limits to each and to define exactly where on be gins and the other ends. Besids I cannot apprehend, where they have soe neare a dependency, what security you can take[d] of their fidelity and obedience from all their oaths and protestation, when that other soverainty they pay homage to is acknowledgd by them to be owner of a power that can acquitt them of all perfidy and perjury, and that will ⟨be⟩[e] ready to pardon and court them to it with dispensations and rewards; and you will have but small reason to repose trust in one who when ever it shall be his interest (which it will always be) shall by deceiveing you not only obteine the name of Inocent but meritorious, who by throwing of his obligations (whereof he will always keep the key himself) shall not only possesse himself of your portion of earth but purchasse aditionall a title to heaven and be Canonized saint at the charge of your life and liberty. and seeing you your self (if I remember aright) make the apprehensions of intrest[f] and the justice of the cause the rule and measure of, constancy to, activity for and obedience under any goverment you can never hope that they should cordially concur with you to any establishment whose consciens. and concearments both for this world and the other shall always biasse them another way. these are those tares started up in my thoughts amongst

[a] *Followed by* (which I consent with you ought to be denid them only in reference to the state) *deleted.* [b] *Doubtful reading.* [c] *MS.* X[an] [d] *Alternative for* have [e] *Word omitted by Locke.* [f] *Altered from* intast?

those better seeds you have sowne there, and possibly are only oweing to the temper of the soile and must grow or wither as you please to order them. Thus you see how I make use of the liberty you allow me out of a beleef that you have as much ingenuity as learning, and tis in this confidence that I appeare perhaps in the head of your assailants but not with the thoughts of a duelist but doubter being resolvd not to be an opponent but

your
Admirer

## *76.* JOHN HOSKINS to [LOCKE?], 13 September 1659 (77)

B.L., MS. Locke c. 11, f. 229. Answered by no. 77. The writer is probably the man of this name who matriculated from Christ Church on 1 April 1656, and who contributed a poem (no. 77) to *Britannia Rediviva*, 1660 (Madan, no. 2466): Foster. This man may have been the future adherent of Shaftesbury: p. 436, n. 9.

There was probably a second John Hoskins at Christ Church during Locke's early time there: Sir John Hoskins, 1634–1705; matriculated from Christ Church 9 December 1650; barrister, Middle Temple, 1653; knighted 1676; second baronet 1680: *D.N.B.* He had no enduring connection with Christ Church.

Oxford Ch: Ch: Sep: 13 1659

Sir,

I finde your Letter addes a Crime to my unhappinesse that by its infection makes it so, for my destiny has spoke me dull, but that neclectfull, the one I may call the poornesse of my understanding, the other the pride of my will: things so inconsistent, that though they create, yet when made, destroy each other, as some unnaturall Creatuers that devouer their young, soone as they are borne: but were my Guilt as greate as is your charge, my sorrow would make me as uncapable to write, as does my nature, and so you would increase the ponishment of heaven, and make me miserable above Invention, sence, or degree; for your anger appeares noe lesse terrible to my thoughts. but if not writing be in mee a crime, 'twas you caus'd it, when you promised to beginne; but bate me Ethikes, and twas but necessarie I should have your Letter, as the Standard whereby to measure, and proportion mine, that though the features, order, and conjunction of the words cannot be so exact, and happy, yet I hope its equall intent (as good dispositions in misshapen and distorted Creatures the mistakes of nature) will excuse its other imperfections. if this can perswade, that you ought not, I cann⟨ot⟩[a] say to Christen, but let it be for once to Pagan my silence by the name of neclect, successe waites upon my designe, and I will end, least I should tempt her inconstancie. I had answer'd your Letter last Tuesday, but the Sun that day had rid halfe his Journie before I had seene it: I finde there many Complements that should be rebounded, but I thinke 'tis better not to answer 'em at'all, then doe it scurviely, therefore I shall disband those greate, common, and tread-beare words that incroach one truth, and render her suspected, and only write my selfe

your reall freind and servant
JO: HOSKINS

Mr Godolphin has not beene here since you went nor is there any newes but what I knowe has alreadie reached your eare

## 77. LOCKE to J H [John Hoskins?], [late September 1659?] (*76*, *528*)

B.L., MS. Locke c. 24, f. 53. Draft. Apparently for an answer to no. *76*.

J H.

Sir

I always suspected my best endeavours clogd with imperfections enough to render me criminall to my freinds, yet I never till now thought that my faults were contagious, or at least that they carried soe unruly an infection as to seize on the best and most sincere part of mankinde. Your letter gives me reason to withdraw from the society of men, and tis time I banish my self out of the world, since after haveing been able (as you say) to make you guilty, who knows what mischeef I may doe, and where will any one finde virtue enough to secure himself against me? yet let me be permitted to say thus much in my owne defence. If any words of mine accusd you they stole from my pen with out my consent and possibly relishd more of the clownery of the country then[b–] anger, though perhaps soe rustick an importunity might not be easily distinguishable from a downe right accusation. give me leave[–b] to

[a] *Page rubbed.* [b–b] *This passage might equally be read as* then anger. though perhaps . . . accusation, give me leave . . . *The word* anger *is substituted for* discontent of the writer would suit with soe delicate a pelat

assure you that I purposd not to throw our country dirt as far as oxford. my inke was never intended to bespott you. noe the Graces of all your actions have to cleare and genuine a beauty to need the assistance of such a foile and the splendor[a] of your vertue wants not the neighbourhood of a cloud to illustrate it. should I accuse you it could be with noe other designe then this, for I have not soe fond a conceit of my oratory as to endeavour to confute a generall opinion and ingage in a cause wherein I am sure to have a whole university against me. Seeing at the same time I shall cast guilt upon you I shall provoke all that are vertuous and all that know you against me, and noe doubt to write ⟨encomiums⟩[b] of a tertian ague (that which the ancients lookd on as one of the miracles and masterpeices of rhetorick)[1] would be an easier taske then to draw up a charge against you. But pray lett us lay by charges acusations crimes and all such unsavory words which are but ill ingredients of a letter at least if one of us must needs be guilty I will be careful to be he, but then you must be content to forgive me. but when you acquitt me pray doe not accuse your self of dulnesse poornesse of understanding want of fine words and neate composure and ignorance in complements and I know not what which noe body will ever discover in you if ⟨you⟩[c] can but keepe your owne councell. certainely if you will spare your self noe body else would make choise of you to write a satyre, against, yet if your genius inclines you to invectives you will always have a fitter subject for them as long as the world holds one man besides your self. all this dissembling will not hide your skill, and you declaime to handsomely against your feigned imperfections to be beleevd, tis pitty you should abuse good language soe and that such[d] treasure[d] should be soe ill imployd, that when there is only one thing in the world which you cannot ⟨persuade⟩[e] me to,[f] you should make choise of that, and are resolvd to torture me betweene the contrary force of your ⟨expressions⟩[g] and my owne knowledg. you see what a churlish[h–] aire I live[–h] in how untoward I am growne, since the losse of your company. I noe sooner [i] but I

[a] *Substituted for* clearnesse [b] *MS.* encomius [c] *Word omitted by Locke.* [d] *Substituted for* your excellent expressions [e] *MS.* persuaded [f] *Followed by* credit *del.* [g] *Deleted in MS.* [h–h] *MS.* churlish I aire I live [i] *Illegible word:* fo. ld, *followed by* accusations *deleted.*

[1] Apparently alluding to Aulus Gellius, *Noctes Atticæ*, xvii. 12. Among the ignoble subjects argued by Favorinus for the sake of practice was a tertian ague.

presently grow querulous and quarlesome (the usual temper of melancholy and discontented men), I reproove my comforter, finde fault with an obleiging letter for being to kinde and ⟨calling⟩[a] your self guilty for my sake and tire you before you come ⟨to the⟩[b] cheife designe of my letter which is to assure you that I am most affectionately

## 78. LOCKE to a lady, 19 September [1659?]

B.L., MS. Locke c. 24, f. 8. Draft or copy. Mr. Cranston regards this as intended for Anne Evelegh: *John Locke*, pp. 50–1. It seems to me not to fit with her preceding or succeeding letters (nos. *71*, *83*). If the draft no. 84 was intended for her the style of this draft implies a different personality. The absence of the initials E A is also against the conjecture. The draft is also unlike those for P E. It is perhaps intended for a third young woman, or even as an exercise in composition. The year is conjectural.

Madam

If the Opinion which tells us that every one hath his *Tutelar Angell* be true, I am confident that You are mine, Seeing that I finde that under the protection of your company, I am not only the happier, but the better too: And that those evills, which assault me in other places, dare not approach me, whilst I am neare you. Tis certaine, had I not mett you in the world, I had lost my journy into it, and my way in it; Since without you, all the rest would have beene but a Croud of Confusion, and servd only to trouble, or misleade me. But (Madam) though you are a *Great Spirit*, yet you daine to live at the rate of one of us ordinary mortalls, and suffer your self to be confind to the limits of place; the misery is, that walls and doors are able to shut us up from your conversation, and a horse and businesse carry us out of your Tuition, the sad effects whereof I have reason enough to complaine of: For I was noe sooner out of your Protection but *Melancholy* with a traine of *Sad thoughts* set upon me. *Unsociablenesse* made its self my companion. *Envie* began to seize me. and *Ill nature* to returne with soe much violence, that I am ready to accuse you of the stay I am like to make in the country. Pray tell me doth not this savour a little of *Distraction* and doe you not begin to thinke that in this little

[a] *Word supplied; MS.* accuseing *del.* [b] *Words supplied; MS.* to that which I de- *del.*

absence, I have made a great deale of haste to be naught, since I dare father my faults on you? and will you not conclude me most perversely malicious, that when you command my speedy returne to my happinesse I should yet dare to impute my delays to you, and make you guilty of my disobedience? But yet I must take leave to tell you, that you have some hand in it, and that if I continue here as I have begun, I shall unavoidably exceed the bounds were set me, not that I finde my businesse like to take up more time, but that you keepe my thoughts soe altogeather with you at[a] Oxford,[a] that my body is here to very little purpose, and a Statue would almost as well dispatch businesse as I, what course will you advise me to in this condition? I would not willingly to noe purpose linger away those howers here, which might be spent with the greatest advantage of pleasure and improvement in an other place. but yet I cannot command the attention of my minde to triviall concearments here, and force it from an happinesse which it only injoys when it contemplates you. for I protest my thoughts finde soe much pleasure in being with you, that it will not be easy for any, but one that hath a more absolute command over them then I, to take them off, and sett them to the drudgery of any other imployment. Doe you not pitty me to see how many evills the want of your company hath involvd me in? and are you not moovd to finde one that you had formerly some good thoughts for, growne on the suddaine. Envious, Melancholy, Sower, Sullen, Stupid and I know not what? But yet I despaire not, but I shall returne to my self againe when I returne to you and that these Goblins will cease to haunt me, when this long night shall be over and I injoy the day againe, for you know I doe not reckon the common way, there is some thing more glorious, and lasting then the sun, that makes my faire days; the brightnesse and beautys of a noble soule, that shine through all your actions, and who ever that brave minde will communicate its rays to, cannot be in the darke at any time. You will see how much I stand in need of that light by these wanderings of my pen, and I feare you will have reason to thinke that like one in darkenesse I have only dreamt you a letter; but if it be a dreame tis too true, too troublesome, and it will become your goodnesse to send me day in your next letter and wake me out of it. In the meane time pray remember that what ever you may thinke of these Resverys of a cloudy spirit, yet you

[a] *Locke has concealed these two words by writing* Fro London *over them.*

ought to beleive this as a reall, serious, and wakeing truth, that I am and always shall be till my long and last sleepe

Madam

Your most faithfull and affectionate freind

L

Pensford 19° Sept:[a]

f. 8v: The words 'for my' are written three times, and 'for' twice, possibly not by Locke.

## 79. Locke to P E [Elinor Parry, later Mrs. Hawkshaw?], [late September 1659?] (74, 80)

B.L., MS. Locke c. 24, ff. 212–13. Draft. The year from Black Hall; the time of year from the apples and the writer's 'a month's absence' from Oxford.

P E:

Sir

Since your vertue is Boundlesse must your empire be soe too and is it not enough that those to whome nature hath given eys and soules to see and admire you should doe you homage but would you captive too those insensible things that Nature intended for roveing, and imprison quills that were designd to be as unconfind as the aire they flye[b–] in, you[–b] might methinks without any disparagement to your power have sufferrd a poore fether or two of mine to be free. but if you are resolvd to exercise your rigor I know not how to help it this I know my pen hath not deservd to loose that liberty you desire to take from it unlesse you thinke none deserves to speake to you or of you but your owne, other wise I thinke you need not feare any weapon[c] in my hand, and I am confident it could run into noe dangerous errours whilst it was persueing your extraordinary qualitys and goodnesse (which indeed would give imployment to many more skilfull pens then mine) except it were in falling short of expressing their excellency and my resentments of and obligations to them. But Sir every body must not hope to write like you, and tis the priviledg alone of your pen never to erre though it should never stand still, and it deserves never to be confind but like the soule that directs it to be always in motion. what ever mistakes mine may have run into it never

[a] *This line is scribbled.* [b–b] *Or* flye in. you*; from* you *on the sentence is interlined or added in margin.* [c] *Or* wepon

adventurd on the boldnesse to describe you and it hath beene always wise enough to know that you are not to be drawn but by your self and it is as difficult to decipher as to imitate[a] you. Noe[b] Sir when you are resolvd to appeare to the world you must like the heavenly bodys dresse your self in your owne beames and with your owne light shew your self to our wonder: a mischeef on my pen, I thinke you are in the right indeed and it ought to be imprisond. I thought to have imployd it in returning thanks for the favour of your letter and those many obligeing things in't and it mindes noething but its owne concearnements and Apologies for its self. I would therefor it were a prisoner in your custody, that since you cannot be ignorant that my thoughts for you are such as you would desire and cannot disapprove, it might learne in your hands to speake them in a language suitable, and[c] I might not always be ashamd to finde those thoughts which I please my self in whilst they remaine in my immagination should appeare soe disadvantagiously to you upon paper, and that I might not still be troubld that I cannot finde words soe good and soe charming as the person they are sent to. But I finde Sir my wishes have not that successe which attend yours which are able to confer happinesse in the midst of sadnesse, and which have soe greate a power in the disposeing of my condition that I beleeve I can never be absolutely miserable soe long as you shall wish me happy. and that I can never be quite undunne till you and Fortune shall consult and agree togeather to ruine me. and yet I have soe greate a confidence of your goodnesse that were Fortune at my disposure I would trust you togeather, I would send her from my self (though she as you know be esteemd very good Company) to wait upon you, and I cannot but thinke how the quickest sighted person in the world and the blindest would agree togeather and whether twould not be judgd that she ought to be guided and directed by you. you were noe stranger to my thoughts when you concluded that Ox: held some persons who make me desirous to see it againe, but certainely the name you set downe was not the first that offerd its self to your thoughts, you willingly mistooke it and though he be a person whose conversation I very much esteeme, and for whome I have a very greate kindenesse, yet you might, (had you not preferd raylery to truth.) you might have found some body else,

[a] *Preceded by a false start.* [b] *Followed by* mad- *del.* [c] *Altered from or to* that

noe lesse attractive, and since there be those there that are able to draw me back you might have placd the end of the chaine in other hands. But seeing you tell me (what ever you know or thinke) that his company is the most pleasing to me in Ox to be quits with you for soe good news (which before I knew not.) I shall desire you to perswade him into a beleef of it, and as often as you see him make it your care to confirme and increase that freindship which you thinke soe deare to me. imploy that tongue in my behalf that uses to be denid noething and let it once for my sake doe wonders and I hope to finde the good effects of it in his next letter and I shall enquire of him whether you remember me when you meet. I would send you those good parts in me you should praise to him, but haveing this evening buried my vertues under a larger supper I cannot at present very well come at them. however you who can at such a distance espie a generosity in me that can make me willing, to forsake my native soile, to leave a Pleaseing walke (where I have the pleasure to read better letters then any I receive in Oxford (over which hangs a tree loaden with apples better then those were once smelt in my pocket at B H: and whereof I never eat one but I wish some body else another) and two or 3 bonny country girles that have not one jot of dissimulation in them, and take a journy of two days mearely for the sake of a new acquaintance, not at all considering my freinds of a longer standing, you I say that could discover such a generosity as this can noe doubt finde allso other good qualitys in me where on to ground your commendation. Certainely I should be very much ravishd if in some convenient place I could but over heare your discourses of me, and twould be no small pleasure to finde you make me a gallanter fellow then I am, and dresse me up in the lord knows what good qualitys the better to put me off. and twould be worth your pains to procure me assureance of his amity, since you know I have the gift quickly to be weary of it and am not soe stupid but can quit and slight an old freind upon the first offers of a new. But Sir to be serious with you am I indeed soe unfortunate as to have noe other freind left[a] in Oxford but Mr T[1] that should indeare

[a] *Interlined before, instead of after,* freind

[1] Tilly may have been, and Towerson was, a visitor at Black Hall; pp. 106, 87. If Mr. T. is the 'new acquaintance' of this letter, he is likely to be Towerson. Locke may have known Dr. David Thomas (p. 283 n.) and James Tyrrell (p. 495 n.) by this time, but neither has any known connection with Black Hall.

my returne to me? I'm sure then I know somebody is to be blamd. is it possible that a months absence should ruine a freindship that I thought everlasting, and that a kindenesse I was formerly acquainted with and was very confident of should of a suddaine be soe decaid ⟨as⟩[a] to have soe little left to put into a letter. What judgment I shall make of my condition I shall know by the next, for jesting I am sure will not always last, and you will not in a frolique make your self sport with tormenting me. I have a great deale more to say but I have beene to long already, but for the rest I shall refer you to your midnights revelation, where in you have a faculty to discover the truth of things at a distance and if you please to imploy it here you will find that I have those thoughts for you which words never yet did or could tell you and that I am more then

## 80. LOCKE to P E [Elinor Parry, later Mrs. Hawkshaw?], [mid-October 1659?] (79, 87)

B.L., MS. Locke c. 24, f. 218. Draft; many deletions; some reconstruction. The 'dissenting factions' could belong to any time between the fall of Richard Cromwell in May 1659 and Monck's establishment in power in February 1660; as Locke writes from Somerset the period is limited to July–December 1659, when he was in the country. I assume that the draft was written about the time of the expulsion of the Long Parliament on 13 October.

P E.

It is but fitt you receive an account of the commands you honourd me with and you will permitt me to tell you that tis as certaine that to the least circumstance of your injunction you are perfectly obeyd in ⟨Somerset⟩[b] as that you ought to be soe every where else. Let not your modesty blame me for giveing soe large a power this will appeare noe hyperbole to any that will allow ⟨virtue⟩[c] a title to empire, and possibly tis the only thing where in all the dissenting factions now in England would agree (viz) that you ought not only to be generall but ⟨Sovereign⟩.[d] Tis true I cannot promise that in this corrupted age every party should have that respect for Virtue that they ought, but this I can assure you that[e–] your authority dos extend its self above 50 miles,[–e] that there are some who take soe much pleasure in obeying you that they know noe place priviledgd from this subjection, and were they willing

[a] *MS.* a *altered from* and [b] *From deleted version of this sentence.* [c] *MS.* virtute [d] *MS.* Sov [e–e] *Interlined above following clause.*

to revolt twould be hard to finde any power in the world that could give protection against your mandamus. But why doe I talke of impossibilitys I shall never grow weary of happinesse, nor soe much oppose your right and my owne inclination as to decline submission. I rather complaine that your orders were of soe easy and short a dispatch, that you gave me not commands that should have beene my every days imployment then me thinks I should have had some reason of being absent and twould have satisfid me some thing for not seeing you that I was about your businesse. But now since I have finishd what you requird of me methinks I have noe more to doe here, all my actions displease me and I can give my self noe account of the spending those hours which might be better imployd at B.H in new lessons of virtue new acquest of knowledg and all those other advantages that are the[a] companions[a] ⟨of⟩ your conversation. all the wellcomes and caresses of my frinds cannot make me relish the country whilst I consider that I might be more happy in another place which would afford me the company of a person embelishd with all sorts of excellent quality and stord with more goodnesse then others can phansy. but pray consider whilst I talke and can only talke of these glorious things how sad an estate I must needs be in in the losse of them and whether all the kindnesse you can putt into a letter be not necessary to support me in a condicon that armes all my former injoyments against me and persecutes me with the remembrance of my past happnesse. This noe doubt will move a heart that is not hard and you will not deny a miserable man the only comfort that his banishment is capable of which is to be assurd that he is some times rememberd by you and that he is sometimes admitted into those thoughts that entertaine noething but noblenesse and excellency, and is still an inmate with virtue in that breast which is her cheifest habitation. I know tis noe meane courtesy I stand in need of yet such as the professions of frendship you have honourd me with will allow me to expect. I hope you will not take it ill that I dare not distrust you, and twill not appeare ⟨a rudenesse⟩[b] to receive those assureances you bestow upon me and repose confidence in them. I could presse your charity with many arguments which[c–] might render your grant as reasonable to you as for me it is

[a] *Substituted for* to be gaind by; *the word* of *supplied.* [b] *MS.* a rude *substituted for* rudenesse [c–c] *substituted for* and possibly extort some words from were I willing *deleted.*

necessary very cautious[-c] to sully the glory of such a favour by oweing it to any other cause then meerely your ⟨goodness⟩,[a] noe M tis to that alone I am willing to be indebted, and I woud not have my happinesse allaid with the mixture of any other considera-con, yet if I may be permitted to plead the high esteeme I shall always have for you if thoughts full of respect honour amity and what ever may be acceptable to you have any value, you shall not complaine of a totall losse of your favours, I mention this now not that I thinke you unacquainted with the temper of my heart, but because I here in give you the greatest assureances of sincerity can be imagind since I am in a country where art hath noe share in our words and actions, you can meet with noething here but what is the innocent product of Nature and you may as well suspect daizies and daffadils to be painted as artefice in anything that comes from hence. this is the only advantage I receive from this place, which I hope will be an Apologie for rudenesse of this letter, aier and genius of the place carrying an antipathy to all things that are elegant and courtly which suffers me not to use ornament and rhetorick but instead thereof reality and truth when I tell you

## 81. LOCKE to TOM [Thomas Westrowe?], 20 October 1659 (82)

B.L., MS. Locke c. 24, f. 182. Apparently the letter written for dispatch but not sent. Both Dr. von Leyden (p. 17, n. 3) and Mr. Cranston (pp. 43–4) suggest that it was intended for Locke's brother Thomas; the absence of family and local news, and the general style, make this improbable. I suggest Thomas Westrowe, with whom Locke was on Christian-name terms: no. *99*.

Westrowe matriculated from Christ Church on 18 March 1657, and was a student at the Inner Temple 1657, as of 'Merstham', Kent: Foster. Merstham is probably an error for Mersham (there is no Merstham in Kent); Thomas Westrow, d. 1625, alderman of London, and sheriff in 1625, had a daughter Dorothy, who married Sir Norton Knatchbull, bart., of Mersham Hatch (*D.N.B.*). Locke's friend is probably a grandson of the alderman. He contributed a poem (no. 59) to *Britannia Rediviva*, 1660 (Madan, no. 2466).

Deare Tom

Your errors as well as intentions obleige me, and I am content you should mistake my letters for Inditements soe long as it gives you occasion to confirme the innocence and integrity of your freindship, Twas your guilt that cast blacker upon my paper then

[-c *See note on previous page.*] [a] *MS.* goods?

my inke, this made you take every messenger for a Pursevant and suspect every call for a Hue and Cry. When I complaine you conceit I accuse you, and your imagination puts a trick upon you, I can not blame you for yeelding to that which is the great commander of the world and tis Phansye that rules us all under the title of reason, this is the great guide both of the wise and the fooleish, only the former have the good lucke to light upon opinions that are most plausible or most advantageous. Where is that Great Diana of the world Reason, every one thinkes he alone imbraces this Juno, whilst others graspe noething but clouds, we are all Quakers here and there is not a man but thinks he alone hath this light within and all besids stumble in the darke. Tis our passions that bruiteish part that dispose of our thoughts and actions, we are all Centaurs and tis the beast that carrys us, and every ones Recta ratio is but the traverses of his owne steps. When did ever any truth settle it self in any ones minde by the strength and authority of its owne evidence? Truths gaine admittance to our thoughts as the philosopher did to the Tyrant by their handsome dresse and pleaseing aspect,[1] they enter us by composition, and are entertaind as they suite with our affections, and as they demeane themselves towards our imperious passions, when an opinion hath wrought its self into our approbation and is gott under the protection of our likeing tis not all the assaults of argument, and the battery of dispute shall dislodge it? Men live upon trust and their knowledg is noething but opinion moulded up betweene custome and Interest, the two great Luminarys of the world, the only lights they walke by. Since therefor we are left to the uncertainty of two such fickle guids, lett the examples[a] of the bravest men direct our opinions and actions; if custome must guide us let us tread in those steps that lead to virtue and honour. Let us make it our Interest to honour our maker and be usefull to our fellows, and content with our selves. This, if it will not secure us from error, will keepe us from loseing our selves, if we walke not directly straite we shall not be alltogeather in a maze, and since tis not agreed where and what reason is, let us content our selves with the most beautifull and usefull opinions. The place I am in furnishes me with noe relations, and my affection must say something to you, though it tell you

[a] *Substituted for* actions and opinions

[1] I have failed to identify him.

but my owne Idle thoughts, Though there be noe harvest nor gleaneings abrode yet my freindship will needs make you a present if it be but of the weeds of my owne garden, had I flowers you should have them too, but those I expect in returne from your more fruitfull and better cultivated minde, where if there be any remains of reason left amongst men I may hope to finde it what ever I have said; bare opinion methinks will not serve my turne, for I shall always have reason to be, and you ought always to know that I am most affectionately

Sir Your cordiall freind

J L

Pensford 20° Oct 1659

## 82. Locke to ——, [Thomas Westrowe?] 8 November [1659?] (81, *99*)

B.L., MS. Locke c. 24, f. 14. Apparently the letter written for dispatch but not sent. The year from the contents. The salutation is exceptional; perhaps to the same person as no. 81.

Pensford 8° Nov:

Deare Freind

I did not guesse that you would finde a prophesye of these new stirs[1] in my last midnights meditations, that was the hower of their birth you might easily finde by the drowsinesse of them and did not this mad world too much justifye them they might well be accounted a melancholy dreame, and conceivd at that time when at least my reason was dormant, But this age is soe frantick that it will make good what ever can be said against it, and I cannot repent the troubleing you with any thoughts of mine which may help to make you slight that world which fosters scarce any reasonable creaturs. I would not have it thought that I arrogantly extoll my self by condemning all others. I am one of the mad men too of this great Bedlam England, and shall thinke my self happy enough if I can but order my fits and frenzys any way to the advantage of my freinds, if my extravagancys can be improvd to your caution or my talkeing idle your pastime, which is the best use you can make of the world its self which with all its frippery is scarce worth a

[1] General John Lambert (*D.N.B.*) expelled the Long Parliament on 13 October. General George Monck (the future duke of Albemarle; ibid.) in Scotland disapproved, and on 3 November Lambert set out from London with some forces.

serious thought. he that pays downe any part of his quiet or content for it hath a hard bargaine, I wonder what evill Genius possesse men now that they are enamourd of this maukin,[1] that they will venture their blood for mire and scramble soe much for dirt, I thinke a very small portion of it is requird to the composition of happinesse, tis a scurvy dull ingredient and at best doth rather clog then cure the stomach, they that feed on it often surfett are never ⟨satisfyd⟩.[a] I thought to have said some thing else to you but being upon this chapter of the world I could not easily leave it. and pray now how doth this phylosophie become a rustick? doe I not grow Stoick apace? me thinkes I finde my self hard and half Iron already and can turne a churlish insensible outside to the world, though my warme affections will still keepe my heart neald[2] soft and pliant to all your commands and ready to receive any impressions from you. tis this tendernesse makes me inquisitive after our affairs, and I cannot but be concearnd for that ship in which you as well as I venter all ⟨our⟩[b] fortunes with which we must either sinke or swim; a ship me thinks is noe improper name for this Iland for surely it hath noe foundation, it is not firme land but hath been floateing these many years and is now puting forth into a new storme ill victuald ill tackld and the passengers striveing for the helme. Oh for a Pilot that would steare the tossed ship of this state to the haven of happinesse! doe not laugh at this expression for I assure you I have learnt it out of the pulpit from whence I heare it every Sunday. you must not misse the next post, nor leave out any tittle of authentick news but tell me what's past present and to come, this you'l say is a hard taske, but tis for a freind, for whome you ought to doe more then every pamphleteer doth for a penny a sheet, here in you will favour not soe much my curiosity as my credit I being the prime Statesman of the place, and the Dictator of intelligence. You would laugh to see how attentive the grayheads be to my reports (of more credit and concearment then Cook's)[3] and how they blesse them selves at my relations, and goe home and tell wonders and prophesye of next years affairs. The

[a] *MS.* satisyd *or* satifyd [b] *MS.* your

[1] Malkin, slut: *O.E.D.*

[2] Tempered, softened, or toughened, by the action of heat; used of metals and glass: ibid.

[3] The *Reports* of Sir Edward Coke, the judge (*D.N.B.*). Publication began in 1600.

Royalists and . . .[a] with all their subdevided interest looke merry or . . .[a] please to imploy their passions and dispense intelli . . .[a]

Sir as I take it this is no meane condition which you ought to continue me in to the best of your power. I thought to have given you in exchange a story of a Quaker but you shall have it by the next for I have not roome enough now, and twould be as incommodiously lodgd here, as a fuddled fellow was lately who mistakeing his quarters and creeping in amongst a company of yoakd piggs, and being wrung with their yoak-sticks,[1] complaind to his bedfellows crying Edg (a proper terme of this country for lye farther)[2] Gentlemen what doe yee goe to bed with your swords on. I am whilst my owne

Yours J L

## *83.* ANNE EVELEGH to LOCKE, 8 November 1659 (*71*, 84)

B.L., MS. Locke c. 8, ff. 79–80. Probably answered by no. 84.

Most accomplished Sir

those generouse expressions and markes of your frindshipe which you have with so much zeale lavished away upon me: makes my dull genious at length produce this ill shaped letter: no Sir I should not thus long have hazared the loss of your good opinion by my silence: had I not feared that my last letter: hath given you new discoveries of my folly and weakenesse: for when I reflect on your genious: and one of so cleare a judgment and quick sighted which can acquiesse in the harts and soon find out there infirmityes: therfore I give you a more plainer way: that I durst adventur to write to one of so cleare intellects: but I have had suficient experience of your worth or else I shuld not thus have exposed my folly to the view of so compleat[3] a Person: no—no mr Lock it is not for want of true respect that I have for you that I have been speechlesse all this while: ⟨it⟩[b] is still beleiveing that you would not have let us bin mourning for your absence: and I was unwilling to expose those commands which I have to lay on you to the thinnes of a sheet paper: no you need not feare of any supplanting you for

[a] *Page torn.* [b] *MS.* is

[1] Yokes: *O.E.D.*
[2] More generally, make room: Wright, which quotes a Somerset example.
[3] In the obsolete sense, fully endowed, accomplished, etc.: *O.E.D.*

it is not possible to finde one in the universe of more merrit then your selfe, but I being conscious to my selfe of my owne unworthynesse: I may justly feare you are willing to be free from such a mistress: but stay Sir I will not part with my hapinesse at so cheape a rate: as to give you your fredome to loose you for ever: for could I once claime that title of being soveraigne my ambition weare at the highest pitch and my thought should be at rest and never thinke of aspiring no farther: I could wish I had that Power over you which you faine would make me beleive: I have I would then indevour to accomplish my desires: that is you should soone be at black hall againe: for I will say with the wise man that the desires accomplished is sweet to the soule:[1] therefore the conclusion is the want of your vertuous conversation is sorrow and bitternesse: for did you really know the resentment of my soule you would there find ingraven the Characters of true frindshipe and high esteem for you and to supply the defect of my unhapinesse, that wee cannot injoy your companie here: I am forced to veiw and reveiw your letter over againe: wherein I find such a grandure of goodnesse and such sweet obliging expressions: which puts me in an extasy: and makes me sigh and that[a] Somersetshire will outvie oxford in ingrosing so exquisite and so vertuous a soule all to themselves: but I cannot blame there prudence but rather aplaud and commend there ingenuity: for being ambitious of a person which can challeng from all the world: nay more, then it is able to bestow: but the heavens will doe justice to your merit: and do more then mortals are able to imagine: as for your happinesse weare it any to be in my thoughts: you need not then feare to be ruined for time nor abscence shall never make me forget the delights of your ingenious conversation: nor there is none more propitious stars which can challeng a greatter esteeme in my thoughts, then your selfe: therefore I beseech you doe not make an ill exposition on a hart which dayly wishes you both spirituall and temporall blesings: and I could wish that would come and make those tedious houres which paseth away with sad and melancholy actions become more pleasant: for those little cupids which you mention flie from me and returne to som beautifull objects which are able to read lectures of love with more ingenuity then I can: for I am not verst in that

[a] *First word of new page.*

[1] Proverbs 13: 19.

science therfore I cannot instruct others: I feare I have committed a crime which will not be veniall, in suffering the extravagancy of my pen to be so tedious: but I pray attribute it not to my weaknesse that with this long and sordid still: I have tired your patience: but make this conclusion: that I know not how to breake of discoursing[1] with you although at a distance yet it is pleasing to me, weare the paper capable of a blush it would then shew its bashfulnesse and slinke into a corner for ⟨shame⟩[a] that so pure a hand and so divine a tongue should peruse it and se the folly which it incloseth: I will sum up all with this incomium: that your returne is hartily desired by all heare and especially by her who is Sir

Your faithfull frind
ANNE EVELEGH

Blackhall the 8 of november 1659:

my father and mother remembers there respects unto you

Address (in a hand other than Anne Evelegh's): For Mr John Locke Junior at Pensford in Sommersetshire Leave these at Mr Thomas Day's house in St Thomas street in Bristow.

## 84. LOCKE to E A [Anne Evelegh?], [*c.* 19 November 1659?] (*83*, *86*)

B.L., MS. Locke c. 24, f. 38. Draft. The initials E A suggest that it was intended for Anne Evelegh; the words 'you disclaime your skill in love' apparently reflect her 'I am not verst in that science' in no. *83*; hence the proposed date. If it was intended for her she appears not to have received any letter based on it by 22 November, when she wrote no. *86*.

E A

That my returnes are not soe quick as yours is not oweing only to an impossibility of sending but to that extasy your excellent letters put me into from which a weeks time is but little enough to recover my self and reduce me to a condition of thinkeing and writeing soberly, your letters are not lik pamphlets to be slightly runne over. I am soe much a freind to my self to enjoy and remuniteate[2] on my good fortune, you send me wrapd up in one sheet

[a] *MS.* same.

[1] In the obsolete sense, conversing: *O.E.D.*
[2] Locke apparently began to write one word and changed to another.

delicates enoug to feast me a whole weeke and I have not leisure to returne thanks in the middle of the banquett. I must confesse did I not finde my name in your letter I should suspect you had misplacd the superscription. the complements in your letter are soe altogether unsuitable to me I professe you have made me soe fine that I scarce know my self and I can not guesse why you should be at the charge to trim me with soe many gaudy expressions, unlesse it be because you thinke it fitt that your servant should were a handsome livery. but yet I cannot thinke it manners to be spruser then my Mistress and I feare those ornamentes will sit but il-favordly on me which are properly yours belong to you however you disowne 'em, will you disrobe your self of all your worth and excellencys to cast them upon me, this is too much charity to high a courtship, I must confesse all is but little enough to cover my deformitys and render me fitt for your service. I but the meane while you are unjust to your self. can you not stroke me on the head and call me good boy unlesse at the same time you quarrell with your self? well if it be impossible that we should be both commendable togeather I feare it will never come to my turne, but I see you are resolvd to disowne whatever you are mistris of and miser like to professe poverty in the midst of riches. I am sorry to finde this humor soe much your favorite to the prejudice of your good qualitys that you indulge it too much. you disclaime your skill in love where in you have beene soe long practisd, this makes you tell me that you have not more and happier servants. I could deny too that I have other M[1] but I doubt whether we should beleeve one another. let us deale ingeniously and not with complements desguise truth which will assure you that if you had 1000 servants and I as many M there cannot be one that is more then I am

## *85.* William Uvedale to Locke, [*c.* 19 November 1659?] (*73*, *105*)

B.L., MS. Locke c. 22, ff. 177–8. Evidently the letter enclosed by Anne Evelegh in hers of 22 November 1659 (no. *86*).

Mr. Locke;

what ever usage wee found in other parts of Somersetshire, I am sure wee had noe reason to complaine of That att Pensford; there

[1] Mistresses. The 'more and happier servants' may reflect the 'little cupids' of no. *83*, the lovers who desert Anne for other women.

being so vast a difference betwixt them, That I can hardly perswade my selfe wee were in the same county; Indeed one such Person as you is able to civilize a whole nation, and they must be very much in Love with Rudeness who can't learne civiliti⟨e⟩[a] when they enjoy soe much Advantage over others as to have you for their Pattern. That I have not yet returned you Thankes for what I soe much admire, I can partly excuse by Those multitudes of little buisnesses I have met with ever since I left you, and you must exercise one part of your goodness more in the Forgiving of itt; For the easyer procuring whereof I have used a litle cuning, and prevailed (I hope) soe farr with your Valentine, and Mistresse[1] as to get them to intercede in my behalfe; as being confident what they say for me will be more powerfull with you, then any thing from your very affect. Friend

W. U.

Waltham in Hampshir⟨e⟩[a2]

Mr. Towerson, and my selfe have met with better success this yeare att All Soules then the last;[3] but I was very much troubled when Mr. Carr[4] told me there, that we must not exp. you untill after winter; If soe I wish it may be a short one.

Address: For his very much respected Friend mr. John Lock These.

## 86. ANNE EVELEGH to LOCKE, 22 November 1659 (84)

B.L., MS. Locke c. 8, ff. 81–2.

most excellent mr Lock

you are not able to imagin with what joy I take a pen to present those respects which my hart oweth you: and which you may justly challeng from me: the cause of my troubling you this time:

[a] *Page torn.*

---

[1] Locke's valentine cannot have been Anne Evelegh, who was Uvedale's: p. 131; and was perhaps Elinor Parry: p. 68 n. His mistress here is perhaps Anne Evelegh.

[2] Bishop's Waltham: p. 74 n.

[3] Towerson's father petitioned Richard Cromwell as Chancellor of the university for a fellowship at All Souls for his son: *Cal. S.P.*, *Dom.*, 1657–8, p. 86 (the date is given there as 'August? 1657').

[4] Carr was elected a fellow of All Souls in 1658: 'The Restoration visitation of Oxford' (p. 151, n. 4 *ad fin.*), p. 33.

is that I received a Letter out of hamsheire: from my valentine:[1] with the inclosed wherein he desireth me to helpe make his apoligie for his silence: I am confident his one Rhetorick hath more power and force over you then any I can use: yet I can say: this much of him that the troublesom buisinesse about alsoules kept him from writing to you but you weare perpetually in his thoughts: for mr udall is a more generous and vertuous soule then to forget his frinds: especially you who merits from all the world a faithfull frindshipe and true respect: I shall not trouble you with the particulars of mr. towerson and mr udall: for I presume you have hard alredy: onely this I must say that the heavens at last hath done justice to mr udals merit: for truly he is a most deserving gentleman: now let me com to my one interest: and say how long shall wee mourne for the absence of the compleatest man that ever the world brought forth: for truly I am so sensable that fortune should still froune on: us in depriveing us all this while of your sweet company: and permite me to tell you: that I envie Somersetshere: for being so covetous to ingrosse all the vertue to themseleves that they will not let the world be sharers to partake of there happinesse: and I have most reason to complaine: for I can have no service done me in your absence: therefore you se I complaine not without a cause: thus with a sad hart I resent my losse: and am still in hopes that fortoune will at last grow weary of persecuting me: and you will returne: to the comfort and satisfaction of all your frinds here at blackhall: for it is beyond termes to expresse the resentment of my soule: and I doe hartily pray for your happinesse: now I must beg you to excuse the excursion of my extravagant pen: and really beleive that I am Sir

Your faithfull and cordiall frind: ANNE EVELEGH

blackhall the 22 of november 1659

all here presents there service to you

Address: For my worthy frind mr John Lock junior. Leave this at mr thomas Dayes in st: thomas street: at bristoll to be sent to Pensford in Somersetsheire these

[1] Evidently William Uvedale.

## 87. LOCKE to P E [Elinor Parry, later Mrs. Hawkshaw?], [early December 1659?] (80, 89)

B.L., MS. Locke c. 24, f. 209. Draft. The date appears to be shortly before an intended return to Oxford; it might be at the close of some other visit to Pensford, either before 1659 or in November 1660.

P E.

When I observe the superscription on the outside and the contence in the inside of your letter I can scarce forbeare to begin thus The Invincible and Unconquerable Stratexanpoquozungus[a] to the high and mighty Generall[b] and Commander ParryoCalistan[c] defiance.[1] The summons that you gave to my Courage by your challenge hath rousd in me such a transcendent resolution that ere the cælestiall Wagoner hath twice 7 times driven his Flamivomous[2] Teame about the terrene globe I will in the Court of Astracan:—I should goe on in this straine but that I finde it not very easy to weild this mighty stile a whole page togeather, and I may be pardond if I cannot finde blustring words to quarrell with one whome I have not the heart to consider as an enemy, and I am cozend if this already hath not cald the bloud into your cheeks and made you ready to lay hold on your fan and draw your bodkin[3] as if you would presently have about at sword and buckler. But knowing what mischeif you are able to doe and how impossible it is to defend ones self against you. I thinke I were not best to put you into a fighting posture, and to be soe wise as to passe over what ever is of stomach and dareing in your letter and take[d] notice[d] only upon the kinde and the comfortable. ⟨give⟩[e] me leave therefor in a more gentle dialect to tell you how sensible I am of the ⟨assureance⟩[f]

[a] *Substituted for* Tangrolipix [b] *Followed by* of hearts *deleted.* [c] *Substituted for* Astrophell [d] *Substituted for* dwell [e] *MS.* gime? [f] *MS.* assureane

[1] Locke derived the name Tangrolipix probably from either Richard Knolles, *The Generall Historie of the Turkes*, first published in 1603, or George Sandys, *A Relation of a Journey*, first published in 1615 (Locke later owned a copy of the 7th ed., 1673: L.L., no. 2553); Sandys (p. 43) probably derived his account from Knolles. Tangrolipix is the Greeks' name for Toghrul Beg (d. 1063), the founder of the Seljuk dynasty. Both writers give Axan, which may have helped Locke to construct Stratexanpoquozungus; and Calizasthlan, which comes close to the later part of ParryoCalistan. Astrophel comes from Sir Philip Sidney, but by 1659 was probably common currency. Toghrul Beg is not connected with Astrakhan, and I have found no romance of which it is the scene.

[2] Flammivomous, 'vomiting or belching flames of fire': *O.E.D.*, quoting J. Bullokar, *An English Expositor*, editions of 1663–76.

[3] A long pin used by women to fasten up the hair: *O.E.D.*

you give me of your freindship and that I cannot but be very much satisfyd to finde that I have still a roome and residence in one of the best and noblest places in the world, is it not soe? could I finde words that were all soft and sweet you should perceive that I could write in a stile not always high and quarlesome and however you call me invincible and unconquerable I can not but yeeld to the[a] assaults[a] ⟨of⟩ kindenesse and stoope to the chains of such obligations. after this I can beare with the railery and chalenges of your letter, yet I wonder that you that can be soe obleigeingly perfectly good when you please as if you were made for noething else, should ever be otherwise, methinks a face that becomes smiles soe well should never put on frouns, tis strange you finde it such a difficulty not to be Crosse even when you tell me you will not. that you should delight to weaken your cordialls by allays surely when you consider how much more noble it is to revive then ruine you should follow the bent of your owne temper and be perfectly generous and I should receive one letter from you full of free and open kindenesse. But since you dare me all that I can answer to your challenge what ever it be is that I shall be as little able as willing to oppose you and that you are sure to be Conquerer in what ever you please. and if you thinke the change of S[1] will give you any advantage I shall subscribe my self

Your H. H. H.

What ever good humor you thinke I was in when I writt this, (as the reading your letter and the thoughts of talkeing with you is able to doe much) doe not doubt but when I am with you I shall be in a farre better, and if you will let me heare from you this returne of the Carrier the next trouble I shall give you shall be to thanke you my self.

## 88. LOCKE to a lady, 12 December [1659?]

B.L., MS. Locke c. 24, f. 19. Draft or copy. The dialect suggests that it was written in Somerset. Locke may have been there in December 1657: no. 37; and there is no information about where he was in December 1656. He was

[a] *Interlined;* of *supplied.*

[1] Style?

probably there about 22 November 1659; he was probably in Oxford in January 1660: no. 91; the date of his journey is unknown.

Zoft harted and vaire condicon zister

Chill tell you what cause made soe bold to write these few lines to your womanship and the rather becase chad zoe vitty a messenger who could vag and zay well, nay and an honest trusty carrier chad noething new god wot to zend you but these tway beans the bag of the place I's doe habit I's doubt not but youl expect it most abominable kindely as though twas the hougest gay Jewell in aule the world or zomerzet shire over tis vor aule the world as cha zeen a zwinging zomerzet sheire bag puding vul of veggs and vat, disclosed in a course, but comparisons are odoriferous wherefor chill condiscend to an end

From ditchet[1] the dozenth day of dezember when the Vokes were goeing to nummet[2]

## 89. LOCKE to P E [Elinor Parry, later Mrs. Hawkshaw?], [mid-December 1659?] (87, 112)

B.L., MS. Locke c. 24, f. 220. Draft. The date is conjectural. If no. 87 is correctly dated Mrs. Parry offended Locke about the beginning of December, when he was preparing to return to Oxford; he thereupon wrote no. 87, in which he asks for an answer by return. The present draft appears to be for an acknowledgement of her answer. There was, however, a further quarrel about April 1661: no. *121*; and there may have been other quarrels.

P E:

Dearest Cosin[3]

Alls well, the Quarrell is ended and we are freinds againe, and I thinke tis very hard for us long to be enemys. but were I stubborne you know how to mollify me, and had I set up my strongest resolution to stand out you have found a way to take me in and bring me to conditions. you cannot doubt the acceptance of what you sent me. Love is too wining a present to be refusd from any one espetiall comeing from a Person that is stord with all those virtus and qualitys that are requird to perfection. But Sir when I

[1] Ditcheat, about 18 miles south of Pensford. The wife of Locke's uncle Peter Locke perhaps came from Wraxhall near Ditcheat: no. *2132*. Locke is not in any other way connected with it; he perhaps selected the name on account of its sound.

[2] A corruption of Noonmeat, a light meal or luncheon: *O.E.D.*; Wright, s.v. Nammet.

[3] This appears to be inserted for concealment.

consider all the circumstances I am ready to conclude (If I conclude a misse pray correct me), that either you have very little love who are forcd to buy it, or that you thinke any good enough for me since you send me that which is soe slight and fadeing and lyes open to every ones purchase. Is it true indeed that your love lyes in the mercers boxes and is measurd out by the pennyworth. I have beene told that tis too noble a thing to be bought and sold or to be made merchandise and that it is the trafic of soules not shops, and that where it goes the heart goes with it, pray send me word whether you sent your heart with this. if you did I shall be very chary of it and be carefull to lodg it in the safest and most suitable place that can be. pray tell me too whether yours be true love or Noe, for our old philosophers say that love is a fire and a flame full of heat and warmth, if it be, certainely tis the coldest that ever was for I dare say if one were coverd all over with this sort of Love twould scarce make one warme, and one might never the lesse freeze and starve to death, pardon me that contrary to my promise I begge the trouble of an other letter, but it very much concearns me to be well assurd in this point, before I resolve to remove hence where every chimny offers the comfort of a warme sunne to a place where it seems fire heates not and flames have noe warmth. and I thinke it would be noe great pleasure to you to see dyeing with coldnesse

## *90.* A lady to [LOCKE?], [1659/60?]

B.L., MS. Locke c. 23, f. 180. It is impossible to suggest either a writer or a date.

Were this inquiry temred unjust by you I should soone silence my penn from requesting any thing that would argue a want of discrestion or kindness in mee by my pressing the knowledg of what would perhaps be the greatest satisfaction imputed, I beg you to a sence of my being concerned in whatsoever relates to you and not a curiosity shall not I then know the reason of that sadness that is visible especialy to me that can perceive it in you as soone as entertained by you deny it not then since a deniall will not hide it but rather agree to a cleare confession and persevere not in[a–] a obstinacie[–a] misbecoming a true frend if you chide pray let

[a–a] *MS.* in a a obstinacie

it com accompanied with counsell to learne wisdome but I tell you your chid⟨in⟩g[a] shall not be ⟨a barre⟩[b] to my admiration but to my tounge now you have power either to satisfie me by revealing or to refuse it if the former my obligation will be the greater, if the latter my punishmet shall be a perpetuall silence to such enquirys you may cause this resolution and withall beleeve my kindness is such that it make me almost forget the civill rule which I ought to follow, and shew to a person that hath beene extreamly liberall thereof to mee, the sens and acknowledgment I shall for ever retaine whilst I am the real hartied

## 91. LOCKE to JOHN LOCKE, sen., [*c.* 9 January 1660] (59, 95)

B.L., MS. Locke c. 24, ff. 175–6. Approximate date from contents.

Honoured Sir

I finde noe disapointment at all in the delay of your treaty with Dr I[c] [1] since I shall not willingly be drawne from hence whilst things are in these uncertaine hurrys, nor thinke to enter upon a steady course of life whilest the whole nation is reeleing. What face soever affaires may weare there it appeares to me here altogether lowering and cloudy and I feare a storme will follow. Divisions are as wide, factions as violent and designes as pernicious as ever and those woven soe intricately, that there are few know what probably to hope or desire, and the best and wisest are faine to wish for the generall thing settlement without seeing the way to it. In this time when there is noe other security against mens passion and reveng but what strength and steell yeelds I have a long time thougt the safest condition to bee in armes could I be but resolvd from whome I ought to receive them and for whome to imploy them, or could be but securd that I should not spend my bloud to swell the tide of other mens fortune or make myself a c⟨ar⟩kas[d] for their ambition to advance its self on. Armes is the last and worst of refuges, and tis the great misery of this shatterd and giddy nation

[a] *Page torn.* [b] *MS.* abarre [c] *Or* Dr J [d] *Blotted.*

[1] Presumably Dr. Ayliffe Ivye: nos. *26*, *97*, 113. If Locke was considering a medical career the negotiation may have been connected with it.

that warrs have producd noething but warrs and the sword cut out worke for the sword, and I can scarce thinke that the drum was ever intended to lull this nation into quiet. I must confesse in this posture of affairs I know not what to thinke what to say. I would be quiet and I would be safe, but if I cannot injoy them togeather the last certainely must be had at any rate. I know it will not become either my condition nor inexperience to offer at advice only I wish that you may not venture your rest, health or estate for ingratefull men as all ambitious are, nor deceitfull, as religious pretenders are, nor tyrants such as are the promisers of liberty. nor giddy such as I had almost said all English men are, You are too well acquainted with the publick faith to lett it run in your debt, and you have had too much experience of their gratitude to be willing to obleige them at your owne cost. I must begg your pardon for this boldnesse, which possibly doth better bespeake my affection then discretion, But this is a time when few men injoy the priviledg of being sober, and I am something excuseable if I cannot consider you steping again into danger without some emotion. If the sword be drawne againe I hope the nation and you too will reape greater advantages by it then either hath donne hither to. The most Authentick news here is, that the Rump hath voted out all the secluded members and made them incapable of being chosen into those vacancys which they intend to fill againe with qualified elections.[1] Lambert is come to London with about forty horse[2] and Munck is sent for whose good affections to the Rump is suspected.[3] Fairfax[4] in armes in the North for a free Parlament and the City not very well satisfyd. What you can spell from this medly I know not, to me it hath noe pleasant meaneing. I intreat to heare from you as often as may be that I may know how you are and things there and which way your armes are like to point.

Address: These present To mr John Locke at Pensford. To be left at mr Thomas Days in st Thomas street Bristoll.

[1] This was voted on 5 January; the vote was erased on 21 February: *C.J.*
[2] Early in January there were various reports about Lambert's attempts to come to London: *Cal. Clarendon S.P.* iv. 508–13. He remained in the north.
[3] The commons voted on 6 January that Monck should be invited to London: *C.J.*
[4] Thomas Fairfax, third Baron Fairfax of Cameron (Scotland), the general: *D.N.B.*

## *92.* WILLIAM CARR to LOCKE, [3 February 1660] (*39*, 93)

B.L., MS. Locke c. 5, ff. 9–10. Date from contents. Answered by no. 93.

Deare John

It is not my intention att this time to lett you know how much I am improved by eating att the Inns of Court and what eloquence I have got by devouring salt-fish within these walls, for to use Rhetorick to an intimate, is to abuse him, therfore I shall forbeare that, and in plaine termes informe you of the newes here in towne; Yesterday there was a very high mutiny among the Common Souldiers divers Commanders being wounded and a Leftenant kild; but their mouths being stoped with monny they are for a time appeased;[1] this day Monke came into London with his whole army; the best foot and the worst horse that ever was seen;[2] before every Regiment there went 2 men playing on bag-pipes. att this time there be severall hundreds of Woster-sheire men with Monke who declare for a free Parliment,[3] Prithee pardon this absurd abruption for Pegg Brook[4] will let me writte no longer being to waite on her abroad. The same cause that makes me so uncivill with you will not give me leave to writt to Jesy[a] Ward,[5] only letting me subscribe my selfe

Yours
W. CARR

if I had time I would write to you in my best hand

Address: For his much Esteemed freind mr John Locke master of Arts and student of Ch: Ch: Oxford these.

Scribbled note (by Locke?): 6739 digitis dic ordine flexis
dic flexos, decados reliquos hos ducit in illos

[a] *Or* Jesay *or* Jefry *?; part rewritten.*

[1] The principal outbreak was on 2 February: Davies, *Restoration of Charles II*, pp. 273–4.
[2] This was on 3 February.
[3] I have found nothing to confirm this statement.
[4] Margaret, *c.* 1640–67, daughter of Sir William Brooke, K.B.; married, 1665, as his second wife, Sir John Denham the poet; mistress of James, duke of York (the future James II): *D.N.B.*, art. Denham, Sir. J.; G. E. C., iii. 350 n.
[5] Apparently Isaiah (Esay) Ward.

## 93. LOCKE to WILLIAM CARR, 5 March [1660] (*92*, 94)

B.L., MS. Locke c. 24, ff. 27–8. Apparently written for dispatch, but there is no trace of a seal; it was probably not sent, Locke sending Carr a letter based on it, but omitting his unwillingness to leave Oxford for Gray's Inn. See further no. 94 n. Answers no. *92*.

March. 5.

Sir

Is there never an Order of Ladys about London whose businesse it is to excuse totall silence as well as half letters? certainely it will very much concearne your credit here to finde them out, and unlesse they adopt you into their sex your silence will scarce be pardonable. the guilt whereof would noe doubt (if you retaine any of that ingenuity you carried from hence) make you blush through a maske were it as thick as buff and your face to boote fencd with a hide of the same hue with the Compounders.[1] In good sooth Sir I have rummagd all my thoughts to finde an excuse for you, but can meet with noe cause that should keepe your hands from writeing unlesse you burnt your fingers with squibs at the late Bonefires,[2] what else should keepe them from runing over a side of paper, you know that lawers lines and scribere cum dassho will quickly arive at I rest yours etc.: this would be noe great pains to a man that had a minde to it and I am well enough perswaded that would you exercise it you have a pretty faculty in these kinde of matters and have a tolerable gift of inditeing and could begin a letter with my love remembred unto you hopeing that you are in good health[3] with as good a grace as any he that had read the Schoole of complements[4] 3 times over and had commencd pidler in Romances, I hope Plowden[5] hath not spoild these good parts yet, and you doe not begin allready to be ashamd of your stile, when feofment Soccage Seisin and a hundred such barbarisms are ready to slip into every sentence and discompose the beauty of your periods. I should be sorry to finde that habendum et tenendum hath ejected me and all your good thoughts out of your memory, and that your head is

[1] The royalists who submitted to the victors in the Civil War and compounded 'for their delinquency by the payment of a sum to be assessed on them towards the relief of the public burdens': S. R. Gardiner, *History of the Great Civil War*, new impression, 1904–5, iii. 197–8. Locke perhaps thought that, with the Restoration in view, they should blush for their submission.

[2] The great nights were those of 11 and 21 February: Pepys, *Diary*.

[3] So in no. 18.

[4] p. 110, n. 1.

[5] Edmund Plowden, 1518–85, the jurist: *D.N.B.* Several editions or abridgements of his *Commentaries* were published about this time.

stufd like a tailers pocket with fragments of parchment and scraps of ould moth eaten leases,[1] this gives me a quarrell to our profession and makes me slow to change a Colledg for an In of Court.[2] If it be the fashon in London neither to thinke of nor write to ones freinds pray send me word, I beleeve I could easily put my self into it, and could without much pains be sullen too, keepe my thoughts on this side Mag: Bridg,[3] and make a shift to dreame of my freinds but once a quarter. I know now, could I lie handsomely, I should tell you a story as dolefull as Queene Didos, what torments I endure in the want of your letters, and how many times a day your neglect racks me, But I have the witt not to tell you, what youl have the witt never to beleeve, But were I a Courtier noe doubt I should feele abundance of paine, but I thanke my stars I am not of their tender makeing; for ought I see I talke, sleepe I and eat too when I can get it as well as ever, I cannot perceive that I pine away and I beleeve I should be able to munch my $1^{d}$ ob commons[4]. though I receivd never a letter this 7 years, what thinke you? and yet all this doth not excuse you, to breake your word is an ungentle crime which I cannot pardon, to be sullen like a pouting girle is unmanly, and should I examine it I should finde a hundred faults in that lazinesse which will not allow you to repay me these few words which tell you that I am

Sir

Your most affectionate freind

J L

Address: Thes present To mr William Carr at Colonel Pophams at Lincolne howse[5] Westminster.

[1] They were used for taking measurements: Sir Walter Scott, *The Antiquary*, ch. v.

[2] Locke was admitted to Gray's Inn in 1656; Carr in 1655: pp. 42 n., 46 n.

[3] Magdalen Bridge, then at the eastern limit of Oxford, and crossed by the road to London. The parish of St. Clements, across the bridge, was not part of the city at this time.

[4] So p. 79. Ob. for obolus: *O.E.D.*

[5] Probably the house of this name in Tothill Street, Westminster: H. B. Wheatley, *London Past and Present*, 1891 (notice dated 1665).

## 94. LOCKE to WILLIAM CARR, 15 March [1660] (93, *166*)

B.L., MS. Locke c. 24, ff. 29–30. Draft, perhaps for an answer to an answer to a letter based on no. 93. Year from contents.

Ch Ch: 15° Mar.

Sir

Your excuse is worse then your fault and I should rather be content to finde you carelesse then not in a condition to write, your Apologie hath given me but very little satisfaction what opinion soe ever you may have of the goodnesse of it, and all the courtesye you have donne me by it, is to change a short and freindly anger into a serious and lasting melanchorly. Pray send noe more such strong arguments[a]– for not writeing,–[a] your letters would be better were your reasons worse. I had rather have you silent then speechlesse, I am not of their envious humor who had rather the sun should be quite eclipsd, then not shine on them. I can not phansie you neare a desease without trembling at the apprehension, and though you should tell me the danger were over, yet I could not presently recover my self, such great stormes even when they are past leave a shakeing behinde them: what thoughts doe you suppose I have, when I consider you besett with Opiats and Apozems Clysters and Cataplasms and a rabble of such stuff the very names whereof would turne ones stomach and make ones head ake; to see you beleagered with pots and pipkins as terrible as cannons ready to discharge upon you, and to this, three or four Ladys persicuteing you with broths and caudles, and a thowsand howdees,[1] certainely Sir these are enough to deject a spirit lesse feeble and sensible then mine. But what a trim occasion would you give me of sorrow, should this proove noe thing but a Westminster desease, such as I have beene troubld with, when I went to schoole there, which we then, who spoke downe right and according to the vulgar cald sloth? I heare you can ride in a coache yet, but that (may be) is only to take the aire; you can whole afternoons entertaine Ladys, but that is a restorative, to sitt at a play[2] 4 howers is

a–a *Substituted for* reasons: for your silence

[1] How-do-ye's, messages inquiring after people's health: *O.E.D.*

[2] There were probably some performances about this time; an order prohibiting them was issued on 23 April: J. L. Hotson, *The Commonwealth and Restoration Stage*, 1928, pp. 197–8. Locke may, however, mean a game.

only a diversion, if you drinke wine tis to recover your spirits and I beleeve that though you eat, drinke, and use all the liberty of those that are well; yet what is our diet is your physick and that you are neverthelesse under a desease, and have only found a better way of cure. I heare there is a Diana a goddesse Diana[1] take heed your devotion to her take you not againe from other company, and keepe you a brode too long; solitariness, and sitting up are naught for sick men. There was a Ball too, Sir John Salsburys Ball,[2] did not the tosseing of that something disable your hand from writeing? The truth is when I consider you every day sporting in the beams of soe many sunns, as constantly appeare in that horizon, I cannot but thinke you may easily be distemperd and if you are as easily to be inflam'd as mr Ward[3] is, there are some days where in you must needs have above three feavers upon you at once. If then there be certaine seasons wherein I must be deprivd of your conversation, I had rather resigne you into the hands of Ladys then Physitians, and If your hand must sometimes shake soe as not to be able to guide a pen, I had rather it should be att the approaches of a mortall beauty, then a Roman goddesse which they were pleasd to call an Ague.[4] yet I would not have you often make use of these subterfuges . . .[a] This gives me a quarrell to our profession, and makes me slow to remove from a colledg to an Inns of Court. and I shall never expect to finde soe much satisfaction at Grays Inne as I doe at Ch: Ch: did I not hope to injoy you there. though I am not very well assurd of that happinesse as long as there is a Lady Anne Digby[5] a Peg Brooke and a Diana Newport[6] soe neare you. These indeed are temptations that human frailety cannot resist. you may submitt without a blush to a faire and

[a] *Here is a passage cancelled by Locke by writing a second version of it over the first. Both the original and the rewritten versions are similar to the passage* you have a pretty faculty . . . old moth eaten leases *in no.* 93.

[1] See below. Locke perhaps alludes to Acts 19.
[2] Sir John Salusbury, d. 1684; fourth baronet 1658: G. E. C., *Baronetage*, i. 128.
[3] Isaiah Ward.
[4] 'Febrem autem ad minus nocendum templis colebant': Valerius Maximus, *Factorum Dictorumque Memorabilium Libri Novem*, II. v. 6.
[5] Anne, *c.* 1646–1716, daughter of George Digby, second earl of Bristol; married, 1665, Robert Spencer, second earl of Sunderland (p. 218, n. 5.): *D.N.B.*, art. Spencer, R.
[6] Diana, d. 1732, daughter of Francis Newport, Baron (later Viscount) Newport, created earl of Bradford 1694; married (i) Thomas Howard, d. 1701, son of Sir Robert the dramatist; (ii) William Feilding, brother of Basil Feilding, fourth earl of Denbigh: O. Manning and W. Bray, *The History . . . of Surrey*, 1804–14, ii. 629–30, 631.

vertuous Lady, since you have the example of Alexander and Cæsar, and they who triumphd over all the world, were in such an encounter made vassalls. Lett us talke while will, and call that Sex the weaker, a Beautifull face and noble soule will still command us. but yet you may keepe some few thoughts for him that is

yours most affectionately

J L

Yesterday your quondam Tutor Mr Dod was chosen Proctor.[1] I hope to see you here within these few days. you will not neglect to lend an hand to the setting on of your owne head:

Address: These present To Mr William Carr at Lincoln howse Westminster:

## 95. LOCKE to JOHN LOCKE, sen., 10 April [1660] (91, 110)

B.L., MS. Locke c. 24, ff. 177–8. Year from contents.

10° Apr.

Deare Father

I perceive that to withdraw from the world is not a sure remedy against its troubles, retirement affords but a slender fence against crosses, and there is noe place soe hidden, noe condition soe solitare where affliction will not finde one out; I had began to arme my self against the evills of the world, but I finde my self wounded in a place ungarded, and twill be but in vaine to endeavour to harden ones self, whilst Nature Virtue and Gratitude will keepe some places continually sensible, The news of the returne of your malady, hath shaken all the constancy I have beene building; which I should not be able to beare up under did I not hope, that it is only such an anuall revolution of your desease, as the assistance of your Physitian could easily remove. The humors at this time of the yeare usually grow tumultuous if not restraind, and you know who is able to doe it. Dr Meara[2] hath too well assured you of this to lett you doubt it, and you may with confidence expect health from that hand from which formerly you have receivd it. Though noe other losse of health but what I have felt in my freinds, which hath beene too often, hath taught me to prize it yet from thence I have learnt

[1] John Dod: p. 203 n. He was chosen for proctor at Christ Church on 14 March and elected there on 26 April; his election was challenged: Wood, *L. and T.* i. 307, 310, 313.

[2] p. 163 n.

that it is the best and most ne⟨cessary⟩[a] of all outward things, to be purchasd ⟨at                    ⟩[a] worth above 5 miles send⟨ing                    ⟩[a] to beccon you to this care of your self, and to point you to the place where he hath laid up this blessing for you, nor is your wellfare alone concearnd in it. the comfort and happinesse of your children are wrapd up in your health. and your country too may have use of it. For my part twill always be to me as necessary as my owne. and 'twill be but a small advantage (espetially to a schollar) to have a sound body with a languishing minde, and I must needs wither whilst the stock I grow on decays. Sir you have not beene wont to refuse me any thing and I hope I shall not now meet with a deniall, when I begg for a father for a brother and for my self, when my desires are for the welfare of a whole family, which makes me thus importunate for the Advice of your Physitian who I hope will soone restore a perfect health to you and comfort to

Sir

Your most obedient sonne

J LOCKE:

The Burgesses for the towne are the Lord Faulkland and Esquire Uxly:[1]

The University hath not yet chosen, the delay occasiond by the High Canvasing of Speaker Lentall (for whome Munck hath appeard and written to us more then once) Judg Hales Dr Mills Can⟨non⟩[a] of Ch: Ch: and Dr Claiton Regius professor of Physick[b2]

Address: These present To my Father.
Endorsed by Locke: To Mr J Locke

[a] *Page torn.* [b] *A word may be torn away.*

[1] Henry Carey, fourth viscount of Falkland (Scotland; G. E. C.) and James Huxley were returned on 5 April: *Oxford Council Acts, 1626–65* (Oxford Hist. Soc., vol. xcv, 1933), pp. 255–6.

[2] Monck refused to be a candidate for the university, but recommended William Lenthall, the Speaker of the Long Parliament (*D.N.B.*). His letters on behalf of Lenthall were read in Convocation on 4 and 7 April; the second was printed (Madan, nos. 2509–10) and 'great canvassing' followed. The election took place on 12 April; the successful candidates were John Milles, D.C.L. 1649; a canon of Christ Church 1648–51 and reinstated on 13 March of this year (Foster); and Thomas Clayton, D.M. 1639; Regius professor of medicine 1647–65; knighted 1661; Warden of Merton College 1661–93 (ibid.): Wood, *L. and T.* i. 311–13. Judge Hales is (Sir) Matthew Hale, 1609–76, the judge (*D.N.B.*); he was a justice of the common pleas from 1654 to 1658, and was a member of parliament for the university in 1659 (Richard Cromwell's parliament). He was not a candidate in the present contest.

## 96. Locke to P A [Col. Alexander Popham], [*c.* April 1660?] (8)

B.L., MS. Locke c. 24, f. 223. Draft. The initials and the contents show that it was intended for Popham; the date is indicated by the allusion to his tenure of office and by the mention of his son.

P A

Sir

The greatest advantage I demand of my studys is an ability to serve you with them, and I shall thinke those years I have spent in Oxford not lost when I perceive they have renderd me any way usefull to him that first placd me there. The Muses deserve better of me then that by my negligence I should disgrace them to their best Patron and make them seeme ungratefull, and I would not willingly give you a reason to thinke that your care of Learning is a fruitlesse thing and such as from whence you must expect noe returne. This maks me diligently eye all occasions that may beccon me to your service, which should I oversee or be lesse carefull to observe it might justly be thought that in a place where all others improve their knowledg and become quicksighted I alone grew blinde and stupid or at least that all the light I have gaind from philosophie hath beene noe other then that of the Quakers which leads men from the sense of curtesy and gratitude. Sir to say that I am obleigd to you is noe more then to professe my self an English man and it cannot passe for a peculiar acknowledgment at a time when the whole nation lookes on you as a defender of their laws and libertys,[1] but besides my share in the common benefit I have receivd many particular favours and owe you not only for my safety and prosperity but my knowledg and reason too, and my private obligations as far exceed the publick (though they be such as the good of 3 nations depends on) as the minde doth the body. if then I have made any acquisitions in learning tis fitt I dedicate them to you as their first author, which I cannot any way better doe, then by offering them[a]– to the–[a] assistance to your sonne.[2] I

[a–a] *Substituted for* my

[1] Popham was appointed a member of the Council of State on 23 or 25 February, and attended meetings between 9 March and 4 May. He was a member of the Long Parliament, which was dissolved on 16 March, and of the Convention, which met on 25 April.

[2] Francis Popham, d. 1674. He matriculated from Christ Church on 13 July of this year; K.B. 1661; M.A. 1662; M.P. 1669–74: Foster.

cannot be content, only to beare part in the generall acclamations and with the people make wishes for you at a distance, but as I have always stood nearer your bounty I cannot but desire to keep the same station in my imployment and whilst others are prepareing monuments, frameing and erecting statues to you,[1] twould be a buisnesse suitable to the sense I have of your favours to have a hand in fashoning that image which must survive you and shew posterity a copy not soe much of your pearson as vertues. It will equally unbecome me either to promise any thing for my self more then a zele to this undertakeing or to prescribe to you what way you shall make use of me. I shall only take leave to minde you that I am an utinsill wherein you have a propriety and lie ready for any imployment you shall be pleasd to honour me with, being ambitious that my actions as well as words should speake me

## *97.* Dr. Ayliffe Ivye to Locke, 20 May 1660 (*26*, 113)

B.L., MS. Locke c. 12, ff. 1–2. A negotiation mentioned in no. 91 suggests that Locke's father had proposed some kind of association between Ivye and Locke.

Worthy Sir,

by this time you may verye well thincke that I have forgotten you; truth is ⟨untill⟩[a] now I could finde noe fitt oppertunitie to send unto you butt now can doe noe less then thancke you for your greate civilitie and kinde remembrance of me and my wife; we will studye requitall when it shall be our happiness to see you in the countrye; I hope Sir, you will lett slippe noe occasion whereby you may better your selfe, and soe me, by your aquaintance with Mr. Boyle,[2] I longe to have an accounte of my Quæries; I made the Panacæa Last weeke and have sent you two dragmes, tis the First preparation calcined via humida, liquore alkahestico[3] then, washed and dryed you may go higher and with spirite of wine acuated[4] etc. drawe off his perfect tincture; but truelye this worketh admirable well and noethinge standeth in his way, and tis most

[a] *MS.* unlill

[1] I have traced nothing to which this can refer.
[2] The Hon. Robert Boyle, 1627–91, the scientist: *D.N.B.*
[3] The alkahest was the universal solvent of the alchemists: J. R. Partington, *A History of Chemistry*, 1961–70, ii. 218–19.
[4] Sharpened: *O.E.D.*

safe to administer it secundum Glauberi modum;[1] I make upp: into pills with sugar one grayne for one pill and soe give it more or less etc. Sir I should be glad to heare from you, In the meane kissinge your hand I am unfaynedlye

Your most humble servant
AYLIFFE IVYE.

Bristleton[2] may the 20 1660.

Address: For his honoured friend Mr John Lock att his Chamber in Peckwater quadrangle in Christchurch College Oxon

## *98.* JOHN STRACHEY to JOHN LOCKE, sen., 24 May 1660

B.L., MS. Locke c. 18, ff. 195–6. Strachey's nearest letters in date to Locke are nos. *55*, *103*.

Sir

The Gentleman of Grays Inn[3] is soe much your servant that hee will not dispute what you object to him as a fault, only hee humbly craves your pardon, if his thoughts were soe carried away in the generall streame of joy, that he neglected what was due to his freind at Pensford. And that you may see how willinge hee is to undergoe pennance for his offence hee is ready to bee laught at in this sheete the same day his crime was told him. Had hee stayde till the returne of Mr Burges[4] you might have had what news this Towne afforded from better hands, wherefore to make himselfe considerable and to allay your passion, hee humbly offers what follows. Tis Currantly reported that the Kinge landed this morninge at Dover, though I have some reason to suspect the trueth, for a Gentleman newly come from the Hague tells mee that the Kinge intended not to take shippinge till this day.[5] Generall Monke is gon to meete him, hee went yesturday noe farther then Rochester,[6] Att his tayle thousands of Starrs as at the Dragons, viz: Sparkes followed, good fayth twas a splendid Trayne, but all the feare is most of them will be forced to uncase when they come to London; but thats nothing to mee; news from Ireland is, one Colonell Ayres hath headed a party of phanaticks and old Rebells, and Colonell

[1] J. R. Glauber, 1604–70, chemist: *A.D.B.*; for his panacea see Partington, ii. 357. Locke possessed a number of books by him (L.L., nos. 1254–70).
[2] Brislington, 2½ miles SE. of Bristol, and 4½ north of Pensford.
[3] Strachey himself.
[4] There are men of the name in nos. 29, 64, etc.
[5] Charles embarked on 23 and landed on 25 May: Pepys.
[6] According to the *Publick Intelligencer*, 28 May, p. 172, he went to Blackheath.

Jones is gon to quell them.[1] Well there may bee some Antimonarticks there, but if you would bid mony, not twenty to bee found in London, and those few by hanging and drowning will caper away very speedily. There is 400 000l to be forthwith raisd by the Pole to stopp gaps,[2] I am glad I am noe Captaine or Esquire; but seriously I shall allwaies bee proud to bee knowne under the degree and quality of

Sir

your humble servant

JO STRACHEY

May 24 60.

Pray remember mee to one of your Sons and bestow a chiding upon the other for forgetting his freinds.

Address: For his much esteemed freind Captaine John Locke at his house in Pensford these.

Leave this with Mr Day a Soape-boyler in the high-streete in Bristoll

Notes by Locke: [references to books and statutes, notes on the Bible, some calculations.]

## *99.* THOMAS WESTROWE to LOCKE, 30 [June?] 1660 (82, *100*)

B.L., MS. Locke c. 23, f. 74. The vote relating to the regicides is that of the commons on 30 June; further, in view of the king's speech on 27 July, Westrowe would scarcely have written as he does about the Act of Indemnity on 30 July.

London July 30th 1660

Honest John,

The slender ocation that they have taken to send for me, affords me so little businesse, that it leveth too much time to malencoly, and the condolings of my want of freinds, and good company, such frinds (I meane) that are good comepany: would I had you here to see in what a[a] malencolly posture I now set: pitty would perswade to stay and be my comforter. But why doe I desire impossibilities, you can not see me in this moode, unlesse I were blind too,

[a] *Altered from* all?

[1] Col. William Eyres or Ayres, an extreme republican: Firth, *Regimental History of Cromwell's Army*, i. 9; Col. Theophilus Jones, knighted *c.* 1644: *D.N.B.* Jones captured Eyres by 24 May: *Parliamentary Intelligencer*, 4 June, p. 366 (news from Dublin, 24 May).

[2] A bill for the tax was ordered on 19 May; it received the royal assent on 29 August: *C.J.*; *L.J.*

and ⟨might⟩[a] not have that sight which would be my imediate cure. The only divertisment this place yeldeth is some halfe hours vist to a freind, whos envi'd businesse so sone snacheth him from my company, then consider what losse I am at, who have nither men nor bookes to convers with, thoughts (the mother of my desease) is then my only refuge, O that some of ye (though ye can not see me in) would see me safe out of this fit. if I can not hope to see you perswade Jack[1] to be your deputy. that being so imployed he may bring me two freinds, and Jack include John. they have long been united in a lesse place, where affection plaseth those freindship joineth. What an unhapinesse, that this (the only good the world can give) should have this evell: that the treue delights of presence should be counterpoised by as reall greefes of absence. But to end my morning and conclude my letter I will tell all newes I heare. which is this small parsel only. the Qeene sudenly comes over, and Prince Robert[2] to give his cosen a visit: this day it pased the house that all those of the Kings judges that came not in shall ⟨be⟩[b] guilty as well for life as estate,[3] the act of indemnity is not like to come out this great while,[4] more then this the wett wether will not let me inquire

Your freind and what more affection can clame
THOMAS WESTROWE

Remember me to Jack esay and Fra. Poppum etc.[5]

I pray[c] desire Mr Fouler[6] to send my linin[c] this weeke and direct them to Mr Howards in fetter lane over against the flower de luce Inne.

On reverse, probably written by Locke:

How hate full is a Locke to some
confineing them within a Roome
But plesant is a Locke to me it
keepes me from bad company

[a] *MS.* migh [b] *Word omitted by the writer.* [c] *Doubtful reading; page rubbed.*

[1] Perhaps John Nourse: pp. 53, n. 4, 153.
[2] These reports are premature: Henrietta Maria came late in October, Prince Rupert late in September.
[3] This refers to a proviso to be inserted in the Act of Indemnity; those of the regicides who had not surrendered themselves within fourteen days in accordance with the Proclamation of 6 June were to be excepted 'out of this Act for Life and Estate'. This proviso was introduced into the house of commons and voted on 30 June: *C.J.*
[4] On 27 July Charles II made a speech to parliament about the need for haste in passing the Act of Indemnity. It received the royal assent on 29 August: *L.J.*
[5] Probably John Nourse and Isaiah (Esay) Ward; Francis Popham.
[6] Perhaps a college servant.

## *100*. [Thomas Westrowe?] to Locke, 19 July 1660 (*99*, *139*)

B.L., MS. Locke c. 23, f. 71. The identification of the writer is based on the initials of the signature, and on the resemblance of the writing and contents to those of nos. *99*, *139*.

Your Humble Servant Sir.

A tired horse doth not Love to goe out of his rode. so weary am I this day with making large preambles to nothing, troting up and down with the affore-said salutations am so founderd as maketh me wish, that I could now at night make feet, as it hath been businesse all day to make ledgs; to ussher in a how would you advise me Sir to this executor, who adviseth to goe to t'other, he to a third; who teleth me law, and frustrats the whole dayes worke with what I don't understand, nor[a]– can be he–[a] satisfied till Mr Jenk: endeth his cervet. these with a dell combersome patienc have so taken up my time that I am unable. to searsh in this wood for the thing I suspect you have not sent, as the nessesary tackling of my profeshion, (when a coachman) or the harnesse, which if you nickname are straps to the two somter trunks, and 4 rings that were in little draer in the cabanet of Glase (where are things worth your saving) these if not here allredy I pray take care to send: the pictures and cabanet are at your servise. excuse me to Mr Fowler tha't I dont answare his letter the post is not so patient as I, who am both

Your Humble Servant Sir

T. W.

July 19 1660

## 101. Locke to J. O., [early August 1660?]

B.L., MS. Locke c. 24, f. 60. J. O. is perhaps the John Oliver mentioned in no. *54*. Date from contents.

To J[b] O

Sir

I am sorry the promise I made you in the country should be[c] forcd[c] into soe neare a resemblance of a complement as to bring

[a–a] can be *is interlined between* nor *and* he [b] *Altered from* E [c] *Substituted for* degenerate

you noe other returne but words for those signall and reall courtesies I receivd from you. and I cannot without discontent see Fortune oppose my serious indeavours in a thing of such concearnment. Certainely your freindship hath made her my enemy and she treats me as one that began to disesteeme her good will upon the first appearance of yours. and one that whilst he injoyd your favour was like to grow carelesse and thinke he stood in noe need of hers. It could not be else that when I had made way to the obteineing any thing in Mr B . . .[a1] study I should misse the second part of Alex: van Suchten:[2] which was supposd to be there. had he had it it had come to you with this paper. and I had beene soe happy as to procure something fit to be logd among those raritys that inhabite your study. But since I was disapointed in that I have adventurd to send in its roome a peice of Glaubers[b] newly arivd,[3] you will finde him as uncoverd, and naked as he was borne, he was soe willing to lay hold of the first oportunity that might convey him to your hands that he would not stay here to be clothd in a new outsid: Though your commendacon of this author and Mr B . . .s[c] prefering him to Suchten might incourge me to present it you yet I consider how ill in the meane time I satisfy my promise. that for a manuscript send a book in print and when I was to procure you something choise and soe rare that only some few were priviledgd to be owners of I offer you a thing that is common to all that ⟨c⟩an[d] read. you will undoubtedly judg that one that was master of any reason should not take such an unsuitable way to make good his word. But Sir you are not to expect that I alone should preserve my reason cleare in a place. where every one hath his clouded and disturbd by noe ordinary feare, you can not looke for a reguler composdnesse in the actions or letters of one ⟨that⟩[e] dwells in a place shaken with continuall earth quakes and is every minute tottering. Oxford now is not a place for serene thoughts and such as should dictate a letter to you.[4] tis to that Sir I must

[a] *Blotted.* [b] *Followed by* (an author that mr B: prefers very much to Suchten) *del.* [c] *The name, apart from the initial B, deleted.* [d] *Page torn.* [e] *Wrongly deleted in MS.*

[1] Presumably Boyle.

[2] A sixteenth-century writer on the secrets of antimony: Partington, *Hist. of Chemistry*, ii. 156; Boyle, *Works*, ed. T. Birch, 1744, i. 323, 574.

[3] p. 147, n. 1. I cannot identify the book.

[4] Locke apparently refers to the Restoration visitation of the university. Proceedings began on 31 July, and continued until 20 August; they resumed on 11 September, and continued at least until 6 November 1662. Most of the expulsions

intreat you to pardon the unhandsomeness of this scribling. the great respects and[a] high[a] esteeme I have for you would undoubtedly have furnishd me at another time with words more suitable to your obligacons and my gratitude, But Sir you will not blame me if my hand shake in a storme. and rather cast burs on my papr then elegancys. and I am to be excusd if my thoughts put not on the gaity of rhetorick when every one else is wrapd in melancholy. I hope likewise this consideration will prevent the ill opinion you might other wise justly conceive of me, and that this first disapointment will not soe blemish me in your thoughts as to render me unfitt for any imployment herafter since there is noe thing in the world that I shall entertaine with more eagernesse then the oportunitys to testify unto you that I am

## *102.* GEORGE PERCIVALL to LOCKE, 29 August 1660 (*109*)

B.L., MS. Locke c. 17, f. 60. George Percivall, 1637–75; youngest son of Sir Philip Perceval (*D.N.B.*); at Westminster School; matriculated from Christ Church 1656; B.A. 1658; M.A. 1660; contributed a poem (no. 75) to *Britannia Rediviva*, 1660 (Madan no. 2466); registrar of the Prerogative Court of Ireland 1661?–75?: J. Anderson(?), *A Genealogical History of the House of Yvery*, 1742, ii. 322–4 and table at ii. 1 (the book is untrustworthy but this passage seems reliable); Barker and Stenning; H.M.C., *Egmont MSS.*, vols. i and ii.

Mr Locke

Since I came into Ireland I have bin so taken up with my freinds here that I have not had time to thinke of thos that I left behinde me. however I have not forgot them, and amongst the rest that I remember, Ile assure you my thoughts are particularly fixed on you, whos acquaintance I value so much, and whose correspondence I so much desire. I write not long since to Mr Lower[1] but have received no answer from him, which makes me beleive that he is in the countrey, and therfore I must beg of you the Oxford intelligence, and what alterations time has produced there, since

[a] *MS.* and I high

were ordered by mid-October 1660: 'The Restoration Visitation of the University of Oxford', ed. F. J. Varley, in *Camden Miscellany*, vol. xviii (Royal Historical Society, Camden 3rd ser., vol. lxxix, 1948).

[1] Richard Lower, 1632–91; at Westminster School; matriculated from Christ Church 1651; B.A. 1653; M.A. 1655; M.D. 1665; the physician: *D.N.B.*

my departure. I would furnish you by way of requitall with irish news were it considerable, or worth the penning, but I think it is not, all that I observe in this country is the pride and hardnes of the irish people, the men will not drive a cart without a long cloake on there backe, and that without any shooes or stockings, the women will stand in the river all day long and wash cloaths, and that as they tell me here, not only at this season but in the midst of winter. I have not had time to looke about me as yet. I have spent my time hitherto in visits and seing of my freinds which are so numerous that really I know not how to pay them that civility which either they expect or I intend them, by reason of my intentions to returne for England suddenly, if my freinds which would otherwise dispose of me, will permit. I am going to morrow to Munster to visit my brother[1] who is very sick, and I beleive will not recover. however if you please to direct your letters to my mothers[2] house upon the Merchants Key of Dublin. I shall safely receive them. my service to all our freinds at Oxford, to Mr Ward,[3] and tell him that Mr Veale[4] was gone for England ere I landed, so that I could not deliver his letter to him. and to Mr Lower, and Mr South,[5] Mr Vincent,[6] Jack Nurse,[7] and all our freinds with you. I wish I were to returne to you to morrow, for I am almost weary of my freinds civilities here. but I hope I shall returne at the farthest next spring unto you, and if my place be in any danger I desire you to secure it for me by giving Sir Tim Terrell[8] timely notice of

[1] Probably Sir John Percival, 1629–65; created a baronet 1661; owner of an estate at Burton, co. Cork: H.M.C., *Egmont MSS.*, vols. i, ii, introductions.

[2] Catherine, d. 1681, daughter of Arthur Usher: *D.N.B.*, art. Sir P. Perceval.

[3] Isaiah Ward.

[4] Identifiable as Edward Veel or Veal, *c.* 1633–1708; matriculated from Christ Church 1651; B.A. 1652; M.A. 1654; fellow of Trinity College, Dublin, *c.* 1653–61; B.D. of Trinity 1661; nonconformist divine and tutor: *D.N.B.*

[5] Robert South, 1634–1716; at Westminster School; matriculated from Christ Church 11 December 1651; B.A. 24 February 1655; M.A. 1657; D.D. 1663; contributed poems to Oxford congratulatory, etc., volumes 1654, 1660, etc. (Madan, nos. 2243 (61), 2466 (114), etc.); public orator (Oxford) 1660–77; prebendary of Westminster 1663: *D.N.B.*; letters below, no. *2229*, etc.; mentioned perhaps as 'little Robin' on pp. 54, 56.

[6] Apparently John Vincent, 'a boon companion': Wood, *L. and T.* i. 361. He contributed poems to two Oxford collections, 1660 (Madan, nos. 2466–7 (26, 49)). He is not identifiable in Foster.

[7] pp. 53, n. 4, 149, n. 1.

[8] Timothy Tyrrell, *c.* 1617–1701; knighted 1643; married, *c.* 1641, Elizabeth, 1620–93, daughter of James Ussher, archbishop of Armagh; they were the parents of Locke's friend James Tyrrell (no. *343*, etc.): W. B. Wright, *The Ussher Memoirs*, 1889, pp. 104, 110–17, etc. Lady Tyrrell and Percival's maternal grandfather, Arthur Usher, were distantly related to one another. Percival alludes to the visitation of the university.

it by a letter, whose acquaintance with the Canons[1] may doe me a great courtesie, and what ever charges my letters to you, or your messages to him may put you to, I desire you to charge upon my name. I shall conclude this present trouble to you by subscribing my selfe in hast

Your affectionate freind and servant
GEO. PERCIVALL

Dublin. Aug. 29. 60

Address: For Mr John Lock At his chamber in Christ church In Oxford England.
In another hand: post payd to London

## *103.* JOHN STRACHEY to LOCKE, 22 September [1660?] (*55, 98, 107*)

B.L., MS. Locke c. 18, ff. 204–5. The year is a guess.

How much easier were it to bee a Man of Letters then Law, to reconcile books then men? besides the pleasure of wrangling to the Worlds end without cost or charge These paper quarrels quickly vanish into smoake whereas mony differensies are as durable as the mettal they concerne. And yett wee have Laws and Judges but the first with a Nose of wax, the others with brazen faces and this Monster can outface the[a] right[a] sub sigillo Legis and make a maske of his Nose. If then the waters are stir'd for a poore Samaritan and a Levite thrusts in before him, hee that went out for a Cure may well returne with a Crutch, and if hee ha'nt faith enough for a miracle may dye a Cripple.[2] This I conceive makes you thinke I am worsted, but hold, the dye is not cast yett, wee came on couragiously, but I understanding what is before intimated fairely sounded a retreate not through a distrust of my owne Strenght (in that I was fully assured from my Champion Lawyers) but in hope of a better day for it. Wee are now drawn off to our winter quarters, but doe still skirmish in the Reare, and much action ca'nt bee expected till the Springe and wee breake forth afresh and then the greate controvercie may bee decided betweene the Pope and Turke, for the Kindred and Pyramid I give you

[a] *Written in margin, possibly after the next words were written.*

[1] Of Christ Church. [2] John 5: 2–9.

thanks but I have not leasure enough to turne Prophet, and I hope you will beleive without revelation that I am

Sir

your freind and servant

JO STRACHEY

Sep 22th.

Pray lett mee begg one litle glass more of C.C.[a]

Address: For Mr John Locke att Christ-Church in Oxford these.

## *104.* GABRIEL TOWERSON to LOCKE, 23 October 1660 (*106*)

B.L., MS. Locke c. 22, ff. 1–2. Gabriel Towerson, 1635?–97; matriculated from Queen's College 1651; B.A. 1654; M.A. 1657; fellow of All Souls 1659–63 (resigned); contributed poems to Oxford congratulatory, etc., volumes 1660, 1661 (Madan, nos. 2466 (126), 2543); rector of Welwyn, Herts., 1662–97; D.D., Lambeth, 1678; author: *D.N.B.*; Martin, *Catalogue of the Archives . . . All Souls*, p. 382.

At this time Towerson and Locke were investigating the Law of Nature. The subject aroused much interest all through the seventeenth century, and more especially after Hobbes's attacks on it in *Leviathan* (1651) and elsewhere. In 1660 (probably in January or February) Robert Sharrock of New College (*D.N.B.*) published his *Ὑπόθεσις ἠθική de Officiis secundum Naturæ Jus* (Madan, no. 2529; for date of publication the probable mentions in Henry Oldenburg, *Correspondence*, ed. A. R. and M. B. Hall, 1965, i. 348, 353, 357, 363), which implies an existing interest in Oxford. Locke may have known Sharrock before his book appeared (so von Leyden, introd., p. 38). There is nothing to show when Locke's active interest in the Law began; there had evidently been some exchanges of views between him and Towerson prior to this letter. Their intercourse and the relation of Towerson's *An Explication of the Decalogue*, 1676, to Locke's 'essays' on the Law of Nature are discussed by Dr. W. von Leyden, introduction to Locke's *Essays*, pp. 82–5. Uvedale also may have been interested in the subject: no. *105*.

Mr. Lock,

I have ever thought it more proper to prevent than wipe of an accusation, and that is the sole occasion of the present addresse. I had taken time enough to consider of a reply to your last, but had so streitned my selfe of time to transcribe it, that I was forc'd to doe it negligently enough, which you I hope will so far excuse as not therfore to condemne my argumentations; you being (I

[a] *Doubtful reading.*

presume) not at all of kinde to him who instead of satisfiing his Creditors bill tooke occasion to quarrell with the fist that scribbled it. I have so much in me of a scholler, as to deferre the doing of any thing till an extreme necessity urge me therunto; but assure your selfe I have so much respect for you as to be willing to be accounted at least in this sense *None*,[a] rather than obtrude upon *you* my sudden and undigested thoughts, who are wont to consider before you refell[1] my papers. And now had I any thing of news worth acquainting you with, I have here roome enough to insert it; but really the winter is a time of as little action in the University as it is in the Campagne; or if any thing be done, the notice therof may freez before it come at me who keep home and expect not to heare any thing till the next spring release me and the now congeald intelligence. One thing only I may not forget, that the Melancholy Knight[2] hath gain'd so much upon the affections of the heads of houses by his last sermon, that he hath bin desir'd by them all to solemnize the 5. of November. This week I expect Mr. Uvedale home, and then perhaps you may heare somwhat of Ca-star-a,[3] and our club. In the meane time it may suffice that *Mrs. Parry*[a4] is as well as you can wish her, and so very much *yours*,[a] that nothing but my sex, and this secret addresse can authorize my subscribing my selfe

Your most affectionate freind and servant

G: TOWERSON

All-Soules. October 23. 1660.

If you have not or doe desire the University verses upon the Duke of Glocester,[5] or D. Pearsons reply to Dr. Burges[6], upon your intimation therof you shall receive them by the next. The latter is but

[a] *Written in large letters.*

[1] Refute: *O.E.D.*

[2] Apparently John Ailmer of New College: p. 158.

[3] Apparently Anne Evelegh: pp. 49, n. 2, 158, n. 1, etc. The name is from William Habington's volume of poems *Castara*, first published in 1634.

[4] Presumably Elinor Parry.

[5] Henry, duke of Gloucester, Charles II's youngest brother; born in 1639; died on 13 September of this year: *D.N.B.* The book is *Epicedia Academiæ Oxoniensis*, etc.: Madan, no. 2467.

[6] *Reasons shewing the Necessity of Reformation of the Publick Doctrine, Worship . . . Church-government, and Discipline*, by 'divers Ministers' and edited by Dr. Cornelius Burges (p. 183, n. 2), was published about 3 August of this year. Dr. John Pearson (p. 193, n. 6) answered it in *No Necessity of Reformation*, published about 20 August. Burges replied; and Pearson responded in *An Answer to Dr. Burges*, published about 20 September. By Pearson's 'reply' Towerson apparently means the *Answer*.

a small thing but will I beleive give you as much content as his former papers did, if not for the contents of it yet for the assurance he there gives of a sudden and just reply to all theire exceptions against the doctrine, discipline, and ceremonies of the church of England. I have lent out my owne, or else you should have had it now.

Address: For his much respected freind Mr. Joh: Lock Jun: at Pensford Leave this at Mr. Tho: Days in St. Tho: street Bristoll

## *105.* WILLIAM UVEDALE to LOCKE, [*c.* 30 October 1660?] (*85*, 158)

B.L., MS. Locke c. 22, ff. 175–6. Nos. *105* and *106* are both addressed to 'Mr. John Lock Jun. at Pensford'. This implies a date before February 1661, when Locke's father died; and, as there is nothing to show that Locke was aquainted with either Uvedale or Towerson before 1659, favours August–December 1659 or September–November 1660. The Law of Nature, mentioned in both letters, suggests 1660 in preference to 1659: no. *104* n.

In no. *105* Uvedale has recently returned to Oxford. In 1659 he returned to Oxford about 7 September: no. *73*; he left later, visited Locke at Pensford, and was in Hampshire about 19 November: no. *85*; he could have returned to Oxford between September and November, but there is no indication that he did so. In 1660 he was expected to return within a week of 23 October: no. *104*; hence the date to which this letter is attributed.

Uvedale's father made his will on 22 August 1660; it was proved on 12 July 1661: *Surrey Archæol. Coll.* iii (1865), 123–4.

Mr. Lock.

I doe not intend to trouble you with any discourse of the Law of[a] nature, or (what is more proper for me) a dispute about the motion of the Diaphragme;[1] my designe att present is meerly to acquaint you with my Returne to oxford and to let you see how readily I embraced those conditions you proposed mee in your Letter; I would send up a wish or two that you might not stay long behind, but that I know tis as impossible to recall you from Pensford yet, as tis to raise a dead man from his Grave; I meane unlesse Scribelia thinke fit to exercise her Power, and worke miracles; I make noe Question but shee hath charmes more powerfull over you, then the

[a] *Followed by* the *deleted.*

[1] To move the diaphragm is to excite laughter: *O.E.D.*, with quotation dated 1629.

Influence of that starr[1] wherewith you threaten mee; And therefore I shall take the boldnesse to conjure for once in her name, which I am confident has soe much of the chaine in it as to pull you back sooner then you intended, if not to draw you back presently; But whensoever you returne, you will be doubly welcome, I mean to the now melancholly Lady (who deserves that name as well as her Knight[a2] did once) and your very affect. Friend.

W. U.

Address: For his much Respected Friend Mr. John Lock Jun. att Pensford. To be left at Mr. Thomas Day's in St. Thomas Streete, Bristoll.

## *106.* GABRIEL TOWERSON to LOCKE, [*c.* 3 November 1660?] (*104*, 108)

B.L., MS. Locke c. 22, ff. 3–4. Printed in von Leyden, introd., pp. 8–9. The letter evidently belongs shortly before 5 November, the year not stated. The reasons for attributing it to 1659 or 1660 are given in no. *105* n. The size to which Towerson's and Locke's controversy on the Law of Nature has grown, and Towerson's interest in a forthcoming 5 November sermon, indicate that no. *106* is a sequel to no. *104*; hence the date given to it here.

Mr. Lock,

The papers that have past between us being now growne so voluminous that I conceive it more difficult to informe our selves of the state of the controversie between us, than to refell what either of us hath said;[3] I shall crave leave for my owne ease and because I would willingly be Mr. Ailmer's Auditor this 5th. of November[4] to respite my answer till the next week, in the which intervall I intend (God willing) to peruse all that hath past between us upon this head, and then on mine owne part to put a period to this controversie, if I find you inclinable therto. Which I no way doubt but you will be, if you consider but these two things which I have now to propose to you. 1. Whether (it being agreed upon

[a] *MS.* K[t]

[1] Presumably the Ca-star-a of p. 156; as she is someone other than Scribelia (Elinor Parry?) probably Anne Evelegh.

[2] Probably Locke; he wrote about his melancholy to P E in letters datable September and October 1659: nos. 72, 74, 79, 80; but perhaps John Ailmer: no. *104* n.

[3] No papers relating to the controversy survive in the Lovelace collection.

[4] John Ailmer (or Aylmer), d. 1672; matriculated from New College 1650; fellow 1652; B.C.L. 1656; D.C.L. 1662: Foster. He was a friend of Robert Sharrock (p. 155 n.), writing a preliminary epistle for Ὑπόθεσις ἠθική.

between us that there is such a thing as a law of nature and one of those arguments which I produc'd for it admitted without any scruple) it were not much more for our advantage to proceed in our enquiry touching the law of nature, then to contend any longer about a second argument 2. I would willingly know of you whether you thinke the being of the law of nature can be evinc'd from the force of conscience in those men who have no other divine law to square theire actions by.[1] If you doe (as for my owne part I doe because I thinke it to be St. Pauls owne argument)[2] I shall then thinke it incumbent upon you, who have engag'd in the same designe with your servant, to answer in short your owne objections. If not, I shall despaire of perswading you, if what I have already said and shall in my next (which will I beleive be all that I can say for it) be not of force so to doe. Sir I am

Your most affectionate freind and servant

G: TOWERSON

Address: For his most respected freind Mr. John Lock Jun. at Pensford Leave this at Mr. Thomas Day's in St. Thomas street Bristoll

## *107.* JOHN STRACHEY to LOCKE, 22 November 1660 (*103*, *117*)

B.L., MS. Locke c. 18, ff. 197–8.

Sir

The litle time I have to write in will only give mee leave to acquaint you that I have received your books and letter, for which I am highly oblidgd to you and could wish my thankes could proportionate those greate pleasures Mounseir Belgerac hath given mee in the reading his book,[3] I have made some inspection into the other two and if they entertaine mee with an equall delight (as hitherto they have) I shall beleive it a better returne of my monie, then any Usurer had of his. Pray afford mee as often as you can the consolation of your letters in this my melancholick retirement and if you meete not with an exact correspondence pray

[1] On these two considerations see von Leyden, introd., p. 83, and Locke, *Essays*, pp. 116/17.

[2] Apparently Romans 2: 14–15. Towerson answers his question in the affirmative in *An Explication of the Decalogue*, 1676, pp. 2–3.

[3] Presumably an English translation from Savinien de Cyrano de Bergerac, either *Satyrical Characters*, etc., 1658 (L.L., no. 279), or, more probably, *Selenarchia, or the Government of the World in the Moon*, 1659.

impute it not either to my negligence or unfreindlinesse, for ile assure you nothinge but the want of meanes can hinder mee from lettinge you know that I am

your very humble Servant
JO: STRACHEY

Nov. 22. 60.

My Mother[1] and Sister[2] remember to you.

Address: For mr John Locke of Christ Church these. Oxon.

## 108. LOCKE to [GABRIEL TOWERSON?], 11 December 1660 (*106*, *115*)

B.L., MS. Locke e. 7, ff. 35–6. Printed in Locke, *Scritti editi e inediti sulla Tolleranza*, ed. C. A. Viano, 1961, pp. 60–1; *Two Tracts on Government*, ed. Abrams, pp. 174–5. MS. Locke e. 7 is a paper book containing Locke's treatise, 'Quest: whether the Civill Magistrate may lawfully impose and determine the use of indifferent things in reference to Religious Worship'; for it see p. 167, n. 3 *ad fin.* The letter, which is appended to the treatise, was struck out, presumably when Locke composed a preface for the treatise. The existence of the treatise was known to Towerson by 12 March 1661 (p. 167), and the letter was almost certainly intended for him. The letter is not printed here, as it will be included among the writings on Toleration.

Viano gives the place from which the letter is dated as Christ Church, which is wrong; Abrams as Pensford. I believe it to be Oxford.

## *109*. GEORGE PERCIVALL to LOCKE, 19 December 1660. (*102*, *126*)

B.L., MS. Locke c. 17, f. 61.

Sir

Since I came out of the country I have received two of yours, and I thinke my selfe very happy that you will so far obleige me as

[1] Elizabeth, d. 1672(?), daughter of William Crosse of Blackmore Farm in Charlinch, Somerset. She married first Samuel Jepp, by whom she had a son Samuel, who died *c.* 1659–60 (p. 168 n.); secondly John Strachey, by whom she was the mother of Locke's friend the younger John Strachey (he was born about 1634); thirdly Edward Baber, *c.* 1585–1645. She bought Sutton Court for her son Samuel Jepp; as he died without male issue she settled it on John Strachey: Wood, *Chew Magna*, pp. 138, 146–8 (unreliable); *Virginia Magazine of History and Biography*, lix (1951), 275–96.

[2] Strachey's only known sister is Mrs. Elizabeth Jepp, the widow of his half-brother: p. 168 n. She calls him her brother in no. *125*.

to let me know how it is with your selfe, and the rest of our good freinds at Oxford. and I should thinke my selfe very ungratefull should I omit my acknowledgment and thanks unto you for your looking after my concerns there, and though I thinke I shall make no more use of my place,[1] yet I am very glad to see my freinds so carefull of my interest there, especially since it is my desire, and shall be my endeavor to enjoy you there againe, though my freinds here are very unwilling to hearken to such a motion. but however I desire you not to divulge any thinge concerning my abiding here, for since it is not yet fully resolved on, and my freinds I know will not detaine me here to my disadvantage, I would not resigne my place; and I doubt not but next terme (if the Courts here be then up) I shall be able to resolve you. my mother has made me totally to renounce the study of physick, and I think I must now have an eye towards the law, for I have an unkle's life in the clarkes office of the king's bench and another in the registers office of the court of wards (which will here certainly be up)[2] and if I can but procure law enough to execute the one, and a deputy for the other. I shall not repent my continuing here. Ireland affords no news, and therfore I hope you will expect none, here is plenty of all things but money. and the colledge here[3] has as much mutton for three halfepence as christch. can afford for sixpence. I was at kingsale not long since, where a poore marchant, had a great losse in his muttons, for driving his sheepe to the seaside over a rock that inclined towards the sea, one chanct to fall in, and all the rest, as sheepe use to doe, followd there leader and lept in, so that I thinke three hundred were drownded. thes and like misschances makes your commons so little, for twenty thousand sheepe a yeare are reckond to goe from one port to England, and ten thousand head of cattle, but fourteen Vessels of them were cast away a month since togather. at the same place was a vessell cast away coming to Ireland with spice and nutmegs, and it being neere the harbour, some Irish found some of the nutmegs, and went to crack them,

[1] At Christ Church: pp. 153–4.

[2] Percivall's uncles are his mother's brother Sir William Ussher the younger, clerk of the King's Bench, Ireland, and brother-in-law Sir Paul Davis, secretary of state and clerk of the council, Ireland, 1661–*c.* 1672: Wright, *Ussher Memoirs*, pp. 139–41; Anderson, *House of Yvery*, ii. 314; *Cal. S.P., Ireland*, 1660–2, p. 525. By 'an uncle's life' Percivall apparently means the tenure of an office during his uncle's lifetime; Davis held the office of clerk and register of the Irish Court of Wards in trust for Sir Philip Perceval, George Percivall's father: H.M.C., *Egmont MSS.* ii. 16. The court was abolished by the Irish parliament in 1662.

[3] Trinity College, Dublin.

but thay prayed for a thousand of st patricks curses to fall upon the merchant for bringing nuts without kirnells in them. if such kind of news doe affect you I could write diurnalls of them. but I will not divert your thoughts too long from better employment, therfore I shall with my service to you conclude this present trouble and rest

Your assured freind and servant
GEO: PERCIVALL.

Dublin. Dec: 19. 60.

My service to all my freinds at Oxford, in particular to dick lower, and tell him next post I will trouble him with a letter, and if white frize would serve instead of good linnen for surplesses, I would send you both some, and if gray did please you, you shall not want it. pray let me know if Ald. lock of Bristoll[1] be akind to you. I could send some to him, and Usquebah too, and the carrier from Bristoll to Oxford could convey it to you.

Address: For mr John Lock st of ch-ch. Thes.

## 110. LOCKE to JOHN LOCKE, sen., 20 December [1660?] (95)

B.L., MS. Locke c. 24, f. 179. Printed in King, pp. 2–3. Year from general contents and Locke's note 'last'.

20° Dec:

Most deare and ever loveing Father

I did not doubt but that the noise of a very dangerous sicknesse here[2] would reach you, but I am alarmd with a more dangerous desease from Pensford and were I as secure of your health as (I thanke god) I am of my owne, I should not thinke my self in much danger, but I cannot be safe soe long as I heare of your weakenesse, and the increase of your malady upon you, which I begge that you would by the timely application of remedys indeavour to remoove, Dr Meara hath more then once putt a stop to its incroachments. the same skill, the same means, and the same god to blesse them is

[1] John Locke, d. 1666; son of Richard Locke of Bedminster; merchant; alderman of Bristol 1640–56, 1660–6; mayor 1641–2: *The Deposition Books of Bristol*, vol. i, ed. H. E. Nott (Bristol Record Soc., vol. vi, 1935), pp. 251–2. Locke's father called him 'my cousin', presumably meaning first cousin or first cousin once removed: Fox Bourne, i. 10 n. He was perhaps father or uncle of Samuel Locke (no. *2598*, etc.).

[2] Wood, *L. and T.* i. 347, 349, 350.

left still, doe not I beseech you by that care you ought to have of your self, by that tendernesse I'm sure you have of us, neglect your owne and our safety too. doe not by a too pressing a care for your children endanger the only comfort they have left. I cannot distrust that providence which hath conducted me thus far. and if either your disapointments or Necessitys shall reduce us to narrower conditions then you could wish, content shall enlarge[a] it, therefor lett not those thoughts deject you, there is noe thing that I have which can be soe well imployd as to his use from whome I first receivd it, and if your convenience can leave me noething else, I shall have a head, and hands and Industry still left me, which alone have beene able to raise sufficient fortunes. Pray Sir therefor make your life as comfortable and lasting as you can, lett not any consideration of us cast you into the least despondency, if I have any refletions on or desires of[b] a free and competent subsistence, it is more in reference to another (whome you may guesse) to whome I am very much obleigd,[1] then for my self, but noe thoughts how importunate soever shall make me forgett my duty, and a father is more then all other relations and the greatest satisfaction I can propose to my self in this world[c] is my hopes that you may yet live to receive the returne of some comfort for all that care and Indulgence you have placd on

Sir

your most obedient sonne

J L:

Address: These present To my Father Mr John Locke at Pensford.

Marked by Locke at head of letter: last

## *111.* DR. EDMUND MEARA to LOCKE, 2 January 1661

B.L., MS. Locke c. 16, ff. 82–3. Edmund Meara, d. 1680; M.D., Rheims, 1636; F.R.C.P. 1664: *D.N.B.*; Childrey, *Britannia Baconica*, pp. 37 *bis*–41.

Bristoll 25 Jan. 1660

Sir

I am still of opinion that Capt: Locke hath the regions of the Liver and mesentery so much out of order that there are little

[a] *Followed by* mine*? del.* [b] *Followed by* an es- *del.* [c] *Altered from* life

[1] The meaning is not clear. Probably Locke's father; the only apparent alternatives are Alexander Popham and Elinor Parry.

hopes of repayreing them, and can scarce resolve on sending any thing to him as well because of his aversion from all things as because I allmost despayre of successe: if you please to cause Gellyes of hartshorne and Ivery to bee made for him with agrimony, liverwort, harts tongue, maidenhayre, raisins, red rose budds, anise seeds, and veale or pullett it will be convenient nourishment for him; and if it can have the effect as to strengthen nature and make him capable of further meanes I shall upon notice make use of the occasion and endevour further to serve him: in the meane tyme I have sent you Sanctorius[1] and shall in what else may lye in my power willingly expresse how much I am

Sir

Your true friend and servant

EDM. MEARA

Address: For mr John Locke these at Pensford

## 112. LOCKE to P E [Elinor Parry, later Mrs. Hawkshaw?], 4 January 1661 (89, 119)

B.L., MS. Locke c. 24, f. 206. Draft.

P E.

4° Jan 60

Sir

What heavinesse soever lyes upon my thoughts they will not be hindered from getting sometimes to Oxford and whilst I attend[a] wholy[a] on the health of my freinds me thinks tis[b–] not besides[–b] my businesse to enquire after yours and sicknesse in my freinds hath made its self soe terrible to me that I feare it every where, could my thought convey Itellegence betweene Oxford and this as easy and as often as they move thither I should need noe other carrier, for all those few minutes of time they can get from a sader imployment are spent with you and I have as much of your com-

[a] *Interlined as alternative to* am intent only [b–b] *Interlined as alternative to* it is part of

[1] Santorio Santorio (Sanctorius), (1561–1636; *Enciclopedia italiana*), *De Statica Medicina*, Venice, 1614; new editions 1624, 1634, 1657, etc. Locke possessed a copy of The Hague edition of 1657: L.L., no. 2546.

pany as melancholy will permit and phansy can help me to. This indeed may seeme but a thin and aery refreshment, compard with those reall injoyments your presenc affords, which are soe rich and pleasing that their very memory is not without some satisfaction, and like the sun your influence reaches[a] and comforts those who are out of your sight ⟨and⟩[b] condemnd to darkenesse. those that have once injoyd your conversation, may reape advantages from it as often as they will but make use of their memory and your company ceases not to obleige those whom you see not nor thinke not on. and though I know not what miracles you can work on others this I am sure the Ideas I have of you serve me as the pictures and shadows of the saint[c] did of old if not to cure at least to alleaviate and ease my distempers as often as I reflect on them but Sir these Lucid and serener intervalls are scarce long enough to write a letter in and sadnesse which hath now but too just a ⟨title⟩[d] to my thoughts ⟨grudges⟩[e] you a long and quiet possession of them, and will not take it well to be excluded by a wellcomer guest. but yet what ever melancorly may dwell in them be assurd they will always be such as you may expect from one that is

At foot of page: What

## 113. LOCKE to DR. AYLIFFE IVIE, 8 January [1661?] (97)

B.L., MS. Locke c. 24, ff. 58–9. Fair copy with address, but no trace of seal; perhaps the letter completed but not dispatched. Year from contents.

Sir

The painefull increase of my fathers weakenesse with the addition of a feavourish distemper last night hath by my perswasions made him not only willing but desireous to see you here this morning. your own eys and enquiry may possibly give you better discoverys of his disease and condition then my descriptions could. I the more earnestly begge this trouble of you, not only because I hope it may be more conduceing to my fathers recovery, but also that when you are in an other place then Bristoll I may finde you of another minde, and you will not in all places put me to the shame

[a] *Doubtful reading.* [b] *Deleted in MS.* [c] *MS.* s[t] [d] *MS.* tile
[e] *MS.* grudes?

of receiveing favours from you, without admitting any offers of returne from the acknowledgment of

Sir

Your most obleiged servant

JO: LOCKE

Pensford 8° Jan

Pray present my humble service to Mrs Ivie

Address: These present To his honoured freind Dr Ivie at Brislington
On another fold: This for Dr Ivie

## *114.* ROBERT CROSSE to LOCKE, 19 February 1661

B.L., MS. Locke c. 7, f. 186. Robert Crosse, *c.* 1605–83; M.A.; B.D.; member of the Westminster Assembly of Divines 1643; vicar of Chew Magna 1653–83; controversialist, etc.: *D.N.B.*

Mr John Locke

Your Paul's-Churchyard[1] I cannot get from the Lady to whom I lent it in the West, but am willing to pay yow for it what yow payd for it, or what yow shall in reason give for another of that kind. that soe I may have Procopius[2] return'd unto me. I lent your Father. Anth: Cade of Justification etc.[3] and two bookes more your Father had of mine from mr Crreentvile[4] to whom I had lent them. And they were a Pamplet touching the Mortality of the soule; and an ingenuous answre by an unknowne hand of that Wild Pamplett.[5] Your Father also had from me a booke of Poems in a large octavo, which I had borrowed of Mr James Longman, but by Mr Longmans leave did lend it to your Father; it is a Miscellany of Poems. and at the latter end, or neer it, there is a song in Commendation of Ale, made (as I have heard) by the great Bishop

[1] Sir John Birkenhead (*D.N.B.*), *Paul's Churchyard: libri theologici, politici, historici, nundinis Paulinis–una cum Templo–prostant venales*, or the enlarged edition, *Two Centuries*, etc., 1653. They are catalogues of imaginary books, the titles satirizing contemporary events, etc. Locke owned a copy apparently of the first edition: L.L., no. 2238.

[2] Probably *The History of the Warres of the Emperour Justinian*, translated by Sir Henry Holcroft, 1653.

[3] Anthony Cade, *A Justification of the Church of England*, 1630.

[4] Grenfeild: p. 24 n.

[5] The pamphlet is *Mans Mortallitie*, 1643, by Richard Overton (*D.N.B.*), or the enlarged edition, *Man Wholly Mortal*, 1655. The answer is probably *The Prerogative of Man*, Oxford, 1645: Madan, nos. 1852–3; it was still in print in 1653: ibid. iii. 396.

of Winchister in his younger days.[1] if yow please to returne these bookes unto me; or the last to Mr Longman whose it is, yow shall doe that which is righteous. if yow send me the price yow putt on that booke which is lost, it shall be payd before[a–] I see[–a] Procopius in my keeping. I have not else to adde, but that I am heartily sorry for the death of your Father[2] and am

Your loving Freind[b]
ROBERT CROSSE

Chue: Feb: 19: 1660

Your Brother Thomas had a peice of Poetry also, which is not returned to me.

Address: For Mr John Locke at Pensford.

## *115.* GABRIEL TOWERSON to LOCKE, 12 March 1661 (108, *118*)

B.L., MS. Locke c. 22, ff. 5–6.

Mr. Lock,

You had heard from me before this had I not had some occasions to goe to London and some avocations since I return'd hither; but this it may be comes time enough because it is like to bring some trouble with it. I heare Mr. Bagshaws booke is so well lik'd of as that it is probable it may passe a second impression; and you may perhaps doe God and the church a peice of seasonable service if you would be pleas'd to print your answer to it.[3] I know not

[a–a] *MS.* before I i see? [b] *Doubtful reading.*

---

[1] The book is perhaps *Sportive Wit: The Muses Merriment*, a collection made by John Phillips, 1656; it is, however, a duodecimo. At pp. 118–19, near the end of the second pagination, there is 'A Song in Praise of Ale', eight stanzas varied or adapted from *The Ex-Ale-tation of Ale*, 1646. Alternatively the book may be *The Academy of Complements*, a collection by John Gough; the edition of 1650, which is also a duodecimo, contains at pp. 241–2 'A Song in Praise of Ale', completely different from the preceding poem, and far superior to it. The great bishop is Lancelot Andrewes (bishop 1619–26; *D.N.B.*), who is unlikely to have had anything to do with any of the poems. *The Ex-Ale-tation* is sometimes attributed to Peter Mews, bishop of Winchester 1684–1706 (no. *532*), but that was hearsay.

[2] The elder Locke died on 7 February and was buried on the 13th: B.L., MS. Locke c. 25, f. 6; Fox Bourne, i. 81.

[3] The book is *The Great Question concerning Things Indifferent in Religious Worship*, by Edward Bagshaw, jun., a student of Christ Church (*D.N.B.*). It was published

whether this may be a fit season to represent this to you,[1] but sure I am I could not satisfie my selfe till I had acquainted you with my request. Uvedale hath lately had a very great fortune fallen to him by the death of a Cosen German and that hath bin the cause he hath so long absented himselfe from the University.[2] All our freinds at Mr. Prats[3] are well and some of them have check'd me for not writing to you before this, and that it may be is one reason why I chuse rather to take a pipe of tobacco at home, though that you know is a convenient place. Sir I am

Your most affectionate freind and servant
G. TOWERSON

Oxon. March: 12. 1660.

## *116.* MRS. ELIZABETH JEPP to LOCKE, 2 April 1661 (*125*)

B.L., MS. Locke c. 12, ff. 15–16. The writer was Elizabeth, daughter of Francis Buckland of West Harptree, 6 miles SW. of Pensford, and widow of Strachey's half-brother Samuel Jepp, who died about 1659–60. It was apparently through Jepp that she was related to Locke. Her daughter Mary married Locke's future friend Edward Clarke of Chipley: Wood, *Chew Magna*, pp. 138, etc.

Nobell Cosen

That which occasined these Impolished Lines wase my promis and the engagment you ware pleased to Impose upon me and tharefore I hope you will not Imput it to a confidnc unbeseeing me I wold mack sum excuse for the raged broken paper which came latly to your hands but I am confident of your good nature and that

about September 1660: B.M., *Catalogue of the . . . (Thomason Tracts)*, ii. 338; and there is a 'third' edition dated 1660. Locke's answer was 'Quest⟨ion⟩: whether the Civill Magistrate . . .' which was completed by 11 December: p. 160 n. He wrote a preface for it after the opening of the new parliament on 8 May: allusion in the preface; *Two Tracts*, ed. Abrams, p. 119. See further nos. *123*, *127*.

[1] Presumably referring to the elder Locke's death.

[2] A cousin german is a first cousin: *O.E.D.*

[3] Probably Richard Pratt, one of the Oxford city bailiffs 1662–90; mace-bearer and chief serjeant 1673–85; probably living on the north side of the High Street near Carfax; *Oxford Council Acts, 1626–65, 1665–1701* (Oxford Hist. Soc., vol. xcv, 1933: new ser., vol. ii, 1939); *Surveys and Tokens*, ed. H. E. Salter (Oxford Hist. Soc., vol. lxxv, 1923), pp. 186, 223.

you think the best of your freinds of which noumber I desier to be accounted for assuredly you have

A Loving cosen in
ELIZABETH JEPP.

Ap: th 2: 61:

Address: these To Mr John Locke present At pensford

## *117.* JOHN STRACHEY to LOCKE, 2 April 1661 (*107, 125*)

B.L., MS. Locke c. 18, ff. 202–3.

Sir

You have beene soe used to bestow pardons and I to deserve them that to fayle on either side would bee equally strange; I must confesse you act the more noble part, but lett mee advise you to lay it aside when you come to that greatenesse to which fortune when it sides with vertue must needes bringe you, for too greate a clemency emboldens delinquents, who, when they find noe punishment, are never wanting to committ such actions as are worthy of it. To make this seasonable, I must desire you to call to mind a former letter, wherein you playde the Pope and dispenct a pardon for all offences past, present, and to come, the feare you should repent of soe greate a goodnesse hath made mee keepe it till a time of neede, which like a cunninge Lawyer I am able to produce whenever I am impleaded. This I thought good in short to acquaint you with, without troubling myselfe to make longe excuses for those faults you lay against mee, you know how sparinge our profession is of words when they bringe noe profitt, and wee seldome write soe much as our names if an Angell doth not guide our hands.[1] A pretty reservd and proud generation indeede wee are (for I begin now to number myselfe amonge them and you will wonder when you see mee next what a greate alteration the litle time I have beene from you hath made in mee, I have putt on a severe countenance, clad myselfe in the robes of gravity, seldome speake without weighing my words in a balance, begin to love mony dearely, and would never by my good will open my hand, but I would have it soe stuft with gold, that I should hardly bee able to shut it againe. I dont speake this to enhaunce the price of these

[1] The angel was a gold coin. So far as is known it was coined last in 1634: B.M., *Handbook of the Coins of Great Britain and Ireland*, 1899, p. 107.

lines, you are my freind, and therefore for this time Ile have noe Fee, but if ever I come to bawle at the Barr, I will drop my words as you doe your silver, yett all that I have hitherto gott by the profession is that it hath afforded matter for this letter, otherwise I should in fewer words have told but ⟨more⟩[a] seriously then all the rest, that I am

Sir

your very loving freind and servant.

J. STRACHEY

Aprill 2th. 61.

Address: For Mr John Locke at his Father's house in Pensford these. Leave this with Mr Day Soapeboyler in High-streete in Bristoll

## *118.* GABRIEL TOWERSON to LOCKE, 9 April 1661 (*115*)

B.L., MS. Locke c. 22, ff. 7–8.

All-Soules. Apr. 9. 1661.

Mr. Lock

Immediately upon the receit of yours of the 15. March I sent to Robinsons the Bookseller[1] to forbid him to send you Highmore[2] but I found it was too late for he had the week before delivered it to the Carrier. And of this you had bin long since certified had not the Carrier fail'd of coming; for I had written an answer and dispatch'd it to the Inne he is wont to lodge at. This day fortnight your freind Mr. B.[3] preach'd at St. Maries and in the close of his sermon insisted upon his old theme, and though he prayed for Archbishops and Bishops yet he tooke away theire power and made it a marke of AntiChrist to impose ceremonies. He had a fling or two at Tho: Peirce[4] for so all interpreted it but I suppose he is not much troubled at it though all the church look'd upon him. for he only said and that too ἐν παρόδῳ[5] where it might very well have

[a] *Word omitted by the writer.*

---

[1] Thomas Robinson, active 1638–63: Madan, ii. 514.

[2] Dr. Nathaniel Highmore (*D.N.B.*), *Exercitationes Duae . . . De passione hysterica . . . De affectione hypochondriaca*, 1660 (about September). Madan, no. 2499; L.L., no. 1451[b].

[3] Identifiable as Edward Bagshaw the younger: p. 167, n. 3.

[4] Thomas Pierce or Peirse, 1622–91; D.D. 1660; President of Magdalen November 1661–72; dean of Salisbury 1675: *D.N.B.* For his dispute with Bagshaw see Wood, *Athenæ*, iii. 946–7; Madan, no. 2433 n.

[5] 'In passing'.

bin spar'd could he have but supprest his anger, that the elect could not fall from grace let Devils doe and men say what they would. You cannot imagine how much Dean Harry[1] was gratified, for he laught upon Dr. W.[2] after his dull manner and could not hold from inviting your freind to dinner, but he was not so vaine as to accept of it, or please himselfe much with so ungratefull an applause. This I thought good to informe you of partly that I might not want matter for a letter and partly too that you might know there may be some necessity that your papers should see the light. All yours are well I meane your freinds and would be very glad to enjoy your company here, but none more than your freind and servant

G: TOWERSON

The letter you mention in your last never came to my hands; if it had you may be confident I would not have bin so backward in returning an answer as to deserve a chiding.

Address: For his much respected freind Mr. John Lock Leave this at Mr. Tho: Dayes in St Thomas street Bristoll

## 119. LOCKE to P E [Elinor Parry, later Mrs. Hawkshaw?], 13 April [1661?] (112, 120)

B.L., MS. Locke c. 24, f. 207. Draft. Elinor Parry appears to have gone to London while Locke was 50 miles away from Oxford. He was probably at Pensford about 9 April: no. *118*; and she apparently in London on 23 April: no. 120; she had presumably gone there some days before. No other year in which Locke's movements are known fits so well as 1661. Locke apparently writes from Oxford.

P E

Apr. 13

I expect a kindenesse and behold a quarrell, I am accusd because I have donne as much as human indeavours could reache, I am chid because I am not inspird with the gift of prophesye and neither the heavens nor you afforded me means to perceive your motion at 50 miles distance[3] and tis ill nature in me which in any

[1] Henry Wilkinson, 1616–90; Presbyterian divine; B.D. 1648; principal of Magdalen Hall from 1648 until his ejection in 1662; called 'Dean Harry' to distinguish him from another Henry Wilkinson, canon of Christ Church ('Long Harry'): *D.N.B.*

[2] I have failed to identify him.

[3] The conventional distance between Oxford and Pensford: nos. 12, 72, etc.

other would be reason to looke for ⟨any thing⟩[a] in the same place it was left in, this I must confesse is a cunning I will not say how kinde a[b] way[b] of acquitting your self by casting guilt on another and I must be content to be faulty because you were silent but this is not all you tell me you intended me some thing of mirth in your letter but with hold it from me only because I am sad, and I must not expect from you any[c–] diversions or remedys[–c] of my melancholy till it be first gonne, this is ⟨as⟩[d] commendable a charity as his who denys a cordiall because his patient faints and will not administer physick till the diseas be remoovd, your letter that I thought should have brought the performance of your word tells me I must not expect it and you adjorne your promise to a day which you doubt whether ever it will come or noe? and you forbid me the hopes of any satisfaction from your letters untill I shall have noe need at all of them and your company againe shall render them uselesse. this usage I receive from an unexpeted hand which[e] I yet kisse whilst it is strikeing me and I cannot but wish all happinesse to that person which detaines frome me a designed comfort in my greatest need of it and at a time when If Freindship had beene silent Pitty would have pleaded for more tendernesse. But yet I know[f] not[f] why you should put my Freindship always upon such hard exercise and[g–] should suffer me to receive noe other advantage from your promise but an unsatisfied expectation.[–g] would you be thought the same in L you were at Ox:[1] and yet deny me that there which you offerd here.

however I will beleeve as long as I can that your thoughts are better then your letter and that your wishes obleige me as much as your words disapoint me, I have hitherto with all the strenght I have supported my spirit against dispondencys and perswaded my self that these are but ⟨the⟩[h] artefices of your kindenesse. but I cannot promise you that my confidence shall always be able to bear up against such contrary appearances and If in your next you thinke me not worthy to receive the effect of your promise, I shall see how willing you are to give me up to the persecution of my owne sad thoughts, and leave me to the mercy of those suspitions which in a minde disposd to melancholy will be ready enough to

[a] *Deleted in MS.* [b] *MS.* away [c–c] *MS. originally* any cures or diversions; *the word* cures *was deleted and* remedys *was interlined after* diversions [d] *MS.* a [e] *MS.* which which [f] *Doubtful reading.* [g–g] *Inserted in margin.* [h] *MS.* te

[1] London, Oxford.

tell me that you intended only to make your self some sport with an afflicted person, that she that is most just and generous to all the world besides can faile her word when I am concernd int and that my reall freindship deserves noething in exchang but railery. though[a]– I might well desire to know what you claime that soe I might have the greater care and esteeme of it in my self and cherish that which you are willing to owne–[a] and though the occasions of mirth could not but be welcome to me from any one espetial⟨ly⟩[b] from you yet I might perhaps with patience digest the delay of this satisfaction but S[c][1] to feel your good intentions in any thing whether merry or serious slacken towards me, to find it possible that your promises should be lesse certaine to me then others performances is a change in our acquaintance which neither you nor I can allow till either you can beleeve that I am not or I can cease to be what I shall be forever.

Madam[d]

## 120. Locke to P E [Elinor Parry, later Mrs. Hawkshaw?], [*c.* 25 April 1661?] (119, *121*)

B.L., MS. Locke c. 24, f. 214. Draft. Date from the coronation. Apparently answered by no. *121*.

P E

Did you require my obedience to the next letter you should write with an intention to write noe more, and did I not in my last appeare to you under a sufficient pressure of sadnesse unlesse you also made an heavy addition by the disapointment of an heithened expectation as if you had purposd only to shew me something which you knew could not but be pleaseing to me with a designe the more cruelly to rob me of it? these are suggestions apt enough to rise in a spirit discomposd with melancholy, but yet my thoughts how much soe ever my persecutors have not beene able to draw me to this suspition, and I will distrust all things before I will beleeve that soe good soe perfect and soe obleigeing a freind would take soe much paines only to mock me, and I know you too generous to trample on one already dejected by soe heavy a stroke of providence. Yet Sir you cannot but imagine some

a–a *Inserted in margin.* b *Page cut.* c *Substituted for* M d *MS.* M[d]

1 Sir substituted for Madam.

part of those thoughts which must needs attend soe unexpected a silence till at my arivall here I found some excuse in your journy, though that plea would scarce gaurd you from my just complaints would I allow my self the liberty of quarrelling with you. But I defend you against all my querulous thoughts and I have been soe always wont to receive favours from you that I am willing to perswade my self that there is a kindenesse in all your actions. I tell my self therefor that the various entertainments of London, the injoyment of freinds and the glorious splendour of a Coronation[1] might easily divert your thoughts from a melancholy object and mak you for a while suspend that claime which you were sure would be good at any time, and[a] when I reade againe those words in your letter in the next you shall know what I lay claime to that you may be just, guesse not but promise what soever it be methinks I perceive a designe of sharpening my desires by some little delay that you might with the greater pleasure satisfy them. I once more tell you that I obey your commands perfectly. I promise without guessing, and doe not allow my thoughts to be busie beyond your commission, but give you leave to supprise me with my happinesse. this you may be sure of I shall always be just to you, you know very well when you requird me to be just that you demanded all I could promise you, for you have long since taken from me all the means of gratitude and courtesy. all that I can doe is confinde barely to justice, and when I grant what ever you can lay claime to I at once engage my whole stock. since you made your self a title to all within my power when firs you made me

On reverse: [a draft written in pencil of the opening passage of the present draft].

## *121.* [ELINOR PARRY, later Mrs. Hawkshaw?] to LOCKE, [30 April 1661?] (120, 122)

B.L., MS. Locke c. 23, f. 181. The writer appears from the handwriting to be Scribelia, here identified as Elinor Parry. The letter apparently answers no. 120; it is answered by no. 122. If the dates here assigned to them are correct the available Tuesdays are 30 April and 7 May. The square brackets are the writer's.

a tusday—5 a clock

Have you [Mr Locke] changed that nature which was thought Excellent ⟨by⟩[b] my self, and can you accuse Innocence itself that

[a] *Followed by* methinks *deleted.* [b] *MS.* my

[1] Of Charles II on 23 April 1661.

is not faulty: tis well since Silenc must be Chid that I am att this distance and that your angry vaine hath a pritty Journie to take before it apeares and then tis Obligeing: Is it possible that my silenc moves your notice, or is my Letter a Happy-ness when I thinke it none: you may be perswaded easeily to be of my mind, and confess with-all it enricheth you not, I am the poorer for tis not in the power of London's gallantry or pleasures you name'd that can furnish me with expressions fitt for a Letter, especally for you: neither can the complement [*of your servant Sir*] be wellcom to you that is better stor'd: yett no other must be expected if I continew Longer Heir: for Ile tell you, the Liveliness of that witt[a]– I Gathered–[a] from you and others wants renewing: my Pen that was ready in obaying formerly is now grown dull as its [*mistress*] and if it could would complaine for want of excersise. this is I thinke a suficent excuse: beleeve it since I have none other, as also that I have *Goodness*: and Charitie for those that needs it, but my memory is convinct freinds want it not, neither is any ones Life conserned did pleasure and forgettfullness take full posesion: [*now I see*] your complement is much stronger then myne, if my wish were so, it would be rather with the Parent[1] then in C: Ch:[2] for I doubt its wellcom: but not mine, but truely I am Ignorant when it will be; not with my Brother,[3] so that whatsoever you win I cleame Half. Lett me know Pray what your wagers are: and Least you should be discourgged I tell you I shall not come yett: for I am not so weary of London as I am with writeing: A strange Change.

adew

Address: these For His Respected freind mr John Locke att Ch–Ch– in Oxford Hast hast

## 122. Locke to P E [Elinor Parry, later Mrs. Hawkshaw?], [early May 1661?] (*121, 185, 193*)

B.L., MS. Locke c. 24, ff. 215–16. Draft. Date by connection with no. *121*, which it answers.

P E

⟨Madam⟩[b]

May I not be credited if I know any thing comparable to your wit but your vertue. you mould our thoughts into what fashon

[a–a] *MS.* witt I / I Gathered [b] *Altered to* Mr —; *the surname illegible.*

[1] Apparently of the wish, Elinor herself. [2] Christ Church.
[3] John or Benjamin Parry: p. 69 n.

you please. there is not an affection or faculty in us which you doe not absolutely command and all our passions are ready to take your part against us and either settle or disturbe ones quiet as you thinke fit to imploy them. Certainly nature had a greate care and kindenesse for man kinde when with this power it gave you a proportionable Goodnesse, which only sometimes permits you to let us see what you could doe had you a will to be mischeivous I must confesse that my courage forsakes me when I consider those bright and irresistible weapons you conquer with, and when I observe that band of Confederates that you have lodging in my breast that will upon the least commission from you turne all into uprore and disorder I dread the thoughts of entring into any contest with you and doe very much wonder that I have beene sometimes soe hardy as to chide you this makes me that I dare not contradict you when you say that your silence is innocent and that your want of wit is a sufficient excuse for it, though give leave to tell you that in the meane time it is very hard to belive it. I had lately an experience of that obedience they pay you, and you cannot thinke how many fits I had in the perusall of your letter, Hope Feare Joy Sorrow, envy and I know not how many more of them tooke their turnes, and that upon soe slight occasions, that upon soberer considerations it was concluded that neither they nor I understoode very much of the whole matter. all that appears clearly intelligible to me is your command to be informd in my wagers, all the rest is beyond my ken and I must confesse my self a dunce in it till you releive me by your comment and make me understand the text which hath a more then ordinary obscurity. In the meantime pray take this inventory of my winings, Mrs Prat[1] for she leads the van hath lost and is to provide the greate Old Sultan Salmon that hath ruld in the Thames this hundred yeare. it must be that very same salmon that knew ⟨when⟩[a] Sir Francis Drake tooke ship, and kept company with him in his voyage round about the world.[2] there must be men imployd to take him, and we intend he shall tell the story of his travells before we eat him if we can get an interpreter for tis thought he doth not speake very good English. if our fishers should misse him which is possible for he is a

[a] *Deleted in MS.*

[1] Probably the wife of Richard Pratt: p. 168, n. 3.

[2] The salmon is short-lived: Bacon, *Historia Vitæ et Mortis*, 1623 (in *Philosophical Works*, ed. J. Spedding, ii. 128). For Drake see nos. 348, 508.

very politique fish a Jole of one of his subjects must serve the turne. Next a Neats tongue a tongue of truth a great rarity and a choise bitt that is not commonly in every ones mouth and will beare witnesse against false ones. To this meat that you may know it to be a womans wager, there is but one bottle of Cider which because it is a winde liquor we have orderd that it shall singe Civy Chase[1] to us all dinner time and soe melodiously spend its breath that way, at little passages to be made on purpose. with this she will alsoe loose all her confidence of wining or laying wagers after it, which till the decision of this she is permitted to keepe. Mr Prat like a good honest fellow findes drinke, which is to be the best Montifiasco[2] such as the Pope drinks himself when he keeps holy-day, I cannot well tell you how much tis, but enough to make us all merry. Mr Uvedall is to serve in a brace of grave Lobsters, which are to be sent over from the King of Spaine armd Cap a pe to denounce warre against England,[3] they will come under water for feare of being intercepted by pirats,[a] how he will get them is beyond my skill but you know he hath an extraordinary tricke as he thinks at diveing at least into secreats. Your Brother[4] hath lost only a dozen of Niteinggals or some such birds, the eggs I thinke are already set to hatching, and you must be sure to come by that time they are fledgd, or else be faine to content your self with ordinary pigeons, and last of all to close our Stomachs the grave Mr Towerson is to provide a Tart, he is to finde out what[b] Apples grew in the hesperides garden that they may be of the same sort that fill his Tart and tis ⟨thought⟩[c] he will find some of them at Carfax,[5] and soe large as may hold all the history of Dido and Æneas and three or fower other Love storys *in pastery Imagery*, which he shall peeke[6] out of his great readeing and will be (as he will contrive the fine workemanship) better then twenty Romances.

[a] *Substituted for* some of our frigots [b] *Perhaps deleted in MS.* [c] *MS.* though

[1] Chevy Chase. Locke treats it as a pothouse ballad in no. 180.
[2] Montefiascone, famed in legend for its wine.
[3] Spain was trying to prevent the marriage of Charles II and Catherine of Braganza, and about the time of this letter the Spanish ambassador was instructed to threaten war if his negotiation failed: K. Feiling, *British Foreign Policy, 1660–1672*, 1930, pp. 38–9. Locke can have known little of this.
[4] p. 175.
[5] This alludes apparently to Richard Pratt's garden and the inmates of the house: p. 168, n. 3.
[6] Apparently a mis-spelling of pick.

This I thinke will be enough for one dinner if not pray tell me and I will win a great deale more. If you finde it something difficult to beleive all this bill of fare pray come and disprove it and if I doe not make these people entertaine you with choiser cates then all your mulbery garden[1] Queasy Cicshows I will give you leave to injoyne me a long Lent for my Penance. I suppose I have fully acquited my self to your command and shall now only desire the explication of some of the remainder of your letter as what is signified by those great burly letters marshald up into the posture of Your Servant Sir and[a] what is to be understood by Complements and when that word or those things began to be in use betweene us and[a] what tis you meane by Change in the ⟨beginning⟩[b] and what by change in the end of your letter and whether it relates to weather or what else. this you that I shall allways beleive to be unchangably good and virtuous cannot deny to him that is

Unchangeably

At foot of page: p P

## *123.* JAMES ALLESTRY to SAMUEL TILLY, 14 May 1661

B.L., MS. Locke c. 3, f. 21. Printed in P. Abrams, ed., Locke: *Two Tracts*, p. 244. James Allestry, d. 1670, was active as a London bookseller from 1652 until his death. On 9 November 1663 he and John Martyn were sworn printers to the Royal Society: H. R. Plomer, *A Dictionary of the Booksellers . . . 1641–67* (Bibliographical Society), 1907; T. Birch, *The History of the Royal Society of London*, 1756–7, i. 328.

London May 14 1661

Worthy Sir,

In answer to yours of the 7th instant, I assure you that the Treatise[2] you left in my hand will be put to the presse to morrow

[a] *Perhaps deleted.* [b] *MS.* beging

[1] The pleasure-garden of this name, on part of the site of Buckingham Palace, was open in 1654 and 1660, but must have closed by 1665; a new Mulberry Garden, on a site near the present Royal Mews, was open in 1668–71: Evelyn, *Diary*, ed. de Beer, iii. 97 n.

[2] Dr. von Leyden (Locke, *Essays*, pp. 23–4) and Mr. Abrams (pp. 11–13; notes, p. 28) identify this as 'Quest⟨ion⟩: whether the Civill Magistrate' (pp. 160 n., 167, n. 3 *ad fin.*). If nos. *127* and *129* relate to this piece, Tilly cannot have been an intermediary for its publication in May 1661, unless he had no knowledge of what he was handling. Further there is an objection based on dates and probabilities. The preface shows that Locke, probably at Oxford, contemplated publication at a time when he knew the contents of the speech delivered by the king on 8 May. If he

and all Expedition used in its dispatch, Wherefore I earnestly entreate you to send mee the Title page and what other additions you shall thinke fitting to adde to make it compleate, by the first opportunity; as also to specify how many Copies you desire, that I may accordingly acquaint my friend who hath undertaken the printing it[1] from whom you may expect all ingenuuos and candid dealing which you shall ever find in

Your respectfull friend and servant
JAMES ALLESTRY.

Address: To his much Esteemed friend Mr. Samuel Tilly at Mr. Prats[2] neare Carfax in Oxford, These

## *124.* DR. JOHN DOLBEN, later archbishop of York, to LOCKE, 17 May [1661?]

B.L., MS. Locke c. 7, ff. 213–14. Date: on 1 June 1661 Locke received £8 16*s.* by Dolben's order on account of Richard Vaughan: B.L., MS. Locke f. 11, f. 7v. Vaughan is presumably the pupil in this letter. Dolben (1625–86; *D.N.B.*) was a chaplain in ordinary in 1663, with May as his month of attendance: Institute of Historical Research (University of London), *Bulletin*, xix (1942–3), 17; he was appointed presumably when the Chapel Royal was re-established in 1660. Vaughan was a son of Richard Vaughan of 'Llantidwan, Cornwall' (? Llantyd or Llantwyd, Pembrokeshire); he matriculated on 12 July 1661: Foster.

Mr Lock

I suppose it may suit well with another charge which the Deane intends you,[3] that you take this youth into your tuition and care; He is one whom I will be answerable for in point of expence. His way of living I would have in the quality of a Commoner. I have

changed his mind in time, a message might reach Allestry soon enough to prevent the compositor's starting work on 15 May; it is difficult to see any reason for such a change of mind. If the compositor started work Locke would presumably have to indemnify him; unless Tilly had made very bad terms with Allestry's friend, it would cost Locke more to stop publication than to go forward; and no valid reason for his withdrawal after work had started has been suggested (in view of Locke's statement to Pembroke in 1684 (no. 797) it cannot be argued that the piece was published though no copy is extant).

[1] I take this to mean that Allestry was acting as intermediary for another bookseller, who would publish the treatise with which Tilly was concerned. Towerson uses the word print in this sense in no. *115*: 'to print your answer'.

[2] pp. 168, n. 3, 177.

[3] John Fell, 1625–86; D.D. 1660; Dean of Christ Church 1660–86; bishop of Oxford 1676–86, holding the deanery *in commendam*: *D.N.B.* Letters to Locke below, no. *303*, etc. The other charge is perhaps another pupil.

sent order to my Tailor to provide him a gowne, and I hope Mr Subdeane will assigne him a Chamber.

I am
Your very freind
J DOLBEN

Whitehall
May. 17.

Address: To my good freind Mr John Lock Master of Arts and Student of Christ Church in Oxon

## *125.* JOHN STRACHEY to LOCKE, with postscript by Elizabeth Jepp, 31 October 1661 (*117*, *128*; *116*)

B.L., MS. Locke c. 18, ff. 206–7.

Sir

I knew a Butcher that runn madding after his knife when all the while hee had it in his mouth, the like it seemd happen'd to you (pardon the similitude though it belongs to you to knock downe hæresy as hee doth a Bullocke) when you rode in quest of an University that you might have found under your owne hatt; I knew likewise or at least heard of an old Sir John[1] who being a litle ⟨dimme⟩[a] sighted did use to saddle his nose with a payre of spectacles, an arch crack had gott these his better eyes and painted thereon certaine flies, when the old Cinquecater[2] went to reade his homily, hee thought they had beene on his booke and much sport there was in his endeavouring to brush them off; even soe—Lett mee not live I dont know how to make it out—but I am sure there was a greate fault in the glasse when you lookt on mee as the Mother of Learninge, that am not worthy to bee cald her Son—I suppose you have by thi time exchangd you Napsack for a Satchell,[3] for the Moths and you are very much of a diett. you feede altogeather on leaves, that you may (as occult Philosophy teacheth) being transplanted into the Country bring forth good

[a] *MS.* dinne

[1] A priest: *O.E.D.*, s.v. John.
[2] Cinquanter; a man of fifty; an old stager: *O.E.D.*
[3] The traveller's and the scholar's bags. This and the opening lines of the letter imply that Locke had recently visited Somerset.

fruit: Madam Jepp[1] hath comanded mee to tell you that the Gentleman you laught at was here with a Grotius[2] in his hand, but being admitted to the sight onely of the Maides, his learning servd him to litle purpose; thi paper spoiles my good meaning, for I would have writt more then barely thi that I am

your faithfull freind and servant
JO: STRACHEY

Octo 31th 61.

I intend to bee at London the next weeke where I desire youre answer and that you would spare the sending the Liturgy[3]

[Postscript by Mrs. Jepp:]

Sir

I thinke it as Lawfull for my brother and I to write as for my mother[4] and I to be written to in one Letter and I wold tell you a tale of a Tinker as well as hee has of a Bucher and a vicar if I know what but this I know and hope you Believe that you have

A very Loving cosin in
ELIZ: JEPP

Address (written by Strachey): For mr John Locke Master of Arts att Christ-Church these. Oxford.

## *126.* GEORGE PERCIVALL to LOCKE, 1 December 1661 (*109, 134*)

B.L., MS. Locke c. 17, ff. 62–3.

Dublin. Dec. the first. 1661.

Sir

I cannot passe by this opportunity of sending my best respects unto you without being conscious to my selfe of a great neglect. nor could I suffer any freind of mine to passe through Oxford without letting him know that I had a freind there too. I have had some account of the alterations in Oxford since my departure, by a student of Christchurch one Mr Okell,[5] who is lately come over

[1] Presumably Mrs. Elizabeth Jepp.

[2] Probably either *De Veritate Christianæ Religionis* or *De Jure Belli et Pacis.*

[3] Probably a copy of one of the reprints (1660 and 1661) of the 1604 version of the *Book of Common Prayer.*

[4] Her late husband's half-brother and her mother-in-law: Strachey and Mrs. Baber.

[5] William Okell; matriculated 1657; B.A. 1660: Foster.

here seeking for preferment, which I feare he may seeke long enough and never find. Ireland being a desolate country that wants people and auditors rather then teachers. and some here are of opinion that a hundred good plowman[a] would doe god and there country more good service then double the number[b] of the black robe.[1] I am very glad you continue your repute in christchurch which you ever had most deservedly, you can doe your selfe no more right then to preserve nor me more right then to beleive that I am

Sir

Your very affectionate Freind and faithfull servant

G PERCIVALL

my very humble service to my Tutor, to Dr Lockey.[2] and the rest of my freinds with you that have a memory of me.

In the perclose[3] of this my letter the enclosed coppy of verses came to mee from sir Peter Pett once fellow of all souls the author of them.[4] I thought fitt to send you them that you may see Ireland has some Muses in it.

Address: For his very affectionate Freind Mr John Lock student of Ch. Ch. In Oxford.

## *127.* SAMUEL TILLY to LOCKE, 5 December 1661 (*36, 123, 129*)

B.L., MS. Locke c. 20, ff. 179–80.

Compton Martin Dec: 5 —61.

Sir

E're this I presume you have concluded either me or those papers lost, that you directed to me, having hitherto receiv'd no return, whence you might conjecture the contrary. And least you now suspect me chargeable with any neglect in not assuring you of the safety of what you were content should run so greate a hazard for

[a] *Or* plowmeen [b] *Spelling doubtful.*

[1] The clergy. [2] p. 48, n. 2.

[3] Variant of parclose, meaning enclosure, etc.: *O.E.D.* Here apparently that formed by folding and sealing the letter.

[4] Sir Peter Pett, 1630–99; knighted *c.* 1661: *D.N.B.*; T. Birch, *The Life of the Honourable Robert Boyle*, 1744, pp. 298–300. Anthony Wood mentions a Latin poem written by him about 1658: *Athenæ*, iv. 576.

my satisfaction, let me tell you, that your letter of the 5th of November came not to my hand until within this fortnight, not through any fault in the conveyance but by reason of my absence from hence, where at my return I found it with your other papers, then which (next to your selfe) nothing could be more welcome to me.[1] And tho' from them even at the first glance my perswasions concerning you made me promise my selfe much yet after a more deliberate perusal I at last found you had out-done my expectation. About a yeare since by the meanes of Doctor Burges[2] I remember I had a sight of your adversarys papers wherin besides those Rhetorical colours where withall his discourse is varnish'd o're I could then observe litle of solidity or substance; nothing that might perswade and very litle that might move an intelligent reader. Indeed the cause he maintains hath so litle of truth in't that it can be no wonder there is no more of strength to be found in his arguments. I have now read it againe together with your answer, with what indifferency I possibly could, and least my affection should render me partial to the later I have consulted the judgments of others, who importune me to improve my interest in you for its publication. I have not yet spoken with the Bishop of Chew[3] but intend very speedily and shall punctualy observe those instructions you gave me. Till then be pleasd to suspend your expectations of receiving your papers which (If I may not be so happy as to see you in the Countrey this Christmasse) shall with a more particular accoumpt of them be carefully returnd you by

Sir

Your unfeigned friend

SAM: TILLY

Present my Cordial respects to those you know are my real friends. My father[4] presents his service to you.

Address: These for Mr John Lock master of Arts and Student in Christchurch in Oxon:

[1] Unless there was some composition by Locke that has disappeared entirely, this passage and no. *129* must relate to Locke's answer to Bagshaw's *The Great Question*, 'Quest: whether the Civill Magistrate . . .': pp. 160 n., 167, n 3. Tilly's language is loose, but suggests that he did not see Locke's 'Question' until he found it with Locke's letter of 5 November.

[2] Cornelius Burges, 1589?–1665; D.D. 1627; preacher at Wells cathedral 1656–60: *D.N.B.*; Matthews, *Calamy Revised*; above, p. 156. There is nothing by Bagshaw in Burges's *Reasons shewing the Necessity of Reformation.*

[3] Apparently Robert Crosse, the vicar: pp. 166 n., 186.

[4] p. 28 n.

## *128.* JOHN STRACHEY to LOCKE, 21 January 1662 (*125, 130*)

B.L., MS. Locke c. 18, ff. 208–9.

Sir

Over bootes, over shoes,[1] This is a pretty proverbe to begin a letter with, but this lay soe patt in my way, that I could not passe it over without shewing a contempt to our antient wisdome—expanded thus—I had committed such a fault in not answering your last, that I had even resolved to have made a greate one and not to have writt att all, but then considering you to bee of a surly nature and one that wo'nt write unless you are writt to, the loss of your letters made mee take upp an old penn and worse paper and scratch these lines; first then I aske pardon for my offence, but with noe promise of amendment, for I know the Divell for stronge and myselfe soe weake that if I made an engagement I should sinn doubly, just as Osborne observes, after marriage single fornication Sprouts into adultery.[2] This quotation hath soe strange a cohærence that I am glad I fall into mercifull hands, I might else bee mistaken for one that is distracted. Secondly I assure you I love you very well, but on my consciene I shall never give any greate testimony of it either in word or action, for I find my nature soe averse to all befitting carriage, that I can nither make good freind nor good Courtier unless it bee in downe right courtesies and those you have noe neede off; But if you want one that will speake well of you in homely language, and words without fluency, dropping like old mens or your nose or one that would venture a bloody one for your sake, I may boldly say heres your man. Thirdly—I would come to a Seaventeenly, but tis a shame to write more then one side, therefore I am

Sir

Your humble Servant

JO: STRACHEY

Janu 21th 61.[a]

Here is news but I protest it cost mee mony.

Address: For Mr John Locke at Christ-Church these Oxford.

[a] *Page torn; a word before* Janu *may be lost.*

[1] Generally 'Over shoes, over boots': *Oxford Dict. English Proverbs.*

[2] Francis Osborne, *Advice to a Son* (p. 55, n. 2), ii. 7.

## *129.* SAMUEL TILLY to LOCKE, 7 March [1662?] (*127*)

B.L., M.S. Locke c. 20, ff. 173–4. In the date '51' is a slip: the mention of the king shows that it dates from after 1660. It should probably be '61', meaning 1661/2: the letter is unlikely to date from 7 March 1661, when Locke was probably in Somerset; by its contents it is associated with no. *127*.

Bristoll. March. 7. —51

Ingenious Sir

I now return your paper's with my cordial thanks for the liberty of their perusal. Although my trespasse have bin over bold in detaining them so long, yet I am now as bold to promise my selfe your pardon; Indeed I was unwilling to expose them to the hazard of this passage, and therefore presuming I should have seen Oxford my selfe ere this I was not over-hastie to return them, before mine owne intended comming; but being now forced to lay by those resolutions until towards the Act,[1] I must therefore transmit them by the hands of the carrier, that I may no longer hinder, upon any private accoumpt, what may be of publique use and concernment; In the perusal of your lines, least my affection might possibly subject my understanding to oversee any failings that might be found in them, I have therefore used other more judicious, and more searching eies then mine owne, to make if it were possible such a discovery; who after an advised and punctual examination of the whole assure me they finde nothing dissonant from truf,[a] much that may tend to publique satisfaction. Your adversary besides many texts of Scripture misapplied, hath many confident assertions that are indeed no arguments (I say) unlesse it be of the weaknesse of the cause maintained by them. I presume you expect not that he should retract what he has written, who seems resolved like him in Plautus that professed dicat quod quisque vult ego de hac sententiâ non dimovebor;[2] some mens intellectuals are so clouded with prejudice that either they can't or at least won't see whats manifestly apparent. The King I hope will shortly answer such arguments,[3] as he did Zenoe's subtilties against the existence of

[a] *Doubtful reading.*

[1] That is, about July.

[2] 'Let anyone say what he likes, I'll not be shaken from this purpose of mine': *Persa*, 373–4. The correct reading is 'demovebor'.

[3] A bill 'for the Uniformity of Public Prayers' was introduced into the house of commons on 29 June 1661; it was brought to the lords on 10 July, but was not read for the first time until 14 January of this year. It received the royal assent on 19 May: *C.J.*; *L.J.*

motion, who confuted them by doing what he pretended could not be done.[1]

If mr Crosses affaires did permit him to peruse your papers by the next I shall be able to give you his judgment concerning them. For myselfe as I have ever entertaind a more then ordinary respect for your person so I can't but highly esteem and value this late obligation of which, when it lies in my power you shall command a like return from

your real and faithfull friend

S. T.

Our friends here present their service to you.[a]

Address: These For Mr John Lock at his chamber in christ-church in Oxford

## *130.* JOHN STRACHEY to LOCKE, 18 March 1662 (*128, 131*)

B.L., MS. Locke c. 18, ff. 210–11.

Sir

Missing your answere at London, I thought to try my fortune in the Country and as luck would have it I noe sooner came hither but your letter mett mee and though it was not directed to mee yet thereby I understood what I desir'd viz: that[b] you[b] were not very much gon in sicknesse, for meethought you spoke sence and did not att all talke light-headed; I was unwilling to bee the Ladys Scribe,[2] but importunity still prevailes with good natures and I did not know how her reputation might suffer in writing to a liquorish Scholar of the University, if your anger riseth at thi expression, I am confident it will bee layde before I see you and then I am out of danger; att the present you must satisfie yourselfe with thankes from her and commendations for the good seede time you have given her, if you are but as fortunate in the harvest, shee will present you with the fruits of your own labour and give you a greate deale of sallad to an Oxford Commons, if it may not bee presum'd that the appetites there want noe provocatives. As for my part I

[a] *This postscript is written immediately beneath the date at the head of the letter.* [b] *MS.* that y[t] you?

[1] Zeno of Elea. It was Diogenes the Cynic who refuted the argument by moving: Diogenes Laertius, *De Vitis . . . Philosophorum*, vi. 39.

[2] Presumably Mrs. Elizabeth Jepp's.

entreate noe seedes from you, a litle paper strowde with black but in intelligible characters (your pen can draw noe other) will lett mee know that you have not forgott mee, and to have a roome sometimes in your memorie when your Studys will give way is the highest aime of

Sir
your humble Servant
JO: STRACHEY.

March 18th 61–

My Mother prayde to bee remembred to you.

Address: For Mr John Locke Master of Artes att Christ-Church these. Oxford.

## *131.* JOHN STRACHEY to LOCKE, [20 April 1662?] (*130, 132*)

B.L., MS. Locke c. 18, ff. 199–200. Mrs. Elizabeth Jepp made her will on 4 April 1662; it was proved on 18 April 1665: Frederick Brown, *Abstracts of Somersetshire Wills*, ed. F. A. Crisp, 1887–90, iv. 107. I assume that she made her will at the onset of her illness.

Sir

I writt to you the last time this Gentleman went to Oxford, and I had writt to you since had not a fatall accident arrested my penn and employd my thoughts about my Sisters sicknesse, which hath now to my greate greife carried her hence to a better place for herselfe. Her disease was the small pocks, her Physitian Dr Peicer, and after all our apprehensions that the danger was past (it being the seaventeenth day shee dyed) her faire soul fled, and hath left mee here to mourne the losse of her company that made Sutton a City. If ever I had serious reflections on death, hers hath given mee them, and I begin to value this body of mine soe litle, that I thinke I could for ever leave it and spend few sighs at partinge. Troth, Freind, I hope to bee much altered in a litle time, and if you will bee grave enough to bee my Confessor, in the next you shall see as in a glasse all my transgressions. I give you thanks for the last booke you sent mee which intruth is a very good one and is the best company I now enjoy, but yett I place it not above the meanest of your letters, since they assure me I have still some roome in your thoughts, which without complement is to mee a high satisfaction. If you have any other Authour that in my melancholy moode I may play withall, I pray send it, I wont tell you I will pay you what you disburse, I conceive you beleive it as likewise that I am

Sir
your faithfull freind and servant
JO: STRACHEY

Sunday night.

Address: For his much respected freind Mr John Locke at Christ Church these Oxford

## *132.* JOHN STRACHEY to LOCKE, N.D. [April/May 1662?] (*131*, *151*)

B.L., MS. Locke c. 18, f. 201. The passage about confession refers to no. *131*; this letter followed it probably within three or four weeks or less.

Sir

My letters are soe litle able to pay you what you spend in reading them, that 'tis noe wonder if I grow soe modest as to bee unwilling to thrust any more upon you, and yett it were noe lie to tell you that I send as often as I can conveniently, which from a lesse candid nature then yours would find small thanks. But I consider that Schollars are a strange sort of Adventurers and all the returne they can expect from their Longe studies is but a patient attention to their learned discourses and perhaps a litle praise. If you are but as conscientious as the rest of your coate, I shall however not bee much in your debt, for I am an exact paymaster in both those, but if you ambition any thing more, to deale freely with you, you'le goe beyond my abilities. I remember in my last I promisd to make confession in my next, my sins are afraide of your rigour, but here you have my weakness much good doe it you. Instead of that suffer mee to bee your Pupill and give you this short account of my reading. Your foure Authors I have allmost lookt over, and in my own thoughts have profited more in the humane then the divine, the first please mee exceedingly and I could wish were it not too greate a trouble for more of the same, the last is a pretty fellow I confesse, but I dont love to trade in divinity, and am soe perfect an enemie to M. Pope that I cant fancy any that would reconcile mee to him.

I am loth to engage on the other side, for feare I should not goe thorough stitch; I will therefore rest satisfied in being

Sir

Your freind and servant

Jo: Strachey.

## *133.* Robert Mandey to Locke, 30 June 1662 (*142*)

B.L., MS. Locke c. 15, ff. 198–9. The writer was apparently a steward or secretary of Lord Berkeley.

Sir

I am very glad that the Bills came safe to your hands as I finde by your letter, I hope the bottle of stilled water[1] for Sir Charles[2] is likewise safe with you beinge sent by Bartlett the Carrier; I have acquainted my Lord and Lady with the remove of Sir Charles to another chamber and that the hangings are become uselesse to him, Their desires are, that they may bee taken downe and that Thomas may have them brushed and well folded up and laid aside in some spare corner with some carelesse cloth throwne over them till it bee certaine whether Sir Charles shall keepe his lodgings hee now is in, for if hee should be put to remove againe then probably those hangings may bee againe of use to him; Thomas must bee carefull that noe rats get into them which is very usuall when they lye by; If they may be spared I will take care to have them to London and ease Thomas his trouble of lookinge to them, which I desire fully to understand when it can certainly bee resolved; I have presented the inclosed letter to the 2. Ladyes Sir Charles his sisters[3] who take it not a little kindly their brothers

[1] Distilled. The water may be a water-like fluid rather than water itself.

[2] Charles Berkeley, 1649–1710; K.B. 1661; matriculated from Christ Church 3 May 1662; created M.A. 28 September 1663; matriculated at Cambridge 30 May 1663; admitted to Trinity College 6 August; M.A. 1663; styled Lord Dursley 1679–98; second earl of Berkeley 1698: G. E. C. He contributed in English to *Domiduca Oxoniensis* (p. 191, n. 1). Letters below, no. *140*, etc. His parents were George Berkeley, 1628–98; ninth Lord Berkeley 1658; created earl of Berkeley 1679; and his wife Elizabeth, d. 1708, daughter of John Massingberd: G. E. C.

[3] Six sisters are recorded; their dates of birth are unknown: Arthur Collins, *Collins's Peerage of England*, ed. Sir E. Brydges, 1812, iii. 620.

affectionate remembrance of them and doe intend to greet him in the like measure; my lady goes for Glocestershire[1] on Munday next; my service to the younge Knight, I am

Sir

your very humble servant

ROB. MANDEY

Dardens.[2] June 30. 1662

Address: Theis For mr John Locke Student in Christchurch in Oxford

## *134.* GEORGE PERCIVALL to LOCKE, 4 July 1662 (*126, 135*)

B.L., MS. Locke c. 17, ff. 64, 64'.

Sir

I received a letter from you the last weeke, by the hands of Mr Meese,[3] whom I have not had the happinesse to see since that time, or I had bin more speedy in a returne of an answer to you, that day I received it from him he went into the country, so that I could not obtaine a narritive of your university affaires, which I earnestly covett. I doe intend this evening, to enquire of his returne at his lodging, and see if I may satisfie my curiosity, without giving you the trouble of being my Intelligencer. I doubt not but this my letter will come safe to your hands, it being designed to meete with you at the Act[4] where it cannot misse of you, and I heartily envy that paper that shall kisse your hands at that time. I shall beg the favour of you to transmitt the remarkable passages of so great a solemnity to me, before you take the benefit of your vacation retirement into the country. and to let as many of my auncient friends as shall be there present know that I am still at there service. I have lately had a sight of your Oxford poetry, amongst which I find your selfe one of the most remarkable poets, and am obleiged

[1] Presumably to Berkeley Castle, the principal family seat.

[2] Durdans near Epsom, the usual residence of the family at this time: Evelyn, *Diary*, ed. de Beer, iii. 15 n.

[3] Probably Nicholas Meese, born *c.* 1630; of St. John's and later of Trinity; M.A. 1652; Proctor 1661–2; B.D. 1663; divine: Foster.

[4] It ought to have been held on 12 July, but this year was cancelled: Wood, *L. and T.* i. 443.

to returne you thankes for that satisfaction which I received in the perusall of your verses. I cannot as yet, (having had but a few howres sight of your domiduca) give my selfe any great accompt of it, only I find in generall that the king at his landing was much more beholding to ch. ch. then I find the queen to bee; but I hope thay have made her some recompence, and though she has fewer poets I hope she finds better poetry, then was so lately presented his majestie.[1] Osborne[2] (to whom the advise of a father to a son doth properly belong) is a lawyer here in Dublin, and is as ingenious a man as his father, and is in some repute amongst the lawyers. I thinke Ireland has none else that come under your knowledge besids my selfe, or if there were I should give you some accompt of them. I must intreate you still to keepe me in your memory, and not let the distance of the place make any seperation betweene us, whome I hope a solemne affection has linked togather. I had write at this present to dick lower[3] but that your letter doth discourage me from it, for I find by you that his practise has calld him in the country, and I doubt an act will not perswade him to forgoe his profit, for his pleasure, unlesse it ware more certaine. and durable. I doubt not but since all the witts are returned to the university againe with the old Senior Masters you have more Ingenuity though worse sermons, then formerly.[4] pray remember me to Dr Lockey[5] and Mr South,[6] both which I wish preferment sutable to there meritt, and I should be very glad my wishes were effectuall. if mr Long[7] be yet in the colledge present my service to him, he has a solitary Unkle that was never married of a very good fortune here, and the expectation of it might tempt him (I am sure it would tempt me) into a worse place then Ireland. I feare I

[1] The book is *Domiduca Oxoniensis: Sive musæ academicæ gratulatio ob auspicatissimum serenissimæ principis Catharinæ Lusitanæ, regi suo desponsatæ, in Angliam appulsum*, 1662: Madan, no. 2578. L.L., no. 2163. It contains 126 poems; about 29 Christ Church men contributed to it. Locke's poem is in English. *Britannia Rediviva*, 1660, for the king (p. 53, n. 4), contains 158 poems; about 43 Christ Church men contributed.

[2] John Osborne, *fl.* 1648–92; B.C.L., Oxford, 1654; barrister, Inner Temple, 1657; Bencher 1689; sometime a serjeant at law in Ireland: Francis Osborne, *Advice to a Son*, ed. E. A. Parry, 1896, introd., pp. xvi–xx.

[3] Lower resided in Oxford usually until 1665, but may have been absent this spring: notices in Wood, *L. and T.*

[4] On the restored men as preachers see ibid. i. 356–7, 360–1.

[5] pp. 48, n. 2, 182.

[6] p. 153, n. 5.

[7] Presumably Walter Long, younger son of Sir Walter Long of Draycot Cerne, Wilts.; born *c.* 1637; matriculated from Christ Church 20 July 1654; B.A. 1657: *Wiltshire Visitation Pedigrees, 1623* (Harleian Soc.), p. 118; Foster. I cannot identify the uncle.

transgresse by my tediousnesse theref⟨ore⟩[a] I shall beg your pardon and conclude this trouble to you by subscribing my selfe

Sir

Your very affectionate freind and humble servant

G. PERCIVALLE.

Dubl. July 4th. 1662.

Address: For his much Respected Freinde Mr John Locke Master of Arts and st. of ch. ch In Oxford.

post paid to England.

Postmark: IY 11

## *135.* GEORGE PERCIVALL to LOCKE, 12 July 1662 (*134, 201*)

B.L., MS. Locke c. 17, ff. 65–6.

Sir

I cannot but be very thankfull to you in sending me a letter by mr Mees, and your favour in it I doe the rather acknowledg in regard it brought me into the acquaintance of so deserving a person, I have made bold to trouble him upon the like errant and to send this my letter by him, though I had rather sent it by another messanger, so we might have the happines of his society here a little longer, his stay in this Kingdome has bin so little, and of that little he has spent so much of his time in the country, that I have not had the opportunity to shew him the least civilitie, for which I must beg your pardon as well as his, and seriously were his stay in the country but some houres longer, he should not leave the place without the civelitie of the country, though I had no other inducement then your recommendation to engage me to it. I doubt not but your act and your annuall solemnity at it, has bin very greate and sutable to the fame of your university, we have had a kind of a mimick act at the University here in Dublin. thay call it a commencement, and I thinke it is most properly so, being made up (as I heare for I was not present) of puns and quibles in imitation of Cambridge.[1] pray doe me the favour as to let me have an account of your proceedings this act, though I am at a great

[a] *Edge of page.*

[1] This refers to the speech made by the prevaricator at Cambridge. In Trinity College, Dublin, as in Oxford, it was made by a *terræ filius*.

distance from Oxford, yet I have it more in my mind then some that are neerer it, and am as much delighted in hearing from my good freinds as others are in enjoying them, my service to mr Bold your proctour,[1] and all my rest of my acquaintance particularly to mr Vernon[2] if he be at Oxford which I desire to know, as also to Mr Bisby,[3] of whose stay at oxford I desire like wise to be informed; Deare Sir let me not want the pleasure of your correspondence since I am deprived of the happinesse of your company, and therin you will further obleige

Your very affectionate freind and most obedient servant.

G PERCIVALLE

Dubl. July 12. 1662.

My very humble service to my Tutor. Dr Lockey and mr Thurman[4] if he be yet among you.

Address: For his very affectionate Freind Mr John Locke M.A. and st. of ch. ch. In Oxford. Thes. England.

## *136.* GEORGE BERKELEY, ninth Lord Berkeley, later first earl of Berkeley, to LOCKE, 27 July 1662

B.L., MS. Locke c. 3, ff. 185–6. For the writer see p. 189, n. 2.

Sir

I feare you wil be surprised (with the Deane)[5] at my so sudden removing my sonne, which is wholly upon Dr persons score,[6] I shal referre you to the Deanes letter to whom I have writ at Large.

[1] Henry Bold, d. 1677; at Westminster School; matriculated from Christ Church 7 July 1651; B.A. 1655; M.A. 1657; B.D. 1664; precentor of Exeter; etc.: Barker and Stenning; Wood, *L. and T.* i. 359, etc.; ii. 389 and n. He was 'your proctor' because it was the turn of Christ Church to provide a proctor in accordance with the proctorial cycle (p. 62, n. 1).

[2] Probably Francis Vernon, d. 1677; at Westminster School; matriculated from Christ Church 10 November 1654; B.A. 1658; M.A. 1660; diplomatist and traveller: *D.N.B.*; pp. 370, 693.

[3] Nathaniel Bisby, 1635–95; at Westminster School; matriculated from Christ Church 10 November 1654; B.A. 1658; M.A. 1660; D.D. 1668; nonjuror: *D.N.B.*

[4] Probably Henry Thurman, d. 1670; at Westminster School; student of Christ Church 1648; B.A. 1652; M.A. 1654; divine: Barker and Stenning; Wood, *L. and T.* i. 359, 369, etc.

[5] Dr. John Fell: p. 179, n. 3.

[6] John Pearson, 1613–86; D.D. 1661; Master of Trinity College, Cambridge, 1662 (14 April)–1673; bishop of Chester 1673; author of *An Exposition of the Creed*, 1659; etc.: *D.N.B.* He was probably for some time chaplain to Berkeley's father and then to Berkeley.

I returne you my harty thankes for your greate care of my sonne, my removing him from you wil not I hope be interpreted any diminution of the extraordinary good opinion and value I have of your parts and piety and your excellent Qualifications for the wel governing youth. I neede say no more, but assure you I shal upon al occasions endeavour to expresse my selfe

Sir

your assured freind to serve you
with great kindnes and reality. BERKELEY

Durdence July the 27th. 1662.

Address: For my much esteemed freind mr Lock Student of Cht. Churche In Oxford.

## *137.* GEORGE BERKELEY, ninth Lord Berkeley, later first earl of Berkeley, to SIR CHARLES BERKELEY, K.B., later second earl of Berkeley, 27 July 1662

B.L., MS. Locke c. 3, ff. 183–4.

Charles:

Dr Pearson is now upon his Jorney Towards Oxford with intention to remove you, which I hope wil not dissatisfie you because it is my Desire. You very wel know what greate Obligation you have to the Doctor, which may prevaile with you to go with him Chearefully. But before your departure Be sure you returne greate and humble Thankes to the Deane, and your Tutor for theire constant care of you. probably you wil expresse it with sighnes of affectionate Duty and Kindnes: which will much become you. I pray God bles you and direct you in al the passages of your life, I pray God direct me to advice you alwaies for the best for his Glory and your Good. so prayeth

your very affectionate father
BERKELEY

Durdence July the 27th. 1662

Address: For the little Kt Sir Charles Berkeley at Cht. Churche In Oxford.

## *138.* HENRY TOWNSHEND to LOCKE, 29 July 1662 (*141*)

B.L., MS. Locke c. 22, ff. 9–10. Henry Townshend of Elmley Lovett, Worcs.: pedigree in T. R. Nash, (*Worcestershire*), 1781–99, i. 378. The son is Roland Townshend, *c.* 1646–85; matriculated from Christ Church 14 May 1662; fellow of All Souls; B.C.L. 1670; D.C.L. 1675: Foster; Wood, *L. and T.* iii. 154; exercises, etc., in Locke's Herbarium (MSS. Locke c. 41; b. 7: *Bodleian Library Record*, vii (1967), 190–3).

Sir

I must acknowledg my self very much engaged for your kind expressions of your Care and tendernes of my sonn, and the hopefull promises yow have of him. I beleeve yow will not be deceaved in your Expectation, unles unfortunatly he deviat from that procedure, which hitherunto with all Easines as Alacrity he hath walked. And give me Leave to speak without flattery, I could never perceav those Boyish Carraidges as Generally youths are given to and practise by him. For his only Delight here was Musick playing, and singing Quire service and Tunes: pritty Diversions for a Retired (yf not Melancoly) spiritt; and so at Recreative howres may be Continued.

Ther is now sent a Bed with all furniture. As for Bedsted, table desk, chayre, or other Accomodations I must wholy Commend and Commit to your discretion to fitt them with furniture, which hapily may be had as well at Second hand as new with less chardg.

I have taken order and sent to him to deliver into your Custody such monyes as is over and above, dischardging his Gown and Surplyce, which he hath at present, unles som small Reserv, which I beleev he wilbe thrifty of. That your sole discretion may have the right manadgment.

Be pleased to Accept this paper as an Entrance to our future Converse one with another. And yow will make his parents happy to heare of his increase and proficiency in learning which will more and more oblidg me to be your (though as yet unknown) affectionat frend and servant.

HEN TOWNSHEND

Worcester. 29th July. 62.

Address: Thes To Mr John Lock at his Chamber in Christchurch at Oxford. deliver

## *139.* THOMAS WESTROWE to LOCKE, 30 July [1662?] (*100*)

B.L., MS. Locke c. 23, ff. 72–3. The year is conjectural. The letter presumably dates from after (or near the time of) Lord Wharton's marriage to Mrs. Popham.

July 30th Fetter Lane

Deare John

I received your letter just as I came to towne, from barnet, where I have scoured myself as a man should scoure a gun, what I poured in at one end I squerted out at the other,[1] but how cleane I am I know not, having yet cause to complaine, but you have none to complaine of my lasinesse, for all the time I was there I was doing my businesse, where if I had sott still to chide you I my self might have been to blame or forsed to have guilt my papper too richly to have sent in disspesure, and made it fitter raither to present then to chide with. let me thefore compound it thus, you shall be content to lose the gifte and I to keepe my anger; I have inquired at my Lod Whartons but am no wiser then before, when she knowes she will send word Mr Carr.[2] I hope shortly ⟨to⟩[a] returne into Kent, therfore direct yours as formery to corne hill and they will be convayed to the hand of your most harty freind

THO: WESTROWE

Address: For Mr John Locke Student of Ch: Ch: Coll: in Oxford These.

## *140.* SIR CHARLES BERKELEY, K.B., later second earl of Berkeley, to LOCKE, [*c.* 17 August 1662?] (*147*)

B.L., MS. Locke c. 3, ff. 189–90. Date based on contents and postmark.

Sir

You know I am no complementer therefore I hope yo will expect none of me I received your kind letter and do blame my self though indeed I had not an oppurtunity for not sending my respects

[a] *Concealed by a blot.*

[1] A medicinal well at Barnet provided an aperient water: A. S. Foord, *Springs, Streams and Spas of London*, 1910, pp. 152–5.

[2] Lord Wharton (Philip Wharton, 1613–96; fourth Baron Wharton 1625) married on 24 or 26 August 1661, as his third wife, Anne, sister of Locke's friend William Carr and widow of Edward Popham: p. 46 n.

sooner to you but I hope you will exccuse me for I was continually enquiring for the post that comes from Oxford to Cambridge but I could not heare of him. so[a]– that at last–[a] I was feigne to send my letter first to London then to Oxford I was at Cambridge when you sent your letter and have bin ever since words are not able to expresse that love respect and affection which I have had for you ever since I knew You therfore I shall not trouble you with any more at this present I shall only desire you to present my service to the Dean and canons and all my acquaintance to name them all in particular would be to much trouble to you.

I rest your loving freind and servant
CHARLES BERKELEY

I prevailed with a lady at court to ask my father that I might return to Oxford but he said it was to late when every thing was removed

Address: For Mr John Lock Master of art student of Christ Church in Oxford These to be left at Oxford posthous to be sent as is above directed
Postmark: –V 19
Postal note: post paid to London forward

## *141.* HENRY TOWNSHEND to LOCKE, 18 August 1662 (*138, 145*)

B.L., MS. Locke c. 22, ff. 11–12.

Sir

Taking the Advantadg of my frend the bearer intended approches to your Colledg, I must be an Intruder upon your patience so farr, as to be informed what little progress my son makes in his studyes for the tyme, and his deligent Application to such work, as yow assign him to; hoping he wilbe so conformable to your Dictats, That his parents may receive incoradgments. And yf that he wants any kind of Materialls, either in Clothing, or Books, which accidentally may be mett with our stationers (and not with yow)[b] who buy many studyes, and soe meet with books of variety of Learning, we shall either indevor to have them, or at least give an Account.

a–a *MS.* so that at/that at last    b *Interlined; not in brackets.*

I will not at present put yow unto any further trouble then to assure you that I am your obliged frend and servant

HEN TOWNSHEND

Worcester. 18° August 62.

Address: Let this be presented to his worthy frend Mr John Locke at Christ Church Colledg in Oxforde.

## *142.* ROBERT MANDEY to LOCKE, 19 August 1662 (*133, 143*)

B.L., MS. Locke c. 15, ff. 200–1.

Sir

yours I have received and sent the inclosed to Sir Charles to Cambridge, who made little stay heere, but went towards Cambridge in Doctor Persons coach the tuesday after hee left Oxford, from whence I have not had one lyne since of his welfare or how hee likes Cambridge.

Our family (I praise God) are all well; my Lord and Lady thanke you for your continued respects and truly affectionate well wishes to Sir Charles; and will bee ready on any occasion to expresse such their thanks to you; I did truly informe both of them how I found all things at Oxford, and were it to doe againe I am most confident it would not bee; It was a surprise indeed upon every one, my selfe havinge noe notice of it till comanded to goe to oxford to meet Dr. Person there; I am confident the younge Knight will place oxford in the upper roome of his thoughts for many reasons, on all occasions, I pray god to send him his health there where hee now is.

I doe not forget what my lorde in honor is to doe still at Christchurch, I meane, to give som thinge towards the buildinge[1] instead of plate, and likewise towards the Library, but wee have been soe full of feastinge of severall great persons as the Duke of yorke and his Dutchesse, and others on severall dayes, that I have no opportunity to presse my lord in it, but will doe it when I finde him at leisure, beinge for the most part at Court at present. The Queen mother dines with us within this fortnight, and such is the pleasure that wee enjoy livinge soe neere the Court.[2]

[1] The north side of the great quadrangle; the work began in 1638 and was completed in 1662–5; Anthony Wood, *History . . . of the Colleges . . . of Oxford*, ed. J. Gutch, 1786, p. 447.

[2] The court was at Hampton Court, about 8 miles from Durdans, from 29 May to 23 August. The duke and duchess are James Stuart, 1633–1701, king as James II

my Lord wrote a letter to the Deane (Dr Felle) with a warrant for a bucke inclosed in it,[1] I sent it by Bartlet the Carrier and doe hope it came safe to mr Deanes hands; Thus ceasinge further to trouble you, I doe againe and againe thanke you for your singuler respects to the younge Knight, upon whome all the hopes of our family depends,[2] desiringe ever to expresse my selfe

Sir

your most obliged and thankfull freind to serve you

ROB: MANDEY

Durdens. Aug: 19. 1662

Address: For my much honoured freind mr John Locke Student in Christs-Church, in Oxford.

To the Posthouse

## *143.* ROBERT MANDEY to LOCKE, 22 August 1662 (*142*) with note from Andrew Crooke to Locke

B.L., MS. Locke c. 15, ff. 202–3.

Sir,

Since I wrote my last to you in answer to yours I have moved my lord about some money to bee sent to the Colledge in stead of plate, and his Lordship hath ordered mee to returne Ten pounds for it, but will take no notice of any booke for the Library, this 10 li. beinge to bee in leiu of plate only; I pressed him to double the somme which I thinke had been little enough dividedly; I have paid the 10 li. to mr Andrew Crooke[3] heere who will returne the payment to mr Thomas Robinson bookseller at oxford[4] to pay it in; I have heard since from Sir Charles by his servant, but before your letter could come to him, I am

Sir

your very Servant

ROB: MANDEY

Durdens. Aug. 22. 1662.

1685–8, and his first wife Anne Hyde, 1637–71; the queen-mother is Henrietta Maria, 1609–69, Charles I's queen 1625. Berkeley entertained most of the royal family at Durdans on 1 September: Evelyn, *Diary*.

[1] Berkeley was keeper of Nonsuch Palace and the Little Park from 1660 to 1669 or 1670: Manning and Bray, *Surrey*, ii. 606.

[2] There was a second son, George, *c.* 1652–94; prebendary of Westminster 1687: (*Westminster Abbey Registers*), ed. J. L. Chester (Harleian Soc., vol. x, 1876), p. 29 n.

[3] A London bookseller active from 1630 to 1674: Plomer, *Dictionary*, *1641–67*.

[4] p. 170, n. 1.

[Postscript by Andrew Crooke:]

Sir the tenn ponds herein mentiond wilbe payd you one the inclosd note by Mr Richard Davis[1] from your humble servant

ANDREW CROOKE

Ag 28. 1662.

Address (written by Mandey): For my much honour'd freind mr John Locke Student in Christs-Church in Oxford

## *144.* ROBERT PICKERING to LOCKE, 19 September 1662

B.L., MS. Locke c. 17, ff. 158–9. The writer, born 1619, was a barrister: G. Ormerod, *History of (Cheshire)*, 2nd ed. (1882), i. 749.

Worthie Sir

As I have great cause soe I give you many thanks for your paines and care of my sonne[2] who I wish may deserve part of the comendations in your lre before your notes came to my hand I hope you had reced some money which I sent by a Carrier what is wanting shalbee returned with speed I hope to see you in November as I goe to London that I may have the opportunity further to expresse my thankfulnes to you The hopes you give mee of my Sonne is an incoureagement to encounter with the foulenes of the Jorney to see you I begg the favour from you to present my service to the Deane with acknowledgment of your great favour I remeyne

Your much obliged friend and servant

RO PICKERING.

Thelwall 19 September 62

Address: For my worthie and much Honoured Friend Mr John Lock Master of Arts at his Lodgings in chchurch in Oxford

## *145.* HENRY TOWNSHEND to LOCKE, 22 September 1662 (*141*, *155*)

B.L., MS. Locke c. 22, ff. 13–14.

Sir

I can no way disallow the Bills of my sonns Accounts, they being reasonable; And I shall never feare other, having so good Overseers. According to your desire their shalbe so much returnd as the Bills

[1] *c.* 1618–93 or later; bookseller in Oxford active *c.* 1646–88: Madan, vols. ii, iii; Wood, *L. and T.*

[2] John Pickering, 1645–1703; matriculated from Christ Church 19 July 1662; barrister: Ormerod; Foster; letter below, no. *700*.

comes, wherby yow may still keep in your hand 10l as a provision[a] and so take with your other pupills, But yow have not sett down for your own payns in Tutoradg, which I desire yow pleas to do, as with your schollers.

I would have sent your monyes, yf I knew how with security. The Carrier asks 4d. per 1l. Return. As yet I have no present frend to Convay it by; But shall use all Expedition and Diligence one way or other to be safly delivered to your hands.

I have no more But to return yow great thanks for your Care of my Son, which obligeth me to be

your affectionat frend to serv yow
HEN TOWNSHEND.

Worcester. 22° Sept. 62.

Our Bishop[1] after 11 dayes great affliction and payn dyed on Sunday last about 2 in the postnoon. A most excelent preacher and pious person: God send us his equall, we cannot expect a better.

Since I wrot, the Carrier Sam. Newman will pay yow 5l and so shall bring up the money by degrees.

Address: This For his especiall kind frend mr Jo. Lock of Christ Church in Oxford.

## *146.* HENRY BARNARD to LOCKE, 29 September 1662 (*162*)

B.L., MS. Locke c. 3, f. 153. The writer is not identifiable.

Sir

My sister Serle bein enformed from mr. william Bowdlye that you are the person designed to be her sonnes tutor hath sent him unto you desireing you willbe pleased to take the chardge of him,[2] I question not but he willbe govern'd by you in all thinges being of a singular good nature, and much given to his Study, shee desires he may be entred a Commoner and willbe willing to allow him 40l. per annum or theire abouts, and hath sent you 20l. for present

[a] *Abbreviated; spelling doubtful.*

[1] Dr. John Gauden, bishop of Worcester since 10 June of this year: *D.N.B.* He is generally said to have died on Saturday, 20 September.

[2] Henry Searle, son of Nicholas Searle of Tadley, Hants, gent., who is described in 1671 as deceased and late of Milbrough Stoke, Salop; matriculated from Christ Church 26 November of this year; barrister, Lincoln's Inn, 1671: Foster; exercise in Locke's Herbarium.

disburcements and when you shall have occasion for a new supply, upon his writing either to his mother or my selfe, I shall take order to have it returned from London, shee further desires that he may goe with my Man to Wincester to see his friends to returne to you once in a weeke or 10 daies. he desired me to entreate you if it maybe to have a double chamber, expecting a schoolefellow of his to meete him theire, whoe probablely you may have the charge of him, being what have for present take leave to remayne

your lo: friend and servant

HEN: BARNARD

Bridgenorth. 29th September 62

Address: These For his honoured friend Mr Locke student of Christ Church in Oxford

## *147.* SIR CHARLES BERKELEY, K.B., later second earl of Berkeley, to LOCKE, [September/October 1662?] (*140*, *150*)

B.L., MS. Locke c. 3, ff. 187–8. The year on general grounds; the season from the fog and mist.

Sir

The last letter which I had from you rejoyced me very much; becaus I heard of the health of my freinds at Oxford. Sir If I should in this letter number up how much ingaged I am to you more especially, and to all my freinds at oxford, it would fill this whoole paper, and as much more. Here I am dayly disputing with the Cantabrigians Præferring Oxford, before Cambridg, there is sccarce one morning among ten but that there is a fogge or mist enough to choake the whole university: which I beleive makes them so dull and stupid. it gives them as it is very proper in the latin pingue ingenium;[1] pray Sir excuse me to mr. Cary[2] for not Answering his letter, I will next post. Thus I rest

Your most Affectionate freind

CHARLES BERKELEY

Address: To my very loving freind Mr John lock at Christchurch in Oxford

[1] 'Thick wits'. The idea is originally from the ancient Greek jeer at the Bœotians, whose climate was supposed to have that effect: 'Bœotum in crasso jureres aere natum': Horace, *Epistles*, II. i. 244. Hardly a quotation, though Ovid has 'pingue ingenium' in another connection: *Metamorphoses*, xi. 148.

[2] Probably Francis Henry Cary, *c.* 1642–1712; at Westminster School; matriculated from Christ Church 22 August 1661; pupil of Locke; B.A. 1665; M.A. 1669; divine: Barker and Stenning; exercises in Locke's Herbarium.

## *148.* JOHN DOD to LOCKE, 7 October 1662

B.L., MS. Locke c. 7, ff. 209–10. The writer, d. 1692?, matriculated from Christ Church 26 Nov. 1650; B.A. 1654; M.A. 1656; B.D. 1663; rector of Hinton, Northants., 1662–92: Foster; p. 143, n. 1.

Neighbor

I should bee glad to heare whether your thoughts are fixt about my chamber; as I told you at Oxford soe I say now, I shall not bate any thing lower, then the thirds,[1] and I leave you still to your liberty whether the goods shall bee mine or yours: if you thinke them worth 8l 13s–4d they are at your service, if not, I will have your freindship though I have none of your money; but if you will pay that summe you may take your owne time to discharge it, to him who is

your Faithful Friend and Humble Servant

JOHN DOD

Hinton Oct. 7. 1662.

Address: These For Mr John Locke at his chamber in ch. ch.

## *149.* [Mrs.] ELLICE PRICE to [LOCKE?], 21 October 1662

B.L., MS. Locke c. 18, f. 7. The writer was presumably a waiting-woman.

Sir

I have bin somtimes the bearer of letters to the post-house directed to you from mrs. Parry, and now I leave one for you there, and from the place I take on me the boldnesse to informe you that Mrs. Parry have in some measure entertained a servant, who is very much in love with her, his name is Bricknocke,[2] and very well liked by mrs. Kingwell[a][3] whome I doe live withall, and know the

[a] *Or* Ringwell

[1] An incomer paid for the furnishings, etc., of college rooms a sum usually assessed at two-thirds of the amount paid by the preceding tenant: *O.E.D.*, s.v. Third, II. 5.

[2] Not identified.

[3] Perhaps Margaret Kingwell, the writer of an undated and unaddressed fragment of a letter, B.L., MS. Locke c. 13, f. 8:

. . . Me . . . betweene you and me, you had . . . shillings of nuts in my absence which I have paid since I com whom, how things are nowe[?], let me know in a private note, if you will have me send your peece downe to you send me word soe, mrs Fisher and mrs Chester Mrs Dorothy Peyton present theyr service to you and soe doth your oblyged servant

. . . MARG: KINGWELL

. . . arry, and to the Doctor . . . er is heare once again

The same woman is perhaps the writer of a letter to Sir Edward Harley 15 April

passages, Sir if this may Concerne you I thought it good to give you notice of it, if it does not pray excuse my boldnesse; how ever pray let me desire you not to discover this to mrs. Parry, I should be glad to here whether this came to your hands or not, this is all from your servantt

ELLICE PRICE

From the posthouse this 21 october 62

if you please to write direct your Letter to mr Jones in the little sentry[1] westminster.

## *150.* SIR CHARLES BERKELEY, K.B., later second earl of Berkeley, to LOCKE, [November/December 1662?] (*147*, *153*)

B.L., MS. Locke c. 3, ff. 201–2. The date from the subscription. The form is the same as that of no. *147*, of questionable date, and is similar to that of no. *153*, whose date is fairly certain.

Sir

I should beg, but that we must both mutually beg and receive pardon, for not writing: and by blaming my self I should accuse you of the same fault. yet Sir I am perswaded you dont write, in Comiseration of me, lest by adding that of writing a letter to your former kindnesses, y⟨ou⟩[a] should heap so many on me that I should sink under the burden, not being able to repay half of them. unlesse your glory is in always giving, and never thinking to receive but I hope your free nature will overcome your pity and you will once more oblige him with a letter who is

Your Most affectionate freind

CHARLES BERKELEY

Address: For Mr John Lock Student of Ch: Ch in Oxford

[a] *Page torn.*

---

1662; if so, she was probably a connection of Col. Maurice (or Matthew) Kingwell: H.M.C., *Portland MSS.* iii. 258, 260, 261; Firth, *Regimental History of Cromwell's Army*, ii. 679–81, 691–2.

[1] Little Sanctuary.

## *151.* JOHN STRACHEY to LOCKE, 31 December 1662 (*132, 163*)

B.L., MS. Locke c. 18, ff. 212–13.

Sir

I know noe greater triall I can make of your freindship, then by committing faults that aske a pardon. I confesse I have received three letters from you ὕστερον πρότερον[1] and have answered nither 'till now, but the same excuses you found out for mee prove to bee very reall, viz. the uncertainty where you were and the woing of a Mistress, who is since turnd to a wife, having lost the name of a Virgin the 17 night of this moneth,[2] I acknowledg I cant handsomly tell you thus much without sending the tokens of Gloves and Favours, but in good faith twould bee very exceptious having bestowde none such on hers or mine owne relations, however I would hazard much for your sake were I in place where, but I am now in Glocester shire, where noe Gloves are to bee had which doe not smell of Cotswool,[3] the best way I conceive is the next occasion you have to buy gloves lett them be worne in commemoration of my marriag, that hath litle trouble and lesse cost in it, (on my conscience I may bee a rich man in time) if you send mee a letter or any thing elce after this unkindnesse lett it bee left with Andrew Morris at the Signe of the Bell in St Thom. Streete, I expect the books according to promise and am

Sir

your very lovin freind

J. S.

Decem$^{st}$ last 62.

Address: For Mr John Locke Master of Arts and Student of Christ Church these Oxon

---

[1] The words are commonly Anglicized, hysteron proteron. Here they mean in the wrong order or the last first: *O.E.D.*

[2] Strachey's wife was Jane Hodges (1643–1727) of Great Wedmore: p. 54 n.

[3] Cotswold.

## *152.* [SIR?] P[HILIP?] HARCOURT to LOCKE, [*c.* 1662/ 1663?]

B.L., MS. Locke c. 11, ff. 140–1. If the writer is Sir Philip Harcourt the date probably falls within the term of his first marriage. Philip Harcourt, d. 1688, of Stanton Harcourt, Oxfordshire; knighted 1660; father by his first wife of Simon Harcourt, first Viscount Harcourt, the Lord Chancellor (*D.N.B.*). He married first, in 1660 or earlier, Anne, d. 23 August 1664, daughter of Sir William Waller, the general (p. 284, n. 1). He remained a widower until about 1671: *The Harcourt Papers*, ed. E. W. Harcourt, 1880–1905, i. 200–7.

Sir

I must first returne you thankes for your last obliging civilitys, when you would draw so great a trouble upon your selfe, at your chamber, as my being there may perhaps have caused, and pay my just acknowledgments of that before I contract a new debt. This last favour, coming unaskt, and unlooked for, has so exceedingly overjoyed and pleased my wife, dos lay so binding an obligation upon me, that if either of us did desire to make those due returnes, which either you may expect, or it deserves, wee must necessarily stay till the suddennes of so unexpected a busness be over, when wee may be able to recollect our selves, and with freer eys behold the effects of that ingenuous spirit, which I did allways judge, and I see now not falsly you were master of. My wife receaved the litle chained prisoner but began to handle him before she had read the latter end of your letter, and thereby found that squirrells have no respecte of persons, I thought to goe more warily to worke, and put on a great thick glove, never thinking that if he could crack a hard nut, he might easily peirce my gauntlet, and so we both came of that service wounded, having a litle smart with our pleasure; I have only told you how my wife was pleased with her present, I must now let you know that she sends you as many thanks as will reach you from hence to Oxford, to which I joyne mine with my desires for and resolutions to improve all occasions, whereby I may tender those respects, and services which are due to you from

Sir

your freind and servant to his power

P. HARCOURT.

Address: These To his much respected freind Mr Lock at his chamb⟨er⟩[a] in Christ Church Oxford deliver[b]

[a] *Page rubbed.* [b] *MS.* đđ

## *153.* SIR CHARLES BERKELEY, K.B., later second earl of Berkeley, to LOCKE, 15 January [1663?] (*150, 156*)

B.L., MS. Locke c. 3, ff. 195–6. The year from connection with other letters from the writer and from the contents.

Sir

I hope you will excuse my slothfulnesse in acknowloging my thanks for those many Letters you have bin pleased to send to me hear are divers of your schoolfellows which are very glad to heare you are well Mr Hill and Mr WRight Mr Bratle and Mr Blomer[1] which will be very glad to see you at the commencement[2] we lateley had two commedies acted at our Colleadg in one of them I had a part one latin called Adelphe the other english calld Albumazar[3] I am to go to London within this fortnight or three weeks I should be very glad to se you there. Pray Remember me to all my freinds at Oxford and tell Mr Cary that I have received his Letter and shall answer it the next oppurtunity.

Your affectionate freind
CHAR: BERK:

T.C.C Jan: 15

Address: For Mr John Lock Mr. of Art student of Christchurch in Oxford.

## *154.* THOMAS HARBORNE to LOCKE, 20 January 1663

B.L., MS. Locke c. 11, f. 139. The writer was of Aylesbury, Bucks.; his son, also Thomas, matriculated from Christ Church on 3 May 1662 aged 17: Foster. Exercises by the son in Locke's Herbarium.

Honnoured Sir

my humble service presented to the worthy Deane and yourselfe, giveinge you hearty thankes for your Care and paines to my

[1] Thomas Hill, D.D. 1670, dean of Ossory 1671–3, or Richard Hill, M.A. 1661, vicar of St. Michael's, Cambridge, 1663; Charles Wright, D.D., 1671, professor of Arabic 1702–11, or Lawrence Wright, M.D. 1666; Daniel Brattell, d. 1694, D.D. 1681; and Thomas Blomer (p. 332, n. 2). All six were at Westminster with Locke and were now fellows, etc., of Trinity College: Barker and Stenning.

[2] p. 212, n. 1.

[3] Two 'comedies', not named in the Junior Bursar's accounts, were performed at Trinity in January 1663. *Adelphe* is almost certainly the unprinted play by Samuel Brooke, sometime Master of Trinity; a copy has a new prologue dated 1662. It was first performed at Trinity in 1612. *Albumazar* is by Thomas Tomkis; it was first performed before James I at Trinity in 1615; editions 1615 *bis*; 1634 *bis*; new ed., revised, 1668: G. C. Moore Smith, *College Plays Performed in . . . Cambridge*, 1923, pp. 66, 67, 71, 89; *D.N.B.*, arts. Brooke and Tomkis.

sonne and humbly desire the continuance of the same and that you would be pleased to keepe him to his Study and that he avoide ill Company. I have sent you by him mony to repay what you have disbursed beinge almost Eight pounds and att the Assizes next I shall waite on you (god willinge). my sonne had Came a weeke sooner but that I have beene from home but I hope his paines and Care in his Study will regaine his Lost Tyme soe haveinge noe more att present but wisheinge us a happy New yeare I take Leave and remaine

Sir

your most obleiged Freind and servant

THO: HARBORNE

20th of January 1662

Address: To his much respected Freind mr John Locke att Christ Church in Oxford

## *155.* HENRY TOWNSHEND to LOCKE, 4 February 1663 (*145*)

B.L., MS. Locke c. 22, f. 15.

Sir

Had the Weather bin open and seasonable to travell your schollar had bin with yow befre this tyme, and although som would advise his further stay, yet he is willing not to loose, but rather improv his tyme for his future good, though it be gotten through Cold and hunger. His mother and I Return yow thanks for your Care over him, and also the Good Character yow are pleased to decipher him out, I pray and wish and hope yow shall rather ⟨receive⟩[a] Creditt, then the Least disparadgment by his outward Conversation or Study. We have perused your Accownts and noats of receits and disbursments, and do beleev have assest them right according to the paper inclosd with allowance for Tutoradg. Only I do not understand why Barbers Landresses and woman to make Beds and swep Chambers or such like should be paid for no service or work don by the quarter, when either one comes up in the midle of a quarter, or are absent a third part or half a quarter together, but[b–] proportionably for the tyme;[–b] I speake not of som few weeks. But the Custom of the Colledg may convince mee. I

[a] *MS.* rec    [b–b] *Interlined.*

have sent 11s to make up the former Accounts even, And also 5l more to remayn in your hands towards this quarter. Thus wishing yow a happy New yeare I remayn

your affectionat frend to serv yow
HEN TOWNSHEND

Worcester. 4° febr. 62.

## *156.* SIR CHARLES BERKELEY, K.B., later second earl of Berkeley, to LOCKE, 14 April 1663 (*153*, *160*)

B.L., MS. Locke c. 3, ff. 191–2.

Sir

It is so long since I wrote to you, that perhaps you may think I forget you: if I should, I should forget to be thankfull, which Ile assure you Sir I shall never do to you; for I can never testify enough how much I owe you. I have for a long time bin at London, and there I have had many occasions to put of my writing: I thougt to write this day, then somthing hinderd me, and I though to doot the next then I was hinderd to, and so at last I stayd till I came to Cambridge again. and now Sir I am In Cambridg as much your pupill and Honorer as I was in Oxford.

Your freind and servant
CHARLES BERKELEY

Pray Remember my service to the Dean and all my freinds.

Aprill 14 1663

Address: For Mr John Lock Mr of Art student of Christchurch in Oxford

## *157.* GEORGE WILLIAMSON to LOCKE, 17 April 1663

B.L., MS. Locke c. 23, f. 98. The writer, *c.* 1599–1685; M.A., Oxford, 1626; perhaps B.D. 1643; canon of Bristol 1643; etc.: Foster. See further no. *159*.

Sir

I have according to my promise sent you up five Pounds for my son Roberts[1] Caution, unto whome I have given order to take an

[1] *c.* 1645–80?; matriculated 22 May of this year; B.A. 1667; M.A. 1669; vicar of Keynsham 1675–80 and rector of Saltford 1679–80 (both in Somerset): Foster; Weaver, *Somerset Incumbents*, pp. 273, 285. His caution is his caution money, a deposit made as a security for good behaviour. Exercises, etc., in Locke's Herbarium.

acquittance of Mr Bowcer for the receit of it. Besides I have sent six Pounds ten shillings more to pay mr Davis[1] the Bookeseller for mine and my sonnes bookes, which commeth in all to 4£ 8s. 6d. and 41s. 6d. for to pay mr Souch[2] for his surplesse which my sonne sent me word in his letter by the Carier was provided; but he like a wise man, at least otherwise, mencioneth not what the surplesse and making came too, so that I was faine to send money by ghesse; mr Souch (If I mistake not) having told me himselfe that it would come to within 40s. If there be any over plus I should desire you and mr Hill[3] to whome I pray present my true affection and respects to drinke a cuppe of wine together, and take Mr Davis along with you, and remember us here if you please. If any thing be wanting to satisfy Mr Souch let Robin make it up, and I shall repay him againe when I write or send up next. Mr Davies his bookes being second hand bookes for the most part me thinkes he might be persuaded to abate something. of his prices. if he may be brought to it you may please to bestow it upon your scholar. Whome I shall now leave to your care and hope that you will so employ him this long Vacation that he may be put in fourme the next Terme. But that I shall referre to your discretion intreating you to put so much imployment upon him as may keepe him out of Idlenes and unnecessary wandring[a] about the towne, which I earnestly desire him to forbeare, and you to suffer. So desireing you to present my humble service to Mr Deane, I commend you to the divine protection and rest

Sir

your very humble servant

GEORGE WILLIAMSON.

Brist. April. 17. being Good-friday. 1663.

you shall receive these monies vz: 11£. 10s by bill of Exchange in Oxon which bill you shall receive here enclosed.

I pray Sir Bid Robin remember my service to mr Souch and thanke him for his curtesies shewed me at Oxford. and to tell him

[a] *Or* wanding

[1] p. 200 and n. 1.

[2] Either John Souch or his son Richard; both of them milliners in Oxford: *Surveys and Tokens*, pp. 436–8; Wood, *L. and T.*

[3] Perhaps Richard Hill, *c.* 1623–95; M.A. 1646; student of Christ Church 1640–8, 1660– ; canon of Salisbury 1683: Foster.

that I was at his house the same morning I returned for Bristoll, but he was not at home.

Address: For his honoured friend Mr. John Locke student in Christ-Church at his Chamber there present in Oxon.

## 158. Locke to William Uvedale, 29 April 1663 (*105*)

B.L., MS. Locke c. 24, ff. 281–2. Apparently the letter sent and returned to Locke.

Sir

I know businesse now wholy possesseth you, and that Chancery lane and Westminster hall share all your time, But when the Lawyers shall have resignd you back again with advantage to the injoyment of your freinds, and you shall have noething else to doe but heare their congratulations, then perhaps it may not be unseasonable to wait upon you, and those who could not assist you in obteining the victory, may yet be permitted to attend your triumph, and rejoyce in your successe. This will be businesse enough to draw me to London, and perhaps to Wellwin (where I shall be sure to meet with one to joyne with me in itt) if you will but doe me the favour to lett me know (a weeke before you goe) the day that you designe your journy thither. I will not then faile to attend you to the learned Rectors,[1] who shall keepe a Thanks-giveing day for your successe, for certainly Astræa[2] returning again to the earth to make you noe inconsiderable present, may well deserve to be enterteind with solemnity, at least with the joynt acclamations of all your freinds. Give me then oportunity to make one upon this occasion and to assure you that I am

Sir

Your most humble and most faithfull servant

J Locke

Ch: Ch: 29° Apr 63.

If you goe not to Welwin yet pray let me know when you goe out of London.

Address: These present To Mr William Uvedall To be left at Mrs Pledwells in New-market street near the new Theater London[3]

Added in another hand: At the George upon Fleet bridg

[1] Gabriel Towerson: p. 155 n. [2] The goddess of justice.

[3] The Theatre Royal in Vere Street, opened in 1660 and superseded on 7 May of this year. Clare Market was called the New Market apparently until 1661 or later: A. Nicoll, *A History of English Drama, 1660–1900*, 1952–9, i. 294–8; Wheatley, *London*.

## *159.* RICHARD WILLIAMSON to LOCKE, 29 April 1663

B.L., MS. Locke c. 23, f. 99. The writer is apparently a son of George and brother of Robert Williamson: no. *157*.

Sir

My Father Comannded me to give you an Accompt of mr. Ayliffes bill of exchange, and of his not sending a letter of Advise to Accompany the bill. Sir I was this Morning with mr Ayliffe and communicated unto him your letter, who upon knowledg thereof, told me possitively, that he did send a letter of advise, and withall in the same letter advised mr. Ayleworth, that if he could not pay the whole monyes, to goe to one mr. Rawlings (if I mistake not his name and one whoe deales with mr. Ayleworth, with said Ayliffe) and to desire him to honour the bill for payment thereof: However Sir mr. Ayliffe hath herein sent you a bill upon mr. Ayleworth for payment of 7l: 10s. and another bill for the foure pownds, to which I referr you. My father as I suppose has writ to my brother that the mony is returned by the Carrier, but I had ordered otherwise before, which I hope will not faile. I have nothing here remarkable to write unto you, at present I begg leave to subscribe my selfe

Sir

your humble servant

RICH. WILLIAMSON 1663

Bristoll the 24th Aprill 1663

Sir mr. Ayliffe hath taken order with the Carrier for payment of the 4l.

Address: For his honoured Friend mr: John Lock Student in Christ Church Present in Oxon.

## *160.* SIR CHARLES BERKELEY, K.B., later second earl of Berkeley, to LOCKE, [late May 1663?] (*156*, *161*)

B.L., MS. Locke c. 3, ff. 199–200. The time of year is fixed by the mention of the Commencement. Berkeley is unlikely to have spent more than about two years in Cambridge; the year 1664 is unlikely for this letter as it cannot have been written shortly before no. *168*, and more than a day or two later would have been too near the Commencement.

Sir

I am now in great hopes that it will not be long before we see one another. tis not above six weekes to the commencement[1] and then

[1] It was held on the first Tuesday in July: E. Chamberlayne, *Angliæ Notitia*, 1674, ii. 315. This year the day fell on the 7th.

if you keep your promise I shall see you and not only I but many more of your freinds will rejoyce very much to se you here and I dare say will endeavor to make you heartily welcom. pray put My lord Anslow[1] and Mr Hogies[2] and mr Cary and all those that promised me in mind of their promise. I do still wait for and expect that happy time when I shall have an opportunity to show how much I am indebted to you and am your

freind and servant
CHARLES BERKELEY

Address (written by someone other than Berkeley): For Mr John Lock Master of arts and Student of Christchurch in Oxfford These

## *161.* SIR CHARLES BERKELEY, K.B., later second earl of Berkeley, to LOCKE, 15 August 1663 (*160*, *168*)

B.L., MS. Locke c. 3, ff. 193–4.

Sir

I think it will be always my fortune to remayn in your debt for your kind letters, I have ought you one a great while, but I hope you will excuse me for I have bin sick and out of town. Mr Hill[3] does acquaint me with that which I knew before your great civility; And I must thanke you for your kindnesse to him my freind, and to my self for Remembring me. I was to go to Glocestershire,[4] and might have gone with my father when he went, but I declined it, and was willing to stay longer so I might come by Oxford and se you and it. which I shall do within this three weekes or month.

I rest
Your freind and servant
CHARLES BERKELEY

August 15 1663

Address: For Mr John Lock Student of Christchurch in: Oxford

[1] James Annesley, *c.* 1645–90; styled Lord Annesley 1661–86; second earl of Anglesey 1686; at Westminster School 1658–60; matriculated from Christ Church 4 December 1661: G. E. C.; etc.

[2] Probably Locke's friend Nathaniel Hodges: p. 260, n. 3.

[3] Thomas Hill or Richard Hill at Cambridge; p. 207, n. 1.

[4] i.e. to Berkeley Castle, as in no. *133*.

## *162.* Henry Barnard to Locke, 20 October 1663 (*146*)

B.L., MS. Locke c. 3, f. 154.

Sir

yours of the 15°. July I received by Cozen[1] Henry Serle, theirby wee are heartly glad to heare of his soe good deportment from you. I hope he will continue the same to your Credit, and his friends Comforts. I observe what monies you received, allsoe what disburcements you had made for him, and that theire remained 6s: 8d. due upon that account, which my Sister Serle desires you to expend on a paire of gloves for your selfe, shee presents her service to you and returnes you many thankes of your care of hers, as my selfe, for the which shall ever remayne

Sir, your Assured friend to serve you

Hen: Barnard

Bridgenorth 20th: Octobris 63

Address: These For Mr John Locke Mastr. of Art, and student of Christ church present in Oxford

## *163.* John Strachey to Locke, 18 November 1663 (*151*, 177)

B.L., MS. Locke c. 18, f. 214. Locke had apparently consulted Strachey as to whether he should accept a living. It was uncertain how long he could retain his studentship at Christ Church as a layman. When a vacancy occurred among the Theologi the senior Philosophus, unless he held a Faculty place, would be obliged to fill it and to qualify himself for it by taking holy orders; should he refuse to do so he would forfeit his studentship: see note on Christ Church, p. 3. Locke wrote in 1666 that he had received several offers of livings: p. 304. He had probably received one recently. On 4 October of this year Fell as Dean of Christ Church, Dr. Edward Pococke (p. 256, n. 1) as sub-dean, and Richard Gardiner, one of the canons, signed a certificate relating to his character, conduct, and orthodoxy: Fox Bourne, i. 88. It is probably to be associated with such an offer.

On 14 November 1666 Charles II granted Locke a dispensation which enabled him to retain his studentship without taking orders: ibid. i. 131. He obtained a Faculty place in 1675: no. *523* n.

Sir

Whilst you accuse mee of a litle complement, you have putt the greatest upon mee imaginable, in asking my advise in this concerne

[1] In the obsolete usage, a collateral relative more remote than a brother or sister: *O.E.D.*; in this case a nephew.

of yours, certainly your owne strenght is greate enough not to neede any forreine succours, and those small auxiliaries I can bringe may possibly share in the glory, not contribute the least in your aid, but since you are pleased to call for my assistance, I will chuse rather to manifest my owne weaknesse then not appeare forward to serve you. And since I must confine my thoughts to this paper, I will not state your case, but suppose that your Genius and Studies doe now crosse your present Interest, and you must necessarily declare your selfe for one; as to your studies (I hope I may speake without flattery) I beleive you and your parts such, that you may bee well said to bee homo versatilis ingenii,[1] and fitted for whatever you shall undertake, but to deale freely I have alwaies lookt on you as one of a higher head then to take covert under a Cottage, and in my opinion the best Country Parsonage is noe more, and although our holy Mother makes better provision for some of her children and bestows titles and preferments on them, yett the expectation is soe tedious, and the observance soe base besides the uncertainty, that it will tire the patience of an ingenious spiritt to[a]– waiht on–[a] such an old doting Grandame, not to meddle with your owne Genius and inclination which is as bad as Helmonts Archeus[2] if once twharted and one were as good hange as contradict it, for what is a restraint but a strangling of nature. This is such a trade as may be tooke to at any time and as longe as there are dunces in the world a man of parts, lett him study but complyance, hee need want noe preferment. The onely thing you can well stagger at is the present losse, but surely you are not of the Simpletons mind in the Gospell that would not lend out his money for feare of loosing it,[3] not forgoe a Colledge Pension out of distrust that you shall neere meete with the like againe, prithee leave that leare shore[4] and putt to sea, Neptune is not soe mercilesse as most men fancy, and if you returne not in a yeare or two

a–a *Interlined.*

1 'A man of versatile mind'. Livy has 'versatile ingenium': XXXIX. xl. 5; but here it is hardly a quotation.

2 Jan Baptista van Helmont, 1577–1644, chemist, physician, etc.: *Biog. nat. de Belgique*. His Archeus is the vital force, the organ of the soul that controls the working of the body; it resides in the stomach and when irritated causes diseases. The treatises relating to it were published in 1648; an English translation, in 1662: van Helmont, *Opera Omnia*, 1707, prefixed key; pp. 38–9, etc.; Partington, *Hist. of Chemistry*, ii. 234–40, etc.

3 Matthew 25: 14–30.

4 Probably a slip for lee shore, one on which the wind blows.

with as rich a Cargoe as the best, Ile neere cast figure more, and the Sea putts mee in mind that a litle outlandish aire would doe mighty well if not for health yett for reputation, and sure as longe as I had ⟨land⟩[a] I would not want money for such a purpose, and if you dont redeeme it againe in a short space, the world would bee a hard Stepdame, You see how ready I am to answer if not to goe beyond your desires, but you know when zeale is up tis a hard matter to keepe it in its due bounds, that it may not turne Fanatick, but I hope you will pardon mee upon the same score that its admirers hope to bee, viz: because tis from a good meaninge and nevertheless take me to be still loyall in

your freindship and service.

JO: STRACHEY.

Novem 18th. 63.

Mr Jo: Blanch Mr Walters man hath his shop whether you may please to send.[1]

## *164.* WILLIAM OWEN to LOCKE, 26 December 1663

B.L., MS. Locke c. 16, ff. 182–3. William Owen, *c.* 1618–72; M.A., Oxford; rector of Pontesbury, Salop, 1641–6, 1660–72: Matthews, *Walker Revised*, pp. 306–7.

Sir

I doubt not in the least of your learned paines and readines to instruct my s⟨o⟩ne,[b2] but whether they have bene answerd in him with that successe which you endeavour and my selfe expect, I should be glad to heare; parents are much concernd for their children; And therefore though impertinently I mind you and desire (which questionlesse you are forward of your selfe) to perswade him to consort himselfe with the most civill and learned company of his standinge, I hope youle pardon me this error, who

[a] *MS.* sand *or* tand [b] *Page torn.*

[1] This was a Bristol address: no. 177, etc.

[2] Corbet Owen, 1646–71; at Westminster School 1658–63; king's scholar 1659; matriculated from Christ Church 3 July 1663; admitted to Lincoln's Inn 1665; B.A. 1667; M.A. 1670; Latin poet: *D.N.B.*; Barker and Stenning; exercises, etc., in Locke's Herbarium.

shalbe ready to gratifie your greate care as far as any, beinge indeed noe more then you may justly expect from

Sir

Your much obliged friend and servant to commaund

WILLIAM OWEN

Sir I hope ere this you have received 20s from mee more then the common allowance for Tutoridge.

iff you please to befriend mee with a line or two in answere to these, direct your lettere for me to bee left at Mr Woods shop mercer in Salop, and it will come safe to my hands.

Pontesbury the 26t. of 10ber: 63.

Address: These To Mr. John Lock master in Arts and student of Christ Church present in Oxon

## *165*. WILLIAM COKER to LOCKE, 31 January 1664 (*169*)

B.L., MS. Rawlinson D 286, f. 6. Copy by Coker. Excerpt printed in C. Bastide, *John Locke: ses théories politiques*, etc., 1907, p. 18. The writer matriculated from Christ Church on 10 April 1663, aged 17; B.A. from All Souls 1666; M.A. 1670; B.M. 1673; D.M. 1678: Foster; exercises, etc., in Locke's Herbarium.

This is a complimentary letter to Locke on his entering office as Censor of Moral Philosophy. Coker sent a copy to Benjamin Woodroffe (*D.N.B.*), the Censor of Natural Philosophy: Locke, *Essays on the Law of Nature*, ed. von Leyden, pp. 12 and n., 235 n. Coker's letter is omitted here, as is his valedictory letter, no. *169*.

## *166*. WILLIAM CARR to LOCKE, 21 February/2 March [1664] (94)

B.L., MS. Locke c. 5, ff. 11–12. Carr's date is presumably new style. Year from contents.

Dear Jacke

If that damnable French spirit will not leave you I will leave writting, For you can not imagine that a man being 9 months in France can indure to heare falss French, much less to see it writte: If Monsieur or Mademoiselle be in your next letter, I proclaime my selfe to be your open ennimie. As for honest Sue I could wish the caractere you give of her were trew, that she pleases att a distance, then I should have my sheare. If Sue's head were upon a Frenchwomans shoulders she would make an excellant mistress; But to speake without partialitie (and not like those that thinke they are obliged to commend all that they see abroade) the Frenchwomens humour is so plesant that it is impossible to be exprest. I had designed both these trifles for Dick Lower,[1] but your desier of one and his avirice togeather, hath maide me seperate them; if they prove not good, send me w⟨ord⟩,[a] and Ile fier the towne they were maide in, because it is famous for nothing else. That 46 thousand men has passd through Lyons to Marselliers and so for Italie, I am an eye-wittness of it and there are more daily passing notwithstanding the articles and the Piramede which is erected in Rome very high for the King ⟨of⟩[b] France and so proude that none but the Italiens would suffer it.[2] within these 3 weekes we are for Ausburge,[3] and have designed Rome for our quarters next winter. as for the Germane tongue I would not learne it to have the Empire although much urged to it by our Governour. I understand so much of your Terræfilius's speeche[4] that I desier no more of it, allthough the question would have maide any ingenuous. Here is a report that my Lord Sunderland and Harrie Savile who went into Spaine togeither are both dead, But he that was the auther of this report is knowne to be a man much given to tell wonders, so that I hope the contrarie.[5] Tell Jefferie[6] I begine to have as ill an opinion of a

[a] *Paper rubbed.* [b] *Page torn.*

---

[1] pp. 152, n. 1, 280, etc.

[2] A riot of the Pope's Corsican guards against the French ambassador in Rome on 20 August 1662, N.S., led Louis XIV to break off relations with the Pope. Negotiations having failed, in November 1663 Louis sent 3,500 troops towards Italy. Fresh negotiations at Pisa led to a treaty signed there on 12 February 1664, N.S. The terms included the erection of a pyramid (or obelisk?) with suitable inscriptions opposite the barracks of the Corsicans; it was demolished in 1669: E. Lavisse, *Histoire de France*, 1901–11, VII. ii. 269–71; L. von Pastor, *Geschichte der Päpste*, 1901–33, XIV. i. 366–83; C. de Mouÿ, *Louis XIV et le Saint-Siège: L'ambassade du duc de Créqui*, 1893, ii. 299–301, etc.

[3] Augsburg.

[4] At the Act of 1663; the speaker was Joseph Brooks of Christ Church: Wood, *L. and T.* ii. 563 etc.

[5] Robert Spencer, 1640–1702; second earl of Sunderland 1643: *D.N.B.* Henry Savile: p. 86, n. 8. They were in Madrid in December 1663; Savile was unwell whilst travelling thither: *Savile Correspondence*, ed. W. D. Cooper (Camden Soc., vol. lxxi, 1858), p. 3.

[6] Presumably Isaiah (Esay) Ward; so perhaps Jefry in no. *92*.

Phisitian's friendshipe as of his religion, prethee, prethee prethee Jack writt constantly

Thine WI CARR.

Lyons Mar 2.

Address: These For mr Locke master of Arts and Student of Ch: Ch: in Oxford.

Postmark: MR 10.

## *167.* CHARLES POWELL to LOCKE, 29 April 1664

B.L., MS. Locke c. 18, ff. 3–4.

Mr Lock,

I am sorry that I missed to answer your letter by the Carryer last weeke, that I might rectify the mistake of Edmund for Edward; I doe acknowledge that you have paide the money to the right person my freind mr Edward Morgan[1] of Queens Colledge and doe thanke you for soe doeing; since the superscription of my letter to him did in A great measur satisfy you which another person probably would not have done it thus with my respects I wish you health and happiness and assure you that I am

Your Reall freind to serve you
CHARLES POWELL

Bristoll the 29th Aprill 1664:

Address: For Mr John Lock at Christ Church in Oxon present

## *168.* SIR CHARLES BERKELEY, K.B., later second earl of Berkeley, to LOCKE, 24 May 1664 (*161*)

B.L., MS. Locke c. 3, ff. 197–8.

Sir

I am ashamed again to use this so often urgd præamble the begging your excuse for my so long silence, yet I must once more ask your pardon for it. I am very glad to heare that you florish so with pupils, for I am so bold as to sharer in your joys; always esteeming my self most happy, when you are so. I have a hope (which I would not have deceive me) that you would trouble your self so far as to come

[1] Matriculated 1662; barrister 1674: Foster.

to Cambridge this commencement, but it is to great a happinesse for me to wish for: therefore I and all Your freinds here (who desire to Remember theire service to you) will petition and beg of ye to come. hoping you will be charitable

I rest Youre freind and servant
CHARLES BERKELEY

tuesday May 24. 64

Address: For Mr John Lock Mr of Arts student of Ch: Ch: Oxford

## *169.* WILLIAM COKER to LOCKE, 14 December 1664 (*165*)

B.L., MS. Rawlinson D 286, f. 6v. Copy by Coker. Here omitted: see no. *165*.

## *170.* LADY (ANNE) ALFORD to LOCKE, 31 January 1665 (*171*)

B.L., MS. Locke c. 3, ff. 5–6. Anne, *c.* 1619–93, daughter of Clement Corbet, LL.D., and widow of Sir Edward Alford of Offington, near Worthing, Sussex, knighted 1632: E. Cartwright, *Parochial Topography . . . Rape of Bramber*, 1830, pp. 30, 36–7 (J. Dallaway, *Hist. of . . . Western . . . Sussex*, vol. ii, pt. ii).

worthy Sir

I doe acknowlege my grat thankfullnes for your civillitys tow me and the grat care you have of my son[1] your letter was a very good cordiall tow revife my weak spirit it joys me much tow heare he is carfull tow keep such cumpany as you are pleased tow wish him tow I beseech god tow blese him that he may prove well and as honest a man as his most worthy father my desirs are he should keep the beast company which is civell and orderly ther he will most advantage him selfe and be lease expeensive, with your prudance and advice I doubt not but he will live as thrivftely as any gentleman ther this last quarter have bine more expencive then the naxt will be by rason of wood and other things for his chamber he wrights me word he shall want a sut againe sumer when you thinke it convenient be pleased tow help him tow by it I doubt the fastions will not be new untill E'ster tearm I am very sencible of this cold wather it much percies my weak body so as I

[1] John Alford, *c.* 1647–91; matriculated from Christ Church 18 November 1664; M.P. for Midhurst 1679, 1680–1; for Bramber 1689–90: Foster; etc.

shall add noe more but this tow desire your furder care of him which shall ever very much oblige me to be

Sir

Your humble sarvent

AN ALFORD

Jan 31 1664

Address: These for my much honnered frend Mr John Loock present

## *171.* LADY (ANNE) ALFORD to LOCKE, 23 May 1665 (*170*, *172*)

B.L., MS. Locke c. 3, ff. 7–8.

Worthy Sir

At the recait of your letter I ⟨was so⟩[a] weak as not able tow wright tow you tow ⟨give⟩[a] you my many thanks for your letter which was as a Cordiall tow me in heareing so good a Carracter of my son which I hop he will desarve from you and all that knows him. Sir I shall thinke my selfe much obliged tow you if you doe still continu your care over him As tow read tow him and give him all such instrouctions which you shall thinke fitt tow make him a religious honest good man which I pray dayly for I have looked over his quarters[b] expences both in your bill as in his own and trouly I doe find things very high as tow his batlings[1] I doe very will like of your preposall to give him a sartaine alowance which I hop will make him a better husband and more thrifty of his mony and then it will doe him good tow set down what he lays out tow mak him parfict in keeping accounts when he coms tow his estat. So if you please tow pay your selfe of what you have layd out in this bill above the 20l sent the remainder of that 5–18–6 which was left in your hands at first I pray pay unto my son and the naxt mounth I shall returne him 10 pounds more which will I hop discharge all his expences untill August when I intend tow send for him hom the next yeare I intend to alowe him a 100 a yeare so he shall pay all and by all his Clothes and living himselfe which is a very grat allowance out of his estat. when he coms tow keep house he will

[a] *Smudged by wax.* [b] *MS.* q[rs]

[1] A verbal substantive formed from battel. It may mean simply food in general or the college accounts for food supplied to members individually, either to battelers, who received no commons, or to commoners as extras: *O.E.D.*, s.v. Battel, *sb.*, etc.

find he cannot live tow spend so much upon himselfe I perceive he is removed tow an other Chamber more conveniant and chaper, which I lik very well of he must be a good husband for he hath a great Charg of Brothers and a Sister[1] tow provid for and noe grat estat tow doe it if god should take me which is more likly then tow hop of recovery his Car will be the gratter so as I doubt not of your discration in advising him for his good and tow soport his poore famely when I am in my grave which if you pleas tow doe me that faver you will furder oblig me tow be

Your sarvent
AN ALFORD

May 23 1665

Address: These for my much honnered freind Mr Locke

## *172.* LADY (ANNE) ALFORD to LOCKE, 13 June 1665 (*171, 173*)

B.L., MS. Locke c. 3, ff. 9–10.

Wort⟨hy⟩[a] Sir

Yours I have received and cannot but acknowledge my thankfullnes for your discreet propossals my desirs are that my Son should have your advise in the managing of all his afaires he being younge and newly com intow the world may have many temtations tow lay out his monys but I hop he is so sober and well inclined as not tow misspend it the trouth is his expences is very high in his backlings[2] which I have shewed tow many of my freinds which thay wonder very much at you and other giving him the Caractur of a civell younge man his fortune is but small and must not live so high in expence as many others which have not so grat a charg tow provide for as my son hath. that mad me desire that he might have[b–] the laying[–b] out of his mony for his backlings himselfe and so pay for it ounce or twice a week while in his memory that he might not be abussed by any in that kind for many parsons in such pleaces doth set doune sum tims more then gentlemen have so if you please

[a] *Page torn.* [b–b] *MS.* have y[e] / the laying

[1] The Alford pedigree (p. 220 n.) mentions one sister but no brothers.
[2] Batlings.

then tow lett him have 40 shillings at a tim in his purse tow paye for his backlings I shall now wright tow him tow give you weekly an account of it and so give him more as you se he expends that well it will doe him good tow keep an account of things and I hop make him consider his condistion not tow be so expencive as now he is in his backlings I much feere gentle men doth not so well fallow ther studdys as ⟨co⟩manly[a] thay spend so much in ther Chambers which ⟨I⟩[a] shall desire your faver tow have an eye tow se my son be non of those but that he may spend his tim well is my ernest prayer at his coming hom I hop tow live tow se a very grat improvement which will incurge me tow send him againe tow you he wrights tow me for mony againe the act[1] which was a time of sum expence, I conceive for those gentlemen which have relations neere that pleace but he haveing none need not be at any expence of intartainment: I shall be willing tow be at any charge tow improve him in any way for his good so not tow exseed his fortune I am still but weake but should be unwilling tow live tow lave a debt behind me I love tow pay all I owe and shall hop my son will barr the sam mind when I am dead and gone which god grant he may doe. Sir which if you please still tow instrouct him in all ways which may advantag his education tow make him a religious honest man you will furder oblige me tow be

Your assured loving frind tow sarve you

AN ALFORD

June 13 1665

Address: These for my very much honnered freind Mr John Locke at Christ Church Oxford[b] present

## 173. LADY (ANNE) ALFORD to LOCKE, 13 July 1665 (*172, 192*)

B.L., MS. Locke c. 3, ff. 11–12.

July 13: 1665

worthy Sir

I blese god my son is com hom very well I give you many thank for you favers and care of him I doubt not but I shall find by him

[a] *Page torn.* [b] *Added in another hand.*

[1] It was due to be held on 8–10 July, but was cancelled on account of the plague: Wood, *L. and T.* ii. 39, 42.

the same caructur which you are pleased tow give him if You had not sent him I did intend tow have sent for him the naxt week My care was so grat for feare of the sicknes[1] being Mr Carter[2] tould a freind wright him word that the Court was expacted at Oxford sudingly god blese the Kind[3] and your uenevercyty from the sicknes Sir I find by your bill I am now in your debt 1–12–4 which you have given me noe order tow send by this berrer or else I should have sent it now I praise god this parts are all free from infaction I could wish ther might be a good occation tow bring you in to this County I should be extramly glad tow se you in the mane tim I must be in your debt for the grat care you have had of my son which I shall studdy to requit if ever I live tow return him back tow you againe the Massenger hast is such as I doe wright so ill as I feare you will have much trouble tow Read it which I desire you tow excuse and belive me tow be

Your assured freind tow sarve you

AN ALFORD

Address: These for Mr John Lock present

## *174.* HENRY FLOWER to LOCKE, 3 August 1665

B.L., MS. Locke c. 8, ff. 141–2. The writer was of Stockwood in Keynsham, about 3 miles north of Pensford.

Worthy Sir

Having taken the best care I can to make my sonne Tom Flower a scholler,[4] my next resolve is (If you please to vouchsafe me the acceptance) to send him upp unto you to Oxford, and in reference to his conveniences there, I pray be pleased to procure him in your Colledge, a Chamber, with a Chamber fellow, suteable, and fitt, for his condition, that he may be made capable of your instruction, and discipline, as his Tutour; Sir If my sonne might be soe happy as to be admitted in some parte of your Chamber to be neare you, I should take it as a greate favour, and will thankfully

[1] The plague. Undergraduates who left Oxford at this time may have stayed away until January 1666: Wood, *L. and T.* ii. 68.

[2] Probably Samuel Carter, vicar of Findon (near Offington) 1662–77: Foster, *Alumni*; see also p. 273.

[3] The king came to Oxford on 25 September and lodged in Christ Church: Wood, *L. and T.* ii. 46.

[4] Thomas Flower, *c.* 1649–90; matriculated from St. John's College 23 March 1666; B.A., Gloucester Hall, 1669; divine: Foster.

requite all your undertakings for him; And the reason of this my request (Sir) unto you is; For that I dare say without ambition, that you will singularly well affect his disposition: Be pleased Sir to give your selfe the trouble by lettre, to advertise me what course I shall steere, for the accomplishing of my desires herein, and my sonns necessary accomodations for the Colledge; which done; You will very much oblidge me to thankfullnesse, and to acknowledge that I am:

Your most affectionate friend and servant
HENRY FLOWER

Stockwood: 3° Augusti 65

Sir If my desires herein may not be accomplished, favour me (I beseech you) with your endevours for a Demies place in Madling Colledge, or a schollers place in Corpus Christi: For that the Bishop of Winchester[1] is my very honourable friend, and hath promised my sonne preferment. I intend to send my sonne up to Oxford about Michaelmus next; And when you send your lettre I pray convey it to Mr. Arthur Start, an Inkeeper at the Bell in Saint Thomas street in Bristoll, to be conveied unto me: Sir the inclosed will tell you that I am very much beholding to Mr: Arundell,[2] and your Sister, Mrs: Lock:[3]

Address: These To his very worthy friend Mr: John Locke at his Chamber in C:h: C:h: present Oxforde Port: paid 6d:

LOCKE'S VISIT TO CLEVES IN 1665–6: nos. 175–84, etc.

In November 1665 Sir Walter Vane[4] was sent on a diplomatic mission to Frederick William of Hohenzollern, elector of Brandenburg ('the Great Elector'),[5] who was then at Cleves, and Locke accompanied him as secretary.[6] Vane's official letters home, written by Locke, are preserved in the

[1] Dr. George Morley, bishop 1662–84: *D.N.B.* The bishop of Winchester is *ex officio* visitor of Corpus Christi and local visitor of Magdalen.

[2] Perhaps the William Arundell who was a witness of Thomas Locke's nuncupative will: Cranston, p. 79.

[3] Dorothy, widow of Thomas Locke. In 1664 she married Robert Taunton, who was probably an organ-maker in Bristol; she apparently married a third husband, George Bowcher, a Bristol merchant, in 1685: *Marriage Bonds for the Diocese of Bristol*, vol. i, 1637–1700, ed. E. Ralph (Bristol and Gloucestershire Archæological Society, Records section, [1952]), pp. 15, 47, 74, 164; no. *3001*.

[4] p. 233, n. 3. His passport is dated Oxford, 11 November 1665; Locke left Oxford on the 13th: B.L., MSS. Locke c. 25, f. 8; f. 27, p. 64.

[5] 1620–88; succeeded as elector in 1640.

[6] Locke owed his appointment probably to (Sir) William Godolphin. Vane was responsible to the secretary of state Lord Arlington.

Public Record Office, S.P. Foreign, German states, vols. 56, 57 (S.P. 81/56, 57); some drafts for them are in B.L., MS. Locke c. 22, ff. 181–9. Locke's copies of the English government's replies, written in a paper book, are preserved in the British Museum, Add. MS. 16272. These letters and answers are excluded from the present publication.

Locke kept drafts or copies of his private letters in a paper book. Of this there survive gatherings B, C, and D, each of sixteen pages, and one leaf of E; but most of the first leaf of B is cut away: B.L., MS. Locke c. 24, ff. 246–58.

England declared war against the United Provinces on 4 March 1665. In June Christoph Bernhard von Galen, bishop of Münster,[1] who had his own grievances against the United Provinces, joined by treaty with England and prepared forces. The Emperor, Leopold I,[2] was more or less favourable. The bishop sought further allies, and among them the Elector Frederick William.

The Hohenzollerns had acquired the duchy of Cleves and the counties of Mark and Ravenstein by inheritance and treaties after the death in 1609 of the last descendant in the male line of the old house of Cleves. Frederick William had his own disputes with the Dutch on account of the garrisons maintained by them in Emmerich and other towns in his territories; moreover he was linked with the house of Orange by marriage, and consequently opposed to the States party, which at this time held power in the United Provinces, and to its leader, Jan de Witt.[3] But he feared French intervention and Roman Catholic intrigue; he wanted to keep war out of the Empire and to support the Protestant United Provinces. When late in 1665 he decided to go to Cleves his course was clear: to work for a general settlement, but to sell his support to the United Provinces for the best terms that he could get. He would not join Charles II; Vane's mission was of value to him chiefly as helping him to raise his price. The various bids for his alliance, his goodwill, or his neutrality, produced a notable gathering of diplomatists this winter in the town of Cleves.

The duchy was remarkable in the Europe of this time for the freedom of worship enjoyed by the members of the Evangelical (Lutheran), Reformed (Calvinist), and Roman Catholic churches, and for the connivance extended to the Mennonites (Anabaptists). The Roman Catholics were unable to hold civil or military office; as they belonged mainly to the lower ranks of society this disability did not affect them greatly; there was no other legal discrimination against them. The Elector was a devout Calvinist. He detested Roman Catholicism: 'Ist Gott lob die Chur Brandenburg undt Pommern, von Pabstlichen groben greulen undt Abgötterey gentzlich befreihet, ausser was die Lutterischen in Ihren Kirchen auss den Pabstumb ahn Ceremonien behalten haben.' In Cleves the Hohenzollerns were bound by agreements ('Reversallen');[4] the Roman Catholics were to be allowed their religion:

[1] p. 229, n. 2.
[2] 1640–1705; emperor 1658: *A.D.B.*
[3] 1656–72; grand pensionary of Holland, etc., 1635: *N.N.B.W.*
[4] By an agreement ('Revers', 'Reversal') made at Duisburg, 4/14 July 1609, the Elector Johann Sigismund of Brandenburg and the Pfalzgraf Wolfgang Wilhelm, duke of Neuburg and of Jülich, engaged to continue, etc., in public use and exercise 'die Catholische Romische / wie auch andere Christliche *Religion*, wie so wol in Römischen Reich / als diesen Fürstenthumb und Graefschap von der Marck ahn einem

'darin ist keine conivens, sondern eine freie zu zu lassung Ihres abergleubischen glaubens bewilliget'; these declarations were to be loyally maintained by the Elector's successors. In general he exhorts them: 'Ewere von Gott untergebene Unterthanen musset Ihr ohne ansehung der Religion als ein rechter Landes Vatter lieben.'[1]

The town of Cleves is situated on a high bank overlooking the flat ground of the lower Rhineland; the ducal castle (Burg or Schwanenburg) is at about the highest part. The population in 1800 was said to be 5,300.[2] The inhabitants spoke Dutch. The surroundings had recently been greatly beautified by Johan Maurits van Nassau-Siegen, stadholder in Cleves since 1647.[3] Frederick William visited it on several occasions during the life of his first Electress (p. 231, n. 5); after her death in 1667 he came only once again, in 1686.

The diplomatic situation is set out by G. Pagès, *Le Grand Électeur et Louis XIV, 1660–1688*, 1905; A. Waddington, *Le Grand Électeur Frédéric Guillaume . . . sa politique extérieure, 1640–1688*, 1905–8, ii. 113–31; Keith Feiling, *British Foreign Policy, 1660–1672*, 1930, pp. 159–62. I have found no general history of the duchy of Cleves at this time; outline in *Handbuch der historischen Stätten Deutschlands*, vol. iii, 1963: Nordrhein-Westfalen, by W. Zimmerman, etc., pp. 345–8. The Elector's conduct towards the Roman Catholics is described and documented in M. L. E. Lehmann, *Preussen und die Katholische Kirche*, vol. i, 1878. Seventeenth-century views of the town and its environs are reproduced, with extracts from contemporary writings relating to the Great Elector's visits and other leading events, in F. Gorissen, *Conspectus Civiæ*, 1964.

## 175. LOCKE to the HON. ROBERT BOYLE, 12/22 December 1665 (197)

R. Boyle, *Works*, ed. T. Birch, 1744, v. 565–7. Though written earlier than no. 177 some part of this letter is based on the experiences narrated there.

Cleve, Dec. $\frac{12}{22}$, 1665.

Honoured Sir,

I look upon it as the greatest misfortune of my journey hither, that it hath afforded me so little worth your notice; and that after having gone so far, and staid so long, I should yet send you so empty a letter. But, Sir, it is not unusual, that a man far in debt, after long delays, should pay nothing. And had I travelled through more fruitful places, and been myself better able to observe, I should

jeden Ohrt'; no one was to be disturbed or molested in his conscience or worship: J. Dumont, baron de Carlscroon, *Corps universel diplomatique*, 1726–31, v. ii. 109.

[1] The quotations are from the Great Elector's political testament, 1667, printed in L. von Ranke, *Zwölf Bücher Preussischer Geschichte*, 2nd ed., 1878, pp. 499–517.

[2] *A Geographical, Historical . . . Description of Germany*, 1800, p. 166 and table xii.

[3] p. 241, n. 4.

still have been in the same condition, and not have been able to return any thing of what I owe to your many and great favours. We are here in a place very little considerable for any thing but its antiquity, which to me seems neither to commend things nor opinions; and I should scarce prefer an old ruinous and incommodious house, to a new and more convenient, though Julius Cæsar built it,[1] as they say he did this the Elector dwells in, which opinion the situation, just on the edge of a precipice, and the oldness of the building seems to favour. The town is little, and not very strong or handsom; the buildings and streets irregular; nor is there a greater uniformity in their religion, three professions being publickly allowed: the Calvinists are more than the Lutherans, and the Catholicks more than both (but no papist bears any office) besides some few Anabaptists,[2] who are not publickly tolerated. But yet this distance in their churches gets not into their houses. They quietly permit one another to choose their way to heaven;[3] for I cannot observe any quarrels or animosities amongst them upon the account of religion. This good correspondence is owing partly to the power of the magistrate, and partly to the prudence and good nature of the people, who (as I find by enquiry) entertain different opinions, without any secret hatred or rancour. I have not yet heard of any person here eminently learned. There is one Dr. Scardius,[4] who, I am told, is not altogether a stranger to chemistry. I intend to visit him as soon as I can get an handsom opportunity. The rest of their physicians go the old road, I am told, and also easily guess by their apothecary's shops, which are unacquainted with chemical remedies. This, I suppose, makes this town so ill furnished with books of that kind, there being few here curious enough to enquire after chemistry or experimental learning. And as I once heard you say, I find it true here, as well as in other places, that the great cry is ends of gold and silver. A catalogue of those books I have met with, some at Antwerp, and some in this town,

[1] For the supposed foundation of the citadel at Cleves see S.V. Pighius (Pighe), *Hercules Prodicius*, 1587, pp. 35–6; for the inscription relating to Caesar, pp. 248–9.

[2] 'The comprehensive designation of various groups on the Continent who in the sixteenth century refused to allow their children to be baptized and reinstituted the baptism of believers'. In England in Locke's time and later the name was more or less opprobriously applied to the Baptists; he applies it here to the Mennonites (*Menisten*), the followers of Menno Simons (1496–1561), a sect originally Dutch, who reject infant baptism and believe in pacifism and non-resistance: *Oxford Dictionary of the Christian Church*.

[3] For similar expressions see no. 75.

[4] Apparently J. Schard: p. 277 n. Chemistry here probably signifies the use of chemical preparations in medicine: p. 284.

I here inclosed send you, and am told by the only bookseller of this place, that he expects others daily from Francfort.[1] The weather is here exceedingly mild, and I have not seen any frost or snow since my coming; but it is an unusual clemency of the air, and the heavens seem to cherish the heat men are in to destroy one another. I suppose it no news to tell you, that the Dutch have forced a surrender of Lochem; there marched out of it two hundred and fifty of the bishop's men.[2] In another rencounter the bishop's men killed and took four hundred Dutch horse: so that this has only shaked the scales, not much inclined them to either side. The States of Cleve and March[3] are met here to raise money for the Elector, and he with that intends to raise men, but as yet declares for neither side: whether he be willing, or will be able to keep that neutrality I doubt, since methinks war too is now become infectious, and spreads itself like a contagion, and I fear threatens a great mortality the next summer, The plague has been very hot at Cologne; there have died there within this quarter of a year above eight thousand. A gentleman, that passed by that town last week, told me, that the week before there died there three hundred and forty eight. I know these little trivial things are as far distant from what I ought to send you, as I am from England: for this I do not only blame my own present poverty, but despair of the future, since your great riches in all manner of knowledge forbid me the hopes of ever presenting you with any thing new or unknown. I should not therefore take the boldness thus to importune you, did I not know, that there is nothing so slight or barren, which you cannot force to yield you something, and make an advantageous use of poor common things, which others throw away. This is that, which gives me the confidence to tell you, that I am,

Sir,

your most obedient, and most faithful servant,

JOHN LOCKE.

[1] At this time Frankfurt was the leading centre for the German book-trade: A. Dietz, *Zur Geschichte der Frankfurter Büchermesse 1462/1792*, [1921], pp. 23–4.

[2] The bishop is Christoph Bernhard von Galen, 1606–78; bishop of Münster 1650: *A.D.B.* He declared war against the United Provinces on 14 September; his forces invaded Gelderland and took Lochem and other places by about the end of the month and for a time threatened Overijssel and Groningen. The Dutch lost a number of men in an encounter near Delden on 9 December but recaptured Lochem on the 14th: L. van Aitzema, *Saken van Staet en Oorlogh*, 1669–72, v. 639–41, 645, 667–8, 669–70 (new-style dates).

[3] The estates, the constitutional assembly: *O.E.D.*, State, *sb.* 23; Estate, *sb.* 6b. The county of Mark had been attached to the duchy of Cleves since 1368.

Since I writ this I met with a Jesuit,[1] who had been in Hungary. I enquired, whether he had seen the mines; he told me, that he had gone down into a copper mine near Neisol[2] (if I mistake not the name) six hundred fathom deep; that at the bottom in a hollow of some bigness, there dropped down water, which they received in a wooden trough, wherein they cast pieces of old iron, which by the water would be turned into good copper. That a piece of iron of the bigness of a man's finger would be changed in three months, and that the mutation began from the superficies inwards with streaks (or to use his word *striatum*;) that he had a horse-shoe, whose exterior part was copper, and inside iron. I asked him, whether it were cold or hot, he told me it was warm enough, so that the workmen were naked from the waist upward, and sweat in working. I had not time to enquire after more particulars, being hastily called away. He belongs to the baron de Goes,[3] envoy here from the Emperor. If you think this relation worth any further enquiry, or that I can any other way serve you here, I should be glad to receive your commands, which either Mr. Godolphin[4] or Mr. Proctor Thomas[5] will convey to me.

*Kercheri Mundus Subterraneus*, fol. 1665.[6]
*Schotti Schola Steganographica*, 4to. 1665.[7]
*Pet. Mich. de Hevedia Opera Medica*, fol. 1665.[8]
*Heldebrandi Magia Naturalis*, 4to. 1664.[9]
*Bauschus Schediasmata curiosa de lapide hæmatite & ætite*, 8vo. 1665.[10]
*Strausius Conatus Anatomicus*, 4to. Giesæ, 1666.[11]
*Licetus de Monstris*, 4to. Amstelodami, 1665.[12]
*Simon Pauli de abusu Tabaci & Theè*, 4to. Argentor, 1665.[13]
*Phil. Jac. Sachs Gammarographia*, 8vo. 1665.[14]

[1] Perhaps F. Raulin: p. 270.
[2] Neusohl on the Gran, about 90 miles north of Buda: Edward Browne, *Brief Account of some Travels*, 2nd ed., 1685, pp. 62, 66–9. It is now Banská Bystrica in Czechoslovakia.
[3] Johann, Freiherr von Goës (or Goëss), 1611–93; cardinal 1686; envoy from the Emperor to the Great Elector 1665–71: *A.D.B.*; etc.
[4] William Godolphin.
[5] Dr. David Thomas: p. 283 n. He was junior proctor in 1665–6.
[6] The principal object of the notes to this list is to facilitate the identification of the books. The *Mundus Subterraneus* is by Athanasius Kircher, S.J.
[7] By Gaspar Schott, S.J.
[8] P. M. de Heredia.
[9] By Wolfgang Hildebrand. First edition, in German, 1610; I have not traced a copy of the 1664 edition.
[10] J. L. Bausch, *Schediasmata Bina Curiosa.*
[11] Laurentius Strauss.
[12] Fortunio Liceti. L.L., no. 1741. First edition, Padua, 1616.
[13] S. Paulli, *Commentarius de Abusu*, etc.
[14] *Gammarologia, sive Gammarorum, vulgo cancrorum consideratio physico . . . chymica.*

*Phil. Grulingii Medicina practica*, 4to. Northusa, 1665.[1]
*Ger. Blasii Medicina Universalis*, 4to. 1665.
*Schookius de Sternutatione*, 12mo. 1664.[2]
*Deusingius de Generatione & Nutritione*, 12mo. 1665.[3]

## 176. LOCKE to WILLIAM (later Sir William) GODOLPHIN, 12/22 December 1665 (66, 178)

B.L., MS. Locke c. 24, ff. 247–8 (pp. 11–13 of Locke's Cleves letter-book). Draft or copy. The first eight lines are largely in shorthand; the rendering here may not be completely accurate. Part of the letter is printed in King, pp. 12–13 (it is preceded by part of no. 181, the two extracts being combined in a single letter).

By what I find here a diligent enquiry things are otherwise then at first apprehended those that are dependants of Br say that he intends to raise forces but he hath reason to thinke it will not be so for I find that Br coffers are not very full and his revenues are usually spent before they come in which is owing to his relations which depend hereat and to the great number of his attendants and to let you see that he is not much before hand give me leave to tell you that since we came hither he sent into hol to buy some things provisions for his kithing and was fain to borrow 2000 rix dollars[4] for that use.[a]

Br demands of the States met here 150000 rix dollers, they after haveing been here almost this month are not resolvd what to give him, (for they meddle with noe other affairs but this subsidie). tomorrow is the day they declare their resolution and if I can learn it before the goeing of the post you shall be sure to receive it but should it come up to his demands by that time the daughter of the old princesse of Orenge (sister to the Electrice)[b] is married to the prince of Semerin, the celebration whereof is designd to be here at Cleve before Easter and at the Elec charge.[5] and other expences

[a] *The rest of the text is in longhand.* [b] *Added in margin.*

[1] P. Gruelingius. L.L., no. 1344. Earlier edition 1648.
[2] Marten Schook. The second edition.
[3] A. Deusingius, *Genesis Miscrocosmi, seu, De generatione foetus in utero dissertatio*, etc.
[4] The rix-dollar was a silver coin issued in various parts of the Empire and in the United Provinces; the value ranged from 4*s*. 4*d*. to 4*s*. 7*d*.
[5] The old princess of Orange is Amalia von Solms, 1602–75 (*N.N.B.W.*), widow of the stadholder Frederick Henry. The Electress was her eldest daughter Louisa

of this Court are defraid there will not be much left for the raiseing of Soldiers, and these that he has already in pay are but sufficient to man those[a] garisons that are requisite for dominions soe scatterd as his are. The men of businesse who are his Counsellors and manage the affairs of the El are only 3. Baron Swerin[1] a man nobly borne a learned and experiencd man that well understands the state of the Empire and has most power with the Elector. Next to him is Mr Jeana[2] a Doctor of law and formerly professor ⟨at⟩[b] Hidelberg he hath been about 6 years of the E councell and is as I am told a knowing and confident man, the other is Mr Blaspell,[3] a man of mean extraction, whose great abilitys lyes in the knowledges of the affairs of Holland he is now there and at his returne I hope to give you an account of his negotion. I[c–] will endeavour to get a more particular knowledg of their parts humors[d] and inclinations.[–c] he is dayly expected, he got into the favour and Councell of the E by means of the Princesse dowager[4] mother to this Electrice and I beleive is much at her devotion. The Baron de Goes Envoy of the Emperor returnd hither last night from the Bishop of Munster.[5] some of his people with whome I talkd told me that the Bishops forces were about 16000, that they all wanted money and the foot clothes, but none of them either courage or victualls, that they were all old stout experiencd soldiers, and they seemd all to prefer them much to the Dutch forces. they told me that many of the French ran over to the Bishop being unwilling to fight against their owne religion[6] that the Bishop usd them kindely gave them leave to depart whether they pleasd but entertaind none of them in his service, being secure of soldiers enough when ever he has mony. they told me too that the beating that party of the Dutch and

[a] *Or* these [b] *MS.* & [c–c] *Added in margin.* [d] *Doubtful spelling.*

Henrietta, 1627–67, who had married Frederick William, the great Elector, in 1647. Louisa Henrietta's youngest sister, Maria, 1642–88, was now to marry Ludwig Heinrich Moritz, 1640–73, Pfalzgraf of Simmern, a nephew of Frederick V of the Palatinate, the Winter King: J. Hübner, *Genealogische Tabellen*, 1727–37, nos. 139, 256. The marriage contract was signed on 14/24 March 1666; the wedding was celebrated on 3/13 September: Gorissen, pp. 57, 58.

[1] Otto Freiherr von Schwerin, 1616–79: *A.D.B.*

[2] Friedrich von Jena, 1619–82; in 1654–5 professor of law at Frankfurt on the Oder: ibid.

[3] W. W. Blaspiel, d. 1681; envoy to the United Provinces 1665–78: ibid.

[4] Amalia von Solms: p. 231, n. 5.

[5] C. B. von Galen: p. 229, n. 2.

[6] Roman Catholicism. French and Dutch troops together captured Lochem (p. 229): Comte G. d'Estrades, *Lettres, mémoires* . . . 1743, iii. 586–7.

takeing those prisoners more then paid for the losse of Lochem a little place and slightly fortified the Bishop now is at Cosfeild[1] a strong place in his owne dominions where they saw some of the cheife of the prisoners he had taken at the last ⟨e⟩ncounter[a] enterteind at the Bishops table. his[b–] forces are dispersd into severall places and there is like to be noe engagement this winter.[–b] They all spoke very highly of the Bishop and more affectionately then I thinke could be merely to comply with that concernment they ⟨might⟩[c] thinke I had in his affairs, whether hence any thinke may be guesd of the inclination of the Germans of the Baron de Goes or of the Emperor I am not able to make any judgment upon soe short a conversation but I shall endeavour to learn, only befor his returne I found the munks of the Covent where the baron lodges[2] wholy inclind to the Bishop. How our affairs stand in this court and what progresse is made you will better understand by Sir Walters[3] dispatches in which whatever shall be found I desire I may be considerd only as a transcriber tied to a copie even to the very spelling and sometimes soe straitend in time that hast maks my hand worse then it would be. If my intelligence be not soe considerable as you may expect you will pardon it to my want of experience and language not of will and endeavour I have yet had but little oportunity to make fit acquaintace for that purpose and there is noe thing I write that I dare assure you soe confidently as that I am

Newbourgs Envoye[4]

## 177. LOCKE to JOHN STRACHEY, 14/24 December 1665 (*163*, 180)

B.L., MS. Locke c. 24, f. 232. This letter and nos. 180 and 182 were written for dispatch, but have no seals or covers. Statements in nos. 188 and 189 show that Locke held back some of his letters to Strachey from Cleves. This one was perhaps dispatched at the time of writing; nos. 180 and 182 were perhaps held back. Incomplete draft or copy, with additional opening

[a] *Page torn.* [b–b] *Interlined.* [c] *MS.* migh

[1] Presumably Koesfeld, about 20 miles west of Münster.
[2] That of the Franciscans (Minorites): p. 235.
[3] Sir Walter Vane, a younger brother of Sir Henry Vane the republican (1613–62; *D.N.B.*); he appears to have been a royalist and was knighted probably by 1654; he was killed in the battle of Seneff in 1674: *D.N.B.*, art. Vane, Sir Henry the elder (1589–1655).
[4] For the duke see p. 252, n. 1. I have not traced an envoy in Cleves at this time.

paragraph, in Locke's Cleves letter-book (B.L., MS. Locke c. 24, ff. 246–58), f. 246v and pp. 13–18. Printed, from f. 232, in King, pp. 21–5. Locke's dates in this letter are old style.

Sir[a]

Dec. 4 This day our publick entertainment upon the Electors account ended[1] much to my satisfaction for I had noe great pleasure in a feast, where amidst a great deale of meat and company, I had little to eate and lesse to say, the advantage was the lusty Germans, fed soe heartily themselves, that they regarded not much my idlenesse, and I might have enjoyd a perfect quiet, and slept out the meale, had not a glasse of wine now and then jogd me; and indeed therein lay the care of their entertainment and the sincerity too, for the wine was such as might be known, and was not ashamd of its self. But for their meats, they were all soe disguisd, that I should have guesd they had rather designd, a maske, then a meale, and had a minde rather to pose then feed us. But the cooke made their Metamorphosis like Ovids, where the change is usually into the worse. I had however courage to venture upon things unknowne, and I could not often tell whether I eat flesh or fish or good red herring, soe much did they dissemble themselves: Only now and then a dish of good honest freshwater fish came in, soe far from all manner of deceit or cheat, as they hid not soe much as their tails in a drop of butter, nor was there any sauce neare to disguise them. What thinke you of a hen and cabbage? or a peice of pouderd beef, coverd over with preservd quinces? these are noe miracles here. One thing there is that I like very well, which is that they have good sallets all the yeare, and use them frequently. Tis true the Elector gave his victualls but his ⟨officers that⟩[b] attended us valud theire service, and one of them had ready in his pocket, a list of those that expected rewards, at such a rate that the attendance cost more then the meat was worth

[a] *In the draft (f. 246v) there is an opening paragraph* if it will not tire you more to reade then it hath donne me to see what this excursion into Germany hath shewne me either new or pleasant I shall frequently give you an account of a person you have soe good a title too, and of those adventures which dureing this errantry I shall be engagd in. you will doe me a kindnesse to lay them aside in some corner of your study till I returne, for I intend to deposit in your hands all the memoirs of my journy, being unwilling to beg [?] about papers, and I hope when we meet they will afford us some matter of discourse and diversion. *The draft then continues* Dec. 4 This day *and so on.* [b] *Page torn; reading from f. 248v.*

[1] Vane arrived at Cleves on 1/11 December.

Dec. 9 I was invited and dind at a monastary with the Franciscan Friers,[1] who had before brought a Latin Epistle to us for releife, for they live upon others charity, or more truly, live Idldly[a] upon others labours. But to my diner. For my mouth waters to be at it: and noe doubt you will long for such another enterteinment when you know this. After something instead of grace or Musick, choose you whether, for I could make neither of it. For though what was sung were Latin, yet the tone was such that I neither understood the Latin nor the Harmony. The begining of the Lords prayer to the 1 petition they repeated aloud, but went on silently to, sed libera nos etc and there broke out into a loud Chorus which continued to the end, dureing their silence they stoopd forwards and held their heads as if they had been listening to one anothers whispers. After this præludium downe we sat. The cheife of the Monks, (I suppose the Prior) in the inside of the table just in the middle and all his breathren on each side of him. I was placd just opposite to him, as if I had designd to bid battle to them all. But we were all very quiet and after some silence, in marchd a solem procession of pease porredg every one his dish. I could not tell by the looks what it was. till puting my spoone in for discovery, some few pease in the bottom peepd up, lookd pittifully, and divd again. I had pitty on them, and was willing enough to spare them, but was forcd by good manners, though against my nature and appetite, to destroy some of them, and soe on I fell. All this while not a word, I could not tell whether to impute this silence to the eagernesse of their stomachs, which allowd their mouths noe other imployment but to fill them, or any other reason: I was confident it was not in admiration of their late musick. At last the Oracle of the place spoke, and told them he gave them leave to speake to enterteine me. I returnd my complement, and then to discourse we went hilter skilter, as hard as our bad Latin and worse pronuntiation on each side would let us: But noe matter we card not for Priscian, whose head sufferd that day not a little.[2] However this savd me from the pease pottage and the pease pottage from me, for now I had something else to doe. Our next course was every one his cut of fish, and butter to boot. but whether it were intended for

[a] *Spelling doubtful.*

[1] The Minorites.

[2] Priscian was a Roman grammarian; 'to break Priscian's head' was to violate the rules of grammar: *Oxford Dict. English Proverbs.*

fresh or salt fish, I cannot tell and I beleive tis a question as hard as any Thomas[1] ever disputed, our third service was cheese and butter, and the cheese had this peculiar in it which I never saw any where else, that it had Caraway seeds in it. The Prior had upon the table by him, a little bell which he rang when he wanted anything, and those that waited never brought him anything or tooke away, but they bowd with much reverence, and kisd the table, The Prior was a good plump fellow, that had more belly then brains, and me thought was very fit to be reverencd, and not much unlike some head of a Colleg. I liked him well for an entertainment, for if we had had a good dinner, he would not have disturbd me much with his discourse. The first that kisd the table did it soe leasurely, that I thought he had held his head there, that the Prior dureing our silence, might have writt something on his bald crowne, and made it sinke that way into his understanding. Their bear was pretty good, but their countenances bespoke better, their bread browne and their table linnin neat enough. After dinner we had the second part of the same tune, and after that I departed. The truth is they were very civill and courteous and seemd good naturd. It was their time of fast in Order to Christmas. If I have another feast there you shall be my guest. You will, perhaps, have reason to thinke, that what ever becomes of the rest, I shall bring home my belly well improvd, since all I tell you is of eateing and drinking. But you must know that Knights Errant, doe not choose their adventures; and those who sometimes live pleasantly in brave Castles, amidst feasting and Ladys, are at other times in battles and wildernesses and you must take them as they come

Dec 10 I went to the Lutheran church, I found them all merrily singing with their hats on. Soe that by the posture they were in and the fashon of the building, not altogether unlike a theater, I was ready to feare that I had mistooke the place. I thought they had met only to exercise their voices, for after a long stay they still continued on their melody, and I veryly beleive they sung 119 psalme, noething else could be soe long, that[a–] that made it a little tolerable was that they sing[–a] better then we doe in our churches and are assisted by an organ. The musick being donne up went the preacher and praid and then they sung again and then

[a–a] *In the draft* but the truth is twas tollerable for they sing

[1] St. Thomas Aquinas.

after a little prayer, at which they all stood up (and as I understand since was the Lords prayer) read some of the bible, and then laying by his booke preachd to them memoriter.[1] His sermon I thinke was in blank verse, for by the modulation of his voyce, which was not very pleasant, his periods seemd to be all neare the same length, but if his matter were noe better then his delivery those that slept had noe great losse and might have snord as harmoniously. after sermon a prayer and then the organ and voices again, and to conclude all up stood another minister at a little deske above the Communion table (for in the Lutheran and Calvinist churches here there are noe Chancells) gave the benediction, which I was told was[a–] this Ite in[–a] nomine domini, crosd himself and soe dismisd them. In this church I observd two pictures one a crucifix, the other I could not well discerne, but in the Calvinist church noe pictures at all. Here are besides Catholicks, Calvinists and Lutherans (which 3 are allowd) Jews Anabaptists[2] and Quakers.[3] The Quakers who are about 30 familys, and some of them not of the meanest, and they increase. for as much as I can learne they agree with ours in other things as well as name and take noe notice of the Electors prohibiting their meetings

⟨Dec. 11⟩[b] I had formerly seene the size and armes of the Dukes gards, but to day I chancd to have a sample of their stomachs (I meane) to eat not to fight for if they be able to doe as much, that way too, noe question but under their gard the Duke is as much in safety, as I beleive his victualls are in danger. But to make you the better understand my story, and the decorum which made me take notice of it, I must first describe the place to you.[4] The place where the Elector commonly eats is a large roome into which you enter, at the lower end by an ascent of some few steps. Just without this is a lobby. As this evening I was passeing through it into the Court, I saw a company of soldiers very close togeather and a

[a–a] *Draft* was this in German ite in . . .   [b] *Page worn; reading from f. 250.*

[1] In England at this time the Anglican divines tended to preach *ex tempore*, the Nonconformist, *memoriter*. Dr. Fell occasionally lapsed into blank verse: W. Fraser Mitchell, *English Pulpit Oratory from Andrewes to Tillotson*, 1932, pp. 17–26, 309–10.

[2] Mennonites.

[3] Apparently an error; there are no other notices of Quakers in Cleves at this time.

[4] The duke is the Elector; he was duke of Cleves. The palace is the Burg (Schwanenburg); account of it in 1698 in T. Dorrington, *Observations concerning . . . Religion . . . some Provinces of Germany*, 1699, pp. 371–3; picture of the interior (copy, 1829, of a seventeenth-century painting) in H. Dattenberg, *Niederrheinansichten holländischer Künstler des 17. Jahrhunderts*, 1967, no. 55.

steame riseing from the midst of them. I as strangers use to be, being a little curious, drew neare to these men of mettle, where I found 3 or 4 earthen fortifications wherein were intrenchd, pease porredg and stewd turneps or apples most valiantly stormd by these men of war; they stood just opposite to the Dukes table and within view of it. and had the Duke been then at supper, as it was very neare his supper time I should have thought they had been set there to provoke his appetite by example, and serve as the cocks have donne in some contrys before battle to fight the soldiers into courage, as certainely these soldiers might eat others into stomachs. here you might have seene the court and camp drawn neare togeather, there a supper prepareing with great ceremony, and just by it a hearty meale made without stoole trencher tablecloth or Napkins and for ought I could see without beare bred or salt, but I staid not long for methought twas a dangerous place and soe I left them in the ingagement:[a] I doubt ⟨by⟩[b] that time you come to the end of this course enterteinment you will be as weary as I am with writeing and therefor I shall refer you for the rest of my adventures (wherein you are not to expect any great matter) to the next chapter of my history

News here is that the Dutch have taken Lochem from the Bishop of Munster and he in thanks has taken and kild 5 or 600 of their men. The French they say run away some home and some to the Bishop who has disposd his men into garrisons which has given the Dutch an oportunity to beseige another of his towns but not very considerable. all things here seem to threaten a great deale of stir next sommer, but as yet this Elector declares for neither side. Remember me to your Lady and mother To my Uncle[1] and his family. I sent him a letter of Atturny (before I left England) to authorize him to dispose of my affairs there and order my estate as he should thinke most convenient, I hope he receivd it. I thinke it best my tenants should not know that I am out of England for perhaps that may make them the more slack to pay their rents. If he tells you any thing that concerns me pray send word to

your faithfull freind

J L

Writ within an hower of Christmas day.

[a] *The draft stops here.* [b] *MS.* be

[1] Peter Locke: p. 288 n.

Direct your letters to Mrs Lichfeilds[1] in Oxford and they will be sent me

Throw by this in some corner of your Study till I come and then we will laugh together, for it may serve to recall other things to my memory for tis like I may have noe other journall

Address: For John Strachy Esq. at Sutton Court To be left ⟨at⟩[a] Mr John Blanches neere the high crosse in High street Bristoll

## 178. LOCKE to WILLIAM (later Sir William) GODOLPHIN 19/29 December 1665 (176, 179)

B.L., MS. Locke c. 39, ff. 11–12. The original letter; it did not belong to the Lovelace Collection. Draft or copy in MS. Locke c. 24, ff. 251v–252v (Locke's Cleves letter-book, pp. 20–2).

Cleve $\frac{19}{29}$ of Dec. 65

Sir

Tis soe hard for a man that wants language, to aske questions, or to learne even open and common things, that you will pardon me, if I give you not soe full an account of things here, as you may expect and I desire; though that be not the only difficulty, I am to strugle with here, but of that when I see you. In the meane time what oportunitys I shall have to make any enquirys or observations I shall be carefull to improve. Mr Blaspell is returnd from the Hage without concludeing the treaty, and I beleive this Elector would not be unwilling to keepe a Neutrality, unlesse the[b–] mony or intrest of France[–b] poize him that way. The reasons why I thinke soe are these, First because 'tis supposd his coffers are not full, for (not to mention what I told you in my last) besides 150000 Rixdolars he owes the Dutch, which they will not remit, and which (by what I can learne) is the great stop to the conclusion of that treaty: he owes besides soe much to other persons, that (I am told) the revenews of Marck and Cleve 3000 Rix dolars per annum, goe to pay the use of it. This debt was contracted by his father anno 1616

[a] *MS.* & [b–b] *Draft* the mony of France

[1] Anne, d. 1671, widow of the first Leonard Lichfield (*D.N.B.*) and, after his death (1657), printer to the university with her son, the second Leonard Lichfield (p. 270, n. 1.): Madan, vol. iii, p. xxix.

and increases dayly rather then deminishes.[1] Soe that notwithstanding the great Levies of forces mentiond here at our first comeing, I can yet finde noe preparation for them, and that talke is over. And the 150000 Rixdolars he demands of the States of Marck and Cleve are not yet granted, and that businesse sticks. Another reason that I guesse may make him wary of declareing for the Dutch, is the feare of haveing his Country, (which lies scatterd and very Obnoxious to incursions) invaded by any of the Catholick Princes of Germany who should joyne with the Bishop,[2] and perhaps the bringing over some of these Catholick princes, as[a–] the house of Austria, or Bavaria,[–a] from whome a more forward assistance to the Bishop might be expected (for I finde that[b–] it is generally apprehended[–b] to be a Warre of Religion) would put a greater stop to his declareing for the Dutch then the offers of mony, where in tis probable (if it be worth doeing) that the French will out bid us. If he take either side, I guesse it will be the Dutch not only because of Neighborhood, and the mixture of many ⟨concernments⟩[c] of towns and other affairs with them. But here are two great persons in this Court (none of those three I mentiond in my former letter to you) who sway him most (and as I am told) wholy, who are at the Devotion of France, and will be sure to check all contrary interests.[3] Besides the Envoye of France[4] returnd hither on Sunday last, and his negotiation is kept very secret. To which the consideration of religion may adde something, for that is supposd the great businesse of the war, and I never faile of guesseing right, of any ones religion, by the affection I finde he has to the Bishop or the Dutch. And there is not one Catholick Prince of Germany, that I can heare, who affords the least assistance to the Dutch, but that they all wish well to the Bishop; and of the Dukes of Lunen-

[a–a] *Draft* as the house of Bavaria or Austria*; these words are interlined in the draft.*
[b–b] *Draft* that here generally tis apprehended [c] *MS.* concerm[ts]

[1] The debt was said to be 100,000 thaler in 1616, and 2,864,000 gulden in 1661: M. Philippson, *Der grosse Kurfürst Friedrich Wilhelm von Brandenburg*, 1897–1903, ii. 47. The debt was incurred by the Great Elector's grandfather, Johann Sigismund, who inherited the duchy of Cleves in 1609. The thaler is the rix-dollar. The Dutch rix-dollar was of 50, the gulden of 20, stivers.

[2] Of Münster.

[3] These two persons were not members of the Elector's council: p. 251. One may have been the Electress.

[4] (Jacques?) Du Moulin; he had been sent to Cleves in November; after returning to France he came again with new instructions dated 17 December, N.S.: *Recueil des instructions données aux ambassadeurs . . . de France*, 1884– , vol. xvi (Prusse), pp. 97–113.

burg,[1] he that is reported the far wiser and more potent of the two, Though his country be all Lutherans, yet being himself a catholick, has not permitted Count Waldeck[2] to make any levies in his Country, nor favourd his designes at all. And the Lantgrave of Hesse[3] a protestant prince and Neigbour to the Bishop of Munster apprehends his Victorys, and feares, that if the Bishop should conquer the Dutch, he himself should not be secure, and that the Bishop would spread his armes farther. Prince Maurice[4] is expected here today, and I know not whether the inclination of this Court, may be guesd by this; that he is at the same time a member of this Court and generall of the Dutch army. and in the absence of the Elector possesses his place here and governs all under him. The mistakes of these conjectures you will excuse in one not versd in affairs of this nature, and hath not all the conveniencys of informeing himself. which yet I should not thinke convenient to write thus, could I have obteind the use of the Cypher, which being denid me, I shall not venture to write thus openly again at least till I heare from you, but I thought it convenient now in this conjuncture of affairs to give you any way what account I could.

The armys are drawne into their winter quarters, The Bishop is safe for this winter. and in a condition rather to doe then suffer. All people say he is strong in horse, and that they are brave men, but that he has not paid them any thing since their listing, which gives occasion to some to talke here, as if he had provided, for a retreat in the Banck of Venice,[5] others say tis not the fashion in Germany to pay their soldiers. The Dutch are as ill paid.

On Sunday last a part of the Dutch and French forces came to take up quarters in Emerick,[6] a towne ⟨within⟩[a] 4 or 5 English miles

[a] *MS.* with

---

[1] The house of Braunschweig (Brunswick)-Lüneburg; Georg Wilhelm, 1624–1705, duke of Celle 1648; and Johann Friedrich, 1625–79, who was converted to Catholicism in 1651: *A.D.B.* They were brothers of Ernst August, the future Elector of Hanover.

[2] Georg Friedrich, 1620–92, prince of Waldeck, count of Pyrmont and Culemborg, the general and friend of William III: ibid.

[3] Wilhelm VII, 1651–70, Landgrave of Hesse-Cassel from 1663. As he was a minor his mother acted as regent; she was Hedwig Sophie, 1623–83, a sister of the Great Elector; married Wilhelm VI, Landgrave of Hesse-Cassel, 1649: Hübner, *Geneal. Tabellen*, vol. i, nos. 178, 209.

[4] Johan Maurits van Nassau-Siegen, 1604–79, 'de Braziliaan'; stadholder in Cleves, etc., from 1647: *N.N.B.W.* He was a second cousin of the Electress.

[5] According to (Sir) William Temple (*D.N.B.*) von Galen had enough money in the Bank of Venice to buy a cardinal's cap: letter from Brussels, 6 Sept. 1665, in *Works* (ed. 1770, i. 232).

[6] Emmerich.

of this place. The Dutch were admitted into the houses but the French forcd to lye in the streets all night. They tooke all the carts wagons, and other moveable fuell they could finde about the towne, to make them selves fires, but that could not hinder some of them from perishing by the cold. They were soe little welcome there that the inhabitants would not sell them any thing for their mony, but the next day they threatend the townsmen to force their houses, if they provided them not quarters, and made bold to borrow some cows belonging to a person of this Court. The towne belongs to the Elector, and the inhabitants are his subjects but tis one of those the Dutch keepe a Garrison in. This Enterteinment makes the French already enquire the nearest way home, and tis supposd many will endeavour to finde it. This I had from an intelligent person that was then in Emerick and was a witnesse of this.

The middle of those 3 persons I mentiond in my last is of the French faction the other two for the Bishop and the last a great enemy to de Witte[1]

I am Sir

Your most humble servant

J L

Address: These present To Mr William Godolphin at Oxford[2]
Endorsed by Godolphin⟨?⟩: Mr Lock from Cleve $\frac{19}{29}$ December –65

## 179. Locke to William (later Sir William) Godolphin 26 December 1665/5 January 1666 (178, 181)

B.L., MS. Locke c. 24, ff. 252$^{v}$–253$^{v}$. (pp. 22–4 of Locke's Cleves letter-book). Draft or copy.

G 5° Jan. S.N.

In my last I gave you at large an account of all those things I could either learne or guesse at here, and they remaine soe much the same in my apprehension that had I not those reasons I mentiond there to be more spareing hereafter in things of that kinde, yet I should finde very little to adde, since Things at Court seeme to stand at the same passe[a] and camp affords little in a season that has

[a] *Or* posse

[1] Jan de Witt. I have not found any confirmation of Locke's statement that Blaspiel was hostile to him.

[2] The court was at Oxford on account of the plague from 25 September until 27 January 1666: *Intelligencer*, 2 October 1665, p. 954; *Oxford Gazette*, 29 January.

forced the armys to their winter quarter, and there is now noe other warre but what the French make in their quarters, where tis said they are not very kinde to their Landlords (whatever they are to their wives) but use them with a great deale of rudenesse and are not spareing of any outrages. The Dutch fore saw this well enough, and therefor have assignd them their winter quarters in the Electors towns they are possesd of upon the Reyne (The [a] of which towns is thus[b] that though the Dutch have garisons in them yet the inhabitants are acknowledg to be the Electors subjects, and all the revenews and profits of those places acrew to him,)[1] how he takes this I cannot learne. But I finde others here to thinke it strange that he suffers it. There lately pasd over the Reine two companys of French and marchd through some parts of the El: dominions without askeing him leave, which I heare he resents. people wonder here that the Dutch should make soe bold with him, at a time when they want and court his freindship, and to me it seems to proceed either from a great confidence or little regard of him. The strong party they have in this Court must give them the first, Or the inclination they finde he has to quiet and neutrality the latter, and methinks they appeare secure that he will be a sure freind or at least not an enemy. What ever it be that makes them soe little tender of disobleigeing him this I finde that the people here guesse our businesse donne, for all that I converse with are frequent in askeing when we goe, when we returne to England as if it were publickly beleivd that we had noe more to doe here. I mention not this that I thinke the common opinion usually gives a true account of things, but only to let you see what are the ⟨apprehensions⟩[c] of most here. Prince Maurice[2] came hither friday last and went yesterday to the Hage. I doe not heare that Count Waldeck stirs and tis ⟨said his⟩[d] levies amount not to above 5000, and that for this winter they are like to bring noe other increase to the affairs of Hol. but of Charges. Betweene Ostend and Bruges I remember we met an agent[e] from the Bishop[f] ready[f] to receive ⟨the ⟩[g] but I cannot finde here any Envoye

[a] *MS.* condition *and* state, *both del.* [b] *Or* this? [c] *MS.* apprehenions [d] *Page torn.* [e] *MS.* age$^{t}$ [f] *MS.* B$^{p}$ to ready [g] *Deleted; second word may be* men *or* mon *or ?*

[1] There were Dutch garrisons in Emmerich, Rees, Wesel, Büderich, and Orsoy: Philippson, *Der grosse Kurfürst*, ii. 45.

[2] Johan Maurits.

from him to procure the freindship of the El or that he hath sent any to any other parts to make him any alliances amongst the Catholick princes of Germany, and they seeme to conclude here, that the next summer he will not be able to subsist by himself and alone defend his country against the joynt forces of Fr and Hol. Though all say if he have mony enough and pay them well he can not want soldiers. whether this may give any reason to credit the report I mentiond to you in my last I shall leave you to judg.

I am informd that he is marching with some of his forces into Frisland[a] what the designe is and what will be the event will not be long ⟨unknown here⟩[b] and when it appears you shall be sure to receive an account of it From

## 180. LOCKE to JOHN STRACHEY, [*c.* 26 December 1665/ 5 Jan. 1666?] (177, 182)

B.L., MS. Locke c. 24, f. 230. The letter written for dispatch but perhaps kept back: see p. 233 n. Draft or copy in Locke's Cleves letter-book (MS. Locke c. 24, ff. 246–58), pp. 18–20, 22, 24–6, 28–31. Printed in King, pp. 13–18. The letter was completed in the week following Sunday 24 December/3 January: see p. 249, n. 1.

Sir[c]

Are you at leisure for half an howers trouble? and will you be content I should keepe up the custome of writeing long letters with little in them? Tis a barren place, and the dull frozen part of the yeare, and therefor you must not expect great matters, tis enough that at Christmas you have empty Christmas tales fit for the Chimny corner. To begin therefor. Dec. *15*. here *25* Christmas day about one in the morning I went a gossiping to our Lady. thinke me not prophane for the name is a great deale modester then the service I was at. I shall not describe all the particulars I observd in that church being the Principall of the Catholicks in Cleve.[1] but only those that were particular to the occasion. neare the high altar, was a little altar for this days solemnity, the Scene was a stable, wherein was an ox, an asse, a cradle, the Virgin, the babe, Joseph, shepheards and angells drammatis personæ, had they but given them motion, it had beene a perfect pupet play. and might

[a] *Spelling doubtful.* [b] *MS.* unknow her [c] *Locke, apparently later, noted at the head of the letter* Cleve 65

[1] The Stiftskirche.

have deservd pence a peice, for they were of the same size and make that our English pupets are. and I am confident these shepheards, and this Joseph are kin, to that Judith and Holophernes which I have seene at Bartholomew faire.[1] A little without the stable was a flock of sheepe cut out of Cards, and these as they there stood, without their sheepheards, appeard to me the best emblem I had seene a long time, and me thought represented these poore innocent people, who whilst their sheepheards pretend soe much to follow Christ, and pay their devotion to him, are left unregarded in the barren wildernesse. This was the shew: the Musick to it was all vocall in the quire adjoyneing: but such as I never heard. They had strong voyces, but soe ill tund, soe ill manag'd, that 'twas their misfortune as well as ours, that they could be heard. He that could not, though he had a cold, make better Musick with Chivy chase[2] over a pot of smooth ale deservd well to pay the reckoning and goe away a thirst. However I thinke they were the honestest singing men, I ever have seene, for they endeavourd to deserve their mony, and earnd it certainly with pains enough: for what they wanted in skill, they made up in loudnesse, and variety, every one had his owne tune, and the result of all was much like the noise at chooseing Parlament men, where every one endeavours to cry loudest. Besides the men there were a company of little Choristers. I thought when I saw them at first, they had dancd to the others Musick, and that it had beene your Grays Inne revells,[3] for they were Jumping up and downe about a good Charcoall fire, that was in the middle of the Quire (this, their devotion, and their singing was enough I thinke to keepe them warme though it were a very cold night). But it was not danceing, but singing they servd for; when it came to their turnes, away they ran to their places, and there they made as good harmony as a consort of little pigs would, and they were much what[4] as cleanly. Their part being donne, out they sallied again to the fire, where they plaid, till their Cue cald them, and then backe to their places they huddled. soe negligent and slight are they in their service, in a place where the nearnesse of adversarys might teach them to be more carefull. But I suppose the naturall tendency of these outside performances, and these

[1] In London; held annually on 23 August and the following days.

[2] p. 177.

[3] The Christmas revels in the Inns of Court are described in Chamberlayne, *Angliæ Notitia* (1674 ed., ii. 258–9).

[4] Commonly muchwhat: *O.E.D.*; frequently used by Locke.

mummerys in religion, would bring it everywhere to this passe, did not, feare and the severity of the Magistrate preserve it, which being taken away here, they very easily suffer themselves to slubber over their ceremonys, which in other places are kept up with soe much zeale and exactnesse, but methinkes they are not to be blamd, since the one seems to me as much religion as the other. In the afternoone I went to the Carthusians church,[1] they had their little gent too, but in finer clothes, and their angels with surplices on, and singing books in their hands, for here is noething to be donne without booke. hither were crowded a great throng of children to see these pretty babys, and I amongst them as wise and as devout as they, and for my pains had a good sprinkle of holy water, and now I may defie the divill. Thus have I begun the holy-days with Christmas Gambols. But had I understood the language, I beleive at the reformed church[2] I had founde something more serious, for they have two sermons at their church each of the 3 first days, for Christmas lasts noe longer here. that which pleasd me most was, that at the same catholick church the next day I saw our Lady all in white linnin dresd as one that is newly laine in, and in her lap something, that perhaps 20 years since was designd for a baby, but now it was growne to have a beard, and me thought was not soe well usd as our country fellows use to be, who though they scape all the yeare are usually trimd against Christmas. They must pardon me for being merry for it is Christmas, but to be serious with you the Catholick religion is a different thing from what[a]– we beleive–[a] it in England and I have other thoughts of it, then when I was in a place that is fild with prejudices, and things are knowne only by heare say. I have not met with any soe good naturd people or soe civill as the Catholick preists, and I have received many courtesies from them which I shall always gratefully acknowledg. But to leave the good naturd catholicks, and to give you a little account of our brethren the Calvinists, that differ very little from our English Presbyterians. I met lately accidentally with a young sucking Divine, that thought himself noe small champion, who as if he had beene some knight errant, bound by oath to bid battle to all comers, first accosted me in courteous wise, but the

[a–a] *MS.* what we be beleive

[1] An error, presumably for the Capuchins. There were no Carthusians in Cleves.
[2] The Calvinist.

customary salute being over, I found my self ⟨assaulted⟩[a] most furiously, and heavy loads of arguments fell upon me. I that expected noe such thing was faine to gard my self, under the trusty broad sheild of ignorance, and only now and then returnd a blow by way of enquiry: and by this Parthian way of flying defended my self till passion and want of breath had made him weary, and soe we came to an accomodation, Though had he had lungs enough, and I noe other use of my ears, the combat might have lasted, (if that may be cald a combat (ubi tu cædis ego vapulo tantum)[1] as long as the warrs of Troy, and the end of all had beene like that, noething but some rubish of divinity, as uselesse and incoherent as the ruins the Greeks left behinde them. This was a probationer in Theologie, and I beleive (to keepe still to my errantry) they are bound to shew their prowesse with some valiant unknowne, before they can be dubd, and receive the dignity of the order. I cannot imagine why else he should set upon me, a poore innocent weight, who thought noe thing of a combat, and desired to be peaceable, and was too far from my owne dunghill to be quarrelling. But tis noe matter there were noe wounds made but in Priscians head, who suffers much in this country. This provocation I have sufficiently revenged upon one of their church, Our Landlord, who is wont some times to Germanize and take a little too much of the creature. These frailtys I threaten him to discover to his pastor, who will be sure to rebuke him (but spareing his name) the next sunday from the pulpet, and severely chastise the liberty of his cups. thus I sow up the good mans mouth, because the other gaped too much, and make him as much feare my tongue as I was punished with the others. But for all this he will sometimes drinke himself into a defiance of divine and discipline, and hearkens only to Bacchus's inspirations. You must not expect any thing remarkeable from me all ⟨this⟩[b] following weeke. for I have spent it in getting a pair of gloves, and thinke too I have had a quick dispatch. you will perhaps wonder at it, and thinke I talke like a traveller: But I will give you the particulars of the businesse. Three days were spent in findeing out a glover, for though I can walke all the towne over in lesse then an hower, yet their shops are soe contrivd, as if

[a] *MS.* assauted [b] *MS.* thes

[1] 'Where you deal the blows and I only take them': Juvenal, iii. 289, with *caedis*, which upsets the rhythm, substituted for *pulsas*.

they were designd to conceale not expose their wares, and though you may thinke it strange, yet me thinks it is very well donne, and tis a becomeing modesty to conceale that which they have reason enough to be ashamd of. But to proceede, the two next days were spent in drawing them on, The right hand glove (or, as they call them here, Handshoe)[1] Thursday and the left hand Friday, and Ile promise you this was two good days worke, and little enough to bring them to fitt my hands, and to consent to be fellows, which after all they are soe far from, that when they are on, I am always afraid, my hands should goe to cuffs one with an other, they soe disagree: Saturday we concluded on the price, computed and changed our mony, for it requires a great deale of Arithmatick and a great deale of brasse to pay 28[a–] stivers and 7 doits.[–a][2] But god be thanked they are all well fitted with counters for reconing, for their mony is good for noething else, and I am poore here with both my pockets full of it.[b] I wondered at first, why the market people brought their wares in little carts drawne by one horse, till I found it necessary to carry home the price of them, for a horse load of turneps would be two horse load of mony. A paire of shoes cannot be got under half a yeare. I lately saw the cow kild out of whose hide, I hope, to have my next pair. The first thing after they are married here, is to bespeake the childs coat, and Truly the Bridegroome must be a bungler, that getts not a child before the mantle be made. for it is far easyer here to have a man made then a sute. To be serious with you, they are the slowest people and fullest of delays that ever I have met with, and their mony is bad. Dec. 22 I saw the inscripsion that entitles the Electors house here to soe much antiquity. It stands at the upper end of a large roome, which is the first entrance into the house, and is as followeth. Anno ab urbe Romana condita 698 Julius Cæsar Dictator hisce partibus in ditionem susceptis arcem hanc Clivensem Fund.[3] I know not how old the

[a–a] *Draft* 29 stivers and 7 doits out of a Rix dolar [b] *Draft adds* the worth of a crowne tires me to carry it

---

[1] Dutch *Handschoen* (German *Handschuh*). See further nos. *610*, 626, 782, and *Some Thoughts Concerning Education*, § 7 (all editions).

[2] Eight duyts made a stiver, which was worth slightly more than an English penny.

[3] Pighius gives a different version of the inscription and writes that it was set up by the old dukes: *Hercules Prodicius*, p. 35. Dorrington gives another version: p. 372. There appears to be no satisfactory evidence for a Roman settlement at Cleves. The Burg is a medieval building.

wall was that bore it but the inscripsion was certainly much younger then I am, as appears by the characters and other circumstances. However I beleived the painter, reverenced the antiquity, and did homage to the memory of Cæsar, and was not averse to a tradition which the situation and antique mode of building made not improbable. The same time I had the favour to see the Kitchin and the Seller, and though in the middle of the first there were made on the floore a great fire big enough to broyle halfe a dozen St Laurenc's, yet me thought the seller was the hotter place, and soe I made hast to leave it, and have little to say of it, unlesse you think fit I should tell you how many Rummers of Rhenish I dranke, and how many bisquets I eat, and that I had there almost learnt to speake High Dutch. Dec 24 At the Lutherans church after a good lusty rattleing High Dutch sermon,[1] the sound whereof would have made one thinke it had beene all a use of reproofe. I had an oportunity to observe the administration of the Sacrament, which was thus. The sermon being ended the minister that preachd not (for they have two to a church) stood up at a little deske which was upon the communion table almost at the upper end of the church, and then read a little while, part of which readeing I judgd to be prayer but observd noe action that lookd like consecration[a] (I know not what the words were) when he had donne he placd himself at the north end of the table, and the other minister that preacht, at the south end, soe that their backs were towards one another, then there marchd up to him on the North side a communicant, who when he came to the minister, made a low bow and kneeld downe, and then the minister put a wafer into his mouth, which donne he rose, made his obeysance, and went to the other end where he did the same, and had the wine poured into his mouth without takeing the cup in his hand and then came back to his place by the south side of the church, thus did 4 one after another which were all that receivd that day and amongst them, was a boy about 13 or 14 years old. They have at this church a Sacrament every Sunday morning. In the afternoone at the Calvinists I saw a christening. After sermon there came 3 men and 3 women (one whereof was the midwife with a child in her armes, the

[a] *Draft adds* of the bread (or wafers) and wine, *and omits the following parenthesis.*

[1] The day is Sunday, 24 December, O.S. The Lutherans were the Elector's German-speaking officials, etc., from Brandenburg.

rest were godfathers and godmothers, of[a–] which they allow a greater number then we doe, and soe wisely got more spoons)[–a] to the table which is just by the pulpet. They taking their places, the minister in the pulpet read a little of the institution,[1] then read a short prayer, then another minister that was below, tooke the child and with his hand poured water 3 times on its forhead, which donne, he in the pulpet read another short prayer, and soe concluded. All this was not much longer then the Lords prayer Creed and 10 Commandements, for all their service is very short besides their preaching and singing, and there they allow good measure.

Address: For Mr Strachy

## 181. LOCKE to WILLIAM (later Sir William) GODOLPHIN 30 December 1665/9 January 1666 (179, 183A)

B.L., MS. Locke c. 39, ff. 13–14. The original letter; it did not belong to the Lovelace Collection. Draft or copy in MS. Locke c. 24, ff. 254v–255v (Locke's Cleves letter-book, pp. 26–8). Part printed from the draft in King, pp. 11–12 (it is succeeded by part of no. 176, the two extracts being combined in a single letter).

Sir

I have by the post continually from time to time, given you my ⟨apprehensions⟩[b] of things here, but since Sir Walter thinks he has reason, to suspect, that some of his dispatches have miscarried, and therefor, has sent an expresse, I shall by him send you again an account of all I can learne. I have hitherto beene of the minde that their councells here tend to the preserveing a neutrality, and the reasons I had to thinke soe were, that I saw noe preparations for warre, noe leavys made, but only talkd of. And besides I was informed, that there is here a great scarcity of mony, That the expences of the Court are great. the debts greater, and the revenews small. And that the Revenews of March and Cleve, (which are wont to pay the use of old debts are now employd in the expences of the houshold dureing the Electors abode here, and the creditors are to be content now without either use or principall. the businesse of 150000 Rixdolars which the El: demands of the Estates of March

[a–a] *Not in the draft.* [b] *MS.* apprhensions

[1] That part of the office of baptism which consists in reciting Christ's words in instituting baptism (the term is also applied to part of the prayer of consecration in the Eucharist): *O.E.D.*

and Cleve moves slowly. And though at our first comeing hither, it was said that it would be granted in two or three days, yet I can not finde that the Deputys are yet come to a resolution, or are like to grant it suddainly. For I am told many of them went home at christmas and that they are not yet returnd. But should that summ be presently granted, and paid. there are other ways, to dispose of it, besides armes, some whereof, I have mentioned to you in my former. The strong party the French and Dutch have in this Court (Amongst which are two, and[a]– those not Councellors,–[a] by whose advice the El. is much swaid) will make it difficult to draw him to the Bishops side, And the consideration of Religion may perhaps a little increase that difficulty, since tis generally apprehended here that the warre is upon that score. And perhaps the feare of haveing some of his scatterd countrys molested by some of the Bishops allies will make him a little cautious of declareing for the Dutch. The use you will finde in this dispatch they make of late news from Ratisbone,[1] I cannot thinke any other then a pretence. Since I am told, that the resolution, that is taken at the meeting there of assisting the Bishop is not soe new, that the Elector could be ignorant of it till now. I beleive there is yet a neutrality, and that at least they are not forward to appeare for either side. And perhaps (since mony seems to me to be here as well as in other places the great souder[b2] of pacts and agreements) they delay the bargaine, to raise the price, and wait for the best chapman. They treat with Hol: They treat with France, and in what termes they stand with us you will see by Sir Walters dispatch but I must not mention. But by the whole, I beleive, you will finde, they either dally with others, or waver themselves. The Dutch have fild the Electors towns on the Reyne with their French soldiers, and they fill them with outrages. which he resents and complains of. But it still continues the same. Whether you will impute this proceeding of the Dutch to their confidence of his freindship, or carelesnesse of his enmity, I know not. Tis said a considerable body of the Bishops army are now marching, if it be upon any feisible designe, he seems to have chosen a fit season, whilst the States are questioning their generalls, for some miscarriages, in the last Campania, and things are out of order in Hol:

a–a *These words are not in the draft.* b *Draft* sodder

---

1 Regensburg, where the Imperial Diet met. 2 Solder: *O.E.D.*

I was told yesterday, that Mr Blaspell was to goe from hence this day to the Duke of Neubourg[1] but his businesse I can not learne. I know there is very little herein, but what I have writt to you formerly: which I should not thus trouble you with the repetition of, did I finde here more that was new: or were I sure my former came safe to your hands. In my first letter from hence, I told you of a booke I had founde here of that kinde you desired. and since perhaps, that may have miscarried, I shall send you, the title once more, and desire to know by this bearer, whether I shall buy it for you. It is too big by half for it is half high Dutch, and soe you must take both languages togeather.[a] The title is

Theatrum pacis. i e tractatuum atque instrumentorum præcipuorum ab anno inde 1647 ad 1660 usque in Europa initorum et conclusorum ⟨Collectio⟩[b] in 4° *1663*.[2] This or any other commands from you will be acceptable to

Sir

Your most humble and most obedient servant

JOHN LOCKE

Cleve 9° Jan: 66. S.N.

Since the writeing my letter I heare from Sir Walter that the King of France hath sent a letter to his Ambasador in Hol:[3] to presse the States to take the feild again presently and fall upon the Bishops Country, and if they will not he gives Order to his Generall Mr Pradell[4] to over run it with the French troups

Address: These for Mr William Godolphin at Court

Endorsed (by Godolphin?): Mr Lock from Cleve January. 9th s: n: 1666

## 182. LOCKE to [JOHN STRACHEY?], [early January 1666?] (180, 184)

B.L., MS. Locke c. 24, f. 231. The letter written for dispatch but perhaps kept back: p. 233 n. Draft or copy in Locke's Cleves letter-book (MS. Locke c. 24, ff. 246–58), pp. 31–4. Printed (from f. 231) in King, pp. 18–20. The letter

[a] *The draft stops here.* [b] *MS.* Collection

[1] The Pfalzgraf Philipp Wilhelm, 1615–90; succeeded as duke of Neuburg and Jülich 1653: *A.D.B.*

[2] By J. A. Endter; published at Nuremberg.

[3] Louis's ambassador in the United Provinces was Godefroy, comte d'Estrades, 1607–86: *N.B.G.* The letter here summarized is not identifiable among those to him from Louis that are printed in his *Lettres, mémoires.*

[4] François de Pradel, d. 1690; lieutenant-general 1657: J.-B. Colbert, *Lettres, instructions et mémoires*, ed. P. Clément, 1861–82, vi. 473 n.

was apparently addressed to Strachey; if so, the 'divinity disputation' probably alludes to the encounter with the 'young sucking divine' of no. 180, and the letter should be dated about a week later than no. 180.

Sir

The old opinion that every man had his particular Genius, that ruled and directed his course of life, hath made me sometimes laugh, to thinke, what a pleasant thing it would be, if we could see little Sprites bestride men, (as plainely as I see here women bestride horses) ride them about, and spur them on in that way, which they ignorantly thinke they choose themselves. And would you not smile to observe that they make use of us, as we doe of our palfrys, to trot up and downe, for their pleasure and not our owne? To what purpose this from Cleve? I'll tell you; if there be any such thing (as I can not vouch the contrary) certainly mine is an Academick goblin. When I left Oxford I thought for a while to take leave of all university affairs. And should have least expected to have found any thing of that nature here at Cleve of any part of the world. But doe what I can I am still kept in that tract. I noe sooner was got here, but I was welcomd with a divinity disputation, which I gave you an account of in my last. I was noe sooner rid of that, but I found my self up to the ears in poetry, and overwhelmed in Helicon. I had almost as rathe[1] have beene soused in the Reyne as frozen as it was, for it could not have beene more cold and intollerable, then the poetry I met with. The remembrance of it puts me in a chill sweat, and were it not that I am obleiged to recount all particulars, being[a]– under the laws of an historian,–[a] I should finde it very difficult, to recall to minde this part of my story. But haveing armd my self with a goode peice of bag puding which beares a mighty antipathy to poetry, and haveing added there to half a dozen glasses of dareing wine I thus proceed. My invisible master therefor haveing mounted me rod me out to a place where I must needs meet a learned Bard,[2] in a thread bare coat, and a hat that though in its younger days, it had beene black, yet it was growne gray with the labour of its masters brains, and his hard study or time had changed the colour of that as well as his masters haire. His breeches had the marks of antiquity upon them, were borne I beleive in the Heroick times, and retaind still the

[a–a] *Draft* haveing undertooke to be my owne historian

[1] Soon. The adverb was obsolete, but survived in dialect: *O.E.D.* See further p. 294, n. 3.

[2] I have failed to identify him.

gallantry of that age and had an antipathy to base pelfe. Stockings I know not whether he had any, but I'm sure his two shoes had but one heele, which made his owne feet goe as uneven as those of his verses. He was soe poore that he had not soe much as a rich face, nor the promise of a carbuncle in it. soe that I must needs say that his outside was poet enough. After a little discourse wherein he sprinkled some bays on our British Druid Owen,[1] out he drew from under his coat a folio of Verses,[a] and that you may be sure they were excellent: I must tell you that they were Achrosticks upon the name and titles of[b] the Elector of Brandenburg. I could not scape readeing of them. When I had donne I endeavourd to play the poet a little in commending them, but in that he out did me clearly, praised faster then I could, preferred them to Lucan and Virgill, shewed me where his Muse flew high, squeesed out all the very juce of all his conceits and there was not a secret Conumdrum which he laid not open to me: and in that little talke I had with him afterwards, he quoted his owne verses a dozen times and Gloried in his works. This poem was designed as a present to the El: but I being Owens country man had the honour to see them before the Elector, which he made me understand was a singular courtesie, though I beleive 100 others had beene equally favoured. I told him the El: must needs give him a considerable reward. he seemed angry at the mention of it, and told me he had only a designe to shew his affection and parts and spoke as if he thought himself fitter to give then receive any thing from the El: and that he was the greater person of the two, and indeed what need had he of any gifts who had all Tagus and Pactolus in his possession, could make himself a Tempe when he pleased and create as many Elysiums as he had a minde to. I applauded his Generosity and great minde, thanked him for the favour he had donne me and at last got out of his hands. but my University goblin left me not soe, for the next day when I thought I had beene rod out only to aireing, I was had to a fodering of chopped hay or Logick forsooth, poore materia prima was canvessed cruelly, stripped of all the gay dresses of her formes and shewne naked to us, though I must confesse I had not eys good

[a] *Draft adds* and blessed me with the sight of his composition [b] *Draft adds* Fredericus Gulielmus

[1] John Owen, *c.* 1560–1622, the epigrammatist: *D.N.B.* At least five editions of his collected epigrams were published in Amsterdam by 1650; there were also editions published at Leipzig (1615, 1622) and elsewhere.

enough to see her, however the dispute was good sport and would have made a horse laugh, and truly I was like to have broke my bridle. The young Munks[1] (which one would not guesse by their lookes) are subtile people, and dispute as eagerly for materia prima, as if they were to make their diner on it, and perhaps sometimes tis all their meale, for which others charity is more to be blamed then their stomacks. The professor of Philosophy and moderator of the disputation, was more acute at it then father Hudebrasse,[2] he was top full of distinctions, which he produced with soe much gravity and applyed with soe good a grace, that ignorant I began to admire Logick again, and could not have thought that simpliciter and secundum quid, materialiter. and formaliter, had beene such gallant things, which with the right stroking of his whiskers, the setling of his hood, and his stately walke made him seeme to himself and me something more then Aristotle and Democritus. But he was soe hotly charged by one of the Seniors of the fraternity, that I was affraid sometimes what it would produce, and feared there would be noe other way to decide the controversy betweene them but by cuffs, but a subtile destinction devided the matter betweene them and soe they parted good freinds. The truth is here hog-sheering[3] is much in its glory, and our disputeing in Oxford comes as short of it, as the Rhetorick of Carfax does that of Belings gate. But it behoves the Moncks to cherish this art of wrangleing in its declineing age, which they first nursed and sent abroad into the world to give it a troublesome idle imployment. I being a brute that was rod thither for anothers pleasure profited little by all their reasonings, but was glad when they had donne that I might goe home again to my ordinary provender and leave them their sublime speculations, which certainly their spare diet and private cells inspire abundantly which such grosse feeders as I am are not capable of.

Reliqua desiderantur

[1] Apparently the Minorites. There were no monks in Cleves.

[2] Hudibras 'could distinguish, and divide
A hair 'twixt South and South-west side';
Ralpho 'had *First Matter* seen undrest'
—*Hudibras*, ed. J. Wilders, 1967, I. i. 67–8, 554.

[3] The term apparently derives from the proverb 'A great cry and little wool, quoth the Devil when he sheard the hog': James Howell, 1659, quoted in *Oxford Dict. English Proverbs*, where earlier forms, *c.* 1475 and 1579, are given. The hog here is the swine; the word is also applied to a young sheep, from the time when it ceases to be a lamb until its first shearing; there appears, however, to be no allusion to the lamb's-wool of the hoods of the bachelors of arts.

## 183. LOCKE to JOSEPH (later Sir Joseph) WILLIAMSON, 16/26 January 1666

Public Record Office, London. State papers, foreign, German states, vol. lvii (S.P. 81/57), f. 30. Excerpt printed in Fox Bourne, i. 121. Joseph Williamson, 1633–1701; at Westminster School; matriculated from Queen's College, Oxford, 18 November 1650; B.A. 1654; M.A. 1657; fellow of Queen's 1657–78; at this time Arlington's principal subordinate; knighted 1672; D.C.L. 1674; secretary of state 1674–8; president of the Royal Society 1677–80: *D.N.B.*

Cleve 26° Jan 66 S N.

Sir

Though the letter Sir Walter sends, leaves me noething worth the sending to you yet the knowledg I have of your civility makes me persevere in the intention I had to write to you, and confidently desire you, that if any letters from any of my freinds in England to me, come to your hands, you would doe me the favour to send them me in the pacquet to Sir Walter. All other ways of conveyance hither, are soe utterly unknowne to me, and give me soe little hopes of receiveing any letters, that you will pardon this request, to a man, that is unwilling to be deprived of the ⟨correspondence⟩[a] of all those freinds and the knowledg of some affairs he left in England, and who hopes the granting of it will not cost you much trouble. I wish there were any thing here where in I might serve you, since there could be noe thing wellcomer to me then your commands, and the oportunitys to assure you that I am

Sir

Your most humble and most obedient servant

JOHN LOCKE

Pray if you see Dr Pocock[1] whilst you stay in Oxford[2] present my service to him, and let him know I writt to him about a fortnight since.

Address: These present To Mr Joseph Williamson at Court

Endorsed: Cleve[b–] Jan 26 166$\frac{6}{5}$[–b] Mr Locke

[a] *MS.* rorrespondence [b–b] *Faded; readings doubtful.*

[1] Edward Pococke, 1604–91, the Orientalist; D.D. 1660; a canon of Christ Church from 1660: *D.N.B.*; see also Locke's account of him in no. 3321. Letter from him below, no. *542*.

[2] See p. 242, n. 2.

## 183A. LOCKE to WILLIAM (later Sir William) GODOLPHIN, 19/29 January 1666 (181)

The Humanities Research Center, The University of Texas at Austin. Transcribed from xerox print.

Cleve 29° Jan 66 S N

Sir

The news was sent hither, that you were gon into Spaine, hath for some time made me forbeare writeing to you. But the returne of Sir Walters man haveing assured me, that you are yet in England, I againe gave you this trouble, and shall constantly write, when I know that you are in a place where my letters may come to you. I was the more easily perswaded to beleive you were gonne with my Lord Sandwich,[1] since though I had writt to you every post I had not received one letter from you since I came hither. Mr Beverling[2] from the States came hither this day seventh night And Mr Colbert[3] from the King of France yesterday. Tis reported that the King of Poland intends to lay downe his Regality and retire into a Monastary and that Saphia the second person in Lubomirski's party and generall in Lithuania is dead. Lubomiski too was reported dead, but that is contradicted.[4] Tis said also that the Emperor has an intention to send twenty regiments to the assistance of the Bishop of Munster, and that he hath intimated to the Dukes of Lunenbourg that if they make a warre in the Empire, he shall be concerned to take notice of it.[5] We heare the Prince of Aurange's interest gets footing every day in Amsterdam, and they begin there to incline very much that way.[6] I finde noe great reason to

[1] Edward Mountagu, first earl of Sandwich, the admiral and general at sea; ambassador to Spain 1666–8: *D.N.B.* He did not leave London until 23 February (sailing from Portsmouth on 2 March); Godolphin accompanied him as secretary: Harris, *Sandwich*, ii. 49–52.

[2] Hieronymus van Beverningk: *N.N.B.W.*

[3] Charles Colbert, marquis de Croissy, 1629–96, brother of Louis XIV's minister; ambassador to England 1668–74; secretary of state for foreign affairs 1679(80)–96: *D.B.F.*

[4] The king is John Casimir (Casimir V), 1609–72; king since 1649; he abdicated in 1668 and became abbot of St. Germain-des-Prés. George Lubomirski, d. 1667, formerly Grand Marshal, at this time in open rebellion. P. J. Sapieha: *Wielka encyklopedia powszechna PWN*, x (1967), 355. On Polish affairs at this time see A.-M. Gasztowtt, *Une Mission diplomatique en Pologne, etc.*, 1916.

[5] I have been unable to check these statements.

[6] William III (William Henry), 1650–1702, prince of Orange from birth, the future king of England. For this movement see S. B. Baxter, *William III*, 1966, pp. 39–40.

alter the opinion I have always had concerning the inclination of this Elector, and beleive it still to be as I formerly writt to you. I am

Sir

your most humble and most obedient servant

JOHN LOCKE

Address: These for Mr William Godolphin at Court

## 184. LOCKE to JOHN STRACHEY, 2/12 February 1666 (182, 186)

B.L., MS. Locke c. 24, ff. 233–4. The letter sent. It was not originally delivered to Strachey, but was returned to Locke, who added the two notes and sent it to Strachey with no. 186 of 22 February.

Cleve. 12° Feb. 66 S.N[a]

Sir

If my letters have not missed their way you will have found, that by goeing into Germany, I have only changed the place, not laid by the custome of our correspondence, though after severall letters I have not beene fortunate enough to receive any one from you. The variety of hands and hazards they must passe in comeing hither makes me beleive that some may have miscarried, for I cannot thinke you would be spareing of your letts, which being always very wellcome to me, must needs be now much more, when I am farther from you, and have noe other way to receive any knowledg of my affairs in Somerset shire. Germany is now at quiet, but though few swords are drawne yet they are all puting them on and the Princes of Germany doe all arme, whether they doe it by imitation or feare of one another, or with designe is not yet know for none of them declare. The Bishop of Munster hath an army strong in Horse and is now recruiting his foote forces. The Dutch too prepare to match him next spring, they have designed *Marshall*[b] *Turin*[1] of France for their Generall and have offered the *Prince*[b] *of Aurange to be Lieutenan Generall* of the horse and Admirall.[2] They endeavour on both sides both Bishop and States[3] to gaine partisans

[a] *Part of letter torn away.* [b] *Over this word the figure* 1.

[1] Henri de la Tour d'Auvergne, vicomte de Turenne, 1611–75; field-marshal 1643: *N.B.G.*

[2] William was to serve under Turenne: Baxter, *William III*, pp. 39–40.

[3] The States General of the United Provinces, the central political body of the Dutch Republic.

in the Empire, but noe body hath hether to declared except the Dukes of Lunenbourg[1] who afford the Dutch some thousands of men but to be paid by the States. This *Elector of Brandenburg*[a] declares himself not to be engaged though I will whisper in your eare that I thinke he leanes to the Dutch and we have but little Hopes of him. The Swedes are marched into Germany, and give every one feare but noebody an account of their designe. The French fill the borders of Flanders[2] with their troups and if they attempt any thing the Emperor hath promised to send aid into Flanders. You may be certaine that the Dutch are full weary of the French that are amongst them and finde them to be soe dangerous and troublesome freinds that I beleive you will finde they will endeavour all manner of ways to be rid of them, the rest, the inclosed printed papers will give you. I am

Sir

your most faithfull and obedient servant

JOHN LOCKE

My service to Mrs Strachy and Mrs Baber[3]

My love to my Uncle[4] and the rest of his family, and desire him to have a care of my affairs there

Send your letters for Me either to Mr David Thomas[5] Proctor of the University, at new Colledg or Else to Mrs Litchfeilds[6] neare the Schools in Oxford, but the latter is safest since Mr Thomas may be out of towne

Address: These for John Strachy Esq at Sutton Court To be left at Mr John Blanch's neare the high crosse in High street Bristoll

Locke's marginal notes:

1 They are scarce yet resolved on a Generall and have beene in great disorder about it

2 The El. of Br: joyns with the Dutch, which they pay for[7]

[a] *Over this word the figure* 2.

[1] pp. 240–1 and n.
[2] The name was applied loosely to the Spanish Netherlands in general.
[3] Strachey's wife and mother respectively. [4] Peter Locke.
[5] pp. 230, n. 1, 283, etc. [6] Mrs. Anne Lichfield: p. 239, n. 1.
[7] The treaty is dated 6/16 February: Dumont, *Corps univ. diplomatique*, VI. iii. 85–103.

## *185.* [Elinor Parry, later Mrs. Hawkshaw?], 'The Oxford Gazett', 13 February 1666 (122, *193*)

B.L., MS. Locke c. 8, f. 62. Scrap, cut down left side and at foot; something may be lost at the foot. Attributed to Elinor Parry principally on account of the handwriting.

The newspaper the *Oxford Gazette* was first issued in November 1665 (probably on 16 November). It continued with this title until no. 23, 29 January–1 February 1666; it then became the existing *London Gazette.*

The Oxford Gazett: feb: the 13

. . . tin[a] Court The Queens miscarriage posesed all: with Greife but new hopes of a prince here after[1]

Ch Ch.

Ch Court In the Absenc of King[2] and Cannons mr Hodges will be Cheife there / he is to be Proctor by the absenc of —— tis said he looses (Honour) in travelling for it[3] —— mr Candish commoner of C:C: is to mari the hansome Terill[4]

(Oxford)

Pococke the book seler came of with Honour from his last enterprise he with a peacefull asault is now posesed of mr Wests daughter. haveing stole her. twas a brave adventure for a crocked peece.[5]

The fresh report now heer is of a Combat betwix Elia and Berelisa tis beleeved for a German that is expected

[a] *Part of a word apparently cut away.*

[1] Queen Catherine lodged in Merton College from 26 September 1665 until 16 February 1666. She was reported to have miscarried on 4 February: Wood, *L. and T.* ii. 59, 67, 68, 72, 73.

[2] Charles left Christ Church on 27 January: p. 242, n. 2.

[3] Nathaniel Hodges, *c.* 1634–1700; matriculated from Christ Church 21 March 1651; B.A. 1654; student of Christ Church; M.A. 1657; proctor 26 April 1666–17 April 1667; professor of moral philosophy 1668–73; prebendary of Norwich, installed 2 May 1673; and of Gloucester, 20 May 1673; the first earl of Shaftesbury's chaplain: Foster; Madan, nos. 2243 (68 and 97), 2466 (36 and 130); Humphrey Prideaux, *Letters . . . to John Ellis, 1674–1722*, ed. E. Maunde Thompson (Camden Soc., new ser., xv, 1875), pp. 159, 161; P.R.O., S.P. 30/24, bdle. 4, no. 236 (list of Shaftesbury's household, Christmas 1672); letters and notices below. In some letters he is called Lysis. The absentee is presumably Locke.

[4] Henry Cavendish, born *c.* 1648; of Doveridge, Derbyshire; matriculated from Christ Church 13 November 1663: Foster. His wife is Mary, daughter of Sir Timothy Tyrrell (p. 153, n. 8): G. Lipscomb, *Hist. . . . of (Buckinghamshire)*, 1847, i. 352–3.

[5] Samuel Pocock, traceable 1659–67; married Elizabeth, daughter of John West of Hampton Poyle, Oxon., armiger: Wood, *L. and T.* i. 119; vol. ii, p. viii; etc.

shortly. Scribelia keeps her valor to disinchant you after your adventures.[1]

Holand

tis soposed the States will not permit the prisoners stay: in consideration of the little service thay will doe them,[2] tis wish't the Germans would doe the like and pack the english from them / where would you be A.[3]

white Hall[4]

the Secretarys Grumble damnably at the tedious dispacthes of those beyond sea, thay say thay are too much taken up with writing to their mristresses thay neglect the greater afares: but in zeal to the publick, all such are to be called Home, you[a–] may be mistaken so brought with the Rest[–a]

Ireland[b]

mr Jo: Parry is in expectation of the deanery tis thought he will be perswaded to acept thereof;[5] his Sister then will Cherish the German.

Denmark

Summons are sent, for the Danes appearing in franc, then home, tis really beleeved t'was a Ladys request in favour of one of them: (which) tis not known[6]

Bristoll

a Belch[7] travelling to Oxford[c] from Germany tooke this way, amazed all, mr Strachy is in his tranc still

[a–a] *This may belong with a lost notice relating to Ireland.* [b] *End of the first page; a notice may be cut away.* [c] *MS.* Ox

---

[1] By their handwriting Elia, Berelisa, and Scribelia, appear to be the same person: above, p. 68 n.; the data are insufficient for certainty. The German is Locke.
[2] I cannot explain the allusion.
[3] Probably Atticus: so no. *214*; as 'Att' in no. *222*; as 'A' in nos. *225*, *232*.
[4] Charles returned to Whitehall on 1 February.
[5] Parry (pp. 69 n., 301, etc.) was installed dean of Christ Church, Dublin, on 5 April of this year: H. Cotton, *Fasti Ecclesiæ Hibernicæ*, 1848–78, ii. 44.
[6] I have not traced the allusion. There were Danish readers in the Bodleian Library in 1663 and 1664: Wood, *Fasti*, ii. 276, 280.
[7] Perhaps meaning an utterance, here a letter.

that is the reason there is no returns to Germany, mrs margaret[1] punished senc it came with the toothache, wee entreat our english friends to keep such Blasts from us, as thay hope for a ransome hereafter

the Plague runs yett about London[a]

## 186. Locke to John Strachey, 22 February 1666 (184, 187)

B.L., MS. Locke c. 24, ff. 235–6. Two passages are printed in King, p. 25.

London 22° Feb. $\frac{65}{66}$

Sir

If the rest of my letters to you out of Germany have had noe better fortune then this inclosed[2] (which I met here at London comeing backe to me to Cleve I suppose by the mistake of Mr Proctor Thomas) I have beene lost to you longer then I was willing, and you will have missed some of those storys Germany afforded me. Though I write from London yet I shall send you out landish news which I am yet better acquainted with then our English affairs, being landed at the downes on Tuesday morning last,[3] at which time Sir Christopher Mings[4] set saile from thence with 15 men of Warre and is goeing for Hamborow with hopes to meet some Dutch and intention to convoy hence some merchants of ours. On Tuesday was seventh night[5] I saw neare Antwerp a regiment of New raised foote of the Bishop of Munsters who were marching towards Holland upon some designe, and I heare since they have beaten some of the Dutch but this I doubt. Things in Germany stand much according as the inclosed tells you with the marginall correction and there has beene a great stir in Holland about makeing a Generall which is not yet resolved on.[6] The French fill their townes towards England and Flanders with Soldiers. But what ever we apprehend I scarce beleive with a designe of Landing in

[a] *Something further may be cut away.*

[1] Perhaps Margaret Kingwell: p. 203, n. 3. [2] No. 184; see further below.

[3] 20 February. The Downs is the roadstead between Deal and the Goodwin Sands.

[4] Sir Christopher Myngs, 1625–66, vice-admiral: *D.N.B.*

[5] Vane had his final audience on Tuesday 6/16 February. Locke appears to have been in Antwerp on his homeward journey on 16/26 February: B.L., MS. Locke f. 27, p. 90.

[6] pp. 258, 259; Baxter, p. 40.

England. The Elector of Brandenbourg joynes with the Dutch and assists them next campania with 12000 men upon their pay and provision as doe the Dukes of Lunenbourg. all the rest of Germany arme but declare not yet. Thus stands the publique in the parts I have visited, what private observations I have made will be fitter for our talke at Sutton then a letter. and if I have the oportunity to see you shortly we may possibly laugh togeather at some German storys. but of my comeing into the Country I write doubtfully to you; for I am now offered a faire oportunity of goeing into Spaine with the Ambasador.[1] If I imbrace it I shall conclude this my wandering yeare, if not you will ere long see me in Somerset shire. If I goe I shall not have in all above ten days stay in England. I am puld both ways by divers considerations and doe yet waver, I intend tomorrow for Oxford and shall there take my resolution. This towne affords little news, and though the returne of the court gives confidence to the timerous that kept from it for feare of the infection yet I finde the streets very thin, and methinks the towne droopes. present my service to Mrs Strachy and Mrs Baber and be assured that I am

Sir

your most faithfull and most obedient servant

John Locke

My love to my Uncle and Aunt and Cosins[2] when you see any of the family

Address: These present To Mr John Strachy at Sutton Court To be left at Mr John Blanch's shop neare the high crosse in High street Bristoll

Postmark: FE 24

## 187. Locke to John Strachey, 28 February 1666 (186, 188)

B.L., MS. Locke c. 24, ff. 237–8. Printed in King, pp. 25–6.

Oxford 28° Feb. 65

Sir

I writt to you from London as soone as I came thither to lett you know you had a servant returned to England, but very likely to

[1] Sandwich, who was now about to leave London with Godolphin as his secretary: p. 257, n. 1. Locke would perhaps have taken Godolphin's place.

[2] Peter Locke had three children living at this time: Peter, *c.* 1653–1674?: p. 288, n. 3; Anne, wife of Jeremy King: no. *733*; and Mary, d. 1678, first wife of William Stratton: p. 567.

leave it again before he saw yow. but those faire offers I had to goe to Spaine have not prevaild with me, whether fate or fondnesse kept me at home I know not or whether I have not let slip the minute that they say everyone has once in his life to make himself I cannot tell. this I am sure I never trouble my self for the losse of that which I never had, And have this satisfaction that I hope shortly to see you and finde at Sutton Court a greater rarity then my travells have afforded me. for beleive it one may goe a long way before one meet with a freind. I long to heare from you pray write by the first and let me know how you doe and what you can tell of the concernments of

Sir

your most affectionate freind

J LOCKE

My service to the Ladys

Address: These present To John Strachy Esq at Sutton Court To be left at Mr John Blanch's shop neare the High crosse in High street Bristoll

## 188. LOCKE to JOHN STRACHEY, 6 March 1666 (187, 189)

B.L., MS. Locke c. 24, ff. 239–40.

Ch. Ch. 6° Mar $\frac{65}{66}$

Deare Sir

yours of the 16th Feb: I received just now, and if at the same pace it had continued on its journy to Cleve it would have arived there sometime the next winter. I am very glad to heare that you are all well and to finde that you still preserved some remembrance and concernment for a poore wanderer, who though in this little excursion he hath met with severall things that have jogd[a] his spleene, yet there hath not beene any thing which he thinks deserves more heartily to be laughed at then what he findes in your letter, that what I intended only for our private mirth, any one should thinke fit to make publick folly. but I take it as a little of your railery and to revenge my self continue to persecute you with soe much of my story as I had prepared at Cleve but brought thus far my self,[1] the rest you shall have when I see you. for I am now

[a] *Doubtful reading.*

[1] See no. 189.

fixt again in England, though I was very likely to have made but a short stay. we have variety of News here but out of it I have not skill to single out what may be most probable. the little account I have beene able to furnish my self with conncerneing the affairs of Germany are either too long or not fit for a letter, and I would faine preserve some thing that might make me wellcome to you when I come to Sutton.

I am very truly
your affectionate freind and servant
JOHN LOCKE

My service to Mrs Baber and Mrs Strachy

Address: These for Mr John Strachy at Sutton Court To be left at Mr John Blanch's shop neare the High crosse in High street Bristoll

## 189. LOCKE to [JOHN STRACHEY?], 13 March 1666 (188, 191)

B.L., MS. Locke c. 24, f. 241. Perhaps a draft. The general style suggests that the letter was intended for Strachey; and the first lines associate it with no. 188.

Mar. 13 $\frac{65}{66}$

Sir

In my last I told you of an inclosed but I kept it here. be pleasd to thinke the mistake businesse or haste or forgetfulnesse or any thing rather, then a reviseing it to fitt it for the presse, and licking it overagain for the publick, it was borne amidst the cups of Germany, and though I had my drinke with the lusty Almans, yet my mirth and company I had only with you, and some of my freinds in England. and was apt to thinke when I was a litle put by[1] my soberer thoughts by their wine, to thinke freindship would make you as good natured as dulnesse did them, and that you would be well enough pleased with my chat though there were noe great matter of witt or novelty in it. I send it now stale and insignificant it is to shew you my remembrance of you abrode and my confidence at home, lay it up some where with the rest in some hole where spiders ⟨may⟩[a] weave it a cover.[2] I am faine you see to make one

[a] *MS.* way

[1] Deprived or cheated of: *O.E.D.*, s.v. By, *prep.*, 16*c*.
[2] Compare the postscript of no. 177.

letter the matter of an other in this scarcity of news. though I heare the Emperor begins to Interest himself in the quarrell of the B of Munster. and hath sent him aid, and tis from good hands reported that the Swedes have declared against the side the Danes take. and have told the French they cannot be of the same part with the Danes.[1] This I beleive, that Germany will be very busy next summer but Sir I am now out of the Politicks, and have noething to be proud of but that I am

your most humble servant

J L

## *190.* JOHANNES GERRART or GERRARD to [LOCKE?], 15/25 March 1666 (*195*)

B.L., MS. Locke c. 10, f. 9. No cover or address. I have failed to identify the writer.

Sir

Yours from Anvers[2] I received, my duty was, to answer to it sooner then I doe, but having no news worthy to write (:because all things being kept very close:) I was forc'd against my wil to forbear writing. But now I send you here the treaties between the Elect: of Branden: and the States of Holl:[3] which I got with a great deal of pains, and with no less danger, having hardly time to copy them.

The General of the French army Pradel[4] hath been at Cleve dyning with the Elect: and many great French Officers, where they did drink the health of the king of French with great glasses, and no less affection.

My Lord Smeising[5] Extraord: Ambas: of the Bishop of Munst: after 4. daÿes staying at Cleve returned again to his Master, but is expected here again every day: There is talked of peace between Holl: and Munster, and to set forth the warre against spain, to make the elder Son of the Elect: (:which is called the Keurprince:)[6] Duc of Gelder, and so the Bishop of Munst: the Elect: of Brandenb:

[1] I have found no confirmation of this report.
[2] Antwerp. Locke was there on 13/23 February: p. 262.
[3] p. 259, n. 7.
[4] p. 252, n. 4.
[5] Matthias Korff called Schmising: Waddington, ii. 129.
[6] Karl Emil, 1655–74, the Electoral Prince (Kurprinz): Waddington, ii. 35–7.

the States of Holl: and the King of French would bee united together to put it (:if possible:) to the effect.

The Extraord: Ambassad: of French My Lord Colbert[1] having been at the Hague and Amsterd: is come again to Cleve, and presented to the Elect: of Brandenb: a present, called in the french tongue *un meublement*, to furnish a chamber withall, worth Seven hundred thousand gul: hol:[2] it was accepted with such a kindnesse, as it was presented with all, I have seen the present, must needs confess it to be very rich.

Prince Maurice[3] as General of the army is come from the Hague, did stay but 4. dayes here, and departed for Wesel, having with him three of the States of Holland.

The Prince of Orange was talked of to bee General of the Infanterie, but the Princesse of orange his grand Mother[4] would not have him to climb up by degrees, but to bee honoured with the dignities of his Father immediatly.

Sir, I hope you wil for this time bee satisfied with this, and bee sure, that I am, and ever shall bee

Your Humble servant
JOHANNES GERRART

Cleve the 25. of March 1666.

The amb: of the Bishop of Munst: arrived at Cleve yesterday. There is expected everÿ daÿ an ambas: of Swedl. and dennemark.[5]

## 191. LOCKE to JOHN STRACHEY, 20 March 1666 (189, *208*)

B.L., MS. Locke c. 24, ff. 242–3.

Ch: Ch: 20 Mar $\frac{65}{66}$

Sir

Could desires and affection have ordered my journys I had certainly steped noe where till I had throwne my self into those armes of yours which I finde soe open to receive me, and where I could be content to meet a period of my wanderings. But I finde at land as well as sea that the Winde and Waves, troubles and businesse (the

[1] Colbert de Croissy: p. 257, n. 3; for the *ameublement* see Pagès, pp. 137–8.
[2] Dutch gulden; at par of exchange slightly over £63,000.
[3] Johan Maurits van Nassau-Siegen: p. 241, n. 4.
[4] Amalia von Solms: p. 231, n. 5.
[5] See pp. 271, 272.

boisterous and imperious Commanders of this great Ocean), will in spight of the gentler fluxes of our inclinations carry us which way they please. I am now pleasd with my late excursion since it afforded me an oportunity of doeing something which you are pleased to thinke kindely of. Though that ought not to be an obligacion to you which was my cheifest diversion, whilst I found more pleasure in your imaginary conversation, then in all the company of the jolly Germans. and since I could not tell how to convey to you any Runletts of Rince and Hockamer.[1] yet I was willing to see how far the effects of it could reach and whether it could make you mery at second hand. I hope very shortly to get out of this towne to you, that I may at last ease you of my long scribblings and with lesse trouble to you assure you that I am

Sir

Your most faithfull freind and servant

JOHN LOCKE

My service to the Ladys.

Address: These for Mr John Strachy at Sutton Court
Endorsed by Locke: J *L* to Mr Strachy *65*

## 192. LADY (ANNE) ALFORD to LOCKE, 9 April 1666 (*173*, *196*)

B.L., MS. Locke c. 3, ff. 13–14.

worthy Sir

I have received your civell kind letter and returne you my many thanks for your favers tow my sonn and your care of his things. he shall wait upon you about that tim you intend tow be at oxford he presents his sarvis tow you and longs for the happines tow be with you having a very grat kindnes for you the tim he is tow stay with you will not be long but I desire your faver tow improve that tim as much as you can for his advantage which shall very much oblige him and me to be

Your humble sarvent

AN ALFORD

Aprill the 9 1666

[1] The former is apparently Rhenish; the latter, more commonly called Hockamore, is Hochheimer, here probably used generically.

I pray be pleased to give his gounes out to his sarvitar tow eaire and brush up clean againe his coming for lying so long it is like thay are muldye

Address: These for my very much estemed freind Mr John Loocke at Christ Church present In[a] oxford[a]
Postmark: AP 19.

## *193.* [ELINOR PARRY, later Mrs. Hawkshaw?] to LOCKE, 10 April [1666?] (122, *185*, *214*)

B.L., MS. Locke c. 8, f. 63. The writer may be not Scribelia (Elinor Parry), but a close associate of hers. Year from contents.

The relations between Locke and Scribelia are shown by two notes written by her in a notebook of his containing memoranda dated 1664–6:

> Doe not sufer the uni: to be unjust to Scribelia but Perswad it to beleeve I value it equall to my Life
>
> be mindfull of your selfe and what you owe Scribelia no: the 12
>
> —B.L., MS. Locke f. 27, f. 93, and inside back-cover.

When you Parted from Berelisa you left her with her reason. but now intends to forfitt it and limit your time of stay from her: she professeth, your Jouiney to Germany did not Create more feares then your now being neer bristoll doth, so that for her quiett and your owne safty you are to return with in the time she once mentioned to you. She tooke a Confident liberty to Open a Paqett that came to her hands the first sheet was a letter from Mr Allestry[1] with notice the Paquett Cost fouer shill:s and ten penc, dated Ap: the 2d; the second sheet held a Papper booke with a language I understand not and a letter which I send you inclosed. which I had from my dear Berelisa to send to you: the Papper Booke she intends for the Schooles for it may be of use to some that visitt them, so that at your return you shall Confess I am a Benefactress to the Scooles: and also that I am as liberall as you are, tis now a 11 a Clocke so that I must end, and goe and dress my self and prapare my self for a visitt either from mr T:[2] or Scribelia and then you may Guess what our discours may be: with a little Complaint of your

[a] *Added in another hand.*

[1] Probably James Allestry: pp. 178 n., 278.
[2] Probably David Thomas (p. 283 n.) or James Tyrrell (no. *343*; see also p. 260) rather than Gabriel Towerson or Samuel Tilly.

unhappyness in the loss of a Pupell, but of that when you see your freinds and the duch

ELIA:

Ap: the 10th

Address: For mr John Locke at Pensford Leave it at mr Thomas Day's in st Thomas street: Bristoll if not Call'd for in a weekes time lett it be sent backe to Ox ford to mr Lichfild[1] in Catt Street.

## *194.* FRANCISCUS RAULIN, S.J., to [LOCKE?], 17/27 April 1666

B.L., MS. Locke c. 18, f. 10. The writer may be the unnamed Jesuit of no. 175. I have not traced him elsewhere.

Perillustris ac generose domine

Promissis et obligationi meæ iampridem fecissem satis, nisi frustra ea expectassem Viennâ, quibus sperabam me gratificaturum generosæ dominationi vestræ. Scribam ipse in Ungariam ad quendam amicum, à quo, si quid singulare habuerit, confido me accepturum, ut quantocyus cum aliqua mei satisfactione ad vestram generosam dominationem transmittam.

Cæterum cum in D. Episcopum Monasteriensem tam multi principes conspirarent, ut resistendo impar fuerit, necessitati cedendum fuit, adeoque cum nemo ferret suppetias tractatibus pacis, in quibus aliquot mediatores adlaborarunt, annuente dubio procul serenissimo Angliæ rege, acquievit, qui hodie ante octo

---

Illustrious and noble Sir,

I would have fulfilled my promises and my bounden duty some time ago if I had not been waiting in vain to receive from Vienna the items with which I hoped to gratify your Honour's wishes. I will write myself to a certain friend in Hungary, from whom I feel sure of obtaining anything remarkable that he may have, so that I may send it on to your Honour as speedily as possible and with some satisfaction to myself.

For the rest, the Bishop of Münster, finding so many princes united against him that he was unequal to the task of resisting them, was obliged to yield to necessity and has accordingly, since no one came to his assistance, agreed to the terms of peace, in which a number of mediators gave their services, and which no doubt had the approval of his Majesty the King of England;

---

[1] Leonard Lichfield the second, d. 1686; printer to the university from 1657: Madan, vol. iii, p. xxix; above, p. 239, n. 1. Cat (Catte) Street ran north from the High Street to the city wall, and had houses on both sides; on the east side for most of its length: maps, etc., in H. E. Salter, *Survey of Oxford*, vol. i (Oxford Hist. Soc. new ser., vol. xiv, 1960).

dies tum a partibus ipsis, tum a mediatoribus subscripti sunt.[1] Si qua in re possem servire v.d.g. imperet, et experietur me generosa ⟨dominatio vestra⟩[a]

suum humillimum in Christo servum
FRANCISCUM RAULIN. S.J.

Clivis 27 Aprilis 1666.

[a] *MS.* dominationem vestram; *both words are abbreviated.*

---

these terms were signed a week ago by the parties concerned as well as by the mediators.[1] If I might be able to serve your Honour in any matter, please command me, and you will find me to be

Your most humble servant in Christ,
FRANCISCUS RAULIN, S.J.

Cleve 27 April 1666.

## *195.* JOHANNES GERRART or GERRARD to LOCKE, 23 April/3 May 1666 (*190*)

B.L., MS. Locke c. 10, ff. 10–11.

Sir

How vigilant I am to gather true intelligence, what means and persons I use to advertise you of the state of things, nevertheless I can get very few, by reason of the close carriage thereof. Though considering the Reputation and Interest of your Great Master, I can not but give you an account of some proceedings here.

The peace between Holland and the Bishop of Munster beeing concluded I wished with all my heart, to could have send you the treaties thereof, which are in Latin, I had the occasion by a certain Gentleman at Court, to read them, but I could by no means get leave to coppy them, though I tried to lock up his hands under a silver seal, but I know, they are send to Sir Walt: Ven,[2] to whom I refer you.

It is secretly whispered in Court, that there are some Regiments on foot of his Electoral High: ready to goe for Denmarck against those that would invade it.

The forrain Ambassadors are departed from Cleve, except The Emperor, France, and Denmark are there still.

[1] The treaty, between the bishop and the United Provinces, was signed at Cleves on 8/18 April: Dumont, *Corps univ. diplomatique*, VI. iii. 106–8.
[2] Sir Walter Vane.

They are very busie and occupied at Court every day in matters of state, the particularities I can by no means decipher, but time and opportunity will bring things together, which were never dreamt of.

His Electoral High: The Prince of Anhalt, and the Duke of Hollstein are going for Holland incognito within this two dayes to see the navie fleet. It is said, as if they were invited of the States of Holland.[1]

The Match between the Prince of Denmark and the Daughter of the Landgrafs of Hessen is sure[2]

Yesterday arrived here an Ambassad: of Swedland.[3]

My Lord Aleveld[4] Ambassad: of Denmark is gone for Holland, if he doth return, it is uncertain.

No more now, but that I am
Your most faithfull servant
JOHAN: GERRARD

Citissim:[5] the 3. of May 1666.

Address: For Mr. John Locke at Christ Church in Oxford.
Note in Locke's hand: Ros Mayalis[6]

## *196.* LADY (ANNE) ALFORD to LOCKE, 30 April 1666 (*192, 202*)

B.L., MS. Locke c. 3, ff. 15–16. Locke wrote to her son John Alford on 12 June: no. 200.

Aprill 30: 1666

worthy Sir

the Sicknes incrasing in London and is much disparsed in severall parts of this Kingdom maks every one feare a sad sumer of sicknes[7]

[1] Frederick William; Johann Georg II, 1627–93, prince of Anhalt-Dessau 1660, Statthalter for Frederick William; his wife, Henrietta Catherina, was a sister of the Electress (*A.D.B.*); and Christian Albrecht, 1641–94, duke of Schleswig-Holstein-Gottorp 1659 (ibid.). The Elector was at The Hague about 3/13 May: Estrades, *Lettres, mémoires*, iv. 274.

[2] Christian V, 1646–99; king of Denmark 1670; married, 25 June 1667 (O.S.?), Charlotte Amalie, 1650–1714, a daughter of William VI of Hesse-Cassel and niece of Frederick William (p. 241, n. 3).

[3] Probably Otto Wilhelm, Graf von Königsmark (1639–88; *A.D.B.*), calling at Cleves on his way to France.

[4] Ditlev Ahlefeldt, 1612–86: *Dansk Biog. Lexikon.* Gerrart here contradicts an earlier statement in his letter.

[5] *Citissime*, very speedily.

[6] May dew, dew gathered in the month of May and supposed to have medicinal and cosmetic qualities: *O.E.D.*

[7] The plague. This year there were outbreaks in the Kentish ports and East Anglia, and some cases in London, but no great epidemic.

it begining so early tow sprad, which hath occationed me to alter my resolution in sending my son any more to oxford for feare of indangering him therfore I shall beg your faver tow receive his caution mony which is teen pounds and tow sell his things in his chamber and tow pay what he oweth in butter which is not much by your bill it was payd June 19 he cam a way July 12 1665 his debt tow the cook is lease for by your bill that was payd July 3. pray pay what he oweth for his Chamber which is all he oweth in the Collage only the 1–12–4 tow your selfe which I desire you tow take out of that monys and what remains be pleased to send me a note of it is a grat trouble tow my son as well as tow my selfe that he cannot com to be ther in any safty I should be glad if ther might be a good occation tow bring you into these parts my son would be very glad tow se you and lett me assuer you that you should be very kindly wellcom to her who is

Your assured freind to sarve you
AN ALFORD

I pray be pleased to send up his 2 trunks of books to Mr Irlands house in whit friers with all his lining. I shall leave a small token with Mr Carter[1] for sum of madling Collage tow bring you which I pray exceapt of as token of my thankfullnes for your favers to my son

Address: These for Mr John Locke at Christ Church in oxford present
Postmark: MA 3.

## 197. LOCKE to ROBERT BOYLE, 5 May 1666 (175, *199*)

R. Boyle, *The General History of the Air*, 1692, pp. 137–41. Reprinted in Boyle, *Works*, 1744, v. 157–8. Answered by no. *199*.

Honoured Sir,

I have been able to do so little in the Attempts I have made to serve you, that I am ashamed to have been so well furnished to so small purpose. The Barometer I had from you was conveyed safe into the Country, and as soon as it came to my Hands, I rode to Minedeep,[2] with an Intention to make use of it there, in one of

[1] p. 224, n. 2. He was a chaplain of Magdalen College from 1660 to 1662: J. R. Bloxam, *Register (of Magdalen)*, 1853–85, ii. 166–7.

[2] Mendip. The principal centres for lead mining appear to have been Chewton Mendip and Priddy: *V.C.H.*, *Somerset*, ii. 362–79.

the deepest Gruffs[1] (for so they call their Pits) I could find: the deepest I could hear of was about 30 Fathom, but the Descent so far either from easy, safe, or perpendicular, that I was discouraged from venturing on it. They do not, as in Wells, sink their Pits strait down, but, as the Cranies of the Rocks, give them the easiest Passage; neither are they let down by a Rope, but taking the Rope under their Arm, by setting their Hands and Legs against the sides of the narrow Passage, clamber up and down, which is not very easy for one not used to it, and almost impossible to carry down the Barometer, both the Hands being imployed. This Information I should have suspected to come from their Fear, had not an intelligent Gentleman, Neighbour to the Hill, assured me 'twas their usual way of getting up and down. For the Sight of the Engine, and my Desire of going down into some of their Gruffs, gave them terrible Apprehensions, and I could not perswade them but that I had some Design: So that I and a Gentleman that bore me Company, had a pleasant Scene, whilst their Fear to be undermined by us, made them disbelieve all we told them; and do what we could, they would think us craftier Fellows than we were. But, Sir, I will not trouble you with the Particulars of this Adventure: but certain it is the Women too were alarm'd, and think us still either Projectors or Conjurers. Since I could not get down into their Gruffs, I made it my Business to inquire what I could concerning them: The Workmen could give me very little Account of any thing, but what Profit made them seek after; they could apprehend no other Minerals but Lead Oar, and believed the Earth held nothing else worth seeking for: besides, they were not forward to be too communicative to one, they thought they had Reason to be afraid of. But at my Return, calling at a Gentleman's House, who lives under Minedeep-Hills, and who had sent out his Son to invite me in; amongst other things he told me this, that sometimes the Damps catch them, and then if they cannot get out soon enough, they fall into a Swound, and die in it, if they are not speedily got out; and as soon as they have them above ground, they dig a Hole in the Earth, and there put in their Faces, and cover them close up with Turfs; and this is the surest Remedy they have yet found to recover them. In deep Pits they convey down Air by the side of the Gruff, in a little Passage from the Top; and that the Air may circulate the better, they set up some Turfs on the Lee side of the

[1] Grooves: mines, mining-shafts, etc.: *O.E.D.*; Wright.

Hole, to catch, and so force down the fresh Air: But if these Turfs be removed to the windy side, or laid close over the Mouth of the Hole, those below find it immediately, by want of Breath, Indisposition, and Fainting: and if they chance to have any sweet Flowers with them, they do not only lose their pleasant Smell immediately, but stink as bad as Carrion. Notwithstanding this ill Success, I had attempted some Trials once more, had not the spreading of the Contagion[1] made it less safe to venture abroad, and hastened me out of the Country sooner than I intended. But I have some Hopes, the next Journey I make into those Parts, to give you a better Account than this that follows. Near the House where I sometimes abode, was a pretty steep and high Hill. *April. 3. hora inter 8 et 9. Matutin.* the Wind West, and pretty high, the Day warm, the Mercury was at 29 Inches and $\frac{1}{8}$, being carried up to the Top of the Hill, it fell to 28 Inches $\frac{3}{4}$, (or thereabouts, for I think it was a little above 28 Inches $\frac{3}{4}$:) Both going up and coming down, I observed that proportionably as I was higher or lower on the Hill, the Mercury fell or rose. At my return to the bottom of the Hill, the Mercury wanted of ascending to its former Height $\frac{1}{32}$ of an Inch, which I impute to the Sun's rarifying some Particles of Air that remained in the upper Part of the Tube, rather than to any other Change in the Air; for I find it harder to clear the Tube of Air perfectly, than at first I thought, or of Water, if that have been put in with the Mercury, and I fear liable to the same Inconvenience with Air inclosed. I know this is far short of what you might have expected, and has, I fear, but little answered your Desires, since I guess it was the perpendicular Height of the Place I made the Experiment in, that you would have had, and perhaps other Considerations of Air, inclosed, and liable to mineral Steams, would have made a Trial in one of the Gruffs more acceptable to you. I do not think any thing in this Letter worthy of you, or fit for the Publick. But since I find by the two last Philosophical Transactions, that Observations on the Torricellian Experiment are much look'd after, and desired to be compared; if for want of better, this should be thought fit to fill an empty Space in the Philosophical News-Book, I shall desire to have my Name concealed.[2] But I fear that

[1] The plague: p. 272.

[2] Locke's account was not published. The Torricellian experiment is that by which Evangelista Torricelli (1608–47; *Encic. italiana*) demonstrated that the atmosphere has weight; the barometer is based on it. The *Philosophical Transactions* is the periodical of the Royal Society; it began in 1665 and still continues.

this very Caution of being in Print, where there is no Danger of it, has too much of Vanity in it. I'm sure 'tis Boldness enough, though allaid with Obedience, to venture such slight things to your Sight. I visited the incrusting Spring I formerly mentioned to you, and could not find any thing incrusted within at least 20 Yards of the Rise of it. The Place where it works most, is about 40 or 50 Yards from the Spring-head, and is at a Fall higher than my Head: there it sheaths every thing with stony Cases, and makes the sides of the Bank hard Rock, and from thence all along its Stream, it covers Sticks, etc. with a Crust; and some so candied I found above this Fall, but not so frequent; whether the mixing of Air with the Water in the Fall, contributes any thing to the Effect, I cannot guess; but that the Fall does, I suppose: for besides that at the above-mentioned Fall, it seems to operate most strongly, I observed, that though I could not find any thing incrusted within a good Distance of the Spring, yet that the Moss above the Spring was a little incrusted, (but not so firmly as at the other Place) for the Water in the Winter, when the Springs are full, runs out also at a Hole two or three Yards above the Place, where now only it rises, and from thence falls perpendicularly into this lower Spring, from whence it runs by an easy Descent to the next Fall. A Gentleman in whose Field it rises, and by whose House it runs, told me upon Inquiry, that he uses it both in his Kitchen and Brew-house, without any sensible ill Effects, he being a pretty ancient, but healthy Man, and long Inhabitant of that Place. It will bear Soap, freezes quickly; and waters his Grounds upon Occasion, with Advantage. All the ill Effects of it, that he can guess, are, that his Horses are usually short-breathed, which he imputes to the drinking of that Water. I brought with me from Minedeepe some Oar, and some Stones; but I think them so inconsiderable, that I shall not judg them worth sending, unless you please to command them.

I am, SIR,

Your most Humble and most Obedient Servant,

JOHN LOCKE.

Ch. Ch. 5° May, 1666.

POSTSCRIPT. I had forgot to mention to you, that in their Gruffs, after burning, (when they meet with hard Rocks in their way, they make a Fire upon them, that they may dig through the easier) they find it very dangerous to go down into them, as long as there remains any Fire or Heat in any Chinks of the Rocks.

## *198.* J. SCHARD to LOCKE, 10/20 May 1666

B.L., MS. Locke c. 18, ff. 62–4. The writer is presumably the Dr. Scardius of no. 175; Dr. Scardysse in no. *204* is probably the same man. Locke entered several of his prescriptions in B.L., MS. Locke f. 27. I have not traced him elsewhere.

The letter is badly written; there are many abbreviations and chemical symbols. I have not tried to reproduce the prescriptions, etc., on the second and third pages. All appear to be medical and to be based on a work (or works) by Ruland; either Martinus Ruland, 1532–1602 (*A.D.B.*), or his son, also Martinus Ruland, 1569–1611 (ibid.); both were physicians and the father, if not the son also, was a follower of Paracelsus.

Clivis 20 Maj

Clarissime Vir

Literas tuas utrasque per D. Akenium Londino allatas et 1 Martii, alteras Bruxellis missas et Oxonii 1 Aprilis datas 10 Mai recte accepi. Speroque ad primas tuas responsionem in quibus de [Mercuriis] variis parandis, sp. [Salis Ammoniaci] cum [spiritu Vini] purgendis [destillandis] et . . . andis, et alia edocui, redditas jam esse ut non necesse habeam paginam supervacanea repetitione implere. Quod si tamen, quod[a] nolim, interiisse intellexem,[b] ⟨denuo⟩[c] mittam. Et confidas de meo in te affectu nihil me habiturum tam secretum quod negaturus tibi essem; saltem, indigites, quibus in rebus tibi gratum munus præstare possem; et in mea potestate sit. Quando Chymeæ dabis operam in iis laborate quæ jam ante communicavi, et labores tuos ad me perscribas tam illos quos susceperis jam quam quos in consilio habes, ut ⟨si⟩[d] opus fuerit, admonitione te juvare possem.

[a] *Abbreviation in MS.* [b] *Or* intellerem*?* [c] *MS.* denua, *altered from* id-
[d] *MS.* se

Cleves 20 May

Distinguished Sir,

I duly received on 10 May both your letters, one brought from London by Mr. Aken, dated 1 March, the other sent from Brussels, dated 1 April at Oxford; and I hope you have already received my reply to your first letter, in which I informed you about the preparation of various mercuries, the purification of spirit of Sal Ammoniac by spirit of wine, its distillation and . . ., and other matters, so that I need not fill a page with superfluous repetition; but if I find that the letter has been lost, which I hope is not the case, I will write it afresh. You may feel assured of my regard for you and that I shall never keep anything so secret as to deny it to you; you have only to let me know in what matters I can gratify your wishes, if it is in my power. When you turn your attention to chemistry you should experiment with those things that I have already told you about and let me know about your work, both what you have already undertaken and what you intend to do, so that if

Pro transcriptis Collyrio et aliis gratias ago maximas. Reposui inter notata mea selectiora et experiar successum imprimis Collyrii quod mihi hactenus non fuit cognitum.[a] Quæ de Butyro [Antimonii] scribes optimum tibi præstabit menstruum in parandis . . .

Ad Rulandi secreta quod attinet. quod scio hic habes. Extractum esulæ ex radice paratur . . .

. . . Hæc sunt quæ mihi ex Rulando nota sunt. Si qua in re amplius tibi gratificare possum, saltem verbo indices. Quæquæ in potestate mea erunt, erunt et tua. Novarum rerum post pactam pacem Monasteriensem nulla sunt. Elector copias suas ad 14000 contrahit, ad expeditionem quæ adhuc in secreto est. Lustrantur hodie prope Lipstadium. Salutant te omnes amici, Uxor mea cum fratre. Hisce te Vir Clarissime valere jubeo

et salvere a tui studiosissimo

J SCHARD

20 Maj 1666

Address: For Mr John Locke at Christ Church in Oxford To[b]– be left at Mr James Alestys[1] in St Pauls Churchyard London–[b]

Postmarks: MA 31; IV 2; postage due mark D 8

[a] *First letters doubtful.* [b–b] *Deleted.*

need be I might possibly assist you with advice. I am most grateful for the transcripts concerning collyrium and other things. I have placed them among my choicer records and shall try for success first of all with collyrium which I had not known of till now. What you will write about butter of antimony will provide you with an excellent menstruum for the preparation of . . .

As to Ruland's secrets, here is as much as I know. An extract of spurge is prepared from the root. . . .

This is as much as I know from Ruland. If I can oblige you further in anything you have only to let me know, and whatever is in my power shall be in yours too. There have been no new happenings since the conclusion of peace with the bishop of Münster. The Elector is assembling his forces to the number of 14,000 for an expedition which is still a secret. They are being reviewed today near Lippstadt. All your friends send you their greetings, as do my wife and her brother. With this, distinguished Sir, I bid you good-bye and good health, from

Your most obedient

J SCHARD

20 May 666

[1] Allestry: p. 178 n.

## *199.* Robert Boyle to Locke, 2 June 1666 (197, 223)

B.L., MS. Locke c. 4, ff. 150–1. Answers no. 197.

Lees[1] In Essex June 2d 1666

Sir

If your Letter had found me at London, this Returne of it would have been brought you much earlyer to Oxford. And though I now write in a place where a Crowd of such Persons whose Quality or Beauty requires a great deale of attendance, reduces me to make this Letter short and hasty;[2] yet I cannot but snatch time to returne you my deservd Thanks for the favour of yours at some passages of which I could not but smile as well as you did, though I was troubled that soe much Curiosity and Industry as you expressd, should by soe grosse a want of it in others be made soe unsuccessfull. But I hope this will not discourage you from embraceing, and seekeing future opportunitys to search into the nature of Mineralls, in order to which, I wish I had time and conveniency to send you some sheets of Articles of Inquirys about Mines in generall;[3] which I once drew up, for the use of some freinds and partly for my owne. My absence from London kept me from receiving your Account of the Barometricall observation, till t'was some days too late to make the use of it you allow. But I hope I may have another occasion to mention it pertinently as it deserves. The Receipt I promisd you is soe plaine and simple a thing that as I would not communicate to every Body a Remedy of that approved Efficacy—soe I should feare that its seeming meanesse would make you dispise it, if the Person t'is now inclosd to, were not lookd upon as a Virtuoso by

Sir Your very Affect: Freind and humble servant

Ro: Boyle

[1] Lees or Leez, now Leighs Priory, the seat of Charles Rich, 1616–73; fourth earl of Warwick 1659. His countess was Mary, *c.* 1625–78, a sister of Boyle: C. Fell Smith, *Mary Rich, Countess of Warwick*, 1901; for Lees, pp. 102–9.

[2] Boyle made a similar complaint in a letter to Henry Oldenburg 13 June: Oldenburg, *Correspondence*, ed. A. R. and M. B. Hall 1965– , iii. 160. The company at Lees was likely to consist of Lord and Lady Warwick, one or two of Warwick's nieces, and occasional visitors. In view of Warwick's illness and Lady Warwick's piety the company was no doubt decorous, but would demand attention.

[3] These articles were probably related to Boyle's 'General heads for a natural history of a country', of which the first part was published in the *Philosophical Transactions* on 2 April of this year: J. F. Fulton, *A Bibliography of the Honourable Robert Boyle*, 2nd ed. 1961, no. 210.

my humble service to Dr. Wallis,[1] Dr Lower,[2] mr Thomas[3] and the rest of my Freinds at Oxford

Address: These To my much Esteemd Freind Mr John Lock A.M. at Christ-Church College Present In Oxford post paid.

Postmark: IV 9.

## 200. LOCKE to JOHN ALFORD, 12 June 1666 (*668*)

East Sussex County Council, County Record Office, Lewes, Shiffner MS. 1561. Copy: ibid., Shiffner MS. 1560 (eighteenth century?). Printed in *Gentleman's Magazine*, 1797, i. 97; Fox Bourne, with incorrect date 12 Jan. 1666/7, i. 134–5. For Alford see p. 220, n. 1.

Ch: Ch: 12° Jun. 66

Sir

I have not yet quite parted with you. and though you have put off your gowne, and taken lea⟨ve⟩[a] of the University. you are not yet got beyond my affection or concernment for you. Tis true, you are now past Masters and Tutors, and it is now therefor that you ought to have the greater care of your self: since those mistakes or miscarriages, which heretofore would have beene charged upon them, will now, if any, light wholy upon you. and you your self must be accountable for all your actions; nor will any longer any one else share in the praise or censure they may deserv⟨e.⟩[a] 'Twill be time therefor, that you now begin to thinke your self a man. and necessary that you take the courage of one. I meane not such a courage, as may name you one of those daring galla⟨nts⟩[a] that stick at noe thing. but a courage that may defend and secure your virtue and religion. for in the world you are now lanching into, you will finde perhaps more onsets made upon your innocence then you can imagine. and there are more dangerous theeves, then those that lay wait for your purse, who will endeavour to rob you of that virtue which they care not for themselves. I could wish you that happynesse, as never to fall into such company. But I consider you are to live in the world and whilst either the service of your country,

[a] *Page torn.*

---

[1] John Wallis, 1616–1703; D.D. 1654; the mathematician: *D.N.B.*

[2] p. 152, n. 1, etc. Although he was practising in London now he visited Oxford this spring: Wood, *L. and T.* ii. 71, 73, 76–7.

[3] p. 283 n.

or your owne businesse makes your conversation with men necessary, perhaps this caution will be needfull. But you may with hold your heart where you cannot deny your company. and you may allow those your civility, who possibly will not deserve your affecti⟨on.⟩[a] I thinke it needlesse and impertinent to dissuade you from vices I never observed you incline⟨d⟩[a] to. I write this to strengthen your resolutions Not to give you new ones. But let not the importunitys or examples of others, prevaile against the dictates of your owne reason and education: I doe not in this advise you to be either a Munke, or Morose: to avoid company, or not enjoy it. One may certainly with innocence use all the enjoyments of life. and I have beene always of opinion, that a virtuous life is best disposed to be the most pleasant. For certainly amidst the troubles and vanitys of this world, there are but two things, that bring a reall satisfaction with them, that is, Virtue and Knowledg. What progresse you have made ⟨in the latter⟩[b] you will doe well not to loose. your spare howers from devotion, businesse, or recreation, (for that too I can allow, where imployment not idlenesse gives a title to it) will be well bestowd in reviveing or improveing your University notions, and if at this distance I could afford your st⟨ud⟩ys[a] any direction or assistance I should be glad and you need only but let me know it. Though your anc⟨e⟩stors[a] have left you a condition above the ordinary rank, yet tis your self alone that can advance your self to it: For tis not either the goeing upon two legs, or the liveing in a greate house, or possessing many acres: that gives one advantage over beasts or other men: but the being wiser and better. I speake not this to make you carelesse of your estate, for though riches be not vertue, tis a great instrument of it, wherein lyes a great part of the usefullnesse and comfort of life. In the right management of this lyes a great part of prudence. and about mony is the great mistake of men; whilst they are either too covetous, or too carelesse of it. If you throw it away idlely, you loose your great support, and best freind. If you hugge it too closely, you loose it, and your self too. To be thought prudent and liberall, provident and good naturd, are things worth your endeavour to obtei⟨n,⟩[a] which perhaps you will better doe, by avoiding the occasions of expences, then by a frugall limiting them when any occasion hath made them necessary. But I forget you are neere your Lady Mother, whilst I give you these advises. and doe not observe that what I

[a] *Page torn.* [b] *Words lost in crease; supplied from old copy.*

meant for a letter begins to grow into a treatise. Those many particulars that here is not roome for, I send you to seeke in the writings of learned and sage authors. Let me give you by them those counsells I cannot now. They will direct you as well as I wish you. and I doe truly wish you well. you will therefor pardon me for this once playing the Tutor since I shall hereafter always be

Sir

Your faithfull freind and servant

JOHN LOCKE

Note in later hand: The foregoing letter of the great and good Mr. Locke was addressed to John Alford Esq son of Sr. Edward Alford Knight of Offington Place near Arundell Sussex.

## *201.* GEORGE PERCIVALL to LOCKE, 27 June 1666 (*135*)

B.L., MS. Locke c. 17, ff. 67–8.

dublin Junij 27° 1666.

Deare Sir

You have obleiged me infinitely in takeing notice of a Freind that seemed to forgett you, for which I neede make no apology since your acknowledgeng of mee is a sufficient assurance of a pardon, though I could tell you that I had not bin guilty of so seeming a neglect, had I not bin informed that you had quitted your station, which I was very apt to beleive when I considered how fitt you were for the world before I left you. But I see you have not thought the world so deserving of you, and have therefore resolved to Cloyster up your selfe, and to impart the benefitt of your selfe to none but your particular Freinds, of whome it is my ambition to bee one, (Deare sir) beleive mee that as I did ever beare a great respect to the place in which I received my education, so I ever had and continue to have a just respect for any person that had one for mee in that place, of whom I am very well assured you are one, And though I have changed my condition and placed my cheifest affections on a person of an other sex,[1] yet have I not so absolutely surrendered my selfe, as not to retaine a kindnesse and value for

[1] Percivall married Mary Crofton, d. 1705, acquiring an estate at Templehouse, co. Sligo, by the marriage. She married secondly Richard Aldworth, sometime King's Remembrancer in Ireland: Anderson (*House of Yvery*), ii. 324; H.M.C., *Egmont*, ii. 61. A son by her first marriage is mentioned below, no. *3511*; by her second marriage she was mother of John Aldworth of Ruscombe (no. *2933*): *Miscellanea Genealogica et Heraldica*, new series, iv (1884), 174.

my former acquaintance, and particularly your selfe, and should be very proud that any opportunity should offer wherin I might shew it; in the meane time lett me begge the continuance of your correspondence togather with such passages of your university as you thinke may be understood by

Sir

Your very affect⟨ionate⟩[a] and Faithfull servant

G PERCIVALL

For mr Lock.

Address: For mr John Lock student of Ch. Ch In Oxford. These England
Postmark: IY 2 (?)

## *202.* LADY (ANNE) ALFORD to LOCKE, 3 July 1666 (*196*)

B.L., MS. Locke c. 3, ff. 17–18.

Worthy Sir

I have received your civell letter with the account of my sons things which I returne you my many thanks for the trouble I gave you in the disposing of them. I doe understand by the account ther is 7–12–04 remaining in your hands still. I have wright tow you before this but I waited upon this oppertunety of my sons bringing it to your hands. I desire you tow exceapt of fortty shillings of that mony and to pay the remainder of it unto my son. Sir I should be very glad to meet with any occation wherin I might exprese my thankfullnes to you for your care of my son who I troust will prove to desarve the good carrictur which you weare pleased tow give of him. wishing all happines may ever attend upon you I am

Your sarvant

AN ALFORD

July 3 1666

Address: These for Mr John Locke present

## *203.* DR. DAVID THOMAS to LOCKE, 9 July 1666 (*204*)

B.L., MS. Locke c. 20, ff. 1–2. Printed in King, pp. 403–4. David Thomas, *c.* 1634–94. Of Preshute, Wilts. Scholar at Winchester School 1646; matriculated from New College on 11 October 1651; B.A., 11 May 1655; M.A. 22 April 1658; proctor 1665–6; licensed to practice medicine 28 April 1666; B.M. and D.M. 17 December 1670: Foster; T. F. Kirby, *Winchester scholars*,

[a] *End of line.*

1888, p. 182. He moved to Salisbury in the first half of 1667, and remained there for the rest of his life. He was attached to Lord Shaftesbury, whose seat, Wimborne St. Giles, is 14 miles SW. of Salisbury. His friendship with Locke continued until his death; he was a friend of James Tyrrell also. In the correspondence he is sometimes called Adrian; his wife (p. 324, n. 1), Parthenice.

Physicians were divided by their views into Galenists, who adhered to vegetable preparations, and chemists, the disciples of Paracelsus and J. B. van Helmont. His letters show that Thomas belonged with the chemists and that he interested himself in the preparation of medicaments. When he writes about chymists he means persons engaged in this work, and not alchemists or chemists in the modern senses, either the scientific or the popular. For the term see *O.E.D.* s.vv. Chemist, etc., Galenist, etc. (the modern term is iatrochemist).

My deare Freind

This towne is very barren of News and therefore you must not expect much. The most considerable is, that commissions are granted for raysing 16 troopes of horse, among others to the Lord Fayrefayx Collonell Inglesby Sir W. Waller[1] etc. The fleete will sett sayle the beginning of the next weeke, if the London bee ready; but not without her, as I am now enformed by a Gentleman of P Ruperts,[2] who came yesterday from the fleete, which he says consists of 89 sayle which are ready, and 18 or as some say 25 fire shipps which wilbe made 30. After all the greate noyse of a presse,[3] I am enformed that not above 2200 men are sent from hence to the fleete: The Gazet will enforme you of more. where[a] in the story of C. Reeves[4] is true; and the K[5] much troubled at it, and hath given order that a Captaine who was to be exchanged for him, be layd in Irons.

I must request one favor of you, which is to send mee word by the next opportunity, whether you can procure 12 bottles of water for my Lord Ashly[6] to drinke in Oxford sunday and munday

[a] *MS.* w$^{r}$

[1] Fairfax, the general (p. 137, n. 4); Sir Richard Ingoldsby, K.B. (*D.N.B.*); Sir William Waller, sen., *c.* 1597–1668, the general (ibid.). These commissions were countermanded: p. 286. Pepys gives a similar report on 13 June 1667: *Diary*.

[2] Prince Rupert, 1619–82, Count Palatine of the Rhine, etc.: *D.N.B.* The ship is the *Loyal London*, 1,134 tons: R. C. Anderson, no. 367.

[3] Notices in Pepys, 30 June–2 July, 6, 10 July.

[4] *London Gazette*, 9 July. Maltreatment by the Dutch of Captain William Reeves of the *Essex*.

[5] The king.

[6] Sir Anthony Ashley Cooper, 1621–83; second baronet 1631; created Baron Ashley of Wimborne St. Giles 1661; earl of Shaftesbury 1672; Chancellor of the Exchequer 1661–72; Lord Chancellor 1672–3; the Whig statesman; Dryden's Achitophel: *D.N.B.*; lives by W. D. Christie, 1871; Louise Fargo Brown, 1933;

morneing;[1] if you can possibly doe it, you will very much oblidge him and mee. I this day spake with C. Grant, and will give you an account of vipers by my next: I am too morrow resolved to goe to the fleete: However let mee receave a Letter by the next opportunity. I am

your affectionate Freind and servant
DAVID THOMAS

Halfe moone in Breadstreet Jul. 9

Give my humble service to my freinds; and to mr Glanvill[2] whom I desire you to wayte on and enforme him of the contents of this Letter.

Address: For Mr John Locke at Christchurch in Oxford These.

Endorsed by Locke: (i) D. *Thomas* 9 Jul. *66*
(ii) T 66 (iii) T.O.U.

## *204.* DR. DAVID THOMAS to LOCKE, 19 July 1666 (*203, 212*)

B.L., MS. Locke c. 20, ff. 3–4.

My deare Freind

I have acquainted mr Perrott[3] with your desire of a Correspondence with Dr Scardysse,[4] and he will, what may be expected of him faythfully performe: he freely offered to convey Letters from and to you as oft as you please. I have bought [antimonii] mineralis lbvi which I am told is hungarian, I will send some of it to mr Boyle to be assured of the truth. Keffeler dyed of the plague last summer;[5] and I cannot heare of any one that grinds glasse stopples in the

K. H. D. Haley, 1968. He was suffering from a suppurating hydatid abcess of the liver (so diagnosed by Sir William Osler from Locke's description: *The Lancet*, 20 October 1900; reprinted in Osler, *An Alabama Student*, etc., 1909, pp. 68–107). According to Lady Masham he came to Oxford to visit his son (p. 293, n. 7) and at the same time to drink Astrop medicinal waters there; she states that he invited Locke to drink the waters with him; when he left Oxford, she continues, he went to Sunninghill, 'where he drank the waters some time', and where Locke joined him: letter to Jean Le Clerc, 12 January 1705.

The present letters suggest that Locke followed Ashley to Astrop, and that Ashley did not drink Sunninghill waters at this time: nos. *205–7*, *209*; for the waters see pp. 287 n., 293 n. 3.

[1] 15 and 16 July.

[2] Probably William Glanville, John Evelyn's brother-in-law: p. 293 n.

[3] Presumably Charles Perrott: p. 289 n.

[4] Presumably Scardius, J. Schard: p. 277.

[5] Apparently J. S. Kuffeler (or Kuffler, etc.), M.D., the son-in-law of Cornelius Drebbel the inventor (*D.N.B.*); he did not die until 1677: *N.N.B.W.*

whole towne. This day I shall goe to the minerys[1] and enquire for Hungarian [vitriol] and minerall [sulphur]. Too morrow I shall receave 6 vipers which if I canne I will send by the Coach: and on tuesday night I will wayte on you: I doubt not but to procure the Lampoone you write for in your last of Jul. 17.[2] As for news Yesterday was kept a fast in the Fleete, which wilbe ready to set sayle within very few days, which how few so ever: This place is much disconted that they are so many; and All people speake very ill of My Lord Arlington. Sir W Coventry and Sir G. Carthwright, And of all the D.Y privy councell for soe they call his Freinds and advisers.[3] Some seamen and wives of seamen with debenturs for pay presseing something rudely on Sir G. Carthwrights doore on tuesday last the sentry dicharged upon them and shott a woman through the thigh which is like to be mortall.[4] All the new Presbiterian troopes to be raysed are like to come to nothing, and the commissions are countermanded. Hither came a trumpeter from Holland about the Body of the late Valiant Captaine Sir W Berkly;[5] and tis sayd that a courrier is sent from the Swedish ambassador to the Dutch about peace, and that the Chancellor is for concluding it;[6] all which I much suspect. I thinke wee know nothing of the Dutch East India Fleete whether on this or the other side the Cape

Since I wrote the first part, I heare 46 troopes of horse are raysed; I saw a cart load of backes brests and head peece for them. This day came an expresse to the King, that the Fleet weighed Anchor about 1 of the clocke yesterday, and that 17 of the Dutch laying in the gunfleete seeing our fleete, stood out to sea to the rest of their fleete. ours about 94 sayle and 18 fire shipps. The Cambridge and Matthias[a] a merchant left behind not fitted.[7] too morrow about noone wee expect to heare the gunns. I cannot yet get minerall [sulphur] or Hungårian [vitriol]

[a] *Or* Metthias

---

1 Presumably the Minories.

2 Perhaps 'The Second Advice to a Painter': M. T. Osborne, *Advice-to-a-Painter Poems*, 1949, no. 10.

3 Sir Henry Bennet, 1618–85; created Baron Arlington 1665; earl of Arlington 1672; secretary of state 1662–74 (*D.N.B.*); Sir William Coventry, 1627–86 (ibid.); Sir George Carteret, *c.* 1610–80 (ibid.); James, duke of York, Lord High Admiral from 1660 to 1673.

4 Carteret was treasurer of the navy from 1660 to 1667.

5 Sir William Berkeley, vice-admiral; killed on 1 June, the first day of the Four Days' Battle: ibid.

6 Edward Hyde, earl of Clarendon, Lord Chancellor from 1660 to 1667: ibid.

7 The *Cambridge* was a third-rate; the *Mathias*, a prize taken in 1653: R. C. Anderson, nos. 370, 177.

Pray give my service to Mr Glanvill, to whom communicate, and let him know that on Munday I dined at Detford[1] and that his freinds there[a] ar well and send their service to him.

I am your affectionate Freind
D. THOMAS

London Jul. 19

Address: For Mr John Locke of Christchurch in Oxford These with speed
Postmark: IY 19

## 205. ROBERT HAMMOND to LOCKE, [early August 1666?]

B.L., MS. Locke c. 11, ff. 137–8. The writer was apparently a member of Lord Ashley's household. While there is no positive evidence that Ashley visited Astrop (p. 284, n. 6 *ad fin.*), this letter and the addresses of nos. *206* and *207* indicate that he did so. The letter was probably written between John Elford's matriculation on 21 July and the arrival in Oxford of Peter Locke's letter of 16 August.

Astrop is in Northamptonshire, 5 miles SE. of Banbury and 17 miles from Oxford. The medicinal spring there was discovered by Dr. Richard Lower in 1664, and within a few years Astrop became a minor watering-place: G. Baker, *History (of Northamptonshire)*, 1822–41, i. 703–5.

Sir

my Lord did understand you intended to bear him companey the[b]–time he shall stay–[b] at the wells. he hath now commanded mee to lett you know he hath a bed at Burston[2] for you and if you can dispence with your owne occasions, desier you would come over to morrow to us. here will be alsoe a horse to carry your worship abroad whither my Lord shall goe: pray forgett not to bring the verses upon the witts[3] with the other coppy you wott on:

this is all from
your faithfull friend and servant
RO: HAMMOND

[a] *MS.* yr    [b–b] *Substituted for* for 3 or fower days

---

[1] Perhaps meaning Sayes Court, the house of William Glanville's brother-in-law, John Evelyn, at Deptford.

[2] Probably Purston, a hamlet about 2 miles north of Astrop: Baker, i. 667–9.

[3] Perhaps 'The Session of the Poets. To the Tune of Cock Laurel': *Poems on Affairs of State*, ed. G. deF. Lord, 1963– , i. 327–37 (the date suggested there is 1668, but the poem appears to have been written before the death of James Shirley in October 1666).

from the wells
wenesday morn:

my Lord desires you to tell mr Stratford[1] he hath been soe Hurried aboute he could not possibly answer his Letter and that he would know John Elfords[2] tutors name Likewise that he shall have a bed sent speedily to him

Address: For his Worthy frend Mr John Lock at his chamber in Christ-church.

## *206.* PETER LOCKE to LOCKE, 16 August 1666 (*211*)

B.L., MS. Locke c. 14, f. 182. The writer, 1607–86, was a younger brother of Locke's father; of Sutton (probably Sutton Wick, 4 miles SW. of Pensford) in Chew Magna, Somerset; probably '*Peter Lock*, a *Tanner*' who was active in the sequestration, *c.* 1646, of Robert Joyner, vicar of Chew Magna: Fox Bourne, i. 3 and n.; J. Walker, *An Attempt . . . Sufferings of the Clergy*, 1714, ii. 64. His wife's Christian name was Anne; she was perhaps a sister or sister-in-law of William Grigge of Bristol (p. 44, n. 1.); she died in 1682. For his children see p. 263, n. 2.

Lovinge Cozen

I Thanke you for your Kind Love to my Son[3] att length I Have spoken with Mr Hollaway Whom I fownd Angry with you for som words In your letter to Him wherin as He saies you used threts which I conseve is nothinge but a knott In a bull Rush[4] the better to execut His Warrant which He said He would do without delay but for the unJust proseedinge against you he saies He cannott healp And after much discourse He would forebeare the execution of His warrant till after Bathe assises[5] and then I promised to Pay the mony he would not tell me In what Shrifes year this amearssment was but I shall know yf He will not tell me by the aquettanc In what yeare it was I did aske the advise of an able Layer who tould me this amearssment must be Paid no avoidinge of it also He Put me In a way How to prevent The like damage In tyme to com I Pray lett me know your mind In your next I belive yf I Had not spoken

[1] Probably Nicholas Stratford, 1633–1707, of Trinity College; D.D. 1673; bishop of Chester 1689: *D.N.B.*

[2] John Elford, *c.* 1651–1706; son of Thomas Elford of Over Winchendon, Bucks.; matriculated from Trinity 21 July of this year; B.A. 1670; incumbent of Pilsdon and Sherborne, both in Dorset, 1672–82 and 1677–82, and of West Bagborough, Somerset, 1682–1706: Foster; Matthews, *Calamy Revised*, p. 182.

[3] Peter Locke, *c.* 1653–74?; matriculated from Christ Church 11 May 1670; B.A. 19 February 1674: Foster; Fox Bourne, i. 220.

[4] Proverbial; it occurs in Terence: *Oxford Dict. English Proverbs*.

[5] 16 August: *London Gazette*, 28 June.

with Him that day which I did a distresse Had bine taken for tayler[1] your frind was then with Him I am sory I can Gett no mony for you att Pensford I Have Rec: only 4l of Pensson who Gives Good words makinge many promises He will Pay the Rest with all speed I have Rec: non from Liance He tells me He heth lost 3 horses more this yeare He desires you to forbeare Him till 29 Sep: next and then He promiseth to Pay altogether for Flory Pore man he is like to dy and I see no Hopes of mony ther as yett for John Flower I am wery to Go to him for mony you see what could comfort this world doth aford it is enough that we can Tak comfort In the Lord yf my cozen Dority[2] doe wantt mony I will God willinge Pay Her for you

I have not seen Her since you wer Heer I Heer (How true it is I know not) shee is like to be maried mine and my wives and childrens Love and Kind Respects to you Hopinge your Health and Happines with my earnest praiers to god for you I Rest

Your Lovinge unkill
PE: LOCKE

Through the Great mersy of god Bristoll and other places Heer about is In a good condition of Health[3]

Sutton this 16th August 1666

Address: For mr John Locke att Ch: Ch: Colledge In Oxford

Added in another hand: To be left with Mr. David Thomas or Mr. Nathanie Hodges at Astrop.

## *207.* CHARLES PERROTT to LOCKE, 21 August 1666

B.L., MS. Locke c. 17, ff. 70–1. The writer is identifiable as Charles Perrott, 1627(?)–77; matriculated from Oriel College 1647; B.A. 1649; M.A. 1653; editor of the *London Gazette* February 1666–70: Foster; Wood, *L. and T.* ii. 372–4; P. M. Handover, *A History of the London Gazette, 1665–1965*, 1965, pp. 14–18.

Whitehall. Aug. 21. 66.

Honest J Lock

Mr Williamson[4] and I were the last night discoursing of you, and of your late Employment abroad: Here is now another opportunity,

[1] The sentence could read 'taken, for Taylor your friend' or 'taken for Taylor; your friend'. I cannot identify Taylor.

[2] His niece by marriage, Dorothy, widow of Locke's brother Thomas: p. 225, n. 3 where her second husband is named.

[3] This refers to the plague.

[4] (Sir) Joseph Williamson: p. 256 n.

offers itt selfe pretty fayrely, which is His Majesty is sending an Envoyè into[a] Sweden,[a] who, we suppose, is not yet fixt upon a secretary for that Employment, if your inclina⟨ti⟩ons[b] are that way, Mr Williamson has promis'd his assistance, and I am confident will easily effect itt for a person of your Meritt. I have nothing more[c] at present but in as much hast as heartines I am

Your faithfull servant
CHARLES PERROTT.

The person designd for Envoyè is (if I mistake not)[d] Mr Thin.[1] I suppose your acquaintance.

Address: For Mr John Lock Master of Arts and Student of Christ Church Oxon To[e–] be left with Mr. David Thomas at Astrop.[–e]

## 208. JOHN STRACHEY to LOCKE, 30 August 1666 (*191*, *215*)

B.L., MS. Locke c. 18, ff. 215–16.

Mr Doctor[f]

For soe I am told you are, though you are willing to conceale your honour from your Friends, yett I was loth to write you soe in the superscription, least it might bee otherwise, I pray lett mee know,[2] I thanke you for your last according to the obligation, and though I am barren in relation to myselfe as to any thing worth the communicating yett Dr Cross[3] is desirous that such things which hee hath received lately from Paris might bee known to you, which I conceive are worthy, hee saith that whilst he was there Antimony was accus'd as hurtfull to Mens bodys, and since the Faculty have consulted and have concluded it not hurtfull, and have pas't it into an Act of Parliament, only Patine the Greate

[a] *MS.* into a Sweden, [b] *Letters apparently omitted.* [c] *Spelling doubtful.* [d] *Closing bracket supplied; MS. has comma.* [e–e] *Added by another hand.* [f] *MS.* M[r] D[r]

[1] Thomas Thynne, 1640–1714; matriculated from Christ Church 1657; second baronet 1680; created Viscount Weymouth 1682: *D.N.B.* He was envoy extraordinary to Sweden from January 1667 to January 1669.

[2] Locke was still only a master of arts; he took the degree of bachelor of medicine on 6 February 1675. He had studied medicine for some years.

[3] Robert Crosse: p. 166 n. He was an Aristotelian and an opponent of the Royal Society; Joseph Glanvill (*D.N.B.*) attacked him in *Plus Ultra*, 1668.

Droll wash't his hands and would not bee found guilty of the blood of the Kings Subjects[1]

One Philip[2] a Hollander hath discover'd a liquour clear like water in the Chrystalline humour about the bigness of a pea conteyned in its own tunicle shown to the Virtuoso's at Mr Bourdelos,[3] (as alsoe a cleare liquour betwixt the Vitreau and Retine) you may make the experiment by putting of a needle into an Oxes Crystalline and you shall see the liquour come out

Mr Steno[4] hath written from Rome to Mr Burdelo (and Dr Croane[5] att London hath received a letter to the same purpose from Steno) that a Tortoice which had his head cutt off liv'd 24 hours after, and beeing prickt on the side did putt forth his foote on the same side to remove the instrument (which alsoe was shewn at Mr Burdelo's) whence he concludes that paine and sence is not communicated from the head

Mr Graff a Hollander hath shewn in the same house that succus pancreaticus mixt with the Bile made a fermentation and afterwards turn'd the Bile into a greene colour, the juice was salt, hence he deduceth intermitting feavers (in confirmation of Dr Cross his Thesis,) to which purpose Graff hath written[6]

In the Jesuites colledge at Paris there was a disputation proving by demonstration Des Cartes way of seeing ⟨light and⟩[a] colours[7]

There was a woman that had a greate tumour on the outside of her thigh, sometimes greate sometimes scarce appearing and a greate

[a] *MS.* and light

---

[1] The use of antimony in medicine was forbidden by decree of the Faculty of Medicine of the University of Paris in 1566. This was rescinded by a decree of the Faculty on 29 March (or shortly after) of the present year. The new decree was registered by the Parlement of Paris on 10 April, and the use of antimony was authorized by the Faculty on 16 April (dates N.S.): *Journal des Sçavans*, 7 June 1666 (Amsterdam ed., 1666, pp. 331–7); J. Lévy-Valensi, *La Médecine et les médecins français au XVII^e siècle*, 1933, pp. 132–57. Its use was especially opposed by Gui Patin (1602–72; *N.B.G.*): *Lettres*, ed. J.-H. Reveillé-Parise, 1846, iii. 86, 608–10, etc.

[2] I have failed to identify him.

[3] Pierre Michon, l'abbé Bourdelot, 1610–84, physician: *D.B.F.* From about 1664 until his death he was the host and leader of an academy, a reunion for scientific discussion, etc.: Harcourt Brown, *Scientific Organizations in Seventeenth Century France (1620–80)*, 1934, pp. 231–53. See also no. *479*.

[4] Niels Steensen (Nicolas Steno), 1638–86, anatomist, etc.; titular bishop of Titiopolis 1677: *New Catholic Encyclopedia*, 1967.

[5] William Croone, 1633–84; M.D. 1662; F.R.S. 1662: *D.N.B.*; *The Royal Society: its Origins and Founders*, ed. Sir H. Hartley, 1960, pp. 211–19; his account of Steno's experiment with the tortoise: Birch, *Royal Society*, ii. 102–3.

[6] Reinier de Graaf, 1641–73: *N.N.B.W.* His book is *Traité de la nature et de l'usage du suc pancréatique*, etc., Paris, 1666. Notice in *Journal des Sçavans*, 2 August 1666 (pp. 445–9).

[7] I have found no other report.

paine on the Region of her ventricle with vomiting, the tumour was opened, and there came out a liquour like chyle or milke in greate quantity, which is one of Mr Burdelos proofs that the chyle is carryed through the whole body betwixt the membranes, the woman is a Nurse and hath noe milke when the tumour appears, and a comparison was made betwixt it and milke and noe difference found.

If your curiosity is any thinge gratified in these relations, I as for my part shall bee glad and the Doctor will bee encouraged to impart what farther shall bee sent to him, and if you know any thinge new hee desires the favour that you would communicate it. I did your business to your Uncle and am

your assured Friend and servant

JO STRACHEY

August 30 66.

Address: For Mr John Locke att Christ Church Colledge in Oxford these.

## *209.* E. BEDEL to LOCKE, 10 September 1666 (*218*)

B.L., MS. Locke c. 3, ff. 164–5. The writer, who was evidently a member of Lord Ashley's household, may have been a woman. A 'Mrs. Bedles' mentioned by Ashley in 1670 (p. 343) may be the same person.

Sir

beffore I reseved yours I was resolved to wright and to inquire of your good health: and to secure my confidence in that Adres. I had my Ladys[1] commition so to doe. you wear offten spoken of with expretions of desire to hear from you: and I dare Asure you that your inclosed was so acsepted that henceforth you need not care ffor A prologe to what ever you pleas to derect to his Lordship: to make mine Acseptabel to you at this time I will tell you that: (Allthoue the destirbance and destruktion of this place has bine very great)[2] yett both thar Honers are very well and all at exeter howse:[3] but the multitude of peopel whearin this sitty Abounded being ffired out so sudenly in all condition. will sartenly occation great bisnes for phitions so that if you pleas to com to theas

[1] Margaret, 1627–93, sixth daughter of William Spencer, second Baron Spencer of Wormleighton; married Ashley as his third wife 1655: G. E. C.

[2] By the Fire of London, which lasted from 2 to 5 September.

[3] On the north side of the Strand, on the site of Burleigh Street and Exeter Street, about opposite the Savoy. It was occupied by Ashley from 1663 or earlier until 1676, when it was demolished: Evelyn, *Diary*, ed. de Beer, iii. 203 n., 624 n.

subarbes (now the sitty is Allmost burnt downe) you will find objects enough to try your skill in performing three cures which must be dun before you be declared A publick docter:[1] I have not heard of docter benitt[2] since but we hear A very Ill report of the park watters[3] that every body which drunk them has bine Ill since

Sir Thomas Draper[4] very like to dye: the marchants meett att Gresham Coledg[5] as thay use to do at the exchang hear is great talke of bilding this sitty Againe finer then ever it was.[6] I besheech present my humble sarvis to Mr: Ashly[7] and if in this place I am capabell of sarving you comand ffreely

your ffrind and sarvant
E BEDEL

Sept xth: 66

Address: For Mr: John Lock att Christ Church in Oxfford

## *210.* WILLIAM GLANVILLE to LOCKE, 22 September 1666 (*1770*)

B.L., MS. Locke c. 10, ff. 12–13. The writer is probably William Glanville, *c.* 1618–1702; barrister 1642; a commissioner of the Alienation Office 1689–1702; his wife, now dead, was a sister of John Evelyn the diarist: Evelyn, *Diary*, ed. de Beer, ii. 539 n., etc. The identification is based on the notice on p. 287.

Kinde Freind

With much adoe uppon my Comming to Towne, I gott a Lodging, and not a day hath past since, wherein I have not thought of your

[1] The writer of the letter misrepresented the requirement. Men desiring a licence from the Royal College of Physicians to practise medicine in London and 7 miles about had to be examined on three separate days in physiology, pathology, and therapeutics: Sir George (N.) Clark, *A History of the Royal College of Physicians of London*, 1964–6, i. 179–80, 408–11; ii. 758–61.

[2] Not traced.

[3] Apparently those from Sunninghill in Berkshire, on the west side of Windsor Great Park: so Lady Masham in her account of Locke. They continued in use in the eighteenth century: J. Merrick, M.D., *Heliocrene*, 1735 and 1756; *A Compendious Gazetteer . . . Places within Sixteen Miles of Windsor*, 4th ed., 1801, pp. 103–4.

[4] He was of Sunninghill; created a baronet 1660; died in 1703: G. E. C., *Baronetage*, iii. 35.

[5] Sir Thomas Gresham's former house, between Bishopsgate Street and Old Broad Street; occupied by Gresham College from 1596 to 1768. At this time it provided accommodation for the Royal Society.

[6] The City asked for a new plan on 8 September, and Wren and other men submitted proposals during the next few days: T. F. Reddaway, *The Rebuilding of London after the Great Fire*, 1940, p. 53.

[7] Anthony Ashley Cooper, 1652–99; styled Lord Ashley from 1672; second earl of Shaftesbury 1683: G. E. C. He matriculated from Trinity College on 2 April of this year; created M.A. 4 February 1667. The use of Ashley as the surname, rather than Ashley Cooper, continued in the next generation.

and Mr Thomas's Civilityes to mee; Freinds since our late Calamity, are not yet United againe, beeing much to seeke how to meete and Converse; I have sent Mr Provost of Queens[1] by this post, a paper of the most Creditable Newes I can pick upp, and lett mee tell you, Newes is now a Commodity hard to come by; I have intreated Mr Provost, that hee will communicate my paper to mr Thomas and then you will see It; I am in some hast called from the Towne, to see a sick freind in Surry,[2] when I meete with Sir Walter Vane, I will doe you right, pray present my affectionate Respects to Mr Thomas, and tell him Doctor Barloe will shew him my paper; could I have stayd in towne and deferd writing till night, perhaps I might have sent somwhat more and fresher; I desire both you and Mr Thomas to beleve, that no person can bee more yours then Is

your affectionate servant
WILLIAM GLANVILLE.

Strand September 22th 8 in the morning 666.

Address: These For his honored freind Mr John Lock Master of Art att his Chamber in Christ Church Oxon post is payd

## *211.* PETER LOCKE to LOCKE, 25 October 1666 (*206*, *213*)

B.L., MS. Locke c. 14, f. 183.

Sutton this 25 October 66

Lovinge Cozen

I Rec: yours of the 13 Instant but 6 minuts to late which Had[a] I Rec but so littill Rather[3] I Had not paid the mony for that unJust Amersment which did so much trouble me but I Returned[b] backe to Mr Hollaway with my Lords warrant[4] And demaned the mony which then I paid 31s but He Refused to Repay it but promised yf the order was Alowed In the Exchequer He would Repay it when

[a] *Doubtful reading.* [b] *Ms.* Retd

[1] Thomas Barlow, 1607–91; D.D. 1660; Bodley's Librarian 1652–60; Provost of Queen's 1658–77; bishop of Lincoln 1675: *D.N.B.*

[2] Richard Evelyn of Woodcote Park near Epsom, the diarist's brother, was ill about this time: Evelyn, *Diary*, 29 September, 8 November 1666.

[3] Earlier or sooner. For the positive of the adverb, rathe, see p. 253; the comparative survived in Somerset dialect until the nineteenth century: *O.E.D.* It occurs again in no. *1448*.

[4] Probably Ashley, who was Chancellor of the Exchequer from 1661 to 1672.

he Returned[a] to bristoll. I could not Give you an Acount to your Last excepte complaints Against your Tenants which I am sure is not pleasinge to you. I Have bine often with them but I Rec: but Little mony. They promise to Pay now att the faire[1] which yf they do not you shall know by the next I Have not Rec: more then formerly[b] I gave you an acompt of. from Penson I beleve nothinge will be gotten by suite of Law. He is very Pore and begs your mersifull forberance and doth promise to Pay som and som as He is able. He Hath Paid His Rent now to your Ante Elinor[2] And shee Hath promised all att the faire. I am Resolved to sew Liance yf He Pay not the next weeke. What you will Have don with John flower writt your mind In the next and Inclose it and leave it to me to seale it He will Pay me nothinge. I Have Rec: 10l from John flory Who Hath promised to Pay The Rest when His Lease is sealed which He promised to Gett made and send to me to that end to send it to you for that purpose. The next day I am att bristoll I am to Pay my Cozen Dority mony but I know not How much shee expects. I doubt I shall cale uppon you for mony about The next springe. I thinke I shall place[3] one or boath my daughters for which I desire your prairs

Mine and my wives and daughters kind love and Respect to you beseechinge The Lord to be Gratious to you and to Teach us to make that Holy and Santifid use of His hevy Hand on our brethren neibours and Nation[4] for is the daily Praiers of

your Lovinge unkill
PE: LOCKE

Address: For mr John Lock These In oxford

[a] *MS.* Retd [b] *MS.* form^r

---

[1] Two fairs appear to have been held each year in Pensford. This one was held apparently in November, after the 4th (no. *3367*) and before the 21st (no. *213*; the tenants mentioned in the present letter have paid their rents). The other fair was held in April: no. *1282*.

[2] Elinor, born Gullock (?), widow of Locke's uncle Edward, who died in 1663; perhaps still living in 1697: Cranston, p. 8; Fox Bourne, i. 3 n.; no. *2167*, etc.

[3] Apparently meaning to give in marriage: *O.E.D.* A grandson (Peter King) was born in 1669.

[4] This refers to the Fire of London, the plague, and the disasters of the war.

## *212.* DR. DAVID THOMAS to LOCKE, 18 November [1666] (*204*, *227*)

B.L., MS. Locke c. 20, ff. 7–8. The year from Locke's and Thomas's addresses: Locke did not know Ashley until 1666, and after June 1667 Thomas was resident in Salisbury.

My deare Freind

I have long expected you, our businesse will require your presence. For now I have made our[a] lute hold drying, and I doubt not but it will endure the fire: If you bring with you [mercurii] vivi lb j vel lb ij wee will make [mercury sublimate] our selves which wilbe much cheaper then to buy it: Pray take the paynes to goe to Mr Sheryn[1] and desire an answer to my letter. For I cannot proceede in that businesse untill I receave his answer. Here is noe news, but that the warre betweene the university and the towne[2] which you will not find concluded when you returne which the sooner shalbe more wellcome to

your affectionate Freind and servant

D. THOMAS

New College. Nov. 18

I have receaved a letter from my Lord of Thanet[3] where in he gives his service to you

Address: For Mr John Locke These. Leave these with the Lord Ashleys porter at Little exceter house[4] in the Strand London.

Postmark: NO 1–

## *213.* PETER LOCKE to LOCKE, 21 November 1666 (*211*, *293*)

B.L., MS. Locke c. 14, ff. 184–5.

Lovinge Cosen

I Rec: your Letter And order And Given you Answeer to it In october but I Heer not from you Therfore I doubt my letter Hath

[a] *Doubtful reading.*

[1] Perhaps R. Sherwyn, described in 1663 as secretary to Ashley: Oldenburg, *Correspondence*, ii. 10.

[2] One of the city serjeants had recently been arrested on a warrant from the vice-chancellor; the resulting dispute continued until 1668: *Oxford Council Acts, 1665–1701*, pp. x, 6, 307; Wood, *L. and T.* ii. 125, 128–9; iv. 70.

[3] Nicholas Tufton, 1631–79; third earl of Thanet 1664; brother of Locke's future friend Thomas Tufton, later the sixth earl (no. *429*): G. E. C.

[4] Apparently the same as, or part of, Exeter House.

miscarid. I now Give you to understand I Paid mr Hollaway 31s for the Amerssment and Gave Him the order you sent[a] he promised to Return[b] the mony to you yf the order be Alowed In the Eschequer your Rents The Gretest parte I Have Rec: and Hopes to Rec the Rest excepte John Flower mr Curtis demands Half a years Rent end the 25 march last which I tell him I believe[b] you paid Him but you know best[1] your Tenant Liance Hath paid me Half years Rent and the other Half yeare is almost out In payments Hee desirs that som other may pay the payments He tells me He is werry of the trouble And I thinke you may be werry too I should be Glad to see you Heer I thanke the lord we be in Health Mine and my wives and all my children Love and Kind Respect to you with my continewall praiers to God for you

I Rest your Lovinge Unkill
PE: LOCKE

Sutton this 21 nov 1666:

Address: For my Lovinge Cosne Mr John Locke These In oxford

## *214.* [ELINOR PARRY later Mrs. Hawkshaw?] to LOCKE, 25 November [1666?] (*193*, 220)

B.L., MS. Locke c. 8, f. 67. The handwriting agrees with Scribelia's, who is here identified as Elinor Parry; the seal is identical with that used by her in 1669 (no. *232*). The year from the mention of Thomas and his name in the address; the writer does not know of his removal to Salisbury. The letter was probably written from Dublin; besides the 'Angiere street' address this is indicated by the interval between the date of writing and that of the postmark.

The attempts at concealment make the meaning of the letter obscure.

Deare Sir

Your former Kindness and helps to that perferment which I Have. hath fixt in me an extroadenary affection to your service, and your concerns, as to any freind, relates to me this you are to reward with the assureanc of your health tis that onely is wisht for heir and tis that onely is beg'd of by me, delay it not then (Sir) least my cosen[2] have some Grownds to beleeve London hath wrought that Change in you: which the severest considerations

[a] *Followed by a short word* R-? [b] *Abbreviated in MS.*

[1] Locke rented some land from Alexander Popham; Curtis was perhaps Popham's agent.

[2] Elinor Parry herself.

formerly could not, you know what thay were you know the unhappyness that parted you, /[a] may thay be no longer a hinderanc to your Happyness/[a].[1] how vaine are those wishes, were you the better for those that are made howerly for you you would be the envied person of the world, and not the absent Mr Lock but /[a]

Sir there is little news heir the most wellcom would be that you send resolve it then as speedily as you can and I promise to return some: to you lett me know of all things and tell me somewhat of my freind Atticus[2] to whom I writt 2 month a goe but I beleeve it came not to his Hands this I hope will bring you a 1000 good Harty wishes from

Sir

Your most obliged servant THO: WILLSON

my Respects to my honist freind mr Thomas of New: Coll: I will after your next tell you my thoughts of your university may it flowrish when I am dead and forgotten farewell. derect yours to my Cosen R: as you did long agoe to be left where I am att Angiere street flanders[3]

No the 25 my true respectes to Atticus:

Address: for mr John Locke att Christ Church in his absenc to be leaft with mr Thomas at new College Oxon paid to Lo.

In another hand: forward 2

Postmark: DE 5

## *215.* JOHN STRACHEY to LOCKE, 27 November 1666 (*208*, *226*)

B.L., MS. Locke c. 18, f. 217. On the reverse is a draft for a letter, here printed as no. 220.

Sir

I doe not know very well whether or noe I was best aske your pardon for not writing before or writing now, for as the first may argue neglect or idleness, soe the last signifies soe litle,[b] that I

[a] *Mark resembling a closing bracket.* [b] *Strachey notes in the margin* obscure.

[1] Almost all our knowledge of Locke's relations with Elinor Parry is derived from the surviving letters between them, letters whose authorship or direction is sometimes questionable, and whose dates are frequently problematical. In any case the letters would not tell the whole story as the couple were frequently resident in the same town. For these reasons the present passage cannot be associated with any passage in the earlier letters.

[2] p. 261, n. 3. [3] Apparently Aungier Street in Dublin.

should choose it much rather then the other, but that I thinke you are willing enough to heare that there is such a thing as I alive in the world, and is noe changeling as to matter of affection towards you, and besides I perceive without I scribble something to you, I am like to have not a tittle from you, and how doe you thinke that in these cloudy times I can steare my course, unless I have some light from you, who are my Polestarr. Fears, Jealousys, Longe knives, Masses, present and future pressures, forrein and Domestick enemies, litle money and less witt doe soe afflict and distract the Country, that I am sometimes afraid, that as the warme weather comes on wee shall breake forth into flame and fury, did I not experience that Beefe, pudding and Bacon and such gross restringents, are most powerfull smotherers of those fiery humours which boile in our Country veines, and yett tis true that some old women like Catts in the Chimney corner, have flew upon and scratcht the faces of some of those that gather Hearth money,[1] and there is a general murmure and discontent against that and other greivances, and what these things may come to, none but the Divines can tell, and I thinke of those not your hoop't ones, for they keepe all in, but the ungirt ones are allways the best Prophets and have most news.[2] (This by the bye leads mee to tell you that Dr Cross is marryed and setled in Bristoll).[3] Sir you that are up to the elbows in State affaires I must beseech to cleare these umbrages with true relations, and excuse these shifts I am putt to, to pene up a letter, whose maine business is to assure you that I am with all sincerity

Sir

your real Friend and Servant

JO. STRACHEY.

November 27. 66.

Address: For his honoured Friend Mr John Locke att Litle Exeter house in the Strand. London.

Postmark: NO 30

[1] A tax of two shillings per annum on every fire-hearth in England and Wales, with exemption for the poor; imposed by statute in 1662 (14 Car. II, c. 10) and abolished in 1689.

[2] The hooped divines are presumably Anglicans, and the ungirt Dissenters. I have not found the expression elsewhere. It perhaps derives from the girdle confining the cleric's cassock: see *O.E.D.*, s.v. Surcingle.

[3] He obtained a marriage licence in 1664: *Marriage Bonds for the Diocese of Bristol*, i. 28. See also p. 399.

## *216.* SIR PAUL NEILE to LOCKE, 1 December 1666 (*628*)

B.L., MS. Locke c. 16, ff. 129–30. Paul Neile, 1613–86; astronomer; son of Richard Neile, archbishop of York (*D.N.B.*); knighted 1633; F.R.S. (Original Fellow), active in the affairs of the Royal Society from the start: *The Royal Society: its Origins, etc.*, ed. Hartley, pp. 159–65; Hudson's Bay Company, *Minutes, 1671–4*, ed. E. E. Rich (Champlain Soc., Hudson's Bay ser., vol. v, 1942), pp. 241–2. He was an associate of Shaftesbury (Ashley), but Roger North's statement about him (*Examen*, 1740, p. 60) is unreliable. It was he who proposed Locke as a candidate for the Royal Society on 19 November 1668: Birch, *Royal Society*, ii. 323–4.

December the 1st. 66.

Sir

by yours of the 28th of November I see the greate care you take of mee. and should bee glad you would lett mee have the bill of your ballsome. that I might gett it made heere. and then I should hope it would cure mee. but as longe. as by these artifices you seeke meanes to keepe your selfe from being cured of the infirmity under which you labour. of never thinking you can oblige those persons enough. that you please to call friends. I can hardly hope you can cure mee. when I see noe persuasions of mine can prevaile to make you cure your selfe. of that which is indeed a disease not only in your selfe but to your friends. that you will not bee contented to oblige them by your advise but you must adde a chardge which I am not willing to receave but the advise I shall at any time verry thankfully. Soe that upon the matter it is in your power by the waie of helping mee to your balsome. to oblige mee or other waies. but now you see I am thus farre in earnest. I hope. you will doe it that waie which will make it most obligeing to mee.

The next convenient oprortunity I shall not faile to acquainte my lord[1] with as much of your letter as I finde by his present temper is nessesary. and in that and all things I shall really endevor to expresse my selfe to bee.

Your most faithfull servant
PAUL NEILE

Address: These to my assured friend mr John Locke a student of Ch: Church in oxford deliver at his Chamber there.

Postmark: DE 1

[1] Presumably Ashley.

## *217.* JOHN PARRY, later bishop of Ossory, to LOCKE, 2 December 1666 (219)

B.L., MS. Locke c. 16, ff. 188–9. For the writer see p. 69 n.; he was now dean of Christ Church, Dublin. Answered by no. 219.

Deare Sir

I returne you thanks for yours by my sister[1] and wish it might ever lye in my way to evidence the esteeme I have for you, in order wherunto my respects and kindeness invites me to make a motion unto you which you may be pleasd to consider of, and to act as you shall finde most for your advantage therin. What your resolutions are as to a calling and whether England be the place you onely intend to fix in I know not; but in case you thinke fitt to venture your fortune with us heere, and take Orders, I shall lay out my whole interest to serve you and doubt not but in a litle time to get you to be Chaplain to my Lord Duke[2] and the first Dignity that falls, especially in my owne Cathederal (and I am not out of hopes suddenly to make way there) I do really beleeve to procure for you so that in a litle time I am confident I shall see you very hansomely provided for, in this place without being a Constant preacher.

This is a very fayre large towne and I do beleeve you would not mislike of a setlement therin. Sir If you finde any inclinations in your selfe to accept of this motion let me heare from you by the very first that so accordingly I may act as things may fall, as also give you my thoughts as to your speedy remove. Being to preach to morrow in Christ church I dare not in large but onely to assure you that if you thinke fitt to hearken heereunto, there shall be none who would more zealously improve all opertunities to serve you there

Deare Sir
Your most assured friend and servant
JO PARRY.

December 2nd 1666. Dublin.

Address: For my Worthy Friend Mr. John Lock at Christchurch These Oxon.

[1] Probably Elinor, but another sister (or sister-in-law?) was also in Dublin: pp. 304, 312. The only other known sister is Mary Flood alias Bulkeley: p. 69 n.

[2] James Butler, first duke of Ormond; Lord Lieutenant of Ireland 1662–9, 1677–85: *D.N.B.*

## *218.* E. Bedel to Locke, 5 December [1666?] (*209*)

B.L., MS. Locke c. 3, f. 166. The year depends on the duration of Ashley's son's residence in Oxford, which appears to have been only a few months: p. 293, n. 7. Locke apparently left London for Oxford shortly before 1 December: no. *216*.

Sir

Since we could no longer retaine your good company I am glad to hear you are well att oxford I have returned your gratitud to my Lord and La: for thar sivilitys to you in towne thay[a] both desir to be kindly remembred to you, his Lordship continews in good health as you left him: but sumtimes has fitts of the Cramp: by all I can truly understand his Lordship will be very well pleased to see you at any time: but this I dout thar will not be Lodging for you in this howse when Mas. Ashley is hear: this I freely tell you that you may (acording to the custom of this world) consider your one conveniency as well as your great sevelity but this I am sure whear you pleas to make your Abode this crismus whether oxford or exeter howse will be hapyer then whear you are not: the young Lady[1] presents her sarvis and thankes to you for the consideration you have of her—shee has bine very Ill in that kind since you left the towne

my cosan bety has lost her: cough and recovered her voyce very well and tells mee if you wear hear she could wisper still to you: but I belive shee has nothing now to whisper but only to tell what use shee intends shortly to make of her voyce. I besheech you to present my cos: bety and my humbel sarvis to Mas Ashley: I cannot conclud this with out A littel quarell to you or rather my Ill memery that you wear not payd for thos things my Lady gave mee order to pay befor you went out of towne all I can say now is I hope youl com or ellce lett me know and ma: south shall pay it. I hope you will exscuse my not writing sooner and belive that I am

your frind and sarvent

E B

Exeter Hows De 5:

[a] *MS* y[a]:

[1] Ashley had no daughter; his son did not marry until 1669.

## 219. LOCKE to [JOHN PARRY, later bishop of Ossory], [*c.* 15 December 1666] (*217*)

B.L., MS. Locke c. 24, ff. 221–2. Draft. Parts of f. 221 soiled and rubbed; some reconstruction. Passages, preceded by passages from no. 220, printed, as a single letter, in King, pp. 27–8. Evidently the draft for an answer to no. *217*; hence the addressee and the approximate date.

The letter I sent by your Sister I perceive came to you by a wellcome[a] hand, which[b] it[b] could not otherwise have deservd soe kind a returne, with[a] which I pay you my thanks and acknowledgment you cannot doubt but I have Inclination enough to be in Dublin without considering the beauty and largenesse of the towne. It being the conversations of those I love and company of my freinds (and how much you are soe your letter shews) that makes any place desirable to me. But Sir he must needs be a very quick sighted or very inconsiderat person that can between the comeing of one post and goeing of the next peremptoryly resolve to transplant himself from a country affairs and studys he has been bread in into all these very distant. upon probability, which though perhaps your interest there may make you look on as certain, yet my want of fitnesse may possibly disapoint, for certainly something is requird on my side, it is not enough for such places barely to be in orders, and I cannot thinke that preferments of that nature will be throwne upon a man that hath never given any proofs of him self nor ever tried the pulpit

would you not thinke it a strange question if I should aske you whether I must be first in those places or in orders, yet if you will consider with me it will not prhaps seeme altogeather irrationall; for should I put my self into order[1] and yet by the meanesse of my abilitys prove unworthy such expectation, (for you doe not thinke that Divines are now made as formerly by inspiration and on a suddain, nor learning caused by laying on of hands) I unavoidably loose all my former studys and put my self into a calling that will not leave me nor keep me, were it a profession from whenc there were any return,[2] (and that amongst all the occurrences of life

[a] *Doubtful reading.* [b] *MS.* which it it *interlined.*

[1] Here probably a slip for orders. The latest occurrence of the singular in this sense quoted in *O.E.D.* is dated 1620.

[2] An Anglican clergyman could not relinquish his orders before 1870: *Oxford Dictionary of the Christian Church*, s.v. Clerical Disabilities Act.

may happn to be very convenient if not necessary) you would finde me with as much forwardnesse imbrace your proposals, as I now acknowledg them with gratitude.

You cannot then thinke it strange if these reasons,[a–] the difference of my studys, with a just feare, sure sight of myself, and the misfortune of altogether, suffer me not[–a] at least soe much on a suddain to resolve on so waity an undertaking, since the same considerations have made me a long time refuse very advantageous offers of severall considerable freinds in England.[1] I am[b] apt[b] ⟨to⟩ flatter my self that the reason of this your kindenesse is yet a very much greater. and which above all things in the world I should be glad to meet in a way wherin[c–]I should[–c] ⟨be⟩ not unworthy of it, and shall be infinitely indebted to any one that shall open such a one to me. but I[d–] can not be forward ⟨to⟩ disgrace[–d] you or any body else by being listed into a place which perhaps I cannot fill and from whence there is noe desending without tumbleing. (If any shame or misfortune attend me it shall be only mine and if I am covetous of any good fortune tis that one[e–] I love[–e] may share it with me.)

But Sir your obligation is not the lesse because I am not in a condition to receive the effects of it. I returne all manner of acknowledgments due to soe great a favour and shall watch all occasions to let you see how sensible I am of it and to assure you that I am

pray present my service to both your sisters.[2]

## 220. LOCKE to [ELINOR PARRY later Mrs. Hawkshaw?], [*c.* 15 December 1666] (*214*, *222*)

B.L., MS. Locke c. 18, f. 217$^{v}$. Draft, written on reverse of no. *215*. A passage, with an opening sentence from elsewhere in the letter, and succeeded by passages from no. 219, printed, as a single letter, in King, pp. 27–8. The draft deals with John Parry's invitation and is for the antecedent of no. *222*; hence the addressee and the approximate date.

Between the writeing and sending of my letter, came to my hand what you had made me expect,[3] wherein I finde my self more and more indebted to your kindenesse, which could make you for my

[a–a] *Partially interlined; the arrangement of the various considerations is uncertain.* [b] *Substituted for* would [c–c] *Interlined.* [d–d] *Altered from* I will not disgrace [e–e] *Substituted for* somebody

[1] See p. 214 n. [2] p. 301, n. 1.
[3] John Parry's invitation. It was perhaps alluded to in Elinor's lost letter written about September: see p. 298.

sake consent that I should take a calling which you your self are not very fond of and in resolutions against which you have been this 7 years confirmeing me. and which before 7 years more be over you will finde twas neithr want of reason or affection made me refuse. Remember what I now tell you. In the meane time pray consider that a mans affairs and whole course[a] of his life are not to be changd in a moment and that one is not made fit for a colling espetially that in a day. and I beleive you thinke me too proud to undertake any thing wherein I should acquit my self but scurvily.[b] I'm sure I cannot content myself with[c–] being amongst the meanest possibly the midlemost of my profession. and you will allow care and consideration is to be taken[–c] not to engage in a ⟨calling⟩[d] wherein if one chance to be a bungler there is noe retreat. at lest more time certainly is requisite for takeing such a resolution then is allowd me. an answer being expected by the first, considering too what I have donne here to the contrary.[1] The proposalls noe question are very considerable for which I owe my thanks and I with discontent reflect upon my misfortune that makes me uncapable of it. O my best are all my pleasant hopes returnd to the same place they were. were[c–] any thing of an other nature offerd me here you should see with what hast I should imbrace it. I long to be with you[e] and only desire to come handsomly soe that we may enjoy one another and ourselves. But I finde I am a little unfortunate and by severall ways am led to the prospect but shut from the possession of my happynesse.[–c] could I speak freely to you without being thought to chide. I should tell you, that you have let me know soe little of the state of your affairs there that I cannot tell how to advise you or my self and am at a losse how to answer some things in your ⟨brothers⟩[f] letter but I have delt according to my humor freely and openly. I wish heartily you had not beene soe much silent: you cannot thinke that since you went I have only slept[g] here and laid noe designes or made me noe concernment; and can you beleive 24 time[h] enough[h] to consider dispose and alter all. But I rest satisfied in your prudence and kindenesse.

[a] *Alternative for* drift [b] *Alternative for* meanely. [c–c] *Some words interlined, etc; conflated reading.* [d] *Deleted.* [e] *Followed by a short illegible word; perhaps* but [f] *In MS. a word ending* -ers*; it is not written in full and the earlier letters are doubtful.* [g] *Followed by* ne (?) *and a deleted and illegible word.* [h] *Interlined.*

[1] On 14 November Locke obtained a dispensation enabling him to retain his studentship at Christ Church without taking orders: p. 214 n.

## 221. LOCKE to —— [late December 1666?]

B.L., MS. Locke c. 24, f. 222v. Written on the verso of part of no. 219. Hence the date; but it may be earlier, Locke using an old blank page for the draft of no. 219.

Sir

Though the greatnesse of your condition and knowledg make it difficult to finde fit presents for you, yet the favour interpretation you have beene pleasd to put on my insignificant endeavours to serve you hath made me ventur to present you with an old almanack, and patch up a new years gift with remnants borrowd from the old. Indeed when I consider, how much you see which lys hid from most eys I begin to be confident that when I informe you which way the wind sit, and assure you that it is cold weather at Christmas I tell you that is as much a secret to you as any thing that not only I but almost any other could have presented you with

## *222*. [ELINOR PARRY later Mrs. Hawkshaw?] to LOCKE [19 February 1667?] (220, *225*)

B.L., MS. Locke c. 8, f. 64. Defective: part of leaf, containing opening of address, torn away. Despite the roundabout language the writer appears to be Elinor Parry. The letter evidently answers no. 220. Shrove Tuesday in 1667 fell on 19 February.

Deare Sir

I perceve my Last in answere to that Letter which you mentioned your intentions and refused a fathers[1] invitations is unluckly miscarried: my Cosen[2] is very sinsible of its misfortune in not meeting with your freind:[3] least he thinks she should forgett the care which she tooke of your Content in afording it by Letters which she is more pleasd with then with silenc, she bids me tell you she repines att this seperation and as Her kindness would perswade Her to patienc and hope for the sight of you, yett Her dispare is greater, and more firmly fix't it tis not Growned on any Hinderances this side as she knows: she is as Hartily reall in Her affection as ever neither doth she now practis that nicity of disowneing it, but that of your Happyness is regarded beyond any Consideration whatsoever, and sinc she is so much Consern'd In your content you must

[1] Her brother's, John Parry. [2] Presumably Elinor herself.
[3] Presumably Locke.

beleeve she neglects not writing: to you, I have Little news to send you and less time, onely I must ⟨tell⟩[a] you from S:[1] that if you are the yett passionatte Att:[2] and the reall one you ever was you will hid nothing from Her, she must share in your Concerns as she has share in your Hart and you must tell Her all things; that you may not question Her reality she wisheth for you Howerly: my Cosen and Scribelia are alwaise the same in their wishes for you: my Cosen is a little Changed since she Left you tis onely in Her Humour that she sees not you as she used, *Heavens* /[b–] *my Best shall I never see you: shall I alwaise Lament your absenc with out any Hopes: if you can send me some I shall Rest better satisfied then I am, now I am unwilling the pacquett should goe without this Lett so that I must Rest your faithfull Ber:*[b3]

Shrove tusday night there is much Companie in the Hous but thay must not hinder a 100 sighs farewell Life

Lett me Heer as soon as you can of all things. my Concerns and yours are owne, a father doth not know of the Corispondencie, I think

Address: . . . . . Oxford paid[c] to London
In another hand: forward 2
Postmark: MR 23
Endorsed by Locke: (i): Sc: *66*; (ii): S *66*

## 223. Locke to Robert Boyle, 24 February 1667 (*199*, 224)

Boyle, *Works*, 1744, v. 567.

Christ Church, Feb. 24, 1666.

Honoured Sir,

According to the directions you gave in your last letter to Mr. Thomas, I have endeavoured to provide paronychia,[4] and I think I shall be able to procure pretty good store of it. The fittest time I suppose to gather it will be, when it begins to be in flower, which will be about a fortnight hence, the spring hereabouts not being over forward. How I shall dispose or order it for you, I must desire

[a] *MS.* fell *or* sell [b–b] *This passage is in larger and rougher writing than most of the rest of the letter.* [c] *MS.* p[d].

[1] Scribelia. [2] Atticus: p. 261, n. 3. [3] Berelisa.
[4] Willow-wort: *O.E.D.*

to be directed. Though by your approving of that way in other like cases, I have some thoughts to pound and seal up some part of it in a bolt head, and so keep it, since the juice being the thing desired; and not being fully acquainted with the way Helmont[1] mentions he made use of to preserve juices, I know not how otherwise well to keep it. In the process of [oil of vitriol] with [spirit of wine] you did me the honour to send me, I must beg this additional favour, to know, whether in each distillation I must draw off the [spirit of wine] of[2] ad ficcitatem; for I find, that if the fire be a little augmented, the volatile [spirit of wine] being pretty well first gone over, the remaining liquor will rise in plentiful very white fumes; but I suspect this too violent a way of proceeding. After having distilled it in this manner, I let it stand above twenty four hours to cool; and though when I took off the head from the body, it had been several hours quite cold, and my nose were not within a foot of the mouth of the body; yet there came out so quick and penetrating a steam, that it made me cry out, and made my eyes run over, but the effects of it quickly ended, and I was soon at ease again; though I dare be confident it is one of the briskest and most pungent steams in nature. Did I not know, how favourably you interpret any poor essays, and slight observations of those, that are willing to learn, I should not venture to importune you with such trifles. But since my design is not (nor can ever be) to instruct you, you will permit me by all the ways I can, to assure you that I am,

Honoured Sir,

your most humble, and most obliged servant,

JOHN LOCKE.

Mr. Thomas presents his humble service to you. He and I are now upon a new sort of chemistry, i.e. extracting money out of the scholars pockets; and if we can do that, you need not fear but in time we shall have the lapis; for he that can get gold and silver out of scholars, cannot doubt to extract it any where else. The truth is, he and I are preferred to be ⟨assessors⟩[a] of the poll-money;[3] and if you do not make haste hither, I believe you will at your next

[a] *Birch has* accessors

[1] J. B. van Helmont: p. 215, n. 2. He mentions a method in his tract 'Natura contrariorum nescia', §45 (*Opera Omnia* (1707), p. 168).

[2] This may be a slip in the rendering or a redundant off.

[3] A graduated poll-tax was to be levied by act of parliament (18 and 19 Car. II, c. 1), which received the royal assent on 18 January.

coming hither find us both beaten out of town, for having had too good thoughts of our neighbours, it being now an injury to believe any one rich, or a gentleman. We return our thanks for your queries by Dr. Lower,[1] and intend some trials on the first opportunity.

## 224. LOCKE to ROBERT BOYLE, 24 March 1667 (223, 228)

Boyle, *Works*, 1744, v. 567–8.

Christ Church, March 24, $\frac{66}{67}$.

Honoured Sir,

I should not have been so slow in returning my thanks for the great favours of your letter, had not the carelessness of the letter-carrier kept it from me two or three days after it came to town. I am concerned that you should believe this truth, and I should be very much ashamed to appear guilty of tardiness, to a person, who thinks his favours need an apology, if they are not as speedy as they are great, who is not content to oblige an undeserving scholar beyond the ordinary rules of kindness, unless he also excuse the excess of his obligations. Had I any skill in the art of speaking, I should on this occasion tell you, that this is to be like the sun, and those other heavenly bodies, who are exempt from the corruption and nigardliness of things here amongst us, and bestow their light and influence constantly, and as it were out of necessity. But, Sir, the pretensions I make to philosophy will excuse my want of rhetorick; and though I have but little of the knowledge, yet I shall make use of the language of a philosopher, and content myself to speak plainly, as I mean honestly; and do therefore with a sincerity due to that profession, tell you, that I have a very great sense and acknowledgment of your favours, however I want words to express it. The warts you speak of, I doubt not but I shall be able to provide you in the place I am going to, though I would be glad to know, whether there hath been any difference observed in the operation of those of stone-horses, geldings, and mares, and whether they are to be taken from live horses, since (if I forget not) Helmont some where says,[2] that if in histerical fits, (for in that disease he commends them) you use those that are taken from an horse, *æstuante venere*, they have different effects from others. I desire also the favour to

[1] He was in Oxford on 23 February: Wood, *L. and T.* ii. 99.
[2] Not identified.

know, how much of [spirits of sal ammoniac] may be thought a large dose, and whether it be that [spirits of sal ammoniac] which is made with [mercury], whereof we have prepared some. The particulars of the process Mr. Thomas has undertaken to give you an account of. Sir, having from a passage in your writings taken the first notice of the time of gathering pæony roots;[1] and since finding it in the observations communicated to Riverius,[2] where the observer says it must be *inclinante luna in ariete existente*, which also F. Wurtz[3] confirms with this addition, that it must be in April, when Sol is in Aries, and at a plenilunium before the rising of the Sun. I rode to a place, where was pretty good plenty of male pæony, and on the 14th instant between ten and eleven in the morning had some of the roots dug up, and am promised others to be dug up on the 30th instant before sun-rising. If there be any advantage in the time of gathering, I owe the knowledge of it so much to you, that I should be an unworthy reader of your writings, if I should not return you my thanks, and offer you some part of those roots, from whom I learnt the usefulness of them; if you please to make trial, whether these have any more virtue than those gathered at another season, I having chosen those times, that I think come nearest to their directions. I intend to go between this and Easter[4] into Somersetshire, where if I can do you any service about Mendipp, or any other way, you will oblige me with the employment. It is so much my concernment to receive your commands, that I shall be sure to give you notice where I am, and how I may receive the honour of your letters. After some little stay in that country, I hope to kiss your hands in London, and I now begin to make wishes, that you will come hither very quickly. I am,

Honoured Sir,

your most obedient, and most obliged servant,

JOHN LOCKE.

Mr. Thomas presents his service.

Having followed your directions the best I could with [spirit of wine], and [oil of vitriol], having drawn [spirit of wine] from it till

[1] This refers to *Certain Physiological Essays* (1661); L.L., no. 439. See Boyle, *Works*, i. 222–3, where Riverius is mentioned.

[2] Lazare Rivière, 1589–1655, physician: A. Hirsch, *Biog. Lexikon der Aerzte*, 1929–35; L.L., nos. 2486–7.

[3] Probably Felix Wuertz, *c.* 1505–*c.* 1590, author of *Practica der Wundarzney*, 1563: ibid. Locke possessed a copy of an English translation, 1658: L.L., no. 3190.

[4] This year Easter Day fell on 7 April.

it comes off sweet, I find the remaining matter when dried retains its acidity, and will not any part of it so dissolve in [spirit of wine] as to pass through a filter, but will easily make a mash with it; but being set to digest it subsides, and leaves the upper part of [spirit of wine] clear; whether it should be so I know not.

## 225. [ELINOR PARRY later Mrs. Hawkshaw?] to LOCKE, [spring 1667?] (*222*, *232*)

B.L., MS. Locke c. 8, f. 65. Defective: strip torn off side, containing some words at end of letter. The grounds for the date are Locke's endorsement '67', which is not completely reliable, and the contents. This could perhaps be the letter mentioned in no. *222* that miscarried, but seems to be later than no. *222*.

my deare A:[1]

It is but fitt I should give my selfe a little pleasure and talke with you: and to doe it I have hid my self from the compane which is now heer to doe it, I am Come my Best—from the Countrey where I have bin this fortnite and my f:[2] att our return he mett yours with the inclosed. but you may guess I stared when there was none for me in answere to my Last, I have a 1000 questions to aske you. but dare not, are you Changed and doe you now think indifferently of the affection you have fram'd in my soule—you see my L:[3] a Chiding will out wheither I will or no I cannot Command my thoughts. but thay must apere out of the confidenc I have my Conserne for you is wellcome to you, prethy tell me is it not so / I doe beleeve it my L: and I must tell you I have breath'd your name often at my Lady Kenidys walkes. and as often Call'd you. but in vaine—my f has mett with a wife there if her father will give Her a good portion which I beleeve he will[4] she then will be my: S:[5] but It tis not yett proposed to her freinds, she is the second daughter and now heere att super. and I and she are very gracious to gether, with out any consideration of my selfe I further it, but when you Come in my thoughts I grone to death but all will be well, as you respect

[1] Atticus.

[2] Father: i.e. her brother John Parry.

[3] Probably Life, as in no. *222*.

[4] John Parry married Constance, daughter of Sir Richard Kennedy, knight, later second baronet: Leslie, *Ossory Clergy*, p. 19; G. E. C., *Baronetage*, iv. 196–7.

[5] Sister.

my Life make much of your self wish me with you. and mine shall meet agreeably with you my Best fare well

my Sister this weeke goes to wales for mony[1] derect yours to me at my—in Angeirs S:[2] burn this Letter tell no one of this I send you I shall if it goes forward send you word to London twill be news Lett me know all things that Conserns you thay Call fare well[a]

Endorsed by Locke: Scribelia 67

## 226. LOCKE to JOHN STRACHEY, 15 June [1667] (*215, 261*)

B.L., MS. Locke c. 24, ff. 244–5. Printed in King, pp. 26–7. Year from contents.

Jun. 15.

Sir

I beleive report hath increasd the ill news we have here. therefor to abate what possibly feare may have rumord I send you what is vouchd here for nearest the truth. The Dutch have burnd 7 of our ships in Chatham. (viz) the Royal James. Royal oake, London. Unity St Matthias. Charles 5th. and the Royal Charles which some say they have towed off, others that they have burnd. One man of warre of theirs was blown up and 3 others they say are stuck on the sands, the rest of their fleet is fallen downe out of the Medway into the Thames. Twas neither excesse of courage in them, nor want of courage in us that brought this losse upon us, (for when the English had powder and shott they fought like them selves and made the Dutch feele them) but whether it were fortune or fate or any thing else let time and tongues[b] tell you. for I professe I would not beleive what every mouth speakes.[3] Tis said this morning, the French fleet are seen off the Isle of weight. I have neither the gift nor heart to prosphesie. and since I remember you bought a new cloke in the hot weather I know you are apt enough

[a] *Parts of the rising letters of some further words follow.* [b] *Doubtful reading.*

[1] See p. 301, n. 1. [2] p. 298.

[3] The Dutch were in the Medway on 12 and 13 June. The *St. Matthias* is the *Mathias*: p. 286, n. 7. In all they burnt eight ships and towed away the *Royal Charles*. The resistance was from Upnor Castle: A. W. Tedder (Lord Tedder), *The Navy of the Restoration*, 1916, pp. 185–6.

to provide against a storme. Should I tell you that I beleive but halfe what men of credit and eye witnesses report you would thinke the world very wicked and foolish or me very credulous. Things and persons are the same here and goe on at the same rate they did before. and I amongst the rest desire to continue

Sir

your faithfull freind and servant

JL

I thinke the hulls of 3 or 4 of our great ships are savd being sunke to prevent their burning totally. Pray remember me to my Unkle and shew him this, for I beleive the report in the Country is worse. We are all quiet here but raiseing of forces apace

Address: For Mr John Strachy at Sutton Court

Endorsed by Locke: JL 15. Jun. *67*

## 227. Dr. David Thomas to Locke, 22 June [1667] (*212*, *229*)

B.L., MS. Locke c. 20, ff. 5–6. Year from contents.

Dear Freind

I had forgot in my last, to tell you that I have taken all the remainder of the materialls to Sarum,[1] but as yet have not opened any thing I brought hither; as thinkeing this not a time for Chymists and therefore cannot tell you what your part comes to: pray let me know whether Turner be payd for the glasses; and if you see James Tyrrell[2] pray pay him for mee—5s—6d I ow him, and I will account to you for it; pray send mee word whether the Dutch have quitted Sheerenesse or fortify it.[3] The militia in this county and hampsheere as well as farther westwards are in armes; and the prebends of winchester have each sent in an horse to Sir John Cloberrys troope[4] and all that towne hath contributed to the buying more horse

[1] Salisbury. The materials are probably chemical or medical preparations, the work of Locke, Thomas, and associates in Oxford, or the raw materials for them: no. *1681*.

[2] No. *343*.

[3] The Dutch captured the fort at Sheerness on 10 June.

[4] John Clobery of Bradstone, Devon, *c.* 1622–87; knighted 1660: Peter Le Neve, *Le Neve's Pedigrees of the Knights* [1660–1714], ed. G. W. Marshall (Harleian Soc., vol. viii, 1873), pp. 66–7; Henry Hyde, second earl of Clarendon, and S. Gale, *The History (of Winchester Cathedral)*, 1715, [pt. ii], pp. 45–7.

and he yesterday mustered betweene 30 and 40 horse. This in hast from

your[a]

Sarum. Jun. 22.

Address: For Dr Locke These Leave these with the Lord Ashleys porter at little Exceter house London

Postmark: IV 24

Endorsed by Locke: D. Thomas. 22 Jun 67

## 228. Locke to Robert Boyle, 12 November 1667 (224, 335)

Boyle, *Works*, 1744, v. 568.

Exeter-house, Nov. 12, 1667.

Honoured Sir,

I know you will pardon the silence of a man, that hath regard to your time, and is loth to importune you with insignificant compliments. And I will assume so much pride to myself, as to believe, that you would not think me so foolish as to venture the loss of your good opinion, or rob myself of the advantage of your letters, by a bare negligence, or for want of writing a few lines. This confidence of your favourable thoughts of me, and an unwillingness to trouble you with reading an empty letter, made me forbear sending to you, though I must confess, I have a long time wished for a fair opportunity to beg some communications from you, without which I shall be able to send but a very ill furnished letter to my friend in Germany.[1] I some time since received from him one of those Scarabei I formerly mentioned to you, which I guess to be the *Proscarabeus fœmina*[2] mentioned by Moufet, Cap. XXIII.[3] and would be very glad to know, whether Jacob Bobart,[4] or any other, have found that kind in England, for he very much commends the use of them in the disease I told you. The place I am at present in, and the remove I am like to make (for I believe I shall once more cross the seas before

[a] *Signature, etc., torn away.*

[1] Probably Schard.

[2] The oil beetle.

[3] Thomas Moffett (Moufetus, *D.N.B.*), *Insectorum sive Minimorum Animalium Theatrum*, 1634, L.L., no. 2059.

[4] Presumably the elder Bobart, 1599–1680, keeper of the Physic Garden in Oxford: *D.N.B.*

I settle) have kept me from attempting any farther experiments in chemistry, though I find my fingers still itch to be at it, and I have not met with any thing worthy your notice. I can only inform you, that I am acquainted with a young gentlewoman, who some years since had the misfortune to have one of her legs cut off, which yet very frequently does so pain her, that I have heard her more than once grievously complain of vehement torture, sometimes in the heel, sometimes in the instep, and at other times in the toes of her dead and buried foot; and she tells me, that sometimes being wakened by the pain, she has (before recollection) put her hand down to feel for the grieved part, as if her leg had not been cut off. I return you my humble thanks for that preparation of Helmont, and the other favours of your letter. The odoriferous oil of vitriol, if it be made by any other or shorter way than by digesting [spirit of wine] on [oil of vitriol], you will do me a favour to let me know it; for for such trials I may perhaps get conveniency this winter, and I would not willingly be idle, where I might be encouraged and directed by so kind and skilful a hand. But I ought not to be begging more, where I am so much indebted already, and have nothing to repay, but an assurance, that I am,

Honoured Sir,

your most humble, and most obedient servant,

JOHN LOCKE.

## *229.* DR. DAVID THOMAS to LOCKE, 29 November [1667] (*227*, *237*)

B.L., MS. Locke c. 20, ff. 9–10. Year from Locke's endorsement.

Deare Freind

The last word in my last was Scardys,[1] and for Ens [Veneris][2] I have cured two Quartans with it, the last of which it cured without any method, the patient mistakeing my directions, and the first time soe that he had noe manner of fitt. I shall this weeke try it in a Double Quartane which was first a quartan, The method I shall proceed is this. the fitt comes at 4 in the afternoone, in the morneing I give pill [Lunares] n 4 and two houres before the fitt

[1] Schard.

[2] 'Sublimation of equal Parts of the calcin'd Powder of Cyprus Vitriol, and of Sal Armoniack': *O.E.D.*, quoting Kersey, 1715.

I give a third part of the folowing Sweateing drinke ℞ Aq. Centaur. min lb i ent. [Veneris] ℈ij vel ℈ijss. the day of the next fit I give in the morneing Conserv Ros ʒi ent. ven gr xij and two houres before the time of the fit the other third part of the drinke and soe before the third fitt etc I doubt not the effect For this gott Scardys his antipodagricum. you shall have the originall of Helmonts febrifuge[1] by the next. I am

your true Freind
D THOMAS

Sarum Nov 29

Address: For Mr John Locke These Leave these with the Lord Ashleys porter at Little Exceter house in the Strand London

Postmark: D– –

Endorsed by Locke: D Thomas 29° Nov *67*

## 230. LOCKE to DE BRIOLAY DE BEAUPREAU, [1668] (*231*)

P.R.O., S.P. 30/24, bdle. 47, no. 2, f. 48. Draft. Covering letter for Locke's account of his treatment of Ashley in June and July 1668. For the treatment see Sir William Osler, as cited p. 284, n. 6 *ad fin.* Answered by no. *231*.

Fox Bourne identifies the person addressed as 'an eminent foreign physician, the Abbé de Briolay de Beaupreau, of Angers': i. 201 n. René de Briolay, abbot of SS. Serge et Bacchus 1629–71, the only *abbé* of the name traceable at Angers at this time (*Gallia Christiana*, xiv. 654), seems unlikely to have been a physician.

Hæc sunt ea quæ in hoc cùm ægro tùm casu minimè vulgari acciderunt observatu digna, qua licet singula summâ fide et qua potui brevitate recensui, optandum tamen esset, ut et tali argumento, et tanto lectore dignior contigisset historicus. Quamvis enim res ægrorum lugubres oratorum flosculos et pigmenta facile deesse

---

The following is an account of what has occurred worthy of note in the treatment of a patient and a case alike out of the common. I have recounted the particulars with complete fidelity and as briefly as I could; yet it was to be wished that a narrator could have been found who was worthier of such a theme and of so eminent a reader. For although the dismal affairs of invalids can easily dispense with flowers and ornaments of rhetoric, yet, when under-

---

[1] J. B. van Helmont, apparently 'De febribus', xiv. 9 (in *Opuscula*, 1707, pp. 139–40).

patiantur, nobilis tamen viri doctrinâ iuxta ac honore ornatissimi alloquia adeuntem deceret comptior et nitidior oratio. Et sane narrationem hanc crassiore filo contextam, et abscessui huic inconcinnè obvolutam, tibi Vir Illustrissime in manus tradere vix auderem, nisi sperandum foret, illum, qui animum altioribus studiis assuetum ad observationes medicas demittere dignatur, velle etiam ignoscere res medicas medicorum more tractanti, qui dummodo sanum integrumque sit corpus, de ornatu minus sunt soliciti, et dum valetudini prospiciunt parùm student elegantiæ. Quantum autem mea in scribendo imperitia defecerit, id omne supplebit et ægroti nobilitas et novitas exempli, cum in morbo reperias quod ingenio tuo placeat, in ægro quod conveniat dignitati, in utroque forsan quod mireris.

Si quid porro sit in hac observatione quod fusiùs explicari desideris (de futuro enim jam pene securi nihil omnino in posterum vel in ulcere vel in medicatione, quæ nulla est nisi qualis esse solet cauteriorum, immutatum iri confidimus) id, cum te velle intellexero, summo studio diligenterque curabo. Quippe mihi pergratum fuerit quodcunque officium quo ostendere possum quanta cum veneratione sum.

Endorsed by Locke: A Monsieur l'Abbé de Beaupreau a Angers. 68

---

taking to address one so notable for learning and holding such a high office, a more elegant and polished style would have been fitting. And indeed I would scarcely presume to put in your hands, most illustrious Sir, the coarsely woven fabric of speech in which the subject of this abscess is awkwardly wrapped, unless there were reason to hope that he who condescends to turn his mind from the higher studies to which it is accustomed to medical observations may also be willing to pardon one dealing with medical matters in the manner customary with physicians; for these so long as the body is sound and whole are not concerned for its adornment, and whilst providing for health have little care for elegance. Moreover any deficiency in my unskilled pen will be amply compensated by the rank of the patient as well as the novelty of the case, since you may find some intellectual interest in the malady, and in the patient what is agreeable to your own position, and in both possibly some matter for surprise.

Furthermore, if there should be anything in this account which you might desire to have explained more fully (for we now have hardly any fears for the future and are confident that there will be no subsequent change either in the ulcer or in its treatment, which is simply the usual kind of practice with cauteries) I will, when I know your wishes, devote all my care and diligence to fulfilling them. For nothing will give me greater pleasure than to perform any service by which I may show with what high respect I am . . .

## *231.* DE BRIOLAY DE BEAUPREAU to —— BROWNE, April 1669 (230, 250)

P.R.O., S.P. 30/24, bdle. 47, no. 2, ff. 20–1. Copy of a translation? Part on treatment of Ashley omitted here. I have failed to identify Browne. Answers no. 230.

Sir

I have read over and over with an extraordinary satisfaction the relation, you were pleased to send me, of my Lord Aschley's sicknes, and in the perusal of it, I can hardly determine my selfe, whether I ought to admire more in it the wise and timely proceedings of my Lords Physitians, or the exactnes of the author of the relation both for the elegancy of his stile, and his judicious remarkes with which he hath illustrated his narrative. I must needs say, though it be to my owne confusion, that I am not able to give Mr. Locke thanks with my owne penne for this favour, and his particular expressions of civility to my selfe towards the latter end of his relation; but must desire him to be contented to receive my just acknoledgment thereof by your mediation: which favour I hope you will not refuse me, because having ended my divinity studes in the yeare 1626 I have not since exercised my selfe in writing the Latin tongue: which upon this occasion would be absolutly necessary, for me in order to the compliance both with my duty and inclination therein

Now as for my Lords disease . . .

Your most humble servant
DE BRIOLAY DE BEAUPREAUX

Endorsed by the copyist: Monsieur de Beaupreaux his letter to Mr. Browne translated into English

Endorsed by Locke: *Beaupre* Apr. *69* Lord Ashleys case

Further endorsement by Locke: My Lord Ashleys case. *69*

## *232.* [ELINOR PARRY later Mrs. Hawkshaw?] to LOCKE, 11 April [1669] (*225, 1152*)

B.L., MS. Locke c. 8, f. 66. Year from Locke's endorsement.

Ap: the 11th

my dear A[1]

How hard is it for you to disguise your soule and hart to one that knows it soe well as I doe and how ill doth such grave councell

[1] Atticus.

becom your pen as you would perswade me to follow, as I know you Generous I could expect no less. but as I know you love me still in spight of al my follys / you have over acted the indifferent part. but twas onely to requite a seeming and mistaken letter too too unhappy since it hath brought us both never[a] to a neerer meeting. I beleeve in the next[b] world[b] sinc we will not in this, but take this truth as it realy is, I did not intend any disturbanc to you. and if you were neer me I could convinc you and for that of 2 years[1] I onely expressed. my dislike to your absenc an impatiency very incedent to love. I vow this was the sens of it, now I beg you to lett al unkind thoughts pass and if you are not better ingaged receve to your breast the kind affection of your Scribelia banish ill thoughts of Her, and consider a woman cannot be alwaise wise, and that she can no otherwise then—

now I entreat you to have a great care of your life as you regard mine. Take all the peac you can posible in the assuranc that I love you tenderly. that I value your Life beyond my owne and that I am certain I shall see you yett unless you take a greater care to be rid of me then to keep me, you se my A I doe not take either the way of a High passionate Humour or an indiffrent one, you may freely guess my proceeding is. beyond al that ever was in this case. but I owe it to my inclination[c] and my Justice to continew. yours S:[2]

I expect an answere to this be as free, and lett your soule dictate it, may you be Happy, as I wish you. truely truely and by al that is good / I am very soberly real, farewell I could with a vow tell you, you have bin faulty, but I forgive

Address: These For mr John Locke at little Exitor Howse on the Strand London

Postmark: AP 26

Endorsed by Locke: Scr 11° Apr. 69.

[a] *Or perhaps* neerer; *blotted and perhaps deleted.* [b] *MS.* next, sworld
[c] *Or* inclinations; *page torn.*

[1] Apparently the letters in 1667, especially no. *222.* [2] Scribelia.

## *233.* JOHN COCKSHUTT to LOCKE [about 1669?]

B.L., MS. Locke c. 6, ff. 193–4. The only means of dating the letter is the identification of the writer. The only traceable John Cockshutt who is likely to be the writer was born about 1641. He was admitted to Caius College, Cambridge, in 1657 and matriculated in 1658. He was admitted to Gray's Inn in 1661, but in his epitaph is associated with the Inner Temple. He travelled in Italy with Sir John Finch. He was closely associated with Dr. Henry More (no. *731*), who wrote his epitaph. He died on 9 March 1670. William Wycherley, presumably the dramatist (no. 407), is named in his epitaph as his executor: J. Venn, *Biog. Hist. of Gonville and Caius College*, 1897–1901, i. 400; *Conway Letters*, ed. M. H. Nicolson, 1930, pp. 304 (not mentioned by name), 307, 334; Manning and Bray, *Surrey*, ii. 574.

Locke is unlikely to have met Cockshutt before he came to London in 1667. In view of the division of the letters to Locke between the Lovelace Collection and the Shaftesbury papers, the letter is likely to be earlier than 29 August 1669.

Sir

I wish I could returne with my owne hands this Manuscript you were pleas'd to entrust me with, that such choice observations might not seeme to be so carelessly scatter'd. If I had beene at my owne liberty I would have deferr'd my journey in hopes of your most ingenious and obliging converse which you againe bestow'd upon me after I had so ungratefully neglected it, by which you have stopt a great many regretts, and blushes which would have flown in my face as often as my incivilitie (which every day grew more, and more beyond excuse) had return'd into my mind. If any service, or affection from me may deserve your freindshippe it shall be always endeavourd. I will not twice hazard the resputation you have given such a scandalous, and extravagant youth[1] as is

Sir

Your most obliged servant

JOHN COCKSHUTT

Saturday

Address: For Mr John Locke

[1] Extravagant here means erratic, not profuse: *O.E.D.* 'Youth' was an elastic term, and could be applied to a man more than twenty years old: see quotation of 1687 ibid. Here it is probably used playfully.

## 234. SIR ANTHONY ASHLEY COOPER, Baron Ashley, later first earl of Shaftesbury, to LOCKE, 29 August 1669 (*235*)

P.R.O., S.P. 30/24, bdle. 4, no. 175. Printed in Christie, *Shaftesbury*, ii. 35.

Wimborn Saint Gyles
August 29th 1669

Mr lock

I hear from my lady Rutland that my lord and his family resolve to be in london the beginning of next month and then finish the marriadge.[1] Soe that I think my Sonne may best come away to me and he shall from london meet his lady as they come up, soe that you must settle an intelligence both for the time and stages of their jorney. I have sent Mawrice[2] to you fully instructed and with another Jewell, I would have my Sonne present his lady with both together a day or two before he goes. my best blessing to my Sonne and respects to you. I rest

Sir
Your most affectionate freind
ASHLEY.

Address (written by an amanuensis?): For his verey worthy Friend Mr John Locke at Bellvoir Castle These

Endorsed by Locke: Lord Ashley[a] 29° Aug. 69

## 235. SIR ANTHONY ASHLEY COOPER, Baron Ashley, later first earl of Shaftesbury, to LOCKE, 6 September 1669 (*234, 236*)

P.R.O., S.P. 30/24, bdle. 4, no. 176. Printed, with wrong date 16 September, in Christie, *Shaftesbury*, ii. 36–7.

September the 6th 1669

Sir

yours of the second instant came to me by Mawrice last night; I am very well pleased with either of my ladyes[3] resolutions, soe

[a] *The words* to Mr Locke *and* Private *added by another writer.*

[1] Locke was now at Belvoir Castle in Leicestershire, the seat of the earl of Rutland, negotiating a marriage between the future second earl of Shaftesbury (p. 293, n. 7) and Lady Dorothy Manners (after 1632–98). Her parents were John Manners, 1604–79, eighth earl of Rutland 1641, and his wife Frances, 1613–71, daughter of Edward Montagu, first Baron Montagu of Boughton: *D.N.B.*; G. E. C.

[2] I have failed to identify him; apparently a servant. [3] Lady Rutland.

the marriadge be dispatcht[a] either at Belvoir or london; I never thouhgt of prescribing any place only begd itt mought receive noe delay, both to satisfy my Sonne and avoyd all uncertaintyes in an affair soe agreable to all my wishes. I have in this pacquett sent two letters to my lord and my lady Rutland to assure them I shall with my wife attend them att Belvoir the 21st of this month,[1] and to beg their pardons that I doe itt not sooner being by the assurance of their comming to london putt soe much back in the ordring my affaires; I have sent Mawrice to london to provide wedding clothes and all other things against that time. My best blessing to my dear Sonne, this letter must serve you both; and desire him to present my most affectionate service to my lady Dorothy, who has highly obliged me in all her carriadge in this affair, having donne all with soe much sweetness and prudence as gives me the assurance of the greatest happiness in her both to my self and family. I hope my Sonne has presented her with the two Jewells I sent him the diamond cross and pendants. My lord and lady Rutland my lord Ross[2] my lord Mountague and his brother the Attorney[3] have all ben most obligeing in this business, soe that it goes on with the most auspicious omens and I hope will be a great blessing to a dutifull sonne.

Sir

you have in the greatest concernes of my life ben so successively and prudently kind to me that it renders me eternally

your most affectionate and faithfull freind

ASHLEY

Address (written by an amanuensis?): For his very worthy Friend Mr John Locke at Belvoir Castle These

Endorsed by Locke: Lord Ashley.[b] 6° Sept. 69.

[a] *Doubtful ending.* [b] *The words* to Mr Locke *added by a second (?) writer.*

---

[1] The marriage ceremony took place on the 22nd.

[2] John Manners, 1638–1711; brother of Lady Dorothy; styled Lord Ros 1641–79; ninth earl, 1679, and first duke, 1703, of Rutland: *D.N.B.*

[3] Edward Montagu 1616–84, second Baron Montagu of Boughton 1644 (ibid.), and William Montagu, *c.* 1619–1706, attorney-general to Queen Catherine 1662–76 (ibid.); they were brothers of Lady Rutland.

## 236. SIR ANTHONY ASHLEY COOPER, Baron Ashley, later first earl of Shaftesbury, to LOCKE, 5 October 1669 (*235*, *247*)

P.R.O., S.P. 30/24, bdle. 4, no. 177. Printed in Christie, *Shaftesbury*, ii. 37.

London October 5th 1669

Mr lock

I shall not fayle to attend your good company att luton[1] wendesday night being the 13th instant with two coaches; and if they want a carriadge for their thinges I will send mine with two horses either to Boughton[2] or luton as you shall direct by the next post, tis much better then any sumpter. I have written to my lady Rutland that I shall not thinke of Salisbury hous[3] att that rate and besides since my comming to towne I am hott on a designe of building and hope that will satisfy my lady Dorothy to endure worse lodgings for a whyle. I am glad to hear they follow my business soe hard I hope to hear of whatt followes shortly; pray tell my Sonne if Mr Heymore[4] with his broken head should butt bye a bed half as long with Mrs Sarah his family would encreas and I hope as well of the Master. My best blessing to them both. I rest

Your most assured freind

ASHLEY

Address (written by an amanuensis?): For his much Esteemed Friend Mr John Locke at Belvoir Castle neare Grantham These Lincolneshire

Postmark: OC 6

Endorsed by Locke: L. *Ashley*. 5° Oct. *69*[a]

[a] *Added by another* (?) *writer* Private.

---

[1] On the road from London to Kettering. None of the families concerned in the Ashley marriage had a seat there.

[2] The seat of the bride's uncle, Lord Montagu of Boughton, 3 miles NE. of Kettering.

[3] On the south side of the Strand, to the west of the Savoy (about the site of Shell-Mex House): Wheatley, *London*.

[4] John Highmore, Lord Ashley's chaplain; matriculated at Oxford 1652; rector of Wimborne St. Giles 1658–84: Foster; Dorset Natural History and Archaeological Society, *Proceedings*, lxxv (1955), 120; Christie, *Shaftesbury*, ii. 215 n., 350–1.

## 237. Dr. David Thomas to Locke, 19 October 1669 (*229, 238*)

P.R.O., S.P. 30/24, bdle. 47, no. 2, ff. 27–8. Excerpts printed in Fox Bourne, i. 249–50.

Deare Freind

I glad you are returned to London and wish much joy to Mr Ashley. I would desire the favor of your company within a month and soe would Parthenice[1] About which time I beleeve wee shalbe married. Pray give me some advice concerneing wedding cloaths and the fashions. I entend to buy two suits one for rideing the other to be fine in on that day

Pray send mee $\frac{1}{4}$ of an hundred[2] of [antimony] 12l of it minerall. I supplyed with[a] [nitre] I have beene this halfe yeare attempting the Tinctura [b] Scardys and find it a d⟨ifficul⟩t[b] though I thinke ⟨not⟩[b] impossible matter. I hope to make ludus Paracelsi described by Helmont[3] in his last chap save two I thinke De Lithiasi and in appendix of the second volume of Glauber.[4] Compare the places.

I know what to say to your gelding but if you keepe him a little while till I canne see him (for I am now goeing out of towne) I will give you my resolution. I am

your true Freind
D. Thomas

[a] *Doubtful reading.* [b] *Page torn or worn.*

---

[1] Honor, sister of John Greenhill, the portrait-painter (p. 391, n. 1): pedigree in *Familiæ Minorum Gentium*, vol. iii (Harleian Society, vol. xxxix, 1895), p. 1137.

The name is one of a set of fanciful names used by Locke, Dr. and Mrs. Thomas, and other friends, at this time and for some time to come, probably in imitation of a French practice common a few years earlier. The names used by them were taken, with perhaps one exception, from Charles Sorel, *The Extravagant Shepherd: or, the History of the Shepherd Lysis. An Anti-romance*, translated by John Davies, 1653; 2nd ed., 1660 (p. 110, n. 1; citations here from the 2nd ed.). The names are Parthenice (above), Sorel, (i) 164, etc.; Hircan (p. 325; perhaps John Greenhill), (i) 92, 93, etc.; Lysis (p. 392; Nathaniel Hodges), throughout; Carmelin (p. 496; Locke), (i) 101, 103, etc.; Adrian (no. 554; Dr. Thomas), (i) 5, 6, etc. Musidore (p. 326; James Tyrrell) occurs as Muzedor and Musedorus, a dog, (i) 111; the source is more likely to be Sorel, *The Comical History of Francion* (1655), bk. v, where Musidorus is a threadbare poet (Parthenice is named casually in *Francion*, bk. v, p. 8; Carmeline, in the French original (ed. E. Colombey, 1858, pp. 243, 427), but in the English is 'the Carmelin' and 'the Carmelite': bk. vi, p. 14; bk. x, p. 28).

[2] Probably a hundredweight: *O.E.D.*

[3] J. B. van Helmont. The Ludus was a solvent for gall-stones: 'De Lithiasi', iii. 28; the reference here is to vii. 20 (*Opuscula*, 1707, pp. 17, 48). See further Partington, *Hist. of Chemistry*, ii. 226.

[4] J. R. Glauber: p. 147, n. 1. I have not identified the book.

Sarum
Oct. 19. 69.

Pray let mee know whethe the grypeing of the gutts[1] of which soe many dy in london and are sicke in the country be Cholera morbus[2] and what way of cure Sydnam[3] useth. my humble service to him. I shall have severall good ⟨tinct⟩ures[a] of [antimony] from crud. the vie . . . . s[a] a cementation of it with lime[b]

Address: For Mr John Locke These Leave these with the Lord Ashleys porter at Little Exceter house in the Strand London

Postmark: OC 20

Endorsed by Locke: D.T. 19 Oct. *69*
*Antimonium*
Tincture [antimony]

## *238.* DR. DAVID THOMAS to LOCKE, [*c.* 18 November 1669] (*237*, *278*)

P.R.O., S.P. 30/24, bdle. 47, no. 2, ff. 29–30. Excerpts printed in Fox Bourne, i. 250. Date from postmark and Locke's endorsement. The expansions of some of the chemical symbols are questionable.

Deare Freind

Parthenice is as well as ever I saw her, and I saw her since Hircan,[4] shee presents her service to you. Pray let me have at least 10 lb of hung[5] [antimony]. If your chymists wilbe Free, enquire for [aqua sulphuris?] which is [sulphide of copper?] of Helmont. I endeavoured to make the antispasmicum of the honorable,[6] which is an extract with [spirit of wine] from the caput mortuum flor the [distillation?] of [oil of vitriol] cum [spiritu vini] but I could procure no tincture. If you were here or could spend this winter a fortnight or 3 weekes in Sarum wee might it may be performe some good operations.

[a] *Page torn or worn.* [b] *Very doubtful reading. Locke notes in margin here* Tincture of [antimony].

[1] Colic.

[2] 'A disorder, attended with bilious diarrhoea, vomiting, stomach-ache, and cramps'; now distinguished as English or summer cholera, etc.: *O.E.D.*

[3] Thomas Sydenham, 1624–89, the physician: *D.N.B.* Locke had contributed a Latin poem to the second edition, 1668, of his *Methodus Curandi Febres*. Letters below, no. *295*, etc.

[4] Perhaps John Greenhill (p. 391, n. 1), but some other common friend of Locke and Thomas is possible. For the name see p. 324, n. 1.

[5] Hungarian.

[6] Robert Boyle. I have not found the formula in his *Works*.

The[a-] Tinctur [antimonij] in Harmans[b] pract. c.[1] ⟨de⟩[c] Podagra is good and will doe. I have formerly told you of my Balsom of [antimony] drawne over the tel . . .[d] from which I drew of the Sp Terebinth and put on Sp vini and have an excellent tinctur though it may be the balsom may be of more worth.[-a] If you find good Cinnabaris nativa buy mee a pound. Enquire an easy way to make [sulphur antimonij] album inflammabile.

This is enough to enquire for some time

I am

your faithfull Freind

D. THOMAS

you send me no news of Musidore[2]

Address: For mr John Locke These. Leave these with the Lord Ashleys porter at little Exceter house in the Strand London

Postmark: NO 19

Endorsed by Locke: D. Thomas Nov. 69

Further endorsement by Locke: *Antimonij* Tinctura et Bals

## 239. LOCKE to [MARGARET BE(A)VIS, later Mrs. Blomer?], [December 1669?] (*240*)

P.R.O., S.P. 30/24, bdle. 47, no. 2, f. 37. Fragmentary draft; some readings doubtful. Printed in Fox Bourne, i. 251–2. Apparently a draft for the antecedent of no. *240* ('hunts abrode for [discontents] in the concernments of others: and rather then want troubles' / 'their [own troubles without hunting] a broade for them in the concernements of others'; 'a femall virtuoso' / 'a shee vertuoso'); hence the date here assigned to it. The person for whom it was intended is determined by its connection with nos. *240* and 241.

Margaret Beavis was an attendant on Lady Northumberland. Probably in the summer of 1670 she married (Dr.) Thomas Blomer (p. 332, n. 2). She and Locke call one another brother and sister as terms of endearment, with no suggestion of kinship. Mr. Beavis (p. 338) may be her father or brother; and A. Beavis, Locke's 'governess' (no. *395*), her sister or sister-in-law ('Mrs. Beavis', Mrs. Ann Beavis, and Mr. Beavis, occur in Locke's Journal, 1679: 31 May, 3 June, 12 July; pp. 96, 97, 117). I cannot explain 'Dor' in Locke's

a–a *Marked by Locke for attention.* b *Doubtful reading.* c *MS.* dr*?*
d *Indecipherable.*

---

1 Johann Hartmann (1568–1631; *N.B.G.*; Partington, *Hist. of Chemistry*, ii. 177–8), *Praxis Chymiatrica*, 1633 and later editions. Locke owned copies of those of 1647 and 1663: L.L., nos. 1396, 1396a.

2 James Tyrrell. For the name see p. 324, n. 1.

note of the addressee of this letter, or BD in the subscription of no. *240*. References to Dr. and Mrs. Blomer occur in the Mapletoft correspondence (see no. 243, etc.) in *European Magazine*, 1788–9, in letters other than Locke's at xvi. 9, 98; see further no. 1121 n.

Lady Northumberland was Elizabeth, *c.* 1646–90, daughter of Thomas Wriothesley, fourth earl of Southampton (*D.N.B.*), and a half-sister of Rachel, Lady Russell; she was a first cousin of the present Lady Ashley. She married in 1662 Josceline Percy, eleventh earl of Northumberland (p. 338, n. 4), by whom she had a daughter Elizabeth; secondly, on 24 August 1673, Ralph Montagu, the future first duke of Montagu (p. 451, n. 3), a first cousin of Lady (Dorothy) Ashley: G. E. C. She was now wintering at Blois: no. 241, address; H.M.C., *Le Fleming MSS.*, p. 67.

have your sighs the vertue to blow away others tears or will your freind the more easily support his misfortune[1] because you droope under it. he that goes about to comfort an other with tears in his owne eys, is a professed dissembler with an ill looke, and at[a–] the same time[–a] by his owne example confuteing his discourse does but confirme the malady he pretends to cure, and is as ridiculously busy as a drunken preaching up temperance. the afflictions of others are but multiplied not lessened by the share we take in them and he that would remove the greif from an others minde by placing it in his owne does as much good as he that to save his neigbours when it is in a flame sets fire on his owne house, where by the mischeif is only made the greater and more uncapable of remedy. I would not be thought by this to perswade you to any indecency or ill nature, but to be wise and carefull of your quiet. Every ones share of misfortunes is heavy enough for his owne shoulders without borrowing lead of his neigbour and he is very fond of discontents that hunts abrode for them in the concernments of other: and rather then want troubles will adopt those of others. I am I know not how fallen into a grave discourse on a subject I thought not on at the begining of my letter but now I am in let me be in earnest with you. I cannot doe you a greater kindenesse then to arme you against all the accidents of life, and since one who has soe many freinds as you and soe reall a concernment for them lies very open to the assaults of fortune whilst a painfull sympathy shall entitle you to their crosses, tis fit you retire more within your self leave as little roome as you can for mishaps sufferance and

[a–a] *Interlined; the incidence might be after* looke

[1] It is not clear whether Locke alludes to a misfortune of his own or to some other source of grief for Mrs. Beavis. See further nos. *240*, 241, 243.

conclude that noe thing ought to afflict that does not really hurt you: I that earnestly wish you ⟨a⟩[a] long injoyment of perfect happynesse cannot but desire and advise that you should feele nothing at all of others misfortunes and as little as you can of your owne. then a great part will be saved of unprofitable pain and sorrow which doubly shortens our lives both by cuting of a good part of the remainder and makeing the present uselesse. By this time I hope I have sufficiently convinced you that a Philosopher of the R.S.[1] may hold discourse with a femall virtuoso without any great danger of Idlenesse and at least I am revenged of you for supposeing that my conversacon with you is losse of time, if you persist in this opinion you may perhaps in my next meet with an other sober lecture hopeing in the meane time that you will be the better for this, for we philosophers are always in earnest and always expect our rules advises should be followed whether they be pertinent or noe, and if mine be not seasonable now tis fortunes fault and let her answer for it, She may make them soe when shee pleases therefor pray lay ⟨the⟩m[b] up till the occasion serves. and then put them in practise

Endorsed by Locke: *J Lo* To *Dor 69*

## 240. [Margaret Beavis, later Mrs. Blomer] to Locke, 14/24 January 1670 (239, 241)

P.R.O., S.P. 30/24, bdle. 47, no. 20. Badly damaged; in the spellings of supplied words I have followed those of the fragments; some readings supplied from version in Fox Bourne, i. 253–6. The authorship is determined by no. 241, which answers it; it itself answers no. 239. It was probably written from Blois: p. 327 n.; the date is new style.

⟨Janu⟩ary[c] ⟨th⟩e 24th: $\frac{70}{69}$

My De⟨are⟩ brother:

I know not how you have got the start of mee, sin⟨ce⟩ you cannot bee better pleased with our ⟨e⟩pistolical converse then I am; When I call myselfe to an account for this, I presently finde my error to proceede from those many hours I dayly spen⟨d wit⟩h

[a] *MS.* an; *succeeding word altered.* [b] *Blotted.* [c] *All words, etc., in angle brackets, except as noted, are for damage.*

[1] Locke was elected a fellow of the Royal Society on 26 November 1668.

you, concluding that when I have do⟨ne so you⟩ can have nothing to reproach mee with ⟨for me⟩thinks you should heare all that I say and be⟨e⟩ in my company when I am in yours, and ⟨that⟩ there should bee something more then ordinary in those imaginary conferances which passe betwe⟨en⟩ us so frequently, for as your conversation was ⟨v⟩ery agreeable and usefull to mee in England, so I finde ⟨w⟩ayes to make you repeate the same discourses to mee here, where my greatest care is to keepe my selfe alive till wee meete where wee first begun that friendship which is above those hazards which useually attend distant friends, and as secure from any decay, as the best natur'd of us can wish. But all this while I forget to tell you how I come to bee ⟨so mu⟩ch in your debt. let ⟨the⟩ cause bee what it will, I am sure it is not ⟨un⟩kindness, and so ⟨l⟩ong my D:B:[1] you may pardon my silence. that which to mee seams most probable, is that when I reade your letters, I think I have sufficientl⟨y p⟩aid you ⟨in⟩ beleiveing all that you ⟨s⟩ay ⟨in⟩ them, and tha⟨t⟩ you are ⟨satisfied, beca⟩use I ⟨am so. b⟩ut upon second ⟨thoughts I b⟩lame ⟨myself a⟩nd a⟨m as⟩ full of repentance as you are of impatience; I pr⟨es⟩ently lay before mee the just rule of doeing as I would bee don by, and that sets us to rights againe; for while I derive my greatest content from my interest in you, and that I receive the perfectst accomplishment of all my wishes in the assurance you give mee of it, I shall alwayes think it fitt for mee to conclude that I deserve it best, when you have least reason to doubt of my being what I ought. and I know no expedient so proper towards the d⟨is⟩charge of my consciance as that which frees you from all uneasy apprehensions; for though railery represents mee delighted with your sufferings, I finde nothing more opposite to my nature. Therefore tis but justice in you (my Deare Brother)[a] to suppose (as you doe) that my practise will surely confute the disguised professions of being pleased with your complaints. When they a⟨re⟩ in earnest I shall never exercise any cru⟨el⟩ty which may not become the strictest and best grounded friendship, for I can with greate securi⟨t⟩y protest, that nature could not have given you a sister that would have been (in her concerne and vallew for you) halfe what I am, Though but an adopted one. This Subject is very insinuating, and such as I could say more on th⟨en⟩ is necessary,

[a] *Closing bracket supplied.*

---

[1] Dear Brother.

considering how few there are ⟨that⟩ have the ha⟨ppy⟩ness to understand ⟨one another better. let us therefore leave our super⟩-fluous protestations to new beginners, and give them, that, to s⟨et⟩ up with which wee doe not want, nor (if I mistake not) never shall. tis not that I meane by this, to lay aside the life of friendship and satisfie myselfe with the oppinion I have of it, that will not answer the felicity wee ayme at, there must bee constant demonstrations added to our confidence, for its most certainly the delightfull'st entertainement in the world, to bee often told what on is willing to heare, and to bee assured at all distances that those are our friends whom wee desire should bee so.

I will not so much as think that I begin to grow teadious, since you have checkt my saying something like it in my Last, but w⟨ith th⟩e impudence of a femall predicatrisse, talke o⟨n⟩ as if I said ⟨th⟩e finest things imaginable and as if you were bound in duty ⟨to he⟩are the impertinancys of a shee vertuoso, which you have en⟨courag⟩ed and entroduced into the society of the wisest amongst th⟨e w⟩itts. ⟨If⟩ the presbyterian praters, were as easily understood as wee women preachers, Their trade would soone faile them, for their ambiguitys are as necessary for their purpose, as our plaine doctrine is usefull to us, since the soundness of ours consists in honest simple truth, and that wee are not sure to bee in the right, till better judges approve what wee assert.

After all this faire weather you must expect a storme and I ⟨am⟩ resolved to winde u⟨p⟩ all in an use of ⟨reproof and ring you an angry peale⟩ at the close of the day.

Pray tell mee what you ⟨me⟩ane by the ⟨me⟩lan⟨ch⟩oly hints you give mee of your retireing out of the bussle of this ⟨l⟩ife; it perplexes mee to heare such dolefull Things come from you, and though there follows a seeming a⟨llay, and⟩ that you say it is only to adorne your letter and make ⟨it à la⟩ mode, yet it is not sufficient to warrent me from those ⟨distur⟩bances which I shall alwayes have, when-ever I suspect any ⟨dis⟩order in you.

I might beleive as you would have mee (th⟨ough⟩ you are in jest) if I did ⟨no⟩t know your care to preserve ⟨my qu⟩iet, and that you are so ⟨ex⟩traordinary a friend that you ⟨ra⟩ther chuse to suffer all your selfe, then lett mee share with ⟨you⟩. tis a considerate kindness in you (my D: ⟨B:) but⟩ that shall not serve your torne no more then it dos myne, I m⟨ust⟩ know more particularly then so, what makes you to quarel thus with the world, and whither

⟨the⟩ admonitions you give mee to prepare mee for the disappointments of it) bee occassioned by any accident which I doe not know. You give mee a greate-deale of ⟨good⟩ advice which I receive with a sense ⟨pr⟩oportionable to the benifit you designed mee in it, let mee know that it has noe relation to your selfe, and I will promis you to follow it as well as I can; but till I am sure of that, I must bee allow'd to feare that fortune intends mee a more severe tryal then that which you seeme to arme mee agai⟨nst⟩. I co⟨nf⟩esse wi⟨th yo⟩u. that wise persons will bee content with their ⟨owne troubles with⟩out hun⟨ting⟩ a broade for them in the concernements of others; b⟨ut⟩ still there are ⟨so⟩me thing⟨s⟩ which may very reasonably Touch them. nay and I know (tha⟨t⟩ even you) my Deare brother) with all your phylosophy) a⟨re⟩ as little able to defend your selfe against such defeat⟨es⟩ (as you are Liable to) as the verryest woman of us all. I know you have more then your share of tenderness, and pray bee not ashamed to owne it, till it m⟨akes⟩ you suffer for an ill cause.

I hope the l⟨at⟩e fir⟨ce⟩ cold has spar'd your Lungs, and that this warme season will prove favourable To you, and consequently To all those who would not have you die as long as they Live. I will consent you should talke of your death and burial, and bee as romantique as my beloved Author,[1] but you are To take notice that whatever you doe with your selfe in my absence, I shall require your appearance when I come To the place where I left you, but now I think on't that was in a dusty high way, for cleanlyness therefore and other ⟨con⟩veniencies, let it bee in the sober dark chamber in the Long galerry, or rather, in the pretty arbour, at the end of the fine garden[2] where wee have spent some hours as agreeably, as (I dare ⟨say⟩) either of us have don since, or shall doe till wee meete there (or some where else) againe;—

wee are here so Idle, that the best improvement wee can make of our time, is to resolve to spend it better hereafter. Cowleys wish[3] is often my contemplation, and when I goe about to fancy my selfe a happyness, I finde it noe where soe well ⟨suited to⟩ my inclinatio⟨n⟩ as in his ⟨choyce⟩, of ⟨a⟩ litle house, a Large gar⟨de⟩n, a few

[1] Locke's answer implies that he is not English. Perhaps Montaigne, referring to *Essayes*, I. xix (in Florio's translation). But Mrs. Beavis alludes perhaps to her fellow-traveller Thomas Blomer.

[2] Perhaps at Northumberland House in the Strand in London. In view of a passage in no. *256* Petworth is unlikely.

[3] Abraham Cowley, 'The Wish', verse 2, in *Works*, 1668, 'The Mistress', pp. 22–3.

friend⟨s⟩, and becaus⟨e⟩ I have not his learning I will lea⟨ve⟩ his many bookes, and take only his retire⟨men⟩t, to which I would add nothing, but some rambling groves, and there would I with the best of the⟨se⟩ few friends, ⟨pitty⟩ Those who flatter themselves with ⟨a⟩n opinion of being happyer then

Your faithfull ⟨and⟩ most affection⟨ate⟩

B D:[1]

our silenced Mr. Blo:[2] has often desired mee to present his service to my friend Mr. Locke and hee would not forgive mee if hee thought that this were the first time of his being mention'd.

I writ to you by Mr Gee[3] 4 or 5 dayes since

Sir C: B: your pupile[4] took this place ⟨in⟩[a] his way home 2 or 3 dayes after but I did not care to say any thing to you by so great a courtier.

Address: For Mr: Locke at Exeter house In the Strand These.

Endorsed by Locke: D 24° Jan $\frac{69}{70}$

## 241. Locke to Margaret Beavis, later Mrs. Blomer, 24 and 27 January 1670 (*240*, *248*)

B.M., Add. MS. 32094, ff. 222–3. Poor condition; badly worn, with some holes. Printed in *The Athenæum*, 9 February 1884, pp. 184–5. The letter is likely to have belonged at one time to George Harbin the nonjuror (1665?–1744; *D.N.B.*; Humfrey Wanley, *Diary*, ed. C. E. and R. C. Wright, Bibliog. Soc., 1966, index): B.M., Catalogue entry for Add. MSS. 32091–6. Harbin was sometime chaplain to Francis Turner, the nonjuring bishop of Ely (no. *820*) and was later an associate of Thomas Ken, the deprived bishop of Bath and Wells. He was perhaps acquainted with Mrs. Blomer and prob-

[a] *MS.* is

[1] Perhaps a combination of Beavis and 'Dor'.

[2] Thomas Blomer, d. 1723; of Cheshire; at Westminster School; admitted to Trinity College, Cambridge, Easter 1653; B.A. 1657; fellow 1658; M.A. 1660; D.D. 1671; prebendary of Canterbury 1673–1706; rector of All Hallows Bread Street 1681–1723: Venn. He is said in July 1673 to be chaplain to Sunderland (p. 218, n. 5): *Letters to Sir Joseph Williamson*, ed. W. D. Christie (Camden Soc., new ser. vols. viii, ix, 1874), i. 131. He may have been related to a man named Blomer, an upholsterer in Cornhill who was married to a half-sister of Sir John King (p. 497, n. 8): Le Neve, *Pedigrees*, p. 296. See also p. 207.

[3] Probably (Sir) Orlando Gee: *D.N.B.*, art. John Gee; E. B. De Fonblanque, *Annals of the House of Percy*, 1887, ii. 639, 641.

[4] Sir Charles Berkeley, K.B.: p. 189, n. 2.

ably with Mrs. Grigg (p. 334, n. 2; he probably owned also Ken's letter to Mrs. Grigg, 7 June 1691, B.M., Add. MS. 32095, f. 387).

The earlier part of no. 241 acknowledges the receipt of a lost letter of 10/20 January that was brought by Mr. Gee; the later part answers no. *240*.

Jan. 24. *69*

My dearest Sister

You must excuse me if beleiveing you an extraordinary person I expect extraordinary things of you. I am sure you have all the qualifications of an excellent ⟨fre⟩ind[a] and yet I would not have you concernd for the calamitys of those I thinke you have a ⟨kind⟩enesse[a] for. I desire you should be (as you are) very good natured: and yet I would forbid you sympathy, and a tender sense of others sorrows. I confesse ingeniously, I know not how in my owne thoughts, to reconcile these difficulties, and can hope only to finde it donne in your actions. and though I cannot tell the way[a] wherein this is to be brought about,[a] yet I doe[a] not much doubt of it whilst I consider you have a soule large enough to be capable of things that seeme to be at a very great distance, and which other people know not well how to put togeather. I allow therefor my sister to be as civill as kinde as gratefull as she please, but if that neare and affectionate relation she ownes brings any disquiet or trouble to my sister I shall not take it very kindely. I have twenty reasons to the same purpose to adde to the preachment you received from me just before the sealeing of your last letter of the 20th instant, which I forbeare to trouble you with here because methinks to a rationall creature one should not need to make use of arguments to perswade her to be happy, the first degree whereof is to be rid of trouble and vexation. If you will doe this, you at the same time cure me of all those misfortunes you apprehended might give occasion to my exhortations. I have noe cause (I thanke god) for melancholy thoughts but what you breed there. and all that I said in that letter, was designed to come before the ill news and to breake the force of that blow which I feard would fall too heavy on you. I knew how much you were concernd and would have beene glad to have prevented the surprise. and fenced you against that affliction. but I hope there needs now noe farther application to a wound: which the vigor of your[a] owne constitution ought before this time to have perfectly cured without leaveing either pain[a] ⟨o⟩r[a] scar. and truly it would be a shame to lye long under cure your self when you

[a] *Page torn or rubbed, making readings doubtful.*

can furnish others with such powerfull remedys at a distance. you have by the compassion, you have shewn, you are ready to afford me in any distresse, armed me against any misfortune, and[a] there are not many calamitys can happen to me, wherein the enjoyment of soe pleaseing a freindship will not make me thinke my self[b] happy and whilst you continue soe kinde, fortune can doe me little harme being never able to reach the tender and sensible part of my soule which you wholy possesse.

The gent: that brought me your letter was very punctuall in obeying your commands and deliverd it him self to me on Saturday last[1] the next day after his arrivall, The businesse you gave me in charge I have beene as carefull of as you could desire, and you could not suspect I would be cold in an affair wherein if it succeeded I was to reape soe great an advantage. I beleive therefor that things will be set agoeing according to your wishes, and I pray successe may attend it. the hand that is designd, and (if I mistake not) resolved to doe the feate is usually a very lucky one, and seldom fails in its attempts. you cannot imagin what satisfaction these hopes flatter me with, and I had little thoughts that I could have contributed soe much to my owne good fortune, Fild with these good thoughts and in a very gay humor I am just now goeing to Leadenhall street[2] with your letter: for there it is that I spend

[a] *Defective, perhaps erased.* [b] *Page torn, etc.*

---

[1] 22 January.

[2] This probably refers to Thomas Grigg, rector of St. Andrew's Undershaft, his wife Anne or Anna, and their son William. The rectory of St. Andrew's was near the church and presumably in Leadenhall Street: Strype's Stow, ii. 72.

Grigg was a Bristol man, perhaps a son of William Grigg, a member of the Bristol Common Council 1646–52 and 1654–61, and an opponent of James Nayler: A. B. Beaven, *Bristol Lists*, 1899, pp. 199–201, 293; p. 44, n. 1. He was born about 1638; matriculated from Trinity College, Oxford, in 1653; B.A. 1656; M.A. 1658; ordained 1661; B.D. 1666; chaplain to Humphrey Henchman, bishop of London (*D.N.B.*); rector of St. Andrew's Undershaft 1664; prebendary of St. Paul's 1666. He died on 2 September of this year and was buried on the 4th, Simon Patrick (ibid.) preaching his funeral sermon: Foster; Wood, *Fasti*, ii. 282–3; Fox Bourne, i. 260–1. He was probably a nephew of Peter Locke's wife: see genealogical table.

Mrs. Grigg was probably a sister of Margaret Beavis, later Mrs. Blomer: Mrs. Blomer mentions her 'sister Grigg': nos. *249*, *256*; and, alluding to her, calls her her sister: no. *248*; Mrs. Grigg mentions her 'brother and sister Blomer': no. *319*. These might be only terms of endearment, but she and her son William occasionally use a seal with the Beavis arms: nos. *533*, etc.; *1883*. In 1671 Dr. John Worthington, sometime Master of Jesus College, Cambridge (*D.N.B.*), considered proposing marriage to her: Worthington, *Diary*, etc., vol. ii, pt. ii (Chetham Soc., vol. cxiv, 1886), pp. 358, 379–80. She was a small woman: nos. *555*, *558*, *707*. Letters below.

Her son is William Grigg, d. 1726; admitted to Jesus College, Cambridge, 1684; matriculated 1685; B.A. 1689; M.A. 1697; D.D. 1717; fellow of Jesus 1696–1714; Master of Clare College 1713–26; etc.: Venn. Letters below.

the happyest howers I have in any company now in England and when I returne you shall know more of my minde and perhaps of other folkes too

I thinke I should scarce have beene drawne of from talking with you by any thing else but the good company I have beene with, who very well deserved to share in the good news of your health, and I made some conscience to delay the delivery of your wellcome letter and the satisfaction I was sure it would bring to them, which would have beene an injury, which judging by my self, I could not have expected easily to be forgiven. The Husband the wife and the child are all very well and I thinke very[a] happy. (Just here I was interrupted by an importunate visitant who kept me soe long in discourse that I lost the oportunity of the last post, and this letter sets out three days later then I intended[1] but to continue on wh⟨ere⟩[a] I left off) The good woman to whome I delivered your inclosed says she will in a few days answer it at large and hopes she shall have occasion soe to doe, in the meane time she bid me tell you that you may doe well to cosinder the affair in Brother Harbins hand[2] since he himself takes noe notice of it. And now haveing given you others commands, I must tell you from my self that you have found out the best way imaginable to excuse your silence. I account my self happyer in the confidence you owne and permitt me to have in our mutuall freindship, then the finest words in the world could make me. I am glad I can finde something in your letters better then the letters themselves, which I am sure to reade there what ever you write, and I can speake to my self in your name though you hold your peace. but yet though discourse be not any cause now, yet letters may well be the enterteinment[3] of our freindship. I presse not this as counting how many you are in my debt, and that there are severall (as you say) unanswerd. If I should come to a reconing with you and trade with you value for value one of yours pays for all mine. This consideration when I looke back, upon the ill stile, scraleing hand, and not very ornamentall black patches where

[a] *Page torn, etc.*

---

[1] The post for Paris at this time left London on Mondays and Thursdays: Chamberlayne, *Angliæ Notitia* (ed. 1674, ii. 243). The days this year fell on 24 and 27 January.

[2] I have failed to identify him. The parentage of George Harbin the nonjuror (p. 332 n.) is unknown.

[3] In the obsolete sense sustenance, support, etc.: *O.E.D.* Locke probably repeats the word from no. *240*, but uses it with a different meaning.

with this paper is set out, makes me begin (notwithstanding all the preference you give to scurvy manuscripts) to be afraid of Cowley and Mrs Philips)[1] for as for your beloved author[2] I never thought to rivall him more, then you to except him. I am abundantly satisfied in being your Brother, and am not much troubled he should be your gallant. But if you doe not thinke me as much the better Freind as he was the better talker: I shall conclude you are partiall to that side the water. But I have really noe suspition or quarrell to you at all in my owne name, only from Philander[3] I must tell you, that he a little grumbles at your commands, and takes it very much amisse that you could finde noe other imployment for him then to be an Executioner, and that a cruell one too, and ungratefull. an Executioner not only of the innocent, but the obleigeing the good and kinde. To shew his resignation he has obeyd your harsh commands, but with this profession that you will doe very ill to require often, such marks of his submission, which is the only one of all your orders that he shall obey with regrett. He says if you are delighted with such executions, you have those there that better deserve such treatment. whose ill lookes and language may if (there were noe other fault) excuse such kinde of usage, before the excellent and the innocent goe to wrack. pray endeavour to comply with him in this point. for I thinke veryly he never disputed the least intimation of your will till now, for when you lay such injunctions on him tis to be doubted whether he or the martyr be the greater sufferer. But I plead noe more for him, being soe very well securd of my owne good condition. the great satisfaction I enjoy in the great concearnment of your freindship makes me easily passe by all little accidents. I know you have reason in all you doe and desire, soe that I know not what I complain of but your absence. Pra⟨y take⟩[a] great care of yourself ⟨and of all those things⟩[a] that may make your life either ⟨long heal⟩thy[a] or pleasant. Tis a misfortune ⟨that⟩[a] I can contribute noe thing to it ⟨but⟩[a] my best wishes but this I doe with all the zeale concearne and sincerity of

My dearest sister
your most affectionate brother
J L

[a] *Page torn, etc.*

---

[1] Mrs. Katherine Philips, 1631–64, the poetess, 'the Matchless Orinda': *D.N.B.*
[2] p. 331 and n. 1.
[3] Perhaps Locke. Lady Masham used the name for him in 1685: no. *830*, etc. What follows may refer to Margaret's lost letter.

Jan. 27.

The old Dutchesse of Albemare has made hast after her husband taking leave of this world on sunday last.[1]

The Lady I once with the Doctor affronted in your chamber by saying noething to her, more then sufficiently revengd her self on me on Saturday last by comeing in and interrupting me in the midle of your letter.[2] all the courtly things she could say not makeing amends for the delay of one of your words. she is certainly my evill angell in a good shape, haveing more then once injurd me by appeareing unseasonably to interrupt either your writeing or my reading. Pr⟨ay⟩[a] tell me whether I were not best s⟨cr⟩atch[a3] her the next time we meet to prevent farther mischeif. but what ever comes on't I am resolved never to be silent in a womans company again, haveing sufferd soe much for this

Address: These present To Mrs Margaret Beavis at the Earle of Northumberlands at Blois.

Endorsed: A Letter of the famous Mr Locks[b]

## *242.* FRANCES MANNERS, countess of Rutland, to LOCKE, 31 January 1670 (245)

P.R.O., S.P. 30/24, bdle. 4, no. 185. Excerpts printed in Fox Bourne, i. 205–6.

Ja: 31, 69

Worthey Sir

I accknowledg the favour of your lettor, allthough an account most unwelcome, yet bless god, that, since it was not sollid she was so soone freed ofe; I am sure, I owe much to your care of my deare child, in this, and favours all manner of ways, for which, shall ever remaine

yours oblidged
FR

excuce this discomposed retorne, present my service with thankes to noble mr ashley for his kind conserne, give my blessing with

[a] *Page torn, etc.* [b] *Presumably written by George Harbin: see head-note.*

[1] George Monck, duke of Albemarle, died on 3 January of this year; his duchess followed him on the 23rd, as here stated.

[2] I have failed to identify her.

[3] It was a common belief that a bewitched person could obtain relief from spells by scratching the witch responsible until blood came: C. H. L'Estrange Ewen, *Witch Hunting and Witch Trials*, 1929, pp. 63–4.

all affectionat prayres to poore doll,[1] and on wedsenday shall (god permitting) write to her, in hope she may be able to read it and begin to follow the advices, which the lord of heaven inable her to doe, to his glorie and all our comforts

Address (written by an amanuensis): For Mr Locke at Exeter house in the Strande These London

Postmark: FE 2

Endorsed by Locke: Countesse of Rutland 31 Jan. $\frac{69}{70}$

## 243. Locke to Dr. John Mapletoft, 10 July 1670 (259)

*European Magazine*, xiv (1788), 321–2. John Mapletoft, 1631–1721; at Westminster School 1645; admitted to Trinity College, Cambridge, 1648; B.A. 1652; fellow of Trinity 1653–62; M.A. 1655. In 1658 he became tutor to Josceline Percy, the future eleventh earl of Northumberland; this was the beginning of a lasting connection with the Northumberland family. He now studied medicine, graduating M.D. of Cambridge in 1667, and was professor of physic at Gresham College from 1675 to 1679. In 1683 he took holy orders, and was vicar of St. Lawrence Jewry from 1686 until his death; he graduated D.D. of Cambridge in 1690: *D.N.B.* He was at present attending Arthur Capel, earl of Essex (no. 561), ambassador to Denmark from May to July. Lady Essex was a half-sister of Earl Josceline.

Exeter-House, 10th July, 70.

Sir,

Though by the good news I meet with here of your suddain returne to England,[2] and it is uncertain where this letter will find you, yet I cannot forbeare with all speed to acknowledg my late mistake, and to send you the good news of Mr. Beavis[3] happy recovery. I know the news of my Lord of Northumberland's death[4] hath given you but too much saddnesse, and you need not be disturbd with any new apprehension. But my too just fears could not be hinderd from speaking themselves to one who was not like to heare them with indifferency. And now the storme is over, if

[1] Her daughter Lady Dorothy Ashley.

[2] Sudden is used here in the obsolete anticipatory sense, shortly to come to pass: *O.E.D.* Essex had his last audience on 19/29 July.

[3] p. 326 n.

[4] Josceline Percy, b. 1644; eleventh earl of Northumberland 1668; died at Turin on 21/31 May of this year: G. E. C.; *The Despatches of William Perwich*, ed. M. B. Curran (Royal Hist. Soc., Camden 3rd ser., [vol. v], 1903), p. 92. Lady Northumberland was in Paris on her way to England on 8/18 June: Perwich, p. 94.

you will allow me to be merry with you, methinks you could not possibly have beene in any country, whither I could with soe much confidence have sent you bad tideings, as that you now are in, where every place soe abounds with antidotes against feare and sorrow; where every meale is designd to drowne the memory of all affliction, and each enterteinment is noe thing but an inundation of Nepenthe. Is it possible one could shrink at the approaches of a sad story, being garded and beset with an army of stout Dutch-bellied rummers?[1] All the doubt is, that you, like others of our profession,[2] were a little squemish towards your remedys, and did not take downe your dose as you ought to doe, and you did not very well accommodate yourself to the new way of takeing physick by the yard.[3] But, however, you were sparing in your cordialls. I hope the ill news I sent you, after that other which was deeply died in blacke, but, like fullers earth laid upon a stain, will, when tis rubd out again, carry away with it some of the former sully, and leave your minde clearer then before;[4] though perhaps it would have wrought more effectually, if it had been soaked in with a due proportion of Hockomear.[5] I know not whether my trifleing may not finde you in thoughts too serious for such a conversation. If it doe, I cannot tell whether it be not as convenient for you to bring your minde a little this way, as for me to joyne my condoling to your sadnesse. Any grave reflection of mine would, I thinke, doe you but little service; and for me to furnish out reasons against sorrow, or to imagin that you had not strength enough to cope with calamitys, were to be ignorant of Dr. Mapletoft, and forgett the person I am writing to. This same sober sadnesse lookes so ill in Mrs. Beavis,[6] and has don her soe little good, that I begin to be out of love with it in myself and all my freinds. Haveing, therefor, begun the correspondence with me, you must endure the disadvantages of a bad bargain, and content yourself with the ratleing of the beads, from one who (as you were assured in my last) had noe more valuable commoditys to barter with you. But, Sir, however I talke

[1] Denmark was regarded as a land of hard drinking: quotations in E. H. Sugden, *A Topographical Dictionary to the Works of Shakespeare*, etc., 1925; R. Molesworth, Viscount Molesworth, *An Account of Denmark*, 1694, pp. 90–1, 93.

[2] Medicine.

[3] For beer-glasses a yard long see *Notes and Queries*, 6th ser. (1880–5), especially v. 368, 456. Physic with Locke may mean medicines in general: so *Some Thoughts concerning Education*, § 29; but the word was commonly used in a specific sense, to mean a purge, and that may be intended here.

[4] There may be an error in transcription in this sentence.

[5] p. 268.

[6] Margaret, the future Mrs. Blomer.

idle upon other occasions, I am very serious and in earnest, when I assure you that I am,

Sir,

Your very humble and obedient Servant,

J. LOCKE.

Dr. Sydenham desires to be kindly remembered to you.

Mrs. Beavis is not yet got soe far either from her French melancholy or English malady, as to dare to trust herself with those thoughts which a letter to you must needs produce in her. This is that only which withholds her hand. You know how soft she is in this part of her soule, too apt to receive and retain such uneasy impressions, toward the defaceing whereof time has hitherto don but litle. But as if they were of lasting monumentall marble, time, as he uses to doe with such peices, is able yet only to strow over those deaths heads she delights to pore on with coverings of dust, which every sigh of her's blows off, and the least reflection that way, brings into full view a croud of melancholy objects. Knowing therefor her temper as you doe, and how apt she is to relaps, I doubt not but you will be glad that she begins to have any care of herself, and is at last soe far concearned for her owne quiet, as to shun occasions which may recall those sorrows under which she has suffered but toe long and too much already.

Address: For Dr. John Mapletoft, at the Right Honourable the Lord Ambasadors at Copenhagen.

## 244. THOMAS BLOMER to LOCKE, [August 1670]

P.R.O., S.P. 30/24, bdle. 4, no. 192. A strip down the right margin of the first page is lost; this affects some words. Quoted in Fox Bourne, i. 258. Date from Locke's endorsement. For the writer see p. 332, n. 2.

Dear Sir

A man that knows how necessary yow are both to yo⟨ur⟩[a] selfe and others must either resolve to bee though⟨t⟩[a] impudent, or bring very good reason why hee us⟨es⟩[a] yow thus; but I hope yow will not dispense with one w⟨ho⟩[a] is of soe tender a conscience, that hee thinkes hee is bound to act against the Laws of modesty herei⟨n.⟩[a] to say the truth yow have made it fit and lawfull ⟨for⟩[a] mee to trouble yow, and it is more ingenuous and pardona⟨ble⟩[a] to pay my acknowledgments rudely, then altogethe⟨r⟩[a] to conceale

[a] *Page torn or rubbed.*

and disowne them, and yow must either renounce your courtesy, or find out some more ungratefull persons to bestow it on, if yow would avoid the inconvenience of such returnes; yow know wee are in an honest ignorant place[1] that does not suggest much of that yow call complement at London, and therefore yow must take this, as it is, for well meant and good natur'd simplicity, for I should bee loath to ingage with yow in the elegant and florid way, besides yow would bee very injurious to your kindnes, and seeme too much a stranger to what yow deserve of mee, to imagine that I aime at any thing herein but the sincere and hearty expression of my just sentiments; yow ⟨may⟩[a] take what course yow please to secure your selfe ⟨f⟩rom[a] such a mischiefe for the future by silence, or prohibition, or with holding your favours, but I'le assure yow this is a trespasse hath no malice for its principle, and which I could not forbeare committing after I had well consider'd the hainousnes of it and that not without pitying yow who were to suffer so much by it; yet sure I cannot forfiet your friendship by all that is uncivill and disobliging herein when it was chiefely undertaken to give yow an account of that charge yow intrusted mee with, the share your dearest Sister[2] hath in it must needs attone for all the rest, for I know yow can indure any thing that brings yow news of her amidst an heap of impertinence; be pleasd to understand then that in order to her health she is enterd into a course of gluttony, for shee is never well but when shee is eating, if yow were here now to write a bill for the kitchen and make father Williams[3] her apothecary, to prescribe a dish of fruit to be taken just before shee goes to bed, and then direct that a certaine composition calld a fricacy should bee ready for her breakfast, shee would say yow were a very skillfull man and knew what was good for her disease; so much hath the air of this countrey inlargd the dimensions of her stomack, and made her very formidable to cold chickens and hot ones too, when her appetite is in a passion, and to say truth the sight of any edible thing does provoke it as much as a Cat does Mrs Rooper; And now, Doctor, before I dismisse yow I must acquaint yow that my Lady[4]

[a] *Page torn or rubbed.*

[1] Probably Petworth, Lady Northumberland's seat in Sussex: no. *248*, etc.

[2] Margaret Beavis. Locke's endorsement to no. *249* indicates that she was married to Blomer by 23 September; the present letter suggests that she was married to him already.

[3] Probably a member of the Northumberland household.

[4] Lady Northumberland.

hath bin pleas'd to recommend my concernes to the patronage of my Lord Ashley, who hath undertaken to bring her requests done unt⟨o⟩[a] her by the next faire wind, or windfall, of opportunit⟨y⟩,[a] but a person that is full of greater affaires may easily let slip so small a matter, and therefore I shall venture to prefer my little interest and recommend the successe of it to your conduct, which will very much need such a remembran⟨ce⟩:[b] my Lady I thinke mention'd onely Windsor, Eaton and Westminster, but it is not fit his Lordship shu'd bee confin'd to places, which are almost all alike where the advant⟨age⟩[a] is equall, especially if they bee within the reach of your conversation, I am your ⟨most affectionate friend and faithfull servant T. BLOMER⟩.[a]

Address: These For Mr Locke at Exceter house in the Strand London.
Endorsed by Locke: T. Blomer Aug. *70*.

## 245. LOCKE to FRANCES MANNERS, countess of Rutland, 23 August 1670 (*242*, *246*)

H.M.C., *Rutland MSS.* ii. 20. Probably answered by no. *246*. Text not available at present.

## *246*. FRANCES MANNERS, countess of Rutland, to LOCKE, 27 August 1670 (245, *251*)

P.R.O., S.P. 30/24, bdle. 4, no. 190. Part printed in Fox Bourne, i. 206. Apparently answer to no. 245.

aug: 27

worthey sir

I am much oblidged to you, for representing unwelcome tidings, with all advantages, to draw consolations from, and blessed be god, her owne hand this day, gives me assurances that your hopes weare not in vaine, the lord preserve her and reward your compassionat cares for her, and so sir, having another discomposur upon me at present, hast to say with ten thousands of thankes, that I am, your faithfull servante

FR

Address: For mr lock
Endorsed by Locke: Countesse of Rutland 27. Aug. *70*

[a] *Page torn.* [b] *End of line.*

## 247. Sir Anthony Ashley Cooper, Baron Ashley, later first earl of Shaftesbury, to Locke, 29 August 1670 (*236*, *297*)

P.R.O., S.P. 30/24, bdle. 4, no. 191. Written by an amanuensis; signed by Ashley. Printed in Christie, *Shaftesbury*, ii. 40–1, with year as 1671; excerpt in Fox Bourne, i. 208–9, also as 1671. Christie and Fox Bourne evidently assumed that 'the little boy' refers specifically to the future third earl of Shaftesbury, who was born on 26 February 1671; Ashley may allude, however, to Lady Dorothy's pregnancy (Hans-in-kelder). The letter for Buckingham fits well in 1670; while nothing is known that makes 1671 impossible for it, the mention of the secretary is against it.

August 29th 70

Mr Lock

I have received yours of the 27th instant with the most welcome news both to me and my Sone of my wives my Lady Dorothys and the little boys Health, we pray Hartily for the Continueing of it unto them all three, but that you may not think us of John Dees humour we wish well to you and mrs Bedles[1] and are content you should be blest and mutiply to if you please, for I am sure that, would be no prodigie but a good omen, Especially to our partes, that may well hope dry grownde might increase as well as dry bones. I hope my wife hath received two letters lately from me, soe that this to you shall excuse me untill next post, I must desire your trouble to dispose of these severall letters according unto theire direction, that for the Duke of Buckingham[2] must be left at one of the secretarys, the letter to my Lord Mountacue[3] I have left open, that when my Lady Dorothy hath perused that, and the letter with it she may seale it up and send it away. I rest

Sir

Your very affectionate friend to serve you

Ashley

Address: For your selfe.

Endorsed by Locke: Lord Ashley 29° Aug. *70*

[1] p. 292 n.

[2] George Villiers, 1628–87; second duke of Buckingham 1628: *D.N.B.* He was sent about the beginning of August on a mission of compliment to Louis XIV and returned in September, arriving at Dover on the 10th. The secretaries here are the two secretaries of state.

[3] The second Baron Montagu of Boughton, Lady Dorothy's uncle: p. 322, n. 3.

## *248.* MRS. MARGARET BLOMER, formerly Beavis, to LOCKE, 12 September 1670 (241, *249*)

P.R.O., S.P. 30/24, bdle. 47, no. 9. Excerpts printed in Fox Bourne, i. 261–2.

My Deare brother

You cannot accuse mee of unkindnes without being guilty of it your selfe, for if at any time I doe any thing that Lookes like it, I assure you it is more my Trouble then yours, Therfore pray forbeare thinking worse of mee then I deserve, since you can hardly bee just if you doe not think my friendship (for you) unalterable, For as I have formerly profes't, noe condition shall ever make mee Loose one graine of that esteeme and real kindness which you have so well deserved from mee: methinks I say more then is necessary upon this score, for I would faine live so with you (my deare brother) as never to Suspect onanothe⟨r⟩,[a] and if I know my owne heart, I am never better pleased, then when I can assure my selfe that Mr. Locke (is not only my best brother) but my sure friend. beleive this Truth and you will never mistake my silence for a willfull neglect, nor harbour any oppinion of mee, that would not become a friend of the first rank. tis fitt I should thank you for your charitable care of the poore little dis⟨c⟩onsolate[a] widow;[1] Though I know you doe not expect it, but as it is the best part of payment it must not bee omitted; the maine reward is to come from him who has given you a mind above other men. how much the Losse of this good man has afflicted mee, is easier for you to imagin then for mee to expr⟨ess.⟩[a] I hope god will support my sister under This severe stroake and make her able To goe through this deplorable change of her condition, I doubt not but shee is The object of all good peoples compassio⟨n⟩[a] (who know her, and what shee has lately Lost) what shee is like to suffer (as to the Provissi⟨o⟩ns[a] of this life) would have be⟨en⟩[a] in a greate measure repaird, ⟨had⟩[a] Mr. Blomer prov'd as successefull ⟨in hi⟩s[a] request to my Lord of London[2] ⟨as hi⟩s[a] designe in it was hearty and kind ⟨to⟩[a] my sister. If there bee yet any hopes of it and that you think his goeing To the Bishop may bee of any significancy. the first summons will produce him. My Lady[3] has not been well since shee

[a] *Page torn.*

---

[1] Mrs. Grigg; Thomas Grigg died on 2 September: p. 334, n. 2.

[2] Humphrey Henchman the bishop: ibid.

[3] Lady Northumberland.

came into the Country. if shee dos not mend, a few weekes may bring us into your ⟨neig⟩hbourhood[a] ag⟨ain⟩[a] and if that doe not prove effectual, I doubt there will bee a necessity for our goeing againe into france—which I cannot think of with any pleasure, in the meane time prepare your selfe against next spring and remember you are to goe with us. Doctor Mapletoft is now here and Laments hee could not see you, but you may probably meete within 8 or 10 dayes, and by him you shall heare againe from

Your most affectionate sister

M: B:

Petworth the 12th September 1670

Endorsed by Locke: M. B. 12° Sept *70*

## *249.* Mrs. Margaret Blomer, formerly Beavis, to Locke, 23 September 1670 (*248*, *256*)

P.R.O., S.P. 30/24, bdle. 47, no. 10. Printed without the postscript in Fox Bourne, i. 263.

Petworth the 23d: september 1670

My Deare Brother

If all the kind things you say in your letter bee not sufficient to make mee amends for the alarme you give mee at the conclusion of it, you may easily imagin (without lessening the vallue I have for your friendship) what my concerne is when you so plainely tell mee that tis france must give you life; this declaration from a man not accu⟨s⟩tomed[a] to represent things worse then they ⟨ar⟩e,[a] cannot but create such apprehensions ⟨in⟩[a] mee, as must of necessity bee very uneasy ⟨and⟩[a] Lasting.[1] I have pleased my selfe with ⟨the⟩[a] Thoughts of goeing to London (upon ⟨n⟩o[a] other account Then that of being within ⟨r⟩each[a] of you) for I neede not tell you that my fondnes for the towne is not greate, and yet I would willingly have endured all the noyse and clutter of so confused a masse to bee where part of my time might bee spent with you; but if that satisfaction faile mee, I shall recall my former opinion that nothing is lasting that pleases, bee it never so allowable, t'is a severe decree

[a] *Page torn.*

[1] Locke had apparently engaged to accompany Lady Northumberland to France in spring 1671: no. *248*.

that will not suffer us to enjoye that Long which wee once begin to delight in.

I Confesse my Deare Brother t'will bee hard for mee to part with that friendship, which I soe heartily bespoake of you (not for my selfe alone) but for all those whom Duty and nature should oblige mee to wish well unt⟨o⟩,[a] I can never say enough of this, till you and I, (and one more) meete, which I hope may bee about a month hence, and then wee intend to perswade you to live longer, for I assure you, you have here two friends that would bee glad you would never forsake them, they have laid a trap for you, and you must helpe them to catch you in it, (upon this confidence) that if our wishes prevaile you shall not think your selfe a prisoner nor the trap wee threaten you with an uneasy tenniment; there shall bee nothing in it but what will study to divert and preserve you; but all this is too obsc⟨u⟩re,[a] and nothing but an entervieu ⟨can⟩[a] cleere it. in the meane time take ca⟨re of⟩[a] your selfe, I know the little Sparke,[1] will fo⟨r⟩[a] the Publique good assist you with her's.

My Deare brother I long to see you, but my greatest impatience will bee to heare that your cough is abated, I can say nothing of my owne health till yours is better: farwell I am

Your most affectionate sister.

M: B:

Mr. Blomer desires you would deliver this letter to Dr Pearson[2] with your owne hand if possible, it may bee very usefull To my sister Grigg, for hee has a greate interest ⟨in⟩[a] the Bishop of London,[3] you may speake freely to him. Mr Theophilos Pearson,[4] his[b] brother,[b] hosier in the new exchange at the signe of the Squerel, will Direct you to the Doctors Lodgings, and tell you what time you may meete with him at home.

Address: For Mr: Locke at Little Exceter-house, In the strand London:
Endorsed by Locke: Mrs Blomer 23 Sept. *70*

[a] *Page torn.* [b] *Words interlined; punctuation supplied.*

[1] Probably a woman member of Lord Ashley's household. Probably not 'our little spark' of no. *256*, who seems to be a child; perhaps the 'little femme' mentioned in no. *256*, etc.

[2] Dr. John Pearson: p. 193, n. 6. [3] Henchman: p. 344.

[4] He died at Downham Market, Norfolk, in 1696: J. Pearson, *Minor Theological Works*, ed. E. Churton, 1844, vol. i, pp. xv–xvi. The New Exchange was on the south side of the Strand, to the west of Salisbury House.

## 250. LOCKE to DE BRIOLAY DE BEAUPREAU, 20 January 1671 (*231*)

P.R.O., S.P. 30/24, bdle. 47, no. 2, ff. 1–2. Draft. The final section appears to be for a covering letter from Ashley to Briolay.

Secundus jam agitur annus ex quo Illustriss Viri Domni Ashley Baronis de Winborne St Ægidii mirandus ille abscessus humorque ad ⟨eam⟩[a] sanitatem deductus est quam etsi omni ⟨modo⟩[b] perfectam non dixeris nihil tamen est de quo nobiliss. vir conqueratur, cum modico luis nec molesti ulceris fluxu quotquot in corpore uspiam enascunt noxii[c] humores continuo per apertam hanc et quasi a natura destinatam sentinam eliminantur et futuri optime præcaventur morbi. Qualis enim erat rerum status cum ad te Vir biennium abhinc literas dederim idem plane ad hunc usque diem immutatus perstat. Cum enim ex præpropera nimis aditus exclusione recrudesceret iterum intus malum metusque esset ne si ulcus consolidare et exterius orificium coalescere paterentur, ex levissima intus relicta labe, (si qua tenuissima pars adhuc non esset sincera) nova fieret puris et saniei collectio, tam felicem non facile inventura exitum, consultius visum est, tubulo argenteo ad ipsum mali fontem munire aditum, et confluentibus vel illic enascentibus sordibus paratum semper transitum præbere. huic consilio nec defuit ratio nec successus. Tubus ille argenteus qui circa medium

[a] *MS.* eum statum deductus est *del.* [b] *MS.* mode. [c] *Substituted for* in corpore

---

It is now the second year since that remarkable abscess and humoral trouble of the illustrious Lord Ashley, Baron of Wimborne St. Giles, was brought to a state of healthiness which one could not call altogether complete, but which leaves the noble lord with nothing to complain of. There is moderate exudation and discharge from the ulcer, which gives him no trouble; by this means any noxious humours that arise anywhere in the body are forthwith got rid of through this open drain, designed as it were by nature, so providing an excellent precaution against future ailments. The state of things has in fact remained the same up to the present day as it was when I wrote to you, excellent Sir, two years ago. For at one time an over-hasty closure of the approach was resulting in a recrudescence of the internal trouble, and there was a fear that if the ulcer were allowed to heal up and the external orifice to become closed there might be some very slight trace of corruption left inside, supposing that some very small part were not yet sound, and that this might produce a fresh collection of pus and corrupt matter, which might not easily find such a fortunate outlet; it therefore seemed wiser to secure access to the actual source of the trouble with a silver tube, and thus to provide a permanent passage for any foul matter that might collect or arise there; this plan proved reasonable and successful. The silver tube, an

Sept. anno 1668 sesqui unciam longus in ulcus immissus est ab eo tempore continuo gestavit sine molestia sive incommodo. alternis solùm diebus ad eluendas sordes extrahitur, et vino ⟨c⟩alido[a] elotus, iterum reponitur, nec omnino differt hoc ulcus a simplici cont⟨us⟩o[b] nisi sede et profunditate qua etsi subjectis vivisque visceribus minari videatur, nihil tamen incommodi jam biennium expertus sensit nobiliss patiens nisi quod hac æstate ex motu nimio vel indebita forte corporis flexura dum se in sphæresterio exerceret vel occasu forsan aliquo parum observato, tubulus loco suo motus et parum circumactus cuspide quæ declivis esse solet sursum versu curvaturâ suâ infernas tenerasque carnes læserat, unde secutus est dolor sanguinisque una aut altera gutta effluentem ichorum tinxerat. Sed fistula argentea loco suo mox restituta ægrotantis dolorem omnem metusque nostros protinus abstulit. hoc quicquid est incommodi semel tantum idque casu in duorum[c] annorum[c] spatio jam passus est. Enimvero[d] etsi ambulet equitet sphæresterio se exerceat omniaque vitae munia more solito promptus et alacer obeat. et hujusmodi noxas a fistulæ diffusione solum expectandas in posterum posse caveri speramus. adeo ut ulcus hoc videatur solum fontanella loco inustitato sita quæ cum vulgares illas brachio-

[a] *Blotted.* [b] *Blotted; substituted for* fonticulo*?* [c] *Carelessly altered from* duobus annis*; the word* spatio *is interlined.* [d] *MS.* Nv.

---

inch and a half long, which was inserted in the ulcer about the middle of September 1668, has been worn ever since then without trouble or inconvenience; all that is done is to withdraw it every other day in order to clear it of any foul matter, after which it is washed out with hot wine and replaced. This ulcer differs in no way from a simple contusion except for its position and depth, owing to which it appears to threaten the healthy flesh lying beneath it; yet the noble patient has experienced no inconvenience during these two years, except that last summer, as a result of excessive movement or perhaps an undue bending of the body whilst playing tennis or possibly some fall which escaped observation, the tube was shifted in its seating and slightly twisted round; the point of it, which is usually inclined downwards, was turned upwards, and being thus bent it injured the tender internal flesh; this was followed by pain, and the watery discharge was stained with one or two drops of blood. But the silver pipe was soon restored to its position, and the patient's suffering and our own fears were immediately relieved. The noble lord has only once suffered this inconvenience, such as it is, in the course of two years, and that by accident, though he walks, rides, plays tennis, and performs all the functions of daily life as usual in a brisk and active manner. These kind of injuries, which are to be expected only from displacement of the pipe, we hope can be guarded against for the future. This ulcer seems, in fact, simply like a fontanel in an unusual situation; it gives hardly as much

rum molestia vix æquet, fluxu parum excedit, usu tamen et beneficio longe superat. Nam A quo primum sisti cæpit morbus et evacuatio quod intus collectum erat putridi humoris spem fecit salutis nihil omnino passus est adversæ valetudinis sed redeunti[a] sensim Vultui oculisque vigore, roboreque nervis restituto, factus est quam per multos annos ante insultum[b] morbi[b] fuerat habilior longe et vegetior, nec jam diutius imbecilitas ventriculi aut cruditates vel icterici languores, terrent omnino aut affligunt. Verum tam prospera et secura usus est valetudine, ut ne semel quidem vel levissimo carthartico vel quovis alio medicamento ipsi opus fuerit. Hunc finem habuit humor ille casusque siquis alius in praxi medicinæ admirandus. Cujus ego fidam ⟨hanc⟩[c] tibi Ill. etsi minime ornatam transmitto narrationem, quam te eodem quo priora nostra hac de re legeras, animi candore admissurum non dubito. quanquam vix auderem tam incultam et proletaria oratione exaratam historiolam tanti viri oculis judicioque subjicere. nisi maxime dicere putarem etiam nobili viro de rebus philosophicis sciscitanti de rebus ipsis nude et aperte respondere.

Servus tuus quam humillimus

J L

[a] *Or* redeuntibus; *last letters perhaps deleted.* [b] *MS.* insultum morbo, *with* infestum morbi *interlined above it.* [c] *MS.* hac

trouble as those commonly inserted in the arms and discharges very little more, whilst it far surpasses them in its useful and beneficial effects. For ever since the malady was first checked and the evacuation of the putrid humour collected internally gave hopes of a cure he has suffered no ill health at all; on the contrary, vigour has gradually returned to his expression and his eyes, his muscles have recovered their strength, and he has become far more brisk and active than he had been for many years before the inimical onset of the disease. He is no longer frightened or afflicted by weakness of the stomach, or attacks of indigestion, or jaundice with periods of lassitude, but has enjoyed such good and sound health that he has not once needed to use even the mildest purgative or any other medicine. Such has been the end of this humoral affection and of a case as remarkable as any in medical practice. I send you this faithful if unadorned account of it, which I have no doubt that you will accept as kind-heartedly as you did our previous reports on the subject when you read them. At the same time I should hardly have presumed to submit a story so unpolished and expressed in such vulgar terms to the eyes and judgement of so eminent a person if I had not thought it entirely becoming to reply in plain and straightforward terms to the inquiries on scientific matters even of one so celebrated as yourself.

Your most obedient and humble servant

J L

20 Jan. $7\frac{0}{1}$

Vna cum hisce meis literis omni officio plenis (Tibi Vir Illustrisse) tradentur aliæ ab eodem authore conscriptæ qui affectus mei historiam literis a se mandatam jam olim tibi perferendam curavit. Cujus (cum a studio rerum medicarum non sit alienus)[a] ab eo usque tempore et in observando diligentia et in narrando fides efficiet ut nequid hoc in casu scitu dignum vel negligentia vel inscitia prætermissum desideres. Maxime enim mihi cavendum censui ut viro tanto tam amice juxta ac docte valetudini meæ pridem consulenti et jam denuo de eadem officiose quaerenti omnia quæ hactenus acciderunt quam ⟨diligentissime⟩[b] perscriberentur. Me vero quod attinet omnia illa a me tibi dicta volo quæ a grato animo proficisci aut debeant aut possint quæque viro doctrina non minus quam loco et genere insignissimo

Endorsed by Locke: A. Mr Beaupre 71 Lord Ashleys case

[a] *Closing bracket supplied.* [b] *MS.* diligentisse

20 Jan. $7\frac{0}{1}$

Together with this letter of mine, which conveys my best respects, illustrious Sir, you will receive another, written by the same person who some time ago sent you an account, composed by himself, of my own malady. This gentleman, who is no stranger to medical studies, will, thanks to his careful observation ever since that time and to his scrupulousness as a narrator, ensure that you miss nothing by its being overlooked through negligence or ignorance. For I felt bound to take care that one of such eminence who had for long taken such friendly interest in my health and had given me such skilled advice on it, and who now once more had made obliging inquiries about it, should receive as careful an account as possible of all that has occurred up to the present. As for myself, I offer you all the expressions that should or could proceed from a grateful heart, when addressed to one so distinguished not less for his learning than for his position and family.

## *251.* Frances Manners, countess of Rutland, to Locke, 7 March [1671] (*246, 252*)

P.R.O., S.P. 30/24, bdle. 47, no. 11. Excerpts printed in Christie, *Shaftesbury*, ii. 39 n.; Fox Bourne, i. 206–7. Year from Locke's endorsement.

Mar: 7

Worthey Sir

I most thankefully accknowledg gods great goodnes to my deare daughter, and am oblidged to owne your justice, that are pleased so amply to make satisfaction for some kind though unwelcome accounts, the lords name be blest and praised for her well doeing and safely bringing that noble familie so hopefull an heire,[1] that early accosts ladies[a] in bed and manages a weapon at 3 days olde to my wonder as joye, Sir these freindly droles, shews your greatly oblidging conserne for this blessing, which most hartyly thanke you for; I am sorrie his lordshipe[2] is indisposed, hope this cordiall will contribut to restore him, I beseech you present my service to him, and it, in all trew thankes to my honored lady[3] for her charitable ministrations to my good child, to the noble father and his sweet sonn my prayres, and Sir for selfe, take all assurances of my remaining

Sir

your much oblidged freind and servante

FR

Address: To Mr Locke at Exeter House in the Strand London this

Postmark: MR 10

Endorsed by Locke: Countesse of Rutland 7° Mar: $7\frac{0}{1}$

## *252.* FRANCES MANNERS, countess of Rutland, to LOCKE, 10 March 1671 (*251*)

P.R.O., S.P. 30/24, bdle. 4, no. 210.

mar: 10 / 70

Sir

this second favour of yours, much advances my account, and with thankes to you, bless god for his gracious dealing with my deare daughter, and that her sweet sonn antony, is made an heire of heaven as borne to st giles,[4] I beseech the lord goe on in mercie to the mother and child; I am glad at last, though too long first, my letter was received, but sorrie, that my lord ashleys goute gives not truce yet, I humbly thanke my lady[3] for such favorable acceptation of a distracted accknowledgment and imperfect though

[a] *MS.* la[s]

[1] Anthony Ashley Cooper, born at Exeter House, on 26 February of this year; styled Lord Ashley 1683–99; third earl of Shaftesbury 1699; d. 1713; the philosopher: *D.N.B.*

[2] Lord Ashley. [3] Lady Ashley.

[4] Wimborne St. Giles, Dorset, Lord Ashley's seat: Hutchins, *Dorset*, iii. 578–82, 598–600, 603–7.

harty thankes, I shall pray ease to all her paines, and reward, for her goodnesses to my daughter, now sir, being come to your oblidging selfe, am at a non plus, being not able thus to pourtraire,[1] as I am,

worthey sir
your faithfull servante
FR

Address (written by an amanuensis): These For Mr: Locke att Exeter house in the Strande London

Postmark: MR 13

Endorsed by Locke: Countesse of Rutland 10° Mar. *70*.

## *253.* ROBERT HUNTINGTON, later bishop of Raphoe, to LOCKE, 1 April 1671 (*382*)

B.L., MS. Locke c. 11, f. 246. The date is probably old style. The writer, 1637–1701, matriculated from Merton College, Oxford, 1652; B.A. 1658; M.A. 1663; D.D. 1683; Provost of Trinity College, Dublin, 1683–92; bishop of Raphoe, 1701: *D.N.B.* He was chaplain to the Levant Company's factory at Aleppo from January 1671 to 1681; and was a correspondent of Locke's friend Dr. Edward Pococke, who had been chaplain there from 1630 to about 1635.

Sir

I can answer your Request, (though I may disappoint your Expectation) and in Complyance therewith have resolv'd upon a Letter to you; which is rather an Accompt of my self, than any observations I have made worthy your knowledge, and telleth you I am well, (which is Newes of my perticular Concern,) and little else. Though wee sayld much in sight of Land, yet sometimes wee had sea-roume enough, to discover how usefull it must needs be in Navigation, to find out the Longitude of the place exactly, in which a ship at any time chanceth to sayle; a Probleme by some suppos'd very easy, allthough I never yet found it attempted with right good and certain successe; And really the advantages of it when known will recompense the labour of any ingenious Person that shall travaile therein.[2] The Variation of the Compass observable in severall places more or lesse, but wee took notice of it nowhere so much as between Rhodes and Cyprus, is a riddle of Nature, and

[1] Apparently portray; the form is not recorded in *O.E.D.*; perhaps the French word.

[2] It was impossible to determine longitude at sea exactly until John Harrison (*D.N.B.*) devised his chronometers in 1735 and later years.

deserveth the search of Curious men to find out a satisfactory reason;[1] notwithstanding the Skill of our mariners, and their Rationall method generally preventeth the inconveniences it might occasion. Indeed I saw not anything more remarquable by Land: As for the flax-stones which once made the Linumvivum or Asbestinum, and might doe so still, they can be no rarity in Europe, since there are rocks of them in Cyprus, out of which the Inhabitants make lint upon occasion for their wounds; which seemeth feaseable enough to be carded and spun and fitted for the loome.[2] The Great Cities once famous through the world, are now fallen into small Townes or Villages, or else quite buryed in their Ruines; and by the crumbling and hollow soyle (as at Ephesus and Antioch) it appeareth that Earthquakes, the deadly Falling-sicknesse of These Places, might very well help on their Destruction. The Country is miserably decay'd, and hath lost the Reputation of its Name, and mighty stock of Credit it once had for Eastern Wisedome and learning: It hath followed the Motion of the Sun, and is Universally gone Westward. May it never sett there: I am still an Englishman; and consequently, to wish all happiness to the Land of my Nativity, and my Friends there, is no more than my Duty, which you may allwayes challenge from

Sir

your faithfull Servant
ROB. HUNTINGTON

Aleppo in Syria Apr: the 1st. 1671

I intended to beg Mr Boyles Commands and Instructions for the right Improvement of my time in these Parts: But the Report of his death (Especially since I understood he was ill before I came away)[3] hath put a stop at present to my Petitions. You know the truth of things and how to act accordingly for my Advantage, that when I shall ramble farther into the Country, I may not only spend so much time in Travaile.

Address: This For Dr John Locke at the Lord Ashley's in the Strand

Endorsed by Locke (twice): Mr *Huntington* 1° Apr. *71*
R Huntington Apr. *71*

[1] This was studied from the time of William Gilbert (1540–1603; ibid.).

[2] Huntington sent a specimen to Dr. Robert Plot (ibid.): *Philosophical Transactions*, xv (1685), 1057.

[3] About June 1670 Boyle had a paralytic stroke, and had not recovered completely in May 1671: Birch, *Life of Boyle*, pp. 207–9.

## CAROLINA AND OTHER COLONIZING ACTIVITIES 1670–4

When Locke entered Ashley's household he became concerned in Ashley's colonizing activities. These fall into two groups, those arising from his membership of colonizing proprietorships and trading companies and those arising from his presidentship of the Council of Trade and Plantations.

In 1663 Charles II granted Carolina to eight proprietors of whom Ashley was one, to be settled and developed by them as a colony. The name goes back to Charles IX of France; the territory granted was everything lying between 31 and 36 degrees north latitude and extending from the Atlantic to the Pacific (approximately from Brunswick, Georgia, to Albemarle Sound; the Pacific is called the South Sea in the charters). In 1665 Charles granted a new charter to the same eight proprietors; the southern and northern limits were increased to 29 degrees and 36 degrees 30 minutes (from Daytona, Florida, to the present boundary between Virginia and North Carolina). The proprietors made little use of their grant until 1669. On 26 April of that year they agreed to pay £500 apiece and to send an expedition to settle Port Royal (about 55 miles SW. of Charleston). Ashley then drew up, with Locke's assistance and the intervention of another proprietor, a constitution for the colony, the document known as the Laws or the Fundamental Constitutions of Carolina; it was sealed by the proprietors on 1 March 1670. From this time onwards many of the Carolina papers in the Shaftesbury collection are endorsed or bear notes by Locke.

On 1 November 1670 Ashley and the five other Carolina proprietors then living were granted the Bahama Islands. No plantation was established. On 4 September 1672 the proprietors entered into an agreement with a company of adventurers to develop the islands (p. 380, n. 1). Locke was a member of this company until 1676 when he sold out his stock.

Ashley was also a member of the Hudson's Bay Company (mentioned in no. *296*) and of the Somers Islands (Bermuda) and Royal African Companies.

On 27 September 1672 a new Council for Trade and Foreign Plantations was established, with Ashley, now earl of Shaftesbury, as its president. The secretaryship fell vacant in September 1673 and Locke was sworn secretary on 15 October. Shaftesbury and Locke continued in their respective offices until the abolition of the Council on 21 December 1674.

The following letters all relate to Carolina or the Bahamas, dealing with the proprietors' business or containing information about the colonies: nos. *254*, 262, *270*, *272*, *274–5*, *279*, *287*, *289–91*, *297*, *300–1*, *305*, *317–18*, *729*. The following (the texts are not printed here) relate to the Council's business: nos. *280*, 281, *288*.

*Bibliography*. South Carolina Historical Society, *Collections*, vol. v, 1897: 'The Shaftesbury papers and other records relating to Carolina and the first settlement on Ashley River prior to 1676', edited by L. Cheves (523 pp.). Most of the documents are printed in full. Cheves did not have access to the Lovelace Collection.

*Calendar of State Papers*, *Colonial Series*, *America and West Indies*, 1669–1674 (cited below as *Cal. S.P.*, *Col.*, vol. vii; the volume enumeration does not appear in the book).

C. M. Andrews, *British Committees, Commissions, and Councils of Trade and Plantations 1622–1675* (Johns Hopkins University Studies in historical and political science, 26th ser., nos. 1–3), 1908.

*English Historical Review*, xl (1925), 93–106 (article on the journals of the councils 1670–4, now in the Library of Congress).

Haley, *Shaftesbury*, pp. 227–65 (Shaftesbury's colonizing interests and activities).

M. E. Sirmans, *Colonial South Carolina*, 1966.

H. C. Wilkinson, *The Adventurers of Bermuda*, 2nd ed., 1958.

B.M., Add. MS. 15640, copy of the Bahamas agreement 4 September 1672 (this copy has marginal notes written by Locke).

M. Craton, *A History of the Bahamas*, 1962.

## 254. SIR PETER COLLETON to LOCKE, [early summer 1671?] (*270*)

P.R.O., S.P. 30/24, bdle. 48, no. 82. Printed in Fox Bourne, i. 244–5; with Locke's notes, in South Carolina Hist. Soc., *Collections*, v (1897), 264–6; calendared in *Cal. S.P.*, *Col.*, vol. vii, no. 714. Date from the notice of Ogilby's *Atlas*; it could be a year earlier.

Peter Colleton, 1635–94; second baronet 1666; F.R.S. 1677; M.P. 1681, 1689–94: G. E. C., *Baronetage*, iii. 161–2; Hudson's Bay Co., *Minutes, 1671–4*, pp. 218–19. His father, Sir John Colleton, was one of the original proprietors of Carolina, and Sir Peter inherited the proprietorship.

Sir

Mr Ogilby[1] who is printing a relation of the West Indias[2] hath been often with mee to gett a map of Carolina wherefore I humbly desire you to gett of my lord[3] those mapps of Cape feare and Albemarle that hee hath and I will draw them into one with that of port Royall and waite upon my lord for the nomination of the rivers etc: and if you would doe us the favour to draw a discourse to bee Added to this map in the nature of a description such as

[1] John Ogilby, 1600–76, miscellaneous writer, bookseller, cartographer, etc.: *D.N.B.* He published his *English Atlas* in 1670 and the following years. The first part, 'Africa', appeared on 28 April 1670. In June he announced that he hoped to publish the second part, 'America', in the following January; in November, that this part was well forward. It was published on 3 November 1671: *The Term Catalogues*, ed. E. Arber, 1903–6, i. 45–6, 50, 63, 94. L.L., nos. 2124–5.

[2] More commonly the West Indies by this time: '*America*, or the new discovered World called *India Occidentalis*, or the *West Indies*': Phillips, 1678, s.v. India; variants in other editions, 1658–1720. The name appears to have been restricted to the islands only late in the eighteenth century: quotations in *O.E.D.*, s.v. West Indies, etc.

[3] Ashley.

might invite people without seeming to come from us it would very much conduce to our speedy settlement[1] and bee a very great obligation to

Your most faithfull frend and servant

P COLLETON

Thursday

Address: To my honnoured frend Mr John Lock present

[On blank pages, there are notes by Locke, 'Writers of Carolina', listing books, authors, travellers, subjects for a note on Carolina, etc.]

## 255. LADY DOROTHY ASHLEY (*veré* Ashley Cooper), later styled Lady Ashley, later countess of Shaftesbury, to LOCKE, 1 [July 1671] (*258*)

P.R.O., S.P. 30/24, bdle. 47, no. 12. Printed in Christie, *Shaftesbury*, ii. 38. Date completed from Locke's endorsement.

Lady Dorothy was perhaps writing from Belvoir; her mother, Lady Rutland, had died on 19 May and was buried on 16 June at Bottesford, Leics., the parish to which Belvoir belongs. Her second son, John, was born on 12 February 1671/2: Hutchins, *Dorset*, iii. 594–5.

Good Sir

I am so much oblidg'd to you, for your letter and kind account; and care of my Deare one;[2] that I am force'd to give you trouble by this letter; and must tell you I doe find so much allteration in my health, and strength that I doe most hartily wish you heare every day; for I am sure this place would at this time doe you all the good in the world; for though I be breeding I have no manner of cough, or heaviness at hart as I had of De: one, but grow both fatt and big; though I eate littell meat but butter, and salletts; and porridg when I can get them; so that I belive being in the sweet aire, I shall have too boys; I wish I was at St Gill's with my Lord and Lady[3]

[1] The account of Carolina occupies pp. 205–12 of the 'America'. It is extremely favourable; at the end, as a special attraction for settlers, it gives a summary of the Fundamental Constitutions of Carolina (p. 395, n. 2). No part of it appears to be by Locke but he probably supplied some of the materials for it on behalf of the Lords Proprietors.

[2] Her son, the future third earl: p. 351, n. 1.

[3] Lord and Lady Ashley.

and then I should se you there; with them for to be with them is much desir'd by

Good Sir
Your most oblidg'd friend to serve you
DOR ASHLEY

the 1

Address (written by an amanuensis): This For mr Lock att Exeter House in the Strand London

Endorsed by Locke: Lady Dorothy Ashley 1° Jul. *71*

Added by another hand: to mr Lock private

## *256.* MRS. MARGARET BLOMER, formerly Beavis, to LOCKE, 10 July 1671 (*249*, *267*)

P.R.O., S.P. 30/24, bdle. 47, no. 13. Excerpt printed in Fox Bourne, i. 266.

⟨Pe⟩tworth[a] the 10th. July 1671

Deare Brother

I Chose To come and say something To you, rather then to take an evening walke with Mr. Blomer and the litle femme,[1] who were very earnest with mee to goe with them; had you been of the Company I should not have disputed the matter.

I hope you have received so favourable a discription of Petworth as to bee incouraged to come and see it especially now that the house swarmes with your friends and humble servants. I could tell you a Thousand fine exploytes of our litle sparke[2] but that shall bee the worke of an other day. My Lady[3] is not so well as I wish her. my owne health is much better[b-] then it[-b] was when I writ to you Last. which I impute a good deale to my takeing of whey these 3 or 4 dayes finding that it agrees with mee (and that Dr. Sydneham is a friend to it I hope I may safely continue to take it (at least till farther order from him) my dos is about a quart and sweetned

[a] *Part covered by sealing-wax.* [b-b] *MS.* better then / then it

[1] She reappears specifically in nos. *267* and 269; she was not Mrs. Grigg and was apparently a member of the Ashley household. She was probably one of the 'two little femmes' of no. 265, and may be 'the little Sparke' of no. *249*.

[2] This is perhaps a Blomer child. The expression seems too familiar for Lady Elizabeth Percy.

[3] Lady Northumberland.

either with sirup of violets or syrup of bugleose, I am willing to get a litle more strength before I take the Phisick which Dr. Sydneham has appointed mee; however (if hee think it fitt I shall delay it noe Longer.) the walkers are Come home and I must now leave you to entertaine them. I am

Your affectionate sister:
M BLOMER

I would faine heare from my sister Grigg[1]

Address: For Mr. Locke at Little Exeter house in the strand These London
Endorsed by Locke: M Blomer 10° Jul. *71*.

## 257. MARGARET COOPER, Lady Ashley, later countess of Shaftesbury, to LOCKE, 14 July [1671] (*747*)

P.R.O., S.P. 30/24, bdle. 47, no. 14. Printed in Christie, *Shaftesbury*, ii. 40. Year from Locke's endorsement.

Petworth[2] 14th. July

Good Sir, though I am very ill, at this exersise in all kinds, yett my ernest inclination to express my gratitude, upon every occation, will not suffer me to ommitt this returne of my thankes to you, for the best of newes, you sent me, of my deare Lord's wellfaer; and of the gallant actions of our Iland adventurers,[3] and allsoe of the old dotteage, and young folly, of the senceless Inglish and Irish contrivance, overthrone by the french experince in Gallentry,[4] all which, in severall wayes, is very entertaining to.

Your faithfull frend to serve you
M. ASHLEY

Address: for Master Lock.
Endorsed by Locke: Lady Ashley 14° Jul. *71*

[1] p. 334, n. 2.
[2] Lady Ashley and Lady Northumberland were first cousins.
[3] Sir Henry Morgan (*D.N.B.*) captured Panama in January; there is a notice of the exploit in *London Gazette*, 6 July.
[4] I cannot explain this.

## *258.* LADY DOROTHY ASHLEY (*veré* Ashley Cooper), later countess of Shaftesbury, to LOCKE, 15 [July 1671] (*255*)

P.R.O., S.P. 30/24, bdle. 47, no. 75. Printed, without the postscript, in Christie, *Shaftesbury*, ii. 39. Date completed from Locke's endorsement.

the 15

Good Sir

I returne you ten thousand thanks for your letter this day; for writeing last weeke to my Lord;[1] and not haveing any word of him; if I had not heard from you; I must have bine in great consearne, with feare he had bine ill; but now tis nothing but business I will be content; till I se, or heare from him; for longer then this day sennight; I cannot stay heare; unless I am commanded[a] by his Lordship, for this 2 or 3 days; I doe find my condition mak's me most unfitting for to be heare, where I find every day so many wounderfull disturbancess; that I must be at rest somewhere; for I finde need to be at ease; for I am now sick every day; and cannot indewer; to waite of my Jar:[2] as I have done till now; so I intend God blesing me; to set out hence next weeke; pray with my humble duty to my Lord; let him know what I write; for without his commands[b] now I have satisfied my Brother[3] by writeing as I did last weeke to his lordship I have nothing to doe; but come as he gave me leave to his sweet St-Gyles; for nothing is more pleasant then the thoughts to se his Lordship, and my Lady and yourselfe too.

Good Sir

your most oblidg'd friend and servant

DOR ASHLEY

Mr Ashley presents[c] his his service[d] and thanks to you Sir and prays his duty may be presented[e] to my Lord and now he is impatient of staying though but this week as if it was an age to be from St Gyles my Neece Juliana Chaw[4] presents[c] you her service[d] if you can Sir let me heare from you this week I shall be glad for else we shall be gon the next and heare nothing

Address: For Mr Lock att Exeter house in the Strand London

Endorsed by Locke: Lady D. Ashley 15° Jul. *71*

[a] *MS.* com[d]. [b] *MS.* com[ds]: [c] *MS.* pre[ts]. [d] *MS.* ser[ce] [e] *MS.* pre[d]:

[1] Ashley. [2] Presumably for journey. [3] Lord Ros: p. 322, n. 2.

[4] Juliana, d. 1692, daughter of Patrick Chaworth, third Viscount Chaworth of Armagh (Ireland), by Grace, Lady Dorothy's elder sister; married Chambre Brabazon, *c.* 1645–1715; fifth earl of Meath (Ireland) 1708: G. E. C.

## 259. Locke to Dr. John Mapletoft, 10 October 1671 (243, 260)

*European Magazine*, xiv (1788), 401–2. The dates of nos. 259 and 260 as given in the *European Magazine* (10 October 1671 and 7 October 1671) are incompatible: Locke did not write to Mapletoft for some time before he wrote no. 259. Both letters may be dated incorrectly, but the *European Magazine* editor was careful, and there is likely to be an error only in one part of one date. Fox Bourne dated no. 259 as '10 October 1670' and no. 260 as 19 October 1671, but Locke appears to have been in London in September and October 1670: nos. *248*, *249*; *Cal. S.P.*, *Col.*, vol. vii, no. 284. The addresses suggest that the letters are fairly close in date; if that view is correct no. 260 is to be dated 27 or perhaps 17 October, and the sequence would be: no. 259 written 10, received 12 or 13 October; Mapletoft writes a lost letter? *c.* 15 October; Locke leaves Salisbury for Sutton *c.* 20 October?; Mapletoft writes again *c.* 23 October?; Locke receives Mapletoft's letter of *c.* 23 October and writes to him on 27 October. But the sequence could be shorter.

Salisbury, 10th Oct. 71.

Sir,

The confidence I have in your freindship hath made me delay soe long to write to you, notwithstanding my promise; and the same confidence makes me now write, haveing noe thing to say to you but of my self. That these are arguments whereby I would pretend to hold a place in your affection, you may be easily persuaded by my past conversacon with you: where in I have donne little more to prevaile with you to be my freind, then by giveing you assureance that I presumd you were and would be soe. But be the inequality what it will, let the obligacon be all yours and the advantage mine, you are not now like to get off this hard bargain, make what profit you can of the honour; it is to bestow the greatest kindeness you can freely, I meane your freindship, for I tell you plainly I am not apt to foregoe the benefit I make by it. I send you, therefor, an account of my self, as of a thing you are obleigd to be concerned for. My first remove was from your towne to Oxford, where either my constantly being abroad in the aire as much as the clouds would permitt, or in good company at home, made me beleive I mended apace, and my cough sensibly abated. From thence I came hither about the middle of last weeke, where I feare the aire will not be soe advantageous to me; for at best I have but made a stand, if not gone backwards, in this watry place,[1] and

[1] Water-courses through the streets were a feature of Salisbury until the nineteenth century: *V.C.H.*, *Wiltshire*, vi. 89–90.

therefor I thinke I shall make but a short abode here. However this is not to give you an excuse for silence, which, if you are but half as lazy as I really am, you will be ready to lay hold of; for if you direct your letter to me, at Dr. Thomas's, in Salisbury, it will finde me wherever I am in this country. You see how confidence begins and ends my letter, and runs through my whole conversacon with you. But let me tell you for your comfort and my excuse, that none but good and generous men use to be treated soe, at least you are one of those few with whome I am willing to use it, as a testimony that I am,

Sir,

Your most humble and most affectionate servant,

J. LOCKE.

Sir,

That on the other side was writt before the receit of yours of the 2d instant, which with all the satisfaction it brought me, made me yet sorry that you bestowd soe many kindenesses upon soe thin a subject. I must conclude my carcasse to be made of a very ill composition that will not grow into good plight in fresh aire, soe much improved by the good wishes of my freinds; and whilst my minde is at perfect ease in soe full an enjoyment of what I most desire, methinkes my body should batten. What will be the issue I know not, but if I should returne that burley man you speake of, I shall put noe thing into your imbraces you will not have a just title to. This I may securly acknowledg to one who is full master of the inward man already. And this I also wish, since as I now am I shall but litle credit my owner, and to confesse truly to you, I finde soe much regret to be at a distance from those freinds you wish me with, that I thinke I may be excused if I am not yet willing to take my last farwell of them. The winter quarters you have provided for me, I thinke not only preferable to the solitarinesse of the grave, but the gaity of courts, or other admired places of the world. All that I am afraid of is, that I shall be noe more fit for that excellent person's company then if I were realy taken out of the grave, and however you have dressed me up to him, you will use your freind the Doctor[1] little better than he that joynd the liveing and the dead togeather. But I perceive you extend your kindeness beyond your profession, and take care I should be better as well as fatter. You have laid such temptations for my returne, that had I noe

[1] I have failed to identify him.

inclination to it of myself, I could not long resist. But I assur you I am soe little pleasd with my absence from you, and the rest of the freinds you mention, that I am often at variance with my body about it; and methinks I purchase health deare at that rate. By the scrip inclosd in your letter I finde you are a punctuall gentleman: much more soe then was necessary in an affaire with one who knew you as well as I doe, and I must crave leave to tell you, whatever you say, that there could not come any thing more unwelcome to me if I thought you tore in peices with that paper all the obligacons I have to be,

Sir, your most humble servant,

J. LOCKE.

Pray tell the Lady that eats applepye in spight,[1] that I shall returne again to London to share with her those good things she taunts me with. My service to Mr. Firmin[2] and his wife, Mrs. Grig, and the applepie-eaters.

Address: These present, To Dr. John Mapletoft, at Mr. Firmin's, over-against the George, in Lombard-street, London.

## 260. LOCKE to DR. JOHN MAPLETOFT, [27?] October 1671 (259, 265)

*European Magazine*, xiv (1788), 322–3. For the date here suggested see no. 259 n.

Sutton, 7th Oct. 71.

Dear Sir,

Though before the receit of your last letter, (which, by my slow progresse hither, I overtook not till this night,) I was very well assured of your freindship; yet the concernement you expresse for my health, and the kindnesse wherewith you presse my journey into France,[3] gives me fresh and obleigeing testimonys of it. This is soe far from an offence against decorum, or needing an apologie on that score, that I thinke the pardon you aske for it the only thing

[1] I have failed to identify her. The apple-pie may be allusive rather than literal; there is what appears to be a similar use in nos. *1821*, etc.

[2] Thomas Firmin, 1632–97, the philanthropist, and his second wife, Margaret, daughter of Giles Dentt: *D.N.B.* He and Mapletoft were kinsmen. Letters below, nos. *1759*, etc.

[3] About September 1670 Locke considered visiting France, apparently in spring 1671: nos. *248*, *249*. He went for a short visit about September or October 1672: nos. 264, 265.

I ought to take amisse from you, if I could take amisse any thing from one who treats me with soe much kindenesse, soe much sincerity. I am now making hast back again to London, to returne you my thanks for this and severall other favours; and then haveing made you judg of my state of health, desire your advice what you thinke best to be donne, wherein you are to deale with the same freedom, since noe thing will be able to make me leave those freinds I have in England, but the positive direction of some of those freinds for my going. But however I dispose of myself, I shall dwell amidst the marks of kindenesse, and shall enjoy the aire of Hampsted heath[1] or Monpelier,[2] as that wherein your care and freindship hath placed me; and my health will not be the lesse welcome to me when it comes by your advice, and brings with it the hopes that I may have longer time in the world, to assure you with what affection and sincerity I am,

Sir,

Your most humble servant, And faithful freind,

J. LOCKE.

Pray give my service and thanks to Mr. Firmin and his lady. To Mrs. Grig let me be ⟨kindly⟩[a] remembred; and let her know that her and my unkle Locke,[3] who is by whilst I write this, remember her. To our Northumberland-house freinds I must not be forgotten.

Address: For his much honoured freind, Dr. John Mapletoft, at Mr. Firmins, overagainst the George, in Lombard-street, London.

## *261.* JOHN STRACHEY to LOCKE, 19 January 1672 (226, 264)

P.R.O., S.P. 30/24, bdle. 4, no. 217. Excerpts printed in Fox Bourne, i. 312.

Sir

I must confesse that I have taken too much time to answer your letter, but I hope the Holydays and Xmas Gambolls may bee my

[a] *European Magazine* kindlely

[1] Hampstead church was about 3½ miles from the nearest part of the built-up area of London. See also no. *760*.

[2] Where Locke spent most of 1676.

[3] Peter Locke. He was apparently related to Mrs. Grigg through her husband.

excuse, which delights although the come very short of a correspondence with you, yett tis a hard matter to shake of Custome, video meliora etc.[1] As to your 3 first reasons why taxes should bee laid on Land, as I write not for dispute but satisfaction, soe I acknowledg myselfe convinc'd, but as to your fourth that all taxes terminate at last on the land,[2] I cannot soe readily subscribe, for methinks your instances doe not reach it, the Excise on Ale not making barley cheaper, but only less Ale is sold for the money and thereby the Drinkers and not the Countriman pay the Tax, indeed if the Statute was putt in Execution which commands such a quantity to bee sold for a penny, then Barley must bee sold cheaper, else the Brewer would not buy it to bee a Looser by the bargaine, but since as the Excise doth rise hee may lessen the quantity of his Ale, I can't see why it should fall on Barley. Soe for the Rest, and although you speake never soe rationally on this subject, the Country will hardly be brought to yeild, I could wish I had your thoughts on a Free Port,[3] for I doubt not but they are very ingenious. I thanke you for Mr Bernie,[4] I am mightily taken with some things in Him. I begg your pardon for this hasty Scribble, I thought it better to doe soe then not to write at all. I am

Sir

your very humble servant

JO. STRACHEY

Janu 19 1671

Address: For Mr John Locke at Little Exceter House in the Strand London

Postmark: IA 22

Endorsed by Locke: Taxes J Strachy 19° Jan 1671[a] Taxes on Land

Further endorsement by Locke: Taxes on Land

[a] *Date altered from* 71; *the figures* 16 *may have been inserted by a later writer.*

---

[1] Ovid, *Metamorphoses*, vii. 20.

[2] Locke published his views in 1692 in *Some Considerations of the Consequences of the Lowering of Interest*, pp. 87–98. (2nd ed., 1696, pp. 88–99). In the preliminary epistle he writes: 'I find not my Thoughts now to differ from those I had near Twenty Years since': p. 4.

[3] No paper by Locke on this subject is known.

[4] The name comes at the end of a line and is probably short for Bernier, i.e. François Bernier: no. 390, etc. Translations of his two books on India (no. *547* n.) appeared in 1671: *The History of the Late Revolution of the Empire of the Great Mogol* and *A Continuation*: *T.C.* i. 66, 86.

## 262. LOCKE to CAPTAIN RICHARD KINGDON, 29 April 1672

P.R.O., S.P. 30/24, bdle. 48, no. 88. Printed in South Carolina Hist. Soc., *Collections*, v (1897), 392; calendared in *Cal. S.P., Col.*, vol. vii, no. 810. Kingdon was a commissioner of Excise from 1665 to 1677.

Exeter house Apr 29: *72*[a]

Capt Kingdon

There is to be within this day or two a meeting of the Lords Proprietors of Carolina. Against which time my Lord[1] desires there may be a perfect state of their accounts, some of them presseing hard for it, and if it should faile to be there, it would discompose their affairs. I desire you when you next come this way to bring my 20l with you and if I be not in the way pray pay it to Mr Stringer[2] or Mr Jones.[3] I am

Sir

Your most humble servant

J LOCKE

Address: For Captain Kingdon at the Excise office in B⟨ro⟩ad[b] street

Endorsed (probably not by Locke): Mr. Lock Letter the 29th. of Aprill about Caraline business 1672

## *263*. WILLIAM ALLESTREE to LOCKE, 16 August 1672 (*271*)

P.R.O., S.P. 30/24, bdle. 4, no. 228. The writer, 1643–90?, was admitted to St. John's, Cambridge, in 1658; matriculated from Christ Church, 27 May 1661; diplomatist: *Genealogist*, new ser. xxxii (1916), 164–71.

Stockholme. Aug: the 16 s:v: 1672.[4]

Sir

Although our journey hath bene tedious and not without danger, yet the good company, and the kindnesse of sir e: wood,[5] made those inconveniences more easy to me, and gave me a reall

[a] *The year was written by Locke, but possibly some time after he had written the letter. Page torn.*

[1] The former Lord Ashley, created earl of Shaftesbury on 23 April.

[2] p. 434 n.

[3] Peter Jones, d. 1674; treasurer and agent of the Lords Proprietors of Carolina: *Cal. S.P., Col.*, vol. vii, nos. 1270, 1402.

[4] The Julian calendar was in use in Sweden until the eighteenth century.

[5] Envoy extraordinary to Sweden 1672–9; he arrived on 24 August, N.S.: Bittner and Gross.

occasion of making me resolve to thanke you for the employment I am now in, as soon as I should come to Stockholme. If there be any newes here, I am as much a stranger to it as to the town, but Mr Clement who giv'es you this, will be able to informe you of the temper of this Court, as being a person that understands it very well. I wish you all happinesse, and am sir

your most oblig'd and most humble servant

W: ALLESTREE

Mr Lock.

Address: For Mr John Lock at Exeter house in the Strand London
Written by another writer: Mr Clement
Endorsed by Locke: W: Allestree 16. Aug. *72*

## 264. LOCKE to JOHN STRACHEY, [mid October 1672] (*261*, 276)

Rand, pp. 77–9, 'from a contemporary copy of the original'. Words in square brackets are supplied by Rand. Date from contents. Perhaps written after no. 265.

Locke had recently accompanied Lady Northumberland to Paris. She left London on 11 September, arriving in Paris on 24 September/4 October: Alfred Morrison, *Collection of Autograph Letters*, 2nd ser.: *The Bulstrode Papers*, vol. i, 1897, p. 249; Perwich, *Despatches*, p. 241. Locke returned to London by 13 October: Fox Bourne, i. 313.

Sir,

If you are as you ought to be at leisure to hearken to the words of a gentleman and a traveller, and which is more thought of a Monsieur, the time is now come that you are to be beatified by the refined conversation of a man that knows the difference between a black and white feather, and who can tell you which side of his two-handed hat ought to be turned up, and which only supported with an audace. I fear you have the unpardonable ignorance not to know what an audace is; to oblige you then, know that what an untravelled Englishman would take to be a piece of ordinary loop lace made use of to support the overgrown brims of a flapping hat has by the virtuosos and accomplished gallants of Paris, when I was there, been decreed to be an audace. And thus you may reap the benefit of what cost me many a step. O the advantage of travel! You see what a blessing it is to visit foreign countries and improve in the knowledge of men and manners. When could you have found out this by living at Sutton Court and eating crammed capons and apple pies? But now I have communicated this to you and enriched your understanding with the notice of a new fashionable French word, let it not make you proud, that belongs to us only that have taken pains and gone a great way for it. If I thought it would not, and being embellished by some scatterings of those jewels I have lately picked up in France you would not be elevated in your own thoughts and at the next sessions laugh at those of the worshipful quorum, which you are not to do till you have been refined with French air and conversation, I would tell you yet better things, and you should (as Don Quixote saw Dulcinea by hear say)[1] see the Louvre, the Seine and Pont Neuf over it, Paris, and, what is the perfection and glory of all, the King of France himself. And is not this do you think well worth a journey of 5 or 600 miles, and are not our people wise when they admire and run even mad after these things and several others, whereof I care not if I give you a little taste, viz., There I saw vast and magnificent buildings as big almost as others dominions preparing only for one man, and yet there be a great many other two legged creatures, but 'tis not the way of that country much to consider them, and so let them go who are in such perpetual motions that they will not much need mansions till they come to their long home. [I saw] there men that had forsaken the world and women that professed retirement and poverty have yet in the ornaments of their buildings and the hatchments of their trinkets all the mighty riches exquisite art could produce of convenience, beauty or curiosity. This I saw and what is more believed that this was to forsake the world and I take it may be allowed to be a heavenly life to have all things with ease and security in a place where labour and vexation enter not. I saw too infinite gay things and gewgaws, feathers and ⟨frippery⟩,[a][2] and to come to you I saw Westminster Hall in epitome,[3] which exceeds ours (how wide mouthed soever it be) a thousand times, in the noise and din. How much it came short in honesty I had not

[a] *Rand* frippers

[1] Pt. i, ch. xxxi.
[2] Rand has 'frippers', presumably a transcriber's slip or printer's error. A fripper was a dealer in old clothes: *O.E.D.*
[3] At the Palais, now the Palais de Justice, and almost entirely rebuilt. As in Westminster Hall there were in the great hall shops for fashionable goods, book-stalls, etc. There were also galleries with shops. See further p. 503, etc.

occasion to know, I thank my stars, but the hum and buzzing of those busy hornets made me suspect the laborious bee did not keep all his honeys to himself. If I should go on with my story, you would find nothing in my letter but I saw, and I saw, and I saw, which not being a very graceful figure nor becoming the eloquence of an accomplished Monsieur, which having been at Paris I hope now to pass for, I will here give off.

Perhaps your mouth will water after other matters, but to stop your longing I am to tell you that the great happiness of this heaven upon earth, Paris, lies wholly in vision too. Eating, drinking, sleeping and the entertainment of the other senses are not there altogether so voluptuous; but those are earthly pleasures for clodpate mortals, and we ⟨ayry⟩[a] men contemn them. And I think a man that hath once tasted the dirty water of the Seine, and smelled the variety of stinks that set off Paris, is thereby privileged to contemn you men of toast and ale and powdered beef, which salt keeps from due haut gout. If the air of the country hath given me but half so much health as it hath vanity, I shall quickly be as strong as I am now conceited. I only wish this puffing up would make me in truth more bulky. But if it do not, 'tis yet a piece of greatness to have been amongst a sort of men that look down on all the world, and to have seen him that tramples on them who undervalues us. To get this gift of undervaluing all on this side the water is (as experience shows) one of the best qualities one can learn amongst them, and therefore do but think how your quondam friend John,[1] now fashionable Monsieur John, abominated damned roastbeef and the other gross meats of England, when his mouth watered at the sweet grapes and insipid or sour bread that those brave men make meals and feast on, and how did he a night's laugh at the drowsy English men when the *punaise* and other creepers tickled him. This accomplishment [you will permit] a man that hath gone so many miles for it, and you will not deny me this privilege of my travels to bring home with me the contempt of my country. I wish you were but here to see how I could cock my hat, strut and shake my garniture, talk fast, loud, confidently and nothing to the purpose, slight you and everybody. I protest it is worth your seeing. But I wish then you would do yourself the kindness to come quickly, for I fear

[a] *Rand* agey

[1] Locke himself; not Mapletoft, as in Rand's note.

my French seasoning will not be so lasting as theirs who receive it in the powdering tub[1] and therefore may in time decay. And therefore if you make not haste, I believe at our next meeting you will find me what I cannot forbear even already to tell you that I am after the old English fashion, *i.e.* in earnest.

Dear Sir,

Your most affectionate friend and humble servant,

J. L.

My humble service to your Lady, Mrs. Baber and my Cousin Jepp.[2]

Endorsed: Copy of Dr. Locke's letter to Mr. Strachey.

## 265. Locke to Dr. John Mapletoft, 19 October 1672 (260, 269)

*European Magazine*, xv (1789), 9–10.

Exeter House, 19° Oct. 72.

Deare Dr.

I want noe thing to compleate all the satisfaction I could expect from a journey that caryed me away from you, but an assurance that you, and the rest of that good company with you, accomplishd yours with as good successe, though I hope with better weather then we did ours.[3] For whether it were that hardships doe naturally attend the undertakings of puissant as well as errant Knights, and that Heaven seldome smiles upon their enterprises; or whether the tutellar angell of the country would not favour the flight of a man that had bilked one of the most considerable men of the place; for what more worthy person then a French taylor? or what greater offence can there be then to goe away in his debt? but what ever was the cause, soe it was, that from the time we tooke horse in Paris, which was within an hower or two after your departure, till we came to Calais, we had not one dry day. And as if all the rain that was stored in the clouds had been laid up there only for us, when we were got within a league of Calais, it fell on us as if it had been powerd downe with buckets; which violence of the storme pursued

[1] The sweating tub for the cure of venereal disease: *O.E.D.*

[2] Mary, d. 1706, daughter of Strachey's half-brother the younger Samuel Jepp (p. 168 n.). She married Edward Clarke of Chipley (no. *682*): Collinson, *Somerset*, ii. 99 (misnumbered 91); letters and notices below.

[3] Lady Northumberland wintered at Aix-en-Provence: nos. *267*, 269.

us till we just got at the gates, and as soone as we were got to shelter it presently broke up, and we had noe rain till after severall days we had been in England. This wet was some of the worst of our story, for we had by the way some adventures worth reciting, which I must adjourne till an other time, that I may doe what is more necessary for me, and may returne those thanks which those obligacons I received when I was with you, call for from me. You know how little skill I have in speeches; and my ignorance in French, which is the very mint of compliment, will excuse a dull oyster if it only gape, and by that you must guesse at my meaning, which is all manner of thankes and acknowledgment to that excellent lady to whose favour I owe my voiage and all the advantages of it. This you are to put into the best words you can finde, and on this occasion you cannot say too much. For if Leoncourt and Chantilly, St. Germans and the Lover,[1] be sights which cannot be sufficiently admired, I'm sure there cannot be enough said in returne for that favour which added a grace even to those fine places, and made me value the sight of them more then otherwise I should have donne. When you are about to doe me this kindnesse, I would not have you reflect upon my declineing to perfect the recovery of my health in soe advantageous a way, and in your company, least you should thinke soe inconsiderate a man unworthy your patronage, and forbeare to say some thing for me which may preserve me from being thought ungrateful even for that health which I have got by goeing soe far, and which I should be glad to imploy in the service of those to whose kindenesse I am indebted for it. But you know that our journey as well as pilgrimage in this world have their setled bounds, and none of us can goe beyond the extent of that tether, which certainly tyes us. In that danceing country, where every one thinkes he may skip up and downe as he will, I know not whether you will admit of this doctrine. But thinke it as extravagant as you will, *I'm sure*, soe I found it; and Mr. Vernon,[2] if he be with you, will justifye this fatall necessity. Pray present my most humble service to Lady Bette.[3]

[1] Liancourt; Chantilly; St. Germain-en-Laye; the Louvre. Liancourt was a notable show-place: Locke's Journal, 10 Sept. 1677.

[2] Probably Francis Vernon: p. 193, n. 2. He was in Paris on 28 September/ 8 October: Perwich, *Despatches*, p. 242.

[3] Presumably Lady Elizabeth Percy, Lady Northumberland's daughter, born on 26 January 1667 (d. 1722) and wife successively of Henry Cavendish, styled earl of Ogle; Thomas Thynne (no. *682*); and Charles Seymour, sixth duke of Somerset (no. *586*): *D.N.B.*, art. Seymour, Charles.

To Mrs. Ramsy,[1] with my service, give an account that her letters were safe deliverd at Northumberland House. Let Dr. Blomer and my sister[2] know that I have a great deale of service for them, and that I deliverd the ones letters and the others tokens. Dr. Tilotson[3] was well satisfied about the bookes, but the two litle femmes[4] are like to goe togeather by the ears which shall have both the sleeves. They have only made a truce for soe long till she can send them word whether there be any French trick to make one sleeve serve for two armes. In the meane time they grumble, and desire her to remember that all the cold in the world (however she be troubled with it) is not in France, and that such scanty clothing will scarce preserve a warme remembrance of her in her freinds in England this winter. Pray also remember me very kindely to my brother Scawen,[5] to whome pray give this inclosed bill, with my service and thankes. I had writt to him my self this turne, had not my chimny been this day on fire, which fild my chamber with soe much company, smoake, and confusion, that I have scarce recoverd breath yet, and shall not bring myself and things in order this good while. But pray tell him I sent his letters away by the post as soone as I came to towne, which was that day seventh night I parted from you, and his token to Dr. Millington[6] I sent away since by a safe hand. And now I come to you beloved, first with a word of informacon that your cosin Collet[7] is well, and his wife well brought to bed the day after I returned. Mr. Firmin and his wife very well. Secondly, with a use of discomfort, because there is yet noe use nor principle to be got. I wish Poole hold stanch, for Mary and Maning I feare are leaky vessells, and hold noe thing but emptynesse.[8] But of this affair your cosin Collet and I will take all

[1] She, Mr. Scawen, and Mrs. Alice, below, were in attendance on Lady Northumberland; they are mentioned again in no. 269.

[2] Mrs. Blomer.

[3] John Tillotson, 1630–94; D.D. 1666; at this time a prebendary of Canterbury; appointed dean on 4 November of this year; archbishop of Canterbury 1691: *D.N.B.* He was a friend of Thomas Grigg as well as of Mapletoft: no. *320*.

[4] One may be Mrs. Grigg; the other is probably 'the litle femme' of no. *256*.

[5] John Scawen, *c.* 1645–95; son of Robert Scawen of Horton, Bucks, a servant and trustee of Earl Algernon; matriculated from Christ Church, where he was a pupil of Locke, 1661; B.A. 1664; M.A. 1667; rector of Horton 1692–5: De Fonblanque, *Annals of Percy*, ii. 638–41; Foster; etc.

[6] Thomas Millington, *c.* 1628–1704; M.D. 1659; knighted 1680; president, Royal College of Physicians, 1696–1704: *D.N.B.*

[7] John Collett, a nephew of Mapletoft's mother; admitted to the Middle Temple 1652; barrister 1659: J. E. B. Mayor, ed., *Cambridge in the Seventeenth Century*, 1855–71, pt. i, Nicholas Ferrar, pp. 377–84; *Middle Temple Records: Minutes of Parliament*, ed. C. T. Martin, 1904–5.

[8] I have not identified these three.

the care we can, and when that is donne, what ever happens, I think you will not have one sigh the more, nor will I have one laugh the lesse. The prorogacon of Parliament till the Spring,[1] I doubt not but you have heard of. Other news we have little, the King being but just returned from Newmarket. I desire to heare from you how you all doe, and where you have fixed, and whether any body went along the journey with you besides your owne company, for we have here noe news of Mr. J. S.[2] who, if he were in England, I am confident would tell us soe. I wish you all maner of happynesse, and am

Your most humble and obedient servant,

J. LOCKE.

My service to Mrs. Alice.

Address: For his much honoured freind Dr. Mapletoft, at the Right Honourable the Countess of Northumberland's, in France.

## 266. LOCKE to WILLIAM PRETTYMAN, 11 December 1672

B.L., M.S. Locke c. 24, ff. 224–5. The letter, with notes on it (written by Prettyman?).

William Prettyman, d. 1688; Remembrancer of the First Fruits and Tenths; an uncle of Mrs. Evelyn, the diarist's wife: Evelyn, *Diary*, ed. de Beer, ii. 538 n.

Shaftesbury was appointed Lord Chancellor on 17 November of this year. He in turn appointed Locke secretary of presentations, with a salary of £300 per annum: Fox Bourne, i. 278. The Lord Chancellor's duties included the bestowal of 'all Ecclesiastical Benefices in the Kings gift under 20*l.* yearly in the Kings Books': Chamberlayne, *Angliæ Notitia* (ed. 1674, i. 151).

Locke kept among his papers (B.L., MS. Locke c. 8, ff. 243–4) a letter from William Fuller, bishop of Lincoln (*D.N.B.*), to Shaftesbury, 27 January 1675, stating that, in accordance with his promise, he had conferred on Dr. John Stillingfleet the prebend of North Kelsey. This Stillingfleet was a brother of the future bishop (p. 373, n. 2). There is nothing to show whether the promise was connected with Shaftesbury's official patronage as Lord Chancellor or whether it was personal. The letter is endorsed by Locke.

Exeter house 11° Dec 1672

Sir

I desire you will doe me the favour to let me know what the Rectory of Lee in Kent is valued at in the King's books.[3] and

[1] Parliament was prorogued by proclamation dated 17 September.

[2] There is no obvious identification.

[3] A man named John Jackson was admitted on 14 December of this year: E. Hasted, *Hasted's History of Kent*, ed. H. H. Drake, pt. i, 1886, p. 229.

whether there be any such Rectory Viaredg or sinecure as St Nicholas in Pembroke shire of what value, and whether in the King's gift.[1] I desire to know, when you or your officers will be soe far at leisure that I may come there to informe my self soe that I may not need to trouble you any more by these kinde of enquirys I am

Sir

your very humble servant

JOHN LOCKE

Lee[a] Rect. Decanat. de Dartford in the Dioc of Rochester per annum } iijl xjs viijd.

Com. Pembr. Decanatus de Pembrooke Vicar. Sti Michaelis Pembrooke per annum } iiijl.

I find noe St Nicholas in the Dioc of St Davids or County of Pembrooke in charge Berwyn

D: Pembr.

Monnckton Vicar Sti Nicholai per annum cs.[b]

Address (in Locke's hand): For his very worthy friend Mr Prettyman at the first fruits office in Hatton Garden.

## *267.* MRS. MARGARET BLOMER, formerly Beavis, to LOCKE, 17/27 December 1672 (*256, 359*)

P.R.O., S.P. 30/24, bdle. 47, no. 16. Excerpts printed in Fox Bourne, i. 314–15.

Aix the 27th. December 1672

Deare Brother.

I am in the first place to give you thankes for the favour you intended us upon supposition of Dr. Stillingfleets removall,[2] and doubt not but the same friendship and kindnesse which employ'd

[a] *Except name* Lee *all this in a hand other than Locke's.* [b] *MS.* Cs.

[1] The vicarage of St. Nicholas was held with that of Granston; it appears to have been in the gift of the bishop of St. David's. There was a new vicar on 29 January 1673: Hist. Soc. of West Wales, *West Wales Hist. Records*, i (1912), 302–4.

[2] Edward Stillingfleet, 1635–99; D.D. 1668; dean of St. Paul's 1678; bishop of Worcester 1689; Locke's future antagonist: *D.N.B.* At this time he held prebends in Canterbury and London; in October he exchanged that of Islington for that of Newington; Mrs. Blomer may refer to this or to some other rumoured promotion. Dr. John Stillingfleet (p. 372 n.) was rector of Beckingham, Lincs.; in 1673 he became rector of South Hykeham, Lincs.: Venn.

your thoughts about that will againe represent our concernes to you on the like occassions, or any other accident that may give you an oppertunity to oblige us; there are few that have a memory so good and faithfull for the absent, or that can preserve a steddy inclination for persons at our distance amidst the throng of so many diligent pretenders; as to the busnes of Northumberland house I suppose I need not say much to perswade you to beleive that my Lady will in this (and all things else) shew her readynes to gratifie the desires of so good a friend as my Lord Chancellour;[1] You will find by Mr. Gee[2] etc. that her Ladyship has given her full consent (as far as it is significant) and I am confident shee wishes shee had had right and authority enough to have made it a compleate courtesy. pray mention mee kindly To Litle femme,[3] and tell her that I hope my chamber and closet will fall to her share. wee shall see how desirous you are to see us for our retorne this summer will depend much on your Lords management and advice. The newes you sent us of Dr. Pearson and Dr. Barrow, was what wee wisht for.[4] may your letters never bring worse tydings To

Your affectionate sister and humble servant

M: BLOMER.

it is expected that either your Lord or Lady should say somthing to my Lady themselves concerning Northumberland house. make use of this hint and let it not bee knowne from whense you have it, though I am not to tell you what the rules of decency and civility are and how far they prevaile with ladys.

Address: For My Brother Locke at My Lord Chancellours.

Endorsed by Locke: Mr Blomer 27 Dec. 72.

## *268.* JOHN AUBREY to [LOCKE?], 11 February 1673 (*1714*)

P.R.O., S.P. 30/24, bdle. 7, no. 493. Printed in L. F. Brown, *Shaftesbury*, p. 206; Cranston, *Locke*, pp. 151–2. The principal reason for believing that the letter was addressed to Locke is the endorsement; its preservation among the Shaftesbury papers and the references to Shaftesbury favour the

[1] Northumberland House was at Charing Cross, with a garden running towards the river; Northumberland Avenue occupies the site. Shaftesbury as Lord Chancellor presumably wanted more or better accommodation than Exeter House provided.

[2] p. 332, n. 3.

[3] No. *256*.

[4] Dr. John Pearson, who was probably a friend of the Blomers (p. 346), was nominated bishop of Chester on 1 December of this year; Dr. Isaac Barrow (1630–77; *D.N.B.*) was appointed Master of Trinity College, Cambridge, on the same day: *Cal. S.P., Dom.*, 1672–3, p. 234.

view, but are not decisive. Aubrey and Locke are likely to have met at meetings of the Royal Society, if not elsewhere.

John Aubrey, 1626–97, antiquary and biographer: *D.N.B.*; Anthony Powell, *John Aubrey and his Friends*, 1948.

Sir!

I cannot but present you my thankes for your great Humanity and kindnes to me; as also for the honour you doe me to peruse my Scriblings.[1] I was at your lodgeing twice to have kiss't your hands before I came out of Towne—to have recommended a MSS or two (worthy of your perusall) of my old friend Mr Th: Hobbes.[2] One is a Treatise concerning the Lawe, which I importun'd him to undertake about 8 yeares since and then in order thereto presented him with my L. Ch: Bacons Elements of the Lawe.[3] All men will give the old Gentleman that right as to acknowledge his great felicity in well defining: and all know that the lawyers especially the common [omnium Doctorum genus indoctissimum][a] superstruct on their old fashion'd Axioms, right or wrong; for great practisers have not the leisure to be analytiques. Mr H. seem'd then something doubtfull he should not have dayes enough left to goe about such a worke. In this treatise he is highly for the Kings Prerogative: Ch: Just: Hales haz read it,[4] and very much mislikes it; is his enemy and will not license it. Judge Vaughan[5] haz perusd it and very much commends it, but is afrayd to license for feare of giving displeasure. 'Tis pitty fire should consume it, or that it should miscarry as I have known some excellent things. I never expect to see it printed, and intended to have a copy, which the bookeseller will let me have for 50s; and God willing I will have one at my returne. He writes short and therfore the fitter for your reading, being so full of Businesse. When you goe by the Palsgrave-head Taverne[6] be pleasd to call on mr W: Crooke[7] at the green dragon and

[a] *Aubrey's brackets.*

[1] Catalogue and description of Aubrey's extant MSS. in Powell, pp. 271–94.

[2] Thomas Hobbes, 1588–1679: *D.N.B.* The treatise was published in 1681 with another book by Hobbes: *The Art of Rhetoric, with a Discourse of the Laws of England.*

[3] Francis Bacon, Viscount St. Albans, *The Elements of the Common Lawes of England*, 1630; later editions 1636–35, 1639.

[4] Sir Matthew Hale, 1609–76; Lord Chief Justice of the King's Bench 1671–6: *D.N.B.*

[5] Sir John Vaughan, 1603–74; Lord Chief Justice of the Common Pleas, 1668–74: ibid. He was a friend of Hobbes and owned a copy of the treatise: Aubrey, '*Brief Lives*', ed. A. Clark, 1898, i. 341–2, 369.

[6] On the south side of the Strand, near Temple Bar: Wheatley, *London.*

[7] William Crooke, active as a bookseller from 1664 to 1694. In succession to his father Andrew Crooke (p. 199, n. 2) he published Hobbes's works from 1671 onwards: Plomer, *Dictionary, 1668–1725.*

remember me to him by the same token I desired Mr Hobbes to give his Workes to Magd: hall[1] and he will shew it to you. I have a conceit that if your Lord[2] sawe it he would like it. You may there see likewise his History of England from 1640 to 1660 about a quire of paper, which the King haz read and likes extremely, but tells him there is so much truth in it he dares not license for feare of displeasing the Bishops.[3] The old gent is still strangely vigorous [85][a] if you see him (which he would take kindly) pray my service to him. God graunt length of dayes to our Illustrious Lord Chancellor,[4] who seriously deserves a Statue for the good he haz already begun. I humbly beg your pardon for giving you this trouble, and to be assured that I am affectionately

Sir

Your most humble servant

JO: AUBREY.

Shrovetuesday, 1672. Essex.

I have writt to parson Browne[5] of Myntye to send you a Token of Remembrance. Myntye is my Lords mannor.[6]

About May I hope to kisse your hands.

Endorsed by Locke: Mr *Aubrey* Feb. *72*

## 269. LOCKE to DR. JOHN MAPLETOFT, 14 February 1673 (265, *314*)

*European Magazine*, xiv (1788), 402–3. Fox Bourne, reprinting the text from the *European Magazine*, silently corrected it at two points: i. 316–17. I have followed him in altering it.

Exeter House, 14th Feb. 72–3.

Dear Sir,

'Petimusque damusque vicissim',[7] is noe unusefull rule in freindship; or if it be, I thinke I have taken a sure course to convince you

[a] *Aubrey's brackets.*

[1] Where Hobbes was entered at Oxford.
[2] Presumably Shaftesbury.
[3] This refers to *Behemoth*. It was first published as *The History of the Civil Wars in England*, 1679 (three editions), and then as *Behemoth*, 1679, 1680, 1682, and in Hobbes's *Tracts*, 1682; the first complete edition, by F. Tönnies, 1889: H. Macdonald and M. Hargreaves, *Thomas Hobbes: a Bibliography*, 1952, pp. 64–7, 74. Hobbes again mentioned Charles II's refusal to license it in his letter to Aubrey, 18 August 1679.
[4] Shaftesbury.
[5] Richard Brown. Not further identifiable.
[6] Probably Shaftesbury.
[7] 'We ask (it) and grant (it) in turn' (of poetical licence): Horace, *Ars Poetica*, 11.

that I was not angry at the slowness of your congratulacon,[1] since I have not been hasty to chide you for it: and things are now come to that passe, that I feare I shall be thought the guiltyer person of the too. I have a great deale to say in my excuse, and should no doubt use a pretence of businesse; the confusion and disorder of new affairs, to a man not versed in the world, and a thousand things of this nature, which you that have noe thing, I hope, to doe but enjoy the faire day of a constant spring, may easily thinke[a-] on: some[-a] such pretences, I say, I should offer to you in defence of my silence, did I not consider you as my assured freind, who were not to be got or lost at the rate of a few words, or would not thinke favourably of me when I did not speake for myself. And I doubt not but you have donne by my acknowledgment as I did by your good wishes, for I assured myself of them before they came, and staid not for the post or the pacquet bote to receive that satisfaction. Could I as easily bring hither all that I value in France, as I could those kinde thoughts, you had perhaps lost now and then a sunshiny day this winter, and would at this moment more want a freeze coat then a parasol: but I will not tell you how fast it snows here now, least you should grow ⟨too⟩[b] fond of Aix, and thinke London an ill habitation. But I hope the sun, who hath made you almost forget your own country, will revenge us on you, and drive such runagates very shortly from his neighbourhood. This I confesse is a little harsh to be said, but what would you have a man doe whose fingers ake with cold whilst he is writing to those who brag of warmth and sunshine, and wantonly reject and repell those rays every day which we see not once a fortnight. But to be serious with you, I rejoyce heartily at the health you have all found in that temperate climate. I wish the whole journy may have the same successe, and returne you safe to us, who long for you in England. I enjoy my part of your delicate evenings, and there is noe thing about me that is not the better for it but my lungs. I know not how they will hold out, but this I found, that my voiage to Paris did not a litle mend them. For that and the kinde intentions farther, I must never forget to pay my most humble thanks to the best Lady in France,[2] which I desire you to doe in your best words,

[a-a] *European Magazine* thinke: on some   [b] *European Magazine* so

[1] On his appointment as secretary of presentations.
[2] Lady Northumberland.

with my service to the little lady.[1] Your cosin Collet, from whome in this pacquet I convey a letter to you, is very well; you are both very much indebted to him for his care in Pool's affaire; we have fingerd some mony, and hope to have more after some time, for we both thought it was better to stay for it then by beginning an uncertain war produce certaine trouble without being assured of the event. We knew you a peaceable man, but perhaps it may not be amisse to send feirce commands to Mr. Collet that you may seeme terrible, and let us alone to mitigate your wrath. Dr. Sydenham and I mention you some times, for we doe not now meet often, my businesse now allowing me but litle leisure for visits: but I hope I shall in a short space bring it to better termes. Here is a freind of mine, troubled with a paralitick distemper, sollicites me to desire you to procure him, from the part of France you are in, some of the Queen of Hungary's Water,[2] which he hears is best made there abouts. If you can get him three or four quarts and send it to London by the way of Marselles, or ship it at any other port, you will much oblige me. The use and effects of it here would be worth your enquiry, and if you can informe your self concerning Bourbon Waters,[3] how to be taken, in what diseases, and with what successe, you may possibly bring home with you a new use of our Bath waters, for which I would thank you. I continue my request to you for some sweets, as gloves, perfumes, out of those parts when you come away, but would not cumber you, for roads and carriage I know will be scarce. My service to all the good company; and be assured that I am,

Dear Sir,

Your most affectionate, sincere, and humble servant,

J. LOCKE.

My humble service to Mrs. Ramsey, Mr. Scawen, Mrs. Alice, Mr. Sherwood, and the rest of my freinds there.

Pray tell the Doctor and his wife[4] that Mrs. Grig and the litle femme[5] are well, and present my service to her.

Address: For my much honoured freind Dr. Mapletoft, at Aix.

[1] Lady Elizabeth Percy.

[2] A distillate of rosemary: A. C. Wootton, *Chronicles of Pharmacy*, 1910, i. 296–8.

[3] At this time the celebrated waters were those of Bourbon-l'Archambault: Evelyn, *Diary*, ed. de Beer, ii. 155 and n.

[4] Dr. and Mrs. Blomer.

[5] No. *256*, etc.

## *270.* SIR PETER COLLETON to LOCKE, 28 May 1673 (*254, 275*)

P.R.O., S.P. 30/24, bdle. 48, no. 90. Excerpts printed in Fox Bourne, i. 288. 292; the whole, in South Carolina Hist. Soc., *Collections*, v (1897), 422–4; calendared in *Cal. S.P.*, *Col.*, vol. vii, no. 1103. For transmission see no. *275*,

Colleton was deputy-governor of Barbados from *c.* 5 April of this year until *c.* 1 November 1674: *Cal.*, as above, nos. 1065, 1372.

Barbados this 28th of may 1673

My deare frend

I have been long expecting to hear newes from you from New england,[1] and my lord Willoughby[2] and I had projects of taking Carolina in our way and viziting of you there, but it hath pleased God to dispose things otherwise, hee is dead you I understand in imployment in England, and I tyed by the legg with an office here, untill his majesty please to release mee, Our frends in Carolina sing the same song they did from the beginning, a very healthy, a very pleasant and fertill country, but great want of victuall, cloathes, and tooles, and I am of opinion the 2 last ought to bee sent them, one suply more of that kind would bee enough, victuall they will bee sufficiently furnishd with this year never to want more, and if wee should omit the other two wee may run a hazzard of loozing all the mony wee have been out, for after Barbados had been setled 6 years, the people who were then upwards of 600 men were leaving of it in a humour, and you see what this Island is come to, and no doubt if wee hould our grownd but Carolina will excell all other English plantations, severall men of Considerable estates will ingage from hence as soon as their is peace and shipping is to bee had,[3] I have sent all the letters I have Received to my lord[4] who I doubt not but will comunicate them to you, I send to Colonel Thornburgh[5] by this conveyance a box of Carolina China root[6] to bee

[1] This appears to be the only extant notice of whatever project Locke may have formed of a journey to New England.

[2] William Willoughby, sixth Baron Willoughby of Parham, governor of Barbados since 1667; he died on 10 April of this year: *D.N.B.*, art. Willoughby, Francis.

[3] Barbados was taken possession of in 1625. The first settlers arrived in 1627. Disputed claims to proprietorship led to local dissensions, and the years 1630 and 1631 are known as 'the Starving Time'. By 1629 the population was between 1600 and 1800: V. T. Harlow, *History of Barbados, 1625–85*, 1926, pp. 3–15. For the then condition of Carolina see nos. *272*, *275*.

[4] Shaftesbury.

[5] Col. Edward Thornburgh, who acted as secretary to 'the Gentlemen Planters [of Barbados] in London': *Cal. S.P.*, *Col.*, vol. vii, no. 413, etc.

[6] Probably the root of Smilax pseudo-China, 'still employed in America as an alterative medicine': *O.E.D.* (1889), s.v. China.

devided between your selfe and a cozen of mine that is a drugster, they tell mee here they are the right sort, and they may bee so for any thing I know, I find I am your partner in the Bahama trade which will turne to accompt if you meddle not with planting, but if you plant otherwise then for provizion for your factor you will have your whole stock drowned in a plantation and bee never the better for it, planting is my trade and I thinke I may without vanity say I understand it as well as most men, and I am sure I am not deceived in this particuler, if other men will plant there, I mean the Bahamas,[a] hinder them not, they improve our province, but I would neither have you nor my lord ingadge in it, I can give reasons I am sure will sattisfye you,[1] I was in hopes to have sent you a jarr of this Islands Tarr[2] by this conveyance but it shall come by the next with what other raritys wee have, in the mean time I desire you to beeleeve that I am most sincerely

your faithfull frend and servant

mr Lock

Address: To John Lock Esquire at little Exeter howse in the Strand London.
Endorsed by Locke: *Bahama* Sir Peter Colleton to JL 28° May. *73*

## *271.* William Allestree to Locke, 16 June 1673 (*263*, *273*)

P.R.O., S.P. 30/24, bdle. 47, no. 17. Excerpts printed in Fox Bourne, i. 320.

Stockholm. June the 16th: 1673.

Sir

If you thinke winter left us here before the 14th of April (which is the date of yours) let me tell you without heat or passion, that you are grosely mistaken; for even upon the first of may it froze so hard, that what juste-au-corps, or vests were that day in fashion

[a] *Clause interlined; punctuation supplied.*

[1] On 1 November 1670 the Bahamas were granted to the Lords Proprietors of Carolina, who entered into an agreement on 4 September 1672 with eleven 'adventurers to Bahamas', a group including Locke, Mapletoft, Thomas Stringer (p. 434 n.), Richard Kingdon (p. 365 n.), Peter Jones (p. 365, n. 3), Edward Thornburgh (p. 379, n. 5), John Darrell (p. 392, n. 6), and William Kiffin (p. 571, n. 2); they were to provide between £1,600 and £2,000 and in return to be granted land in New Providence and the other islands and to enjoy various rights for 31 years: B.M. Add. MS. 15640; Fox Bourne, i. 289–93; Brown, *Shaftesbury*, pp. 167–8.

[2] Its properties are set out in no. *275*.

at Hide-Parke I know not, here I am sure good furr coats were all a la mode. I acknowledge myselfe very happy in that warmth which you assure me remain's still in your breast towards me, and though my heart be as full of heat and zeal for your service as any, yet in spite of it, my nose end (at which place none but whelps and beasts make love) is yet very cold. As for the pleasures of winter, here are but few for strangers, since they consisting principally in drinking, coursing, and shooting, wee who cannot do these things, must stay at home: besides, that that cold which they call fine briske weather would as surely kill us poore tender chickins, as they do Pheasants: 'tis true, the clearnesse of the heavens and the whitenesse of the Earth, is a pleasant sight even to our Eyes which are hurt by the reflexion of its light, but when wee vent're out a sledging the aire is so sharp, and the motion of the sledge so swift, that if honest Squire Argus himselfe with his 100 Eyes were here, were they all as tender as my two, hee might staire as long as hee pleas'd, but it would be to as little purpose as ever the blind-Bard Homer did; and hee would soon have as much need of a Dog and a bell for his conductour as that old Tost[1] had when hee went whining out his songs from doare to doare for bread and cheese. But what is yet worse, wee are forc'd to keep our selves so warme within our chambers, that wee can hardly come out, without taking cold; whereas the very Children of this country will come piping hott out of their stoves, and after having play'd and tumbl'd awhile upon the snow, go in again. You may see souldgiers here, who will take as sound a nap upon a fleece of snow, as you can upon a bed of Down, and who when they rise and shake their Eares find not their haire full of feathers (as our Loobyes in England do) but well tagg'd round with Iceiccles,[a] and such as these are Gothes and vandalls.

As for the witches, to whom you desire to be better known, I have no acquaintance with them, because they (as upon examination they confesse) cannot possibly get in to Stockholme, and I am resolv'd not to go out to them. I am promis'd a copy of the last Tryall of them, which if I obtain, as soon as it can be translated, you shall have it. Things of this nature are har⟨d to b⟩e[b] got, as being forbidden to be communicated, upon the account that the

[a] *MS.* Ice- / iccles [b] *Page torn.*

[1] An old toast, a soaker: *O.E.D.*

silly commonalty which will still be reading them, oft phansy's from thence things tending to its own prejudice.[1]

I have a mapp to send you wherein is represented by picture the manner how the Laplanders worshipp old nick, with severall other customes in use amongst them.[2] The History of Lapland hath lately bene writ in Latin by a Priest who liv'd long in that country, but you will easilier get it in England, then I can here, for it is now printing at Franckfort.[3]

It is not only in Lapland but also in these parts, that the country people drinke the healths, of God the Father, of their King, and that of their wives, and then whilst one drinke's, the rest of the company sing these words, If these three be our friends, wee care not for our Enemyes.

Sir Ed: wood (who is your humble servant) will be my witnesse, that before I receiv'd this letter of yours, I was preparing to send you what you aske for, and therefore give me leave to tell you, that I do not thinke you are so great a stranger to witches and Familiars as you would passe for, since you have so opportunely enter'd into his thoughts who think'es none so well employ'd, as those which tend to prove him in his very soule,

Sir

your most devoted servant

WM: ALLESTREE.

Address: For John Lock Esquire Secretary to my Lord High Chancellor of England London.

Endorsed by Locke: Mr. Wm *Alestree* 16 Jun. *73*

## *272.* JOSEPH WEST to LOCKE, 28 June 1673 (*318*)

P.R.O., S.P. 30/24, bdle. 48, no. 91. Printed in South Carolina Hist. Soc. *Collections*, v. 424–5; calendared in *Cal. S.P., Col.*, vol. vii, no. 1113.

Joseph West, *fl.* 1669–85; acting governor or governor of Carolina 1671–2, 1674–82, and 1684–5; an associate of Shaftesbury and apparently the most

[1] There were several investigations into alleged cases of witchcraft about this time; in 1669 23 men were condemned to death, and 15 of them were beheaded and burnt; in 1675 71 were condemned, and 9 beheaded and burnt: G. P. Hallenberg, *Dissertatio de Inquisitione Sagarum in Svecia, an. 1668–1677*, 1787.

[2] See no. *277*.

[3] See no. *282*. The author, J. G. Scheffer or Schefferus, 1621–79, was not a divine; he was appointed professor of oratory in the university of Uppsala in 1648 and honorary professor of the Law of Nature and Nations in 1665: *A.D.B.*; *Biografiskt Lexikon . . . Svenska Män*, 1843–90. He derived his information about the Lapps from the local clergy and government officials. For another book by him see no. *1525*.

active man in the colony: *Dict. American Biography*; *D.N.B.*; Haley, *Shaftesbury*, pp. 248–50, etc.

Sir

Allthough I have writt severall times to you, both by way of Berbados, and Virginia, and by Mr Portman[1] who latly went from hence by way of Bermuda, in the ship Blessing,[2] yett I could not Omitt this opportunity, to present you with this my humble servis, and to Intreat your Assistance by Impertuning the Earle of Shafts Bury, to hasten a ship from England, with more People, and supplyes of Cloathing, and Toole, etc; for the People are not able to subsist long without they are supplyed by the Lords Proprietors, and there is nothing butt the Lords Proprietors Assistance can preserve the settlement from falling, which in time I am Confident will Come to something, and If timely supplyed will Answer every mans expectations of it, and for the Advantage of healthfullness, and pleasantness, I beleeve noe plantation settled by the English in America doth aford the Like, and if we ware butt Once stocked with Cattle, that we might fall uppon English Husbandry it would quickly be a very plentyfull Place, I suppose before this you have heard of our Extream wants of provisions this year, which now God be praised we have Allmost overcome, for about a Monthe hence we shall have Corne Enough of our owne Groweth, and hope we shall never fear wanting Indian Corne againe, for this Want will doe much good in the Countrey, by teaching people to be better Husbands, and more Industrous, for the futter, and not depend any more uppon supply, Butt I being straightned for want of time, I shall Refer you to the Report of the Barer Mr: Miles Man,[3] who I hope will truly Informe you of all things here noething elce I am

Sir, your Most humble servant to Command

JOSEPH WEST

Charles Towen one Ashly river
June 28th: (73

Address: To John Locke Esquire at Littell Exeter house In the Strand present London

Endorsed by Locke: *Carolina* Jos: West to JL 28° Jun. *73*

[1] Christopher Portman: p. 386; South Carolina Hist. Soc., *Coll.*, v. 330 n., 331, etc.

[2] She reached Carolina on 14 August 1671 and apparently now returned to England: ibid., p. 318 n., etc.

[3] Apparently sent to Carolina in 1672 either for public work or for work on Shaftesbury's own plantations: ibid., pp. 375–6, 406. He was perhaps a kinsman of Col. Miles Man, who served under Monck in Scotland in 1659–60: Firth, *Regimental History*, pp. 515–18, etc.

## 273. William Allestree to Locke, 14 July 1673 (*271, 277*)

P.R.O., S.P. 30/24, bdle. 5, no. 254. Excerpt printed in Fox Bourne, i. 321.

Stockholm: July the 14th :–73.

Sir

This honest marchand whose name is Bedall hath seen the map of Lapland which I designe to sent you, and if hee had comne all the way by sea, hee had certainly brought it with him. I will send it you by the first good occasion. I have a Relation of witches in the Swedish Tongue, but for my life cannot get it translated. As much as I am able to comprehend of it, it contain's as extravagant storyes as ever were told in a chimney corner by an old woman in winter nights in England. Sir John Worden hath the same relation as I have, and (as I am told) hath gott it translated and printed in English.[1] I will give you as good an account of this as I can when I send you the map. The Bearer of this will be able to give you a good account of witches as living very near Norway, where the witches are as learned as in Lapland.

I have no newes to send you but that these people though Mediatours, wish as little successe to us as to the Hollanders, and if wee can get nothing by our Armes, wee must not expect much from their Intermission.[2] The Envoy[3] Kiss'es your hands, I wish you from my very soul all health and happinesse, and remain Sir

your most oblig'd and ever obedient servant

Wm Allestree[a]

Address: For John Lock Esq secretary to the Lord High Chancellor of England at Exeter house London

Endorsed by Locke: mr *Allestree* 14 Jul *73*

[a] *Beneath the signature there is a note, written not by Allestree and only questionably by Locke* Mr Bedall at the Blew bell in Waping.

---

[1] Sir John Werden was envoy extraordinary to Sweden from 1670 to 1672: *D.N.B.* I have not found his translation. An account of an examination of some alleged witches in Sweden in 1669 and 1670, translated by Anthony Horneck (ibid.), is appended to Joseph Glanvill, *Saducismus Triumphatus*, 3rd ed., 1689.

[2] In the war between the English and French on the one side, the United Provinces on the other, the Swedes were acting as mediators; a congress opened at Cologne on 8/18 June 1673: Lavisse, *Hist. de France*, VII. ii. 318.

[3] Sir Edward Wood.

## *274.* ISAAC RUSH to LOCKE, 15 July 1673 (*291*)

P.R.O., S.P. 30/24, bdle. 49, no. 5. Quoted in Fox Bourne, i. 293.
New Providence is one of the Bahamas. Rush was Shaftesbury's deputy there: *Cal. S.P., Col.*, vol. vii, no. 963; for him see L. F. Brown, *Shaftesbury*, pp. 168, 175. He was evidently a Quaker.

Newe Providence the 15th of the 5th moneth caled Ju⟨ly⟩[a]

Doctor Lock

Being informed by my very good friend Roger Knowles[1] of thy respects in prefering mee to the Lord Chancelors favor:[2] I could in civility doe noe les then signify my acknowledgment by a fewe lynes in returne: of my thankefull axceptance: I hope my indeavors in the discharge of my duty and trust by the Chancelor will noe way blemish the reputation of those who weeare instrumentall in my preferment: By Thomas Hasted[3] I have sent the two shugar loves as an earnest of my future gratitude which I shall by all opertunities take advantage to signify especially if it may sute with thy desier of houlding coresspondsy with mee I shall be glad to be any way servisable to thee or thy intrust wheareby it may Apeare that I am

Thy friend to serve the in any office of love

ISAAC RUSH

Address: These To Doctor John Lock present

Endorsed by Locke: *Bahama* Isac Rush to JL 15° Jul. *73*

## *275.* SIR PETER COLLETON to LOCKE, 12 August 1673 (*270, 279*)

P.R.O., S.P. 30/24, bdle. 49, no. 3. Written mainly by an amanuensis. Excerpts printed in Fox Bourne, I. 326–7. For transmission see no. *279*.

Sir

I wrote you by his Majestys Ship the St: David which Letter I hope came safe to your hands.[4] Since then wee have had newes from

[a] *Page torn.*

[1] A man of this name was a warden of the Barber-Surgeons' Company in 1688–91 and Master in 1693–4: S. Young, *The Annals of the Barber-Surgeons of London*, 1890, p. 10. He may be the Mr. Knollys who is said to have operated on Shaftesbury under Locke's direction in 1668: Haley, p. 205. See also no. *1627*.

[2] Shaftesbury.

[3] Probably not — Hastede of no. *279*.

[4] The letter is no. *270*. The *St. David* was a fourth-rate, 646 tons, 54 guns, built in 1667: R. C. Anderson, no. 430. She brought Lord Willoughby's body to England: *Cal. S.P., Col.*, vol. vii, no. 1098.

Carolina of the 28th of May where the poor people had been exposed to very great misery and hardship's for want of supplyes one vessel by which they expected them was 7 months on a voyage that might have been performed in two Months, the other was taken by a Caper,[1] they have sent home Mr Christopher Portman[2] to make their condition known to the proprietors, and they must be fair spoken at this Instant or they may chance to quitt the Collony in a humour and wee loose all the money wee have been out, In this nick it hath gone hard even with those that are best able, for fraught being here at 12 l. per tonn wee could not get a vessel to goe there, to carry the supplys that were ready in this place to be sent, Inclosed is, a Letter from Mr Owen[3] by which you may perceive what tune the people sing, they have now lanched two vessells there, and I have bought another to ply there which will be a help to them, if wee can but make them stand untill the warr be over, wee need not doubt the comeing to them of most of the people Northward of them, they should presently have a supply of tools cloathes and amunition sent them.

By the last Fleet I sent you a parcell of Carolina China Root, which was directed to Colonel Thornburgh for you, by this I send you a Jarr of this countrey Tarr, which I think is Oyl of Bitumen[a] of whose sanative quallity some here talke wonders, I have Known the Oyl of it helpe the sciatica, and it with white lilly root hath cured the Glanders in severall of my horses, I also send you a pott of Tarara root,[4] which is the root which cures the wounds made by the Indians poysoned Arrows, which was first discovered by Major Walker a Kinsman of mine, and now a Captain in the princes Regiment of Dragoons,[5] an Indian that had accidentally prick'd his Thumb with an arrow being at Sea, and having none of this root gave him self over for dead, and his hand swell'd extreamly, Major Walker being with him found a mongst his things a small piece of the root at the sight of which the Indian rejoyced extreamly, and chewing and applying some of it to the wound and swallowing

[a] *Word written by Colleton.*

[1] A privateer: *O.E.D.* [2] p. 383.

[3] William Owen, one of the more important colonists in Carolina: South Carolina Hist. Soc., *Collections*, v. 196 n. and *passim*.

[4] I have not found the name elsewhere. Apparently snake root or something similar: see *O.E.D.*

[5] Presumably James Walker of the Barbados Regiment of Dragoons, under the command of Prince Rupert: *Cal. S.P., Col.*, vol. vii, nos. 791–2.

another part put a stop to the swelling, and when he came on shore being brought to a garden where Walker had formerly planted some, by the fresh Juce of that root quite cured his Thumb in a very short time, I find amongst the people it hath an extream hygh reputation, but our Doctors who think it not for their proffit that any should have the power of healing but themselves, are Infidells, yet some have confessed to me that the sediment of the Juce dried and powdred is a most forcible diaphoretick,[1] Colonel Codrington[2] my Lord Willoughbys deputy in this place, hath assured mee that he hath by giveing the Juce inwardly cured gonorheas[a] in his Negros so virulent, and Coroding, that bloud hath Issued mingled with the usual Flux of that distemper, nor hath any accidents hapned upon the suddan stopping of that flux, it cures the yawes in our negroes, which I think is a disease between the Leprosy and the pox, a grave Gentleman a Judge and neighbour of mine tells me that a Negroe of his hath had a sore legg 17 years, which was so bad the Surgeons would have cutt it off, which the Negroe refuse-ing to suffer they left him as Incureable, this Gentleman hath caused the arrow root to be tryed on his negroe, of the Juce of which he drinks and hath it applyed outwardly to his legg also, which hath almost brought the ulcer to a perfect cure, and tells me he doth not doubt it will make him quite well, One story more I must give you to shew that there is a vertue in this Drug I have not heard of in any other, Major Kingsland[3] sayes he had an old Bull that was so weak he could not stand, and giveing him over for dead, he was resolved to try what this tarara root would do on him, and gave him a good lusty draught of the Juce mingled with wine, and in an hourr after the bull riseth and finding a Cowe of his acquain-tance by, getts upon her back and did the feat very well with her, if this root have the vertues I have written I have sent you a treasure, however if it be not I wish it weare[b] and I desire you to beeleeve mee to bee most sincerely

your very faithfull and humble servant

P Colleton

Barbados this 12th of August *1673*

[a] *Word written by Colleton.* [b] *The rest of letter and the address are written by Colleton.*

[1] A sudorific.

[2] Christopher Codrington, sen., 1640–98, deputy-governor of Barbados 1669–72: V. T. Harlow, *Christopher Codrington, 1668–1710*, 1928, pp. 11–37.

[3] Nathaniel Kingsland of Barbados: *Cal. S.P., Col.*, vol. vii, no. 44, etc.

I have sent the Tarr and the roots to Colonel Thornburgh for you

Address: To my honnoured frend mr John Lock at my Lord Chancellors present London

Endorsed by Locke: *Medicina* Sir Pet: Colleton 12 Aug. *73* Tar and Tarara root

## 276. LOCKE to JOHN STRACHEY, 16 September [1673] (264, 284)

University Library, Basel. Transcribed from photostat. Printed in Rand, p. 80. Year from contents.

Exeterhouse 16 Sept:

Sir

Since my last I had an oportunity to speake with Sir Walter Vane[1] who is ⟨unkle⟩[a] to the young Knight Sir Nicholas Pelham,[2] who received the proposition concerning my Cosin Jep[3] very kindely, and told me that now goeing out of towne into the Country where he should see his Nephew he would talke with him of it and I should heare from him in a few days, The estate he tells me goes for 1000l. and is really now in the abatement of rents worth 900l. per annum, and the young Knight himself is realy as sober and pretty a man as any I know. I am extreamely glad the physick wrought soe well on the man that came to your house as soon as I had left it. I desire you would persuade him to give it effectually to others in the like case, for it will be very much for their health and good. This I will be answerable for and a better physitian of my acquaintance here, who you know is in that malady for miled and gentle physick, and hath a great care not to hurt his patients that are troubled[b] with this disease, pray see that this bee donne with good effect. and you will be usefull to your neighbours[c] in this sickly season. I cannot approve of the aire of Bath, but you that are soe neare a neigbour to it will I hope be carefull to make what

[a] *MS.* unke [b] *Or* trubled [c] *Or* neigbours

[1] p. 233, n. 3.

[2] *c.* 1651–1739; a younger son of Sir Thomas Pelham, second baronet, of Laughton, Sussex, by Margaret, sister of Sir Walter Vane; knighted 1661; matriculated from Christ Church 1665; M.P. 1671–8, etc.: Foster.

[3] p. 369, n. 2.

observations you can and improve the knowledg of one who is yet but a young practitioner in physick. You are a very lucky man for I had bespoke, and bid mony for a periwig the morning before you writt to me, but we agreed not in the price and soe that bargain is saved. I will take care about your belt, have given your message to Mr Stringer[1] and am

Sir

most affectionate humble servant

JOHN LOCKE

My service to the Ladys

Address: For John Strachy Esquire at Sutton Court. To be left at Mr Codringtons[2] shop in High street Bristoll

Postmarks: SE —; defective receiving-office mark.

## 277. WILLIAM ALLESTREE: notes on a picture showing Lapp life, 16 September 1673 (*273*, *282*)

B.L., MS. Locke c. 31, ff. 13–14. The original picture is probably lost; it appears to be reproduced in a pair of coloured drawings and in an engraving.

The drawings, the summer and winter pictures separately, are in B.M., Add. MS. 5253, ff. 6–7, and are accompanied by a manuscript copy of the present notes. The volume containing them, an album of drawings, belonged formerly to Sir Hans Sloane (no. *788*), who acquired the natural history and other collections of William Charleton (or Courten; p. 508 n.). In 1687 Locke sent to Charleton a set of drawings of 'Indians' made by his servant Sylvester Brounower (p. 628, n. 4): no. 951; these are almost certainly a set in the album, and it is likely that the present drawings also were made by Brounower and given by Locke to Charleton; the likeliest date is in 1689 or shortly after (the drawings are very unlikely to be the two parts of the original picture sent to Locke in 1673).

The engraving is by F. H. van Hove (Thieme, *Lexikon*) and is in Moses Pitt's *English Atlas*, vol. i, 1680 (p. 583, n. 5). The summer and winter pictures are shown one above the other; the plate bears the arms of the first earl of Shaftesbury and is accompanied by a slightly varying version of the present notes. The arrangement of some of the scenes or figures differs from that in the drawings; there are divergences in the dresses and the background. In general the drawings appear to be fairly faithful reproductions of the original, and the engraving to give an elaborated version; the dresses in the drawings are far closer than those in the engravings to those shown in the cuts in Scheffer's *Lapponia* (p. 397, n. 1; the alterations in the engraving would have been in van Hove's powers).

[1] p. 434 n.

[2] The name occurs from time to time as that of a Bristol shopkeeper or merchant; it is not clear whether it is the one man throughout.

If the drawings are fairly faithful the original was probably fairly crude, the work of an amateur and not of a professional artist. Though some of the figures are similarly occupied there is no obvious artistic relationship with the cuts in Scheffer. Some of the scenes are probably fictitious, and notably the brandy at the church-door: G. Ahlström, *De Mörka Bergen*, 1966, pp. 16–17; information from Dr. Ahlström.

The Lives and manners of the Laplanders.

Going from your Right Hand to your Left,

The upper part represent's their summer. where first you see

A church for those who are converted to the Lutheran Religion, at the Entrance of which in lieu of a Bason of Holy water, there stand's one full of Brandywine with a spoon in it, of which every one who com'es to church tak'es a supp to encourage and warme his zeal. The first man you there see represent's the Priest, the next the best man of the parish, Then follow'es a Bride attended upon by two Bridemaids, after whom com'es the Bridegroom and other Friends.

The next is their manner of making Baskets, which is their greatest Trade.

The two next figures represent their way of carrying and of Rocking their children.

The manner how the young children grown up, suck the Rine-Deer.

The man and wive's way of Lying in Bed.

Above that, you have Their houses for keeping their provisions, Themselves in the coldest part of winter lying in Tents.

The next is their manner of Eating.

Then the Priest's way of Baptizing, and the clark'es bringing of water.

Above which you have.

Their way of drawing wire which is much us'd amongst them for adorning of Lapp's Boots and coats.

Then amongst those who are not yet converted to the Christian Religion you have, Their way of Sacrificing, Their three Gods stand uppermost, and under each of them upon each Altar ly three pieces of the sacrific'd Rine Deer, after which follow'es Their way of praying to them.

Then, Their way of buriall. Then

Their way of praying to Death herselfe that shee would be pleas'd to spare them awhile.

In the second part you have their Winter.
where going from the left hand to the Right you find First,

Their manner of bringing Their Taxes consisting of severall sortes of Skins, and dry Fish, to the Kings Commissioner. which being pay'd, each one tak'es a larg Spoonfull of Brandywine which stand's at the End of the Table, and so away.

Above which you see the Commissioner's Tent,

Their way of travelling in Sledges drawn by Rine Deer, (which by the by, do agree with those barren countryes so well, that if you do but bring them into this of Sweden (which yet is none of the most fertil) they dye in a short time).

Their way of Carrying their Goods.

Their manner of Ruling their Rine Deer with a whip or line.

Their way of Shooting them.

Their taking Tobacco, which they prize above meat.

Their Speaking in the Ear of their Rine-Deer, telling them what they should do, or whither they should go, (which as I am here credibly inform'd, They will observe exactly).

Their manner of gelding them.

Their way of laying their heads under a Drum, which the Devil beats, and from thence the man learn's what successe hee shall have in his affairs.

His giving the man the hammer, and leting him beat.

Address: This Paper and Picture are for Mr Lock Secretary to the Lord High Chancellour of England; sent him by his most
Humble Servant
WILLIAM ALLESTREE.

Stockholm
Sept: 16. 1673

Endorsed by Locke: LAEI *Lapland* Explicacon of the picture *73*

## *278.* DR. DAVID THOMAS to LOCKE, 29 September 1673 (*238, 345*)

P.R.O., S.P. 30/24, bdle. 5, no. 263.

Deare Freind

My Brother Greenehill[1] is very much troubled that such a report should be raysed on him who meant nothing lesse as will appeare

[1] John Greenhill, *c.* 1640/5–76, the artist, Mrs. Thomas's brother: *D.N.B.*;

by his answer to mee inclosed, by which if you are satisfyed pray let him know soe much and likewise consider whether that report may not be raysed by some other to make a difference betweene you he drawing my Lord Chancellors picture[1] pray present my Service to Dr Sidneham and Lysis.[2] Parthenice[3] send hers to you all. I am

your Freind and Servant
D THOMAS

Sarum
Sept 29 73

Endorsed by Locke: D: *Thomas* 29 Sept 1673

## *279.* SIR PETER COLLETON to LOCKE, [about October 1673] (*275*, *287*)

B.L., MS. Locke c. 6, ff. 215–16. Text written by an amanuensis. Date from mention of no. *275* and by reckoning from the postmark.

Sir

I wrote you by Captain Hailes[4] of which Inclossed I send you the copy least the Originall should have miscarryed and you think me more negligent towards you then I am, by that Ship I sent you a Jarr of this country tarr and a pot of tarara root which I hope came safe to your hands. Since then is arrived here the Bahama Merchant[5] whom Captain Dorrell[6] hath luckily sent here to seek a fraught and I hope he will make upwards of 1000ld: fraught of what he takes in here, I find the people in providence did not well brook the adventurers being jealous they would turn to a company like that of Bermuda[7] at first but being satisfied of the contrary have

B.M., *Catalogue of British Drawings*: vol. i, *XVI and XVII centuries*, by E. Croft-Murray and P. Hulton, 1960, pp. 338–9. For his portrait of Locke see appendix.

[1] Presumably the portrait of Shaftesbury now at Wimborne St. Giles.

[2] Nathaniel Hodges: p. 260, n. 3. For the name see p. 324, n. 1.

[3] Mrs. Thomas.

[4] The letter is no. *275*. Captain Peter Hales or Hayles of the *African*: *Cal. S.P.*, *Col.*, vol. vii, nos. 1058, 1131, 1233.

[5] Mentioned again in no. *291*.

[6] Captain John Darrell or Dorrell of Bermuda, who was active in the settlement of the Bahamas in 1666: H. C. Wilkinson, *The Adventurers of Bermuda*, 2nd ed., 1958, p. 337, etc.; *Cal. S.P.*, *Col.*, vol. vii, nos. 153, etc. (Two men of the same name, perhaps father and son, may be concerned.)

[7] For the adventurers see p. 380, n. 1. The 'company . . . of Bermuda' refers probably not to the Somers Island Company, the proprietors of Bermuda, but to the Company of Adventurers for the Plantation of the Islands of Eleutheria. This originated in 1647 when exiles or refugees from Bermuda, mainly Independents, made plans for a settlement in the Bahamas; it was to be a republic and enjoy freedom of conscience and was called Eleutheria (Freedom). The settlement declined

at length submitted, but what great proffitt this trade will bring unto us I must confesse I cannot see unlesse you can set up the whale fishing. and that turn to accompt or that by haveing all the Brasiletto wood[1] in your hands you can raise the price of that and whether that will doe it you may easily be informed, if you Inquire amongst the Dyers whether Brasiletto be of absolute necessity for the dying of any couller, or whether onely to helpe when Logwood[2] is deare, for if it be onely used in that case, or as I am Informed ground and mingled with Log-wood by the Salter[3] to cheat the dyer, the price is not like to rise for the English haveing found the way to cutt Logwood themselves which was formerly onely done by the Spaniard in the uninhabited places about the Bey of Campeache have reduced the price of that wood from 60l: per tonn to under 20ld: as I am Informed it ought also to be inquired whether their comes no Brasiletto wood but from the Bahama Islands for if there doe, you shall no sooner rise your price but the markett will be cloyd with that wood from other places, I am Informed that Braseletto is not now worth in England above 10ld: per tonn It cost you 5ld and that Ship that shall fetch it from the Bahamas for under 7ld: per tonn will not save by the voyage so that at this rate you will loose 40s: per tonn. as to Ambergrice the quantity found is not much nor can you be at certainty to have all that is found Nor will the Seader[4] turn to any great accompt, it will helpe to save the charge of a Ship when nothing else offers, this what I write Dorrell Knowes well enough therefore wisely sent the Ship hither with not much more Brasiletto in her then will serve for dunnage[5] for the sugar taken in as I am Informed by Captain Halstead[6] Intends for the future to make it his practice to

after two or three years. New settlers came after the Restoration and about 1666 occupied New Providence. By 1671 the population of the Bahamas was said to be about 1,100, of whom 443 were slaves: M. Craton, *A History of the Bahamas*, 1962, pp. 56–64, 70; Wilkinson, *Adventurers of Bermuda*, pp. 266, 270, etc.; Wing, C5583. The new settlers presumably wanted more support from England than the Eleutherians had obtained. (Colleton is unlikely to refer to the Providence Adventurers, a company which maintained a settlement on Catalina Island (Dominican Republic) from 1631 to 1641: Wilkinson, pp. 215–17, 226–33.)

[1] A species of dye-wood inferior to Brazil-wood: *O.E.D.*

[2] Another species of dye-wood: ibid.

[3] Drysalter, a dealer in dye-stuffs, etc.: ibid.

[4] Presumably cedar.

[5] Light or less valuable materials stowed among or beneath the cargo of a ship to keep it from injury by chafing or wet: ibid.

[6] Identifiable as Captain Mathias Halsted or Halstead of the *Blessing* (p. 383): South Carolina Hist. Soc., *Collections*, v. 318 n., 331, etc.; *Cal. S.P., Col.*, vol. vii; no. *296*.

load the Ship with wood for this Island and shee to unload her wood here and to take in a fraught of Sugar etc: and to load her wood wood on board other Ships, which will be some Improvement of your trade, for I beleeve your wood by this meanes may be sent home from hence for 20s per tonn, In times of peace, but you must not expect alwayes the same rate for fraught you have now, for In times of peace the usuall rate here is from 3ld to 5ld: per tonn as Ships are more or few in port: Dorrel gives me some hints in his Letter of hopes of a private trade with the Spaniards[1] and referrs me to hastede[2] for further Information but he can tell me nothing, if that can be efected something great may be done, with wise management, but you must be secret in it, if you fall upon a plantation its my opinion you will loose your stock for besides the disadvantage that country hath by the nature of its Soyle compared with the other English settlements, I never yet knew any man that setled a plantation by the management of any other but himself that ever saw his money again, If I judge right in what I have written I shall have the reputation to have foreseen what came to passe, if I mistake and the trade prove proffitable I shall get my share, Dorrell hath the reputation of a cunning Snap[3] amongst his countrymen and you ought to have a strict eye upon him.

The want of the supply of cloathes and tooles I desired might be sent to Carolina when I left England, hath been much felt there, to which hath been added a great want of victualls, occasioned by miscarriage of their supplyes from a broad, which hath made them suffer much misery, In so much that two of the councell and the Surveyor generall are run away, by which you may see what great reason the Lords Proprietors have to strive who shall have the disposure of the Offices since men run from them,[4] I doe Intend to Perswade Andrew Norwood[5] of Bermudas to goe theire and take the office upon him he is an Ingenious man and I shall endeavour to make him understand the drift of the Lords as to lyeing out of the

[1] Shaftesbury tried to establish trade with the Spaniards in 1674: *Cal. S.P., Col.*, vol. vii, nos. 1284, 1287. The Spaniards occupied little more than points along the east coast from St. Helena in South Carolina to Cape Florida.

[2] Probably Captain Mathias Halsted rather than Thomas Hasted (p. 385).

[3] A sharper or swindler; a sly or treacherous fellow: *O.E.D.* See *Cal. S.P., Col.*, vol. vii, no. 1262.

[4] South Carolina Hist. Soc., *Collections*, v. 424 n., 425–6.

[5] The elder son of Richard Norwood, the surveyor of Bermuda (*c.* 1590–1675; *D.N.B.*; Wilkinson, *passim*); Wilkinson, p. 373 n.

countrey, I finde all men that are come from thence to agree, that the country is extream healthy and pleasant, and the understanding planters say its very fertill, but better further up then where they are Setled, which is soe near the barren sands of the Sea shore, I am very sure that if we overcome the want of Victuall, all the English planted northward will come into us for in new England the greatest ⟨part⟩[a] of the summer labour of the husbandman, is spent to p⟨rovide⟩[a] fother[1] to Keep his cattle alive in the winter, Its the same at new Yorke, and in Virginia and Mary-land where they are not soe carefull in doeing it, they lost above two thirds of their cattle the last winter, whereas the cattle of Carolina were beef all the while, and will never need to be fothered, which advantage added to our being able to produce many commodityes that they cannot, and all their owne cheaper then they can, must force them in time all to come to us, and that this hopefull countrey may not be lost and that that excellent forme of Government in the composure of which you had soe great a hand may speedily come to be put in practice[2] I earnestly desire you to solicit my Lord Chancellor[3] that the supply of cloathes and tooles may be sent them togather with the 1000 bushells of pease I have writt about which may put them past want of Victuall any more and about 600ld: will effect it, there is gone home one mr Man[4] whom the councell have sent

[a] *Page torn.*

---

[1] Fodder, an obsolete form: *O.E.D.*

[2] This refers to 'The fundamental constitutions of Carolina', sometimes called 'The laws of Carolina'. The surviving draft, bearing 21 July 1669 as the date on which the document was to be sealed, is in Locke's hand throughout. It was written probably in association with Shaftesbury. Much of it is a more detailed and more formal statement of matter contained or implicit in the two charters granted to the Lords Proprietors of Carolina in 1663 and 1665 and in the concessions granted by them to the colonists in 1665. Though some of the language, and even some of the matter, may have been supplied by Locke, Shaftesbury is to be regarded as the author and Locke as his assistant. The draft was revised by another of the Lords Proprietors; the date for sealing is 1 March 1670. This version was printed; there is no date of printing, but it was probably shortly after sealing in order to provide an inducement for prospective colonists to settle in Carolina and as guidance for the governors of the colony; a printed version is mentioned on 3 October 1674: South Carolina Hist. Soc., *Collections*, v. 453. Mentions below in no. *354*, etc. show that copies were then available. The constitutions never came into full effect. There were two later versions in 1682 and a third in 1698: texts in *North Carolina Charters and Constitutions, 1578–1698*, ed. M. E. E. Parker, 1963 (The Colonial Records of North Carolina, new ser., vol. i), pp. 74–240 (the 1670 text, with two small corrections, is reprinted in *A Collection of Several Pieces*, pp. 1–53); the Constitutions are discussed in Haley, *Shaftesbury*, pp. 242–8. See further no. *878*.

[3] Shaftesbury.

[4] p. 383, n. 3.

with their Letters by whom you will be Informed at large of all things.[a] I am

your faithfull frend and servant
P COLLETON

Address (written by Colleton): To John Lock Esqr at the Lord Chancellors London

Postmark: DE —

Endorsed by Locke: *Colleton* Sr Pet 73

## *280.* JOHN RICHARDS to LOCKE, 23 October 1673

P.R.O., S.P. Col., vol. xxx, nos. 72, 72I. Calendared in *Cal. S.P.*, *Col.*, vol. vii, no. 1153. The writer is identifiable as the clerk of the Council of Trade and Plantations, a post which ended in December 1674. The Shaftesbury connection suggests that he is the same man as the writer of no. *675* but there is no positive evidence (a John Richards in Sir Joseph Williamson's office about this time and later in Arlington's service appears to have been another man). Locke was sworn in as secretary to the Council of Trade and Plantations on 15 October 1673.

[Forwards news from Middelburg.]

## 281. LOCKE to SIR HENRY BENNET, earl of Arlington, 6 January 1674

P.R.O., S.P. Col., vol. xxxi, nos. 2, 3. Calendared in *Cal. S.P.*, *Col.*, vol. vii, no. 1197.

[Council of Trade business.]

## *282.* WILLIAM ALLESTREE to LOCKE, [7] January 1674 (*277*, *285*)

P.R.O., S.P. 30/24, bdle. 5, no. 275. Printed in Fox Bourne, i. 321. The day in the date from Locke's endorsement.

Stock: Jan⟨uary 7⟩th:[b] 167$\frac{3}{4}$

Sir

I had acknowledg⟨ed th⟩e[b] receit of yours of Octob: 9th. long since, had I not bene tril'd on[1] in a constant expectation of being

[a] *The rest is written by Colleton.* [b] *Page torn.*

[1] Fox Bourne modernized tril'd as 'trilled'; the sentence is quoted in *O.E.D.*, s.v. Trill, v.[1] 1b, as an example of the word to trill, meaning to roll or trundle (a

brought acquainted with the first magistrate appointed for the judging of witches, from whose information I hoped in some measur⟨e⟩[a] to be able to answer your demands concerning them; But Hee continuing still up in the country, I cannot learn any thing certain here, where the storyes and opinions about those things are so different. The History of Lapland which treats of what you desire to be inform'd, is now out, written by Dr[b] Schafferus, and printed in quarto at Franckford.[1] What Hee sayes there concerning the Devil and witches, is collected out of this Kings own library, and the most authentick papers of that nature. If you cannot find the booke in London, let me but know it, and I will send you it from hence. I hope you have before this time, receiv'd the Picture and Laps-boots[2] sent to my Lady Wood, for you, from, your most obedient servant Wm. Allestree

Address: For John Lock Esquire at Exeter house London

Endorsed by Locke: Mr. *Allestree* 7 Jan. 7¾

## *283.* Lady Ann Howe to Locke, 15 January [1674?]

P.R.O., S.P. 30/24, bdle. 6B, no. 410. The year must be after 1672, the year of the writer's marriage, and before 1676, when Locke was abroad. The likeliest year is 1674 because in 1673 Lady Anne should have designated Shaftesbury as Lord Chancellor, and in 1675 he was out of favour at court.

Lady Anne Manners, born *c.* 1655, youngest daughter of Lord Rutland (p. 321, n. 1) and sister of Lady Ashley, made a runaway marriage with Scrope Howe (1648–1713; created Viscount Howe (Ireland) 1701; *D.N.B.*) in April 1672. She died between 1682 and 1698.

Haddon jan: the 15

Good Sir

The occassion of my giveing you this trouble, is to desier the favour of you, to acquaint my Lord of Shafsbury, that since my Father will not be satisfied, as to what was agreed on conserning

[a] *Page torn.* [b] *Doubtful reading.*

ball, hoop, etc.), here used figuratively. It is more likely to be a false or variant rendering of drilled; to drill a person is to lead him on: *O.E.D.*, s.v. Drill, v.[1] 3. This obsolete use occurs again in no. 2376; other uses of to drill and to drill on occur in nos. *377* and 2182.

[1] J. G. Scheffer, *Lapponia*, 1673. See p. 382. An English translation was published at Oxford in the autumn of 1674: Madan, no. 3023. Locke owned a copy of the French translation, 1678: L.L., no. 2566.

[2] Scheffer, English trans., pp. 102 (figure), 105; pp. 390, 401.

me at his Lordships, from any other hands his owne and has write to him aboute it, I must beg, his Lordship will oblige me soe much, as to give my Father a particular account of it as soon as with convenience he can, I pressume his Lordship will both name to my Father the sume then fix'd on, and the usse from that time till the whole was payed, soe I have onley to desier, the favour of his Lordship nameing the Plate with the Griffins Head, and it will be a very great obligation to

Sir
Your assured servant
ANNE HOWE

my humble service I pray Sir to Lord and Lady Shafsbury

Address: These To Mr Locke at the Earle of Shafsburys att little Exceter House in the Strand to be sent as directed with care London.

Postmark: IA 17

Endorsed (not by Locke): The Lady Anne How's Letter.

## 284. LOCKE to JOHN STRACHEY, 17 or 18 January 1674 (276, *286*)

New York Public Library: Berg Collection. Published by permission of the Trustees of the Berg Collection. Transcribed from photostat. The page is torn for a seal. Printed in Rand, pp. 81–2. The contents show that Locke's year is old style; the date of the postmark makes the day of writing questionable. Answered by no. *286*.

Exeter house 18° Jan. 73

Sir

By the last post I gave you a short account of what you will finde here inclosed more at large. The estate he tells me was by his father left entailed, but he hath by a fine and recovery cut it off of half of it that it might be free for joynture or any other setlement he shall have occasion to make. In the values set downe he assures me he hath not set the highest, and in some places noe other then as it is accounted in the poores booke, and in the woods he hath only valued the Copice wood, without any consideration of the timber, which he hath upon his estate to some value. There is noe debt, nor sisters portions charged on any part of the estate, what is in joynture to his mother the paper shews. He farther tells me (That he may leave noe thing concealed which he thinkes in these cases is by noe means faire) that for the furnishing his house, and ⟨to pay⟩[a] the charges of his Election into the house of Commons[1] he hath been forced to take . . .[a] which his mother and he are bound, but he hath not set this downe, because his . . .[a] purchased some land not mentioned in the particular which is setled upon him in r⟨e⟩version,[a] and is of more value then his debt. He hath only one Sister who is maried.[2] and his elder brother by another Venter Sir John Pelham[3] is a man of 3 or 4000l per annum. He is a very sober young Gent: and a good husband which is a rare thing in this age. But for his Character I had rather Mr Stringe⟨r⟩[b] should informe him self from the Gent: of that Country, and give it you then that you should depend on my opinion, who yet have noe temptation to be mistaken on that side.

The journal of the proceedings of the House of Commons comeing into my hands I could not but send you it.[4] This I suppose is a better payment of a desperate debt then ever you lookd for, and in such a lump of news at once you will be satisfied for the litle you have received from me this long time. I am not wise enough to comment or prognostick, this I'm sure I pray for a happy conclusion that all things may be setled to the best advantage. I am

Sir

Your most affectionate humble servant

JOHN LOCKE

Pray present my service to your Lady and my Cosin Jep. and tell her that I am very diligent in the Commission she gave me, and as an effect of it hope shortly to see her a Lady and my neighbour.

Address: For John Strachy Esq at Sutton Court To be left at Dr Crosses in Cornestreet Bristoll[5]

Postmarks: IA 17; OFF 4

[a] *Page torn.* [b] *End of line.*

[1] Sir Nicholas Pelham was elected M.P. for Seaford on 23 February 1671.
[2] Philadelphia, 1654–85, wife (8 July 1673) of Francis Howard, 1643–95, fifth Baron Howard of Effingham 1681: G. E. C.
[3] *c.* 1623–1703; third baronet 1654: G. E. C., *Baronetage*, i. 9.
[4] Apparently a manuscript version. Parliament met on 7 January; since then the Commons had attacked Buckingham and Arlington.
[5] See p. 299.

## *285.* WILLIAM ALLESTREE to LOCKE, 2 February 1674 (*282, 292*)

P.R.O., S.P. 30/24, bdle. 47, no. 19. Cited in Fox Bourne, i. 321.

Stockholm: Feb: 2d. 167$\frac{3}{4}$:

Sir

The present season of the year would take it ill, and might expresse its anger by robbing me of some joynt or other, should I endeavour to entertain you of any thing but her. Know then, that this winter here is acknowledg'd by all to be one of the severest that this country hath know within the memory of the oldest persons living,[1] of which I shall give you some instances. Severall of the country pesants (who generally are well garded against cold) have bene found dead upon the road, The very aire and breath they drew in, having so congeald and frozen the blood in the passages of their lungs, that all circulation hath bene suddainly stop'd and they in a moment depriv'd of life.

The yound Lord Douglas[2] going abroad the other day with the King, Had his brains perfectly frozen, who after a phrensy fitt, and a violent accesse of the feavour dy'd mad. I going out the other day in my sledge, escap'd well enough, though my footman is yet in danger of loosing one ear, and one finger; and this within a quarter of a mile of the town.

now let me tell you a story from the mouth of Sir Ed: woods houskeeper. There was not many dayes since a larg piece of Beife to be roasted, and a fire made proportionably for it, The fatt which fell from it, froze under it in the dripping pan, and did not only coole there like grease, but had a perfect ice upon it.

There was a piece of beife which had been some time salted, which after having boild full two howers was found tender on the outside, but within it was as hard as iron, and as bloody as if it had bene just brought from the shambles.

After all this, you will wonder that any man should either desire to come or stay in these parts, but yet let me tell you, That Sir E: wood doth talke of leaving the country, Hee hath bene and is still very kind to me, as having acquainted me freely with all his businesse, I shall willingly serve him how long soever hee may stay

[1] This part of the winter was extremely cold in northern Europe: Easton, *Les Hivers*.

[2] He was probably a Swedish nobleman of Scottish descent.

here: I have some reason[a]– to believe–[a] hee will endeavour to leave me here under some small publick Character.[1] I can without vanity say, I understand in some measure this court and the businesse England hath with it, and I have made some considerable acquaintance in it. I only tell you this, knowing you are my friend, and that I do not displease you in giving you an occasion of shewing your kindnesse to me. Mr S: Coventry[2] will be the man of power in this businesse who hath alwayes bene kind to me. If you can help me, I am confident you will, but pray you, let it not come as a thing propos'd by me, but as proceeding from your selfe, upon the bare love you have bene pleas'd alwayes to expresse to

Sir

your most humble servant

WM: ALLESTREE.[b]

By what I have lately heard from England, I have reason to hope that you have receiv'd the Picture of Lapland which I sent you, but as for the Lapps-boots I fear you will never see them, since the ship they were sent in, nam'd the Samson, hath suffer'd shipwrack upon the coasts of France, though it is believ'd most of the goods may be sav'd. But of this my Lady wood will tell you more.

Sir E: Wood p⟨res⟩ents[c] his most humble ⟨ser⟩vice[c] to y⟨ou⟩[c]

Address: For John Lock esquire at Exeter-house in the Strand London.

Endorsed by Locke: Mr *Allestree* 16 Feb. $7\frac{3}{4}$[3]

## *286.* JOHN STRACHEY to LOCKE, 10 February 1674 (284)

P.R.O., S.P. 30/24, bdle. 47, no. 18. Printed in Fox Bourne, i. 329–30. Answers no. 284.

Sir

I have received your three letters, and it was not through neglect but choise that I made noe speedier an Answer, for it was till now

a–a *MS.* reason to / to believe  b *MS.* Alt[e].  c *Page torn.*

---

1 Wood continued as envoy in Sweden until 1679.

2 Henry Coventry, 1619–86; secretary of state 1672–80: *D.N.B.* He was envoy to Sweden from 1664 to 1666, and ambassador in 1671–2.

3 Presumably a date of receipt, though it seems quick.

before the young Lady[1] could come to any resolution, and truly as the Case stands with Mr Co:[2] Shee is not at all blameworthy, for though Shee might bee fixed against the Marriage, yett Shee thought it would have been very inhumanely don to have been instrumentall to his relaps, but now Shee thinks that hee is able to endure a deniall, Shee intends to breake through all difficulties and to lett him know what hee must trust to, as for the younge Knight[3] Shee likes his Character and doth not except against the Particular nither doth her Uncle Buckland[4] whoe was here this day, but whether they may like one another upon the interview is hard to prophesy, I find her backward to goe to London, least it bee thought Shee goes a woeinge, otherwise you know Shee intended it, but I can't imagine how you will satisfy Her in that Scruple of honour. The Particular of her Estate I shall not now send you, because I am a Person too much concernd, there beeing some questions in Law betweene us, but that they may bee fairely ended I intend to bring my writings to London and to stand to the Judgment of the best Lawyers, yett I doe not say but that I may doe more then what the Law will force mee to, and truly I doe not exactly know her Concerne at Sydcott[5] and therefore I thinke Mr Buckland would bee the fittest Man to send a Particular, in summe I beleive her fortune may well answer the Knights Estate and I shall speake with Mr Buckland and informe you better hereafter, this is all at present from

Sir

Your most humble Servant

JO: STRACHEY

Febr. 10th 1673

Address: For Mr John Locke at Exeter House in the Strand London

Endorsed by Locke: Mr Strachy 10 Feb $7\frac{3}{4}$

[1] Mary Jepp.

[2] Not identifiable.

[3] Sir Nicholas Pelham.

[4] A man of this name died in 1678: p. 672; John Buckland of West Harptree, 3 miles SW. of Sutton Court, in 1696: Collinson, *Somerset*, ii. 143.

[5] Sidcot is a hamlet in Winscombe near Axbridge, about 8 miles west of West Harptree.

## *287.* SIR PETER COLLETON to LOCKE, 3 March 1674 (*279*, *289*)

B.L., MS. Locke c. 6, ff. 213–14. Text written by an amanuensis.

Barbados this 3d: of March: 1673

Sir

Inclosed is the Copy of my last unto you since which I have Received Letters from the Governor of Providence[1] and mr. Dorrell[2] the Copys of which I have here inclosed sent unto you that you may see what newes I have from thence and that I was not mistaken in the Incomodiousness of that soyle for planting, the Vessell that brought me these letters I am Informed was Loaden with Brasiletto but for whose accompt I have not yett learnt but shall make it my Endeavour.

The last week I Received a Letter ffrom Collonel West[3] of Carolina by whom and from some come from thence I am Informed the people there have at length quite mastred the want of graine, which the next yeare will Infallibly compleat and I hope they will shortly bee alsoe in a good condition as to other sorts of provizions and then and not beefore they will bee able to make tryall what comoditys that Country will produce for men have little hearts to try Experiments whilst they are in a feare of being sterved, they want Cloathes and Tooles Extreamly for want of which and the dispayre of beeing suplyed, many have Endeavoured to run thence. I have written to my Lord Chancellor[4] about it and I desire you to put him in minde of it, less then 250l. will doe it and this will bee the last in my opinion they will neede, They Continue still extreame healthy and have latly made new discoverys of new Rivers, the best of which washeth one side of Lock Island.[5] I have sent Wests Letter to my lord by which you may bee Informed more at large.[a] I am

Your most humble and faithfull servant

P COLLETON

Endorsed by Locke: *Colleton* Sir P: 3° Mar. *73*

[a] *The rest is in Colleton's hand.*

[1] John Wentworth, governor of Providence and the rest of the Bahama Islands 1671–6: *Cal. S.P.*, *Col.*, vols. vii, ix.

[2] Captain John Darrell or Dorrell: p. 392, n. 6.

[3] Joseph West: p. 382 n.

[4] Shaftesbury was dismissed on 9 November 1673. Presumably the news had not yet reached Colleton.

[5] A projected new settlement on the Edisto River; instructions to the governor, Andrew Percival (no. *317*), were issued on 23 May of this year. The project failed. The area is now called Edisto Island: South Carolina Hist. Soc., *Collections*, v. 439–45; further, ibid. pp. 445–8, 466, 468.

## *288.* JOHN COOKE to LOCKE, 16 June 1674

P.R.O., S.P. Col., vol. xxxi, no. 46. Calendared in *Cal. S.P., Col.*, vol. vii, no. 1306.

[Forwards orders from Secretary Coventry.]

## *289.* SIR PETER COLLETON to LOCKE, 22 July 1674 (*287*)

B.L., MS. Locke c. 6, ff. 217–18.

Barbados this 22th of July 1674

I have Just now received yours of the 26th of Decemb: with the aditions of the 18th and 27th of may which is all I ever received from you, though you mention a former, wee have been sufficiently informed here of the great love and Esteem the people in Generall have for the Earle of Shaftsbury, nor hath his courage industry and care for the good of the nation outgone my expectation, I confesse I am amazed at the variety of newes I have Received from England, and am like a man who sees people danceing at a distance and not hearing the Musick, wonders what they are doeing,[1] when I heard of the disasters of our statesmen I fancyed my lord of Shaftsbury like a man who had gotten to the upper round of a ladder, and those who were next to him were endevour⟨ing⟩[a] to Breake the Round on which hee stood, upon which hee Articles to quit his Station, upon condition, he might have liberty to goe downe himselfe, but assoon as hee is safe upon the ground, falls a shakeing the ladder and brings all the rest downe headlong.[2]

I am glad to heare there is a suply of cloathes and tooles gone to Carolina, and I hope amunition is not forgott, this will Establish the settlement; for they have at length mastred the want of victuall, I am sorry to heare Yeamans[3] is out of the Goverment, for his family is a sixth part of the whole collony, and his cattle a third of

[a] *Page rubbed.*

---

[1] The comparison occurs in Calderon, *El pintor de su deshonra*, act I (speech of El Príncipe).

[2] Shaftesbury was dismissed from the office of Lord Chancellor on 9 November 1673. In January and February of this year his three surviving colleagues were attacked in the house of commons and were discharged from office or deprived of power.

[3] Sir John Yeamans, 1611–74; created a baronet 1665: *D.N.B.*; *Dict. American Biog.* He was appointed governor first in 1665; again in 1672; and was superseded by a commission to Joseph West, issued in London on 25 April of this year: *Cal. S.P., Col.*, vol. vii, no. 1265.

the whole stock of Carolina, I have been informed of his selling Rum and molasses to pore people, for their provizions, at extravagant rates, and detested him for it, but by what I have heard since am at a stand whether to Impute it to coveteousnesse, or to great wisdome, and foresight, for the people by their want have been made good husbands, and I am informed by mr Smith[1] who is now with mee, that the same man afterwards gave seed corne gratis to all that wanted, and distributed provizions that hee had sent for from Virginia to those in distresse, and required but the same quantity againe, when they had produced it from their owne labours, though they offred him three for one, saying he came not there to traffick, and though hee made vastly chargeable propositions to the Lords,[2] I Judge them rather to proceed from a designe to buoy up the peoples spirrits with hopes of vast suplys and thereby win them to patience, (who were under all the discouragements that want of victualls cloathes and tooles could give, and in dispayre of beeing suplyed were ready to quit the collony,) than any hopes hee had the lords would send them, however if hee quit not the Collony in discontent all is well enough, one damd fault hee has hee hates to put pen to paper, and thereby leaves people dissattisfyed, I have had but once letters from him since I came hither, by the Inclosed to my brother James,[3] you will perceive hee had put the people upon planting tobacko for the payment of the proprietors, this letter Smith brought who was comeing out of Carolina in Company of the Lady Yeamans in february last, whose vessell could not gett over the barr the wind scanting upon her so cast anchor within, that which Smith was in beeing out beefore stood away, and was taken by a caper, who plundred them, but restored the Vessell, the lady Yeamans is not since heard of, in her vessell were my letters and those to the proprietors

I have sent a pott of tarrara root to Collonel Thornburgh for you, the pot hath a wooden cover fitted to it which is covered all over with pitch, and canvas over that, which will keep out the ratts as I conceive, I have never seen any of it dryed, nor doe I know whether it will that way bee preserved, one thing I must observe to you of it that the Juice taken in to great a quantity at a time and to long continued, is suposed hath inclined some people to a palsy, but hath worne of againe upon discontinuance

[1] Not identifiable.

[2] The Lords Proprietors of Carolina.

[3] James Colleton: *South Carolina Hist. and Geneal. Magazine*, i (1900), 329–31.

I aprove of the Articles signed by the lords proprietors,[1] and will either come speedily my selfe and signe them or Impower Collonel Thornburgh who writes mee hee will pay in my money when demanded, when I goe hence I intend to take Carolina in my way to England, severall Inhabitants of this place say they will goe with mee, haveing intent if they like the place to transport their familys to it. pray present my service to Doctor Barrow[2] and bee assured that I am

Your very affectionate humble servant
P COLLETON

I am Just now informed that the Juice of the Tarara root aplyed warm gives Instant ease to the gout.

Endorsed by Lock: Sr P *Colleton* 22 Jul. 74

## 290. RICHARD LILBURNE to LOCKE, [6 August] 1674 (300)

P.R.O., S.P. 30/24, bdle. 49, no. 5. Excerpt printed in Fox Bourne, i. 328–9. The date is Locke's interpretation of that given by the writer. He received the letter shortly before 20 May 1675, when he sent a quotation from it to Henry Oldenburg: p. 423.

Fox Bourne quotes part of a letter from Lilburne to the Bahamas Adventurers, 9 August 1674: i. 327–8. I have failed to trace him elsewhere. A man named Robert Lilburne was governor of the Bahamas from 1682 to 1687: Craton.

Providence the 6th A° 1674

Sir

I took notice of your desires to the Governor[3] concerning the Papers sent to him by way of Carolina Bermudas etc that soe haveing a veiw of all those which were sent you might take care to supply what was defective, he made answer there was none received by him onely by this ship and those I presume you don't require; I gave him an account[a] of it in the same terms that was in your letter that there might be no mistake: I have not met with any rareities worth your acceptance though I have been dilligent in

[a] *MS.* acc°:

[1] The articles concluded on 6 May and signed by the six other proprietors: South Carolina Hist. Soc., *Collections*, v. 431–5; calendared in *Cal. S.P.*, *Col.*, vol. vii, no. 1270.

[2] Apparently Dr. Isaac Barrow: p. 374, n. 4. [3] John Wentworth: p. 403, n. 1.

inquireing after them, of those which I have heard of one seems strange to me: the fish which are here are many of them poysonous bringing a great pain o⟨n⟩[a] their joynts which eat them and continues soe some short time and at last with 2 or 3 dayes itching the pain is rub'd of, those of the same species, size, shape, collor, taste are one of them poyson the other not in the least hurtfull and those that are, onely to some of the Company; the distemper to men never proves mortall; Dogs and Catts sometimes eat their last: men which have once had that disease upon the first eating of fish though it be those which are wholsom the poysonous ferment in their bodie is revived thereby and their pain increased. I think you spoke to me for some oyle of souldiers[1] and I have indeavoured to procure it but this being the time of their spawning non can be drawn from them: when opportunity presents it self I shall be ready to serve you in that or any thing el⟨se that you⟩[a] will command

Your ⟨ humbl⟩e[a] servant

⟨RICHAR⟩D[a] LILBURNE.

Sir, since my writeing this letter I received from the Governor the Instructions[2] he formerly received by this ship which I have got a Coppie of and sent directed to your self

RICHARD LILBURNE

Address: For Mr: John Locke at Exceter-house in London

Endorsed by Locke: *R. Lilburne* 6 Aug. 74

## *291.* ISAAC RUSH to LOCKE, 10 August 1674 (*274, 301*)

P.R.O., S.P. 30/24, bdle. 49, no. 5. I have omitted Rush's vindication of his conduct.

New Providence the 10th of the 6th Month caled August 74

Doctor Locke

And my loving friend by the Bahama merchant[3] I received thy lynes and token for which I returne my thankes not forgeting thy

[a] *Page torn.*

[1] Soldier-crabs or hermit-crabs. For oil of soldiers see p. 424. It is mentioned by Lionel Wafer in *A New Voyage and Description of the Isthmus of America*, 2nd ed., 1704 (Hakluyt Soc. edition, 1934, p. 67).

[2] The only extant instructions to Wentworth are those of 30 December 1671: *Cal. S.P., Col.*, vol. vii, no. 712.

[3] p. 392.

kindnes in prefering mee to the good opinion of the Earle of Shaftsbery: not doubting but that I shall by the faithfull discharge of my duty in that trust to mee comited by him render my selfe an honest and upright man acording to his desier and thy expectation: and soe consequently aquit the of bearing part of that shame which by any underhand dealing of mine might fall upon thee: and theirfore shall speake something to the perticulars which I am informed the lords suspects mee for . . .

[There follows a vindication of Rush in which Locke is mentioned incidentally.]

to conclude as thou art somewhat engaged for my creadat soe thou art obleiged to indeavor my vindication soe farre as truth is on my side and as I in part know my acusation soe I would willingly know my acusers which would doe mee an axceptable kindnes and obleige mee ever to continue

thy Loving friend
ISAAC RUSH

Endorsed by Locke: *Bahama*.
Endorsed by another writer: New Providence Aug 10th *1674* Isaac Rush to Dr John Locke

## *292*. WILLIAM ALLESTREE to LOCKE, 23 September 1674 (*285*, *298*)

P.R.O., S.P. 30/24, bdle. 5, no. 279. Excerpts printed in Fox Bourne, i. 321–3, 325–6.

Stock: Sep: 23d. 1674.

Sir

yours of April the 14th, came to me on the 17th of Sept: by which you will judge, that either the Laps had no power to hasten it, or that they are no friends of mine, nor I at all in their book'es, who would deprive me so long of so great a kindnesse.[1] I could have wish'd, that as this, though late, came at lengh, the Laps-boots had had the same conveyance to you, and if they were lost in the sea, you may see, that though their makers are accounted witches because the⟨y⟩[a] cannot sinck, yet the boots who did so, were honest.

[a] *Page torn.*

[1] Lapland witches were traditionally reputed to be able to command the winds; Scheffer attributes the power to the Finlappers and Finlanders of Norway: English trans., p. 58.

If the ship whic⟨h⟩[a] carri'd them had not let in water, I am confident they would have held it out, and had the vessell bene in them, it had bene safer, then they were, being in it. For they were made of an Elk'es skin with the hair outwards, which doth defy both wett and cold, and tho⟨ugh⟩[a] the ill successe I have hitherto had in addressing things to merchants doth discourage me, yet, if in a short time I can find no particular person to send them by, I will convey a pair of them, together with Schafferus, by Mr Sowton,[1] to you. The short Relation[2] (which I kindly thanke you for) is I believe, a very good one, since as to some things it relat'es I know them to be true, which mak'es me guesse the rest may be so too. Sir Ed: Wood and I went lately about halfe a mile from hence to see a colony of 40 Laps who with their Elkes under a mossy Rock, have bene planted here all this summer, but they will shortly be trudging, as fearing the moderate winter of this climate, may do them harme. The French Ambassador[3] would willingly have kep't two of their boyes, but the parents would by no means suffer it, as looking on all service to be slavery, and they will rather with their own hands, cut their childrens throats, then leave them here behind them. I saw two of them fight the other day, their way of challenging, and entring into the lis,[4] was, each of them with a stick drew a line upon the ground before him, which hee who pass'd over first did thereby give the signal to warr, and so enter into the *champ de battaille*, being thus advanc'd, the parties on both sides, let the combatants singly[b] determine the warr without meddling with them in the least, which was done by the younger of them becoming conquerer, who triumph'd over his vanquish'd foe by leaping and schrieking, and all other expressions of joy imaginable, whilst the standers by sided all wi⟨th⟩[a] the victor, laughing, shouting, and hanging upon his neck, especially the women, and left the unfortunate warrier alone, to bewail his miserable defeat, and ruminate upon his losse of honour: I will do my utmost, to

[a] *Page torn.* [b] *Doubtful reading; word altered.*

[1] See p. 421.

[2] Not traced under this title; probably a copy of Pierre Martin de la Martinière, *A New Voyage into the Northern Countries*, which was advertised in February of this year: *T.C.* i. 162; it includes accounts of the Lapps in Norway and Russia, but not of those in Sweden. The French original was published in 1671; Locke owned a copy of the second edition, 1676: L.L., no. 1928.

[3] Isaac de Pas, marquis de Feuquières, d. 1688; ambassador in Sweden 1673–82: *N.B.G.*

[4] Probably a slip for list, a place of combat: *O.E.D.*

inform you, and myselfe more, concerning their witchcrafts,[1] though the Gent: from whom I was to expect it, is gone with the army into Germany,[2] and you cannot conceive, how closely they keep up all relations of that nature here, much apprehending the hurt they might do, if once divulg'd amongst the common people. That person by whom ⟨I⟩[a] was to have bene inform'd, speaks French, so that could I have mett with him, I should have had the whole relation by word of mouth, but now, I have no other, but one given me in Swedes; which I cannot get translated, there being no English man here who hath time, and Swedes enough, to do it in, as being at the least 8 leaves in folio, and I perswaded one to undertake it, who after some dayes brought it me back again, and swore the very reading of it, had so frighted and disturb'd his rest, that for the whole world hee would not undertake the translating it. Of the two Lap's pictur'es, I sent you one, and Sir Ed: sent my Lady the other:

now let me tell you, that as to my desire of staying here in some small publick character after Sir Ed's coming away, it purely proceed's from dispair of Employment in any other way any where else, and from an opinion, that few persons being ambitious of the place, so underserving an one as myselfe, may the more easily obtain it: Had I but the least shaddow of hopes of any preferment in England agreeable to my inclinations as well as my Education, I would be as far from that desire, as I am now from home; but rather then come to London, and there be out of businesse, or go to Oxford, and there be press'd to enter into a profession, which the very reverence I have for it, perswad'es me to decline,[3] I would stay here, and like the Lapps, enjoy that poor content in a cold climate, which is not to be had in a more moderate one. This is my last refuge, which yet I persist rather to embrace, then to be uncertain of any Employment when I come home. If therefore it must be so, I can furnish you with no other arguments to plead for me, but only my having bene acquainted three years with the businesse of this Court, and the Examples, not only of many other

[a] *Page torn.*

---

[1] Probably those not of the Lapps but of the Swedes, and apparently the proceedings in 1674: pp. 421–2.

[2] Sweden at this time held the western part of Pomerania, the duchies of Bremen and Verden, and other territories in Germany. See further below.

[3] Allestree evidently feared the predicament in which Locke had been in 1666: p. 214 n.

Secretaryes, but particularly, of the King of Sweden's Envoy now in England, who after having bene there in ⟨the qua⟩lity[a] of Secretary, was left Resident, and since, is made Envoy.[1] There can be no secular fortune in England which may be fitt for me, or I for it, which (though of a very moderate value) I should not much rather embrace, then this which I here propose, and I would employ diligence and faithfullnesse in the Execution of it, but if I should be out of the Kings service here, or out of all businesse at home, I may be press'd to the bad choise of either taking orders, or loosing what I possesse in Ch: Ch:

As for newes from hence, This Kings roving in the Country whil⟨st⟩[a] the season will permitt, robbs us of it, and let's us know nothing but only, That hee hath this year, transported considerable forces into Germany, which about a weeke since, were follow'd by the Great Constable[2] himselfe. notwithstanding all which, opinions as to their entring into action are very different, for as on the one side, it is believ'd, that they have transported more men already, then their own countryes in those parts, are able to nourish, (which must oblige them to seeke other quarters) so it is thought, they will not easily enter into a warr with their neighbours, which would deprive them of the honor, and those advantages which they propose to themselves by a mediation.[3] The French Ambassador encourages them both by fair promises, and monyes, and hath sent a Gent: along with them as Commissary, who hath Bills upon Hambourg for Eight hundred thousand crowns. And though the season for war be pass'd with others, yet they will find themselves fresh, and their neighbours harrass'd with the summers service, and it is observ'd of Swedes, that they fight best, when they can see their own breath.

[a] *Page torn.*

[1] Pehr Larsson Sparre, Baron Sparre, ambassador to England 1672, 1674–6: *(Svenskt) Biog. Lexikon.*

[2] Carl Gustaf Wrangel, 1613–76; Great Constable (*Riksmarsk*) 1664: ibid.

[3] Swedish foreign policy was temporizing and evasive. In order to retain an alliance with France without active participation in the European war, Sweden acted as mediator at the congress at Cologne, which lasted from June 1673 to April 1674. By July of this year the Great Elector was a belligerent; Louis XIV feared that he would attack the French forces on the Rhine. Feuquières therefore persuaded or bribed Charles XI of Sweden and his advisers to send considerable forces into Sweden's German territories; as these districts could not maintain them they were likely to invade the Brandenburg territories. Sir William Temple, writing from The Hague on 26 October, N.S., declared that Sweden still wanted to act as a mediator: F. F. Carlson, *Geschichte Swedens*, vol. iv, 1855 ('Geschichte der europäischen Staaten'), pp. 583–97; Temple, *Works*, 1770, iv. 54, 75–8.

I thanke you for your seasonable present of usquebah,[1] which is very Excellent, and by warming both me and my friends may save Sir Ed: a great deal in firing. I really acknowledge all your favours, and as I looke upon it as the best marke of my judgment and good sense, that I esteem and honour you, so I never put any value upon myselfe, but when I consider you have bless'd me with your friendshipp, and thereby have made me so eminent in the world, as to be,

Sir

your most oblig'd and obedient humble servant.

WM: ALLESTREE.

Sir Ed: kiss'es your hands.

Address: These For John Lock Esq at Exeter house Strand London

Endorsed by Locke: Mr Alestry 23° Sept 74
Received 19° Oct.

## 293. LOCKE to PETER LOCKE, 14 October 1674 (*213*, 294)

B.L., MS. Locke c. 24, ff. 180–1. This consists of Locke's copies of extracts from three of his letters to his uncle; it is here divided as nos. 293, 294, and 296. Locke's marginal citation on these notes and no. 294 apparently relate to Peter Locke's answer, which is answered by no. 296.

A Copy of a letter to my Unkle 14° Oct 74

1 John Anthony for the rent of Mich. *72* paid me a noble[2] lesse then my rent. I remember you sent me word he pretended he laid it out for makeing a hedg. I know noe such allowance I was to make him by our bargain nor doe I thinke it usuall. I remember when I let it him he complaind the hedges were bad to which Robert Harol answerd, he should leave it as he found it and soe it was agreed pray Unkle enquire into it and let me have right don me.

2 Robert Harol for his rent at Mich *73* paid but 8l–11s–4d and I cannot finde any where how he discounted the rest. I desire you would call for it from him and send it me

3 He was also speakeing to me to have some time in the liveing,[3] I desire to know what terme and at what rent

4 Thomas Summers's $\frac{1}{12}$ of all the taxes etc which were paid in $\frac{1}{2}$ year ending at our Lady day *74* is –01–2s–$5\frac{1}{4}$d

[1] Usquebaugh, whisky.

[2] A gold coin worth 6*s.* 8*d.* It was last coined during the reign of Henry VIII.

[3] In the obsolete sense, a holding (of land), a tenement: *O.E.D.*, s.v. Living, *vbl. sb.*, 4b.

5 William Smith for $\frac{1}{2}$ year ending at Mich. *73* paid but 6–7–11. I desire also to know the particulars of his abatements.

4 William Gullocks $\frac{1}{6}$ of taxes and burthens etc: for $\frac{1}{2}$ yeare ending at Lady day last is –0l–4s–10$\frac{1}{2}$d

6[a] My Aunt Lockes[1] account stands thus

| El: Locke Dr 1673 | | |
|---|---|---|
| Mar 25 | For $\frac{1}{2}$ years rent for the Stags head and common mead——— | 4–18–0 |
| | For Lokiers——— | 0–0–6 |
| Sept 29 | For $\frac{1}{2}$ years rent for Stags head Common mead and Lokiers— | 4–18–6 |
| | 1674 | |
| Mar 25 | For $\frac{1}{2}$ years rent for Common-mead and Lokiers——— | 1–18–6 |
| Sept 29 | For $\frac{1}{2}$ years rent for the same——— | 1–18–6 |
| | | 13–14–0 |

| El: Locke Cr 1672 | | |
|---|---|---|
| Sept 29 | By payment towards the next half year | 0–7–8 |
| | 1673 | |
| Aug 12 | By mony paid you | 4–0–0 |
| | 1674 | |
| Aug 11 | By mony paid you | 2–0–0 |
| 18 | By mony paid me | 1–0–0 |
| | | 7–7–8 |
| | Due to Ballance | 6–6–4 |

Soe that now at Mich *74* she owes me 6l–6s–4d which I desire you to get as soon as you can

7 Kent owes me for 3 half years now at Mich *74* –6s

8 Floury is at Mich last in arrear for 2 whole years 8s. If they will not pay I desire to destraine for at this rate the longer it goes the harder it will be to get. I desire to know also who at present is owner of that house.

9 For the house also that I sold Mrs Hopkins there is this Mich. 2 years in arear for which Branch owes at least till his wives death and since that he or El: Hopkins. If it be not paid the same course also must be taken here

10[b] Pray Unkle enquire also what Edward Taylor hath donne in the Coleworks at Beluton.[2] I have received noething since August *73*

[a] *This item is distinguished by a marginal note* v 26 Oct. 74. [b] *This item is distinguished by a cross and a marginal note* vid. 26° Oct 74.

---

[1] Mrs. Elinor Locke: p. 295, n. 2.

[2] Beluton (Belluton) is a hamlet in Stanton Drew parish: Collinson, *Somerset*, ii. 433; in legal documents about 1683 Locke describes himself as of Beluton. Pensford is about the centre of a coalfield; there is an account (1719) of the coal found at Sutton in *V.C.H., Somerset*, ii. 383–4.

11 You let the Grounds to A: Barnes for 5l per annum But I finde the last yeare he paid but 4–16–0. I desire to know how it comes to passe

12 I desire Unkle that when you receive any bill for disbursements you would see that the times be set downe in the severall sums were laid out and that when you send me any account of your receits or payments you will also set downe the particular time wherein each was made

13 James Atkins paid for ½ yeare due at Mich 73 but 1–2–0. I desire to know why it was a shilling lesse then it used to be and also whether 4s per annum to the poor there be not too high

14[a] I desire to know whether Sampson Silke hath taken all the remainder of Flourys time in the Furzes or how that stands.

## 294. LOCKE to PETER LOCKE, 17 October 1674 (293, 296)

B.L., MS. Locke c. 24, ff. 180–1. See no. 293, head-note.

Extract out of a letter to him of 17° Oct 74

I[b] desire to pay to Mr Strachy all he hath of mine in his hands except the 50l I lend him he being Debtor to me 24° Aug 74 73l–4s–7d

To send me a note of his receits and disbursements since 24° Aug 74

To take care of the Publoe rates as setled by the Justices

Propose[b] to have Pools synopsis[1] at the rate it cost him and his grandson King[2] to have them at the same rate of me again when I die or he needs them

a *This item is distinguished by a marginal note* vid. 26° Oct. 74. b *This item is distinguished by a marginal note* v.26 Oct.74.

1 Matthew Poole (*D.N.B.*), *Synopsis Criticorum Aliorumque Sacrae Scripturæ Interpretum*. Vols. i–iii appeared in 1669–73; vol. iv in two parts, in 1674 and 1675. L.L., no. 2369. Locke bequeathed his copy to Peter King.

2 Presumably Peter King, 1669–1734; knighted 1708; created Baron King of Ockham 1725; Lord Chancellor 1725–33: *D.N.B.* From about 1696 he occupied a large place in Locke's affections; many letters between them are printed below.

## 295. Dr. Thomas Sydenham to Locke, [about November 1674?] (*337*)

P.R.O., S.P. 30/24, bdle. 47, no. 2, ff. 11–12. Excerpts printed in Fox Bourne i. 334–5; the greater part by Dr. K. Dewhurst in *The Practitioner*, clxxv (1955), 315; in his *Dr. Thomas Sydenham*, 1966, pp. 167–8.

All the known papers that belonged to Locke and came into the Shaftesbury collection date from between 1667, when he entered Shaftesbury's household, and November 1675, when he went to France. His earliest recorded illness in this period belongs to September 1670. He appears to have had little regular business on hand before Shaftesbury became Lord Chancellor in November 1672 and was perhaps not fully occupied until he became secretary of the Council of Trade and Plantations on 15 October 1673. This employment ended when the Council was abolished on 21 December 1674. Locke apparently contemplated visiting France in May 1675 and by about the end of October had decided to go there: pp. 438, n. 3, 433. He was then troubled by his cough (asthma); the present letter appears to relate to some other illness.

The letter was written about the approach of winter. In 1670 and 1671 Locke could scarcely be described as 'broken with business'. In October 1672 he was pleased with his condition: no. 265. In October 1673 he accepted fresh office. In the autumn of 1675 he was preparing for his journey. This leaves the autumn of 1674 as the most suitable date. Fox Bourne suggests this date, but does not give any reason for doing so.

your age, ill habitt of body, and approach of winter concurring, it comes to pass that the distemper you complaine of yealds not so soone to remidies as it would doe under contrary circumstances. However you may not in the least doubt but that a steddy persisting in the use of the following directions (grounded not on opinion but uninterrupted experience) will at last effect your desired cure. First therfore in order to the diverting and subducting allso the ichorose matter, 'twill be requisitt to take your pills twice a weeke as for example every Thursday and Sonday about 4 a clocke in the morning, and your Clyster in the intermitting dayes about 6, constantly till you are well. In the next place forasmuch as there is wanting in bodyes broaken with business and dispirited upon the before mentioned accounts, that stock of naturall heat which should bring the matter quickly to digestion 'twill be highly necessary that you cherish your selfe as much as possibly you can by going to bed very early at night even at 8 a clocke, which next to keeping bed that is unpracticable will contributt more to your reliefe then can be imagined. As to diett all meats of easy digestion and that nourish well may be allowed, provided they be not salt sweet or spiced and allso excepting fruits, roots and such like. For wine a totall forbearance therof if it could possibly be and in its steede the use of very mild small beer such as our lesser houses doe afford, would as neare as I can guess be most expedient, for therby your body would be kept coole and consequently all accidents proceeding from hott and sharpe humors grating upon the part, kept off. As to injections, in your case these things disswade the use of them. First your more then ordinary both naturall tenderness and delicacy of sence. Then the blood that twice allready hath bin fetched by this operation, which if we are not positively certaine (as how can we be) that it proceeded not from the hurt of the instrument, will (if often repeted) endanger the excoriating the part and making it liable to accidents. Besides they have bin allready used (perhapps as often is wont to be don) and this is not a remidy to be long persisted in by the confession of every body. Sure I am as I have over and over sayd to you and you know it to be true by my written observations which you have long since seen, that I never use any, where I am concerned alone, there being noe danger nor less certainty of cure in the omitting; and in relation to this business I have now asked myselfe the question what I would doe, and have resolved that I would lett them alone.

This is all that I have to offer to you and I have thought of it, and all circumstances relating to your case, with the same intention[1] of mind as if my life and my sons were concerned therin.

T: S.

Notwithstanding that by this way the cure is certainly to be effected yet nevertheless I observe that in ancient bodyes, especially in the declining part of the year, some little kind of gleeting or moisture (but voide of all malignity) will now and then appear by reason of the weakness of the part and will scarce totally vanish till the returne of the warme spring.

Address: For Mr. Locke

Endorsed by Locke: Dr Sydenham.

[1] In the obsolete sense, the action of straining the mind or attention to something: *O.E.D.*

## 296. LOCKE to PETER LOCKE, 3 November 1674 (294, *306*)

B.L., M.S. Locke c. 24, ff. 180–1. See no. 293, head-note.

3° Nov. 74

Tel him Mr Strachy hath paid me 23–4–7.
Desire to know whether he allows the account I sent him downe 17 Oct. 74
Desire Harol and Smiths bill of Mich. ½ year 73
Desire my aunt Elenor[1] to pay what she owes me forth with

Bills to be regular

Propose my unkle to pay for Synopsis 3 first volumes and I the 2 last and my cosin K to have all when I die I to use them in the mean time[2]
Desire a bond or bill for my 50l to be paid L day[3] next. the bond or bill to be left in Mr Strachys hand who hath the bill to give up, but I depend on the mony in the mean time if I have occasion.
Tel him I write to Robert Harol about J: Anthonys cuting my trees.
Desire his advice about leting Beluton for a terme.
Tell him that R Harol hath noe reason to desire abatment for time past, for I have not been backwards to him

Endorsed by Locke: P Locke Extract of my letters to him 74

## *297*. SIR ANTHONY ASHLEY COOPER, first earl of Shaftesbury, to LOCKE, 23 November [1674] (*247*, *322*)

B.L., MS. Locke c. 7, ff. 69–70. The greater part written by an amanuensis. Printed, omitting a passage, in King, pp. 33–6; complete in Christie, *Shaftesbury*, ii. 60–4; excerpts in Fox Bourne, i. 277–8, 293, 332–3, 423. The year from the passages relating to Halsted and to Locke's annuity.

St Giles Novemb the 23th

Mr Locke

I write onely to you and not to Mr Stringer,[4] because you write me word Hee is ill for which I am exceedinglie sorry, and pray heartily for his recovery, as being very much concerned both in friendship and interest.

As for Capt: Halsteed's affaire I have this day received this

[1] Mrs. Locke: p. 413.
[2] Poole's *Synopsis*; Cousin King: p. 414.
[3] Lady Day, 25 March.
[4] p. 434 n.

inclosed letter from Him, which when you have reade you will beleive I have reason to desire to be freed from his Clamour, therfore pray speake with Him againe and Tell Him, that Mr Stringer being sick I have desired you to appeare fore me before the Referrees, and that whatever they shall award I have given order to pay my proportion, and that according to his desire I have written as effectually as I Can to the other Lords that they would doe the same. pray keepe his letter and let me have it againe.

I have here withall sent you an answer to the Lord Craven, and the rest of the Lords letters which I have not seald that you may read it, when you have read it you may seale it your selfe[1]

I desire you would speake with Mr Hawkeings about our ships at Hutsons Bay and what hopes there is of either of their returneing this yeare,[2] and pray let me know what you heare of our Bahama ship

I desire this inclosed to Mr Wake may be Carefullie and speedilie delivered and that Mr Burch send his daughter upon any Termes. I will take care we shall not differ upon any thing thats reason.[3]

Pray let Mr Ball the Gardener at Brandfoord[4] have this inclosed note and be pleased to get some one to take care that the things be pact up and sent downe for me.

I desire you to speak to South at the Custome house that He would buy me one busshell of the best sort of Chesnuts, it is for planting, and send them downe by the Carrier.

You guesse very right at the designe of the Pamphelet you sent me,[5] tis Certainely designed to throw dirt at me, but is like the

[1] On 20 November William Craven, first earl of Craven (*D.N.B.*), and two further Lords Proprietors of Carolina wrote to Shaftesbury about the state of the plantation; they also complained about the importunity of 'that idle fellow Halsted': South Carolina Hist. Soc., *Collections*, v. 454–5; *Cal. S.P.*, *Col.*, vol. vii, no. 1388. Shaftesbury's answer is lost. For Halsted see p. 393, n. 6.

[2] Richard Hawkins was treasurer of the Hudson's Bay Company. The two ships, the *Prince Rupert* and the *Shaftesbury*, sailed about June of this year and returned in September: Hudson's Bay Co., *Minutes*, *1671–4*, pp. 114–16, 212, etc. Shaftesbury held stock in the company from 1668 to 1679, and was deputy-governor in 1673–4: Haley, pp. 231–2.

[3] Identifiable as Samuel Birch and his daughter Elizabeth. The father, an ejected nonconformist divine, was chaplain to Lord Wharton (p. 46 n.) and kept a school at Shilton, Oxfordshire. The daughter was a member of Shaftesbury's household in 1675 as governess of the future third earl; she was said to have spoken Greek and Latin: later she apparently kept a school at Clapham in association with a Mr. Tanner, who was probably a brother-in-law: Matthews, *Calamy Revised*, pp. 56–7; Christie, *Shaftesbury*, ii. 211; A. A. Cooper, fourth earl of Shaftesbury, life of his father in *The Life . . . of Anthony, Earl of Shaftesbury*, ed. B. Rand, 1900, p. xix; notices below.

[4] Apparently Brentford. Syon House belonged at this time to Lady Northumberland.

[5] I have failed to identify this pamphlet; it may have been in manuscript. It evidently charged Shaftesbury with originating the Stop of the Exchequer.

great Promoters of it, foolish as well as false, it labours onely to asperse the Originall Authour of the Councell, which it will have to be one person and therefore seemes to know; and never Considers that it is impossible that any stats man should be soe Mad as to give a Counsel of that Consequence to a juncto or Number of Men, or to any but the king Himselfe who tis not to be imagined will ever be come a Witnes against any Man in such a Case, especially when he hath approved the Counsell so far as to Continue the stop ever since by a new great seale every yeare, besides I am very well armed to Cleare my selfe, for tis not impossible for me to prove what my opinion was of it when it was first proposed to the Councill. and if any man Consider the Circumstance of time when it was done, that it was the prologue of makeing the Lord Clifford Lord Treasurer,[1] he will not suspect me of the Councill for that busines, unles he thinkes me at the same time out of my witts; besides if any of the Banckers doe enquire at the Clerckes of the Treasurie with whom they are well acquainted, they will find that Sir John Duncome[2] and I were so little satisfied with that way of proceeding as from the time of the stop we instantlie quitted all paying and borrowing of Money and the whole transaction of that part of the affaire to the Lord Clifford, by whom from that time forward it was onely Managed, I shall not deney but that I knew earlier of the Counsel and foresaw what necessarily must produce it sooner then other Men haveing the advantage of being more verst in the Kings secret affaires, but I hope it will not be expected by any that doe in the least know me that I should have discovered the kings secrets or betrayed his busines whatever my thoughts were of it. This worthy scribler if his law be true or his quotations to the purpose should have taken notice of the Combination of the banckers who take the protection of the Court and doe not take the remedie of the law against those upon whom they had assignements, by which they might have been enabled to pay their Creditors, for it is not to be thought that the king will put a stop to their legall proceedings in a Court of justice. besids if the Writer had been really concerned for the Banckers He would have spoken a little freelier against the continueing of the stop in a time of peace as well as against the

[1] Sir Thomas Clifford, 1630–73; created Baron Clifford of Chudleigh 1672; appointed Lord High Treasurer on 28 November 1672: *D.N.B.*

[2] Sir John Duncombe of Battlesden, Beds., Chancellor of the Exchequer, 1672–6: Evelyn, *Diary*, ed. de Beer, iii. 442 n. He, Ashley, and Clifford were commissioners of the Treasury when Charles II ordered the Stop of the Exchequer.

first makeing of it in a time of War, for as I remember there were some reasons offered for the first that had their weight viz that the Banckers were growne destructive to the Nation especially to the Country Gentleman and farmer and their interest. that under the pretence and by the advantage of lending the king Money upon very great use they got all the ready money of the kingdome into their hands so that no Gentleman Farmer or Merchant Could without great difficulty Compasse money for their occasions unlesse at almost double the rates the law allowed to be taken: that as to the kings affaires they were growne to that passe that twelve in the Hundred did not Content them but they bought up all the kings assignements at 20 or 30 per Cent. profit. so that the king was at a fifth part losse in all the issues of his whole Revennue, besids in support of this Councill, I remember it was alleaged, by those that Favoured it without dores for I speake onely of them that the king Mought without any dammage to the subject or unreasonable oppressure upon the Bancker pay them six in the hundred interest dureing the war and three hundred thousand pound each yeare of their principall assoon as there was peace, which why it is not now don the learned writer I believe hath friends can best tell Him. this I write that you may shew my friends or any body else, the Messenger staying for me I have written it in hast and not kept a Copy therefor I pray loose not the letter[a]

I am sorry you are like to fair soe ill in your place,[1] but you know to whom your company is ever most disirable and acceptable pray lett me see you speedily and I shall be ready to accomodate you in your annuity at seaven yeares purchase if you gett not elswhere a better bargain for I would have you free from care and thinke of living long and at ease;[2] this from

Deare Sir

Your truely affectionate freind and servant

SHAFTESBURY

Address (written by the amanuensis): These For his much esteemed Friend John Locke Esquire

Endorsed by Locke: E: *Shaftesbury* 23° Nov. 74

[a] *The rest of the letter is written by Shaftesbury.*

[1] Probably alluding to Locke's secretaryship to the Council of Trade and Plantations. The Council was abolished on 21 December.

[2] On 25 December of this year Thomas Stringer gave Locke a receipt for £600 in cash and a bond of Shaftesbury's for a loan of £100 formerly made him by Locke,

## *298.* WILLIAM ALLESTREE to LOCKE, 14 April 1675 (*292*)

P.R.O., S.P. 30/24, bdle. 5, no. 285. Excerpts printed in Fox Bourne, i. 323–5.

Stockholm. April. 14th. 1675.

Sir

In October last, by a ship call'd the St nicolas order'd to mr Sowton, I sent you a pair of Lapps-boots, and the history of Lapland in Latin.[1] They were put up in a wooden case, in the which there was also another pair of Lapps boots design'd for my Lady wood. From the marchand here who sent away the vessell, I understand that hee hath long since receivd newes of its arrivall at London, which makes me hope you may with it, have receiv'd what I sent. Mr Sowton is every day to be found in the Eastland walke upon the Exchang, or at his Father in-Law Sir William Riders house in Broadstreet;[2] This I tell you, to the end that if the things be not come to your hands, you may send for them; These marchants are a sort of people who promise fair, and undertake readily, but who seldom perform, but where there is something to be gott. I told you in my last, that I would endeavour to procure the Relation of the examination of witches who were jud'g'd in the latter end of the past year 1674.[3] It was given into my hands in Swedes yesterday, and I hope to have it in English within a week'es time; if my former things sent to you have miscarried, I shall hardly find a way of conveying it to you, though I will be sure to embrace the opportunity which shall be the most unlikely to fail. The Relation is but short, and though I have not spoke with the judg, who is yet up in the country, yet I have lately talk'd with one who hath discours'd the thing at larg with him. I find the judg is of opinion, that very few or none of them, are really possess'd with the Devil, but that all their ⟨extravagancyes⟩[a] proceed, from a distemper'd

[a] *MS.* extavagancyes

the whole being £700 paid by Locke to Shaftesbury 'for a Lease of the Farme and Mannor of Kingston in the County of Dorsett for 99 yeares determinable on the death of the said mr Lock, and to Commence from the day of the date of these presents': B.L., MS. Locke c. 19, ff. 114–15. The lease was to be the security for an annuity of £100 to Locke.

[1] Scheffer, *Lapponia*; pp. 397, 409.

[2] The father-in-law is Sir William Ryder or Rider, d. 1669; knighted 1661; sometime Master of Trinity House: Le Neve, *Pedigrees*, pp. 128–9; Pepys, *Diary*. Samuel Sowton of the parish of St. Peter le Poer was licensed in 1674 to marry his daughter Anne: J. L. Chester, ed., *London Marriage Licences, 1521–1869*, 1887.

[3] See p. 382, n. 1. Presumably the trial leading to the execution of nine men in 1675.

brain, ill diet, and a constant conversation amongst themselves wherein they prepossesse their phansies with the discourses of Devils and witchcraft. The pretended possess'd are generally young children who say the Devil is brought to them, and they bewitch'd by old women in the neighbourhood, which they name, who when they are both confronted before the judg, talke of a Gent: in pantoloons who uses them kindly, of great feasting, of flying about in the aire, and resting sometimes upon weathercocks, and such like things as some of our students in Bedlam relate. But this is observable, that neither the young nor the old ones do any hurt either to man or beast, but are a sort of pour silly people who have taken up a very beggery trade. Formerly upon this subject, I told you, the Devil had declar'd hee had not power to come into this town, but the great want of provisions in the country I am afraid hath forc'd him hither. For the other day under my window there was a great young strapping jade who play'd the possess'd, by howling, kicking, sprauling, and makeing wry faces, whilst three of the plot who were with her, kept her down, and lying upon her brest endeavour'd either to crush the Devil out again, or make his lodging uneasy. By this time a great croud of people were gather'd about her, who immediately began to sing Psalmes, which being a musick Satan likes not, hee left his prize, which yet seem'd not to be fully herselfe again, till most of the company had given her monyes, to dispossesse her pocket; which had so wonderfull an effect, that shee look'd as merrily as if by that means shee had conquer'd the Enemy of all mankind. But I hear since that time she is sent to the correction house, and then I leave it to you to thinke how well the Devil will like whipping. and:

I beg the continuance of your former kindnesses and friendship, and remain

Sir

your very much obligd and humble servant

Wm: Allestree.

Sir Ed: Wood presents his humble service to you.

Endorsed by Locke: W: Allestree 15 Apr. *74*

## 299. LOCKE to HENRY OLDENBURG, 20 May 1675

The Royal Society, MS. L 5–6, no. 90, Printed in *A Collection of Several Pieces*, pp. 249–51. Henry Oldenburg, *c.* 1618–77; secretary of the Royal Society from 1662: *D.N.B.*; Oldenburg, *Correspondence.* He read the extract from Lilburne's letter (no. *297*) at the meeting of the Royal Society on 27 May: Birch, *Royal Society*, iii. 220; it was printed in the *Philosophical Transactions*, x. 312.

Exeter house 20 May 75

Sir

I here with send you an account I lately received from New Providence one of the Bahama Islands concerning fish there, which is as followeth

> I have not met with any rarityes here worth your acceptance though I have been diligent in enquireing after them; of those which I have heard of this seems most remarkeable to me. The fish which are here are many of them poisonous bringing a great pain on their joynts who eat them, and continue soe some short time, and at last with 2 or 3 days itching the pain is rubd off. Those of the same species, size, shape, colour, taste, are one of them poyson, the other not in the least hurtfull; and those that are, only to some of the company. The distemper to men never proves mortall. Dogs and Cats sometimes eat their last. Men who have once had that disease, upon the first eating of fish, though it be those which are wholsom, the poysonous ferment in their body is revived thereby, and their pain increased.

Thus far the ingenious person from whome I had this relation, who haveing been but a very litle while upon the Island when he writ this, could not send soe perfect an account of this odde observation as one could wish, or as I expect to receive from him in answer to some Quæres I lately sent him by a ship bound thither. When his answer comes to my hand if there be any thing in it which may gratifie your curiosity I shall be glad of that or any other occasion to assure you that I am

Sir your most humble servant

JOHN LOCKE.

Address: For Mr Henry Oldenbourg at his house in the Pall Mall

Endorsements, etc.: (i) (by Oldenburg?) Mr Locks letter entred N.7/1675.
(ii) Mr Locks letter to Mr Oldenburg concerning a poisonous fish about the Bahama islands.
(iii) Mr Lock about fish in the Bahama Islands / entred N.7.
(iv) Read May 27: 75. Enterd L B. 7. 234. Printed Trans: 114.

## *300.* RICHARD LILBURNE to LOCKE, 12 August 1675 (*290*)

B.L., MS. Locke c. 13, ff. 175–7.

New-Providence August 12th 1675

Sir

This place affording no curious naturalists and my studies never being inclin'd that way hinders me from giveing you soe good an account as by a curious inspection many things here might admitt of, but if you please to give acceptance to what I can inform you I shall serve you in it to the furthest of my knowledge; as to the Souldiers[1] if you had given me a further hint of what had been remarkable it's like by what I might have observed here I might have given you a confirmation: all which I have taken notice of in that creature is that according to their growth they provide themselves still with shells suitable, either which they beat other souldiers out of or else a sort of Wilks which they pull out of their houses, of which they take possession for their own use and draw about with them till by their growth they find themselves too much pent up and then they make inquiry for a new habitation, which either they procure by force or else perhaps meet with a tenement thats forsaken either wilk or mother of pearl or any shells which wind after that manner, in which he secures the softer part of his body and weaker claws all being cover'd by a great and strong claw which lies out just at the entrance into his Cabbin, and alwayes open ready to defend himself against any assailant: the oyle of Soldiers is much esteem'd here and difficult to be got they reckon it here a very soveraign thing for any aches and pains either in the limbs or joynts and many other things of which I beleive you may be better inform'd in England than here for I have little judgement in these affaires. here is Snakes oyle Guana's[2] and Aligater's which last I hear is an admirable remedie for the Gout and I remember was sent by Sir Thomas Linch[3] Governor of Jamaica to a freind as an admirable present. I desire your advise particularly of what your judgement is concerning these things there is one who I imploy'd at Andrews Island[4] to get some Souldiers and try them in the Sun who hath sent down word he hath procur'd some which if it come

[1] Hermit-crabs.

[2] Iguana; an old form of the word: *O.E.D.*

[3] Sir Thomas Lynch, later a correspondent of Locke; lieutenant-governor of Jamaica 1671–5; governor 1681–4: no. *634*.

[4] Andros.

before the Ship goe away I shall send it otherwise I will take care to doe it by the first opportunity. there is but this season in the year that it can be procur'd your particular queries I have answer'd in a peice of paper inclosed. I am Sir

Your most humble servant
RICHARD LILBURNE

[Enclosure:]

Answers to the Queries propos'd according to the best account, and observations which I could meet with here

1 All sorts have not any poysonous quallity

2 The poysonous which I could get account of is Rock-fish, Parcudas,[1] Amber-fish, Hogg fish, Snappers etc

3 Some of these are poysonous in other places as Amber fish but some are not and differ much from the nature of the pains which they cause here seeming by what I have heard rather to be a surfet than any thing else

4 There is not any here yet which have made a perfect discoverie but in some sorts of fish they observe them to be most innocent which have a clear and fresh collour about the head and those which are blew about the head are found most dangerous

5 In hog-fish the Boar is observ'd allwayes to be the wors't in other sorts there is not any certain observation yet

6 In May and June they find them wors't the weather nor time of the moon is not found to cause any alteration

7 The women children and weakest constitutions are soonest infected yet they often find when $\frac{1}{2}$ a doz: eat of the same fish some are poyson'd others not though there appear but little difference in the constitutions

8 The Symptons are first a tingling in the nose like those who have got a great cold next a pain and ache in the bones which will remove suddenly from 1 part to another as from the armes to the legs which is not found in the body allsoe a great heat in the breath and scalding[2] with difficulty and stoppage of urine, with a faintness in the body then a violent itching in all parts with severall intermissions: the distemper continues according to the quantity of the fish or poyson which they have taken and according to the different constitutions the itching many times continues for

[1] Presumably barracudas.

[2] Read '. . . and scalding, with difficulty and stoppage . . .'.

6 months together hindring them from their rest and sleep the other pains are generally removed in 2 or 3 dayes or a week

11 The best remedie found here is a dose of Ambergreece in Brandy or Rumm and to use strong drink

12 Dogs die with a great quivering groaning and itching soe that some have been known to claw their throats bare to the windpipe. Hogs have fed upon the same fish and are never known to receive any prejudice.

13 after their first sleep they are generally sensible of some symptons

The lean fish of those sorts which are poysonous are alwayes found to be soe

This relation the greatest part of it I had from one who had been 20 times poyson'd but now not sensible in the least any way of the effects thereof and I look upon the information I received to be very certain

By Copulation the women though before free yet if there husbands be troubl'd are made sensible of the same pain which their husbands have and procures pangs to them much like those which they have In travell and with as great extremity, as I am inform'd by a woman a sober and discreet person and one who hath been generally assistant to women in labour here

Sir, If from the symptons, accidents, and effects above-mentioned you can propose any remedie it may be much to the benefit of the Inhabitants here and an ingagement to

Sir

Your most humble servant

RICHARD LILBURNE

Address: For Mr: John Locke at Exceter house in London

Endorsed by Locke: R *Lilburne* 12 Aug. 75

## *301.* ISAAC RUSH to LOCKE, 19 August 1675 (*291*)

B.L., MS. Locke c. 18, ff. 45–6.

N Providence Mon 6th: Day 19th: 1675

Doctor Lock

By Richard Lillburne the Adventurers Agent I received thine of May 17th: 75 and acording to thy words found by the inclosed that the Earle of Shaftsbury continues his good opinion of mee and his favors to mee: I am glad as well for my friends sake as my owne (of which I must acknowledg thee not the least) that those evill reports of mee are seased and that noe blame or blemish hath happned to them on my Acount which encourages mee to desier a continuance of thy recomendation: by way of Newe England I sent the a letter dated the 6th of instant[1] whearein acording to thy desier I gave the best acount I could of the nature of our poyson fish and as I can farther informe my selfe shall aquaint thee theirewith, I understand Richard Lillburne hath given the an acount likewise who is better acomplished for that purpose and a more curius observer of such things: by the next I will indeavor to procure some Gwyana and some snakes oyle, which is reported to be of greate use: I have directed a small box to thee with some shells and other trifles in it for the earle of Shaftsbury and a dosen for thy selfe and ½ dosen for my friend Roger Knowles[2] his wife. I have not Received any lines from him this time neither can I learne by any meanes wheather he be living or not pray remember mee to him if he be living. I should be glad to receive some lynes from him, who hath bin and I hope will continue my good friend. I shall be very much encouraged by a continuance of thy Corospondence and hereafter indeavor more to demonstrate how much I am obleged to thee, and Remaine

Thy very friend
ISAAC RUSH

Address: To Doctor John Lock at Exceter house present
Endorsed by Locke: J. Rush 19 Aug. 75
In another hand (T. Stringer?): letters to mr Lock

## *302.* W. FANSHAWE to LOCKE, 14 September 1675

P.R.O., S.P. 30/24, bdle. 5, no. 290. In bad condition.

The writer is perhaps William Fanshawe of Great Singleton, Lancs., *c.* 1640/3–1708: Ann, Lady Fanshawe, *Memoirs*, ed. H. C. Fanshawe, 1907, pp. 316–18; H.M.C., *Bath MSS.* ii. 158, 162, 165.

When it was rumoured that Col. Giles Strangeways, one of the knights of the shire for Dorset, was to be made a peer, the question of a successor arose (Strangeways did not become a peer, but died in July; a new writ was order on 13 October). Shaftesbury wanted a friend named Freke (? Thomas

[1] Lost. [2] p. 385.

Freke, M.P. for Dorset 1679–1700) to stand, but he refused to do so. Therefore when Shaftesbury met an agent of Lord Digby, who had announced his candidacy, he told him that he knew of no opposing candidate, and at a county meeting some days later showed his willingness to support him. Then, learning that Digby was connected with the Court party, he brought forward a candidate who would support the Country party. The meeting at Tregonwell's house followed on 27 August. Digby said that Shaftesbury was against the king and for a commonwealth; Shaftesbury denied having pledged himself to Digby, and complained that he had behaved disingenuously. Eventually Shaftesbury obtained an apology from Digby's father, George Digby, second earl of Bristol (*D.N.B.*), for words uttered by him in the House of Lords; and in an action against Digby was awarded £1,000 damages: Christie, *Shaftesbury*, ii. 214–23; Haley, *Shaftesbury*, pp. 386–7; pp. 436, 446, 448.

Whitehall Tuesday the 14th. of September 75.

Sir

The occasion of this trouble is my desire to be satisfyed in a Scandalous and I am confident a false report raised heere by my Lord Shaftsburyes Enemyes and told all over the towne to his Lordships disgrace. The tale they tell is that my Lord Shaftsbury upon the death of Collonell Strangewais[1] made a visit to my Lord Digby[2] and did perswade him to stand to be knight of the sheire offering Lord Digby his interest, upon which Lord D. told him he would accept of his kind offer and to that en⟨d⟩[a] writt to all his freinds and prepared himself accor⟨ding⟩ly[a] after which my Lord Shaftsbury thought fitt to sett up one Moore[3] a man of ill principles to the Government and writt ⟨divers⟩[a] letters in his behalf some of which comeing to Lord Digbyes hands he thought fit to take notice of it to my Lord Sh⟨a⟩ftsbury[a] and theire Lordships meeting by accident up⟨on⟩[a] an invitation at mr Tregonnills Lodge,[4] my Lord ⟨D⟩igby[a] calls to my Lord ⟨Shaf⟩tsbury just . . .[b] withdrawne aside he told him, my Lord Shaftsbury you promisd me your interest towards makeing me knight of the Shire and I now heare

[a] *Page torn.* [b] *Nearly two lines, at foot of page, lost, apart from fragments o words.*

---

[1] Giles Strangeways, 1615–75; of Melbury, Dorset; royalist; M.P. for Dorset from 1661: Hutchins, *Dorset*, ii. 663, 665, 681.

[2] John Digby, *c.* 1635–98; styled Lord Digby 1653–77; third earl of Bristol 1677 G. E. C.

[3] Perhaps Thomas Moore, M.P. for Lyme Regis 1680–1.

[4] Fernditch or Verditch Lodge in Wiltshire, about 6 miles north of Wimborne St. Giles: Christie, ii. 215. John Tregonwell of Milton-Abbey and John Tregonwell of Anderston are listed in R. Blome, *Britannia*, 1673, p. 369. Both places are south of Blandford.

you intend it for another. you are a gentleman and I see you weare a long fighting Sword I hope you will give me satisfaction, my Lord Shaftsbury upon this told him he would serve him as he promisd him and therefore hopd he would not take any thing ill; Upon this my Lord Digby shewd him a letter under his owne hand in behalf of Moore and thereupon told him he was a knave and he should fight with him or he would cutt his throate adding divers other opprobrious words whereupon the Company parted them. The greatest part of this story I am sure must be false and ⟨tis⟩[a] now my request to you that you will oblige me with a ⟨true⟩[a] relation of it and presenting my most humble servis to my Lord Shaftsbury my Lord Ashley and both their Ladyes let my Lord know that I desire his leave to justify him according ⟨to that⟩[a] which I shall receave from you. Be pleasd to direct your letter to My Lord Pembrooks[1] house in Channell Row[2] in Westminster for

Your most faithfull humble servant

W FANS⟨HAW⟩[a]

Address: F⟨or m⟩y[a] worthy freind Mr Locke at the Earle of Shaftsburyes house at St Gyleses nere Cramborne in Dorsetshire

Endorsed by Locke: W: *Fanshaw* 14° Sept. 75[b]

## Spurious: LOCKE to ——, 29 September 1675

Messrs. Maggs Brothers, Catalogue no. 445, 1923, item no. 2650 and pl. xv.

[The letter begins: 'The great number of books I intend to consult . . .'; it runs later: 'The more science will be known, the more methods shall be improved, and libraries lose of their importance. I should feel very happy if my essay was destined, a day or other, to throw into the dark and oblivion the eighty works I have a mind to consult.' This is altogether unlike Locke, whatever is meant by 'the essay'; for the books see no. 886. The handwriting also differs from his.]

[a] *Page torn.* [b] *Noted by another writer* relative to Digby.

[1] Philip Herbert, 1653–83; seventh earl of Pembroke 1674; brother of Locke's friend Thomas Herbert, the eighth earl: *D.N.B.*, art. Philip Herbert, fourth earl.

[2] Now Cannon Row. At this time it extended south to New Palace Yard. Until the formation of Parliament Street (1739–50) it was more important than it is now; there were several noblemen's houses in it: Strype's Stow, vi. 63.

## *303.* DR. JOHN FELL, Dean of Christ Church (later bishop of Oxford) to LOCKE, 8 November 1675 (*544*)

B.L., MS. Locke c. 8, ff. 103–4. Printed in King, p. 153.

For the writer see p. 179, n. 3. Locke was now about to go to France for his health. He left London for Gravesend on the evening of 12 November. See further p. 434 n.

Sir

I am sorry for the occasion of your voiage but wish you success in it, and by no means expect you should add to it, by a journy hither upon the score of ceremony. Tis that which I by no means expect from my friends, and I hope the rest of the Chapter[1] are of the same mind. When we have occasion to meet next, I shall propose your concern to the Company, and with my affectionate remembrances remain

Sir

your Assured friend and servant

J. FELL.

Nov. 8.

Address: To His esteemed Friend Mr: John Lock these D.

Endorsed by Locke: Fell 8° Nov. 75

## *304.* SAMUEL THOMAS to LOCKE, 11 November 1675 (*439*)

B.L., MS. Locke c. 20, ff. 128–9.

Samuel Thomas, *c.* 1627–93; son of William Thomas, rector of Ubley, Somerset, about 7 miles SW. of Pensford; B.A., Cambridge, 1649; at this time chaplain or petty canon of Christ Church; vicar of Chard, and prebendary of Wells, 1681; deprived as a Nonjuror 1691: Foster.

Ch: ch: Nov. 11. 75

Mr Lock

Since mr Wall's departure[2] and to whom I pray my services your goods are put into my custody. viz: 2 Large Trunkes. 2 little

[1] The Dean and canons, forming the governing body of the college.

[2] There were at this time students of Christ Church named George Wall and George Walls; seventeenth-century writers do not always distinguish between the two surnames. The present man is George Wall, *c.* 1646–81; of Gloucester; matriculated from Christ Church 6 April 1663, aged 17; pupil of Locke; left Oxford probably on Monday 8 November; with Locke in France until about July 1677; died January 1681; Foster; p. 501; Prideaux, *Letters*, p. 49 (where the date is fixed by the New College robbery); Wood, *L. and T.* ii. 514. Exercises, etc., in Locke's Herbarium. For George Walls see p. 613 n.

Leather-boxes, 7 Firre-boxes.[a] A bundle of Papers. A chymicall Glasse. with 2 other Glasses. 4 Glasse-bottles. A Barometer. A Thermometer and a Large Mapp of France. All but the two large Truncks I can very well dispose of in my owne chamber and study. And those too are in my chamber at present. But if you thinke fitt to consent I would remove them into the roome that's within the study belonging to our common-Fire-roome,[1] where I have already some Truncks of my owne. and which is a much safer place, if Fire or any such mischief should happen, and of which our Deane[2] onely Keepes the Key. A Line or two from you concerning your thoughts of this proposall will be very acceptable to

your cordiall Friend and humble servant

SAM: THOMAS

your Coll: money and chamber-rent for the last Quarter are it seemes still due. and I shall receive it when your Tenants and the Treasurer will pay.[3]

Address: For Mr John Lock at little Exeter house in the Strand this.

Postmark: NO 12

Endorsed by Locke: S. Thomas 11° Nov. 75

## *305.* DR. HENRY WOODWARD to LOCKE, 12 November 1675

B.L., MS. Locke c. 23, ff. 102–4. The letter is mentioned by Locke in his Journal, 7 June 1679 (p. 99). The writer was active as a surgeon and explorer between 1666 and 1686. He visited the Westo Indians in the autumn of 1674: South Carolina Hist. Soc., *Collections*, v. 188 n., 456–62.

Sir,

I have made the best inquiry that I can concerneing the religion and worship. Originall, and customes of our natives. especeally among the Port Royall Indians amongst whom I am best accquainted. they worship the Sun and say they have knowledge of

[a] *Or* Fiere-boxes?

[1] The room beneath the west end of the hall, fitted up about 1667, and later known as the masters' common-room: H. L. Thompson, *Christ Church*, 1900 ('College Histories' series), pp. 232–4.

[2] Fell.

[3] For Locke's income from Christ Church from 24 June 1675 to 25 December 1679 see no. *523*.

Spirits who appeare often to them. and one sort there is who abuses their women when he meets them opportunely in the woods, the which women never after conceive. they acknowledge the sun to bee the immedeate cause of the groth and increse of all things whom likewise they suppose to be the cause of all deseases. to whom every year they have severall feast and dances particularly appointed. they have some notions of the deluge, and say that two onely were saved in a cave, who after the flood found a red bird dead: the which as the pulled of his feathers between their fingers they blew them from them of which came Indians. each time a severall tribe and of a severall speech. which they severally named as they still were formed. and they say these two knew the waters to bee dried up by the singing of the said red bird. and to my knowledg let them bee in the woods at any distance from the river they can by the varying of the said birds note tell whether the water ebbeth or floweth. they seeme to acknowledge the immortality of the soul in alloweing to those that live morally honest a place of rest, pleasure and plenty: and contrary wise to the others a place were it is very cold and they are fed with nothing but nuts and acornes setting upright in their graves. they say they had knowledge of our comeing into these parts severall yeares before wee arrived, and some of them in the night have heard great noise and as it were falling of trees. one sort of them pretend to cure deseases by sucking the part affected which is but a Fallacy they makeing their owne mouths bleed pretend to have sucked the said blood from their patients. another sort doe accquire great knowledge in hearbs and roots, which they impart onely to the next akin. had I not bin upp in the maine I should have sent some know, but shall by the next oppertunity. another sort have power over the ratle snakes soe farr as to send one severall miles over rivers and brooks[a] to bite a particular Indian which has bin don since our being here. and the said doctor kild by the relations of the other at whose death severall snakes came and liked up his blood. the westoes[1] amongst whom I now am worship the ⟨de⟩vel[b] in a carved image of wood. they are seated in a most fruitfull soyle and are a farre more ingeneous people then our coast indians. I hope before my returne to

[a] *Doubtful reading; page rubbed.* [b] *Page torn.*

[1] The town visited by Woodward was on the Savannah river near the present Augusta, Georgia: J. R. Swanton, *Early History of the Creek Indians and their Neighbours* (Smithsonian Institution, Bureau of Indian Ethnology, Bulletin 73, 1922), pp. 306–7.

effect that which will bee worth my tarrying. and shall give you a farther account by the next.

Yours to command
HENRY WOODWARD

From Westoe towne November 12. 1675.

Address: To Dr: John Lock Att Exiter House in the Strand present these In London England

Endorsed by Locke: H Woodward 12° Nov. *75*

## *306.* PETER LOCKE to LOCKE, 13 November 1675 (296, *403, 443*)

B.L., MS. Locke c. 14, ff. 186–7.

Sutton 13 nov: 75

Dear Cosen

Yours of the 2 nov: I Rec: not till this day. it was sorrowfull newes to me to Heer of the Return of your cough the Lord Give Good Succses In your Intended viage or Jurmey In to france In order to your Health. I did writt to you by mr Jones[1] but I thinke he was not In town when your letter was dated

I Have In my Hands of Lady dais Rent 22l–07s–06d which I shall Return to London the next opertunity. I Have in my Hands a smale matter of one mans Rent of the last ½ yeare which I am not willing to Returne because I would keep the ½ years Rent to Gether

Yf you Goe this Jurney I desir the Lord to blesse and preserve you In it and bring you safe back unto your native contry In health with Grace In your soule to live to His Glory for which is the daily prairs of your a sured

Lovinge unkill
PE LOCK

On reverse of f. 187: 1674/5 Lady dais Rent of the Rents In partiquler within mentioned [a statement.]

Address: For mr John Lock att exeter Howse these or In his absence to mr Thomas Stringer In London

Postmark: NO 22

Endorsed by Locke: P. *Locke* 13° Nov. *75*

[1] Perhaps Richard Jones of Stowey: p. 73, n. 2.

## *307.* THOMAS STRINGER to LOCKE, 25 November 1675 (*308*)

B.L., MS. Locke c. 19, ff. 116–17. On the inner side of the cover there are an address written by Locke 'For Mr. Thomas Stringer at Exeter house in the *Strand* London' and a fragment of Locke's seal. Excerpt printed in King, 1830, i. 70 n. *ad fin.*

Nothing is known of the writer's origin or when he entered Shaftesbury's service. He became his steward, but was not so concerned in his political activities as to be victimized by the government after Shaftesbury's death. On 19 June 1675 he was licensed to marry, at St. Clement Danes, Jane Barbon, *c.* 1654–1740, of Wimborne St. Giles, daughter of James Barbon of St. Paul's, Covent Garden. He bought an estate at Bexwells (sometimes Bexfields) near Chelmsford, Essex, in 1675; between 1682 and 1688 he moved to Ivy Church in Alderbury, near Salisbury, where he died, aged 63, on 6 May 1702. His widow subsequently married Jon. Hill of Cholderton, Wilts.: epitaph in Sir Thomas Phillipps, ed., *Monumental Inscriptions in the County of Wilton*, 1822, South Wilts., p. 49; P.R.O., S.P. 30/24, bdle. 4, no. 236; Chester, *London Marriage Licences*; Mrs. Hill's letter, 1734 (?), to Lady Elizabeth Harris, in Christie, *Shaftesbury*, vol. ii, app., pp. cxxiii–cxxix (Stringer's fragmentary memoir of Shaftesbury, 1672–3, is printed ibid., pp. xxii–xlv); Stringer's letters to Locke below; notices, etc., in Christie.

It was probably at this time that Locke began to keep a regular Journal, commencing with a note of his journey to Gravesend on the evening of 12 November 1675. The part relating to France includes, besides a travel diary, drafts or copies of original essays (or letters) of Locke's, medical notes and prescriptions, extracts from books, and notes of loans. Selections comprising the travel diary, 1675–9, and some related material, have been published by Professor J. Lough as *Locke's Travels in France*, 1953 (here cited as Lough; it supersedes the extracts published by Lord King). Bibliographical statement in the introduction, above, where other collections of excerpts are listed.

November 25th: 1675

Deare Sir

I have received both your letters, and am very Glad to heare you mett with soe good a Passage, and had the happynes of my Lord Embassendors Protection.[1] Your friends here are mightily Concerned for your welfare, and desires to see you returne in perfect Health. My Lord[2] beggs the kindnes that you will deliver this inclosed wherein is the Copie of this note for Trees, that which his Lordship desires is that you will gett some Person there to pay for

[1] John Berkeley, 1607–78; created Baron Berkeley of Stratton 1658; one of the Lords Proprietors of Carolina: *D.N.B.* He was now going as ambassador to France. Locke crossed from Dover to Calais on 14 November, apparently in the yacht provided for Berkeley, and continued with him as far as Abbeville: Locke's Journal; p. 440; Evelyn, *Diary*, 14 November 1675.

[2] Shaftesbury.

them and gett them Packed up and sent to Some merchant here in London, and to send me word whoe it is that you shall think fitt to direct them unto, And alsoe to settle a Correspondence with some Person there that my Lord upon any occation may write to him for more, and have them payd for and sent in like manner; Here is little alteration in affaires sinc you went from hence, but that upon the difference between the two houses, the House of Commons order'd a vote to be posted up against any Commoners Appealing to the Lords, which was taken soe very ill by theire Lordships that a motion was made for an Addresse to the King to dissolve the Parliament, and this debate was carryed on soe strong that when the house came to devide upon the question the Duke[1] and 40 the greatest Lords was for it, and seven proxyes, and 21 Lords 13 Bishops (which were all that were in the house) and 16 Proxyes against it, and soe it was lost by 2 proxys, which occationed a Protestation with reasons for theire dessolution, whereupon the Parliament was Prorogued untill the 15th of Feb: next come twelvemonth. I am in great hast and have the remembrances of all your friends here and many others to present you with but at present I can only tell you that none is mor hartily your friend and servant

Than

T:S:

Address: For my worthy friend John Lock Esqr These

Endorsed by Locke: T. Stringer 25° Nov. 75

## *308.* THOMAS STRINGER to LOCKE, 10 February 1676 (*307, 309*)

B.L., MS. Locke c. 19, ff. 118–19. Excerpt printed in Christie, *Shaftesbury*, ii. 220.

London: Feb: 10th. 1675.

Deare Sir

I have received all your letters from Callais, Paris, Lyons and I beleive Monpelleire,[2] and am sorry to heare mine have not reached your hands, I observed your directions in sending of them and doe finde you have sinc made some alteration, but me thinks not Considerable enough to make them all miscarry, and therefore by this

[1] James, duke of York. Stringer recounts the events of 19, 20, and 22 November: A. Browning, *Thomas Osborne, Earl of Danby*, 1944–51, i. 182–4.

[2] Locke arrived at Montpellier on 25 December/4 January.

time I presumme you have heard from me, however for more Certainety I shall againe acquaint you that your two bills of Exchange, (vizt that of 20l from Paris and 100l from Lyons) were Punctually Complyed with, and your letters of Creditt againe made good for what further summe you shall have occation off at Lyons.[1] Your Goods at Oxford are secured by mr Thomas[2] there according unto your owne desire, though as yett I have received noe money from theare, by reason as mr Hodge[a][3] tells me the Colledge is bare, and those that are absent are to be last payd. I have received 6l from your uncle[4] and have a bill of Exchange for 16l more, but cannot yett receive it. Your other things are all safe and well that you left at Exceter House, where yett we all are besides my wife whoe is settled at Bexwells in Essex;[5] and hath the happines of Enterteyneing me there once in a weeke; My Lord S:[6] and Lady I thank God are in very good health, though my Lord hath lately been violently afflicted with the Gout. The Cause proceeds vigorously against Digby. and will come to a tryall by a jury of Wiltshire Gent in Easter Terme.[7] Your boy Jack Continus still in my Ladys favour, and is much the better beloved for his old masters sake; be sure to remember sending word when you wilbe back at Paris that Sir William Cooper,[8] mr Hoskins[9] and my selfe may have an oper-

[a] *Last letter doubtful.*

---

[1] Locke had obtained a letter from E.(?) Margas in Paris, 2/12 December, to Simon Peloutier, merchant, at Lyons, requesting him to furnish Locke with money up to 976 livres (approximately £73) in return for Locke's bills of exchange on London: B.L., MS. Locke c. 15, ff. 224–5. Margas was a Protestant and Peloutier perhaps also: H. Lüthy, *La Banque protestante en France*, 1959–61, i. 68; E. and E. Haag, *La France protestante*, 1846–59 (and 1877–88), s.v. Pelloutier, S.

[2] Samuel Thomas.

[3] Nathaniel Hodges: p. 260, n. 3.

[4] Peter Locke.

[5] For Mrs. Stringer see p. 434 n. Letters from her below. Bexwells, formerly Bekeswell, is generally called Bexfield. It was a manor in Chelmsford formerly belonging to the Mildmay family; 'the mansion house is at the entrance of Gallowwood common, on the right hand side of the road that leads from Cheltenham to Billericay': P. Muilman, (*History*) *of Essex*, 1769–72, i. 102–9. Stringer bought a house here (the manor-house?) from Richard Langley on 17 June 1675; he leased it on 6 May 1682 to Andrew Wharton of Chelmsford; release, 14 September 1683, to William Kissen (Kiffin?; no. *382*) and Henry Kissen his only son: documents at Wimborne St. Giles (information from Professor R. Voitle).

[6] Shaftesbury.

[7] See pp. 427–9, etc.

[8] William Cowper, d. 1706; second baronet 1664; father of the first Earl Cowper, the Lord Chancellor: G. E. C., *Baronetage*, ii. 160. He was a political associate of Shaftesbury, but apparently not a kinsman.

[9] Presumably John Hoskins of Oxted, Surrey, *c.* 1640–1717. Probably the John Hoskins who matriculated from Christ Church in 1656: p. 112 n. He was an adherent of Shaftesbury, perhaps a kinsman and probably his solicitor: F. Blomefield, (*History*) *of Norfolk*, 1805–10, viii. 19; R. Clutterbuck, *History . . . of* (*Hertfordshire*), 1815–27,

tunity of meeting you there. Here are aboundance make daily inquiry after you, and are soe harty in theire good wishes, that I hope suddainly to heare of your perfect recovery. Pardon my hast which is at this time very great and be Confident that I am and ever shalbe

my deare friend
Yours as mine owne
T:S:

Address: A Monsieur Monsieur Lock Gentilhome Anglois. Chez Monsieur Puech mr Apotecaire a Monpellier[1]
post paid to Paris

Postmarks: (fragmentary) OFF 4; (a blurred circular mark, perhaps) FRANCHES

Endorsed by Locke: T: Stringer 10 Feb. 75

## *309.* THOMAS STRINGER to LOCKE, 17 February 1676 (*308*, *311*)

B.L., MS. Locke c. 19, ff. 120–1. In margin is a ruled line, divided into inches and described as 'halfe a foote'. Extract printed in Christie, *Shaftesbury*, ii. 220–1.

London Feb: 17th: 1675.

Deare Sir

I just now received your six hundred forty and fifth lett⟨er⟩[a] and shewed it to my Lord,[2] whoe beleives you are almost as good as John Cooke at Numbers. But I am very much troubled that all mine, mr Hoskins and mr Terrills[3] letters are at such a losse in finding you out, it is some strange Corner you are crept into, that your owne directions cannot trace you. My Lord (whoe I thank god is very well) was very well pleased with the news of those vines, and seeds you have promised him, and hath pockett up your letter for the improvement of his understanding in those matters, both him and my Lady are very much concerned for you, and hopes in a little time to see you here againe Perfectly recovered. A great misfortune hath

[a] *End of line.*

iii. 132; Manning and Bray, *Surrey*, ii. 386, 391; Rachel Russell, Lady Russell, *Letters*, ed. [Lord John Russell], 1853, i. 107, 136; ii. 143, 217; *Cal. S.P., Dom.*, *1677–8*, p. 235. See also below nos. *528*, 753; etc.

[1] Jacques Puech, a Protestant: Lough, p. 16 n.

[2] Shaftesbury.

[3] Probably James Tyrrell: no. *343*.

lately befalen the Bankers, which hath streightened all, and proved very fatall to some, Especially 3 of the Forths.[1] Sir Stephen Fox hath soe long been toyled in buisnes that the T: thought Convenient he should now take his Ease and retire from those troublesome imployments and young Kingdon succeeds in those undertakings.[2] I have by great accident gott the payment of the bond you left in my hands which went towards the satisfaction of your bill of Exch: on Sir Patience Ward.[3] that letter of Creditt is Confirmed if you have occation of any more money at Lyons. Sir Robert Payton[4] is alsoe eased of all his troublesome Comissions, and a Friend of ours is advised to goe into the Country, but a Law suit and some other buisnes is like to hinder it.[5] Doctor Sydenham[a] presents his

[a] *Or* Sydenhum

[1] This probably refers to a government scheme for the reduction of expenditure, adopted by order dated 28 January 1676. The brothers John (1625–78) and Dannet Forth were aldermen of London; they, with associates, were farmers of the Excise. John was a son-in-law of the younger Sir Henry Vane; a daughter of Dannet was married to Francis St. John, son of Oliver St. John the Lord Chief Justice: Browning, *Danby*, i. 186–7, iii. 19–21; Woodhead, *Rulers of London*; Hudson's Bay Co., *Minutes 1671–4*, pp. 225–6.

[2] Sir Stephen Fox (1627–1716: *D.N.B.*), Paymaster of the Forces since 1660, was dismissed on 19 January at Danby's instance (Sir Thomas Osborne, successively earl of Danby, marquis of Carmarthen, and duke of Leeds; Lord High Treasurer ('the T') 1673–9: ibid; Browning, *Danby*). His successor was Sir Henry Puckering (previously Newton; *D.N.B.*), but the latter's position was a sinecure; the work was done by the Deputy Paymaster Lemuel Kingdon: Browning, i. 195–6.

[3] 1629–96; merchant; alderman of London 1670; knighted 1675; Lord Mayor 1680–1; an adherent of Shaftesbury; he was tried for perjury in 1683, and fled to the United Provinces, where he remained until *c.* 1687: *D.N.B.* He gave Locke a letter of credit in May 1675:

London 2 May 1675

Sir if one Doctor Lock an English Gentleman have occasion of twenty pounds sterlin I pray you to furnish it him and take his bill on me for soe much wherein you will oblige

Sir
Your assured [?] friend [?]
P. WARD

Address: To mr Nicolas Lee merchant In Nantes.

Endorsed by Locke: Sir P. *Ward* 2 May *75*

—B.L., MS. Locke c. 23, f. 61.

[4] Robert Peyton, d. 1689; of East Barnet; knighted 1670; sometime one of the two Examiners in Chancery; an extreme Whig; M.P. for Middlesex 1679, 1680, until expelled on account of intrigues with James duke of York; later a refugee in the United Provinces; took part in William III's expedition to England: F. C. Cass, *East Barnet* (London and Middlesex Archeol. Soc., 1885–92), pp. 70–1; Le Neve, *Pedigrees*, p. 239; *Correspondence of the Family of Hatton, 1601–1704*, ed. E. Maunde Thompson (Camden Soc., new ser., vols. xxii–xxiii, 1878), i. 203; C. Dalton, ed., *English Army Lists and Commission Registers, 1661–1714*, 1892–1904, ii. 246; nos. *528*, *874* n. below. Peyton may also have been a notable London merchant.

[5] Sir Joseph Williamson was sent to Shaftesbury to advise him to retire to the country: Haley, *Shaftesbury*, pp. 404–5; Browning, *Danby*, i. 196.

service to you and is now Printing his booke.[1] here are many remembers you but none are more affectionately

Your servant then

T:S

Address: A Monsieur Monsieur Lock Gentilhome Anglois Chez Monsr: Puech mr apoticaire a Montpellier
post paid to Paris
Postmark: (fragmentary; probably) FRANCHES
Endorsed by Locke: T. Stringer 17 Feb. 75

## 310. LOCKE to ——, 1 March 1676

B.L., MS. Locke c. 25, ff. 19–20. Draft. Unfinished; the writing breaks off in the upper part of f. 19ᵛ. Excerpts printed in King, pp. 41–3; the whole, in Lough, pp. 276–81. Locke had presumably sent an earlier letter to the present correspondent, narrating his adventures as far as Boulogne. The date may be old style, or the writing may have extended over several days: see p. 442, n. 1. I have checked the distances by M. L. R. (C.-M. Saugrain), *Nouveau voyage de France*, dernière édition, 1723, p. 424.

*3*

Montpellier 1 Mar. 167$\frac{5}{6}$

We left our two Combatants with their hands lift up. (As you know Mr Scudery and other good authors our predecessors often doe)[2] and holding each one the end of a sheet in them. and if the French feircenesse carry it not sooner yet at least the blaze of the faggot quickly goes out, their heat cooles and the English man at last is laid on his back, from which captivy he is releived early next morning at the command of Sultan Messenger[3] who is cheife commander in all these castles where he comes; and sure is a very happy prince, for though his subjects goe through many hardships, yet they usually obey all his commands willingly. Are they summond be fore day to rise? course and stinkeing lodging makes them forward. Are durty heavy boots to be put on? want of slippers takes away all reluctancy. Is leane ill dressed meat to be eat? a good stomach bids it wellcome. Are you to be dismounted and thrust into a rascally Inne 4 or 5 in a chamber? ten or eleven leagues on a dull hobling

[1] *Observationes Medicæ circa Morborum Acutorum Historiam et Curationem*, 1676. It is advertised in May: *T.C.* i. 238. L.L., no. 2814.

[2] This recalls *Don Quixote*, pt. i, ch. viii. Madeleine de Scudéry (1607–1701; *N.B.G.*) used her brother Georges's name (1601–67; ibid.) as a *nom de guerre*.

[3] The *messager*, who, besides conducting a carrier service, contracted with travellers on certain routes to provide them with transport, food, and accommodation for their journeys.

jade will make you glad of it. But though I remember where we left our combatants, I have almost forgot where I left you. I thinke it was some where in the way between Bologne and Montriel.[1] tis all one where, for all the way is made up of plains hills and dales, and those coverd all with corne or wood, unlesse it be some barren hills of sand that beare noe thing unlesse it be now and then a Mosse trooper. In a very convenient wood 2 or 3 leagues out of Boulong we lookd for our freinds of St Omars. but the Dons were affraid of the French, or us, or their trumpeter, (for I dare not doe the gentlemen the injury to imagin they had any aversion to our mony) and soe we saw noe more whiskers.[2] After we were passed this terrible place, those that had mony thought it their owne, and beleived their clothes might last them to Paris, where the Taylors lye in wait to strip you of your old clothes, and pick your pockets, and I know not yet, whether a taylor with his yard and sheirs; or a trooper with a sword and pistol in his hand be the more dangerous creature. From this wood we marchd on merrily to Montriel the remainder of this days seven leagues, and arrived there Saturday 30 Dec[3] in good time. Supper was ready before our boots were off and being fish almost as soon digested, our lodging something better then Boulogne

1 Dec: early in a frosty morning we were with all the train on our March to Abevil 10 leagues[a-] from Montreel.[-a] Abevil is a large towne seated on the river of Amiens.[4] Here his Excellence dismissed his St Omers trumpeter.

2 Dec. The Ambasador resolveing to goe by Amiens, our Governor the messenger was willing to goe the ordinary rode by Poy,[5] which we, who went to seek adventures beyond Paris, easily consented to, we therefor plodded on the carriers rode and pace our 9 leagues to Poy, and though that way of travailing tires an Englishman sufficiently, yet we were noe sooner got into our chambers,

[a-a] *MS.* leagues from from Montreel.

---

[1] Boulogne and Montreuil-sur-Mer.

[2] St. Omer formed part of the Spanish Netherlands at this time. France and Spain were at war from 1673 to 1678. Whiskers are moustaches: '**Whisker**, a tuft of Hair on the Upper Lip of a Man': Phillips, 1706.

[3] A slip for 30 November, N.S.

[4] Abbeville on the Somme. The distance from Montreuil is given as 8 leagues in the road-books. The French league (*lieue*) varied from province to province, ranging roughly from $2\frac{1}{3}$ to $3\frac{1}{2}$ miles.

[5] Poix; 8 leagues from Abbeville. Locke had presumably spent a night there in 1672.

but we thought we were come there too soone, for the highway seemd the much sweeter cleaner and more desireable place. had I not been of old acquainted with this memorable lodging, I should have suspected that General Messenger had been leading us against the Germans, and that now we had been just on those frontires which both armys had pilaged at the end of the last campagne,[1] and had left this castle garisond not with horse, but an other sort of 6 legd creature to defend it against the next comers. It being decreed we must stay there al night, I cald, intreated, and swaggerd a good while, (for necessity multiplys ones French mightily) for a pair of slippers, at last they were brought, and I sat me down on the only seat we had in our apartment, which at present was a forme, but I beleive had been heretofore a wooden horse,[2] but the legs being cut shorter and the ridg of the back taken down to the bredth of ones hand it made a considerable part of the furniture of our chamber. my boots being off I thought to ease my self of my seat by standing, but I assure you with noe very good sucsesse, for the soles of my Pantofles being sturdy timber had very litle compliance for my feet. and soe made it some what uncomfortable for me to keepe my self (as the French call standing) on one end.[3] This smal tast of Sabots, gave me a surfet of them and left such an aversion to them in my stomach, that I shall never make choise of a country to passe my pilgrimage in, where they are in fashion. Tis possible they may be very necessary to the aiery people of this country, who being able to run, skip, and dance in these, would certainly mount into the aire, and take most wonderfull frisks, were there not some such clogs at their heels, but I beleive a dul heavy Englishman might be as soon brought, to dance a jig with a pair of stocks about his ankles, as to walke the streets in such brogues as these, though they were never soe curiosly[a] carved as I have seen some of them. Of these crabtree soled slippers we had two pair between three of us, and there could never happen a nicer case in breeding, then there was then between us three, to know whether one were bound by the rules of civility, to take ones self, or offer to an other, or refuse the offer of a pair of these slippers, it being still a doubt to this day, and like to remain

[a] *Spelling doubtful.*

[1] The principal French campaigns in 1675 were in Alsace and on the Moselle.
[2] It was an instrument of punishment, chiefly military: *O.E.D.*, s.v. Wooden.
[3] *Se tenir debout.*

soe, whether barefoot in a ragged brick floore, or these slippers on, were the better posture. However to shew that we profited by our travails, and were willing to improve our manners into the courtlynesse of the country, we made it a matter of complement. many good things, I assure you, were spoke on the occasion, we had shuffled favour, civility, obligacon, honour, and many other the like words (very usefull in travaild and well bred company) forwards and backwards in severall obleigeing repartees: and this fashionable conversation had lasted longer had not supper come, in and interrupted us. Here the barefoot gent thought to finde comfort in his humility, and the others in the stocks to divert their pain, but we quickly found that a supper of ill meat, and worse cookery, was but an insignificant sound, and served ill to fill ones belly. soup and ragoo and such other words of good savour, lost here their relish quite, and out of 5 or 6 dishes were served up to us, we patchd up a very untoward supper, but be it as rascally as it will and meane, it must not faile in the most material part to be fashionable, we had the ceremony of first and second course besides a disert in the close, for were your whole bill of fare noe thing but some cabbage and a frog that was caught in it, and some haws of the last season, you would have a treat in all its formalitys, and would not faile of three courses, the first would make a soope, the second a good fricasie (of which I have eaten) and twas not long since that preserved haws were served up for a disert to me and some others of my country men, who could not tell what to make of this new sort of fruit, they being some thing biger then ordinary, and disguised under the fine name of pomet de Paradise, till the next day on the road our Voiturin shewd us, upon what sort of tree this, that made soe fine a wett sweetmeat grew.[1] After supper we retreated to the place that usually gives redresse to all sorts of moderate calamitys, but our beds served but to compleat our vexation and seemd to be ordeind for antidotes against sleepe. I will not complain of their hardnesse, because tis a quality I like, but the thinnesse of what lay upon me and the tangible qualitys of what was next me, and the savour of all about me, made me quite

[1] Locke was given 'Pomett de Paradise' at Balaruc near Montpellier on 4 March, N.S.: Journal. *Pommette* is the common name in the south of France for the azarole, the fruit of the Neapolitan medlar; it looks like a haw but is larger: P. Larousse, *Grand dict. universel du XIX*e *siècle*, 1866–76; J. Evelyn, *Silva*, ed. A. Hunter, 1776, p. 184 n. The *voiturin* let horses to travellers and accompanied them as guide; the word was used only in the provinces of France near Italy: Richelet, 1740. Wet sweetmeats are those preserved in syrup: *O.E.D.*, s.v. Wet, *a.* 11.

forget my slippers and supper, and twas impossible I should have lasted in that strong perfume till morning, had not a large convenient hole in the wall at my beds head powerd in plenty of fresh aire. As good luck would have it, we had a long journey of twelve leagues to goe next day, which made our stay here the shorter; we were rousd before day, and I heard nobody complain of it; we were glad to be released from this prison (for tis impossible to beleive, freemen should stay themselves here) and willingly left it to those miserable soules were to succeed us. If Paris be heaven (for the French with their usuall justice extol it above al things on earth) Poy certainly is purgatory in the way to it

3 Dec: we dinde at Bauvais 9 leagues from poy, where I saw not any thing very remarkeable, but the quire of a church very high and stately, built as they say by the English, who it seemes had not time to compleat the whole church, nor have the French it seems thought fit ever since to finish it;[1] were there a body of the church added to this peice, answerable to it, it would be a very magnificent structure, but as far as I have observed of the churches of both countrys, to make them every way exact, we ought to build, and they to adorne them. Hence wee went three leagues to Tiliard to bed.[2] Good mutton and a good supper here, cleane sheets of the country, and a pretty girle to lay them on (who was an angell compard to the Feinds of poy) made us some amends for the past nights sufferings. Doe not wonder that a man of my constitution and gravity mentions to you a handsome face amongst his remarks, for I imagin that a travailer, though he carrys a cough with him, goes not yet out of his way, when he takes notice of strange and extraordinary things.

4 Dec: we din'd or rather breakefasted at Beaumond 5[3] leagues from Tiliard. This being the last assembly we were like to have of our company, 'twas thought convenient here to even some small account had happend upon the road. One of the French men who had disbursd for our troope was by the natural quicknesse of his temper carryed a good deale beyond the marke, and demanded for our shares more then we thought due whereupon one of the English desird an account of particulars not that the whole was soe considerable but to keepe a certain custome we had in England not to

[1] According to Saugrain Beauvais is 10 leagues from Poix. I do not know Locke's source for his statement that the English built the cathedral; it is incorrect.

[2] Tillard, 5 leagues from Beauvais.

[3] Beaumont, 3 leagues from Tillard.

pay mony without knowing for what. Monsieur answered briskly he would give noe account, and the other as briskly that he would have it, this produced a reconing of the severall disbursments and an abatement of $\frac{1}{4}$ of the demands and a great demonstration of good nature for Monsieur Steward shewd more civility and respect to the English gent who had been warme with him after this litle contest then he had donn all the journey before

## *311.* THOMAS STRINGER to LOCKE, 6 April 1676 (*309, 312*)

B.L., MS. Locke c. 19, f. 122. Excerpts printed in Christie, ii. 221–2.

Aprill 6th. 1676.

Deare Sir

I have received your letter of the 17th of March, and I beleiv⟨e⟩[a] all those that you writt before, but by this last I am very sorry to heare that your Cough doth increase upon you. Sir Paul neile[1] is still of an opinion that to come into Engl: and marry a young woeman is the best Remidy. My Lady[2] hath received your box of oreng Trees and valews them as a very Choyce present from one of her best friends. She hath sent for Serjeant Stephens[3] whoe is a man of great delight in Gardens, and he hath undertaken to mannage them for her. My Lord is alsoe pleased Exceedingly, with his present of vine Cuttings, and hath taken the best care he can to preserve them, they doe both amongst other of your friends hartily desire your recovery, and long to see againe in England. I thank god they are both in very good health but in some trouble where to take another house because we have now disposed of Exceter house to builders,[4] and are to remove from thence by midsomer next, but at our remove I shall take care of all your things.

[a] *End of line.*

[1] p. 300 n.

[2] Lady Shaftesbury. Presumably the trees bought by Locke on 15 February, N.S.: Journal.

[3] Robert Stephens, 1622–4 November 1675; serjeant-at-law 11 February 1675: R. Bigland, (*Gloucestershire Collections*), 1791–2, i. 540. He was a brother-in-law of Sir Edward Harley (no. 1792).

[4] See p. 292, n. 3.

## *311. T. Stringer, 6 April 1676*

Our friend mr Thompson[1] and his Partners have lately been soe hard pressed for money by theire Creditors that they are forced to abscond, though sinc they have summoned theire Creditors, and have propose in 3 years time to pay them all theire money and Interest, if they will give them that liberty to fetch in theire Estates which is all out in Trade and most of it beyond sea, the Creditors upon Examining theire books and finding there is 38000l. more then will pay all theire debts, have most of them alre⟨a⟩dy[a] Co⟨ns⟩ented[a] thereunto, and there is a probability that the rest will not stand off, where there is soe faire a shew of theire satisfaction. A great Duke[2] hath lately declared himselfe a discenter from the Church of England and Divers great Lords are following his Example. My Lord Ashley and Lady were lately in Towne, and tells us the Children are all very well, Mrs Clerke[3] (whoe often enquires after you) is as bigg as she can Tumble, and a friend of yours in Essex[4] is growing very fast after she had your letter, and must Answere for her selfe why did not Answere you. mr Hoskins and mr Hodges we expect in Towne this weeke, and Doctor Tho:[5] the next, and then you may expect a further accompt of matters in the mean time I rest

my dearest friend
Yours as mine owne
T:S:

Endorsed by Locke: Stringer 6 Apr. *76*[b]
Also marked by Locke: Dedicatory *76*

[a] *Page torn.* [b] *Altered from* 79.

[1] On 10 March Richard Thompson (d. 1713?), Edward Nelthorpe, and others, merchant bankers, summoned their creditors to a meeting, and failed to satisfy them. Thompson and Nelthorpe were kinsmen or connections of Andrew Marvell (*D.N.B.*) and William Popple (no. *1140* n.); Shaftesbury may have invested money with them; they may have been nonconformists and probably shared his political views: *Notes and Queries*, cciv (1959), 204–7.

[2] On or shortly before 23 March James duke of York declared that he would no longer accompany the king to Anglican services: Marchesa Campana de Cavelli, *Les Derniers Stuarts à Saint-Germain en Laye*, 1871, i. 166–7; Evelyn, *Diary*, 24 March 1676.

[3] Perhaps Locke's cousin Mrs. Mary Clarke, formerly Jepp: p. 369, n. 2; p. 448 below, etc.

[4] Mrs. Stringer at Bexwells.

[5] Dr. David Thomas.

## *312.* THOMAS STRINGER to LOCKE, 5 June 1676 (*311, 315*)

B.L., MS. Locke c. 19, ff. 123–4. Excerpts printed in Christie, ii. 222–4. This is probably the letter of '15' June mentioned by Locke in his Journal, 3 August, N.S.

June 5th. 1676[a]

My deare Friend,

I have received your letter of the 15th of May, and alsoe the paquett you sent by mr Nevock,[1] he not comming himselfe, but sending that paquett likwise by the post and thereby I perceive my former letter about 3 weeks sinc is not come to your hand, which gives you an accompt of our Tryall, with my Lord Digby. Even from digbys owne Evidence that tryall was the greatest vindication of my Lord in that Concerne of the Election, that could be imaginable, the Lord Digbys Wittnesses making forth to a high degree what we most harty wished for Witnesses to prove, that had the jury given noe damages that very Examination in soe Extreame Crowded a Court was a most honourable Justification, but the Jury were pleased to give a further evidence of it by theire verdict of one thousand pownds damages, but they did declare to the Judge whoe tooke theire Privy verdict, that the did Consider how the E of Bristoll was still living, that Digby had but a small estate in hand, and that they were not willing to Perpetuate a feiwd between two noble Familys, otherwise they woud have given much greater Damages; Digbys Councill afterwards moved in arest of Judgement upon a pretended Error in the declaration, which Exception the last terme was argued by the Counsell on both sides and the Judges the Satyrday last, gave theire opinions on that Error, which was that it was noe Error and that my Lord of S: ought to have his Judgement, this being the unanimous opinion of the Court. I am this afternoon to tax the Costs of the suit and make forth the Execution, you may imagin what favour a man is like to finde that did at first begin and ever sinc carry on his affront, with soe high provocation.[2] I long sinc sent you 3 of Doctor Sydenhams books and directed them just as you directed, which I pre-

[a] *Locke adds* rec[d] 29° Jun

---

[1] Locke, Journal, 10 May, N.S.
[2] See pp. 427–9, 436; *Hatton Corr.* i. 123–4, 126.

sume before this are come to your hands.[1] I heare sinc by mr Hoskins you desire one of Doctor Stillingfleets,[2] which I shall take an opertunity to send you by mr Hunts sone[3] being come in the Charge of mr Man to Paris[4] and afterwards under the care of a mayde to you at montpellier, and by[a–] her you will likewise receive[–a] a note for the 25l you desire. I suppose they wilbe with you about a fortnight after you shall receive this they intending to sett forward from hence on Fryday next. here was a Gent left a little paper of Red berrys, but I could never heare whoe it was, neyther have yet had any letter to tell me what they are.

Wee are yett at Exceter house, but about a weeke or ten days hence my Lord and Lady are removing to St Giles[5] and the Exceter house wilbe forsaken, our Goods are to ⟨be⟩[b] carryed to a house which we have taken in St Martins Lane, where our Family will settle all the next winter. The seeds you mention to have sent by mr Nevock are not yett come to hands. Your friends here are very Glad to heare that you are soe well recovered we all earnestly desire the ayre of that Place wilbe soe favourable to perfect your cure: The Cheife Justice Hales hath layed downe his place and Rainsford is sworne Cheife Justice in his Roome,[6] the Lord Cheife Baron Turner is dead and mr Atturney Mountague is sworne into his Place.[7] Sir John Duncomb is turned out, and Sir John Earnle is Chancellor of the Exchequer.[8] My Lord Ashley and his Family are

[a–a] *MS.* by her you will likewise you will receive [b] *An illegible deleted word in MS.*

[1] Probably three copies of the *Observationes Medicæ* (p. 439, n. 1). Locke apparently gave copies to Drs. Brouchier and Barbeyrac (pp. 451, 515; the mentions on pp. 492 and 515 may, however, refer to a later transaction).

[2] Identifiable as *A Defence of the Discourse concerning the Idolatry practised in the Church of Rome*, 1676, which Locke was reading on 22 December, N.S.: Journal; *T.C.* i. 255 (November 1676); L.L., no. 2775.

[3] Apparently a boy. The father is identifiable as Maurice Hunt, whose maid Ann Osby was in Paris in 1678: Locke, Journal, 18 June, 6 July; see also nos. *430*, 770 n. The Mr. Hunt of no. 566, etc., whose son died at Montpellier in 1680 is probably the same man.

[4] Perhaps John Mann, M.P. for Melcombe Regis 1673–8: Haley, *Shaftesbury*, pp. 293, 316, 318.

[5] Lord and Lady Shaftesbury; Wimborne St. Giles.

[6] Sir Matthew Hale (p. 375, n. 4) resigned on 20 February; Sir Richard Rainsford (*D.N.B.*) was appointed on 12 April to succeed him.

[7] Sir Edward Turner (ibid.), Lord Chief Baron of the Exchequer since 1671, died on 4 March; William Montagu (p. 322, n. 3) was appointed on 12 April to succeed him.

[8] Duncombe (p. 419, n. 2) was dismissed on 21 April; Sir John Ernle was sworn in on 8 May: Browning, *Danby*, i. 196–7; for Ernle see Evelyn, *Diary*, ed. de Beer, iv. 533 n.; S. B. Baxter, *The Development of the Treasury, 1660–1702*, 1957, pp. 32–3.

goeing from St Giles, only mr Anthony[1] is to remaine with his Grandfather, by agreement and to be educated by him. mrs Clerk[2] is delivered of a young Sone, and my[a] thinks looks prettily for a mother. I have lately received a letter and a bill of Exchange from your Uncle[3] for 24l, but as yett I heare nothing from Oxford, though I desired mr Hodges to Enquire a little into that affaire. mr Hicks the Tayler hath buryed both his wife and daughter.[4] Here are divers shells and strange things sent you From the Bahamas which my Lord hath Communicated to mr Boyle. they are now before the Royall Societie, and I doubt not but in some short time you will have a learned lecture upon them. I suppose now I have made amends for my short letters. My Wife being just come to Towne and I not seen her this fortnight, I am soe much in arreare to her, that I must reserve the rest for you untill the next opertunity; I have just now been and taxed 152l for Costs (besides the Damages) on my Lord Digby. My Wife commands me to present her kinde service to you and soe doth aboundance more of your very good friends. I am

Deare Sir

Your most affectionate humble servant

THO: STRINGER

Address: A Monsieur Monsieur Lock Gentilhome Anglois Chez Monsr: Peuch mr Apoticaire a Montpellier
Post paid to Paris

Postmark: (blurred; perhaps) FRANCHES

Endorsed by Locke: Mr Stringer 5 Jun. *76*
[and elsewhere:] 5 Jun.

[a] *Altered from or to* me

---

[1] The future third earl of Shaftesbury. [2] p. 445.
[3] Peter Locke.
[4] John Hicks, with whom Locke perhaps lodged in 1679 (he used Hicks's lodgings as an address for letters for some time: no. *469*, etc.). Mrs. Hicks was buried on 11 January; a married daughter, on 26 March: *Registers of St. Paul's Church, Convent Garden*, vol. iv (Harleian Soc., Register section, vol. xxxvi, 1908), pp. 71, 72.

## *313.* MRS. ANNA GRIGG to LOCKE, 28 June 1676 (*319*)

B.L., MS. Locke c. 10, f. 118. For the writer see p. 334, n. 2.

Sir

I must not pevishly tell you that you are not in all things a man of your word, but rather honestly confess that I am oblig'd to you for remembering me as you doe, since I cannot pretend to meritt it; And now Sir as a marke of my respect you must be contented to receave an account of my great travells; I am but newely return'd from Bristoll where I had the satisfaction of meeting my Uncle Locke and cousin Stratton[1]—I will not possetively say their greatest designe was to enquir of your health; I satisfied them as well as your silence would give me leave, and could I have bin assur'd of your safety I should have bin inclin'd to make a little mischief, but great concerne, and a little good nature overpower'd my colerick resentments, and I was willing every body should foregive you upon condition you could sends us glad tidings at the last. Mr Stringer tells me you are returning, And you must pardon me if I answer I am sorry for it, since I cannot understand that you have conquer'd your distemper. Would not another winter perfect and settle your recovery? and too quick a returne defeate your owne and all your friends hopes? but I must not pretend to be a counceller in so grave an affair but doe as I use to doe wish most heartyly that all may succeed prosperously. I will not undertake to entertaine you with newes, the french understand our condition so well that you may informe us how we doe, we like neither their fire nor Dagers,[2] and if they love us as we feare they doe, None are so safe as those who are consumptive and forc'd to vissitt Mompellier; I have as you may imagin bin pratting with tmerous and mellancholy persons, and that must be my excuse for writting so sillyly I hav⟨e not forgotten⟩[a] how many wayes I am indebted to you, nor doe

[a] *Page torn.*

---

[1] Peter Locke and Mary or William Stratton: p. 263, n. 2; no. *543*, etc. The wording shows that Mrs. Grigg was a niece or niece by marriage of Peter Locke or his wife; as she never calls Locke cousin the relationship must have been through Mrs. Locke.

[2] In this month there were rumours about French incendiaries and perhaps about large purchases of knives: *Cal. S.P., Dom.*, 1676–7, pp. 142–3, 161, 174, 185.

I intend to love myself if I rudely neglect any respect is due to you from

Your most obliged friend and humble servant

ANNA GRIGG

London June the 28th 76.

Address: To Mr Locke

Endorsed by Locke: A Grig. 28 Jun. *76*

## *314.* DR. JOHN MAPLETOFT to LOCKE, 28 June 1676 (269, 339)

B.L., MS. Locke c. 15, ff. 205–6.

Mapletoft was Professor of Physick at Gresham College from 1675 to 1679.

Gresham Colledg Jun 28. 76.

Deare Sir

The Letter you were pleased to favour me with in February came not to my hands in a long time after, neither did your last of May 9 arrive till the beginning of this Month, so that this is the first in which I had any opportunity of complying with your desires in setling that Monthly Correspondence in the manner you propose, which I esteem a mark of your particular Friendship and value myselfe upon it accordingly. In pursuance of your Commands I acquainted Dr. Sydenham with all that relates to your health, of which I found you had given him a later account then mine was. He threatens to write to you himselfe but in the mean time desires me to tell you That he lays the main stresse of your Cure upon Alteresty[1] as he calls it, and would therefore advise you to give yourselfe up to the Dyet of the Country you are in, eating and drinking as they doe, without which he doth not expect much from the aire. he thinks you should drink Wine and Water together, as they doe, rather ⟨than⟩[a] the Pure Element, and that you should rather forbear Milke then make so constant use of it He mislikes not your having bled once, but doth not advise to repeate it, nor take any kind of Physick. I hope you will find all the advantages you could propose to yourselfe in your journy and that you will shortly return to us

[a] *Word omitted by Mapletoft.*

[1] The word is not in *O.E.D.* It was apparently coined from the questionable or late Latin word *alterare*, to vary.

in perfect good health. I am glad you found Dr. Brouchier[1] so much the Man I promised you, he expresses great satisfaction in you likewise, so that I pretend to have served you both. Dr. Coxe laments your not coming with his Son, but owns his obligations to you for the kindnes you did him whilst you were together.[2] My Lady Northumberland hath been at Bristoll and Bathe and drunk of both those Minerall Waters, but without any great effect. I beleive she will try Bourbon in the fall, Mr. Mountague being designd (as the King says) to goe Embassador into France in the room of Lord Barclay.[3] But he is no surer of it then I tell you, and hath a Mighty Dutches at Court his Enemy.[4] Dr. Blomer and his Family went for Canterbury this morning.[5] They give you their hearty service, as doe all your Friends here that know of this opportunity. Mr. Firmin is in Holland with his Eldest son whom he means to leave there for some time.[6] Dr. Sydenham's Book runs the

[1] Dr. Claude Brouchier: pp. 560–2. Locke met him when he was at Aix in April. Brouchier gave him some prescriptions and continued:

Si Monsieur Locke me veut honnorér de ses commandements, les addresserá á paris á Monsieur Vilj docteur en Theologie au temple pour faire tenir á Monseigneur le cardinal grimaldij archeveque d'aix et au dessoubs la susdite enveloppe y mettre la suivante

A Monsieur Brouchier professeur en medecine medecin de Monseigneur le cardinal *grimaldi* archeveque d'aix á aix.

Monsieur aura, s'il luy plait, la bonté de dire á monsieur mapletoft de faire la mesme addresse, monsieur Revolat n'estant plus á Paris.

Endorsed by Locke: Dr Brouchier 76

—B.L., MS. Locke c. 4, ff. 163–4.

Locke copied the whole, except the last paragraph, in his Journal, 19 April, N.S. He evidently expected to return to England shortly: so no. *313* and Mapletoft above. Brouchier was appointed professor of chemistry in the University of Aix in 1669 when the chair was founded: P. J. de Haitze, *Histoire de la ville d'Aix*, 1880–92, vi. 65. For the cardinal see p. 560, n. 3.

[2] The father is Thomas Coxe, 1615–85; M.D., Padua, 1641: *D.N.B.* He was already advising the younger Sir William Waller (p. 515, n. 5), and was called a Whig in 1683: Locke, Journal, 14 November 1676, N.S.; Wood, *L. and T.* iii. 76. There were at least two sons, one, probably Thomas, being at Montpellier on 14 February, N.S., of this year: Locke, Journal. Letters from Thomas and Dr. Coxe below, nos. *321*, *383*; see also no. 386.

[3] On 24 August 1673 Lady Northumberland (p. 327 n.) married as her second husband Ralph Montagu, *c.* 1638–1709; a first cousin of Lady Ashley; succeeded as third Baron Montagu of Boughton 1683; created earl, 1689, and duke, 1705, of Montagu: *D.N.B.* He was appointed ambassador to France in September, in succession to Lord Berkeley of Stratton (p. 434, n. 1). Bristol waters are those of the Hot Well at Clifton: Evelyn, *Diary*, ed. de Beer, iii. 103 n. Bourbon is Bourbon-l'Archambault: p. 378, n. 3.

[4] Louise-Renée de Penancoët de Kéroualle, 1649–1734; created duchess of Portsmouth 1673; Charles II's mistress: *D.N.B.* Montagu had intrigued against her in the spring: Browning, *Danby*, i. 223.

[5] They apparently accompanied Lady Northumberland to France: p. 459.

[6] For Firmin see p. 362, n. 2. This son died about 1690: *D.N.B.*

Gauntlet luckily enough here with us.[1] Mr Stringer tells me he beleives your Books are with you and I presume you have obliged Dr. Brouchier with one as you told me you intended. If in any thing I can serve you here I hope I need not request you to make use of the right you have in

Deare Sir

Your most Faithful Humble Servant

J MAPLETOFT.

Address: A Monsieur Monsieur Locke Gentilhomme Anglois chez Monsieur Puech A Montpellier
Franc pour Paris.

Postmark: (fragmentary; probably) FRANCHES

Endorsed by Locke: Dr. Mapletoft. 28° Jun *76*

## *315.* THOMAS STRINGER to LOCKE, 8 July 1676 (*312, 333*)

B.L., MS. Locke c. 19, ff. 125–6. Excerpts printed in King, 1830, i. 70 n. *ad fin.*; Christie, *Shaftesbury*, ii. 224. Locke mentions the letter in his Journal, 3 August, N.S.

Bexwells July 8th. 1676.[a]

My Deare Friend

I have received your letter of the 26th of may and doe beleive that none of yours have miscarryed to me, and doe presume that none of mine can miscarry to you if they are carfully delivered into the Post, but the multitude of buisnes I have lately had, (Occationed both by my Lord Digbys obstinacy, and our owne removeing from Exceter house) that I have been forced to trust somtimes some other Persons and not see them delivered my selfe, that I feare the money[b] which they cost to Parris doe make them miscarry to the Post, and upon this Consideration I have adventured once more to direct them bare faced to you, and thereby to trust the Post with that, which I will none of our owne People againe, and by this you will have the news of all our removall from Exceter House, the Gentleman whoe hath taken it being Comming this weeke to pull it downe and rebuild it all into Smal Tenements. My Lord A: and

[a] *Locke adds* Recd 1 Aug. [b] *MS.* mo

[1] The *Observationes Medicæ*.

his Lady with theire two younger sones are gone to Haddon[1] to spend the remainder of this Sommer and ensuing Winter there to save Charges and gather a good stock that the next Spring they may begin Houskeeping at Martin.[2] St Giles being Empty my Lord of S, and his Countesse are gon thether to visitt mr Anthony whoe is left to theire care and tuition and a little after Michaelmas they resolve to come againe to London, but to what house is yett uncertaine, for at present we have taken one in St Martins lane to hold the goods, but they are seeking after an other for theire habitation, and where about his Lott will fall I am not able to Guesse, though Russell house in Southampton[a] Square we have all a minde to, and mr Atturney is willing to parte with it, if we can agree the Terms.[3] I have in our removall taken great care of all your things and sent them to mr Hicks, whoe hath lately gott him a new landlady, and would noe longer live the life of a disconsolate widdoure, Mr Clerke and his Lady in Hatten Garden are very well but have lately buryed theire young sone, which hath been a great trouble to them, and she was the more unwilling to parte with him because it cost her soe much payne and difficulty to bring him into the world.[4] Our good friend mr Hoskins hath been somwhat indisposed, which hath kept him in London behinde my Lord and Lady, but his distemper being pretty well over, he intends to prepare his body for travelling in Harfordshire the next weeke that he may be

[a] *MS.* South

[1] Lord and Lady Ashley; apparently Haddon Hall, Derbyshire, which belonged to Lord Rutland, Lady Ashley's father. The two younger sons are John Ashley Cooper, 1672–93, and Maurice Ashley Cooper, 1675–1726.

[2] Presumably the Hampshire village, about 6 miles NE. of Wimborne St. Giles.

[3] Russell House appears to be the former Southampton House, later Bedford House, on the north side of the former Southampton, now Bloomsbury Square. At this time it belonged to Lady Rachel Vaughan (later Lady Russell), who was a daughter of the last earl of Southampton and a half-sister of Lady Northumberland, and to her second husband William Russell, later Lord Russell, who was executed in 1683 (no. 561). Mr. Attorney is identifiable as Sir William Jones (p. 73, n. 2), who was Attorney-General from 1675 to 1679; he lived in Southampton Square in 1682, and presumably at this time; he may have been empowered to negotiate. On 15 July Shaftesbury wrote to Stringer: 'I am not rich enough to buy Mr. Attorney's house'; that could scarcely apply to an ordinary house in the square: *London Topographical Record*, xvii (1936), 55–7, etc.; Christie, *Shaftesbury*, ii. 225.

[4] The wife is evidently the Mrs. Clarke of pp. 445, 448; and the Mr. and Mrs. Clarke of p. 499 are likely to be the same couple. They are probably Edward Clarke of Chipley and his wife Mary (Jepp), Locke's cousin: p. 369, n. 2; no. *682* (where there is an account of Clarke). The identification here is based on what is known of Clarke's later life. No other man of the name is known among Shaftesbury's adherents about this time.

able undertake a jorney to St Giles the next after, he did me the favour but a little while sinc to accompany my Lord and Lady here at my house, where they Continued from Satyrday untill teusday in great delight, and you may be sure whoe was Pleased to see her Guests soe well satisfyed with the Place and her enterteynements.

The boy doe begin to thump now as though he was willing to be out of his box and wanted more roome to Play, it hath brought me into these partes on purpose to expect his appearance and bid him welcome to Bexwells. it makes me laugh to think how enterteyning his mother and he wilbe of one an other. After I have had a little Pleasure of it which I feare will not be untill the latter end of next month, I have promised to undertake a jorney into Dorsettshire to acquaint mrs Mary[1] how good it is to have a husband. I have yett received noe money from Oxford but have lately had 24l more from your uncle. I hope long ere this[a-] you have[-a] received the 25l you writt for, it being long sinc ordered to be payd you at Montpellier, by mr Man, whoe is alsoe upon the Road thether. Pray henceforward direct your letters to be left at mr Samuel Lownds[2] for

My good friend
Your most faithfull humble servant
T:S:

Address: A Mounsieur Mounsieur Lock Gentilhome Anglois Chez mounsieur Peuch mr Apoticaire a Montpellier
post paid to Paris
Endorsed by Locke: Mr Stringer 8° Jul. *76*

## *316*. SAMUEL (later Sir Samuel) EYRE to LOCKE, 11 July 1676.

B.L., MS. Locke c. 8, f. 92.

Samuel Eyre, 1633–98; barrister 1661; serjeant-at-law 1692; judge, King's Bench, 1694; knighted 1694; of Newhouse, Wiltshire, 7 miles SE. of Salisbury: *D.N.B.* (where he is said to have been befriended by Shaftesbury);

a–a *MS.* this you/you have

[1] Perhaps Mrs. Mary Percival: p. 456 n.
[2] He is probably not connected with William Lowndes, the future secretary to the Treasury (no. *1949*).

Sir R. C. Hoare, *History of Modern Wiltshire*, 1822–44, v. ii (Frustfield), 56. Letters from his widow and from his son (Sir) Robert, below, nos. *2552* etc.

Newhouse July 11th 1676.

Sir

This is first to enquire of your health, Then to know if you resolve to continue long out of England, and if so, Whether or no you will take the charge of a young gentleman of 15 yeares of age, who is designed for some Academy[1] in France for two or three yeares and afterwards to travell. It is my neighbour Mrs Pierpoynts son. He is grandson and heire to Mr William Pierpoynt, and likewise heire to the Marquesse of Dorchester, and shall be (if he lives) Earle of Kingston.[2] There is nothing will be thought too much for his good Education, and the Lady his mother hath importuned me, to advise her to some person to whom she may safely committ him. I am sure I could not wish her better, and am confident (if you are willing to take upon you such a charge) you will receive much sattisfaction in this, having to do with persons of so much honour and worth, and a young gentleman, of good naturall parts and temper and untainted, not inclinable to any manner of Vice, bred at Winchester Schoole, and well beloved, and thought off there. I beg your suddain answer herein

My Lord of Shaston[3] is well at St Giles's and all his. I am

Sir

Your faithfull freind and servant

SAM: EYRE

Endorsed, probably not by Locke: Samuel Eyre July 1676

Note written by Locke: Rings and Twist for a Hat

## *317.* ANDREW PERCIVALL to LOCKE, 10 August 1676 (*729*)

B.L., MS. Locke c. 17, f. 58.

Several persons surnamed Percival are associated with Shaftesbury: (i) 'my servant James Percivall', 1646: Shaftesbury's diary in Christie, vol. i, app.,

[1] Probably one of the Paris academies—finishing schools where young noblemen and gentlemen were taught horsemanship, military subjects, dancing, and deportment: Evelyn, *Diary*, ed. de Beer, ii. 134 and n.

[2] Robert Pierrepont, *c.* 1660–82; succeeded his great-uncle Henry Pierrepont, marquis of Dorchester, as third earl of Kingston, 1680. His mother was Elizabeth, 1639–99, daughter of Sir John Evelyn of West Dean, Wilts.: G.E.C.; Evelyn, *Diary*, ed. de Beer, ii. 557 n. West Dean is about 3 miles north of Newhouse.

[3] Shaftesbury.

pp. xxxii, xxxiii, xxxvi; (ii) Mrs. Mary Percival, a member of his household: p. 517, n. 1; (iii) Peter Percival, goldsmith or banker: no. *529* etc.; he is said to have been Shaftesbury's banker, but the statement is not documented; he and Mrs. Mary Percival were brother and sister or, less likely, sister-in-law: Locke, Journal, 1692, pp. 37–8; (iv) Andrew Percivall, writer of the present letter. He is said, probably in error, to have been a kinsman of Shaftesbury. In 1674 he was sent to Carolina to take charge of Shaftesbury's own plantation of St. Giles; secretary of the province 1680; died in London *c.* 1695?: South Carolina Hist. Soc., *Collections*, v. 440 n., 456 and n., 464–5; Haley, *Shaftesbury*, p. 250, etc.

These persons are probably not connected with the Irish (earl of Egmont) family to which Locke's former friend George Percival belonged.

St: Gileses the 10th august 1676. Carolina[a]

Honoured Sir

I returne youe my most hearty thankes for the favor of kising your hand by a line from youe, with account of my relations. Sir I thanck God I have been, and am, amply well satisfyed as to my comeing to Carolina[a] and doubt not but in some measure to answer my Lordes expectation haveing I thanck God hitherto found nothing so dificult but that a dilligent care with some trouble hath overcome it. but I refer you wholly to my Lordes letter where youe may be amply well satisfyed as to the fertillyty of the Country, the healthynesse of the Clymate, and our present state with Indians, and for the religion, morrality, or Customes of Indyans together with theire physicall Charmes I wholly referr youe to Dr Woodward[1] who is the barer of theise and will doubtlesse abundantly satisfy youe I remayne Sir Your most assured freind and

humble servant

ANDREW PERCIVALL

Sir per Dr Woodward have sent youe a gallon of Bares oyle which the Ind use both Inwardly and outward especially for aches burnes and such like.

Address: To his honoured Freind Dr John Lock present theise. Exeter house

Endorsed by Locke: A Percival 10° Aug. *76*

[a] *Abbreviated in MS.*

[1] p. 431 n.

## *318.* JOSEPH WEST to LOCKE, 4 September 1676 (*272*)

B.L., MS. Locke c. 23, ff. 69–70. Written by an amanuensis apart from the date, signature, and address.

Sir

your Letter of the 10th of June (75) came Safe to hand which I answered by way of Bermuda and do now present you with the best account I can gett Concerning the Natives here hopeing it may give you or any other Gentle Man some sattisfaction for the Present. The Relations I had from Mr Mathewes[1] and do not doubt but hee tooke all the Care he could to Informe mee. Sir did I know where to gett any dressed Deare Skins worth Your acceptance, I should Gladly present them to you, for it is a difficult thing to gett any at all now from our Neighbour Indians.

Sir my urgent nessecity maketh me Intreat you to speake in my behalf to my Lord of Shaftesbury, that the Bills I have now drawn upon his Lordship and the ⟨rest⟩[a] of the Lords Proprietors may be paid, to supply my present wants, for I am not able to live any longer in this Condition. I will appeal to any person that hath beene in other Plantations, how a man in my Place can Live with out Servants, Cloathing etc. and what an Inconsiderable Summ a hundred pounds is to supply mee for Seaven yeares, which is all as I have yet Received from the Lords Proprietors, having truly and faithfully served them and brought my self to povertie by keeping close to their business and Indeavouring to promote their Intrest. Still hopeing I should have sixty pound per annum paid mee in England, as was promised mee by my Lord of Shaftesbury and Sir Peter Colleton. but now I finde my Lord Doth intend I shall be paid here out of the Peoples, old debts. but what Commoditty they will pay in (that will yeeld mee something in an other Place to Releive my wants) I cannot tell. besides, I do know these people so well, that If they can any wayes a void it, they will not pay the Lords Proprietors a penny, So that If I am thrown upon them, I do expect little or nothing, no man but my self knows the Trouble and Clamour I have had with them from time to Time and more especially since the arrivall of my Lord Shaftesburys Familie,[2] because

[a] *MS.* rst

[1] Maurice Matthews, sometime surveyor-general of Carolina: South Carolina Hist. Soc., *Collections*, v. 332 n.

[2] Presumably the settlers at St. Giles: p. 456.

Mr Percivall and Dr Woodward doth Trade with the upland Indians. If I had Complyed with the Advice of some persons to disturb those Indians as they came down to Mr Percivall. I am confident the Settlement would have been prejudiced by it. but my greatest Care hath beene alwaies to preserve Unity in the whole Plantation. I presume Captaine Godfrey[1] suddenly comes for England to informe Sir Peter Colleton of the Advantage my Lord of Shaftesbury hath by the Indians Trade, and if he can will persuade Sir Peter to settle a Plantation at the head of the Coopper River on purpose to Encourage a Trade with the Northrne Indians. Sir If Captaine Godfrey should Importune the Lords Proprietors to be survayer Generall, I do assure you he is no fitt person for such an Imployment. If the Lords Proprietors do appoynt any person to be the survayor untill a man be found quallified in all Respects fitt for such an office I think Mr Stephen Bull[2] is the most fitt person now in the Countrey. Sir I have desired mr James Smith[3] to Address him self to you for advice and assistance to gett some monys of the Lords Proprietors for mee. If you doe me any kindeness therein I hope shall not be ungratefull to you. So wishing you that happiness which all men in this world ought to seeke after I am

Sir, your very Humble Servant

JOSEPH WEST.

Charles Towen September 4th (*76*

Address: To Mr: John Locke at Exeter House In the Strand London

Endorsed by Locke: J: West 4 Sept 76

## *319.* MRS. ANNE GRIGG to LOCKE, 13 September 1676 (*313, 320*)

B.L., MS. Locke c. 10, ff. 119–20.

Sir

There is noe reason why I should be half so well pleas'd when I write to any Man besids yourself for none makes me so good returnes, most persons overlooke my meaning and treate me as if I were in

[1] John Godfrey, d. 1691; twice acting governor of Carolina; father-in-law of Dr. Henry Woodward: South Carolina Hist. Soc., *Collections*, v. 229 n.

[2] Died *c.* 1707. He 'was, after West, the mose useful man in all duties of the settlement'; surveyor-general 1685: ibid., p. 192 n.

[3] A man of this name possessed land in Charles Town (Charleston) in 1672: ibid., p. 408.

love with cros purposses: when I honestly speak a civil or gratfull thing they as good as tell me that I am a hypocrite, and rejecting their owne right when I pay it they have all most mard my manerly humer and taken off my heart from all those expressions that use to looke well in letters, I cannot but complaine of this as an affront to my owne inclinations, for I love to be not onely Esteem'd in thought but in word also, And I begin to think that you are best aquainted with my Ambitious mind, who so generously reward and interpret every thing I doe or say

And like a most ingenious friend
Will find out something to commend[1]

Mr Cowley having so luckely help'd me to a rime that fitts this occasion I wish some courteous Genius would furnish me with as proper and handsome words wherby I might expres the desire I have that France or Italie may be as benificiall to your health as you have bin to mine in its greatest dangers; but you can in spite of my very silence (I hope) assure yourself that I have a very sincere concerne for you, And that I faile not to wish you very well; You have many friends in England I doubt not who long for your prosperous returne, but none more faithfully values your company then myself though I begg your Absence (tell the Doctors (who advise your continuance abroade) call you back againe) And yet I am sensible that my Brother and sister Blomers March after you[2] agravates the sense of your being so many hundred Miles off, for in a world that admits of very few substantiall friends, tis being allmost undon to loose two or three at once, but ile recall myself and consider you as onely retired that you may apeire againe with greater advantage. I bless God I am in good health without taking too much care or paines aboute it, onely at present my sisters farwell makes me looke a little sulenly, and somewhat infects my temper, which for ought I know may provoke those that have most of my company to wish I were transported (and I asure them were I a man I would without much intreaty make my leg and be gon) but now I must studie to sweeten my adversityes by a little disemulation.

[1] He lov'd my worthless *Rhimes*, and like a *Friend*
Would find out something to *commend*.

—'On the Death of Mr. William Hervey', stanza 8, in Cowley, *Works*, 1668, first pagination, p. 17.

[2] Dr. and Mrs. Blomer probably accompanied Lady Northumberland to Paris; they were there by June 1677: p. 489.

Mrs Foxcroft[1] to whose governement you resigned me is a very tyrant, she knows well enough the pride of my heart and yet afords me no gentler language, then goe foolish thing what are you good for,[2] And now I can gues by what tricks I make every[a]-body (as–[a] you say they doe) love me having the old proverbe at hand fooles have fortune,[3] however I desire to be imagin'd a better (tho not a more) luckey thing. Our friends in and about Bristoll salute you as they are oblig'd, your letter in the Spring was receaved and answred. Honest Will[4] is at Bristoll where he prospers mightyly, I intend to leave him there till he be fit to busle with the hardships of a bording scoole, in the meane time he goes to a very good Master who speaks well of the child, and indeed I have great reason to bless God for giving me so hopefull a son, he often mentions you as his friend and I fancy when you see him you will not grudge your being so, for he is ingeneus and sweet humerd, all this you are bound to believe because his mother saies it, however admire my couradge in leaving him (And wish that I may not secretly pine after him) Methinks I am now a Nun indeed (and I may as well fancy myself at Montpelier conversing with you through a Grate) the affair you settled for me is as you wish, and those three friends you perticularly remember returne their thanks and service: Sir Paul[5] was very neir leaving us to keepe you company (since I receavd your letter) his phesitian ordering it as the last remedie for his threatning illness, but contrary to all Expectation he is neither in his grave nor in any present danger, and a whole regement of Learned men conclude (as his father wishes) that he may safely live in England, but I persevere to wish in my heart that he were with you. I am runing to Clapham[6] where I will indulge innocent

a–a *MS.* every (body as

---

[1] Identifiable as Elizabeth, sister of Benjamin Whichcote (p. 626, n. 3) and wife of George Foxcroft. Her husband was mathematics lecturer at Cambridge in 1658, was in Ireland in 1663, and was agent of the East India Company at Fort St. George from 1665 to 1672. During his absence Mrs. Foxcroft resided with Anne Conway, Viscountess Conway (*D.N.B.*), at Ragley, Warwickshire. She was probably in or near London by 1673, and by April 1677 was living at Clapham. Dr. John Worthington (p. 334, n. 2.) married a niece of hers: Worthington, *Diary*; *Conway Letters*, ed. M. H. Nicolson, where two letters to her from Dr. Henry More (no. *731*) are printed.

[2] Not identified.

[3] A variant of 'Fortune favours fools' or 'God sendeth fortune to fools'.

[4] Her son: p. 334, n. 2.

[5] Identifiable as Sir Paul Whichcote, 1643–1721; knighted 1665; succeeded as second baronet 1677: G.E.C., *Baronetage*, iii. 22. If the identification of Mrs. Foxcroft is correct, he was her nephew.

[6] See n. 1.

thinking and endevor to be a tolerable little Animall that you may never be reproach'd for your civilityes to me, nor have any just cause to shut me out of your plesant reveries

Your most faithfull friend and humble servant

A G

Sept: the 13th 76.

This rambling letter will trie your patience and perplex me till you assure me that you pardon it

Address: A Monsieur Monsieur Locke Gentilhomme Anglois chez Monsieur Puech Maistre Apotecaire a Montpelier

Endorsed by Locke: A G 13 Sept. *76*

## *320.* MRS. ANNE GRIGG to LOCKE, 12 December 1676 (*319*, *533*)

B.L., MS. Locke c. 10, f. 121.

December the 12th 76.

Sir

Tho I have of late medetated on the excellency of humility and in some fits of zeal allmost resolved to resist pride as the bussiest and worst Divill, yet so subtle is this spirit that it finds a way into my heart through the wisest friendships I can make upon Earth, for having a passion (not by every body understood) for those I call friend they have power to make me believe all they say, this best relation being onely able to command my attention and assent, what care are you obliged to, that too much kindness on your part doe not puff me up and make me concaipt myself to be better then I am in reality? Tis no difficulty to be Deaf when an ordenary or triffling tongue speaks with a designe to flatter and please me; but when such a man as Mr Locke treats me with perticular markes of esteeme tis than I am bewilldred and in danger to forget who I am. You cannot imagin how apt I was to be transported when you fancyed great prittyness in a Soul so placed as mine is but I wonder how I should be so vaine when every thing I doe is imperfect enough to convince me that I am not onely a woman but a very silly on to. Since then I have not ingenuity enough to thrive by the most gentill methodes, pray so order the matter that I may be able againe to converse with common mortalls, for methinks your letter has made me an ilfavoured hauty thing, and though our

Nunns[1] love me yet they know not why, if I should once in my vapouring moudes say as you doe that I have a manly Soul they will not endure me so great is that fondness we here have for our femenin simplicity, however in secret I will converse with that stronger spirit that instructs me to value that intrest I have in your favour beyond what I will undertake to expres, and having all this while say'd I know not what, tis time to speak with my understanding befor I take my leave, and first I dare assure you I rejoyce to hear that your health increases, may it become perfict, then your friends will not pin at the rememberance of your being some time longer from them; My wellfair being that which you have allwayes endevord, since you knew me, tis fit I should let you know that I have a long time ben very well, and as chearfull as you would wish, and to be more just then I was in my last to mrs Foxcroft I must owne that she is not a little pleas'd with ⟨ev⟩ery[a] thing that looks kindly upon me, she is as mild as may be and wonderfully your servant. Sir Paul is well againe and neir matrimony.[2] I wish him as well in bonds as you are out of them, ⟨when⟩[a] I write next I will have less noyse about my Ears and then write better sense. Your humble Ser:[b]

if you and I should die before Willy be of age pray leave him to the Deane of Canterbury[3] or some such man who loved his father.

Endorsed by Locke: A G 12 Dec. 76

## *321.* THOMAS COXE to LOCKE, 22 February 1677

B.L., MS. Locke c. 7, ff. 180–1. The writer is probably Thomas Coxe, son of Dr. Thomas Coxe: p. 451, n. 2.

London. 22d February. 1676. stilo vetere.

Sir

I am desired by Sir John Banks to make this Adresse to You Concerning his onely Son, a young Gentleman who, as I remember, is not unknowne to You; and for my owne particular I have had the happynesse to be knowne to him these many yeares, and have

[a] *Page torn.* [b] *The writer's initials may be torn away.*

[1] 'Methinks I am now a Nun indeed': Mrs. Grigg, in no. *319*. At a later period she is apparently called an abbess: no. *815* n. Here she perhaps refers to Mrs. Foxcroft and her household.

[2] Sir Paul Whichcote married on 14 June 1677. [3] Tillotson: p. 371, n. 3.

allwayes thought him such a Person as was worthy of the best Advantages of Education, which his Father is earnestly desirous, and very well able to give him. If I mistake or forgett not the good Correspondence that was betweene my Lord Shaftsburys and Sir John Bank's familys, during your Relation to the former, I shall not neede to say much to You concerning Mr. Banks.

I thinke Sir John's present designe is to send his Son into France, and in Order to his doing that to his better satisfaction, I believe he will endeavour, by a Letter to You this Post, to entreate your favour in the Assistance and Conduct of this young Gentleman, so farre as it shall be Consistent with your Consent, and the Posture of your affaires. It will not be proper or decent for me to enter farther into Particulars with You upon this Matter, Or to take any Part of it out of Sir John's owne hands, farther then to acquitt my selfe of my Commission, which was to undertake the Adressing of a Letter to You; and for that I hope to obtaine your Pardon.[1]

You will have heard from much better hands then mine, of the Committment of the Duke of Buckingham, E. of Shaftsbury, E. of Salisbury, and Lord Wharton close Prisoners to the Tower, and the Causes of it;[2] the Revocation of our Forces in forreigne Service,[3] the purging the house of Roman Catholick Members,[4] the granting 600000ll. for the building of ships, as designed;[5] with the farther Expectation of an Additionall-Summe, and Perpetuating the Excize etc. On which I shall not presume to enlarge, But hoping from your goodnesse a forgivenesse of this fault, Pray for your health, and assure You that I am

Sir

Your most humble servant.

THOMAS COXE.

[1] The father, Sir John Banks, 1627–99; created a baronet 1661; businessman, interested especially in the East India Company; M.P. 1654–9, 1679–98; of London and Aylesford, Kent; married, 1654, Elizabeth, *c.* 1636–96, daughter of Sir John Dethick, Lord Mayor of London 1655–6. The son is Caleb Banks, 1659–96; admitted to Gray's Inn 1675; M.P. 1685–90, 1691–6. For the family see D. C. Coleman, *Sir John Banks*, 1963.

[2] On 15 February, the opening day of the new session of parliament, Buckingham (p. 343, n. 2) moved that, as a result of the length of the interval since the last session, parliament was dissolved. He was supported by Shaftesbury, James Cecil, third earl of Salisbury (*D.N.B.*), and the fourth Lord Wharton (p. 46 n.). The house regarded the motion as an insult and next day sent the four peers to the Tower.

[3] A bill was read in the commons for the first time on 19 February; second reading 22 February: *C.J.*

[4] Inquiry concerning Sir Thomas Strickland, 16 and 19 February: ibid.

[5] Voted 21 February: ibid.

My Father and Brother present You with their very humble service.

Address: A Monsieur Monsieur Püesch Maistre Apothicaire, pour faire tenir à Monsieur Lock Gentilhomme anglois à Montpelier.
Endorsed by Locke: T. Cox 22 Feb. 7$\frac{6}{7}$

## 322. Sir Anthony Ashley Cooper, first earl of Shaftesbury, to Locke, 23 February 1677 (*297*, *532*)

B.L., MS. Locke c. 7, f. 71. Written by an amanuensis (apparently Thomas Stringer) apart from the last words. Printed in Christie, *Shaftesbury*, ii. 235. Probably the letter forwarded by Banks on 26 February: p. 466.

Feb: 23d. 1676.

Sir

Sir John Banks my intimate good friend is sending his Sonne into France to travell about that Country for foure or five months. he hath already learned the French Tongue, but is only willing to lett him see the manners of those people. Sir John intends to send him over to Paris about a fortnight hence in the Custody of Sir Richard Dutton[1] whoe is goeing thether and then is very desirous if you will undertake that Charge to have him recommended to your care. In order thereunto he beggs the kindnesse of you, to come and meet him at Paris where Sir Rich: Dutton is to deliver him up to your care. As for the Charges of your Travels Sir John is to defray and will otherwise as he sayth give you such a reward as becometh a Gentleman. I am[a]

Your most affectionate freind and servant
SHAFTESBURY

Address (written by a third hand): Thesse To mr Locke
Endorsed by Locke: E. Shaftesbury 23 Feb. 7$\frac{6}{7}$

[a] *The rest is written by Shaftesbury.*

---

[1] Soldier and adventurer; governor of Barbados 1680–5: Dalton, *English Army Lists*, i. 90, etc.; Harlow, *Hist. of Barbados*, pp. 241–59.

## 323. SIR JOHN BANKS to LOCKE, 26 February 1677 (*324*)

B.L., MS. Locke c. 3, ff. 66–7. For the writer and his son see p. 463, n. 1. In his letters Banks abbreviates words frequently, using a general form to indicate abbreviation, regardless of spelling. These words are as a rule expanded silently here.

Sir

It is my great present concerne to let my son spend 5 or 6 months in France to see and observe what soe short a time may permitt and then that he may if it shall please God returne well home. And give me leave to say it will be a very great satisfaction to me and my wiffe to have him duringe his stay there under your freindship and Conduct, which hath at last inclined us both to answer my sons desire, which occasyons me to give you this trouble. to request that you will please to come to Paris, assoone as you can. For soe it falls out that sir Richard Dutton goes for his health thither this day fortnight and havinge soe good an opertunity that he may be delivered safe into your hands I have entreated one of the kings Yatchts. to passe them over: I have desired mr Stringer to speake to my Lord Shaftesbury and acquainte him this my intention and he very much approves of it and promised to give a line to you: I have alsoe Consulted sir Robert Southwell,[1] Dr Cox, mr Pepys,[2] with whome my son hath spent 2 or 3 months[a] to weane him from home. And in dependance upon your favor (for soe I shall ever owne it) upon consideration with my freinds and what Mr Stringer tells me from my Lord, I doe make this adventure, and doe thinke I have reason to blesse God, that your name came into my thoughts, assuringe you that I have not only a very great honnor for you, but confidence in you. and doe hoope that both you and I shall finde a good issue of this matter thro Gods blessinge, And give me leave to say my son is not given to any extravigancy,[3] but I hoope you will finde him a person, of that temper and conversation, that you will be pleased with and in althings submittinge to you, the french tounge he hath perfect and is a reasonable scholler. and doe thinke it best that he spend most of his time in travellinge as you shall see

[a] *MS.* m[b]

[1] 1635–1702; knighted 1665; diplomatist etc.; F.R.S. (Original Fellow); President, Royal Society 1690–5: *D.N.B.*; I.H.R., *Bull.* xx (1945), 48–9.

[2] Samuel Pepys, 1633–1703, the diarist: *D.N.B.*; etc. He was interested in Caleb's progress, and wrote to him and to Locke about it: Pepys, *Further Correspondence . . . 1662–79*, ed. J. R. Tanner, 1929, pp. 306–7, 318–25 *passim*; no. *405*.

[3] In conduct, not necessarily in expenditure: p. 320, n. 1.

best, for his stay will be short of which shall heerafter say more. And you shall heare of my son at the house of Monsieur Guliame de Voulges[1] at Paris. / And I doe presume to send my son, before I have your answer not only in dependance upon your grantinge my request. but mr Stringer tells me you are intended to be speedily at Paris, which alsoe encourages me the more, and give me yet leave to say, that I shall not only owne your kindnesse in complyinge with my request as a very great favor, but reckon my selfe bound to render the same fully satisfactory to yourselfe. who with the tender of my humble services doe remaine

Sir

Your assured freind and servant

JOHN BANKS

Lincolns Inn feilds
26 Feb. 1676.

Address: A Monsieur Monsieur Piiesch Maister Apothecary, pour faire tenir A Monsieur Lock, Gentilhomme Anglois A Montpelier France
Post payd to Paris

Postmark: (fragmentary; probably) FRANCHES

Endorsed by Locke: Sir J: *Banks.* 26 Feb. 7$\frac{6}{7}$

## *324.* SIR JOHN BANKS to LOCKE, 5 March 1677 (*323*, *325*)

B.L., MS. Locke c. 3, ff. 68–9.

[The letter opens with a copy, not in his hand, and with insignificant verbal alterations etc., of Banks's letter to Locke of 26 February; Banks continues in his own hand:]

Ady. 5 March. 76.

Sir, The foregoinge is copy of my last which I hoope is come safe to your hand, inclosed I sent my Lords letter[2] who is in health, and I have not more to add then the continuation of my request as abovsaid, and in dependance upon your Goodnesse to meete my son at Paris and take him into your protection, I have given way that he take his passage in the Portsmouth[a] Yatch[3] for Deepe[4] on the 14th of this moneth, and I hoope God will bring you well to meete at Paris and preserve you in your travells and bring you in

[a] *MS.* Portsm$^{u}$.

[1] See below, pp. 487–8, etc. Locke mentions him in his Journal, 2 June, 2 September 1677, N.S. [2] Shaftesbury's; presumably no. *322*.
[3] R. C. Anderson, *English Ships*, no. 568. [4] Dieppe.

savety to your owne home, and be assured it will be such an obligation layd on me and myne, as I must ever owne and shall make it fully satisfactory to yourselfe. and I have remitted monnys to meete you at Paris, and shall fully supply all your occations on my sons accompt, and I shall write you more at large to Paris by him to meete you there. in the meane time let me say he is of that good and governable temper as you may be assured he will be at your disposall, as well as my selfe who truly am.

Sir

Your assured freind and servant

JOHN BANKS

Address (written by the copyist): A Monsieur Monsieur Lock Gentilhome Anglois Chez Monsiur Puesch Maister Apothecary A Montpelier

Post paid to Paris

Postmark: (fragmentary; probably) FRANCHES

Endorsed by Locke: Sr J: Banks 5 Mar. 7$\frac{6}{7}$

## *325.* SIR JOHN BANKS to LOCKE, 12 March 1677 (*324, 330*)

B.L., MS. Locke c. 3, ff. 70–1.

[The letter opens with a copy of no. *324*, written by the same amanuensis as the copy in no. *324* and with insignificant verbal changes. Banks then continues in his own hand:]

Ady. 12th Ditto.

My former letters are well I hoope with you, and as I have acquainted, soe My son doeth intend his journy God willinge for Paris this weeke, and in relyance upon your takinge him into your protection, and in trust thereto, I have made no other provition for him, And in case these should yet find you at Montpellier, I doe entreate you will assoone as possible there receave him into your care wherein you shall ever oblidge

Sir

Your assured freind and servant

JOHN BANKS

Sir I doe write to you at large by my son. and after I have told you my minde I shall leave it to yourselves to spend 4 or 5 months in such course as you judge best, which shall very well satisfy

Sir yours J. B.

Address: (not in Banks's or the copyist's hand): A Monsieur Monsieur John

Lock Gentilhomme Anglois, chez Mr. Puesch Maistre Apothecaire à Montpelier
Port paÿé Jusqu'a Paris.
Postmark: (fragmentary; probably) FRANCHES
Endorsed by Locke: Sir J: Banks 12 Mar. $7\frac{6}{7}$

## *326.* Dr. Denis Grenville to Locke, [*c.* 3/13–5/15 March 1677] (*327*)

B.L., MS. Locke c. 10, ff. 64–5.

The dates of nos. *326–9* are problematical. Grenville's three letters were written in March 1677, N.S., and in a place where he expected Locke to spend some time. The only appropriate place is Montpellier. Grenville was there on 26 and 31 December 1676, N.S.: Locke, Journal; and presumably continued there. Locke was absent on a short tour from 16/26 February until Thursday 1/11 March; he left finally for this year on 15/25 March. Sir John Banks wrote to him, asking him to take charge of his son, on 26 February/8 March; this letter (no. *323*) is unlikely to have reached Locke before Monday 12/22 March, but Coxe's of 22 February/4 March (no. *321*) might have reached him four days earlier. Locke wrote to Banks, presumably in answer to no. *323*, on 13/23 March: p. 479.

Locke, whose health was good at this time, apparently expected to return to England this summer: pp. 481–2, 488–9. He may have decided to leave Montpellier, as the first stage of his journey; or his departure may have been due to a change of plan following the receipt of Banks's letter.

No. *329*, written on Monday morning, can be satisfactorily dated 12/22 March: 5/15 March is too early for Banks's letter; and, as Locke left Montpellier on 15/25 March any later Monday is too late. The opening lines of no. *326* mention a general report of Locke's impending departure on a Wednesday; that must be either 7/17 or 14/24 March. No. *327* apparently belongs to a later date, when Locke had told Grenville on what day he intended to leave Montpellier. Locke's answer, no. 328, lacks a covering letter; it was apparently written almost immediately after Locke had received no. *327*. The 'feather' in no. *329*, a letter from Locke received by Grenville on Sunday 11/21 March, relates either to no. 328 or to a lost earlier answer to no. *327*. The former is the better alternative. In that case no. *326* dates from about 3/13–5/15 March; no. *327* two or three days later, say about 6/16–8/18 March; no. 328 about 9/19–11/21 March (it might take two or three days to compose); and no. *329* from 12/22 March.

Denis Grenville, 1637–1703; D.D. 1671; dean of Durham from 1684 until his withdrawal in December 1688; deprived 1691; Jacobite: *D.N.B.* He was now living in France probably on account of his debts. He was accompanied by his sister, Lady Joanna Thornhill (p. 521, n. 4), stepmother of Sir John Banks's friend Henry Thornhill (p. 478, n. 1), and her daughter Mary. Among Locke's papers there is a report on him by Dr. Brouchier of Aix (p. 451, n. 1), 17 April 1679, N.S.: B.L., MS. Locke c. 10, ff. 56–7, endorsed by Locke 'Mr *Grenvils* case'. For Mrs. Grenville see no. *486*. Collections of Grenville's correspondence and papers are published in Surtees Society, vol. xxxvii,

1861, *Miscellanea* (the first section is 'The remains of Denis Granville, D.D.'; here cited as '*Remains*'), and vol. xlvii, 1865, *The Remains of Denis Granville, D.D., . . . being a further selection . . .* (here cited as '(*Further*) *Remains*').

Sir

I did hope (notwithstanding your Designe to returne into England) to have injoyed the felicity of that Freindship, which you are pleased to allow mee, for some weekes before you had left this Place, but being, since I saw you, scared with a Report of your departure next Wensday, I cannot forbeare to give you the trouble of this Paper, and A Blunt Demand, Vizt To know, whether your Resolution to Returne bee unalterable, if soe, I shall not give you the disturbance of using any arguments to the contrary. But if this Determination of yours should happen to bee otherwise, give mee leave, I beseech you, to make an assault on you with all mine owne strength, and that of my Family,[1] to interrupt you in this your Designe, and prevaile with you if it bee possible, to Continue somewhat longer in these parts of France. Sir I set soe great a value on your Worthy Freindship, and Excellent [Edifying][a] Conversation, that I am willing to purchase it at any rate, and may possibly bee capacitated to make some proposalls (in order thereunto) that A Wise Man may prudentially enough comply with, The particulars whereof, with the true Condition of my selfe, and affaires, I shall at leasure Communicate to you. This I send away hastily to you, to prepare you, and prevent (if it comes not too late) your Intentions from passing into an Absolute Decree. Were it not an unseasonable time and a post night I could not refraine from giving you the farther Disturbance of a visit, and the Discussing of all my thoughts, which I shall not long delay to doe, if you please to vouchsafe mee an Opportunity, In the meane time have charity, (notwithstanding any ill appearance of my hasty attempt, or abrupt discourse) for

Deare Sir

Your most unworthy FREIND, but faithfull and affectionate humble servant

DE. GRENVILLE.

9. clock

Address: A Monsieur Monsieur Lock

Endorsed by Locke: D: Grenvill Mar. 77

[a] *Grenville's square brackets.*

[1] His household, not his kindred in a wider sense.

## *327.* DR. DENIS GRENVILLE to LOCKE, [*c.* 6/16–8/18 March 1677] (*326*, 328)

B.L., MS. Locke c. 10, ff. 66–7. For the date see p. 468 n. Answered by no. 328.

I[a] cannot Content myselfe (Sir) to loose one of those few dayes you intend to stay, without making some Improvement of your Freindly Compliance with my desires. And therefore without any more adoe, (having received, both *in scriptis*, and *vivâ voce*, noe small Incouragement) shall begin to set you to Worke. But least you may bee scared at my Importunity, I doe declare that I shall not presse to bee allowed more than one houre, of your pretious time, each day, for the penning downe your thoughts on such particular things, as I shall present you with in Writing, in which Method I shall desire, (if you please to give me leave,) to proceed; first for the better securing your thoughts, secondly for the helpe of my Infirmity in not being able otherwise easily, and clearely to ex-presse mine. The subjects concerning which I shall in order write, and desire you to discourse, are five. *1.* Recreation. *2.* Buisnesse *3.* Conversation. *4.* Study. *5.* Exercise of Devotion.[1] I begin with the first, and shall thinke my selfe very happy if wee can but fully discourse that one point before wee part, it being of noe small importance to mee (as you will finde when I have said all) to bee set right, but, in this particular; soe far am I, poor fellow, from being advanced above your good Counsell and advice in other matters of greater moment. It is since I entred into holy Orders about 16. yeares,[2] (which obliged mee to bee a Guide to Others,) during which time I cannot deny but that I have been buisy about discharging my Office (how Imperfectly soever I have performed itt) and may have been usefull possibly (through Gods Blessing) to some, as to Counsell, in those very matters concerning which I have needed it myselfe, having in my nature, sometimes, somewhat of the Infirmitie of the Great Dr. Reynolds, who, when hee had

[a] *At head of letter a numeral(?)* 1, *presumably written by Locke.*

---

[1] It was perhaps as a result of this request that Locke wrote on 26 March and in the following weeks an essay on Study: Journal, pp. 87–140 *passim*; printed in King, pp. 90–109. See further nos. *372*, *421*.

[2] Grenville was ordained at the same time as William Beveridge, bishop of St. Asaph, who was ordained deacon on 3 and priest on 31 January 1661: Grenville, *Remains*, pp. 235–6; *D.N.B.*, art. Beveridge.

convinced his adversary, could not Confirme himselfe.[1] To Indulge to somuch thoughtfullnesse as my Temper Inclines mee to, may perchance hurt my Body or Braine; and to Divert this Temper with the ordinary Recreations which some Christians, and Divines (nay (I might add) Bishops) use, as Hunting, Shooting, Angling, chesse, cards, or Tables[2] etc. is dangerous, (as I finde) and often hurtfull to my spirit. I have therefore thought it the safest way to quit these and all such Recreations for many yeares together, nay most of my seculars Buisnesse too (for the same Reason) and give my selfe up to Solitude and Contemplation, according to the desires and necessities of my Minde, and which, I Blesse God, is still soe pleasing to mee, that I could with great Delight Continue soe to doe my whole life. But having seen some sad Consequence thereof in Others, of stronger heads and constitutions (in all appearance) than my selfe, (tho. I was never sensible of any inconvenience of my owne Course) have returned for some while to some of the former Divertisements as Chesse, or Angling, the most Innocent that I could pick out abroad, or at home, till I found my boyish temper Revive in mee, which made mee too intent upon them, and some times Immoderate in Consumption of time; which hath made mee with fresh Force and Resolution recoyle back to my studies and Retirements, feeling the Truth of Honest Tho. a Kempis his beloved Motto vizt. *In omnibus Requiem quæsivi, et nusquam Inveni nisi Angello cum libello.*[3]

From which pleasing Course I have been againe soon pulled of by the Importunities of Freinds, who have thought it Injurious to mee, and that it might bee of ill Consequence. Thus have I long been, and am still, tossed between the Feares and Inconveniences accompanying one Extreame or the other, and can not tell how to establish myselfe, tho I often afford some freinds assistance in these particulars. I humbly beg your Judgement, in this particular, where to set Bounds to my Retired studies, and Divertisements abroad. I am of the minde that it is the best and wisest Course to leane to the Excesse of study, and Devotion, rather than that of Recreation;

[1] Dr. John Rainolds, 1549–1607; President of Corpus Christi College, Oxford, 1598–1607: *D.N.B.* Grenville alludes probably to the epigram by W. Alabaster printed in Anthony Wood, *Historia et Antiquitates Universitatis Oxoniensis*, 1674, ii. 139.

[2] Backgammon; formerly the usual name: *O.E.D.*

[3] 'I have sought repose in all things and nowhere found it except in a little nook with a little book.' The saying occurs in the life of Thomas à Kempis by Franciscus Tolensis (F. de Bakker, called Artopæus, *fl.* 1570; van der Aa) which is prefixed to some editions of his works and of *The Imitation of Christ*.

It being more eligible, methinks, to *hazard the hurting* the mind by Imployment soe good and acceptable to God, than *certainly hurting* itt with Recreation, or at least Indisposing itt for Spirituall Imployment thereby. I would faigne hit the Meane if I could tell how. It is my earnest prayer to the Wise God, that I, at last, may. Which prayer is in some sort heard, by Directing mee to soe discreet a Freind, (when I was in search of one) as your selfe, whoe doe Evidence by your discourse and Carriage that you are above the poor difficulties I struggle with and soe very well quallified to assist mee. Which makes mee repeat my Request and desires to you, to Continue the Exercise of your Freindship this way, in familiarly penning downe your thoughts upon such subjects as I shall recommend to your Consideration, which thoughts of yours, how meane an Opinion soever you have of them, can appeare soe to noe other person. I am sure for my owne part I shall have soe great regard to all such papers that you shall oblige mee with, as to peruse them oftner then some large volumes, (which make a great noise in the World,) and I noe wise doubt but with more proffit. I beseech you, Sir, then lay aside all that Shame which you mention in your letters, and use all liberty immaginable in declaring your thoughts of what you *read*, or *see*, in Relation to my selfe, whoe will never bee ashamed to learne of One, who seemes to bee more expert than my selfe in mine owne Trade

Endorsed by Locke: D Grenville Mar: 77 Recreation

## 328. Locke to Dr. Denis Grenville, *c.* 9/19–11/21 March 1677 (*327*, *329*)

B.L., MS. Rawlinson D 849, ff. 144–7 (this and other letters from Locke in this volume are parts of a collection of Grenville's papers preserved by his servant John Proud). Printed from the copy in Locke's Journal (see below) in King, pp. 323–5, and thence in Fox Bourne, i. 388–90. Part of an answer to no. *327*; Locke's covering letter is lost. For the date see p. 468 n. The surviving part begins by repeating a passage from no. *327*, 'The subjects concerning which I shall in Order write . . . It is my earnest prayer to the wise God that I at last may'. This passage and a covering note probably written by Proud are omitted here.

Locke obtained a copy of this surviving part (or part of it) from Grenville in November 1678: pp. 633–4; and copied it from 'As for my Recreation thus I thinke' to the end in his Journal, heading it 'An essay concerning Recreation in answer to D G's desire Mar 77'; it occurs, and was evidently written, between the entries for 2 and 5 December 1678 (pp. 351–7. The draft for

## 328. *Dr. D. Grenville*, *11 March 1677*

Locke's letter to Grenville, 26 November/6 December 1678 (no. 426) also occurs between these two entries).

As for my Recreation thus I thinke

That Recreation being a thing ordeind not for it self but for a certain end. That end is to be the rule and measure of it

Recreation then seemeing to me to be the doeing of some easy or at least delightfull thing to restore the minde or body tired with labour, to its former strength and vigor and thereby fit it for new labour it seems to me

1 That there can be noe generall rule set to *divers persons* concerning the time, manner, duration or sort of recreation that is to be used, but only that it be such that their experience tells them is suited to them and proper to refresh the part tired

2 That if it be applied to the minde it ought certainly to be delightfull because it being to restore and enliven that which is don by relaxing and composeing the agitation of the spirits, that which delights it without imploying it much is not only the fitest to doe soe, but also the contrary i e what is ungratefull does certainly most discompose and tire it

3 That it is impossible to set a standing rule or recreation to ones self, because not only the unsteady fleeting condition of our bodys and spirits require more at one time then another, which is plain in other more fixd refreshments as food and sleepe, and likewise requires very different according to the imployment that hath preceded, the present temper of our bodys and inclination of our mindes, but also because variety in most constitutions is soe necessary to delight, and the minde is soe naturally tender of its freedome, that the pleasantest diversions become nauseous and troublesome to us when we are forced to repeat them in a continued fixd round

It is farther to be considerd

1 That in things not absolutely commanded or forbiden by the law of god, such as is the materiall part of Recreation he in his mercy considering our ignorance and fraile constitution, hath not tied us to an indivisible point, to a way soe narrow that allows noe latitude at all In things in their owne nature indifferent there is the liberty of great choise great variety within the bounds of innocence

2 That god delights not to have us miserable either in this or the

other world, but haveing given us all things richly and to enjoy we cannot imagin that in our recreations we should be denied delight which is the only necessary and usefull part of it

This supposd I imagin

1 That recreation supposes labour and wearynesse and therefor that he that labours not hath noe title to it

2 That it very seldome happens that our constitutions (though there be some tender ones that require a great deale) require more time to be spent in recreation then in labour

3 That we must beware that custome and the fashon of the world or some other by interest doth not make that passe with us for recreation which is indeed labour to us though it be not our businesse, as playing at cards for example though noe otherwise allowable but as a recreation is soe far from fiting some men for their businesse and giveing them refreshment, that it more discomposes them then their ordinary labour

Soe that god not tieing us up to exact nicetys of time, place, kinde etc in our recreations, if we secure our main duty which is in sincerity to doe our dutys in our calling as far as the frailty of our bodys or mindes will allow us (beyond which we cannot thinke any thing should be requird of us) and that we in truth designe our diversions to put us in a condition to doe our dutys we need not perplex our selves with too scrupulous an enquiry into the precise bounds of them, for we cannot be supposd to be obleiged to rules which we cannot know. for I doubt first whether there be any such exact proportion of recreation to our present state of body and minde. that soe much is exactly enough and what soever is under is too litle what soever is over is too much. but be it soe or noe this I am very confident of, that noe body can say in his owne or an other mans case, that thus much is the precise dose hither you must goe and noe farther. Soe that it is not only our priviledg but we are under a necessity of useing a latitude, and where we can discover noe determined precise rule it is unavoidable for us to goe sometimes beyond, and sometimes stop short of that which is, I will not say, the exact but nearest proportion, and in such cases we can only governe our selves by the discoverable bounds on one hand or other, which is only when by sensible effects we finde our recreation either by excesse or defect serves not to the proper end for which we are to use it. Only with this caution, that we are to suspect our selves most on that side to which we finde our selves most inclined. The cautious devoute studious man is to feare that he allows not himself enough. the gay, carelesse and idle that he takes too much.

To which I can only adde the following directions as to some particulars

1 That the properest time for recreateing the minde is when it feels it self weary and flaging, it may be wearied with a thing when it is[a-] not yet weary of it[-a]

2 That the properest recreation of studyous sedentary persons whose labour is of the thought is bodyly exercise. To those of bustleing imployment sedentary recreations.

3 That in all bodily exercise those in the open aire are best for health

4 It may often be soe orderd that one business may be made a recreation to an other, as visiting a freind to study

These are my suddain extempory thoughts upon this subject, which will deserve to be better considerd when I am in better circumstances of freedome of thought and leisure

## *329*. DR. DENIS GRENVILLE to LOCKE [12/22? March 1677] (328, *357*)

B.L., MS. Locke c. 10, ff. 62–3. For the date see p. 468 n. Apparently answers no. 328.

Munday Morning 7. clock

Deare Sir

I give you thankes for the *Feather* (as you call itt) which you were pleased yesterday to bestow on mee, which I esteeme such, that I will not put it in my Cap, I doe assure you, nor imploy it to make Flyes to catch Trouts, (tho my beloved Recreation) but Lock it up (With a Lock upon Lock notwithstanding it may bee false Heraldry) as securely, as the Feather that came from Compostella,[1] which did (as they say) soe many Miracles, not doubting but to doe many more with mine, than are told of in the story of the sanctified Hen

[a–a] *Locke's copy in his Journal reads* is not weary of it

[1] Grenville alludes probably to a miracle usually attributed to St. James: *Acta Sanctorum*, Venice, 1734– , July vi. 46–7.

(or Capon, I cannot tell which) which was there raised to Life, and Flew out of the platter. But to bee serious, Sir, I am infinitely satisfyed, that I have secured that which I did soe greedily desire. In reallity you have bestowed on mee what I thinke a great Jewell, the virtue whereof I shall dayly more and more study, to make suitable applications thereof, for my owne advantage, assuring myselfe that I shall every day make farther discovery of more and more hidden good quallities.

In order to which I beseech you (tho I cannot oppose at all your Compliance with Sir J. Bankes his Desires) to deferre your Journey, for but 15. 10. or 7. dayes, that wee may be a litle better acquainted before wee part. And then I can very well dispence with you for a while to soe a good a purpose, especially since you give mee such an Intrest in you, as to presume to cut out some worke for you, whereof I may have a good account at meeting againe in these parts; which I hope may bee in three, or foure, monthes at most, and which I conceive noe way inconsistent with the Designe of Sir John Banks, nor unsuitable to your Health, nor Temper, which I perceive Loves Motion.

The Thing I mainly aime at, is, to bee within a days Journey of you, at least, during my stay in France (if wee cannot bee together in the same towne allwayes which I hope wee shall bee the Winter season), in order to some frequent Communication of thoughts by letter or otherwise (which a dayes Journey shall never keep mee from) and once in every three monthes to make some Toure together for 15. dayes or three weeks, or the like, And lastly, if possibly, to make One for three Monthes before wee leave France, I meane, that of Italy. And if such a felicity as this did not Commence at present, but at the End of foure, or five Monthes after you had dispatched your other pupill, I should thinke myselfe extraordinary happy, since the other day I looked on the happinesse I now enjoy, as irrecoverably gone, (imagining that some indispensable affaires of obligation had called you into England) till you were pleased to make mee an Offer, and since give mee an assurance, of your Freindship. In returne to which I doe reassure you of mine, soe far, as to promise you not only an Intrest in my *Breast*, but in my *Barne*, I meane, shall have a Considerable share (if you please) in those goods (of Fortune as men call them) which I doe, and am likely to, enjoy, as I have related, far beyond my Desert, and whereof (tho I gave you a Tedious) I gave you not a perfect account. soe good Luck have I, among the Fortunate Fooles of the World. And for which large portion, I can noe way better quallifye my selfe, than by Gods Blessing, and such a Companion, (as I beleive you are) during my Retirement (give mee leave to call it) here abroad from the hurry of my affaires, and distractions in England.

I shall impose nothing on you (*Worthy Freind*) meane, or ungratefull to you, unlesse one Imployment bee thought soe (not unusuall to men of your profession) which in short is (by the good Leave of Dr. Hinton)[1] to set you up for a *man-Midwife*. But it will bee, I assure you, to bring forth the Fruit of my Braine, not of my Body. For which meridian, you seeme, soe well calculated, that I had mocked God, if I had let slip this occasion of Arresting you, after soe many Earnest desires to him, to direct mee to such a person, as you seem to bee, and with which thoughts of you, I find nothing to Jarre. In reallity, Sir, without some such person, as I have an Idea of, and hope I have found, I am like to perish in Travell, and never be Capacitated to bring forth. I have a Confused head very full of thoughts and notions about vertue and vice, and our Demeanour here in this life, in order to a better, (And which thoughts I now begin to bee found of since I find that they doe allmost allwayes Jump with yours) which if I could once happily unburthen my selfe of, and methodise and reduce into practice, I should bee at great Ease, and become (in some small measure) usefull to my Generations espetially being placed by a kind and Benigne Providence in soe advantagious a Poste, that the Weakest person, if honest, may doe great things. I pray doe but informe mee, and assure mee (under your hand, if you please, rather than by word of mouth) of your willingnesse to accept of this new Imployment, and I shall not faile speedily to summon you, by my shreekes and Groanes to my Labour and assistance. I am

Sir

Your true and affectionate Freind.

DE. GRENVILLE.

Endorsed by Locke: Dr Grenville Mar. 77

[1] Sir John Hinton, *c.* 1603–82, M.D., who specialized in midwifery: *D.N.B.* Munk, as cited there.

## *330.* SIR JOHN BANKS to LOCKE, 25 March 1677 (*325*, *331*)

B.L., MS. Locke c. 3, ff. 72–3.

Sir

These are intended you by my son who goeth hence this day, by the Portsmouth Yatch. accompanyd with my very worthy good freind Mr Thornehill,[1] who hath done me the honnor to come on purpose with him, to give him safe to your hand, and as I hoope God will give them a good passage, soe I am abundantly satisfyed that he comes to your care, in respect to soule and body: And I doe beleive you will finde him to be of that temper to be ruled very willingly in what you shall direct: I doe not intend his stay above 5. or 6 months: he hath the French languadge. and duringe his stay at Paris, let him be imployed with such diversion as you see best; I am in longinge expectation to heare of your arrivall at Paris, and then shall write you more at large, but I know ⟨not⟩[a] what to say more then to leave him wholy to yourselfe to spend that time at Paris and in such travell as you see best for him to such places and in such company[b] as you see Good. but I thinke the les he keepes company with the English may be the better. which I leave to you, assuringe you I shall ever appeare to be

Sir

Your very humble servant JOHN BANKS

Dover. 25 March 1677.

Sir I have delivered my son. byls for 120l. I pray let him keepe an account of Expences and I shall from time to time supply you with byls to answer both your occasyons, I cannot tell how to limitt your expences. my son is not profuse, and I would have him have what you shall see necessary, and I know he will be governd by your advise.

Address: To his Honnod freind John Locke Esqre prsent At Paris

Endorsed by Locke: Sr J: Banks 25 Mar. 77

[a] *Word omitted by Banks.* [b] *MS.* comp$^{a}$

---

[1] Identifiable as Henry Thornhill, d. 1689?, of Olantigh, in Wye, Kent; surveyor to Queen Catherine *c.* 1682–9; his stepmother was Joanna, sister of Denis Grenville (p. 521, n. 4): E. Hasted, *The History . . . of Kent*, 1778–99, iii. 170, note u, 179, note m; Chamberlayne, *Angliæ Notitia*, editions of 1682, etc.; Coleman, *Banks*, pp. 127 (as Richard Thornhill), 141–2 etc. Letter below, no. *509*.

## *331.* SIR JOHN BANKS to LOCKE, 2 April 1677 (*330*, *334*)

B.L., MS. Locke c. 3, ff. 74–5. Answered by no. 336.

Sir

I have the Honnor of yours of the 23th March expressinge your very great kindnesse, to the abundant satisfaction of my selfe my wiffe and freinds, And we shall thinke our son very happy under your conduct, and am very glad my desire met you soe timely at Montpelier, that my request was not prevented, the Grauntinge wherof, I must owne solely to your owne goodnesse. and that you will excuse my attemptinge the same, for that as I have said my son is my great concerne, and that tho. I have been very backward for many reasons to send him abroad, Yet discoursinge your and my freinds and findinge I had hoopes to prevaile with you (in whose care and prudence give me leave truly to say I can trust all I have) I did give way to my sons goinge abroad; and if I have surprized you, soe as not to give you much time for consideration, I may say that was part of our designe, for I shall ever owne this favor of yours, not as in a customary way to those who performe this office for Gentlemens sons. but owne my selfe and myne more particularly oblidged to you; Nor indeed could I have adventured my son under such a conduct, or any but yourselfe: For as my son is, (I have good reason to beleive not only free from all vice, or I may say was never in his life acquainted with ill men or ill things, soe I doe account the first impressions he shall have abroad, will much abide with him, and therfore you will I hoope pardon me, that I have made choice of yourselfe for his guide. and I doe trust you will finde him very obequious to all your directions, he is I hoope of that temper that he will not disoblidge you, nor me.

I have had some thoughts of marryinge my son, but have still found his inclination was first, to spend some time abroad, and consideringe his years I was the more ready to answer his desire, and have thought my selfe the more concerned to have a sutable companion for him abroad, and as it pleaseth God soe to order althings, that they seeme to concurr as we have desired for his good, I doe hoope and am very well satisfyed that I shall see (by your mannagment) a good returne of this adventure, to our comforts and yours. I doe forebeare to offer any advice how to direct your course. Shall only say my intention is to keepe my son abroad for about six months. And I doe wholy leave it to you. to contrive the spendinge that time as you conceave may be to the best advantage For exercise, travell, and readinge, he hath French well, and rides and dances, and I hoope well in Latine, therfore please yourselves upon your owne consultation, and I have writt my son. to be directed by you.

I did Give my son at his goinge hence Ginnes. 50:– and byl exchange for 120l:– and told him he must keepe particular accounts of all his expences and pay all charges of himselfe and you: and I will from time to time supply what you and he shall desire, I know he will not, under your care espetialy be profuse, and I would on the other hand let him have a plentifull supply, that he may appeare as becomes a Gentleman, and yet with all good frugality, for as his stay is shorter, I doe reckon his expence will be the more: The next weeke I doe send him byl to receave 100l– more. and have ordered him to present you with 50l– to equipp yourselfe with what you have occation for your necessary accommodations in accompanyinge of him;

Our honnoured[a] freind[1] continues in health and I have some litle hoopes that things may be better. but since I had your letter I could not have the opertunity to speake with him, or my Lady, but by the next I shall Give you a better accompt, assuringe you I am

Sir

Your ever oblidged freind and servant

JOHN BANKS

Lincolns In feilds 2 Apr. 77

Address: To John Locke Esqre present At Paris

Endorsed by Locke: sir J Banks 2 Apr. 77

## *332.* JACQUES SELAPRIS to LOCKE, 4/14 April 1677 (*419*)

B.L., MS. Locke c. 18, ff. 69–70. The text of the letter is written by an amanuensis.

Jacques Selapris, d. 1681, and his partner, Jacques Horutener, who attended to Locke's affairs in Lyons, were bankers of Swiss origin, the names being Schlappritzi and Hochreutiner; Lüthy, *La Banque protestante*, i. 52 n. They appear to have been Protestants. Selapris became a friend: letters and notices below; Locke, Journal, 10, 12 November, 2 December 1678, N.S.

[a] *MS.* honno[d]

[1] Shaftesbury, a prisoner in the Tower.

On 19 August 1695 a payment of £1 was made on Locke's behalf to a Mr. Selaperis in London: Locke, Journal. He was presumably related to the present writer.

In some of his letters Selapris is apt to insert apostrophes generally after the first letter of a word: e.g. 'J'e N'ay pas voulu L'aisser partir vostre L'aquay . . .': no. *419*. I have suppressed them silently.

A Lyon ce 14me. avril 1677.

Monsieur.

Appres vous avoir salué et asseuré de mes Respects je vous prye d'agréer Lincluse petitte lettre de Recommandation sur mrs. Caillanel et Casez marchands de Tholoze[1] qui sont de mes amys, si vous avés besoing de quoy que ce soit je vous prye de me faire la faveur de vous addresser a eux et de leur Rendre la lettre cy Joincte en main propre, jay beaucoup de Resentiment des biens que jay receu par cy devant de vostre Chere personne, ainsy que de Monsieur Charleton[2] mon tres cher Compere. cest pourquoy voyéz en quoy je vous puis estre utille soit pour l'acheminement de vos lettres pour angletterre ou autre part, ou en tout ce que je vous pourray servir, et si vous me faictes cest honneur que de m'addresser vos lettres il vous plairra mettre a Jacques Selaperis laisné marchandt Rue de larbre secq a Lyon, enfin je vous offre tout ce qui Depend de moy et suis plus que personne du monde avec grand attachement

Monsieur

Vostre tres humble et tres obeissant serviteur

JACQUES SELAPRIS l'aisné

Address: A Monsieur Monsieur Locq gentilhomme anglois depresent a Tholoze.

Endorsed by Locke: *Selaperis* 14 April 77

## *333.* THOMAS STRINGER to LOCKE, 9 April 1677 (*315*, *344*)

B.L., MS. Locke c. 19, ff. 129–30. Passages printed in King, 1830, i. 70 n.; with an additional sentence and wrong date, 9 August 1677, in Christie, *Shaftesbury*, ii. 236–7.

London. Aprill. 9th. 1677.

Deare Sir

I received your letter from Tolouse, and am glad to heare you are soe farr in your Jorney towards us. I should be mighty glad all things

[1] Locke was at Toulouse from 19/29 to 21/31 March this year, and not again until September/October 1678.

[2] p. 508 n.

would soe far concurr that we might be soe happy to see you perfectly well in England this summer and this is not only the desire of your friends at Bexwells, but of many others that I meet with up and downe in my travailes whoe seem to be very much concerned for you. My Lord is yett in the Tower with the other three to accompany him, but wee Expect this[a-] weeke a[-a] Prorogation and then the Prisoners wilbe enlarged.[1] there have been great endeavours against our little Friend, but the ayre is now growen very cleare, and the season towards the end of a stormy winter, putts us in expectation of Faire weather at hand.[2] we heare of noe other discourses concerning your 2 other friends mr H: and S:[3] but that this fine month of Aprill that gives life and Freshnes to all other things, will send them out of a dirty stinking ayre from ill meaning base and despicable Company, into a sweet and Pleasant Country to receive the delightfull imbraces of theire wives and mistrisses. Sir John Banks is very much satisfyed with your takeing upon you the Charge of his sone, he Concludes hime as well with you as though he was under his owne care, and I am very well pleased you have soe faire an opertunity to Close your travailes this summer. I have lately heard from your Uncle,[4] by whome I finde your friends in those partes are in good health, he hath sent me up a bill to receive some money for you, but I have given him notice not to pay it in the Country, because I feare the man will not be able to answere it here in Towne. mr Tho: of Christ Church[5] hath some time sinc returned me 50l for you, from that Colledge, which is well settled for you. I am disturbed by some Persons just now come in upon me and have only time to tell you that I am

Dearest Sir

Your most Faithfull humble servant

T:S:

Address: A Mounsieur Mounsieur Lock Gentil home Anglois

Endorsed by Locke: T. *Stringer* 9° Apr. 77

[a-a] *MS.* this weeke/weeke a

---

[1] p. 463, n. 2. Parliament was adjourned on 16 April, and again from time to time; it was not prorogued until 13 May 1678. The other three peers were released about July 1677; Shaftesbury on 26 February 1678, only after complete submission in the house of lords.

[2] 'our little Friend' is probably Shaftesbury, who was small. The weather presumably is political.

[3] Probably Hoskins and Stringer.

[4] Peter Locke.

[5] Samuel Thomas: p. 430 n.

## *334.* SIR JOHN BANKS to LOCKE, 3 May 1677 (*331, 336*)

B.L., MS. Locke c. 3, ff. 76–7. Answered by no. 336.

London 3 May 77

Sir

Mr Stringer being now with me, refreshes me with the last letter of yours, wherin you are pleased to say you were soe recovered as to undertake your kind designed journy for Paris, wher my son hath with much longinge desire, as well as my selfe. hooped for your good conduct. And doe leave all things to your and my sons guidance, I did finde him inclinable to an accadem[1] for 2 or 3 months, which I leave to your consideration, I perceave since mr Thornhils comming away my son hath had the company of one Monsiur Roseman,[2] who was left only to keepe him company til your arrivall. the person I know not, but heare him to be an honest man, but I suppose noe scholler; I doe not doubt but you will finde my son very desirous to improve himselfe in whatever you shall advise and both my selfe and wiffe present you our humble services and are abundantly satisfyed with the hoopes that you are with our son, whose wellfare and yours we earnestly wish and I remaine

Yours JOHN BANKS

Address: To his ever Honoured John Locke Esqre present

Endorsed by Locke: Sir J. Banks. 3. May 77

## 335. LOCKE to ROBERT BOYLE, 25 May/4 June 1677 (228, 397)

Boyle, *Works*, 1744, v. 568–9. Locke arrived in Paris on 23 May/2 June: Journal. The date is apparently new style.

Paris, June 4, 1677.

Honoured Sir,

If in an absence, longer than I thought when I set out, I have not once writ to you after so many obligations, that I have to seek all occasions to testify my respects to you: you will not, I hope, impute

[1] p. 455, n. 1.

[2] There was a Huguenot family named Rosemond, including J.-B. de Rosemond, the translator of Burnet's *History of the Reformation*: Haag.

it to want of knowledge in me, or a willingness to decline your commands. I am not so insensible of your favours as to be guilty to that degree. And if my omission be culpable, it was only out of consideration, that being in a place, where I had no prospect of any service I could do you, I forbore to give you the trouble of an idle letter. Now I am come to this place, which is one of the great magazines of things and persons of all sorts, I thought, that perhaps there might be something, wherein I might be here in a condition to serve you. And though I believe you are not much concerned to know, whether broad or narrow brim'd hats be like to carry it this summer, or which is the newest alamode cut of pantaloons; yet in this universal mint of new things, there are some others, that possibly you will think worth your enquiry and knowledge. In something of this kind I would be glad to have the honour of your commands; and methinks whilst the press furnishes every day new books to St. Jaques Street,[1] the observatoire,[2] laboratories, and other officinæ of the virtuosi here are so busy to produce something new, I should not be without some employment from you. I dare undertake for myself, that I shall be a very faithful and diligent factor; and you cannot blame me for desiring the employment, since I may inrich myself in it very honestly, without at all lessening any part of your returns. And to confess the truth, I have besides this another private interest of my own in it; for who ever served you in any thing without being an extraordinary gainer by it? I would beg the favour of two or three lines from your hand, to recommend me to the acquaintance of any one of the virtuosi you shall think fit here. I know your bare name will open doors, and gain admittance for me, where otherwise one like me without port[3] and name, that have little tongue, and less knowledge, shall hardly get entrance. Pardon, I beseech you, this freedom I take; your goodness hath taught it me, and however faulty it may be, let it pass under the plausible title of *libertas philosophica*. They talk here of a little brass globe three or four inches diameter, that being wound up once a month, shews all the motions of the heavens.[4] I am so newly come hither, and am since my late ague so ill a walker, that I have not

[1] Near the Sorbonne; it was noted for its bookshops: G. Brice, *Description nouvelle . . de Paris*, 1684, ii. 73–4; no. *465* n.

[2] The Observatoire Royal, built in 1667.

[3] Probably in the obsolete sense, style of living, rather than external deportment, bearing, etc.: *O.E.D.*, Port, *sb.*[4]

[4] It is described in *Journal des Sçavans*, 24 May 1677 (pp. 164–6).

yet seen it.[1] But I hope in a little while my legs will come again to themselves, and be able to carry me about lustily; and then I shall be trudging up and down in quest of new discoveries. Excuse, I beseech you, Sir, the trouble and confidence of this letter, and give me leave to assure you, that I am,

Honoured Sir,

your most humble, and most obliged servant,

JOHN LOCKE.

Your letters will find me, if they be directed to me, Chez Monsieur Charas[2] maistre apothecaire rue de Boucherie[3] dans le Fauxbourg St. Germain à Paris.

## 336. LOCKE to SIR JOHN BANKS, 30 May/9 June 1677 (*334*, *338*)

B.L., MS. Locke c. 24, ff. 20–1. Locke began to write this for dispatch, and then treated it as a draft. Answers nos. *331*, *334*; answered by nos. *340*, *341*.

Paris 9° Jun. 77

Sir

By the last post I gave you an account of my arrivall here and that I found Mr Banks very well. Since that haveing had time to revise[4] the letters you have beene pleased to write to me, and considerd them togeather with the two last you sent to your son, I finde that you are inclineable to have Mr Banks spend yet some time here in Paris and are apprehensive of his removeing in the great heats. Tis certainly fit I always follow your directions in the disposall of your son, and tis certain I shall very readily comply with any desire of yours, espetially when (as in this case) your inclinations direct to that which I upon the place should have chosen without any influence from you. But yet I must crave leave soe to interpret such

[1] Locke fell ill at Agen on 23 March/2 April, suffering from fever (ague) and a pain in his head due to an accident. He reached Bordeaux on 26 March/5 April and was ill there for some time. He had probably recovered by 29 April/9 May; he resumed his journey on 8/18 May; but he was still in poor health on 12/22 and 14/24 May: notices in Journal.

[2] Moïse Charas, 1619–98; a Protestant, forced to abjure by the Inquisition in Spain between 1684 and 1689; author of *Pharmacopée royale galénique et chimique*, 1676 (L.L., no. 664; new editions 1682, 1691, 1753; English translation 1678; Latin 1684), and other works: *D.B.F.*

[3] Correctly rue des Boucheries; now widened to form part of the boulevard Saint-Germain.

[4] In the obsolete sense, to re-examine (with no intention of improving): *O.E.D.*; p. 94, n. 1.

intimations so as to reconcile it with other parts of the commission you give me in your letters and to beleive that if I finde any reason to remove it is your will and suitable to my trust still to follow our greatest conveniencys or avoid any danger, that may appear, either by goeing or staying, where perhaps you have not particularly directed. Only this you may be sure that when ever we remove from this or any other place I shall take care to doe it in such ways or at such seasons, as the intemperance of the weather may not endanger Mr Banks's health. Of this my newly[a] recoverd[a] disease, and yet crazy body will always be a pledg. And haveing soe lately sufferd by travelling in unseasonable weather you may be sure that for my owne sake as well as upon Mr Banks's account I shall be very wary how I venture a second time. I finde by your letters to him as also by your sons discours that he had formerly mentiond some inclination he had to put himself into an Academy. But before I came here, he had changed his minde and at my arrivall I found him off from it, and that upon soe just reasons that I could not but allow of them. And though he rides in one of them yet I thinke he does better to continue out soe that we both concur in that as I hope we shall doe in all other things, and upon what grounds it is that I am of this opinion I shall satisfie you if you desire a more particular account.

I cannot but thinke my self obleiged to returne you my thanks for the 50l you designed me for the equippeing my self at my comeing hither, though I have not yet received it. Your son not haveing hitherto mentiond it to me, I have not thought it convenient to say any thing to him of it, and I shall desire you would not take notice of it to him. It being better to be donne any other way, then by repeating your order to him, which however gently donne cannot but carry some kinde of rebuke with it. And I who have always thought that those who have to doe with young gentlemen of his condition mistake their businesse quite, and put them selves out of a capacity of doeing them that good they might, if they doe not get their freindship and affection, for without that all their authority will availe but litle. I say I should be very unwilling that any such dissatisfaction upon my account should arrise at the begining of our acquaintance. the impressions that are first made being apt to bias the minde for a long time after, and sometimes it happens that they never are got out again. And

[a] *Substituted for* late

perhaps the provisions he hath made for him self hath not left him furnishd with mony enough to follow your directions for the supply of mine. However you may thinke it a great part of my businesse as certainly it will be to looke after and manage the expences whilst we are abroad. I have yet made noe enquiry into his past expences or the stock of mony he hath at present by him, and perhaps it is best that[a]– I should not medle at all with what is past: though the knowledg of any ones expences gives one the surest insight into his temper inclination, and gives one an oportunity to apply fit remedys. but I would not appeare too curious to him in lookeing backwards, the mony which for the future will passe to him through my hands will serve well enough to instruct me, and by the mony he shall imploy hereafter in his private expences which I shall always let him have as he shall demand without difficulty or restraint (for I beleive he will not by any mistakes force me to hold my hand at any time to prevent or remedy some visible inconvenience) out of the cash shall be in my hands will afford me opportunity enough to observe his conduct to discourse with him about the regulation of his expences, and take occasion to insinuate such remarkes upon his company exercises diversions as may be necessary and usefull to him.–[a] Mr Banks complains a litle of Monsieur de Voulges payments. and if you thinke any measures of the man are to be taken from such litle matters I will tell you that haveing writ to Mr Banks a letter from Bourdeaux[1] and two others

[a–a] *This substituted passage is largely rewritten, and is to some extent reconstructed here; Locke's alterations in it are not recorded here. The original passage runs* that I never doe it. But whether for the future you will not thinke it most convenient that all the mony should passe through my hands even what he has for his private use as well as what is to be managed for the publique [*altered to* common] charge of our litle family I leave you to consider. Not that hereby I would have his allowance either stinted or come to him with more difficulty (for I have observed many young gentlemen heirs to considerable fortunes miscarry for want of soe liberall an allowance as they might justly expect as suitable to their condition) But hereby I shall always have (if there should be noe other use of it) an oportunity to observe his conduct, and to discourse with him about the management of his expences which always when known give a great light into the temper and inclination. and give occasion to observe the company and courses that any one follows. I know too well the inconveniencys that attend an honest man in receiveing and paying others mony. to be covitous of that part of the imployment. But haveing taken upon me a trust which cannot well be dischargd without takeing upon me also that troublesome and dangerous part of manageing another bodys mony, I would not decline any thing that might be necessary to my main businesse. Though to travell, eat and drinke without the trouble of reconing, accounts, or telling of mony be much more for ones ease, and lesse hazardous for one who intends not nor has leave of his conscience to make any advantage that way.

[1] See p. 485, n. 1.

from severall places on the road, which I addresd to Monsr de Voulges not ⟨knowing⟩[a] any other way to direct them to Mr Banks, when I came to Paris I found all my three letters in Monsr de Voulges window he haveing not sent one of them to your Son. And for the single letter of half a sheet you sent to him to lye there for me till I cald for it he made me pay twentipence. Litle things in some circumstances soe discover the temper of men, that I desire the bills you send me may be rather upon some other man. And I thinke our Bankier here should be one to whom you might addresse your letters when we remove from hence, with confidence that he would take care to send them forward to us according to the advice we shall from time to time give him of the places where we are. I am

Sir

Your most humble servant

JOHN LOCKE

Pray present my most humble service to my Lady.

Address: These present To Sir John Banks at his house in Lincolns-Inne-feilds London

Endorsed by Locke: J L to Sir J Banks 9 Jun. 77

## 337. DR. THOMAS SYDENHAM to LOCKE, 4 [June] 1677 (*295*, *363*, *398*)

B.L., MS. Locke c. 19, f. 163. Printed by K. Dewhurst in *The Practitioner*, clxxv (September 1955), 318, with date as 4 January 1678; in his *Sydenham*, p. 169. The month from Locke's endorsement.

Sir,

I am glad to heare that you are advanced so farr on your way homewards that we may hope to see you here shortly, but I stand amased at your taking bloud and as much at the purging you have allready used and that which you further intend after your Ague, which latter would here infallibly returne it upon you or bring on worse mischiefe.[1] I conceave (and I would my selfe take the same course) tis your best course to doe nothing at all. But in point of diett twill be convenient that you drinke somewhat more liberally wine then before and ride as much as possibly you can. The symptoms you complayne of you ought not to be concerned att, for they

[a] *MS.* know

[1] Locke notes his treatment in his Journal, pp. 143–6.

are noe other then what are usuall after agues, and endeed if you shall so mind them as to obviatt each particulare one you will create to your selfe great danger. they all depending upon one cause viz the weakeness of your bloud by the ague, which I am sure nothing will reduce but time and exercise, and even a Clyster of milke and sugar will make worse. If you would but ride on horsbacke from Paris to Calis and from Dover to London, upon that and drawing in this aer your symptoms will vanish. Since your going hence I have had multiplied experiences of riding long and persisting journies in England, which hath cured more inveteratt distempers then ever yours was, I meane of the longues.[1] I have bin and am still very ill of the gout, pissing of bloud etc. more then a quarter of an year; and having so many distempers broaken in upon very impayred and ill body I dispaire of being evr well agayne, and yet I am as well content as if I were to live and be well. My service to Dr. Bloamer and his Lady. I am most heartily

Sir

Your humble servant and very affectionat friend

THO: SYDENHAM

⟨June⟩[a] 4° 1677[b]

Address: A Madame Madame Blomer chez son excellence l Embassadeur d Angleterre[2] al Hostel de Turenne[3] á Paris. pour faire tenir a Mr. Locke a Paris

Postmark: IV—

Endorsed by Locke: Dr Sydenham 4 Jun 77

## *338.* SIR JOHN BANKS to LOCKE, 5 June 1677 (336, *340*)

B.L., MS. Locke c. 3, ff. 78–9.

Sir

Your welcome lines of the 4th instant have made us much at ease, becaus it is what was first designed, and we are abundantly satisfyed in your care and conduct, and when you come to have considered matters to gether. I hoope your resolution will prove to the best: And my son will follow your advice, but my thinks I

[a] *Part of the date is torn away; MS. has* -ny(?) *deleted here.* [b] *Locke adds at the end of the letter* The time and place

[1] Lungs. [2] Ralph Montagu: p. 451, n. 3.

[3] In the Marais; its site is occupied by St. Denis-du-St.-Sacrement: Piganiol de la Force, *Description de Paris*, new ed., 1742, iv. 262.

am not soe willinge to confine him to an Academy. he may as well I hoope improve his time at Paris, and lodge els where as now he doth; My Lord[1] is well I did see him Yesterday, but his liberty will not yet be granted

Sir I wish your owne health and with the tender of myne and my wives services doe remaine

Sir Your very humble servant

JOHN BANKS

London. 5 June: 1677

Address: A Monsieur Monsieur Locke A Paris

Endorsed by Locke: Sir J. Banks 5 June. *77*

## 339. LOCKE to DR. JOHN MAPLETOFT, 12/22 June 1677 (*314*, *347*)

*European Magazine*, xv (1789), 10–11. An excerpt ('If either absence . . . comfortable habitation') is printed in Dr. John Ward (*D.N.B.*), *The Lives of the Professors of Gresham College*, 1740, pp. 275–6; there are slight variations from the *European Magazine* text (for Ward's access to other letters from Locke to Mapletoft, see pp. 503 n., 625 n.). Answered by no. *347*.

Paris, 22 June 77.

Dear Sir,

If you make not use of the same goodnesse in excuseing my silence, as you use to doe in affording me your letters, I shall be in great danger of your hard thoughts, and you will in appearance have reason to imagin that I know not how to value either your freindship or correspondence as I ought. When I thinke on the particular accidents and considerations that have caused this neglect in me, methinks I have some thing to say for my self, but when I looke on the length of time all at once, me thinks noe thing is enough to excuse it. However I will not enter upon the long story of my vindication, I choose rather to throw my self wholy upon your mercy. I know your kindenesse will stand a greater shock then this, and you will not be much angry with me for a fault wherein I have been the sufferer as well as the guilty. If I thought it were necessary to say any thing more then this, I would refer you to the inclosed. But I phansy with my self that is some kinde of merit of your pardon, that I dare expect it of you, without troubling you with a long story, which for my vindication I have thought

[1] Shaftesbury.

necessary to tell one, who yet I thinke a very good freind and very good-naturd.[1] I arrived here about the beginning of this month, with the remains of a very untoward ague upon me, which seizd and kept me a good while upon the way; but I thanke God have now pretty well recoverd my strength, soe that if you had any commands for me here I might hope to execute them. But I have litle expectacon of any from you; you, that when you were here your self, and breathd the aire of this place, which seemes to me not very much to favour the severer sects of philosophers, were yet soe great an one as to provide for all your necessitys with the expence only of a crown or two, will not, I guesse,[2] now you are out of the sight of all our gaudy fashionable temptations, have much imployment for a factor here. But yet if either absence (which sometimes increases our desires) or love (which we see every day produces strange effects in the world) have softend you, or disposd you towards a likeing of any of our fine new things, 'tis but saying soe, and I am ready to furnish you, and should be sorry not to be imploid. I mention love, for you know I have a particular interest of my owne in it. When you looke that way, noe body will be readier as you may guesse to throw an old shoe after you,[3] much for your owne sake, and a litle for a freind of yours. But were I to advise, perhaps I should say to you, that your lodgings at Gresham colledg were a very quiet and comfortable habitation. I know not how I am got into this chapter of love, unlesse the genius of the place inspires me with it. For I doe not finde that my ague hath much inclind me to the thoughts of it. My health, which you are so kinde to in your wishes, is the only mistris I have a long time courted, and is soe coy a one that I thinke it will take up the remainder of my days to obteyn her good graces and keep her in good humor. She hath of late been very wayward, but I hope is now comeing about again. I should be glad that my constant addresses should at last prevaile with her, that I might be in a better condition to enjoy and serve you; being with all sincerity,

Deare Sir,

Your most humble servant,

JOHN LOCKE.

[1] I cannot identify this friend unless it be Mapletoft himself.

[2] This appears to be the earliest known occurrence of Locke's use of the locution; for it see *O.E.D.*, Guess, *v.* 6.

[3] To wish you well, especially on the occasion of your wedding: *O.E.D.*, s.v. Shoe, *sb.* 2a.

My service I beseech you to all my freinds in your walke, particularly Dr. Sydenham. The spell held till I had left Montpellier, for by all the art and industry I could use, I could not get a booke of his to Montpellier till the weeke after I had left it.[1] I shall be glad to heare that it every day gains ground, though that be not always the fate of usefull truth, especially at first seting out. I shall perhaps be able to give him an account what some ingenious men thinke of it here; though I imagin he is soe well satisfied with the truth in it, and the designe that made him publish it, that he matters not much what men thinke. And yet there is usually a very great and allowable pleasure to see the trees take and thrive in our own time, which we our selves have planted.

Address: For Dr. John Mapletoft, at his lodgings in Gresham Colledg, London.

## *340.* SIR JOHN BANKS to LOCKE, 14 June 1677 (*338*, *341*)

B.L., MS. Locke c. 3, ff. 80–1. Answers no. 336.

London. 14 June 77

Sir

Havinge been for these 8 days out of towne at my returne this eveninge finde your severalls of the 9 and 12 instant, to which I cannot now give my particular answer, but have thought it necessary to let you know that I shall doe it by the next. I doe thinke you have well ressolved to stay at Paris for the present. Mr De Vulges hath not done well and that he will finde, but my son is not to blame in that matter for I did direct him to Mr Vulges with direction to trust him therin, which I thought might be done, but his ill usage in detension your letters, I doe as illy resent as this of the Exchange, and my son did formerly complaine of this losse by mr Devulges and is very sensible therof. but I shall remytt him 100l–on Munday and take care of his supply that he nor I may be any more prejudiced in this kinde, Sir my humble services to yourselfe, not doubtinge of your care to my concernes who truly am

Yours J BANKS

Address: These To John Locke Esqre present Paris

Endorsed by Locke: Sir J. Banks 14 Jun. 77

[1] Apparently Sydenham's *Observationes Medicæ*: pp. 446–7, 452, and nn.

## *341.* SIR JOHN BANKS to LOCKE, 18 June 1677 (*340, 342*)

B.L., MS. Locke c. 3, ff. 82–3. Answers no. 336.

Sir

The last thursday night comminge late to London, I could not give that full answer to your severalls of the 9 and 12 instant which I did intend, havinge since none of yours nor any from my son. Sir as I am very sensible of your care and kindnesse in takinge soe great a journy, to receave my son into your conversation and conduct, soe I do and ever shall returne you my hearty acknowledgment thereof. And now it hath pleased God to bring you together. I doe thinke you have done for the best in ressolvinge to stay at Paris a while longer espetialy til towards September when the weather may be cooler, and that my son doe continue to use those exercises. as alsoe imploy himselfe in those studys. readings and improvements as you and he shall thinke fitt with respect that I doe intend his comminge home about xmas. God willinge, and you will have the opertunity of better knowinge each other. and my son will I am confident be advised by you: but I doe not yet finde by you that you and my son are in one lodginge, which if you were I should hoope you would be more satisfyd in each others conversation then by yours and my not havinge any thing this weeke from my son; it doeth seeme to me you are, You may be assured, that as I have all honnor for yourselfe, soe let me say that while my son was heer I did much observe him and have I blesse God had good satisfaction in him, and I hoope nothing appears in him to you to the contrary, and I have had noe ground to feare anything of profusenes in him, but that he might be trusted—Yet my desire was as I did acquainte you to have soe good a companion with him as your selfe (and indeed was one great inducement to my adventringe him abroad) to bring him more to the knowledge of men and things, and that you might live easy together, knowinge my sons temper; and that he might be more encouraged to appeare and converse with others—and havinge the languadge that he might presently rall to observe the cariages of others and those advantages which he could not soe well have under my roofe because there is that naturall temper and modesty in him, not to be perhaps overfree in his parents presence, tho. I have always treated him as my Companion as well as my son. And soe I did many moneths since take him of his tutor and give him more liberty, and at his goinge hence did prevaile with my worthy freind mr Thornehill to be his Companion to Paris, and committed the Purse to my son as I alsoe wrott you. which I should not have done without consideration, nor indeed was he desirous of it, but I did let him see I would as well give him trust abroad as I had done at home, he never havinge disoblidged me, and all circumstances considered, and havinge given me noe occasion to be jealous of him since he hath been abroad, I cannot give him any ground to thinke that I am in any thing scrupulous of him, and as opertunity offers I pray doe you improve it to make him sensible of my kindnes and trust that he may be the more oblidged to me. and let me try him in this time of your beinge with him as I have hitherto done, and I doe assure my selfe that when you are together you will be very easy in althings. And my wiffe who presents her services to you, is abundantly satisfyed that you doe stay at Paris till hott weather be over. Sir, my son doeth not write me that he wants mony, but if you know of any occasyon he hath I should be glad to be informed, that I might supply him and advise him accordingly: I doe intend to remyt him 100l– next post however to supply his and your occasyons; he might have made use of that credit on Mr Devulges 2 months sooner but he wrott me he shold not need it, til your arrival, and indeed I am only to blame for that unkindnes shewed by Mr Devulges, for Givinge him so much trust: and I thought I might have trusted him, but I shall make use of another. which you shall know by the next.

Sir, Thus I have with all freindship and plainenesse told you my minde, knowinge you will give me leave soe to doe considringe my concerne, yet havinge as great honnor for you as confidence in my son. whose stay or comminge home may be 2 or 3 months more or les as you shall advise with respect to your owne affaires and him, and I shall ever appeare to be

Sir Your oblidged humble servant

JOHN BANKS

Lincolns In feilds. 18 June 77

Address: These To Mr Locke present

Endorsed by Locke: Sir J Banks 18 Jun. 77

## *342.* SIR JOHN BANKS to LOCKE, 25 June 1677 (*341*, *346*)

B.L., MS. Locke c. 3, ff. 84–5.

Sir

My last to you was the 18th instant, since which have none of yours, and doe wayte in hoopes of your answer to myne by the first post. And I shall be abundantly satisfyed to finde things to your and my sons Content. whom I have always bread in a way of freedome, and in many things as a companion, findinge it most sutable to his temper. notwithstandinge all the ill's of this towne and if your health permitt I shall hoope your further acquaintance will make things pleasinge to you both; and that he will pay all dew respect to you, beinge well satisfyed you have a true kindnesse for us both. and if I have put to much trust in my sons hand, as things stood in your absence it could not be avoided, and I have all reason to beleive he will demeane himselfe well to you himselfe and me to, which is the desire of

Sir Your assured freind and servant

JOHN BANKS

Lincolns in feilds 25 June 77

Address: To John Locke Esqre present

Endorsed by Locke: Sir J: Banks 25 Jun 77

## *343.* JAMES TYRRELL to LOCKE, [*c.* 3 July 1677] (*554*)

B.L., MS. Locke c. 22, ff. 36–7. The date is a few days after the death of Sir John King: p. 497, n. 8.

James Tyrrell, 1642–1719, historical and political writer. Son of Sir Timothy Tyrrell and his wife Elizabeth, daughter of Archbishop Ussher (p. 153, n. 8). Matriculated from Queen's College, Oxford, 15 January 1657; M.A. 1663. He told Lady Masham that he made Locke's acquaintance in 1658. He lived mainly at Oakley, near Brill, Bucks., and later at Shotover, near Oxford. His principal writings are: *Patriarcha non Monarcha*, 1681, a reply to Sir Robert Filmer's *Patriarcha*; *A Brief Disquisition of the Law of Nature*, 1692, largely derived from Richard Cumberland's *De Legibus Naturæ Disquisitio Philosophica*; *Bibliotheca Politica*, thirteen dialogues, 1692–4, republished collectively 1694, etc.; and *The General History of England, both Ecclesiastical and Civil*, 3 vols. (all published), 1697–1704: *D.N.B.*; Wright, *Ussher Memoirs*, pp. 104–17 (mainly genealogical). About 1681–3 he and Locke collaborated in notes on Edward Stillingfleet (p. 373, n. 2), *The Mischief of Separation* (1680) and *The Unreasonableness of Separation* (1681): B.L., MS. Locke, c. 34; and it was he who took charge of Locke's books, or some part of them, when Locke went to the United Provinces in 1683. Many letters below.

## 343. *J. Tyrrell, 3 July 1677*

Tyrrell's handwriting is careless and untidy, with sprawling and badly formed letters, and punctuation that is frequently doubtful. In the present transcription there are probably some wrong and many doubtful renderings of the punctuation, and occasional wrong renderings of spellings.

Dear Carmelin[1]

I perceive by yours of the 25th: of June that mine which I writ in answere to yours upon the road never came to your hands, though I sent it to meet you at Paris, and directed it as you appointed Mr: Stringar and Mrs: Blomar, at my Lord Embassadors.[2] so that I give it over for lost, which vexes me a little because you may there see the concerne your Freinds had for your indisposition, and the Joy they receiv'd upon the hopes of your recovery: besides which there was an account of the proceedings in Parliament before the last adjornment,[3] which was the onely crime that I know it could be guilty of to make it miscarry: but I shall not offend in hast in the same kind in writeing of news, since I shall not see London againe 'till next Terme[4] at soonest being goeing a great Journey to morrow into Cheshire, and to stay in those parts for about six weeks my wife goeing downe to see her relations there;[5] and whether this will meet you at Paris, I perceive is uncertaine since I suppose your new Charge will carry you out of Towne for some monthes, how-ever I will venture once more, and send up this to honest J.H.[6] to be directed to you; and wish it may have better successe then the former, but now 'tis time to say something in answere to your kind letter which I received very lately: I can onely tell you I am sorry your Freinds have lost your good company so long, and are like to be recompenced with so small a returne of health, as you tell us you are like to bring over, though I hope great part of it onely proceeds from melancholy, and dissatisfaction in not haveing this voyage fully answere your expectation, and your Freinds desires: and I hope for all this you will be well enough to come over this Autumne or at Spring at farthest: but not to make you reflect longer on this melancholy subject I must now tell you I am extremely pleased with the Account you give me of Versales,[7] which

[1] The name is taken from Sorel's *The Extravagant Shepherd*: p. 324, n. 1.

[2] Ralph Montagu.

[3] The houses were adjourned until 16 July on 28 May.

[4] Michaelmas term, 23 October–28 November.

[5] Mrs. Tyrrell was Mary, *c.* 1645–87, daughter of Sir Michael Hutchinson, of Fladbury, Worcs.: *Westminster Abbey Registers*, p. 5.

[6] John Hoskins.

[7] Locke visited Versailles on 13/23 and 14/24 June: Journal.

is a great deal in a little; and as for the Waterworks there it is no wonder that he who endeavors to be Monarch of the Ocean, should make a perfect conquest over some petty Water Nymph. I am so much taken with your description of the place, that I desire you would doe me the favour as to buy me the prospects of that pallace and Gardens, and of those in and about Paris and other parts of France, they are as I take it done by one Nanteul and are of a small volume, and cost about 20s, or 30s, though they are much dearer here.[1] I desire likewise you would lay out for me, (or let me know how I may returne you) 40s, or 50s, more to buy me some French books which I leave to your discretion, provided they be not Mezeray,[2] nor the life of Henry Le Grand,[3] nor Montaign, nor Charron[4] for those I have already: but I would have Reserche de la verité, in two parts;[5] and some of the best translations out of Greek, or other History what you think good. I am not in hast provided you doe it at any time before you leave Paris. I have no more (but leaveing all matters of news to J.H. being here a perfect Recluse from the noyse of the World)[6] shall give you a short account of as much as I know of our Freinds. Lisis[7] is still by the banks of Sabrina, the stream of Isis not pleaseing him about Act time. I suppose since ill news flyes apace. J.H. will have certifyed you of the death of our good Freind Sir John King whom a Feavor the news of which to my great Greif J.H. sent me to day.[8] and I doe not doubt but you will receive it with all the resentment which the losse of so dear, and worthy a man, can deserve: he is highly lamented by all

[1] Robert Nanteuil (Thieme, *Lexikon*) was the great engraver of portraits; no engravers of views of this name are known. Tyrrell probably has in mind N. or A. Pérelle or Israël Silvestre.

[2] François Eudes de Mézeray (no. *470*), author of *Histoire de France depuis Faramond jusqu'à maintenant*, 1643–51.

[3] Probably that by H. de Beaumont de Péréfixe (1605–71; *N.B.G.*), first published in 1661.

[4] Pierre Charron (1541–1603; *D.B.F.*), author of *De la sagesse*, first published in 1601 and frequently reprinted. L.L., nos. 672–4a.

[5] Nicolas Malebranche (no. *642*), *De la recherche de la vérité*, first published in 1674–5. Locke possessed copies of several editions, 1675, 1677–8, 1678–9: L.L., nos. 1875–6, 1883–3a.

[6] Tyrrell probably wrote from Oakley.

[7] Nathaniel Hodges, who was a prebendary of Gloucester: p. 260, n. 3; for the name, p. 324, n. 1. Sabrina is the Severn.

[8] Born in 1639; lawyer; attorney general to James, duke of York; knighted 1674; died on 29 June: *D.N.B.* He may have been connected with Dr. Blomer; his half-sister married a man of that name: p. 332, n. 2. Edward Clarke and his wife, when in London between 1682 and 1688, lodged with a Lady King, who was probably Sir John's widow: no. 683 etc. His two sons and his daughter Mrs. Gelsthorpe are mentioned about 1692–4: nos. 1476, *1649*, etc.

good men, and in him I have lost the best Freind I had of his Robe, who was designed if he had lived to as much Greatnesse as such vast parts, and Industry would deserve: but I see there is nothing but incertainty in this vain life. if a man does not take paines he signifyes nothing, and if he does, 'tis 10 to one he lives not half his dayes. but you know the old saying Immodicis brevis est etc.[1] and so haveing made my self melancholy and godly I have nothing els left to conclude this scribble but my prayers for your health and our happy meeting, since a true freind in this corrupt Age is hard to find, and as hard to keep when a man hath him, and such a one I cannot be too much concerned for, which makes me the better know how to value those I have left. I wish there be roome to wr⟨ite⟩[a]

MUSIDORE[b2]

My wife presents her service to you. all my small Family is well God be thanked.

Address (written apparently by John Hoskins): A Madam Madam Blomer chez son excellence l Ambassaduer d Angleterre a l Hostel de Turenne a Paris Pour fair tenir a Mr: Lock

Endorsed by Locke: J. Tyrrell 77

## *344.* THOMAS STRINGER to LOCKE, 13 July 1677 (*333, 351*)

B.L., MS. Locke c. 19, ff. 131–2. Short excerpt printed in King, 1830, i. 70 n. *ad fin.* Mentioned by Locke in his Journal, 24 July/3 August.

July 13th. 1677.

Deare Sir

I am mightily troubled that we have been soe very unfortunate in our letters, this now is sent in the reare of severall others that are gone before some of which I presumme are come safe to your hands. I have been prevented taking that course you directed to leave them with Sir John Banks because of his being soe little and soe very uncertaine in Towne, he is under the misfortune of building

[a] *Page torn; followed by* Lisis *expunged.* [b] *Written over* Lisis*?*

[1] 'Immodicis brevis est aetas et rara senectus': Martial, VI. xxix. 7. 'The most gifted have but a short life and rarely reach old age.'

[2] p. 324, n. 1.

in the Country,[1] that I doe not see him once in two months to gether, and those which I have left with his servant I perceive have failed of reaching your hand. I have had the good fortune of meeting mr Wall,[2] by whome I heare you are much recovered sinc your Ague and if you finde noe other benefitt in the French ayre then mr Wall hath done, it is great pitty wee should want your Company any longer here in England. I don't see but he hath brought home the same thin body he carryed away, though to deceive his friends he was beholding to some fine ladys to stuffe his breeches with sweet Gloves that he might appeare the more bulkye. I have at length with much adoe gott away your box from the Customhus[a] and all your things I hope are well secured in it. it is nayled up and I intend to keepe it soe untill your returne, which I hope will now be shortly. if you can make a guesse I should be glad to have the time named. your bill of Exchange on mr Barley[3] and likewise the 10l due upon that bill, as alsoe the 15l due from mr Wall, I have received and gott your Flaning[4] shirts in a redinesse, and the first opertunitye I can meet with to send them you shall not faile to receive them from me. I shall take care to doe your devoyer to mrs Kirby,[5] in all respects as you desire. The two bottles you mention of the Queen of Hungarys water[6] to be sent by mr Upton[7] I have not yett received, neyther doe I heare any news of them, but I shall make it my buisnes to Enquire of them. mr Wall was gone forth of Towne before I could cleare your box at the Custom house, that I could not putt any seeds into his hands, neyther have I yett opened it to see what is in it, nor will not if I heare you wilbe here in any short time. me thinks I doe now begin to think the time long untill I see you. mr Clerk and his Lady[8] are at Tunbridge for her health, where the poore Lady hath been surprized with a miscarriage. our old friend[9] is still in limbo and now Closer Confined then

[a] *End of line.*

---

[1] At the Fryers, Aylesford, Kent: Coleman, p. 124.

[2] George Wall of Gloucester: p. 430, n. 2; the identification from p. 501.

[3] 'Mr Ed Barkly in Angell Court Throgmorton Street': Locke, Journal, 2/12 May.

[4] Flannel: *O.E.D.*

[5] Mr. Kirby was established at Bordeaux, and attended to Locke's business there. Mrs. Kirby probably died there in 1682: Locke, Journal, 15, 24 September 1678, N.S. (the name as Kerby); no. *736*; etc.

[6] p. 378, n. 2.

[7] He was at Montpellier in 1676 and early this year: Locke, Journal, 9 May 1676, 13 February 1677, N.S.

[8] Probably Edward Clarke of Chipley and his wife: p. 453, n. 4. Tunbridge is probably Tunbridge Wells.

[9] Shaftesbury.

ever mr Hoskins my selfe and all but two or 3 that are necessary to his Person are Excluded from seeing him, and for what reason we know not. I am forced and end with my Paper but shall for ever remaine

Deare Sir

your most affectionate humble servant

T:S:

Address (not in Stringer's hand): A Madam Madam Blomer chez son Excellence l Embassaduer d Angleterre a l Hostle de Turenne a Paris Pour fair tenir a Mr. Lock.

Endorsed by Locke: T. *Stringer* 13. Jul. 77

## 345. Dr. David Thomas to Locke, 21 July 1677 (*278*, *514*)

B.L., MS. Locke c. 20, ff. 11–12. Fragment; the lower part of both leaves is torn away.

Sarum Jul 21: 77

Deare Freind

I heare you are arrived at Paris and hope to see you in England before the Summer is over that if you stay longer the winter favor not your cough and soe like a Monseur you like not your owne country. I have sent into Holland for Ammiani Marcellini Histor⟨ia⟩[a] cum notis Henrici Vallesii[1] but cannot get it. If you canne find it at Paris where it was printed pray ⟨bu⟩y[b] it for me and bring it ⟨with yo⟩u[b]. If . . .[b] wellcome as from your owne relation which is earnestly expected and desired by

your affectionate Freind and servant

D Thomas

My wife sends her service to you and enformes you that as well as the rest of our children your godson[2] is well

Address (apparently not written by Thomas): For Mr. Lock chez Mr: Charas Apothecaire rue de Boucherie Fauxbourg St: Germain a Paris

[a] *Edge of page.* [b] *Page torn.*

[1] Published in Paris, 1636. The editor is Henri de Valois (1603–76; *N.B.G.*). L.L., no. 1897.

[2] Identifiable as John Thomas, who was born about 1675 or 1676: no. *1278*. There were at least two other sons, William and Henry (nos. *572*, *646*, etc.), and a daughter (no. *1138*, etc.).

## *346.* SIR JOHN BANKS to LOCKE, 23 July 1677 (*342, 349*)

B.L., MS. Locke c. 3, ff. 86–7.

Sir

I had your former and now yours of the 24th instant, and my beinge in the Country prevented my sooner takinge notice therof. I can only say that I am abundantly satisfyed in all things, and have only to request that you doe soe contrive matters that my son and you may be in one house, that he may be in your good company nocteque dieque:[1] and as you have done me the honnor to take your journy thither purposely to have him under your care, soe I doe hoope to finde the good effects therof. that he doe more espetialy endeavor to improve in the exercise of the minde, then in those other of the body Ridinge etc. which are in their kinde good for a season. but the other to perpetuity, and now is his only time, and I doubt not but your good example and councell will prevaile upon him, who doth alsoe seeme to me very desirous of all improvements. and if there be roome for that of the Mathematicks I wish he may attend the same, but I will particular none beinge fully pleased he is under your conduct, and will be governd by you. and therfore let him spend his time as you see best, and to regayne what hath beene a litle lost there, to which purpose I have writt to him.

Sir

I cannot advise my sons Goinge often to the Embassadors,[2] but constantly to the Protestant church,[3] and to eate at ordinarys wher he hath opertunity of conference with all sorts. This I say not knowinge but that you doe act the same things, and doe leave all to you. Your Pupill mr Wall[4] was pleased to call on me and give me the accompt of your and my sons wellfare, much to our content: I did tell my son I should remitt no more mony till he gave me notice and that he must doe it timely. Yet I doe intend to remytt next weeke 100l– to supply your and his occations; and if you judge it best to goe up the river Loer[5] and spend October and November in travellinge, I shall be governd as I heare from you: but I doe not write to him, becaus I would kepe him intent to the studys you

[1] 'Night and day.'

[2] Ralph Montagu; perhaps his chapel.

[3] Presumably the French Protestant church at Charenton. Locke mentions dining at Charenton on 10/20 June: Journal; he mentions it again in a notebook, 26 February 1679, N.S.: Lough, p. 258 n.

[4] George Wall of Gloucester: p. 499, n. 2.

[5] Loire.

shall now put him on: Sir, Your freinds are in health and I can say no more but that I shall ever be

Sir, most assured freind and servant J BANKS

Lincolns in feilds 23 July 77.

I direct my letters as formerly becaus you Give me no other notice

Address: These To mr Locke present

Endorsed by Locke: Sir J: Banks 23 Jul. 77

## 347. DR. JOHN MAPLETOFT to LOCKE, 25 July 1677 (339, 348)

B.L., MS. Locke c. 15, ff. 207–8. Answers no. 339; answered by no. 348.

Gresham-Colledg Jul. 25.77.

Deare Sir

As little a Monsieur as you are pleased to make a man that equipped himselfe fine enough to see the French King with lesse then 3 crowns charge,[1] I shall give you to understand that I am at least too faire a Duellist to take any advantage even where 'tis most allowable. The little hast this hath made to kisse your hands justifys my Pretence to this piece of Gallantry, and putts us upon the levell of Veniam petimusque damusque vicissim.[2] But your last bringing me the good News of your returning Health was, I must confesse, more wellcome to me then halfe a dozen would have been which had told me that you continued ill. For as there are some things of which wee may be safely Ignorant, so there are others of which one would chuse to be so, viz where knowledg can only contribute towards our own trouble and nothing to the cure. I hope your next will sett a time for your return to your Friends on this side the Ditch, and that you will as well for your own sake as ours take care to be with us before the Thrushes and Field-fares.[3] To quicken your diligence I think fitt to advise you that I have 2 or 3 Mistresses harboured for me, but whether I shall like, or if I doe, shall master the Game, Time will try. For if when (as Tom Bagnall learnedly sings) he thought her as sure as a gun, She sett

[1] Mapletoft presumably saw Louis XIV in or about 1672.

[2] p. 376 and n. 7.

[3] The fieldfares are winter visitors to England, arriving in late September, old style. The song-thrushes and mistle-thrushes are mainly residents, but some immigrate to the east coast in the autumn.

up her scutt and away she run,[1] what great hopes can there be for a man who will not goe much either out of his way or his pace, and builds upon this Fundamentall Maxime, That she that saith No and stands to it will never doe him harm:[2] but is not so sure what I Elizabeth (c.gr.)[3] take thee John may come to. But if that be in fatis,[4] I shall be glad to swerve from the wholsome advice you give me To think Gresham Colledg a quiet place and as Comfortable as amy other Importance,[5] to give you the advantage of taking it yourselfe; and shall both in that affaire, and all other instances give you the best Assurance I can of my Being au dernier point, as you Gallants speake,

Deare Sir

Your most very humble Servant

J. Mapletoft.

Dr. Sydenham who hath been laid up with the Gout about 20 weeks hath spent 5 or 6 of them at Hatfield where he still is. A letter from him yesterday tells us that he begins to find his Limbs again, and hopes to be with us here in a forthnight and to fall to his busines again.

If you could gett me a faire Tully's works in Fol. of Robert Stephen's Edition[6] and bring over with your Books you would oblige me more then with all the Garnitures etc. au palais.[7]

Address: For John Lock Esquire

Endorsed by Locke: Dr Mapletoft 25 Jul. 77

## 348. Locke to Dr. John Mapletoft, 30 July/9 August 1677 (*347*, *356*)

*European Magazine*, xv (1789), 89–90; the second part corrected from a copy (which omits the postscript) made by or for Dr. John Ward (p. 490 n.),

[1] Quoted, with scutt in place of taile, from 'Dr. Smith's Ballet' in Sir J. Mennes and J. Smith, *Musarum Deliciæ*, 1655, p. 89. The preceding poem is 'Tom Bagnall's Ballet'.

[2] Perhaps varied from the proverb, 'If you always say "No", you'll never be married': *Oxford Dict. English Proverbs*, s.v. Always.

[3] The usual abbreviation for 'cum grano' in prescriptions.

[4] 'Destined to happen.'

[5] Andrew Marvell attacking a book by Samuel Parker (no. *957*) and finding in it the phrase 'in matters of a Closer and more Comfortable Importance to himself and his own Affairs', decided that Parker's 'comfortable importance' could only be 'a Female', and made merry with it: *The Rehearsal Transpros'd*, second impression, 1672, pp. 7–8, 186, etc. The expression was current for some years; Locke uses it in no. 348; it occurs below in nos. *1401*, *1559*.

[6] Robert Estienne (1503–59; *N.B.G.*) published his folio edition of Cicero in 1538–9.

[7] p. 367, n. 3.

B.M., Add. MS. 6194, pp. 245–8 (Ward does not say how he obtained access to the originals of this letter and no. 417, or the copies of them, but he corresponded with John Mapletoft, Dr. Mapletoft's son, in 1743–5: B.M., Add. MS. 6226, pp. 64–6, 88–91); the substantive divergences are noted. Answers no. *347*; answered by no. *356*.

Paris, 9° Aug. 77.

Sir,

When I doe not heare from my freinds in a long time, I presently conclude that either their's or my letter hath miscaried, and soe betake my self to the known remedy of writeing again. I have been now here above these two months, and though you that could doe all your markets here your self for two or three crowns, will not, 'tis likely, much need a factor, and soe I can hope for noe imployment from you; yet you must consider that I need to heare from you: and haveing lost lately two very considerable freinds in England, Sir John King[1] and Dr. Barrow,[2] you will not blame me if I enquire a little earnestly what is become of the rest. The place you have given me in your freindship, and the great concernment it is to me to preserve that advantage, allow me to be inquisitive. You must therefor excuse my importunity. I who love my ease, even to a great degree of lazynesse, cannot take it amisse that you should be indulgent to yours. But since you have charity enough sometimes to have your rest broken for the releife of others, permit me also to apply my self to you for a paine which you only can remedy, and let me know by the first that you are well, and preserve me in your memory. I understand, both from himself and others, that our good friend Dr. Sydenham hath of late been very ill of more then one maladye. I hope he is by this time well recoverd, and returnd again to his old thoughts and practice of physique. I am very much concerned for it, both for the publique and my owne particular interest. Pray remember me very kindely to him, and in your next doe me the favour to let me know how he also does.

I am,

Deare Sir,

Your most affectionate Humble servant,

JOHN LOCKE.

Your letters will still finde me, chez Mr. Charas, apothecaire, rûe de Boucherie, Fauxbourg St. Germaine.

[1] p. 497, n. 8.

[2] p. 374, n. 4. He died on 4 May of this year; his epitaph was written by Mapletoft, who was a friend of his: *D.N.B.*

## 348. *Dr. J. Mapletoft, 30 July 1677*

Dear Sir,[a]

I had noe sooner don my letter on the other side but I found it answerd by yours of Jul. 25. And though it hath satisfied me, that you are very well, and given me new proofs, that you are very much my freind; yet it hath put new doubts into me, and methinks I see you goeing to loose your self. I will say noe worse of it, not knowing how far the matter is gon, else I would aske you, whether she were young, old, or midle agd, each of which is sure to meet you with the hornes of a dilemma. I see you are, what ever you think, hot upon the scent; and if you have noething else to defend you, but those maxims you build on, I feare the chase[b] will lead you, where you your self will be caught. For be as grave and steady as you please, resolve as much as you will never to goe out of your way nor pace for never an hey trony nony[c] whatsoever, you are not one jott the safer for all this sturdynesse. For beleive it, Sir, this sort of game haveing a designe to be caught, will hunt just at the pursuers rate, and will goe noe farther before, then will just serve to make you follow; and let me assure you upon as[d] good authority as honest Tom Bagnall's, that *vivus vidensque pereo*[1] is the lamentable ditty of many an honest gentleman. But if you or the Fates have determin'd (for the poor[d] Fates are still to be accus'd in the case) if your mettle be up, and as bold as Sir Fr. Drake, you will shoote the desperate gulph;[2] yet consider, that though the riches of Peru lie that way, how well you can endure the warme navigation of the *Mare de Zur*,[3] which all travellers assure us is nicknamed pacificum. But hold, I goe to far. All this perhaps, notwithstanding your ancient good principles, will be heresie to you by that time it comes to England; and therefor I conjure you by our freindship to burne

[a] *Ward's copy begins here. It is headed by the date, presumably that at the beginning of the letter and not a repetition of it at this point by Locke.* [b] *European Magazine* close [c] *European Magazine* a hey nony nony [d] European Magazine *omits.*

[1] 'I'm perishing while still alive and seeing': Terence, *Eunuchus*, 73 (spoken by a despairing lover).

[2] The Straits of Magellan. 'Sir Francis Drake's going through it gave birth to that famous old wives' saying, viz. that Sir Francis Drake shot the gulf; . . . as if there had been but one gulf in the world': Defoe (1725), quoted in *O.E.D.*, s.v. Gulf, *sb.* 2c.

[3] The South Sea, the Pacific, lying to the south of the Isthmus of Panama, from which it was first seen by Europeans. Locke may have in mind a passage in *The World Encompassed by Sir Francis Drake*, 1628; he owned a copy of the edition of 1635: L.L., no. 994. The '*Mare del zur*' is named, and 'the South Sea (called by some *Mare pacificum*, but proving to us rather to be *Mare furiosum*)': ed. W. S. W. Vaux (Hakluyt Soc., vol. xvi, 1854), pp. 79–80, 82.

this as soon as you have read it, that it may never rise up in judgment against me. I see one is never sure of ones self, and the time may come when I may resigne my self up to the empire of the soft sex, and abominate my self for these miserable errors. However, as the matter now stands, I have discharg'd my conscience, and pray doe not let me suffer for it. For I know you lovers are a sort of people that are bound to sacrifice all to your mistrisses. But to be serious with you, if your heart does hang that way, I wish you good luck. May Hymen be as kinde to you, as ever he was to any body; and then I'm sure you will be much happyer, then any forlorne batchelor can be. If it be like to be, I beg you to continue your care of my interest in the case, and remember it is for one, that knows how to value the quiet and retirement you are goeing to quit. You have noe more to doe for me, then what lovers use to doe upon their owne account, viz. keepe the matter as secret and private as you can, and then, when it is ripe and resolvd, give me but notice, and I shall quickly be with you, for it is by your directions I shall better governe my motions, then by the flight of thrushes and feildfares. Some remains of my cough and something like a charge is fallen into my hands lately here,[1] will, if noething else happen, keepe me out probably longer then the time you mention. But not knowing whether the aire of France will ever quite remove my old companion or noe, I shall neglect that uncertainty upon the consideration of soe comfortable an importance; and for the other affaire I have here, if you please to let me hear from you some times, how matters are like to goe, I shall be able to order that well enough, to come at the time you shall thinke seasonable. Whatever happens, I wish you all the happinesse of one or t'other condition, for I am very perfectly,

Deare Sir,

Your most humble And obedient servant,

JOHN LOCKE.

I am very glad to heare that Dr. Sydenham is getting out of this long fit. Pray remember me kindely to him. My service also to Mr. Firmin, and the rest of my freinds at your end of the town.

I shall take care of your Tully, and be very glad of any other commands from you.

Address: These For Dr. John Mapletoft, at his lodgings in Gresham Colledg, London.

[1] Caleb Banks.

## *349.* Sir John Banks to Locke, 9 August 1677 (*346*, 352)

B.L., MS. Locke c. 3, ff. 88–9. Perhaps answered by no. 352.

Sir

I am very sensible of your great indulgence to my son, and as it was my great designe to have had him first in your care, which it pleased God to prevent, soe now I doe not question but you will doe what you judge best and that he will be guided by you, which he franckly assures me in all his letters and I doe say that I doe most value the internall improvements.

It would abundantly gratify my wiffe as well as my selfe, that you contrive such way and means at such time as you thinke best for your being in one Lodginge, I speake not in distrust my son, but know it must be his advantage: My son hath sent me his account Expences, and I am satisfyed therin, and have sent him a letter of Credit this post. from sir Natha. Herne[1] upon the Widow Herring[2] and Son, which I did take for 500l, yet to be payd as I shall order. and I have now ordered her to pay my son 100l, for your accommodation: I did take it for soe large a summe not to have the trouble of a fresh credit, nor yet to be profuse, it being to be payd as I shold order. And to tell you the truth I did finde my son desirous to make the Tour,[3] and goe further, and I did intend this credit your supply soe much as was needed, which I have had by me since the 27 July but have forborne to send it, becaus I finde my wiffe cannot beare the thoughts of any such undertakinge, which I have hinted to my son, and tell him Paris answers all; and I hoope he is now come into the road of a serious aplication of his time in a regular way to such studys as you have advised, and I doe beleive my wiffe may be content to let him stay out til springe, Wherefore myne and my wives particular request to you is, being doubtfull least our sons inclination, to the leavinge of Paris for a while may be a little more earnest, then the benefit he can expect from it in soe little a time as I designe his stay abroad, can compensate, and beinge indeed greatly concerned for my wives satisfaction, whom I finde in

[1] *c.* 1630–79; merchant; sheriff of London 1674–5; alderman 1676–9: Woodhead, *Rulers of London*.

[2] Locke generally writes Herinx: Journal, 13 May 1678, N.S.; etc. There was a banker named Herins in Paris in 1692: Lüthy, *La Banque protestante*, i. 76.

[3] The round of France. 'Ceux qui venants en France, pour faire le tour de ce noble Royaume . . .': C. de Varennes, *Le Voyage de France*, 1639, Voyage, p. 1.

noe degree inclined to his goinge further from thence, then may stand with her havinge an easy and certaine account of his health at least once every weeke. besides the consideration that you conceave all that is to be obtayned for the delightinge or adorninge a yong Gentleman by travel in France is to be found at Paris, and the visitinge the places of note within easy journys from it, the mannagment wherof I submitt to your prudence, but doe in confidence of your concurrence with me, recommend it to your mannagment to divert my son from the desire of goinge further, wither by proposinge any other methods of entertaininge himselfe wher he is, that may be to his content, without givinge his mother that occasyon of disquiet which I cannot bear, nor if he were heer would he expose her to: Newes heer is none, If any letters come for you to me they shall be timely sent forward, My wives ⟨and⟩[a] my most humble services to you assuringe you I doe owne m⟨y⟩[a] selfe to be

Sir Your oblidged humble servant

JOHN BANKS

Lincolns in feilds 9 Aug. 77

Address: To Mr John Locke Thesse

Endorsed by Locke: Sir J. Banks 9 Aug. 77

## 350. LOCKE to WILLIAM CHARLETON, 16/26 August 1677 (353)

Houghton Library, Harvard. Transcribed from photostat.

The person addressed is William Courten, 1642–1702, a grandson of Sir William Courten (1572–1636: *D.N.B.*); owing to the involved state of his grandfather's and his father's affairs he lived abroad for some time and called himself Charleton. He was an ardent collector, especially of coins and medals and of natural history specimens, and after his final return to England about 1684 established a private museum in his chambers in the Temple. He bequeathed his collection to Sir Hans Sloane (no. *788*), from whom it passed to the British Museum: *Biographia Britannica*, ed. A. Kippis, 1778–93, iv. 334–53 (mainly the family fortune); *D.N.B.* (as Courten); E. St. John Brooks, *Sir Hans Sloane*, 1954, pp. 58, 132, 177–9. I have used the name Charleton throughout.

Locke met Charleton at Lyons on 11/21 December 1675; they apparently travelled together to Montpellier.

[a] *Page torn.*

## 350. *W. Charleton, 16 August 1677*

Paris 26 Aug. 77

Sir

The inclosed I received from Mr Diggs[1] the last post and he tooke this way to send it you I imagin hopeing it might come safe to your hands, for he tells me he hath writt four letters to you without haveing receivd any one from you. I perceive by what he says to me that his matters goe very well in England for which I am heartily glad. He thanks me in his letter for the discourse I had with him at Montpellier. I tell you this that when you write to him you may continue still to refresh those good advices of yours to which I doubt not but in a great measure he owes the good successe of his affairs, for you see they are not lost upon him. And I wish him soe heartily well that I would have all things contribute to continue him in the same course you soe wisely directed him to and he has with soe good successe begun. But Sir I need not minde you of any good offices to your friends. It will better become me and my obligations to you to bethinke my self of returneing my thanks for those infinite favours I have received from you my self: were they of an ordinary sort perhaps I might finde words that might expresse my sense of them, but exceeding as they doe the common rate of civilitys and those things men extoll as courtesys you must not blame me if I want words when languages them selves doe. for words being signes[2] suited to mens conceptions and experiencys of things, 'tis noe wonder they should not yet have found out names for what is soe seldome met with in the world a generosity and way of obleigeing their freinds, like yours. The seeds you did me the favour to send me are I doubt not by this time in Oxford, though I have not heard a word from Mr Wall[3] since he went by whom I sent them. But I doubt his letters have miscaried as I suspect they doe alsoe sometimes between this and Montpellier, for haveing writ to you about a month since and received never a letter from you since I suspect that either yours or mine hath misd its way. If it be mine it is noe great matter soe you will but beleive I faile not in my respects to you. But the losse of yours I count at an other rate, for there being noe thing more valuable to me then the marks of

[1] Probably Col. Edward Digges, a member of the Digges family of Chilham Castle near Canterbury: Hasted, *Kent*, iii. 130; p. 575, n. 3; no. *509*.

[2] 'Our words . . . are the signs that every man makes use of to stand for his own particular complex idea': Locke, *Essay*, draft B, §76 (ed. Rand, p. 154). The thought is fully developed in *Essay*, III, ii. 1.

[3] George Wall of Gloucester: p. 499, etc.; the seeds, ibid.

your kindenesse and freindship tis one of the most sensible displeasures Fortune can doe me to rob me of those you designe me. I have only this comfort that I place your freindship it self amongst those good things she cannot deprive me of. and you have taught me confidently to beleive, that haveing bestoud it on me without any desert on my side, the same goodnesse will continue it me still and my want of merit will not make me loose it. Holding therefor soe great a favour from you it cannot seeme strange if I interest my self in your affairs espetially those that may concerne your safety, and conjure you for a while to lay aside the thoughts of your Spanish journey. The plague there is soe spread and soe hot that you cannot without manifest danger of your life venture your self into a country soe infected and where the great danger that accompanys that disease is soe much increased by that want of that assistance one usually findes in other parts. I should be glad I confesse to see you in that part of France this winter, but however wellcome that would be to me it has noe part in this story. I never impose upon my freinds for any buy respect[1] of my owne, nor is this a flying report raisd here in an Enemy Country. I saw lately the account of it sent hither from England which speaks of it as of a great mortality that has alarmd them to that degree that they are very strict in their towns upon their Quarantine and other cautions of health; which admitting there were noe danger would yet certainly make the journey very dangerous. I beg you to excuse this Liberty as ⟨c⟩omeing[a] from one who never balances circomstances nor ceremonys when he meets with any occasion where in he thinks he may assure you that he is in reality

Deare Sir

Your most affectionate humble servant

JOHN LOCKE

Pray present my humble service to Sir John Chichley.[2] All the news I have for him and you is that Sir Ellis Laiton upon a summons of a privy seale sent him hither hath renderd him self in England

[a] *Edge of page cut away.*

---

[1] Locke wrote similarly 'a Pretence made use of to cover some other By-Interest': *A Third Letter for Toleration*, 1692, p. 167.

[2] Sir John Chicheley, d. 1691, admiral: *D.N.B.*; I.H.R., *Bull.* ii (1925), 94 (where Lady Chicheley is identified). For his residence at Montpellier see Lady Newton (E. Legh), *Lyme Letters*, 1925, pp. 69–72.

and is sent Prisoner to the tower.[1] The prince of Orange being recruited with 5.000 fresh men is marching again towards the French army. The King went yesterday from Versailles to Fontainbleau where he will ⟨s⟩tay[a] about 20 days The D of Monmouth is expected here every day.[2]

Pray present also my humble service to my Lady Chichley[b] and Mrs Fines.[b3]

Address: A Monsieur Monsieur Charleton gentilhomme Anglois á Montpellier

## *351.* THOMAS STRINGER to LOCKE, 16 August 1677 (*344, 354*)

B.L., MS. Locke c. 19, ff. 133–4. Printed, with slight omissions, in King, 1830, i. 70 n. *ad fin.*

Thanett House[4] August 16th. 1677.

Deare Sir

Our friend mr Hoskins being just takeing of a jorney unto Bath hath desired me to take care of the enclosed from himselfe and mr Terrill,[5] the others came by other means to my hands. I thank God our friends at the Tower and here are in very good health, they want nothing but liberty and that is not like to be had untill the next Prorogation.[6] his Lordships desires you will gett him the best mapps of Champaigne, Loraigne, Luxenburge, and the Country between the River Sambre and Luxenburg. because the warr in probability will come there againe. And likewise he desires you to

[a] *Edge of page cut away.* [b] *The lower part of the name is cut away.*

[1] Sir Elisha Leighton, d. 1685, courtier and political intriguer: *D.N.B.* He was sent to the Tower on 1 August: H.M.C., *Le Fleming MSS.*, p. 139.

[2] James Scott, 1649–85; created duke of Monmouth 1663; of Buccleugh (Scotland) 1663; Charles II's eldest acknowledged son: *D.N.B.*

[3] Lady Chicheley was Isabella, d. 1709, daughter of Sir John Lawson (ibid.); her first husband was Daniel Norton, d. 1666, whose mother was probably Elizabeth, daughter of William Fiennes, first Viscount Say and Sele (ibid.): Le Neve, *Pedigrees*, pp. 112, 234. Mrs. Fiennes was probably a first cousin of Daniel Norton.

[4] A large early seventeenth-century house in Aldersgate Street belonging to the Tuftons, earls of Thanet. Shaftesbury was a tenant from this year until his death; it then reverted to the Thanet family and was divided into tenements; Shaftesbury Place is on or near the site: Wheatley, *London*, s.v. Aldersgate Street; for the character of the street, Strype's Stow, iii. 121.

[5] James Tyrrell.

[6] Of the four peers sent to the Tower in February (p. 463) Shaftesbury alone remained there; the others were released in July: p. 482, n. 1. Stringer may be thinking of the members of Shaftesbury's family at Thanet House who would want his company.

enquire and lett him know what books the dolphin[1] was first innitiated withall to Learne latine. he apprehends there are some books both latine and French, eyther Janua linguarums, or Colloquies, and alsoe he desires to know what Grammers, this he conceives may be best learned from those two Printers that Printed his books: having your order I opened your box of things and have furnished him with those books you sent over. he hath engaged to be very carefull in restoring them and in order thereunto hath gott a box to keepe them in aparte from all other things, and it proves a very good entertainment in this time of Close Confinement, when his friends are not permitted to see him without Particular order under the hand of one of the secretarys,[2] whoe are Generally very kinde and deny none that aske for leave, as I doe heare off. amongst those books his Lordship findes a Printed Paper of all the Generall officers of the King of France for the yeare 1675.[3] if there are any such Papers Printed for the yeare 1676. and 1677 he desires you will give your selfe the trouble of sending them unto him. I have your shirts ready wayting for a Passage and the first opertunity you shall not faile of receiveing them from me. in the mean while I am not willing to keepe you longer from reading the enclosed but in great earnest subscribe my selfe

Dearest Sir

Your most affectionate and faithfull servant

T:S:

Address: A monsieur monsieur Lock Gentilhome Anglois Chez monsr. Charas Apothecaire rüe de Boucherie Fauxbourg St Germaine a Paris

Endorsed by Locke: Mr Stringer 16. Aug. 77

## 352. Locke to Sir John Banks, 18/28 August 1677 (*349, 365*)

Puttick and Simpson, sale-catalogue, 28–30 April 1859, no. 332. Extracts. The same extracts sent by the Revd. J. E. Jackson, canon of Bristol, the owner, to Fox Bourne; printed by him with modernized spelling, i. 378. Present ownership unknown. Described in the catalogue as 'Copy of a

[1] The Dauphin, Louis, 1661–1711, 'Monseigneur'. His tutor, Bossuet, composed a Latin grammar for him; it was not printed: A. Floquet, *Bossuet précepteur du Dauphin*, 1864, pp. 57–60. On 21/31 October Locke sent Stringer for Shaftesbury Tannegui le Fèvre, *Methode pour commencer les humanites grecques et latines*, Saumur, 1672, and *Examen de la manière d'enseigner le latin par le seul usage*, 1668: Journal; L.L., nos. 1082[b], 1114.

[2] The secretaries of state.

[3] I have failed to identify this; apparently a single sheet rather than *L'Estat de la France*, the political almanack. See further p. 545.

letter in [Locke's] own hand . . . to Sir John Bankes, Paris, August 28, 1677, endorsed by him [Locke?] "J. L. to Sir J. B., 28 Aug 77."' It is said to be from Lord King's papers. It apparently referred to a passage in a letter from Banks (no. *349*?) in which 'Sir John and his Lady disagree as to whether their son shall remain in Paris, or travel through France', and continued:

As to the improvements of travell I think they are all comprehended in these four—Knowledge, which is the proper ornament and perfection of the minde: Exercise, which belong to the body: Language and Conversation. Of all these, Exercise only is that which seems to perswade the spending his time in Paris. . . . I grant some parts of Mathematiques might be learnt here, but methinks he is not yet ready for those sciences. For to engage one in Mathematiques who is not yet acquainted with the very rudiments of Logique is a method of study I have not known practised, and seems to me not very reasonable. . . . They who imagine that the improvements of forain conversation are to be sought by making acquaintance and friendships abroad, seeme to me wholy to mistake the matter, and it appears to me quite another thing. The great benefit to be found by travell is by constant changeing of company, and conversing every day with unknown strangers is to get a becomeing confidence and not to be abashed at new faces—to accustome ones self to treat every body civilly, and to learne by experience that that which gets one credit and recommends one to others, is not the fortune one is borne to, but the riches of the minde and the good qualities one possesses. And were it not for this one thing I know not why young gents should not be sent for breeding rather to the Court of England than the Inns and Eating Houses of France.

## 353. LOCKE to WILLIAM CHARLETON, 31 August/10 September 1677 (350, *369*)

Present ownership unknown. Text here from facsimile of first page in J. A. Stargardt (Marburg), sale-catalogue no. 554, collection of Dr. Robert Ammann, Aarau, pt. i, 16 November 1961, item no. 419; and from Messrs. Maggs Brothers, *Catalogue*, no. 616, 1935, item no. 982, corrected by fragments printed in Ammann sale-catalogue; an additional sentence from fragments in Mr. Paul C. Richards (Brookline, Massachusetts), *Catalogue* no. 5 (1962), item no. 127.

The Messrs. Maggs Brothers item consists of excerpts from six letters of Locke's, of which five are to William Charleton (not Dr. Walter Charleton, as stated in the catalogue) and one to the College (Edward Clarke and John Freke). The remaining excerpts for Charleton belong to nos. 415, 465, 972, and 996; that for the College, to no. 2048.

Paris 10 Sept. 77

Sir

If in my last to you I mentiond a former I had writ it was not to claime a debt But to prevent the suspition of my negligence. For haveing noe thing to returne to you for the many signall favours I have received but now and then a few words of acknowledgments I would not be thought to faile in soe slight and easy a kinde of gratitude And I ought to be sedulous in this litle ⟨performance⟩[a] to let you see that in occasions of greater importance you should not finde me backwards. If you consider this as the reason and duty of my letters you will not thinke it necessary to make excuses for your silence. And though (to confesse the truth and lay open to you the inside of my heart) there is always a concerne[b] there that makes me secretly wish to heare often of your health and that you reteine me in your kinde thoughts. yet I would not importune you with it Satisfying my self with an assureance of your freindship even when you say noe thing to me of it. I have this only to beg of you, that you will not soe interpret either my words or thoughts as to thinke them too partiall to you, I have a thousand instances in my particular besides the consent of all the world that knows you, to justifie them And I beseech you to beleive that earnestly desireing as I doe to preserve with you a lasting and solid freindship I have noe intention to enterteine you with empty words and aery complements, but with the truth and sincerity that becomes and is necessary to that Relation. I thanke you for your kinde remembrances of me with Mr Selaperis,[1] If they did you noe harme then they doe me I assure good now a great while after. and I doe not know in the whole extent of this great monarchie two others that I had rather be remembred by. As often as I thinke of Mr Selaperis I returne you thanks for him in my minde. Tis only for you to make such presents as these to your freinds, whom[c] yet by this title I count my self to have soe sure an interest in that had I any affaires at Lyon I should with as much confidence trouble him as if you your self were there. I beg you, when you write to him, to assure him of

[a] *MS.* performance [b] *Last letters doubtful.* [c] *Interlined; preceded by* with *or* which *apparently deleted.*

[1] p. 480 n.

this; And also to let him know that if, where ever I am, he doth not use me with the same freedome in all occasions that may be serviceable . . .[a]

I know not yet how my motions will be ordered this winter it depending not wholly on myself . . .[b]

. . . I was very much concerned for Sir John Chichleys sickness when I received the first news of his being ill, but was less frighted when I heard it was the Jaundice than I should have been had it been any returne of his old malady, hoping that this woud passe over without any danger of his life I am glad to finde by your letter that I was not mistaken in my prognostick. I shall be glad to heare that he is perfectly recovered. Pray present my most humble service to him, my Lady and Mrs. Finnes. And pray returne my respects and service to those other persons you mention in your letter who oblige me by their kinde remembrance. Pray doe me the favour to present my service to Dr. Barbyrac[1] and tell him I should be glad to receive his sentiments concerning Dr. Sydenhams book which I presume ere this time he has read.[2]

Here is talke of preparations to beseige Ipre[3] some thinke it to be in good earnest others to alarme the enemy. The D. of Monmouth is here in town he came hither the last week from Fountaine bleau, where besides other marks of welcome he received from the K.[4] his picture set with diamonds tis said to be of a very considerable value. He goes hence for Diepe and soe for England thursday next. The last week being in a shop I saw one passe by in a coach whom I imagined to be Sir William Waller[5] and accordingly I saluted him with my hat which he returned. But hearing no more of him and there being a lady in the coach with the gent. I saluted, I thought I might be mistaken. Yesterday by chance I being at tother side

[a] *The Ammann facsimile ends here; the next sentence from the Richards catalogue.*
[b] *The rest from the Maggs catalogue apart from the subscription, which is from a facsimile in the Ammann catalogue.*

[1] Charles de Barbeyrac, 1629–99; M.D., Montpellier 1649; as a Protestant incapable of holding any professorship, etc.: *D.B.F.*; Haag. Locke knew him by 28 January 1676, N.S.: Journal. In 1702–4 his nephew Jean Barbeyrac corresponded with Locke: no. *3141*, etc.

[2] Presumably the *Observationes Medicæ*: pp. 439, n. 1, 492.

[3] Ypres.

[4] The king.

[5] Died 1699; son of the general (pp. 206 n., 284, n. 1); informer, etc.: *D.N.B.* He was in Montpellier on 14 November 1676, N.S., when Locke treated him for fits, and on 26 and 31 December: Journal. I have failed to discover the date of his knighthood and to identify Lady Waller and her sister. Further notices below, no. 991, etc.

the towne I was told that Sir William Waller was hard by where I was, but was just going out of towne where indeed I found him as they said just going to Rouen, where he tells me he expects his lady and sister Hester with her about a month or 6 weekes hence and then he intends to settle for this winter about Orleance. Pray tell my lady Chichley this. He came as he told me from Rouen hither with my Lady Meath who is going forward to her Lord to Bourbon.[1]

Your most humble and obedient servant

J LOCKE

## *354.* THOMAS STRINGER to LOCKE, 7 September 1677 (*351, 355*)

B.L., MS. Locke c. 19, ff. 135–6.

Sept. 7th. 1677.

Deare Sir

Yours of September 8th. came last night to my hands. I am very sorry I am soe very unfortunate to write soe many letters and soe few of them come to your hands. I lately sent you a Paquett of severall letters from diverse of your friends here, and amongst others from mr Hoskins mr Terrill Doctor Thomas etc. I therein acquainted you that my Lord[2] had a request to you to gett him the best mapps of Loraigne Luxenburg Champaigne and the Country between the River Sambre and Luxenburg, and likewise that you would enquire what books the Dolphin was fist taught for him to learne latin, and what way of Grammer, and alsoe if there be any Printed Papers of the K: of Frances Generall officers for the yeares 1676. and 1677. because he hath a desire to see them, if you can Conveniently Convey them over to him. I will take care to enquire after Sir John Banks sending that by that messenger you may receive your Flaning shirts and alsoe the Constitutions of Carolina.[3] Sir John and my selfe have bin soe much in the Country this Summer that I have not seen him above these foure months. Your friends here I thank God are in very good health. they wilbe Exceeding Glad to see you, when you shall think fitt to visitt England

[1] William Brabazon, *c.* 1635–85; third earl of Meath (Ireland) 1675; and his countess Elizabeth, sister of Thomas Lennard, earl of Sussex: G. E. C. Bourbon-l'Archambault: p. 378, n. 3.

[2] Shaftesbury. This passage repeats part of no. *351*.

[3] p. 395, n. 2; presumably a printed copy.

againe. mrs Mary Percivall[1] bid me tell you that they will nurse you up with soe many Good things that she will undertake you shall thrive better in theire hands then amongst the French Folks. I am sure I doe most hartily wish you well ⟨wherever⟩[a] you are, and not body shalbe gladder to see you in England then

Your most Faithfull humble servant

T:S

Address: A monsieur Monsieur Lock Gentilhomme Anglois Chez monsieur Charas. Apothecaire rüe de Boucherie Fauxburg St Germaine a Paris

Endorsed by Locke: Mr Stringer 7 Sept. 77

## *355.* THOMAS STRINGER to LOCKE, 5 October 1677 (*354*, *378*)

B.L., MS. Locke c. 19, ff. 137–8. Excerpts printed in Christie, *Shaftesbury*, ii. 250.

Thannett House October 5th. 1677.

Deare Sir

I have received your letter of the 6th of October and am glad to heare that mine have at length found out the way to you. I hope there will not now be any more danger of miscariages. I will take care to enquire after the mapps you have sent by Sir Tho: Armstrongs daughter for they wilbe of great use unto my Lord, his Cheife devertisment being in books, mapps, and Papers.[2] I have according unto your order enquired after the books you mention for monsieur Briott.[3] As for the Treatys between England and other Countrys they are very scarce and voluminous, and soe wilbe very Chargeable, but a Perfect Collection I finde is impossi⟨ble⟩[b] to gett especially in lattine which was the languadge they were generally signed in, but if you desire to have me gett

[a] *MS.* wherevery    [b] *Page torn.*

[1] pp. 454, n. 1, 456 n. She was one of the principal members of Shaftesbury's household in 1675, sitting with Stringer and others at the steward's table for meals: P.R.O., S.P. 30/24, bdle 5, no. 286.

[2] Sir Thomas Armstrong, born *c.* 1624, a follower of Monmouth, hanged, drawn, and quartered in 1684 for his presumed complicity in the Rye House Plot: *D.N.B.* He had two or more daughters. The maps for Shaftesbury were ready on 20/30 September, and 'Mrs. Armstrong' took them two days later: Journal.

[3] Pierre Briot, d. 1678, translator from the English; perhaps a member of the Protestant family of this name. His library, sold in 1679, contained, apart from others, 320 English books: Haag; G. Ascoli, *La Grande-Bretagne devant l'opinion française au XVIIe siècle*, 1930, ii. 19, 23, 57–8, etc.; p. 632 and no. *594* below; notices in Locke's Journal.

as many as I can I will make it my buisnes to doe it, and doubt not but I may meet with many of them in English.[1] Doctor Cudworths book is not yett Printed, it hath been Printing these 3 or 4 yeares, and it was at one time feared it would not come forth at all, but now it is thought it may be finished about halfe a yeare hence. the reason of the delay it is sayd doth proceed from the Doctors great alterations, even in the Printed sheets that they are forced to give them severall reprintings.[2] There hath been noe new impression of the Seamans Dictionary,[3] Soe that I have not bought that because I perceive mr Briot hath one of those already, but for the Philosophicall Transactions[4] being 8 in number at 5s. Tract de Tartaro:[5] 3s. Dr Stillingfleets Answere etc.[6] 5s: 6d. Duke Hambletons Memoires[7] 10s. 6d. the whole being 24s. I have gott the Packed up, and sent to mr Barksteed[8] in Spittlefeilds with such direction to mr Briot as you desire, and alsoe hath putt up amongst them the Fundamentall Constitutions of Carolina for you. As for the other books you desired me only to enquire about you may take this account of them That Olearius[9] is growing very scarce, it being at first hand about 20s and at second hand at 15s. Puffendorp De jure Naturæ et Gentium[10] about 10s, and his Officium hominis[11] etc. about 3s, they

[1] No general collection of treaties, so far as is known, was published in England until 1686.

[2] Dr. Ralph Cudworth (p. 642), *The True Intellectual System of the Universe: The first part*, a folio of 899 pages apart from the preface, etc. The imprimatur is dated 29 May 1671; the book is dated 1678 and was advertised in May of that year: *T.C.* i. 312. L.L., no. 896.

[3] By Sir Henry Mainwaring; first published in 1644; later editions 1667, 1670.

[4] The Royal Society's periodical. The price in 1669 was 6*d.* for each issue: *T.C.* i. 14.

[5] Perhaps Daniel Ludwig (Hirsch, *Aerzte*), *De Volatilitate Salis Tartari Dissertatio*, Gotha, 1674. L.L., no. 1833.

[6] Probably *An Answer to Several Late Treatises*, 1673, part of Stillingfleet's attack on the Roman Catholic Church. The price is given in the Term *Catalogue* as 3*s.* 6*d.*: *T.C.*, i. 134.

[7] Gilbert Burnet (the future bishop of Salisbury; no. *506*), *The Memoires of the Lives and Actions of James and William Dukes of Hamilton*, 1677. It had appeared very recently: T. E. S. Clarke and H. C. Foxcroft, *A Life of Gilbert Burnet, Bishop of Salisbury*, 1907, p. 150.

[8] A silk merchant: Locke, Journal, 10 August 1678, N.S.

[9] Adam Olearius (1603(?)–71; *A.D.B.*); probably his travels to Russia and Persia, which were first published in German as *Offt begehrte Beschreibung der newen orientalischen Reise*, Schleswig, 1647; enlarged edition 1656; English translation as *The Voyages and Travels of the Ambassadors sent by Frederick Duke of Holstein, to the Great Duke of Muscovy, and the King of Persia*, 1662; 2nd ed., 1669. The price of the latter, bound, is given as 18*s.* in *Mercurius Librarius*: *T.C.* i. 22. Locke possessed copies of the first edition of the translation and of the French translation, the editions of 1656 and 1679: L.L., nos. 2128–30.

[10] Samuel, Freiherr von Pufendorf (1632–94; *A.D.B.*), *De Jure Naturæ et Gentium Libri Octo*, 1672. Locke owned two copies of this edition: L.L., no. 2401.

[11] *De Officio Hominis et Civis juxta Legem Naturalem Libri Duo*, 1673. L.L., no. 2403.

are all very scarce but yett are to be mett with if you desire them. Your 2 Flaning shirts I have this day sent to Sir John Banks whoe hath undertaken to send them to his Sone by one of my Lord of Feravershams servants[1] that is comeing over to Paris, if you please to speake with mr Banks about them, for they will come to his hands first, without any directions to you upon the Paper any other then my seale; My Lord of Shaft. hath had a fitt of the Gout lately, but otherwise he is better in his health, fresher in his Complextion and fatter in his body then Ever I saw him in my life, which I doe impute to his temperance and well ordering of himselfe where he is. My Lady and the rest of the Family I thank God are Exceeding well, and John Whilock is become a Principall officer about my Lord;[2] My Lord Mohun is lately deceased of his wound, to the great affliction of all his friends.[3] mr Hoskins is suddenly Expected home againe whoe hath been rambling a great while out of Towne. I am now preparing for a jorney out of Towne to morow soe farr as Bexwells and soe shall at present take my Leave with an assurance that I am

Deare Sir

Your most faithfull and devoted servant

T:S:

Address: A Monsieur Monsieur Lock Gentilhome Anglois Chez Monsieur Charas Apothecaire rüe de Boucherie Fauxburg St Germaine á Paris

Endorsed by Locke: Stringer 5 Oct. 77

## *356.* Dr. John Mapletoft to Locke, 11 October 1677 (348, *358*)

B.L., MS. Locke c. 15, ff. 209–10. Answers no. 348.

Gresham-Colledg Oct. 11. 77.

Deare Sir

My long absence from town and indisposition since my return have made me trespasse upon all my friends: I know you have both goodnes and compassion enough, and more then I hope I shall need upon this occasion. I am not sorry at your designd longer

[1] Louis de Duras, *c.* 1638–1709; succeeded as second earl of Feversham 16 April of this year: *D.N.B.* He was sent to Paris on a diplomatic mission in November.

[2] John Wheelock: nos. *1500*, etc., below. It was in his arms that Shaftesbury died.

[3] Charles Mohun, born *c.* 1645; third Baron Mohun of Okehampton 1665; wounded as a second in a duel 17 November 1676; died 29 September of this year: G. E. C. He was an associate of Shaftesbury's: Haley, *Shaftesbury*, p. 383, etc.

absence since I beleive it will be for the advantage of your health; nor perhaps will you think Gresham-Colledg motive great enough to make you quitte la belle France an hour sooner then you intend otherwise. But that you may know at what rate some men value the little concern I have there I shall acquaint you with an overture lately made to me by a good Friend of mine, who suspecting I might be more inclinable to Matrimony then formerly came on purpose to tell me, That when I designd to leave he will take it as a favour if I would accept 200ll. from him, and assist him in being my Successor, which he doubts not of Compassing almost by his own interest, but thinks himselfe very sure if I joyn mine. He frankly told me he had offred another Professor 300ll. to resign to him, and that if I desired more he would give it. I told him what obligation I had to you (though without naming you) and that I could promise nothing till I knew your mind: but did beleive you would not value it at the rate he did, which is the top of his hopes. He offers me too the use of my Stables and Coach-house rent-free as long as I please, and will stick at nothing that I can reasonably demand. I need not tell you after this that he is a very young man (wholly designd to live) res ipsa loquitur. When I receive your answer I shall know what to say to him. In the mean time I need not desire you to say nothing of all this to any person whatever. For though I am well enough satisfyed there is neither Simony nor any thing that deserves an ill name in the case, yet perhaps some others may be of another opinion. Besides that a thing of this nature if it takes wind is probably spoyled.[1] But I durst trust you with a greater secret then this, who am, Deare Sir

Your Faithfull humble Servant

J M

Dr Sydenham is pretty well recovered again. I shall be glad to receive your answer as soon as you please, though I assure you I am not in hast to alter my condition, and think I have never yet seen the Person that will occasion it, but perhaps may shortly for all the grave counsell you can give me, or I myselfe.

Address: For his Honoured Friend Mr. John Lock.

Endorsed by Locke: Dr *Mapletoft* 11 Oct. 77

[1] Tancred Robinson is said to have been an unsuccessful candidate for the succession to Mapletoft: Ward, *Lives of the Gresham Professors*, p. 279. As he was born about 1658 and did not graduate M.B. until 1679 he is unlikely to have been the present aspirant: *D.N.B.*; Venn.

## 357. Dr. Denis Grenville to Locke, 9/19 November 1677 (*329*, *366*)

B.L., MS. Locke c. 10, ff. 68–9.

Aix Nov: 19th 1677.

Sir

I did in Sept. last, upon my Returne to Montpellier, give you an account of all our Jumbling up and downe (during the spring and summer,) from our leaving of that place till the Date of my letter, together with some Relation of our Good Fortune in finding a very Convenient Refuge from the Heates during the Month of August (till which time wee were not fixt) at the Duke de Lesdigueres his Castle a la Tour D'Aigues,[1] where wee were to remaine till wee tooke up our winter quarters at Aix, which wee had pitch'd on for that purpose and for our Remaining stay till the Spring. And in the same letter I said all that I could to excuse my silence, and to assure you of the Extraordinary value and esteeme I continue to have for you. I shall not repeat what I then writ (tho I have some Jealousy the letter hath not met with you) designing cheifly at present to informe you of our Removall into Aix, where wee have settled our selves till the season and waies invites us hence. It will bee but a piece of Justice to your selfe, to informe you that the cheif Reason, why wee make soe long abode, here at Aix, is our great Happinesse in the acquaintance of worthy Dr. Brouchier,[2] (for which I thinke wee are beholden to you, you first Recommending him to Mr. Walls[3] as hee to us) one of the honestest physitians, and hearty civill men, that I ever met with in my life. Soe usefull a person to us in all Respects, that wee are contented to swallow downe the many Inconveniences occasioned here by the Bigottry and Dearenesse of the Country, and want of English; which wee could not endure had wee not soe good an Allay (tho I must confesse to bee Just to Aix, the Towne is very fine, and our Treatment very good.) as this Excellent and Obliging physitians Company; whoe becomes all things to us, and supplyes all Defects. My sister[4]

[1] A village near Pertuis (Vaucluse), some miles north of Aix. Some notes made by Grenville while residing there in December 1678 are printed in (*Further*) *Remains*, pp. 30–2. The duke is François-Emmanuel de Bonne de Créquy, 1645–81; duke and governor of Dauphiné from 1 January of this year: Saint-Simon, *Mémoires*, ed. A. de Boislisle, 1879–1930, iii. 17; xii. 6–7; and nn.

[2] p. 451, n. 1.

[3] George Wall of Gloucester: p. 430, n. 2; etc.

[4] Joanna, 1635–1709 (1708?), widow of Col. Richard Thornhill and stepmother of Henry Thornhill (p. 478, n. 1); from 1675 styled Lady Joanna; sometime one of Queen Catherine's dressers: Evelyn, *Diary*, ed. de Beer, iv. 9 n.

cannot complaine of her Doctor here for want of Respect or visits. Shee is fitted according to her owne hearts wish. For this kind man comes to us, most commonly, foure times a daye of his owne accord, in the Quallity of a freind, being soe great a Shunner of Fees; that, I thinke, there is not a person in the Whole World, on whom it is more difficult to Fasten a Fee, then himselfe; except one Mr. Lock, whom my sister had once the happinesse to meet withall at Montpillier. In reallity I thinke hee spends all his time with us; but what he bestowes on his patients; whom hee doth not neglect neither, for I find none that complaine of him, being loved and valued by all. It is well for him that hee hath studied well heretofore; for if hee had many such patients, on whom hee bestowed soe much of his time, hee was not like to increase his learning; hee gratyfying us (I thinke in good earnest) with all the time that hee usually imployes to that purpose.

And by this you may Judge (as my sister orders mee to tell you) how much wee are obliged to you for your acquaintance; since wee reape somuch advantage from it even in your absence, and at soe great a distance. My sister commands mee farther to let you know, that if shee did not meet with any of these fresh memento's, shee could never forget your extraordinary kindnesse to her selfe, and troublesome child[1] last winter. The last time I saw our good Doctor I talke of, hee gave mee Commission allsoe to give you his humble service, with this assurance, that if any more freinds come here in Mr. Locks name, they shall meet with noe lesse Respect. Our litle Demoiselle (tho much worse humoured than when I last writ) is ashamed to bee soe monstrously il-natured, as not to acknowledge her obligations to soe great a benefactor, wherefore shee saies, shee presents you with her service, and thankes for your Favours, and many such fine words; but to tell you the plaine truth, I feare there is noe great sincerity in them. For shee hath discovered much hypocrisy, since the last favourable character I gave you of her, to my sisters and my great Trouble; For after some Demure and tollerable carriage, (since I brought her from Montpelier) shee is apostatized into much Rebellion. I know you soe kindly concerned for my poore sisters Quiet and wellffare, as to pardon the impertinency of this Relation I give of her. And soe

[1] Presumably Mary Thornhill, but there may have been a second child in Grenville's party: Grenville, (*Further*) *Remains*, pp. 33, 34. She is the 'little demoiselle' below, and 'Miss' in some later letters.

charitable and Devout, as to add to the many good Counsells you have given, your good wishes and prayers for her Amendment. Hearing noe newes of my last letter (wherein I made request to know where you intended to winter) I will not venture this the same way (tho in that, If I mistake mee not, I followed your owne Direction in your last letter) but convey it to you, according to the advice you gave mee in a former, and send it to Mr. Rosemond,[1] whom I have desired to find you out. I gave you my Reasons, in the last letter I mention to have written to you, why I did not send you a lusty packet of papers, I designe for you, which I shall still suspend till I have the happinesse to heare from you, and bee informed which way you intend to steere, when you leave Paris; if this way, as a Report made us once beleive, I shall have lesse cause to disturb, and torment you, at soe great a distance, when you are like to have a sufficient share of trouble at meeting. There bee few Blessings in this world, I doe assure you Sir, that I desire more, being most sincerely according to (nay beyond) all my past professions

Sir

Your most faithfull and affectionate Freind, and humble servant

DE GRENVILLE

Endorsed by Locke: Dr Grenvil 19 Nov. 77

## *358.* DR. JOHN MAPLETOFT to LOCKE, 22 November 1677 (*356*, 360)

B.L., MS. Locke c. 15, ff. 211–12.

Gresham-College Nov. 22. 77.

Deare Sir

I think you are much in the right when you resolve not to buy a Wife, and doubt not but most of the marryed men in England will be on your side and perhaps for a reason or two more then either you or I yet know of. But I am not in so much hast as you suppose to putt on the Yoke, be the Terms what they will, and beleive that in the Spring you will find me in Statu quo, and not advanced at the most above the degree of a Seeker. Only I could not well refuse the importunity of a Person that I am obliged to, and desires to make me

[1] p. 483, n. 2.

more so, and when he hath done will think himselfe still in my Debt. This very afternoon I had a glimpse of Mr Charas at the Royal Society, and only just time to salute him.[1] If he would have stayed a little longer wee could have shewed him about 200 animalls, by Dr. Wallis's computation, in the fifth or sixth part of a drop of Water. Wee had such storys written us from Holland and laught at them as perhaps you may doe at this But seeing is beleiving and to that I referre you.[2] I made your Complement to Dr. Sydenham who would return it under his hand but that he cannot prevayl with himselfe to write A Monsieur Monsieur which he rayles at as a very impertinent way of adres. I thank you for the Tully[3] the Doctor and you have provided, and if you will take the trouble of adding to it a Plutarch Gr. and Lat. of the best Paris Edition[4] faire and well-bound (which will cost here 4ll. sterl.) and bring both with your Bookes you will yet farther oblige him whom Matrimony itselfe shall never make other then

Deare Sir

Your most Assured Friend and Servant

JOHN MAPLETOFT.

Address: A Monsieur Monsieur Lock Gentilhomme Anglois chez Mr. Charas maistre Apothecaire dans la ruë de Boucherie aux Fauxbourg St. Germain A Paris

Endorsed by Locke: Dr. Mapletoft 22 Nov. 77

## *359.* MRS. MARGARET BLOMER to LOCKE, [22 November/2 December 1677] (*267*)

B.L., MS. Locke c. 4, f. 12. Identifiable as the note received by Locke between 6 and 7 p.m. on Thursday, 2 December, N.S. (as he was in constant attendance on the next two days there would be no occasion for another summons). Lady Northumberland was suffering from trigeminal neuralgia.

[1] Robert Hooke (p. 621 n.) says that Charas (p. 485, n. 2) this day presented to the Society his *Pharmacopée royale*: *Diary, 1672–80*, ed. H. W. Robinson and W. Adams, 1935, p. 329. No minutes exist for this day's meeting: Birch, *Royal Society*, iii. 352 n.

[2] The animals in 'pepper water', etc. (infusoria), were shown by Hooke; Wallis is the mathematician: p. 280, n. 1. Mapletoft alludes to two letters from A. van Leeuwenhoek (1632–1723; the microscopist; *N.N.B.W.*) which were read to the Society on 1, 15, and 22 February and 5 April, and printed in *Philosophical Transactions*, xii. 821–31, 844–6. There was evidently much discussion, which was resumed in October and November: notices in Birch.

[3] p. 503. The doctor is Blomer: Locke, Journal, 10 February 1678, N.S.

[4] The only recorded complete edition in Greek and Latin published in Paris prior to 1677 is that of 1624, in two volumes, folio.

The diagnosis is based on Locke's notes on the case, which were given by Lord King to the Royal College of Physicians (Fox Bourne, i. 384 n.); on the succeeding letters; and on his Journal, 2–16 December, N.S. The case is described by Dr. Dewhurst in *Journal of the History of Medicine*, xii (1957), 21–36.

My Lady sends you now her coach and desires you would come in it, and bring with you the best blistring plaister you can thinke on for a violent rume in her teeth which puts her to very greate torment, and shee is not willing To try any more french experiments, haveing found them all ineffectual. her Ladyship will have the better oppinion of the plaisters if you see them made which you may doe, haveing the Coach at your dispose to waite at the apothycarys till you have don.

Your servant
M: BLOMER

Address: pour Monsr Locke–
Endorsed by Locke: Mrs Blomer 3 Dec. 77

## 360. LOCKE to Dr. JOHN MAPLETOFT, 24 November/ 4 December 1677 (i) (*358*, 361)

*European Magazine*, xv (1789), 185–6. Locke this day sent Mapletoft three letters or two letters and a note; the note failed to arrive by 3 December, O.S., and is now lost: nos. 361, *363*. This is clearly the first of the two surviving letters. They arrived probably on 29 November, as Mapletoft and Sir Charles Scarborough discussed them on the morning of the 30th. Answered by no. *363*.

Paris, 4 Dec. 1677.

Sir,

I never had a more unwelcome occasion of writing to you than now, believing I can scarce send you more unacceptable news than that of the illnesse of a person whom not only you and I, but all the world have soe just reason to esteeme and admire. On Thursday night last I was sent for to my Lady Ambassadrice, whom I found in a fit of such violent and exquisite torment, that (though she be, as you know, a person of extraordinary temper, and I have seen her even in the course of this distemper endure very great pain with a patience that seemd to feele noe thing) it forced her to such cries and shrieks as you would expect from one upon the rack, to which I beleive her's was an equal torment, which extended itself all over the right side of her face and mouth. When the fit came, there was, to use my Lady's own expression of it, as it were a flash of fire all of a suddaine shot into all those parts, and at every one of those twitches, which made her shreeke out, her mouth was constantly drawn on the right side towards the right eare by repeated convulsive motions, which were constantly accompanied by her cries. This was all that appeard outwards in these fits according to the exactest observation I could make, haveing had but too many oportunitys to doe it. These violent fits terminated on a suddaine, and then my Lady seemd to be perfectly well, excepting only a dull pain which ordinarily remained in her teeth on that side, and an uneasinesse in that side of her tongue which she phansided to be swollen on that side, which yet when I lookd on it, as I often did, had not the least alteration in it in colour, bignesse, or any other way, though it were one of her great complaints that there was a scalding liquor in her fits shot into all that half of her tongue. She had usually a presentation of the fit by a little throbing upon her gum of the lower jaw, where she had this summer a tooth drawn; and a like throbing in the upper jaw, just over against it. In all this time of her being ill she has not found the least pain in all the other side of her face or teeth, which hath soe wholy possessed the right side that it went even to the very tip of her tongue, and the last tooth before on that side.—With all this torment that she endurd, when the fit was over there was not the least appearance of any alteration any where in her face, nor inflamation or swelling in her mouth or cheeke; very little defluction of rhewm more then what the contraction of those parts in those fits might cause. Speaking was apt to put her into these fits; sometimes opening her mouth to take any thing, or touching her gums, especially in the places where she used to finde those throbings: pressing that side of her face by lying on it were also apt to put her into fits. These fits lasted sometimes longer, sometimes shorter; were more or less violent, without any regularity, and the intervals between them at the longest not halfe an hower, commonly much shorter. It being night when I was cald, I saw noe roome for any thing else to be done but to endeavour to give her present ease by topical anodyn applications to those parts of her gums where the first beginnings of her fits appeare, which had soe good an effect that that night she had two or three howers rest togeather without any fits, besides some other litle intervalls of sleepe. But the next day[1] the fits returning, tho' not altogeather

[1] Friday, 3 December N.S.

soe frequent and violent as they had been, yet bad enough to make us feare they might, I thought it necessary to purge her Honour, for besides that I saw noe indication for bleeding. My Lady had beene soe often and soe much bleeded on the like occasion this sommer, without any reliefe, that there was litle to be hoped from it, and I thought it ought to be very waryly made use after soe much taken already. The purge wrought seven or eight times, the fits continuing still by intervalls after her purge; soe at night, as you know is usuall, she tooke a quieting cordial. The first part of the night she had her fits very severely, but the latter part hath been more favourable, and till about nine or ten of the clock that I write this,[1] there remains only an ordinary tooth acke, the violence of those fits being ceased; but whether we are not to apprehend their returne in this extraordinary case I cannot be over confident, two or three days of ordinary tooth acke having preceded them. I wish with all my heart you were here, both to assist my Lady by your better skill, and to ease me of a part of that sollicitude I am under, haveing the care of a person of her consideration wholy upon me; she haveing had soe litle successe with the French phycitians here this summer, in the like case, wherein for eight days togeather their applications did her noe good, that she is resolved to trie them noe more. If I durst interpose my opinion in a case soe extraordinary as this, I should aske whether you did not thinke this to proceed from some affections in the nerves in the place where the tooth was drawn, which draws all the rest into consent and convulsive motions on this side, and that perhaps some sharpness in her blood may contribute to it. I beg your opinion, and of whoever else of the ablest of our phycitians you shall think fit to consult with, but I wish much more for your company, than your opinion without it. I am, Sir,

Your most humble Servant,
JOHN LOCKE.

There is some mixture of vapours I also apprehend with the other symptons.

My Lady Harvey[2] thinks it very convenient Dr. Scarborough[3]

[1] On Saturday morning, 4 December N.S.

[2] Elizabeth, *c.* 1639–1702, sister of Ralph Montagu and widow of Sir Daniel Harvey, the ambassador to Turkey: *Miscellanea Genealogica et Heraldica*, 2nd ser. iii (1890), 331; L. Petit, *La Fontaine et Saint-Evremond*, 1953, pp. 44–59, etc.

[3] p. 533, n. 1.

should be consulted, and certainly you cannot consult an abler man.

I beg your pardon for my ill writing, it is in haste and in feare. The weather here is very cold.

Address: For Dr. John Mapletoft, at Gresham Colledg, London.

## 361. Locke to Dr. John Mapletoft, 24 November/4 December 1677 (ii) (360, 362)

*European Magazine*, xv (1789), 186, which includes the two notes. See no. 360 n. Answered by no. *363*.

Paris, 4 Dec. 77.
At One in the Afternoon.

You will certainly thinke me in great distraction, when after a letter and note that I sent you already this morning, I now send you this third. But it is to tell you, that my Lady upon a little increase of her paine, apprehending the violent returne of her fits, hath since the writing my last note, had a blistering plaster put on to her neck.[a] In a litle fit she had since, the violence of the pain not being soe great as it usually is, she had the liberty to shew me her tongue, which she had some reason to imagine swollen, all the left side of it being drawn up dureing the fit, and soe seemd thicker as if it were swollen; but as soon as ever the fit is over, it returnes to its natural state, and there is noe discernable difference between the sides of it, nor the least impediment in my Lady's speech, or alteration in her voice. She has, especially when the fits are most violent, a drinesse in her lips more than ordinary[b]. It may not perhaps be amisse to let you know also, that during all the pain and disorder my Lady has suffered, her temper[1] has been as good and her pulse as equall, sedate and regular, as that of any one in the best health, only sometimes the violence of her pains puts her into a litle sweat, but as soon as that leaves her, she returns presently to her ordinary good temper. I am willing you should know as

[a] *Addition by Locke?* Inter scapulas. [b] *Added by Locke* And my Lady Harvey tells me, that several days before the comeing of these fits, finding this unusual drieness of her lips, she apprehended she should have them, she having particularly observed this symptome to accompany those fits she had in the sommer.

[1] Her bodily condition: *O.E.D.* Locke uses the word also with the significance state of mind, temperament, as on p. 576.

much as I doe of all the circumstances of her case. And I should be glad you knew better what would perfectly cure it, tho' I wish heartily it may be over before your answer come. I am, Sir,

Your most humble Servant

J. L.

## 362. Locke to Dr. John Mapletoft, [25] Nov./[5] Dec. 1677 (361, *363*)

*European Magazine*, xv (1789), 273. In the date the day from the contents and by comparison with Locke's Journal. Received by Mapletoft on 3 December, O.S. Answered by no. *363*.

Paris, Sunday night, . . .[a] Dec. 77.

Sir,

I wish this would make so much hast as to come to you before the ill news I sent you yesterday; at least, I hope it will not leave you long under that paine which I know you will be in till you receive better. It is therefore with great satisfaction that I tell you, that notwithstanding my Lady's feares yesterday, upon a little returne of some, though not of the violent sort of fits, and my apprehension (for who in soe extraordinary a case, and for soe extraordinary a person, would not apprehend all things) it hath pleased God soe to blesse those things my Lady hath used, that she had very good rest the last night, and her sleepe, which nature itself voluntarily offerd, was very seldome interrupted by any pains that made her complaine. The progresse of this day hath not been unsuitable to the precedent night. My Lady continues to get ground upon the distemper, which now, for the most part, is not much more then the grumbling of the tooth-ach, with now and then some shootings, which reach now but from that part where the tooth was formerly drawn to the fore teeth on that side; soe that I hope by the next oportunity I shall be able to send you word that she is perfectly well. I must beg your pardon for the many faults in my yesterday's writing, which hast and hurry made me commit; for both my letter and myself being cald for whilst I was writeing the first of the three, I was affraid I should misse the post, and I was faine to hudle up things with lesse method and order then was necessary in such a case. But since I hope it will be of noe

[a] *Presumably a defect in the manuscript.*

ill consequence to my Lady, and that the businesse will be over before your advice can arrive, I promise myself your excuse and favourable interpretation.

I am, Sir,
Your most humble servant,
JOHN LOCKE.

Notwithstanding these present good circumstances, yet I continue my request to you to hasten away the best advice you can send me, whatever may happen; for one cannot be too well fortified against such an enemy, who hath already made more then one assault, and after a cessation returnd.

*363.* DR. JOHN MAPLETOFT to LOCKE, 3 December 1677 (362, 364), with four enclosures: Dr. J. Micklethwaite: advice on Lady Northumberland's case; Sir Charles Scarburgh, Dr. E. Dickinson, and Dr. T. Sydenham, letters to Mapletoft 30 November–3 December 1677.

B.L., MSS. Locke c. 15, ff. 213–20; c. 19, f. 164 (Sydenham's letter). Sydenham's letter was printed by Dr. K. Dewhurst in *The Practitioner*, clxxv (September 1955), 317–18; in his *Sydenham*, pp. 169–71; Mapletoft's letter and all four enclosures, in *Journal of the History of Medicine*, xii (1957), 28–34. From Mapletoft's postscript to it Sydenham's letter is likely to have been enclosed with the other three. Answers nos. 360–2; answered by no. 364.

Gresham-College Dec. 3. st.v. 77.

Sir

Upon the receit of your 2 Letters dated Dec. 4 (for the Third you mention came not to my hand,) My Lord[1] commanded me to advise with the now President Dr. Micklethwait, Sir Charls Scarburgh, and Dr. Dickinson, the result of whose thoughts upon my Ladys case I send you inclosed in their own hands, all which are left to your Discretion and Skill to manage as you think best. I am very glad to find that you have been so successfull allready as your last,[2] which I received this day, acquaints us to the great joy of those that honour my Lady and love you, and that you are like to have so little need of the Auxiliarys I herewith send you. When you have

[1] Ralph Montagu, styled 'My Lord' as ambassador. He was in England on a short visit at about this time: Browning, *Danby*, i. 255–6; ii. 297–9.

[2] No. 362.

presented my humble duty to my Lady I desire you to lett her know that I read your last letter this morning to my Lady E. Percy[1] who had the good fortune you wished me, to heare of my Ladys recovery before she did of that Extremity she had been in, of which I afterwards gave her some account. I write you no news save what you will not, I beleive, receive from other hands and you are a little concernd in, viz That on St Andrew's day which was Friday last Sir Joseph Williamson was chosen President of the Royall Society,[2] Dr. Grew and Mr. Hook Secretarys (Mr. Oldenbugh being dead as you have heard I presume)[3] and Mr. Hill Treasurer in the room of Mr. Colwall, who had held it 11 yeares and yet bought never a foot of Land, either in Parnassus or elsewhere.[4] My Lord Brouncker was not present being lame of the gout.[5] An Annuall choice, they say, is like to be kept up and a new one every yeare to be chosen. Sir Joseph had 27 votes and my Lord only 13. Pray be so kind as to requite this little piece of News with what will concern us both more, the health of our Honoured Lady, of which I desire an account, if you please by the next opportunity. My service, I pray, to the good Doctor and his Wife[6] to whom I wish a good houre if it be not past allready. When you look on this you will find you have no great need to make excuses for ill writing, and for the future I will abate you that line upon condition of your pardon which I shall allways need but never mean to ask more, nor to need upon any other occasion, as being

Sir

Your most Faithfull humble Servant

JOHN MAPLETOFT.

Address: A Monsieur Monsieur Lock chez Monseigneur L'Ambassadeur du Roy d'Angleterre a l'Hostel de Turenne. à Paris

Endorsed by Locke: Dr. Mapletoft 3 Dec. 77

[1] Lady Northumberland's daughter: p. 370, n. 3.

[2] St. Andrew's day, 30 November, is the day on which the Society holds its anniversary meeting. Williamson (p. 256 n.) was elected as a result of the fellows' dissatisfaction with the then state of the Society: Evelyn, *Diary*, ed. de Beer, iv. 125 and n.

[3] Nehemiah Grew, M.D., 1641–1712: *D.N.B.*; Robert Hooke: p. 621. Oldenburg (p. 423 n.) died probably on 5 September: Hooke, *Diary*.

[4] Abraham Hill, 1635–1721, scientist, collector, etc.: *D.N.B.*; he had been treasurer from 1663 to 1665. Daniel Colwall, d. 1690, scientist and philanthropist; treasurer since 1665: ibid.

[5] William Brouncker, *c.* 1620–84; second Viscount Brouncker (Ireland) 1645; mathematician: ibid. He had been president of the Society ever since his nomination in its first charter in 1662.

[6] Dr. and Mrs. Blomer.

## *363. Dr. J. Mapletoft, 3 December 1677*

[First enclosure (Micklethwaite):][1]

Upon consideration of the Case of that most excellent Lady soe very well stated, it seemes cleer, that the blood is not in fault, but some pungent vapor or serum or both that affects the nerves to qualifie which is our great business. I doe not apprehend any necessity of bleeding and but litle of purgeing which in case of vapors will rather aggravate paine. but if by reason of the antecedent Cause it be thought necessarie, it must be done by such purges as make the least commotion in the humours and best take of their acrimonie, consideration being had to such as usually have best agreed with her Honor heertofore. quære de usu Calomel in Cons ros pallid. 4to vel 5to quoque die. dieb intermittentibus sumet dec. amar cum sen et agar ana ʒ i coct. and all along use decoct sars chinæ, ras c c eboris, santal alb glycyr, salv; pro potu Con vel quantum poterit. but because the paine is the most urgent, it will be necessarie to give opiates inwardly and apply litle sponges or linnen dipt in spir of Castor and liquid laudanum to the part pained. and apply large blisters under the eare and near the armepit of the side affected and if there may be gott ashes of the barke of ash and put them into a very fine cloth and dip it in vinegre and binde it to the place you would blister it many times raises a blister in $\frac{1}{2}$ or $\frac{1}{4}$ of an hower. this decoction is also good. ℞ Cortic radic hyosycami ℥iss seu eiusdem ʒ iii pyrethri rad ℥ ss Caryophyllorum ℈vss seu Coriander ʒ iii Coq in aq font ad lib i ss Colaturæ adde acet opt ℥ ii take Cochleari calidé sæpius and after a while held in the mouth spit it out. I would commend to her honor the frequent use of sage in pouder ad ʒ ii cum sacchar vel sine bis in die I meane ʒ i pro dosi as her Ladyshipp can get it downe and often, trahato fumus succini ore et naribus. Let her Honor have a care of all things that sharpen the blood and juyces or raise vapor. and lastly I desier her Ladyshipp to make an issue in the arme of that side she is most afflicted. I pray God Almighty add his blessing.

JOHN MICKLETHWAIT

Nov 30 77

Endorsed by Locke: Dr Micklethwait 30 Nov. 77 Dentium dolor convulsivus

[1] 1612–82; M.D. 1638; president of the Royal College of Physicians 1676–81; knighted 1679: ibid.; H.M.C., *Lindsey MSS.*, p. 30.

[Second enclosure (Scarburgh):][1]

November the 30th. 1677.

Sir

The Case of the Countess of Northumberland, which this morning we read togeather, although it be extraordinary, yet I have severall times met with the like, though not in all points the same. Undoubtedly some peculiar disaffection of the nerve of that part from whence the tooth was drawn is a great cause of those sharp and scalding pains, though not the only one, for that Her Honour was before much vexed with the tooth-ach. So that the main original is seated in the blood and nerval juices. The application of vesicatories in the paroxysme was proper and necessary, and ought to be as near the part affected as may be. As upon the vertebraes of the neck and back, and chiefly behind the ears and so downwards along the sides of the neck, as large as may be conveniently made, and kept running as long as well can be. And indeed those behind the ears may be continued from time to time in the nature of an issue, and very likely to a considerable benefit. Besides in the extremity of a fitt Cupping glasses may be used, either with scarification or without. Also leeches to the Gumme it self, which is very often found a present relief. If these prevail not, the last and I think most sure remedy is to cauterize the gumme downe to the very bottom, where the tooth was fixed, and, upon its drawing, the nerve lacerated, or otherwise offended, perchance by a fissure of the loculus of the tooth. The way of cauterizing is by such a kind of instrument as is frequently here used in the cauterizing of the Tonsills of the throat, and without any offence to the adjacent parts. This Sir, is the summe of what at present I can think most usefull in respect of the part it self. For as to other applications of ointments, ol: Succini etc. outwardly, or waters proper to be taken into the mouth upon those convulsions, which the letter mentions, I think needless to prescribe to that gentleman now attending, and of such excellent knowledge and judgement. For it cannot be certainly determined whether hot cephalick waters as Aq. Lavendulæ comp. Aq. Pæoniæ comp. Tinct. Castorei or the like may agree, though they are commonly used and relieve the brain and nerves in convulsions. Yet I should advise to make use of such by way of Gargle, either simply by themselves or els diluted with milder waters at discretion. Now for the temperating of the blood and humors of

[1] 1615–94; M.D. 1646; knighted 1669: *D.N.B.*

the body I conceive a constant diet drink to be necessary after this kind of form.

℞ Sarsæ parill. ℥ iiij. Rad. Chinæ. Santali albi ana ℥ iss. Ras. Corn. Cerv. Eboris ana ʒ x. Infund in lb. x Aq. fontanæ per noctem super ciner: calidos, vase probè obturato, deinde mane coquantur, addendo Passularum integrarum et mundatarum ℥ iiij, ad consumptionem partis mediæ circiter, subque finem injiciendo Santali rubri concis. ʒ ij. Trajiciatur liquor per manicam, et per subsidentiam depuretur ad lb. iiij. atque in lagenis condatur pro potu ordinario, Quo utatur per dies Quadraginta. Besides purgations at seasonable times will be convenient. And because I suspect that in this case much may be Hysterical I should advise such a sort of familiar pil. ℞ Aloes rosat. Pil. Aggregat. Galbani colati ana gr. ix. Castorei. pul. gr. ij vel iiij. Ol. succini chym. gutt. iiij. Misce. Fiant pil. numero iiij. sub horam somni sumendæ bis vel ter in septimanâ, Cum levi custodiâ. Lastly Issues are to be considered, if this malady continue. And because bleeding hath been often administred with little or no success, I dare not at this distance pronounce any wayes concerning it. Only I think that leeches may be safely applyed to the Temples and behind the ears in extremities. Worthy Sir, this is all at present I can with safety and reason say in a case but once related to me, and concerning so honorable a person to whose state of body I am wholy a stranger, yet alwaies an honorer of herself and family, and most ready to serve Her Ladyship to the utmost. Sir I am

your most humble Servant
CHARLES SCARBURGH.

Address: For his much honoured Friend Dr Mapletoff. These.
Endorsed by Locke: Sir: C. Scarburgh 30 Nov. 77 Dentium Dolor convulsivus

[Third enclosure (Dickinson):][1]

Decemb. 3. 77.

Sir

From the Hystory of the Symptoms, I conceive the distemper of the right Honorable the Countess of Northumberland is not of a Sanguineous, but Nerval kinde; and doth depend partly on the weakness of the Nerves branching to the left side of the Face; and partly on the pravity of the Nerval juice.

[1] Edmund Dickinson, 1624–1707; M.D. 1656: *D.N.B.* Letter below, no. *1632*.

The weakness of those Nerves seeme to have it's Origine from the streeching[a] and tearing of some Nerves in the drawing of a tooth on that side.

The pravity of the Nerval matter may be occasion'd by the dyscrasy of Liver, or Spleen.

The same il-condition'd matter was formerly the occasion of the frequent difficulty and shortness of breathing to which her Honour hath bin soe much inclind:

The Releife is to be attempted by strengthning of the weak'ned Nerves; and by altering of the deprav'd matter in them.

For the strengthning of the Nerves I recommend the use of the Queen of Hungary's water, by bathing that side of the Face often with it; and by often holding some of it in the mouth. Aqua Lavendulæ composita may be us'd in the same. I præferr the Hungary water if well made. being an efficacious, and more sweet and cleanly remedy.

For the altering and sweet'ning of the acid and sharpe matter in the Nerves, I propose the use of Bezoardicum minerale solare made according to the description of it by Hartman[1] and Schroder,[2] which being rightly made, is a pleasant and efficacious remedy, eight or tenn granes of it given every night att bed-time, and (at the least) two houres after a light Supper, in two spoonfulls of Cowslipp and sage water æqually mixed, another spoonfull being dranck uppon it. This remedy is to be continued a good while.

The Nerves will be the sooner strengthned, and the matter in them better alterd, if it be less'ned by a Blyster behinde the Eare on the weake side, which must be kept running as long as may be. I have in the like Case made an Issue behind the Eare, and have seen it very effectuall.

And if some proper Purgation of it be made once in a month, (or of'tner as need shall be) by the Resin of Jalap, or Scammony finely powdered and mixed with a spoonfull of the Syrup of violets, or Cowslipps. fifteen granes of either of them (more or less according to her honour's strength) may be soe given.

E DICKINSON

Endorsed by Locke: Dr Dickinson 3. Dec. 77 Dentium dolor convulsivus

[a] *Doubtful reading; rewritten and perhaps deleted;* and *also perhaps deleted.*

[1] Presumably Johann Hartmann, *Praxis Chymiatrica*: p. 326, n. 1. For bezoar see no. *3057*.

[2] Presumably Johann Schroeder, M.D. (*A.D.B.*), *Pharmacopeia Medico-chymica*, 1641 and later editions. Locke possessed a copy of the fourth, 1656: L.L., no. 2590.

[Fourth enclosure (Sydenham):]

Dear Doctor

At your earnest request I have thought on the case of the Lady, the fomes[1] of whose distemper I doe not judge to be any ulcer or any venenatt quality else upon the gumm (where it may be supposed some laceration of a nerve was made by that operation) but to be a hystericall quality in the bloud discharging its selfe entirely upon that place and side, where occasion was given by the drawing of the tooth, together with the payne of the operation and the apprehension therof, for all the raies to be contracted, after the manner of a Clavus[2] in the head, or that other distemper like it, of a violent and exquisitt paine about the temporall a⟨rtery⟩[a] which is wont to come and goe and may, as ⟨with a⟩[a] Clavus, be covered with a shilling.

As to what is to be don. I conceave that ⟨while⟩[a] bleeding and purging are immediatly contraindic⟨ated⟩[a] in that they encrease the tumult in the m⟨ ⟩[a] both are absoluttly necessary in respect of ⟨ob⟩teyning[a] the quieting and settling those vapo⟨urs which⟩[a] otherwise very often will not admitt therof, as I know by certaine experience: but after such evacuation easy quieters will doe it. Wherfore were she one of those poor people whom my lott engages me to attend (for I cure not the rich till my being in the grave makes me an Authority) I would take the following course. I would take 8 ounces of bloud from the arme of the affected side. The next morning would give the following pills. ℞ mass. pil. coch. ma: ℈i. mercurii dulc. gr. xv. resinæ Jalapii gr. iiij. balsami Peru. gutt. iij. ms. f. pil numero iiij. Cap. summo mane. Not stirring out of her bedd that day. That night quiett not with Laud. liq. but with Mathewes Pills, they being much better in that they cause a mador[3] the next morning, and so a profitable discharge. The same I would give every night for 3 weekes. The dose is from 14 to 18 graines and are as saff as butter I would keepe her to milke and water, watergruell, roasted apples and such like fleshless diett for 8 or 10 dayes, to destroy the ferment the sooner. Take heed of

[a] *Page torn.*

[1] Touchwood or tinder, the Latin word. It was used figuratively in English in the seventeenth century; in the eighteenth it denoted the morbific matter of a disease (earliest quotation 1773): *O.E.D.*

[2] A corn, whitlow, area of hard flesh, etc. The Latin word.

[3] Sweat: ibid.

irritating the gumm, but rather in extremity of paine lett her hold a pledgett imbued with some dropps of laudanum liq. keeping it between her teeth halfe an houre and then taking in an ⟨o⟩th⟨er⟩[a] till her payne cease, which will not be long. If she hath bin allready sufficiently purged, to bleed only may be sufficient and then to come to quieting. When she is out of the fitt lett her guard agaynst the impulse of the disease upon her jawes, by dabbing them with ragg wett with Planten water wherin hath bin dropped spiritt of vitrioll to make itt a little sharp, which by its astrictoriness will defend the part from the deflux better then any thing else; but this must not be don till she hath bin a pretty while well of her fitts. This is my opinion, of which make what use you please. I am very affectionattly

Your humble servant
THO: SYDENHAM

Pell-Mell Dec. 1º 1677.

[Postscript by Mapletoft:]

I thought it not best to mention these our Friend's directions for reasons you may know,[1] yet I beleivd you would not be displeased to have his opinion too in a case of this difficulty and concernment, which you may make use of as you find cause. I have sent by Mr. Hill ℥i. of Mathew's Pill which I have superscribed Philon. Angl. ℥i. and directed to you. If you think the name will prejudice the advise you may take it upon yourselfe. He advises also a Galbanum plaster to the navell.

Address (by Mapletoft): For yourselfe. Lege solus.

Endorsed by Locke: *Dentium* Dolor Dr. Sydenham 1º Dec. 77[b]

[a] *Page torn and rubbed.* [b] Dentium Dolor *written with different pen and ink from the rest.*

---

[1] Sydenham was on bad terms with the College of Physicians; there is no precise information and the causes of the divergence are unknown: Dewhurst, *Sydenham*, p. 43; Clark, *Royal College*, i. 319.

## 364. Locke to Dr. John Mapletoft, 12/22 December 1677 (*363*, *368*)

*European Magazine*, xv (1789), 273–4. Answers no. *363*, fourth enclosure; answered by no. *368*.

Paris, 22 Dec. 77.

Haveing gotten another litle parcel of time before the post goes, I cannot but tell you, upon reading our friend's letter, I was ready to cry out, The spirit of the Prophets is upon the Sons of the Prophets;[1] I haveing in what I have done here not only proceeded by the same method, but used the very remedys he directed as to the maine; for besides pil. cochia and mercurius dulcis, which was the purge I used, though I had not phil. Anglic. yet by adding some volatile salts to laudan. I provided for sweating. Bleeding I should perhaps have used in another patient; but it not being necessary here, I forbore soe much as to mention it, and that upon several considerable reasons. For prevention, I like mightily the plantain water and spirit of vitriol. I had proposed to my Lady something to the same intention before, which was often washing her mouth and gums, her temples, eyes, and behinde her ears with cold water: this I thought likelyer to harden and strengthen the nerves and parts then any of those hot oyles and spirits which are commended, and which I cannot but think likelyer to doe harme then good in this case. Indeed I had not thought of any acid spirits in the water; and perhaps the feare of irritation hinderd me from thinking beyond soft innocent spring water; for he that had seen her in these fits, and how touchy the parts were upon almost any application, (for there was but that one which he mentions which did not upon triall provoke a fit that I saw) would be apt to apprehend any thing that was pungent; but since I read it in his letter I have reflected on it, and thinke it the most proper thing that can be used. I have proposed also a totall abstinence from wine, light suppers, and early going to bed, and great care of taking cold; which I thinke is not to be donne by keeping herself very warme (which in my opinion is the readyest way to get colds), but by being and exercising frequently in the aire; and as a meanes to obleige her to that, as well as for its owne sake, I propose the takeing a slight dose of Goddard's drops, viz. gt. vi. every other morning, and walking after it in the open aire, or at least as often as the weather shall be seasonable for

[1] Apparently varied from 2 Kings 2: 15: 'And when the sons of the prophets . . saw him, they said, The spirit of Elijah doth rest on Elisha.'

such walking. This I thinke might strengthen the genus nervosum. For however I am fully satisfied that hystericall vapours joyn in to increase the tumult and disorder in the nerves on that side, and that I believe the drawing of those two teeth, especially the last, hath injurd some nerve, and soe makes it very apt to be provoked, and draw its neighbours into consent; yet by what my Lady has informd me, since the violence of her pains have been over, I have reason to suspect there is an ancienter fault in the nerves of that side: and I know not whether an excrescence she has on the ⟨amygdalus⟩[a1] on that side may not occasion or contribute to it, considering what communication there is between the nerves and glandules, this fault in that glandule being of an ancient standing. For having asked her diverse questions concerning her teeth a great way backwards, she told me that she hath heretofore, long before any of these fits, been frequently troubled with extreme violent itching in her gums on that side (which she hath had now since the fit is gon) and sometimes twitchings, which seem to me to be from some fault in the nerves, or succus nervosus, which you please, on that side. I have proposed also the avoiding the evening aire about sun seting, and at least an hower after, which I thinke very apt to cause defluxions; and I suspect what would cause an ordinary tooth-ach in another, or heretofore in my Lady, will put her into these fits. I desire you two to consider of these things togeather, and give me your opinion upon these, and your advice of any thing else that you can thinke on, as probable to secure as much as may be the future. Pray remember me very kindely to him, for I am both his and your very affectionate freinde and humble servant,

J. LOCKE.

## 365. SIR JOHN BANKS to LOCKE, 27 December 1677 (352, 367)

B.L., MS. Locke c. 3, ff. 90–1. Answered by no. 367.

Sir

I have receaved yours of the 22th instant, from whence (however I may want it in reference to any other point les worthy my givinge

[a] *The printed text leaves a blank space; word supplied from Locke's Journal.*

[1] The almond of the ear, 'a small lymphatic gland over the mastoid process or below the external ear': *O.E.D.*, svv. Amygdal, Almond.

either you, or my selfe any further trouble about) I have at length the Content of hearinge from you, that you are now fully satisfyed in all that concernes your owne particular, it beinge that which (whatever caution you seeme still to beare about you in reference to mony) I shall never thinke my selfe in danger of payinge to deare for, soe long as I remaine under my present assurances of havinge the charge of your satisfaction from me, amply answered by as great to my selfe from you, with regard to my sonn, on whose behalfe (least he may have omitted it) I doe by the inclosed endeavor to answer your francknesse, in the makinge him privy to the last of yours; Desyinge (that since by his request, I am freed from the apprehension I had, of it's becomminge matter of discouragement, to him) you will admitt of his request of deliveringe up to you the care of receavinge and disposinge of the whole monnys which the occations of both of you shall call for, by which, and that entire resignation of himselfe to your direction, which he promises in his said letter, and I question not his full complyance with, nothinge will I hoope remaine that should make me doubtfull of that successe of your care and kindnesse I have ever promised my selfe, and rest now more then ever assured of on his behalfe, remaininge with the tender of my wives and my humble services, and desyringe as oft as your affaires permit we may have the account of your wellfares,

Sir Your assured freind and servant

JOHN BANKS

Lincolns in feilds 27th. December. 1677

Address: To Mr Locke Thesse Paris

Endorsed by Locke: Sir J: Banks 27 Sept. 77

## *366.* DR. DENIS GRENVILLE to LOCKE, 29 December 1677/8 January 1678 (*357*, *372*)

B.L., MS. Locke c. 10, ff. 70–1.

Aix. Jan. 8th. 167$\frac{7}{8}$

Deare Sir

I cannot have soe much patience as to delay the signifying to you the Great satisfaction I have in the receipt of yours of the 22th of last month soe long time as to dispose in order and make up the large packet I have threatned you with and still designe you. Espetially Dr. Brouchier and my sister, (whoe are at my Ellbow and exceeding Joyfull to heare of you.) pressing mee to write by this first post (tho I have litle time) the one to inclose his letter; and the other to repeat the sense of your Favours and her thankefull acknowledgements, which if I did performe according to her mind and Order, would bee in more words, and more approaching to Complements, than I am willing to use to soe good a freind. I am very much troubled that you did not receive my letter which I writt you in Sept: last; It would have given you some satisfaction, that I had reteined as great an Esteem for you, notwithstanding a summers silence, as if I had persecuted you with letters. I shall not now give you the trouble of any Repetition, since your letter tells me, that you did not suspect any unkindnesse, which I hope I shall never give you any just Occasion to doe, tho I will not sweare but that I may tumble into such an ill appearance as some months silence. For I will not Conceale from one whom I desire to make a *Bosome freind* that I have been sometimes guilty, as well as often accused of the like Fault. Namely, that, tho I doe write in a yeare as many lines, as most men alive in my Circumstances, to freinds, yet I come still short, of what they expect, and I intend. I troubling them some whiles with too many (as is like to bee your case ere long) and other whiles with too few. Tis one of the things that I designe to learne of you, I meane, somewhat of more Evennesse, and steadinesse in my Correspondences, as well as Actions. You will finde mee, (when you know mee better,) sometimes very soon distracted, and disordered, and even allmost unfitted (with small crosses) for reading, writing, or indeed any kind of Imployment, And at other times Bustle thorough a series of Distractions, able to crack a stronger Braine than mine owne. Sometimes appeare to my freinds, (that may least know mee), a litle negligent of them; and at other times prove my selfe Freindly (if it bee possible soe to bee) even to Excesse. To bee speake the truth I am made up in a manner of Contradictions; and know not well yet what to terme my selfe. When you and I are better acquainted I hope better to understand my selfe; This is all I can boast of, that tho I am full of great Faults (wanting the Magnæ virtutes to Ballance) I have had the good luck to have been rejected by none of those Excellent persons (and I thanke God I have met with some such for Freinds) whoe have once owned mee. I promise my selfe, that my Fate will not bee worse in reference to your selfe. And I desire this favour from you, vizt. That you will continue of the same mind, which you seeme to bee of in your letter, when you say *that you doe never Conclude your selfe abandoned of your freinds till they tell you soe.* If you please to stay till that time, applying it to mine owne particular, and all will bee sure enough. Had I had the happinesse to have enjoyed you personally till this time; I doubt not but to have fortified you against worse appearances than last summers fault. I will terme it a fault though I have enough to say for my selfe (were wee Bouche a Bouche, as the french man saies, I take it) to evince that it is not an unpardonable one. Doe but pardon the Extreame I may run into, on the other side, before wee have done, and all will bee well. I doe not intend, I doe assure you, Sir, to leave you soe. Noe, Remember, I must have my booke out of you first. My Judgment is the same that it ever was of mr Lock. I value not only his lines, but ordinary talke, more than most I reade. And if I have not been over forward to send my long threatned packet to tempt you to a Returne of thoughts; it is really out of Consciousnesse of my owne defects, fearing that they may not rellish soe well at a great Distance, as when in the same citty, or province. This advantage I have from mine owne ommissions; I have some Experience of your goodnesse towards mee; all expressions whereof will bee ever treasured up carefully by

Sir

Your faithfull freind and most humble servant

DE. GRENVILLE

I pray Sir present my humble service to my Lord Donnegall[1] and Mr Herbert;[2]

My sister mends, tho but slowly, but I feare it is her owne fault.

Wee are much allarummed here with the declaring of warr on the Convention of our parliament. I would willingly understand the truth thereof. you that are neare[a] our ambassadours, may oblige mee at this Juncture, with a litle newes; tho I am not at all times fond

[a] *Word altered; spelling doubtful.*

[1] Sir Arthur Chichester, d. 1678; second earl of Donegall (Ireland) 1675: G.E.C.

[2] Identifiable as Thomas Herbert, the future eighth earl of Pembroke: p. 668 n. Locke met him at Montpellier on 2 October 1676, N.S., and attended him for fever from 15 to 26 November, N.S., of this year: Journal.

thereof.[1] I should bee glad to heare what is become of our freind Mr. Walls.[2]

Address: A Monsieur Monsieur Lock Gentilhomme anglois chez Monsr. Charas Apothecaire Rue de Boucherie Fauxbourg St. Germain A Paris

Endorsed by Locke: Mr Grenvill 8 Jan. *78*

## 367. LOCKE to SIR JOHN BANKS, 5/15 January 1678 (*365*, *370*)

B.L., MS. Locke c. 24, f. 22. Draft. Answers no. *365*.

Sir

I have great obligation to you for the care you expresse of my satisfaction which yet I cannot enjoy to that degree I hoped as long as you let me understand there is any point wherein you want it and it begins presently to be a burthen to me as soon as it comes within the mention of being a charge to you: for I cannot but thinke you pay to deare for it if it costs you any thing. Tis upon this as well as severall other considerations that the caution I seeme to beare about me in reference to mony is very much in earnest and I beg the favour of you that the current of our expences may run in the same channell it has donne hitherto and the mony be still continued in Mr B hands. If in the receit or disbursement of it or any matter of accounts here my assistance may be usefull he may be assurd by what is past that it shall not be wanting to him and if you shall thinke fit at any time to give me any direction concerning our way of liveing or management of expences I shall endeavour the best I can to conduct them in that method that you shall order. For ⟨haveing⟩[a] besides those good wishes I have always very seriously had for M.B. this late unexpected obligation to him you may be satisfied I shall not be bacward in any care or pains that may be serviceable to him or assure you that I am

Endorsed by Locke: JL to Sir J: Banks 15 Jan. *78*

[a] *Deleted in MS.*

[1] Parliament met and was adjourned on 3 December (and again on 15 January). It was widely expected that, as a sequel to the marriage of William III, prince of Orange, to Mary, daughter of James, duke of York, England would join the allies against France.

[2] George Wall of Gloucester: p. 430, n. 2.

## *368.* DR. JOHN MAPLETOFT to LOCKE, 10 January 1678 (364, *371*)

B.L., MS. Locke c. 15, f. 221. Excerpt printed by Dr. K. Dewhurst in *Journal of the History of Medicine*, xii (1957), 35. Answers no. 364.

Gresh: Coll. Jan. 10. $7\frac{7}{8}$

Deare Sir

I had not presently an opportunity of speaking with our Friend.[1] to whom I have shewed both your Letters to which he only answers That you are in a very good way and ought to prosecute what you so rationally design. I am glad to heare the good news of my Ladys health confirm'd by later accounts, and wee entertain hopes of her being shortly with child. Wee are full of Rumors of Warrs here and consequently in expectation of seeing you all sooner perhaps then you desire: but I doe not heare that any resolutions are yet taken, and it may be you may know more then wee doe, and I carry coales to New-castle.[2] Wee desire to see no French-men in your company (our Ladys being in great feare of being ravished) but a Wise Greek and Roman will both be very wellcome. and more then the great Hector of Europe himselfe.[3] I am glad to heare Mrs. Blomer is gott off so very well and wish the Doctor and her much joy of their little acquest. Mrs. Grig, as I am inform'd, hath fortifyd herselfe in her resolutions of continuing in her desolate State and the Doctor her late Gallant must begin a fresh siege where he may hope to speed better. I am still where I was, and like to be, for ought I know, till you come over, and perhaps seven yeares longer. However in all places and states I shall ever be

Deare Sir

Your Affectionate Faithfull Servant

JO: MAPLETOFT

Endorsed by Locke: Mapletoft 1° Jan $7\frac{7}{8}$

[1] Sydenham.

[2] See p. 543, n. 1.

[3] The Greek and Roman are Plutarch and Cicero: pp. 524, 503; the Hector is Louis XIV.

## 369. WILLIAM CHARLETON to LOCKE, 22 January/1 February 1678 (353, *379*)

B.L., MS. Locke c. 5, ff. 22–3.

Montpellier the 1th: February $167\frac{7}{8}$

Deare Sir

upon my returne from waiting on sir John Chichley to see Mr. Selapris at Nismes[1] (where he treated us with Geneva Cappons and a Troutte of that Lake of 45lb. weight)[2] the verry night I came hither I received yours of the 17th: past, with no small Content-ment, since it imparts to me your health and the Continuance of your freindship which I have as I ought a verry great value for. I have written to mr. Selapris this post to procure me a printed list of the officers that are to serve this Campagne[3] and if it be to be had I doubt not but I shall send it you, his resolutions of going for England towards the middle of the next month about a Concern of sixteen thousand crownes betwixt him and one Monsr. L'En-gendre[4] a French merchant of London made me take the liberty of giving him your adresse at Paris, and of desiring you to favour him with a letter of recommendation to some one of your freinds at London who may be able to put him in a way of procuring his right from Mr. L'Engendre in case that they should not Come to an amicable Conclusion. I beg a thousand times your excuse for the trouble I give you, and desire since he presses me for letters to some freinds of mine there, that when you see him you will be pleased to give him an account of my Condition which I had not Confidence enough to do my self. Sir John Chichley having perse-cuted me about my returning for England at the time we were with mr. Selapris to avoide the giving mr. Selapris as I fear'd he would jealousy, by some expressions that fell from him I was forc't to discover my self to Sir John who at the same time assur'd me he would be verry secret, and expressed a great deale of kindnesse to me.[5] John ha's at length left me and Mr. Selapris ha's given me another in his roome who I hope will prove a verry good servant being John's Countreyman and one whom Mr. Selapris ha's trusted for severall yeares with greater summes then I am likely to have at

[1] Selapris lived in Lyons.

[2] See Evelyn, *Diary*, ed. de Beer, ii. 523 n.

[3] p. 512, n. 3.

[4] Jean Le Gendre: p. 629, etc.

[5] This perhaps refers to Charleton's reasons for living under an assumed name: p. 508 n. He appears to have been in trouble with it again when he required a pass-port: p. 568.

a time in my Custody. you cannot imagine how much I am concern'd that I cannot be serviceable to him in this journey, and therefore beg of you once more to give him all the assistance you can. you see Sir how troublesome I am to you but nothing but a freinds concern could have prevailed with me to use so great freedome, though I know no person to be more readdy to serve his freinds then your self, and wish that my misfortunes had not put me out of a capacity of answering the obligations I have to you as I ought since I am

Sir

Your Infinitely obliged servant

WILLIAM CHARLETON

Sir John Chichley presents you his service and ha's received your letter and I presume will answer it shortly he desires the favour of you to acquaint Mr. Brisban or his Lady[1] that he sent them a small chest of wine and another of olives, he would be verry glad to know whether they are received.

I spake with Dr. Barbyrac who gives you his service and Commends extreamely Dr. Sydenham's book.

Mr. Tufton[2] ha's tooke a journey into Provence, where I heare my Lady Thornhill and Dr. Grenville intend to stay another yeare.

we have at present in towne one mr. Wildman[3] a widdower and one mr. Stoel an Irish Gentleman and I heare this morning there is another English man Come to the white horse but I know not his name.

2 regiments of English and Irish have their quarters in Dauphiney[4]

Address: A Monsieur Monsieur Locke Gentilhomme Anglois chez monsieur Charas apoticaire rüe de boucherie Fauxbourg St. Germain a Paris

Endorsed by Locke: Mr. *Charleton* 1 Feb. *78*

[1] John Brisbane, *c.* 1638–84; secretary to the Admiralty 1680–4; and his wife Margaret, d. 1706, who succeeded as Baroness Napier (Scotland) in 1686: Evelyn, *Diary*, ed. de Beer, iv. 178 n. Brisbane was a diplomatic agent in Paris from 1676 to 1679, but was at present in England: p. 547. Locke mentions him in his Journal first on 8 October 1677, N.S.; they moved in the same French intellectual circle.

[2] Identifiable as Thomas Tufton, the future sixth earl of Thanet: p. 652 n.

[3] Perhaps John Wildman the politician (nos. *1149*, *1366*) or a son.

[4] In view of the ostensibly hostile relations between England and France Charles II and Louis XIV were now negotiating disingenuously about the return of the English, Scots, and Irish regiments in French service. Douglas's regiment (Scots) was ordered to Dauphiné in January; Dongan's, later Richard Hamilton's (Irish), was at Aix about March and April: Ruth Clark, *Anthony Hamilton*, 1921, pp. 67–9; Browning, *Danby*, ii. 416; see further p. 567.

## *370.* SIR JOHN BANKS to LOCKE, 24 January 1678 (*367*, *373*)

B.L., MS. Locke c. 3, ff. 92–3.

Sir

I have receavd your severall letters for which I thanke you, and shall be glad as oft as your affaires permitt to be informed from you, of your owne and my sons wellfare, And at present have only to say, that I perceave by my son his cash is at an end, wherefore doe heer remitt order to receave of Widow Herringe and son. 200l– which you may please to take as occasyon requires and give her my sons receipts, the credit being to him. And doe desire that, as I have formerly said, you doe please, now to add this to your accompt and to keepe the same for such expences as shall be betwixt you. I cannot willingly give any limitation in all of the expences. but leave the same to your prudence, that my son may live as becomes a sober and frugall gentleman. and when further supply is desired you shall be accommodated therwith: I have made a visite to mr Brisban[1] who Gives me good satisfaction concerninge my son and your great kindnesse to him, which is much to the Content of

Sir, Your assured freind and servant

JOHN BANKS

Lincolns in feilds 24 January 77

Address: Monsieur Monsieur Locke A Paris

Endorsed by Locke: Sr J: Banks 24 Jan $7\frac{7}{8}$

## *371.* DR. JOHN MAPLETOFT to LOCKE, 26 February 1678 (*368*, 417)

B.L., MS. Locke c. 15, ff. 222–3.

Gresham-College Feb. 26. $\frac{77}{8}$

Deare Sir

I am very glad that your Method succeeds so well where wee are all concern'd that you should doe soe. I advised with our Friend[2] about the contents of your last, who thinks you are in a very good way, approves of the Herbes you propose, whose juices he would have taken now the Spring comes on, but insists upon Bleeding

[1] He returned to Paris about March or April: Browning, *Danby*, ii. 346, 349, etc.

[2] Sydenham.

and Purging both as requisite to prevent a Storm which he feares may otherwise ensue. Your conjecture of the excrescence of the Almond[1] on the side affected seems to be very probable, and the Succus Nervosus cannot, I think, be acquitted. Wee know no more rationall ways then those you propose for the redres of all, and therefore can only second you with our good wishes. I desire you Sir to spare for no cost in the Purchase you are to make for me, which commission I should not give you for any Commodity in the Palais,[2] nor in the Indies neither, where they have nothing better then Gold, Pearls, and Diamonds, and such like Womens and Childrens wishes. But not a word of this parmi les dames, for feare you spoyl my marriage. Wee talke of nothing here but Taxes and Pole-mony, and are like to pay more for one head then an hundred can be sold for, unlesse their owners are first Bandited.[3] Wee mean also to live and dye and be buryed in our Woollen Manufactures, and to beat France by drinking none of their wines, and neither wearing their silkes, nor linnen. All the good I expect from this Warre is that wee shall see our Friends so much the sooner, to whom I beseech you give my particular service, who am,

Deare Sir

Your most Faithfull humble Servant

JO: MAPLETOFT.

You know I presume, that my Lord Shaftsbury is at liberty again.[4]

Address: A Monsieur Monsieur Lock Gentilhomme Anglois chez Monseigneur L'Ambassadeur du Roy d'Angle-terre al'Hostel de Turenne A Paris

Endorsed by Locke: Dr Mapletoft 26 Feb $7\frac{7}{8}$

## *372.* DR. DENIS GRENVILLE to LOCKE, 2/12 March 1678 (*366*, 374), with three enclosed papers by Grenville.

B.L., MS. Locke c. 10, ff. 72–9. Answered by no. 374.

Aix March 12th $167\frac{7}{8}$

Deare *Freind.*

I am resolved to advance a step above *Deare Sir*, I assure you. Notwithstanding I have long threatned you with a Lusty Pacquet,

[1] p. 539, n. 1. [2] p. 367, n. 3.
[3] Proscribed: *O.E.D.* The taxes and regulations were in view of the expected war. See further p. 566. [4] He was released this day: p. 482, n. 1.

yet I cannot prevaile with my selfe to disturb you at soe great a distance, with more than the three papers, which accompany this, (picked out of above 40 which your eyes might see were wee once more together): nay soe doth my scrupulosity (which I complained of on another account) haunt mee even on this, that I am not well satisfied to send any soe far, after all my talke and designes to that purpose. Meethinkes it lookes like setting a value on what ought[a] bee matter of great shame. That after neare 20 yeares I have appeared on the stage in a Cassock to helpe others, I should bee soe litle established my selfe.[1] But this temptation I thanke God, I have thus far gott over; soe far as to assault you with some of my Bolts, (Foolish enough, I trow, tho they have been long a shooting) hoping they will procure for mee my desired game. three sheets of the same proportion towards the making up of my booke; which designe I am very fond, tho I have been thus dilatorily in this as I am in most things I undertake. I could willingly now fall a Railing on my selfe one halfe houre; to provoke you to such another excellent letter, as you favour'd mee with a while since, to my extraordinary satisfaction; though I have reeled back into my Rude negligence, soe as not to acknowledge your Freindlinesse therein. Your Candour, (for which I dearely hug you) may bee possibly with soe ill ⟨a nature⟩[b] as mine a temptation to make bold with you thus in further neglects. But I should not have done it on that account, were there not somewhat else here in the case. Which when I begin to take this freindly liberty will not bee preposterous to hint to you. Really my hands and head here are exceedingly full and constantly imployed. My sister out of a too melancholly humour shunning all English Company creates a horrid deale of trouble to mee, poor feeble agent and Conductour. And her temper of her soule being as delicate as that of her body, I am at my witt's end allmost how to act; having not such a freind as you at my Elbow. Of this more at another time. Take this hint (inter nos) for the present. Mr. Brouchier is wonderfully serviceable to mee, as well as my sister; but yet however I want a Mr. Lock, on this account as well as many other. Wee have noe summons from our Freinds in England, notwithstanding all Rumours and preparations of war; which they have promised us, and wee expect before wee make

[a] *Interlined.* [b] *MS.* anature

[1] Grenville was ordained in 1661: p. 470, n. 2.

any for our Journey home. Mr. Brouchier gives you his service and will performe all you desire about the manner of ordering the prunelles, and sending the slips, concerning which you shall have account in time.[1] Hee begs your pardon for not writing. You would gratifye him, I perceive, if you would bee pleased to procure, and send him, the book which your Land-lord Monsieur Charas hath printed, called la pharmacie de Monsieur Charas.[2] I did deliver your Letter, and attempted with my poor french to assist you in a Complement, as you hinted, till Monsieur Brouchier afforded mee a view of your notable french veine, whereby I found you abused your poor freind Grenville; in putting such a youngster upon an attempt in french when you are soe much a greater master. however I freely forgive you upon Condition you will continue to beare with the manifold Infirmities of

Sir

Your faithfull Freind and humble servant

DE. GRENVILLE

My sister is very humble servant and very well at present. Miss saies soe too; but I beleive her in nothing.

Endorsed by Locke: Mr Grenville 12 Mar. $7\frac{7}{8}$

[Enclosures:]

2. About Temporall Buisnesse.[a3]

As it hath been allwayes a difficult to mee to know how to attend (seasonably) to Devotion on the one hand, and Recreation on the other, without exceeding in either; soe it hath been allwayes a difficulty to mee, to keep the meane between ones spirituall Concerns, and secular buisnesse.

There is noe One whatsoever, that can have soe great spirituall Obligations (publick, or private), as to bee wholy exempted from some secular ones. As there is noe One that can bee exempted by his secular Obligations (in whatsoever Circumstances hee may bee) from some regard to his spirituall Ones.

But how to set the bounds, so as to regulate my selfe, or another, I am at a great losse. And I shall bee very glad of noe worse discourse, here, on this point; than I had once, on that of Recreation.

[a] *Dated by Locke* 12 March $7\frac{7}{8}$

[1] No. *375*.

[2] The *Pharmacopée royale*: p. 485, n. 2.

[3] The first of this series of papers was that on Recreation: nos. *327*, 328.

As for my owne part, since I have been first convinced, that there was due Care to bee had of my soule, I have usually leaned to that which I thought the best extreame; Allwayes when I found it difficult to attend to both, neglecting the affaires of this world, rather than those which related to the Other.

But many times upon a Review, I have discerned a great fault, in having neglected buisnesses, tho secular, yett of Reall obligation and which good Conscience bound mee to, as well as mine Intrest, and Reputation.

Hereupon my Conscience hath smote mee; whereupon I have endeavoured to stop my mind in her spirituall Carreer, and have applied my selfe in some measure to the mannaging of my Temporalls.

But very soon after, I have discerned my selfe run into a very much worse extreame; in having neglected the great Worke of my soule, to the great prejudice of my spirituall estate, if not to the scandall of Good men; and yet for all this could never effectually doe my buisnesse, nor regaine my Repute with the World; soe as to bee thought a man that minded my buisnesse; but am condemned by all as one most notoriously Negligent unto this very day.

Hereupon seeing all my Endeavours soe fruitlesse; as neither to doe my buisnesse to the purpose, noe nor soe much as to salve my Reputation, I have Returned againe to my old spirituall Imployment, minding that with such Intention,[1] as my soule seemed to require, to make sure of that part of my duty, since I did not find my selfe, soe happy, as to succeed well in both.

But it hath not been long, againe, till I have been awakened by my Conscience, and the Clamours of the *World*, to Remember that it was some part of my Duty, to look to that; wherewith I have complied, till I have found the forementioned Inconveniences, and of much worse Consequence.

Then after this I have quitted buisnesse againe, and fallen to devotion; and as soon after abated in Devotion; and fallen againe to Buisnesse; Indeed, have done both soe often that I am ashamed to mention. And yet, God knows, all this while, deserve not to bee termed either a *man of Buisnesse*, or of *Devotion*; Having not succeeded in Either. Both my temporall and spirituall estate, being in great disorder; I cannot well tell which is in most. Thus have I been neare 20 yeares tossed with these difficulties, (sometimes to

[1] In the obsolete sense, attention, application: p. 416, n. 1.

the Incredible torment of my soule) allwaies to my great hindrance either in my spirituall progresse, or Temporall mannagements.

O may that God, whom the Wind and the sea doe allwayes obey, calme all stormes and tempests in his poor servants breasts, and bring us safe at last, through all our Difficulties and dangers, to our Wish'd for Port; even that of salvation.

Amen.

Endorsed by Locke: Mr Grenville 12 Mar. $7\frac{7}{8}$ Businesse

3. Concerning study[a]

My distractions and difficulties in this respect are not lesse than the former.

For besides the time, which my devotions, my buisnesse and my Recreations call for, and aptitude in my nature to bee immoderate in Each, I meet with here many new disturbances.

And which seeme to bee occasioned by three weaknesses whereto I have been allwayes very subject. vizt. 1. Some Darkenesse in my Understanding, which makes mee long in Judging what is fit to bee undertaken. 2. Some Inconstancy in my Temper, which hinders mee from going through with my Undertakings; and 3. lastly Some scrupulosity in my minde, which makes mee feare, that what I have undertaken at any time, is not the most propper; causing mee to change that sort of study for some other, or to prosecute it, flaggingly, and lesse effectually.

In the first place, I must owne my selfe soe subject to disputes with my selfe, concerning the fitnesse of the study I am going about; that I have spent more dayes in Consideration what to study next, then would bee[b–] sufficient to[–b] make a very Blockhead, if they were put all to gether, a much better schollar than my selfe. And after all such consideration and dispute have lighted on the wrong, or lesse propper, and seasonable course and Method.

Secondly when I have determined and set to any Course or method, I am soe soon disturbed, if not quite broke of by my owne Inconstancy, or weaknesse to resist the temptations I meet with all, that I never succeed in any to the purpose; nay will confesse (to soe good a freind), that I never went roundly through any one method, which I begun, in my life. And then Judge you, what kind of Freind you have got in mee; as to Book-learning.

[a] *Dated by Locke* 12 March $7\frac{7}{8}$ [b–b] *Interlined; preceded by* would *wrongly repeated.*

Thirdly When I have after much adoe well-begun, and proceeded too for some while, I am often disquieted with Jealousies and feares (deeply rooted in my nature) that what I am about, is not the most suitable and proffitable course; soe that I either sitt still, or advance very ineffectually, and much to the Disturbance of my minde.

I have been soe clogged with these and the like difficulties for many yeares past; that I am in a manner discouraged from most undertakings, as to such studies which men in my Circumstances usually doe applie themselves to. And have in a manner quitted all hearty study; but the Immediate study of the Bible. And could bee very well Contented, if I Could Comfortably goe on with this, (which too many of us ministers are wanting in) without equall difficulty and disturbance.

But reallity through mine owne fraill nature and malice of the Devill, I meet more and greater here; too many to be Comitted to paper designed to bee sent soe many leagues.

These will bee enough to evince that I need not only the Counsell of my Freinds, but their pitty and praiers; having soe great reason to improve all meanes and methods for bettering my parts (Considering the station I am placed in, and charges I have undertaken) and being soe much obstructed in doing thereof. A word in season as to this particular would doe good service, and well deserve place in my Designed Book.

Endorsed by Locke: Mr Grenville 12 Mar. $7\frac{7}{8}$ Study

4. Concerning Conversation.[a1]

The difficulties allsoe which I meet with in mine ordinary Conversation are soe many; that I am thinking sometimes to quitt all conversations that are not absolutely necessary, except that with some choice Freinds. At least not to appeare soe much in publicke, and upon such triviall accounts as too many of mine owne Coate doe frequently.

Surely preists antiently, when people had great veneration for them, did seldome appeare abroad but when 'twas visible that their Duty did oblige them to it.

Whereas wee doe too often now adayes by fidling and frisking up and downe (sometimes more scandalously than (the graver

[a] *Dated by Locke* 12 Mar. $7\frac{7}{8}$

[1] In the obsolete sense, social intercourse: p. 101, n. 3.

sort of) Lay-men) render ourselves very cheap, and contemptible, and doe often too much Invalidate thereby our Counsells and reproofs.

Hereby I am often stop'd from that free kind of Converse which some expect from mee; and give my selfe up to my solitude and Retirement. But when I consider againe, how much proffit I might receive, my selfe, from choice Conversation; and how much proffitt others may receive from mee, provided I could (as I ought) live to Edification, I quit my Cell (where I could very contentedly dwell allwayes, were I only to please my owne minde) and attempt againe a more active Life (to speake in the Language of asceticks) but with litle advantage (that I can perceive) to others, and lesse to mine owne soule. For when I returne to review my past deportment. I too often find my selfe wounded, and my Brother scandalised.

One of the maine difficulties I meet with in Conversation, is, to know how to exercise that fraternall Duty of Reproof; which as is some wayes Incumbent on every One, must bee more espetially on those whoe weare Christs livery.

To heare my *Lord and Master* dishonour'd and despised grates my very soule, and yet how reproove effectually requires more prudence and Charity than I can pretend to

The Circumstances of my Family, and office Calls for a great Measure of both, to make mee really live to Edification; but how to secure a sufficient stock for that purpose is not very easy; nor will bee effected, I feare, till my Noddle bee a litle better fraught with philosophy, and my heart with true Devotion.

I am strongly perswaded that some Considerable Conversation with one Mr Lock, would bee by Gods Blessing very effectuall to the aforesaid Ends.

I doe assure you such Conversation, I should never abandon

God Grant mee againe such another prize as was in my hands (itt seemes the hands of a foole) the other winter at Montpelier; and forgive mee my Over-Wisdome, and Cautiousnesse, in being soe long before I ventured on Contracting a freindship with him. If it please God to afford mee such another Opportunity of Communication of thoughts, I shall prefer it before study, and never trouble my head with any Intricate methods and Courses to become Monsieur Literatus

The more I consider Mr Locks acquired and naturall Parts and Temper; The more hee seemes Calculated (meethinkes) for my

Meridian, And the only man, that I ever mett withall yet in the world for the polishing, if not new-making his humble servant

D.G:

Endorsed by Locke: Mr Grenville 12 Mar. 7⅞ Conversation

## *373.* SIR JOHN BANKS to LOCKE, 11 March 1678 (*370, 376*)

B.L., MS. Locke c. 3, ff. 94–5.

Sir

I am very much oblidged for your severalls of the 19 Feb. and 5 March. And upon full consideration shall governe my sons returne as you shall advise, as well in respect to the improvements of him, as the rumors of warr, for I doe beleive there is noe danger in his stay soe long as our Embassador[1] continues there, Sir I pray write me freely what you thinke best, in regard to my sons returne or longer stay and how long. and I shall advise with my wiffe therin, who will desire to put in for a share in this matter.

I perceave you had receavd 100l and let the other lye till further occasyon, and that you thinke good to continue things in the old channell, and I pray let my son as you have well directed spend what time he can in the Mathematiques and such other imployments[a] of the minde as you thinke best. My wiffe presents you her humble services. and I shall ever appeare to be

Sir, Your oblidged humble servant

JOHN BANKS

London 11 March 77/8

Address: To Mr Locke Thesse

Endorsed by Locke: Sir J: Banks 11 Mar 7⅞

## 374. LOCKE to DR. DENIS GRENVILLE, 13/23 March 1678 (*372, 377*)

B.L., MS. Rawlinson D. 849, ff. 148–9. Draft in Locke's Journal for 1678 (B.L., MS. Locke f. 3), pp. 69–79, dated 'Sunday Mar 20'; printed from this

[a] *Altered from or to* improvements; *abbreviated.*

[1] Ralph Montagu.

draft in King, pp. 109–13. Copy in B.M., Add. MS. 4290, ff. 109–14; printed from this copy in Fox Bourne, i. 390–3. Answers no. *372*.

Sir

Shall I not passe with you for a great empirick if I offer but one remedy to the three maladies you complain of? Or at least will you not thinke me to use lesse care and application then becomes the name of freind you honour me with if I thinke to make one short answer serve to the three papers you have sent me in matters very different? But yet if it be found as I imagin it will that they all depend on the ⟨same⟩[a] causes I beleive you will thinke they will not need different cures.

I conceive then that the great difficulty, uncertainty, and perplexity of thought you complain of in those particulars arises in a good measure from this ground, that you thinke that a man is obleiged strictly and precisely at all times to doe that which in it self is absolutely best, and that there is always some action soe incombent upon a man, soe necessary to be donne preferable to all others, that if that be omitted, a man certainly failes in his duty, and all other actions whatsoever otherwise good in themselves, yet comeing in the place of some more important and better that at that time might be donne are tainted with guilt, and can be noe more an acceptable offering to god then a blemished victim under the law.[1]

I confesse our duty is sometimes soe evident, and the rule and circumstances soe determin it to the present performance, that there is noe latitude left, noe thing ought at that time to come in the roome of it. But this I thinke happens seldome. At least I may confidently say it does not in the greatest part of the actions of our lives wherein I thinke god out of his infinite goodnesse considering our ignorance and frailty hath left us a great liberty

Love to god and charity to our selves and neighbours are noe doubt at all times indispensibly necessary. But whilst wee keepe these warme in our hearts, and sincerly practise what they upon occasions suggest to us I cannot but thinke God allows us in the ordinary actions of our lives a great latitude. Soe that two or more things being proposed to be donne, neither of which crosses that fundamentall law but may very well consist with the sincerity

[a] *MS.* sames

[1] The Law of Moses: Leviticus 1:3; etc.

wherewith we love god and our neighbour. I conceive tis at our choise to doe either of them

The reasons that make me of this opinion are

1° That I cannot imagin that God who has compassion on our weaknesse and knows how we are made, would put pore man nay the best of men, those that seeke him with sincerity and truth under almost an absolute necessity of sining perpetually against him, which will almost inevitably follow if there be noe latitude alowed us in the occurrences of our lives; But that every instant of our being in this world has always incumbent on it, one certaine determinate action exclusive of all others. For according to this supposition the best being always to be donne, and that being but one it is almost impossible to know which is that one. There being soe many actions which may all have some peculiar and considerable goodnesse, which we are at the same time capeable of doeing: and soe many nice circumstances and considerations to be weighed one against an other before we can come to make any judgment which is best, and after all shall be in danger to be mistaken. The Comparison of those actions that stand in competition togeather with all their grounds motives and consequences as they lye before us being very hard to be made. And which makes the difficulty yet far greater is that a great many of those which are of moment and should come into the reconing always scape us, Our short sight not penetrateing far enough into any action to be able to discover all that is comparatively good or bad in it: Besides that the extent of our thoughts is not able to reach all those actions which at any one time we are capeable of doeing. Soe that at last when we come to choose which is best, we makeing our judgment upon wrong and scanty measures we cannot secure our selves from being in the wrong. This is soe evident in all the consultations of mankinde that should you peeke[1] out any number of the best and wisest men you could thinke of to deliberate in almost any case what were best to be donne, you should finde them make almost all different propositions, wherein one (if one) only lighting on what is best, all the rest acting by the best of their skil and caution would have been sinners, as misseing of that one *Best*. The Apostles themselves were not always of a minde

[1] Probably meaning to pry out, to find out by prying: *O.E.D.*, s.vv. Peek *v.*[1] and Pry, *v.*[1] 3b; but no exact parallel is quoted.

2° I cannot conceive it to be the designe of god, Nor to consist with either his goodenesse or our businesse in the world, to clog every action of our lives, even the minutest of them (which will follow if one thing that is best be always to be donne), with infinite Consideration before we begin it and unavoidable perplexity and doubt when it is donne. When I sat downe to write you this hasty account, before I set pen to paper I might have considerd whether it were best for me ever to medle with the answering your questions or noe. My want of ability; It being besides[1] my businesse; The difficulty of adviseing any body and the presumpsion of adviseing one soe far above me would suggest doubts enough. Next I might have debated with my self whether it were best to take time to answer your demands or as I doe set presently to it. 3° Whether there were not some what better that I could doe at this time. 4° I might doubt whether it were best to read any books upon those subjects before I gave you my opinion, or to send you my own naked thoughts. To these a thousand other scruples as considerable might be added which would still beget others, in every one of which there would be noe doubt still a better and a worse, which if I should sit down and with serious consideration endeavour to finde and determin clearly and precisely with my self to the minutest differences before I betake my self to give you an answer, perhaps my whole age might be spent in the deliberation about writeing half a sheet of paper to you. And I should perpetually blot out one word and put in another, raze to morrow what I write to day. For it is not an easy matter even when one is resolved to write to know what words, expressions, and arguments are the very best to be made use of. Whereas haveing this single consideration of complying with the lawfull desire of a freind whom I honour and whose desires I thinke ought to weigh with me, and one who perswades me too that I have an oportunity of doeing him some pleasure in it, I cannot thinke I ought to be scrupulous in the point or neglect obeying your commands, though I cannot be sure but I might doe better not to offer you my opinions which may be mistakes, and probably I should doe better to imploy my thoughts how to be able to cure you of a quartan ague or to cure in my self some other and more dangerous faults, which is properly my businesse. But my intention being respect and service to you, and all the designe of my writeing comporting with the love I owe to god

[1] The preposition, in the obsolete sense beside, beyond the compass of: *O.E.D.*

and my neighbour I should be very well satisfied with what I write could I but be as well assurd it would be usefull as I am past doubt it is lawfull, and that I have the liberty to doe it, and yet I cannot say, and I beleive you will not thinke it is the best thing I could doe.

If we were never to doe but what is absolutely the best all our lives would goe away in deliberation and we should never come to action

3° I have often thought that our state here in this world is a *State of Mediocrity* which is not capeable of extreams though on one side or other of this mediocrity there might lie great excellency and perfection. Thus we are not capeable of continuall rest nor continuall exercise, though the later has certainly much more of excellency in it. We are not able to labour always with the body nor always with the minde. And to come to our present purpose, we are not capeable of liveing altogeather exactly by a strict rule, nor altogeather without one. not always retird nor always in company. But this being but ⟨an⟩[a] odde notion of mine it may suffice only to have mentioned it, my authority being noe great argument in the case. Only give me leave to say, that if it holds true it will be applicable in severall cases and be of use to us in the conduct of our lives and actions. But I have been too longue already to enlarge on this phansy any farther at present

As to our actions in generall this in short I thinke

1° That all negative precepts are always to be obeyd

2° That positive commands only sometimes upon occasions. But we ought to be always furnished with the habits and dispositions to those positive dutys in a readynesse against those occasions

3° That between these two i e Between *Unlawfull* which are always and *necessary* quoad hic et nunc[1] which are but sometimes there is a great latitude, and therein we have our liberty which we may use without scrupulously thinkeing ourselves obleiged to that which in it self may be Best.

If this be soe, as I question not but you will conclude with me it is, the greatest cause of your Scruples and doubts I suppose will be removd and soe the difficultys in the cases proposd will in a good measure be removd too

[a] *Word omitted by Locke.*

[1] 'With respect to the present time and place'; 'in the present circumstances'.

When I know from you whether I have guessed right or noe I may be incouraged to venture on two other causes which I thinke may be concernd also in all the cases you propose but being of much lesse moment then this I have mentioned here, may be deferd to another time, and then considerd en passant before we ⟨come⟩[a] to take up the particular cases seperately I am

Reverend Sir

your most humble servant

J LOCKE

Paris 23 Mar. 78

## 375. DR. CLAUDE BROUCHIER to LOCKE, 23 March/2 April 1678

B.L., MS. Locke c. 4, ff. 165–6. For the writer see p. 451, n. 1.

Ce 2. avril 1678 aix

Monsieur

Comme Madame thornheill et Monsieur de grenville son frere sont des personnes extraordinaires par leur vertu, ils le sont d autant plus en gratitude, puisqu'ils ont eu la bonté de vous faire mention des petits offices que je leur puis Rendre en cette ville, vous protestant, Monsieur, avec toute la sincerité possible que Je trouve plus de satisfaction á les leur rendre, qu'eux de les recevoir, ainsi Monsieur, ne m'en fassies pas, si'l vous plait, des remerciements, puisque je vous dois Reiterer les mesmes que je me suis donné l'honneur de vous faire, de m'avoir procuré celuy de leur connoissence. Jugés par la du desplaisir que J'ay d'entendre dire qu'ils pensent á s'en retournér en anglet⟨erre⟩[b] ce mois de may prochain, J'ay receu le livre de corde,[1] dont je vous Rends tres humbles graces, J'avois prié Monsieur Villy[2] ageant de s'E.[3] de l'allér prendre ches vous, auquél Monsieur Charras á Respondu que vous ne logiès plus ches luy, et au lieu du traicté de corde, luy á donné, sellon qu'il á escrit, un autre livre, dont il luy á faict payér six livres, Il y á de l'apparence que c'est sa pharmacopeé,[4]

[a] *Word omitted by Locke.* [b] *End of line.*

[1] Identifiable as Richard Lower (p. 152, n. 1), *Tractatus de Corde*, first published in 1669; new editions 1670, 1671 (and 1680). L.L., no. 1815 (ed. 1669).

[2] p. 451, n. 1.

[3] Son Éminence; Jerôme de Grimaldi, 1597–1685; cardinal 1621; archbishop of Aix, nominated 1645; confirmed by Papal bull 1655: *N.B.G.*

[4] pp. 485, n. 2, 550.

mais il n'avoit pas ordre de demandér aucun livre á Monsieur Charras, ny celuy cy de luy en donner aucun, en effect Monsieur de grenville m'a dit vous avoir escrit pour cela; ainsi si vous l'avés achepté, J'en auray[a] deux.

puis le 23 du mois passé J'ay envoyé de l'ordre d'un mien amy, un bouc[1] d huylle á Monsieur gousnél[b] Rüe des petits champs, vis á vis le palais mazarin,[2] et luy ay aussi envoyé deux boittes des prunes pour vous, l'ayant prié de vous les envoyér ches Monsieur Charras, mais comme Je n'ay pas l'honneur d'estre conneu de luy, il pourroit le negligér, ainsi vous y pourrés envoyer un vallet pour sçavoir lorsque le muletier sera arrivé et les prendre, elles ne sont pas si belles que celles que vous me fittes la grace d'accepter á aix parceque nous sommes dans la derniere saison, et qu'elle en á esté sterille, mais J'espere qu'elles ne seront pas moins bonnes, et que vous excuserés la liberté que Je prens de vous envoyér semblables bagatelles, si nous n'avons pas guerre, vous en recevrés en angleterre, si Je puis trouver quelque Commodité par mer, aussi bien que des petits arbres s'il est possible. il faut les faire pelér bien delicatement, et les enfillér dans des petits bastons, qui ne soint pas plus gros qu'une petite plume, apres qu'elles sont a demy seiches, faut tirer le noïïau, aprés les Rendre plattes avéc les doigts de la maniere que vous voyés qu'elles sont, en moüillant tant soit peu les doigts, pour esvitter que la viscosité des prunes s'attachant aux doigts n'empesche qu'on ne les puisse pas bien proprement accommodér, apres cela vous les faictes entierement seichér sur une table.[3] Si vous estes encore ches Monsieur charras, et que vous ayés quelque confience avéc luy, je vous auroy[a] obligation, si vous me faictes la grace, de luy donnér quelques bonnes Impressions de moy, par ce qu'il se pourroit rencontrér quelque occasion, dans laquelle je pourrois me servir de son ministere pour parlér á Monsieur d'aquin,[4] mais il y trouveroit son advantage, je vous supplie portant ne luy en faire aucun semblant. Jugés, Monsieur, par ma maniere d'agir, de celle avéc laquelle, vous pouvez vous

[a] *Or* aurois [b] *Or* gousnét

[1] 'Bouc, (la peau du Bouc où l'on met du Vin *ou* de l'huyle) *a Borachio*, or *Bouget of Leather*': Boyer, 1702.
[2] The Palais Mazarin is now the Bibliothèque Nationale.
[3] Further accounts of the process in no. *385* and in Locke's Journal, 15 August 1678, N.S.
[4] Probably Antoine d'Aquin, 1620?–96, physician of Louis XIV: *D.B.F.*

servir en mon endroit, et estre persuadé que je suis sans Reserve et sans façon, mais pourtant avéc Respect,

Monsieur

Votre tres humble et tres obeissant serviteur

BROUCHIER

Address: A Monsieur Monsieur Loke Gentilhome Anglois Ches Mr Charras Me apothiquaire rue boucherie fauxbourg St germain a paris

In another hand, elsewhere on page: Revolate de Marseilles[1]

Endorsed by Locke: *Brouchier* 2 Apr. *78*

## *376.* SIR JOHN BANKS to LOCKE, 1 April 1678 (*373*, *381*)

B.L., MS. Locke c. 3, ff. 96–7.

Lincolns in feilds 1 Ap. 78

Sir

I have receavd yours of the 30th ultimo and am well satisfyed you may stay att Paris as long as our Embassador,[2] and have considered with my wiffe who presents you her services and is willinge with my selfe that my son spend 2 or 3 months more abroad, as you judge most to his advantage, as I have formerly said, if the Warr doe not occasyon, sooner returne, and your affaires may admitt the same.

If you have occation of further supply of mony for your selfe or my son. I pray give me your timely advice, and you shall have a sutable returne. and beleive me to be

Sir, Your oblidged humble servant

JOHN BANKS

Address: A Monsieur Monsieur Locke A Paris

Endorsed by Locke: Sir J: Banks 1 Apr. *78*

## *377.* DR. DENIS GRENVILLE, to LOCKE, 3/13 April 1678 (374, *411*)

B.L., MS. Locke c. 10, ff. 80–2.

Aix. Aprill 13. 1678

Sir

I sent you last week a great Troublesome packet about my secular Concernes. You give mee soe large an Intrest in, and soe much

[1] p. 451, n. 1. [2] Ralph Montagu.

assurance of, your Freindship upon all accounts, that you see I advance in boldly Imploying of you. I will not spend time in Complementing and begging pardon. For Really I have very little, being not got perfectly out of the Hurry, which I mentionned in my last letter I was then in, and which was much increased by the buissy season (for us parsons) which my sisters hasty Resolutions fell out in, being Passion weeke.[1] My spiritualls clashing together with those other affaires (the Consequence of my sisters determination) put mee into great Disorder as to my weake Noddle. And a litle thing, God Knowes as I have told you, is sufficient sometimes to doe that. Without farther Complement, then, I must repeat my Request to you, that you will bee pleased Immediately after the Receipt of this letter to undertake a second trouble of going to my Banker Mr. Pierre Heusche[2] Rue de St. Denis, (if hee did not gratifye you and mee in your former motion) pressing him with any fresh arguments you can find in your budget for a Freind, to returne mee both the summes for which I have given him bills (or one at least) by the first post (if possible) our Journey having been determined on, and the beginning of May prefixed by my sister for the time of setting Forth. And if I doe not receive both these summes before the 1st of May, I shall bee put more to my Trumps than I have ever in my life been. Whereof I have now some Apprehension; for I have just now this morning (together with a letter of yours of Apr: 4th) received a letter from Mr. Heusche my Banquier (in answer to twoe of three letters which I sent him about the first hundred) where hee tells me that he hath received my twoe first letters with the bill I sent him in March drawn on my freind in England, and that he will not faile to returne mee the value thereof, when hee shall have the money returned him out of England. Which is a strange surprising answer to mee, considering his usuall practice, past Civility, and the method which I had established with him (by the Helpe of Dr. Du Moulin)[3] when I left Paris. Upon then given him a bill on the same person (drawne in the same forme) hee paid mee the value in hand, and gave mee hopes (as Mr. Du Moulin and I understood him) to doe the same for mee while I was abroad. At least this I am sure I have depended on (though I did not thinke often to have made use of his kindnesse)

[1] The new-style Easter day fell this year on 10 April; the old style, on 31 March.

[2] Michel Heusch is mentioned in 1675; Pierre in 1692 and 1705: Lüthy, *La Banque protestante*, i. 69, 76.

[3] Probably Peter du Moulin, D.D., 1601–84, prebendary of Canterbury: *D.N.B.*

and shall bee extreamely Incommoded if he failes mee now at this pinch, as well as my poor sister will bee if I faile her in being ready at the prefixed time for setting forth. I beseech you Sir to Oblige mee here in by pressing him to doe it as effectually as you can. You may bee as successefull it may bee as Mr. Du Moulin was, whoe hath transacted my buisnesse with him hitherto. Hee hath ever found mee an honest man, and my Agents in England very punctuall with his Correspondent at London, both now and during my former abode in France.[1] And that hee should now begin to act suspitiously and lesson his sivilities, is a litle strange. Perchance hee doth not well understand my miserable french, and not throughly apprehend my necessities from my letters, which for wanting of language were very short. To supply which defects, and to prevent future Inconveniences; I did Commend the trouble of my last bill to your Care; hoping that you could say what I could not write, and Remove any scruples hee might have of advancing the money. I cannot Remember whether I did mention in my former to him, or you, that hee might not only allow him the ordinary provision, and frais,[2] but allsoe deduct for the advance proportionnably. Perchance here may bee the Rub; pray Sir endeavour to remove it some way, or other. I am willing to bee imposed on, and give unreasonnably rather than want my money at the time mentionned. I may chance to drill[3] my sister into a weeks delay (for that if I have an effectuall answer in the first weeke in May, it may bee pretty well; but to stay till Mr. Heusch shall have received my money out of England, quite destroyes all my designes and methods. For the bills being drawne at A Months sight, it will bee June before I can possibly receive my money, nay the End of may before my Banker can receive it, for the letters will not bee at Durham till towards the End of this month. For Gods sake (if you can) draw mee out this Confusion. I dare not say any thing to my sister; whose head is too full of trouble allready. Whom I cannot make use of in matter of money at present for many Reasons, which I shall communicate to you at Paris where I hope to find you. It is not Impossible but that my sister (being *a*[a] *woman*[a]) may change her mind.

[a] *In large writing.*

[1] Grenville was in France probably in 1673, when physicians at Blois and Angers wrote reports on Mrs. Grenville: no. *486* n.

[2] Charges, expenses; the French word.

[3] Draw or entice: *O.E.D.*, s.v. Drill, *v.*[1], 4. For other uses of to drill see p. 396 and nos. 2182, 2376.

But there is a necessity for mee to bee ready to depart with her, (which I cannot bee without this 200l sterling mentionned in my twoe bills) for if I should bee the cause of her stay (shee being bent on going) it will give her a deep wound. And I dare not communicate to her soemuch as my needs of money; tho some Irregular courses and determinations of her bee the cause of itt. Somuch I dare owne to soe good a freind as Mr Lock. But these Inconveniences are Inavoydable. My sisters mind and body are both like a Venice glasse, and breake with the least Contradiction. Insomuch that I undergoe many expences and troubles for her which I keep to my selfe, to avoide the disturbance of her mind. I want soe prudent a freind as you at my Elbow, to direct mee how to steere in reference to my sister; whoe tho an Excellent woman, is overy[1] difficult to bee conducted by another, shee being very Extraordinary both as to body and soull. I doe not neglect to Consider the subject of your late paper[2] (which I much prise) tho I cannot make any returne thereto, till these my temporalls are settled. and soe you see my shattle-braine,[3] Inconstant, Temper verified in this Instance. But God blesse and continue mee as good a freind as your selfe and I will not dispaire of a Cure in time. I am and Ever will remaine

Your

D: Gr:

I confesse that when I came abroad I did not thinke to have spent soe much money as I have done, nor desire soe much credit from Mr Lucy at London (thinking to have had some helpe from my sister) but as the case is (my sisters Infirmities of body and sometimes of mind) increasing my Expences) I must have it; and I thanke God there is at Durham a Freind. Pray improve what is said as you may.

Endorsed by Locke: Mr Grenvill 13 Apr. *78*

[1] Not found elsewhere; presumably a slip for over or overly.
[2] Presumably no. 374.
[3] Correctly shittle brain; shittle means inconstant, flighty, etc.: *O.E.D.*

## *378.* THOMAS STRINGER to LOCKE, 15 April 1678 (*355, 389*)

B.L., MS. Locke c. 19, ff. 139–40.

Aprill 15th. 1678.

Deare Sir

Sinc my Comming to Towne I saw a letter from you to mr Hoskins wherein you complaine of not hearing from us. what that Gent hath done I know not but this is the third or fourth letter I have sent sinc I received any from you, besides that with the bill of Exchange from mr Herbert[1] by this time I suppose you have an accompt that the money is received thereupon, mr Cholmly[2] readily Complying therewith, but a Clause lattly passed in the Act of Poll Money, to Prohibitt all kinde of Trade with France, hath hindred any shipps from importing any thing that is of the Growth, Manufacture, or Product of France sinc the 20th of the last month,[3] whereby none of those things you mention to have sent by mr Herbert or mr Phrasier[4] is brought on shore, notwithstanding mr Herbert hath very much solicited for the Clearing of it. The mellon seeds you sent me is received and delivered both unto my Lord[5] and Sir Paule[6] according unto your order. I gave you an account of my enquiry after Major Sallaway,[7] whoe is now in London and in prety good health, he hath bin here these 7 or 8 weekes, hath had somthing of a Cold sinc his coming to Towne, but it is indifferently well gon off. I have enquired of my Lord if he desires an more books or mapps, whoe tells me he cannot yett tell whether he shall want any others or noe, unlesse he knew what other mapps were to be had, or whether the warr is likely to turne this Summer. The mapps you sent by Mrs Armstrong came to mr Hoskins hand and by him were presented to my Lord, but for the 2 bottles of the Queen of Hungarys water you formerly sent by mr Upton, I could never yett heare of them. I have bought Sir William Temples State

[1] Probably Thomas Herbert, the future eighth earl of Pembroke: pp. 542, 668 n., etc.; Locke, Journal, 12 March, 2 May 1678 N.S.

[2] John Cholmeley at the Golden Anchor opposite St. Dunstan's church: ibid. 1678, p. 64.

[3] p. 548. The act, 29 and 30 Car. II, c. 1, received the royal assent on 20 March. Stringers refers to § 70.

[4] A variant of Fraser. Perhaps James Fraser: no. *2149*.

[5] Shaftesbury.

[6] Probably Sir Paul Neile (p. 300 n.) rather than Sir Paul Whichcote (p. 460, n. 5).

[7] Identifiable as Major Richard Salwey, 1615–85, the parliamentarian: *D.N.B.*; p. 675, n. 3.

of Holland[1] but cannot finde an opertunity of sending it to you, the very first I have you shall not faile to receive it. I presume you have heard of the death of mr Peter Locks daughter Stratton,[2] which is a great affliction to him; Your friends are very Glad of the hopes you give them to see you in a little time here in London, I thank God in our Family they continue very well, and wilbe Extreamly glad to bid you wellcome home, and amongst them all none can be better pleased to shake you by the hand then

Dearest Sir

Your most Faithfull and affectionate servant

T: S:

Address: A mounseur Mounseiur Lock Gentilhome Anglois Chez Monsr: Charas Apotecaire rue de Boucherie a Fauxbourge St Germaine a Paris.

Endorsed by Locke: T: Stringer 15 Apr. *78*

## *379.* WILLIAM CHARLETON to LOCKE, [*c.* 21 April/1 May 1678] (*369, 380*)

B.L., MS. Locke c. 5, f. 34. Corner of a letter. The authorship from the handwriting. Approximate date from the movement of Hamilton's regiment. What remains of the letter, here omitted, concerns Mr. Tufton. A fragmentary postscript runs:

Colonel Hamilton's Regiment is march't . . .
at Ville Franche in Rouergue.[3] Captain Digby . . .
is here with his Company of above 100 English me . . .
incorporated into the Prince of Furstemberg's Regi . . .[4]
present you their service, we dine all of us once . . .
Earl of Meath Sir John Chichley and mr. Butle . . .[5]

[1] Sir William Temple, *Observations upon the United Provinces of the Netherlands*, first published in 1673; new editions 1673, 1676; later editions 1680, etc.

[2] p. 263, n. 2.

[3] Apparently a mistake for Roussillon, near the Spanish border. Villefranche in Rouergue had no garrison; Villefranche in Roussillon was an important military post; Col. Richard Hamilton's regiment was sent there from Aix about May: Clark, *Anthony Hamilton*, p. 69. Richard Hamilton, d. 1717, was a brother of Anthony Hamilton, the author of the *Mémoires de Grammont*.

[4] See Clark, *Anthony Hamilton*, p. 69.

[5] A Mr. Butler is mentioned on p. 676.

## *380.* WILLIAM CHARLETON to LOCKE, 30 April/ 10 May 1678 (*379, 385*)

B.L., MS. Locke c. 5, ff. 24–6.

Montpelier the 10th: may 1678

Deare Sir

I see I must be uncivill and not returne you one word of thankes for all the kindnesses I receave from you for feare it might looke like a Compliment but you will have it so and I am resolved not to disobey, but I am sure of this though I dare not say so, that I thinke my self extraordinaryly obliged to you, and if I had a mistress here and that she were but half so kind as you are, I should be verry solicitous if a war should happen not to be deprived of her Conversation, but that is none of the reasons why I would stay. The Inclosed will give you the state of my Condition, and I presume a passeport will not be refused, the lesse restrictive it is the better both as to time and place, for I would not be Cooped up at Montpellier, nor obliged by haveing to short[a]– a time–[a] to renew it often, which will be both troublesome and Chargeable, but I must not be my own Carver.[1] I have tryed to obtain the sight of one but though I have made enquiry of severall persons whom I thought must needs have knowen the form's of them, I find they are as much in the dark as my self but I beleeve that may be learn't of one of Mr. Pompone's Secretary's.[2] if a passeport can be procured (though I know not whether it be usuall or no) before the declaration of war I should desire you to get one although it prove of no use, for the expence is not so Considerable but that I should willingly hazard such a summe fearing least if there be a rupture it may be more difficult to obtaine, I have taken care Sir to have 5 Louis d'ors Lodged at Mr: Guillemart's Banquier rüe Simon Le franq and to discover how little I compliment you I have so ordered it that you will be put to the trouble of fetching them. be pleased to draw a bill upon me for the value receaved, payable

a–a *MS.* short a / a time

---

1 The enclosure is lost; it presumably contained Charleton's reasons for living in France under an assumed name: p. 545. A passport at this time was a safe-conduct granted by a competent authority to a stranger passing through, or, as here, residing in a country, and not, as now, a certificate granted to a traveller by the government of his own country.

2 Simon Arnauld, marquis de Pomponne, 1618–99; secretary of state for foreign affairs 1671–9: *N.B.G.*

to his order at Montpelier according to the Inclosed Coppy. If you send Sir William Temples book[1] I shall be verry Carefull in the delivery of it to the Cardinall[2] or of doing anythinge else whereby I may assure you without a Compliment of my being

Sir

Your most Affectionate humble servant

WILLIAM CHARLETON

Sir

Since the writing of my last I have heard from Mr. Selapris who is resolved to pay his creditors sooner then it was agreed on, and to that end intends to sell part of an estate that he ha's at St. Gall[3] so that I beleeve by the 2 next payments (as they call them at Lyons) that is to say within 6 months he will have clear'd all scores.

I presume you may have heard of Mr: Clovis' imprisonment for having wounded Mr. Ryan with 2 blows on the head with a pocket pistoll, the bussinesse is now accomodated and he at liberty, and the other recover'd of his wounds. It ha's cost him about 8 Louis d'ors and 6 or 7 days confinement in the Common prison. this accident I hope will make him wiser for the future.

[Enclosure; by Charleton:]

a Paris le may 1678 pl

a veue vous payera par cette seule lettre de Change a monsr. Jean Bonnel au a son ordre la somme de —— pour valeur receue Comptant de Monsr. Guillemart rüe Simon le franq et metterez a Comte suivant l'avis

A De

Guillaume Charleton
a Montpelier

Address: A Monsieur Monsieur Locke Gentilhomme Anglois chez mr: Charas Apoticaire rüe de boucherie Fauxbourg st. Germain a Paris

Endorsed by Locke: Mr *Charleton* 10 May. *78*

[1] p. 567, n. 1. Two different French translations were published in Paris and The Hague in 1674.

[2] Pierre de Bonzi, 1631–1703; bishop of Béziers 1659; employed as diplomatist *c.* 1662–71; cardinal 1672; archbishop of Toulouse 1669–73; of Narbonne 1673–1703; president of the Estates of Languedoc 1673–1703: *D.B.F.*

[3] The Schlappritzi family (p. 480 n.) belonged there: *Dict. hist. et biog. de la Suisse.*

## *381.* SIR JOHN BANKS to LOCKE, 13 May 1678 (*376, 384*)

B.L., MS. Locke c. 3, ff. 98–9.

Sir

I perceave my son hath made use of 100l– upon the last credit, and the exchange[a] it is true runns very high, yet is I thinke noe more then the common course

I did write to my son last post, as I have done by this, that findinge by his letters he was desirous to be some longer time abroad, that he would give me the reasons of his such desires, and how and where he would improve that time to his better advantage for 2 or 3 months—I would satisfy him, in what might be to his most improvement, which he might in such a time accomplish, the which I did alsoe desire him to acquainte you.

I am glad my son hath his health soe well, and I doe hoope he makes a sutable improvement of his time, and doe alsoe hoope you will finde more benefit to your owne health by the growinge worme weather, I doe expect my sons answer which I hoope to have in 10 days with your opinion and shall then give you my further thoughts, who remaine

Sir, Your oblidged freind and servant

JOHN BANKS

London. 13 May. 1678.

Address: Thesse To Mr Locke

Endorsed by Locke: Sir J: Banks 13 May. *78*

## *382.* ROBERT HUNTINGTON, later bishop of Raphoe, to LOCKE, 22 May 1678 (*253*)

B.L., MS. Locke c. 11, ff. 247–8. The date is old style presumably. For Huntington see further no. *716*. Letters from Mrs. Huntington below, no. *2532*, etc.

Sir

Whoever 'twas you gave your Letter to of March the 3d at Paris, he has discharg'd his Promise; for last week it came to hand: And I make an Acknowledgment by the same Conveyance, altho tis not unlikely I might hav found a safer way, than your way of Marseilles. But I wont loose the advantage of your Correspondence, nor giv occasion to suspect my satisfaction in the thoughts of it: Especially

[a] *MS.* ex[a]

since without the usuall shifts, of miscarrages, want of opportunities, and the like, you very ingeniously produce the tru caus of your former silence. Yet Sir I was not without the effect of your Good Wishes, those arriv'd happily which you sent by the way of heaven, (and severall Gentlmen of my Acquaintance gave me such an Information) I hav enjoyd a proportion of Welfare greater than my expectation, far greater than my deserts: And tho' I may be justly accused for loosing the best part of my time, and the greatest opportunities of preferment, by being so long in a distant and no very desirabl Country: yet whilst I am in my employment and can be content, I hav enough to silence my own Conscience, if not others accusations. Now I scarce know which way to come home, and the late change of Affaires makes me at a loss how to take my measures: For I would not leav such a Glorious place as France without the circuit of my Rambles. I am glad you recovered your health there, may you continue it in England: And so much you may hope for, if God shall vouchsafe to hear the Prayers of a sinner

Sir

your very humble Servant

ROB. HUNTINGTON

Aleppo, May the 22d 78

Pray salute Dr John Master,[1] and those you know of my Friends.

Address: For Mr John Locke at Mr Kiffins[2] a Merchant in Austin Friers In London

Recommended to Mr Edwin Browne by his much obliged servant R.H.

Endorsed by Locke: R. Huntington 22° May. *78*

## *383.* DR. THOMAS COXE to LOCKE, 2 June 1678 (386)

B.L., MS. Locke c. 7, f. 182. Answered by no. 386. For the writer and his sons see p. 451, n. 2.

Lo⟨ndon.⟩[a] Jun. 2. 1678.

Sir

Since my sons Infelicity of parting with you at Montpellier, I have had very little Heart to trouble you with any letter from hence,

[a] *Page torn.*

[1] Matriculated from Christ Church on 20 July 1654; B.A. 1657; M.A. 1659; D.M. 1672; honorary fellow of the College of Physicians 1680: *D.N.B.*, art. William Master.

[2] Probably William Kiffin, 1616–1701, merchant and Baptist minister: ibid.; pp. 380, n. 1, 436, n. 5.

though I have not bin unsensible of your kindenes to him there, and of the obligation that I stand in to you for your Concerne for him, which[a]- I wish-[a] he had bin soe happy as to have understood when Time was.

Monsr Charras[1] brought mee your letter of Recommendation for himselfe, and renewed respects and kindenes to mee; which truly I intended to have answerd by him, but slipt the opportunity. By this I take the opportunity of giving you an account of frequent discourses that have past betweene Sir John Bankes and his Lady and my selfe, in Relation to Mr Caleb Bankes. My Lady has bin passionately desireous for a long while that her son should returne without any further delay. Sir John has bin content to gratify him in his desire of staying some longer Time there. I thought it had bin noe way amisse to let him have pass't two or three monethes in a slow and graduall making that which they call the little Tour of France,[2] beginning to leave Paris and to advance forwards in that expedition about three monethes since; and to have bin backe at Paris about this time, or at farthest about the Middle of this moneth. This would not then be hearkened to by my Lady, though I pressed it very much. It is now againe in Consideration whether this may not be done at this time. The truth is, I can hardly say now what I should advise. I heartily wish that Mr Bankes his Inclinations might be complied with; provided that you make but easy and leysurely motions, because of the Heate of the Season. I wish you by any meanes not to goe Crowded in a Coach, but to take a Coach to your selves onely, and to take your owne time, in going forth and Comming to your Inne. A few dayes Rest will be necessary at all the Considerable places; till you come to the place where you intend to passe the most of your Time. Tis two to one whether, when you are come to some good place that you like well, you will be willing your selves to goe on forwards, or to returne, till the heates shall be a little abated. Bloys, Saumur, Angiers, Poitiers, are all good places; and it will be best to please yourselves.

The chiefe Inconvenience uppon the River of Loyre, is the multitude of young unexperienced youths of our owne Nation and

a-a *MS.* which I/I wish

---

[1] p. 485, n. 2, etc.

[2] For the 'Tour' of France see p. 507, n. 3. The 'Petit Tour' embraced the towns on the Loire, Rennes, La Rochelle, Bordeaux, and thence by Poitiers to Paris; the 'Grand Tour' extended nearly to the frontiers: M.L.R. (C.-M. Saugrain), *Nouveau voyage de France*, 1723, 'Au Lecteur'.

Germans, that flocke thither; whome for your peace and ease I know you will indeavour to avoyd. Let mee againe put you in minde of not taking one Hurrying Journy, nor in the Heates, uppon what occasion soever; nor (if it can be avoyded) to lodge and eate where any other company but your selves are; I meane that you take onely furnished lodgings, eating either alone, or at publick places according as you understand the humour of others that eate there. As for going to see the Army, Flanders, Holland etc. the discourse of it may be respited till your Returne to Paris; which god send you to doe in safety. Uppon the Supposition of a Peace, which now on all handes is taken for granted, the greate thing pressed by the Commons is that the Army be speedily (or as they would have the word—forthwith) disbanded.[1] I doubt not but it will ere long be done; though tis generally thought that some Regiments will be continued, especially towards the North. other particulars you will have from better handes. My eldest son wrote to Mr Bankes by the Poste about a fortnight since. we all joyne in the Tender of our humble service to Mr Bankes and yourselfe. Hoping to see you heare in due season in Health and safety I remaine

Sir your ever most faithfull and most affectionate friend

and humble servant

THO: COXE

Address: A Monsieur Monsieur Locke gentilhomme Anglois a Paris

Endorsed by Locke: Dr Coxe 2 Jun. *78*

## *384.* SIR JOHN BANKS to LOCKE, 3 June 1678 (*381*, *387*)

B.L., MS. Locke c. 3, ff. 100–1.

Sir

I am oblidged unto you for yours of the 28 May and the freedome of your advise, wherin I perceave my son desires rather to goe southward then come home by way of Holland etc. And to answer his request which I suppose to be with your concurrence, I have consulted with my wiffe and other freinds, and doe desire that my son, havinge the benefitt of your good conduct and company[a]

[a] *MS.* comp[a].

[1] '*Resolved*, etc. *Nemine contradicente*, That all the Forces that have been raised since the Twenty-ninth of *September* last . . . be forthwith paid, and disbanded': vote of 30 May: *C.J.*

may spend 2 months upon the Loire and makinge as much of the little tower of France[a] as you see best. I doe leave the manner and method of your proceedinge wholy to yourselvs, The weather is hott: and I know your good prudence, will consider, the doinge what you doe intend with most conveniency, and I pray God preserve you both: I thinke that 4 or 5 days in any place may be sufficient but I doe leave the whole matter to yourselvs. I pray write to us by all opertunities, which you may I hoope doe altho. we cannot soe certaine write to you:

For your supply of mony I pray take creditt from mrs Herrings to all places as customary and as you shall need more money[b] shee shall have direction to supply you. and valew her selfe on Sir Na. Herne. My wiffe presents you her services—And I doe thinke it may doe well to passe thro. flanders and Holland in your returne home, of which pray give your opinion. Sir, I remaine

Your oblidged freind and servant

JOHN BANKS

Lincolns in feilds 3 June 78

Address: To Mr John Lock present[c]

Endorsed by Locke: Sir J: Banks 3 June. 78

## *385.* WILLIAM CHARLETON to LOCKE, 4/14 June 1678 (*380*, 407)

B.L., MS. Locke c. 5, ff. 27–8. Locke copied the passage about curing plums in his Journal, 24 June, N.S.

Montpellier the 14th. June 1678

Deare Sir

The Asseurance of a peace with this crowne and Holland, and the uncertainety of my letters meeting you at Paris, since yours of the 23th. past mention'd your being ready to put foot in stirrop, made me continue thus long silent, but not hearing of your being yet gone I hazard this letter to returne my thankes for the trouble you have taken about my security in case of a warr, I shall not venture to tell you how much I am obliged to you for former favours for feare of being chide, though I thinke you use me a little unkindly in finding fault with me for endeavouring to perform my duty, I shall only tell you that I fully concurre with you

[a] *MS.* ffr[a]. [b] *MS.* m[o]. [c] *The address was written by an amanuensis.*

in what you hint as to my desisting from procuring a passeport as yet, but if occasion requires hereafter I may possiblely make bold to make use of the Interest you have procur'd me with your freind.[1] Sir I remember you were pleased to lay your Commands upon me in case I past Brignol[2] to give you an account how they cure their plums, by Information that I have received it is in this manner. They gather them when they are fully ripe and having stript them of their skinns they stick them upon scures of about 6 Inches long not to close to one another, the scures are fastened one above another either in a cane or rope of straw like a rope of onions, and as we hang them up in our houses to keep, so do they these in the sun to dry, when they are once a little hardned they take out the stones and pressing them together again they spit them a second time and expose them to the sun till they are roasted enough, the best plums are those that grow at Brignoll but the greatest quantyties Come from other parts, my freind that gave me this account sent me some dryed with the stones in them which I know not whether you have ever eaten of, if not and that there be a free commerce betwixt the 2 nations if I may be favoured with your adresse I shall send you some for a tast, The newes of mr. Digg's perferment is verry welcome to me though the Inclosed you was pleased to send me takes no notice of them, but that his father and mother are extreame kind and have setled upon him a verry plentifull fortune.[3] Mr Selapris presents you his service and I am sure will be verry ready to expresse how much he is your servant if you please to adresse any of your freinds that go that way this he ordered me to acquaint you with, if you meet with Mr. Tufton upon your returne for London assure him of my being his most humble servant, My humble service I pray to Sir John Chichley and his Lady and Madam Fines and beleeve that I must cease to be when I do not avow my self

Sir

Your most faithfull and most obliged humble servant

WILLIAM CHARLETON

[1] Locke now had several French friends, including Toinard (p. 579 n.) and Justel (no. *472*); and was friendly with John Brisbane, the diplomatist (p. 546, n. 1).

[2] Brignoles, 35 miles east of Aix. For another account of the method of curing plums see p. 561.

[3] Probably Col. Edward Digges: p. 509, n. 1. The appointment of Lt.-Col. Digges as a deputy-lieutenant for Kent was approved on 23 May: *Cal. S.P., Dom.*, 1678, p. 185. The father is Thomas Digges, d. 1687; matriculated at Oxford 1626: Foster. See further no. *509*.

I feare sir John chichley will be to free to discourse of me and my Concern's, if you can find a Convenient time pray give him a hint to the Contrary.

Address: A Monsieur Monsieur Locke Gentilhomme Anglois chez Mr: Charas Apoticaire rüe de boucherie fauxbourg st. Germain a Paris

Endorsed by Locke: Mr *Charleton* 14 Jun. *78*

## 386. Locke to Dr. Thomas Coxe, 13/23 June 1678 (*383*)

B.L., MS. Locke c. 24, ff. 33–4. Draft. Answers no. *383*.

Paris 23 Jun. 78

Sir

I had soe litle oportunity to doe your son any service in a place where he was more at home then I that 'tis with shame I receive your thanks for it and I have noe thing to defend me from the utmost confusion in the case but the disposition I owne of serveing him or you or any one belongs to you in all occasions that will allow it. I finde that Sir John Banks is now come to the execution of that which was the thing proposd when he sent him into France and to that purpose desires that he should spend yet some time abroad. I confesse were I to speake freely my opinion concerning what is best for the young gent (as I thinke I may to you) I[a]– should considering his temper besides many other reasons thinke, as I have a long time don, travelling better for him then resting at Paris, where a young english gent, (espetially if he be naturally bashfull) will be sure to flee the conversation of strangers and to heard always with his country men, and soe have litle of the advantages with all and more then all the risques of a forain country.–[a] But to you I need not mention these things who know them soe well your self and as to those[b]– who are more concernd–[b]

[a–a] *Substituted for* I should perhaps say that, considering his temper and what he most wants, (besides a great many other reasons) frequent change of company and new faces as much as might be would be of most use to him, and therefor wandering up and downe at ease from town to town would improve him more then double the time spent at Paris, for I can not see the advantages Paris has over London to a young English gent, (espetially if he be naturally bashfull and fears strange faces) who will be sure to heard always with his owne country men and soe have litle of the advantages with all and more then all the risques of a forain country whereof there are but too many examples. [b–b] *Substituted for* Sir John

haveing had but ill successe in the[a]– first offers I made to advise what I thought necessary upon a view of things here upon the place I have ever since thought it good manners to forbear being wiser in other peoples concernes then comes to my share. Though I must allow my self the vanity to say that when I have the oportunity to discourse to you the scheme I had laid downe in my head of Mr Banks spending his time abroad. you will be of opinion that neither Sir J: nor his son would have had reason to repent if it had been followd.–[a]

I am perfectly of your minde that when you proposd it, it was much a fitter season to make a Tour in France. But the constant tenor of our letters from home seteing but short limits to our stay, And the Spring being the proper time for my returne into our English aire, I never dreamt of his going farther but thought we should have been in England before this time where I had prepard all my freinds and some businesse to expect me. But being I know not how fallen into this affair the respect I have for Sir J: and his family makes me consent to make my litle affairs give way to the designe he hath for improveing his son, and perhaps the relation, that the world will thinke I had to him, makes me more then a litle cautious that noe hast of mine should cut him short of any improvement that longer time abroad might afford him. For if the critical world can finde any thing to lay hold on at his returne I know where the censure will light, lett the fault be where it will. I thanke you Sir for your good advice concerning our method of journeying both as a concerne of Mr Banks's and mine too, and altogeather agree with you in it. I thinke our businesse will not require us to make any long and wearysome journeys nor in incommodious weather. I shall not be for any thing but what may be very consistent with all manner of precautions in reference to health, and some regard to ease too. Where convenience and curiosity enterteine us best we will make longest stay, and when we have thus dispatchd our businesse at one towne we will take our oportunity for removeing to the next soe as always to be masters of our owne time and stages and by this meanes I hope we may with safety to the young gent whose heart is set upon it visit what is proposd in this journey. But tis not fit to lead you any

[a–a] *Substituted for* the propositions I at first thought my self obleiged to make surveying things upon the place, It is long since I have given off to thinke my self capeable of giveing advice concerning the disposal of Mr Banks whilst abroad.

farther in it, the length of my letter has already made it a journey to you. To dispose you to pardon me I beg you to consider how very naturall it is to forget ones self when one is talkeing with a person for whome one hath that esteeme wherewith I am

My service to Sir

## *387.* Sir John Banks to Locke, 20 June 1678 (*384, 391*)

B.L., MS. Locke c. 3, ff. 102–3.

Lincolns in feilds 20. June 78

Sir

This day brings me yours of the 22 instant. perceavinge you are pleased to oblidge me in accompanyinge and conductinge my son for the Loire, which is very much both to my wives and my owne satisfaction, And doe wholy leave the disposinge your selvs and all matters relatinge to this voyage to yourselvs, beinge assured my son hath that great kindnesse and respect for you that you may dispose him as you please, which I am fully satisfied will be in what you know to be most to his advantage. I have desired Sir Na. Herne, 10 days agoe, to write to Madam Herinx to give you what further Credit, you desired, and before the next post goe, I shall speake to him againe, yet I pray take that freedome to pas your byls on me from any place, where you finde a necessary supply. and they shall be dewly payd, and you may not only shew this my order for your voucher, but I shal send you a further from some other freind at my first leasure and you may expect to be more reasonably supplyd by your owne byl direct for London then by freinds at Paris, but as your stay will require noe Great supply yet it your care I doe see to be supplyed on the best termes and I have writt alsoe to my son that a prudent frugality becomes any Gentlemen

I perceave your kind care, to have all my sons concernes discharged at Paris, before you move thence, for which I thanke you. and he will I hoope have sent me the account of his Expences to his goinge thence, for I would have him keepe the same exact: and if you shall please to keepe the same forward, I doe hoope as it will be an ease to him soe it will be much more convenient unto you both.[1] For other matters I may write more by the next opertunity, assuringe you that I shall ever owne my selfe to be

Sir, Your very obligded freind and servant

JOHN BANKS

Mr Finch[2] presents you his humble services

Address: A Monsieur Monsieur Locke.[a]

Endorsed by Locke: S^r J. Banks 20 Jun. *78*

TOINARD

Locke met Nicolas Toinard at Henri Justel's house at some date between June 1677 and April 1678; he mentions Justel on 7 October 1677 for the first time, and the meeting may have taken place slightly earlier; he mentions Toinard for the first time on 21 April 1678. The two became friends. Though they did not see one another again after May 1679, they corresponded frequently. The correspondence was interrupted by the Nine Years' War and ended with the outbreak of the War of the Spanish Succession apart from a single unwelcome letter from Toinard that Locke received in 1704. At the outset Toinard had much to tell Locke about the activities of their common friends; in later letters he is more concerned with his own interests.

The usual and correct spelling of his surname is Thoynard; Nicolas adopted the form Toinard as part of his scheme for improving French orthography, but apparently remained Thoynard in legal documents (the *privilège* for his Harmony of the Gospels). The family was armigerous. The earliest known member, Nicolas Thoynard, was a *bourgeois* (freeman or burgess) of Orleans in 1550. Some of his descendants held office locally. Toinard's father, another Nicolas, was a magistrate (*Président au bailliage et siège présidial*); his mother, Anne de Beauharnois, was a member of the family to which belonged the first husband of the Empress Josephine. Toinard is said to have

[a] *Address written by an amanuensis.*

[1] How Caleb spent part of his time in Paris is suggested by a letter from an unidentifiable writer:

Sir

I did not think you had ben so ill bred as to denid a lady so small a faver sa that was I desier of you but sin you ar so uncind I am resalf to wat of you as soun as my Clos is mad wich will not be long forst I am suer you ar the worst naterd man in the world suer your corig is not so litell as to be dantd by a wonen I hop the sit of me would not a fritid you mouch bout rather then a disableg you I would a pot on a mask I hat my self when I think that ever I should have the lest of pasion for won that hats me nou far well the worst of men

Address: Thes For Mr Banks thes Preset

Endorsed by Locke: to C. Banks *78*

—B.L., MS. Locke c. 23, ff. 198—9.

[2] Identifiable as Heneage Finch, *c.* 1649–1719; created baron of Guernsey 1703; earl of Aylesford 1714; he had married Banks's daughter Elizabeth on 16 May of this year: *D.N.B.*

been born on 31 March 1628; he was baptized at Orleans on 5 March 1629. With a view to succeeding his father he studied law, but, disliking the subject and having sufficient private means, devoted himself to scholarship. In 1652 he was introduced to the Jesuit Father Denis Petau (p. 662, n. 2) and henceforward moved freely in learned circles in Paris and Orleans. In 1661 and 1662 he travelled in Spain and the Netherlands. In 1666 he accompanied Cardinal d'Estrées (no. *884*) to Portugal. He is said to have visited England in 1667. Thereafter he remained in France, residing by turns in Paris and Orleans. He did not marry. He died in Paris on 5 January 1706.

Toinard's great ambition was to compose a harmony of the four Gospels, using the Greek texts. He was a devout Catholic. He was acquainted with Bossuet, but appears not to have been a regular member of Bossuet's *petit concile*, a group for the study of the Bible that met weekly from 1673 to 1681.[1] He printed a version of his harmony in 1678 for his own use (no. 428). Although the French clergy wanted it he refused to publish it. He had a fertile and ingenious mind and constantly devised fresh improvements; industrious and conscientious as a scholar, he failed to concentrate his interest sufficiently to complete his work. There were not only the subsidiary studies for the harmony, including notably chronology and numismatics. For a few years he was eager to produce other harmonies, of parts of the Old Testament, of the Apocrypha, and of Josephus. But there were wider interests. Henri Justel (no. *472*) held at his house meetings of scientists and men interested in science, and perhaps of the learned in general. Catholics and Protestants, Frenchmen and foreigners, were alike welcome. Toinard appears to have been a mainstay of these gatherings. He was greatly interested in voyaging and exploration; he collected explorers' narratives and maps, and made some use of his knowledge. It is questionable whether he appreciated properly the achievements of the scientists of his time. He was captivated by new inventions, regardless of whether they were capable of realization or likely to prove useful, and was ready to improve whatever came his way; later on, as his fortune dwindled, he hoped to restore it by some new project. In addition to his superficiality he was apt to be facetious.

Toinard published only a very few small pieces; apart from some notes on Lactantius' *De Mortibus Persecutorum*, mainly dissertations on particular coins or medals. The history of his harmony of the Gospels is uncertain. Besides the complete version printed in 1678, one, two, or perhaps three, other versions appear to have been set up in whole or in part. It was published posthumously in 1707 as *Evangeliorum Harmonia Græco-Latina*.

Toinard's work on it broke new ground. Earlier compilers, from Tatian onwards, were concerned probably in most cases primarily with edification; the work was to be done properly; the reader was to be presented with a reliable composite narrative. Toinard was concerned primarily with historical scholarship; scholars were to be presented with the materials so arranged that they could construct a composite narrative for themselves. To this end he devised a new layout. The texts of the four Gospels were placed in four parallel columns; each text was set out continuously, but broken into verses,

[1] Floquet, *Bossuet, précepteur du Dauphin*, pp. 420–51; for Toinard's position as regards the *petit concile*, the letter, pp. 438–9.

sentences, phrases, or single words, as required by the texts in the other columns; hands ('fists') directed the scholar from one column to another (part of St. Matthew is displaced in order to bring it into the same chronological sequence as that of the other Gospels). An additional column provided a Latin summary narrative; at the head of the page the place and date are set out, the latter according to the various epochs, the consular and regnal years, the years of the life and ministry of Jesus. An opening of what appears to be an alternative version of the Harmony shows how the scholar would use it. In this version there is a complete Latin conflated narrative, the Gospels from which it is drawn being indicated; another column contains the discarded variations. This alternative version (if that is what it is) is over-elaborate and too cumbersome. The earliest version—that of 1678—performs its task adequately; the posthumous publication is an amended reprint of it. Given the premiss that the Gospels are susceptible of verbal integration in a composite narrative, Toinard's *Harmonia* is a masterly achievement. For his general conduct and the treatment of detail he had models in the work of other scholars. Some of his chronology is questionable; there is some superfluous if not useless information; and there may be other weaknesses. The peculiar excellence of the work lies in the marshalling of the material; in this respect it may well have proved influential far beyond the limits of its own subject.

*Authorities.* The principal materials for Toinard's life are the letters from and to him. He kept many letters addressed to him. The collection appears to have been preserved intact until the mid-nineteenth century. The bulk is now in the Bibliothèque Nationale, MSS. Nouvelles acquisitions françaises, nos. 560–3. Some portions were detached and apparently went into the autograph market. The majority of the letters from Locke were in the collection of J.-C. Brunet and were sold at auction by E. Charavay in 1868. Most of the letters in this sale were acquired by the British Museum, which acquired also modern copies of some other letters. Ollion printed thirty-two items from the Museum's holding in his *Notes sur la correspondance de John Locke*, 1908 (here cited as Ollion, *Notes*); then in the *Lettres inédites de John Locke*, 1912 (here cited as Ollion), fifty-nine letters, all except one apparently from originals or copies in the Museum's holding. Letters from other correspondents to Toinard are printed in the *Bulletin du bibliophile*, 1888 and 1908, and by E. Du Boys, 1890.

The letters from Toinard to Locke in the Bodleian Library form the most important collection of those that survive. There are about fifty-five letters from him to J. G. Grævius in the Royal Library in Copenhagen. A few letters to Leibniz have been published. There are single letters or small holdings elsewhere.

Jean Le Clerc, who had himself composed a harmony of the Gospels, published a notice of Toinard's *Harmonia* in *Bibliotheque choisie*, xv. 247–90; this is probably the most important estimate of Toinard as a scholar. His standing as an antiquarian and numismatist is shown in notices in *Bibliotheque universelle*, XXI. ii. 130–2, and F. Perez Bayer, *De Numis Hebræo-Samaritanis*, Valencia, 1781, p. 106. The best modern account of him is that by Charles Cuissard in

Société archéologique et historique de l'Orléanais, *Mémoires*, xxviii (1902), 33–57, in which his will and other documents and a bibliography are printed (cited below as Cuissard). Ollion follows this; he makes some additions, largely from Locke's letters: pp. 1–13.

Locke's set of leaves of the 1678 Harmony is now in the Mellon Collection at Upperville. There are a number of leaves of this version in a volume in the Bodleian Library (shelf-mark E 4. 4 Th.); this volume also contains the single opening (begins Matthew 4: 21) mentioned above of what appears to be an alternative version (for a tentative identification see no. *545* n.).

Locke listed the contents of Toinard's letter of 12/22 July 1678 (no. *392*) by inserting in the margins single-word notes of the subjects of the various passages and then repeating these words in the endorsement. He did this habitually for Toinard's letters from June 1679 (no. *477*) until the interruption of their correspondence, at least so far as it is extant, in June 1682 (no. *721*). He made no attempt to continue the practice when their correspondence resumed in 1684 except perhaps in the first letter (no. *778*). There are occasional irregularities, such as the omission of one or more marginals from the list in the endorsement; he sometimes amplifies them, as in no. *501* where 'Baudran' becomes 'Geographie de Baudran'. Sometimes there is no list; sometimes there are no marginals; sometimes, as in no. *594*, what is in effect a marginal is on the back of a sheet. The course adopted in printing is in general to discard the marginals and to retain and amplify the lists. Marginals omitted by Locke from the lists are inserted in their due places; they are distinguished by square brackets. Other irregularities are noted as they occur. The amplifications are not recorded, nor are insignificant changes of spelling between the marginals and the lists; changes of language are recorded.

Locke adopted the same practice for some letters from Justel (no. *534*, etc.); it is recorded as it occurs.

## 388. Locke to Nicolas Toinard, 29 June/9 July [1678] (390)

Boston, Massachusetts, Public Library. Published by courtesy of the Trustees. Single sheet. Copy, made *c.* 1871, in B.M., Add. MS. 28,836, f. 14. Printed from the copy in Ollion, *Notes*, p. 28; Ollion, p. 14. Year from contents.

Paris 9 Jul.

Monsieur

En ouvrant ce papier je trouvé la herbe dont je vous a parlé. Jé suis bien aise que j'ay le moien de ne pas manquer a ma parole devant que partir de Paris[1] parceque je suis

Monsieur

Vostre tres humble et tres obligé serviteur

J Locke

Address: Pour Mr Toynard

[1] Locke left Paris on either this or the following day: Journal.

## *389.* THOMAS STRINGER to LOCKE, 3 July 1678 (*378, 403, 430*)

B.L., MS. Locke c. 19, ff. 141–2. Mentioned by Locke, 11/21 July: Journal.

July 3d. 1678.

Deare Sir

I received your letter dated Midsomer last[1] at my coming to Towne on Munday night, which is the only letter I have had from you these 3 months. I am very glad to heare you are at length on your jorney homwards, though it be the farthest way about, I hope we shall see you heare in a short time. I have not had any money from mr Thomas[2] a long time, but have write tenderly to him as you desired about it, though I have not yett received an Answere. I have alsoe writt to your Uncle[3] for an accompt of your affaires out of Somersettshire that by your returne home I Expect I shalbe able to give you satisfaction. Your sister in Law[4] I never heard from sinc your departure, but for the silks by good fortune they are all turned into money, and the money is out at Interest upon a morgage. The Attlas you mention I finde is intended more to gett money by it then for a publiqe benifitt that I am told by some booksellers I shall by it much Cheaper out of a Booksellers hands then it will cost the subscribers.[5] I have just now Received your letter of the 6th of July, with your bill on Sir John Chitchley which I shall take care in, the former bill on mr Beamont[6] I received long sinc. Your things sent by mr Herbert are not yett cleared out of the Custome house, though mr Cholmley tells me he is in great hopes of doeing it Every day, as well for you as mr Herbert they being there together. I am at some dispute whether it is the improvements you have made by your Travells in Strength and Vigour, or the thoughts of old age ⟨and⟩[a] infirmitys which makes a man consider of living honest, ⟨th⟩at[a] putts you in minde of getting a wife, but bee it which it will in hopes that a wife will fetter you by the heeles and make you live soberly amongst us I will promise you shall not want my helping hand nor the Assistance

[a] *Page torn.*

[1] Probably 14/24 June.
[2] Samuel Thomas: p. 430 n.
[3] Peter Locke.
[4] Mrs. Dorothy Taunton: p. 225, n. 3.
[5] Moses Pitt, the publisher (*fl.* 1654–96; *D.N.B.*; no. 544), advertised in the Term *Catalogue*, 22 June of this year, proposals for *The English Atlas*: *T.C.* i. 324. The completed parts were published in 1680–2: Madan, no. 3253. See further pp. 389 n., 615.
[6] Charles Beaumont: Locke, Journal, 4 June 1678.

of mr Hoskins whoe will most Chearfully Contribute his ayde in helping you both before you have gott her, and after you have her to, in[a-] case your need shall require it[-a] be assured you shall not want friends upon such an occation, nor any other incouragement that may forward your inclinations in soe good a designe. And if you will think the Experience of a friend of any weight to forward it, I doe assure you there is noe satisfaction like it, which will readily be attested by the hand of

Dearest Sir

Your most Faithfull affectionate servant

T: S:

Address: A monsieur Monsieur Lock Gentilhomme Anglois Chez Madam Herinx et mr Sonfils banquiers a Paris

Endorsed by Locke: Mr Stringer 3 Jul. *78*

## 390. Locke to Nicolas Toinard, 4/14 July 1678 (388, 390A)

B.M., Add. MS. 28,728, ff. 1–2. Printed in Ollion, *Notes*, pp. 28–30; Ollion, pp. 14–17. Answered by no. *392*.

Orleans. 14 Jul. 78

En verité Monsieur vous etez á craindre, mais vous etez ausi beaucoup davantage á aimer. Quand on est hors de la portée de vos fuzils,[1] pour excellents qu'ils soient, on n'est pas hors de la portée de vos obligations, et a trent lieus (je parle seulement de cela que j'ay eprouvé) de vous, vous savez bien atteindre ceux sur lesquels vous avez dessine. Aprez tant des obligations que vous m'avez faites á Paris je me trouve icy á Orleans de nouveau accablé des bienfaites par les maines de vos amis auxquels vous m'avez fait l'honeur de m'addresser. Mr de Rebours[2] a qui j'ay rendu vostre livre m'a recu avec grand civilité. Mr Perot[3] me montra l'execution

[a-a] *Altered from* in case you shall have occation

[1] Locke describes guns, etc., invented or improved by Toinard: Journal, 1678, pp. 108–10, 113–15, 165–6; later notices, Journal, 1678, p. 383; B.L., MS. Locke d. 1, p. 101 (printed in Lough, p. 285); p. 606; no. 467 n.

[2] François de Paule de Rebours: Ollion, p. 15 n.

[3] Bernard Perrot, d. 1710; of Italian origin (Bernardino Perotto); glass manufacturer at Orleans from 1668: ibid.; A. Du Pradel (N. de Blegny; no. *497* n.), *Le Livre commode des adresses de Paris pour 1692*, ed. E. Fournier, 1878, ii. 44 and n., 45, n. 3. Locke recorded his visit to the glass house, and the 'glasse bottles with glasse stoppers that scrued in', in his Journal, 12 July. Toinard tried to exploit his invention later: no. *589* etc.

de vostre belle invention des vers á vice et toutes les autres curiositez de son metier dont on trouve quantite chez lui en leur perfection, et je croy qu'il ne lui manque rien que un peu de vostre aide pour porter cette art a sa plus grande hauture. Mr Godefroy[1] me fit tout l'acuile possible, méme il me fit l'honeur de m'inviter a soupper mais mon compagnion m'attendoit á soupper au logis ce que m'obligea de m'en excuser. Mr L'Abé Gendron,[2] quoique a ce que je crois un de premiers hommes de son seicle, estoit le dernier que j'avois l'honeur de voir, et ayant eté deux ou trois foiz a sa porte sans reussir j'avois peur que comme ce pauvre attendant á Bethesda[3] je demeurerois inconsolable faute de queque un pour me faire entrer en ce lieu de santé. Je scavois bien que son garçon qui venoit a la porte n'estoit pas un bon ange parceque il ne vous connoissoit pas, ce que lui fit me dire toutjours que son maistre etoit a la campagne. Mais a la fin vostre letre ouvrit la porte et j'y suis entré avec bien de la joy. Mais au lieu d estre gari[4] du desire que j'avois de connoistre cet excellent homme, je le trouvé par sa conversation beaucoup augmenté. Il me montra votre petit moulin[5] de grand effect, ou je trouvois les marques de votre Grand Genie dans cette admirable simplicité. Il me donna un de ses livres et un de ses excellentes remedes et m'en expliqua ausi la composition. Cest á vous Monsieur que je dois les obligations de tant d'honétes gens et c'est a vous ausi á les en remercier, il surpasse tout ce que je peu. Et pourtant je vous avoue que avec tout cela vous ne gainez rien sur moy parceque je ne peu pas etre plus que je ne suis

Monsieur

Votre tres humble et tres acquis serviteur

JOHN LOCKE

Je croi partir aujourduy pour Blois[6] ou je serois infinement ravi de recevoir de vos nouvelles et de la progresse del harmonie. Si je ne part pas aujourdui j'auray l'honeur de voir Mr L'Abé Gendron encore une fois

[1] d. 1686; he was a doctor of medicine at Orleans: no. *884*; Journal.

[2] François Gendron, 1618–88; trained as a surgeon; lay assistant ('*donné*') with the Jesuit mission to the Hurons 1643–50; ordained priest 1652; treated Anne of Austria for a tumour on the breast 1664–5; commendatory abbot of the Cistercian abbey of Ste. Marie de Maizières (near Beaune) 1665; resident at Orleans from 1671: *Dict. Canadian Biography*; Royal Society of Canada, *Proc. and Trans.*, 3rd ser., vol. vi (May 1912), i. 35–83. Frequently mentioned below.

[3] John 5: 2–9. [4] 'guéri'. [5] Journal 13 July; later notice 23 July.

[6] Locke did not leave Orleans until 20/30 July.

Je baise les maines tres humblement a Mr l'Abé Fromentin[1] et Mr Bernier,[2] á qui je suis faché de n'avoir pas peu dire adieu avant ma sorti de Paris comme je tachois en vous quittant

Si vous me faitez l'honeur de m'ecrire, vous me pourriez addresser vos letres chez Madame la Vefve de Mr Simon Fesneau á Blois ou je resteray trois ou quatre jours au moins

Address: A Monsieur Monsieur Toynard á la teste noire
rue Mazarin
Fauxbourg st Germain
á Paris

Endorsed by Toinard: 14.Juil.78.

## 390A. Locke to Nicolas Toinard, 11/21 July 1678 (390, *392*).

B.L., MS. Locke c. 39, ff. 21–2. Answered by no. *392*.

Orleans aux trois Empereurs
21 Juil. 78

Dies jam aliquot sunt quod ad Te (Vir Ornatissime) Gallico, ut potui, sermone scripsi, vereor autem ne non agnoscas vernaculam tuam calamo meo inscité exaratam. sed tuæ est, nec dubito, humanitatis, agnoscere animum gratitudinis et observantiæ plenum (qualem ego meum erga Te profiteor) sensa sua male exprimentem. Tua Aurelia Tui similis non cito dimittit quos semel amplexa est. Mora hæc, dum Tuis careo literis, quas me authore

---

Some days ago I wrote to you, most distinguished Sir, to the best of my ability in French; but I am afraid you will not recognize your own native tongue when it is clumsily set down on paper by my pen. But with your usual kindliness you will recognize, I am sure, a mind full of gratitude and respect, such as I declare mine to be in regard to you, however badly it expresses its feelings. Your city of Orleans is like you: it does not readily let go those whom it has once taken to itself. This interval of delay, during

---

[1] Raymond Formentin, 1631–1703; canon of Ste.-Croix of Orleans 1665. He is frequently mentioned below, often as 'le Capitaine Formentin', and so on, probably because his father came from Barfleur; no other connection with the sea is known. He was educated for holy orders, but never took more than deacon's orders: notice, with his letters to Toinard, in B.N., N. Acq. fr. MS. 561; Soc. archéol. et hist. de l'Orléanais, *Mémoires*, xxxviii (1902), 140–1. The identification of the Abbé and the Capitaine is fully established in no. *2693*: 'le Triumvir Capiténe de Marine est alé à Rome avec son patron m. le Card. de Coislin.'

[2] François Bernier, 1620–88; M.D. of Montpellier, traveller and philosopher: *D.B.F.* Locke mentions him first on 8 October 1677: Journal.

Blæsas missas credo, mihi maxime tædio fuisset nisi obstitisset Optimi et doctissimi viri Domini Godfroy frequens et amica consuetudo. Si tamen verum fateri liceat, non mirandum est, si mihi inter ingenuos optimosque viros híc versanti Tui restat desiderium. nec enim plures Tui similes una in urbe, etsi Tua sit, reperiendi; cum plures ejusmodi vix unum producat sæculum. Dominum Abatem Gendron semel tantum ex quo hic commoratus sum videre contigit, etsi sæpe foribus ejus adsum importunus cliens. sed, ut opinor, aut ægrotantium negotia, aut otium, sibi curisque suis debitum, ⟨difficiles⟩[a] reddit aditus. Sed dum meum hac in re doleo infortunium, illius laudo humanitatem, et gratus agnosco beneficia. In primo enim illo congressu ultra spem meritumque meum, sed tui causa me locupletatum medicamento, scientiâ auctum ⟨dimisit⟩.[b] Animi tamen parum grati esse existimo, et ingenuo indignum, eo insalutato abire. Et ut dicam quod res est, molam istam tuam portatilem[1] cum per moram hic licet, velim libenter, si permissum esset, accuratius contemplari. meretur enim ut non currente oculo,

[a] *MS.* deficiles [b] *MS.* demisit.

---

which I have been without letters from you (I believe they were sent to Blois on my instructions), would have been very tiresome to me if the frequent and friendly company of the excellent and learned Mr. Godefroy had not prevented it. However, if I may admit the truth, it is not surprising that, though I move about among high-minded and excellent men here, I should still continue to miss you. For not many men like you are to be found in one city, even in your own city, since scarcely a whole century produces more than one of that stamp. It has chanced that during the whole of my stay here I have seen M. l'Abbé Gendron only once, although I have often presented myself at his door as a persistent client. But I imagine that the affairs of his patients, or even the leisure which is due to him and to his constant concern for them, has made access difficult. But, while I lament my own bad luck in this matter, I commend his regard for his fellow-men, and I gratefully recognize all he has done for me. At that first meeting of ours he exceeded my expectations and my deserts and out of deference to you he sent me away enriched with medicine and enlarged with knowledge. I think it would show ingratitude, and would be unworthy of a gentleman, to go away without taking leave of him. And, to tell the truth, I should like very much—and my delay here makes it possible—to examine if you give me leave that portable mill of yours with greater care. For it deserves more than the passing

---

[1] The Latin word is unusual. It occurs in a book-title, *Bibliotheca Compendiosa & Portatilis*, a duodecimo list of books and authors for law-students entered among the new books in *Journal des Sçavans*, 1703. Locke may have been influenced by the English word, occurrences of which from 1657 onwards are quoted in *O.E.D.*

uti factum est, sed ut singulae ejus partes earumque symetria per otium et defixo in eas animo observentur. Nondum hinc decessurus sum, Adeoque spero, ante decessum, me certiorem ex tuis literis fieri, et te bene valere et voluptatem magnam capere ex facili et non impedito magnæ illius Tuæ harmoniæ progressu.[1] Vale et me ama

Tui observantissimum
J Locke

Dominum Fromontin et Dominum Bernier rogo ut meo nomine salutes

Address: A Monsieur Toynard á la Teste noire rüe Mazarine Fauxbourg St Germain á Paris

Endorsed by Toinard: 21. Juil. 78–

---

glance I have given it: it deserves that each separate part, and the ways in which the parts are proportioned one to the other, should be studied at leisure and with attention concentrated on them. I am not likely to leave here yet, and I hope very much that before I do I shall learn from a letter from you that you are well and are deriving great pleasure from the smooth and unhampered progress of that great 'harmony' of yours.[1]

Good-bye and hold me in affection as your most dutiful
J. Locke

I ask you to give my greetings to Mr. Fromontin and Mr. Bernier.

## *391.* Sir John Banks to Locke, 11 July 1678 (*387, 396*)

B.L., MS. Locke c. 3, ff. 104–5.

Lincolns in feilds 11. July. 1678

Sir

I have receavd yours of the 9th instant from Paris and 14th from Orleans, and note you were upon your intended perambulation, in which doe wish you both your good healths, The weather proves heer very hott. and as I am very well pleased by what I finde in your letters at my sons being out of Paris for this season. soe I

[1] Toinard showed Locke 'his Harmony of the Evangelists printed in a new method' on 21 April of this year. This was probably sheets from the version of which Locke received a complete set by December: no. 428. Toinard gave him some sheets before he left Paris as he packed 'Harmonia Toynardi' in a trunk that he left in Paris: Journal, 21 April, 2 July. See pp. 589–90. The printing was not completed before Locke left Paris.

Toinard experimented with a second version in 1680 (no. *545*) and appears to have made some progress with one or more further versions (no. *1777*, etc.). The work was published in 1707 after his death as *Evangeliorum Harmonia Græco-Latina*.

hoope will he be to returne home when he hath ended this journy and satisfyed himselfe therin; wherin I wish you both good successe.

Sir, I did send a weeke since to Madam Herinx a fresh credit from Sir N. Herne to supply you what ever you should desire. It was my hap to be from home, els I had sent you a Gen. credit, but I doe not doubt. but you will finde supply. and your byls shall be dewly payd, as all yet have beene, and I thinke it now to late to send you other creditts, I have writt to Madam Herinx prayinge her care to your supply, My Lord Shaftesbury and other your freinds there are in health. The enclosed I receavd 2 days since. My Wiffe is abundantly satisfyed in the account you Give of her sons health; and his brother and sister Finch present him and yourselfe their salutes. as doth alsoe

Sir, Your assured freind and servant

JOHN BANKS

Address: Monsieur Monsieur John Locke

Endorsed by Locke: Sir J: Banks 11 July. *78*

## *392.* NICOLAS TOINARD to LOCKE, 12/22 July 1678 (390A, *393*)

B.L., MS. Locke c. 21, ff. 1–2. Answers nos. 390 and 390A. Answered by no. 394.

+

A Paris ce 22. Juill. 78.

Il y a non seulement des jours heureux mais aussi des heures heureuses, car hier au meme tems que j'obtins a laudience du Parlement un Arrest a la confusion de l'avocat de notre partis, vous songiez en moy, Monsieur, puisque vous m'ecriviez. Je ne veux pas tarder davantage a vous en temoigner ma reconnoissance, et quoique je sois pressé par l'heure du courier je crois avoir assez de tems pour vous remercier de l'honneur de vos premieres qui etoient tres bien eccrites en notre langue. La latine que je reçois me rend votre obligé en deux manieres. Je ne me suis point donné lhonneur de vous ecrire a Blois parceque jetois allé voir un amy a trois lieües dici quand la votre ariva, et a mon retour je suputé que vous seriez parti de Blois, et je trouvai ici matiere de m'exercer dans un emploi odieux, car nos parties firent une nouvele chicane inouie, et il me falut solliciter, de maniere que je n'ay eu que deux pages de l'harmonie depuis celles que vous avez veües, encore y en a til une dont les sommaires ne sont pas encore faits; J'aprehende d'avoir peus de repos devant la fin du Parlement qui est au commencement de Septembre, parceque nous poursuivons un Arrest definitif que nos parties eludent depuis huit ans. J'ay bien songé des fois aux Loix de la Carolina au sujet des persecutions que lon nous fait parceque la chicane est ici un metier.[1] Je fus encore heureux hier en ce qu'un de mes amis me montra un Hygrometre le plus sensible et le plus simple du monde qu'il a inventé, et lui coute quatre sous argent content. Il le tient encore secret, et il en pretend faire un mouvement perpetuel, parcequ'y ajoutant quelque chose il fera qu'une pendule se monte d'elle meme.[2] Il etoit venu trois ou quatre fois me voir pendant que vous etiez ici, et sil m'avoit trouvé il me l'auroit montré des lors et jaurois bien obtenu de lui la meme chose pour vous. Il dit qu'il a aussi une invention pour rectifier les pendules, mais lheure me presse. jecris a monsieur Gendron. cachetez lincluse devant que de la rendre, et faites porter le moulin chez celui qui la fait. Il est bon de lui dire que je vous ay dit bien du bien de lui, car les ouvriers veulent etre flatéz. Il est serrurier et demandez le sous ce nom la dans son cartier, mais par honneur je luy donne cete autre qualité. Vous verrez dans le petit livre de monsieur Gendron une ortografe particuliere dont je vous rendray conte une autre fois.[3] faites moi la justice, Monsieur, de me croire Votre tres humble et tres obeissant serviteur

TOINARD

Avec votre permission je salueray monsieur Godefroy. Je savois bien que vous le gouteriez fort. Faites moi la grace si vous alez chez monsieur Perrot de lui dire qu'il m'envoie les essais de poudriers dont je luy ay ecrit, parceque jen suis pressé, et excusez ma liberté.

Address: A Monsieur Monsieur Locke Gentilhomme Anglois demeurant aux trois Empereurs A Orleans

Endorsed by Locke: Mr Toinard 22 Jul. *78*
Hugrometre Pendul Handmill Gendron.

[1] The document called alternatively the Fundamental Constitutions of Carolina: pp. 395, n. 2, 516. Toinard probably alludes to § lxiv: 'No Cause shall be twice Tried in any one Court, upon any reason or pretence whatsoever.'

[2] The inventor, Jacques de Hautefeuille (p. 632, n. 4), devised a new form of hygrometer; he attached a clock to it in such a way that the movements of the hygrometer served to wind the clock: see further p. 591.

[3] Gendron's book is perhaps *Principaux remedes*: L.L., no. 1237; no. *910*. No copy is known. The peculiar orthography was probably an example of one of Toinard's reforms: see p. 595.

## *393.* NICOLAS TOINARD to LOCKE, 14/24 July 1678 (*392*, 394)

B.L., MS. Locke c. 21, ff. 3–4. Answered by no. 394.

+

A Paris ce 24. Juill. 78.

Etant allé hier feliciter Monsieur Brisban sur son Inter-Ambassade (car je crois que vous savez qu'il fait les afaires d'Angleterre en l'absence de l'Ambassadeur)[1] il prit part a la joie que j'avois de ceque notre ville vous possedoit encore, et me temoigna qu'il etoit en peine de vous faire tenir une letre: Je m'ofris, monsieur, de lui rendre ce petit service, et a vous aussi; et le priay d'ajouter mes plaintes de ceque vous avez par votre absence deconcerté l'Harmonie. il s'en aquite par cete incluse que je vous remets de sa part, a laquelle je lui ay dit que vous pouviez repondre des demain. Vous devriez bien, Monsieur, retourner prontement ici pour voir le mouvement perpetuel executé par un Hygrometre. Je ne veux pas vous en dire autre chose sinon que l'Inventeur est aussi d'Orleans qui trouva jeudi une letre de vint un mille cent quarante livres paiable au porteur, et que nous cherchons chacun de notre coté celui a qui elle apartient, qui a sans doute lui seul plus dinquietude que ce mien amy et moy n'en avons tous deux; car si lon alloit au banquier qui la doit paier a Paris, on pouroit en composer avec lui, et cete somme seroit perdue pour celui qui l'a conteé. Un certain comte d'Albi, Irlandois (Wit en son nom qui signifie blanc) home intrigant, fut areté vendredi au matin et mené a la Bastille au retour d'un voiage de la Rochelle. Il y a desja eté mis deux ou trois fois, et a des freres a Vienne, Madrid et Munic, tous gens d intrigue etc.[2] Je commence a esperer de la paix, au moins qu'il n'y aura point rupture avec l'Angleterre parceque Monsieur Brisban fait faire un beau carosse. Il souhaite que vous veniez l'etrenner. Vous verrez en meme tems l'efet prodigieux

[1] Ralph Montagu returned to England without leave about the beginning of July: Browning, *Danby*, i. 286–7. When, on 3 July, O.S., his credentials were revoked, Brisbane was empowered to act as agent; although a new ambassador was sent to Paris in July, Brisbane was not recalled until June 1679.

[2] Andrew White, Count d'Alby, was sent to the Bastille on 31 July, N.S., charged with espionage for Spain; he was kept there for eight years. The most prominent of his brothers was Ignatius White, marquis of Albeville, James II's ambassador to the United Provinces: below, no. *974*. For the brothers see *English Hist. Review*, xlv (1930), 397–408.

d'un microcospe simple et nouveau que Mr Hugens a raporté d'Hollande, et dont il fut fait hier experiences a l'Academie.[1] lon y a vu entre autres choses de petis animaux dans de la semence, et cest avec un pareil microscope que Mr Sammerdam[2] a donné l'ovarium du pou. Je m'en vais porter l'Inventeur du mouvement perpetuel a[a] publier prontement sa machine, parceque je scay que des gens a qui il la communiquée, veulent le prevenir; et cest pour cela que dans les assemblées je dis que lon verra bientost cete machine afin de se precautioner contre les plagiaires. J'ay salue de votre part monsieur Bernier qui vous salüe aussi. Pour le capitaine de marine a[a] la[a] Sorbonne[3] il est a la campagne. Tout le monde vous regrete fort ici, monsieur Auzout[4] m'en parloit encore hier. Monsieur Roemer[5] et moy salüons monsieur Godefoi. croiez toujours, monsieur, quoique vous ecrivant a batons rompus que je seray regulierement votre tres humble et tres obeissant serviteur

THOYNARD

Address: A Monsieur Monsieur Locke Gentilhomm Anglois aux trois Empereurs A Orleans

Endorsed by Locke: Mr Toinard 24 Jul. *78*

Further note by Locke:

| | |
|---|---|
| | 6–0 |
| | 1–10 |
| | 9–0 |
| | 16–10 |

[a] *Doubtful reading; word altered, etc.*

[1] Christiaan Huygens, 1629–95, styled of Zuylichem until 1687; '*the Great*—Huygenius': *N.N.B.W.*; Locke, *Essay*, Epistle. His description of the microscope was published in the *Journal des Sçavans* of 15 August (pp. 352–4).

[2] Jan Swammerdam, 1637–80, the naturalist: *N.N.B.W.*

[3] Presumably Formentin.

[4] Adrien Auzout, 1622–91, physicist and astronomer: *D.B.F.*; M. Lister, *A Journey to Paris*, 1699, pp. 28, 99–100.

[5] Olaus Rømer, the astronomer: no. *463*.

## 394. Locke to Nicolas Toinard, 16/26 July 1678 (*393*, 399)

The Pierpont Morgan Library, New York. Transcribed from Xerox print. Answers nos. *392* and *393*.

Orleans 26 Jul. *78*

Vir Colendissime

En tibi tandem literas jam triduum destinatas, quas nunc retinendas nunc mittendas suasit ⟨itineris⟩[a] nostri incertitudo, nollem enim ego incertæ sedis, earum libenter remittere fructum amplissimum, tuarum scilicet spem. Ita enim in ambiguo nostri hinc decessus consilium, ut an hic an Blæsis tuas ego expectarem literas, quibus carere non possum, nondum constat. Hisce me agitatum dubiis iisque otiosé immorantem tua heri excitavit epistola et oficii memorem fecit; nec ulterius differenda est gratiarum actio cum non solum tuas sed amicorum etiam tibi debeam literas. Quod de communi nostro amico Domino Brisban, mihi prorsus inscio et harum omnium rerum utique ignaro, scripsisti: De Legato nostro rumusculos aliquos hic aliquando audivi, sed cum quasi in transitu, et incerto authore dicti, et cito transierant, vanos credideram. siqua inde nostro fiat aut honoris accessio aut ad ampliora gradus gratulor. Quamprimum tuæ 22° datæ, mihi traditæ fuerunt, Domi-

[a] *MS.* iteneris

---

Orleans 26 Jul. 78

Honoured Sir,

Here at last is the letter I have been meaning to send you for the last three days; the uncertainty I was in about my movements made me at one time think it better to keep it back and at another to send it, for as I was not sure where I should be I would not have wished, if I could help it, to miss the best reward I might hope for from it, namely a letter from you; so in this uncertainty about my departure from here I have not yet made up my mind whether to wait here or at Blois for your letter, which I cannot do without. Such was the state of doubt in which I was idly loitering when I was yesterday roused by your letter and reminded of my duty, and I must thank you without further delay, as I am indebted to you not only for your letter but for those of friends. As to what you tell me about our common friend Mr. Brisbane, I was quite unaware of it, and in any case I know nothing about all those things. I heard some gossip here from time to time about our ambassador; but it was only in passing, as it were, and not on any certain authority, and as it soon died down I thought there was nothing in it. If it means a more honourable position for our friend or a step to greater things I congratulate him. As soon as I received your letter of the 22nd I went to see Mr. Perrot; he told me that

num Perot adii, qui tibi vitra quæ postulasti cum jam parata essent eodem se die ad te misurum promisit. Si te crederem ignarum pulveris, ejusmodi clepsydris commodissimi tenuissimique, qui ex stanno fit, ejusdem præparationem tibi mitterem. digna sane res quæ microscopio isto, cujus mentionem fecisti, oculis objiciatur, cum enim subtilissimus sit pulvis, cujus granula maximam partem rotunda sint, et polita, mire jucundum est in tantillo speculo integram fenestram imo totas ædes quasi in puncto ope microscopii contemplari. De hygrometro quod dicis magnum est, et optime et tum amico tuo et tum literato orbi consulis dum protinus promulgandum suades, ne quis alius alienis inventis inhians egregiam hanc sibi præripiat laudem, debitam ingeniosi inventoris mercedem, majora etiam meriti. Si autem (quod te narrante dubitare non possum) satis habeat virium ad alia movenda pondera, nec inconstantiâ aliquando fallat, magnum author afferet humanis laboribus solatium et rebus mechanicis complimentum, vix[a] enim aliud majus numerari potest inter iam diu desiderata, quam mobile perpetuum. Sed cum mihi certum sit posteros multa reperturos quæ nobis non solum incognita sunt, sed etiam impossibilia videntur de eo etiam sæculo in quo te et tui similes videmus nil desperan-

[a] *Preceded by* p *deleted?*

---

the glasses you asked for were now ready and promised to send them to you the same day. If I had thought you did not know of the most convenient and finest powder for hour-glasses of that sort, which is made from tin, I would have sent you the method of preparing it. It is certainly an object worth looking at under that microscope you mentioned, for the powder is very fine, its granules being mostly round and smooth, so that it is wonderfully pleasing to study in such a minute mirror a whole window, or indeed a whole house, as it were, in a single spot with the aid of the microscope. What you tell me about the hygrometer is important, and you are doing the best thing both for your friend and for the learned world in advising that it should be made public immediately, in case anyone else with a covetous eye on other people's discoveries should snatch for himself the signal credit of this invention, which is the due reward of the ingenious inventor, who deserves even greater things. If moreover, as I cannot doubt from your description, it is powerful enough to move other weights and is not liable to fail at times through irregular working, the originator will be affording a great relief to human labours and making a contribution to mechanics, for nothing greater can be counted among our long-felt wants than perpetual motion. I am sure, indeed, that those who come after us will discover many things that are not only unknown to us but even seem impossible; yet we need not despair even of the present age, in which we see you and those like you. I congratulate myself and

dum. Gratulor mihi et literariæ reipublicæ nuperam tuam forensem victoriam, male actum est cum bonis viris si tibi diutius eo in pulvere versandum sit, sed uti spero Deus O. M. cui viri boni curæ sunt hisce curis litibusque te totum eximet, otioque tuo literario te iterum tradet[a]– istis molestiis–[a] solutum. Molinam tuam affabre factam iterum iterumque intus et extra magna cum voluptate contemplatus sum, nec unquam tam parvo in corpore tantam vim eos præsertim ad usus mihi adhuc videre contigit, experimentum in eo nullum feci, nec opus est, nam cum autopsia res constat, quid est quod ultrá experiri velis, harmoniæ hic etiam actum est, et visu res probatur. Qua ego voluptate Domini Abatis Gendron librum perlegi vix potes concipere non solum ex argumento quod mira continet, sed scripturæ methodo, pronuntiationi accomodata, ex quo enim hic in Gallia sum aliquid super ea re animi causa commentatus sum, in quo jam mihi met placeo, cum rem ipsam tibi non displicere sentio, quo authore audebo fortassis aliquando orthographiæ heterodoxæ nostra etiam in lingua dare specimen. quid enim scientiam rerum, sermone et scriptura facili propagandam doctis hujusmodi et inutilibus nugis impedimus? ⟨sed⟩[b] de his hactenus, vereor enim ne garulitate nimius sim, et

[a–a] *MS.* tradet istis/istis molestiis [b] *MS.* se

---

the commonwealth of learning on your recent victory in the courts; good men are badly treated if you are to be involved any longer in the dust of that conflict; but Almighty God, who is concerned for good men, will, I hope, relieve you entirely of these cares and wranglings and will restore you to your learned leisure free from these troubles. I studied your ingeniously constructed mill again and again both inside and outside with great pleasure; I have never yet had the opportunity of seeing so much power, especially for those uses, in such a small body. I have not tested it in any way nor is there any need, for one is certain of it simply by looking at it; why should one want to make any further trial? here too is a product of harmony, and the thing approves itself on sight. You can hardly imagine with what pleasure I read the Abbé Gendron's book, not only for the subject-matter, which includes some remarkable things, but for the spelling of words, which is adapted to their pronunciation; for since I have been here in France I have amused myself by composing some thoughts on that subject. I now feel satisfied with myself about it, as I believe that you are not unsympathetic in this matter; so with your support I may possibly venture some day to give a specimen of heterodox orthography in our own language as well. Why must the propagation of knowledge, which demands easy language and writing, be hindered by such pedantic and useless futilities? But enough of this; I am afraid I am too talkative and a greater nuisance than even the lawyers; you must pardon

ipsis causidicis[a] magis molestus, ignoscas animo qui dum de te cogitat se totum effundere vellet, urbanitatis fortassis et decoris immemor, verum et si minus scité, sinceré tamen omnia loqui scias. Nemo enim omnium est quem ⟨majoris⟩[b] æstimo, magis amo, quam te; nemo a quo magis cupiam amari. Vale

Tibi devotissimus
J Locke

Notum tibi non dubito Hygrometrum simplicissimum sed et valde ⟨sensibile⟩[c] ex barba avenæ fatuæ constructum, quale sæpe expertus sum.

Rogo ut mihi indices locum aliquem Parisiis quo mitti possint, etiam te absente, res aliquæ tibi destinatæ. Scripturus enim sum ad amicum quendam Londini quo curante ad te mitti velim librum istum de duplicata proportione[1] de quo olim locuti sumus, et siquid aliud iis ex regionibus desideras. Nam certior factus sum aliquem mihi notissimum huc in Galliam venturum, qui res ejusmodi cum cura asportabit.

Decessus meus ex hac urbe nondum adeo certus quin tuas hic

[a] *Or* causedicis [b] *MS.* magioris; *word badly altered from* magis [c] *MS.* sensible

---

a soul that would like to pour out all it contains when it thinks of you, perhaps forgetting courtesy and seemliness; but even if I show little skill, you may nevertheless be sure that all I say is said sincerely; for there is no one in the world whom I esteem and love more than you, or by whom I would more desire to be loved. Good-bye.

Your most devoted
J. Locke

Doubtless you know a very simple but highly sensitive form of hygrometer, that which is made of a beard of wild oats; I have often found it so in practice.

Please tell me of some place in Paris to which any things intended for you could be sent even when you are away. I am about to write to a friend in London through whose agency I should like the book on duplicate proportion[1] that we spoke about some time ago to be sent to you, as well as anything else you want from those parts; for I am informed that someone I know very well, who will bring such things with him carefully, will be arriving here in France.

I am not yet so certain about leaving this city that I cannot still hope to

---

[1] Sir William Petty (no. *470*), *The Discourse made before the Royal Society 26 Nov. 1674, concerning the Use of Duplicate Proportion*, 1674. L.L., no. 2281.

sperare adhuc possum literas, quas saltem si Domino Godfroy mittas, curabit credo, ut quocunque abiero ad me perveniant.

Tuis ego hic cumulor beneficiis, et hac ipsâ horâ Dominus Abbas alterum secretorum suorum ⟨δραστικωτάτων⟩[a] mihi communicavit. Ipse te salutat; te illi gratias agere meo nomine impensé rogo, brevi ad te literas daturum dicit

Dominum Bernier et bonum nostrum Navarchum saluto. Qui ut ut strenuus sit nunquam tamen erit, uti auguror, nisi bonorum Authorum pirata, ex quorum ⟨spoliis⟩[b] ditescere mire habilem credo

Address: A Monsieur Monsieur Toynard á la Teste noire, rue Mazarin Fauxbourg st: Germain á Paris

[a] *MS.* δραστικοτάτων [b] *MS.* spolii

---

get a letter from you here; at any rate if you send it to Mr. Godefroy I am sure he will see that I get it wherever I may have gone.

I am heaped with your kindnesses here; this very moment M. l'Abbé has communicated another of his potent secrets to me. He sends you his greetings; I beg you particularly to thank him from me; he says he will be writing to you shortly.

Remember me to M. Bernier and to our good friend the Captain; however strenuous he may be, yet he will never, I predict, practise piracy except on good authors; I believe he has a wonderful knack of enriching himself with the plunder he gets from them.

## 395. MRS. A. BEAVIS to LOCKE, 22 July/1 August 1678

B.L., MS. Locke c. 3, ff. 162–3. The writer was probably related to Mrs. Blomer: p. 326 n.

Paris Agust the 1: 78

Sir

I must confess I am not concerned att our returne: into Ingland tho I should have bin better pleased if it had bin tow months sooner: for severall reasons that I will not trouble you with now but leave it to stats men:[1] I have received your Letter by mr Brisband and your orders for your treasurs which were at his house: I have it in my charge now till wee pack up and then I will lett it shift for it selfe in the wide ocian with the rest of my Lords Plate: my Lady says you, are very lazey to be noe farther then orleans all this while, shee hope to be in Ingland long before you gett to bloys if you make

[1] This refers to Montagu's dismissal: p. 591, n. 1.

noe more hast then you have yett shee is very well and soe is Deare mistres Anne:[1] shee gives you her humble servis and say shee is not in hast ⟨for⟩[a] her gloves since they cannot come time enough to goe with her: for wee shall goe from Paris in ten days if all continue well: now I hope like a good Pupile you will belive I will be very carfull of your standish and candlesticks and if you have any more servis for mee I shall very willing purforme it: till then I am

Sir

Your most humble servant and Governesse A B.

all our famely are your very humble servants. But Mr Cole[2] is very sick and in continuall swetts that hee looks like a dead creatur.[3]

Address: A Monsieur A Mr Lock: Chez madam La vefve de mr Simon fesneau:[b] A Blois

Endorsed by Locke: Mrs: Beavis 1 Aug. *78*

## *396.* SIR JOHN BANKS to LOCKE, 25 July 1678 (*391, 404*)

B.L., MS. Locke c. 3, ff. 106–7.

Sir

I am glad to understand by you of my sons well recovery I pray God continew both your healths. and I doe not doubt of your care and kindnesse to him in all his concernes. and doe assure you it is

[a] *Word omitted at end of page.* [b] *Spelling doubtful.*

[1] Probably Anne, d. 1742, daughter of Ralph Montagu and Lady Northumberland; married, first, Alexander Popham, d. 1705, of Littlecote, son of Sir Francis Popham, K.B. (p. 145, n. 2.); secondly, General Daniel Harvey, d. 1732, of Combe, Surrey, a grandson of Sir Daniel Harvey the ambassador (p. 527, n. 2): J. Burke, (*History*) *of the Commoners*, 1836–8, ii. 200; etc.

[2] Nathaniel Cole: P. S. Lachs, *The Diplomatic Corps under Charles II and James II*, 1965, p. 192. I have failed to identify him further.

[3] An undated statement of account by Mrs. Blomer may relate to Locke as it is endorsed by him:

| | |
|---|---|
| two head dresses $7\frac{11}{W}$ | 21:00:00 |
| one head dress of petit point | 20:00:00 |
| one Girdles cap | 03:00:00 |
| for a fann | 33:00:00 |
| £: | 77:00:00 |

I had like (by a mistake in the shop keepers bill) to have cheated, you or my selfe, of 5l. your point de france is in the caps. the box cost 7 sols, and all your things are put up in it very securely:—

Endorsed by Locke: Blomer *78*

—B.L., MS. Locke c. 4, f. 13 (a scrap). £: for *livres*.

noe great satisfaction to me and my wiffe who presents you her humble services

I have spoken to Sir Na. Herne and he hath promised to write to mrs Hering. but if he doe not, the credit is to my son or his order, and his direction to mrs Herrinx will be sufficient.

I have not time to write to my son, pray tell him we are all well. and hoope he and you will sute your returne before winter, for the last news of his not being well maks his mother more desirous of his cominge home, and we feare his travell this worme weather. but know you will dispose all matters the best you can, my son Finch and daughter present you both their humble services and beleive me to be

Sir, your oblidged humble servant

JOHN BANKS

Lincolns in feilds 25 July 78

I pray let my son write as oft as he can to us

Address: A Monsieur Monsieur Locke.

Endorsed by Locke: Sir J: Banks 11 Jul. *78*

## 397. LOCKE to ROBERT BOYLE, 27 July/6 August 1678 (335, 478)

Boyle, *Works*, 1744, v. 569–70.

Blois, August 6, 1678.

Honoured Sir,

You will not wonder, that I lay hold on so fair an occasion of presenting my service to you, when you reflect on the many great obligations I have to you, and that I should be very unworthy of the honour I have to be known to you, did I pass by any opportunity to express my acknowledgments. I should think it a great advantage to me, whilst I am abroad, if you would honour me with any of your commands. And if in this part of France I am now rambling, your curiosity had any enquiries to make, I should with great satisfaction embrace the commission, and be sure to give you an exact account. I have news from Paris, from an ingenious acquaintance of mine there,[1] that a friend of his hath found out a very

[1] Toinard: see pp. 590, 591.

sensible hygrometer, which, besides marking the moistness of the air, will also be improved to wind up a pendulum; which, if it succeeds, will be a kind of perpetual motion. And a watch-maker I know there[1] sends me word, that he is now at work upon a movement, that the air will wind up; which, I suppose, is the execution of the design my friend (who is a very good mechanick, besides an admirable scholar) sent me notice of. He also mentioned to me the extraordinary goodness of a microscope Mr. Huygens has brought with him out of Holland. But these things having happened in Paris since I left it, I cannot give you so perfect an account of them, as I desire. When I was there, I saw in the Charity a boy about eighteen years old, who had a kind of horns grew out in the place of his nails of almost all his fingers or toes; some of them were four or five inches long. I have a large piece of one of them, which was broke off in my presence, and the whole history of the case amongst my things at Paris. This accident began to grow upon him, after the small pox, about two or three years since. Enquiring for him a little before I came away, I was informed, that he was cured and gone.[2] Some other things worth observation I have also light on, which would be too long to trouble you with here. And, amongst other things I have a small quantity of a medicine given me, which I believe to be of great efficacy to certain purposes, whereof perhaps you will not be displeased to see the effects. I was extremely well pleased to hear, that the things were sent me from the Bahamas were put into your hands; they could not have been placed any where so much to advantage, and to my desire. For I shall always be exceeding glad, if any thing I have or can may serve to testify the respect and esteem, wherewith I am,

Honoured Sir,
your most humble servant,
J. LOCKE.

If at any time you design me the honour of a letter, it is but sending it to Sir John Banks's in Lincoln's-Inn-Fields, and it will find the way to me.

[1] Perhaps J. Oury, or Ouri, whom Locke met on 1 September 1677: Journal; below, no. *563* etc.

[2] The Charity is La Charité, the hospital. See the fuller account in no. 478.

## *398.* DR. THOMAS SYDENHAM to LOCKE, 3 August 1678 (*337, 363, 496*)

B.L., MS. Locke c. 19, ff. 165–6. Parts of the letter have been cut away in three places (this was presumably done by Locke in order to maintain the secrecy of the new treatment of ague). Printed by Dr. K. Dewhurst in *The Practitioner*, clxxv (September 1955), 319; in his *Sydenham*, p. 171.

Dear Doctor

understanding how much Tabor, now knighted here, hath bin admired for his skill in curing Agues,[1] I thought fitt to lett you know a way if you have not allready observed it in my book, page 99:[2] Tis thus. The fitt being for example on Sonday, lett that fitt pass, (it being dangerose to checke the aguish matter that is now ready to be discharged by a paroxisme) and give 2 dramms . . .[a] monday morning, 2 drams monday night, 2 tuesday morning, 2 tuesday night, and you shall be certeyn twill miss comming wensday. Or thus ℞ . . .[a] ℥j. syr.ros.sicc. ℥ij aut q.s. Take it at 4 times as before in the intermitting dayes, drinking a draught of wine after it. If it be a double quartan run over the bastard fitt and give notwithstanding. As in a quartan so in a tertian, begin at[b] morning or at night as soon as the fitt is over and be sure the next fitt will not come. If a child, then boyle 3 Dramms . . .[a] in a pint of Clarett and give 2 or 3 spoonfulls every third houre. Now to prevent a relaps, be sure to give it agayne ether within 8 or 9 dayes, or if you will, the day after the missing of the first fitt, as thursday morning, thursday night, friday morning, fryday night.

Thus you shall be sure to cure, for I never affirmed any thing to you which failed. Sic vos non vobis.[3] I never gott 10l. by it, he hath gott 5000. He was an Apothecary in Cambridg wher my booke of practise have[c] much obteyned. Thanke you for my Patient Mr. Robinson.[4] I am most cordially and sincerely

Your true friend and affectionate servant

THO: SYDENHAM

Pall-mall Aug. 3° 1678.

[a] *Page cut away.* [b] *Blotted, perhaps for deletion.* [c] *Doubtful reading.*

---

[1] Robert Tabor or Talbor, *c.* 1642–81; knighted on 27 July of this year: *D.N.B.* He improved the method of administering quinquina or cinchona bark, otherwise called Jesuits' bark and Cortex Peruvianus, or simply the bark, the substance from which quinine is extracted. See further nos. 656 n., *948* n.

[2] *Observationes Medicae.*

[3] 'Sic vos non vobis mellificatis apes': *Anthologia Latina*, ed. F. Buecheler and A. Riese, 1869–97, pt. i, no. 257.

[4] Identifiable from no. *459* as William, 1655–79, son of Sir John Robinson, bart. (Lord Mayor of London, 1662–3); knighted 24 November of this year: G. E. C.,

If the Ague be a new one twill be fitt to purge before you give the powder or stay till it has worn it selfe a little, but if an old one begin presently. I am I thank god perfectly well of my pissing bloud, gout etc. and understand my trade somwhat better then when I saw you last, but am yet but a Dunse.

Address (presumably not written by Sydenham): A Monsieur Monsieur Locke, chez Madam Herinx, et Monsr: son fils, banquiers, A Paris

Postmark: AV 3

Endorsed by Locke: Dr Sydenham 3. Aug. *78*

## 399. LOCKE to NICOLAS TOINARD, 10/20 August 1678 (394, *402*)

B.M., Add. MS. 28,836, ff. 1–2. Copy, made *c.* 1871. The original was at that time in the collection of B. Fillon at Fontenay-le-Comte (Vendée); later, with Messrs. Maggs Brothers: *Catalogue*, no. 433, Christmas 1922, item no. 3444. Printed from the original in Alfred Morrison Collection, *Catalogue*, vol. iii, 1888, pp. 182–3. Printed, from the B.M. copy, in Ollion, *Notes*, pp. 32–3; Ollion, pp. 17–18. Answered by no. *402*.

Angers 20 août 78.

Monsieur

Quoique vous m'ayez préparé partout des amies les plus honests et les plus scavants, ce qui pouvoit bien contenter un homme qui auroit l'esprit un peu réglé, Je ne peu pas pourtant m'empecher de vous avouer que parmi les beautés du meilleur pays de France et le bon aceuil de vos amis, aux quells vous m'avez fait l'honeur de m'adresser, je n'ay pas un contentement parfait, puisque je n'ay point de vos nouvelles. Je confesse que cela est bien importun; mais pour le guerrir, il faut que vous ayez moins d'amitié, moins de merit. Quand cela arivera, on sortira peut etre de Paris sans avoir plus de regret de quitter un monsieur Toynard, que toutes les belles choses qui y attire tout le monde, et on goutera mieux les plaisirs qu'on cherche dans les provinces. Mais, comme vostre maniere d'agir ne donne point d'espérance de cette sorte, trouvez bon, je vous prie, que je vous demande le soulagement qui me rest

*Baronetage*, iii. 53 n.; epitaph in Le Neve, *Monumenta Anglicana . . . 1650–79*, 1718, p. 193. Locke treated him for dysentery, etc., between 26 November 1677 and 14 April of this year: Journal, *passim*.

de recevoire quelque foie de vos letres. J'arivay icy hier au soir, et, aujouduy, j'ay eu l'honeur de voir Mr l'Abbé Froger.[a] En vérité Monsieur, vos Abbés sont extraordinairs, Et si touts les Abbés en France seroient comme ceux dont vous m'aves donnée la conneissance, a Orléans, et a Angers, et a Paris, il n'y auroit rien de si excellent que cette sorte de gens. Je n'ay pas eu le temps encore d'aller voire Mr de Juignié-Locé,[1] et d'ailleurs on croit qu'il n'est pas présentement en ville. Je crois partir d'icy on moins de huit jours pour la Rochelle. On parle en ces quartiers de Rochefort comme d'un place qui merit le mieux d'estre veu de toutes les places en France, et, comme vous avez beaucoup de cognoissance avec les gens de marine, (ausi bien qu'avec nostre bon Capetain Fromontin, dont je suis le très-humble serviteur), vous me ferez grand plaisir de m'adresser à quelqu'un à Rochefort, qui me pourroit faire voire quelque party de ces belles choses la. Vos letres me troveront à La Rochelle chez Mr Jean Raullé.[b]

Mais si vous avez des amis ou non, je vous supplie de ne manquer pas de m'y donner de vos nouvelles. Vostre santé, vostre *Harmonie* sont des choses auxquelles j'ay trop d'interest (et, puisque vous me permettez cett honeur, vostre amitié ausi) pour ne pas en attender des nouvelles avec impatience. Pardonnez-moy cette liberté, s'il vous plaist, parceque je suis avec toute sorte de recognoissance

Monsieur

Vostre très-humble et tres acquis serviteur

J LOCKE

Je baise les maines très humblement a Mr l'Abé Fromentin,[2] Mr Bernier, et Mr Auzot.

On parle icy de la paix comme faite;[3] j'en suis bien aise.

Dans ma derniere d'Orlèans, je vous priay de me mander vostre adresse à Paris en votre absence, parceque il y a un de mes amis

[a] *The Alfred Morrison text reads* Troger, *as did Fox Bourne.* [b] *Badly written; read by Ollion as* Raulté. *The correct reading is given in B.L., MS. Locke f. 28, p. 44, and in the address of no.* 402.

[1] Probably a member of the Angevin family Le Clerc de Juigné-Verdelles: F. A. A. de la Chenaye-Desbois and Badier, *Dictionnaire de la noblesse*, 3rd ed., 1863–76, v. 817–26. Ollion suggests Jacques Le Clerc, seigneur et baron de Champagne, de Juigné, de Lande, etc.

[2] Despite the repetition the Capitaine and the Abbé are the same man.

[3] The treaty between France and the United Provinces was signed on 10 August N.S.

qui viendra de Londres à Paris cett automne, qui peut vous apporter le livre de duplicate proportion, dont je vous a parlé,[1] et toute autre chose que vous souhaitez d'Angleterre. Aiant point reçu de vos letres depuis, je répéte icy la même priere.

Je serois bien aise d'antendre que le dessein du mouvement perpetuel a bien reussi.

Address: Monsieur Monsieur Toynard a la teste noire dans la rüe Mazarine Fauxbourg St Germain a Paris.

## 400. LOCKE to DE JUIGNÉ-LOSÉ, 12/22 August 1678

B.M., Add. MS. 28, 836, f. 2$^v$. Copy, made *c.* 1871; written badly. The original was at the time in the archives of the de Juigné family. Printed, apparently from the B.M. copy, in Ollion, *Notes*, p. 34; Ollion, p. 19. Excerpt, translated, in Fox Bourne, i. 400, where the letter is said to be addressed to Toinard.

Angers, 22 aoust 1678.

Monsieur

Un ami de M. l'abbé Froger m'a engagé de passer par Thouars, Fontenay et Marans, me rendant à la Rochelle. Ceste route est, suyvant lui, à préférer à l'autre que j'avois résolue de suyvre, et ce qu'il m'a conté des richesses de Mr le duc de la Tremouil a comencé à me faire faire reflection en sa faveur.[2] Il ne tient qu'à vous, Monsieur, de me diriger par un chemin ou par l'autre, ayant resolu de me remettre à vous sur ce point, partant d'icy. Une route cahoteuse ne me deplaist point, pourveu que le pays soit plaisant sans fascheuse rencontre. Je veux bien employer mon voyage à conoistre les provinces, où je seray passé, et ne pas négliger ce qu'elles ont de Curieux et de rare, comme il arrive aux estrangers mal conseillers, ou du tout, par des tuteurs généreux. Si M. l'abbé Froger n'eust quitté Angers pour une journeè ou deux, il vous auroit espargné la peine de cest itinèraire, mais, à son deffaut, les recomandations de M. Toynard et de M. l'abbé de Gyvé,[3] m'ont fait le devoir de m'adresser à vous, dont j'ay deja receu bon acueil, et la responce

[1] Petty's *Discourse*: p. 596, n. 1.

[2] The duke is Charles-Belgique-Hollande, duc de la Trémoille, 1655–1709; succeeded as duke 1672: la Chenaye-Desbois and Badier, xix. 194. There is a notice of Thouars in C. de Varennes, *Le Voyage de France*, ed. 1667 (L.L., no. 3068), p. 158. Locke took the alternative route by Richelieu and Niort: Journal.

[3] Ollion suggests a member of the Gyvré family of Poitou.

que j'attende augmentera encore ma recognoissance. En attendant, croyés sans plus que je suis,

Monsieur, vostre tres humble et obeissant serviteur,

J LOCKE

## *401.* MME M.-L. BRUNYER to LOCKE 12/22 August 1678

B.L., MS. Locke c. 4, ff. 193–4.

De Blois ce 22ᵉ Aoust 1678

Monsieur

Je fits partir hier une douzaine de paires de gans double pour Madame la Comtesse de Northumberland Lesquels Mr. houri[1] a a dressés a Mr. son frere suivant vostre ordre et Jay remis es mains du dit sieur houri vingt et une livres Les quelles Jointe avec les dix ecus que Jay payés pour La douzaine de paires de gans font la somme de cinquante et une Livres Laquelle vous mavies mise entre les mains si Javois peu obliger le marchand a tout reprande je Laurois fait mais il na voulu reprande que la douzaine de simple Je souhaite quils puissent estre bien tost entre les mains de celle pour qui ils ont esté faits et quelle Les trouve a son gré afin que vous en ayes le contantement que souhaite celle qui est

Monsieur

Vostre tres humble servante

M L BRUNYER $ $

Address: Angers A Monsieur Monsieur Locke gentilhomme Anglois chés Monsieur de la riviere Huet[2] A Angers

Endorsed by Locke: Me Brunier 22 Aug *78*

## *402.* NICOLAS TOINARD to LOCKE, 17/27 August 1678 (399, 418)

B.L., MS. Locke c. 21, ff. 5–6. Answers no. 399.

+

A Paris ce 27. Aoust. 78

J'ay bien de la joie, Monsieur, de la satisfaction que vous avez eüe de mes amis, cela tiendra un peu lieu de compensation pour les

[1] Perhaps a rendering of Ouri: p. 600, n. 1.

[2] A banker: B.L., MS. Locke f. 28, p. 38.

mauvaises heures que vous passez avec moi. Il ne manque plus qu'une page a l'harmonie, et même elle se peut suppleer car cest st Jean qui parle seul. Ma santé seroit bonne si j'avois la tranquillité necessaira a mon genre de vie, mais aiant a solliciter deux ou trois procez dans le debris du Parlement qui finit au 7. du prochain mois jugez quel regal cest pour moi. Le nouveau fusil qui se charge par la relasse est entierement fini, et je l'ay tiré douze fois pour lessaier; quoiqu'il soit ovalé il ne repousse point du tout. Il m'est tombé entre les mains un cahier manuscrit de secrets en Anglois dont vous serez l'interprete. Quand vous repasserez par Orleans je pourray avoir l'honneur de vous y revoir. L'une de ces incluses en Portugais est pour un tres honete home qui a eté principal Ingenieur a Angole pendant huit ans, et de la passa a Buenos ayres. il vous en contera bien. Il est frere de monsieur de ste Colombe l'un de nos plus celebres Ingenieurs principalement pour les choses de la marine.[1] Je vous prie de salüer Madame sa femme de ma part. C'est par galanterie que j'ecris en portugais a mr Massiac et le fais re-souvenir de cequi m'ariva a Lisbonne ou les Portugais lui dirent en confidence parlant de moi; *que cela etoit pitoiable qu'aiant d'ailleurs quelque sens, je l'avois perdu jusques au point de passer la mer pour leur demander des nouvelles des couleuvres du Bresil.*[2] Le souvenir de ce conte, qui est veritable, le divertira, et je lui dis que vous avez la même manie pour nos bonnes amies les couleuvres de les Empacaçes d'Angola,[3] et que c'est expressement pour cela que vous etes venu d'Angleterre à Rochefort. Je me suis aquité de ceque vous m'ordonniez envers mss Fromentin, Bernier et Auzout, qui mont aussi prié de vous assurer de leurs services. Lautre letre est pour monsieur de la Touche[4] secretaire de monsieur de Meun Intendant de la marine.[5] Il est de Toulon et cest le plus honête provençal que je connoisse.

[1] The brothers are Barthélemy de Massiac, still living in 1684, and Pierre de Massiac, sieur de Ste-Colombe, d. 1682, 'ingenieur ordinaire du Roy de France', who planned the fortifications of Brest (1677): P. Levot, *Hist. . . . de Brest*, 1864, i. 149–59, 170–2; ii. 8 n., 9, 21. Massiac and de la Touche (see below) showed Locke and Caleb Banks the sights of Rochefort on 8 and 9 September: Journal. Ste-Colombe is mentioned frequently in Toinard's correspondence with Locke, Massiac occasionally; and both occasionally in the Journal.

[2] Toinard was at Lisbon in 1666: Cuissard, pp. 37–8.

[3] The *empacassa* or *pacaça* is a kind of buffalo found in Angola.

[4] He was a Provençal as distinct from a Frenchman.

[5] Honoré-Lucas de Demuin sometimes called de Muin, intendant at Rochefort from 1674 to 1683; he was a convert from Protestantism and was active and harsh in the attack on the Protestants: L. Pérouas, *Le Diocèse de La Rochelle de 1648 à 1724*, 1964, p. 304, etc.; Colbert, *Lettres, instructions*, ii. 365 n., vi. 127 n., etc.; Élie Benoît as quoted by Lough, p. 235 n.

Aussi est il fils d'un françois qui s'habitua la, et cela fait voir que le sol ne change pas en une seule generation le bon fonds du naturel. Vous pouvez vous souvenir que nous nous sommes autrefois entretenus la dessus sur l'ouverture que vous en fîtes, et que nous en demeurames d'acord par plusieurs inductions. Vous trouverez ici une letre ou il y a bien des machines proposées. l'Auteur est de notre ville. Vous pouvez parler de nos armes a Mess Massiac et de la Touche. Il m'est venu en pensée depuis trois jours une maniere bien simple et seure pour charger des canons par la relasse. ce seroit d'un grand usage sur mer et sur terre. au moins pour les moindres pieces. Je ne m'ennuye jamais avec vous present ou absent, il est neantmoins tems que je vous dise manque de papier que je suis Monsieur, Votre tres humble et tres obeissant serviteur Toinard

Apres avois cacheté les letres incluses, Vous prendrez la peine de vous informer si ces messieurs qui sont des gens peripateticiens en guerre plus qu'en philosophie sont a la Rochelle ou a Rochefort.

Mr Talbor febrifuge est arivé. Je souhaite n'avoir point besoin de lui, neantmoins il est bon de le connêtre

Address: A Monsieur Monsieur Locke Gentilhome Anglois chez Monsieur Jean Raullé A la Rochelle
Endorsed by Locke: Mr Toinard 27 Aug. *78*.

## *403.* PETER LOCKE to THOMAS STRINGER, 21 August 1678

B.L., MS. Locke c. 14, ff. 188–9. Peter Locke's nearest letters to Locke are nos. *306*, *443*; Stringer's are nos. *389*, *430*.

Sutton Ag: 21 1678

Sir

I Rec: Letters from you one of 2 July and now 8 of this month I could not well Give you an ansueer sooner for I Have not been well this month or six weekes as for my Cosen tanton His sister en law[1] I know nothing of any anewity nor ever Had any order to pay any thing to Her. Yf my Cosen Hath a mind to Give Her I should be willing to Pay Her what He shall Apoynt for she is a pore widow.

[1] Mrs. Dorothy Taunton: p. 225, n. 3.

as for the accounts between us I Have Heer In Inclosed as fare as I can Goe till I Have a Rent Role from Him my love and service to your selfe and mrs Stringer

I am your lovinge frend
PETER LOCK

Pray Sir lett me desir you to send this In closed letter to my Kinsman

Address: For mr Thomas Stringer att Thannett House In Aldersgate Street In London *altered by another hand to* Att Bexwelles near Chellmsford Essex

Postmark: AV 24(?)

Endorsed by Locke: P. Locke to T Stringer 21 Aug. *78*

## *404.* SIR JOHN BANKS to LOCKE, 29 August 1678 (*396*, *406*)

B.L., MS. Locke c. 3, ff. 108–9.

Sir

My last to you was the 15th instant, since which none of yours—My Lady Northumberlands goods[1] are not yet arrived, nor is Mr Cole in towne. I shall take all possible care therin

Your byl I have accepted and shall be dewly payd as have all beene this weeke that you had Given to Madam Herinx at your leavinge Paris, being but now dew. I doe finde my son very importunate to Goe to Thaloes[2] from Morlaix,[3] which I presume to be with your consent I meane that you thinke it convenient for him, to whom you have shewed soe much kindnesse. And therfore doe leave it to your prudence, who are best judge of his health and what may be to his best satisfaction and advantage, to doe in althings as you see best with respect to his returne with as much conveniency as may be, which will be much to our satisfaction, both his Mother and my selfe thinking his stay long.

I doe wish both your Good healths. and hoope to see you both well heer. yet nothing is more to my satisfaction then that my son in under your care, wither ever he goes—and I pray will you

[1] pp. 597–8. [2] Toulouse.
[3] Presumably Banks's mistake for Bordeaux.

alsoe respect your owne Conveniency as my sons desire of spendinge a litle more time abroad. and beleive me to be

Sir, Your oblidged humble servant
JOHN BANKS

Lincolns in feilds 29 Aug. 78

I have writ to my son to Bordeux under mr Pepys Cover. as he directed These come by Paris that you may see which comes first

Address: Monsieur Monsieur Locke

Endorsed by Locke: Sir J: Banks 29 Aug. *78*

## *405.* SAMUEL PEPYS to LOCKE, 29 August 1678

Samuel Pepys, *Further Correspondence, 1662–1679*, ed. J. R. Tanner, 1929, p. 320. Copy made by or for Pepys in his letter-book. The original was sent by Pepys with a letter from himself to Caleb Banks: copy, ibid., pp. 318–19; and a letter from Sir John Banks to Caleb: no. *404*. For Pepys and his interest in Caleb see p. 465, n. 2.

29 *August*, 1678.

The time I have taken for acknowledging the favour of yours of 26 June has wiped off a great deal of the score which you (in your generosity rather than any strictness of justice) are pleased to charge yourself with towards me, and for the remainder of the reckoning, shall with your leave turn Mr Bankes over to you for it towards the discharging of an account wherein I stand debtor to him in the same specie.

This will I hope find you well arrived at Bourdeaux, to which I inclose Mr Bankes the addition of one way-bit more, I mean to Tholouse and, could it have stood almost with humanity towards my poor Lady Bankes, I would with much more pleasure have sent him a commission for a greater length; nor possibly should I have wholly forborne my offers at it, had I had any certain knowledge how you stood affected to it and Mr Bankes (more or less) solicitous for it. But, I say, under my imperfectness in this, and being a daily witness of the uneasiness of my Lady's life under the apprehensions of her son's going still further from home, I do think Mr Bankes may reasonably bound his desire of travel at Tholouse, and from thence make his coming back as delightful and instructive as by your directions he can; giving his mother at length the just satisfaction of contemplating him with his face homewards.

For what respects yourself, I have upon ample grounds been long your honourer, making you (with my beloved Mr Bankes) a great piece of my care . . .

## *406.* SIR JOHN BANKS to LOCKE, 5 September 1678 (*404, 408*)

B.L., MS. Locke c. 3, ff. 110–11.

London. 5. September 78

Sir

My last to you was the 28 ultimo. Since which have yours of the 30, and of my sons of the 4 September from Rochelle.[1] wher I perceave you have spent time to your good contents, I doe hoope my former letters have given both you and my son satisfaction in our concurrence that he doe proceede for Thaloes. it pleasinge God to Give you your healths and more seasonable weather, Therfore I doe not now write to my son, and pray tel him we are all I praise God in health, altho. it be a very sickly time and many dye, in and about London. And I may tell you your byl for the L. 400. taken at Angers shall be dewly payd, and soe shall all others be that you doe pas on me. who doe remaine

Sir,

Your oblidged and humble servant

JOHN BANKS

I doe send my letters under Madam Herinx cover to Paris, and yours come as well the one way as the other

Address: A Monsieur Monsieur John Locke

Endorsed by Locke: Sir J: Banks 5 Sept. *78*

## 407. LOCKE to WILLIAM CHARLETON, 9/19 [September] 1678 (*385*, 415)

The Houghton Library, Harvard. Transcribed from photostat. The correct month from Locke's journal and the dates of the letters mentioned in the text.

Bourdeaux. 19 Aug. *78*

Deare Sir

The slownesse of my journey hither rather then of my thanks has put me in debt to you for the favour of two of your letters one

[1] The last two dates are new style.

of 13th Aug and the other of 5th instant which brought an inclosed with it from Mr Selapris, which I looke on as an increase of my score to you: For tis to you I owe the civilitys I receive from him, as well as those that come immediately from your self, amongst which are the pains you have taken to enquire me out people that have correspondence at London, and the care you have taken to informe me of it. But for these and those other numberlesse obligations I have to you twill be the businesse of my life and not of a letter to render my thanks. and therefor I shall here only beg you to beleive that I am extrem sensible of them, and that I looke on your friendship not only as the greatest advantage has happend to me here in France, but one of the greatest happynesses I can enjoy in this world. Haveing, as without complement I have, this thought dwelling vigorously[a] upon my minde, thinke what pleasure I have to consider my self once more neare you again, with hopes to have the satisfaction in a few days of seeing you and of throwing my self into the armes of a freind who has soe just a right to dispose intirely of me, and where I thinke my selfe soe safe and soe happy. This addes a wellcome to the good news your last letter brings me that all feare of the sicknesse is over, for I would not, now I know you are there, have any thing hinder my journey to Montpellier, And I hope by this time the raines there as well as here have restord the town to a very good state of health and the air to a good temper.[b] Sir John Chichley writ me word of his designe to returne to Montpellier again this winter before I left Paris, and would it not be strange if we three should meet there again. I thought when I left Languedoc that we might have sooner met at Constantenople, and there togeathe have drunke healths to our friends of Christendome in Sherbet and Coffé. The complement I found in your letter from Mr Witcherly[1] mightily surprised me with great satisfaction, not that I thinke it strange that one of his great civility and good nature should remember an old acquaintance, but haveing since I left Paris with great concerne heard of and regreted his death it was altogeather unexpected to heare news of him in these parts, for whatever they tell us of Old Orpheus a long time since, and though

[a] *Or* vigerously [b] *Altered from* temperature.

[1] William Wycherly, 1640?–1716, the dramatist: *D.N.B.* Locke perhaps met him through John Cockshutt: p. 320 n. He was at Montpellier on account of his health. He had published all his plays already, but no poems.

I thinke Mr Witcherlys poetry as powerfull and as charming as his, yet I feare that trick is lost, and doe not expect that any poetry should have power enough in our days to make a man that goes under ground in England rise again in Languedoc. Pray tell him I finde it much better to goe twise to Montpellier then once to the other world and that I shall be exceeding glad to kisse his hands there. I have here inclosed made a shift to write a French letter such as it is to Mr Selapris in thanks for the favour of his. I must beg you to correct it for me to make it intelligible before you seale it and send it him, and pray assure him that my meaning is good though my French be ill. I will not trouble him nor you any farther about the matter of returns[1] till I[a] come to Montpellier. Here arrived yesterday fower Dutch vessels but tis said under the protection of passes rather then the free liberty of peace, which is yet talked doubtfully of here.[2] I begin now to be impatient till I see you For I am perfectly

Deare Sir

Your most humble most affectionate and most obleiged servant

J. LOCKE

My service to Mr Cheny[3] and Mr Pasty[4]

If any letters come to Montepellier for me before I come I beg the favour of you to take them up and keepe them for me

Address: A Monsieur Monsieur Charleton Gentilhomme Anglois au Petit Paris á Montpellier

Endorsed by Charleton: Bourdeaux—1678
Mr: Lock—19. August

[a] *Altered from* we

---

[1] Perhaps relating to drafts drawn by Locke on them.

[2] See p. 603, n. 3.

[3] Oliver Cheney. He may have been Irish. The address of no. *411* and mentions on pp. 653 and 676 suggest that he occupied lodgings at Montpellier large enough for him to take in lodgers and that he acted as a travelling tutor. Letters from him below, nos. *2416*, *3191*.

[4] Locke's French tutor at Montpellier: Journal, 14 May 1676; mentioned without his name 9 January; see also 27 February. He wrote some French exercises for Locke, and perhaps gave him some other notes: B.L., MS. Locke c. 31, ff. 173–5, 182–3.

## *408.* SIR JOHN BANKS to LOCKE, 12 September 1678 (*406*, *410*)

B.L., MS. Locke c. 3, ff. 112–13.

Sir

These 14 days have receavd none from my son nor any of yours, which puts us out of sorts, until the next post, which will I hoope give us satisfaction, in the meane time may tell you I did waite on Mr Cole, and offered him my assistance with the Lord Threasurer[a 1] to pas your matters at the Customhouse, but he did thinke it best to take them up as they came, with my Lords concerns, which I did agree to be best. and they are this day brought to my house. being 4 parsells, and wither you will have me open the bales, or let them lye til you come, pray give me your direction—Heer is a discourse of much hurt done at Blois by a Great haile, I would pray the certainty of it. I pray will you let us know when you thinke we may expect you and my son heer; I doe not write to him this post. but we are all very well I praise God, altho it be a very sickly time, and remaine

Sir, Your ever oblidged freind and servant
JOHN BANKS

Lincolns in feilds 12 September. 1678

Address: A Mounsier Mounsier Locke

Endorsed by Locke: Sir J: Banks 12 Sept. *78*

## *409.* GEORGE WALLS to LOCKE, 21 September 1678 (*422*)

B.L., MS. Locke c. 23, ff. 29–30.

George Walls, *c.* 1645–1727; son of William Walls of Rock, Worcs.; at Westminster School; matriculated from Christ Church 3 July 1663; B.A. 1667; M.A. 1670; B.D. 1682; D.D. 1694; chaplain at Hamburg of the Company of English Merchants trading to Hamburg 1682–9; prebendary of

[a] *Abbreviated in MS.*

[1] Danby: p. 438, n. 2. By this time he was hostile to Montagu: Browning, *Danby*, i. 287.

Worcester 1694–1727; of St. Paul's 1695–1727: Barker and Stenning. For George Wall of Gloucester, Locke's travelling companion, see p. 430, n. 2.

Christ Church Sept. 21th. =78

Sir

I am much troubled that yours of the 30th of April came soe late to my hands; both because I was thereby made unable to satisfie you as to any thinge therein mention'd, as alsoe to returne my acknowledgements for the chagrin[1] booke you were pleas'd to bestow on mee; for the trouble of provideing which I longe before knew I was indebted to you, but did not understande the other and greater parte of my obligation, till your letter instructed mee. I have alsoe receiv'd that from Blois of the 2d of Aug; which came to mee into Worcester shire where I have beene payinge a longe and melancholy respecte to a deare relation, that died last weeke;[2] which absence hinder'd my answer to yours, and my late returne makes it an imperfecte one. You may please to know that I founde Ralph Townson[3] missinge at my comeinge home, and tis conceiv'd Mr Stanton[4] will have his facultie, hee haveinge noe rivall; for my Lord[5] doth soe drive us into orders, that theres noe livinge without them, and lesse when wee have them. Dr South[6] is parson of Islip, and Mr Penny[7] his curate. Dr South shoulde have bought a nagge of Mr Hodges,[8] histoire la dessus. Mr Hodges is now at Glocester and many times out of order. Mr Jones[9] is not much satisfied with his greate liveinge in Wales, and others as little that they cannot get one. I have not yet taken your concerns into my hands, but offer'd my selfe to mr Thomas[10] to doe it, now unhappily discoveringe my greate likelyhood to continue in the Colledge. I thinke it unseasonable to mention it againe to him consideringe his correspondent at London hath beene some what faultie in payinge some moneys accordinge to his order; soe that at this time to ease him of his employment would looke like distrust of your

[1] Shagreen: *O.E.D.*

[2] Probably Walls's brother William, who died about 1678: *The Visitation o, (Worcestershire), 1682, 1683*, ed. W. C. Metcalfe, 1883, p. 98.

[3] Student of Christ Church; he died on 8 September of this year: Foster; Wood, *L. and T.* ii. 415.

[4] Probably Robert Stanton; King's scholar, Westminster, 1661; matriculated from Christ Church 3 July 1663; sometime a pupil of Locke; B.A. 1667; M.A. 1670: Barker and Stenning; etc.

[5] Fell, bishop of Oxford since 1676: p. 179, n. 3.

[6] p. 153, n. 5.

[7] James Penny, *c.* 1650–94; matriculated from Christ Church 1665; B.A. 1669; M.A. 1672; vicar of Great Budworth, Cheshire, 1682: Foster; Prideaux, *Letters*, p. 130.

[8] p. 260, n. 3.

[9] I cannot identify him.

[10] Samuel Thomas: p. 430 n.

stewarde. Dr Stanley[1] of new College is lately deade. Dr Dolben Bishop of Rochester hath absolutely refus'd the primacie of Irelande,[2] and tis reported that the bishop of Chichester[3] stands fowle for it haveinge the Dutchesse of Portsmouth[4] on his side. The great tryall (that hath made such a noise in Oxon) betwixt Mr Vernon formerly of Allsoules and Mr Wills of Trinitie concerninge the formers symoniacall promotion to a liveinge call'd Boreton of the Waters in Glocester shire did not goe on last assize at Glocester, the records beinge withdrawn the morninge before twas to bee try'd.[5] Whereas you mention your desire to know the sense of those here concerninge Moyses Pitts Atlas;[6] the information that I yet have gotten is very different, but find not that men have the same expectations of the advantage of the booke if done as formerly they had. If things shal bee hereafter put in a more probable way for effectually answeringe the expectations of those in Oxon that I believe are fitte Judges of a usefull undertakeinge and the means of its accomplishment, you shall not fayle to heare of it. The difference betwixt the towne and univercity is not yet compos'd, and scarce any but the poorest sorte of tradesmen and mechanicks feele the effects of our dislike; some would quitte their[a] mercers willingly if they were not afraid of the vicechancellours courte.[7] I have both thought and enquir'd and cannot possibly gaine any thinge of news to sende you. I have deliverd your commendations to your friends, and am desir'd by many to returne you thanks and service. Charls Pococke[8] deserves not your remembrance, beinge the worst

[a] *Or* your *or* the; *abbreviated.*

---

[1] Roger Stanley, b. *c.* 1642; D.C.L. 1675; died on 17 September: Foster; Wood, *L. and T.* ii. 415.

[2] John Dolben: p. 179 n. He was bishop of Rochester from 1666 to 1683. The primacy of Ireland fell vacant by the death of James Margetson, archbishop of Armagh (*D.N.B.*), on 28 August of this year.

[3] Ralph Brideoake, b. 1613; bishop 1675; died 5 October of this year: ibid.

[4] p. 451, n. 4.

[5] George Vernon, 1637–1720; M.A. 1660; sometime chaplain of All Souls; rector of Bourton-on-the-Water, Gloucestershire, 1667–1720: *D.N.B.* His antagonist is John Willes, *c.* 1647–1700; M.A. 1669; fellow of Trinity 1669; D.D. 1685; prebendary of Lichfield 1688–1700: Foster.

[6] p. 583, n. 5.

[7] The dispute began on 4 August 1677, when a townsman was summoned to appear in the Vice-Chancellor's court; there was no Act this year on account of it; at a hearing in Westminster Hall on 30 October the two sides were ordered to compromise: Wood, *L. and T.* ii. 381–4, 408, 421; iv. 76; p. 641 below. Quit here probably means acquit or requite.

[8] Son of Dr. Edward Pococke (p. 256, n. 1); baptized 22 January 1661; matriculated from Christ Church 22 March of this year; B.A. 1681; M.A. 1684; rector of Cheriton Bishop, Devon, 1690: Foster; *D.N.B.*, art. Pococke.

temper'd boy to all relations I ever yet met with, and were hee not that goode mans son I would soone determine what to doe with him. good Sir believe mee very sensible of all your favours, and ready to approve my selfe

Your most affectionate servant
GEORGE WALLS

There has beene a strange malignant feavour in Wheatly, and in many parts of the country; but Oxon has beene (God bee thanked) free.

Address: For Mr John Locke This To be left at Sir John Banks his house in Lyncolnes Inne fields London

Postmark: SE 2–

Endorsed by Locke: Mr Wall 2 Sept. *78*

## *410.* SIR JOHN BANKS to LOCKE, 30 September 1678 (*408, 414*)

B.L., MS. Locke c. 3, ff. 114–15. This was enclosed, with a letter from Sir John to Caleb Banks, in a letter from Pepys to Caleb of this date: Pepys, *Further Correspondence*, pp. 323–4. It probably reached them at Montpellier after 8/18 October: p. 622. They left Montpellier on 20/30 October.

Sir

I have yours of the 24 instant, perceavinge you were intended for Tholose the next day[1] and that you had accommodated your selves with horses and other necessarys which had occasyoned you to draw some byls, which shall be dewly payd, being well satisfyed you doe husband althings to the best advantage; And now I finde by my sons to Mr Pepys. and his mother (in which you are alsoe concurringe), that he is desirous to Goe for Italy,[2] and I confesse my inclination hath somtimes beene formerly for it, but findinge my wiffe soe much concerned if the post doe not every weeke bring letters, I can then thinke of nothing but his returne, but Sir I must say you have layd a good project. which I beleive will be much to my sons satisfaction and I hoope your owne to, and doe beleive you may well accomplish the same within the time limited and be at home in the spring. Therfore I doe perswade his Mother to trust

[1] Locke left Bordeaux on 16/26 September.

[2] Caleb wrote to Pepys on 9/19 and 11/21 September; Pepys's answer (26 September) shows that he had already expressed his desire to go to Italy: *Further Correspondence*, pp. 321–2.

Providence and wee shall Grant his request upon your assurance that he come home in the springe. we hoope in Aprill, and this I say becaus my son hath still been pressinge further and further. You know it is but to stay the les time in a place. but pray you write by every post. nor should we give way to this designe but that we are abundantly satisfyed in your kindnes to my son as well as your care of his health. Soe I doe leave things wholy to your owne Conduct, to proceede accordinge to your owne method and to returne at your time desired:[a] and shall committ you both to the Lords Protection, knowinge you will alsoe consider my sons youth that he may be constantly in exercise and avoyd those temptations which are so often layd, and which youth and nature are prone to, as alsoe to keepe him well in principles of religion.

Sir, I doe assure you the Consideration of your owne health hath beene often in my thoughts. and that you might not returne at an inconvenient time to your owne health after all your time spent abroad in respect thereto, and I must confesse I did not intend nor cold I expect your comminge over neither in respect to yourselfe or my son til springe and that you might have spent time at Paris— where you had beene nearer home, but as I am fully satisfyd you may husband your time to much better advantage in the way you have proposed, soe that you may alsoe compas the same within the time you have limited, and therfore proceede I pray with all alacrity, And for your further supply of monys. I have desired Sir Na. Herne to write to his freinds Mr George Legatt and Mr Giles Ball at Genoa.[1] and I have alsoe writt to my Good freinds Mr Robert Ball and Francis Gosfright at Legorne, to supply you with what you shall desire, and I pray assoon as you shall arrive at either of the said places make your aplication to them and you may there alsoe expect letters from me. who wish both your wellfares and remaine

Sir, Your affectionate freind and servant

JOHN BANKS

Lincolns in feilds 30. September 1678

Address: A Monsieur Monsieur Locke

Endorsed by Locke: Sir J: Banks 30 Sept. *78*.

[a] *Word interlined.*

---

[1] George Legat was English consul in Genoa about 1667–76: P. Fraser, *The Intelligence of the Secretaries of State*, 1956, pp. 72, 154; Chamberlayne, *Angliæ Notitia*.

## *411.* Dr. Denis Grenville to Locke, 14/24 October 1678 (*377*, *412*)

B.L., MS. Locke c. 10, ff. 83–4.

a la Tour D'aigues le 24me 8bre 1678

I cannot satisfie my selfe with the single Title of, Sir, (My deare and worthy Freind) after soe long an intervall of Correspondence; noe more than I can content my selfe to omit writing till another post; taking penne in to hand immediately after the receipt of yours to assure you that I thanke that Providence in a very particular manner that hath brought us againe thus unexpectedly neare one another, hoping that the same will bee noe lesse kind in granting my next wishes; namely that wee may not only *see*, *but Injoy*, one another a litle before any other Considerable separation. Since you are soe very freindlily charitable, as not to doubt of my freindship, though you have cause to Complaine of my silence since your last letter, (which I received neare about your leaving Paris) I will not spend time (having but litle at this Instant) soemuch as to goe about to excuse it. But rather improve this moment to beseech you, that if it bee possible wee may have an Interview. Wherefore if you cannot bee allowed liberty to see Provence, nor I have time to Come to Montpillier, let mee have an intimation to meet you on the Roade, any where between this and Lions. I hope a better Fate; but if not, for Gods sake, let me not want this satisfaction, tho you have never soe speedy a summons. My sister, whoe is much better than when you saw her, did never till now repent her leaving Montpellier, as she sayes, loosing thereby some satisfaction in Injoyment of your Conversation. Which, however, she sayes, shee will not despaire of; not doubting but that Mr. Banks, whoe hath had the liberty to make soe great a Tour; will not affront Provence, for which shee is a great Champion, soe much as to passe it by; Shee and wee all are I thank God in Good[a] health, and will continue according to our professions

Your servants and honourers.

and I in another Capacity ever I hope *Your Freind*, as well as

Sir

Your faithfull humble servant

De. Grenville

[a] *MS.* God *?*

My very humble service to Mr. Charleton, Mr. Cheny[1] and any of our Country with you as well as to Mr. Banks in particular manner.

I shall speedily more at leasure, and large write to you.

This post hath astonish⟨ed⟩[a] us with a dismall relation of another Iesuiticall plot to kill our King, newly discovered, as Sir Tho. Higgons[2] writes. Foure or 5. Preists, and others are secured and sent to New-gate: They are English Jesuites that are accused. From whose Rage Good Lord deliver us.

If this generation of vipers will not bee quiet; wee will raise up againe Monsr. Pascall to Confound them.[3]

You will see by this scribble that I am in hast, and straitned in time.

Address: A Monsieur Monsieur Lock Gentilhomme anglois Chez Monsr Cheny Gentilhomme Anglois demeurant proche l'Eglise de St. Pierre A Montpelier

Endorsed by Locke: Mr Grenvill 24 Oct. *78*

## *412.* DR. DENIS GRENVILLE to LOCKE, 18/28 October 1678 (*411, 416*)

B.L., MS. Locke c. 10, ff. 85–6.

a la Tour D'aigues le 28me 8bre 1678

I will not yet, Sir, send any packett (tho I have one in store)[4] being soe impatient of seeing you speedily, that if your owne designes and method bring you not here into Provence, it will bee impossible to keep mee long from Montpelier. Butt rather repeat my request to you by last post, that if you should bee summond to goe strait to Paris, I may have some intimation from you in due season to meet, or at least to pursue you tho it bee as farre as Lions. I should thinke myselfe the most unhappy man in the World, if I should misse of seeing you, being in Circumstances that I greatly need the Counsell and advice of A wise and Faithfull freind; soe that besides

[a] *Page torn.*

[1] Oliver Cheney: p. 612, n. 3.

[2] The Popish Plot, the perjured fabrication of Titus Oates. The first arrests were made during the night of 28/29 September: J. P. Kenyon, *The Popish Plot*, 1972, p. 69. Sir Thomas Higgons, 1624–91, diplomatist: *D.N.B.* He was a brother-in-law of Grenville.

[3] Alluding to the *Lettres provinciales*.

[4] No. *421*.

our paper Conferences, I would now allsoe faigne have some verball ones. I doe thinke some Good Angell hath brought you back to doe mee a good turne. And from this unexpected piece of Providence (I meane your returne into these parts and our stay) I promise my selfe great successe and a happy Issue in all my designes I have upon you; which are not a few, as you will soone experience if wee once more meet, in the same towne, if not under the same Roof. My sister with her faithfull humble service, bidds mee minde you of the severe Winter that there was at Montpelier, this time twoe years, and to assure you that there hath not been these twoe past Winters any snow at all at Aix; soe that if you will winter here (if you stay in these parts of France) you have noe reason to feare the tumbling downe of any houses. I have many arguments of mine owne allsoe to add (though I am not soe great a champian for Provence as my sister) to perswade you to take up this for your Winter Quarters. But I will omitt them and avoid the giving you any farther trouble till I have the happinesse to receive another letter from you, which I much long for; being in great suspense till I know, how, when, and where I may see you. With my very humble service to Mr. Charleton and Mr. Chenay etc I rest

Sir

Your very faithfull freind and most humble servant

DE. GRENVILLE

Mrs. Thornehill,[1] whoe is imprisonned for her old and new Iniquities, would bee very glad that Mr. Locke, would come now and deliver her from a Convent; as hee did once from a Ague. A Desperate desease hath occasionned this desperate Remedy; wherein I am only passive.

Wee have received noe more newes from England. If you have any particulars of the Jesuiticall plot I pray Communicate them. God save the King.

Address: A Monsieur Monsieur Locke Gentilhomm anglois chez Monsieur Chenay Gentilhomme anglois demeurant vis a vis la grande Eglise de St. Pierre A Montpelier

Endorsed by Locke: Mr Grenvill 28 Oct. *78*

[1] Probably Mary Thornhill: p. 522, n. 1. The convent is no doubt figurative.

## 413. LOCKE to ROBERT HOOKE, 19/29 October 1678

The Royal Society, L. 5–6, no. 91. Probably sent with no. 417. The account of the eclipse was written probably by a Frenchman. Robert Hooke, 1635–1703, the scientist; secretary of the Royal Society 1677–82: *D.N.B.*; etc. Locke entered a copy of the account of the eclipse in his Journal, 29 October (pp. 317–18).

La lune étant elevée de 18 degrés, peu moins, a 6 heures 45 minut. de nos montres a paru sensiblement eclipsée, de sorte quon peut conter le commencement de l'Eclipse depuis 6 heures 42 minutes. a 7 heures 48 minutes nous avons eté asseurés que tout son disque etoit dans l'ombre, mais comm'il y avoit des nuages qui la cachoint de tems en tems, il peut etre que tout son disque etoit dans l'ombre toute entiere, quelques minutes plutot que nous ne l'avions estimé. la lune estoit pour lors eslevée de 27 degrés.

La lune estant elevée de 44 degrés et demy, a 9 heures 29 minut. de nos montres, a commencé de sortir de lombre.

a 9 heures 58 minutes la lune avoit recouvré sa lumiere dans tout la moitié de son disque

a 10 heures 28 minutes la lune estant élevée de 53 degres et demy, l'Eclipse finit entierement.

[Written by Locke:]

Montpellier 29 Oct 78

Sir

Being invited by a very good astronomer a freind of mine of this town[1] to be at a place where he intended to observe an eclyps of the moon which was to be this evening I was hinderd by some occasions that I could not be there all the time. However I send you the copy which was given me of the observation he made which I imagin will not be unacceptable to the Royal Society nor to you. I was there at the time that the moon was totally eclypsed, and I thinke according to the best observation I could make that it began to be soe at 7 and 47 minutes, but the clouds made it a litle difficult to observe the exact time when it lost all its light. I thinke I have some where amongst my papers his observations of an eclyps of the sun which he made when I was formerly at Montpellier, but being now at a distance from my papers I cannot send them you. I should

[1] Identifiable as Pierre Jolly (or Joly?); M.D., Montpellier, 1669; a Protestant; abjured; pensioned in 1686: Lough, p. 100; Locke, Journal, 29 Oct., etc.

be glad of any other occasion whilst I am abroad to render any service to the Royal Society, or to assure you that I am

Sir

your very humble servant

J LOCKE

Your neighbour Dr Mapletoft[1] by whose hand I convey this to you will informe you how to send to me if you or the Society have any commands for me

Address: For Mr Hooke at Gresham Colledg

Endorsements, etc.: (i) containing[a–] observation on an[–a] Eclipse of the Moon[b] at Montpellier, 29 Oct. –78. / Lr 12 / NP. / P. because Cassini observed the same at Paris in L.A. V. 1. p. 320.

(ii: at foot of letter) Read December 12: 78.[2]

## *414.* SIR JOHN BANKS to LOCKE, [*c.* 22 October 1678] (*410, 425*)

B.L., MS. Locke c. 3, ff. 116–17. Locke's endorsement is probably a date of receipt. Sir John says that he wrote to Leghorn 'three weeks since' to arrange credit for Locke and Caleb there; he wrote on or shortly before 30 September: p. 617. He could scarcely have received Caleb's letter of 8/18 October from Montpellier much before 22 October O.S.; if Locke received the present letter before he left Lyons on 5/15 November, it cannot have been written much later.

Sir

I now am with yours of the 15. and my sons of the 18th October from Montpellier and as we are Glad of your good healths soe doe hoope your next will give us the account of your and my sons havinge receaved to your satisfaction and his, our willingnesse to gratify his desire to Goe see part of Italy, which I doe assure you could not have beene done by any means but yourselfe, not only upon the consideration of your assurance for both your returns in the springe, which I doe absolutly depend on, but the enjoyment of your good conversation and company was alsoe a great inducement. and I must entreate you to beleive me, that I doe desire his returne in the springe and as early as convenient, All the bylls passed on me have beene payd and I have 3 weeks since, given notice to Mr George Legatt and Mr Giles Ball at Genoa, as alsoe to

[a–a] *Words added probably by the writer of no. (ii).* [b] *In MS. the symbol* ☾.

[1] The Royal Society occupied rooms in Gresham College.

[2] At the Royal Society's meeting: Birch, *Royal Society*, iii. 448.

Mr Robert Ball and Mr Robert Gosfright at Legorne to supply your occations when ever you shall make use of mony. and to vallew themselvs on me, which as the Exchange rules is the best and surest way for you, and their bylls shall be payd.

I am in hoopes you will meete mr Thomas Tufton[1] at Lon, and probably Sir John Chicheley, Mr Tufton doth ressolve for Italy, and in your company, and it is very probable you will alsoe have Sir John Chicheley with you, which will alsoe please his Lady from whom I did the laste weeke send you her letter under my sons cover to Lyon.

My Lord Shaftesbury was pleased to honnor me with his company yesterday, and is pritty well as he saith but my thinks very thinne and lame, and presents you and my son his freindship. I pray remember us to my son and let him know we are all well. If you meete mr Tufton I pray make use of any my credits or freinds to serve his occations and let him draw on me whatever he wants which upon all considerations is better then to remitt mony to Legorne, as the Exchange rules. and doe me the favor to present my humble services and let him know what I say for he is a person to whom I am oblidged with other brothers of that family. Sir, havinge now wrott to you, my son may excuse me, tho I cannot excuse him to omitt any post. and your letters come uncertaine, The remainder is myne and my wives humble services who truly am

Sir, Your assured freind and servant JOHN BANKS

Address: A Monsieur Monsieur Locke A Lyon

Endorsed by Locke: Sir J: Banks Nov. *78*

## 415. LOCKE to WILLIAM CHARLETON, 26 October/5 November 1678 (407, *445*)

Present ownership unknown. The bulk of the text from Messrs. Maggs Brothers, *Catalogue* no. 616, 1935, item no. 982 (for this item see p. 513 n. above); the date and additions from Messrs. Sotheby and Co., sale catalogue, 18 November 1974, lot no. 391.

[Locke acknowledges Charleton's letter of 1 November.]

. . . My comeing away from Montpellier soe quickly being the most unacceptable thing has happened to me all my journey.[2] Since

[1] pp. 546, n. 2, 652 n., etc. Besides the present earl of Thanet (p. 296, n. 3) he had three or four brothers now living.

[2] Locke left Montpellier on 20/30 October and arrived at Lyons on 25 October/4 November.

it tis like to produce nothing but the vexation of leaving a place where I might have longer enjoyed a friend whom I infinitely value to carry me to a place where amidst the noise and bustle of it I shall still carry about with me this uneasinesse of haveing soe soon lost this occasion of conversing with you, which was the great pleasure I proposed to my self in this journey. For all the imaginations you will have till this letter comes to you of my being on the other side the Alpes, will be but soe many castles of your building on the other side the Pyrenes. We are the first of those that are come too late to passe the mountaines this winter. An English gent. that came over Mount Senné[1] about 8 or 10 days since found the passage very good but there fell soe much snow as soon as he was over that the very men that brought over his things for five pistols[2] told him they would not carry them back again for an hundred, and tis concluded here with reason that abundance more snow has fallen since that time, since the cold and hard windes we had in our faces almost all the way hither has the last weeke coverd. the tops of the hills as I came along. Tis beleived that carriers may passe, and that for a need with ventureing to have only legs frozen, with good luck one might bustle through. But considering that I am not passing over the hills for a warm benefice to thaw me again on tother side and that Mr Bankes is not the popes nephew, and soe has noe necessity at any rate to get to Rome to make his fortune, I have thought it more reasonable to stay on this side and soe have nothing to doe but to wish my self with you and to ride to Paris which is like now to be my winter quarters.[a]

## *416.* DR. DENIS GRENVILLE to LOCKE, 27 October/6 November 1678 (*412*, *421*)

B.L., MS. Locke c. 10, ff. 87–8.

a la Tour D'aigues Nov. 6 1678

Deare Sir

Yours of the 29th of last month hath mortified mee above measure. I have not mett with any disappointment soe much to

[a] *For additional paragraph, see p. 703.*

[1] The Mont Cenis.

[2] The pistole was a gold coin in use in Italy and Spain; in France the name was applied to the corresponding coin, the louis d'or. The value according to Sir Isaac Newton (1700) was 16*s.* 9*d.*

my dissatisfaction these many years. I had extraordinary reasons to have consulted a wise and vertuous freind more particularly than by letter. But since God will not have it soe, I know it is my duty to submitt; which I endeavour to doe with Christian Patience; wishing you with all my heart a prosperous Journey, and beseeching you, if you stay long enough in any one place in Italy, to write, and to receive an answer, to favour me with a letter, and an addresse how to direct mine. My sister (whoe is very well) seemes troubled as well as my selfe at this great disappointment; but it cannot afflict any soe sensibly, as

Deare Sir

Your very faithfull and affectionate freind and most humble servant

DE. GRENVILLE

Had I been assured to have seen you, I would have gon to Lions rather than failed of it. My service to Mr Banks.

My sister is your servant etc.

I write in haste

Address: A Monsieur Monsieur Locke Gentilhomm Anglois chez Monsieur Jaques Selapris l'aisné A Lion

Endorsed by Locke: Mr Grenville 6 Nov. *78*

## 417. LOCKE to DR. JOHN MAPLETOFT, 29 October/8 November 1678 (*371*, 450)

*European Magazine*, xv (1789), 353. Copy, omitting the postscript, made by or for Dr. John Ward (p. 490) in B.M., Add. MS. 6194, pp. 248–50.

Lyon, 8 Nov. 78.

Deare Sir,

If all the world should goe to Rome I thinke I should never, haveing been twice firmely bent upon it, the time set, the company agreed, and as many times defeated. I came hither in all hast from Montpellier (from whence I writ to you) with the same designe: but old father Winter, armed with all his snow and isecles, keeps gard on Montsenny, and will not let me passe. But since I cannot get over the hills, I desire your letters may not; they may now keepe their old road to Mr. Charas's, where I hope in a few days to see and be acquainted with your friend Dr. Bugden,[a1] and soe

[a] *In B.M. copy* Budgen

[1] Perhaps Budgen the physician who was in Paris about June 1680: nos. *549*, 556. I have failed to identify him.

haveing seen the winter over at Paris returne to you early in the spring. Were I not accustomed to have fortune to dispose of me contrary to my designe and expectation, I should be very angry to be thus turnd out of my way when I imagined myself almost at the suburbs of Rome, and made sure in a few days to mount the Capitol, and trace the footsteps of the Scipios and the Ceesars; but I am made to know 'tis a bold thing to be projecting of things for to-morrow, and that it is fit such a slight buble as I am should let it-self be carried at the phancy of winde and tide without pretending to direct its own motion. I thinke I shall learne to doe soe hereafter: this is the surest way to be at ease. But hold; I forget you have quitted Galen for Plutarch; and 'tis a litle too confident to talke philosophie to one who converses dayly with Xenophon.[1] I cannot tell how to blame your designe, but must confesse to you I like our calling the worse since you have quitted it; yet I hope it is not to make way for another, which, with more indissoluble changes, has greater cares and sollicitude accompanying it. If it be soe, you need be well prepard with philosophie; and you may finde it necessary sometimes to take a dram of *Tully de Consolatione*. I cannot forbear to touch, *en passant*, the chapter of matrimony, which methinks you are still hankering after; but if ever you should chance soe to be given up as to marry, and like other loving husbands tell your wife who has dissuaded you, what a case shall I be in? All my comfort is, that 'tis noe personal malice to the woman, and I am sure I have noe-thing but friendship for you; for I am, with sincerity,

Sir,

Your most affectionate humble servant,

J. LOCKE.

The inclosed should have been sent from Montpellier, but I suppose it will doe well enough cold.[2] My service to our friend, and the rest of our friends, and amongst them to good Dr. Witch-cock,[3] Mr. Fowler,[4] and Mr. Firmin, when you see them; and all

[1] Locke sent Mapletoft copies of Plutarch and Xenophon: pp. 524, 544; Journal, 1678, pp. 65, 126, 144. Mapletoft retained his Gresham professorship until 10 October 1679; married on 18 November 1679; and was ordained in 1683.

[2] Probably no. 413.

[3] Probably Benjamin Whichcote, 1609–83; D.D. 1649; vicar of St. Lawrence Jewry from 1668: *D.N.B.* His sister and nephew are mentioned above, p. 460, nn. 1, 5.

[4] Probably Edward Fowler, the future bishop of Gloucester: p. 83, n. 1; he was a friend of Firmin and of Mrs. Grigg.

our Northumberland freinds, particularly my Governesse, Mrs Beavis, and aske her what I shall doe with my Lady Bloy's gloves,[1] since I shall not come over till Spring.

## 418. Locke to Nicolas Toinard, 29 October/8 November 1678 (*402, 420*)

B.M., Egerton MS. 22, ff. 228–9. Answered by no. *420*.

Lyon 8 Nov. *78*

Monsieur

Je vous escrivis de Bourdeaux pour vous remercier des honestites que vos amies me firent a Rochefort d'une maniere tres obligeant dont je me souviendray toute ma vie. mais depuis ce temps la je n'ay point eu de vos nouvelles ce que me mette beaucoup en peine. J'avois le dessein de vous ecrire de cette ville cy en tout cas, mais c'est a cettheure de vous dire que d'icy je retourneray vers Paris, et que l'esperance de vous y revoire et d'avoire l'honeur de vostre compagnie me soulage pour la perte de tout le plaisir qu'on trove en le voiage d Italy, que j'ay manqué de faire faut du temps, ayant arivé icy un peu trop tard pour passer les Alpes deja tout couvertes de neige. Mais en verité quand je fais reflection sur cet amas de belles choses et tousjours des nouvelles que se rancontrent dans vostre conversation Je conclus que ce changement de mon voiage moy sera bien avantageus, et que je passeray meux cette hyver a Paris, pourveu que vous y soiez, que je n'aurois fait en Italy. parceque à mon avis on passera bien meux son temps avec un honest homme vivant en qui se trouve toutes les bonnes qualites des ancients Romaines, que parmi les monuments magnifiqus de tants des braves gens deja long temps trepasses. je vous dis cela avec toute la sincerite de mon ame, et parceque il m'import beaucoup davantage de vous revoire que toute autre chose que je peu faire icy en France je passeray expres par Oleans afin que je ne peu pas manquer de vous rencontrer ou a Paris ou a Orleans, parceque il ny a pas homme au Monde que vous soit tant redevable que moi, et que doit avec tant de soin cherche les occasions de vous

[1] Presumably a transcriber's slip for 'my Lady's Blois gloves': p. 605.

temoigner sa reconnoissance et ses tres humbles respects, parceque je suis

Vostre tres humble et tres acquis serviteur
JLOCKE

Dans ma derniere je marquay que le livre Anglois de duplicate proportion[1] pour vous devroit estre adressé pour vous chez Mr Justel[2] avec un peu de semence pour le pere Ange Capucin d'Orleans,[3] je vous repete cela icy croyant cette lettre la perdue

Address: A Monsieur Monsieur Toynard a la Teste noire dans la rue Mazarin Fauxbourg st Germain a Paris

## *419.* JACQUES SELAPRIS to LOCKE, 7/17 November 1678 (*332, 419A, 423*)

B.L., MS. Locke c. 18, ff. 71–3, with enclosure, f. 74. The latter, not printed here, is a corrected copy, written by Locke, of a power of attorney empowering Thomas Stringer to demand and receive money from Jean LeGendre, merchant, of London, or to take action against him on behalf of 'Sieur Jacques Christophe Selapris [and] Sieur Jacques Horutener et compagnie marchands bourgeois a Lyon'. Locke forwarded the original to Stringer on 23 November/3 December: no. *430*.

Lyon ce 17º Novembre 1678.

Monsieur mon tres Cher Amy

Je N'ay pas voulu Laisser partir vostre Laquay Silvestre Brounawer,[4] sans L'acompagne de La presente, pour vous asseurer de mes treshumbles services et Respects, et pour vous dire que Le deplaisir de vous avoir quité m'a esté tres sensible et me l'est encore fort, et Cela à plus forte Raison, d'autant que vostre agreable sejour, ne M'a procuré auqune ocasion à vous Rendre Ny à Monsieur Banqs (a qui je suis aussy treshumble serviteur) le moindre service. Je vous prie donc tres humblement me vouloir faire Naistre les Ocassions, et je fairay mon debvoir et Come vostre dit Laquay n'entend pas encore bien la langue, de Crainte que vos hardes en souffrissent par l'ocassion des Canaille quil

[1] pp. 596, 604.
[2] p. 580 n.; no. *472*.
[3] Died 1679; he gave Locke some medical notes: no. *489*; Journal.
[4] Sylvester Brounower, a Swiss, whom Locke took into his service on 4/14 November: B.L., MS. Locke f. 28, p. 24. He continued with him until 1696 and died about December 1699. Locke usually calls him Syl.

pouroit avoir dans le Coche, jay fait embaler le tout ensemble, et l'ay ádressé á Monsieur Charas, auquel jescris Ce jourduy par la poste, affin quil aye soin de Retirer les hardes et le garçon selon vostre ordre.[1] Je fairay aussy partir demain la Boite de Montpellier par la diligençe d'autant qu'on m'a promis la Rendre demain matin. Jen done par Cest ordinaire[a] avis á Monsieur Marchal[2] auquel jenvoy la vostre. Cy joint une de nostre bon Amy Monsieur Charleton lequel m'adressé vostre boite.

Je prends la liberté de vous envoyer aussy sy Joint la procuration pour Monsieur Thomas Stringer, pour retirer de Monsieur Jean Le Gendre marchant de Londres aveuglement Ce quil Luy voudra Compter, et de l'y en faire un Reçeu de la valeur et sil peut le faire sans le entierement desobliger, en retirer un Compte, et Nous faire la graçe de nous l'envoyer. vous voyés Monsieur Come je Agis et Come je ne fais auqune fasson d'acepter le belles offres que me faités, vous supliant au Non de dieu, de faire en vers Moy de Mesme. Sy Joint une Letre pour le dit Legendre par laquelle je ly mande avoir envoyé procure et quil ne manque pas á ly satisfaire, au refus je prie pour un Mot d'avis. J'ay fait racomoder la Cosaque[3] de Livrée pour vostre dit Laquay qui ly va fort bien. L'on ne prand presentement pas moins de vingt Livres pour persone par le Coche.[4] Sy je puis loger le dit à l 18 Je le fairay et ly doneray le surplus de l'argent pour vous en rendre Compte, jespere quil vous servira fort bien, et Cest ce que je ly ay tres bien recomendé, et ne doubte pas quil ne le fasse, mais sy par malheur il oublioit à faire son deboir, je vous prie de ne le pas flater, et ne ly pardoner pas une à ma Considration, d'autant, que je ne le faisois pas moy mesme n'estant pas la Coustume des Suisses qui vous serve pour avis sil vous plaist.

[a] *MS.* ord[re]

---

[1] The letter is printed as no. *419A*.

[2] 'Mr. Marshal a la ville de Venise rüe de Bussy': B.L., MS. Locke, f. 28, p. 46, with the year [16]79; on p. 186 there are notes of payments to him or his man, apparently on behalf of Caleb Banks. He is mentioned below in nos. *474*, *533*, *602*. The Ville de Venise was 'a famous pension for the English' from 1643 or earlier until 1660 or later; the sign is recorded in 1687: Evelyn, *Diary*, ed. de Beer, ii. 90 n.; H.M.C., no. 79: *Lindsey MSS.*, *Supp.*, p. 292.

[3] *Casaque*, cassock, etc.

[4] The *coche d'eau* was a boat; it provided the cheapest service between Lyons and Paris; about 1723 the fare was 35 *livres*, that for the *diligence* being 75 *livres*; the journey took ten days: M. L. R. (Saugrain), *Nouveau voyage*, p. 106.

Sy vous avéz la Bonté de vous souvenir de Jean[1] me fairéz Bien de graçe, et serois oise pour l'amour de luy qu'il fust bien placé.

Ma feme vous asseure et Moy de Nos humbles Respects, et elle vous remerçie encore fort de vostre Tres Beau present. Nous souhaiterons avoir l'ocassion de Nous Revenger. Monsieur Banqs trouvera aussy avec vostre permission l'asseurançe de Nos Respects, Nous laguissons d'aprendre vostre heureuse ariveé à Paris Le plus haut vous veille bien acompagner Cest le souhait Monsieur de

Vostre plus humble et plus obeissant serviteur

J SELAPRIS L'aisné.

quoy que mayéz ordoné de ne point afranchir vos hardes pour Paris je l'ay pourtant fait, Car l'on ne les à pas voulu prendre autrement[a]

Address: A Monsieur Monsieur Loke Gentilhome Anglois Chéz Monsieur Charas apoticaire au fauxbour St. Germin Rue de Boucherie à Paris.

Endorsed by Locke: Mr Selapris 17 Nov. *78*

## *419A.* JACQUES HORUTENER and JACQUES SELAPRIS to MOÏSE CHARAS, 7/17 November 1678

B.L., MS. Locke c. 18, f. 68. The postscript apparently written by Selapris.

A Lyon ce 17 Novembre 1678.

Monsieur

Nous Vous avons Envoye ce jourdhuy Un Ballot dans lequel trouveres trois pacquet a scavoir Une masle Un paire de saqhoches et un Estuy de Chapeau le tout Remply Dhardes apartenant a Messieurs Locke et Banckes Gentils Homes Englois les quels nous ont Laisse ordre de Vous les adresser et a celle fin que rien ne ses-gare L'avons fait Emballer Ensemble, Il y va aussy le garçon de Monsieur Locke avec, qui Est allemand et nattend point la langue, dont vous prions quand Le Coche DEau arrivera Le faire amener chez son maistre il porte Une Casaque Bleuf avec un petit galon d'argent et vous En Rendra Une Lettre, pour meilheure Cognois-

[a] *Followed by an illegible word, partly abbreviated (a signature?).*

[1] Perhaps Charleton's servant John: p. 545.

sance il vous faire avoir Le ballot qui Est marque come cy bas Voicy ce quil soffre a vous dire Vous saluons et somes

Monsieur

 N° 1 Vos tres humbles serviteurs

Horutener et Selapris

P.S. Le valet sapelle Silvester et ne scauroit se retirer du Coche sy quelqu'un ne le va Chercher de vostre part. Nous somes fachéz de vous Cauzer tant de peines, dispozéz de Nous par Contre en toute fasson sil vous plaist.

Address: A Monsieur Monsieur Charas Maistre Apothecaire En Rue de Boucherie au faux bourg St. Germain A Paris.

Endorsed by Locke: Mr. Selapris a Mr Charas 17 Nov. *78*

## *420.* NICOLAS TOINARD to LOCKE, 11/21 November 1678 (418, 424)

B.L., MS. Locke c. 21, ff. 7–8. Answers no. 418; answered by no. 424.

+

A Paris ce 21 November 78

cest avec une extreme joie, Monsieur, que j'ay apris non seulement le bon etat de votre santé, mais même que l'on etoit sur le point de vous posseder bientost ici. L'Harmonie y a un notable interest et vous pouvez reparer par une revision ce qu'elle a perdu pendant votre absence. ce sera pour elle un grand restaurant aussi bien que pour son autheur qui a eté fort languissant depuis votre depart. Vous pouvez penser, Monsieur, que ce ne lui sera pas un petit deplaisir de n'avoir pas l'honneur de vous recevoir dans un lieu qui a produit une personne qui vous est entierement aquise par toutes sortes de considerations. Je prie Monsieur Godefroi de suppleer a mon defaut et neantmoins de ne vous pas retenir trop long tems parceque je perdrois par le sejour que vous feriez a Orleans les avantages de la communication de Paris d'ou je dois partir en peu de tems. Monsieur Justel me remit avant hier un paquet ou etoit le petit livre de Monsieur Petti avec un petit paquet de graines. Come le tems n'est pas de semer cellescy je les garderay jusques a votre retour ou a votre ordre, cependant j'ay regalé Monsieur Thevenot[1] de la lecture de l'ouvrage de Mr Petti dont il me dist

[1] Melchisédech Thévenot, c. 1620–92; keeper (*garde*) of the Royal Library 1684–92: *N.B.G.* His principal publication is *Relations de divers voyages curieux*, four parts, 1663–72.

hier de choses considerables. j'aymerois bien mieux vous avoir pour interprete que tout autre, et je vous ay promis a tant de gens sur votre parole que vous etes obligé a degager prontement la mienne. Vous m'avez autrefois oui parler d'un Abbé que je cherissois selon toute l'etendüe de son merite qui n'avoit point de bornes. Il m'est arivé une nouvelle afliction a son occasion: *Ingemui enimverò quum sub hastâ positum vidi Harmoniæ meæ græcum exemplar, quod à me charissimus amicus dono acceperat paulò antequam Italiam* peteret. neque parum non dicam pecuniæ *sed laboris impendi, ut illa quæ tres ministerii CHristi annos complectuntur tentamina, è barbaris licitatorum manibus redimerem. Id autem contigit quoniam præstantissimus Abbas famulo suo ac Gerontocomio Parisiensi facultates suas omnes bipertitò legavit*, adeoque auctione divendenda fuerunt omnia. Sentio te sentire quæ tum temporis sensi.[1]

---

Nous avons perdu ici mr Briot[2] en moins d'un jour. Un anglois qui est a Paris, et qui a demeuré six ans constantinople nous a dit chez mr Justel qu'il a envoié a Londres une tres anciene bible hebraique et onze manuscrits grecs du N.T. dont il y en a un de 900 ans. Ce sera un bel appendix de V.L. pour la nouvele edition d'Oxfort. Cet illustre voiageur promet une relation du mont Athos qu'il a parfaitement vu.[3]

Dites a mr Godefroy qu'il vous fasse connoitre mr de Hautefeuïlle qui a proposé le nouvel Hygrometre et autres curiositez dans un ecrit qu'il vous donnera.[4] Vous pourez le salüer de ma part, et

[1] 'I groaned indeed when I saw put up for sale a Greek copy of my Harmony, which a very dear friend had received as a present from me shortly before he left for Italy. Nor did it cost me little, I will not say money but, labour to recover those essays, which comprise the three years of Christ's ministry, from the barbarous clutches of the bidders. This happened because the Abbé left all his effects to be shared between his famulus and a hospital for old people in Paris, so that everything had to be sold by auction. I feel that you must feel what I felt then.' This probably relates to printed sheets of the Harmony.

[2] p. 517, n. 3.

[3] The traveller is Dr. John Covel: no. *471*, etc. He was in Turkey from 1670 to 1677, and was now on his homeward journey. Some of his New Testament manuscripts are said to be in the British Museum. He gave some information about Mount Athos to (Sir) Paul Ricaut (*D.N.B.*), who incorporated it in his account in *The Present State of the Greek and Armenian Churches*, 1679, pp. 216–63.

The Oxford New Testament is identifiable as Fell's edition, 1675, which already gave *variae lectiones* from more than a hundred manuscripts: Madan, *Oxford Books*, nos. 3087–9; L.L., no. 2865. John Mill was already at work on his text: below, no. 640, etc.

[4] The abbé Jean de Hautefeuille, 1647–1724, horologist and inventor; his inventions were marked by ignorance and lack of judgement: *N.B.G.*; C. Huygens, *Oeuvres complètes*, 1888–1950, vii. 437 n. For the hygrometer see above, pp. 590, 591. His book is *Pendule perpetuelle*, etc., 1678. L.L., no. 1401. Notice in *Journal des Sçavans*, 5 September 1678 (pp. 392–4).

lui donner une copie de l'observation de la derniere eclipse de Luna que j'envois a mr Godefroy pour vous en faire part. Elle a eté faite a cete canardiere d'Etoiles qui est au bout du faubourg st Jaques.[1]

Il y a ici un nouveau curieux de Gascogne qui veut paroitre sur l'horizon. Il a quelque chose pour la memoire locale dont il fait grand cas, mais il na gueres gagné a me connoitre car j'ay decouvert son secret ou un equivalent dont quelques personnes se servent desja mieux que lui meme. Il vouloit passer pour savoir de l'Hebreu mais je ne l'ay pas voulu lui nuire dans les rencontres. Lon a seulement bien rit lorsque se vantant d'avoir une infinité de secrets et plusieurs autres, je lui dis qu'il y en avoit un que lon n'avoit point encore trouvé et qui seroit bien de saison dans Paris, qui etoit un Talisman de poche contre les crotes.[2] Vous me ferez justice, Monsieur, de croire que dans l'impatience ou je suis de vous embrasser je demeure avec passion et sincerité Votre tres

J'oubliois a vous dire que j'ay fait de l'harmonie tout le reste que je voulois faire et qu'il ny en aura peutetre jamais autrechose

Endorsed by Locke: Mr Toynard 21 Nov. *78*

## *421.* DR. DENIS GRENVILLE to LOCKE, 11/21 November 1678 (*416*, 426)

B.L., MS. Locke c. 10, ff. 89–91, with enclosure, ff. 92–3. Answered by no. 426.

a la Tour 9ber 21th. 78

My Worthy Freind

I will call you soe in spight of your teeth, run away as far as you please from mee: nay will hold fast your freindship which you have given mee, tho I cannot catch your person. The inclosed papers will testifie the reality of these my threats, and shew that I take you to your word, and am resolved to serve my selfe the best I can of you at a distance, since I cannot as I have a mind to by personall conversation. In pursueance whereof I doe now renew my spirituall intercourse with you; which I have for a while omitted; having here (with a Copie of the paper you gave mee at Montpelier

[1] The Observatoire. The *canardière* here is probably the hide used for shooting duck: *Le Grand Larousse de la Langue françoise*, 1971– (the earliest occurrence given there of the meaning a duck-gun is dated 1794). Later Toinard uses *canarder*, to shoot from concealment: no. *470*; etc.

[2] Generally *crottes*; dung or dirt.

which you desired in a letter you sent mee last Aprill)[1] sent you the fifth and last of those papers which I promised according to the proposed method writt downe before our parting.[2] Soe that now you have some of my thoughts (such as they are) on all those five heads, whereon I doe soe earnestly desire your Reflections. namely, *Recreation, Conversation, buisnesse, study, and Devotion.* To each of which papers of mine, I doe expect one of yours. I will not bate you an Ace, I am resolved on itt; espetially since you serve mee such slippery Tricks: as this last *Goe-by*; raise mee up for some dayes in to a Fools paradise, to make mee more sensible of my misery. You (or Sir John Banks) I have a minde to vent some of[a] spleen against him) have dealt with mee, as some that I have been told of did once with the Tinker, whom, after they had made dead Drunk, laid in a princely bed, afforded royall fare and attendance, till hee began to fancy himselfe a Prince, they made againe Drunke the second time and deprived of his imaginary Principality, leaving him againe in his old Greazy leather doublet, and tatterd hose; Thus I thought my selfe a Mighty Man at soe unexpected good Fortune; as the having soe good a freind, blown unexpectedly by Boreas (with whom I have been well acquainted at Durham) from the Loyer to the Estang of Monpelier,[3] and before any reall injoyment by some worse Air than the Marine blowne away from me againe allmost as far as the lake of Geneva. And this you say is Sir John Banks. Truly wee are litle beholden to him: Hee might have found out some other employment for you, and his money; than to have sent you after soe great Tour here soe neare to mock us; nay downe-right to affront us; as if wee have sett up our station for eighteen months in a Country that doth not deserve looking on. I am really soe angry with his worship, that were I sure hee would pay for this packet, I would write on till toomorrow night and fill up a halfe dozen sheets of paper with mere rayling, and send them accompanied with twice as many old Gazets, to cause him to pay twoe or three crowns postage. But to bee serious, I doe assure you, Sir, that this sudden and unexpected disappointment, after soe sudden and unexpected a Joy, proves a greivous affliction to mee, even grateing upon my spirit, soe as might doe mee prejudice, did I not turne of

[a] *End of line.*

[1] Locke's letter is lost; his paper is that on Recreation: no. 328.
[2] At Montpellier about March 1677: p. 470.
[3] Apparently part of what is now sometimes called the Étang de Maguelonne.

this trouble, as I usually doe others of the like nature with a fitt of drollery; which is my usuall physick for such maladies. Insomuch that when you find mee a litle extravagant in that, you may conclude that some trouble of minde hath preceded itt. And this advertisement by the way I make bold to send you (without which practice I had long since broke my poor braines) for the better understanding of mee for the future. In good earnest, Sir, I was transported with very much Contentment when your letter brought mee the Intelligence of your being at Monpelier, and concluded soberly that the heavens were very kinde to mee, in complying with some very earnest desires of my soule. There being very few things which I desired more than Worthy Mr. Lockes company. And this unexpected providence of having you strangely brought about soe neare, gave mee greater hopes of successe, in reference to my choice of soe good a freind, and designes on him, than if I had beene gratified in my first motion to have detained him at Montpelier. But this more strange disappointment and deprivall of you, when I thought you sure in my Embraces, much disorders as a bad omen my scrupulous soule, representing a great many feares and *Jealousies* to my spirit; disheartenning mee in some flatterring thoughts which I had of appearing noe small fellow in the sight of the world before I died, if I could have secured such a freind, (as you appeare to me,) neare mee to support my weaknesses and supply my defects. Since I first had any notion of *Freindship*, there hath noe-body hit my Fancy in all respects, as your selfe. And whether you thinke your selfe soe Considerable, as I doe, it is noe matter; you are not like to prove the worse freind, or lesse usefull to mee. I am Contented with you, such as you are, and with your Counsells, and reasonnings, call them *Docks*, or *nettles*, or what you please; and am willing with all my heart to take you (if I know how to catch hold of your right hand againe) as people doe their wives, for better for worse etc till Death us doe part. But least I returne into my old streine of drollery, forgetting my boyish Theme of Ne quid nimis,[1] I will stop while it is well, and reply to what you required of mee before you left Paris, in order to the drawing up of 3. distinct papers, to those 3. which I sent you: namely whether you had *hit right* in those your Emperick Prescriptions (you may thanke yourselfe for the Epithet)[2] in assigning one cause, and sending one remedy or way of Cure, for

[1] 'Do nothing to excess': Erasmus, *Adagia*, I. vi. 96.

[2] See no. 374.

all those my troubles. In very good earnest, Sir, you have *hitt right*, very right, even hit the nayle on the head. (You handle a hammer, I see, very well.) That is you have found out the *Originall*[a] cause of my *Mallady*,[a] namely that which drove mee into that disconsolate condition, (whereof I have given you the relation in my 5. paper,) and which, being not perfectly removed, clogs mee strangely in my Christian carreer after Grace and usefull knowledge. In my *Infancy*[a] of *Devotion*,[a] I thought my selfe allwayes guilty of a *Mortall*[a] *Sin*,[a] if I came short of doing what I beleived to bee the very *Best*,[a] making every *Scruple*[a] (where of my mind did abound) soe weighty a matter of *Conscience*,[a] that I had at last created to my selfe a *weight*[a] soe insupportable, that I was forced to sink under itt for some while, as you have heard in the aforesaid paper. And now, tho I have had allwayes, I blesse God since my delivery out of those sad perplexities, *Light* and *Strength* enough to discover, and defend my selfe against, the crafts and assaults of my subtle and mighty adversary, soe as hee cannot reduce mee to such miserable streights, but is forced to suffer mee to goe on my roade with lesse trouble to my selfe and others; yet I have too inconsiderable a measure of Either to ⟨Correspond⟩[b] to my present obligations, and accomplish what I aime at, and have in my Eye; and which I cannot satisfye my selfe without attaining, unlesse some one satisfye mee that there is some fault in my sight. Reason mee therefore I pray, Sir, (I must repeat my old request) either into more vertue, or into more quiet: (which you please); and I will extoll your *Apothecary's*[a] shop, before any Divines study which I have yet mett with all

Yours etc.

DE. GR:

posts.[c]

The other matters which made mee soe extreamely earnest, at this nick, to have some personall discourse, were some difficulties in reference to the Conduct of my Deare Sist: and the child[1] (one of the hardest undertakings that I have ever yet been ingaged in, in my whole life), which I dare not yet Commit to paper, nor desire you at a distance to reply to. I have noe Countryman hereabout to Consult with. I beseech God to supply my want of Freinds, as

[a] *These words are written large for emphasis; the other italicized words in this letter are underlined in the manuscript.* [b] *MS.* Correspondend [c] *Dated at head of page by Locke* 21 Nov. 78

[1] Probably Mary Thornhill.

well as all other my defects. That I may bee the better quallified to guide others; I beseech you to hasten the foure papers I expect for the better settlement of mine owne soule. I shall bee very well Contented to receive one a weeke, and in as familiar a stile and method as you were wont to talk in my sisters chambers at Monpelier.

If you please to returne mee the 5 papers of mine owne which occasiond yours, tho in one packet, I shall willingly pay the postage. for having noe copies, I cannot otherwise have the full benefit of yours. what ever way you stere, I beg the favour of the 5. papers of reflections, wherewith I will rest Contented till next Opportunity of more particular Correspondence.

I pray give my humble service to Mr. Banks. My sister gives you, both, hers

I have received yours from Lions. I wish there were some mountains of snow in the road to Paris allsoe.

If you rescue all papers which I shall send you from the usuall fate of their betters; that of the bum; I shall thanke you.

Address: A Monsieur Monsieur Jacques Selapris l'aisné pour faire tenir s'il luy plaist a Monsieur Locke Gentilhomme Anglois A Lions

Note (by Selapris?): J: Selapris est fort[a] vostre serviteur et vous Baise fort les mains.

Endorsed by Locke: Mr Grenvill 21 Nov. *78*

[Enclosure:]

5: paper, concerning Exercise of Devotion.[b]

Tho I have had these 20 yeares severall notions and distinctions concerning Devotion,[c]– as namely–[c] the Externall, and Internall performance of devotion; sensible and rationall, Devotion etc; neither[d]– have been ignorant how–[d] a good worke, or action, was better than a long speech to God on our knees, and that whosoever did truly *mortifie and Die dayly, did pray continually etc.* and hereby have been sometimes helpefull to Others in my discourses, yet my weaknesses and troubles in reference to this particular have not beene lesse, or fewer, than those heretofore mentioned in reference to the Other matters. As I have been very unhappy in

[a] *Doubtful reading.* [b] *Dated by Locke* Nv°. 21. 78 [c–c] *Interlined. In what follows I have not recorded the smaller interlineations.* [d–d] *Interlined; substituted for* and, *which is not deleted.*

Consuming my time in disputing with myselfe (whereof the former papers sufficiently informe[a] you) throughout my whole Conversation, yet never more than here in this. And as I have been tossed up and downe by my unsetled thoughts, concerning *Recreation, Converse, buisnesse and study*, soe I have been, and am still; here in reference to the Exercise of Devotion. And besides the difficulties that doe arise from this, as clashing with all the Former, there doe arise a multitude from the bare performance of the thing it selfe. I know that true Devotion is only the Imployment of the Soule, and that Externall performances are only to begett, stir up, preserve, or increase such Inward and spirituall temper of Soule as God shall at any time bestow on any of us to[b–] capacitate us to act vertue in our lives;[–b] and yet I cannot disentangle my selfe from the over sollicitous Care, about a nice and punctuall performance of outward Exercises, namely[c] such and such certaine formes and methods of meditations and prayers etc at such and such prefixed times, and houres, in such and such postures of body etc thus often missing of the End by such excessive concernement for the meanes. And on the other side, afterwards I have been tired out with the Inconveniences of this Extreame as[b–] to the Exteriour,[–b] tho I am very sensible of the usefull nesse, expediency (nay necessity (in some cases) of Externall meanes, formes, and methods, yet I doe, under pretence of zealously prosecuting internall[d] Devotion[d] (which is the end of them all) to my great prejudice very often too much neglect them, if not wholly quitt them (as to private). But it is not long till I feele the Inconveniences of such a liberty to[d] bee[d] more in number, and of more dangerous consequence than the former, and soe returne to the outward[d] exercises[d] which I quitted too soon, and am soon constreined to returne to. And which I am however[d] like to quit againe upon the same account, and upon[b–] the same account[–b] like to returne to againe, for the future. Thus (reeling[b–] from one extreame to another)[–b] am I tossed up and downe between my Externall and Internall Exercises of Devotion; as I am between my Exercise of Devotion in Generall and all my other forementioned buisnesses of my life, discoursed of in former papers. Should I particularise my scruples here I should indeed write a volume and perfectly tire you out. I shall only therefore informe you in Generall, that that scrupulosity which I complaine of to bee in my nature (and with which I have been struggling these

[a] *Or* informd [b–b] *Interlined.* [c] *Doubtful reading.* [d] *Interlined.*

20 yeares but cannot perfectly overcome) is here to mee in this respect of all others most troublesome and pernitious; and proves the great clog which cheifly hinders mee in my spirituall progresse, and detaines mee in soe low a pitch, and imperfect[a] state of Vertue and[a] Learning[a]. And here, I thinke, it is a proper time to declare to you the lamentable effect which it once had on mee (for I must conceale nothing from him whom I consult as a spirituall physitian) in plunging mee into a sad and most disconsolate condition. When I was about 21 yeares of age, at Oxford,[1] I began to have some serious thoughts, more than ordinary, of becoming a sober Christian. Whereupon I began to have a very earnest desire to partake of the holy Sacrament (which by the unhappinesse of the times of Rebellion together with mine owne negligence I had been deprived of till that time) and to the same end and purpose hastned up to London to receive it in an Episcopall Congregation, having suckt in with my milke some affection to the Church of England. This obliging mee to a strict inquiry into my past life, and the acquainting my selfe with the particulars of Christian Duty, there did present themselves unto mee such a multitude of difficulties (occasion'd by my ignorance wherein true vertue did consist and the scrupulosity of my nature) that I thinking it impossible to gett through them fell into soe great Dispondency, that, it being much increased by melancholy, I sate downe in dispaire, and quitting all duty; The Reflextion on which drove mee into farther dispaire, and into soe great distresse of Conscience, that I often attempted to make my selfe away; But were preserved by many speciall acts of Gods providence, (too large to relate thus) and at last were delivered out of those snares and Fetters of Sathan, by some sudden light and Comfort darted into my soule, which discovered to mee the Delusions of my Adversary, and my owne weaknesse and folly, and thereby representing a Christian life more possible and practicable, and caused mee to sett up new Resolutions, and set about new endeavours. this I prosecuted for some yeares with much sensible sweetnesse and satisfaction, being soe well pleasd with the life and Dutie of a Christian, which I did at first thinke soe burthensome (nay Impossible) that I could not satisfye my selfe with the

[a] *Interlined.*

[1] Grenville was born on 13 February 1637 and was admitted to Exeter College on 22 September 1657: *Remains*, p. viii.

ordinary obligations to live the bare life of a Christian, without putting my selfe under those much higher and Indispensable ones of A minister, goeing through then with those Resolutions, that had for some while fluttered in my mind, of *Devoting*[a] my selfe to the *Church*:[a] (and this was in the yeare 1659), which I putt in execution soon after the Kings returne, entring into Deacons orders in the yeare 1661.[1] since which time (tho I have wanted that first heat, light, and comfort which did usually accompany my first exercises of Repentence and Devotion, and which some mistick writers terme *Fervor Novitius*) I have allwayes injoyed (Blessed bee God) that solid, rationall contentment both in my Generall and particular Calling, as never to repent of Either; but on the Contrary have in some such measure attended to both, that, if I were vaine, and foolish enough to beleive the words, or compare myselfe with the life and actions, of the generality, I should thinke my selfe a famous Christian and considerable minister. But I am too sensible of the rottennesse of such foundations to build on them; I would faine have a litle better testimony in my owne Conscience. And that is the thing which I am now seeking, and crave your freindly helpe in. Pray, Sir, teach mee some art either to stop the mouth of my clamourous Conscience, or helpe mee up to that pitch of Christian and ministeriall Duty, which it requires of mee.

Soli Deo Glori⟨a⟩[b]

## 422. George Walls to Locke, 11 (?) November [1678] (*409, 459*)

B.L., MS. Locke c. 23, ff. 31–2. Year from Locke's endorsement and contents. The second digit of the day is so written that Locke could read it as 7; but is not very like 7 as written by Walls elsewhere and in view of the postmark is to be regarded as 1.

Christ Church Novemb: 11th.[c]—⟨78⟩[d]

Sir

Immediately uppon my returne out of the Country, I return'd you my thanks for the favour of yours from Blois; and had wrote againe before this time but that either there is nothinge new at Oxon, or if there bee through greate and earnest expectation of

[a] *These words are written large for emphasis; the italicized words below are underlined in the manuscript.* [b] *End of line.* [c] *Badly written; perhaps* 17th. [d] *Page torn.*

[1] p. 470, n. 2.

somewhat more considerable elsewhere, wee doe not observe it. however you may please to know that your friends are well and frequently enquire after you. that Dr Marsh formerly of Exeter, and since principle of Alban hall, is sent over by the bishop of Oxon to bee provost of Trinitie Colledge in Dublin, Dr Warde, the former provoste, beinge made bishop of Ossery.[1] tis said Mr Levet will succeede him in his hall, it beinge much more like a residence to keepe two parsnidges and live at Alban hall, than at Nimeguen.[2] Mr Alestry has beene lately with us after his sixe yeeres stay in Sweden, whither hee is to returne with the character of residente.[3] Tom of Christchurch has beene speechlesse for some time, and the bell-founder has lately miscarried in casteinge of him, many hundred weight of mettall beinge wanteinge to complete him.[4] The greate controversie betwixt the univercitie and towne is now ended, the records beinge withdrawne the morninge before twas to bee try'd. The mayor and aldermen promissinge not to dispute the jurisdiction of our courte, which was all wee contended for. I have not discours'd Mr Thomas[5] concerninge your affayres farther then I mention'd in my last, and shall not doe it till order. Mr Hodges is at Norwich, where hee tells mee hee hath beene ill. Mr Weelkes of C C C is gone to live with my Lord Grey of Werke, Mr Pyndar beinge lately deade of that feavour that has beene almost everie where but at Oxon. his salary is an hundred pounds per annum, Mr Thornton was so neare haveinge that prefermente that Mr Weelks and many others had wish'd him Joy of it.[6] it has beene confidently

[1] Michael Ward, d. 1681, President of Trinity College, Dublin, since 1674, was nominated bishop of Ossory on 25 October of this year in succession to Benjamin Parry (p. 69 n.); he was translated to Derry in 1680: Leslie, *Ossory Clergy*, pp. 21–2. In July, in case the presidency should fall vacant, Dr. Fell recommended for it Narcissus Marsh, 1638–1713, principal of St. Alban Hall 1673–8, the future archbishop of Armagh; he was sworn in as president on 24 January 1679: *D.N.B.*; H.M.C., *Ormonde MSS.*, new ser. iv. 166–7.

[2] William Levet, *c.* 1644–94; matriculated 1659; B.A. from Christ Church 1664; M.A. 1667; D.D. 1680: Foster. He was connected with the Hydes: Prideaux, *Letters*, p. 29. He presumably accompanied Laurence Hyde (the future earl of Rochester) to the peace conference at Nijmegen (later he acted as agent for Henry Hyde, the second earl of Clarendon, in his suit against Anthony Wood). He did not become principal of St. Alban Hall, but was principal of Magdalen Hall from 1681 until his death.

[3] William Allestree: p. 365 n. The notice appears to be incorrect.

[4] The bell was recast in 1680 and brought into use again apparently in 1682: W. G. Hiscock, *A Christ Church Miscellany*, 1946, pp. 146–8.

[5] Samuel Thomas.

[6] Lord Grey is Forde Grey, 1655–1701; third Baron Grey of Warke 1675; created earl of Tankerville 1695: *D.N.B.*; mentions below. William Pindar, of University College, M.A. 1670, his chaplain, died on 23 September of this year: Wood, *Fasti*, ii. 319. His successor was John Weeks, of Exeter College; B.A. 1673; vicar of St. Eval,

reported that a principle, and a master of a Col amongst us are —— what none that knows theire learninge will allow them to bee.[1] Twas confidently said (as Mr Tyrrells news) that you were comeinge for England, but I have this against the beliefe of it that tis winter. If there bee any other little matters here, they concerne men you doe not know, and they are of the nature I have alreadie mention'd, and soe you lose nothinge by the concealement. Tis not yet known who will bee bishop ⟨of⟩[a] Chichester.[2] I know who was.[b] Tis said by some that Chester[3] will bee remov'd. others say that Dr Cudworth[4] of Cambridge will bee the man. Mr Rosewell is prebende of Windsor,[5] and I am

Deare Sir.

your most humble servant

GEORGE WALLS

If you chance to meet with one Mr Pelham[6] at Paris, or else where (who is lately gone into France uppon the great errande) I most earnestly begge you will doe him what kindnesse his circumstances seeme to want. or if hee bee gone to Montpelier (and you can without trouble know it,) and if you continue your correspondence with Monsieur Berbeyrac,[7] I desire that youle mention him to him

Address: For Mr John Locke This. To be left at Sir John Banks his house in Lyncoln's Inne fields London.

Postmark: NO 15

Endorsed by Locke: Mr Wall 17 Nov. *78*

[a] *MS.* o [b] *Followed by a hole in the paper, apparently due to the biting of the ink of a blotted letter.*

---

Cornwall, 1684. The rival was William Thornton, of Wadham College; M.A. 1666; principal of Hart Hall 1688–1707: Foster.

[1] This alludes principally to Obadiah Walker, 1616–99; M.A. 1638; Master of University College 1676–89: *D.N.B.* About this time he and the principals of New Inn Hall and St. Mary Hall were reputed to be Roman Catholics: Wood, *L. and T.* ii. 421.

[2] The see was vacant by Brideoake's death on 5 October: p. 615, n. 3.

[3] Pearson: p. 193, n. 6; etc. He was not translated.

[4] Ralph Cudworth, 1617–88; D.D. 1651; Master of Christ's College, Cambridge, 1654–88; author of *The True Intellectual System of the Universe* (p. 518, n. 2); father of Locke's friend Damaris Cudworth, later Lady Masham: *D.N.B.*; genealogical information in J. Peile, *Biographical Register of Christ's College*, 1910–13; see further nos. *677*, *731*, etc.

[5] John Rosewell, d. 1684; B.D. 1667; fellow of Eton; installed at Windsor 26 October in succession to Brideoake: Foster.

[6] Perhaps John Pelham, a son of Sir John Pelham, third baronet, of Halland in Laughton, Sussex; he matriculated from Christ Church in 1674: Foster.

[7] p. 515, n. 1.

## *423.* JACQUES SELAPRIS to LOCKE, 13/23 November 1678 (*419, 419A, 427*)

B.L., MS. Locke c. 18, ff. 75–6.

Lyon Ce 23e.[a] Novembre 1678

Monsieur Mon tres Cher Amy, Salut

Je veux Esperer que avent la reception de Cellyçy ma pressedente vous sera bien parvenue par vostre Laquay Silvestre, qui partit le 17. du Courant par le Coche, Je Manday à Monsieur Charas Apoticaire que javois fait embaler toute⟨s⟩[b] vos hardes ensemble et aussy dit, la marque, le priant les vouloir retirer avec le garçon franc de tout, Come aussy à Monsieur Marchal de ly avoir adressé par la deligençe un ballot d'hardes quil avoit envoyé sy devent, aussy franc de tout, ne les voulant prendre autrement. Car ny le Coche Ny la deligençe ne prenent plus d'hardes que franches, pour Cest effect je n'ay suivy vos ordres. Cy Inclus trois Letres pour vous, dont deux me sont ádresséz par Monsieur De Charleton, qui vous Baise fort les mains.

Monsieur Wicherley[1] doibt estre icy au premier Jour, pour sen aler à Paris, Je ly ay aresté plaçe dans la deligençe qui vous serve d'avis. Ma feme et moy vous asseurent de Nos humbles ⟨res⟩pects,[c] et vous Remerçions encore treshumblement de toute vos bontéz Amitie Presents et grandes honestetéz, ne souhaitant autre Chose que de trouver l'ocassion pour Nous pouvoir revenger. Monsieur Bancqs trouvera avec vostre permission l'asseurance de nos humbles Respects. Je finis en vous asseurant quil n'y à Persone qui vous soit plus que Moy

Monsieur

Vostre tres humble et vray obeissant serviteur

JACQUES SELAPRIS L'aisné.

tout presentement il m'en souvient que J'ay oublié aven vostre départ de vous doner la Recete pour faire l'ongent pour faire Croistre promptement la corne des Chevaux il faut prendre Ce qui suit—

$\frac{1}{2}$ lb.[d] sire Jaulne

$\frac{1}{4}$ lb.[d] de la Poïs de Cordonier Noire pour dix sols termentine—

[a] *Date altered from 22; this is Locke's reading.* [b] *End of line.* [c] *Page torn.* [d] *Contracted in MS.; the expansion is doubtful.*

[1] pp. 611, 654.

½ lb.[a] de l'a graisse qui est entre la fente des pates des Beufs ou vaches, que l'on trouve vers les tripiers

½ lb.[a] de Moile de Beuf, et sil se peut d'un Beuf Rouge. faités Boulir une bone demy heure tout Cela ensemble, en le bien remuant avec un petit Baston, ápres laissé le Refroirdir, et vous en pouvéz vous en servir un heure apres. se fait asseurement un ongant qui est Exelent pour le susdit sujet.[1]

Address: A Monsieur Monsieur Charas Maistre Apoticaire Rue Boucherie au faubourg St. Germain Pour Rendre a Monsieur Monsieur Loke Gentilshome Anglois loge Chés luy à Paris.

Endorsed by Locke: Mr Selapris 23 Nov. *78*

## 424. Locke to Nicolas Toinard, 16/26 November 1678 (*420*, 428, 432)

Lady Charnwood (D. M. Benson, Lady Charnwood) collection: B.M., Loan MSS. 60, vol. ii, no. 3 (1). Printed, incompletely, in Alfred Morrison Collection, *Catalogue*, vol. iii, 1888; reprinted, from that, in Ollion, p. 148; completely, in Lady Charnwood, *An Autograph Collection*, 1930, pp. 246–7. Answers no. *420*.

Orleans 26 Nov. '78

Monsieur

Comme vous me menacez de vostre depart bien tost de Paris, il ne faut pas m'arester icy plus long tems, quoique la conversation et les amitiés que vous m'avez procurés icy feroient un long sejour en cette ville et bien agreable et bien utile. Mais il y a quelque chose davantage en vous, c'est pourquoy je part même avant cette billete; mais comme elle va plus viste que moy c'est pour vous dire que je seray bien malheureux si vous partirez de Paris le jour de mon arrivé qui sera, s'il plaist a dieu, Lunedy.[2] Au reste ce n'est pas l affaire d'un petitte billette même d'une grande letre de vous temoigner la reconnoissance que je vous ay, a pein tout le rest de ma

[a] *Contracted in MS.; the expansion is doubtful.*

[1] Locke copied the prescription into his Journal, 2 December.
[2] 28 November, N.S.

vie souffira a cela, mais vous pouvez vous assure que je suis perfaictement

Monsieur
vostre tres humble et tres oblige serviteur
J. LOCKE

Address: A Monsieur Monsieur Toynard à la teste noire dans la rüe mazarin Fauxbourg st Germain a Paris

## *425.* SIR JOHN BANKS to LOCKE, 25 November 1678 (*414*, 431)

B.L., MS. Locke c. 3, ff. 118–19. Answered by no. 431.

Sir

I have your severalls with your last from Orleans of the 24 November and of your and my sons being well (thanks be to God) come thither. And as I doe acknowledge your very indulgent care and kindnesse to my son, and therin to us. in your soe consideratly declininge, your intended designe for Italy, for the reasons you mention, soe I doe yet beleive you will more and more finde that the layinge those thoughts aside, will be to your best satisfactions as well as to ours heer. And you may be assured that I shall not be against my sons cominge home thro. Holland when the season of the yeare permitts, if it doe alsoe sute your affaires, and could wish it were now a fit season for your beinge there, but doe thinke you have very prudently made choice of spendinge this winter at Paris, in those exercises and improvements which you thinke most to my sons advantage, and as I doe wholy leave the mannage therof to your prudence, soe I doe not at all doubt my sons ready complyance with what you shall advise, being not only well satisfyed of the kindnesse you beare to him, but of his respects to you—Nor would I confine you to Winter at Paris, if you can offer any place more desirable, in respect to your owne healths and advantage.

I had made a supply at Genoa and Legorne[a] to answer all your affaires, and now I presume Madam Herinx will accommodate what monnys you desire, and desire your byls come on me as the Exchange rules becaus I would not give that trouble to Sir Nathaniel Herne. And I pray Sir will you be free to take to yourselfe what you

[a] *MS.* Leg°.

desire for your owne particular accommodation. My Lord Shaftesbury is better in health then usuall I thinke. I pray will you and my son make much of one another. and keepe together. that he may have the benefitt of your conversation as much as may be, which will be most for his security as well as our satisfaction. but I will say noe more, for you have given that large testimony of your kindnesse as I shall ever acknowledge my selfe to be

Sir Your reall freind and servant

JOHN BANKS

Lincolns in feilds
25 November 78

Address: A Mounsieur Monsieur Locke—A Madam Herinx et fils A Paris

Postmark: G

Endorsed by Locke: Sir J: Banks 25 Nov. *78*

## 426. LOCKE to DR. DENIS GRENVILLE, 26 November/6 December 1678 (*421*, *447*)

B.L., MS. Rawlinson D. 849, ff. 150–1. Draft in Locke's Journal for 1678 (B.L., MS. Locke f. 3), pp. 358–67; not dated, but occurs between the entries for 2 and 5 December, N.S.; the composition continues to p. 378, but on p. 367, at 'with fresh vigour and activity', Locke notes, 'Hactenus 6 Dec.'; printed from this draft, as far as 'well grounded steps', in King, pp. 113–15. Copy in B.M., Add. MS. 4290, ff. 115–19; printed from this copy in Fox Bourne, i. 394–7. Answers no. *421*. There is nothing to show whether Locke sent the remainder of his composition to Grenville; a letter of 27 January 1679, N.S., mentioned in no. *447*, is lost.

6. Dec. 78

Sir

By Yours of 21 Nov you assure me that in my last on this occasion I hit right on the Originall and principall cause of some disquiets you had had in yourself upon the matters under consideration, I should have been glad to have known also, whether the cure, I there offerd at, were any ways effectuall: or wherein the reasons I gave came short of that satisfaction and establishment as to that point. (*viz That We are not obleiged to doe always that which is precisely best*) as was desired

For I thinke it properest to the subdueing of those enemys of our quiet Fears Doubts, and Scruples, to doe as those who designe the conquest of new terretorys, viz cleare the country as we goe and leave behinde us noe enemys unmasterd, noe garisons unreducd, noe lurkeing holes unsearchd which may give occasion to disorders and insurrections or excite new disturbances

If therefor in that or any of my other papers any of my arguments and reasonings shall appeare weake or obscure: If they reach not the bottom of the matter; are wide of your particular case; or have not soe cleard up the question in all the parts, and extent of it, as to setle the truth with evidence and certainty: I must beg you to doe me the favour to let me know what doubts still remain, and upon what reasons grounded. That soe in our progresse we may looke upon those propositions that you are once throughly convinced of, to be setled, and establishd truths, of which you are not to doubt any more, without new reasons, that have not been yet examind. Or on the other side, by your answers to my reasons I may be set right, and recoverd from an Error. For as I write you noe thing but my own thoughts (which is vanity enough but you will have it soe) yet I am not soe vain as to imagin them infallible; and therefor expect from you that mutuall great office of Freindship, to shew me my mistakes, and to reason me into a better understanding. For it matters not on which side the truth lies, soe we doe but finde and imbrace it

This way of proceeding is necessary on both our accounts. On mine because in my freindship with you, as well as others, I designe to gaine by the bargain that which I esteem the great benefit of freindship, the rectifying of my mistakes and errors: which makes me soe willingly expose my crude extempory thoughts to your view, and lay them such as they are naked before you.

And on your account also I thinke it very necessary. For your minde haveing been long accustomed to thinke it true that *The thing absolutely in it self best ought always indispensably to be donne.* you ought, in order to establishing your peace, perfectly examin and cleare up that question, soe as at the end of the debate, to reteine it still for true; or perfectly reject it as a wrong, and mistaken measure, and to setle it as a maxim in your minde, that you are noe more to govern your self or thoughts by that false rule, but wholy lay it aside as condemned without puting your self to the trouble, every time you reflect on it, to recall into your minde, and weigh again all those reasons upon which you made that conclusion. And soe also in any other opinions or principles you have had when you come once to be convinced of their falshood.

If this be not donne it will certainly happen that the above mentioned principle (and soe of the rest) haveing been for a long time setled in your minde, will upon every occasion recur, and the reasons upon which you rejected it not being soe familiar to your thoughts, nor soe ready at hand to oppose it, This old acquaintance will be apt to resume his former station and influence and to disturb that quiet which had not its foundation perfectly establishd

For these reasons it is that I thinke we ought to cleare all as we goe and come to a plenary result in all the propositions that come under debate before we goe any farther. This has been usually my way with my self to which I thinke I owe a great part of my quiet. And I beleive a few good principles well establishd will reach farther and resolve more doubts then at first sight perhaps one would imagin. And the grounds and rules on which the right and wrong of our actions turne and which will generally serve to conduct us in the cases and occurrences of our lives in all states and conditions lie possibly in a narrower compase, and in a lesse number then is ordinarily supposed. But to come to them one must goe by sure and well grounded steps—

This being premised I come to make good my promise to you in mentioning what I guesse may be an other cause of your doubts unsteadynesse and disturbances in the points under consideration. And that I suppose is, that you thinke those things inconsistent that in themselves I judg are not soe. Viz Worldly businesse and Devotion, Study and conversation; and Recreation with all. As if the most material of these soe deserved; or the present and most presseing soe possessed the whole man, that it left noe roome, noe time for any of the other

This if it has had any influence upon your minde to disturb it (as it seems to me by some passages in your papers it has) is not yet of that weight and difficulty as that I before mentioned: And I am apt to think that a few easy and naturall considerations will be sufficient to remove it, And to get quite rid of this, (if any,) ground of disturbance and scrupule, or ⟨unsetlednesse⟩.[a] And for this we need only reflect a litle upon the state and condition that it hath pleased god to place us in here in this world

1 We are not born in heaven, but in this world, where our being is to be preserved with meat drink and clothing and other

[a] *MS.* ustedlednesse.

necessarys that are not borne with us, but must be got and kept with forecast care and labour: and therefor we cannot be all Devotion, All Prayses and Halilujahs and perpetually in the Vision of things above, that is reserved for another state and place. Had it been otherwise, god would not have put us in a condition, where we are obleiged to use all meanes to preserve our selves, and yet those meanes of preserveing our selves in that condition (i e this life) not to be had without thoughtfulnesse and turmoile; without imploying upon the search of them the greatest part of our time and care. For at a lesse rate the greatest part of mankinde can hardly subsist in this world, Espetially this civilized world wherein you are obleiged to keepe your rank and station, and which if by mismanagement or neglect of your temporall affairs you fall from, you by your own fault put your self out of a condition of doeing that good and performing those offices requird from one in that station.

2 We are not placed in this world to stay here for ever, or without any concernment beyond it. and therefor we are not to lay out all our thoughts, and time upon it, and the concernments of it. The author of our being, and all our good here, and the much greater good of another world, deserves and demands frequent addresses to him of thanks prayer and resignation; and our concernments in an other world make it reason, wisdome and duty soe to doe

3 We are borne with ignorance of those things that concerne the conduct of our lives in this world in order to atteining what we desire, or is usefull to us in this world; or we hope in the next; and therefor enquiry, study, and meditation is necessary, without which a great part of Necessary knowledg is not to be had. espetially in some callings.

4 We are borne with dispositions and desires of Society, we are by nature fited for it, and Religion increases the obligation. We are borne members of common wealths, beset with relations, and in need of freinds, and under a necessity of acquaintance, which requireing of us the mutuall offices of familiarity freindship and charity, we cannot spend all our time in retired devotion or study, nor in ploding or takeing care of our worldly affaires i e that viaticum which is to serve us (or those we are to provide for) through this pilgrimage, or some thing in order to it.

5 We are soe framed, soe constituted that any imployment of minde, any exercise of body, will weary, and unfit us to continue longer in that imployment. The springs by which all our operations

are performed are finite and have their utmost extent; and when they approach that, like watches that have gon till their force is spent, we stand still, or move to litle purpose, if not wound up again, and thus after labour of minde or body we have need of Recreation to set us agoeing again with fresh vigor and activity

This is not all on this subject but tis time to release you till another season. tis enough to satisfie you that I am

Yours
J LOCKE

## 427. JACQUES SELAPRIS to LOCKE, 26 November/6 December 1678 (*423*, *436*)

B.L., MS. Locke c. 18, ff. 77–8.

Lyon Ce 6. decembre 1678.

Monsieur Mon tres Cher Patron et Intime Amy Salut.

Je Me trouve avec vostre Tres Chere et Agreable du 2d. du Courant, et suis esté tres Ravy d'aprendre vostre heureuze ariveé à Paris avec Monsieur Banqs, et que vous avéz trouvé vostre Laquay Silvestre arivé un jour devent vous et par Contre suis au desesspoir de Ceque me ditéz n'avoir pas reçeu en mesme temps vos hardes, lesquels sont partis le mesme Jour, et Come javois Crainte que les Billets ne segarrassent desus les Males valize et Estuiits, et le garçon ne scachont pas parler, je vous ay dit, les avoir tout fait Embaler ensemble dans une bale Marqué W.s L.L. et la letre de voiture adressé á Monsieur Charas Maistre Apoticaire[a] selon que vous m'avéz ordoné et franc de tout, Ce que je vous Confirme, Je vous diray en reponce, que jay aussytost esté au Coche et ay fait toute les plaintes possibles, Le Maistre M'a fort asseuré quils sont party le mesme Jour, et que asseurement vous les auréz reçeu du depuis, il m'a mesme fait voir Cela sur le livre, j'espere que la Chose sera de la fasson, Ce que je seray bien aize d'aprendre, Come aussy la Reçeption du Ballot par la deligençe. Il faut ádvouer que je suis bien Malheureux de Ne vous servir que en mal reuissant, et vous proteste en Conscieņçe que Ce n'est pas affaute de bien recomendér les Chozes, mais plustost par je ne sçay quoy, qui me Rend sy Malheureux. Sy par une Malheur de tout les malheurs il n'estoit pas arivé encore, j'espere demain avoir avis par une de vostres, pour faire toutes les Protestations imaginables.

[a] *MS.* M[e] Apo[te]

Vous N'avéz pas sujet de Remerçier sy fort pour N'avoir rien reçeu, Cest Nous qui somes vos tres redevables. Ne vous plaignéz plus du debours, quand le Compte sera un peu plus grand je vous l'envoyeray, puisque vous le vouléz ainsy.

Je vous Remerçie tres humblement du soin que vous vouléz prendre pour Nostre petit affaire en Engletere,[1] et de M'aviser en son temps. Je vous suis et seray obligé eternellement. Monsieur Bancqs trouvera avec vostre permisson icy mes humbles Baisemains, Ma feme et moy vous asseurons de Nos humbles Respects et suis toute ma vie

Monsieur

Vostre Tres humble et Tres obeissant serviteur

JACQUES SELAPRIS L'aisné.

Address: A Monsieur Monsieur Loke Gentils home Anglois Logé Chéz Monsieur Charas Maistre Apoticaire Rue Boucherie au faubourg St Germain à Paris.

Endorsed by Locke: Mr Selapris 6 Dec. *78*

## 428. LOCKE: Inscriptions on sheets of Toinard's *Evangeliorum Harmonia*, 3/13 December 1678 (424, 432)

Toinard, *Evangeliorum Harmonia Græco-Latina*, interleaved set of sheets in Mr. Paul Mellon's collection (L.L., no. 2934). Draft in B.L., MS. Locke c. 27, f. 53. Besides the two inscriptions there are on the sheets some corrections or additions by Locke, in part from E. Merillius, *Notæ Philologicæ in Passionem Christi*, 1657 (L.L., no. 1969), in part from Toinard's letters.

[On p. 1:]

Ex dono viri optimi Authoris eruditissimi Amici colendissimi Domini Nicolai Toinard Aurelianensis

Liber Jo: Locke

[Following colophon of final pagination:]

Dominus Nicolaus Toinard Aurelianensis.[a] Vir optimus. moribus antiquis iisdemque suavissimis. ingenio acutissimo et sagacissimo,

[a] *The draft begins*: Dominus Nicolaus Toinard Aurelianensis. Nomen suavitate ingenii acumine eximius. Vir optimus et undequaque doctissimus. Literis præsertim Græcis et Hebræicis . . . *The words* Nomen–eximius *may be an alternative for the following sentence.*

---

Monsieur Nicolas Toinard of Orleans: the best of men, graced with virtues of the old school yet of great charm, with a most acute and shrewd intellect,

---

[1] The proceedings against Legendre.

omni scientiarum genere ornatus, Literis Græcis Hebræisque nec non Chronologia eruditissimus, uti patet ex hac harmoniâ ab ipso novis fundamentis superstructa, nova methodo composita, novoque artificio concinnata. Unde plurimis in locis sine explicationibus aliunde petitis ex ipso solum intuitu, historiæ Evangelicæ suus constat nitor ordo et sensus. Amicus insuper pluribus nominibus colendissimus hoc gratissimo munere quantivis non redimendo me ornavit et Locupletavit 13 Dec: 1678

---

with learning of every kind, deeply versed in Greek and Hebrew scholarship, and in chronology too, as is clear from this Harmony, built up by him on new foundations, composed by a new method, and arranged on a new system; by which in many places, without explanations sought from elsewhere but simply by inspecting the Gospel narrative, its proper clarity, order, and meaning are made evident; moreover a friend greatly to be cherished on many accounts: furnished and enriched me with this welcome and priceless gift. 13 Dec. 1678

## 429. THOMAS TUFTON, later sixth earl of Thanet, to LOCKE, 7/17 December 1678 (*448*)

B.L., MS. Locke c. 22, ff. 26–7. The writer, born in 1644, succeeded as sixth earl of Thanet in 1684, and died in 1729: G. E. C.

I am very gladd to learne by y⟨our le⟩tter[a] which this night I recieved of your arrivall at Paris, I had not made this delaye in returning my acknowledgement to mr Locke had I knowne where a letter could have found him and I am soe much satisfied your concerne for my welfarre is soe reall that I would not misse this Post in letting you know after your concerne and care you was pleased to take in restoring my health in that wicked towne called Lyons that I shall hereafter avoyed as a Place infected, the weather was soe favourable that my journy by water was not unpleasant and I am now dayly improving a health here being Lodged at one Monsieur Poittevins[1] very well with Sir James Rusworthe[2] who returnes his service to

[a] *Page torn.*

---

[1] There appears to have been a Protestant family of this name at Montpellier: Haag.

[2] Locke mentions 'Sir J. Rushworth' in his Journal, 18 March 1676. No knight or baronet of the name is recorded in this period. The present man is probably the same as the 'Sir James Rushot' mentioned by Charleton, pp. 676, 686, and the 'Chevalier Russot' mentioned by Selapris, pp. 663, 690. If the identification is

you and is very sorry hee had not the good fortune to meet you, to tell you how much I misse and regrett the not having your Compagnie this winter is but what most people expresse I shall only desiere opportunityes of seing you and shall leave it to you to judge if I have not that estime of it as I aught for I thanke God I have sence enough to know and value those men that make my life happy, if you will favour mee sometimes with a letter, give mee they hopes that wee maye passe next winter where wee intended this, which I now mighttely repent my sicknesse should disappoint mee of what I soe much desiered I believe never 3 people were more fixed one that voyage and had done it with more pleasure then wee should have done[1] at least flatter mee with they hopes that wee maye meet againe one that designe and I will promise you not to bee sicke any where but at Lyons, they affaires of England are soe uncertainly represented to us that I resolve to have Patience till farder time dicovers to us what I believe is not perfecly yett knowne there, I am wishing my self there though I know not in what I could bee serviciable and am certaine should not enjoye that measure of health I here finde for wee have had they finnest weather and they tell mee this is like to bee the favorablest winter here hath bine this manny yeares, this daye Sir John Chichely who Lodgeth at mr Cheannyes,[2] mr Charleton who is not to bee removed from his sweet Chamber at the Petit Paris,[3] Sir James Rushworthe and I walked to Sellneufe[4] where wee dinned in comming home they sonn was to hott this wee doe once or twice a weeke, wee doe eat once or twice a weeke at Chianeyes and endeavor by change of Places to divert our selves as others doe by changing other Creatures,[5] Mr Beaumont[6] is newly come from Beaurdeaux still something weake though hee findes amenment here, here is no other Englishe but Sir james 2 Nephews and mr Morice[7] you saw at Lyons who are all Lodged at Pioches,[8] this Post I recieved a letter from my good Cousen

correct he is Sir James Rushout, *c.* 1644–98; created a baronet 1661: G. E. C., *Baronetage*, iii. 210. Locke mentions him as Rushout in his Journal, 24 March 1679; letter to Locke below, no. *1514*.

[1] Locke's proposed visit to Italy.

[2] Oliver Cheney: p. 612, n. 3.

[3] Where Charleton lodged in September: p. 612, address. According to Locke it was exposed to the winds from the sea: Journal, 7 January 1676.

[4] Celleneuve, a village about 6 miles from Montpellier, where Locke spent the summer of 1676.

[5] 'Food and other things which minister to the material comfort of man'; the alternative, intoxicating liquor, is less likely: *O.E.D.*

[6] Charles Beaumont: p. 583.

[7] Probably Mr. Morris of no. *531*.

[8] Perhaps Jacques Puech: p. 437, n. 1, etc.

allington[1] who at last is gone with a third part of his hundred pound, the honnest Gentleman is soe well reconcilled to our Land Ladye wee fell out with one his account that hee gave himself the trouble to write mee a letter I must not prevent Englishe going thither to bee as ill used as wee were I finde hee is in Charittye with all, my service to my fellow Traveller mr Bankes and to mr Wicherly[2] and tell him I wishe him and you such weather as wee have. I am as unwilling to end here as to part with you at Lyons, yours faithfull and obliged Servant

THO TUFTON

Sir John Chichely presents you his service I will tell you mr Charleton does the same though I have not seene him,

Montpellier the 17 of december 78.

Address (written by W. Charleton): A Monsieur Monsieur Lock gentilehomme Anglois chez Monsieur Charas maistre Apotecaire rue de Boucherie Fauxbourg St Germain a Paris.

Endorsed by Locke: Mr Tufton 17 Dec. 78

## *430.* THOMAS STRINGER to LOCKE, 8 December 1678 (*389, 403, 529*)

B.L., MS. Locke c. 19, ff. 143–4.

London December 8th. 1678.

Deare Sir

I have received your letter of the 3d of this instant December with mr Selapris letter of Atturney etc inclosed,[3] and doe assure you, that you may Confidently rely upon any service I may be any ways Capable of doeing eyther for you or your friend, and when I shall serve you to the Uttermost of my power I must still acknowledge it is the least I owe you. I shall make it my buisnesse to finde out mr Legendre and as matters happen in that Concerne I shall not faile from time to time of giving you an account. I long sinc gave you an account of the receipt of 10l. 4s. 10d. from Sir John Chitchley, but the books from mr Hunts mayde[4] I never yett mett with, nor

[1] William Alington, d. 1685; third Baron Alington of Killard (Ireland) 1660; created Baron Alington of Wymondley 1682: G. E. C. His and Tufton's paternal grandmothers were sisters, daughters of Thomas Cecil, first earl of Exeter.

[2] pp. 611, 643. [3] p. 628 n. [4] p. 447, n. 3.

that from Sir John Chitchley nor mr Herbert,[1] neyther did you Ever lett me know what books they were that I could aske for them by name, or could they remember of any you sent by them. as for mr Herbert indeed there may be some Excuse, because his things lay neare two months at the Custom house before he could gett them cleared, and in the mean time was much tumbled and disordered. mr Tho:[2] in July last sent me a bill for 50l, but the money to this day cannot be received, the Person on whome it is Charged delaying with promises without any keeping of his word, and mr Tho: as yett not being willing to have any severer Course taken with him, then Continuall Duning him, and on the other side I doe remember what you formerly hinted, and am not willing to doe a thing that may disobleige your friend, at Oxford, but I shall take care in the mannagement of it that if the Person or Money miscarry, noe blame nor damage may fall upon you. I am forced to Conclude my Paper and time ending together, but I shall never faile of Expressing my selfe

Your most faithfull and affectionate servant

T: S.

Address: A Mounsieure Mounsieure Lock Gentlehome Anglois Chez mr Charas Apothecaire rue Bouchiere Fauxbourg St Germaine a Paris

Endorsed by Locke: T. Stringer 8 Dec. *78*

## 431. LOCKE to SIR JOHN BANKS, 11/21 December 1678 (*425*, *433*)

B.L., MS. Locke c. 24, f. 23. Perhaps commenced as a letter and kept as a draft. One large corner is cut or torn away. Answers no. *425*; answered by no. *434*.

Paris 21 Dec. 78

Nov:

. . . approve of our returne to Paris. The place
. . . cause I supposed it most suitable to your
. . . improvements. For since you have been
. . . ch confidence I shall not faile as long as we
. . . shall judg most advantageous to him

[1] Thomas, the future eighth earl of Pembroke: pp. 542, n. 2, 668 n., etc.
[2] Samuel Thomas; see no. *439*.

. . . siderations of my businesse[a]– in France–[a] I should
. . . thern parts of it. Not that I much feare
. . . ll to me haveing had the experience of it
. . . to flatter my self that my lungs are pretty well[b]
. . . that they will beare the sea-cole smoke of London at my returne, I shall make double advantage of my journey in that with the gaineing my health it hath given me also the oportunity of rendering you some as you . . .[c] tell me not unacceptable service. It is not altogeather without reason that you make me a party in your perswasions to lay aside all thoughts of Italy, for since you guesse soe right (as I finde by Mr Banks's letter you doe) I will not dessemble to you that I was not unwilling to have seen Italy when I was soe neare it, and had I been at Lyon by my self at the time we were there, I doubt not but I should have venturd a step farther over the hills, for though the first falling of the snow had made the passage mighty inconvenient and pretty dangerous, yet I found afterwards that the faire weather had much mended it, and that people went and came without any great difficulty. This I durst not tell Mr Banks haveing concluded that he was not to[d]– venture himself where I could not answer it to you my Lady or my self to suffer him;–[d] and that his, not being every bodys case I was to keepe him on the safer side, haveing soe many reasons for it that I have already told you and some others that I shall tell you when I have the honour to see you. But Sir however true it be that the consideration of Mr Banks was the only thing that kept me on this side the Alpes when I was got soe far as Lyons on the way which otherwise the snow that lay in the road would hardly have donne, being soe neare Italy at the begining of a winter which was necessarily to be spent abroad, Yet I doubt whether I ought to owne this to some freinds I have in England who in favour to my health haveing taken upon them the care of my litle affaires dureing my absence, will thinke that either I have health enough to returne and ease them of their trouble or else not care enough of that litle I have, when they shall know that I would have venturd my self in a passage that I did not thinke reasonable nor altogeather safe for an other. But that being now wholy over I hope they will be satisfied that I am now a good way off of Lyons and soe out of the

[a–a] *Substituted for* owne health [b] *This word from left-hand margin of page; it is followed by an illegible fragment of a word.* [c] *Two illegible words.* [d–d] *Originally* to be ventured where ther might be danger, *which was altered to* to venture himself where there might be danger to him

temptation and that ⟨my⟩[a] thoughts being set wholy northward I hope w[b] . . .
In the time that Mr Banks shall spend at . . .
refresh what[c–] is most usefull . . .[–c] former exercise . . .
again ever since our returne, and after . . .
greatest inclination I finde is rideing of which . . .
with others finde soe litle use that I thinke . . .
great wast of time it makes, for to you I . . .
consideration, and to me who perhaps may w . . .
other things necessary to Mr Banks condition . . .
of[d–] much more importance[–d] which will[e] need that time and more too if he had . . .
as misimploid by one in his circumstances . . .
that matter.[f]
since you refer soe much to my choise and direction in these matters to tell both you and him plainly my opinion. I am very much sensible of your kindenesse in Chargeing your thougths with the care of supplying me for my particular accommodations. The mony I had of my owne when I came hither and the supplys I have since had by your order are not yet quite out, and I doe not foresee any such great occasions I am like to have for the remainder of the litle time I imagine I shall now be abroad that I thinke I shall need draw any particular bill on you. when all my stock is out I presume I may furnish my selfe from Mr Banks for my litle occasions and if any great ones should happen I shall make use of the freedome you allow me and in the meane time return you my thanks for the favour

Endorsed by Locke: To Sir J: Banks 21 Dec. *78*

## 432. Locke to Nicolas Toinard, 16/26 December 1678 (424, 428, *466*)

The Henry E. Huntington Library, San Marino, California. Formerly in Alfred Bovet collection; facsimile in É. Charavay, *Lettres autographes . . . Alfred Bovet*, 1887 (pp. 413–14; item no. 1129). Later in Alfred Meyer Cohn

[a] *Word omitted by Locke.* [b] *The right hand part of this and the following lines is cut or torn away.* [c–c] *substituted for* his [d–d, e] *Interlined.* [f] *Followed by* I thanke you Sir for your . . . *deleted.*

collection: *Die Autographen-Sammlung* . . ., Berlin, 1906, 2. Teil, p. 207, no. 2338 (date as '1778'). Transcribed from photograph.

Lundi 26 Dec *78*

Monsieur

Je vous a promis à Mr Brisban aujourdhui à diner. N'est il pas bien hardi de disposer de vous sans vostre permission? Mais, si je ne me trompe pas, je suis d'intelligence avec vostre inclination, et pour des affaires on n'en fait point de cas dans ces jours des festes. Au moins je ne dispose pas de vous que avec moi meme, et nous courrerons le meme risque ensemble. Je viendray donc s'il vous plaist chez vous environ le midy pour vous amener au rendevous, parceque ce n'est pas chez lui mais icy dans le fauxbourg que nous dinerons.

Je suis
Monsieur
Vostre tres humble serviteur
J LOCKE

Address: A Monsieur Monsieur Toinard à la teste noire rüe Mazarin. Fauxbourg St Germain à Paris

## *433.* SIR JOHN BANKS to LOCKE, 16 December 1678 (431, *434*)

B.L., MS. Locke c. 3, ff. 120–1. The address is written by an amanuensis.

Sir

My Last to you was the 25 November under cover to Madam Herinx, which hoope you have receaved, since which I am with yours of the 3d and my sons of the 7 December, and Glad to finde your well arrivall at Paris, and that you had soe pleasant a journy; I confesse I was willinge to gratify my sons desire to goe for Italy findinge it to be with your concurrence, and inclination, but in respect to us heer, we are abundantly satisfyed in your returns to Paris, and that you did forbeare your Voyage to Italy. upon very prudent and kinde Considerations; That which now remaines is as you say, to spend the time you stay in Paris, to the most advantage, and to take the first opertunity of returninge through Flanders, if the weather shall permitt in any reasonable time, els we shall be desirous of your returnes home directly, assoone, as you shall judge it seasonable.

I have not remitted any monnys to meete you at Paris, becaus I depend on Madam Herinx supply, she hath beene as I perceave very civil to your concernes. and for which I shall Give her my acknowledgment, but the Exchange is now low and I shall remytt monnys, what you doe desire, I pray will you take to yourselfe what you please for your owne accommodation: I doe not doubt but the 1900 Livres were well disposed and that I shall one day finde a good returne therof and of the other summ, so: I pray make much of yourselvs. and what ever you doe shall be with many thanks approved of by

Sir, Your assured freind and servant
JOHN BANKS

Lincolns in feilds 16 December 1678

I did remyt mony to Gosfright and Ball at Legorne, which I have drawn backe with little losse, and if the Exchange come from Paris answerable as it Goeth hence which is 53½ per crowne,[1] it is much best to draw on me, for then I can pay it but once

Address: A Monsieur Monsieur Lock Chez mr Charas Apothecaire rue de Boucherie Fauxbourg St. Germain A Paris

Endorsed by Locke: Sir J: Banks 16 Dec. *78*

## *434.* SIR JOHN BANKS to LOCKE, 23 December 1678 (*433, 437*)

B.L., MS. Locke c. 3, ff. 122–3. The address is written by an amanuensis. Answers no. 431.

Sir

Since my last I have yours of the 21th and my sons of the 16th instant. And as I have formerly wrott you I am very well satisfyed in your returne to Paris for the reasons you have given, and when opertunity offers we may discourse further of that affaire, That which now remaines is as you mention, my sons improvinge the time there, to the best advantage, and as much as may be to recover the first losse, and I shall heerin leave the whole matter to your conduct, and soe I have writt to my son: That in espetiall manner he minde the improvements of the minde, above any Exercises of the body, for which if he have time to spare these short

[1] That is, pence for the *écu* of 3 *livres* or 60 *sous*. The par of exchange was 54*d*. for the *écu*.

dayes for his diversion it may doe well, but would have nothing to impede, those better exercises of the minde, the usefulnesse whereof I hoope he is sensible to be above any other, and to abide longest, and that he is to husband his time now, the best he can. which he will never recover againe.

Sir, My son writes his desire to goe to Flanders and Holland in his passage home, but I doe not remember you say any thing therof. and therfore I pray be free to Give me your advise therin and how it may be sutable to your owne affaires, for I shall depend on your government, resolvinge that he come home with you, and then wither he spend a month or les abroad I shall not be soe much concerned, although my desire is that he come home assoon as you shall thinke convenient for him and yourselfe to, in respect to the season of the yeare: Therfore I will give you my thoughts which when you have considered I pray will you alsoe give me yours and advice with my son, and I shall submitt to your method. If you Goe to Flanders and Holland, I doe thinke it not convenient to be there till May, in respect their winter lasts long. And I doe not thinke it worth while to spend time in Paris in order to goe thither from thence, and I suppose the passage is not only very dirty and inconvenient til about May, but even then the travell is dangerous in respect to the pillage by souldiers[1]—Therfore If you doe first come home and Goe hence to Holland in the month of May, if you thinke that journy necessary, it may be the most convenient way: And now I pray let me know how long you would advice me, in respect to my son, considringe how long he hath beene abroad, that he should abide at Paris and what advantages he may finde there, that he cannot have heer, as alsoe what time you doe judge most convenient as well in respect to yourselfe as him for your returne to us, for I must consider both. and would willingly you were now both well at home, and yet am not willinge to disapoynte your time in any method that you have thought of, for the ordering yourselves there, in those studys and exercises that you have resolved on. or may thinke necessary, when I shall know the same, being very Confident my sons intrest is your whole designe, and that you doe thinke of returninge assone as convenient, and therfore doe desire to heare your opinion on the whole matter and I shall governe my selfe accordingly. My Wiffe presents you her humble services and thanks for your kinde letter to her and will

[1] pp. 440, 670–1.

write you by the next and is very sensible of your indulgent respect to her son. which shall be ever owned both by her and me who truly am

Sir, Your faithfull freind and servant
JOHN BANKS

Lincolns in feilds 23 December. 1678.

I did send forward your letter to Mr Wall[1] at Oxford. My Lord[2] is as well as I have knowne him some years. and as briske.

Address: A Monsieur Monsieur Lock, Chez mr Charas Apothecarie rue de Boucherie Fauxbourg St. Germain A Paris

Postmark: G

Endorsed by Locke: Sir J: Banks 23. Dec. *78*

## *435*. EDWARD BERNARD to LOCKE, 24 December 1678 (*453*)

B.L., MS. Locke c. 4, f. 1. Edward Bernard, 1638–96; D.D. 1684; critic and astronomer: *D.N.B.* He probably met Toinard while he was in Paris about 1677 as tutor to the duke of Grafton.

Honoured Sir

You doe me a great kindnesse in promoteing the Edition of Josephus,[3] particularly by adviseing of the Aide from Monsieur Tonnar:[4] I therefore entreate you to assure him that having receivd lately very good helpe to a correct Text of that historian I shall make a specimen of the Edition with the beginning of the Year approaching, which I pray God make happy and peacefull to you and to us all. I againe commend Josephus to your encouragement and counsell, and am

Your obligd servant
E. BERNARD.

Xmas Eve. *1678*.

Le Moynes purpose at Leyden will not impede our Edition: but I hope may occasion its bettering.[5]

[1] Probably George Walls of Worcestershire.
[2] Shaftesbury.
[3] For this project see *Biographia Britannica*, 1747–66, ii. 755, note G.; P. Bayle, *Choix de la correspondance inédite*, ed. E. Gigas, 1890, pp. 429–30 (Labrousse, no. 524). Further mentions below. Bernard did not complete his edition; parts of it were printed at Oxford in 1686–7 and were published in 1700: *D.N.B.*
[4] Toinard.
[5] Étienne Le Moyne, 1624–89; professor of theology at Leyden *c.* 1677–89: Haag. On his project see Bayle to Minutoli, 26 May 1679 (Labrousse, no. 158).

Pray consult with my Everhonoured freind Mr Justell touching the MSS. of Josephus, which may perhaps be reservd in the Kings, or Monsieur Colberts, or Especially Chancellor Sequiers' Library.[1] Without doubt some amongst the many Excellent Scholars at Paris have travayld in that Author: Adieu.

Pray advise me whether Epiphanius be now reprinting at Paris: and if not, whether the Notes of a very learned Person there, may be purchasd.[2] Mr Justell, I beleive may certifye in this matter: which is of some concerne to me.

My love to Mr Justell, acquainting him that the ArchBishop of *Samos*[3] now with us, hath a *Νόμμον*[4] of the present usages of the Greeke Church, a small booke.

Address: For my loving Freind Mr Lock

Endorsed by Locke: Mr Bernard 24 Dec. *78*

## *436.* JACQUES SELAPRIS to LOCKE, 25 December 1678/4 January 1679 (*427*, *438*)

B.L., MS. Locke c. 18, ff. 79–81.

Lyon Ce 4e. Jenviere 1679.

Monsieur Mon tres Cher et Tres honoré Amy

Je suis tres Mary ne mestre trouvé en ville, lors que vostre à moy tres Chere letre est ariveé, je Ne l'ay que depuis hier, et vous diray en Reponçe que je suis fort estoné de Ce quon vous á fait payer le port de vos hardes, veu que mon home en á payé onze lives en Ceste ville, Monsieur Ragon n'ayant point voulu se Charger des hardes sans quon le payast, ainsy vous Ne devés avoir payé auqun sols,

[1] For the three libraries see Brice, i. 73–82, 87–8, 100–1; A. Franklin, *Les Anciennes Bibliothèques de Paris*, 1867–73. Colbert is Louis XIV's minister. Sequier is Pierre Seguier, 1588–1672; *chancelier* of France 1635–72: *N.B.G.* Toinard answers this inquiry in no. *469*.

[2] Denis Petau, S.J. (Petavius; 1583–1652; chronologer and theologian; *N.B.G.*), published an edition of the *Opera omnia* of Epiphanius at Paris in 1622; a new edition of Petau's edition, edited by H. de Valois (p. 500, n. 1), was published at Cologne in 1682.

[3] Joseph Georgirenes, author of *A Description of the Present State of Samos*, etc., 1678: Sir Steven Runciman, *The Great Church in Captivity*, 1968, pp. 296–300.

[4] Presumably for *Νόμος* (but here in the accusative), a religious Regula (Rule). Georgirenes intended to print a liturgical work for the Greeks resident in England, but, instead of doing so, raised money for building a Greek church in London: no. *515*.

Ny pour Celluy, ny par Celuy de la deligençe, et fairéz tres bien de vous faire rendre vostre argent, Car vous ne ly debvéz rien. et Come Nous avons Començé une Nouvelle anneé je N'ay pas voulu Manqué de vous la souhaiter heureuze, acomply de toute sorte de Benediction du Ciel, que vous pourés souhaiter vous mesme, et vous offre avec la Nouvelle anneé de Nouveau mes Tres humbles Respects et services. Ma feme Vous asseure de Mesme, et vous prie avec Moy vouloir aussy souhaiter de Nostre part une heureuze Année á Monsieur Banqs, avec une Maistraisse a son souhait. Nous ly somes fort oblige de son souvenir. Excuséz de tont de peine que je vous done, disposéz par Contre de Moy en tout ou vous Me jugeréz Capable, vous me demandéz par quelle voy je juge estre plus propre pour envoyer une boite à Lyon, Je vous diray en reponçe que sy Cela nest pas de grand poids, Ce le plus seur par le Messager,[1] et Croy quil Couste le moin, vous n'avéz qua l'adresser à moy et je vous le fairay venir la ou vous l'ordoneréz.

Au-reste Mon Cher Monsieur ne me parléz auqunement d'auqune obligation Ny Choze semblable, sil vous plaist, mais reconoissant tres bien, que je vous en ay un Nombre Infiny au dela, il me sufit que je ne m'en pouray jamais revenger.

Il faut que depuis Monsieur Shinger[2] aye parlé à Legendre, Car il me Mande en quatre ligne quil me prie de Necrire plus en Angletere, quil m'envoyera mon avençe par le premier ordre, et que je revoque les ordres, Ceque je Ne fairay pas, puis que je Ne Crois rien de Ce quil dit. Sy par hazard Cela arivoit je vous en donerois avis. Je puis assés Conoistre par la, Come quoy vous recomandéz bien, et que vous tenéz à Coeur Ce qui me touche, et vous asseure que sans vous Nous ne sortirions Jamais de Cest affaire, Voyéz Mon Cher Monsieur quel grandement je vous suis obligé, Je vous le suis tant que je ne m'en degageray Jamais Mais je seray toute ma vie

Monsieur mon veritable Amy

Vostre trop oblige et plus obeissant serviteur

J. SELAPRIS L'aisné.

P.S. Monsieur Charleton me ordone de vous saluer et me mande que Monsieur Tuffton et Monsieur Chevalier Chicheley et Russot[a][3]

[a] *Doubtful reading.*

---

[1] p. 439, n. 3.

[2] Stringer.

[3] Presumably Sir James Rushout: p. 652, n. 2.

se portent bien—sy joint une letre pour Silvestre Je vous souhaite quil vous serve bien.

Address: A Monsieur Monsieur L'ocke Gentils home Anglois logé Chéz Monsieur Charas Maitre ápoticaire Rue Boucherie au faubourg St. Germain à Paris.

Endorsed by Locke: Mr Selapris 4 Jan. *79*

## 437. Sir John Banks to Locke, 26 December 1678 (*434, 442*)

B.L., MS. Locke c. 3, ff. 124–5.

Sir

I did write to you last munday[1] since which have none of yours. In short I doe expect to heare from you, that I may know how you have ressolved to spend this winter at Paris, or how much therof, That I may governe my selfe for your returne, wether it be a month sooner or later, as I shall be advised by you. being very well assured, as[a] that you have had this experience of my son and way of conversation, soe you will franckly tell me what you thinke best. wherin you shall more and more oblidge

Sir, Your assured freind and servant

John Banks

Lincolns in feilds 26. December: 78

I pray remember me to my son, his sisters[2] have writt to him and I wrott to him 3 days since, soe I doe this time ⟨omitt⟩[b]

Address: A Monsieur Monsieur John Locke Chez mr. Charas Apothecarie dans la rue de Boucheria au Faubourg St Germain A Paris

Postmark: G

Endorsed by Locke: Sir J: Banks 26 Dec. *78*

[a] *Word interlined.* [b] *MS.* oritt?

[1] 23 December; no. *434*.

[2] Mrs. Finch (p. 579, n. 2) and Mary, who married John Savile of Methley in 1693: Coleman, *Banks*, pp. 134–5, etc.

## *438.* JACQUES HORUTENER and JACQUES SELAPRIS to LOCKE, 4/14 January 1679 (*436, 440*)

B.L., MS. Locke c. 18, f. 82. The postscript written by Selapris. For Horutener see p. 480 n. I have brought the letters signed by him and Selapris into the same series as those signed by Selapris alone.

A Lyon ce 14 Ja⟨nvier⟩[a] 1679.

Monsieur

Nous avons Receu Deux Diverses fois Lettres de nostre Debitteur Jean LeGendre de Londres Lequel nous Escrit avec promesse de nous doner sattisfaction d'un ordinaire a L'autre, mais, jusques a present n'a point heu Encore de suitte, et puis que vous avons ⟨c⟩harge[a] de ceste Importunite a nous vouloir faire la Grasse et de nous faire Retirer nostre Deub nous vous prions de Rechef cher Monsieur de Recomander lafaire a vostre amy a Londres, de ne le point quiter, ny se Laisser apaiser, avec parolles et Promesses, ains le tenir bien de court et nous obligeres Infinement, vous demandant mille Perdons de tant de peine Vous Saluons de bon Coeur et Somes

Monsieur

Vostres Humbles Serviteurs

HORUTENER et SELAPRIS.

P.S. Ma feme et Moy vous saluent et vous asseurent de Nos humble Respects vous souhaitant Come à Monsieur Banqs une tres heureuze anneé Excusez de tant de Peine que je vous donons et suis jusques au Tombeau Monsieur

vostre tres affectione serviteur

J. SELAPRIS l'aisnéz.

Address: A Monsieur Monsieur Locke Gentils home Anglois Logé Chez Monsieur Charas Maistre apoticaire Rue Boucherie faubourg St. Germain à Paris.

Endorsed by Locke: Selapris and Horutener 14 Jan. 79

[a] *Page torn.*

## *439.* Samuel Thomas to Locke, 4 January 1679 (*304, 523, 708*)

B.L., MS. Locke c. 20, ff. 130–1.

Ch: ch: Jan: 4. 78.

Sir,

I have now a second Letter from you of thankes for the care you suppose me still to have of your affaires here. and I wish heartily that you had had occasion to conclude this as you did your former with the owning your having receiv'd a second 50lı of your Ch: ch: money, which had beene given you if m. Prowd had continu'd to deale as fairely and squarely with mee as heretofore he was wont.[1] The truth is that upon notice from m. Stringar in July last that a returne of moneys to you would not be unwelcome, I soone sent him a Bill of 50lı drawne upon m. Prowd which I made no question but hee would have discharg'd (as formerly) in a short time after the receipt of it; but tho he accepted the bill, he payd it onely by faire promises putting off m. Stringar with them from time to time and forcing him to make applications to him in vaine; whereupon I wrote severall Letters to urge him to make good and speedy payment. In answer whereunto I had at last one from him (of September 21) wherein he told me he had beene sick of a Fever but hop'd to be abroad in a few dayes, and then he would forth with discharge it. Soone after I urg'd him in another letter to be as good as his word, and withall sent him another Bill of 10lı more to be payd by him to m. Stringar on your account. But tho I have since that time importun'd him by letters and threatn'd to use severer methods if he still delayd payment, yet this day I have receiv'd by mr Hodges[2] (newly come from London) another from mr. Stringar. which complaines that the money is not yet payd, but tells me that if I will give him order to take such course as the Law allowes for the recovery of it he'ill be glad to serve me in it, and does not doubt but by such a vigorous prosecution to force his complyance. which course therefore I shall not onely permitt but request him to take that so you may have your money, and he, and I may be freed from farther trouble; and I desire you to believe that this is the onely considerable trouble your concernes here have occasion'd mee. which I hope I shall shortly give you a better account of as to this 60lı. and in the meane time m. Hodges having left 17lı with

[1] See no. *430*. [2] Nathaniel Hodges.

m. Stringar in hopes of receiving it here (on your score) I have accordingly payd it him this afternoone. I acquainted Mr Bernard[1] with your message to which besides thankes you will I presume receive a returne[a] under his owne hand together with this. I am oblig'd to you for your friendly inviting mee to employ you in procuring for mee any thing which Paris affords and I have a mind to. and I promise you to consider how I may give you the opportunity of farther obliging mee, if so be our owne ill condition doe not by degrees grow so much worse then tis at present as to force us of the Protestant clergy to think of making up owr owne packs and shifting for ourselves.[2] which that God would avert is the hearty prayer of

Sir your reall Friend S. TH:

Address: For Mr John Lock this.
Endorsed by Locke: Mr Thomas 4 Jan. *78*

## *440.* JACQUES SELAPRIS to LOCKE, 12/22 January 1679 (*438*, *446*)

B.L., MS. Locke c. 18, ff. 83–4.

A Lyon Ce 22e Jenvier 1679.

Monsieur Mon tres Cher Amy

J'ay Reçeu vostre tres Chere en date du 15e[a] Jenvier, et veu par içelle vostre Continuelle affection, dequoy je vous suis Infiniment redevable et le seray toute Ma vie. et vous suis obligé, de Ce que vous M'en donneréz avis Lors que Mr Shinger[3] vous Escrira de Nostre affaire, depuis Ma derniere Monsieur Legendre ne ma point Escrit, dieu nous done bon Issue de Cest affaire.

Je suis estoné que l'on ne vous aye pas voulu renbourser le port de vos hardes, icy mr Ragon Ne veut pas Croire qu'on l'aye payé un autrefois à Paris, Cest pour quoy sy vous vouléz m'envoyer le Reçeu, Je m'en fairay Rembourser, Celuy Cy me dit avoir Escrit Ce quil faut à Paris, et ne m'a point voulu doner un Reçeu, sexcusant d'une fasson ou d'autre, sans Cela je vous l'aurois envoyé.

Puis que vous le vouléz Come cela, je vous envoyeray un petit Compte de Ceque je puis avoir déboursé pour vos hardes ou Celles

[a] *Doubtful reading.*

[1] Edward Bernard. [2] This refers to the Popish Plot. [3] Stringer.

de Monsieur Banks, vous declarant que vous estéz trop Exact à vos Amis en Cest Egard, sy je doibz Compter sy Exactement Ce que je vous doibz je me trouveray bien Court, Je vous suplie de dispozer de moy par Contre en toute Choze. Par le premier Coche qui partira je vous envoy un petit Barill Musquat franc de tout seulement pour vous le faire gouster à Paris, ou il est plus rare quisy, je scay tres bien que vous N'en beuvéz guiere ny Monsieur Banks, Cest pourquoy jay mis le Barill petit, Excuséz de la Liberté que je prend, disposséz de Moy en tout rencontre, et ne regardéz la petite Choze, mais plus tost la bone volonté. Sy Joint un petit livre que je vous ay promis, je N'ay jusques apresent point peu avoir l'autre, sy je puis je vous l'envoyeray aveq le Musquat. Ma feme et moy vous somes fort obligé et A Monsieur Banks de vostre bon souvenir, et vous asseurons tout deux de Nos humbles Respectz. et serions Ravy (Mon Cher) de vous faire voir une foiz par Effect que Nous somes tout à vous sur tout moy qui vous suis de Coeur et d'ame sans auqune Reserve

Monsieur Mon tres Cher Amy

Vostre plus humble et plus obeissant serviteur et fidel Amy

J: SELAPRIS L'aisné.

P.S. Jay remis le Barill au Coche il est marque J.L. pour avis.

Address: A Monsieur Monsieur L'ok Gentilz home Anglois Chéz Monsieur Charas Maistre Apoticaire Rue Boucherie au faubourg St. Germin à Paris.

Endorsed by Locke: Mr Selapris 22 Jan *79*

## *441.* THOMAS HERBERT, later eighth earl of Pembroke, to LOCKE, 18 January [1679] (*452*)

B.L., MS. Locke c. 11, ff. 187–8. Year from Locke's endorsement. Not received by Locke for some time: no. *452*.

Thomas Herbert, *c.* 1656–1733; eighth earl of Pembroke 1683: *D.N.B.* He was 'a man of eminent virtue, and of great and profound learning, particularly in the mathematics: this made him a little too speculative and abstracted in his notions: he had great application, but he lived a little too much out of the world, though in a public station; a little more practice among men would give him the last finishing: there was somewhat in his person and manner that created him an universal respect; for we had no man among us whom all sides loved and honoured so much as they did him': Burnet, *History of my own Time*, 1833, iv. 361–2. 'His character for probity was so high, and the esteem of him . . . so general, that his acceptance of employments was a credit to the government; and his own indifference as to them made him the more easily to be removed from them. He was very firm to the government and constitution, but had no particular attachment to ministers or parties; and in that he preserved the dignity of his rank': Arthur Onslow, the Speaker (*D.N.B.*), note to Burnet. He was a Tory, and remained faithful to James II until James fled; voted for the Regency in the Convention; and then transferred his allegiance completely to William and Mary and their successors.

He matriculated from Christ Church on 18 March 1673 and took part in the Encænia in 1674: Foster; Wood, *L. and T.* ii. 288.

The surviving correspondence between him and Locke does not represent their friendship adequately. When Locke was in London in July 1701 he dined with Pembroke: R. Thoresby, *Diary*, ed. J. Hunter, 1830, i. 337. Presumably he visited Pembroke on earlier occasions when he was in town.

London January 18.

Sir

I've been this three Months at Wilton[1] and am but now return'd to London which made me I would not trouble you with a letter not knowing but that you were return'd into England having not heard from you (till now) since I writt last: I've lately had the misfortune to bury my youngest sister;[2] I suppose you may have heard that my Lord Dunagall and my Cosin Roper are dead:[3] pray when the time comes that I shall have the happiness of seeing you here will you bring me those Bucles and sword, I suppose you remember the third tome of Recherche de la Verité, and if there be any Critiques or Answers to it bring them all;[4] likewise all the Journal des Scavans[5] printed since February last (i.e.) since I left Paris; all Naudæus's works except Bibliotheca ⟨instituenda⟩[a] which I have:[6] My mind is alter'd from living in the Temple, my Brother[7] being so kind to me that he will not let me live long from him (though he lets me doe what I will and indeed does little without

[a] *MS.* institueda

[1] The seat of the earls of Pembroke. It is about 3 miles west of Salisbury.

[2] Perhaps Anne, who died unmarried.

[3] Donegal (p. 542) died on 26 October 1678 in Ireland. Samuel Roper, b. 1633, barrister, a second cousin of Pembroke's mother, died on 1 November 1678: R. E. C. Waters, *Genealogical Memoirs of . . . Chester of Chicheley*, 1878, pp. 586, 595. Locke met him at Bordeaux on 12 May 1677: Journal.

[4] p. 497, n. 5. Vol. iii appeared in 1678. A criticism of the first two volumes by Simon Foucher, 1675, was answered in the same year by R. des Gabets.

[5] There were 38 issues in 1678, an exceptionally large number.

[6] Gabriel Naudé, 1600–53: *N.B.G.* The book mentioned is *Advis pour dresser une bibliotheque*, 1627; new edition 1644. No Latin translation at this date is known; Herbert appears to be writing loosely.

[7] Philip Herbert, seventh earl: p. 429, n. 1.

asking my advice.) pray don't hinder me long from your good company who am Your servant to command

T. HERBERT

Address: A Monsieur Monsieur Locke, gentilhomme Anglois, chez Madame Herinx et Monsieur son fils Banquiers. A Paris.

Postmark: G

Endorsed by Locke: Mr Herbert 18 Jan. *79*

## *442.* SIR JOHN BANKS to LOCKE, 20 January 1679 (*437*, *444*)

B.L., MS. Locke c. 3, ff. 126–7.

Sir

The latter end of last weeke I did receave yours and my sons of the 14th instant. (the post comminge more uncertaine then usuall.) And upon good consideration had of what you have soe well stated, together with your obligation that my son may see Flanders eta. As in the first place I doe assure you, my intent is to performe your promise and answer his desire. soe I know in the next place both you and he will consider, which may be the most convenient time to answer your end in that journy; you will easily conceave that our desire is to have my son home assoone as the season permitts which I propose to bee in March. God willinge, that he may come from Paris, or sooner if convenient; and I doe allow that if he come thro Flanders and Holland it may be a months more expence of time, Now it must lye before your dew consideration wither this may be a sutable season to answer your desires in that journy, Or wither it may not be a choice rather to be made first to come home and give us a visite in march and take the first opertunity to goe hence for Holland either this springe, or the end of Aug. and there neede be noe mistrust of his disapoyntment in soe short a tripp, to occasyon any inconvenience, For as I cannot as yet thinke it Good to prolong your being in Paris in order to your comminge home thro Flanders and Holland, soe doe say that I am very willinge to please my son in seeinge of Flanders, eta as beleivinge those places and people as well worth his notinge, as France. if the season of the yeare permitt: I shall omitt to say any thing of the present sicknesses of those places and the danger of the pillageing soldiers, where the Armys have beene, becaus I know you will be well satisfyed if you doe proceede in those and such like matters—But upon the whole it will desirve your and our good consideration wither to come directly home in march, or then to begin your journy for Flanders in order to your comminge home that way, and however that you prepare to leave Paris in march, and pray you let me have your opinion by the first, for I doe take this to be a matter to be better by you determind, who may perhaps finde there more encouragement to such a journy then at this time we can, and being on the place may better know the conveniences or inconveniences that may at this time offer in this journy, and wither it be as advantageous and safe to make the same now as at any other time, and I shall be much governed thereby havinge the Good experience of your great affection, care and kindnesse to me and myne who truly am

Sir, your assured freind and humble servant

JOHN BANKS

London. 20 January 78.

My wiffe presents you her humble services

I doe thinke it best that you doe supply your occations with mony by Madam Herinx as formerly

Address: A Mounsieur Mounsieur Locke chez Mounsier Charas, apothecary dans la rue de boucherie fauxbourgh St Germaine A Paris

Postmark: G

Endorsed by Locke: Sir J Banks 20 Jan 7$\frac{8}{9}$

## *443.* PETER LOCKE to LOCKE, 22 January 1679 (*306, 403, 511*)

B.L., MS. Locke c. 14, f. 190.

Sutton 22 Janary 78

Dear Cosen

I receaved yours of 30 dec: I desir to be thankfull to the Lord that I Heer from you and of your Health and Hopes of your recovery from your destemper, but I am much troubld that so many letters which I Have sent Hath miscarid one I sent about the begining of the sommer after the sad stroke of the death of my daughter Mary

Stratton[1] another about the 20 of August last with a paper written of all the acounts between us to be sent to you by mr Stringer therin to lett you know How ill som of your tenants Hath dealth with you yf mr Stringer Hath not sent it you He Hath not dealth well with you and worse with me for He sent me 2 letters wherin He write your earnest disir to see my acount of your afairs Heer. another letter I sent In november last uppon this occasion the men of Publow Hath Renewed their suit of Raising your payme Hath Had many meettings about it som tyms be fore the Gent: and som tymes otherwise but it cam to this Isue before Sir Thomas Bridges[2] that your pay sould be as formerly for 3 mounthes (which was then to begine abut the 15 of nov:) but yf you com not in that tym then they will Raise your pay your frind mr Buckland[3] is dead long sinc about the begining of winter Sir Thomas Bridges and Mr Jones[4] are your frinds In this busnes I disir you would Hasten your Return unto your native country that I may see your face my only Kinsman and neer Relation before I dy which will not be longe I am now entering In to a Great debtt. I Have bought further estat In my estatt Heer In Sutton which doth cost 350l I am not a little troubled that my wife[5] is so much Grived att it because we must borow som mony to Pay for it I Hope the Lord will enable you to lend us som when you com or about the end of the next summer your unkill John Keen and Richard Keen are boath dead[6] we live In a ding world the Lord prepare us for a better life and a better world pray Cosen make it your chifest busines to be fitted and well prepard for your eternall stat In the Hiest Heavens and take Heed of doing any thing which may unfitt you for eternall Glory because I love you I cannot chuse but put you In mind of these things I Hop the Lord will bring you Hom better in soule and body then when you went from us for I conseave it to be a Great afliction to you to Goe so fare In to another Country for your Health and a Great mersy to obtaine it. Pray Rem: what Job said In his afliction when I am tried I shall com forth as Goold.[7] The Lord blesse you and keep you the Lord lift up the light of His countenanc and Give a Great

[1] p. 567.
[2] *c.* 1617–1707; of Keynsham; knighted 1641: Le Neve, *Pedigrees*, pp. 37–8; no. 574.
[3] See p. 402.
[4] Probably Richard Jones of Stowey: pp. 73, n. 2, 433.
[5] Her Christian name was Anne; she died in 1682.
[6] Apparently brothers of Locke's mother. Locke mentions his cousin Keen in Journal, 1679, p. 108, etc.
[7] Job 23: 10 rendered loosely.

Measure of Grace And fitt you for everlastinge life In the Kingdom of Heaven, for which is the daily prairs and disirs of

dear nepew
your Lovinge Unkill
PE: LOCK

My wife presents Her kind love to you and so doth my son Stratton[1]

Address: For mr John Lock These

Endorsed by Locke: P Locke 22 Jan $7\frac{8}{9}$

## 444. SIR JOHN BANKS to LOCKE, 23 [January 1679] (*442*, *455*)

B.L., MS. Locke c. 3, ff. 128–9. Month and year from Locke's endorsement and contents. The letter is preceded, on the same sheet, by a copy of no. *442* as far as 'governed thereby'. The copy was written by an amanuensis, but the date and some corrections, by Banks.

Ady. 23 Ditto[a]

Sir, Since the abovsaid I have receaved my sons of the 25 January, findinge he had beene some time without any from us, and indeed the posts are uncertaine, I doe alsoe perceave that you have drawne £100: more on me, which shall be dewly payd as shall what else you shall have neede of.

I doe alsoe finde his inclinations are to come home thro. Flanders eta. notwithstandinge he submitts it. And I can say noe more then what I have done, for I am as willinge he doe see the cheife places in Flanders and Holland, if he may have your good company, as France: The only sticke with us, is the season of the yeare and savety in travell: For I doe desire his comminge from Paris the first opertunity that may be by you thought fit. and I would not spend longer time, then soe, there, lingeringe for a Flanders journy: If therfore you be there satisfyed, that you may begin that journy in March or sooner with savety, thro. Gods providence, you may please to order your affaires accordingly and proceede, on that journy—for if the weather should be open and seasonable. I would not have any time delayed in expectation of a further reply from me, becaus the posts are uncertaine—Mrs Herringe may give

[a] *MS.* D°

[1] No. *543* n.

you creditts to Amsterdam and there Mr William and John Vandervoorts will supply you, or I shall send my letters to meete, you at Antwerpe. My Lord Shaftesbury hath had a very lame fitt of the Goute, but is on recovery—My wiffe gives you her humble services and I am

Sir, your oblidged humble servant
JOHN BANKS

The enclosed hath by mistake layn some time, but came not to my hand til now.

Address: A Mounsieur Mounsieur Locke, chez mr Charas apothecary, dans la rue de bouchery Fauxbourgh st Germaine A Páris

Endorsed by Locke: Sir J: Banks 23 Jan. $7\frac{8}{9}$

## 445. WILLIAM CHARLETON to LOCKE, 4/14 February 1679 (415, *449*) with two enclosures.

B.L., MS. Locke c. 5, ff. 29–31, and c. 25, f. 29. The enclosures are identified by their dates. The second appears to be the *lettre de voiture* mentioned by Charleton.

Montpellier the 14th: February 1679

Deare Sir

Having perform'd as well as I could the Commission I received from you, I must now tell you that the 18 Bookes you left with me and all the seeds I could get are at present in Mr: Verchan's custody,[1] who ha's promised me that they shall come to you by the 15th: of the next month at farthest, Inclosed you have the Catalogues, Though you gave me the liberty of troubling you with some things of mine, yet I feare I have sent to many, there being no fewer then 50 bookes, and 3 boxes with curiosities and seeds all contained in the large box, My seeds have been to long gathered to be fit for sowing, otherwise I should desire your acceptance of them, amongst yours, those that are mark't with red lead have the reputation here to be verry rare, though I know not how they may be esteemed of in England, at the bottom of the box are some cutts

[1] Verchan is identified by Professor Lough as Henri Verchant, a Protestant apothecary of Montpellier who also spent time in Paris: p. 113 n. He is perhaps 'le Sieur Verchant devant saint Honoré' who was selling perfumes, etc., from Provence and Montpellier in Paris in 1692: Blegny, *Le Livre commode*, i. 175. Locke went to lodge with him at Montpellier on 17 October 1676; on 10 December he attended to Locke's teeth: Journal. Further mentions in the Journal, etc.

and about 5 peices of painting. if you find that there will be any difficulty as to the importing of the bookes[1] be pleased to sell them at Paris, for I should be verry sorry to create you the least Inconvenience, the Box in which your things are is mark't No: (1) mine No (2) I have pay'd the carriage, they are accompanyed with Mr: Selapris his picture which I entreate you to keep till I have the hapynesse to see you, if I have never that advantage I know he is so much your servant and you his freind that you will keep it for his sake, as I desire you would the rest for mine. Coppy of the letter of Voiture Comes herewith. I hope you will excuse my not writing sooner not only upon the Consideration that Maitre Jaques[2] promised me severall fine seeds, (which he never gave me and which I do at present not expect) but by reason that I was verry willing to give you notice at the same time I wright of my having lodge'd your things in Mr: Verchand's hands. Sir My freinds the 2 brothers you met at Tarara[3] at their arrivall here followed punctually your orders and lay at the White horse,[4] and I designed to have waited on them as far as Marseille, Intending to take a litter to that end, but they telling me that they were obliged to go Post I was forc't to alter my resolutions, but no post horses being to be had, they were nescessitated to make use of those of the Bureau Royal,[5] and I accompany'd them unhappyly as I conceave no farther then St. Gill's[6] 8 leagues on their way, being so ill mounted that I could not indure the fatigue, this I feare ha's occasion'd a coolenesse on the Majors part having write 3 letters to which I have received no answer nor to 5 that I sent his

[1] This probably refers to the English Customs, but books brought into Paris had also to be examined: nos. 465, *474*.

[2] Locke calls him 'the gardiner at the physic garden': Journal, 3 April 1676; he mentions him several times. The garden is the Jardin du Roy.

[3] Edward and Thomas, two of the five sons of Major Richard Salwey (p. 566): pedigree in John Burke, *(History) of the Commoners*, 1836–8, i. 154. Charleton later calls them his 'Cousin Salweys': p. 685, but that appears to be incorrect; Major Salwey's maternal uncle Sir Edward Littleton, bart., and his first cousin Sir Richard Knightly, K.B., were married to Charleton's aunts Hester and Anne Courten: T. Wotton, *The English Baronets*, 1727, i. 287; Noble, *Protectoral-house of Cromwell*, ii. 95–7; *D.N.B.*, art. Courten, Sir W. The brothers wrote to their father from Montpellier probably on 13/23 November 1678, and from Marseilles on 17/27 November; they were on their way to Smyrna, where they probably worked as merchants: H.M.C., *Rep. x*, App., pt. iv, pp. 413–15. Locke spent the night of 15 November at Tarare: Journal.

[4] p. 546.

[5] I have not found a definition. On the regulation of horse-hire for travellers in France at this time see E. Vaillé, *Histoire générale des postes français*, 1947–55, iv. 181–99.

[6] St.-Gilles. It is about 33 miles distant from Montpellier. The *lieue* varied in length in the various provinces of France.

son.[1] Maitre Andrew saw the young gentlemen safe at Marseille from whence I received a verry civill letter from them dated the 2 December wherein they promised me upon their arrivall at Leghorne to write to me, they were to embarque within 2 or 3 day's upon a french vessell, and I have not heard from them since, which do's extreamely trouble me. Sir as yet I find not the Effects of Sir John's frailty,[2] no person having had any notice of my Concern's as I can learne but Mr: Tufton, mr: Beaumont[3] went on Saterday for Marseille from whence he Intends for Avignon, and so to Lyons, and thence to Paris, where he intends to waite on you, and he gives you his service, to which I must ad mr: Tuftons, and Sir John Chichley's, who are all in verry good health. Montpelier aire nor Dr. Barbyrac's skill have not as yet effected any thinge as to the bettering Mr: Butlers[4] health, who is still alive but not like to Continue long. Madam Rochemore and her husband are at length got together againe. Mr: Chiney ha's order from Sir John Champants[5] to Conduct his son to Ireland towards Aprill and my Lord Meath[6] hires Mr: Chiney's lodgings and dyetts himself, he ha's write to his Lady to come to him Mr: Tufton, Sir John Chichley, and Sir James Rushot,[7] move not hence till towards the begining of Aprill, but I thinke I shall continue all the summer here or hereabouts but shall certainely go towards October next (God willing) but am not yet Certaine whether for England, or else where. I wish you all manner of felicity and am

Sir Your

Most affectionate and most assured humble servant

WILLIAM CHARLETON.

My most humble service to Mr: Bankes.

Sir

The weather here ha's been excessive Cold and continues verry Sharp still, your Thermometer having been this morning betwixt

[1] Probably John or Richard Salwey. For John see Henry Hyde, earl of Clarendon, *Correspondence*, ed. S. W. Singer, 1828, i. 303 n.

[2] Charleton had entrusted Sir John Chicheley with his private affairs a year earlier: no. *369*.

[3] Nos. *389*, *429*.

[4] Probably the man mentioned in no. *379*.

[5] Sir John Champante, d. 1708; of Italian descent (Ciampante); settled in Ireland where he was knighted by the Lord Lieutenant in 1674; sometime deputy-treasurer of Ireland: P. Le Neve, *Pedigrees*, pp. 6, 219; J. Le Neve, *Monumenta Anglicana, 1700–15*, 1717, p. 163; Shaw, *Knights*; H.M.C., *Egmont MSS.* ii. 38. He had at least three sons: Venn.

[6] p. 516, n. 1.

[7] Rushout: p. 652, n. 2.

the Howers of 8 and 9 but at 5 degrees. I beg your pardon that I have not been so exact in observing the change of the weather as I ought to have been. those day's that I have found set downe in my table booke are these

13th December at 8 in the morning it was at 6 degrees
14 ——— at 8 ——— it was at 5 ———
15 ——— at 9 ——— it was at 7 ———
17 ——— at 8 in the morning it was at 8 ———
18 ——— at 8 ——— continued at 8 ———
19 ——— at 8 ——— continued at 8 ———
20 ——— at 9 in the morning ——— at 6 degrees
21 at 8 in the morning at 4 degrees
22 at 8 ——— at 4 ———
26 at 9 being a snowy morning at 7.
28 at 9 ——— 2.
29 at 9 ——— at 1.
30th at 9 ——— at 1.
January the 2. at 8 in the morning at almost 4 degrees.
the 3. at 7 in the morning at almost 3 & $\frac{1}{2}$
5 at 8 ——— at 5 ———
8 at 8 ——— at 3 ———
9 at 8 ——— at 3 degrees $\frac{1}{2}$
10 at 8 ——— at 2 degrees
11 at 8 all gone
16th. at 9: in the morning—at 4.

[First enclosure:]

A catalogue of Seeds etc
your
Colutea vesicaria
Genista Hispanica
[etc.]

[Second enclosure:]

a Montpelier ce 14. fevrier 1679

Monsieur

A La garde de Dieu et par la voye du Sieur Verchand parfumeur je vous envoye trois caissettes marquées comme cy contre et contenant les choses cy bas, les quelles ayant receües dans son tempz bien conditionnées ne luy payerés rien pour la voiture, seulemant luy rembourcerés la douäne et aux droitz, Je suis

Monsieur

I.L.

| | | | |
|---|---|---|---|
| | No. 1. | contient 4 petites boettes de diverses semences pesant | £–4– |
| brut 60łł | | Et dixhuict livres reliés pesant —— | £–26– |
| | No. 2. | une boette diverses semences | £–6– |
| | | une boette peaux de serpentz | £–4– |
| brut | | une boette avec de lezards | £–3– |
| 67łł | | un paquet Estampes | £–3– |
| | | Et cinquante livres reliés pezant | £–31– |
| | No. 3. | un tableau avec son cadre pezant | £–57– |

Vostre tres humble serviteur

Endorsed by Locke: ***Inventory*** A note of things sent from Montpellier 14 Feb. *79*

Locke notes: 60łł.
67łł.
57łł.
184łł.

Address: A Monsieur Monsieur Locke Gentilhomme Anglois Chez monsieur charas Apoticaire rüe de Boucherie fauxbourg St: Germain a Paris

Endorsed by Locke: (i: on cover): Mr *Charleton* 14 Feb. *79*;[a] (ii: on enclosure): 14 Feb. *79*

[a] *On f. 30 there are some notes of members of parliament by Locke:*[1]

| | |
|---|---|
| Maidston | Sir John Tufton |
| | Sir John Dorel |
| Canterbury | Mr Hales |
| | Dr Jacob |
| Rochester | Sir R Hed |
| | Sir John Banks or Sir Fr: Clark |
| Quinbourg | Sir Ed: Hales |
| | Mr Herbert |
| Kent | |
| Sandwich | Sir Jam: Oxendine |
| Hide | Sir Ed. Deering |
| London | Sir Rob: Claiton |
| | Sir Tho: Player |
| | Ald: Pilkington |
| | Ald: Low |

[1] They are all members of the new parliament that met on 6 March 1679.

## *446.* JACQUES HORUTENER and JACQUES SELAPRIS to LOCKE, 9/19 February 1679 (*440, 451*)

B.L., MS. Locke c. 18, f. 85. Written by an amanuensis.

A Lyon ce 19 fevrier 1679.

Monsieur

Nous avons Veu par la Chere vostre quil vous a plú Escrire a monsieur Selaperis ce que luy dittes touchant nostre Debitteur Legendre, de quoy vous en Remercions fort, et come il nous met asses en peine pour le procede que Voyons, nous Vous prions Instamment, Monsieur, nous Vouloir faire la faveur et Descrire a vostre Amy pour Sinformer un peu de ses affaires, Voir sil est en bon Estat sil y peut avoir a Craindre quelque Chose ou non, affin que suivant ce quaprendrons le puissions poursuivre et nous obligeres Grandement, vous Demandant par[a] un Million de fois Excuse de La Liberte que prenons et sil par Contre nous Juges Capable pour vos Services Comandes nous que somes avec affection

Monsieur

Vos tres humbles serviteurs

HORUTENER et SELAPRIS.

Mr. Selaperis vous asseure de ses Respets. a cause dun grand Rume il ne vous Escript pas luy mesme, Vous faires la Responce a luy mesme sil vous plaist

Address: A Monsieur Monsieur Charras Maistre apoticaire Rue Boucherie, au fauxbour St. Germain pour Rendre a Monsieur Lock Gentilhome Englois. a Paris.

Endorsed by Locke: Selapris and Horutener 19 Feb. *79*

## *447.* DR. DENIS GRENVILLE to LOCKE, 10/20 February 1679 (426, *458*)

B.L., MS. Locke c. 10, ff. 94–6.

A la Tour D'aigues. le 20.me Feb. 1679.

Deare Sir

I have received yours of Jan. the 27th[1] as well as the former ones which you mention (with the inclosed from Sir John Bankes) but

[a] *Or* pour; *abbreviated in MS.*

[1] This may have contained the later part of Locke's essay on the Exercise of Devotion: see p. 646 n.

if you will not forgive mee my intollerable negligence I cannot blame you; for in reallity I cannot forgive my selfe; nether will you, I feare, pardon another fault, when I tell you that tho I have forgotten soe good a freind as your selfe, and some of your wise Councells, yet I have imployed my braines so much these last three monthes, that they have been in truth a litle in danger. I must confesse to you, as a physitian, as well as spirituall freind, that I had of late by some indiscreet, immoderate, intense thoughtfullnesse soe Heated my Head that I was in some danger of falling into a fitt of Frenzy, or somewhat like ⟨i⟩tt[a] had not my experience of the unhappinesse of a deare freind[1] (whoe in my house did really fall into one in the like manner) made mee a litle knowing in the Approaches of itt. I finding my sleep leaving mee (whoe am ordinarily one of the truest sleepers alive) and raving thoughts arise in my braine with some more pleasure than usually, (the thing which my freind after his recovery caution'd mee against) I presently consulted a physitian in this place (I did not dare dally soe long as to send to Dr. Brouchier) whoe bled mee once, twice, prescribing mee a glister, with a Julep, and since cooling bouillons, which by Gods blessing did soe well settle and Compose mee (and all silently without divulging my feares, and his, to any body but our selves) that I have reason now to hope my selfe as well as ever I was in my life; and a litle wiser, I hope, in reference to the use of my braine; which I begun to imagine a litle better proof (having made some other indiscreet trialls of it heretofore) than I find it. I beg Gods pardon for my sin, and folly, (I must soe terme itt) in imploying it as I have done by fitts of Devotion, to make amends for other fitts of sloth; which is not the way I now experience to become either a learned man, or a good Christian. I was somewhat the sooner perchance insnared into this Fitt (with some mixture of melancholy) by the trouble I conceived at the disappointment of the great satisfaction I proposed to my selfe in your conversation upon your arrivall at Montpelier. My great needs of some more particular, and familiar advices, (and they repeated againe and againe to mee) than letters can commodiously make mee partaker of, made mee more than ordinarily fond of you, (whom I Judged in my armes) and Consequently the disappointment had

[a] *Page torn.*

[1] Apparently a man and not Mrs. Grenville.

some more than ordinary effect on mee. I hope, I am gotten out of one of the Divells snares (God deliver mee from the rest) and have learned to resigne up to God, among other of my Darlings, *my freind as mine owne soule*, when soever hee shall bereave mee of him for the future, (and in reference to which I can shew you at meeting a faithfull record of my soule:) which (I hope) will bee in aprill, wee intending (God willing) to set forth for paris as soon as wayes are fit, which are very bad by reason of a very severe winter. If you should bee once more snatched from mee (for I doe thinke you againe allmost sure) it will bee a new temptation to mee, and a very sore exercise of my patience, but I am I blesse God now a litle better prepared for it; I am not soe great a stranger as I have been to the Exercise of that Excellent and necessary vertue. The thoughts which I have written downe during these last three months (designed for your view) are growne to such a bulk (noe lesse than 50 sheets of paper) that I am at as great a losse, how to pick out the most proper ones to send you, as you are at ranging of your papers whereof you speak: soe that I am afraid that I shall not bee able to come to any resolution what draught I ought to send you while I stay; whoe am now about to change my more pleasant distractions about study and devotion, into those which of all things are most irksome to mee; the preparations for a Remove, and a long Voyage; which God carry us all well through. My sister hath weatherd this winter to awonder; shee gives you her service, (soe doth Misse and all) whoe desires mee to tell you that they have made amends now to Mr. Thornhill for their long silence in having sent a proportion of lines enough to supply for 5. monthes negligence; a fault which may possibly have been increased by my example. And indeed under which I doe groane; there being noe failing that I doe soe much despaire of Curing as that of my unpunctuality in Correspondence. I write more lines I am sure (if not letters) than most men, to the Justling out of more important things; and yet all my freinds have just reason to Complaine. I have made a thousand resolutions to write shorter, and a greater number of letters; but still am insnered into a breach of them, by my unseasonably, over fruitfull, Confused working braine. I resol⟨ved⟩[a] now to have written you but t⟨e⟩n[a] lines, (and if I had thought to have written more I had not medled with pen and paper; and yet I am unawares cheated into this greater number, of new thoughts; which would

[a] *Page torn.*

have been sufficient to have answered all the particulars, to which I ought to have replied, and yet have said nothing. And now after Warming my Noddle; to breake of without writing another sheet is to me an incredible paine; the feare of this makes mee dilatory in setting about writing letters. Meethinks I am a very intollerable, not only freind, but fellow. God forgive mee, and helpe mee. Your Plaisters are admirable, I feele them soe; but I have a hatefull quallity of rubbing them of; I doe dispaire therefore of[a] a[a] perfect Cure till I am neare you to bind them on.

Yours most faithfully
DE GRENVILLE

I cannot forbeare to tell you in a postscript that the Combustions which the Jesuite hath put our Church and Kingdome in at home[1] hath contributed somewhat to the warming my bloud here at this distance. For that affaire alone was enough to fill and buisy my hands, head, and Heart.

I pray give Mr. bankes my humble service. I pray continue your earnest prayers for mee. I doe assure you, I want them, as well as your Counsells.

Address: A Monsieur Monsieur Lock Gentilhomme anglois chez mr charas apothicaire Rue de Bouchèries au Fauxbourg St.Germain A Paris

Endorsed by Locke: Mr Grenville 20 Feb. *79*

## *448*. THOMAS TUFTON, later sixth earl of Thanet, to LOCKE, 11/21 February 1679 (*429*, *454*)

B.L., MS. Locke c. 22, ff. 28–9.

Mr Locke

I recieved your last letter dated the 27 of jannuary and should bee very gladd this place could allow mee any other opportunity in giving you the assurence that when I misse any occation of improving the Frendship you are pleased to expresse for mee I will then allow you to declare you were mistaken in placing favours one a man that could not bee sensible of them, I will make you no other

[a] *MS.* of I a

[1] The Popish Plot.

expression then to lett you know as mr Charleton shall witnesse how I repented not having your Compagnie this winter and I cannot but please my self with the thaught that wee shall spent next in Italy not reflecting that England is the next voyage you are to thinke of, where old and Good Frends will unwillingly Part with you, I can only lett you know the voyage of Italye with mr Locke would bee very pleasant, and in a letter from sir John Bankes last weeke hee reproches mee for not going and that I was the occation his sonne made not that journy and tells mee if hee can perswade him to goe next september hee shall give mee another meetting at Lyons but I feare to here mr Locke will bee to much pleased and believe Englande maye bee as good a Country as Italie, I doe continue resolved to staye next winter out of England and can thinke of passing it noe where else for though I am here among they Frendliest best sorte of people in the world yett change is the sicke mans ease, Mr Charleton is here who not only presents his service but letts you know your things are one the waye to Paris hee hath recieved 2 of your letters which hee will enswer next Post, My service to mr Bankes by Sir Johns letter I finde you will soun bee gonne from Paris, if you will not come and meet mee at Lyons whenever it Pleases God that I returne into old England you shall not bee the last of my Frends that I shall enquire after.

I shall now tell you wee have great hopes our Frost which hath bine very sharp for above 2 monthes is ended this daye being warme weather, wee have had Cleere weather though very Cold and windes that are not to bee endured, if the spring make us no recompence ⟨I⟩[a] finde Montpellier is not a Paridise alwayes.

Since you are pleased to enquire after a health which you did recover and was the occation that I gott soe soun out of that unhappy town of Lions, for the first monthe I was here wee had very fine weather and I mended much, the ill weather a little checked my Carreer though I thanke God I am this day better then I thinke I ever was, the only ilnesse I finde is my stomacke for though I never lived so regularly nor more to my content being Lodging with Sir James Rusworthe[1] a Gentleman who is leaving mee much to my regrett, I did lett them all know you presented your service to them, Mr Beaumont left us 10 dayes since to make the Tower

[a] *MS.* f

[1] Presumably Rushout: p. 652, n. 2.

of Provence and will finde you at Paris, the Post is going which only allow mee time to assure you that I shall ever desiere to prove

your faithfull Frend and servant

TUFTON

montpellier the 21 of February 79.

letters this night confirme your news to mr Charleton that I must no longer value myself as one of the Canaille or in Englishe as a member.[1] I hope all our proceeding will end well

Address (written by William Charleton): A Monsieur Monsieur Locke Gentilhomme Anglois chez monsr: Charas Apothicaire rüe de boucherie fauxbourg St. Germain A Paris

Endorsed by Locke: Mr *Tufton* 21 Feb. *79*

## *449.* WILLIAM CHARLETON to LOCKE, 18/28 February 1679 (*445*, 465) enclosing a catalogue of grapes and a note from Dr. P. Magnol.

B.L., MSS. Locke c. 5, ff. 32–3, and c. 31, ff. 166, 26. The enclosures identified by handwriting, contents, and date. The 'catalogue of grapes that grow in or about Montpellier' is not printed here.

Montpellier the 28th: February 1679

Deare Sir

My last of the 14th: Instant gave you an account of my having put your things with some of mine into Mr: Verchand's hands to be sent you to Paris together with Mr: Selapris his picture, the cariage thither is payed, so that you are only to receave them, they were sent away the same night I write, and he assur'd me that they would be with you at the middle of march at the farthest, your bookes which are to the number of 18 and those seeds which I could procure are in the Box No: (1) the catalogues of both went Inclosed and I hope they have reached your hands, in that letter of mine I mention'd to you (and againe desire) that if the bookes be in the least troublesome you will be pleased to sell them, for I shall meet with most of them in England if ever I returne. I have now 2 of your letters before me of the 6th: and 10th: Instant and I beleeve I should forfeit the good opinion of any persons but yours for my remissenesse not only in not having thanked you, for them,

[1] The Cavalier Parliament was dissolved on 24 January, O.S. Tufton had been a member for Appleby since 1668.

but for not having performed what you ordered me by them till now, you see the effects of being so good and kind a freind, I should not have taken the same Liberty with any one else, though I ought to have taken lesse with you. Inclosed you have the catalogue of grapes that you desired, and Dr. Magnol's opinion in his owne hand writing touching the Botanists.[1] I have enquired of him as to the position of the planets and state of the moone in reference to the gathering and sowing of seeds, setting, and removing of plants, and he tells me that he ha's sowed and gathered seeds, set and removed plants, at all times of the moon, and that he could never find that She had Influence upon them. I have sent you as you desired a pretty large quantity of Sabina Baccifera berry's. I received lately another letter from Mr. Selapris[a-] in which[-a] he expresses himself extreamely obliged to you for the Care you have taken of his bussinesse, I shall neither to him nor any other mention what you enjoyned me as a secret,[2] I wish I could say the like of our freind Sir John Chichley whom I commended to soon in my last for I have found him since failing, but though it be the same thinge as to the prejudice it do's me in my Concerns, yet truly I thinke he meanes no ill, I have taken the liberty to chide him in a freindly manner and he ha's promised me hereafter to be more Cautious. I told you in my last how much I was Concern'd that I had not heard from my Cousin Salweys, and I have since received the afflicting newes of their having embarqued on a ship of St. Malo's of 20 guns bound for Leghorne that was unfortunately engaged by a Mayorquin who after 6 howers fight the Captain being killed and 2 french passengers (whom I verry much feare may prove my poore Cousins) was caryed into Mayorque,[3] yet I was told in the same letter that they went from that Island to Port Mahon in the Island of Mynorca to get passage for Leghorne but he do's not tell me that he had received any letter from them. The letter that gives me this advice is dated the 14th: Instant from a Merchant of Marsilia, but I have heard nothing since, nor have I received one word from England. The major having write to me that he wished I had been at Paris to have accompanyed his sons to marsilia, and I having in my answer

[a-a] *MS.* Selapris in / in which

---

[1] Pierre Magnol, 1638–1715, botanist; a Protestant; abjured; and appointed professor of medicine at Montpellier 1694: *N.B.G.*; Haag. He gave Locke his estimate of some of the botanists named in the enclosure on 20 October 1678: Journal.

[2] This perhaps refers to Locke's intended visit to Italy: p. 656. [3] Majorca.

to him told him that I should have been verry glad to have been at Calais at their landing, and not having gone more then one day's journey with them of their way from hence to marsilia (though I had gone somewhat further if they would have permitted me,) this I beleeve is the cause that I heare neither from him nor his son (as I formerly wrote you) if they had been my brothers I could not in the state I was in, and the hast they were in to get thither ride so fast upon so bad horses without I would have hazarded not only my health but my life, and my going thither or not going would not at all have Contributed to their security but I aprehend if they have miscarryed the major will never forgive the omission, and withall will make me the cause of their unhapynesse, alleadging that had it not been on the score of their designing me a vissit they had never tooke that way, though the plaine English is that they tooke this way to avoide going through the Straits.[1] but be it as it will I know my owne Innocency, and the reall Intentions I have had all along to acknowledge the favours I have received from him, nor have I been altogether ungratefull already, nor will, let what will happen and let him be as unkind as he sees fit if I am in a capacity. Sir I have my heart and head so full of this concern that I hope you will pardon my entertaining you so long with a discourse of this nature, but I shall put an end to it though never to the affection with which I shall indeavour to aprove my self

Deare Sir

Your faithfull and obedient servant

WILLIAM CHARLETON

You have the services of mr: Tufton Sir James Rushot and Sir John Chichley presented to you.

Sir James hopes to see you shortly having left this place yesterday.

Mr: Tufton told me that 2 posts since he acquainted you from me that your things went the 14th. Instant for Paris.

Sir I am sorry that I knew not sooner that you had a mind to have the Combs you wrote for to Sir John else I had sent them you with the rest of your things if it be not to late let me know and I shall send them.

Endorsed by Locke: Mr *Charleton* 28 Feb. *79*

[1] Of Gibraltar.

[Enclosure:]

Pour lhistoire universelle des plantes Jean Bauhin[1] a plus travaillé qaucun autre, Les plantes quil a veues en estat Il les a tres bien descrites mais la plus part de ses descriptions sont faites sur des plantes seches, ses figures ne sont pas bonnes et mesmes Il y en a grand nombre de transposées

Le Pinax de Caspar Bauhin[2] est un fort bon livre quoy quil y aist grand nombre de fautes, mais Il faut estre scavant en botanique pour le lire

Il y a beaucoup dautres bon autheurs botanistes qui ont tres bien escrit quoy quils nayent pas fait une histoire universelle ayant seulement mis Ce quils avoient Veu Comme Clusius[a3] qui est un tres bon livre dont les figures et descriptions sont bones, Lobel[4] aussi est fort bon a bien travaillé. Le Mattheole de Caspar bauhin[5] aussi, Cæsalpine[6] quoyque son livre soit sans figures estoit scavant botaniste, Comme aussi fabius Columna,[7] de qui les figures sont bonnes quoyque petites

Ceux qui ont bien parlé des vertus des plantes entre[b] les autres sont dodon, Mattheol, tragus etc[c8]

Endorsed by Locke: Botanici 79

## 450. Locke to Dr. John Mapletoft, [*c.* 1/11 March 1679] (417)

*European Magazine*, xv (1789), 90–1. The letter dates from not earlier than November 1678, when Locke hoped to meet Dr. Budgen: p. 625. When he wrote it he expected to return to England shortly. He apparently wrote to

[a] *Doubtful spelling.* [b] *Doubtful reading; word altered.* [c] *Locke adds* Dr Magnol

[1] J. Bauhin and J. H. Cherler, *Historiæ Plantarum Generalis . . . Prodromus*, 1619 (see L.L., no. 225 n.); new edition as *Historia Plantarum Universalis*, 3 vols., 1650–1.

[2] *Πίναξ Theatri Botanici*, 1623 (L.L., no. 225); new ed. 1671.

[3] Charles de l'Escluse; probably his *Rariorum Plantarum Historia*, 1601.

[4] M. de l'Obel (Lobelius); either his *Plantarum seu Stirpium Historia*, 1576, or his *Plantarum seu Stirpium Icones*, 1581, with new edition, *Icones Stirpium*, etc., 1591.

[5] Pietro Andrea Mattioli (Matthiolus), *Opera, quæ Exstant, Omnia*, ed. C. Bauhin, 1598; new editions 1674, etc.

[6] Andrea Cesalpino, *De Plantis Libri XVI*, 1583, and Appendix, 1603.

[7] Fabio Colonna; probably his *Φυτοβάσανος sive Plantarum Aliquot Historia*, 1592.

[8] Rembert Dodoens (Dodonæus); probably his *Histoire des plantes*, 1557, a French translation of his *Cruÿde boeck*, 1554; Mattioli (see above) wrote a commentary on Dioscorides, 1565 (L.L., no. 1939); H. Bock (Tragus), *De Stirpium . . . Usitatis Nomenclaturis*, etc., 1552, a translation of his *Kreuterbuch*, first published in 1539.

Denis Grenville to that effect on 14 March, N.S.: pp. 697–8; and this letter must date from about then.

Deare Sir,

I am exceeding glad you have paid me my letter. Not that I think I put you in my debt by mine, but yet I tell you 'tis still a satisfaction to have to doe with people that goe . . .[a] one's reach, nor doe not run their country. I am therefor pleased to finde you still at Gresham Colledg . . .[a] count a much better lodging, not only than the finest church-yard in London, but even then the best house in Montpelier; and I should have taken it mighty ill of your lungs to have sent you of an errant thither, especially at a time when I had patched up mine soe well as to hope they would hold your strong London air, and allow me again the happyness of your conversation after another fashon than this nigardly way of letter. You obleige me by the promise you give me that I shall finde you plump at my returne. I desire it may not be interpreted by comparing yourself with me, for I doubt whether all the ortilans in France be able to communicate to me one grain of their fat, and I shall be well enough at my ease if when I returne I can but maintaine this poore tenement of mine[1] in the same repaire it is at present, without hope ever to finde it much better. For I expect not that Dr. Time should be half soe favourable to my crazy body as it has been to you in your late disease. 'Tis a good marke, but may have other dangers in it; for usually those whom that old winged gentleman helps up the hill, are not yet got out of the reach of the winged boy who does such mischief with his bow and arrows. You see I conclude you keep your word, and that you are by this time not only well but in good plight. I intend very speedily to come and see, so that if you have any more commissions for me here, I beseech you send them by the first opportunity, which I hope to give you a good account of without the convoy of 5000 to guard me home:[2] and, to tell you truly, I have such an esteeme for the gent. on this side the water, and their country, that I would not have them give themselves the trouble to come and see me in our vilanous country of England, but stay at home and enjoy the paradise they have *chez eux*. Dr. Bugden is very well all

[a] *Page torn.*

[1] A variant of the house of clay, etc.: p. 101, n. 1.
[2] This perhaps alludes to fears that a French invasion was imminent.

but his old maladie, which he has some little but not violent fits of some times. He presents you his service. The ——[a] you have with you, may be, for aught I know, a very able man.[1] But this is certaine he is modest too, and does not over-value himself, since he would pass for another; for he is one I never yet saw in my life, and therfore you may believe 'tis not he that was treated with for Dr. Bugden. He is here in town, and I saw him but yesterday, and here inclosed I have sent you his address which he gave me himself. My service to our good friend,[2] when you see him; I writ to him since I came to Paris, but have not heard from him. My service also to our friend in Southampton fields.[3] I am perfectly,

Sir,

Your most affectionate Humble servant,

J. LOCKE.

## 451. JACQUES SELAPRIS to LOCKE, 2/12 March 1679 (*446*, *457*)

B.L., MS. Locke c. 18, ff. 86–7. The text of the letter is written by an amanuensis; the signature and postscript, by Selapris.

A Lyon ce 12e mars 1679.

Monsieur

Je me trouve Honoré de vos 3 agreables Lettres du 3e du passe premiere et 3e. mars par les quelles me marques avoir Receu le Barill Vin Muscat, mais quil Estoit asses mal Condittione des quoy Je suis bien fache et puis bien dire Estre un des plus malheureux voyant les Contrariettes qu'arivent En Voulant servir mes Intimes Amis, Je nen doubte point qu'ils n'ayent, non seulement perce le Barill, mais Encore Le falcifié, ce qui Est domage et asses Cruéll de la maniere quils traittent les pauvres Estrangers, et come lon ne scauroit avoir Raison de ces Bruttals il faut s'armer de Pattience, toutes fois mon Cher Monsieur Je vous suplie de maviser, sy vous faires Encore sy long Sejour a Paris, pour avoir le bien de Vous

[a] *This may represent a defect in the manuscript or a name deliberately omitted by Locke.*

[1] I cannot identify him.

[2] Probably Sydenham.

[3] Presumably Mrs. Beavis or another member of Lady Northumberland's household. Ralph Montagu acquired a site in Southampton Fields (now part of Bloomsbury) in 1675, and began to build immediately; the house was now nearly complete. The British Museum now occupies the site: *London Topographical Record*, xvii (1936), 56, 58–9; Evelyn, *Diary*, ed. de Beer, iv. 90 n.

Envoyer Un autre, que Je feray sy bien accomoder, quasseurement il vous parviendroit bien Condittione et sans falcifié, et mobligeres.

Mr. Legendre alafin nous a Envoye Compte Les quelles somes apres de Verifier, dont vous en donerons avis du bien Estre, ou ce que trouverons, cepandant nous vous prions puis que vous aves Vous voulu doner la peine de vous Informer de son Estat et affaires, men aviser, ce que pourres avoir aprins[1] De luy. Je vous Demande au Reste mille pardons de Limportunitte que Je vous done et vous Prié mon Cher Monsieur En Revange ne mespargner en Rien de vos agreables Services. nos Corespondents et amis a Callais sont messieurs Les freres Molliens aux quels pourres Delivrer et adresser ce quaures a Envoyer a monsieur Charleton sous nostre adresse, et Je luy le fairay tenir avec soing, attendent Lhoneur de vos Comandemens Je vous Baise les mains et vous Demeure ajamais

Monsieur

Vostres humbles Serviteur

J SELAPRIS

Monsieur Charleton vous Baise fort les Mains, Monsieur de Beaumond et Monsieur le Chevalier Russot sont party depuis Cinq Jours pour Paris par la deligençe. sy vous les voyéz je vous prie les asseurer de mes Respectz Come Mr Banqs s'il vous plaist, Legendre nous á remis deux petite Letre de Change Nous vous donerons avis du suivy—Mr. Horutener et ma feme vous saluent profondement.

Address: A Monsieur Monsieur Jean Locke Gentil home Englois Chez monsieur Charras maistre Apoticaire Rue Boucherie au fauxbourg st. Germain a Paris.

Endorsed by Locke: Mr Selapris 12 Mar. *79*

## *452.* THOMAS HERBERT, later eighth earl of Pembroke, to LOCKE, 2 March [1679] (*441, 795*)

B.L., MS. Locke c. 11, ff. 189–90. Year from Locke's endorsement.

London March 2d.

Sir

T'other day I receiv'd your letter by which I'm sorry to heare that you did not receive mine in answer to your former, wherein I

[1] 'Apprins. *as* Appris': Cotgrave.

told you of the death of my Lord Dunaghall and my Cosin S. Roper and that I had then the misfortune to bury my youngest Sister; my Brother is so very kinde to me that he desiers I would live with him att Wilton alwayes when he is there (not pressing me in the least to drinke)[1] so that I did not thinke it fit to buy any Chambers att the Temple, but however have taken a house in Pell Mell where I've settled my bookes and things, and do hope in a little time to enjoy your good company there; I've sent a Note all which or as many as you can find you will oblige me very much to bring over with you, and if you have money with you only for your owne occasions, pray let me know how much will be wanting and I'l send you a Bill by the next Post. The Parliament meets next Thursday.[2] a Member of which I was chosen last munday for Wilton, who am

Your servant to command
T. HERBERT.

Address: A Monsieur Monsieur Locke, gentilhomme Anglois. chez Madame Herinx et Monsieur son fils Banquiers. A Paris.

Postmark: G

Endorsed by Locke: M: Herbert 2 Mar. *79*

## *453.* EDWARD BERNARD to LOCKE, 8 March 1679 (*435, 1228*)

B.L., MS. Locke c. 4, ff. 2–3.

Honoured Sir

I entreate you to be a freind to me and the Bishop of Chester and Dr Gale and Dr Vossius in the conveyance of the Guift of Mr Huëtt, his late Noble worke, unto me in England by a native or sure hand, if not by that which is the best, and yet I beleive more useful to your freinds than your selfe.[3] Tarrying or returning I wishe you

[1] Philip, the seventh earl, was notorious for heavy drinking and for violence when drunk; he killed several men either when he was drunk or as an outcome of drunken quarrels.

[2] Thursday, 6 March.

[3] Dr. John Pearson: p. 193, n. 6; Thomas Gale, D.D., *c.* 1636–1702, high master of St. Paul's School 1672–97, dean of York 1697: *D.N.B.*; Isaac Vossius, D.C.L., 1618–89, canon of Windsor 1673: ibid.; no. *1207*. The donor is Pierre-Daniel Huet, 1630–1721; bishop of Avranches 1689: *N.B.G.* His gift is identifiable as copies of his *Demonstratio Evangelica*, 1679; notice in *Journal des Sçavans*, 9 January (pp. 7–12); L.L., no. 1531[a].

all health and happinesse. Pray let Josephus be obliged to your favour as to the French MSS. or Notes: The charge, whatere it be of Transcripts or Letters or the like, shall be thankfully discounted to your Order.

The enclosed I humbly beg you to give by the soonest to Monsieur Huëtt: wherein I have acquainted him with the good opertunity your visite affords for the Transmission of his 4. Copyes, or what else he designs for me.

The Harmony of the Evang. by Monsieur Tonnar is soe good a worke, that I will either desire the use of your Copy, or else one from him by the first occasion. It will be very usefull to a disigne of mine:[1] as the 6. sheets I have by me of it, doe assure me.

My service to Mr Justell, and Mr Marsham (Sir Jo. Marsham's son),[2] who by his power with Carcavi may doe me a kindnesse in the Royall Library.[3] I would present Bullialdus with Mr Halyes Hemisphere, if any person went hence for Paris:[4] as alsoe Mr Justell with Mr Wase's Freeschooles, as he desird.[5]

When you meete at Mr Justells, pray give my service to Mr Thevenote,[6] and enquire there, as alsoe of Mr Huëtt, whether there be in the Kings, or Seguiers, or any other Library a Copy of the Apostle Barnabas his Catholic Epistle either in Latine or Greeke, (besids the Greeke of Sirmondus and the Latine of the Corbeian[a] Abbey: whence Menardus's Edition came) because it is here reprinting.[7]

[a] *Or* Korbeian*; word altered.*

---

[1] I cannot identify this.

[2] Sir John Marsham, 1602–85, the scholar (*D.N.B.*), had two sons, John and Robert, later second and fourth baronets: G. E. C., *Baronetage*, iii. 283–4. The present man may be either.

[3] Pierre Carcavy, d. 1684, who was in charge of the Royal Library from about 1661 to 1683: *D.B.F.*

[4] Ismael Boulliau, 1605–91, astronomer: ibid.; *N.B.G.* Edmond Halley, 1656–1742, the astronomer (*D.N.B.*), had returned from St. Helena in October 1678. On 7 November his planisphere and description of the stars of the southern hemisphere (*Catalogus Stellarum Australium*, 1679; listed in Term *Catalogue*, 6 December 1678: *T.C.* i. 335) were shown to the Royal Society: Birch, iii. 434.

[5] Christopher Wase (*D.N.B.*), *Considerations concerning Free-Schools, as settled in England*, 1678: Madan, no 3198. For the term free school see p. 56, n. 1.

[6] p. 631, n. 1.

[7] The manuscripts and editions of the Epistle of Barnabas are described or listed in the prolegomena to the edition by O. von Gebhardt and A. Harnack, 1878. Jacques Sirmond, S.J. (*N.B.G.*), gave N.-H. Ménard (ibid.) a copy of a Greek manuscript; Ménard also used the Corbie manuscript of the Latin translation to establish the text; his edition was published posthumously in 1645. The Oxford edition appeared in 1685.

Mr Finch and one Dr Edgebury of Brasennose are Burgesses for this Univ⟨ers⟩ity,[a1] and Mr Vernon of Ch.Ch. and Sir . . . Exton for Cambridge.[2] Pray what is become of the papers of Mr Vernons brother who dyd in Persia.[3]

The specimen of Josephus,[4] dispose, I pray, to the best advantage of the worke, where you please.

I am your Everobligd
E.B.

Oxon March. 8 167$\frac{8}{9}$

Address: For Mr Locke, att Sir John Banks his house in Lincolns Inne Fields In London

Postmark: MR 10

Endorsed by Locke: Mr *Bernard* 8 Mar. 7$\frac{8}{9}$

## *454*. THOMAS TUFTON, later sixth earl of Thanet, to LOCKE, 11/21 March 1679 (*448*, *530*)

B.L., MS. Locke c. 22, ff. 30–1.

Mr Locke

I recieved your kinde letter last Post of the 10 of marche and am satisfied you will before you know whither I deserve it misse no occation to expresse to mee what the rest of your Frends share in and though I should bee very uneasye not to have it in my Power to make what returnes I could wishe you shall alwayes finde I shall esteeme your Frendship as I aught, Sir I have only time to lett you know 15 dayes since I wrote to Sir John Bankes to desiere him to returne mee a 100 pound in two bills of eache 50 a piece to his Marchant at Paris if they Passe through your hands I desiere you will leave one of them with your Landlord or place it where Sir John Chichely maye finde it when hee comes to Paris which will bee the beginning of maye who will laye it out for mee in Close the other Bill I would have sent to mee as I maye draw the other 50

[a] *The word is perhaps abbreviated rather than incomplete.*

[1] Heneage Finch, Sir John Banks's son-in-law, now solicitor-general; John Edisbury, D.C.L., a Master in Chancery 1684–1708: Foster; for the election see Wood, *L. and T.* ii. 440–3.

[2] James Vernon, the future secretary of state: no. *616*; and Sir Thomas Exton, LL.D.: *D.N.B.*

[3] Francis Vernon: pp. 193, n. 2, 370.

[4] No. *435*.

pound to Bourbon[1] or where I may want it I thinke of Decamping from hence about the 10 of next Monthe and will bee the Beginning of maye at Bourbon and what Clothes Sir John Byes mee at Paris shall meet mee there in case my Bills should not come before you leave Paris if you dare trust mee in contriving or ordering your Marchant to furnishe Sir John with that some you would oblige mee, if my letters should hiether after the 10 of Aprile and not find mee my Frend Charleton will send them after mee I showed him the part of your letter where hee was concerned hee returnes you thanke and letts you know the joyfull News of his 2 Couzens[2] arrivall at Lygorne is come to him from England which has revived us all for wee all suffered for his apprehensions who was not to bee comforted, if you should bee gone Sir John will expect to finde your direction and order to your marchant at Paris but hee would bee gladd to here when you depart for hee hath thaught of directing some portmantle to you hee would have mee mention this to you, I hope my Frend Sir James Rusworthe[3] found you, hee is gone with as much expedistion as ever young man did to his mistrise and left mee alone to regrett the losse of soe Good a Compagnion hee told mee hee desiered to renew his acquainttance with you which you will not dislike for hee is a worthy man and Good Frend, I suppose my Frend Beaumont will begon with him else I would send my service and good wishes to him wee were here very happy in there Compagnie and I believe you would not have repented had you passed some time with them, the want of a Frend this sommer will bee my misfortune the only advantage I shall finde will bee to know how to value your Compagnie the better whenever you will allow it to

your faithfull Frend and servant

TUFTON

Montpellier the 21 of marche 79.

Address (in Tufton's hand): AMonsieur Monsieur Locke Gentillhomme Anglois Chez Monsieur Charas Apothicaire ruë de Boucherie Faubourg St Germain

Endorsed by Locke: Mr Tufton 21 Mar. *79*

[1] Probably Bourbon-l'Archambault: p. 378, n. 3.

[2] Edward and Thomas Salwey.

[3] Here identified as Rushout.

## 455. Sir John Banks to Locke, 12 March 1679 (*444, 456*)

B.L., MS. Locke c. 3, ff. 130–1.

Sir

I must confesse. that I have beene prevented writinge to you. by some affaires that kept me in the country, but I did at large give you my concurrence, to gratify my sons desire, (and alsoe thinkinge it very convenient that he doe come home thro. Flanders and Holland) and the rather at this time, now he is abroad and hath the opertunity of your good conduct great care and kindnesse. with him. which I can truly say gives me and my wiffe great satisfaction, then to make another voyadge from home. And doe leave it to yourselvs to begin your journy from Paris assoone as you shall judge the weather and time of the yeare seasonable. for to undertake the same, for altho. I doe wish you were from Paris, yet would not have you goe thence 'til your selves see fitt in respect to your convenient passage. consideringe the Country you goe to: And I doe alsoe leave it to yourselves soe to order this journy, and for such places, as you shall judge best, and I should be glad you could soe dispose of all things as to be at home, God willinge, in May, but I doe not limmitt you. to 20 days. becaus I doe beleive you are alsoe desirous to be at home assoone as you can; doe only let you know, that as I am willinge you should take soe much time as answers your end in this journy, soe I doe alsoe desire you will have respect unto your makinge all convenient hast in your returne home. and I pray God preserve you both.

I shall next munday send you creditts for Flanders and Holland at large, and Madam Herrinx will accommodate what you desire to discharge Paris — Dr Cox is now with me and presents you and my son his humble services— We are in health and my Lord Shaftesbury and his family, and my Lord much better I thinke then he hath beene of late My wiffe presents you her humble services and beleive me ever to be

Sir, Your oblidged humble servant

John Banks

Lincolns in fields 12th March. 78

The great packet I had sent by Mr Savill[1] 14 days agoe, but by

[1] Henry Savile: p. 86, n. 8. He had recently been appointed envoy extraordinary to France.

my servants omition was left behinde and not knowinge its concerne doe send the same by post.

Address: To mr Locke These

Endorsed by Locke: Sir J: Banks 12 Mar. $7\frac{8}{9}$

## *456.* SIR JOHN BANKS to LOCKE, 20 March 1679 (*455, 460*)

B.L., MS. Locke c. 3, f. 132. Copy by an amanuensis prefixed to no. *460*. The original may have failed to reach Locke: see no. *461*.

London 20th. March 1678

Sir

Since the abovesaid[1] I have one from my son and a bill drawne for Lv 402 which I have alsoe accepted, which I suppose is to discharge your engagements. Heere inclosed send you letters Credit for Flanders, and doe desire you and my sonn doe send me an abstract of all the moneys which you have drawne on mee since hee went hence, That I may compare the same with Sir Nathanael Herne and my account

I pray will you take such Credit from Madam Herinx also as you see needfull, and doe desire that you doe give mee notice where to direct my letters to you in Flanders and in Holland, at Amsterdam you may please to addresse yourselves to Mr William and John Vandervoorts to supply you what money you desire. I wish you a good journey and safe returne. I pray remember me to my sonn and tell him wee are all well I blesse God who with the tender of my humble service doe remaine

## *457.* JACQUES SELAPRIS to LOCKE, 22 March/1 April 1679 (*451, 507*)

B.L., MS. Locke c. 18, f. 88. Text of letter written by an amanuensis; only the signature and a few other words, by Selapris.

a Lyon ce premier Avril 1679.

Monsieur

Tout Presentement Je viens de Recevoir Lagreable vostre avec Lincluse de Vostre Amy dont vous men advises Lentiere Conoissance des affaires de Mr. Legendre de quoy J⟨e⟩[a] vous Remercie

[a] *MS.* Jvous, *the* J *being added after* vous *was written.*

[1] The original letter was apparently preceded by a copy of no. *455* or of a lost letter, just as this letter precedes no. *460*.

fort et vous Diray quavec cest ordinaire J'ay done avis a mes Asocies, dont vous en Escriray a son temps leur sentiment Vous supliant m'adviser en Responce ou Je pourois avois Lhoneur de vous Escrire et adresser Les Lettres pour ne vous point manquer et mobligeres.

Je voys aussy que desires avec ampressement scavoir Le peu de Chose que Jay Desbourcé pour Monsieur Barck et Vous dont en trouveres specification cy bas montant l14. .8. .9 que vous serve Davis, Sil se presente occassion a vous Rendre Service en ces quartiers ayés sil vous plaist souvenence des protestations que sy soventes fois Je vous ay faites et Comandes moy Librement puis que Je suis et Demeure de bon Coeur—

Monsieur mon[a]– tres Cher Amy–[a]
Vostre tres humble et tres affectione Serviteur
JACQUES SELAPRIS L'aisné.

| | |
|---|---|
| Pour port dune Boete de la Diligence a la maison | l—. . 5. .— |
| Pour port chez le messager – – – – – – – – – | —. . 5. .— |
| Pour Droits a la doana – – – – – – – – – – | 3. . 5. . 9 |
| Pour port de la dite Boete de Montpellier Icy – | 2. .17. .— |
| Pour port dun paquet par la dilligence a Paris – | 6. .—. .— |
| Pour port de lettre dun paquet – – – – – – – | 1. .16. .— |
| | l14. . 8. .9[b] |

Ma[c]– feme et moy vous asseurons de Nos humbles Respectz Come à Monsieur Banqs.–[c]

Address: A Monsieur Monsieur Jean Lock Gentilhome Englois chez Monsieur Charras maistre apoticaire En Rue Boucherie au fauxbourg St. Germain A Paris.

Endorsed by Locke: Mr Selapris 1 Apr. *79*

## *458.* DR. DENIS GRENVILLE to LOCKE, 22 March/ 1 April 1679 (*447*, *468*)

B.L., MS. Locke c. 10, ff. 97–8.

Aix Apr. 1st Easter Eve 1679

Deare Sir

Tho we are within aweek of our departure, yet I have liberty enough to give you an account of the receipt of yours of the 14th

a–a *Words added by Selapris.* b *Locke adds a note* Paid to Mr Menard 11 Apr. *79*
c–c *Postscript written by Selapris.*

of last month and of the Extraordinary trouble which it brought with it to me, in allaying my hopes of seeing you at Paris, where wee are hastening (my sister sayes that shee will set forth the weeke after Low-Sunday)[1] and where I wish I had wings to flye, that I might have a litle personall injoyment of mee. Really it would prove to me a very Considerable peice of Providence to have an Opportunity of exposing my soule to the view of A wise and faithfull freind before I exposed my selfe anew to the sundry difficultyes of my Calling which await mee in England. God grant me this satisfaction, if hee sees fit; or a fuller Resignation of my selfe unto him, in parting with what is most deere unto mee; which is, A bosome freind. Thanking you for your Excellent spell, or preservative, I rest, Sir,

Your most humble servant and faithfull *Freind*

DE. GRENVILLE

My sister is your humble servant and soe sayes misse likewise.

My service to Mr Bankes.

The Intelligence from England doth much disquiet our soules. Da pacem Domine etc.[2]

Endorsed by Locke: D. Genville 1 Apr. *79*

## *459.* GEORGE WALLS and NATHANIEL HODGES to LOCKE, 22 March [1679] (*422, 540; 527*)

B.L., MS. Locke c. 23, ff. 33–4. The year may have been supplied by Locke.

[Walls:]

Ch Ch March the 22d[a]

Sir

When I was abroade I thought there must somewhat extraordinary constantly happen at Oxon, and soe judg'd my selfe hardly dealt with that I had not notice of it; and I possibly lie under the same censure of yours that my friends did of mine; but in earnest and not to excuse any lazienesse or omission things are as much the same here and like to bee soe, as your table, or I like to

[a] *Followed by* $7\frac{8}{9}$, *probably added by Locke.*

---

[1] The Sunday after Easter; this year 9 April in the Gregorian calendar, 27 April in the Julian.

[2] Probably from the Liturgy: 'Give peace in our time', etc.

continue senior[a] master.[a] however (Sir) you shall have what I thinke most like news. the candidates at our Election were Mr Solicitour Finch, Dr Lamphire, and Dr Edisbury (brother to him that liv'd at Vigan[b]) of which Dr Lamphire did not succeed.[1] The bishop of Lyncolne hath reprinted an account (that was not but with great difficultie to bee met with) of the powder plot, with a preface of his owne, and the addition of some papers of Sir Everard Digby's that were found in Warwickeshire about the time of the first discovery of the plot.[2] Mr Oates hath a sermon lately come out.[3] Sir William Robinson (formerly your patient) died not long since in Oxon.[4] my Lord Donegall is deade.[5] this day died our univercitie Oratour (one Mr Cradocke of Magdalene College) of the small pox, and mr Wyatte of Christ Church is likely to succeede him.[6] Dr Boucher is principle of Alban Hall.[7] Serjeant Gregory is speaker of the house of Commons,[8] and 44 Christ Church men members of it. Mr Herbert burgesse for Wilton.[9] the bishop of Peterborough is deade, and wee can spare more.[10] your affaires accordeinge to your pleasure are manag'd by mr Thomas.[11] you have had a constant tenant for your chamber. the vicechancellour[12] has scons'd you 20s. as prior opponent in a phil: disputation.[13] I

[a] *MS.* señ m^r.  [b] *Doubtful reading.*

---

[1] See p. 693. John Lamphire, M.D.; Principal of Hart Hall 1663–88: *D.N.B.* Edisbury's brother may be Joshua Edisbury of Denbigh, who matriculated from Brasenose in 1653: Foster. I cannot identify Vigan.

[2] The bishop is Dr. Thomas Barlow (p. 294, n. 1). His book is *The Gunpowder-Treason*, 1679, in which he reprints *His Majesties Speach* of 9 November 1605, which includes an account of the discovery of the plot, 1605, and *A True and Perfect Relation of the Whole Proceedings against the Late Most Barbarous Traitors, Garnet*, etc., 1606. The appended letters of Sir Everard Digby (*D.N.B.*) were perhaps contributed by Dr. John Tillotson (p. 371, n. 3): Evelyn, *Diary*, ed. de Beer, iv. 157 n.

[3] Titus Oates, the perjurer (no. *488*), *A Sermon Preached at St. Michael's, Wood-Street*, 1679. The date of delivery is not stated, but it was licensed for printing on 11 March.

[4] p. 601, n. 4. He died on 16 February.

[5] p. 669, n. 3.

[6] Thomas Craddock, orator since 1677, died on 22 March; his successor, William Wyatt, matriculated from Christ Church 1659; B.A. 1662; student and M.A. 1665. He held office until 1712: Foster; Wood, *L. and T.* ii. 446.

[7] Thomas Bouchier, D.C.L., in succession to Narcissus Marsh (p. 641, n. 1): Foster.

[8] William Gregory, 1624–96; serjeant-at-law 1677; elected Speaker on 15 March; appointed a judge on 1 May and knighted on 26 July of this year: *D.N.B.*

[9] p. 691.

[10] Dr. Joseph Henshaw, bishop since 1663; he died on 9 March: *D.N.B.*

[11] Samuel Thomas.

[12] Dr. John Nicholas, warden of New College 1675–9: Foster.

[13] This is probably one of the Lenten disputations, in which candidates for the degree of Bachelor of Arts had to take part: the Laudian statutes of the university (Madan, i. 179), Tit. VI, section 2, ch. 6; Madan, no. 3291.

quarrell'd with him about it; the reason for my soe doeinge you shall know and will approve of hereafter. my Lord Lexington[1] is design'd at his returne from travell to live with us at christ church: and my request to you is that if hee bee in Paris, and you have opportunity that youle please to recommende mee to that relation that some student must customarily have to him. as our affaires now stande the protection of a gentleman seems more eligible then some other uncertaine preferments. twas not in my thoughts[a] to lay any snare for your kindnesse, when I formerly desir'd the favour of you to buy mee a table booke;[2] and I cannot certainely now bee suspected to requeste any thinge but the trouble of it, if I begge that youle bringe mee another somewhat larger, when you come over, which I hope will bee very suddenly. all at Dr Pocock's sende you service and thanks for your kindnesse to Charls,[3] whom I wish to deserve it. Mr Thomas is your servant, and Mr Hodges will assure you that hee is soe in a whole page. I am glad to heare of your successe in your designe in goeinge abroade, and wish the greatest improvement (or continuance if it bee perfecte) of your health. I am

Deare Sir

Your most oblig'd servant.

GEORGE WALLS.

[Hodges:]

Dear Sir

I need not tell you how little apt I am to write; you know very well what zeal I have ever had for the pulpit, and cannot but remember what a freind of yours once observed of me, That it was nothing but perfect lazinesse, and fear of a number of pains that deterred me from the sacred function of matrimony. I shall not fear to tell you that a man is a sort of engin, and finds it hard to move otherwise than his inward springs will let him, For I doe not fear that you will be like to passe the same censure upon me that a learned Doctor of our Church lately did, That I was a Calvinist, for delivering[b] the same Doctrine. I will make no other excuses to you, for to confesse ingenuously and to follow nature in my

[a] *Or* thought [b] *Abbreviated in MS.*

[1] Robert Sutton, 1662–1723; second Baron Lexington (Lexinton) 1668: *D.N.B.* I have not traced him at Christ Church.

[2] A pocket memorandum book: *O.E.D.* [3] Charles Pocock(e): no. *409*.

defence as well as in my fault, I had not put on this peice of activity, but that Mr Tyrrel told me you were so very kind as to enquire after my state of health, and that he could make no answer to that question, because he had not seen me before the writing of his Letter. And I thought therefore I had a more pressing and indispensable obligation upon me, judging every man upon the strongest force of reason to be bound to give a more particular accompt of himself to those, who as they have a peculiar right to dispose of him and his faculties, so have so much goodnesse as to own an interest in both. And I wish I could tell you that I had as much strength of body as willingnesse of mind to serve you. The plain truth is my bloud hath been exceedingly depauperated ever since my often letting bloud at London and drinking of water, and since my Feaver at Salisbury hath grown worse and worse, but more especially since Feb: was twelve Moneth hath shewed it self in more afflicting symptons. I have had all the dismall effects of that the Learned call the spleen, but that which I take most notice of because it hath made deepest impressions upon me, hath been a constant giddinesse, swimming, dizzinesse, noise and suddain turns and touches in my head that have made me almost a perfect prisoner for the greatest part of the time: Because with in doores I can generally converse pretty well at ease, but I walk with very little assurance, and but for a very little while; motion causing a stirring of wind in my side, and then it is immediately in my head. I ride sometimes very well, and as soon again I can not bear it att all. I find all the specifiques for the head have done me no good, if not harm, and am now leaving all to God Almighty and nature. I have not been behind hand in sollicitous enquiry after your health, and have been so often pretty well satisfied therein and fed with frequent hopes of your return that possibly if I had been more addicted to writing than I am, my more pleasing expectations of seing you would have prompted me to think it unnecessary to tell you in the manner I now doe That I am

Your true faithfull servant

N.H.

Address (f. 34v.; written by Walls): For Mr John Locke This To bee left at Sir John Banks his house in Lyncoln's Inne fields London.

Postmark: MR 24(?)

Endorsed by Locke: M. Hodges 22 Mar. $7\frac{8}{9}$

## *460.* SIR JOHN BANKS to LOCKE, 27 March 1679 (*456, 461*)

B.L., MS. Locke c. 3, ff. 132–3. The letter is preceded by a copy, written by an amanuensis, of Banks's letter to Locke of 20 March. This copy is here printed separately as no. *456*.

Ady. 27th Do. Since the abovsaid I have none of yours, nor any, from my son. which I am in expectation of: When you shall come to Amsterdam I pray addresse your selves to Mr Benjamine Poulle. marchant there, who will not only supply what you desire, for monnys. but assist you with all conveniencys. The enclosed I had 2 days since, I pray remember me to my son who remaine

Sir, your humble servant

JOHN BANKS

The House have impeached the Earle of Danby, and he is absented.[1]

Address (written by the amanuensis who copied no. *456*): A Monsieur Monsieur Lock Chez Monsieur Charas Apothecarie dans la rue de Boucherie Fauxbourgh St. Germaine A Paris

Endorsed by Locke: Sir J. Banks 27 Mar. *79*

## *461.* SIR JOHN BANKS to LOCKE, 31 March 1679 (*460, 464*)

B.L., MS. Locke c. 3, ff. 134–5.

Sir

I have yours of the 29th instant and doe perceave you were some time without any of myne. I doe rather much incline to my sons comminge home by way of Flanders and Holland, then to have thoughts of his goinge after he is once come home: and shall be glad it may soe sute your affaires, I have not opertunity to say more at present. Only send this enclosed creditt for Amsterdam. and pray remember me to my son who truly am

Sir

Your most affectionate freind and servant

JOHN BANKS

London. 31 March 1679.

Address: A Monsieur Monsieur Lock Chez Mr Charas Apothecarie rue de Boucherie Fauxbourg St. Germaine A Paris

Endorsed by Locke: Sir J: *Banks* 31 Mar. *79*

[1] Danby was impeached in December 1678; the proceedings were revived on 20 March, and early on 24 March he went into hiding: Browning, *Danby*, i. 321, 323.

## *Addition to Letter no.* 415 *on p. 624*

[Locke will be unable to get Dr. Magnol[1] the book he wanted in Italy but will search Lyon for it; he has seen Mr. Tufton, who is going to winter in Montpellier, 'soe that when Sr John [Chicheley] comes there is like to be a good knot of you'; last night he wrote urgently to Charleton to send directions about 'our box of clothes', but when in his anxiety he asked the messenger to confirm that he had the letter 'the ill naturd rogue denyd it to me'; the box should be sent to Mr. Selapris, who has been overwhelming Locke with kindness, 'he haveing sent me and Mr Tufton a present of wine and gelly'; in Paris he wishes to see Mr. Regis,[2] whose address Mr. Pasti[3] will have; he also refers to other friends.]

[1] Sale catalogue: Maynol. See p. 685.

[2] Probably Pierre Régis, 1656–1726, a physician: *N.B.G.*; Haag. Locke met him at Montpellier in 1676: Journal.

[3] Sale catalogue: Putti. See p. 612.

# INDEX OF CORRESPONDENTS IN THIS VOLUME

THIS index is by the numbers of the letters, italics being used as in the text to indicate letters not by Locke. A bracketed number is either for a letter between persons other than Locke, in which case it appears under the names of both writer (or writers) and person addressed, or for an item other than a letter. If there is correspondence in later volumes between Locke and a person in this index it is indicated by the citation either of the next volume in which any of it occurs or of the next letter.

The citation immediately following a name is that of a biographical note on the person. For persons concerned with only one or two letters the citation is omitted sometimes if the biographical note occurs in the head-note and is insignificant.